Christopher J

CW01496123

ALBERT EINSTEIN

THE
INCORRIGIBLE
RACIST

TABLE OF CONTENTS:

1 EINSTEIN DISCOVERS HIS RACIST CALLING

In 1919, Albert Einstein rose to international fame for predicting that the gravitational field of the sun would deflect rays of light. Eclipse observations confirmed this prediction. Newspapers around the world covered the story and declared that Albert Einstein had surpassed the genius of Copernicus, Kepler, Galileo and Newton. It seemed that all was right with the world—but then everything went tragically wrong.

"The way I see it, the fact of the Jews' racial peculiarity will necessarily influence their social relations with non-Jews. The conclusions which—in my opinion—the Jews should draw is to become more aware of their peculiarity in their social way of life and to recognize their own cultural contributions. First of all, they would have to show a certain noble reservedness and not be so eager to mix socially—of which others want little or nothing. On the other hand, anti-Semitism in Germany also has consequences that, from a Jewish point of view, should be welcomed. I believe German Jewry owes its continued existence to anti-Semitism."—ALBERT EINSTEIN[1]

"This accounts for the fact that there are many anti-Semites there who are not really anti-Semitic in the sense of being Jew-haters, and who are honest in their arguments. They regard Jews as of a nationality different from the German, and therefore are alarmed at the increasing Jewish influence on their national entity. [***] But in Germany the judgement of my theory depended on the party politics of the Press[.]"—ALBERT EINSTEIN[2]

"While he lived in Germany, however, Einstein seems to have accepted the then-prevalent racist mode of thought, often invoking such concepts as 'race' and 'instinct,' and the idea that the Jews form a race."—JOHN STACHEL[3]

1.1 Introduction

Racist physicist Albert Einstein became internationally famous in 1919 when newspapers around the world reported that he had correctly predicted that the gravitational field of the sun would deflect rays of light. The press promoted the virulently racist and segregationist Zionist, Albert Einstein, as if he were the world's greatest mind, a mind that had surpassed the genius of Copernicus, Galileo and Newton.

In April of 1921, Albert Einstein took advantage of his newly found fame and traveled to America. He promoted racist Zionism to the Jews of America, while raising money for the Eastern European Zionists who had made him famous. Einstein championed the racist doctrine of Theodor Herzl, that Jews were a distinct race of human beings, who could not assimilate into any Gentile society and therefore ought to segregate themselves and form a nation in Palestine. Einstein also believed that there ought to be a world government. However, Einstein thought that Israel ought to be a distinct nation. Though he described himself as non-religious, Einstein's racist views, and his concurrent call for a world government and a segregated "Jewish State" mirrored Jewish Messianic prophecies.

Einstein raised money in America for the Hebrew University in Jerusalem. He also tried to popularize the racist Zionist cause. The news media enthusiastically covered his trip to the United States. Mainstream news media claimed that all of Einstein's critics were anti-Semites, but did not criticize Einstein for his rabid racism or his segregationist politics.

Prof. Arvid Reuterdahl of St. Thomas College, in St. Paul, Minnesota, responded to Einstein's aggressive self-promotion. With reference to the notorious circus promoter P. T. Barnum, Prof. Reuterdahl dubbed Albert Einstein the "Barnum of the Scientific World". He publicly challenged Einstein to a debate over the merits of the theory of relativity and publicly accused Einstein of plagiarism.

Einstein refused to debate Reuterdahl. Einstein stated that his sole purpose for coming to America was to raise money for the Hebrew University in Jerusalem and that he could not be bothered with issues related to "his" theories. Even before coming to America, Einstein had earned an international reputation for hiding from his critics. His favorite tactic to avoid debate was to accuse his critics of being "anti-Semites", while refusing to address their legitimate accusations of his, Einstein's, irrationality and plagiarism. Like most bullies by bluff, Einstein was a coward, who hid behind the power of the racist Jews who attempted to shield him from criticism through well-orchestrated smear campaigns in the international press.

In spite of this, or perhaps because of this, Einstein generally had a hard time in America. Due to his incompetence, and the tribalistic racism he and his Jewish friends exhibited, Einstein faced scandal after scandal. Though Einstein had arrived to a triumphant welcome in New York City, he left the United States an utter disgrace. Though Einstein had accepted many honors from American universities, he publicly ridiculed American scholars and Americans in general in a widely published interview he gave after he had returned to Europe. The grapes had turned to sour gripes.

1.2 The Manufacture and Sale of St. Einstein

Isaac Newton believed that light is composed of matter converted into tiny "corpuscles". Newton predicted that the gravitational attraction of other matter would attract light corpuscles, just as it attracted everything else made up of matter. Einstein repeated Newton's prediction that gravitational fields would deflect light.

Like countless others before him, Einstein had proposed a non-Newtonian law of gravity. In Einstein's gravitational theory the deflection of light rays was twice as great as in Newton's gravitational theory.

In 1918-1920, the British astronomers Frank Watson Dyson, Charles Davidson and Arthur Stanley Eddington collaborated with Albert Einstein, and his friends Alexander Moszkowski, Max Born, Erwin Freundlich and Hendrik Antoon Lorentz to promote and sensationalize contrived reports that eclipse observations had confirmed Einstein's prediction. The astronomers had attempted to photograph stars which could be seen near the edge of the Sun during a full eclipse. The images of these stars might indicate that the path of the rays of light coming from stars behind the Sun had curved when passing near the Sun, thereby displacing the images of the stars from the position they would otherwise have had on the pictures, had not the gravitational field of the sun altered the path of light coming from the stars behind the Sun. Johann Georg von Soldner (in 1801) and Albert Einstein (in late 1915) predicted that the deflection would be twice the amount the Newtonian theory of gravitation predicted. This factor of two distinguished their theories from Newton's. Though it was Newton who first predicted the effect, and it was Soldner who first correctly predicted the amount of the deflection for light rays, it was Einstein who took credit for both predictions.

Dyson, Davidson, Eddington and Einstein misrepresented the photographic evidence, which was of poor quality and, therefore, inconclusive. They falsely claimed that the photographs taken during eclipse of the Sun proved not only that the deflection of light had occurred, but that it was twice the Newtonian value, in accord with Einsteinian (Soldnerian) theory. However, this is not what the photographs had shown, and it is doubtful that the photographs could in any case have been conclusive. The effect was exceedingly small and the equipment the astronomers employed was primitive and did not have the precision needed to accurately record the predicted effect.

The press promoted these falsified reports and told the general public that Newtonian theory had been overthrown and that Einstein was a great genius, who was at least the equal of Copernicus, Kepler, Galileo and Newton. Newspapers asserted that Einstein had introduced a new world view, one that was true no matter how strange it appeared to be, with its "warped space-time", "hundred foot poles in fifty foot barns", and other "paradoxes". The press reported that Einstein's unique insight was so sophisticated and enlightened that only twelve men in the world could understand it. Reporters told the people of the world that a dramatic revolution in science had taken place—though this magnificent and unprecedented revolution, so deserving of international attention and praise, had changed nothing in their lives and they had no need, nor reason, to try to understand it.

The sensational reports created a mass hysteria for Einstein in America, one which culminated in Einstein's visit to the United States in the spring of 1921. Einstein's trip came shortly after Einstein had endured a series of public humiliations in the scientific community in Germany in 1920. He was hiding from the German scientists who had informed the public that he was a fraud. Whenever Einstein faced overwhelming problems in Germany, he wisely traveled to other nations, in part for publicity purposes to promote Zionism—which gave him undeserved publicity and paid for his trips—and which gave him the means to hide from his many critics. Einstein went to Spain and to Japan, continually promoting himself by being seen in the company of royalty, heads of state and international celebrities.

In spite of all the humiliating defeats Einstein met in the scientific world, a pro-Einstein press stuck by him and unfairly smeared those who legitimately criticized him. Some of his critics were highly respected Nobel Prize winning physicists, but this did not inhibit the pro-Einstein press from attacking their reputations merely because they had dared to disagree with the racist Zionist Albert Einstein, on purely scientific matters.

1.2.1 Promoting the "Cult" of Einstein

In an epiphany of "Jewish Saint" Einstein, Jewish journalist Alexander Moszkowski wrote to Albert Einstein on 1 February 1917,

> "Regardless of what happens, I would like to continue the 'cult'; for you it is secondary, for me it is of paramount importance in life. Additionally, I have the encouraging feeling that, with my modest writing abilities, I may also serve the cause once in a while."[4]

Moszkowski used his writing talents to make Einstein a superstar. In October of 1919, Moszkowski fulfilled his promise to Einstein to promote the "cult" of Einstein, and began the international "Einstein mania", which peaked in November and December of 1919.

Einstein knew that the newspaper hype was disingenuous and distasteful, but he blamed the public for the hype his racist Jewish friends had manufactured. In mid-December, 1919, Einstein wrote to his friend and confidant Heinrich Zangger,

> "The newspaper drivel about me is pathetic; this kind of exaggeration meets a certain need among the public. Really, a harmless ideology."[5]

On 24 December 1919, Einstein wrote to Zangger and justified the lies as "harmless tomfoolery",

> "[T]his business reminds one of the tale of 'The Emperor's New Clothes,' but it is harmless tomfoolery. [***] The disparity between what you are and what others believe, or at least, say about you, is far too great."[6]

When Albert Einstein's critic physicist Ernst Gehrcke made similar statements, race baiter Einstein called him "anti-Semitic". Zangger received yet another letter from Albert Einstein dated 3 January 1920, in which Einstein stated, among other things,

> "As for me, since the light deflection result became public, such a cult has been made out of me that I feel like a pagan idol."[7]

Again, when Einstein's critic Ernst Gehrcke made similar statements, hypocritical Einstein called him "anti-Semitic".

The press claimed that Einstein was the greatest and most original thinker that the world had ever seen. No one knew better than Einstein himself that the press was deliberately lying to the public. Albert Einstein wrote to Hendrik Antoon Lorentz on 19 January 1920,

> "Nevertheless, unlike you, nature has not bestowed me with the ability to deliver lectures and dispense original ideas virtually effortlessly as meets your refined and versatile mind. [***] This awareness of my limitations pervades me all the more keenly in recent times since I see that my faculties are being quite particularly overrated after a few consequences of the general theory stood the test."[8]

1.2.2 The "Jewish Press" Sanctifies a Fellow Jew

Adapting his title from a poem by Adelbert von Chamisso,[9] Kurt Joël promoted Albert Einstein in the *Vossische Zeitung* morning edition on 29 May 1919.

"Die Sonne bringt es an den Tag?
Eine Himmelsentscheidung in der Relativitätstheorie.

Von
Kurt Joël.

Sonnenfinsternisse sind sicherlich nichts Seltenes. Wiederholt sind in den letzten hundert Jahren wissenschaftliche Expeditionen ausgerüstet worden, um sie zu beobachten und die Ergebnisse dieser Beobachtung zu verarbeiten. Und doch sieht man der Verfinsterung unseres Zentralgestirns, die heute, am 29. Mai, eintritt und 3 Stunden 17 Minuten währt, mit besonderer Spannung entgegen. Nicht etwa wegen der langen Dauer dieser Finsternis, die mit der schmalen Zone ihrer Totalität das nördliche Brasilien und Mittelafrika durchschreitet und zu deren Erforschung von England aus zwei Unternehmungen — die eine mit dem Standort in S o b r a l (Brasilien), die andere nach der Insel I s l a d o P r i n c i p e, etwa 180 Kilometer von der afrikanischen Küste — ausgerüstet worden sind. Nicht bloß die Astronomen, auch Physiker, Mathematiker, selbst Philosophischen harren auf die endgültigen Ergebnisse dieser

Himmelsbeobachtung, da sie mittelbar helfen sollen, eine der wichtigsten neueren physikalischen, ja erkenntnistheoretischen Fragen, die E i n s t e i n s c h e   G r a v i t a t i o n s t h e o r i e, zu beantworten.

Nach der Einsteinschen Relativitätstheorie muß ein Strahl, der von einem Stern aus tangential zur Sonne verläuft, um 1,74" abgelenkt werden und die Ablenkung für andere Sterne umgekehrt proportional diesem Abstand vom Mittelpunkt der Sonne sein. Beeinflußt nun wirklich die Sonne den Lichtstahl und damit die scheinbaren Oerter der Sterne? Diese Frage sollte bereits im August 1914, wo ebenfalls eine Sonnenfinsternis stattfand, entschieden werden, jedoch hat der Krieg die Arbeit der meisten Expeditionen gestört. Welche Entscheidung wird nun der Himmel für Einsteins Theorien bringen?

Schon einmal hat dieser Forscher den Himmel zum Zeugen für die Richtigkeit seiner Theorie angerufen. Es handelte sich um die P e r i h e l b e w e g u n g   d e s   M e r k u r, die bis dahin den Erklärungsversuchen der Physiker und Astronomen getrotzt hatte. Das Perihel (der Punkt der Sonnennähe) erfährt im Sinne der Bewegung des Planeten eine sehr geringe, aber ganz sicher nachgewiesene Bewegung, die in hundert Jahren auf den freilich nicht übermäßigen Betrag von 43 Bogensekunden wächst, sich aber aus den Grundlagen der von Newton begründeten klassischen Mechanik nicht hat ableiten lassen. Der Astronom L e v e r r i e r   hat durch Rechnung gezeigt, daß diese Abweichung der Beobachtung von der Rechnung bei Zugrundelegung der Newtonschen Mechanik nur durch die Annahme unbekannter Massen erklärt werden könne. Aber nach solchen Massen hat man bisher vergeblich gesucht. Da verband Albert Einstein die Gravitation mit seiner Relativitätstheorie; die gewonnenen Bewegungsgleichungen lieferten in ganz überraschender Weise für den Umlauf eines Planeten um die Sonne eine Bewegung des Perihels, die für den Merkur vollständig mit der beobachteten übereinstimmt, während sie bei den entfernteren Planeten einen so geringen Betrag ausmacht, daß sie auch da mit den nicht mit völliger Sicherheit ermittelten kleinen Bewegungen übereinstimmen würde.

Bevor wir uns der hohen wissenschaftlichen Bedeutung der heutigen Sonnenfinsternis zuwenden, wollen wir in wenigen Sätzen das Wesen des Relativitätsprinzips erläutern. Unstreitig sind alle Beobachtungen und Wahrnehmungen relativ, d. h.

abhängig von den Bewegungs- und Geschwindigkeitsunterschieden, die zwischen dem beobachteten Vorgang und dem Beobachter bestehen. Betrachten wir z. B. den freien Fall eines Körpers auf der Erde und nehmen wir an, daß diesen Vorgang einmal jemand beobachtet, der ruhig auf der Erde steht, und das andere Mal jemand, der sich etwa mit 100,000 Kilometer in der Sekunde von der Erde fortbewegt. Dann ist es ohne weiteres klar, daß beide Beobachter verschiedene Fallzeiten und Räume feststellen würden. Einstein hat nun gezeigt, daß eine Zeitangabe niemals etwas Absolutes und für alle Orte in gleicher Weise Zutreffendes ist, sondern nur in Verbindung mit dem Bewegungszustande eines Körpers einen bestimmten Sinn haben kann.

Nachdem er so klargelegt hatte, daß man den Begriff der Zeit und der Länge relativieren, d. h. abhängig von dem Bezugsystem annehmen muß, ist er weiter dazu übergegangen, auf den Zusammenhang zwischen Gravitation und Trägheit im Lichte dieser Relativitätstheorie hinzuweisen. Er veranschaulicht das durch folgende Betrachtungen. Wenn ein irgendwo in der Welt in einem geschlossenen Kasten befindlicher Physiker beobachtete, daß alle sich selbst überlassenen Gegenstände in eine bestimmte Beschleunigung geraten, etwa stets mit konstanter Beschleunigung auf den Boden des Kastens fallen, so könnte er diese Erscheinung auf zwei Arten erklären: Erstens könnte er annehmen, daß sein Kasten auf einem Himmelskörper ruhe, und den Fall der Gegenstände auf dessen Gravitationswirkung zurückführen. Zweitens aber könnte er auch annehmen, daß der Kasten sich mit konstanter Beschleunigung nach „oben" bewegt; dann wäre das Verhalten der „ fallenden" Gegenstände durch ihre Trägheit erklärt. Beide Erklärungen sind genau gleich möglich, jener Physiker hat kein Mittel, zwischen ihnen zu entscheiden. Nimmt man an, daß alle Beschleunigungen relativ sind, daß also ein Unterscheidungsmittel prinzipiell fehlt, so läßt sich dies verallgemeinern: an jedem Punkt des Universums kann man die beobachtete Beschleunigung eines sich selbst überlassenen Körpers entweder als Trägheitswirkung auffassen oder als Gravitationswirkung, d. h. man kann entweder sagen: „das Bezugsystem, von dem aus ich den Vorgang beobachte, ist beschleunigt" oder: „der Vorgang findet in einem Gravitationsfelde statt". Die Identität der trägen und der gravitierenden Masse ist, wie M. Schlick in seinem Schriften „Raum und Zeit in der gegenwärtigen Physik" ausführt, der eigentliche Erfahrungsgrund, der uns erst das Recht gibt zu der Annahme oder der Behauptung, daß die Trägheitswirkungen, die wir an einem Körper beobachten, auf den Einfluß zurückzuführen sind, den er von anderen Körpern erleidet. Einstein ist es nun wirklich gelungen, ein Grundgesetz aufzustellen, das Trägheits- und Gravitationserscheinungen in gleicher Weise umfaßt.

Denken wir wieder an den beschleunigten Kasten und nehmen an, daß er an seiner Seitenwand ein Loch habe. Welchen Weg legt nun ein Lichtstrahl, der senkrecht zur Bewegungsrichtung in den Kasten fällt, gegenüber dem Kasten zurück? In einem gleichförmig bewegten System läuft er geradlinig, in einem beschleunigten System wird ein quer zur Bewegungsrichtung lausender Lichtstrahl demnach zurückbleiben. Sind nun die Gesetze der Schwerefelder wie die bewegter Systeme, so muß auch im Schwerefelde der Lichtstrahl in der Richtung der Schwerkraft aus der geraden Bahn abgelenkt werden. Das folgt aus Einsteins Theorien, und diese Folgerung hat auch der Forscher gezogen. Auf der Erde selbst ist eine solche Messung nicht durchzuführen, da ihr Gravitationsfeld nicht stark genug ist. Wohl aber könnte das Gravitationsfeld der Sonne dazu ausreichen. Das Licht eines Sternes, das sehr nahe an der Sonne vorbeikommt, müßte durch ihr Gravitationsfeld um 1,74" aus seiner Bahn abgelenkt werden. Die Beobachtungen der Astronomen bei der heutigen Sonnenfinsternis — die Sonne ist infolgedessen genügend abgeblendet, um eine Beobachtung des reichen Feldes von Sternen in ihrer Nähe zuzulassen — sollen nun den Beweis erbringen, ob Einsteins Voraussage richtig ist. Damit wäre zugleich eine neue experimentelle Stütze für die Relativitätstheorie geschaffen, die berufen ist, unsere bisherigen Raum- und Zeitbegriffe wesentlich zu beeinflussen."

Carrying on the tradition of the literary tributes paid to Newton in Edmund Halley's *Ode to Newton*,[10] and Voltaire's *Letters Concerning the English Nation*, Alexander Moszkowski promoted the cult of Einstein with a tribute to Albert Einstein in the *Berliner Tageblatt* (which Jewish racist Zionist Theodor Herzl called a "Jewish paper"[11]), Volume 48, Number 476, on 8 October 1919,

"Die Sonne bracht' es an den Tag!

Von

Alexander Moszkowski.

Sie wurde befragt, sie hat Antwort gegeben, und das Echo ihres Orakels wird durch die Jahrhunderte klingen. Wir Menschen von heute stehen dem Ereignis selbst noch zu nahe, als daß wir dessen weitreichende Bedeutung vollkommen ermessen könnten. Aber wir erinnern uns der Ansage des Goetheschen A r i e l :

> Phöbus' Räder rollen prasselnd,
> Welch Getöse bringt das Licht!
> Es trometet, es posaunet,
> Auge blinzt und Ohr erstaunet!

Es wird des Erstaunens kein Ende sein über diese Sonnenbotschaft, die sich an das Zentrum menschlichen Denkens wandte. Wir wollten wissen: Ist die Verfassung der Welt begreiflich? Und Phöbus sprach: Sie ist es, ist dem menschlichen Verstand zugänglich, wenn die neue allgemeine Relativitätslehre E i n s t e i n s aller Betrachtung zugrunde gelegt wird.

Am 29. Mai dieses Jahres wurde die Sonne zur Zeit einer totalen Bedeckung befragt. Ihre Antwort bestand zunächst nur in einigen Lichtpunkten auf photographischen Platten. Aber in diesen Punkten lag die Erklärung des Geheimnisses beschlossen. Es bedurfte noch allerfeinster Messungen, um diese Punktierschrift in eine gültige physikalische Erklärung zu übersetzen. Zwei englische Expeditionen, nach Brasilien und nach Innerafrika, hatten es übernommen, dies zu entwickeln, zu messen und auszudeuten. Vor wenigen Tagen traf die Bestätigung ein: Die Lichtbotschaft steht in v o l l s t e m E i n k l a n g mit der Annahme jenes Weltsystems, wie es von E i n s t e i n s Lehre gefordert wird. Und diese selbst, aus Gedankenexperimenten entsprossen, ist nunmehr auch durch das sinnlich erfaßbare, astronomische Experiment unerschütterlich bewiesen.

Nur mit wenigen Worten sei das Wesen dieses Experimentes andeutungsweise erläutert. Nach Einstein begeben sich die kosmischen Ereignisse in einer vierdimensionalen Raumzeitwelt, innerhalb deren die Newtonsche Bewegungslehre der Himmelskörper nur eine Annäherung darstellt. Zur Erfassung der allgemeinen Vorgänge bedarf es der Einführung einer Ueber-Euklidischen Geometrie, deren Ermittelung von „Weltlinien" im Raumzeitlichen und der Aufgabe jeder Fernwirkung, deren Annahme eigentlich dem menschlichen Denken widerspricht. Die zuerst so verwirrende, mathematisch verwickelte und deshalb überaus schwierige Lehre verwandelt sich, je mehr man in sie eindringt, in die denkbar lichtvollste V e r e i n f a c h u n g des gesamten Weltbildes, in eine wirklich restlose Erfassung der letzten kosmischen Fragen.

Schon einmal hatte diese Lehre in einem früheren Stadium ihrer Entwicklung eine sichtbare Kreuzprobe bestanden, damals, als es ihr gelang, gewisse, sonst ganz unerklärliche Anomalien in der Bahn des Planeten Merkur als durchaus normal und mit der Berechnung übereinstimmend zu erweisen. Aber hinter dieser Kreuzprobe stand eine zweite, die den Lichtstrahl selbst auf seiner Wanderung durch die Welt verfolgen sollte. Eine Ungeheuerlichkeit tat sich auf: Bestand diese Lehre zu Recht, dann mußte sich in sehr starken Gravitationsfeldern — also etwa beim Durchgang in Sonnennähe — eine merkliche K r ü m m u n g der Lichtstrahlen herausstellen. Und eben hierauf waren die Anstrengungen der beiden englischen Expeditionen gerichtet. Es galt die A b b i e g u n g der Lichtstrahlen zu erweisen, die, von Fixsternen ausgesendet, an der verdunkelten Sonne vorbeistreichen, um unser Auge oder — experimentell sicherer — die photographische Platte zu erreichen. Fand diese Abbiegung wirklich statt, so mußte sich dies dadurch offenbaren, daß auf der Platte die Sterne weiter auseinanderstanden, als man nach ihrer wirklichen Position erwarten konnte.

Um wieviel wohl? Die Berechnung verlangte unglaubliche Feinheiten des Ausmaßes. Man stelle sich den ganzen Himmelsbogen vor, in Grade eingeteilt: dann ergibt eine Mondbreite etwa einen halben Grad. Hiervon der dreißigste Teil, eine Bogenminute, ist noch gut vorstellbar. Aber hiervon wiederum der sechzigste Teil, die Bogensekunde, entzieht sich nahezu aller sinnlichen Erfaßbarkeit. Und auf dieses Kleinmaß kam es an: denn die in reiner Gedankenarbeit entwickelte Theorie sagte eine Ablenkung von ein und sieben Zehntel Bogensekunde an. So stand diese Größenordnung auf dem Papier, vorläufig ohne Bewahrheitung durch astronomische Praxis, aber festverankert in einem System unheimlicher

Gleichungen, die in ihrer Gesamtheit die wahre Ordnung des bewegten Universums verkündigen.

Wirklich, es war etwas viel verlangt von den fernen Welten, denen nunmehr ein blinkendes Zeugnis abverlangt wurde. Sie hatten sich zur Zeit einer totalen Sonnenfinsternis so rundum zu gruppieren, daß sie eben noch leuchtende Lichtpünktchen entwarfen, deren Stellung mit Ja und Nein für die vorausberechnete Größenordnung einstehen sollte. Und zwar mit einem Zeugnis, das im Bejahungsfall eine durch Jahrtausende überlieferte Grundanschauung des Menschenhirns überwältigte.

Wie denn? Ein Sternstrahl soll krumm werden können? Widerstreitet daß nicht dem Elementarbegriff der geraden, der kürzesten Linie, für die wir ja keine anschaulichere Vorstellung besitzen, als eben im Strahl? Hatte doch Leonardo da Vinci die Gerade direkt so definiert, so benannt als die „*linea radiosa*"!

Aber für diese vermeintliche Selbstverständlichkeit ist in der vom Forschergeist Einsteins durchstrahlten Welt kein Platz mehr. Die am 29. Mai befragte Konstellation hat die Entscheidung geliefert. Mehr als ein Vierteljahr hat es gedauert, ehe die Punktrunen genügend entziffert waren. Jetzt ist die Bestätigung eingetroffen: die Sternstrahlen werden tatsächlich im Schwerefelde der Sonne abgelenkt, sie zeigen eine Krümmung mit der Hohlseite zur Sonne gewendet, so daß sich der scheinbare Abstand der geprüften Sterne vergrößert: und dies innerhalb gewisser Beobachtungsgrenzen, die Einsteins vorausgesagter Größenordnung entsprechen. Was nur dann möglich ist, wenn das Fundamentalgerüst Einsteins, die allgemeine Relativitätstheorie, als die wahre Verfassung des Universums angesprochen wird.

Galt dies dem mathematischen Denker, dem strengen Physiker schon vorher als Gewißheit, so wird fortan auch für den Erkenntnistheoretiker der letzte Zweifel die letzte Zuflucht zu räumen haben. Ja, man darf voraussagen, daß der größte Gewinn aus der jetzt völlig sichergestellten Einsicht dereinst dem Philosophen zufallen wird, der darauf ausgeht erkenntnistheoretisch das allereinfachste, mit allen Beobachtungstatsachen restlos harmonierende Weltbild zu entwerfen. Er wird auf Kant fußend, aber über Kant hinauswachsend die Idealformen der Anschauung in Raum und Zeit erhöhen und emporläutern zum vierdimensionalen Ordnungsschema, in welchem der letzte Restsinnlicher Schlacke

abzufallen hat vor der reinen Erkenntnis des wahren raumzeitlichen Weltgefüges. Wenn dereinst ein bestimmter
Augenblick bezeichnet werden soll als historisches Zeichnen für
die große Wandlung in menschlicher Anschauung gegenüber
dem Universum, so wird manch einer den zuvor genannten Tag
als das deutlichste Merkdatum wählen. Und wenn er ihn nennt,
so wird er hinzufügen, daß eine letzte Wahrheit entschleierbar
war über Galilei und Newton, über Kant hinaus, bestätigt durch
einen Orakelspruch aus der Tiefe des Himmels, in lesbarer
Strahlschrift. Das Uebereinstimmen einer Menschenforschung
mit der Wirklichkeit des Weltgeschehens — *„Die Sonne bracht'*
es an den Tag!"'"

Shortly after this article appeared, Heinrich Zangger wrote to Albert
Einstein on 22 October 1919,

"I already filled the official's heads with the bent light, years
ago.—Proclaimed Galileo-Newton-Einstein—so if you want the
appointment, or keep it, resp., it would be a joy to all."[12]

Friedrich Karl Wiebe[13] alleged in 1939, that the press in post-World
War One Germany, and with it public opinion, was largely controlled by
traitorous Jews who cheapened the medium with sensationalism—by
Jews who allegedly only cared about Jewish interests and who would
pursue those perceived self-interests at the expense of other Germans.
Jews have long been noted for making judgments based on selfish
interests to the exclusion of broader societal interests, or pure principles,
or a sense of fairness, as is typified by the common racist Jewish
expression, "Is it good for the Jews?"

Though Wiebe only incidentally mentions the publisher Julius
Springer, a man who was very influential in promoting Einstein and who
sought to discredit Einstein's critics, Wiebe does name the publishing
house of the Jewish brothers Ullstein, and the publishing house of the
"Eastern Jew" Rudolf Mosse. Wiebe states that the *Berliner
Morgenpost*, which he alleged had the largest circulation of any German
newspaper, was controlled by Jews, as was the politically influential
Vossische Zeitung, under editor-in-chief Geog Bernhard. The *Berliner
Tageblatt*, which served as spokesman for Germany abroad and was
often quoted in America and England, was led by editor-in-chief
Theodor Wolff, and the *Acht-Uhr-Abendblatt* also had a Jewish chief
editor. One might, together with Theodor Herzl,[14] add the *Frankfurter*

Zeitung to the list of "Jewish newspapers". Many of these papers promoted Einstein and personally attacked his critics. Wiebe alleged that Jews ran the *Reichverband der Deutschen Presse* and the *Verein Berliner Presse*. Wiebe names Georg Bernhard, Theodor Wolff and Maximilian Harden as Jews who had "stabbed Germany in the back" following World War One. He noted that historian Friedrich Thimme dubbed Harden, "the Judas of the German people". Harden was a politically active Zionist Jew.[15]

Germany had been very good to the Jews. German Jews were the wealthiest people in the world. In the years following the First World War, the Germans resented the fact that the Jews, Einstein being their chief spokesman, had stabbed the Germans in the back during the war, and then twisted the knife at the peace negotiations in France, where a large contingent of Jews decided Germany's fate, and reneged on Woodrow Wilson's Fourteen Points, one of which assured Germany that it would lose no territory. The Germans had thought that Wilson's pledge would be honored after the Germans had surrendered in good faith. Had not the Germans received this promise of the Fourteen Points, they would not have surrendered and were in a position to continue the war. The promise was broken by Jews and their agents.

In addition, the Allies insisted that Germany pay draconian war reparations that would forever ruin the nation. Leading Jews in Germany sided with the Allies against their native land. It was obvious that leading Jews were profiteering from the war in every way possible, at the expense of the German nation and its People. Jewish leaders instigated crippling strikes in the arms industry, which left German troops without adequate armaments. Jewish revolutionaries took advantage of Germany's weakened state, which Jews had deliberately caused for the purpose, and created a Soviet Republic in Bavaria and overthrew the monarchy. Civil war and revolutions were always a Jewish strategy to turn Gentile brother against brother (*Judges* 7:22. *Haggai* 2:22). German-Jewish bankers cut off Germany's access to funds. German-Jewish Zionists moved to London and brought America into the war on the side of the British at the very moment Germany was about to win the war. Those arms which were produced were often substandard and were peddled by Jews to Jews in the German Government, which also left the German troops without adequate arms, while making Jews immensely wealthy. German-Jewish bankers conspired with German arms manufacturers to produce weapons for both sides. The German-Jewish press, which had initially beat the war drums louder than anyone else, teamed up with leading Jews in the German

Government at the end of the war and demanded that Germa,
to the demands of the Allies, give up vast territories and m.
reparations payments. The German-Jewish press and Jews in
German Government, many of whom were the same persons who h.
most boisterously called upon the German People to go to war, insisted
that the Germans accept responsibility for causing the war, though they
had not caused it. Etc. Etc. Etc.

While millions of Germans were starving to death, top Jews in
Germany had never known better times. Whenever anyone revealed the
truth of what was happening, the Jewish press immediately smeared
them by calling them "anti-Semites". The situation was similar to,
though even worse than, the situation in America today.

In 1933, the Jews Abraham Myerson and Isaac Goldberg alleged
many of the same facts Wiebe would later allege, though they offered an
entirely different perspective on the same issues. Myerson and Goldberg
wrote, in 1933, in their book, *The German Jew: His Share in Modern
Culture*,

> "The circles of criticism and of journalism in Germany were,
> up to the incursions of Hitler, predominantly Jewish. Julius Bab,
> Alfred Kerr, Fritz Engel, Felix Holländer, Felix Salten (author
> of *Bambi*), Siegmund Freund, Emil Faktor. . . the roster is long;
> nor have we mentioned critics from the professorial fold, such as
> Richard M. Meyer.
>
> Publishing in Germany has largely been built up by a Jewish
> passion for commercial pursuits that parallels the passion of
> intellect so freely evidenced in the Jew. Through such powerful
> interests as those of the Lachmann-Mosse family and the estate
> of Leopold Ullstein, the largest publishing firm in Germany, the
> press and the magazine world have been controlled by German
> Jews. Before it was 'coordinated' into the Nationalist régime, the
> house of Ullstein employed almost eight thousand persons, and
> issued almost a hundred newspapers and periodicals. Ullstein
> (1826-99) passed the fast-growing business on to five
> industrious sons.
>
> Rudolph Mosse (1843-1920) founded the *Berliner Tageblatt*
> in 1872. It was, until the descent of Hitler upon the Jews, one of
> the great newspapers of the world, known to all journalists as a
> palladium of liberalism. . . . Naturally, although these
> newspapers and their allied interests employed a host of Gentile
> workers, there were countless Jews in their offices. Among

ist Calling 19
ny submit
ke the
the

alistic powers were to be found such gifted
imilian Harden and Theodor Wolff. The
hat the Jewish mind, for reasons that have
other artistic and literary pursuits, engages
lism and criticism. Even so anti-Semitic a
ܒ.. ܕ।eurich von Oppeln-Bronowski has been quoted as
blaming, not the Jews, but the inertia of his fellow-Germans.
'The outcry of the conservative press against the literary
incursions of the Jew reminds me of the clamour raised by the
inferior business man against his more clever, ' unfair'
competitor. Instead of making complaint, it had better improve
itself. If it is true that the Jews have assumed so disproportionate
a role in journalism, we can undoubtedly connect the fact with
their exclusion under the old régime from the higher
governmental positions.' [*Footnote:* See I. E. Poritzky: 'The Jew
in the Intellectual Life of Germany,' *Menorah Journal*, Vol. XII,
No. 6 (1926). I refer to this article those who are in search of
many Jewish names.]

In book-publishing the Jew has become a power in Germany
since 1910. It is interesting to observe that at about this same
time the Jew in the United States was entering upon a
distinguished career in the publication of belles-lettres. In
Germany the house of S. Fischer, founded in 1886, may stand
for a quasi-hegemony that includes such important firms as Drei
Masken, Bruno Cassirer, Kurt Wolff, Paul Zsolnay, Felix Bloch
Erben, and Oesterheld & Company.

Incidentally, the famous Universal Edition, Vienna, publisher
of modernist scores, though by no means confining itself to the
musical advance guard, is presided over by Dr. Alfred Kalmus.

One can, therefore, understand the exaggerated outcry of
Herr Bartels—though hardly sympathize with his bigoted
implications—when, after descanting upon the prominence of
Jews in the art and the business of letters, he is suddenly led to
exclaim: 'There is no doubt that on the eve of the war our entire
German life was no longer German in temper.' The situation, to
him, appeared so critical that, instead of commending the
universality of outlook displayed by all these Jewish
publishers—can it be only a commercial accident that the Jewish
firms in other countries display a like interest in publishing
works of international spirit and origin?—Bartels hinted at some
sort of apostasy on the part of those Gentile writers who allowed

themselves to be published by Jews. These leading publishers were not only providers of books; at times they were the supporters of movements.

It is only half metaphorical to declare that, whether in the higher reaches of literature or in the forum of journalism, the German Jew has mingled his blood with printer's ink in the service of German culture. The cruelty of a régime may hold the Jew at once excommunicated and incommunicado; not by fiat, not by a conflagration of books, can it exterminate the past. Books burn; men burn; passions and ideas are immortal."[16]

With Einstein's blessing, the Jewish litterateur Alexander Moszkowski published a sensationalistic and hagiographic book, which advertised Einstein to the public in an unprecedented and shameless way: *Einstein Einblicke in seine Gedankenwelt Gemeinverständliche Betrachtungen über die Relativitätstheorie und ein neues Weltsystem Entwickelt aus Gesprächen mit Einstein*, Hoffman und Campe, Hamburg, (1921); in English translation, *Einstein: The Searcher*, E. P. Dutton, New York, (1921). This book recorded Moszkowski's self-aggrandizing conversations with Einstein, and presented Einstein to the public as if he were a god condescending to speak to mere mortals.

The public was vulnerable to such hype. Heike Kamerlingh Onnes wrote to Albert Einstein on 8 February 1920, as if Einstein were the law giver Moses,

"In my imagination I can already see you at our university's venerable rostrum that was born of the struggle for freedom of conscience,[2] smiling down at us and telling us about your communion with the gods and about the fine interplay of harmony by which hints of Nature's laws are revealed, your kind eyes sparkling with delight!"[17]

Though Jewish litterateurs were infamous for overrating Spinoza's philosophy, Mendelssohn's music, Marx's and Lasalle's political philosophies, Theodor Lessing's *Nathan der Weise*, Bergson's philosophy, etc.; that shameless self-glorification did not begin to approach the magnitude and the absurdity of the promotion of the Jewish racist Albert Einstein. Many leading scientists found such unprecedented advertising for Einstein distasteful. In 1924, Ernst Gehrcke preserved conclusive evidence that Moszkowski's book was promoted in the daily newspapers as part of an overall plan to promote Albert Einstein to the gullible public through an intensive advertising.[18]

As revealed in their letters to Albert Einstein,[19] the Jewish physicist Max Born and his Jewish wife Hedwig knew that this unprecedented and tasteless self-promotion would occur and that it would vindicate Einstein's critics. The Borns, who were apostate Jews, went to the extremes of threatening Einstein in order to prevent the publication of Moszkowski's book. Max Born even requested permission from Einstein to sue Moszkowski in order to block the publication of his book. The Borns had experience with Moszkowski in the past, and they knew that he would shamelessly hype Einstein for personal profit—profits the Borns wanted all to themselves. The Borns knew that Moszkowski's book would serve as proof for the outspoken Einstein critics Paul Weyland, Ernst Gehrcke and Philipp Lenard that Einstein was shamelessly advertising himself to the public. The Borns, who were peddling a book of their own, *Einstein's Theory of Relativity*,[20] and who were themselves seeking to profiteer off of the Einstein brand, failed in their efforts to prevent the release of Moszkowski's work.

The press and elements of the Physics community did indeed create an "Einstein 'brand'" which has lasted. Peter Rogers, editor of *Physics World*, stated in his editorial in the August, 2004, issue of *Physics World*,

"His legacy as the greatest physicist of all time is guaranteed, despite the regular claims that 'Einstein was wrong' or that he stole his ideas from someone else. The real opportunity presented by 2005 is the chance to sell Einstein and physics to the young. Physicists have to realize that physics needs the 'outside world' more than it needs physics. [***] Physics as a subject is lucky in having Einstein as a 'brand'[.]"[21]

Rodgers wrote, in September of 2003,

"[. . .]Einstein developed the special theory of relativity in 1905. This potted history is true, of course, but it overlooks the contributions of Poincare and Lorentz. However, if every article had to give full credit for every advance in the history of physics, there would be little room for what is going on today."[22]

Rodgers also stated, in November of 2003,

"Fabrication,   plagiarism   and   a   range   of   other offences—duplicate submissions, conflicts of interest and referee misconduct—were among the topics discussed at a recent workshop on scientific misconduct [***] Failure to cite the work of others adequately is also an offence [***] [J]ust one more major case of fabrication or plagiarism would be very bad news for our subject."[23]

The Einstein brand was already established and used to market products in January of 1920, shortly after the press hyped Einstein and the theory of relativity in November and December of 1919. Alexander Eliasberg, a Jew who wore his Jewishness on his sleeve, wrote to Albert Einstein on 27 January 1920,

"This new type of monthly, which will serve a very large readership, is characterized by its emphasis on the sciences—of which your illustrious name serves as a symbol[.]"[24]

In letter to Albert Einstein, Paul Epstein described Alexander Eliasberg, who was Epstein's cousin, in the following terms, in the hopes that it would impress the Jewish racist and segregationist Albert Einstein,

"Eliasberg is a Jew of nationalistic bent, who stresses his Jewishness at every opportunity that presents itself. His name is emblazoned on the cover of the Jewish monthly *Jüdische Monatshefte*; furthermore, he has published a library's worth of translations from Yiddish."[25]

The Borns had a vested interest in maintaining the "Einstein myth". Einstein, himself, wrote,

"There you [Max Born] are, giving relativity lectures to stave off bankruptcy of the institute[.]"[26]

Hedwig Born's father delighted in the attention paid to Einstein in the press, because it made him proud as a Jew and as a German to see the world's scientists bow down to Einstein. Viktor G. Ehrenberg, Hedwig's father, wrote to Einstein on 23 November 1919,

"So it uplifts the heart and strengthens one's faith in the future of mankind when one sees the researchers of all nations prostrating themselves before a man of Jewish blood, who thinks and writes in the German language, in full recognition of his greatness."[27]

Paul Oppenheim also took pride in the fact that a Jew and a German was receiving a great deal of positive public attention. He wrote Albert Einstein,

"The purpose of these lines is to congratulate you from the bottom of my heart and to express quite artlessly the pure joy that we have such a man among 'us'—in the double sense."[28]

Alexander Moszkowski was a Jewish litterateur and journalist. It had often been alleged that Jews were guilty of self-advertisement, sought to control professorships in Germany and dominate entire fields of research through corrupt means, and that there was alliance between literary and journalistic Jews—like Moszkowski—and professors—like Einstein—to market themselves to the public. For example, the primary exponent of the modern racial anti-Jewish sentiments that evolved among Hegelian revolutionaries, Zionists, Socialists and Communists in the Eighteenth and Nineteenth Centuries;[29] Eugen Karl Dühring wrote in the 1880's, decades before Moszkowski published his hagiographic book sanctifying Einstein:

"The harmony of professors and Jews is characteristic for both parts. Incidentally, the Jews also press industriously towards university professorships; for they know that there is in this sphere something corrupt to capitalise on. Ruin allures them here too, as everywhere. In turn, the professors make use of the Jews to let the rotten structure be displayed through bold advertisement as a most highly upright and strong one. They even flirt with the literary Jews and flatter them already so that the latter may, through their press and their journals, give to the little professorial authority the varnish which these people appointed to the lectern need very much indeed. The Jews for their part, however, make a business once again through this habilitation in society. In this way they exploit for themselves not only the parties but also one of the most important branches of administration in which they become most harmful, namely that of higher education. [***] But the Germans would, however, indeed not like to forget, in the long run, their ancient forests in which they settled affairs with the Romans, to dutifully let Sinai and the Jewish blood rule. They have too much organic politics of action, and the politics of the Jews consists always only of one thing, namely of the advertisement for their people. This has revealed itself even in Messieurs Gambetta and Disraeli. [***] If the Jews in the newspapers cannot push any longer for the bad products of their people and of their comrades into the advertisement-organs and, at the same time, silence the good and suppress it through distortion, the Jewish or judaised literature will no longer appear anywhere with its wretchedness. It must, as an artificial product of the Jewish advertisement, fall into nothing, if the support of this insolent Jewish advertisement is removed which, where it suits it, raises the most inadequate daily publication to the heavens. Such Jewish advertisement manages to proclaim a subordinate Jewish litterateur or parliamentarian as a great publicist or politician, who exercises a most decisive influence on the development of at least an entire field if not indeed of the entire culture. In general, all other advertisements are strongly affected if the newspaper Jews do not have them any longer in their hands. What sort of advertisement has not been made by the latter in the newspapers, for example, for the most recent German legislation procedure of Jewish stamp, and how these press-Jews have glorified everything to the public before its introduction and, afterwards, when everybody could grasp tangibly its uselessnesses, extenuated it according to their ability! If the newspaper power remains a Jewish power, then in literature and politics, indeed even in the actual science, the most shameless advertisement is made for everything which emerges either from the Jews themselves or from those who side with the Jews, thus from actual Jewish comrades. On the contrary, the really preferable and in general everything good and honorable—to which the Jews already have an aversion from inherited instinct even when it does not have the least to do with pro or con in relation to the Jews—is basically and in an artificial way thrown aside. That however which produced from the character of the modern peoples and so is an especial honour for the nations is in every case devalued where it cannot be silenced. If the nations therefore wish that among them a public word may still be possible for the appropriate evaluation of their best people, they must free themselves from the Jewish press."[30]

Dühring gave his accounts credence by citing Jewish British Prime Minister Benjamin Disraeli, who knew in 1844 that the European revolutions of 1848 were about to occur under Jewish leadership. Disraeli wrote,

"'You never observe a great intellectual movement in Europe in which the Jews do not greatly participate. The first Jesuits were Jews; that mysterious Russian Diplomacy which so alarms Western Europe is organized and principally carried on by Jews; that mighty revolution which is at this moment preparing in Germany, and which will be, in fact, a second and greater Reformation, and of which so little is as yet known in England, is entirely developing under the auspices of Jews, who almost monopolize the professorial chairs of Germany. Neander the founder of Spiritual Christianity, and who is Regius Professor of Divinity in the University of Berlin, is a Jew. Benary, equally famous, and in the same University, is a Jew. Wehl, the Arabic Professor of Heidelberg, is a Jew. Years ago, when I was in Palestine, I met a German student who was accumulating materials for the History of Christianity, and studying the genius of the place; a modest and learned man. It was Wehl; then unknown, since become the first Arabic scholar of the day, and the author of the life of Mahomet. But for the German professors of this race, their name is Legion. I think there are more than ten at Berlin alone.[']"[31]

Einstein's correspondence is filled with discussions about professorships and other positions of influence—as one would expect from a very well-connected professor, regardless of his or her ethnic origin. However, Einstein, who was a racist Zionist, stated that he preferred Jews for his friends and he also stated that he considered all Jews to be his brothers.[32]

Stephen G. Bloom wrote in his book *Postville: A Clash of Cultures in Heartland America,*

"Yet despite the lack of Jewish worship and observance, and my family's total assimilation into everything American and secular, we were thoroughly Jewish. Our perspective was Jewish, as was our very essence. The world was split into two distinct halves: Jews and gentiles. Jews were always sought in business or social dealings over gentiles. A common expression used by Jews to describe a slow, dense person was—and still is—'He's got a *goyisher kop*,' which literally means 'He's got a gentile head' but figuratively means 'slow-witted.' First question when I came home and boasted of making a new friend always was 'Is he Jewish?' 'God forbid!' (my father's expression) if I should ever go out with a gentile girl, and *'Oy vey!'* (which literally means 'Oh pain!') if I ever got serious with her. All my parents' friends were Jews. They all shared the same role models: Sandy Koufax, Bernard Baruch, Bess Meyerson, Sam Levinson, Hank Greenberg, Arthur Goldberg, Golda Meir, Albert Einstein—these were people to be admired. And that poet with the beard, Allen Ginsberg, so smart, but the *faygeleh* (homosexual) business, such a waste!"[33]

In 1930, some German Jews recognized the danger of Zionist racism and demanded that Albert Einstein stop using his scientific fame to promote racism, disloyalty and "interracial" strife. *The New York Times* reported on 7 December 1930 on page 11,

"The National German-Jewish Union, a small group of extreme nationalist and anti-Zionist Jews, protested against Professor Einstein using his world-fame as a scientist for 'propagating Zionism.'"

After the Second World War, some Jews again criticized Einstein for his nationalistic Zionism. Einstein responded,

"In my opinion condemning the Zionist movement as 'nationalistic' is unjustified. [***] Thus already our precarious situation forces us to stand together irrespective of our citizenship."[34]

Einstein believed that "affirmative action" was needed and justified to balance the discrimination Jews allegedly faced in Europe. He was especially concerned that a "Jewish university" be founded in Palestine to provide an opportunity for higher education to the Jews of Eastern Europe. Einstein and his friends attempted to fill universities, and the editorial staff of publications, with Jewish professors and lecturers who would be agreeable to his personal scientific and political views. Einstein agreed with Dühring that "Jews" exercised an undue influence in the press and Einstein stated that relativity theory was advertised, or rejected, in the press based on political bias. Leading Jews in the press and at the universities had organized to silence Dühring and to destroy his career. They did the same to composer Richard Wagner. The campaign to muzzle Dühring only legitimized Dühring's beliefs and fueled him on to publish several very influential works against Jews.

1.3 In a Racist Era

There was a panic in the western world following the violent Bolshevik Revolution in Russia in 1917. *The New York Times* in the late teens and early twenties published numerous articles warning of the dangers of Bolshevism. Many conservative German newspapers also tried to rouse public apprehensions over the dangers of the Communist revolution and Einstein was widely seen as an anarchist and a Communist.[35] Max Born wrote, "Einstein was well known to be politically left-wing, if not 'red'."[36] Einstein put his name to Communist and Socialist causes and both groups actively sought his support, with varying degrees of success.[37] When Einstein wanted to visit the United States in the early 1930's many protested against his admission into the country on the grounds that he was a Communist, an anarchist and a Socialist. *The New York Times*, on 4 December 1932, on the front page, stated,

> "The board of the National Patriotic Council in a statement today termed Dr. Einstein 'a German Bolshevik' and said his original theory 'was of no scientific value or purpose, not understandable because there was nothing there to understand.'"

The Patriot of 22 December 1932 published an article "The Visa of Professor Einstein" detailing the objections raised to the granting of a visa to Albert Einstein,

> "Professor Einstein has informed the world, through the Press, of his difficulty in getting an American visa in Berlin, owing to the U. S. Consul having been warned that he is an undesirable alien by the American Women's Patriotic Association. In the end the professor got his visa, and chuckled over the fact that the sentries of America had not given heed to 'the wise, patriotic ladies,' but had forgotten the occasion when 'the Capitol of mighty Rome was once saved by the cackling of its faithful geese.' The fact is that the patriotic American women had as substantial a reason for giving warning as had the Roman geese.

The Patriot has given many instances in which Americans had as much right to object to the meddling of Professor Einstein in revolutionary movements on his visits to the U. S. as we have to protest against the Bolshevik finger in the preparation of revolution by British Communists."[38]

The *Patriot* article continued with extracts from the law and from the charges, which proved that Einstein was a member of several Communist front organizations and encouraged illegal activities, and that he could not be lawfully admitted into the United States of America. Einstein had influential friends and his record was ignored. The protests that he should not be allowed a visa to come to the United States were ultimately unsuccessful.[39] Einstein expressed himself in Marxist terms and his friends as well as his foes recognized the Socialistic tones in his statements in the early 1920's.[40] In 1949, Einstein published an article in the *Monthly Review* in which he advocated Socialism.[41] Since both world wars weakened the nations of the world, both wars created an atmosphere where Communism could flourish.

There were vocal advocates of anarchism, Communism, and Socialism in many Jewish communities. Many such individuals were romantic, very good-natured humanitarian people who sought social justice for the poor, and we today enjoy many benefits from their sacrifices. Others were mere opportunists who used Communism as a front to promote themselves into positions of dictatorial power. Perhaps most outside of Bolshevik dominated countries were not the murderous material that the genocidal tyrants Lenin and Stalin were. However, in many circles all Communists were seen as dangerous propagandists for imposed atheism, murderous revolution and a conspiracy to rule the world in a unified reign of tyranny led by the Jews.

There certainly were Communist elements in the world striving for the horrific goals of imposed atheism, murderous revolution and a conspiracy to rule the world by a "proletariat" which was in reality an obedient army of the subjugated. Mass murderers like Vladimir Ilyich Lenin, Béla Kun, Joseph Stalin and Mao Tse-Tung, did the biding of Jewish financiers who placed them in power to ruin Gentile nations, destroy Gentile religions and capture Gentile wealth. These assertions will be proven further on in this text. These were murderers whom Einstein admired for their political savvy, while disagreeing with some of their ideals.[42] Though the lower level Communists can be forgiven as deceived Utopian idealists, the upper levels Jews who financed and directed them were out to fulfill horrific Jewish prophecies, and the childish ideals of Communism were but bait in a vile trap. The worst of the Communists were those directly under the control of Jewish bankers, the openly genocidal Bolsheviks who had already slain tens of millions of Slavic Christians by the early 1920's. Einstein wrote to Hedwig and Max Born on 27 January 1920 that he found the Bolshevists not unappealing.[43]

Bolshevik atrocities shocked the free world. The Bolsheviks mass murdered tens of millions of innocent people and criminalized Christianity. The Bolsheviks were conspicuously and predominantly led and financed by Jews. Many have tied the dogmatism and cruelty of Communism to the dogmatism and cruelty of Judaism. The primitive and dogmatic dictator cults of personality, which are common to Communist régimes, mirror obeisance to a vengeful and jealous Jewish God and the ascendence of the Jewish King as the Messiah.

Jews have been praying for thousands of years for a Jewish Messiah to arrive and wipe out the Gentile nations, religions, cultures, and, eventually, peoples. The fact that leading Jews were accomplishing these Jewish Messianic ends through Communism concerned many people around the world. Just as the Jewish religion asserts that there can only be one God to rule the universe, the Jews have chosen themselves to rule over mankind and to destroy it. The relevant religious passages which evince these facts will be quoted later on in this text. When responsible persons voiced their legitimate concerns about Jewish Bolshevik destruction, they were often smeared in the Jewish press around the world as if "anti-Semites".

Some argue that Jews in general have an indoctrinated tendency to stifle progress and restrict disputes to dogmatism. This is an effect of Judaism, which demands obedience to an arbitrary and absolute law. One cannot speak out against, or argue with, the one true God, or with those chosen to represent him and chosen to kill off the unchosen. Some, including Eugen Karl Dühring, Friedrich Nietzsche and Houston Stewart Chamberlain, have argued that Judaism is a slavish religion which inhibits human creativity. The ancient religion has little respect for personal choice and places in its stead absolute obedience to God and to God's laws, and to God's chosen people. Since Judaism is more political than it is religious, the effects of this authoritarianism lingered even in the writings of many German Jews who were supposedly atheists, including Karl Marx, Moses Hess and Ferdinand Lasalle.

This same charge was also made by philo-Semites like the famous cultural Zionist Ha'am. Ha'am wrote of the Jews as a slavish "people of the book" who suffered under the "long-standing disease" of the "tyranny of the written word" which forbade individual thought for the sake of absolute obedience to arbitrary dogmatic laws.[44] Chaim Nachman Bialik's speech at the opening of the"Hebrew University" provides us with a good example of the religious zealotry and of the dogmatic and intolerant worship of the Torah and Talmud of some Jews—probably a very small percentage of Jews today.[45] Jewish children learn Hebrew and Judaism through a process of mindless repetition, which inhibits their ability to reason and think independently. Jewish leaders are often arrogant, absolutist, intolerant and dogmatic. In 1944, David Ben-Gurion cried out "for absolute allegiance to the Jewish revolution", which he defined in the Messianic terms of *the complete ingathering of the exiles into a socialist Jewish state.*[46] Ben-Gurion believed that Jews should lead the Gentiles of the world to adopt Jewish religious mythologies and conduct "world revolution". Violent revolution, and the dictatorships imposed under the illusion of Utopian dreams, have been longstanding Jewish traditions. Reality and science give way to religion and childish delusion.

Like many before him, Albert Einstein believed that Jews had lived in darkness while Gentile Europeans had born reborn.[47] Judaism had inhibited the progress of science among Jews, who attempted to stifle free thought among their own people. When the Jewish community marketed the new Jewish heroes Karl Marx, Albert Einstein and Sigmund Freud to the general public in the Twentieth Century, the old habits remained and a new international dogmatism, like that of the old lawgiver Moses, emerged. No one dare question the pseudo-Messiahs, who had allegedly found ultimate truths that were not open to debate. The old Jewish traditions of hero worship and dogmatism carried on in a new age of mass suggestion through intensive advertising and a controlled and propagandistic press. To question a Jewish hero was to question a Jewish God, and therefore to be anti-Semitic, *per se.*[48]

This largely ended free and open debate, and with it normal scientific progress in these fields. Several nations were forced into the slavery of Communism under the false promise and childish premise of a Jewish Utopia to come. Physics degenerated into mysticism. Psychology reaped tremendous profits for its practitioners, while doing little for its patients that time alone would have otherwise accomplished. Each of these mythologies and advertised heroes could only survive in a climate where dissent was suppressed, and suppression and dogmatism were ancient traditions in the Jewish community. Anatole Leroy-Beaulieu wrote in the 1893,

"Far from emanating from the Synagogue, the new ideas had great difficulty in making their way into it. The Synagogue had, so to speak, stopped up all the chinks and crannies in its traditions; in Poland, Hungary, and even in Germany, in fact, almost everywhere it had proceeded after the fashion prevalent in cold countries, where at the beginning of winter the windows are fastened down with cement to keep the outer air from entering. Its most illustrious children were anathematised by the Synagogue; the *Herem*, with its awful imprecations, was hurled at whoever attempted innovations. Baruch Spinoza was excommunicated in the eighteenth century by the most enlightened community on earth; Moses Mendelssohn, who served as a model for Lessing's *Nathan the Wise*, had in that same century to see his German Pentateuch and Psalms condemned by German and Polish rabbis. The synagogue of Berlin rejected books written in the vernacular; it expelled one of its members for having read a German book. The bulk of Jews of both classes, the *Askenazim* and the *Sephardim*, abhorred the philosophers and their precepts. They held profane sciences in suspicion. [*Footnote:* See, especially, the autobiography of the rabbi-philosopher, Solomon Maimon, published in 1792-93, by R. P. Moritz, under the name: *Salomon Maimon's Lebensgeschichte.* Cf. Arvède Barine's *Un Juif Polonaise* (*Revue des Deux Mondes*, of October 15, 1889).] While the salons of Paris were discussing the philosophy of Descartes, or the approaching regeneration of man, the Jewish communities of Eastern and Central Europe were dreaming of cabalistic utopias, yielding themselves up to the craze of Hassidism, and growing fanatical over the rival claims of false Messiahs, such as Franck and Sabbatai. [*Footnote:* The Seventeenth and eighteenth centuries were, in fact, the age of false Messiahs and also of the diffusion of Hassidism or neo-cabalism, still prevalent in a number of communities. See Graetz's *Geschichte der Juden*, vol. x., chap. vi.-xi.]

III.

Everywhere, in the East as well as the West, it was from the outside, and thanks only to the lamps of the *goim*, that the new ideas, 'the light,' penetrated into the alleys of the Ghetto and pierced the gloom of the *Judengasse*. Could it, indeed, have been otherwise, after centuries of sequestration and debasement! However great may be Israel's elasticity, her mainspring seemed to have been broken. She was weighed down by the double load of her heavy talmudic traditions, and the hatred of a hostile society."[49]

Communists, Zionists and Nazis likewise have been notorious opponents of personal choice and viciously punished dissent and free speech. Each of these movements were led and financed by Jews and by crypto-Jews. The hero worship of figures like Einstein, Freud and Marx, which has led in many instances to a dogmatic stagnation of science and to fanatical personal attacks on dissenters, has been called a "Jewish trait"—the continuance of a persistent habit of intolerance after the abandonment of one religious Jewish creed for another, and the shameless perpetuation and proselytizing of a childish religious creed through the obstruction of open debate, and the self-aggrandizing advertising of Jewish cult figures.

On the other hand, many leading Jews have been very cosmopolitan and cultured people, who were eager to assimilate. They, too, fall victim to a fairly large contingent of racist Jews who wish to quash disagreement with their views by slandering and libeling anyone who brings the facts to the fore by calling them "anti-Semitic" for daring to argue with Jewish racists.[50] This is a highly vocal and well-organized minority in the Jewish community, which is mostly composed of racist Zionist Jews. Albert Einstein, who was himself a vocal racist, is a hero to other racist Jews. Racist Jews often have no regard for individual rights or democratic principles. They insist that everyone obey them, or face death. This charge is not made lightly or whimsically. Other Jews are by no means immune to the attacks of racist Jews, in fact they are the most common target of racist Jewish intolerance, totalitarianism and violence.

Though many early Socialists helped to organize labor unions, which developed the middle class, and were pursuing their Utopian dreams before the genocidal purges of Lenin, Stalin, Kun, Mao and other "Communist revolutionaries" would forever stigmatize the political agenda and ideas of Socialism, Bolsheviks were rightfully seen as terribly dangerous in 1919 and Germany was one of their primary targets. Peter Michelmore wrote in his biography *Einstein: Profile of the Man*,

"But there was another, more sinister, reason. November 7[, 1919] was the second anniversary of the Bolshevik Revolution in Russia and Communist Party agents all over the world had in their hands a secret manifesto saying that this was the day when workers should be incited to overthrow governments, assassinate public officials, bomb army barracks and establish dictatorships of the proletariat. Berlin was a prime target. The amateur republican government of former basketmakers and blacksmiths was in daily danger of collapse under pressure from both extreme left and extreme right."[51]

Einstein, himself, wrote to Emil Zürcher on 15 April 1919 that he knew for certain that Bolshevik leaders were stealing the wealth of the Russian Nation and were "systematically" mass murdering everyone who did "not belong to the lowest class."[52]

In the 1920's, there were many theories about Jewish people, even (one might say, *especially*) in the conservative academic community, who should have been more enlightened. Einstein happened to fulfill many stereotypes. One such stereotype was the belief that Jewish people were genetically incapable of profound intuitive thought, but could only think "logically", *i. e.*, repetitively, deductively and mathematically. Philipp Frank wrote,

"The members of the Jewish community had often been compelled to hear and to read that while their race possessed a certain craftiness in business pursuits, in science it could only repeat and illuminate the work of others, and that truly creative talents were denied them."[53]

In the 1893, Anatole Leroy-Beaulieu wrote,

"There are two opinions current with regard to the Jew. One ascribes to him a spirit, if not a genius, foreign and antagonistic to our race, and calls it the 'Semitic' spirit. The other—often held by the very same persons—asserts that the Jew is utterly lacking in individual genius, in originality. According to this opinion he has never invented anything, and is in art and science, as everywhere else, capable only of adjusting and adapting. 'Look at them,' said one of my friends to me, 'see how quickly and with what monkey- or squirrel-like agility they climb the first rungs of any ladder; sometimes they even succeed in scaling its top, but they never add to it a single round.' Granted; but how many of us really add a single round to that mysterious ladder which we have set up in vacant space, and which reaches toward the Infinite?

Men who consider the remnants of Israel as an ethnic element distinct from all others, insist that they have never displayed any originality, either in art, poetry, or philosophy. The Jew, in their opinion, is utterly lacking in creative power. It is this that is said to distinguish the Semitic, from the Aryan, spirit. The Semite is sterile; neither his brain nor his hands can produce anything new. He is content to appropriate the labour of others, in order to put it to use; he makes the most of ideas and inventions, as of dollars; he combines them and puts them into circulation; in short, he always subsists on others; one might almost say that he is the parasite of arts and sciences.

This is, approximately, the theory of Wagner [*Footnote:* Wagner's *Das Judenthum in der Musik.*] with regard to music, the art most cultivated by the Jews; according to him, Jews like Mendelssohn, Meyerbeer, and Halévy, although indeed able to compose a German symphony or a French opera, have not been able to invent a new form in art. But, is it necessary to invent new forms in order to be an original artist? And does this lack necessarily imply that Jewish genius consists entirely in a faculty for combination? Absence of creative power, of spontaneity and of originality, is said to be the mark of the Jew everywhere. Israel, it is asserted, displays ill this respect something of a woman's nature. The Semites are said to be a feminine race, possessing to a high degree the gift of receptivity, always lacking in virility and procreative power. From which it would seem to follow that they are, after all, an inferior race.

If this be indeed so, it suggests a reflection: If the Jew is merely an imitator, a copyist, a borrower, how can his race possibly denationalise our strong Aryan races? But, are we justified in regarding this lack of originality as a racial feature, the stamp impressed on Israel and the Semite by the hand of ages? As for myself, I must confess that if any of the ancient races seemed to possess originality, it was this race. Even those who have denied it a creative imagination [*Footnote:* Renan's Histoire Générale des Langues Sémitiques: 'The eminently subjective character of Arabian and Hebrew poetry is due to another trait of the Semitic spirit, to its complete lack of creative imagination and to the consequent absence of fiction.] have agreed that it gave the world religion—an invention that holds its own with any other."[54]

Even some of Einstein's staunchest supporters believed in this theory that Jews were genetically inferior to the creative intellect of Gentiles. Einstein tried to portray himself in opposition to intuition and against inductive reasoning, which unscientific stance fit the stereotype of the Jewish mind.[55]

The following letter to the editor, which appeared in *The New York Times* in 1919, captures the spirit of the times, both the commonplaces of the time and the prevailing influence of racialist thought and nationalism in academic circles in the 1920's:

"Einstein and His Theory.
To the Editor of The New York Times:
On the first day of the Autumn meeting of the National Academy of Sciences (New Haven, Nov. 10) Einstein's relativity theory was discussed by two brilliant men from Massachusetts. Perhaps some of your readers may be interested in two remarks made by the speakers. The first speaker, a brilliant mathematician, came to the conclusion that Einstein's theory is mere philosophy, which he explained by the fact that Einstein is a Jew. The second speaker, whom, as he said humorously, physicists look upon as a mathematician and mathematicians consider a physicist, had a good word to say for the theory of Einstein, namely, that he, the speaker, heard in Paris that Einstein, who was and still is a member of the Kaiser Wilhelm's Academy in Berlin, expressed a laudable wish that the Germans should be beaten. Accordingly, Einstein's theory may be unscientific because Einstein is a Jew; on the other hand, the theory ought to be correct because Einstein was an anti-Hun. Undoubtedly the mental rays of some of our scientists suffered a more or less perceptible deviation from the normal, brought about by the course of Mars in the last four years.
                         SAMUEL JAMES MELTZER.
New York, Nov. 11, 1919."

Judaism, Jewish tribalism, and Jewish racism gave the Jews a bad name. However, Jews were often able to intimidate most scholars out of publicly condemning these behaviors, and from publishing examples of them, and conducting research into their causes. The tribalism itself provided racist Jews with a means to quash most public condemnation of Jewish racism and Jewish tribalism. Edward Alsworth Ross, a Professor of Sociology at the University of Wisconsin, wrote in his book, *The Old World in the New: The Significance of Past and Present Immigration to the American People*, The Century Co., New York, (1914), pp. 143-167, Chapter 7, "The East European Hebrews",

"CHAPTER VII
THE EAST EUROPEAN HEBREWS

IN his defense of Flaccus, a Roman governor who had 'squeezed' his Jewish subjects, Cicero lowers his voice when he comes to speak of the Jews, for, as he explains to the judges, there are persons who might excite against him this numerous, clannish and powerful element. With much greater reason might an American lower his voice to-day in discussing two million Hebrew immigrants united by a strong race consciousness and already ably represented at every level of wealth, power, and influence in the United States.

At the time of the Revolution there were perhaps 700 Jewish families in the colonies. In 1826 the number of Jews in the United States was estimated at 6000; in 1840, at 15,000; in 1848, at 50,000. The immigration from Germany brought great numbers, and at the outbreak of the Civil War there were probably 150,000 Jews in this country. In 1888, after the first wave from Russia, they were estimated at 400,000. Since the beginning of 1899, one and one-third millions of Hebrews have settled in this country.

Easily one-fifth of the Hebrews in the world are with us, and the freshet shows no signs of subsidence. America is coming to be hailed as the 'promised land,' and Zionist dreams are yielding to the conviction that it will be much easier for the keen-witted Russian Jews to prosper here as a free component in a nation of a hundred millions than to grub a living out of the baked hillsides of Palestine. With Mr. Zangwill they exult that: 'America has ample room for all the six millions of the Pale; any one of her fifty states could absorb them. And next to being in a country of their own, there could be no better fate for them than to be together in a land of civil and religious liberty, of whose Constitution Christianity forms no part and where their collective votes would practically guarantee them against future persecution.'

Hence the endeavor of the Jews to control the immigration policy of the United States. Although theirs is but a seventh of our net immigration, they led the fight on the Immigration

Commission's bill. The power of the million Jews in the metropolis lined up the Congressional delegation from New York in solid opposition to the literacy test. The systematic campaign in newspapers and magazines to break down all arguments for restriction and to calm nativist fears is waged by and for one race. Hebrew money is behind the National Liberal Immigration League and its numerous publications. From the paper before the commercial body or the scientific association to the heavy treatise produced with the aid of the Baron de Hirsch Fund, the literature that proves the blessings of immigration to all classes in America emanates from subtle Hebrew brains. In order to admit their brethren from the Pale the brightest of the Semites are keeping our doors open to the dullest of the Aryans!

Migrating as families the Hebrews from eastern Europe are pretty evenly divided between the sexes. Their literacy is 26 per cent., about the average. Artisans and professional men are rather numerous among them. They come from cities and settle in cities—half of them in New York. Centuries of enforced Ghetto life seem to have bred in them a herding instinct. No other physiques can so well withstand the toxins of urban congestion. Save the Italians, more Jews will crowd upon a given space than any other nationality. As they prosper they do not proportionately enlarge their quarters. Of Boston tenement-house Jews Dr. Bushee testifies: 'Their inborn love of money-making leads them to crowd into the smallest quarters. Families having very respectable bank accounts have been known to occupy cellar rooms where damp and cold streaked the walls.' 'There are actually streets in the West End where, while Jews are moving in, negro housewives are gathering up their skirts and seeking a more spotless environment.'

The first stream of Russo-Hebrew immigrants started flowing in 1882 in consequence of the reactionary policy of Alexander III. It contained many students and members of scholarly families, who stimulated intellectual activity among their fellows here and were leaders in radical thought. These idealists established newspapers in the Jewish-German Jargon and thus made Yiddish (*Jüdisch*) a literary language. The second stream reached us after 1890 and brought immigrants who were not steeped in modern ideas but held to Talmudic traditions and the learning of the rabbis. The more recent flow taps lower social strata and is prompted by economic motives. These later arrivals lack both the idealism of the first stream and the religious culture of the second.

Besides the Russian Jews we are receiving large numbers from Galicia, Hungary, and Roumania. The last are said to be of a high type, whereas the Galician Jews are the lowest. It is these whom Joseph Pennell, the illustrator, found to be 'people who, despite their poverty, never work with their hands; whose town. . . is but a hideous nightmare of dirt, disease and poverty' and its misery and ugliness 'the outcome of their own habits and way of life and not, as is usually supposed, forced upon them by Christian persecutors.'

OCCUPATIONS

The Hebrew immigrants rarely lay hand to basic production. In tilling the soil, in food growing, in extracting minerals, in building, construction and transportation they have little part. Sometimes they direct these operations, often they finance them, but even in direst poverty they contrive to avoid hard muscular labor. Under pressure the Jew takes to the pack as the Italian to the pick.

In the '80's numerous rural colonies of Hebrews were planted, but, despite much help from outside, all except the colonies near Vineland, New Jersey, utterly failed. In New York and New England there are more than a thousand Hebrew farmers, but most of them speculate in real estate, keep summer boarders, or depend on some side enterprise—peddling, cattle trading or junk buying—for a material part of their income. The Hebrew farmers, said to number in all 6000, maintain a federation and are provided with a farmers' journal. New colonies are launched at brief intervals, and Jewish city boys are being trained for country life. Still, not over one Hebrew family in a hundred is on the land and the rural trend is but a trickle compared with the huge flow.

Perhaps two-fifths of the Hebrew immigrants gain their living from garment-making. Naturally the greater part of the clothing and dry goods trade, the country over, is in their hands. They make eighty-five per cent. of the cigars and most of the domestic cigarettes. They purchase all but an insignificant part of the leaf tobacco from the farmers and sell it to the manufacturers. They are prominent in the retailing of spirits, and the Jewish distiller is almost as typical as the German brewer.

None can beat the Jew at a bargain, for through all the

intricacies of commerce he can scent his profit. The peddler, junk dealer, or pawn broker is on the first rung of the ladder. The more capable rise in a few years to be theatrical managers, bankers or heads of department stores. Moreover great numbers are clerks and salesmen and thousands are municipal and building contractors. Many of the second generation enter the civil service and the professions. Already in several of the largest municipalities and in the Federal bureaus a large proportion of the positions are held by keen-witted Jews. Twenty years ago under the spoils system the Irish held most of the city jobs in New York. Now under the test system the Jews are driving them out. Among the school teachers of the city Jewesses outnumber the women of any other nationality. Owing to their aversion to 'blind-alley' occupations Jewish girls shun housework and crowd into the factories, while those who can get training become stenographers, bookkeepers, accountants and private secretaries. One-thirteenth of the students in our seventy-seven leading universities and colleges are of Hebrew parentage. The young Jews take eagerly to medicine and it is said that from seven hundred to nine hundred of the physicians in New York are of their race. More noticeable is the influx into dentistry and especially into pharmacy. Their trend into the legal profession has been pronounced, and of late there is a movement of Jewish students into engineering, agriculture and forestry.

MORALS

The Jewish immigrants cherish a pure, close-knit family life and the position of the woman in the home is one of dignity. More than any other immigrants they are ready to assume the support of distant needy relatives. They care for their own poor, and the spirit of coöperation among them is very noticeable. Their temper is sensitive and humane; very rarely is a Jew charged with any form of brutality. There is among them a fine *élite* which responds to the appeal of the ideal and is found in every kind of ameliorative work.

Nevertheless, fair-minded observers agree that certain bad qualities crop out all too often among these eastern Europeans. A school principal remarks that his Jewish pupils are more importunate to get a mark changed than his other pupils. A settlement warden who during the summer entertains hundreds of nursing slum mothers at a country 'home' says: 'The Jewish mothers are always asking for *something extra* over the regular kit we provide each guest for her stay.' 'The last thing the son of Jacob wants,' observes an eminent sociologist, 'is a square deal.' A veteran New York social worker cannot forgive the Ghetto its littering and defiling of the parks. 'Look at Tompkins Square,' he exclaimed hotly, 'and compare it with what it was twenty-five years ago amid a German population!' As for the caretakers of the parks their comment on this matter is unprintable. Genial settlement residents, who never tire of praising Italian or Greeks, testify that no other immigrants are so noisy, pushing and disdainful of the rights of others as the Hebrews. That the worst exploiters of these immigrants are sweaters, landlords, employers and 'white slavers' of their own race no one gainsays.

The authorities complain that the East European Hebrews feel no reverence for law as such and are willing to break any ordinance they find in their way. The fact that pleasure-loving Jewish business men spare Jewesses but pursue Gentile girls excites bitter comment. The insurance companies scan a Jewish fire risk more closely than any other. Credit men say the Jewish merchant is often 'slippery' and will 'fail' in order to get rid of his debts. For lying the immigrant has a very bad reputation. In the North End of Boston 'the readiness of the Jews to commit perjury has passed into a proverb.' Conscientious immigration officials become very sore over the incessant fire of false accusations to which they are subjected by the Jewish press and societies. United States senators complain that during the close of the struggle over the immigration bill they were overwhelmed with a torrent of crooked statistics and misrepresentations by the Hebrews fighting the literacy test.

Graver yet is the charge that these East European immigrants lower standards wherever they enter. In the boot and shoe trade some Hebrew jobbers who, after sending in an order to the manufacturer, find the market taking an unexpected downward turn, will reject a consignment on some pretext in order to evade a loss. Says Dr. Bushee: 'The shame of a variety of underhanded methods in trade not easily punishable by law must be laid at the door of a certain type of Jew.' It is charged that for personal gains the Jewish dealer wilfully disregards the customs of the trade and thereby throws trade ethics into confusion. Physicians and lawyers complain that their Jewish colleagues tend to break down the ethics of their professions. It is certain that Jews have commercialized the social evil, commercialized the theatre, and done much to commercialize the newspaper.

The Jewish leaders admit much truth in the impeachment. One accounts for the bad reputation of his race in the legal profession by pointing out that they entered the tricky branches of it, viz., commercial law and criminal law. Says a high minded lawyer: 'If the average American entered law as we have to, without money, connections or adequate professional education, he would be a shyster too.' Another observes that the sharp practice of the Russo-Jewish lawyer belongs to the earlier part of his career when he must succeed or starve. As he prospers his sense of responsibility grows. For example, some years ago the Bar Association of New York opposed the promotion of a certain Hebrew lawyer to the bench on the ground of his unprofessional practices. But this same lawyer made one of the best judges the city ever had, and when he retired he was banqueted by the Association.

The truth seems to be that the lower class of Jews of eastern Europe reach here moral cripples, their souls warped and dwarfed by iron circumstance. The experience of Russian repression has made them haters of government and corrupters of the police. Life amid a bigoted and hostile population has left them aloof and thick-skinned. A tribal spirit intensified by social isolation prompts them to rush to the rescue of the caught rascal of their own race. Pent within the Talmud and the Pale of Settlement, their interests have become few, and many of them have developed a monstrous and repulsive love of gain. When now, they use their Old World shove and wile and lie in a society like ours, as unprotected as a snail out of its shell, they rapidly push up into a position of prosperous parasitism, leaving scorn and curses in their wake.

Gradually, however, it dawns upon this twisted soul that here there is no need to be weazel or hedgehog. He finds himself in a new game, the rules of which are made by *all* the players. He himself is a part of the state that is weakened by his law-breaking, a member of the profession that is degraded by his sharp practices. So smirk and cringe and trick presently fall away from him, and he stands erect. This is why, in the same profession at the same time, those most active in breaking down standards are Jews and those most active in raising standards are Jews—of an earlier coming or a later generation. 'On the average,' says a Jewish leader, 'only the third generation feels perfectly at home in American society.' This explains the frequent statement that the Jews are 'the limit'—among the worst of the worst and among the best of the best.

CRIME

The Hebrew immigrants usually commit their crimes for gain; and among gainful crimes they lean to gambling, larceny, and the receiving of stolen goods rather than to the more daring crimes of robbery and burglary. The fewness of the Hebrews in prison has been used to spread the impression that they are uncommonly law-abiding. The fact is it is harder to catch and convict criminals of cunning than criminals of violence. The chief of police of any large city will bear emphatic testimony as to the trouble Hebrew lawbreakers cause him. Most alarming is the great increase of criminality among Jewish young men and the growth of prostitution among Jewish girls. Says a Jewish ex-assistant attorney-general of the United States in an address before the B'nai B'rith: 'Suddenly we find appearing in the life of the large cities the scarlet woman of Jewish birth.' 'In the women's night court of New York City and on gilded Broadway the majority of street walkers bear Jewish names.' 'This sudden break in Jewish morality was not natural. It was a product of cold, calculating, mercenary methods, devised and handled by men of Jewish birth.' Says the president of the Conference of American Rabbis: 'The Jewish world has been stirred from the center to circumference by the recent disclosures of the part Jews have played in the pursuance of the white slave traffic.' On May 14, 1911, a Yiddish paper in New York said, editorially:

'It is almost impossible to comprehend the indifference with which the large New York Jewish population hears and reads, day after day, about the thefts and murders that are perpetrated every day by Jewish gangs—real bands of robbers—and no one raises a voice of protest, and no demand is made for the protection of the reputation of the Jews of America and for the life and property of the Jewish citizens.'

'A few years ago when Commissioner Bingham came out with a statement about Jewish thieves, the Jews raised a cry of protest that reached the heavens. The main cry was that Bingham exaggerated and overestimated the number of Jewish criminals. But when we hear of the murders, hold-ups and burglaries committed in the Jewish section by Jewish criminals, we must, with heartache, justify Mr. Bingham.'

Two weeks later the same paper said: 'How much more will Jewish hearts bleed when the English press comes out with descriptions of gambling houses packed with Jewish gamblers, of the blind cigar stores where Jewish thieves and murderers are reared, of the gangs that work systematically and fasten like vampires upon the peaceable Jewish population, and of all the other nests of theft, robbery, murder, and lawlessness that have multiplied in our midst.'

This startling growth reflects the moral crisis through which many immigrants are passing. Enveloped in the husks of medievalism, the religion of many a Jew perishes in the American environment. The immigrant who loses his religion is worse than the religionless American because his early standards are dropped along with his faith. With his clear brain sharpened in the American school, the egoistic, conscienceless young Jew constitutes a menace. As a Jewish labor leader said to me, 'the non-morality of the young Jewish business men is fearful. Socialism inspires an ethics in the heart of the Jewish workingman, but there are many without either the old religion or the new. I am aghast at the consciencelessness of the *Luft-proletariat* without feeling for place, community or nationality.'

RACE TRAITS

If the Hebrews are a race certainly one of their traits is *intellectuality*. In Boston the milk station nurse gets far more result from her explanations to Jewish mothers than from her talks to Irish or Italian mothers. The Jewish parent, however grasping, rarely exploits his children, for he appreciates how schooling will add to their earning capacity. The young Jews have the foresight to avoid 'blind alley' occupations. Between the years of fourteen and seventeen the Irish and Italian boys earn more than the Jewish lads; but after eighteen the Jewish boys will be earning more, for they have selected occupations in which you can work up. The Jew is the easiest man to sell life insurance to, for he catches the idea sooner than any other immigrant. As philanthropist he is the first to appreciate scientific charity. As voter he is the first to repudiate the political leader and rise to a broad outlook. As exploited worker he is the first to find his way to a theory of his hard lot, viz. capitalism. As employer he is quick to respond to the idea of 'welfare work.' The Jewish patrons of the libraries welcome guidance in their reading and they want always the best; in fiction, Dickens,

Tolstoi, Zola; in philosophy, Darwin, Spencer, Haeckel. No other readers are so ready to tackle the heavy-weights in economics and sociology.

From many school principals comes the observation that their Jewish pupils are either very bright or distinctly dull. Among the Russo-Jewish children many fall behind but some distinguish themselves in their studies. The proportion of backward pupils is about the average for school children of non-English-speaking parentage; but the brilliant pupils indicate the presence in Hebrew immigration of a gifted element which scarcely shows itself in other streams of immigration. Teachers report that their Jewish pupils 'seem to have hungry minds.' They 'grasp information as they do everything else, recognizing it as the requisite for success.' Says a principal: 'Their progress in studies is simply another manifestation of the acquisitiveness of the race.' Another thinks their school successes are won more by intense application than by natural superiority, and judges Irish pupils would do still better if only they would work as many hours.

The Jewish gift for mathematics and chess is well known. They have great imagination, but it is the 'combinative' imagination rather than the free poetic fancy of the Celt. They analyze out the factors of a process and mentally put them together in new ways. Their talent for anticipating the course of the market, making fresh combinations in business, diagnosing diseases, and suggesting scientific hypotheses is not questioned. On the other hand, an eminent savant thinks the best Jewish minds are not strong in generalization and deems them clever, acute and industrious rather than able in the highest sense. On the whole, the Russo-Jewish immigration is richer in gray matter than any other recent stream, and it may be richer than any other large inflow since the colonial era.

Perhaps *abstractness* is another trait of the Jewish mind. To the Hebrew things present themselves not softened by an atmosphere of sentiment, but with the sharp outlines of that desert landscape in which his ancestors wandered. As farmer he is slovenly and does not root in the soil like the German. As poet he shows little feeling for nature. Unlike the German artisan who becomes fond of what he creates, the Jew does not love the concrete for its own sake. What he cares for is the *value* in it. Hence he is rarely a good artisan, and perhaps the reason why he makes his craft a mere stepping-stone to business is that he does not relish his work. The Jew shines in literature, music and acting—the arts of expression—but not often is he an artist in the manipulation of materials. In theology, law and diplomacy—which involve the abstract—the Jewish mind has distinguished itself more than in technology or the study of nature.

The Jew has *little feeling for the particular*. He cares little for pets. He loves man rather than men, and from Isaiah to Karl Marx he holds the record in projects of social amelioration. The Jew loves without romance and fights without hatred. He is loyal to his purposes rather than to persons. He finds general principles for whatever he wants to do. As circumstances change he will make up with his worst enemy or part company with his closest ally. Hence his wonderful adaptability. Flexible and rational the Jewish mind cannot be bound by conventions. The good will of a Southern gentleman takes set forms such as courtesy and attentions, while the kindly Jew is ready with any form of help that may be needed. So the South looked askance at the Jews as 'no gentlemen.' Nor have the Irish with their strong personal loyalty or hostility liked the Jews. On the other hand the Yankees have for the Jews a cousinly feeling. Puritanism was a kind of Hebraism and throve most in the parts of England where, centuries before, the Jews had been thickest. With his rationalism, his shrewdness, his inquisitiveness and acquisitiveness, the Yankee can meet the Jew on his own ground.

Like all races that survive the sepsis of civilization, the Hebrews show great *tenacity of purpose*. Their constancy has worn out their persecutors and won them the epithet of 'stiff-necked.' In their religious ideas our Jewish immigrants are so stubborn that the Protestant churches despair of making proselytes among them. The sky-rocket careers leading from the peddler's pack to the banker's desk or the professor's chair testify to rare singleness of purpose. Whatever his goal—money, scholarship, or recognition—the true Israelite never loses sight of it, cannot be distracted, presses steadily on, and in the end masters circumstance instead of being dominated by it. As strikers the Jewish wage earners will starve rather than yield. The Jewish reader in the libraries sticks indomitably to the course of reading he has entered on. No other policy holder is so reliable as the Jew in keeping up his premiums. The Jewish canvasser, bill collector, insurance solicitor, or commercial traveler takes no rebuff, returns brazenly again and again, and will risk being kicked down stairs rather than lose his man. During the Civil War General Grant wrote to the war department regarding the Jewish cotton traders who pressed into the South with the northern armies: 'I have instructed the commanding officer to refuse all permits to Jews to come South, and I have frequently had them expelled from the department, but they come in with their carpet sacks in spite of all that can be done to prevent it.' Charity agents say that although their Hebrew cases are few, they cost them more than other cases in the end because of the unblushing persistence of the applicant. Some chiefs of police will not tolerate the Hebrew prostitute in their city because they find it impossible to subject her to any regulations.

THE RACE LINE

In New York the line is drawn against the Jews in hotels, resorts, clubs, and private schools, and constantly this line hardens and extends. They cry 'Bigotry' but bigotry has little or nothing to do with it. What is disliked in the Jews is not their religion but certain ways and manners. Moreover, the Gentile resents being obliged to engage in a humiliating and undignified scramble in order to keep his trade of his clients against the Jewish invader. The line is not yet rigid, for the genial editor of *Vorwaerts*, Mr. Abram Cahan, tells me that he and his literary brethren from the Pale have never encountered Anti-Semitism in the Americans they meet. Not the socialist Jews but the vulgar upstart parvenus are made to feel the discrimination.

This cruel prejudice—for all lump condemnations are cruel—is no importation, no hang-over from the past. It appears to spring out of contemporary experience and is invading circle after circle of broad-minded. People who give their lives to befriending immigrants shake their heads over the Galician Hebrews. It is astonishing how much of the sympathy that twenty years ago went out to the fugitives from Russian massacres has turned sour. Through fear of retaliation little criticism gets into print; in the open the Philo-semites have it all their way. The situation is: Honey above, gall beneath. If the Czar, by keeping up the pressure which has already rid him of two million undesired subjects, should succeed in driving the bulk of his six million Jews to the United States, we shall see the rise of the Jewish question here, perhaps riots and anti-Jewish legislation. No doubt thirty or forty thousand Hebrews from eastern Europe might be absorbed by this country each year without any marked growth of race prejudice; but when they come in two or three or even four times as fast, the lump outgrows the leaven, and there will be trouble.

America is probably the strongest solvent Jewish separatism has ever encountered. It is not only that here the Jew finds himself a free man and a citizen. That has occurred before, without causing the Jew to merge into the general population. It is that here more than anywhere else in the world *the future is expected to be in all respects better than the past.* No civilized people ever so belittled the past in the face of the future as we do. This is why tradition withers and dies in our air; and the dogma that the Jews are a 'peculiar people' and must shun intermarriage with the Gentiles is only a tradition. The Jewish dietary laws are rapidly going. In New York only one-forth of the two hundred thousand Jewish workmen keep their Sabbath and only one-fifth of the Jews belong to the synagogue. The neglect of the synagogue is as marked as the falling away of non-Jews from the church. Mixed marriages, although by no means numerous in the centers, are on the increase, and in 1909 the Central Conference of Jewish Rabbis resolved that such marriages 'are contrary to the tradition of the Jewish religion and should therefore be discouraged by the American Rabbinate.' Certainly every mixed marriage is, as one rabbi puts it, 'a nail in the coffin of Judaism,' and free mixing would in time end the Jews as a distinct ethnic strain.

The 'hard shell' leaders are urging the Jews in America to cherish their distinctive traditions and to refrain from mingling their blood with Gentiles. But the liberal and radical leaders insist that in this new, ultra-modern environment nothing is gained by holding the Jews within the wall of Orthodox Judaism. As a prominent Hebrew labor leader said to me: 'By blending with the American the Jew will gain in physique, and this with its attendant participation in normal labor, sports, athletics, outdoor life, and the like, will lessen the hyper-sensibility and the sensuality of the Jew and make him less vain, unscrupulous and pleasure-loving.'

It is too soon yet to foretell whether or not this vast and growing body of Jews from eastern Europe is to melt and disappear in the American population just as numbers of Portuguese, Dutch, English, and French Jews in our early days became blent with the rest of the people. In any case the immigrant Jews are being assimilated outwardly. The long coat, side curls, beard and fringes, the 'Wandering Jew' figure, the furtive manner, the stoop, the hunted look, and the martyr air disappear as if by magic after a brief taste of American life. It would seem as if the experience of Russia and America in assimilating the Jews is happily illustrated by the old story of the rivalry of the wind and the sun in trying to strip the traveler of his cloak."

Einstein's racism and tribalism provoked a "racial" debate over his personality and the theory of relativity. Counterattacks predictably followed Einstein's ethnic slurs and Einstein's reckless and racist defamations of his legitimate critics. For example,

"NOTES BRÈVES
Einstein, plagiaire.
Le **Juif** d'Allemagne Einstein est un plagiaire. La presse américaine en avait déjà (v. n° **225**) fourni la preuve. Le *Dearb. Independent*, 25.3, y revient avec de nouveaux documents.

Il montre les « découvertes » du Juif suivant pas à pas, et ses publications suivant volume par volume, les découvertes et les publications d'Arvid Reuterdahl, Américain d'origine suédoise, doyen de l'Ecole d'architecture et de mécanique au collège Saint Thomas (St. Paul, Minn.). Le *Raum-Zeit-Kontinuum*, les *Raum-Zeit-Funktionen* et *Raum-Zeit-Koordinaten* du Juif ne sont que des démarquages du *Space-Time Potential* de l'Américain, grossièrement camouflés.

Les Juifs ne sont jamais que des plagiaires. Mais la stupidité des *goyim* leur permet de s'introduire dans la peau des hommes de génie à la manière de Chéri-Bibi. Et la presse de tous les pays, moyennant une poignée de dollars ou de *crasseux*, assassine de silence les vrais savants pour revêtir de leur gloire le gorille du Ghetto."[56]

THE *DEARBORN INDEPENDENT* published an article on 30 July 1921, on page 14, (American Jews successfully organized many large fund raising drives, as represented in the pages of *The New York Times*, especially during the First World War) which ridicules Einstein's anti-

American interview upon his return to Europe:

"*Relatively Unimportant, Extremely Typical*

ALBERT EINSTEIN, who maintained a pose of dignified silence in the face of his scientific accusers while in the United States, has broken into most undignified speech immediately upon his return to Europe.

Knowledge of what he is and the traditional ill-manneredness of which he is an heir, this exhibition of boorishness was not unexpected.

Disgust with Einstein is somewhat an old thrill, because his plagiarism is so manifest and his fame is so directly the result of the circus-advertising instinct of his race. But a new emotion divides it now: What about those nose-led Americans who, in obedience to the swarthy New York ruling race, bowed down and worshipped Einstein and chanted loudest in the chorus of his praise?

Their position is most humiliated. And rightly so. Every white man, who bows down to the swarthy ruling race of New York and elsewhere, gets his nose rubbed into it sooner or later. It is the traditional repayment which that race—and all inferior races—renders when a superior race makes a fool of itself.

Mr. Einstein was gloriously received in the United States. Even the cold photographs retain the glow of passionate occasions. Literally over 150,000 persons by comptometer count, swarmed round him on his arrival. He had not done anything for science, for the easement of human pain nor for the solution of life's pressing problems, yet he was received as a royalty of the realm of reason, while others who have found the way to healing or achievement for the common man have been allowed to enter and leave New York unheeded. Mr. Einstein, by the way, *left* New York unheeded—there were half a dozen persons on the piers —which should, perhaps, be borne in mind.

Mr. Einstein was given the freedom of New York, under protest, and was refused the freedom of Boston, but the universities received him gladly and decked him with their doctorates. The press, in response to swarthy local committees, shouted itself hoarse. Clothing lofts poured out their Red intellectuals by the thousand, and taking it all in all the publicity manager of Mr. Einstein's stunt did a good job—until—scientists began to ask Einstein questions.

The only recorded answer which Einstein made to any but adulatory remarks while in the United States, was, 'See my secretary.' American collegians and scientists, philosophers and literary men besought him; others with the 'goods on him' openly challenged him; but surrounded by a swarthy ring that made everybody believe that a slight to Einstein was equal to sacrilege against the Holy of Holies on Mt. Zion, he maintained his silence and, supposedly, his dignity. That last, however, is not known. He left the United States rather unexpectedly.

THE DEARBORN INDEPENDENT is glad to say that it was one—perhaps not the only one—of the papers that were not taken in by the Einstein publicity managers. It is glad to remember also that it gave much-needed space to a scientific critic of Einstein's theory, who had been refused space elsewhere. A roster of the publications which were afraid of the swarthy crowd around Einstein gives much food for publication.

Therefore, perhaps, THE DEARBORN INDEPENDENT is not so embarrassed as are the Einstein devotees by the attack upon America which the professor has made. Not so embarrassed as, say, the *Scientific American.*

Mr. Einstein's charges are as follows: (1) That America is too exaggerated in its enthusiasm. 'This exaggerated enthusiasm for me and my work struck me as being a genuinely and peculiarly American phenomenon'; (2) that Americans are bored; (3) that America suffers from poverty in intellectual things; (4) that most American men think of nothing but work; (5) that the rest of the men are mere lap dogs for indolent women; (6) 'that women dominate the entire life of America' ; (7) that our excitement over the theory of relativity was 'comic'; (8) that the only real American scientist lives in Chicago and is a Jew!

As complete a slap in the face as the swarthy tribe has ever handed a white people!

Mr. Arthur Brisbane, pen-sentinel of the tribe, who held Mr. Einstein up as an example too lofty for Americans to emulate, yet to be worshipfully gazed upon as a distant and unattainable star, was plainly up against it.

Many people think that Mr. Brisbane is himself distantly

connected by racial ties with people of Mr. Einstein's type, but others are assured that he is not. It is unfortunate, if he is not, because his admiration of the tribe is so great that assertion of his belonging to it would not be construed by him as an insult, but rather as a high compliment. Some people have commented on the name 'Brisbane,' saying that its Hebrew form is Brith Ben, or 'son of the covenant.' The name Einstein is not as Hebrew as is Brisbane; Einstein is German for 'one stone.'

It was rather hard, therefore, after standing sponsor for Einstein in all the Hearst papers and before the American public, to have Einstein hurl his insult across the sea. What did Mr. Brisbane do then, quoth the little bird? Did he turn to his ever-present Hebrew secretary for inspiration as he often has done before? History may never know.

But it is certain that something stirred within Mr. Brisbane's breast, something American, something angry and tipped with truth; and there hurtled through his mobile mind with the clarifying turbulence and light of an electric storm, this luminous thought: 'No wonder Einstein thinks thus of America; *all that Einstein saw of America was the Jews*!' (Wild shrieks of 'pogrom! pogrom!' ringing through the darker recesses of Brisbane's brain!) 'That's it—that's how to explain it; he didn't see America at all—he just saw Jews.'

Lest the reader should think that statement too great a strain on his credulity, we hasten to offer, what we always have on hand in these matters, the evidence. Behold it!

Today

Einstein's Views.
What of the 5,000,000?
Valuable 'Devil's Finger.'
Hopeful Mr. Herrick.
—By ARTHUR BRISBANE—
Copyright. 1921.

Prof. Einstein, of the relativity theory, returned home, says:

First, he is amused by the wild enthusiasm of the entire American nation in greeting him. What Prof. Einstein saw, without knowing it, was the extremely enthusiastic welcome of his co-religionists. Our citizens of Jewish blood delight at another demonstration, in Einstein's person, of the ability of their race. It was Jewish enthusiasm that the professor witnessed, and there is no greater enthusiasm than that. It is a good explanation of the whole Einstein criticism.

It is a good explanation of the whole Einstein criticism.

Moreover, it is true. Outside an occasional university president and Senate, the white mayors and governors en route, once the President of the United States, the professor did not meet many Americans. He did not greatly want to meet Americans. Americans are inclined to sit in judgment first, and that spelled danger.

He has simply made the same error which others have made, in not properly distinguishing between racial strains of blood.

Einstein's charge about the comic enthusiasm is absolutely true; scores of photographs confirm the facts. But who furnished the enthusiasm? A little more candor on Einstein's part would have made that clear. As a long, long benefit of the doubt, it may be agreed that perhaps Mr. Einstein may have mentioned his co-nationalists in this respect, and it may have been changed to 'Americans.' But probably not. If it had been changed to 'Americans' from an original other, it would have made it rather difficult for certain newspapers who bow the knee to the tribe; especially in view of the tact that 75 per cent of the advertising in United States newspapers is paid for by the tribe. Jack Lait once said, 'The department store is the bulwark of free speech!' And he ought to know.

The tribe did make fools of themselves over Einstein. They made a fool of him, too. Now he makes a fool of both by describing the tribal defects and ascribing them to 'Americans.' What a plot for screaming farce by Morry Gest!

Mr. Brisbane is right. He is wrong on nearly everything else he tries to say on the related subject, but he is right in his analysis of Mr. Einstein's sources: Mr. Einstein's opinion of America is the result of his having seen only Jews. Some foreign governments are suffering from the same mis-view of us.

The Brisbane explanation of the Einstein theory of Americans may be applied all down the line. 'The intellectual poverty' he noticed is also due to the fact that all he saw of American intellect was Jewish. The tribe does not originate ideas; it grabs them and exploits them. The tribe is not at home in the study, but on the stage. In art it simply steals ideas and elaborates them. In music it performs, but does not create. In law, it manipulates, but does not clarify great principles. In politics it is opportunist. Intellectual bankruptcy may coexist with a very pert knowledge of what the schools teach, and the tribe is quite expert at possessing itself of that—all white man's knowledge, by the way.

And so on through the charges. The Brisbane explanation is hereby unanimously adopted: Prof. Einstein thinks what he does and says what he did because what he saw was not America but Jews. He couldn't see America for the swarthy swarm that smothered him. And what is worse, hundreds of thousands—millions—of that swam have never seen America either, and never will, for the same reason.

The Jews are strangely silent on the criticism. Rabbi Stephen S. Wise—in the Yiddish papers they spell it correctly, Weisz—refuses to comment. The tribal elders of the New York Board of Aldermen who fought for the freedom of the city for Mr. Einstein just as boldly as they fight for legally imposed social equality where they are not wanted, don't like to discuss it either.

Prof. Rautenstrauch is rather gentle in his comment 'His visit

If funny stories fill your head
    And you would but amuse,
Why keep them laughing by all means,
    But not about the Greeks.

Fill up the page with anecdotes,
    Tell anything that's new
But let no story that you tell
    Poke fun at any Syrian.

You'll only tire your massive brain.
    Your time you'll surely lose,
If you submit to Editors
    Stories on the French.

I'm greatly hampered in my work,
    My stuff they all refuse,
Because the stories that I tell
    Are often on the Swiss.

I should be paid for what I write,
    My lawyer says to sue,
And that is what so puzzles me
    For he, too, is a Belgian.
    —New York Herald, July 3,1921.

LATER BULLETIN—Word comes from Amsterdam that Prof. Einstein did not say it. He is still dazed by the good will of America, still has the glory of America in his eyes, and so on. The difference is that the first story came under the names of responsible correspondents and through the channels of responsible newspapers; while the second story comes orphaned— probably from the Jewish Telegraph Agency, which is the associated press of international Jewry. The agency has not been functioning very much of late, the principal reason being that it cannot send long and harrowing dispatches about 'pogroms' and be believed any more, because there are too many neutral observers in the 'pogrom zone.' There are no pogroms [see: "Pogroms in Poland", The New York Times, (23 May 1919), p. 10; where the report claims that Germans may have fabricated myths, and spread rumors of Jewish pogroms in order to vilify their enemies.—**CJB**], but there is this: There is the sale for money of goods bought by the charity of the American people, mostly the American church people. The agency, however, doesn't deal in facts of that kind.

It is rather singular that none of the tribe's dailies doubted the first Einstein report. They knew how delightfully and characteristically racial it was, how perfectly natural. They took it for granted.

However, the Einstein matter is a mere speck on the racing river of events yet it shows something of the tendency of the river. No one has a license to feel badly over it, except the scientific publications that didn't have the intestinal integrity to challenge the man in the name of science; the universities that did not dare keep him off their list of honors; the society people who fêted the rather mangy lion; and the plain and more honest members of the tribe who thought Einstein might generously reflect a little glory on them. He hasn't."

Einstein apparently did not respond directly to many of the genuinely race-based attacks made against him, such as those above, which were made in no uncertain terms. He preferred to mischaracterize some of the scientific objections to his theories, and the legitimate concerns raised about his plagiarism, as if they were "anti-Semitism" *per se*. When Einstein arrived at America's shores, *The New York Times* emphasized the fact that theory of relativity was widely criticized,

"The man was Dr. Albert Einstein, propounder of the much-debated theory of relativity that has given the world a new conception of space, and time and the size of the universe."[57]

Before Einstein stepped off the ship, he lied and "played the race card" in order to smear anyone who would dare to criticize him in America,

"Professor Einstein was reluctant to talk about relativity, but when he did speak he said most of the opposition to his theories was the result of strong anti-Semitic feeling."[58]

The article continued,

"He was asked about those who oppose his theory, and said:

'No man of culture or knowledge has any animosity toward my theories. Even the physicists opposed to the theory are animated by political motives.'

When asked what he meant, he said he referred to anti-Semitic feeling. He would not elaborate on this subject, but said the attacks in Berlin were entirely anti-Semitic."[59]

Among those highly knowledgeable and cultured physicists and philosophers who actively opposed relativity theory, as it was expressed by Einstein, many of whom were Jewish—who, according to Einstein's assertions, must have been uncultured, ignorant anti-Semites—we find Hendrik Antoon Lorentz, Max Abraham, Alfred North Whitehead, Ernst Mach, Albert Abraham Michelson, Friedrich Adler, Henri Bergson, Oskar Kraus, Melchior Palágyi, [etc. etc. etc.]. Clearly, Einstein lied about a very serious matter, and, what is worse, Einstein was himself a racist instigator and a political agitator; and, therefore, a hypocrite and a deliberate inciter of "racial" discord.

Einstein and his friends' (especially Einstein's *Shabbos Goy* Max von Laue's) wanton and reckless charges of anti-Semitism only served to intensify and provoke it, as evinced above, which was their goal. Einstein expressed the bizarre belief commonly held by racist Jews, that anti-Semitism was a positive thing because it kept Jews segregated from Gentiles. Einstein argued that Jews should not mix with Gentiles, due to "racial" differences. Responding to the truly race-based attacks would have tended to discredit anti-Semitism, and with it racist political Zionism. However, Einstein and Max von Laue's tactic of mischaracterizing legitimate arguments about science and priorities issues as if "anti-Semitism" only inspired anti-Jewish sentiment—much to their delight.

Einstein was allegedly scarred by childhood traumas.[60] Being a coward by nature, he hid behind reckless defamations in order to avoid legitimate criticism.

Hubert Goenner observed,

"Nevertheless, Kleinert (1979, 501-6) and Elton (1986, 95) documented that [*Albert Einstein*] *was first* in referring to anti-Semitism in public, well before any of his adversaries in the campaign against him [*Footnote:* Einstein soon regretted his statement.] [. . . .]"[61]

Einstein's accusation that no one but an anti-Semite would disagree with him was a smear against scientific dissent heard round the world—obviously meant to stifle the debate. It was an open threat to anyone who would challenge him on the facts—anyone who dared to tell the truth and expose him. These smears were accompanied by alarmist (and shifting) misrepresentations of the audience's actions, and the proceedings, at the Berlin Philharmonic when Paul Weyland and Ernst Gehrcke lectured against the theory of relativity. This had a chilling effect on the debate over the facts, with some fearing to challenge Einstein, knowing full well that they would be accused of "anti-Semitism" in the international press no matter what they actually did, said or thought. Einstein's tactics served to provoke and intensify extant anti-Jewish feelings and to numb the ears of the world when the truly rabid and murderous NSDAP rose to power.

As was his habit, Einstein used alarmist tactics and sought to alienate anyone, including Jews, who dared to disagree with him. Most German Jews felt a deep love for, and loyalty to, their present nationality, and wanted nothing of what they thought of as Einstein's archaic Zionist bigotry.[62] Einstein was a simplistic person and he sought to narrowly define people of diverse backgrounds and beliefs,[63] and he sought to intimidate everyone into following his course, by degrading Jews who sought to assimilate and intimating that they were somehow traitors to a religious cause—a religious cause which he, himself, truly found ridiculous. Einstein stated,

"I am neither a German citizen, nor is there in me anything that can be described as 'Jewish faith.' But I am happy to belong to the Jewish people, even though I don't regard them as the Chosen People. Why don't we just let the Goy keep his anti-Semitism, while we preserve our love for the likes of us?"[64]

Einstein was reciting the Herzlian brand of racist Zionism he had embraced as a route to personal fame. Theodor Herzl revealed his core beliefs when recalling a conversation he had had with racist Zionist Max Nordau:

"Never before had I been in such perfect tune with Nordau. [***] This has nothing to do with religion. He even said that there was no such thing as a Jewish dogma. But we are of one race. [***] 'The Jews,' he says, 'will be compelled by anti-Semitism to destroy among all peoples the idea of a fatherland.' Or, I secretly thought to myself, to create a fatherland of their own."[65]

The rabid nationalism Herzl and Einstein embraced, and the anti-Semitism they believed benefitted the Jews by uniting and segregating them, began to become very dangerous in the 1920's—much to the delight of the Zionists. Einstein's hypocrisy, his anti-Nationalism versus his Zionism, remained yet to be resolved in the minds of the naïve. For those who grasped the import of Judaic Messianic myth, Einstein was consistently obedient to the racist and genocidal Jewish prophets of old. In 1938, Einstein stated in his essay "Our Debt to Zionism",

> "Rarely since the conquest of Jerusalem by Titus has the Jewish community experienced a period of greater oppression than prevails at the present time. [***] Yet we shall survive this period too, no matter how much sorrow, no matter how heavy a loss in life it may bring. A community like ours, which is a community purely by reason of tradition, can only be strengthened by pressure from without."[66]

Einstein continues in his essay in an effort to justify the illogical and immoral conflicts in his political philosophy, but without success. Einstein also reveals that his early assertions of the racial purity of Jews were nonsense employed for political effect—the political effect of deliberately bringing the Nazis into power in order to herd up the Jews of Europe and chase them into Palestine—the political effect of discrediting Gentile nationalism, while justifying Jewish nationalism. Zionist are today using the same tactics to discredit Islamic nationalism and promote Jewish nationalism. They delight in the fact that they are killing off large numbers of innocent Gentiles in the process.

Einstein and the Zionist Fascists were carrying on a long tradition of European and Judaic ethnocentrism and racism spanning the middle ages and reaching far back into antiquity. The hatred was directed in both directions—much to the delight of racist Jews.

In Einstein's day, Jews and Gentiles were finally becoming integrated. Racist Einstein and his Zionist friends artificially created a rise in anti-Semitism and demanded segregation. Einstein thought that anti-Semitic attacks and segregation were the best means to preserve the "Jewish race" from the "fatal assimilation" brought on by better relations between Jews and non-Jews.

2 THE DESTRUCTIVE IMPACT OF RACIST JEWISH TRIBALISM

Jews have an ancient tradition of racism and of deliberately segregating themselves from all other peoples. Jews even segregate each other into separate subdivisions of Sephardim and Ashkenazim. Sephardim have traditionally considered themselves to be more "racially pure" than Ashkenazim, and, therefore, "racially" superior to Ashkenazim. Ashkenazim have traditionally viewed themselves as "racially" superior to Gentiles. Since they cannot claim "racial" superiority over the Sephardim, the Ashkenazim use tribalistic politics to kill them off.

"Jews have not troubled themselves to justify, on any rational ground, the tenacious fight of their race against the storms of nineteen centuries of persecution. The fight has been its own justification. Obviously, a race that has endured what theirs has withstood must have some glorious mission to perform; to define that mission would be an element of positive weakness, since their enemies would then have a chance to meet them on the ground of reason, where their peculiar virtues, tenacity, single-mindedness, and pliant heroism, would avail them nothing."—RALPH PHILIP BOAS

"The position of the Jews is unique. For them race, religion, and country are interrelated, as they are interrelated in the case of no other race, no other religion, and no other country on earth. By a strange and most unhappy fate it is this people of all others which, retaining to the full its racial self-consciousness, has been severed from its home, has wandered into all lands and has nowhere been able to create for itself an organized social commonwealth. Only Zionism—so at least Zionists believe—can provide some mitigation of this great tragedy."—ARTHUR JAMES BALFOUR

2.1 Introduction

In the United States in the early 1920's, scholars became increasing concerned by the invasion of racist and tribalistic "Russian or Polish Jews", who had been pouring into America since the 1880's. These immigrants allegedly sought to take over American universities and to Judaize American society. Harvard University opened the question of whether or not it was in the best interests of American society to allow Jews from Poland to obtain majority control over highly influential American colleges and universities.

In 1917, Ralph Philip Boas, who was himself Jewish, discussed the tribalistic, segregationist and racist attitudes common among Jews of the era—and throughout history,

> "DESPITE the fact that we are ceasing to persecute people who disagree with us in religion or politics, we only dimly realize that one of the greatest evils of persecution is the fact that it saves its victims the trouble of justifying themselves. Persecution begets martyrdom, a glory as lacking in reason as its progenitor. Whether Sir Roger Casement was right or not is now only an academic question; his execution, by enshrining him forever in the Pantheon of Irish martyrs, makes the heart rather than the mind his judge. So it is with the Jews. Jews have not troubled themselves to justify, on any rational ground, the tenacious fight of their race against the storms of nineteen centuries of persecution. The fight has been its own justification. Obviously, a race that has endured what theirs has withstood must have some glorious mission to perform; to define that mission would be an element of positive weakness, since their enemies would then have a chance to meet them on the ground of reason, where their peculiar virtues, tenacity, single-mindedness, and pliant heroism, would avail them nothing.
>
> It is, therefore, a happy chance for the American Jew that his age-long persecution has either ended or has degenerated into petty social discrimination. For he must now realize that the day has gone when he could justify himself by recalling his heroic miseries. In other days and other countries he faced only the problems of existence. New ideas and opportunities could not pass the walls of the ghetto; custom made adherence to old ceremonies and beliefs not only easy but imperative. The Sabbath was the one day on which the Jew could be a man

instead of a thing; the recurrent holidays gave him his one outlet for the emotions rigidly suppressed in daily life; the study and analysis of the Law and the Talmud furnished the intellectual exercise that his eager mind was denied in the schools and the learned circles of the country which tolerated him. The very fact that he was confined within a pale, therefore, made it easy for him to keep his race a distinct entity.

But now, if he is unable to find a rational ground for his religious and racial unity, he will meet a foe more insidious than persecution—the gradual disintegration of race and religious consciousness within the faith. Ironically enough, what pales, pogroms, and ghettos could not accomplish, freedom promises to bring to pass. So the time has come when the Jew in America must decide what he is going to do with and for himself; his enemies can no longer save him the effort of decision.

[***]

What is true of Europe is true also of the United States: the Jew occupies a position the importance of which is out of all proportion to his numbers. Hence the problem of Judaism is of real interest in America, because the influence which the Jew can have upon social life and the current political and financial situation depends almost entirely upon his mode of life and manner of thought. [***] What the Jew is going to do with this self-consciousness may, to Christians, seem of little moment. It is not of that loyal kind which moves men to blow up munition factories, or to plant bombs in steamships. For others, doubtless, its implications are not of great importance. For himself, however, they are everything. His self-consciousness colors his whole point of view. It is not a simple thing. It is compounded of many factors. It is both racial and religious; it makes him both hopeful and despondent; it gives cause both for pride and for a feeling of inferiority; it makes him clannish, and it makes him long for a wider field of acquaintance. [***] Judaism is clannish. Jews undoubtedly hang together. The combination of persecution with its inevitable concomitant, self-justification, acts as a centripetal force in driving Jews upon themselves. Just as Jews have the almost grotesque notion that a man will make his philosophic and religious convictions 'jibe' with his birth, so they have the wholly grotesque notion that a man should choose his friends and his wife from the small group among whom he happens to be born, though later education and environment may move him a thousand miles away. The results of this clannishness are paradoxical. For instance, the average Jew is sure that the chief reason why Anti-Semitism is everywhere ready to show its ugly head, is jealousy of the splendid history and the extraordinary business ability of the race. At the same time he subconsciously assumes the inferiority which has long been attributed to him, covering his feelings, however, by uncalled-for justification and bitter opposition to all criticism. It is torture to him, for example, that *The Merchant of Venice* should be read in the public schools. Who can blame him? For Shylock, although undoubtedly an exaggerated character, nevertheless makes concrete those qualities the portrayal of which hurts because it bears the sting of truth.

The development of committees 'On Purity of the Press' in Jewish societies, and the extraordinary wire-pulling over the Russian treaty and the Immigration bill, show to what lengths this consciousness can go. It is impossible for the Jew to be entirely at ease in the world. He is introspective and suspicious, often unhappy, always sure that, for good or ill, he is a marked man among men.

There are three attitudes which Jews in this country take toward their problem—a few as a result of having thought it through, the majority as a result of the forces of inertia, environment, or chance, forces of which they themselves are perhaps not aware. Some Jews attempt to get rid of their self-consciousness by separating from the group. They deliberately set out to convince themselves that there is no difference between them and other men, and that they can act and live in all respects like other American citizens. A second group find their fellow Jews entirely satisfactory. They are conscious of a difference between themselves and others, but, living as they do in large cities where the Jewish community numbers hundreds of thousands, they feel no need of association with non-Jews other than that which they get in business. They are rich, or at least well-to-do; they have all the comforts that money can buy; they occupy fine streets and build expensive synagogues. They are willing, not only to accept their group-consciousness, but to develop it to the fullest extent by means of societies and fraternal orders. In the third place, there is a small group of Jews keenly conscious of their race, who would like to make Judaism vital as a great religion and a great tradition. They differ from the second group in that they not only accept their individuality but try to justify it. It is not sufficient for them that there should be enough Jewish organizations and undertakings to make a respectable year-book: they are interested in showing why such organizations should exist They not only *are* Jews, but they *want to be* Jews; they want to feel that Judaism really has a mission to fulfill and a message to carry to the questioning world.

The Jew who attempts to solve his problem by separating from his community must leave the great centres of Jewish life and go to some small town where he may make a fresh start. There he will find himself in an anomalous position. He will have neither the support that comes from rubbing elbows with one's own kind, nor the mental and moral stiffening that comes from active opposition. He will be simply an odd fish, and as such will be subject, not to antagonism, but to curiosity. What cordiality he meets with is the cordiality of curiosity. He is a strange creature, similar—on a far lower scale of interest—to a Chinese traveler or a Hindu student. He is engaged in conversation on the 'Jewish problem,' or Jewish customs and history, until he sickens with trading on the race-consciousness that he is striving to forget. With cruel kindliness his friends impress upon him that his Judaism 'makes no difference,' with the result that he finds himself anticipating every imminent friendship by a clear statement of his race, lest the friendship be built upon the sands of prejudice. His social relations must be above reproach. A hasty word, an ill-considered action, in other men to be put down to idiosyncracy, in him is attributed to his birth. Even when there exists the frankest and most open friendship, he is continually seeing difficulties. The fathers have eaten a sour grape and the children's teeth are set on edge. The self-consciousness that he learned in youth reappears in maturity. Whether he will or no, a Jew he remains.

If he finds his situation intolerable he may, of course, utterly and completely deny his Jewish affiliation. He may consort with Christians, join a Christian church, marry a Christian wife, and tread under foot the old associations that will occasionally cast a disagreeable shadow across his life Unfortunately for such a solution, a cloud still hangs about the idea of apostasy. Such a refuge seems to a man of honor despicable. It is a cowardly procedure, surely, to deny one's birth and sail under false colors, the more so since, though it does no harm to others, it gains advantage for one's self. Why ii should it be treason for a Jew to abandon his religion and forget his birth any more than for a Frenchman or a Swede to do so? Probably for the reason that no one cares whether a man was born in France or not, whereas in certain circles it makes a great deal of difference if a man was born in Jewry. Furthermore, Christians feel strongly that the Jew who forsakes the religion into which he was born, does so, not because his eyes have been opened upon the truth, but because he sees in apostasy definite material advantages. The Jew who would take this means of obtaining peace, therefore, would find himself cursed by an irrational idealism which can disturb while it cannot fortify and achieve.

If, however, he returns to some great centre of Jewish life and attempts to affiliate with his own people, he is in a perilous position. He is more than likely to meet with distrust where he seeks sympathy. Jews are so extremely sensitive to criticism and so keenly conscious of the social discrimination which they encounter from Christians, that they can hardly believe that a man who seems to have lived for several years on an equal footing with Christians has not either denied his birth, in which case he has been a traitor, or has not certain qualities of mind which, since they have been palatable to Christians, must be severely critical of Jews.

And, indeed, they have, perhaps, a measure of justice in their position. It is impossible for a Jew to live apart from his race for several years without looking upon his people with a new light. For one thing, distance has enabled him to focus. He has learned to sympathize more than a little with those hotel-keepers whose ban upon Jews is a terrible thorn in the flesh of the man whose money ought to take him anywhere. He has come to see that the clannishness of Jews serves only to intensify what social discrimination may exist, and to make present in the imagination much that does not. He has realized that persecution is not necessarily justification, and that because a Jew was blackballed at a fashionable club does not prove that he was a man of first-rate calibre. And finally, he has perceived that there is an arrogance of endurance as well as an arrogance of persecution, and that for a man to be continually assuming that people are taking the trouble to despise him for his birth, is to postulate an importance that does not exist.

On the other hand, he has, because of his distance, idealized

Judaism. In his retirement he studied the history of his people; he thrilled with their martyrdom; he marveled at their tenacity and their fortitude. He built up for himself on the cobweb foundation of boyhood memories, visions of the simple nobility of Jewish ritual and ceremonies, and vague ideals of an inspiring religious faith. He may, perhaps, have met, far more frequently than ill-will, a sentimental and unbalanced adulation of Jews. The cult of the new is with us, and the history, the folk-lore, the literature, and the customs of Judaism have, for many people who pride themselves on their social liberality, the fascination of novelty. It is the easiest thing in the world for a Jew to yield to this sentimental tolerance, and to view his people in a rosy light.

It is, therefore, something of a shock to him when he reënters a great Jewish community, for he finds that the great mass of American Jews have sunk into a comfortable materialism. What persecution could not accomplish, success in business has brought to pass. The innate qualities of the Jew could not save him from the fate of the Christian who has become rich in a hurry—grossness and self-conceit. That Jeshurun waxed fat and kicked is as true now as it ever was, and there is little reason to expect that the race which was hopelessly cankered by national prosperity in the days of Solomon can escape a similar fate in the twentieth century. [***] The sad result is that in prosperity the Jewish self-consciousness ceases to be religious and becomes merely racial.

[***]

The number of immigrants, or children of immigrants, from countries where for centuries they have been trained in an atmosphere of slavish cunning and worship of money, who become rich, is almost incredible. In Russia, Galicia, or Roumania, they cultivated a self-respect by rigid adherence to dignified and beautiful customs; in America the florid exuberance of newly acquired wealth cannot be dignified. Clannishness, exclusion from circles of good taste and good breeding, the infiltration of the parvenu East-European Jews, and imitation of the most obvious aspects of Americanism—its flamboyant and tasteless materialism—all combine to make the thoughtful Jew sadly question what hope lies in the bulk of the Jews who live in the great American cities.

[***]

[Zionism] is actuated by a spirit of helpfulness and by an ideal of racial unity. [***] Aided by persecution and poverty, [American Judaism] furnished admirable discipline to a race naturally stubborn and tenacious. Persecution, poverty, and discipline gone, what is left?—an indistinct monotheism joined to an ethical tradition never formulated into a system, and only vaguely defined. None of the great Jewish philosophers ever succeeded in establishing a Jewish creed; indeed, there was no need of one when common suffering wrought so effectual a bond. [***] At all events it must be remembered that, since the problem of Judaism comes from intense self-consciousness, persecution and sentimental tolerance are both bad for the Jew. The one saves him the trouble of seeking out his reason for existence; the other flatters him into a belief that there is no necessity for the search. If men will treat Jews like other people, instead of nourishing their age-long notions of peculiarity, they will make it easier for time to settle the Jewish problem as it settles all others."[67]

In 1845, an article appeared in *The North American Review*, which revealed that governments were concerned by Jewish Messianic aspirations and the resultant disloyalty of Jews,

"The Jews in Russian Poland have lately been subjected to military service; and to the soldier's oath the government has added, for Israelitish recruits, the following clause: 'I swear to be faithful to my standard, and never desert it, even should the Messiah come upon earth.'"[68]

Frankist Jews in Poland asserted in the 1700's and throughout their later history that the Messiah had arrived in the person of Jacob Frank. They formed revolutionary and destructive bands, which tore apart Polish society. Frank began a dynasty of Messiahs, whose soul alleged migrated from one Messiah to the next through the process of Metempsychosis. Jews have long believed in the transmigration of souls and the perpetual reign of the seed of King David through reincarnation, as opposed to purely through reproduction.[69] It was the duty of the Messiah to utterly destroy the Gentile world.

2.2 Do Not Blaspheme the "Jewish Saint"

When Einstein arrived in America in early April of 1921, shortly after

Einstein, himself, declared that anyone who disagreed with him must *ipso facto* be anti-Semitic, the Board of Aldermen of the City of New York met to vote on a proposal to grant Chaim Weizmann and Albert Einstein the "freedom of the city". Alderman Bruce M. Falconer voted against the proposal and was immediately assaulted, threatened with severe retaliation and smeared as an "anti-Semite"—an accusation he emphatically denied. *The New York Times*, which was owned by a Jewish publisher named Adolph S. Ochs,[70] published Alderman Falconer's name, occupation, and home address, on the front page together with the charges of anti-Semitism, a description of the assault against him, and a report of the threats to destroy him, as well as his denials of any prejudice.

Several stories describing the spectacle appeared in *The New York Times*, beginning with 6 April 1921,

"HOLDS UP FREEDOM OF CITY TO EINSTEIN

Alderman Falconer Blocks Move to Grant Official Honors to Two Scientists.

NEVER HEARD OF HIS THEORY

Alderman Friedman Shakes Fist in Face of Opponent and Calls Action an Insult.

There is at least one man in New York who never heard of Professor Albert Einstein, whose theory of relativity has been discussed for many months in newspapers and magazines. He is Alderman Bruce M. Falconer, whose lack of acquaintance with Professor Einstein's fame caused a row in the Board of

Aldermen yesterday and resulted in the freedom of the city being temporarily refused to both Professor Einstein and Professor Chaim Weizmann, chemist and inventor of the high explosive trinitrotoluol.

At the request of Aldermanic President LaGuardia, Mayor Hylan has called a special meeting of the Board for next Friday at 1:30 P. M., to take action on the resolution.

'I am expressing the feeling of the entire Board when I ask you to call this meeting in order that the desires of the people of this city may be carried out in extending this call to these distinguished people,' he said to the Mayor.

Professor Weizmann is President of the International Zionist Organization, and, with Professor Einstein, M. M. Ussischkin and Dr. Benzion Mossinson, is here to confer with American Zionists. They were received at the City Hall yesterday by Mayor Hylan and a committee of citizens. More than 5,000 Zionists filled the plaza in front of the City Hall.

It was thought that the granting of the freedom of the city to the two visitors would be a mere formality. So it would have been but for Alderman Falconer, who is a lawyer and lives at 701 Madison Avenue. After the ceremony the Aldermen went to their Chamber and a resolution was introduced by Alderman Louis Zeltner, Moritz Graubard and Samuel R. Morris in honor of the visitors. Every one was ready to vote favorably when Alderman Falconer arose. He confessed that until yesterday he never had heard of either Professor Einstein or Professor Weizmann. He asked to be enlightened, but nobody offered to explain the theory of relativity. Mr. Falconer said that he thought the freedom of the city had been too often granted, and, although his objection had nothing to do with racial or religious prejudices, he believed that caution should be exercised.

A storm broke about Alderman Falconer's head. Laughter and protests came from every side, and several members tried to tell him the records of the two men, but their recital made little impression upon the Alderman.

Rules Committee Dodges.

A motion that the resolution be made a general order for next week when it could be passed over Alderman Falconer's protest precipitated a parliamentary row, and in a few minutes the board was tangled up in rulings. President LaGuardia came in and took the chair. He ruled that the point of order to make the resolution a general order was debatable, and about this time the Committee on Rules, led by Alderman Kenneally, slipped out of the room.

Alderman Falconer was obdurate, and at the end of the debate the Rules Committee came back and an attempt was made to get around his objection. It was moved to suspend the rules, when the resolution could be passed over his objection. But Alderman Falconer suspected the purpose of the motion, and objected. Alderman Friedman then asked that the resolution be withdrawn.

After the incident was officially closed there were angry arguments in the boardroom. Alderman Friedman shook his fist under Mr. Falconer's nose and said that his action was an insult and that he would carry the issue into Mr. Falconer's district. Judge Gustave Hartmann tried unsuccessfully to tell Mr. Falconer what Professor Einstein had done in science.

After the adjournment of the meeting Judge Hartman charged Alderman Falconer with having made his objection to the resolution because of purely anti-Semitic motives. This brought a denial from the Alderman and when Judge Hartman repeated his charge Mr. Falconer said: 'You're a liar, I am most certainly not opposed to the Jewish people as a race.'

'I will not let this matter drop,' said Judge Hartman. 'Not only will I bring the matter before the people of the city and the intelligent Jewry, but I will also press this matter in the council of the Republican Party. I am firmly convinced that your attitude in this matter was prompted by anti-Semitism, and I will not be satisfied until you are retired from public life.'

When Professors Weizmann and Einstein arrived at the City Hall, accompanied by their wives and other members of the delegation, they were escorted to the Mayor's office by James F. Sinnott, Secretary to Mayor Hylan, and the Committee of Welcome led by Magistrate Rosenblatt.

'As Mayor of this city, which is the home of more than one-third of all the Jews in America,' said Mayor Hylan, 'I gladly join in felicitating those who have already accomplished so much toward the restoration of Palestine. The success thus far achieved may be regarded as a happy augury that continued endeavor will result in the final and complete attainment of the hope and aspiration of the Zionist organization.

'May I say to Dr. Weizmann and Professor Einstein that in New York we point with pride to the courage and fidelity of our Jewish population, demonstrated so unmistakably in the World War.'

George W. Wickersham, former Attorney General, also spoke of the achievements of the two leaders of the delegation.

Professor Weizmann thanked the Mayor and Mr. Wickersham for their welcome, which he accepted as showing sympathy for the cause he represented.

Mrs. Einstein lost a gold lorgnette with a chain attached during the reception at the City Hall. It was an heirloom."

Intimidation, threats of retaliation and retaliatory actions are common practice among Einstein advocates. The judge threatening and smearing the attorney was and is not unique to the legal profession and political life. American Zionism was headed by United States Supreme Court Justice Louis Dembitz Brandeis and represented by Judge Julian William Mack of the United States Circuit Court of Appeals for the Seventh Circuit. There have been accusations of Jewish American judges allowing guilty Zionist criminals to go free and otherwise preventing justice.[71] The Talmud and other Judaic literature encourage Jews to favor one another at the expense of Gentiles and to forgive crimes Jews commit against Gentiles. For example, *Sanhedrin* 58b states that a Gentile who strikes a Jew must be killed, because striking a Jew is like striking God. Yet according to *Sanhedrin* 57a, a Jew who murders a Gentile without cause will not be put to death and is not civilly liable for the crime.[72] Furthermore, a Jew may steal from a Gentile and may keep the stolen goods with both criminal and civil immunity under Jewish law.

Numerous physicists of international renown have complained directly to your author that their works in opposition to relativity theory, and which expose Einstein's career of plagiarism, have been refused publication without grounds and are often met with angry personal attacks and threats of retaliation as well as reactionary and unjustified accusations of anti-Semitism. Some peer reviewed journals and scientific conferences regularly refuse to even consider works and lectures which question relativity theory, or Einstein's originality. Even Jewish opponents are attacked as if *ipso facto* anti-Semites for daring to utter a syllable of truth about Einstein's plagiarism and the fallibility of "his" theories. Helen Dukas (Einstein's secretary) and Bannesh

Hoffmann wrote,

"Einstein had become a figure of enormous symbolic importance to Jews. In 1923, when he visited Mount Scopus, the site on which the Hebrew University was to rise, he was invited to speak from 'the lectern that has waited for you two thousand years.'"[73]

Dennis Overbye tells the story of Ilse Einstein's letter to Georg Nicolai of 22 May 1918 in which she complains of Albert Einstein's perverse sexual advances towards her. Albert Einstein was conducting an incestuous and adulterous relationship with her mother, Else Einstein, at the time. Albert Einstein was related to his cousin Else through both his mother and his father. Einstein was perhaps dissuaded from his perverse wish to marry Ilse Einstein by his uncle Rudolf Einstein's (Rudolf Einstein was Elsa Einstein's father and Ilse Einstein's grandfather, as well as Albert Einstein's uncle and father-in-law) dowry of 100,000 Marks, which Albert Einstein accepted when he married his cousin Else—Albert thereby continued to have access to Ilse.[74] Albert Einstein was behaving like a Frankist Jew.

Overbye states that Wolf Zuelzer preserved the letter,

"despite pressure from Margot Einstein, Helen Dukas, and lawyers representing the Einstein estate to surrender it or destroy it. The tale, an example of the difficulties scholars have faced in telling the Einstein story, is preserved in Zuelzer's correspondence in the American Heritage archive at the University of Wyoming."[75]

It is rather embarrassing for an ethnic "Saint" and national hero to be exposed as a pervert and a plagiarist, and Einstein had become both an ethnic saint and a national hero for Jews. Bruno Thüring used these facts to characterize Einstein as a rabid nationalist, who used his pacifistic preaching as a front to promote his Zionist agenda. Thüring recounted that the *Jüdische Rundschau* quoted the Zionist David Yellin's welcoming address to Einstein in the name of Jerusalem on 15 March 1929 and Einstein's response:

",,Du hast den Namen ‚Gaon' verdient, den das jüdische Volk seinen erwählten geistigen Führern gibt — dies aber nicht nur wegen deiner genialen Leistungen in der Wissenschaft,

wiewohl wir sie recht zu schätzen wissen — noch mehr aber bist
du uns ein Gaon, weil du die Fahne der nationalen Wiedergeburt
hoch in der Hand hältst und die hebräische Universität in
Jerusalem gefordert hast.''
    Und Einstein antwortete darauf:
    „Der heutige Tag ist der größte meines Lebens. Heute ist das
wichtigste Ereignis in meiner Lebensgeschichte geschehen. Im
Laufe meines Lebens lernte ich die Verirrung der jüdischen
Seele, die Sünde der Selbstverleugnung des Volks-Jüdischen
kennen. Und so freue ich mich, daß Israel seine Bedeutung in der
Welt wieder zu erkennen beginnt. Diese Tat, die Befreiung der
jüdischen Seele, wurde von der zionistischen Bewegung
vollbracht."[76]

Einstein wrote to Paul Ehrenfest on 12 April 1926,

"I do believe that in time this endeavor will grow into something
splendid; and, Jewish Saint that I am, my heart rejoices."[77]

The German Consul General in New York reported on 21 March
1931,

"Es ist ein Charakteristikum für die New Yorker Volkspsyche,
daß die Persönlichkeit Einsteins, ohne daß deutlich erkennbare
Gründe dafür anzuführen wären, Ausbrüche einer Art
Massenhysterie auslöste, und zwar nicht nur bei den hierfür
besonders veranlagten Gruppen von „Friedensfreunden'' und
den schwärmerischen Phantasten neu entstandener mystischer
Religionsgesellschaften, sondern auch in relativ so kühlen
Kreisen, wie z. B. bei den amerikanischen Förderern des
Palästinawerkes. Inwieweit hierbei der Umstand eine Rolle
spielte, daß sich unter den sieben Millionen Einwohnern New
Yorks annähernd zwei Millionen Juden befinden, und ob in der
Wechselwirkung zwischen Presse und Publikum erstere ihre
zahllosen Spezialartikel über Einstein brachte, weil die Leser
sich begehrten, oder ob letztere sich hierfür interessierten, weil
die Zeitungen dieses Interesse schon vor Einsteins Ankunft
erweckten und alsdann wachhielten, wird schwer zu entscheiden
sein. Nicht ganz belanglos erscheint in letzterer Beziehung aber
vielleicht das Scherzwort eines Rundfunkredners zur Zeit des
Höhepunktes der Einstein-Begeisterung, daß wohl nicht 50

Personen wüßten, warum der Gelehrte überhaupt hier sei . . . Einsteins Ausführungen brachten die Anwesenden in einen Begeisterungstaumel, der sich auch darin äußerte, daß zahlreiche Personen Einsteins Hände und Kleidungsstücke küßten."[78]

Philipp Frank wrote,

"The Jewish population of America itself regarded Einstein's visit as the visit of a spiritual leader, which filled them with pride and joy. The Jews felt that their prestige among their fellow citizens was raised by the fact that a man of Einstein's generally recognized intellectual greatness publicly acknowledged his membership in the Jewish community and made their interests his own."[79]

Chaim Weizmann recalled his visit with Einstein to New York in 1921,

"We had reckoned—literally—without our host, which was, or seemed to be, the whole of New York Jewry. Long before the afternoon ended, delegations began to assemble on the quay and even the docks."[80]

The ethnic, racial and religious prejudice of Einstein and his followers, even if in the understandable and forgivable form of misguided pride, has no place in science. Many unscrupulous individuals have disingenuously smeared any person who dares to question Einstein or the theory of relativity as an "anti-Semite", in order to change the subject from the critic's legitimate arguments, to a disingenuous personal attack against the legitimate critic, which evokes powerful emotions. They inhibit the progress of science and the accurate portrayal of history.

The saga of Alderman Falconer's exercising of his rights to oppose the award of the "Freedom of the City" to Weizmann and Einstein continued across the pages of *The New York Times* and newspapers around the world. *The New York Times* reported 7 April 1921,

"RELATIVITY AT CITY HALL.

Alderman FALCONER wants everybody to understand that when he said he had never heard of Professor ALBERT EINSTEIN he didn't know it was the famous EINSTEIN, the destroyer of time and space. The Alderman's reasoning is intelligible even if its result was rather unhappy. Two gentlemen were coming up to be formally endowed with such freedom as can still be granted in this well regulated city. Who were they? Mr. EINSTEIN and Mr. WEIZMANN. And how was any one to know—unless he had read the papers—that this EINSTEIN was the celebrated EINSTEIN? He was coming to New York not as a scientist but as a Zionist, in which capacity he hasn't been working long enough to become celebrated. Any nobody would have suspected that a Mayor hostile to art artists would be asking the freedom of the city for a couple of mere science scientists.

So Alderman FALCONER was led into the blunder in which he is now trying to justify himself. He says EINSTEIN is a German. True, he is German-born, and recently he spent a year or two in Berlin. But genuine blown-in-the-glass Germans of the Reventlow type would fling their hands and howl if they heard EINSTEIN called a German. One of the reasons for his leaving Berlin, apparently, was the attacks made on him by some of the reactionary monarchist organs. They had three counts against EINSTEIN—he is a Swiss citizen, a Jew and a democrat. Nobody but the Staats-Zeitung can seriously believe that 'hatred of the Germans' is behind this opposition to EINSTEIN.

But the professor probably felt quite at home in the City Hall, with or without freedom. Relativity was being practiced in those quarters long before EINSTEIN discovered it as a theory. The rays of logic emanating from the Mayor's office are bent as badly as EINSTEIN's rays of light. EINSTEIN proved that things are not where they seem to be, but that is no news to gentlemen elected on a program of economy who have raised the city budget to unheard-of figures. And a man who has annihilated space may be able to provide our municipal Government with some happy thoughts on the rapid-transit problem.

And perhaps Alderman FALCONER has done no real harm. Mrs. EINSTEIN, emerging from the crowd which had gathered for the reception at the City Hall, missed a valuable gold lorgnette; so no doubt she and her husband are vividly impressed, already, with the freedom of our city."

Einstein and his advocates would sometimes flip-flop on the issue of Einstein's citizenship over the course of many years, often to avoid fulfilling national or political duties, or purely to allege bigotry, arbitrarily changing Einstein's status to fit the accusation and to emphasize and aggravate social divides for political profit.[81] Einstein was also dishonest about his religious status and misrepresented it to suit the occasion and encouraged his friend Paul Ehrenfest to do the same. Ehrenfest had more character than Einstein and Ehrenfest stood by his convictions.[82]

Smear tactics were routine for Einstein apologists. *The New York Times* reported,

"EINSTEIN TO HAVE FREEDOM OF STATE

Senate Passes Resolution Honoring
Visiting Scientist—Measure
Before Assembly Today.

Special to The New York Times.

ALBANY, April 6.—The Board of Alderman having failed yesterday to extend to Drs. Albert Einstein and Chaim Weizmann, the Zionist emissaries, the freedom of the City of New York, the Senate today, by unanimous vote, extended to the distinguished visitors the freedom of the entire State of New York.

The resolution on which action was taken was sponsored by Senator Nathan Straus Jr. of New York, who characterized the failure of the Alderman to act on the Zeltner resolution as 'a disgrace.'

The text of the Straus resolution follows:

'Whereas Albert Einstein of Switzerland and Chaim Wezmann of Great Britain are now visiting our State; and

'Whereas the purpose of their visit is to cement the bonds of unity between the United States and her neighbors abroad in the great struggle for human progress and happiness, and especially to unite the old world and the new in establishing a cultural centre for the Jews of the World in Palestine; and

'Whereas the achievements of Dr. Einstein in the spheres of physics and astronomy have commanded the attention and the admiration of the entire civilized world, and the record of Dr. Weizmann as a chemist during the World War has made the people of the allied and associated powers his debtors, and,

'Whereas it the desire of the Commonwealth of New York to make these distinguished visitors feel that every true American heart goes out to them in cordial welcome; therefore,

'Be it resolved that (if the Assembly concurs) the people of the State of New York extend to Dr. Einstein and Dr. Chaim Weizmann and their associates the handclasp of fellowship and a heartfelt welcome.'

Senator Bernard Downing, another Democrat member from New York City, warmly eulogized the two Zionists and extolled their services to science and to mankind.

The Assembly had adjourned for the day when the Straus resolution was adopted, but upon reconvening tomorrow will have the measure before it for concurrent action.

FALCONER IS DENOUNCED.

Owasco Club Condemns Alderman
for Blocking Welcome to Einstein.

Resolutions denouncing Alderman Bruce Falconer for his action in blocking the resolution in the Board of Aldermen offering the freedom of the city to Professor Albert Einstein and his colleagues were passed at a meeting of the Owasco Club, the Democratic organization of the Seventeenth Assembly District, yesterday.

'The conduct of Alderman Falconer manifests a spirit of bigotry, narrow-mindedness and intolerance, and displays him as a champion of anti-Semitism, which is only a stepchild of anti-Americanism,' said the resolution."

The Judge found political opportunists who sought to make good on his threats and repeat his smears. One can only conclude that such hysteria in New York, such vicious and highly publicized smears and vindictive opportunistic attacks, must have had a chilling effect on the debate over relativity theory and Einstein's alleged originality. Such was the ignoble birth of the modern myth of St. Einstein's infallibility and to this country was of too brief duration and his contacts while here were too narrow.' Second half of answer is right. It doesn't take long to know Americans: 10 minutes is the average time for striking up a real human kind of acquaintance here, and Einstein was with us weeks and weeks— but—'his contacts while here were too narrow.' For reference, Mr. Brisbane's comment again.

Einstein's tribalists cannot answer; it is an outbreak of bad manners, rank contemptuousness and untruth which is indefensible. Einstein never was a great scientist; now we know he is not even an ordinarily passable individual.

What puzzles the Washington *Post* is the reason for Einstein staying on in the country after he had found what a detestable place it was; and why he went on accumulating university degrees and other academic honors when he had formed so low an opinion of our institutions, and when the only scholar he could find in the United States was a Jew out in Chicago.

It's a somewhat honest wail the *Post* puts forth:

'Why did Prof. Einstein not discover after a few days' stay in America his impressions and then make a speedy return to his haven? Why did he accept the attentions and awards from municipalities and educational institutions if he questioned their sincerity?'

The answer is simple, but the *Post* doesn't give it.

The answer is given in 'blank' verse by a poet on this page.

Things One Cannot Print
(Obviously done in blank verse.)
in writing for the Editors
   Telling funny news,
Omit from all you chance to say
   Mention of the South Americans.

Whene'er you feel the writing urge
   Why write whate'er you choose,
Except you must not write at all
   About our friends the Italians.

If verses fill your soul with song
   Turn fondly to your Muse,
But do not let her lead you far;
   Sing not about the British.

originality—opposition was too often shouted down by smear tactic and intimidation—even by formal decree.

Falconer tried to calm and reassure the hysterical mob, who defamed him and sought to destroy his life. *The New York Times* reported on 9 April 1921

"FREEDOM OF CITY GIVEN TO EINSTEIN

Alderman Honor Relativity Discoverer
and Prof. Weizmann
Despite Falconer's Protest.

HE DEFENDS ADVERSE VOTE

Cites Courtesies to Dr. Cook, De
Valera, Mannix and Mrs.
MacSwiney as Mistakes.

Professor Albert Einstein, the noted mathematician and discoverer of relativity, and Professor Chaim Weizmann, British chemist now have the freedom of New York City. It was voted to them yesterday at a special meeting of the Board of Aldermen, made necessary by the refusal of Alderman Bruce Falconer to consent to the passage of the resolution when it first came up on Tuesday, when the two scientists were welcomed by Mayor Hylan at City Hall.

Alderman Falconer cast the only negative vote yesterday, and in so doing said he was not actuated by race prejudice, but that he had in mind the dignity of the honor which has been given to some of the greatest Americans, and thought it should not be conferred on any one unless he were known to every person in the city. He said his first ancestor in this country came as secretary to Lord Cornbury, the first person to receive the freedom of the city, in 1702.

Alderman William T. Collins, leader of the Democrats, seized upon the mention of Alderman Falconer's ancestors with avidity and ridiculed it.

'We on this board are just as proud of our city and of the conferring of the freedom of the city on guests as is Alderman Falconer,' he said. 'It was only narrowness and bigotry that made the one member of this board object to granting the freedom of the city to Dr. Weizmann and Professor Einstein.'

Alderman Falconer said that Alderman Friedman did him a great injustice in saying that his objection was based on race prejudice, and said that his private physician is a Jew and that many of his friends are Jews.

'In 1909,' he said, 'the keys of the city were unfortunately given by the Board of Alderman to Dr. Cook, who pretended to have discovered the North Pole, but were afterward officially withdrawn from him. After that the freedom of the city was not again extended for ten years, until the second year of the Hylan Administration, when it was given to Eamon de Valera, at a meeting which occurred when I happened to be away from the city.

'Since that time it has been extended to Cardinal Mercier, King Albert of Belgium, the Prince of Wales, Archbishop Mannix and Mrs. MacSwiney. At the time the resolution was suddenly proposed in connection with Archbishop Mannix, I did not vote in favor of conferring the honor upon him.

'The next and last individual upon whom this honor was conferred was Mrs. MacSwiney. I did not vote for it, and if I had had a proper chance would have objected.

'I have been assured,' he said, 'that Professor Einstein was born in Germany and was taken to Switzerland, but returned to Germany prior to the war. He is consequently a citizen of Germany, of an enemy country, and might be regarded as an alien enemy.'

Alderman Friedman told Alderman Falconer that Professor Einstein was not a citizen of Germany, but of Switzerland, and Alderman Vladeck, leader of the Socialists, also said that Professor Einstein was far from being a German citizen.

Alderman Ferrand, the Republican leader, in moving the question, said:

'For what has occurred I make no apology to this board or to the citizens of the city. It can be charged to no party. It can only be charged to an individual who is arrogant and ignorant. We will have to take it from whence it comes.'

Professor Einstein visited the College of the City of New York yesterday, and attended a class in mathematics and physics, where he listened to an explanation of his theory by Prof. Edward Kasner of Columbia University. President Sidney Mezes, of the City College, and a number of advanced students were present. Prof. Einstein, who understands English, although he does not speak it well, complimented Prof. Kasner on his presentation of the subject, and later made a twenty minute talk.

It was announced at Princeton University yesterday that Professor Einstein would be the guest of the University from May 9 to 15 and would give five lectures in that time on relativity."

On 11 April 1921, *The New York Times* began to see that Falconer had made a good point,

"A Ceremony
in Need
of Revision.

Now that the implacable FALCONER has been beaten and Dr. EINSTEIN possesses formally and officially the 'freedom of the city' that actually is granted to anybody from almost anywhere, it might be well to abandon the use of a phrase that long since ceased to have any meaning even remotely related to the words composing it. Then the ground would be cleared for its replacement by a designation indicative of a special municipal welcome, accorded to visitors made worthy of it by great achievements or honorable services.

With the ancient ceremony thus revised and brought into accord with modern conditions, Dr. EINSTEIN certainly would be among those thus honored by an appreciation not less honorable to those who manifested it, and at least it is to be hoped that the honor less often would be cheapened, as 'the freedom of the city' has been cheapened several times in recent years, by giving it to persons who—well, to persons whose claims for admiration and respect, unlike his, were not firmly founded on the unanimous opinion of competent judges."

It is noteworthy that the same newspaper which had called Einstein's theory "much-debated" on the front page on 3 April 1921, claimed one week later that there was unanimous support for it.

When Einstein visited Boston, they refused to award him the freedom of the city. *The New York Times Index* does not name any stories covering this event under "Einstein". All they list were their articles of May 18th and 19th of 1921. From 18 May 1921:

"EINSTEIN SEES BOSTON; FAILS ON EDISON TEST

Asked to Tell Speed of Sound He Refers Questioner to Text Books.

Special to The New York Times.

BOSTON, May 17.—There was a large crowd at the South Station this morning to greet Professor Einstein of relativity fame and his party. From the station the visitors made an unexpected automobile tour through the north and west ends, Boston's Jewish quarters, and then proceeded to the Copley Plaza Hotel, where they sat down to breakfast with Governor Cox, Mayor Peters and some 75 distinguished guests.

Mrs. Weisemann, wife of Dr. Chaim Weisemann, of the visiting party, surprised the party when it came time to pass around the cigars by calmly producing a cigarette and lighting it. Her action was welcomed by the men. They wanted to smoke but hesitated to do so in the presence of Mrs. Weisemann and Mrs. Einstein, the only women present. Mrs. Weisemann's action in 'lighting up' paved the way and the men lit their cigars.

Professor Einstein gave out through his secretary the following message for Bostonians:

'I am happy to be in Boston. I have heard of Boston as one of the most famous cities of the world and the centre of education. I am happy to be here and expect to enjoy my visit to this city and Harvard.'

Of course the famous visitor had run into the ever-present Edison questionnaire controversy. He did not tackle the whole proposition but so far as he went failed and thereby became one of us. He was asked through his secretary, 'What is the speed of sound?' He could not say off-hand, he replied. He did not carry such information in his mind but it was readily available in text books.

Professor Einstein took issue with the famous inventor's contention that a college education is of little value. Professor Einstein said he believed education was a good thing. If a man had ability, he thought, a college education helped him to develop it. He stated he had not had an opportunity to study the Edison list of questions. He had heard of the American inventor in connection with the invention of the phonograph and electrical appliances.

Mrs. Einstein said that while Edison was an inventor who dealt with practical and material things, her husband was a theorist who dealt with problems of space and of the universe."

Einstein's "secretary" was Simon Ginsburg (a. k. a. "Salomon Ginzberg" and "Schlomo Ginossar"), who was the son of "Usher Ginsburg" (a. k. a. "Asher Ginberg" and "Ahad Ha'am"), who published under the *nom de plume* "Achad Ha-am". Ginsburg the elder was the secretary for the Odessa Committee for Palestine.

On 19 May 1921, *The New York Times* reported,

"Einstein Honored at Boston.

BOSTON, May 18.—Professor Albert Einstein, the scientist, and his associate, Professor Chaim Weizmann, were guests of Governor Cox at luncheon today. Professor Einstein had spent the forenoon at Harvard University, where he was received informally by President Lowell and members of the faculty. At his request he was escorted through the various college laboratories and museums."

In marked contrast to the long front page story *The New York Times* published upon Einstein's arrival to America, the notices of his departure were far more humble. On 30 May 1921, *The New York Times* wrote on page 8,

"EINSTEIN SAILS TODAY.

**Dr. Weizmann Will Remain In
Interests of Zionism.**

Professor and Mrs. Einstein will sail for Europe today on the Celtic, leaving behind them some puzzled academic minds. Since he came to this country several weeks ago in the interests of the proposed University of Jerusalem Professor Einstein has been the centre of attraction for scientists who have heard him lecture on his famous theory of relativity. He has spoken at several universities and had the order of Doctor of Science conferred on him by Princeton University.

Dr. Chaim Weizmann of the World Zionist Organization and other members of the commission will remain here for a short time. Mrs. Weizmann, who is President of the Women's International Zionist Organization, which is trying to raise $5,000,000 for welfare work among Jewish women and children in Palestine, appealed yesterday for Jewish women to contribute their jewels and treasure, 'gold and silver, new and old,' to the fund."

and buried back on page 14 of the *The New York Times* of 31 May 1921 was,

"Prof. EINSTEIN SAILS.

**Says Relativity Theory Is Receiving
'Sympathetic Dealing' Here.**

Professor Albert Einstein, who has been lecturing in the United States for several weeks on his theory of relativity, sailed for Liverpool yesterday on the Celtic. In lieu of an interview, he gave out a formal statement in which he said:

'I would like to add that the respect and admiration that I always felt for American scientists have been greatly increased as a result of my personal contact with them. I have seen a sympathetic dealing with the theory of relativity and a truly detached scientific interest in it.'

Professor Einstein announced that he had refused to accept an invitation to be the guest of Lord Haldane in London, but gave no reason for his action. Mrs. Clara Louise Weizmann, wife of Chaim Weizmann, President of the World Zionist Organization, also was a passenger. Others who sailed were P. S. Hill, President of the Universal Leaf Tobacco Company; Martin Vogel, formerly Assistant United States Treasurer; Toscha Seidel, violinist; Karonongse, Siamese Minister to the United States; M. Ussichkin, Secretary of the World Zionist Organization, and Dr. George E. Vincent, head of the Rockefeller Foundation."

The joke was on those who had made such a show of defending Einstein's "honor" and who went to such extraordinary lengths to cater to Einstein during his visit to America. Instead of exhibiting due gratitude, Albert Einstein ridiculed them and slandered America upon his return to Europe. He specifically attacked the American scientists whom he had earlier praised in his apparently scripted press statement quoted immediately above. This spectacle did not go unnoticed in the foreign press.

While it is true that some of Einstein's critics were closet (unknown to Einstein) or public anti-Semites, it is also true that many were proud Jews, or Gentiles without any anti-Semitic feelings. While anti-Semitism, which was common in Europe and America in the 1920's—even Einstein was an anti-Semite, was likely to bias its adherents and foster resentment in them of Einstein's public success, it did not in and of itself render legitimate scientific and philosophical non-race related arguments wrong, nor should it render such legitimate arguments taboo. The very bias of "race" prejudice provided an incentive for some to expose Einstein and the exposure of Einstein's plagiarism and irrationality is a good thing, even if "race" prejudice is not.

Einstein should not be pardoned and science should not be stagnated merely because Einstein was criticized by some who may have had more than one motive for exposing him. If the racism of important historical figures, in word or deed, should make it impossible for present day scholars to rely upon their non-race related arguments, we must burn the Bible, the Constitution of the United States of America, the Declaration of Independence, as well as the other writings of many of the Founding Fathers of America, and the works of Aristotle, Herbert Spencer, Albert Einstein, and countless others. Any "race" prejudice some of Einstein's critics may have had did not grant Einstein the license to plagiarize and deceive the public. Nor did it grant him the privilege to hide from debate over the merits of the theory of relativity. Prejudice did not convert

Einstein's plagiarism into non-plagiarism, nor did it turn Einstein's irrationality into rationality. In addition, nothing prevents a person who has expressed a racist bias on one occasion, from making a true statement on another occasion. Einstein, who was himself an anti-Jewish and anti-"Gojisch" racist and a complete hypocrite, took the coward's way out to cover up his misdeeds, but that does not mean that it was untrue when he claimed to have been descended from Jewish parents. It is certainly true that Einstein had no integrity as a scientist, as a man, or as a Jew, but the truth remains the truth regardless of the source.

While racist bias is a factor to be considered when weighing the value of an opinion expressed by an individual, it by no means excludes the possibility that a given expression of opinion or fact is legitimate, logical and factually correct. To pretend otherwise is to supplant logic and truth with reactionary and irrational emotion. To pretend otherwise is to be biased against reason and fact, and amounts to the irrational assertion that dislike of the messenger gives one a right to discount the truth of the message when it is convenient to do so. It is the fallacy of *ad hominem* attack. A debtor might as easily and irrationally pretend that her dislike of a creditor gives her a right to refuse to pay off a legitimate debt. A true fact becomes no less of a true fact merely because it is iterated by someone with a bias or an ulterior motive for expressing it. A debt legitimately due is not paid back by a mere expression of dislike, even if the dislike is warranted.

Some well meaning individuals have been duped into believing that it is a good thing to suppress a legitimate criticism made by any person who has ever uttered an untoward word towards a "race", and to bar every other person from repeating the same legitimate criticism, or to ridicule the criticism itself as a matter of course, even if made before adopted by a person with a known bias. No doubt most of these dupes are rather selective in their sanctions, privileging and excusing some racists like Einstein, while exaggerating the degree and the impact of the statements of others. That aside, such dupes ought to recognize the proven danger of excusing corrupt Jews from criticism by any method, including the method of pointing out that a given critic of corrupt Jews has iterated a generally anti-Jewish sentiment. This practice provides corrupt Jews with an incentive to create and sponsor anti-Semitism and to create a class of professional anti-Semites, whose pronouncements shield corrupt Jews from criticism. Ultimately, the practice of inhibiting the criticism of corrupt Jews, or any Jewish icon, or even any Jew, sponsors Jewish corruption and will inevitably lead to a backlash against all Jews.

It is not surprising that Jewish critics criticize obvious examples of corruption by Jews. That does not place Jews above criticism. Nor does it mean that a non-racist person becomes a racist by noticing and commenting upon the same corruption by a corrupt Jew, which a known anti-Semite has criticized. Nor does it mean that a non-racist criticism of a corrupt Jew becomes racist if noticed and encouraged by a racist. If such were the case, a corrupt Jew could hire another person to pose as an anti-Semite and criticize the corrupt Jew, and then be shielded for life from criticism. More broadly, corrupt Jewish leaders and corrupt Jewish organizations could hire stooges and *agents provocateur* to pose as anti-Semites and make ridiculous anti-Semitic statements, together with legitimate statements of fact, and thereby stigmatize legitimate expressions of criticism as if the expression of "race hatred", *per se*. Such things have happened. Corrupt Jewish financiers paid Hitler's way,[33] and many who have legitimately criticized corruption by Jewish financiers have been likened to Hitler, who was paid by those same corrupt Jewish financiers to criticize them. Are we forbidden to criticize the financing of Adolf Hitler?

2.3 Harvard University Asks a Forbidden Question

In 1921, Ralph Philip Boas discussed a proposed quota system meant to prevent Jews, a small minority in America, from obtaining majority control over leading American universities. Boas employed racist apartheid arguments favoring Jewish domination of the universities, by attributing Jewish success in the colleges and universities to the alleged superiority of the Jewish "race". Boas largely ignored the controlling effects of circumstance, religion and culture. Limiting Jewish enrollment to proportional numbers would have opened the door to more representation by Blacks and other minorities—whether or not those doors would have remained open is a separate issue. Boas wrote in his article, "Who Shall Go to College?", *The Atlantic Monthly*, Volume 130, Number 4, (October, 1922), pp. 441-448, at 443-448:

"Such methods of admission have been in use in many of the larger colleges during the last few years, quietly and effectively; there is little reason to believe that they would have roused public discussion, had not Harvard, with candor worthy of her motto, thrown her cards upon the table and invited the country to discuss openly the question, Who shall go to college?
[***]

III

With the later immigration, however, the case was different. The great Jewish immigration, which began in the eighteen-eighties and still continues to the limit of the law, settled chiefly in the Eastern cities, especially, as it chanced, in or near the very cities where were the largest colleges: Philadelphia, New York, New Haven, and Boston. They brought with them an inherited tradition of education, intellects trained for centuries in the sharpest analysis and dialectic, a natural bent toward the professions, and—what, perhaps, is most important—the repression for years of their attempts to give these desires and characteristics free play. In time they acquired the economic independence necessary to send their children to college; where financial independence was lacking, those children undertook the burden of self-support with the tenacity of the race. There were no Jewish colleges founded for Jewish boys and girls, as with the Catholics, because there was no organized religious body to undertake their founding, and also because Jews have no desire for separation in anything except race and religion.

Now, it happened that Jews began to flock to the colleges at precisely the time when the colleges began to grow unwieldy in numbers and ill-assorted in membership. With the turn of the century, the old college simplicity began to disappear. Old buildings were supplemented by costly modern edifices. The fraternity house and the private dormitory were established to ease the pressure upon the college building funds. Athletics began to develop their present overwhelming importance. Fraternities established hundreds of new chapters. It became necessary to harmonize the differences between rich and poor, between the yearning for scholarship and the cultivation of useful leisure. It was the time when the colleges were violently criticized for their organization, their curricula, and their student life.

Added, therefore, to a burden of cares, came the problem of racial equilibrium. The number of Jews in the eastern colleges gradually increased, until to-day Jews would, were they permitted, in many cases form as much as fifty per cent of the students. The problem of what to do with other groups—negroes, Armenians, Italians—is as nothing when compared with the problem of the Jews.

In the first place, other groups have not the Jewish desire for education. At one remove from the immigrant quarter, other groups do not go to college. Success does not come to them with great rapidity, nor have they the same racial background of learning and scholarship which is, in some degree, in every Jew's blood. Then, too, other groups have not the Jew's adaptability. The Ethiopian cannot change his skin; but Jewish boys and girls differ from their Gentile companions often only in a racial tie so faint that insistence upon it is but a galling reminder of a difference that seems almost academic. Moreover, Jews themselves are the most incoherent of racial groups, varying from the most cultivated, who have acquired the most conservative traditions of Americanism, to the most blatant, who know no traditions except those of oppression. And the urban environment of Eastern colleges has a full case of Jewish types, with the more noticeable, as always, setting the standard of judgment of the race as a whole. Finally, the Jew is the most successful of the newer groups in college. The success of Jews in scholarship is a byword. Rarely a list of honors appears which does not contain Jewish names. When a Jew puts his mind upon achievement, he usually secures what he aims for. He pursues success in scholarship with an intensity and a singleness of purpose which make him at least noticeable. What his hand finds to do, he does with all his might. Fatal gift! If only Jews would be content with mediocrity, the 'Jewish problem' might automatically disappear.

It is not the mere number of Jews, nor their undoubted prominence in scholarship, which complicates the problem. The American college is not, and never has been, an institution primarily for the acquisition of knowledge or the attainment of degrees. It is a social organization, with a very highly organized social structure. In most colleges this structure rests upon a basis of fraternities and clubs, with unwritten rules more rigid than those which govern the most exclusive society, administered with all the relentlessness of youth. It is hard to believe that young men have any inherent objection to their Jewish fellow students as individuals. But the organizations to which they belong have an inherent objection to Jews in the mass. In the admission of Jews they see the subtle undermining of a social prestige which they must preserve, or perish. So far as the classroom is concerned, Jewish students are one thing; but at the 'prom,' or the class-day tea, the presence of Jews and their relatives ruins the tone which must be maintained if social standing is not to collapse. The result of the presence of a large number of students who are themselves not any too welcome at college affairs, and whose relatives are positively impossible, is necessarily disunion and strife within the social life of the college. Jews are naturally clannish, and the social discrimination which they constantly feel makes them doubly so. Isolated as they are, at a time of life and in an environment where isolation is poison, they create a group always sore, always aloof, always a thorn in the side of deans and presidents, who want unity above everything. Where Jewish fraternities and clubs are permitted, the situation becomes worse. Discontent, the gnawing sense of being unjustly treated, the rancor of a brilliant mind forced into social inferiority—these things become articulate and even vociferous; a sense of injustice crystallizes. Then too, the Jewish fraternities necessarily exclude some Jews, and there is left a poor, struggling, often unpleasant remnant, suffering from an aggravated inferiority complex, which makes them mere hangers-on of the collegiate society; men who are using the college for the financial gain of a college degree, men who make neither useful citizens of the college community nor alumni of whom the college can be proud.

The thought which comes into the mind of every right-thinking person is the essential injustice of the situation. In most cases Jewish students are men of good character and fair scholarship. As far as can be learned, they give no trouble to the disciplinary officers. Being what they are, they are despised and rejected; and, being despised and rejected, they develop all their worst traits instead of their best. Were charity, friendliness, forbearance, and kindliness the outstanding characteristics of college men, students of unpleasant personality could be made better college men and better citizens. But these characteristics are no more true of college men than of any group of people. Rather less so, indeed, for young people are notoriously snobbish, hero-worshiping, and intolerant of eccentricity. College authorities, however good their will may be, have not the power to reform the social prejudices of college students. Hence arises a dilemma: either the social nature of a college body must be changed and a new point of view adopted—which seems impossible; or the groups of students who interfere with the harmonious functioning of this social nature must be limited—which rouses a storm of protest.

Those who know the colleges of the East will have little doubt of the outcome: it is easier to endure a storm of protest than to change a point of view. It must be remembered that the point of view has been the slow development of years, and is held alike by trustees, faculties, and alumni.

IV

If the American college were an institution which aimed to find the sharpest brains of the country and to cultivate them, the problem of the limitation of enrollment would be simple. Jews would have nothing to fear from such a system. The bright minds would be admitted; the dull minds would be rejected; and among the successful would unquestionably be the high percentage of Jews who always succeed in an open competition where brains count most.

But, for good or ill, the endowed colleges are not looking for the sharpest brains. In general they would probably like to think of themselves as worthy of Hilaire Behloc's praise:—

Here is a House that armours a man
  With the eyes of a boy and the heart of a
    ranger,
And a laughing way in the teeth of the world
  And a holy hunger and thirst for danger:
Balliol made me, Balliol fed me
  Whatever I had she gave me again:
And the best of Balliol loved and led me,—
  God be with you, Balliol men.

It is obvious that such a conception of college means a careful selection of students to form a type. It means scholarship, to be sure; but it means also, as the presidents of Brown and Bates have stated publicly, that scholarship shall be only one qualification for candidates. Character, personality, the chances of the student's being a leader in life, social adaptability, the power to make friends, eligibility to social circles, conformity to discipline and to accepted thoughts and usages—these formally become the important criteria of admission, as they have been informally, in many cases, for several years. It is needless to say that such a conception of educational eligibility would exclude a large proportion of Jewish students, all negroes, and most members of other immigrant groups; and, with an ever increasing number of candidates for admission, would put a premium upon training in the great private schools.

Once accepted, this idea marks an epoch in American education, the full significance of which most people can hardly recognize, especially when it is remembered that, as the college is, so are large numbers of schools. It means the abandonment of scholastic achievement as the criterion of collegiate success; it means the creation of 'gentlemen's' colleges, as we have had, for a long time, 'gentlemen's' schools; it means the establishment of state universities which will be consciously for the masses, as opposed to 'aristocratic' groups; and it means that the colleges which, though perhaps grudgingly and even unconsciously, have been a powerful agent in Americanization, will now give up that work.

The matter of justice does not enter into this discussion, provided state and municipal colleges are called into existence to give the education which is the right of every qualified youth in a democracy. It is education which counts as a right, not education in any specific college. If Harvard, Yale, Princeton, Columbia, and other endowed colleges feel that social homogeneity is the most important thing in the world for them, they have the right to secure that homogeneity, so long as they maintain no monopoly of college education. It may matter intensely to the alumnus of a great college that his son should go to that college in the same environment which he enjoyed; the young man of immigrant stock, to whom that environment means nothing, ought not make the gratification of that desire impossible, so long as he personally can get his education elsewhere, and so long as the great graduate schools are free to all comers who are properly qualified. It is the thing which matters, not the place in which the thing is obtained. If, for good or ill, colleges wish to stand apart from the incoherencies and the clashings of our changing social life, they have a right to do so, as long as they encourage the founding and maintenance of new institutions which will provide an education for all qualified candidates. It is well to remember, however, that in the past the endowed colleges have opposed the establishment of state universities, and that some of them have already undertaken a policy of exclusion of Jews without informing the public, and without giving a thought, apparently, to the question where the rejected students are to be educated. One of the bad features of the present discussion is the reticence of most college authorities, who permit rumors and sensational news reports to take the place of frank and open discussion, so that the public mind is befogged and confused by anybody who chooses to start a sensational story.

Though the question of justice may be put aside, the question of wisdom may properly enter into the discussion. The important thing is, after all, not what charters permit colleges to do, but what their self-respect, their desire to serve their students and their community, and their best interests in the future tell them they ought to do. Under a policy of exclusion of certain racial groups, of preferring the development of social qualities to active scholastic competition, the colleges are bound to lose more than they will gain. They may be pleasanter places to live in, but they will no longer really represent the eager, heterogeneous, varied amalgam which is America. Young men will be protected from the presence of new Americans at the very age when they ought to be making contacts which will give them real knowledge of actual civic life. There is something disquieting, too, in the thought that their enthusiasm for democracy is so slight that they demand shelter from its perplexities and from its dangers. American college life, surely, ought to be more than a pleasant interlude; it ought to be a stirring achievement.

Most disquieting of all, however, is the feeling that, in the perpetual fight against bigotry, superstition, racial intolerance, and inverted nationalism, the colleges seem to be abandoning the side of the angels. It may be hard to see one's college harboring strange men with alien ways, to see the happy spirit of youthful friendship weakening beneath the fierce and relentless pursuit of knowledge which, to these strangers, is the whole of college life; but it is harder to see one's college the fostering mother of hates and racial dissensions, the parent of bitterness which for years will be a canker in the minds of men. Colleges will doubtless say that, in selecting their students in their own way, they have no such purpose. However, what usually matters is not the purpose of an act, but its result."

Einstein claimed that anti-Semites were correct to be believe that Jews exercised undue influence in Germany. Einstein wrote in the *Jüdische Rundschau*, on 21 June 1921, on pages 351-352,

"This phenomenon [*i. e.* Anti-Semitism] in Germany is due to several causes. Partly it originates in the fact that the Jews there exercise an influence over the intellectual life of the German people altogether out of proportion to their number. While, in my opinion, the economic position of the German Jews is very much overrated, the influence of Jews on the Press, in literature, and in science in Germany is very marked, as must be apparent to even the most superficial observer. This accounts for the fact that there are many anti-Semites there who are not really anti-Semitic in the sense of being Jew-haters, and who are honest in their arguments. They regard Jews as of a nationality different from the German, and therefore are alarmed at the increasing Jewish influence on their national entity. [***] But in Germany the judgement of my theory depended on the party politics of the Press[.][84]

Einstein also stated,

"The way I see it, the fact of the Jews' racial peculiarity will necessarily influence their social relations with non-Jews. The conclusions which—in my opinion—the Jews should draw is to become more aware of their peculiarity in their social way of life and to recognize their own cultural contributions. First of all, they would have to show a certain noble reservedness and not be so eager to mix socially—of which others want little or nothing. On the other hand, anti-Semitism in Germany also has consequences that, from a Jewish point of view, should be welcomed. I believe German Jewry owes its continued existence to anti-Semitism."[85]

Nazi Zionist Joseph Goebbels, sounding very much like political Zionist Albert Einstein, was quoted in *The New York Times*, on 29 September 1933, on page 10,

"It must be remembered the Jews of Germany were exercising at that time a decisive influence on the whole intellectual life; that they were absolute and unlimited masters of the press, literature, the theatre and the motion pictures, and in large cities such as Berlin, 75 percent of the members of the medical and legal professions were Jews; that they made public opinion, exercised a decisive influence on the Stock Exchange and were the rulers of Parliament and its parties."

Max Born knew that a Albert Einstein and his sycophantic Jewish promoter Alexander Moszkowski would be used as examples to justify a Dühring-style general vilification of Jews—which could also hurt the sales of Born's book and spoil his efforts to profit from the Einstein name in the desperate times which followed the First World War. Eugen Karl Dühring, who wrote important historical treatises on Physics which are on a par with those of Ernst Mach, including an analysis of space-time theories and the underlying principles of what was to become the general theory of relativity, promoted racial anti-Semitism to modern Germany and inspired Theodor Herzl's racist political Zionist movement.[86] Dühring was a Socialist who combated Lasalle, Marx and Engels over the future of Socialism in Germany. The Socialists Dühring, Lasalle and Marx each used the tactic of Jew-baiting for political gain. Engels, in at least one instance, spoke out against it.[87]

Shrill cries of "anti-Semite!" and "dirty Jew!" increasingly filled the air in both political and scientific debates, and were most often the product of those Jewish minds who wanted to deflect interest from the facts, and who wanted to keep Jews segregated from non-Jews. Anti-Semitism was a favorite tool of racist Jews to manipulate both Jews and Gentiles, and it was racist Jews who deliberately caused most of the anti-Semitic persecutions of Jews throughout history, either by posing as anti-Semites, or hiring or otherwise recruiting Gentiles to pose as anti-Semites. As fantastic as it sounds, this is easily proven, and will be proven later in the text.

The context of the polemic battles between these Socialists is given in the endnote,[88] which reprints an important and quite readable history of the Socialist movement in Germany in the Nineteenth and early Twentieth Centuries found in Robert Herndon Fife, Jr.'s book, *The German Empire Between Two Wars*, which was published in 1916. Fife also analyzed contemporary German newspapers, and provides the modern reader with an understanding of the background which gives context as to why Einstein was often viewed as a Socialist and Communist agitator. Fife also documents the unabashed political partisanship of the contemporary newspapers in Germany. According to Fife, Socialists tended to be rigidly dogmatic and vicious to those with whom they disagreed. They tended to be very intolerant of dissent and/or mere disagreement.

Einstein had many Socialist friends in the press and publishing business. Most of them were ethnically-biased Jews, who were prone to make personal attacks against Einstein's critics through their journals and newspapers. These pro-Einstein Socialists often called Einstein's critics "anti-Semitic" without grounds. Socialists in the Dühring camp were in turn vicious to Einstein and to Jews in general.

Communists were also rigidly dogmatic[89] and murderous to their critics. Communists are notorious for manufacturing patently false historical revisionism and for suppressing the truth, which false revisionism favors their equally notorious penchant for creating cults of personality around megalomaniacal and genocidal dictators like Lenin (born Ulyanov), Trotsky (born Bronstein) and Stalin (born Djugashvili). Socialists and Communists created personality cults around Marx and Lasalle and used anti-Semitism for political gain, as did the German Jews Karl (born Mordecai) Marx (whose family name was originally Marx Levi) and Ferdinand Lasalle (born Lasal), who promoted anti-Jewish hatred as a means to promote crypto-Jewish Socialists and Jewish Communists into power.[90] The Communist German-Jewish agitator Ferdinand Lassalle wrote to Marx on 24 June 1852,

". . .Party struggles lend a party strength and vitality; the greatest proof of a party's weakness is its diffuseness and the blurring of clear demarcations; a party becomes stronger by purging itself. . . ."[91]

2.4 Jewish Dogmatism and Control of the Press Stifles Debate

If Robert Herndon Fife, Jr.'s book, *The German Empire Between Two Wars: A Study of the Political and Social Development of the Nation Between 1871 and 1914*, Macmillan, New York, (1916), at pages 177-199 and 359-388, bore a political bias, it appears to have been a pro-Socialist bias tending toward Marxist Socialism, though certainly not anti-Semitism. His book is dated in its relevance to Einstein by two factors: the founding of the Weimar Republic, and the interjection of politics into scientific matters practiced by Einstein and his advocates, as well as his opponents. In matters related to Einstein, the normally responsible scientific reporting of the German press surrendered ground to their typically irresponsible political reporting.

Just as a terrible propaganda machine had evolved in Germany, which apparatus of propaganda truly became a monster during the war, Lord Northcliffe and many others had established numerous propaganda outlets in Great Britain and America to promote Allied interests, often with outrageous lies.[92] After the war, these highly advanced propaganda factories consolidated to promote Einstein to the world. They successfully brought him undeserved fame and defamed and largely silenced his critics. Their vitriolic and racist attacks on Einstein's critics, coupled together with organized campaigns to destroy the careers of any scientists who would speak out against the theory of relativity, had the desired chilling effect on the effort to expose Einstein to the public as an irrational plagiarist.

Sir Gilbert Parker, who was in charge of British propaganda in America, revealed the organized power of the highly developed art of propaganda at the time, in *Harper's Magazine* in March of 1918. Parker discussed many of the corrupt tactics that were put to use soon afterwards to promote Einstein and to attack his critics and suppress dissent against Einstein, against Einstein's self-promotion and against Einstein's irrationality,

"Perhaps here I may be permitted to say a few words concerning my own work since the beginning of the war. It is in a way a story by itself, but I feel justified in writing one or two paragraphs about it. Practically since the day war broke out between England and the Central Powers I became responsible for American publicity. I need hardly say that the scope of my department was very extensive and its activities widely ranged. Among the activities was a weekly report to the British Cabinet on the state of American opinion, and constant touch with the permanent correspondents of American newspapers in England. I also frequently arranged for important public men in England to act for us by interviews in American newspapers; and among these distinguished people were Mr. Lloyd George (the present Prime Minister), Viscount Grey, Mr. Balfour, Mr. Bonar Law, the Archbishop of Canterbury, Sir Edward Carson, Lord Robert Cecil, Mr. Walter Runciman, (the Lord Chancellor), Mr. Austen Chamberlain, Lord Cromer, Will Crooks, Lord Curzon, Lord Gladstone, Lord Haldane, Mr. Henry James, Mr. John Redmond, Mr. Selfridge, Mr. Zangwill, Mrs. Humphry Ward, and fully a hundred others.

Among other things, we supplied three hundred and sixty newspapers in the smaller States of the United States with an English newspaper, which gives a weekly review and comment of the affairs of the war. We established connection with the man in the street through cinema pictures of the Army and Navy, as well as through interviews, articles, pamphlet etc.; and by letters in reply to individual American critics, which were printed in the chief newspaper of the State in which they lived, and were copied in newspapers of other and neighboring States. We advised and stimulated many people to write articles; we utilized the friendly services and assistance of confidential friends; we had reports from important Americans constantly, and established association, by personal correspondence, with influential and eminent people of every profession in the United States, beginning with university and college presidents, professors and scientific men, and running through all the ranges of the population. We asked our friends and correspondents to arrange for speeches, debates, and lectures by American citizens, but we did not encourage Britishers to go to America and preach the doctrine of entrance into the war. Besides an immense private correspondence with individuals, we had our documents and literature sent to great numbers of public libraries, Y. M. C. A. societies, universities, colleges, historical societies, clubs, and newspapers.

It is hardly necessary to say that the work was one of extreme difficulty and delicacy, but I was fortunate in having a wide acquaintance in the United States and in knowing that a great many people had read my books and were not prejudiced against me. I believed that the American people could not be driven, preached to, or chivied into the war, and that when they did enter it would be the result of their own judgment and not the result of exhortation, eloquence, or fanatical pressure of Britishers. I believed that the United States would enter the war in her own time, and I say this, with a convinced mind, that, on the whole, it was best that the American commonwealth did not enter the war until that month in 1917 when Germany played her last card of defiance and indirect attack. Perhaps the safest situation that could be imagined actually did arise. The Democratic party in America, which probably would not have supported a Republican President had he declared war, were practically forced by the logic of circumstances to support President Wilson when be declared war, because he had blocked up every avenue of attack."[93]

After the war ended, both the media of the Allies and that of the Central Powers were applied to making Einstein a celebrity and the fine art of controlling public opinion, which had become so refined during the war, was applied to the task of making Einstein famous. The methods learned and employed in wartime were also used to suppress and quash open debate on important scientific and ethical questions related to Einstein's plagiarism, the fatal flaws in the theory of relativity and the misrepresentation of the physical evidence used to justify the theory.

Many were struck by the speed with which Einstein became famous. No scientist had ever become so famous so quickly. Many were skeptical and suspicious that something unseemly was taking place.

In his book, Alexander Moszkowski recounts Albert Einstein's assuredness as to the results of the eclipse observations that made Einstein famous—*before the photographs of the eclipse had been taken*, an assurance that worried Max Planck and struck Heinrich Zangger as odd.[94] Einstein was absolutely confident that the results of the eclipse observations would confirm "his" prediction. Einstein's apparent knowledge of the results before they were obtained leads one to believe that the published conclusions of the eclipse observations, no matter what the evidence actually showed or was capable of showing, was a foregone conclusion arrived at in collusion, not through experimentation and observation. Moszkowski wrote,

"In no sense did Einstein himself entertain a possibility of doubt.

On repeated occasions before May 1919 I had opportunities of questioning him on this point. There was no shadow of a scruple, no ominous fears clouded his anticipations. Yet great things were at stake.

Observation was to show 'the correctness of Einstein's world system' by a fact clearly intelligible to the whole world, one depending on a very sensitive test of less than two seconds of arc.

'But, Professor,' said I, on various occasions, 'what if it turns out to be more or less? These things are dependent on apparatus that may be faulty, or on unforeseen imperfections of observation.' A smile was Einstein's only answer, and this smile expressed his unshakeable faith in the instruments and the observers to whom this duty was to be entrusted.

Moreover, it is to be remarked that no great lengths of time were available for comfortable experimentation in taking this photographic record. For the greatest possible duration of a total eclipse of the sun viewed at a definite place amounts to less than eight minutes, so that there was no room for mishaps in this short space of time, nor must any intervening cloud appear. The kindly co-operation of the heavens was indispensable—and was not refused. The sun, in this case the darkened sun, brought this fact to light.

Two English expeditions had been equipped for the special occasion of the eclipse—one to proceed to Sobral and the other to the Island of Principe, off Portuguese Africa; they were sent officially with equipment provided in the main by the time-honoured Royal Society. Considering the times, it was regarded as the first symptom of the revival of international science, a praiseworthy undertaking. A huge apparatus was set into motion for a purely scientific object with not the slightest relation to any purpose useful in practical life. It was a highly technical investigation whose real significance could be grasped by only very few minds. Yet interest was excited in circles reaching far beyond that of the professional scientist. As the solar eclipse approached, the consciousness of amateurs became stirred with indefinite ideas of cosmic phenomena. And just as the navigator gazes at the Polar Star, so men directed their attention to the constellation of Einstein, which was not yet depicted in stellar maps, but, from which something uncomprehended, but undoubtedly very important, was to blaze forth.

In June it was announced that the star photographs had been successful in most cases, yet for weeks, nay for months, we had to exercise patience. For the photographs, although they required little time to be taken, took much longer to develop and, above all, to be measured; in view of the order of smallness of the distances to be compared, this was a difficult and troublesome task, for the points of light on the plate did not answer immediately with Yes or No, but only after mechanical devices of extreme delicacy had been carefully applied.

At the end of September they proclaimed their message. It was in the affirmative, and this Yes out of far-distant transcendental regions called forth a resounding echo in the world of everyday life. Genuinely and truly the 1.7 seconds of arc had come out, correct to the decimal point. These points representing ciphers, as it were, had chanted of the harmony of the spheres in their Pythagorean tongue. The transmission of this message seemed to be accompanied by the echoing words of Goethe's 'Ariel':

'With a crash the Light draws near!
Pealing rays and trumpet-blazes,—
Eye is blinded, ear amazes.'

Never before had anything like this happened. A wave of amazement swept over the continents. Thousands of people who had never in their lives troubled about vibrations of light and gravitation were seized by this wave and carried on high, immersed in the wish for knowledge although incapable of grasping it. This much all understood, that from the quiet study of a scholar an illuminating gospel for exploring the universe had been irradiated.

During that time no name was quoted so often as that of this man. Everything sank away in face of this universal theme which had taken possession of humanity. The converse of educated people circled about this pole, could not escape from it, continually reverted to the same theme when pressed aside by necessity or accident. Newspapers entered on a chase for contributors who could furnish them with short or long, technical or non-technical, notices about Einstein's theory. In all nooks and corners social evenings of instruction sprang up, and wandering universities appeared with errant professors that led people out the three-dimensional misery of daily life into the more hospitable Elysian fields of four-dimensionality. Women lost sight of domestic worries and discussed co-ordinate systems, the principle of simultaneity, and negatively-charged electrons. All contemporary questions had gained a fixed centre from which threads could be spun to each. Relativity had become the sovereign password. In spite of some grotesque results that followed on this state of affairs it could not fail to be recognized that we were watching symptoms of mental hunger not less imperative in its demands than bodily hunger, and it was no longer to be appeased by the former books by writers on popular science and by misguided idealists.

And whilst leaders of the people, statesmen, and ministers made vain efforts to steer in the fog, to arrive at results serviceable to the nation, the multitude found what was expedient for it, what was uplifting, what sounded like the distant hammering of reconstruction. Here was a man who had stretched his hands towards the stars; to forget earthly pains one had but to immerse oneself in his doctrine. It was the first time for ages that a chord vibrated through the world invoking all eyes towards something which, like music or religion, lay outside political or material interests.

The mere thought that a living Copernicus was moving in our midst elevated our feelings. Whoever paid him homage had a sensation of soaring above Space and Time, and this homage was a happy augury in an epoch so bare of brightness as the present.

As already remarked, there was no lack of rare fruits among the newspaper articles, and a chronicler would doubtless have been able to make an attractive album of them. I brought Einstein several foreign papers with large illustrations which must certainly have cost the authors and publishers much effort and money. Among others there were full-page beautifully coloured pictures intended to give the reader an idea of the paths pursued by the rays from the stars during the total eclipse of the sun. These afforded Einstein much amusement, namely, *e contrario*, for from the physical point of view these pages contained utter nonsense. They showed the exact opposite of the actual course of the rays inasmuch as the author of the diagrams had turned the convex side of the deflected ray towards the sun. He had not even a vague idea of the character of the deflection, for his rays proceeded in a straight line through the universe until they reached the sun, where they underwent a sudden change of direction reminiscent of a stork's legs. The din of journalistic homage was not unmixed with scattered voices of dissent, even of hostility. Einstein combated these not only without anger but with a certain satisfaction. For indeed the series of unbroken ovations became discomfiting, and his feelings took up arms against what seemed to be developing into a star-artist cult. It was like a breath of fresh air when some column of a chance newspaper was devoted to a polemic against his theory, no matter how unfounded or unreasoned it may have been, merely because a dissonant tone broke the unceasing chorus of praise. On one occasion he even said of a shrill disputant, 'The man is quite right!' And these words were uttered in the most natural manner possible. One must know him personally if one is to understand these excesses of toleration. So did Socrates defend his opponents."[95]

Albert Einstein marveled at the spurious evidence which had made him a cult figure. Moszkowski informs us that,

"A copy of this photograph had been sent to Einstein from
England, and he told me of it with evident pleasure. He
continually reverted to the delightful little picture of the heavens,
quite fascinated by the thing itself, without the slightest
manifestation of a personal interest in his own success. Indeed,
I may go further and am certainly not mistaken in saying his new
mechanics did not even enter his head, nor the verification of it
by the plate; on the contrary, he displayed that disposition of the
mind which in the case of genius as well as in that of children
shows itself as *naïveté*. The prettiness of the photograph
charmed him, and the thought that the heavens had been drawn
up as for parade to be a model for it."[96]

We know that Eddington was biased, and that photographs taken in
1918 failed to show any displacement—though it is difficult to believe
that any photographs taken in that era were accurate enough to measure
such things. The Annual Meeting of the British Association for the
Advancement of Science, Bournemouth, 1919, in its "Transactions of
Section A", Friday, September 12, pages 156-157, reported:

"1. *Photographs taken at Principe during the Total Eclipse
of the Sun, May 29th. By* Professor A. S. EDDINGTON,
F.R.S., and E. T. COTTINGHAM, *followed by a
Discussion on Relativity, opened by* Professor
EDDINGTON, *F.R.S.*
Professor Eddington gave an account of the observations
which had been made at Principe during the solar eclipse. The
main object in view was to observe the displacement (if any) of
stars, the light from which passed through the gravitational field
of the sun. To establish the existence of such an effect and the
determination of its magnitude gives, as is well known, a crucial
test of the theory of gravitation enunciated by Einstein. Professor
Eddington explained that the observations had been partially
vitiated by the presence of clouds, but the plates already
measured indicated the existence of a deflection intermediate
between the two theoretically possible values 0.87" and 1.75".
He hoped that when the measurements were completed the latter
figure would prove to be verified. Incidentally Professor
Eddington pointed out that the presence of clouds had resulted
in a solar prominence being photographed and its history
followed in some detail; some very striking photographs were

shown.

Following on this account Professor Eddington opened the discussion on relativity, and referred again to the bending of the wave front of light to be expected from Einstein's new law when the light passes near a heavy body. It should be possible to test experimentally this law, which demands that the speed of light varies as 1—2Ω where Ω is the gravitational potential. He showed that whether Einstein's solution of the problem be correct or not, it has at any rate given a new orientation to our ideas of space and time. Sir Oliver Lodge regarded the relativity theory of 1905 as a supplement to Newtonian dynamics by the adoption of the factor

$$\left(1 - \frac{v^2}{c^2}\right)$$

and its powers necessitated by experimental results; but he did not consider this dependence of mass and length on velocity as entailing any revolutionary changes of our ideas of space and time, or as rendering necessary the further complexities of 1915. He compared the difficulties involved with the case of measuring temperature, defined in terms of a perfect gas, and made with gases which only approximate to this ideal state. Dr. Silberstein pointed out that Einstein's theory of gravitation predicts three verifiable phenomena, *i.e.*, a shift of spectral lines, the bending of light round the sun and the secular motion of the perihelion of a planet. In the neighbourhood of a radially symmetric mass, such as our sun, the line element *ds* is given by:—

$$ds^2 =$$

$$\left(1 - 2M/c^2r\right)c^2dt^2 - \left(1 - 2M/c^2r\right)\left(dx^2 + dy^2 + dz^2\right).$$

The coefficient $c^2\,dt^2$ gives by itself a lengthening of the period of oscillation for a terrestrial observer in the ratio

$$\left(1 + M/c^2r\right) : 1,$$

demanding a shift of spectral lines of about .01 Å.U. Secondly, the path of rays of light is obtained by putting $ds = 0$, and the first and second coefficients give jointly a bending which, for rays almost grazing the sun, is 1.75". Thirdly, Keplerian motion is predicted with a progressively moving perihelion which in the case of Mercury turns out to be 43" per century. He drew attention to the fact that St. John's results in 1917 showed no shift of the spectral lines, a fact which in itself would overthrow the theory in question. Father Cortie pointed out that Campbell's photographs, taken in 1918 and measured by Curtis, gave no trace of any displacement of the images of 43 stars distributed irregularly round the sun."

Regarding this meeting and the evidence against general relativity which was known to Freundlich and Einstein, *see also: Nature*, Volume 103, (1919), p. 394; and *The Observatory*, Volume 42, (1919), pp. 298-299, 361-366; and the letter from E. Freundlich to A. Einstein of 15 September 1919, *The Collected Papers of Albert Einstein*, Volume 9, Document 105, Princeton University Press, (2004); as well as Einstein's response to Freundlich on 19 September 1919, *ibid.* Document 106.

On 9 October 1919, Albert Einstein reported in *Die Naturwissenschaften* (J. Springer), Volume 7, Number 42, (17 October 1919), p. 776,

"Zuschriften an die Herausgeber.
Prüfung der allgemeinen Relativitätstheorie.

Nach einem von Prof. *Lorentz* an den Unterzeichneten gerichteten Telegramm hat die zur Beobachtung der Sonnenfinsternis am 29. Mai ausgesandte englische Expedition unter *Eddington* die von der allgemeinen Relativitätstheorie geforderte Ablenkung des Lichtes am Rande der Sonnenscheibe beobachtet. Der bisher provisorisch ermittelte Wert liegt zwischen 0,9 und 1,8 Bogensekunden. Die Theorie fordert 1,7.

B e r l i n ,   d e n   9 .   O k t o b e r   1 9 1 9 .
A. Einstein."

Lorentz followed his telegram with a letter of 7 October 1919. Einstein delighted in Lorentz' news and forwarded the information to numerous friends and family.[97]

Vossische Zeitung began actively promoting Albert Einstein at least as early as 26 April 1914.[98] On 23 July 1918, *Vossische Zeitung* reported,

"Das Weltbild des Physikers.
Professor Einstein über die Motive des Forschens.
Anläßlich des 60. Geburtstages von Max P l a n c k , dem

Schöpfer der Quantentheorie, veranstaltete die Deutsche Physikalische Gesellschaft eine besondere Sitzung, in der Plancks Verdienste um die Wissenschaft in Ansprachen hervorragender Physiker gewürdigt wurden. Diese Ansprachen liegen jetzt gedruckt vor. (C. F. Müllersche Hofbuchhandlung, Karlsruhe). Der Frankfurter Physiker M. von L a u e schildert Plancks thermodynamische Arbeiten, der Münchener Physiker A. S o m m e r f e l d zeigte, wie Planck zur Entdeckung der Quanten kam, E i n s t e i n , der Physiker der Berliner Akademie, untersuchte die Motive des Forschens und kommt dabei auf das Weltbild des theoretischen Physikers zu sprechen. Dieses stellt die höchsten Anforderungen an die Straffheit und Exaktheit der Darstellung der Zusammenhänge, wie sie nur die Benutzung der mathematischen Sprache verleiht. Aber dafür muß sich der Physiker stofflich um so mehr bescheiden, indem er sich damit begnügen muß, die allereinfachsten Vorgänge abzubilden, die unserem Erleben zugänglich gemacht werden können, während alle komplexen Vorgänge nicht mit jener subtilen Genauigkeit und Konsequenz, wie sie der theoretische Physiker fordert, durch den menschlichen Geist nachkonstruiert werden können. Höchste Reinheit, Klarheit und Sicherheit auf Kosten der Vollständigkeit. „Was kann es aber für einen Reiz haben, einen so kleinen Ausschnitt der Natur genau zu erfassen, alles Feinere und Komplexe aber scheu und mutlos beiseite zu lassen? Verdient das Ergebnis einer so resignierten Bemühung den stolzen Namen „Weltbild"? Ich glaube, der stolze Name ist wohlverdient, denn die allgemeinsten Gesetze, auf welche das Gedankengebäude dr theoretischen Physik gegründet ist, erheben den Anspruch, für jegliches Naturgeschehen gültig zu sein. Aus ihnen sollte sich auf dem Wege reiner gedanklicher Deduktion die Abbildung, d. h. Theorie eines jeden Naturprozesses einschließlich der Lebensvorgänge finden lassen, wenn jener Prozeß der Deduktion nicht weit über die Leistungsfähigkeit menschlichen Denkens hinausginge. Höchste Aufgabe des Physikers ist also das Aufsuchen jener allgemeinsten elementaren Gesetze, aus denen durch reine Deduktion das Weltbild zu gewinnen ist. Zu diesen elementaren Gesetzen führt kein logischer Weg, sondern nur die auf Einfühlung in die Erfahrung sich stützende Intuition . . . Die Entwicklung hat gezeigt, daß von denkbaren theoretischen Konstruktionen eine einzige jeweilen sich als unbedingt allen anderen überlegen erweist. Keiner, der sich in den Gegenstand wirklich vertieft hat, wird leugnen, daß die Welt der Wahrnehmungen das theoretische System praktisch eindeutig bestimmt, trotzdem kein logischer Weg von den Wahrnehmungen zu den Grundsätzen der Theorie führt. Mit Staunen sieht der Forscher das scheinbare Chaos in eine sublime Ordnung gefügt, die nicht auf das Walten des eigenen Geistes, sondern auf die Beschaffenheit der Erfahrungswelt zurückzuführen ist; dies ist es, was Leibniz so glücklich als „prästabilierte Harmonie'' bezeichnete."[99]

On 15 April 1919, *Vossische Zeitung*, evening edition, reported,

"Grundgedanken der Relativitätstheorie.

Professor Einstein am Vortragstisch.

Nicht nur in der Politik, auch in der Wissenschaft wird der Fortschritt aus der Not geboren, so begann Professor E i n s t e i n , das an Jahren jüngste Mitglied unserer Akademie, der Mitschöpfer der modernen Relativitätstheorie, seine Betrachtungen über diese Theorie. Da der Redner bei der überaus zahlreichen Zuhörerschaft, die sich in der Aula der Viktoria-Luisen-Schule auf Einladung des sozialistischen Studentenvereins zusammengefunden hatte, weder auf besonders mathematische, noch physikalische Vorkenntnisse rechnen konnte, so verzichtete er fast völlig auf das anscheinend unentbehrliche mathematische Rüstzeug. Auch die grundlegenden physikalischen Experimente konnten nur kurz in ihren entscheidenden Endergebnissen herangezogen werden.

In seinen Betrachtungen geht Einstein von der Relativität der Bewegung aus, wie sie Galilei und Newton gelehrt haben. Er zeigt, daß wir eine absolut gleichförmige Translationsbewegung in keiner Weise definieren können. Zwei sich gleichförmig gegeneinander bewegende Bezugssysteme (Koordinaten-Systeme) sind mechanisch vollkommen äquivalent. Es sind Aussagen von vollkommen gleichem Inhalt, wenn wie einmal das eine System als ruhend und das andere als bewegt ansprechen oder umgekehrt. Es kommt gar nicht darauf an, welches Bezugssystem das ruhende, welches das bewegte ist. Dieses Relativitätsprinzip der Mechanik läßt sich aber nicht ohne weiteres auf die Vorgänge beim Licht, oder allgemeiner, auf die elektrodynamischen Erscheinungen anwenden. Dem widerspricht anscheinend der Fizeausche Versuch. In einer mit gleichförmiger Geschwindigkeit strömenden Flüssigkeit möge sich Licht in Richtung der Strömung fortpflanzen. Nach dem Relativitätsprinzip Galileis müßte ein im Strom treibender Beobachter die gleiche Fortpflanzungsgeschwindigkeit wahrnehmen, wie wenn die Flüssigkeit ruhte. Der außenstehende Beobachter müßte also die Fortpflanzungsgeschwindigkeit des Lichts um die volle Geschwindigkeit der Flüssigkeit vermehrt finden. Das ist aber nicht der Fall. Auch im luftleeren Raum pflanzt sich der Lichtstrahl mit derselben Geschwindigkeit fort. Michelson hat versucht festzustellen, ob die Bewegung der Erde einen Einfluß auf die Lichtgeschwindigkeit hat, aber sowohl seine Experimente, wie die seiner Nachfolger verliefen so, als ob das Relativitätsprinzip der Mechanik auch in der Optik gilt, während das nach dem Fizeauschen Versuch nicht der Fall war. Wie läßt sich dieser Widerspruch lösen? Er liegt, wie Einstein weiter ausführt, [??? *three words illegible*] Voraussetzungen unserer Ueberlegung. Wenn der nicht mitbewegte Beobachter einen Einfluß der Bewegung für den mitbewegten Beobachter festzustellen meint, den dieser selbst nicht wahrnimmt, so liegt das daran, daß beide Beobachter mit verschiedenem Maße messen, daß es verschiedene Dinge sind, die sie als identisch bezeichnen, gleiche Zeitintervalle und gleiche Längen ansprechen. Was gleichzeitig in bezug auf das eine Bezugssystem ist, ist nicht gleichzeitig auf ein anderes Bezugssystem, ebenso ist der Begriff der Länge ebenfalls relativ. Bewegte starke Körper und bewegte Uhren verhalten sich anders als ruhende. Der bewegte Körper verkürzt sich. Eine Uhr, die vom nichtbewegten System aus beurteilt wird, läuft langsamer. Der bewegte Beobachter beurteilt mit seinen Instrumenten die bewegte Welt anders, als der unbewegte Beobachter.

In der knappen Zeit von 1½ Stunden ist es unmöglich, die ganze Gedankenarbeit auch nur in kurzen Umrissen zu schildern, die zur heutigen Relativitätstheorie geführt hat. Aber man erhält doch einen Einblick, wie die Physiker die gedanklichen und physikalischen Schwierigkeiten zu beseitigen versuchen. Wir sehen, wie das moderne Relativitätsprinzip dazu zwingt, die Beziehungen zwischen wägbarer Masse und Energie neu zu gestalten, wie nach dem Relativitätsprinzip jede Energiezunahme auch eine Massenzunahme zur Folge hat. Tatsächlich haben die neueren Untersuchungen über die Elektronen diese Forderung bestätigt. Auch die Perihelbewegung des Merkur bestätigt die Relativitätstheorie, auch die Aberration des Lichts der Fixsterne dient zu ihrer Stütze. Ende dieses Monats soll ein neuer experimenteller Beweis für sie geführt werden. In Brasilien will man die S o n n e n f i n s t e r n i s daraufhin beobachten, ob eine Ablenkung der Sonnenstrahlen entsprechend dem modernen Relativitätsprinzip stattfinden.

K. J."

On 13 May 1919, *Vossische Zeitung* reported,

"**Sonnenfinsternis und Relativitätstheorie.** Die am 29. Mai stattfindende Sonnenfinsternis, deren Totalitätszone sich in einem nach Süden offenen Bogen von Arequipa an der Westküste von Südamerika bis etwa nach Mikindani, an der Ostküste von Afrika erstreckt, gewinnt dadurch eine ganz besondere Bedeutung, daß sie durch ihre lange Totalitätsdauer für die Prüfung der E i n s t e i n s c h e n Theorie besonders geeignet ist. Zu ihrer Beobachtung haben, wie die „Naturwissenschaften" nach englischen Quellen berichten, die Engländer zwei Unternehmungen ausgerüstet. Die eine unter Crommelin geht nach Sobral in Brasilien (etwa 130 Kilometer landeinwärts von der Küste), die zweite unter Eddington auf die portugiesische Isla do Principe (etwa 180 Kilometer von der afrikanischen Küste). Abgesehen von der langen Totalitätsdauer ist diese Sonnenfinsternis durch das reiche Feld an Sternen rings um die Sonne bemerkenswert, und es ist die Aufmerksamkeit auf die dadurch gegebene, überaus günstige Gelegenheit gelenkt worden, die Einsteinsche Relativitätstheorie zu prüfen. Nach diesen muß ein Strahl, der von eiem Stern aus tangential zur Sonne verläuft, 1,74" abgelenkt werden und die Ablenkung für andere Sterne umgekehrt proportional ihrem Abstande vom Mittelpunkte der Sonne sein. Fällt die Entscheidung für Einstein, so würde das zusammen mit seinem Erfolge in der Erklärung der Bewegung des Merkurperihels, genügen, um seine Lehre als das wirkliche System des Universums anzunehmen. Auch ihre endgültige Widerlegung aber würde von Nutzen sein, da sie die Verschwendung weiterer Kraft auf ihre Ausarbeitung verhindern würde, obwohl diese Theorie, wie die „Nature" bemerkt, als scharfsinniges System idealer Geometrie noch immer unsere Bewunderung verdienen würde."

On 21 July 1919, *Vossische Zeitung* reported,

"Die Sonnenfinsternis am 29. Mai. Wie die englische Zeitschrift „Nature'' vom 5. Juni meldet, hat die englische Expedition, die in Sobral in Brasilien arbeitete, günstiges Wetter gehabt. Die gestellten Aufgaben ließen sich befriedigend durchführen. Alle zu erwartenden Sterne sind auf den photographischen Platten herausgekommen. Auch die nach Eddington an der Küste Westafrikas gesandte Expedition ist mit ihren Erfolgen zufrieden. Beide Expeditionen sollten, wie schon gemeldet, die dicht bei der Sonne stehenden Sterne photographisch aufnehmen, um die Einsteinsche Theorie zu prüfen. Die Aufnahmen während der Sonnenfinsternis dienen zum Vergleich mit Aufnahmen derselben Himmelsgegend bei Nacht, um eine etwaige Verschiebung zu entdecken, die man auf die Anwesenheit der Sonne in diesem Feld als Ursache zurückführen kann."

On 15 October 1919, *Vossische Zeitung* reported,

"Sonnenfinsternis und Relativitätstheorie. Nach einer Mitteilung des neuesten Heftes der „Naturwissenschaften'' hat die zur Beobachtung der Sonnenfinsternis am 29. Mai ausgesandte englische Expedition die von der allgemeinen Relativitätstheorie geforderte Ablenkung des Lichtes am Rande der Sonnenscheibe beobachtet. Der bisher provisorisch ermittelte Wert (die Durchrechnung der Beobachtungsresultate ist noch nicht beendet) liegt zwischen 0,9 und 1,8 Bogensekunden, die Theorie fordert 1,7.

Eine der wichtigsten Folgerungen der Einsteinschen Theorie ist die Abhängigkeit der Lichtgeschwindigkeit von dem sogenannten Gravitationspotential, und die sich dadurch ergebende Krümmung eines Lichtstrahles bei seinem Durchgang durch ein Gravitationsfeld. Die Theorie ergibt für einen dicht an der Sonne vorbeigehenden Lichtstrahl, der z. B. von einem Fixstern herkommt, eine Krümmung seiner Bahn. Infolge der Krümmung muß man den Stern gegen seinen wahren Ort am Himmel um einen Betrag verschoben sehen, der am Sonnenrande 1,7 Sekunden beträgt und proportional dem Abstande vom Sonnenmittelpunkte abnimmt. Da aber die photographische Aufnahme des an der Sonne vorbeigehenden von einem Fixstern herkommenden Lichtes nur dann möglich ist, wenn das alles überstrahlende Licht der Sonne am Eintritt in unsere Atmosphäre gehindert wird, so kommen nur die seltenen totalen Finsternisse für diese Beobachtung und die Lösung der Aufgabe in Betracht. Die Sonnenfinsternis am 29. Mai dieses Jahres, während der die Engländer auf zwei Beobachtungsstationen im Hinblick auf dieses Problem photographische Aufnahmen gemacht haben, hat das erforderliche Material zur Entscheidung geliefert."

On 18 November 1919, *Vossische Zeitung* reported,

"Einstein und Newton.
Die Ergebnisse der Sonnenfinsternis vom Mai 1919.

Wie erinnerlich hatte England eine Expedition ausgesandt mit der Aufgabe, die Erscheinungen der Sonnenfinsternis vom 29. Mai d. J. photographisch festzuhalten. Als geeigneter Ort hierfür war Sobral in Nord-Brasilien bezeichnet worden. Es wurde damals telegraphisch gemeldet, daß die Abordnung ihre Aufgabe voll erfüllen konnte. Inzwischen sind die Mitglieder der Expedition nach England zurückgekehrt und haben der britischen Astronomischen Gesellschaft Bericht erstattet.

Professor C. D a v i d s o n von der Greenwich-Sternwarte sprach sich des näheren einem „Times"-Redakteur gegenüber über diese Ergebnisse aus. Davidson bestätigte, daß die im Augenblick der totalen Verfinsterung der Sonnenscheibe an Kappa 1 und Kappa 2, nahe dem Sternbild der Hyaden, angestellten Beobachtungen die vollständige Richtigkeit der Ablenkung der Lichtstrahlen durch die Schwerkraft der Sonne ergeben haben. Auf den vom Professor R e w a l l von der Universität Cambridge erhobenen Einwand, daß diese Ablenkung durch eine noch unbekannte Sonnen-Atmosphäre von ungeahnter Ausdehnung und noch unbekannter Kraft verursacht sein könnte, erwidert Professor Davidson: „Das ist nicht möglich, denn um eine derartige Ablenkung hervorzurufen, müßte eine Atmosphäre vorhanden sein, die jeder bisherigen Theorie und Beobachtung widerspricht. Ueberdies sind Kometen beobachtet worden, die in einem, den Sonnenraum fast streifenden Abstande von der Sonne ihre Bahn ohne jede Störung verfolgt haben." Davidson trennt sich demnach nicht von der Anschauung, daß die Entdeckung einer Lichtquelle, die sowohl Gewicht als Körper besitzt, einen Fortschritt für die Auffassung bedeutet, daß außhalb des drei-dimensionalen Raumes, wie wir ihn heute kennen, noch besondere Bedingungen vorhanden sind. Professor Einsteins Theorie, so bemerkte Davidson, verlangt u. a. eine Verschiebung der Spektrallien nach dem Rot hin. Diese Forderung hat auch Dr. St. John auf Mount Wilson in Amerika nachgeprüft, doch bisher ohne jeden Erfolg. Nichtsdestoweniger sind gewisse Abweichungen in dem Verhalten der Spektrallien vorhanden, für die, nach Meinung einer großen Zahl von Gelehrten, eine befriedigende Erklärung gefunden werden könnte. Was aber jene in Brasilien gemachte hauptsächlichste Entdeckung anbelangt, so pflichtet Professor Davidson voll der Meinung bei, daß das Newtonsche Prinzip umgeworfen worden sei und daß Professor Einstein wenigstens bezüglich zweier seiner drei Voraussagen recht hat. Seine Vermutung bezüglich des Spektrums, versicherte der Greenwicher Professor, bleibt noch den Beweis schuldig. Betreffs der Lichtablenkung aber haben die in Brasilien vorgenommenen Beobachtungen ergeben, daß an Stelle einer Ablenkung von 0,87 Bogensekunden am Sonnenrande, wie man sie nach dem Newtonschen Gesetze allenfalls hätte erwarten können, diese Ablenkung 1,75 betrug, wie sie nach Einsteins Theorie auch sein sollte."

Vossische Zeitung continued to promote the eclipse observations and Einstein on 8 December 1919, 27 January 1920, 7 February 1920, and 24 February 1920. On 30 November 1919, Erwin Freundlich, a Jewish man who considered himself to have been Einstein's friend, though Einstein had ridiculed him behind his back,[100] and a man who had a personal interest in the promotion of the eclipse observations, published an article in the morning edition of *Vossische Zeitung*, which promoted Einstein. Freundlich had been the brains behind Einstein's plagiarism of the general theory of relativity from Marcel Grossmann and David Hilbert, though Einstein took all of the credit.

Freundlich was trying to advance his career and increase his salary and his success depended on the acceptance of the general theory of relativity by German astronomers. Times were hard in Europe after the First World War. Einstein's friends desperately needed money and believed they could not succeed without promoting Einstein. Einstein's friends often complained to him that they needed money and asked for his help in furthering their careers. Freundlich sought to profit from a book he had published on relativity theory, and from its translation into English—as did Einstein's acquaintance Moritz Schlick—and they had Einstein intervene with the publishers to increase their profits.[101] Freundlich was corrupt through and through, as were Einstein and Schlick.

Freundlich's article is notable for many things. "Einstein's" theory was not initially popular—in fact it was very unpopular in the scientific world. Freundlich was keenly aware that his own institution would not back him due to the lack of support for relativity theory. The majority of physicists and astronomers opposed the general theory of relativity. He also knew that there was strong evidence against the general theory of relativity.[102] Einstein wrote to Freundlich on 19 September 1919,

> "You are entirely right that getting you a position in Potsdam should not be attempted *for the present*. The Gen. Th. of Rel. must win acceptance among astronomers beforehand."[103]

Einstein and his friends knew that they needed a public following and the acceptance of astronomers in order to be successful in setting aside the "old" ideas—in order to forward their careers. Knowing that they had plagiarized it, they nevertheless speciously promoted the theory of relativity as a completely new approach, one which was unique to Einstein and one which he allegedly thought up in his head without any empirical inspiration. They did this in part to deceive the public and make a hero out of Einstein. They also were forced to do this, because Einstein had plagiarized the works and failed to reference his sources.

Note that Freundlich lauds Einstein; but the names of Poincaré, Mach, Bateman, Hilbert, Gerber, Maxwell, FitzGerald, Larmor, Cohn, Lorentz, Minkowski, etc. are conspicuously missing from his piece; such that one must conclude that it was not the ideas which were considered significant, because they were not considered significant under the pens of Einstein's predecessors, but it was instead the promotion of Albert Einstein as a hero that was foremost on Freundlich's mind. Freundlich was also able to blackmail Einstein as a means to promote himself, Freundlich, because Freundlich could have exposed Einstein as a plagiarist and a fraud at any time.

Furthermore, it would have been impossible to have advertised Einstein the way Einstein's friends sought to advertize him, and to still have named a just handful of Einstein's predecessors—the historical facts and the circus promoter's fancy simply did not agree. For example, the perihelion motion of the planet Mercury was taken as proof that Einstein was correct and the implication was that Einstein had predicted a previously unknown effect with a non-Newtonian theory of gravity premised on the belief that gravity propagates at light speed. In fact, the perihelion motion of Mercury was observed long before Einstein was born. The equations Einstein used to describe it in 1915 were first published by Paul Gerber in 1898. Gerber believed that gravity propagates at light speed and attempted to prove it with Mercury as an empirical example. Einstein and Freundlich were aware of these facts and deliberately lied to the public.

Einstein, himself, admitted that the hype promoting him was unfounded,

"'There has been a false opinion widely spread among the general public,' [Einstein] said, 'that the theory of relativity is to be taken as differing radically from the previous developments in physics from the time of Galileo and Newton—that it is violently opposed to their deductions. The contrary is true. Without the discoveries of every one of the great men of physics, those who laid down preceding laws, relativity would have been impossible to conceive and there would have been no basis for it. Psychologically, it is impossible to come to such a theory at once without the work which must be done before. The four men who laid the foundations of physics on which I have been able to construct my theory are Galileo, Newton, Maxwell, and Lorenz.'"[104]

When physicist Ernst Gehrcke made similar statements, Einstein called him "anti-Semitic".

So powerful was the initial propaganda of self-interested liars like Alexander Moszkowski, Erwin Freundlich, Max Born, and the others, so vulnerable and gullible are his admirers, that nothing can shake off their religious fervor for the man. They are eager to excuse his sadistic mistreatment of his family and friends, his career of plagiarism, his irrationality, his racism, his misogyny, and his nationalistic segregationist bigotry. Nothing can make them fall out of love with their shaggy-haired comic book hero. What is worse for them is the fact that Einstein has been so shamelessly overrated for so long, that for them to admit to the truth is to admit to their past gullibility, or deliberate dishonesty and, often, racist philosemitic bias.

Similar hero worship had attended the cults which arose around

Aristotle, Spinoza, Copernicus, Des Cartes and Newton. Einstein and his Jewish promoters knew their history and knew how to manufacture a "star-artist cult" around Einstein, which they could then use to promote a theory with no practical implications (believed by them at the time), which would make Einstein a powerful political force in the international arena, who could then do great good—in their eyes, by promoting Zionism.

R. S. Shankland stated,

"About publicity Einstein told me that he had been *given* a publicity value which he did not *earn*. Since he had it he would use it if it would do good; otherwise not."[105]

Albert Einstein stated on 27 April 1948,

"In the course of my long life I have received from my fellow-men far more recognition than I deserve, and I confess that my sense of shame has always outweighed my pleasure therein."[106]

Albert Einstein told Peter A. Bucky,

"Peter, I fully realize that many people listen to me not because they agree with me or because they like me particularly, but because I am Einstein. If a man has this rare capacity to have such esteem with his fellow men, then it is his obligation and duty to use this power to do good for his fellow men."[107]

Einstein "had been *given* a publicity value which he did not *earn*" so that he could promote political Zionism among Jews. Political Zionism is a racist movement among Jews meant to segregate Jews in Palestine in order to end the assimilation of Jews into other cultures and "races". In 1919, most Jews opposed this racist movement and the Zionists needed a famous spokesman to help overcome this resistance to Zionism among Jews.

Albert Einstein confided to his old friend and confidant Michele Besso, on 12 December 1919, that he planned to attend a Zionist conference dedicated to founding a Hebrew university in Palestine. Einstein wrote,

"The reason I am going to attend is not that I think I am especially well qualified, but because my name, in high favor since the English solar eclipse expeditions, can be of benefit to the cause by encouraging the lukewarm kinsmen."[108]

In his book *The Jewish State*, Theodor Herzl laid emphasis on the need of celebrity and publicity to promote Zionism. The same is true of his diary. In 1897, Theodor Herzl told the First Zionist Congress,

"We Zionists wish to urge self-help on the people; thereby no exaggerated and unsound hopes will be awakened. On this ground, also, publicity in dealing with this point is of the highest value. [***] The confidence of the State, which is necessary for a settlement of large masses of Jews, can only be gained by publicity and by loyal action."[109]

Paul Ehrenfest wrote to Albert Einstein on 9 December 1919,

"I hear, for ex., that your accomplishments are being used to make propaganda, with the 'Jewish Newton, who is simultaneously an ardent Zionist' (I personally haven't *read* this yet, but only *heard* it mentioned). [***] But I cannot go along with the propagandistic fuss with its *inevitable* untruths, precisely *because* Judaism is at stake and *because* I feel myself so thoroughly a Jew."[110]

Most people probably think that we today are the most politically sophisticated generation of all times, having the benefit of the recorded history of all other times to guide us. I do not think we today are, in general, nearly as politically sophisticated as the Europeans of the early Twentieth Century. The reasons for this are many, and I suspect include the overspecialization of today's students, which does not give them a broad enough knowledge of many fields of study to gain the insights needed to absorb the fuller meanings of what they are told, and they too often lack the willingness and ability to judge all aspects of the information presented to them as if facts. Many too often succumb to the opinions of others based on their credentials alone and are reluctant to rely upon logic and research, and instead submit to authority. Physicist Ernst Gehrcke noted that this was already becoming a problem in the 1920's, and Sociologist Max Weber's concerns over the bureaucratic control of human behavior have since been justified. Another problem is the fact that the internationalization and attendant standardization of thought has diminished competition in the arena of ideas and replaced it with cult figures who dominate the debate, not through talent, but through relentless commercial promotion.

At any rate, Einstein's friends were very sophisticated politically. Einstein was himself manipulative. Einstein had a good teacher in his mother on how to manipulate people and circumstances. His friends in the scientific community, and in the press, came to his aid in a most corrupt fashion whenever he needed their help. It appears odd that these scientists were determined to promote Einstein as if a revolutionary figure in the popular press, when they knew that he was not, until one realizes that they were his friends and had selfish interests in promoting and perpetuating the cult of Einstein for personal profit.

Article after article appeared in the popular press aggrandizing and sanctifying the man, but nothing was written about how "his" theory allegedly changed everyday life so as to make it deserving of the abundant *news* coverage that it received—all of which is why Reuterdahl dubbed Einstein the "Barnum of the scientific world". While others made important discoveries that benefitted humanity in unprecedented ways, it was Einstein who was aggressively promoted in the press. The wealthy internationalist Richard Fleischer wrote to Einstein on 21 December 1919 offering grant money for research into any practical applications the theory of relativity might have, with the goal of promoting international cooperation in the sciences. The best Einstein could offer was a self-serving experiment on spectral lines by Grebe and Bachem meant to eliminate the doubts cast on the general theory of relativity by the experiments of St. John and others.[111] This had no practical implications to the man on the street.

The astronomer W. J. S. Lockyer was quoted in *The New York Times* on page 17, 10 November 1919,

"The discoveries, while very important, did not, however, affect anything on this earth. They do not personally concern ordinary human beings; only astronomers are affected."

The New York Times later reported on 25 November 1919, page 17,

"The effects on practical astronomy of the verification of Einstein's theory were not very great. It was chiefly in the field of philosophical thought that the change would be felt."

Einstein was quoted in *The Chicago Tribune* on 4 April 1921 on page 6,

"Whatever the value of relativity, it will not necessarily change the conceptions of the man in the street, said Prof. Einstein. 'The practical man does not need to worry about it,' he said."

Erwin Freundlich, in his article which follows, does not acknowledge the fact that the empirical basis of the theory was known before the theory was developed and applied to it, and that the alleged experimental confirmations and predictions were known beforehand, or were corrupted and misrepresented to fit the theory. Freundlich, as a scientist, must have known that his declarations were, at best, incorrect and premature.

The fundamental belief of science is that of generalization. A non-Newtonian theory of gravitation which describes the known motion of the perihelion of Mercury automatically leads to a non-Newtonian prediction of the deflection of a ray of light grazing the sun, and a shift in the spectral lines, and vice versa. The inductive analysis of one of these known problems leads to generalizations which deduce the solution to the other, such that there was no great insight in clarifying the known problems with known solutions, which is to say that geometrical laws circularly defined to describe one motion ought to describe all of Nature, if Nature is truly uniform, *cæteris paribus*.

A key facet (and specious *fecit*) of the modern propaganda promoting Einstein is the myth that he had thought up the physical problems in his head and derived their solutions by himself with original thought experiments. The solutions and approaches, contrary to Moszkowski and Freundlich's self-serving propaganda, were developed before Einstein by Voigt, FitzGerald, Lorentz, Larmor, Poincaré, Poisson, Gerber, Cohn, Minkowski, Bateman, Varičak, Grossmann, Hilbert, Schwarzschild, and many others; and the physical problems were known through the research of Soldner, Leverrier, Michelson and *Freundlich*, among many others, before Einstein.

Freundlich, of course, knew most of this, though he failed to disclose these facts to the public. Freundlich himself worked on the eclipse idea and Eddington expressed regret that Freundlich was not the first to experimentally test the theory, though he was "first in the field"—a comment which caught Einstein's attention.[112] As is proven by a letter from Max Born to David Hilbert dated 23 November 1915,[113] Erwin Freundlich knew that David Hilbert had first derived and discovered the generally covariant field equations of gravitation of the general theory of relativity, which Freundlich and Einstein plagiarized from Hilbert on 25 November 1915—Freundlich likely being the true primary author of the subsequent paper on the field equations of gravitation attributed to Einstein.[114]

Fruendlich, Born and Moszkowski were but a few of Einstein's many dishonest friends. Max Planck and Max von Laue were well aware that Poincaré had anticipated Einstein, which we know because they cited Poincaré's work in their early works on Poincaré's principle of relativity. In 1905 and 1906, Paul Ehrenfest considered Lorentz' 1904 paper[115] on special relativity and Poincaré's 1905 Rendiconti paper[116] on space-time to be the most significant work (both historically and scientifically) on the subject of the principle of relativity. Ehrenfest and his wife Tatiana attended David Hilbert's 1905 Göttingen seminars on electron theory, which described Lorentz' and Poincaré's work on special relativity. In 1911 in a long and well-referenced paper[117] written in consultation with Lorentz on the principle of relativity, space-time and the perihelion motion of Mercury; Willem de Sitter extensively cited Poincaré, but did not mention Einstein, and de Sitter knew that Lorentz and Poincaré had created the theory of relativity before Einstein. Minkowski, at times, took credit for many of Poincaré's insights, and falsely credited Einstein with Poincaré's ideas on time in Minkowski's most famous lecture "Space and Time" of 28 September 1908 delivered in Cologne. David Hilbert must have been aware of these facts—we know that Minkowski was, because he acknowledged Poincaré's work in earlier statements. Arnold Sommerfeld, whom Einstein characterized as deceitful,[118] was aware of this, and, according to Lewis Pyenson,

"Sommerfeld was unable to resist rewriting Minkowski's judgment of Einstein's formulation of the principle of relativity. [***] Sommerfeld also suppressed Minkowski's conclusion, where Einstein was portrayed as the clarifier, but by no means as the principal expositor, of the principle of relativity."[119]

Lorentz and Sommerfeld failed to include any of Poincaré's work in their famous collection of papers *Das Relativitätsprinzip* of 1913, though they included Einstein's papers and Minkowski's lecture "Space and Time". No scientist would today dare to try to lay claim to all that preceded her the way that Einstein and his friends did, even if she assembled specific known empirical facts and predictions with known theory the way that Einstein and his friends did—often with mistakes and contradictions.

Note Feundlich's overblown title and bear in mind that it was written soon after Germany's defeat in the First World War. Freundlich wrote in the 30 November 1919 morning edition of *Vossische Zeitung*:

"Albert Einstein.
Zum Siege seiner Relativitätstheorie.

Von
Erwin Freundlich, Neubabelsberg.

In Deutschland hat ein wissenschaftliches Ereignis von außerordentlicher Bedeutung noch nicht den Widerhall gefunden, den es seiner Bedeutung nach verdient. Anläßlich der Sonnenfinsternis am 29. Mai dieses Jahres haben englische Astronomen eine wichtige Voraussage der Einsteinschen Relativitätstheorie, nämlich die Ablenkung eines Lichtstrahles im Gravitationsfelde der Sonne, bestätigt gefunden und damit eine Erkenntnis sichergestellt, die von ausschlaggebender Bedeutung für unsere Auffassung von Raum, Zeit und Materie in der Physik ist. Es ist keine Uebertreibung, wenn wir dieses Ereignis als einen Wendepunkt in der Geschichte der Naturwissenschaften feiern, nur zu vergleichen mit Epochen, welche mit den Namen Ptolemäus, Kopernikus, Kepler und Newton verknüpft werden.

Wenn es auch nicht möglich ist, an dieser Stelle die Grundzüge der Einsteinschen Theorie darzulegen, so will ich doch versuchen, die große Linie in der Entwicklung der Physik bis zur Einsteinschen Relativitätstheorie aufzuzeichnen, um die volle Würdigung seiner genialen Leistungen zu ermöglichen.

Das Weltbild, welches sich das Altertum gebildet hatte, ist durch den Umstand gekennzeichnet, daß in den Mittelpunkt der Welt der Mensch, d. h. die Erde, gesetzt wurde, um welche alle Himmelskörper in Kreisen sich bewegen sollten, Gäbe es keine Planeten, so wäre die Durchführung dieser Auffassung nicht auf solche Schwierigkeiten gestoßen. Da tat K o p e r n i k u s um 1543 den ersten großen Schritt. Er entthronte die Erde und erhob die Sonne zum Mittelpunkt der Welt. Diese Tat stellt wohl den entscheidendsten Fortschritt in der Gestaltung unseres Weltbildes dar; doch hafteten ihr zu Anfang noch mannigfache Schwächen an, bis K e p l e r seine bekannten Gesetze aufstellte.

Was die Entwicklung bis dahin charakterisiert, ist der Umstand, daß man sich noch nicht bemühte, durch Aufstellung allgemeiner Prinzipien zu einer einheitlichen Auffassung der mannigfachen auch auf der Erde beobachteten Bewegungserscheinungen fortzuschreiten. Den Beginn mit einer so vertieften Naturbeschreibung machte G a l i l e i , als er den Begriff der Trägheit schuf und den Grundsatz aufstellte: Jeder bewegte Körper behält infolge seiner Trägheit eine einmal gewonnene Geschwindigkeit bei, es sei denn, daß eine bremsende Kraft sie allmählich verringert. Als Galilei seine Bewegungsgesetze aufstellte, stand ihm vielleicht eine einheitliche Erfassung aller Bewegungsvorgänge, auch der der Himmelskörper, als fernes Ziel vor Augen. Zu diesem führte uns aber erst Newton hin. Er verschmolz die Fallerscheinungen auf der Erde mit den Bewegungsvorgängen der Planeten und Monde, indem er neben dem Begriff der Trägheit den der Schwere eines Körpers schuf und sein mathematisch außerordentlich einfaches G r a v i t a t i o n s g e s e t z aufstellte. Auf seinen Aufsätzen baut sich die „k l a s s i s c h e" M e c h a n i k auf, die in einer Kette unerhörter Erfolge alle Bewegungsvorgänge im Sonnensystem mit einer solchen Genauigkeit zu verfolgen erlaubte, daß viele glaubten, hier sei man zu einer ganz endgültigen Theorie der Bewegungserscheinungen gelangt, die in ihren Fundamenten niemals erschüttert werden können. Und doch nagte schon damals der Wurm an den Wurzeln des hochgeschossenen und weit verästelten Baumes; und niemand verspürte vielleicht tiefer die angeborenen Schmächen der Theorie als ihr Schöpfer, Newton, selbst.

Die Newtonsche Mechanik arbeitet nämlich mit verschiedenen Grundbegriffen, über deren physikalische Bedeutung und Beziehung zueinander man nie so recht ins Reine kam. Z. B., obwohl wir ausschließlich die Bewegungen von Körpern relativ zueinander wahrnehmen, tritt doch in der Newtonschen Mechanik der l e e r e Raum als ein physikalisches Ding auf, welches für das Auftreten der Zentrifugalkräfte, die wir auf rotierenden Körpern feststellen, verantwortlich gemacht wird. Schon Newton empfand das physikalisch Unbefriedigende einer solchen Auffassung. Oder, um noch ein Beispiel anzuführen: in die Newtonsche Mechanik werden zwei von einander unabhängige Grundattribute eines jeden Körpers, nämlich seine Schwere und seine Trägheit, eingeführt. Als man an die Messung der Beträge dieser beiden Größen heranging, entdeckte man das anscheinend mit aller [??? *Three to five words illegible on my photocopy.*], daß die träge und schwere Masse aller Körper stets absolut gleich sind. Sollte diese Uebereinstimmung ein reiner Zufall sein? Oder ist nicht vielmehr zu vermuten, daß eine Theorie wie die Newtonsche, in welcher dieses Grundgesetz für alle Materie keine tiefere Begründung findet, in ihren Grundlagen verfehlt ist?

Schließlich stieß man sogar auf eine zahlenmäßige Abweichung zwischen Theorie und Beobachtung, nämlich beim Planeten M e r k u r, die sich im Rahmen der Newtonschen Theorie nicht beheben ließ. Ihre sonstigen Erfolge waren jedoch so groß, daß man lange Zeit nicht glauben konnte und wollte, daß sie in ihren Grundlugen einen Todeskeim trage. Den Anstoß zu ihrem Zusammenbruch erfuhr sie auch nicht von innen heraus, sondern von seiten der Elektrodynamik. Als nämlich diese dazu überging, die elektrischen Vorgänge bei bewegten Körpern zu studieren, geriet man in eine äußerst mißliche Lage. Es zeigte sich nämlich, daß uns die bestehende Physik nicht die erforderlichen Hilfsmittel zur befriedigenden Beschreibung solcher Erscheinungen an die Hand gab. Nachdem man sich einige Zeit vergeblich abgemüht hatte, den fühlbaren Mangel befriedigend zu beheben, trat A l b e r t   E i n s t e i n im Jahre 1905, damals noch ein junger, 26jähriger, unbekannter Physiker, hervor und zeigte, daß in den ganz prinzipiellen, tiefliegenden Schwächen der Newtonschen Theorie der Grund der Schwierigkeiten zu suchen sei. Und nun begann er in einer Folge groß angelegter Arbeiten, die in den letzten Jahren einen gewissen Abschluß gefunden haben, ein ganz neues Gebäude der theoretischen Physik von so unerhörter Kühnheit aufzuführen, daß er sicherlich nicht so schnell Mitarbeiter und Anhänger gefunden hätte, wenn nicht folgende drei Momente jeden objektiv Forschenden gewonnen hätten. Erstens, die grundsätzlichen begrifflichen Schwierigkeiten der Newtonschen Theorie, von denen wir schon einige andeuteten, waren unbestritten vorhanden. Dadurch, daß Einstein seine Theorie frei von diesen Schwächen begründete, kam er einem lang empfundenen Bedürfnis entgegen. Zweitens, schon die ersten Ansätze im Anschluß an die Probleme der Elektrodynamik lieferten eine so befriedigende Darstellung aller Beobachtungen, daß man an der Fruchtbarkeit seiner neuen Gesichtspunkte nicht zweifeln konnte. Drittens, in mutiger Verfolgung der letzten Folgerungen seiner allgemein durchgeführten Ideen hat Einstein n e u e E r s c h e i n u n g e n v o r a u s g e s a g t, die sich bisher alle fast restlos haben bestätigen lassen. Wer es weiß, wie furchtlos, ohne sich gewissermaßen durch Geschwindigkeit seiner Ansätze einen Rückweg zu sichern, Einstein seine Theorie begründet und aufgebaut hat, der vermag die Bedeutung dieser praktischen Erfolge zu würdigen.

Zum Ausgangspunkt seiner Reform wählte Einstein d a s R e l a t i v i t ä t s p r i n z i p   d e r   N e w t o n s c h e n M e c h a n i k. Dieses Prinzip fordert, daß in den Bewegungsvorgängen z. B. auf der Erde, deren, in jedem Augenblick mit genügender Annäherung, geradlinig gleichförmiger Bewegungszustand mit bemerkbarwird. Diese durch die Erfahrung gesicherte Tatsache äußert sich mathematisch in den Formeln der Mechanik darin, daß die Bewegungsgleichungen ihre Gestalt bewahren, ganz gleich, auf welches System die Raum-Zeit-Messungen, die den Vorgang festzulegen und zu verfolgen erlauben, bezogen werden, solange man sich auf geradlinig gleichförmig gegeneinander bewegte Systeme beschränkte. Transformationsformeln, welche den Uebergang von den Raum-Zeit-Messung eines solchen Systems zu denen in einem anderen bewerkstelligen sollten, hatte man abgeleitet und lebte in der falschen Vorstellung besangen, diese Formeln seien die einzigen, die diesem Zweck dienen könnten. Da zeigte Einstein als erster, daß, wenn man den Uebergang von einem System zu einem anderen [*about seven words are illegible on my photocopy*: perhaps Bewegungssystem und insbesondere eine neu gewonnene Erfahrung,] nämlich die besondere Bedeutung der Lichtgeschwindigkeit in der Natur in Rücksicht zieht, man gezwungen ist, a n d e r e Transformationsformeln als die bisher üblichen zu verwenden, und ein neues Relativitätsprinzip formulieren muß. Diese neue Erkenntnis war von geradezu revolutionärem Charakter. Denn einmal folgte aus den neuen Formeln, daß wir unsere Anschauungen über das Wesen der Raum-Zeit-Messungen von Grund auf ändern müssen, da nach ihnen die Länge eines Gegenstandes, der Zeitpunkt eines Ereignis ihren absoluten, d. h. unabhängig vom Bewegungszustand des Beobachters geltenden Wert verlieren. Sodann aber zeigte sich, daß die Gleichungen der Newtonischen Theorie dem neuen Relativitätsprinzip entsprechend umgestaltet werden mußten. Dafür behob aber Einsteins Neugestaltung des Relativitätsprinzips für geradlinig gleichförmig bewegte

Systeme mit einem Schlage alle Schwierigkeiten, auf die die Elektrodynamik gestoßen war. Dies war die erste Etappe auf seinem Wege zur Neubegründung der Physik.

Bis hierher folgten ihm bald viele, sobald man die Richtigkeit und Ueberlegenheit seines Standpunktes erkannt hatte. Und während schon fleißige Hände und Köpfe an die Aufgabe gingen, die Gleichungen der Newtonschen Mechanik dem neuen sogenannten „s p e z i e l l e n" Relativitätsprinzip anzupassen, da war Einstein, in voller Klarheit über die begrenzte Leistungsfähigkeit der bis dahin gewonnenen Erkenntnisse, in seinen Gedanken seinen Mitarbeitern einen großen Schritt voraus. Er war sich darüber im klaren, daß der Boden für die Neubegründung der Mechanik noch nicht erreicht war. Mit der Erkenntnis der Relativität der der beschleunigten Bewegung ein tieferes Erfassen der Gravigeschwindigkeit war wohl e i n e Schwäche der bestehenden Theorie aufgedeckt, aber vielleicht keineswegs ihre fundamentalste. Ein Anpassen der Mechanik an die spezielle Relativitätstheorie wäre ein Stehenbleiben auf halbem Wege gewesen.

Einstein übersah sofort, daß eine Reform der Newtonschen Mechanik nur in einer radikalen Umgestaltung derselben in eine solche bestehen konnte, welche ausschließlich Aussagen über Relativbewegungen enthielt und den Begriff des absoluten Raumes ausschaltete. Er erkannte auch sofort, daß eine Berücksichtigung der beschleunigten Bewegungen ein tieferes Erfassen der Gravitationserscheinungen erforderte. Und hier tritt besonders eindringlich eine Besonderheit der Einsteinschen Forschungsart zutage, die, trotz des ausgesprochen philosophischen Grundzuges seines Wesens, ihn als reinen Naturforscher kennzeichnen. Zwei alte Erfahrungstatsachen, die wir alle in der Schule gelernt haben, an denen wir aber alle mehr oder minder gedankenlos vorübergegangen sind, nämlich die Gleichheit der trägen und schweren Masse aller Körper und die völlige Unabhängigkeit der Fallbeschleunigung von der physikalischen und chemischen Beschaffenheit des fallenden Körpers, diese gewannen durch Einstein erst Leben und tieferen Sinn. Er erkannte, daß diese zwei Tatsachen uns im wesentlichen alle erforderliche Erkenntnisse liefern, um eine Mechanik der Relativbewegungen der Massen und eine Theorie der Gravitationserscheinungen aufzubauen. Allerdings hatte die letzte Säule unserer Anschauungen über das Wesen von Raum-

Zeit in der Physik zu fallen.

Durch die „spezielle" Relativitätstheorie war der absolute Charakter der Raum-Zeit-Messungen zwar beseitigt worden. Doch behielt immerhin jedes System das Recht, eine Messungen nach den Formeln der euklidischen Geometrie auszuwerten. Bei der Ausgestaltung der allgemeinen Relativitätstheorie kam aber die schon im Jahre 1854 von dem genialen Mathematiker Bernhard R i e m a n n ausgesprochene Erkenntnis zutage, daß die E r f o r s c h u n g   d e r   g e o m e t r i s c h e n V e r h ä l t n i s s e   i n   d e r   m a t e r i e l l e n   W e l t   e i n G r u n d p r o b l e m   d e r   P h y s i k sei und nicht eine rein mathematische Angelegenheit. Ganz unabhängig gelangte Einstein zu derselben Einsicht, fand aber zugleich als erster eine Lösung für diese tiefliegende Problemstellung. Er zeigte, daß die Erforschung der geometrischen Zusammenhangsverhältnisse der physikalischen Welt gleichbedeutend ist mit der Erforschung ihrer Gravitationsverhältnisse.

Auf Fundamente von solcher Tiefe und Breite baute Einstein seine neue Mechanik auf; immer, trotz aller Abstraktheit der Gedankengänge und trotz der schwierigen neuen mathematischen Hilfsmittel, die er heranzog, immer bestrebt, durch beobachtbare Folgerungen seiner Ansätze ihre Ueberlegenheit über die früherer Theorie zu erweisen. Er schuf neue Bewegungsgesetze für die Planeten und zeigte, daß sie nicht nur dasselbe leisten wie diejenigen der Newtonschen Mechanik, sondern darüber hinausgehend, sofort die beim Merkur beobachtete und oben erwähnte Bewegungsanomalie restlos deutete. Seine Theorie ergab, daß die Eigenschaft der Schwere und Trägheit, bisher von uns als spezifisches Merkmal der Materie aufgefaßt, auch jeglicher Energie, also Licht, Wärmestrahlung usw. zukommt. Daraus zog er sofort die für die neue Auffassung entscheidende Folgerung, daß ein in unmittelbarer Nähe an der Sonne vorübergehender Lichtstrahl eines Sternes abgelenkt werden müsse. Zwei englische Expeditionen, die am 29. Mai dieses Jahres speziell zur Prüfung dieser Folgerung der Einsteinschen Theorie ausgerüstet worden waren, haben seine Voraussage vollauf bestätigt gefunden. Auch eine dritte Folgerung seiner allgemeinen Relativitätstheorie, ein Einfluß der Schwere auf die Lage der S p e k t r a l l i n i e n ist, wenn auch nicht sicher erwiesen, doch schon heute in hohem Grade wahrscheinlich gemacht.

So hat die beispiellose Gestaltungskraft eines Mannes in 15 Jahren die Physik auf eine ganz neue Grundlage gestellt, so daß wir am Beginn einer ganz neue Epoche der Naturbeschreibung stehen, geknüpft an den Namen E i n s t e i n , so wie frühere an die Namen Ptolemäus, Kopernikus und Newton geknüpft werden. Er hat die Physik vor ganz neue Probleme gestellt, die Mathematik vor die Aufgabe, die neuen mathematischen Hilfsmittel auszubauen, die benötigt werden, da seine Theorie die bisher üblichen Formeln der euklidischen Geometrie verläßt; die Philosophie vor die Notwendigkeit, unsere Anschauungen über Raum — Zeit — Materie einer gründlichen Revision zu unterziehen, und die Astronomie vor die Ehrenpflicht, die Prüfung der letzten Konsequenzen der neuen Theorie an der Erfahrung durchzuführen."

The *Berliner Illustrirte Zeitung*, Volume 28, Number 50, (14 December 1919), printed a large portrait of Einstein on the cover with the following caption,

"**E i n e   n e u e   G r ö ß e   d e r   W e l t g e s c h i c h t e :   A l b e r t   E i n s t e i n ,**
dessen Forschungen eine völlige Umwälzung unserer Naturbetrachtung bedeutet und den Erkenntnissen eines Kopernikus, Kepler und Newton gleichwertig sind."

Einstein's acquaintance Max Born wrote in the *Frankfurter Zeitung und Handelsblatt* (which Zionist Theodor Herzl called a "Jewish paper"[120]), first morning edition, on 23 November 1919 (*see also: Frankfurter Zeitung und Handelsblatt*, first morning edition of 30 September 1919, for an article on the eclipse expeditions):

"Raum, Zeit und Schwerkraft.
Von Professor Dr. M. Born.

Am 29. Mai dieses Jahres fand eine Sonnenfinsternis statt, die einen schmalen Streifen der südlichen Erdhälfte einige Minuten verdunkelte, in Europa aber unsichtbar blieb. Mit diesem unscheinbaren Ereignis ist einer der größten Siege verknüpft, die der Menschengeist der Natur abgetrotzt hat, kein Triumph dröhnender Technik, sondern des reinen Erkennens: die B e s t ä t i g u n g   d e r   E i n s t e i n s c h e n   T h e o r i e   d e r   G r a v i t a t i o n   u n d   d e r   a l l g e m e i n e n   R e l a t i v i t ä t .

Zur Beobachtung der Finsternis war eine englische Expedition unter dem Astronomen E d d i n g t o n ausgeschickt worden; ihre Aufgabe war nicht die Aufzeichnung und Messung jener glänzenden Erscheinungen, die jede totale Verfinsterung so eindrucksvoll machen, wie Protuberanzen, Corona, Fackeln, sondern die Messung der Stellung einiger Fixsterne, die während der Finsternis in unmittelbarer Nähe des Sonnenrandes standen und nur während der Verdeckung der alles überstrahlenden Sonne durch den Mond dem Auge und der photographischen Platte zugänglich waren.

Der Zweck dieser höchst mühseligen, schwierigen Messung war die Prüfung, ob diese Sterne die von der Einsteinschen Theorie geforderte scheinbare V e r s c h i e b u n g zeigten. Der beschränkte Raum gestattet nicht, die Entwicklung dieser Theorie hier darzustellen. Nur soviel sei gesagt, daß es zuerst E r f a h r u n g e n   b e i   o p t i s c h e n   u n d   e l e k t r i s c h e n Präzisionsmessungen waren, die sich mit Hilfe der überkommenen Vorstellungen von Raum, Zeit, Bewegung nicht deuten ließen, und die Einstein veranlaßten, eine Revision dieser Grundbegriffe vorzunehmen.

Der Hauptinhalt seiner Lehre ist folgender: Man denke sich einen Beobachter, der sich mit seiner Umgebung geradlinig und gleichförmig durch den Raum bewegt; dies ist tatsächlich unsere Situation auf der im Weltenraum dahineilenden Erde, wenn man von der schwachen Krümmung der Erdbahn absieht. Richtet der Beobachtet seinen Blick auf andere Körper, die an seiner Bewegung nicht teilnehmen (etwa auf entfernte Gestirne), so wird er an der allmählichen Verschiebung dieser Körper merken, daß sein Standpunkt sich gegen sie bewegt. Die Frage ist nun aber, ob er seine Ortsveränderung auch feststellen kann, wenn er nicht fremde Körper beobachtet, sondern sich auf Messungen in seinem Laboratorium mit seinen mechanischen, elektrischen, optischen Apparaten beschränkt. Die klassische Mechanik gibt darauf die Antwort, daß ihm seine Bewegung verborgen bleiben muß; denn die mechanischen Gesetze in g l e i c h f ö r m i g und g e r a d l i n i g   b e w e g t e n Systemen von Körpern stimmen vollständig mit denen überein, die im Falle der R u h e dieser Körper gelten, daher funktionieren alle mechanischen Apparate, wie Pendel, Wage usw. genau so, als wenn sie sich auf ruhender Grundlage befänden. Versagt also die mechanische Apparatur, so wird der Beobachter die elektrische, magnetische und optische zum Nachweise seiner Bewegung heranholen. Hier könnte man zunächst ein positives Ergebnis erwarten, denn als Träger der elektromagnetischen und optischen Erscheinungen gilt der Weltäther, und wenn das ganze Laboratorium des Beobachters auf der Erde mit der gewaltigen Geschwindigkeit dieses Planeten von etwa 30 Kilometern in der Sekunde durch den Aether rast, so müßte ein heftiger Aetherwind durch das Laboratorium wehen, entsprechend dem Gegenwinde, den der Automobilfahrer bei schneller Fahrt spürt. Der Aetherwind würde mancherlei Wirkungen ausüben, z. B. Lichtwellen verwehen, ihre Richtung und Geschwindigkeit ändern; man hat nun mit den schärfsten Meßmethoden versucht, diese Wirkungen nachzuweisen, aber immer vergebens: Der Aetherwind existiert nicht, die Lichtwellen laufen auf der b e w e g t e n Erde gerade so, als wenn sie ruhte, und von allen elektrischen und magnetischen Vorgängen gilt dasselbe. Das heißt aber nichts anderes als daß auch mit elektromagnetischen und optischen Messungen die Feststellung einer absoluten gleichförmigen und geradlinigen Bewegung durch den Raum nicht möglich ist. Feststellbar sind nur relative Bewegungen eines Körpers gegen den anderen.

Diese Tatsache ist aber, wie das Bild des Aetherwindes zeigt, mit der gewöhnlichen Auffassung von Raum, Zeit, Bewegung vollständig unbegreiflich. E i n s t e i n faßte nun den kühnen Gedanken, zugleich mit der Vorstellung des absoluten R a u m e s auch die der absoluten Z e i t, als einer physikalisch meßbaren Größe, auszugeben. Auf diese Weise gelang es tatsächlich, alle elektromagnetischen und optischen Erfahrungen ebenso gut wie die mechanischen mit der Relativität in Einklang zu bringen.

Diese erste Einsteinsche Relativitätstheorie vom Jahre 1906 heute die „spezielle" genannt, war noch ziemlich harmlos zwar brachte sie außer der Auflösung der überlieferten Begriff von Raum und Zeit noch zahlreiche umstürzende Gedanken wie den, daß die Masse keine konstante Eigenschaft der Materie sondern von ihrer Geschwindigkeit und ihrem Energieinhalt abhängig sei, aber es bedurfte nur weniger Jahre, um so ziemlich alle Physiker zu Relativisten zu machen. Denn diese spezielle Relativitätstheorie hatte eine große Anzahl von Konsequenzen, die sich durch Versuche prüfen ließen, und nachdem ein Experiment nach dem anderen zu ihren Gunsten entschied mußten selbst hartnäckige Verfechter des Absoluten die Waffen strecken.

Die Beschränkung auf gradlinige und gleichförmige Relativbewegung ist für den auf Allgemeinheit der Erkenntnis gerichteten Geist zweifellos ein Stein des Anstoßes. Aber primitive Erfahrungen scheinen dafür einzustehen, daß diese Beschränkung wesentlich ist. Hierher gehören die bekannten Erscheinungen, auf Grund deren man die Rotation der Erde durch irdische, nicht astronomische Messungen nachweist; z. B. die Drehung der Schwingungsebene des Foucauldschen Pendels oder die Zentrifugalkraft, durch die eine scheinbare Aenderung der Schwerkraft mit der geographischen Breite und der Abplattung der Erde an den Polen erzeugt wird. Nach der klassischen Mechanik sind das alles Erscheinungen, die auf die Widerstande der Massen gegen Geschwindigkeitsänderungen (Beschleunigungen), der sogenannten Massenträgheit, beruhen. Durch die Rotation der Erde werden solche Trägheitswiderstände hervorgerufen; obwohl die Mechanik behauptet, die gleichförmige und geradlinige Bewegungen gegen den absoluten Raum nicht feststellbar sind, hält sie daran fest, daß ungleichförmige oder nicht gradlinige Bewegungen, z. B. Rotationen, gegen den leeren Raum bestimmte physikalische Wirkungen hervorbringen. Auch wenn die Erde allein im Weltraume schwebte, müßten die Menschen ihre Drehung etwa mit dem Foucauldschen Pendel oder durch Beobachtung der Abplattung der Erdkugel feststellen können, also eine Drehung gegen den leeren Raum, gegen das N i c h t s. Vor Einstein haben nur wenige Denker an diesem Unding des im leeren Raume bewegten Körpers Anstoß genommen, so vor allem Ernst M a c h, der Physiker und Philosoph, der ausdrücklich eine Revision der mechanischen Grundgesetze zur Beseitigung jeder absoluten Bewegung forderte. Aber erst Einstein besaß die Kraft der Abstraktion, die zu einer solchen Leistung notwendig war. Der Schlüssel für die Lösung war die Entdeckung des Zusammenhangs zwischen dem Raum-Zeit-Problem und dem Problem der Gravitation oder allgemeinen Schwerkraft. Eine sehr sicher begründete, aber wenig beachtete Erfahrung besagt, daß alle Körper (im luftleeren Raume) gleich schnell fallen. Man denke sich einen Beobachter in einem allseits geschlossenen Kasten mit allerlei Gegenständen untergebracht, und dieser Kasten falle herab, dann wird der Beobachter, da alle Dinge im

Kasten gleich schnell fallen, feststellen können, daß die Dinge ihre Schwere verlieren. Hier erkennt man die Brücke zwischen der Bewegungslehre und der Gravitation. Der Widerstand, den die Masse der Körper einer Beschleunigung entgegensetzt, und die Anziehung einer schweren Masse durch die andere werden zwei Erscheinungsformen desselben Grundgesetzes. Nun ist die Massenanziehung offenbar eine relative Wirkung zweier Körper; somit muß auch der Beschleunigungswiderstand relativiert werden, auch er ist nur vorhanden, wenn andere Körper zugegen sind, nicht aber im leeren Raume. Die zum Nachweis der Rotation der Erde gebrauchten Erscheinungen der Massenträgheit, z. B. die Abplattung der Erde, sind nach Einstein Wirkungen fremder Massen, nämlich des Systems aller Himmelskörper, vor allem des Heeres der Fixsterne, und sie würden verschwinden, wenn die Erde allein im Weltenraume schwebte. Das Argument der im leeren Raume allein rotierenden Erde ist für Einsteins Wirklichkeitssinn nichtig; für ihn ist nur reell, was feststellbar ist, also relative Oerter, relative Zeiten, relative Bewegungen. Aber der Weg, der ihn von dieser subjektiven Ueberzeugung bis zur objektiven Behauptung der a l l g e m e i n e n Relativität a l l e r Bewegungsvorgänge, a l l e r physischen Vorgänge führte, war ein Anstieg auf steilsten Hängen, über Hindernisse, die jeden andern abgeschreckt hätten.

Nur einer vor ihm hatte ähnliche Pfade eingeschlagen, der Mathematiker Bernhard R i e m a n n, doch war seine Zeit (Mitte des 19. Jahrhunderts) noch nicht reif, die Summe der Erfahrungen zu beschränkt. Die Durchführung der allgemeinen Relativität erfordert nämlich nicht mehr und nicht weniger als den Verzicht auf die allgemeine Gültigkeit der Euklidischen Geometrie, die seit 2000 Jahren als der Grundstein allen Wissens gilt, und ihre Ersetzung durch die von Riemann zuerst entworfene a l l g e m e i n e R a u m l e h r e. In dieser gibt es weder gerade Linien noch ebene Flächen, die nach Euklid wie ein starres Gerüst den Raum durchziehen. Am besten kann man sich eine Vorstellung von dieser Riemannschen Geometrie machen, wenn man an die Geometrie auf einer krummen, komplizierten Oberfläche, etwa einer Alpenlandschaft, denkt; auch da kann man keine geraden Linien von beträchtlicher Länge auf dem Erdboden ziehen, und ein Feldmesser, der nur mit der Meßkette, ohne optische Visierinstrumente ausgerüstet wäre, hätte eine heillose Mühe:

und doch würde er die Aufgabe bewältigen. Er würde, von irgend einem Netz von Fixpunkten ausgehend die kürzesten Wege zwischen irgend zwei Punkten mit der Meßkette festzustellen suchten, dann die Krümmungseigenschaften der Berge, Täler und Sättel ausmessen und so allmählich eine Aufzeichnung des Geländes herstellen, die von dem zugrunde gelegten Netze von Fixpunkten unabhängig ist und nur die tatsächlichen Beziehungen der Oertlichkeiten enthält. In ganz ähnlicher Lage ist der Mensch im Raume, wenn man diesen nicht von vornherein als Euklidisch voraussetzt, sondern ihn ohne Voreingenommenheit mit der Meßkette ausmißt.

Das ist der Standpunkt Riemanns, den Einstein, durch Einbeziehung der Zeit auf das physikalische Geschehen übertragen hat; zur Meßkette muß dann noch eine Uhr treten. Gestützt auf ein beliebiges Gerüst physischer Fixpunkte sucht man durch Messung die den Dingen eigentümlichen Raumgesetze zu ergründen, die in unserm Bilde den Krümmungsverhältnissen der Erdoberfläche analog sind. Die Einsteinsche Theorie führt dann zu der Vorstellung, daß der Raum nur da „ungekrümmt", „Euklidisch" ist, wo keine merkbaren Massen sind; in der Nähe der Massen aber z e i g t er Abweichungen von den Euklidischen Gesetzen „Krümmungen", und auf diesen beruhen die Krümmungen der Bahnen bewegter Körper, die in der klassischen Mechanik als Wirkungen der Schwerkraft angesehen werden.

Man sieht, wie diese auf dem Boden der Erfahrung gewachsene Theorie hinübergreift über die Grenzen der Naturwissenschaft und die Philosophie zur Stellungnahme herausfordert.

Für die tatsächliche Gültigkeit der Einsteinschen Theorie konnten bislang nur wenige Tatsachen der Astronomie angeführtwerden. Die klassische Himmelsmechanik N e w t o n s ist nämlich vom Standpunkte der neuen Theorie nur näherungsweise richtig und muß in der Nachbarschaft großer, gravitierender Massen, wie der Sonne, in bestimmter Weise korrigiert werden; in der Tat konnte Einstein auf diesem Wege eine bisher unerklärte Abweichung des sonnennächsten Planeten Merkur von seiner Newtonschen Bahn quantitativ genau erklären. Außerdem fordert die Einsteinsche Theorie gewisse Verschiebungen der Spektrallinien des Lichtes der Sonne und der Fixsterne; auch diese Erscheinung ist heute sicher nachgewiesen. Endlich sollen Lichtstrahlen, die nahe an der Sonne vorbeistreichen, von dieser abgelenkt werden; dies zu prüfen, war die Aufgabe der englischen Finsternis-Expedition. Nach einer Mitteilung in der Zeitschrift „die Naturwissenschaften" [*Footnote:* 7. Jahrg., Heft 42 vom 17. Oktbr. 1919. S. 775.]) hat nun Einstein ein Telegramm des holländischen Physikers L o r e n t z bekommen, wonach die von Einstein vorhergesagte Ablenkung der Lichtstrahlen im vollen Betrage (1,7 Bogensekunden) wirklich vorhanden ist.

Ist es nun aber nötig, das ganze Gebäude der tausendjährigen Geometrie einzureißen, um diese winzige, unauffällige Erscheinung zu erklären?

Sicherlich wird der, der nichts anderes als diese eine Uebereinstimmung kennt, ein solches Beginnen töricht nennen; gibt es doch genug physikalische Kräfte, die man ersinnen könnte, um die Lichtstrahlablenkung durch die Sonne zu erklären. Aber wer das ganze System der allgemeinen Relativitätstheorie gründlich durchdacht hat, der ist hinreichend vorbereitet, um an sie zu glauben, sobald ein schlagendes Experiment den Einklang des Gedachten mit dem Wirklichen beweist. Darum kann man dem Vorsichtigen, Ungläubigen nur sagen: geh hin und studiere, die Mühe lohnt; du wirst eine geistige Befreiung erleben, vergleichbar der, die Kopernikus der Menschheit bereitet hat.

Es steht wohl außer Zweifel, daß die physikalischen Wissenschaften sich in Zukunft streng relativistisch einstellen werden. Für die Philosophie aber bedeutet die Einsteinsche Lehre den Sturz der räumlichen und zeitlichen Kategorien von der Höhe des *a priori* in die Niederungen der „platten Empirie". Die Behauptung K a n t s, daß die Urteile über Raum und Zeit synthetische Urteile *a priori* seien, stützt sich auf die zu seiner Zeit geltende Ansicht, daß man an der W a h r h e i t der geometrischen Erkenntnisse in der überkommenen Form Euklids nicht zweifeln dürfe, daß es vielmehr die Aufgabe der Philosophie sei, die „Möglichkeit" einer solchen Erkenntnis nachzuweisen, die Gründe für sie aufzusuchen. Da nun die Möglichkeit solcher objektiven und vollkommen genauen Urteile weder auf reiner Logik (analytisch Urteile *a priori*) noch auf Erfahrung (synthetische Urteile *a posteriori*) beruhen konnten, so entstand die Vorstellung einer besonderen Erkenntnisquelle, die „synthetische Urteile *a priori*" ermöglichen soll. Raum und Zeit sind nach Kant „Formen der Anschauung" und ihre Gesetze *a priori* gültig. Inzwischen hat die Entwicklung der Geometrie die Sonderstellung der Euklidischen Geometrie durch die Entdeckung von logisch widerspruchsfreien „nicht-Euklidischen" Geometrien durchbrochen, sodann hat die Physik die allgemeinste Form dieser übergeordneten Geometrien, die Riemannsche, ihrer Darstellung der Wirklichkeit zu Grunde gelegt. Natürlich bleibt davon die logische Sicherheit des Euklidischen Systems von S ä t z e n unangetastet; aber daß die A x i o m e Euklids, aus denen diese Sätze folgen, die adäquate Darstellung der räumlichen Beziehungen der Dinge sind, das leugnet die heutige Physik. Damit ist die Grundlage der kantischen Lehre von der Unantastbarkeit der geometrischen Wahrheiten durchbrochen. Die Empirie hat sie verworfen und sich allgemeinere Grundlagen geschaffen. Ob die „Formen der Anschauung" Kants als Ausdruck gewisser psychologischer Eigenschaften des m e n s c h l i c h e n G e i s t e s eine Daseinsberechtigung haben, das zu prüfen ist nicht Sache des Physikers. Allerdings steht die Exaktheit der geometrischen Sätze zu der Verschwommenheit aller psychologischen in krassem Widerspruche.

Wer diese Entwicklung miterlebt hat, der wird sich des Zweifels am apriorischen Charakter auch anderer Kategorien des Denkens nicht erwehren können. Einstein selbst steht in seinen philosophischen Ueberzeugungen den größten unter den exakten Naturforschern nahe, einem Gauß, einem Riemann, einem Helmholtz, die sich alle trotz Kant zum Empirismus bekannten und unmittelbar an Hume anknüpften.

Die relativistischen Ideen sind zuerst in deutscher Sprache gedacht und aufgezeichnet worden; das *Experimentum Crucis* haben englische Forscher durchgeführt. Ein so kostspieliges Unternehmen wie die Finsternis-Expedition zu rein Theoretischen Zwecken beweist eine starke Teilnahme der Oeffentlichkeit an wissenschaftlichen Problemen. Großen Anteil daran hat die berühmte, im besten Sinne populäre Zeitschrift „The Nature", die unter Mitwirkung der ersten Gelehrten erscheint und ungeheuer verbreitet ist. Auch wir besitzen ähnliche, nach denselben Grundsätzen geleitet Wochenschriften, vor allem die schon genannten „Naturwissenschaften"; doch spielen sie noch nicht die gleiche Rolle im Geistesleben der Nation wie in England. Erst wenn die Kenntnis der wissenschaftlichen Probleme das Interesse an ihnen geweckt hat, kann die Opferwilligkeit entstehen, die für ideelle Ziele Mühe und Geld nicht scheut."

It is interesting to observe how Einstein's followers like Max Born, Robert Daniel Carmichael[121] and Moritz Schlick[122] tried to justify Einstein's many fallacies of *Petitio Principii*. These fatal fallacies were obvious to Einstein's critics Robert Drill (whom Born had attacked),[123] and more significantly Franz Kleinschrod[124] and Hugo Dingler.[125]

Albert Einstein, Karl Marx and Sigmund Freud were each plagiarists promoted by the "Jewish Press" and each lacked the ability to form rational theories which proceeded from fundamental principles to logical conclusions. They and their defenders argued in circles—redundancies, and stagnated science with their irrational dogmas. When relativity critics pointed out the fatal flaws in the theory of relativity, they were told that the theory was irrefutable and that it was the finest example of logical perfection in the history of science. Redundancies are not theories and it is irrational to state conclusions as premises, which is what Einstein did in order to mask his plagiarism.

Nobel Prize laureate Friedrich August Hayek encountered the same type of irrational devotees defending the irrational dogmas of Marx and Freud, as those who defended the similarly irrational dogmas of Einstein. Hayek stated,

"The two chief subjects of discussion among students of the University of Vienna in the years immediately after the war were Marxism and psychoanalysis, as they were to become much later in the West. I made a conscientious effort to study both the doctrines but found them the more unsatisfactory the more I studied them. It seemed to me then and has so appeared ever since that their doctrines were thoroughly unscientific because they so defined their terms that their statements were necessarily true and unrefutable, and therefore said nothing about the world. It was in the struggle with these views that I developed views on the philosophy of science rather similar to, but of course much less clearly formulated than, those which Karl Popper formed from much the same experiences; and it was only natural that I read his views when he published *The Logic of Scientific Discovery* in 1935, some years before I made his acquaintance. [***] Karl Popper is four or five years my junior, so we did not belong to the same academic generation. But our environment in which we formed our ideas was very much the same. It was very largely dominated by discussion, on the one hand, with Marxists and, on the other hand, with Freudians. Both these groups had one very irritating attribute: They insisted that their theories were, in principle, irrefutable. I remember particularly one occasion when I suddenly began to see how ridiculous it all was when I was arguing with Freudians, and they explained, 'Oh, well, this is due to the death instinct.' And I said, 'But this can't be due to the death instinct.' 'Oh, then this is due to the life instinct.' Naturally, if you have these two alternatives available to explain something, there's no way of checking whether the theory is true or not. And that led me, already, to the understanding of what became Popper's main systematic point: that the test of empirical science was that it could be refuted, and that any system which claimed that it was irrefutable was by definition not scientific. I was not a trained philosopher; I didn't elaborate this. It was sufficient for me to have recognized this, but when I found this thing explicitly argued and justified in Popper, I just accepted the Popperian philosophy for spelling out what I had always felt."[126]

Max Born's condescending tone when addressing Einstein's critics is perhaps reflective of his insecurity surrounding his overblown claims. His strikingly incomplete and nationalistically biased history is one example of his duplicitous character. Note that Poincaré's name is conspicuously absent from Born's article.

Max Born was educated at the Göttingen Academy and this was typical of their attitude toward their mathematical and national rival Henri Poincaré, as Jules Leveugle has shown.[127] Hilbert and Minkowski, both of Göttingen, lectured Born in 1905 on the works of Hertz, Voigt, FitzGerald, Larmor, Lorentz, and Poincaré,[128] the real founders of the theory of relativity; and Born would later acknowledge their contributions—after Einstein had died. While Einstein lived, and after Whittaker had completed the second volume of his *A History of the Theories of Aether and Electricity*, which disputed Einstein's priority for the theory of relativity based upon the facts and primary sources, Born felt obliged to write to Einstein to emphatically deny that he had helped his very good friend Sir Edmund Whittaker to write it. Born then later endorsed Whittaker's and G. H. Keswani's view that Lorentz and Poincaré published the special theory of relativity before Einstein, in a letter Born wrote to Prof. Keswani. Born's early papers on what he, like many others, sometimes called the "Lorentz-Einstein principle of relativity",[129] did not emphasize the work of Einstein, but instead emphasized the work of Lorentz and Minkowski, to the exclusion of Poincaré.[130] Minkowski, like Born, was Jewish and many thought that Lorentz was also Jewish. It should be noted that Felix Klein was an important figure at Göttingen and that Arnold Sommerfeld kept close ties to the Göttingen community.

Note also that David Hilbert's name is not to be found in Born's article. Born, who at one time was Hilbert's lecture assistant, knew that Einstein had plagiarized the generally covariant field equations of gravitation of the general theory of relativity from Hilbert. Max Born wrote to David Hilbert on 23 November 1915,[131] two days before Einstein submitted a paper which plagiarized Hilbert's equations. Max Born knew that Hilbert had the equations before Einstein, and that Einstein and Freundlich copied them from Hilbert.

Einstein's sycophantic friends, Moszkowski, Freundlich, Born, Planck, Laue,[132] etc. had a vested interest in the Einstein image and they desired to make fortunes from it. Moszkowski, Laue and Born were especially greedy. This explains Nobel Prize laureate Max von Laue's disingenuous attempts (which are reprinted later in this text) to change the subject from Einstein's sophistry, self-promotion, plagiarism, and the evidence against the general theory of relativity; to racially charged personal attacks on Einstein's critics Paul Weyland, Ernst Gehrcke and Philipp Lenard, which vicious attacks shocked Nobel Prize laureate Lenard, who had been completely objective in his criticisms of relativity theory and had treated Einstein with great respect.[133]

Lenard was assistant to Heinrich Hertz, who was half-Jewish, and Lenard posthumously edited Hertz' works. Lenard was perhaps himself of Jewish descent,[134] though he later publicly espoused Nazism after Einstein and Einstein's friends had smeared him with lies in the international press and had refused to retract their admitted lies. The financial and egotistical interests of Einstein's friends also explains Planck's corrupt methods at the Bad Nauheim debate, and the deceptive articles by the experts Freundlich and Born which gave credence to the promotional campaign for Einstein in the press, promotions tainted with the foul smell of highly unethical ethnic and political bias.

Born attempted to obstruct Moszkowski's efforts to profiteer off of the Einstein brand Moszkowski had created, by blocking publication of Moszkowski's book *Einstein, the Searcher; His Work Explained from Dialogues with Einstein*. Born feared that the publication of this shameless book would confirm Weyland, Gehrcke and Lenard's accusations that Einstein was a sophistic, plagiarizing, publicity-seeking egomaniac and that many wished to profit from his name. Born, Einstein and others believed that the unprecedented Einstein hype by Einstein's Jewish friend Moszkowski revealed that Jews and Jewish-owned media interests were manufacturing an Einstein legend for the purposes of profit and self-promotion. Hedwig and Max Born wanted to calm this rising storm and protect their financial interests.

The "Magazine Section" of *The Minneapolis Journal* reported on 24 October 1920,

"Dr. Einstein at the present is meeting a wave of opposition in Germany. Professors and scientific men recently have banded together in a campaign against him. They accuse him of fostering a great propaganda with the aid of Jewish funds to put himself on the pedestal of fame. They go so far as to call his work plagiarism and his theories sophistry.

The Tidende of Bergen, Norway, prints in detail the record of a meeting in Germany in which the name Einstein was hooted by the assembly. A writer sent to interview the famous doctor disagreed with the tales of modesty attributed to him and characterized Einstein as a man having a very exalted opinion of himself."

The Literary Digest wrote in April of 1921,

"There are two men in Germany to-day who are traditionally inaccessible to newspaper men, Mr. Tobinkin notes. One is the financier, Hugo Stinnes. The other is Einstein. We are told:

Einstein has been greatly abused by a section of the German press, and he therefore shuns publicity."[135]

Einstein confirmed that Moszkowski wanted to profit from the Einstein brand Moszkowski had created, and that Einstein approved of the profiteering, while attempting to quash legitimate criticism of the theory of relativity by the world-famous physicists Philipp Lenard and Willy Wien. Einstein wrote to Max Born in 1920,

"However, I still prefer [Moszkowski] to Lenard and Wien. The latter two squabble because of a passion for squabbling, while the former does it only to earn money (which is, after all, better and more reasonable)."[136]

Einstein interceded on behalf of Erwin Freundlich and Moritz Schlick in an effort to help them profiteer from the Einstein brand on 27 January 1920.[137]

Max Born was peddling a book of his own, *Einstein's Theory of Relativity*.[138] Born, who was eager to prevent the public disclosure of the truths carelessly revealed in Einstein's conversations, wrote many desperate letters to Einstein trying to prevent the publication of Moszkowski's book and stated, *inter alia*,

"It seems that you are less excited about it than your friends. My wife has already written to you saying what I think about this affair. (She is already regretting that she, too, has tried to turn your name into gold by sending me to America; women, poor creatures, carry the whole burden of existence, and grasp at any relief.) You will have to shake off [Moszkowski], otherwise Weyland will win all along the line, and Lenard and Gehrcke will triumph. [***] Forgive the officiousness of my letter, but it concerns everything dear to me (and Planck and Laue, etc.) You do not understand this, in these matters you are a little child. We all love you, and you must obey judicious people (not your wife). Should you prefer to have nothing further to do with the whole business, give me *written* authority. If necessary, I will go to Berlin, or even to the North Pole."[139]

Bear in mind that Einstein was, at that time, just a friend of these men and not the awe inspiring superhero of science they made him out to be through their deceptive self-aggrandizing promotion. They knew that they were lying to the public, and they constructed the modern myth from their lies and misrepresentations. Born later changed his opinion of Moszkowski's book when he read it many decades later, seemingly having come to believe in his own mythologies. However, Max Born conceded in 1962 in the preface of the revised edition of his book *Einstein's Theory of Relativity* (first edition 1920), that the chief cause of interest in the eclipse expeditions, which made Einstein famous in 1919, was deliberate sensationalism—and he was himself a very active participant in that campaign to promote Einstein,

"This text was originally an elaboration of a series of lectures given at Frankfurt am Main to a large audience when a wave of popular interest in the theory of relativity and in Einstein's personality had spread around the world, following the first confirmation by a British solar-eclipse expedition of Einstein's prediction that a beam of light should be bent by the gravitational action of the sun. Though sensationalism was probably the main cause of this interest, there was also a considerable and genuine desire to understand."[140]

Born states that the first edition of his book of 1920 resulted from a series of lectures given to large audiences. Born's lectures, which were promoted in the *Frankfurter Zeitung*,[141] might have been polemic, as well as promotional. Born states in his book,

"There are opponents of the principle of relativity, simple minds who, when they have become acquainted with this difficulty in determining the length of a rod, indignantly exclaim, 'Of course, everything can be derived if we use false clocks; here we see to what absurdities blind faith in the magic power of mathematical formulae leads us,' and then condemn the theory of relativity at one stroke."[142]

Born did indeed profiteer from the Einstein name,

"At that time a wave of interest in Einstein and his theory of relativity was sweeping the world. He had predicted the deflection, by the sun, of light coming from a star. Several expeditions, amongst them a British one under Eddington, had been sent out to tropical regions where a total eclipse of the sun was visible and the deflection could be observed. Now after laborious measurements and tedious calculations the conclusion was arrived at that Einstein was right, and this was published under sensational headlines in all the newspapers. It caused a tremendous stir in the civilized world, as I have already described in another chapter. There was an Einstein craze, everybody wanted to learn what it was all about, and he became the victim of a publicity racket. I used this for my own purposes. I announced a series of three lectures in the biggest lecture-hall of the University of Einstein's theory of relativity and charged an entrance fee for my Department. It was a colossal success, the hall was crowded and a considerable sum collected. My friends in the Frankfurt business world told me that I would have done even better if I had sent out private invitations to a lecture in the most expensive hotel, in evening dress and with cocktails, and

had asked for an assistance fund. But that was not in my line.
The money thus earned helped us for some months, but as
inflation got worse, it evaporated quickly and new means had to
be found. One day I met a friend of the Ehrenberg family who
told me that he had been engaged for years to an American girl
from whom he had been separated by the war, and now he was
going to New York to be married. I said jokingly: 'If you find a
German-American who is still interested in the old country, tell
him I need dollars for important experiments in my Department.'
I had quite forgotten this remark when a few weeks later a
postcard arrived, signed by this man: 'I am happily married and
have found your man. Write to Henry Goldman, 998 Fifth
Avenue, New York.' At first I took it for another joke, but on
reflection I decided that an attempt should be made. With Hedi's
help a nice letter was composed and despatched, and soon a most
charming reply arrived and a cheque for some hundreds of
dollars which helped us out of all our difficulties."[143]

Felix Ehrenhaft also sought to profiteer from the Einstein name and
wrote to Einstein on 6 December 1919 requesting that he lecture for the
Chemical-Physical Society of Vienna, stating, "[. . .]I would expect
extraordinary profit[. . . .]"[144]

Albert Einstein's Jewish racism justified his theft from Gentiles and
his stubborn refusal to give them adequate credit for their work. In
addition to his hatred for his first wife for being a Gentile, Einstein
believed, due to his racism, that he was entitled to steal from her.

The Jews rallied around Einstein out of greed, tribal loyalty and
racist Jewish hatred of Gentiles. Jews have long taught that a good Jew
never speaks out against another Jew, and a good Jews does not praise
a Gentile unless such praise results in even greater praise for a Jew. Jews
even have an expression, "[do only what is] good for the Jews!"

We sometimes see Jews deigning to give mild and grudging praise
to Hendrik Antoon Lorentz and Jules Henri Poincaré, or to Mileva
Marić; but it is almost always so that they can lavish far greater praise
on an undeserving Jew, Albert Einstein. *Leviticus* 19:17-8 states,

"17 Thou shalt not hate thy brother in thine heart: thou shalt in
any wise rebuke thy neighbour, and not suffer sin upon him. 18
Thou shalt not avenge, nor bear any grudge against the children
of thy people, but thou shalt love thy neighbour as thyself: I am
the LORD."

In this religious admonition, "neighbor" refers only to fellow Jews. Jews are also taught to cover up the sins of fellow Jews, lest the tribe suffer as a whole. *Numbers* 16:22 states,

"And they fell upon their faces, and said, O God, the God of the spirits of all flesh, shall one man sin, and wilt thou be wroth with all the congregation?"

Israel Shahak wrote in his book *Jewish History, Jewish Religion: The Weight of Three Thousand Years,*

"There is also a series of rules forbidding any expression of praise for Gentiles or for their deeds, except where such praise implies an even greater praise of Jews and things Jewish. This rule is still observed by Orthodox Jews. For example, the writer Agnon, when interviewed on the Israeli radio upon his return from Stockholm, where he received the Nobel Prize for literature, praised the Swedish Academy, but hastened to add: 'I am not forgetting that it is forbidden to praise Gentiles, but here there is a special reason for my praise'—that is, that they awarded the prize to a Jew."[145]

Rev. I. B. Pranaitis wrote in his book *The Talmud Unmasked: The Secret Rabbinical Teachings Concerning Christians*, Eugene Nelson Sanctuary, New York, (1939),

"In Abhodah Zarah (20, a, Toseph) it says:

'Do not say anything in praise of them, lest it be said: How good that Goi is!' [Footnote: Maimonides (in Hilkhoth Akum X, 5) adds: 'Moreover, you should seek opportunity to mix with them and find out about their evil doings.']

In this way they explain the words of Deuteronomy (VII, 2) . . . and thou shalt show no mercy unto them [Goim], as cited in the Gemarah. Rabbi S. Iarchi explains this Bible passage as follows:

'Do not pay them any compliments; for it is forbidden to say: how good that Goi is.'

In Iore Dea (151,14) it says:

'No one is allowed to praise them or to say how good an Akum is. How much less to praise what they do or to recount anything about them which would redound to their glory. If, however, while praising them you intend to give glory to God, namely, because he has created comely creatures, then it is allowed to do so.'"[146]

The Jewish book of *Deuteronomy* 2:7 states,

"And when the LORD thy God shall deliver them before thee; thou shalt smite them, and utterly destroy them; thou shalt make no covenant with them, nor shew mercy unto them:"

The Jewish Old Testament Torah book of *Deuteronomy*, chapter 15, verse 6, states that the Jews should use usury, the theft of money, to ruin and rule over Gentiles:

"For the LORD thy God blesseth thee, as he promised thee: and thou shalt lend unto many nations, but thou shalt not borrow; and thou shalt reign over many nations, but they shall not reign over thee."

Deuteronomy, chapter 23, verse 20 states:

"Unto a stranger thou mayest lend upon usury; but unto thy brother thou shalt not lend upon usury: that the LORD thy God may bless thee in all that thou settest thine hand to in the land whither thou goest to possess it."

Deuteronomy, chapter 28, verses 12-13:

"12 The LORD shall open unto thee his good treasure, the heaven to give the rain unto thy land in his season, and to bless all the work of thine hand: and thou shalt lend unto many nations, and thou shalt not borrow.

13 And the LORD shall make thee the head, and not the tail; and thou shalt be above only, and thou shalt not be beneath; if that

thou hearken unto the commandments of the LORD thy God, which I command thee this day, to observe and to do them:"

In the very first book of Old Testament, *Genesis*, chapter 47, verses 1-31, the Jews state that they enslaved the Egyptian People by contracting the money supply:

"1 Then Joseph came and told Pharaoh, and said, My father and my brethren, and their flocks, and their herds, and all that they have, are come out of the land of Canaan; and, behold, they are in the land of Goshen.

2 And he took some of his brethren, even five men, and presented them unto Pharaoh.

3 And Pharaoh said unto his brethren, What is your occupation? And they said unto Pharaoh, Thy servants are shepherds, both we, and also our fathers.

4 They said moreover unto Pharaoh, For to sojourn in the land are we come; for thy servants have no pasture for their flocks; for the famine is sore in the land of Canaan: now therefore, we pray thee, let thy servants dwell in the land of Goshen.

5 And Pharaoh spake unto Joseph, saying, Thy father and thy brethren are come unto thee:

6 The land of Egypt is before thee; in the best of the land make thy father and brethren to dwell; in the land of Goshen let them dwell: and if thou knowest any men of activity among them, then make them rulers over my cattle.

7 And Joseph brought in Jacob his father, and set him before Pharaoh: and Jacob blessed Pharaoh.

8 And Pharaoh said unto Jacob, How old art thou?

9 And Jacob said unto Pharaoh, The days of the years of my pilgrimage are an hundred and thirty years: few and evil have the days of the years of my life been, and have not attained unto the days of the years of the life of my fathers in the days of their

pilgrimage.

10 And Jacob blessed Pharaoh, and went out from before Pharaoh.

11 And Joseph placed his father and his brethren, and gave them a possession in the land of Egypt, in the best of the land, in the land of Rameses, as Pharaoh had commanded.

12 And Joseph nourished his father, and his brethren, and all his father's household, with bread, according to their families.

13 And there was no bread in all the land; for the famine was very sore, so that the land of Egypt and all the land of Canaan fainted by reason of the famine.

14 And Joseph gathered up all the money that was found in the land of Egypt, and in the land of Canaan, for the corn which they bought: and Joseph brought the money into Pharaoh's house.

15 And when money failed in the land of Egypt, and in the land of Canaan, all the Egyptians came unto Joseph, and said, Give us bread: for why should we die in thy presence? for the money faileth.

16 And Joseph said, Give your cattle; and I will give you for your cattle, if money fail.

17 And they brought their cattle unto Joseph: and Joseph gave them bread in exchange for horses, and for the flocks, and for the cattle of the herds, and for the asses: and he fed them with bread for all their cattle for that year.

18 When that year was ended, they came unto him the second year, and said unto him, We will not hide it from my lord, how that our money is spent; my lord also hath our herds of cattle; there is not ought left in the sight of my lord, but our bodies, and our lands:

19 Wherefore shall we die before thine eyes, both we and our land? buy us and our land for bread, and we and our land will be

servants unto Pharaoh: and give us seed, that we may live, and not die, that the land be not desolate.

20 And Joseph bought all the land of Egypt for Pharaoh; for the Egyptians sold every man his field, because the famine prevailed over them: so the land became Pharaoh's.

21 And as for the people, he removed them to cities from one end of the borders of Egypt even to the other end thereof.

22 Only the land of the priests bought he not; for the priests had a portion assigned them of Pharaoh, and did eat their portion which Pharaoh gave them: wherefore they sold not their lands.

23 Then Joseph said unto the people, Behold, I have bought you this day and your land for Pharaoh: lo, here is seed for you, and ye shall sow the land.

24 And it shall come to pass in the increase, that ye shall give the fifth part unto Pharaoh, and four parts shall be your own, for seed of the field, and for your food, and for them of your households, and for food for your little ones.

25 And they said, Thou hast saved our lives: let us find grace in the sight of my lord, and we will be Pharaoh's servants.

26 And Joseph made it a law over the land of Egypt unto this day, that Pharaoh should have the fifth part; except the land of the priests only, which became not Pharaoh's.

27 And Israel dwelt in the land of Egypt, in the country of Goshen; and they had possessions therein, and grew, and multiplied exceedingly.

28 And Jacob lived in the land of Egypt seventeen years: so the whole age of Jacob was an hundred forty and seven years.

29 And the time drew nigh that Israel must die: and he called his son Joseph, and said unto him, If now I have found grace in thy sight, put, I pray thee, thy hand under my thigh, and deal kindly and truly with me; bury me not, I pray thee, in Egypt:

30 But I will lie with my fathers, and thou shalt carry me out of Egypt, and bury me in their buryingplace. And he said, I will do as thou hast said.

31 And he said, Swear unto me. And he sware unto him. And Israel bowed himself upon the bed's head."

In the Jewish Old Testament book of *Exodus* 3:21-22; 11:2; 12:35-36, the Jews borrow the Egyptians gold and silver and steal them, then the Jews boast that they ruined the Egyptians economically in this way. The Egyptians likely used loops and rings of gold and silver as money. By stealing the Egyptians' money, the Jews contracted the Egyptians money supply and thereby ruined them economically:

"3:21 And I will give this people favour in the sight of the Egyptians: and it shall come to pass, that, when ye go, ye shall not go empty: 3:22 But every woman shall borrow of her neighbour, and of her that sojourneth in her house, jewels of silver, and jewels of gold, and raiment: and ye shall put them upon your sons, and upon your daughters; and ye shall spoil the Egyptians. [***] 11:2 Speak now in the ears of the people, and let every man borrow of his neighbour, and every woman of her neighbour, jewels of silver, and jewels of gold.

11:3 And the LORD gave the people favour in the sight of the Egyptians. Moreover the man Moses was very great in the land of Egypt, in the sight of Pharaoh's servants, and in the sight of the people. [***] 12:35 And the children of Israel did according to the word of Moses; and they borrowed of the Egyptians jewels of silver, and jewels of gold, and raiment:

12:36 And the LORD gave the people favour in the sight of the Egyptians, so that they lent unto them such things as they required. And they spoiled the Egyptians."

The Jews are taught to pool their money and concentrate it in the hands of a few obscenely wealthy Jewish bankers, so that these money kings can exercise their power most efficiently and effectively. The Jewish Old Testament book of *Proverbs* 1:13-14 states:

13 We shall find all precious substance, we shall fill our houses

with spoil: 14 Cast in thy lot among us; let us all have one purse:"

From start to finish, the Old Testament tells the Jews that they should steal the wealth of non-Jews, enslave non-Jews, murder non-Jews and come to own all the property of the Earth. The Talmud justifies these inhuman and genocidal doctrines by claiming that God offered the Goyim the Law when Moses accepted it on behalf of the Hebrews on Sinai, but the Goyim refused the Law and failed to obey even the Noahide Laws, and therefore God gave the Jews all of the wealth of the Goyim as their prize for being God's chosen People.

In its article "Gentile", under the subheading "Rabbinical Modification of Laws", *The Jewish Encyclopedia* states (note that "B. M." signifies the tractate "Baba Mezia" in the Babylonian Talmud and "B. K." is tractate "Baba Kamma" of the Talmud):

"With regard to the text 'This is the law when a man dieth in a tent' (Num. xix. 14), they held that only Israelites are men, quoting the prophet, 'Ye my flock, the flock of my pasture, are men' (Ezek. xxxiv. 31); Gentiles they classed not as men but as barbarians (B. M. 108b). [***] The barbarian Gentiles who could not be prevailed upon to observe law and order were not to be benefited by the Jewish civil laws, framed to regulate a stable and orderly society, and based on reciprocity. The passage in Moses' farewell address: 'The Lord came from Sinai, and rose up from Seir unto them; he shined forth from Mount Paran' (Deut. xxxiii. 2), indicates that the Almighty offered the Torah to the Gentile nations also, but, since they refused to accept it, He withdrew His 'shining' legal protection from them, and transferred their property rights to Israel, who observed His Law. A passage of Habakkuk is quoted as confirming this claim: 'God came from Teman, and the Holy One from Mount Paran. . . . He stood, and measured the earth; he beheld, and drove asunder [{Hebrew deleted} = 'let loose,' 'outlawed'] the nations' (Hab. iii. 3-6); the Talmud adds that He had observed how the Gentile nations steadfastly refused to obey the seven moral Nachian precepts, and hence had decided to outlaw them (B. K. 38a)."[147]

From the earliest recorded dealings of the Tribe, the Jews have been money manipulators, who have been working to steal all of the wealth of the non-Jews. They believe they have a religious obligation to steal all of the gold and silver in the World and horde it in Jerusalem. The Jewish Old Testament book of *Haggai* 2:7-8 states:

"7 And I will shake all nations, and the desire of all nations shall come: and I will fill this house with glory, saith the LORD of hosts. 8 The silver is mine, and the gold is mine, saith the LORD of hosts."

Rabbi Higger wrote in his *The Jewish Utopia* that the Jews will come to possess all possessions of the Gentiles:

"All the treasures and natural resources of the world will eventually come in possession of the righteous. This would be in keeping with the prophecy of Isaiah: 'And her gain and her hire shall be holiness to the Lord; it shall not be treasured nor laid up; for her gain shall be for them that dwell before the Lord, to eat their fill and for stately clothing.[Isaiah 23:18]'[20] Similarly, the treasures of gold, silver, precious stones, pearls, and valuable vessels that have been lost in the seas and oceans in the course of centuries will be raised up and turned over to the righteous.[21] Joseph hid three treasuries in Egypt: One was discovered by Korah, one by Antoninus, and one is reserved for the righteous in the ideal world.[22] [***] Gold will be of secondary importance in the new social and economic order. Eventually, all the friction, jealousy, quarrels, and misunderstandings that exist under the present system, will not be known in the ideal Messianic era.[319] The city of Jerusalem will possess most of the gold and precious stones of the world. That ideal city will be practically full of those metals and stones, so that the people of the world will realize the vanity and absurdity of wasting their lives in accumulating those imaginary valuables.[320],[148]

The history of this ancient Jewish plan to steal the wealth of the World predates the Old Testament and likely began in Babylon, where the Apiru (Hebrews) departed from Ur taking with them their knowledge of money and how to use it to enslave the Goyim and rob them of their wealth. See: David Astle's *The Babylonian Woe*. When the Jews appear, their banking systems either immediately precede them, or soon follow them. The Jews destroyed the monarchies and began the reformation movements in part to allow them to overcome the Roman Catholic Church's opposition to usury. In Islam, the Jews exploited the Muslims' objections to usury to become the bankers of the Muslims.

2.4.1 Advertising Einstein in the English Speaking World

Ernst Gehrcke's *Die Massensuggestion der Relativitätstheorie: Kulturhistorisch-psychologische Dokumente*, Hermann Meusser, (1924), is a valuable reference for newspaper and journal articles promoting Einstein as well as criticisms of Einstein up until 1924. I am only able to reproduce some of the articles cited in Gehrcke's important work and add a few others I have found.

The London Times wrote on 7 November 1919,

"REVOLUTION IN SCIENCE.

NEW THEORY OF THE UNIVERSE.

NEWTONIAN IDEAS OVERTHROWN.

Yesterday afternoon in the rooms of the Royal Society, at a joint session of the Royal and Astronomical Societies, the results obtained by British observers of the total solar eclipse of May 29 were discussed.

The greatest possible interest had been aroused in scientific circles by the hope that rival theories of a fundamental physical problem would be put to the test, and there was a very large attendance of astronomers and physicists. It was generally accepted that the observations were decisive in the verifying of the prediction of the famous physicist, Einstein, stated by the President of the Royal Society as being the most remarkable scientific event since the discovery of the predicted existence of the planet Neptune. But there was difference of opinion as to whether science had to face merely a new and unexplained fact, or to reckon with a theory that would completely revolutionize the accepted fundamentals of physics.

SIR FRANK DYSON, the Astronomer Royal, described the work of the expeditions sent respectively to Sobral in North Brazil and the island of Principe, off the West Coast of Africa. At each of these places, if the weather were propitious on the day of the eclipse, it would be possible to take during totality a set of photographs of the obscured sun and of a number of bright stars which happened to be in its immediate vicinity. The desired object was to ascertain whether the light from these stars, as it passed the sun, came as directly towards us as if the sun were not there, or if there was a deflection due to its presence, and if the latter proved to be the case, what the amount of the deflection was. If deflection did occur, the stars would appear on the photographic plates at a measurable distance from their theoretical positions. He explained in detail the apparatus that had been employed, the corrections that had to be made for various disturbing factors, and the methods by which comparison between the theoretical and the observed positions had been made. He convinced the meeting that the results were definite and conclusive. Deflection did take place, and the measurements showed that the theoretical degree predicted by Einstein, as opposed to half that degree, the amount that would follow from the principles of Newton. It is interesting to recall that Sir Oliver Lodge, speaking at the Royal Institution last February, had also ventured on a prediction. He doubted if deflection would be observed, but was confident that if it did take place, it would follow the law of Newton and not that of Einstein.

DR. CROMMELIN and PROFESSOR EDDINGTON, two of the actual observers, followed the Astronomer Royal, and gave interesting accounts of their work, in every way confirming the general conclusions that had been enunciated.

'MOMENTOUS PRONOUNCEMENT.'

So far the matter was clear, but when the discussion began, it was plain that the scientific interest centred more in the theoretical bearings of the results than in the results themselves. Even the President of the Royal Society, in stating that they had just listened to 'one of the most momentous, if not the most momentous, pronouncements of human thought,' had to confess that no one had yet succeeded in stating in clear language what the theory of Einstein really was. It was accepted, however, that Einstein, on the basis of his theory, had made three predictions. The first, as to the motion of the planet Mercury, had been verified. The second, as to the existence and the degree of deflection of light as it passed the sphere of influence of the sun, had now been verified. As to the third, which depended on spectroscopic observations, there was still uncertainty. But he was confident that the Einstein theory must now be reckoned with, and that our conceptions of the fabric of the universe must be fundamentally altered.

At this stage Sir Oliver Lodge, whose contribution to the discussion had been eagerly expected, left the meeting.

Subsequent speakers joined in congratulating the observers, and agreed in accepting their results. More than one, however, including Professor Newall, of Cambridge, hesitated as to the full extent of the inferences that had been drawn and suggested that the phenomena might be due to an unknown solar atmosphere further in its extent than had been supposed and with unknown properties. No speaker succeeded in giving a clear non-mathematical statement of the theoretical question.

SPACE 'WARPED.'

Put in the most general way it may be described as follows: the Newtonian principles assume that space is invariable, that, for instance, the three angles of a triangle always equal, and must equal, two right angles. But these principles really rest on the observation that the angles of a triangle do equal two right angles, and that a circle is really circular. But there are certain physical facts that seem to throw doubt on the universality of these observations, and suggest that space may acquire a twist or warp in certain circumstances, as, for instance, under the influence of gravitation, a dislocation in itself slight and applying to the instruments of measurement as well as to the things measured. The Einstein doctrine is that the qualities of space, hitherto believed absolute, are relative to their circumstances. He drew the inference from his theory that in certain cases actual measurement of light would show the effects of the warping in a degree that could be predicted and calculated. His predictions in two of three cases have now been verified, but the question remains open as to whether the verifications prove the theory from which the predictions were deduced."

The London Times wrote on 8 November 1919,

"THE REVOLUTION

IN SCIENCE.

EINSTEIN v. NEWTON.

VIEWS OF EMINENT
PHYSICISTS.

Wide interest in popular as well as in scientific circles has been created by the discussion which took place at the rooms of the Royal Society on Thursday afternoon on the results of the British expedition to Brazil to observe the eclipse of the sun on May 29. (These were referred to in an interview with Sir Frank Dyson, the Astronomer Royal, which appeared in *The Times* of September 9.) The subject was a lively topic of conversation in the House of Commons yesterday, and Sir Joseph Larmor, F. R. S., M. P. for Cambridge University, on arriving at a lecture before the Royal Astronomical Society last evening, said he had been besieged by inquiries as to whether Newton had been cast down and Cambridge 'done in.'

Mr. C. Davidson, of Greenwich Observatory, one of the astronomers who took the photographs of the sun's eclipse at Sobral, in Northern Brazil, last May, in conversation with a representative of *The Times* last night, said he agreed that the observations taken of Kappa^1 and Kappa^2, near the constellation of Hyades, at the moment of totality, were conclusive of the deflection of their rays by the gravitation of the sun. In reply to the suggestion made by Professor Newall, of Cambridge, that the deflection might be due to an unknown solar atmosphere further in its extent than had been supposed and with unknown properties, Mr. Davidson said:—'That does not seem possible, because to produce such a deflection there would have to be an atmosphere of a kind unknown to theory and observation. Moreover, comets have been known to pass within grazing distance of the sun without any apparent retardation in their motion.'

Mr. Davidson was also prepared not to dissent from the view that the discovery of light possessing weight as well as mass might mark progress towards a conception of conditions outside three-dimensional space as we at present know it. 'Professor Einstein's theory', he remarked, 'demanded a good deal more of the dimensions existing in space than can be at present mathematically proved. It requires the curvature of space, variable time, and the displacement of the spectral lines towards the red. The latter has been very carefully tested by Dr. St. John at Mount Wilson in the United States, but so far without success. Nevertheless, there are some anomalies in the behaviour of the spectral lines which a good many scientific people believe may have compensations to explain them.'

On the main discovery, however, Mr. Davidson fully endorsed the opinion that the Newtonian principle had been upset, and that Professor Einstein had been right in at least two of his three predictions. 'His surmise with regard to the spectrum,' Mr. Davidson said, 'remains to be demonstrated. As to the phenomena of light, the Brazil observations have established that instead of a deflection of .87 of a second of arc at the sun's limit which would have been expected by the application of Newton's law, it was 1.75, which accords with Professor Einstein's theory. Our observations also proved that the outstanding discrepancy in the perihelion of Mercury can now also be accounted for.'

THE ETHER OF SPACE.

SIR OLIVER LODGE'S CAUTION.
TO THE EDITOR OF THE TIMES.

Sir,—To avoid misunderstanding, permit me to explain that my having to leave the meeting, reported in your issue of to-day (Friday), was due to a long-standing engagement and a 6 o'clock train.

The eclipse result is a great triumph for Einstein; the quantitative agreement is too close to allow much room for doubt, and from every point of view the whole thing is of intense interest.

I have more to say about it, and your excellent report gives a good idea of the general position; but I must deprecate the notion that last February I ventured on anything so serious as a prediction concerning the probable result.

I was rash enough to express a hope for a result equal to half Einstein's value. But the double-valued result can be assimilated and specified in various ways, one of which is the ponderability of light coupled with a definite effect of motion on the Newtonian constant of gravitation, an effect which the behaviour of Mercury and other planets has already rendered probable; while another is the vaguer suggestion that one of the two etherial constants, responsible for the velocity of light, is affected by a gravitational field, so as to cause a kind of refraction.

In any case, I would issue a caution against a strengthening of great and complicated generalizations concerning space and time on the strength of the splendid result: I trust that it may be accounted for, with reasonable simplicity, in terms of the ether of space.

Meanwhile I heartily congratulate Professor Einstein, and also the skilled and painstaking observers who have so admirably verified his striking and original prediction.

Yours faithfully,

OLIVER LODGE.

Llwynarthan, Castleton, Cardiff, Nov. 7.

DR. ALBERT EINSTEIN.

Dr. Albert Einstein, whose astronomical discoveries were described at the meeting of the Royal Society on Thursday as the most remarkable since the discovery of Neptune, and as propounding a new philosophy of the universe, is a Swiss Jew, 45 years of age. He was for some time Professor in Mathematical Physics at the Polytechnic at Zurich, and then Professor at Prague. Afterwards he was nominated a member of the Kaiser Wilhelm Academy for Research in Berlin, with a salary of 18,000 marks (£900) per annum, and no duties, so that he should be able to devote himself entirely to research work.

During the war, as a man of liberal tendencies, he was one of the signatories of the protest against the German manifesto of the men of science who declared themselves in favour of Germany's part in the war, and at the time of the Armistice he signed an appeal in favour of the German revolution. He is an ardent Zionist and keenly interested in the proposed Hebrew University at Jerusalem, and has offered to cooperate in the work there."

Note that *The London Times*, which had been one of the Director of British War Propaganda Lord Northcliffe's wartime propaganda organs, wanted to stress that Einstein opposed "Germany's part in the war". It also emphasized the claim that Newtonian theory had been overthrown. This drew harsh criticism from the nationalistic British, who took great pride in Isaac Newton. *The New York Times* emphasized the idea that Einstein's theory was incomprehensible to all but twelve persons in the world.[149] This myth aided Einstein, in that it allowed him to avoid criticism by claiming that anyone who criticized the theory of relativity did not understand it. The myth also enthralled a gullible public, which found the notion of incomprehensibility intriguing, and felt no need to try to judge the merits of the theory for themselves. In the introduction to the abridged version of the collection of some of Einstein's statements entitled *The World As I See It*, it says, among other things,

"Einstein, therefore, is great in the public eye partly because he has made revolutionary discoveries which cannot be translated into the common tongue. We stand in proper awe of a man whose thoughts move on heights far beyond our range, whose achievements can be measured only by the few who are able to follow his reasoning and challenge his conclusions."[150]

The New York Times wrote on 9 November 1919 on page 6,

"ECLIPSE SHOWED GRAVITY VARIATION

Diversion of Light Rays Accepted as Affecting Newton's Principles.

HAILED AS EPOCHMAKING

British Scientist Calls the Discovery One of the Greatest of Human Achievements.

Special Cable to THE NEW YORK TIMES.
LONDON, Nov. 8.—What Sir Joseph Thomson, President of the Royal Society, declared was 'one of the greatest—perhaps the greatest—of achievements in the history of human thought' was discussed at a joint meeting of the Royal Society and the Royal Astronomical Society in London yesterday, when the results of the British observations of the total solar eclipse of May 29 were made known.

There was a large attendance of astronomers and physicists, and it was generally accepted that the observations were decisive in verifying the prediction of Dr. Einstein, Professor of Physics in the University of Prague, that rays of light from stars, passing close to the sun on their way to the earth, would suffer twice the deflection for which the principles enunciated by Sir Isaac Newton accounted. But there was a difference of opinion as to whether science had to face merely a new and unexplained fact or to reckon with a theory that would completely revolutionize the accepted fundamentals of physics.

The discussion was opened by the Astronomer Royal, Sir Frank Dyson, who described the work of the expeditions sent respectively to Sobral, in Northern Brazil, and the Island of Principe, off the west coast of Africa. At each of these places, if the weather were propitious on the day of the eclipse, it would be possible to take during the totality a set of photographs of the obscured sun and a number of bright stars which happened to be in its immediate vicinity.

The desired object was to ascertain whether the light from these stars as it passed by the sun came as directly toward the earth as if the sun were not there, or if there was a deflection due to its presence. And if the deflection did occur the stars would appear on the photographic plates at measurable distances from their theoretical positions. Sir Frank explained in detail the apparatus that had been employed, the corrections that had to be made for various disturbing factors, and the methods by which comparison between the theoretical and observed positions had been made. He convinced the meeting that the results were definite and conclusive, that deflection did take place, and that the measurements showed that the extent of deflection was in close accord with the theoretical degree predicted by Dr. Einstein, as opposed to half of that degree, the amount that would follow if the principles of Newton were correct.

Dr. Crommelin, one of the observers at Sobral, who spoke next, said that eight exposures of twenty-eight seconds each were made during the totality of the eclipse. Seven of these plates showed seven stars in each. One showed no stars, owing to the presence of a thin cloud, but gave well-defined images of the inner corona of the sun and of great prominence. Seven exposures of the same star field were made for comparison between July 14 and July 18 in the morning sky, the sun being then 45 degrees or more away from it. The results reduced to the sun's limb were 2.08 seconds and 1.94 seconds respectively. The combined result was 1.98 seconds, with a probable error of about 6 per cent. This was a strong confirmation of Einstein's theory, which gave a shift at the limb of 1.7 seconds. The evidence in favor of the gravitational bending of light was overwhelming, and there was a decidedly stronger case for the Einstein shift than for the Newtonian one.

Though the results were fairly conclusive, Dr. Crommelin said the question of the revision of Newton's law of gravitation was one of such fundamental importance that consideration was already being given to the next total eclipse in September, 1922, visible in the Maldive Islands and Australia.

Two of the consequences of Einstein's theory, he continued, namely, the motion of Mercury's perihelion and the bending of light by gravitation, might now be looked on as established, 'at least with great probability.' There was, however, a third predicted consequence, which was a shift of the lines in the spectrum toward the red in a strong gravitational field. The effect in the solar spectrum would amount to one-twentieth of the Angstrom unit, the same as that due to a motion of one-half kilometer per second away from the sun. Dr. St. John had looked for this effect without success. If this failure were taken as final it would mean that parts of Einstein's theory would need revision, but the parts already verified would remain.

The effects on practical astronomy, Dr. Crommelin said, of the verification of Einstein's theory were not very great. It was chiefly in the field of philosophical thought that the change would be felt. Space would no longer be looked on as extending indefinitely in all directions. Euclidian straight lines could not exist in Einstein's space. They would all be curved, and if they traveled far enough they would regain their starting point.

Sir Joseph Thomson, summing up the discussion, said:

'These are not isolated results that have been obtained. It is not the discovery of an outlying island, but of a whole continent of new scientific ideas of the greatest importance to some of the most fundamental questions connected with physics. It is the greatest discovery in connection with gravitation since Newton enunciated that principle.'"

On page 17, 10 November 1919, *The New York Times* reported:

"LIGHTS ALL ASKEW IN THE HEAVENS

Men of Science More or Less Agog Over Results of Eclipse Observations.

EINSTEIN THEORY TRIUMPHS

Stars Not Where They Seemed or Were Calculated to be, but Nobody Need Worry.

A BOOK FOR 12 WISE MEN

No More in All the World Could Comprehend It, Said Einstein When His Daring Publishers Accepted It.

Special Cable to THE NEW YORK TIMES.

LONDON, Nov. 9.—Efforts made to put in words intelligible to the nonscientific public the Einstein theory of light proved by the eclipse expedition so far have not been very successful. The new theory was discussed at a recent meeting of the Royal Society and Royal Astronomical Society, Sir Joseph Thomson, President of the Royal Society, declares it is not possible to put Einstein's theory into really intelligible words, yet at the same time Thomson adds:

'The results of the eclipse expedition demonstrating that the rays of light from the stars are bent or deflected from their normal course by other aerial bodies acting upon them and consequently the inference that light has weight form a most important contribution to the laws of gravity given us since Newton laid down his principles.'

Thomson states that the difference between theories of Newton and those of Einstein are infinitesimal in a popular sense, and as they are purely mathematical and can only be expressed in strictly scientific terms it is useless to endeavor to detail them for the man in the street.

'What is easily understandable,' he continued, 'is that Einstein predicted the deflection of the starlight when it passed the sun, and the recent eclipse has proved a demonstration of the correctness of the prediction.

'His second theory as to the anomalous motion of the planet Mercury has also been verified, but his third prediction, which dealt with certain sun lines, is still indefinite.'

Asked if recent discoveries meant a reversal of the laws of gravity as defined by Newton, Sir Joseph said they held good for ordinary purposes, but in highly mathematical problems the new conceptions of Einstein, whereby space became warped or curled under certain circumstances, would have to be taken into account.

Vastly different conceptions which are involved in this discovery and the necessity for taking Einstein's theory more into account were voiced by a member of the expedition, who pointed out that it meant, among other things, that two lines normally known as parallel do meet eventually, that a circle is not really circular, that three angles of a triangle do not necessarily make the sum total of two right angles.

'Enough has been said to show the importance of Einstein's theory, even if it cannot be expressed clearly in words,' laughed this astronomer.

Dr. W. J. S. Lockyer, another astronomer, said:

'The discoveries, while very important, did not, however, affect anything on this earth. They did not personally concern ordinary human beings; only astronomers are affected. It has hitherto been understood that light traveled in a straight line. Now we find it travels in a curve. It therefore follows that any object, such as a star, is not necessarily in the direction in which it appears to be astronomically.

'This is very important, of course. For one thing, a star may be a considerable distance further away than we have hitherto counted it. This will not affect navigation, but it means corrections will have to be made.'

One of the speakers at the Royal Society's meeting suggested that Euclid was knocked out. Schoolboys should not rejoice prematurely, for it is pointed out that Euclid laid down the axiom that parallel straight lines, if produced ever so far, would not meet. He said nothing about light lines.

Some cynics suggest that the Einstein theory is only a scientific version of the well-known phenomenon that a coin in a basin of water is not on the spot where it seems to be and ask what is new in the refraction of light.

Albert Einstein is a Swiss citizen, about 50 years of age. After occupying a position as Professor of Mathematical Physics at the Zurich Polytechnic School and afterward at Prague University, he was elected a member of Emperor William's Scientific Academy in Berlin at the outbreak of the war. Dr. Einstein protested against the German professor's manifesto approving of Germany's participation in the war, and at its conclusion he welcomed the revolution. He has been living in Berlin for about six years.

When he offered his last important work to the publishers he warned them there were not more than twelve persons in the whole world who would understand it, but the publishers took the risk."

On 11 November 1919, on page 17, *The New York Times* reported:

"ACCEPTS EINSTEIN GRAVITATION THEORY

Prof. Currier of Brown University
Calls Eclipse Demonstration
Great Achievement.

SOME SCIENTISTS CAUTIOUS

They Want Full Reports from the
Observers Before Forming Their
Final Conclusions.

Special to The New York Times.
PROVIDENCE, Nov. 10.—The two expeditions which went out from the Royal Observatory at Greenwich, England, in connection with the total solar eclipse of May 29, accomplished one of the greatest scientific achievements of modern times, Clinton H. Currier, Professor of Astronomy at Brown University, declared tonight in commenting on the results recently announced at the joint meeting of the Royal Society and the Royal Astronomical Society in London.

As the result of the observations made by these scientists in Sobral, Brazil, and on the island of Principe, in the Gulf of Guinea, Professor Currier said, the Einstein relativity theory had apparently been confirmed.

Professor Currier pointed out that, according to Newton's

theory, gravitation would not affect the direction of a ray of light. With the development of the electro-magnetic theory of light, however, it was asserted that gravitation would bend a ray of light as if it were a material projective moving at the same rate.

'It was not until 1915,' he said, 'that the four-dimensional theory of the universe, with time as a fourth dimension, was definitely conceived. This was contained in Einstein's famous relativity theory.

'According to Einstein, a ray of light is deflected by gravitation, the amount of deflection being twice that predicted by the electro-magnetic theory. The only way yet devised to test these theories is by means of stars near the sun at the time of a total eclipse of the sun. At such a time, a ray of light from a distant star passing close to the sun would be bent, according to these theories, causing the star to appear displaced from the position it normally occupied.'

This apparent displacement, according to recent dispatches from London, was observed by the scientists last May.

Special to The New York Times.

POUGHKEEPSIE, Nov. 10.—Miss Caroline Ellen Furness, Ph. D., Professor of Astronomy and Director of the Observatory at Vassar, says:

'Einstein's theory is one of the most difficult parts of mathematical physics. As yet I have not followed strictly its application to astronomy. Its results are remarkable and are such that they must be accepted. Since it was made from a study of photographs taken May 29, 1919, it ought to be easily verified by study of photographs of previous eclipses. At the time of every eclipse photographs are taken to see if there are any planets between Mercury and the sun. It ought to be possible to use these for this purpose.

'This phenomenon means that light does not travel in straight lines; that a ray from a star passing near another body of matter is slightly deflected from its original course.

'Ordinarily the positions of the stars are not affected by their nearness to the sun. They cannot be seen when near the sun except at an eclipse. The course of a star may be deflected many times, according to the new theory, and the true positions of stars will be confused for a while,' Professor Edna Carter of the Department of Physics says:

'This is the first positive proof for Einstein's theory of gravitation. It is of great importance. Einstein claimed that light was constant only when in uniform gravitation, and that when it came in the field of the sun it was deflected somewhat. His theory affects the theory of gravitation with relation to generalized relativity. The proof for Einstein's new theory seems indisputable.'

Special to The New York Times.

HANOVER, N. H., Nov. 10.—John M. Poor, Professor of Astronomy at Dartmouth College, said concerning the Einstein theory:

'If, as reported in the daily papers, Einstein's theory has received confirmation as a result of observations of photographs made at the time of the recent eclipse, it represents another approximation to the ultimate truth which the scientist is continually seeking. The Newtonian mechanics will need modification. That will be a matter which for the present, at least, will concern the student in mathematics and pure science. But what the ultimate effect will be on practical life cannot now be foretold.'

Astronomers and physicists and other scientific men in New York are much interested in the news from London that British observations of the total solar eclipse of May 29 bore out the theories of Dr. Einstein, Professor of Physics in the University of Prague, which, in effect, would bring about a revision of Newton's law of gravitation. They are reluctant to express an opinion on the deductions from the observations until they have full information. However, they regard the discovery as important; but one prominent physicist said that he would not regard it as being of such importance as to revolutionize the accepted fundamentals of physics.

Another said that he did not doubt the correctness of the observations, but that he would not be willing to accept the conclusions until it had been more definitely shown that the bending of light from stars passing close to the sun on its way to the earth was not due to the refraction of light gases surrounding the sun. He said that the theory was probably all right, but pointed out that it was one very hard of proof."

Numerous other articles appeared in the period from 1919 through 1921 and those interested in these articles are encouraged to reference the *New York Times* and *London Times* indices, as well as Gehrcke's *Die Massensuggestion der Relativitätstheorie*.

2.4.2 Reaction to the Unprecedented Einstein Promotion

Sir Oliver Lodge was one of Einstein's many critics. *The New York Times* published some of Sir Oliver Lodge's comments on 25 November 1919,

"A NEW PHYSICS, BASED ON EINSTEIN

Sir Oliver Lodge Says It Will Prevail, and Mathematicians Will Have a Terrible Time.

SPACE OF FOUR DIMENSIONS

In Which Gravity Ceases to be a Force and Becomes a Quality.

ATTEMPT TO MEASURE IT

Its Radius Put at 16,000,000 Light-

Years, or 80 Times the Distance to Farthest Star Cluster Known.

Copyright. 1919, by the New York Times Company.
Special Cable to THE NEW YORK TIMES.
LONDON, Nov. 24.—To a small and distinguished gathering at Lord Glenconner's residence tonight, Sir Oliver Lodge explained the theory of Einstein, whose predictions were recently partially confirmed by the solar expedition and given to the world by the Astronomer Royal.

So complicated has this revolutionary theory proved that even some of the most learned have been confounded. Sir Oliver gave the foundation of the theory in this way:

'So long as matter is stationary with matter, its motion with respect to the ether produces no sort of optical effect, though this effect has been sought by observers in the last half century. Hence Einstein said 'let us assume that it is impossible to observe motion through the ether, but that the compensation will always be complete and let us work out a physics on that hypothesis. We do not know,' he said, 'whether the earth is moving a thousand miles a second or only an inch an hour. All our attempts to measure such ideas of motion are frustrated by some compensations influences which are embedded in the ether.'

'So in 1905 Einstein virtually said: 'We must assume that we shall never be able to get anything about the motion of matter through the ether, and we can only make deductions from the relativity of other motions of matter.' '

Hence the new physics, declared Sir Oliver, required four co-ordinates, not merely length, breadth, and thickness, but time. Gravity, too, ceases to become a force but becomes a quality in a fourth dimensioned space.

'The death knell of ether has been sounded,' he said, 'and there come strangely varying properties out of emptiness. Einstein's theory is not dynamical. Euclid becomes incorrect when applied to existing realities. Either there is boundary to space or there is not, but personally I cannot conceive either, though we must assume that one of these theories is right. To my mind, the great achievement of Einstein is his discovery of gravity in its relation to other forces.'

Sir Oliver concluded with the prediction that the new physics would dominate all other physics, and that the next generation of mathematical professors would have a terrible time of it, at which there was laughter.

'For university courses and for all purposes of scholastic instruction,' he said, 'we shall have the Galilean and Newtonian dynamics, but they would reign as a 'limited monarchy,' and, sooner or later, the Einstein physics would influence the intelligent man.'

Replying to Dr. Schuster, who voiced the thanks of the company, Sir Oliver said that the younger scientists of today were pursuing Einstein's path with brilliant success.

'Some day,' he remarked, 'I think that perhaps gravitation will give up its secret, but I must leave all the 'transcendental' methods to the young men.'

More Details Made Known.

The observations confirmatory of 'the Einstein theory' were made during the total eclipse of the sun on May 29 last, by two British expeditions, one sent to Principe on the west coast of Africa, the other to Sobral, in North Brazil. The results of these observations were communicated to a joint meeting of the Royal Society and the Royal Astronomical Society in London on Nov. 6. Perhaps the clearest and fullest account was supplied by Dr. A. C. Crommelin of the Royal Observatory at Greenwich, who was one of the observers with the Sobral expedition.

Dr. Crommelin said that the purpose of the expeditions was to test whether the light of the stars that are nearly in a line with the sun is bent by its attraction, and if so, whether the amount of bending is that indicated by the Newtonian law of gravitation (viz., seven-eighths of a second at the sun's limb), or the amount indicated by the new Einstein theory, which postulates a bending just twice as great. The fact that the new theory explained the anomalous motion of the major axis of Mercury's orbit impressed astronomers with a sense of its truth, and they took advantage of the recent eclipse to test it further. Two cameras were employed by the party at Sobral.

The first had a lens of 4 inches aperture and 20 feet focus; this camera and its coelostat were lent by the Royal Irish

Academy. It was with this instrument that the best results were obtained. Eight exposures of 28 seconds each were made during the totality of the eclipse; seven of these plates showed seven stars each; one (the sixth exposure) showed no stars, owing to the presence of thin cloud, but gave well-defined images of the inner corona of the sun and of a great prominence. Seven exposures of the same star field were made for comparison between July 14 and 18, in the morning sky, the sun being then 45 degrees or more away from it.

The results, reduced to the sun's limb, were 2.08 and 1.94 seconds respectively. The combined result was 1.98 seconds, with a probable error of about 6 per cent. This was a strong confirmation of Einstein's theory, which gave a shift at the limb of 1.75 *seconds*. The results from the individual stars were consistent, and incidentally they confirmed the theoretical law that the shift ought to vary inversely as the distance from the sun's centre. If the shift were due to refraction produced by a gaseous envelope round the sun, it would vary according to a less simple law. The second camera used at Sobral was the object-glass of the Greenwich astrographic equatorial, of aperture 13inches (which was reduced to 8 inches, as it was found to improve the definition), and focal length 11¼ feet, mounted in a steel tube, and supplied with light from a 13-inch coelostat. The focus was obtained by photographs of Arcturus. Unfortunately the images secured were not good, evidently owing to the coelostat mirror not being flat, for the quality of the object-glass was known to be very good.

Observations at Principe were much interfered with by clouds; however, five stars were recorded on some plates. No comparison plates of the field could be taken here; the observers did not arrive early enough to obtain them before the eclipse, and it was impossible to wait long enough to obtain them after it. The plan adopted was to photograph a check field near Arcturus. Both this field and the eclipse field had been photographed with the same object-glass at Oxford (without using the coelostat) and the Oxford plates enabled the eclipse field to be connected with the check one.

The shift at the sun's limb came out 1.60 seconds, with a probable error of about 0.30 second. It could be seen that the mean of this result and that of the four inch at Sobral exactly agreed with the value predicted by Einstein. The evidence in favor of gravitational bending of light was overwhelming, and there was a decidedly stronger case for the Einstein shift than for the Newtonian one. Though the results were fairly conclusive, the question of the revision Newton's law of gravitation was one of such fundamental importance that consideration was already being given to the next total eclipse, in September, 1922, visible in the Maldive Islands and Australia.

Two of the consequences of Einstein's theory, viz. the motion of Mercury's perihelion and the bending of light by gravitation, might now be looked on as established (at least with great probability). There was, however, a third predicted consequence, which was the shift of the lines in the spectrum toward the red in a strong gravitational field. The effect in the solar spectrum would amount of 1-20 of an Angstrom unit, the same as that due to a motion of ½ kilometre per second away from us. Dr. St. John had looked for this effect without success. If this failure were taken as final it would mean that parts of Einstein's theory would need revision, but the parts already verified would remain.

The effects on practical astronomy of the verification of Einstein's theory were not very great. It was chiefly in the field of philosophical thought that the change would be felt. Space would no longer be looked on as extending indefinitely in all directions; if they went far enough they would re-enter the same ground. Euclidian straight lines could not exist in Einstein's space. They were all curved, and if they traveled far enough they would regain the starting point. Mr. de Sitter had attempted to find the radius of space. He gave reasons for putting it at about 1,000,000,000 times the distance from the earth to the sun, or about 16,000,000 light-years. This was eighty times the distance assigned by Dr. Shapley to the most distant stellar cluster known. The fourth dimension had been the subject of vague speculation for a long time, but they seemed at last to have been brought face to face with it."

The New York Times published numerous articles which mentioned Sir Oliver Lodge. Lodge was a vocal critic of Einstein's work.[151] The New York Times published the following on 26 November 1919, on page 12,

"Bad Times for the Learned.

It must indeed have been 'a small and distinguished gathering' that Sir OLIVER LODGE addressed in London, this week, if they were helped toward an understanding of the Einstein theory when he presented, as its foundation, the statement that 'so long as matter is stationary with matter, its motion with respect to the ether produces no sort of optical effect.'

So darkling and so seemingly irrelevant to anything in particular is that statement that one refrains with difficulty from suspecting a cable operator of having edited the dispatch. By no means all of it, however, was incomprehensible, even to the wayfaring man, and some of it even he could enjoy. Nothing could have been simpler, or pleasanter, for instance, that Sir OLIVER'S admission of his personal inability to conceive of space either as having a boundary or as not having one, though obviously it either is or is not unlimited. Some of us cannot see how anybody can conceive space otherwise than as going on and on, forever and forever. At least to do so is vastly easier than to elude the natural question, What except more space can there be beyond the place where space ends, if it does end? If Sir OLIVER can, he is lucky, or queer, or something.

Thoroughly human was his prophecy that as a result of the Einstein discoveries 'terrible times' are coming for the mathematicians—at any rate the tone of satisfaction in which he said it was thoroughly human. Mathematicians have caused so many other people to have terrible times so often and so long that it's only fair for them to have their own troubles at last. Not one woman in a hundred will give them any sympathy, whatever their suffering may be, and innumerable boys and girls will simply gloat if the mathematicians are forced to admit the wrongness of their haughty pronouncements. Their infallibility had been admitted long enough, and those of us who always thought there were errors in the multiplication table, especially where it deals with sevens, eights, and nines, at last are to be brilliantly vindicated."

On 15 December 1919, *The New York Times* wrote on page 14:

"Obviously a Rash Prophecy.

As it was before the Royal Society that Sir OLIVER LODGE last week discussed atomic energies and the possibilities they offer, it is to be presumed that he spoke with some care. Yet, when he prophesied that within a century the power now derived from burning 1,000 tons of coal would be obtained by setting free the force latent in two ounces of some unnamed substance, one cannot help remembering that Sir OLIVER has two personalities—that he is an eminent scientist and a credulous listener to 'mediums.'

That the atoms, instead of being mere ultimate divisions of dead matter, are alive with force nobody now doubts, but it seems hardly scientific to emphasize as Sir OLIVER did the astonishing velocity at which move the missiles which some atoms shoot out without at the same time calling attention to the size of the missiles. He knows, of course, the formulae relating to speed, mass, and momentum, and that to get any appreciable amount of 'work' done by the radium particles he described it would seem that they would have to move far more rapidly than they do. And a way to harness them is hardly imaginable, as yet.

Curved Space Before Einstein.

To the Editor of The New York Times:

In so far as concerns Einstein's 'new theory' that space is curved, which carries with it implications necessarily overturning current scientific dicta that parallel lines can never meet, that astronomical parallaxes cannot be relied upon for giving approximate distances of faraway stars, it may be interesting to note that Einstein is a late investigator in this field of speculative research.

For instance, Professor A. E. Dolbear in his 'Matter, Ether and Motion' (edition of 1892, page 57) says:

'We are assured that, for all we know, and therefore for all we can reason from, space itself may be curved so that if one were to start in what we call a straight line, in any direction, and travel in it on and on he would find himself after a long time coming to his starting point from the opposite direction; that what one would see if his sight were prolonged in any direction would be the back of his own head much magnified. * * * If the space we live in and the geometric relations are only practically true upon a small scale; if we may have a kind of space of four or more dimensions, whether we can now conceive of it or not, then should one understand that spaces and distances and velocities, and all computations formed upon them, though practically true, for all our experience, must not be pushed up into statements that shall embrace all things in the heavens as well as on the earth.'

It will appear from the above that one of our own foremost American physicists, one who is credited as having antedated Marconi in all the theoretical possibilities of wireless telegraphy, had covered, nearly three decades ago, all the essentials of what is now being attributed as a 'new theory' of the universe to Dr. Einstein.

GEO: H. HADLEY.

Fairfield, Conn. Dec. 12, 1919."

Sir Oliver Lodge believed in the utility of atomic energy. Contrary to popular modern myth, Albert Einstein opposed the idea of atomic energy. It turns out that Lodge was right and Einstein was wrong; but, amazingly, it is Einstein, and not his predecessors, who is today considered the father of atomic energy, which is an idea Einstein had found silly. The modern association of Einstein and the formula $E=mc^2$ with atomic energy and the atomic bomb probably originally stems not from Einstein, but from Pflüger and Moszkowski, as will be shown further on in this text.

Charles Lane Poor was another outspoken critic of Einstein and of the disingenuous promotion of the man. *The New York Times* wrote on 16 November 1919:

"JAZZ IN SCIENTIFIC WORLD

Prof. Charles Lane Poor of Columbia Explains Prof. Einstein's Astronomical Theories.

WHEN is space curved?
When do parallel lines meet?
When are the three angles of a triangle not equal to two right angles?

Why, when Bolshevism enters the world of science, of course!

It is thus that Charles Lane Poor, Professor of Celestial Mechanics at Columbia University, explains the extraordinary cable announcements from London about Professor Albert Einstein's theories, which some suppose to have been verified by observations of the recent total eclipse of the sun. These observations were assumed to show that the rays of stars were deflected as they passed the sun, which led to the Q. E. D. that they were subject to the attraction of the sun, that is to gravitation: and from this premise it was easy to jump to the conclusion that Sir Isaac Newton's theory had been knocked to smithereens.

Well, Sir Isaac, after he saw the apple fall in his gardens at Woolsthorpe, and evolved therefrom his theory of gravitation, couldn't prove it for a long time. He made his calculations from a wrong estimate of the radius of the earth; and it was not until years later, when another scientist had corrected the figure for the radius, that he was able to give the gravitational principle to a shocked and incredulous world. Once the incredulity had evaporated in the light of proof, and the theory had become an established fact, it still was not immune from mistaken attack, as Professor Poor points out.

'For some years past,' Professor Poor said the other day, after reading the cable dispatches about the Einstein theory, 'the entire world has been in a state of unrest, mental as well as physical. It may well be that the physical aspects of the unrest, the war, the strikes, the Bolshevist uprisings, are in reality the visible objects of some underlying, deep mental disturbance, worldwide in character. This mental unrest is evidenced by the widespread intent in social problems, by the desire, on the part of many, to throw aside the well-tested authors of Governments in favor of radical and untried experiments.

'This same spirit of unrest has invaded science, and today there is just as great a conflict in the realm of scientific thoughts as there is in the realm of political and social life. There are many who would have us throw aside the well-tested theories upon which have been built the entire structure of modern scientific and mechanical development in favor of psychological speculations and fantastic dreams about the universe.

'Whenever a new observation is made which apparently does not directly fit into the old-time theories these modern disciples of scientific unrest rush into some weird explanation involving psychological speculations as to the constitution of matter or our fundamental concepts of mathematics.

'The eclipse observations reported to have been made on May 29 last are a case in point. If these observations are as reported (and such seems unquestionably to be the case), then these explanations, under present accepted theories, may be difficult, but such observations certainly do not warrant the acceptance of the speculations of Einstein.

'It may be that history is merely repeating itself. When Newton's theory of universal gravitation was given to the world in 1685 it was received with incredulity, especially among scientists on the Continent of Europe. Observations were adduced which these scientists asserted proved the fallacy of the Newtonian ideas. One by one these observations were shown to be in harmony with the law, to be direct consequences of it.

'Nearly one hundred years later (1770) Euler, one of the greatest mathematicians of the age, who had devoted a lifetime to developing and perfecting the Newtonian theory, in discussing the observed motion of the moon, wrote:

''There is not one of its equations about which any uncertainty prevails, and it now appears to be established by indisputable evidence that the secular inequality in the moon's motion *cannot* be produced by the forces of gravitation.'

'The essay in which this statement was made appeared during a time of profound mental and political unrest, such as now pervades the world. It won the prize of the Paris Academy of Sciences. To explain this peculiar motion of the moon, the greatest scientists of that age adopted theories involving a resisting medium in space, or introduced a time element into gravitation. Yet only a few years later Laplace found a full and complete explanation in certain intricate relationships between the motion of the moon and the varying shape of the earth's orbit, which had been overlooked by Euler and his followers, and found that this motion was a direct result of the forces of gravitation.

'Now, the so-called Einstein theories, or rather speculations, are such as completely overthrow not only the law of gravitation, but the fundamental conceptions on which all geometry and physics rest. And to sustain such a complete overturning of the entire basis on which scientific thought has been built, two—just two—observed facts are quoted; the motion of the perihelion of Mercury and certain displacements of stars when photographed near the sun.

'There is no need to go outside the law of gravitation to explain the motion of Mercury's perihelion. The explanation may well be in some term of the most complicated formulas which the mathematicians have overlooked or in some distribution of matter near the sun which the astronomer has hitherto failed to properly note. As a matter of fact, in order to make their equations usable, the mathematical observer assumes that the sun is a perfect sphere and that the space between the sun and the planets is empty. Yet both these assumptions are known to be false; the well-known sun spots and the many photographs of its corona prove the sun to be not perfectly spherical and to be surrounded by an irregular and changeable mass of matter. The real trouble is that the mathematicians have not yet been able to introduce the effects of these into their equations and to deduce their possible effects upon the motion of Mercury.

'The displacement of the stars noted in the recent eclipse photographs may be a phenomenon analogous to the refraction of light. All rays of light, when they pass from one medium to another, from air to glass, for example, are bent or refracted. Upon this principle are based the ordinary eyeglass, or the telescope. When the rays from the stars enter the earth's atmosphere they are bent and travel in curved paths. Now, the sun is surrounded by an envelope of gases of irregular shape and of varying densities, an envelope which certainly extends to the orbit of the earth, and probably, millions of miles beyond. Would it not be in accord with all known laws of optics if the rays of light from distant stars were bent and refracted when passing through such an envelope?

'The fact that such a bending effect has now been measured is of great scientific importance, and the results may change some of the hitherto accepted ideas as to the density and distribution of matter near the sun, but I fail to see how such an observation can prove the existence of a fourth dimension, or can overthrow the fundamental concepts of geometry.

'I have read various articles on the fourth dimension, the relativity theory of Einstein and other psychological speculation on the constitution of the universe; and after reading them I feel as Senator Brandegee felt after a celebrated dinner in Washington. 'I feel,' he said, 'as if I had been wandering with Alice in Wonderland and had tea with the Mad Hatter.''"

2.4.3 The Berlin Philharmonic—The Response in Germany

It was often difficult for scientists in Germany to publish their works in opposition to relativity theory or their condemnation of Einstein's plagiarism. Paul Weyland and Hermann Fricke organized a group of scientists to stand up against the suppression of dissent. They called themselves the *Arbeitsgemeinschaft deutscher Naturforscher zur Erhaltung reiner Wissenschaft*. Their plan was to publish the facts surrounding the promotion of Einstein and the theory of relativity and to hold public meetings exposing Einstein as a fraud and the theory of relativity as a "mass suggestion" imposed on the world public by the press. Einstein knew well the power "of coercive manipulation of public opinion"[152]. Einstein wrote to Lorentz on 21 September 1919 in the context of his, Einstein the Zionist's, hatred of the German People's loyalty to their nation,

"Those on the outside have no conception of how difficult it is to escape mass suggestion."[153]

The first meeting of the *Arbeitsgemeinschaft deutscher Naturforscher zur Erhaltung reiner Wissenschaft* was held in the Berlin Philharmonic on 24 August 1920. Einstein attended the meeting with his stepdaughter Ilse,[154] who was a reluctant member of Albert Einstein's "small harem".[155] Young Ilse Einstein wrote to Georg Nicolai about Albert Einstein's sexual advances toward her,

"I have never wished nor felt the least desire to be close to [Albert Einstein] physically. This is otherwise in his case—recently at least.—He himself even admitted to me once how difficult it is for him to keep himself in check."[156]

At the meeting, Paul Weyland and Ernst Gehrcke publicly exposed Einstein as a sophist and a plagiarist and discredited the evidence taken to support the theory of relativity. After the meeting, Einstein was convinced that all of German science knew he was a fraud. Panicked, Einstein wanted to run away from Germany without another word. A few days later, Einstein learned that his friends and friendly newspapers had instigated a smear campaign against Einstein's critics. Learning that there were others dishonest enough to defend him, and knowing that he would not have to defend himself, but instead would be defended by more competent persons than himself, Einstein decided to join in the fray with an article he published in the *Berliner Tageblatt*. He threw an undignified fit, which juvenile rant found a ready outlet in a pro-Einstein "Jewish newspaper".

Hendrik Antoon Lorentz and Paul Ehrenfest had been trying to persuade Albert Einstein to move to Leyden. Einstein refused because he knew that Lorentz would quickly discover that Einstein had no talent for original thought. Ehrenfest realized this and wrote to Einstein on 2 September 1919 to reassure him that they were not interested in Einstein's work, but merely wanted to use his name,

"No one here expects any accomplishments, all simply want you nearby."[157]

Soon after the press began to promote Einstein as if he were a new Newton, Albert Einstein wrote to Lorentz (whose work Einstein had plagiarized in 1905) about Lorentz' offer to join him in Leyden, or at least to spend a couple of weeks a year in Leyden. The press claimed that Einstein was the greatest and most original thinker the world had ever seen. Einstein wrote to Lorentz on 19 January 1920,

"Nevertheless, unlike you, nature has not bestowed me with the ability to deliver lectures and dispense original ideas virtually effortlessly as meets your refined and versatile mind. [***] This awareness of my limitations pervades me all the more keenly in recent times since I see that my faculties are being quite particularly overrated after a few consequences of the general theory stood the test."[158]

Pacifist Lorentz was very interested in the success of the eclipse observations as an opportunity for *rapprochement*, as were Einstein's supporters Arthur S. Eddington,[159] and Robert W. Lawson and Hans

Thirring, who were apparently friends.[160] Thirring, like Einstein, never doubted the results of the eclipse expeditions. Bertrand Russell, Georg Friedrich Nicolai and Romain Rolland were also Socialist Pacifists, who supported Einstein. Russell profited from a popular book he published on the theory of relativity, which helped to promote the theory, Einstein, and Russell.[161] As so often asserted by the researchers themselves, the eclipse observations were a publicity stunt to advertise a *rapprochement* between British and German science.

When this stunt was exposed, Einstein, in cooperation with a few pro-Einstein newspapers, tried to change the subject to anti-Semitism from Einstein's plagiarism, Einstein's misrepresentations of the scientific evidence, and the exposure of the contradictions in Einstein's theories. Certain papers made it quite clear to all, that anyone who criticized Einstein would be viciously smeared as if anti-Semitic, no matter what the nature of their complaint might be, and whether or not they had made any anti-Semitic statements—even Nobel Prize winning physicists were smeared around the world. There was no to be no fair hearing for Einstein's many critics. There views would not be made known to the public through the major press outlets of the world. This, of course, had a chilling effect on the debate, and when the press had effectively silenced all but a few of Einstein's many critics, the press disseminated the lie that no scientists of renown had ever disagreed with Einstein.

Einstein was right to run from his critics. He had been exposed as a plagiarist and a fraud. However, the proven threat of public smears undoubtedly quieted many who opposed Einstein and the theory of relativity, which group constituted the majority of scientists at the time. The pro-Einstein papers were especially vicious to Paul Weyland, probably because he had dared to accuse them of what they were doing—of shamelessly hyping Einstein, of misrepresenting the facts, and of making false accusations of anti-Semitism in a cowardly attempt to change the subject.

After an exchange of newspaper articles between Max von Laue and his opponents, and after the pro-Einstein press misrepresented the events at and surrounding the meeting in the Berlin Philharmonic, Paul Weyland printed his Philharmonic speech and reprinted several newspaper articles in the second volume of works published by the press of the *Arbeitsgemeinschaft deutscher Naturforscher zur Erhaltung reiner Wissenschaften.* The anti-Einstein press (Einstein used the term "pan-German press"[162]) and Weyland were generally fair to the extent that they allowed both sides of the argument to be heard. Such was not,

and is not, the case with the pro-Einstein press.
Paul Weyland's brochure:

Schriften aus dem Verlage der Arbeitsgemeinschaft deutscher
Naturforscher zur Erhaltung reiner Wissenschaft e. V.
Heft 2.

Betrachtungen

über

Einsteins Relativitätstheorie

und die Art ihrer Einführung

von

Paul Weyland

Vortrag gehalten am 24. August 1920 im großen Saal der Philharmonie
zu Berlin

Berlin 1920

Verlegt bei der
Arbeitsgemeinschaft deutscher Naturforscher zur Erhaltung reiner
Wissenschaft e. V. Berlin N 113.

Als sich die Arbeitsgemeinschaft deutscher Naturforscher
zur Erhaltung reiner Wissenschaft gründete, um als eins ihrer
Hauptziele die Auswüchse der Allgemeinen Relativitätstheorie
einerseits und die Art ihrer Propaganda andererseits zu
bekämpfen, waren sich die Gründer von vornherein darin klar,
daß es hier nicht glatt gehen würde. Der Umstand, daß Herr
Einstein zufälligerweise jüdischen Glaubens sei und seine

Gegner, die sich z. T. in der genannten Arbeitsgemeinschaft zusammenfanden, auch Christen aufweisen, ließ die Vermutung begründet erscheinen, daß, wenn sachliche, von den Rednern der Arbeitsgemeinschaft angeführte Gegengründe nicht sachlich erwidert werden können, diese zu schimpfen anfangen und dann mit dem Rettungsanker, dem Vorwurf des Antisemitimus kommen.

Diese Vermutung, die allerdings erst für die eigentlichen, späteren Vorträge erwartet wurden, hat sich überraschender Weise schon beim ersten Abend bestätigt — ein Umstand, der deutlich beweist, wie schwach man sich auf der Gegenseite fühlt.

Es ist nicht meine Absicht gewesen, meine, ausdrücklich als die Vorträge einleitenden Bemerkungen und Begrüßungsworte an das Auditorium, im Druck erscheinen zu lassen. Ich glaubte meiner polemischen Taktik dadurch Genüge getan zu haben, daß ich einige Artikel in die Tagespresse lenkte. Im übrigen war es — und ist es noch heute — mein Standpunkt, daß nur die Widerlegung des Themas selbst nötig und erwünscht sei. Ich bin eines besseren belhrt worden. Ein Teil jener Presse, die ich als „gewisse" Presse bezeichne, beginnt, sich deutlich abzuheben und durch entstellte Berichte den Wert einer Aktion in den Augen der Öffentlichkeit herabzusetzen, für die sie bestimmt sind. Ich durchbreche deshalb in diesem Falle mein Prinzip nur unbedingt wissenschaftlich zu sein, indem ich mich mit der Technik der Einsteinschen Regie befasse. Immerhin trösten mich die in dieser Schrift angeführten Tatsachen: Der genaue Nachweis der Methode, wie die Einsteinleute arbeiten, ist vielleicht kein wissenschaftlicher Gewinn, aber doch wohl [*4*] Mittel zum Zweck, uns solchem Gewinn näherzubringen. Denn bisher ist es m. E. noch nicht belegt worden, wie systematisch und skrupellos man dort zu Werke geht.

Der Leser möge nun ja nicht glauben, daß ich die „kritischen" Glanzleistungen des „Berliner Tageblatt", der „Vossischen Zeitung", des „Vorwärts" oder des „8-Uhr-Abentblattes" für ernst nehme, daß ich ihnen die Ehre eines Abdruckes zolle. Mein Zweck ist ein anderer. Da, wie gesagt, vermutet wurde, daß die Gegenpartei alles aufbieten wird, um der Aktion zu schaden, so haben wir zunächst auf sachliche Einwände gewartet. Diese sind ausgeblieben Man schimpft. Man kommt mit dem schwarzen Mann, dem Antisemitismus. Was hat der schon bei schiefen Situationen helfen können! Ich will dem interessierten Publikum nun Gelegenheit geben, selbst zu urteilen, wer „Zur Sache" zu rufen ist. Jene Skandalmacher, die um jeden Preis stören wollten, oder ich in meinem Vortrag, der a l l e s, was er behauptete, ausgiebig bewies. Daß ich speziell nicht sprach, habe ich gleich in den ersten einleitenden Worten betont und auf die spezielle Behandlung an einem späteren Termin hingewiesen.

Ich übergebe deshalb meinen Vortrag der Öffentlichkeit in der Hoffnung, daß er dem edlen Zweck, dem die Vortragsreihe dienen soll, ein weiterer Baustein sei. Mit dem Erkennen der Einsteinschen Methode ist schon ein gewichtiger Schritt zum Erkennen der wahren Sachlage gedient. Daß aber die Gegenpartei derartig schnell die Flinte ins Korn wirft und in unsachgemäßes Schimpfen verfällt, hat sich selbst der kühnste Optimist auf unserer Seite nicht träumen lassen. Mein Vortrag ist genau wörtlich nach dem Konzept abgedruckt. Wo es mir wichtig erschien, habe ich Ergänzungen gemacht, diese aber als Fußnoten angebracht.

Vorher jedoch die Abdrucke der klassischen Beispiele objektiver Berichterstattung: Zunächst das Tageblatt vom 25. August 1920, Morgenausgabe. (Nr. 398, Ausgabe A Nr. 210):

Die Relativitäts-Theorie.
Von Dr. V. E n g e l h a r d t (Berlin-Friedenau)

Gestern begann die „A r b e i t s g e m e i n s c h a f t d e u t s c h e r N a t u r f o r s c h e r", über deren Zusammensetzung uns Näheres nicht bekannt ist, in der Philharmonie eine Reihe von Vorträgen, die sich gegen Einsteins „R e l a t i v i t ä t s - T h e o r i e" richten sollen. Obwohl diese Art öffentlicher Polemik gegen einen [*5*] Forscher von der Bedeutung Einsteins uns wenig angemessen erscheint, werden wir über den Eindruck des ersten Abends sachlich berichten. Damit aber die Leser zunächst auch wissen, worum es sich eigentlich handelt, sei in den folgenden Zeilen der Versuch gemacht, über den Sinn der Relativitäts-Theorie einiges in populärer Form zu sagen. Daß ein Problem von dieser Tiefe in dem begrenzten Raum einer Tageszeitung auch nicht annähernd erschöpft werden kann, wird jedem Nachdenklichen klar sein.   Die Redaktion.

Es folgt nun ein Einstein-Artikel.

Erst bekommt also das Publikum schnell eine Einstein-Spritze. Die „sachliche" Entgegnung sieht folgendermaßen aus: (Berliner Tageblatt, Nr. 399. Ausgabe B Nr. 189, Mittwoch, 25.

August 1920, abends).

Die Offensive gegen Einstein.

E. V. Nachdem die Gegner Einsteins und seiner Relativitätstheorie sich in einer „Arbeitsgemeinschaft deutscher Naturforscher" organisiert hatten, erfolgte gestern abend in der Philharmonie der erste Vorstoß. Die beruhigende Erklärung des einen Forschers und Gelehrten, daß entsprechende Maßnahmen getroffen seien, um Skandalmacher an die Luft zu setzen, mußte den rein wissenschaftlich interessierten Besucher, der gekommen war, einer gelehrten Auseinandersetzung, einer streng sachlichen Beweisführung zu lauschen, etwas eigenartig berühren. Immerhin scheint die Erkenntnis, daß Stuhlbeine als Gegenargumente nur bedingten Wert haben, auch in dieser Arbeitsgemeinschaft deutscher Naturforscher vorhanden zu sein. Obwohl P r o f e s s o r   E i n s t e i n, in einer Loge sitzend, eine bequeme Zielscheibe bot, wurde er doch nur mit solchen kleine Invektiven wie „Reklamesucht", „wissenschaftlicher Dadaismus", „Plagiat" usw. bombardiert.

Auf die bibelfesten Naturforscher, die einst so wild gegen Darwin vom Leder zogen, sind die gesinnungstüchtigen Naturforscher gefolgt, die jetzt dem wahrscheinlich höchst prinzipienlosen Relativitätsprinzip zuliebe wollen. Gesinnung ist etwas sehr Schönes, aber es wirkt immer ein wenig komisch, sie in der Mathematik verwendet zu sehen; sie hat die Eigentümlichkeit, den aufgestellten Lehrsatz nur mangelhaft zu beweisen. Das ehrlichste im wissenschaftlichen Kampf bleibt doch immer das *argumentum in rem*. Die *argumenta in personam* sind außerdem ein zweischneidiges Schwert, und als einzige Gesinnung des Angreifers entpuppte sich schon öfter der Neid. Und wenn Namen von so glänzender Unbekanntheit sich erheben, so haben sie doch unbedingt nötig, sich mit Beweisen zu legitimieren.

Daß Herr P a u l   W e y l a n d mit seiner Volksversammlungsrede die sogenannte „Einsteinsche Relativitätstheorie" zu Fall gebracht hätte, kann auch der stärkste Mann der Wissenschaft, ja selbst Herr Weyland nicht behaupten. Er wandte sich auch lediglich gegen die Person Einsteins und „seine Reklamepresse", [*6*] und verfehlte dabei nicht, für die eigene Presse gebührend Reklame zu machen. Sein Ton war nicht überzeugend, bisweilen aber peinlich. Wenn man dem Gegner unlautere Propaganda seiner Idee vorwirft, sollte man diese Idee nicht mit unlauterer Propaganda bekämpfen. Und wenn man dem anderen die Suggestion der Massen nicht verzeihen kann, so sollte man selber nicht auf die Gasse laufen.

Vornehmer und wissenschaftlicher war der Vortrag von Professor G e h r c k e, und sein Spott auf die „junggeschüttelten Organismen" und andere „Experimente" der Relativität der Bewegung und der Relativierung von Zeit und Raum wäre vielleicht sehr treffend

gewesen, wenn er in den Bildern nicht so stark aufgetragen hätte. Was
er über die Beweise der Rotverschiebung der Spektrallinien und über
die Perihelbewegung des Merkur vorbrachte, wird hoffentlich
Professor Einstein zu wissenschaftlichen Entgegnungen reizen.

Von gleichem sachlichen Geist zeugt der Bericht der
„Vossischen Zeitung'', die schon leise zum Rettungsanker des
Antisemitismus schielt:

Der Kampf gegen Einstein.

Der Feldzug gegen die Einsteinsche Relativitätstheorie oder wohl
mehr gegen Einstein selbst wurde gestern Abend in der Philharmonie
ziemlich temperamentvoll eröffnet. Eine zahlreiche Zuhörerschaft
hatte sich eingefunden, darunter namhafte Mitglieder der
Gelehrtenwelt, auch P r o f. E i n s t e i n sah man in einer Loge, an
seiner Seite die Tochter und nicht weit von ihm P r o f. N e r n s t. Der
angegriffene Forscher folgte mit gelassener Ruhe, mitunter sogar leise
lächelnd, den Ausführungen der Redner oben auf der Bühne.

Mit schwerem Geschütz rückte H e r r P a u l W e y l a n d, der die
Kampagne eröffnete, an. Er wandte sich gegen die „sogenannte
Einsteinsche Relativitätstheorie'', die „Einsteinschen Fiktionen'', ohne
auch nur mit einem Worte zu erklären, worin diese eigentlich
beständen. Daneben machte er wacker Reklame für Schriften, die im
Vorraum käuflich seien; um deren Absatz zu befördern, wurde sogar
bald eine einviertelstündige Pause eingelegt. Daneben wurden
Physiker, die für Einstein eintraten, gehörig verdächtigt, dieser selber
beschuldigt, daß er und seine Freunde die Tagespresse und sogar die
Fachpresse zu Reklamezwecken für die Relativitätstheorie eingespannt
hätten. Da man immer noch nicht erfuhr, worum es sich eigentlich
handelte, erscholl wiederholt der Ruf: „zur Sache!'' H e r r P a u l
W e y l a n d erwiderte auf diese freundliche Aufforderung: „Es sind
entsprechende Maßnahmen getroffen, um Skandalmacher an die Luft
zu setzen.'' Nach etlichen Ausfällen gegen die Professorenklique,
wobei der Redner bei Schopenhauer fleißige Anleihe machte, wurde
über die geistige Verflachung unseres Volkes geklagt, selbst der
D a d a i s m u s wurde herangezogen und Herrn Einstein und seinen
Anhängern wissenschaftlicher Dadaismus vorgeworfen. [*7*]
Daneben klang ganz schwach eine antisemitische Note an und zum
Schlusse Herrn Einstein ohne weiteres vorgeworfen, daß seine
Formeln über die Perihelbewegung des Merkur einfach von G e r b e r
abgeschrieben worden sei.

Eine ganz andere Tonart schlug der nächste Redner, P r o f.
G e h r c k e, ein. Er bemühte sich, völlig sachlich seinen gegnerischen
Standpunkt gegen die Relativitätstheorie klarzulegen. Diese sei eine

geistige Strömung; ob gesund oder verhängnisvoll ist eine andere Frage. Er geht kurz auf die Relativität der Bewegung ein, bemüht sich sodann, zu zeigen, wie Einstein seine Relativitätstheorie mehrfach geändert habe; was er als Schwankungen bei Einstein bezeichnete, würden vielleicht andere als eine Entwicklung auffassen. Dann geht G e h r c k e auf die Relativierung von Zeit und Raum ein. Nicht ohne Humor sucht er die Einsteinschen „Organismen", die sich der relativierten Zeit anpassen müssen, zu verspotten. Die Relativierung der Zeit führe, so meinte der Kritiker, zur Relativierung des Seins und damit zum physikalischen Solipsismus. Wie stehe es nun mit den Folgerungen, die Einstein aus seiner Theorie gezogen hatte? Es seien freilich nur winzige Effekte zu erwarten, aber die Rotverschiebung der Spektrallinien hat sich nicht feststellen lassen. Die Perihelbewegung des Merkur sei auch auf andere Weise zu erklären, ebensowenig seien die Ergebnisse der letzten Sonnenfinsternis-Beobachtung ein zwingender Beweis für den Einstein-Effekt. Zum Schluß meint G e h r c k e, daß auch die Gedanken der Relativitätstheorie, nämlich die Idee der Union von Zeit und Raum von einem ungarischen Philosophen schon im Jahre 1901 ausgesprochen sei. Die heutigen Vorträge können noch keine abschließende Antwort über die Einsteinsche Relativitätstheorie gehen. Im übrigen möge sich jeder selbst ein Urteil bilden, die Grundlagen dazu werden die späteren Abende, die dieser Theorie gewidmet sind, liefern.

K. J.

Der freundliche Leser wolle sich an Hand meines Vortrages genau überzeugen, wo ich bei Schopenhauer Anleihe machte und ob zum Thema geredet wurde oder nicht.

Seiner Tendenz entsprechend besitzt der Vorwärts das größte Maß an Unverfrorenheit, der die Veranstaltung sogar für Vorgänge verantwortlich macht, die sich auf der Straße abspielen. Jedes Kind weiß, daß man in dieser herrlichen Republik nicht in seinem Haufe kommandieren kann, daß also auch bei Veranstaltungen, Theatern usw. Zeitungs- und sonstige Verkäufer in dan Pausen bis in die Säle dringen. Daß Zigarettenverkäufer, „Freiheits''-Zeitungshändler ebenfalls da Publikum belästigen, hat der wackere Vorwärtsmann natürlich nicht gesehen. Es entfließt folgender Erguß dem Gehege seines Schreibtisches:

Der Kampf um Einstein. Gestern Abend entbrannte in der Philharmonie der Kampf um Einstein. Die Arbeitsgemeinschaft deutscher Naturforscher zur [*8*] Erhaltung reiner Wissenschaft hatte geladen. Der Anfang war häßlich und hatte mit Wissenschaft nichts zu tun, weder mit „reiner‘‘ noch mit „unreiner‘‘. Am Tore wurden Hakenkreuze verkauft — solche, die man die Rockklappe stecken konnte. Der erste Vortrag des Herrn W e y l a n d paßte zu diesem Empfang. Er versprach eine wissenschaftliche Bekämpfung der Relativitätstheorie und mußte fortwährend zur Sache gerufen werden. Die höchst „sachliche‘‘ Entgegnung des Vortragenden war die Versicherung, daß man auf solche Zwischenrufe gefaßt sei und Vorsorge getroffen hätte, unliebsame Störenfriede an die Luft zu setzen. Jedenfalls auch eine Methode, um wissenschaftliche Fragen glatt zu lösen!

Doch genug von diesem Schmutz, der schließlich in persönlichen Angriffen das höchste leistete. Der nachfolgende Redner, P r o f. G e h r c k e, ein in der physikalischen Welt anerkannter Forscher, hatte nach dieser ihm scheinbar unerwarteten Einleitung sichtlich mit Befangenheit zu kämpfen. Bald aber festigte sich seine Stimme und er brachte in wohltuend ruhiger Weise seine Bedenken gegen die Relativitätstheorie vor. Die Widersprüche dieser Theorie sind nach G e h r c k e nur zu lösen, wenn wir uns auf den Standpunkt eines „physikalischen Solipsismus‘‘ stellen und behaupten, daß jeder Mensch in seiner eigenen Welt lebt, die mit der des anderen gar nichts zu tun hat. Die Schwierigkeiten, welche die Relativitätstheorie unserem Denken bereitet, liegen wohl darin, daß wir immer und immer wieder unser gefühlsmäßiges „Zeiterlebnis‘‘ mit dem exakt definiertem „Zeitmaß‘‘ Einsteins verwechseln. Die Einwendungen G e h r c k e s gegen die Relativitätstheorie gingen ebenfalls von dieser „erlebten‘‘ Zeit aus, die mit dem physikalisch definierten Zeitmaßnichts zu tun hat — und können darum nicht stichhaltig genannt werden. Über den Ausfall der experimentellen Prüfung der Theorie wurde etwas einseitig berichtet. Die Akten sind hier noch nicht geschlossen. Den Stimmen gegen Einstein stehen ebenso gewichtige für Einstein gegenüber. Erst die Zeit wird lehren, ob Einsteins Theorie die experimentelle Fenerprobe wirklich besteht.

Am entzückendsten und sachlichsten äußert sich das „8 - U h r - A b e n d b l a t t‘‘, das Blatt der Dezimeter großen Überschriften, anerkannter Sachlichkeit, pp.:

Ein Einstein-„Kenner‘‘.
Der Kampf gegen die Relativitätstheorie.

Ein Herr W e y l a n d, dessen Verdienste um die Wissenschaft weitesten Kreisen bisher verborgen geblieben sind, versprach gestern in der P h i l h a r m o n i e einen Vortrag über „Einsteins Relativitätstheorie eine Massensuggestion‘‘. Als der Vorleser aber

immer wieder von einer „gewissen Presse'', die für Einstein Reklame
machte, sprach, aus dieser „gewissen Presse'' ihm passende
Artikelstellen zitierte und dann aber selbst für einige
„g e s c h ä ft l i c h e Mitteilungen" Gehör [*9*] verlangte, wurde der
Vorleser aus der Mitte des Saales lebhaft „Zur Sache!'' gerufen. Aber
Herr Weyland hatte darauf nur zu erwidern, daß dafür g e s o r g t sei,
Skandalmacher an die frische Luft zu befördern. Diejenigen, die
wirklich Eintrittsgeld gezahlt hatten und nicht als persönliche
Leibgarde des Herrn Vorlesers erschienen waren, hatten — so dünkt
uns — doch einen Anspruch darauf, zu verlangen, daß gehalten werde,
was in den Ankündigungen versprochen worden war. Tatsächlich sah
man im Auditorium neben einigen wenigen ausgesprochenen
Gelehrtenköpfen — E i n s t e i n selbst saß in der Nähe von N e r n s t in
einer Loge — eine Anzahl junger handfester Burschen, deren ganzes
Gehaben deutlich zeigte, in welchem Zusammenhang sie mit der
Einsteinschen Lehre stünden. Schon beim Betreten des Saales wurden
ja die berüchtigten antisemitischen Hetzbroschüren und blätter laut
angepriesen. — Der Vorleser gedachte nicht mit einer Silbe der
Genialität Einsteins, die von seinen w i s s e n s c h a ft l i c h geschulten
Gegnern ohne weiteres anerkannt wird. Dafür erwähnte er aber die
„sogenannte Einsteinsche Relativitätstheorie'', die einen Umsturz in
den Massen hervorgerufen habe, und prompt sagte eine hinter mir
sitzende biedere Frau zu ihrem Mann: „Nu siehste, ick habe dir doch
jesagt, daß er een Bolschewist ist." Der Mann nickte resigniert. Als der
Vorleser dann, ohne es zu beweisen, von der „gewisse Presse'' sprach,
die vollkommen im Dienste Einsteins stünde, und man im Saal
„Verleumdung Beweise!'' rief, war es das biedere Ehepaar, das Herrn
Weyland am begeisterten Beifall klatschte! Wollte man Herrn
Weylands Ausführungen für ernst nehmen, dann müßte man
folgerichtig die Universitätsfakultäten und Akademien, die Einstein
mit Ehrenprofessuren und anderen akademischen Würden
auszeichneten, für Reklameorganisationen von Stümpern und Idioten
halten. Als der Vorleser schließlich eine Brücke zwischen Einsteins
Lehren und dem Dadaismus zu schaffen sich anschickte, brachte ihm
dies aus meiner Umgebung Kosenamen ein, die ich aus Höflichkeit
hier lieber nicht wiedergeben möchte. Sie sind auch recht
unparlamentarisch. Nach dieser vielversprechenden und
verheißungsvollen Ouvertüre glaubte ich der Fortsetzung dieser
eigenartigen Veranstaltung nicht weiter beiwohnen zu müssen. Diese
taten desgleichen: ergriffen mit der einen Hand ihren Hut, mit der
andern die — Flucht.   K. M.

Hoffentlich nimmt der glänzende Vertreter einwandfreier
Berichterstattung am 2. September Veranlassung, alsdann mit
der anderen Hand sitzen zu bleiben, and jenem 2. September, wo

speziell begonnen wird, Einsteins Theorie zu zergliedern.
Inzwischen erscheint — zur Verwendung für diese
Broschüre nicht mehr geeignet — im Berliner Tageblatt (Nr. 402
Ausgabe A Nr. 212) vom Freitag, den 27. August, Morgen-
Ausgabe, Einsteins Antwort. Hier sei nur soviel bemerkt, daß
Herr Einstein sachlich ebenfalls nichts [*10*] hervorbringt und
ganz offen hinter dem Antisemitismus Schutz sucht. Es ist also
soweit gekommen, eine sachliche Erklärung von ihm nicht zu
erlangen. Er fertigt seine Gegner als kleine Geister ab, hat aber
doch soviel Respekt vor ihnen, daß er schleunigst ins Ausland
geht, statt sie mit seinen „erdrückenden" Beweisen zu schlagen.
Nicht einmal den ersten der s p e z i e l l e n Vorträge hat Herr
Einstein abgewartet! Die ersten allgemeinen Ausführungen
genügten vollständig, ihn zum Rückzug zu veranlassen!
Ich lasse meinen Vortrag folgen:

Meine sehr verehrten Damen und Herren!
Ich habe die Ehre und das Vergnügen, Sie heute mit einigen
einleitenden Worten zu einer Reihe von Darlegungen zu
begrüßen, die sich mit der sogenannten Einsteinschen
Relativitätstheorie befassen. Es handelt sich darum, kritisch zu
untersuchen, ob die Einsteinschen Fiktionen eine konkrete Stütze
durch die Wissenschaft, insbesondere die Naturwissenschaft
erfahren kann, oder philosophische Punkte zu ihrer Bestätigung
anzuführen hat.
Meine Damen und Herren! Es übersteigt den Rahmen der
uns heute zugemessenen Zeit, daß ich Ihnen in diesem erten
V o r t r a g eine gründliche Kritik der Einsteinschen
Relativitätstheorie vom speziellen Standpunkt aus gebe. Diese
Darstellung wird später mathematisch erfolgen. Ich habe mich
heute lediglich damit zu befassen, zu untersuchen, wie es kam,
daß die Allgemeine Relativitätstheorie seit geraumer Zeit die
Massen in Aufruhr versetzen konnte. Ehe ich mich jedoch dieser
einleitenden Aufgabe entledige, möchte ich einige geschäftliche
Bemerkungen vorneweg schicken. Es wird mir soeben mitgeteilt,
daß die Druckerei den heutigen Vortrag des Herrn P r o f e s s o r
D r . G e h r c k e fertiggestellt hat und eine gewisse Anzahl
Exemplare noch heute hierher senden wird. Ich werde diese
Bücher im Foyer aufstellen lassen, wo selbst diese nach dem
Vortrage käuflich zu haben sind. Ebendort wird eine Schrift des
Heidelberger Physikers P . L e n a r d ausgelegt, die ich allen

denen, die sich über den Wert der Einsteinschen Relativitätstheorie in wirklich sachlicher Weise informieren wollen, recht empfehlen möchte. Das Buch erfreut sich nach meinem Dafürhalten neben strenger Wissenschaftlichkeit ungemeiner Eindringlichkeit und Gemeinverständlichkeit.

Meine Damen und Herren! Wohl selten ist in der Naturwissenschaft [*11*] mit einem derartigen Aufwand von Reklame ein wissenschaftliches System aufgestellt worden, wie bei dem Allgemeinen Relativitätsprinzip, daß sich bei näherem Zusehen als höchst beweisbedürftig entpuppte. Dieses System, das unter Heranziehung aller möglichen Philosopheme, mit Mathematik verbrämt, teils in reiner Abstraktion, teils in konkreten Abstrusitäten als Relativismus oder allgemeine Relativitätstheorie bezeichnet wird, wollen wir uns im Verlaufe der vorliegenden Vortragsreihe unter der Führung von Spezialforschern etwas näher ansehen.

Es handelt sich um ein System, welches beansprucht, die alleinige Wahrheit zu bringen über alle Vorgänge des Naturgeschehens. Es soll uns die tiefste Wahrheit über das, was in der Erfahrungswelt geschieht, enthüllt werden. Wie begründet nun aber der Erfinder der Relativitätstheorie diese, seine Absicht. Er sagt: „Es ist mein Hauptziel, meine Theorie so zu entwickeln, daß jeder psychologische Natürlichkeit des eingeschlagenen Weges empfindet.'' Statt uns mit Tatschen zu kommen, statt Beweise zu bringen, wird uns „die psychologische Natürlichkeit der Theorie'', „empfindend'' nahegelegt, an anderen Stellen „die Schönheit der Theorie'', in noch anderem Falle „die Kühnheit der Theorie'' angepriesen. Meine Damen und Herren! Kühnheit des Gedankens ist sehr wohl eine Notwendigkeit des erfolgreichen Forschers, nur hat diese Kühnheit sich selbst Grenzen zu ziehen, die im menschlichen Taktgefühl und in wissenschaftlicher Einsicht begründet sind. Treffender kann sich niemand über diesen Punkt äußern als P. Lenard [*Footnote:* P. Lenard, Über Relativitätsprinzip, Äther, Gravitation. Verlag von S. Hirzel, Leipzig 1920. Preis M. 6.—] in seiner kleinen Schrift. Ich möchte Ihnen diese Stelle hier nicht vorenthalten. Lenard sagt zu diesen Punkt auf Seite 1 folgendes:

„Den Tatsachen kühn voraneilen wollen — Hypothesen machen — gehört dabei dennoch immer zu den schönsten, auch nützlichsten Vorrechten des Naturforschers. Aber er darf auch hierbei nicht rücksichtslos verfahren, sondern muß jeden Augenblick bereit sein, vor Tatsachen sich zu beugen, und er muß nie vergessen, daß er wirklich nur Zufall ist; wenn eine seiner Hypothesen dauernd die Probe an der Wirklichkeit besteht und also einen Fund bedeutet, und daß er also, will er gewissenhaft sein, nur zögernd das, was ursprünglich Hypothese, Dichtung des Geistes war, als Wahrheit auszugehen oder anzuerkennen wird bereit [*12*] sein dürfen. Je „kühner" ein Naturforscher sich gezeigt hat, desto mehr Stellen finden sich im allgemeinen in seinen Veröffentlichungen, die nicht dauernd standhalten; man kann dies mit Beispielen aus alter und neuer Zeit (besonders leicht aus letzterer) belegen. Deshalb verdient die Kühnheit des Naturforschers auch lange nicht die Hochschätzung wie die des Kriegers; denn letzterer setzt mit seiner Kühnheit sein Leben ein, während ersterer meist bequeme Nachsicht und Vergessenheit für seine Fehlschläge findet. Manchmal scheint die Naturforschern zugeschriebene „Kühnheit" wirklich nur darin zu bestehen, daß ziemlich skrupellos zu Ungunsten der Gediegenheit der Wissenschaftliteratur von vornherein auf eigene Schadlosigkeit gerechnet wird. Deutsche Eigenschaft ist **diese** Kühnheit nicht.''

Meine Damen und Herren! Es ist eine ganz auffallende Erscheinung, daß die Einstein-Presse und -Literatur sich mit ganz geringen Ausnahmen in einer derartigen überschwänglichen Lobhudelei gefällt, wie ich sie oben angeführt habe, daß aber diesen Phrasen nicht das geringste Positive entgegensteht. Ich könnte noch stundenlang in der Aufzählung solcher Äußerungen fortfahren — alle aus Einsteins oder seiner Anhänger wissenschaftlichen Veröffentlichungen, aus Arbeiten — die in den Annalen der Physik, in den Sitzungsberichten der Preußischen Akademie und in vielen anderen ernsten wissenschaftlichen Zeitschriften gedruckt worden sind.

Diese Redensarten, die nun schon in der Fachpresse auftraten, werden durch die Veröffentlichungen, welche sich an ein breiteres Publikum wenden, noch erheblich übertroffen. Es soll Einsteins Theorie einen „Wendepunkt des menschlichen Denkens und der menschlichen Kultur" bedeuten. „Die großen Genies der Vergangenheit Kopernikus, Kepler, Newton verblassen gegenüber der alles überstrahlenden Theorie von Einstein!'' „Abgrundtiefe eisige Höhen'', „höchste Gipfel'',

„gewaltigste Gedankenarchitektur" — das sind die Beiworte, die dieser Fiktion gezollt werden. „Die wissenschaftliche Welt beugt sich vor der siegenden Kraft, vor dem glänzenden Triumph des menschlichen Geistes der an theoretischer Bedeutung noch die berühmte Errechnung des Planeten Neptun durch Leverrier und Adams in den Schatten stellt. Von überraschender Folgerichtigkeit, physikalisch und philosophisch gleich befriedigend ist der Bau des Alls, den die allgemeine Relativitätstheorie vor uns enthüllt. Überwunden sind alle Schwierigkeiten, die auf Newtonschen Boden erwuchsen, alle Vorzüge jedoch, durch die das moderne Weltbild sich [*13*] über die engen antiken Anschauungen erhob, strahlen im reineren Glanze als zuvor. Die Welt ist durch keine Grenzen eingeengt und doch in sich harmonisch geschlossen, sie ist vor der Gefahr der Verödung gerettet! Von neuem erkennen wir die erlösende Kraft der Relativitätstheorie die dem menschlichen Geist eine Freiheit und ein Kraftbewußtsein schenkt, wie kaum eine andere wissenschaftliche Tat sie je zu geben vermochte!"

Meine Damen und Herren! Was ich Ihnen hier eben erzählte, sind nicht etwa von mir ausgedachte Parodien, sondern wörtliche Zitate aus der Einstein-Presse, die ich Ihnen hundertfältig ergänzen könnte und die in unzähligen Auflagen in einer wahren Massenflut auf die bedauernswerte Öffentlichkeit losgelassen wurde.

Wenn man sich diese Ausprüche vergegenwärtigt, so drängt sich dem kritisch veranlagten Geist unwillkürlich die Frage auf: „Sollte hier nicht etwas vorliegen, was mit ernster wissenschaftlicher Arbeit und Sachlichkeit nichts zu tun hat? Wie will ein heute lebender Mensch imstande sein, eine menschliche Entdeckung oder Erfindung in eine Linie mit den Taten eines Kopernikus, Kepler oder Newton zu setzten, von denen uns heute Jahrhunderte trennen? Wie will der heutige Mensch irgend einer wissenschaftlichen Neuheit heute schon ansehen können, daß sie sich dereinst in Jahrhunderten aus dem Getriebe der Zeit so herausheben wird, wie dies bei den großen Namen der Vergangenheit der Fall ist? Spricht bei solch exaltierten Ausdrücken wie wir sie soeben gehört haben, überhaupt noch der nüchterne wissenschaftliche Verstand, oder sind wir hier in einem Gefühlsrausch hineingeraten, der vor anderen Räuschen nur das voraus hat, daß es sich auf die Wissenschaft bezieht? Solche überschwänglichen Ausdrücke sind jedenfalls in der wissenschaftlichen Welt etwas ungewöhnliches und lassen deutlich eine gesuchte Beeinflussung mit Reklamemitteln vermuten, wo durch strenge Sachlichkeit nichts erreicht werden kann.

Aber nun wird behauptet, der Erfinder der Relativitätstheorie habe mit allen diesen Dingen nichts zu tun. Ihn kümmerte nur der weitere Ausbau seiner Theorie und die reine Wissenschaft in stiller Gelehrtenzurückgezogenheit. Ein Büchlein [*Footnote: Max Hasse, Das Einsteinsche Relativitätsprinzip, Magdeburg, Selbstverlag des Verfassers.*] dem ich einen Teil der Lobeshymnen entnommen habe, schreibt nun in seinem Vorwart: „Der Verfasser nahm sich die Freiheit, die Druckbogen Prof. Dr. A. Einstein [*14*] einzusenden, der ihn mit folgender Antwort erfreute: „Ihre populäre Darstellung scheint mir in der Tat dem Geiste des Nicht-Physikers in glücklicher Weise entgegenzukommen. Ich sende Ihnen die Korrekturbogen mit einigen Randbemerkungen zurück, d a m i t   S i e   e i n i g e   k l e i n e   B ö c k e   d a r a u s   e n t f e r n e n   k ö n n e n."

In einem Zeitungsartikel verwandte ich diese Niedlichkeit und werde von einem hervorragenden Berliner Physiker darauf mit folgenden Worten angegriffen:

In Nr. 171 dieses Blattes ereifert sich Herr Weyland gegen Einsteins allgemeine Relativitätstheorie; gegen die Art ihrer Verbreitung in der größeren Öffentlichkeit sowie gegen ihren Inhalt. Es liegt mir durchaus ferne, alles das decken zu wollen, was kleinere Geister bei der Verbreitung der neuen Lehre durch Ungenauigkeiten, Übertreibungen und Geschmacklosigkeiten gelegentlich gesündigt haben, und die im besonderen herangezogenen Äußerungen von Archenhold und Max Hasse kann ich nicht beurteilen, weil ich sie nicht kenne. Zu einem solchen Angriff auf Einsteins Persönlichkeit, wie ihn Herr Weyland macht, bieten diese Dinge aber doch nicht den mindesten Anlaß.

Demgegenüber möchte ich festellen, daß Herrn Einstein die Mitwirkung der jetzt abgeschüttelten kleineren Geister doch wohl höchst angenehm war, denn sonst hätte er sich nicht zu der soeben verlesenen Antwort veranlaßt gefühlt. Aber einen Menschen, der in seiner Naivität und Unkenntnis des Themas soweit geht, daß er noch ausdrücklich in seinem Vorwort hervorhebt, nicht mehr einen Satz der euklidischen Geometrie beweisen zu können, vor seinen Wagen zu spannen, ist nach meinem Dafürhalten Reklamemache um jeden Preis — oder Unwissenschaftlichkeit. Wenn Herr Einstein gewollt hätte, diesem Geschreibsel ein Ende zu machen, hätte er jahrelang Zeit gehabt. Durch eine einzige Äußerung, durch der mit seinem Kreise vorzüglich in Verbindung stehenden Presse hätte er es erreichen können, daß der ganze Schwall von Verherrlichung und Bewunderung ein Ende findet, das hat Einstein nicht gewollt, sonst hätte er sich dementsprechend geäußert und was noch wichtiger ist, dementsprechend gehandelt. Das ist die systematische Massensuggestion zum Preis und Ruhm eines Einzelnen, der die breite Öffentlichkeit bitter notwendig hat, nachdem ihm sachlich Opposition über Opposition erwächst. Aber auch in wissenschaftlichen Kreisen wird das Äußerste versucht, um Beweise für die Relativitätstheorie an den Haaren herbei zu ziehen. [*15*] Da es um die Frage der Rotverschiebung still geworden ist, [*Footnote:* Wer sich über den neuesten Stand der Rotverschiebung informieren will, dem sei die Schrift von L. C. Glaser, Über Versuche zum Beweise der Relativitätstheorie (Heft 3 der vorliegenden Sammlung) empfohlen.] schaut man nach anderen Objekten aus und findet leider recht dürftige Ausbeute. Da setzt dann nun an gewissen Stellen, wo man die Beziehung und die Macht hat, die Taktik des Totschweigens ein. Einsteins ständige Referenten geben von Forschungsberichten auf anderem Standpunkt stehender Gelehrten in ihren Referaten entweder gar keine oder durch einschränkende Bemerkungen entstelle Berichte, z. B. werden solche Forschungsergebnisse gegenüber den Einsteinschen „Axiomen" stets als unbewiesene offene Fragen behandelt. [*Footnote:* Unter einem Referat versteht man gemeinhin die Wiedergabe der Meinung eines Autors, ohne daran einschränkende Kritiken zu knüpfen. Die „Physikalischen Berichte", deren Redaktion durchaus unter Einsteinschen steht, wendet diese nicht übliche Praxis der indirekten Stimmungsmache an, wo es absolut nicht zu vermeiden ist, über gegenteilige Ansichten zu referieren.] So wird eine Arbeit von Sir Oliver J. Lodge mit folgenden Worten abgefertigt: „ Es wird in dieser g a n z k u r z e n N o t i z v e r s u c h t, das Wesen der Ablenkung eines Lichtstrahles, nach der allgemeinen Relativitätstheorie eine Folge der Schwere der Energie, a u f Grund f r ü h e r e r A n s c h a u u n g e n p l a u s i b e l z u m a c h e n.

Weiter heißt es (Physik. Ber. 1920, Heft 15, S. 947) J. v. Kries: Über die zwingende und eindeutige Bestimmbarkeit des physikalischen Weltbildes. Die „Naturwissenschaften", 8, 237-44, 1920: Kries wirft die Frage auf, ob das Weltbild der modernen Physik zwingend und eindeutig genannt werden kann, und vertritt die Anschauung, daß diese Forderung für das Weltbild der Relativitätstheorie nicht durchgeführt ist, diese also nur als eine mögliche Erscheinungsform unter vielen anderen erscheint. Für den Physiker, dem die Relativitätstheorie heute als der befreiende Weg aus den Dunkelkammern der bisher klassischen Wissenschaften erscheint, muß diese Auffassung befremdend anmuten usw.

Einen anderen, noch instruktiven Fall finden Sie in der letzten Nummer der Naturwissenschaften. [*Footnote:* Die Naturwissenschaften 1920, Heft 34, Seite 667-673. Der Bericht der englischen Sonnenfinsternisexpedition über die Ablenkung des Lichtes im Gravitationsfeld der Sonne. Von Erwin Freundlich.] In dieser Zeitschrift, die nicht nur [*16*] von Fachleuten gelesen wird, sitzen die Eistein-Leute besonders fest. Von dort aus wird quasi als deren Hauptquartier Stimmung für ihn gemacht.

Es werden in einem langen Artikel die Untersuchungen der englischen Sonnenfinsternisexpedition, die nach Brasilien gesandt wurde, Herz und Nieren geprüft, ob sich etwas für das Relativitätsprinzip günstiges herauspressen ließe. Dabei kann der Referent — natürlich ein Freund Einsteins — nun nicht umhin, sich den Schein der Objektivität zu geben. Er zitiert ausdrücklich die Bedenken der Expeditionsleiter **gegen** eine Annahme einer Bestätigung im Sinne des allgemeinen Relativitätsprinzipes, wo es heißt:

Die Aufnamen mit dem 8zölligen astrographischen Objektiv, die ebenfalls in Brasilien gewonnen wurden, liefern zwar auch einen Hinweis für die vermutete Lichtablenkung, aber die Sternbilder auf den Patten sind nach den Angaben der englischen Beobachter so unscharf und diffus, daß die aus ihnen abgeleiteten Resultate nur ein geringes Gewicht haben. Anscheinend hatte sich der Coelostatenspiegel infolge der Sonnenstrahlen stark verworfen und die Abbildungen verdorben. Es ergibt sich für den Wert von a am Sonnenrand der Wert

0",93. **Nimmt man aber an,** daß der Skalenwert auf den Finsternisplatten in Wahrheit nicht weiter verändert war, als er es nach dem Einfluß der Refraktion und Aberration sein mußte — **eine sehr wahrscheinlich richtige Annahme,** denn die Unschärfe der Bilder rührte wohl kaum von einer reellen Änderung der Fokusierung des Objektivs her —, so resultiert für *a* der Wert 1",52 am Sonnenrand.

Und was macht der Einstein-Mann aus dieser deutlichen Einschränkung?

Er leitet daraus folgendes ab:

„Zusammenfassend kann man sagen:
„Die Sonnenfinsternisplatten in Sobral wie in Principe offenbaren unzweideutig eine systematische Verlagerung der Sternbilder, wie sie zutage treten müßte, wenn das Licht im Gravitationsfelde der Sonne abgelenkt würde. Diese Ablenkung verläuft dem Betrage nach durchaus [*17*] so, wie sie von der Relativitätstheorie vorausgesagt worden war." [*Footnote:* Die Frage der Refraktion, die, w e n n ein Effekt in Frage kommt, sowie der sogen. Eberhard-Effekt, der jedem Astrophysiker bekannt ist, wird hier nicht berührt. Falls Opponenten hier die Beobachtungen auf Principe für sich in Anspruch nehmen, verweise ich auf Heft 3 dieser Sammlung: Dr.-Ing. L. C. Glaser: Über Versuche zum Beweise der Relativitätstheorie, wo dieser Einwand vornherein widerlegt wird.]

Gegenüber solchen Unglaublichkeiten versagt einem Menschen normaler Denkungsweise das Ausdrucksvermögen. Ein Kaufmann hat dafür den treffenden Ausdruck: Bilanzverschleierung.

An diesen kleinen Beispielen, die sich, wie die oben angeführte Lobhudelei in beliebigem Maße fortsetzen lassen, können Sie ersehen, daß auch hier die Macht des Einsteinschen Armes wirkt und die Beeinflussung in diesem Falle der wissenschaftlichen Welt genau so versucht und durchgeführt wird, wie der breiten Öffentlichkeit gegenüber. Wo es absolut nicht geht, die berühmte Konjugation, über die sich bereits Schopenhauer in seiner Abhandlung über die Universitätsphilosophie in so satyrischer Weise ausgelassen hat, anzuwenden, nämlich nach der Formel: ich schweige tot, du schweigst tot, er schweigt tot — wir schweigen tot, ihr schweigt tot, sie schweigen tot außer Kraft zu setzen, da beginnt die indirekte Methode, nämlich Forschern, die sich durch räumliche Entfernung oder sonst wie nicht gleich zur Sache äußern können, den Wert ihrer Abhandlungen durch einschränkendes oder kritisches Referat herabzusetzen.

Warum hat nun Einstein Veranlassung, mit seinen Hypothesen die breiten Massen und die Wissenschaft zu beeinflussen zu versuchen? Wohl nur deshalb, weil ihm in wissenschaftlichen Kreisen dauernd Gegner erwachsen — Tatsachen, die man gern verschweigt und, wenn sie gedruckt werden sollen, gern unterbindet durch die Beziehungen, die man hat. Noch ein in den letzten Tagen erscheinenes Buch eines gewissen Harry Schmidt (Verlag Hartung, Hamburg) erkühnt sich, alle Gegengründe gegen Einsteins Theorie, ohne die Spur eines Gegenbeweises anzutreten, abzuweisen, unglaubliche Unrichtigkeiten und Unsachlichkeiten in das Publikum zu werfen und, was das Unverschämteste an dieser Arbeit ist, B e w e i s e a l s g e s i c h e r t a n z u g e b e n, w o d a s [*18*] G e g e n t e i l   e i n w a n d f r e i   f e s t s t e h t. [*Footnote:* Das Schmidt'sche Buch werde ich an anderer Stelle behandeln.] Aber nicht nur in der Literatur, sondern auch in öffentlichen Vorträgen wird die Massensuggestion im Einsteinschen Sinne emsig betrieben, ohne daß die interessierte Öffentlichkeit den wahren Stand der exakten Naturforschung zu hören bekommt. So hielt kürzlich ein Berliner Popularastronom im Blüthner-Saal einen Propagandavortrag, [*Footnote:* Während der Pause nahm Herr Archenhold Veranlassung, mich im Künstlerzimmer aufzusuchen und sich erregt über meinen Angriff auszusprechen. Herr Archenhold erklärte, daß er den Vortrag aus eigener Iniative hielte, Einstein ebenso gut und schlecht kenne, wie mich. Ferner machte Herr Archenhold Bemerkungen darüber, daß er an der Treptower Sternwarte mit seinem Herzen hängt und genau so arm einst aus ihr herausgehe, wie er hineingekommen ist. Diese zum Thema nicht gehörige Bemerkung möchte ich dahin berichtigen, daß es mir erstens nie eingefallen ist, gegen die verdienstvolle und ehrwürdige Persönlichkeit des Herrn Archenhold auch nur in irgend einer Form vorzugehen, Was Herr Archenhold auf s e i n e m Gebiet — nämlich für die Popularisierung der Astronomie — geschaffen hat, bin ich der letzte, nicht anzuerkennen. Ich verwahre mich aber s a c h l i c h mit Entschiedenheit dagegen, daß er seine große Popularität dazu benutzt, die Einsteinsche Relativitätstheorie zu interpretieren, die er, wie sein Vortrag bewies, in ihren Prinzipien und Konsequenzen nicht erkannt hat. Und w e n n er sie erkannt hätte, wäre es verdammte Pflicht und Schuldigkeit des ernsten Forschers gewesen, sich über die Qualität des referierten Gebietes zu überzeugen, ehe er es kritiklos dem bedauernswerten Publikum vorsetzte. Herr Archenhold trug aber nur Einstein-Literatur vor. Der Arbeiten von Hale, Silberstein, St. John, Evershed, Davidson, Eddington u. a. Forscher, die gewichtiges Material gegen Einstein anführen, gedachte er keines Wortes. Selbst wenn hier, was ich im Interesse des Herrn Archenhold annehme, Gutgläubigkeit vorliegt, so ist doch diese Gutgläubigkeit im vorliegenden Falle u n b e d i n g t verwerflich. Meine kritische Bemerkung war in diesem Falle also sachlich durchaus gerechtfertigt. Gerade Herr Archenhold hat sich durch die Eigenart seiner Position doppelt vorzusehen, unfertige Wahrheiten zu behandeln, denn er spricht vor einer Gemeinde die ihm unbedingt glaubt.] den er nebenbei bemerkt vom Einsteinschen Standpunkte aus betrachtet, schlecht genug interpretierte. Auch hierbei wurde das Publikum in mehr als fragwürdiger und unsachlicher Weise über den Wert der Einsteinschen Relativitätstheorie unterrichtet und bewiesene Gegengründe nach bewährter Methode einfach totgeschwiegen.

[*19*]

Meine Damen und Herren! Es liegt mir heute ob, zu ergründen und nachzuweisen, wie es kam, daß diese sogenannte Hypothese, die sich bei näherer Prüfung als glatte Fiktion herausstellte, die Welt dauernd in Atem halten konnte. Wissenschaftlich genommen, ist dieses leicht erklärlich. Durch die Verbrämung verschiedener wissenschaftlicher Disziplinen mit einander ist es dem Spezialforscher nicht möglich gewesen, sich in ein ihm fremdes Gebiet, schnell genug hinein zu finden. Gründliche Forscherarbeit und Prüfung erfordert eben Zeit.

Aber noch ein anderer Grund spricht hier ein wichtiges Wort mit. Wohl nicht zum geringsten Teile hat diese Erscheinung ihre Ursache in der mehr oder minder geistigen Verflachung, in die uns die gegenwärtige Zeit versenkt hat. Wir haben erst kürzlich erleben können, mit welchem Aufwand von Reklame heutzutage Wissenschaft gemacht wird. Es ist leider soweit gekommen, daß die Wissenschaft nicht mehr Selbstzweck ist, sondern Mittel zum Zweck, gewissen Personen mit dem Glorienschein wissenschaftlicher Päpstlicher zu umgeben. Sie alle, meine Damen und Herren haben es mit eigenen Augen gesehen und mit eigenen Ohren gehört, in welchem Tiefstand sich die geistigen ethischen, und moralischen Qualitäten derer bewegten, die uns die gegenwärtigen Zustände brachten. Das schlimmste Übel war eine gewisse Presse, die die neben einer bereits bestehenden wie Pilze aus der Erde schoß, die alle moralischen und sittlichen Werte im deutschen Volke erstickte, um aus dem geschaffenen Trümmerhaufen für sich brauchbares herauszuscharren. Um diese Presse gruppierten sich Abenteurer jeder Art, nicht nur in der Politik, sondern auch in Kunst und Wissenschaft. Genau wie die Herren Dadaisten mangels jeden Erfahrungsgedankens in ihrer Kunst- und Weltanschauung, Aufbau, Entwicklung und Reife vermissen lassen und dieses unreife Zeug durch einen Teil der alten, hauptsächlich aber die neue Literatur propagieren lassen, weil sie geistig nicht imstande waren, sich selbst durchzusetzen, genau so vollzieht sich in der Einstein'schen Relativitätstheorie als ein völliges Analogon das Hineinwerfen der Relativitätstheorie in d i e M a s s e n. A u c h h i e r l i e g t b e w u ß t e   A b l e h n u n g   e r f a h r u n g s m ä ß i g e r K e n n t n i s s e u n d E r k e n n t n i s s e v o r. W i r s t e h e n b e i d e r B e t r a c h t u n g d e r E i n s t e i n s c h e n I d e e n g e n a u   v o r   d e m s e l b e n   G e d a n k e n c h a o s   d e r D a d a i s t e n,   d i e   w o h l   e t w a s   w o l l e n   u n d w ü n s c h e n,   e s   a b e r   n i c h t   b e g r e i f l i c h   m a c h e n u n d b e w e i s e n k ö n n e n.

[*20*]

Meine Damen und Herren! Niemand wird sich wundern, wenn gegen diesen wissenschaftlichen Dadaismus eine Bewegung entstanden ist, mit dem Ziele, die Öffentlichkeit aufzuklären, was denn eigentlich an der Einsteinschen Relativitätstheorie ist, und was man vor allen Dingen unter Fortschritten der Wissenschaft zu verstehen hat. Es sollen in einer Reihe von Vorträgen andere Gesichtspunkte und Anregungen zur Geltung kommen, als sie bisher in allzu einseitiger und aufdringlicher Weise der Öffentlichkeit geboten worden sind. Zu Einzelheiten wissenschaftlicher Art mich zu äußern bin ich heute noch nicht an der Reihe. Den Herren, die schon lange in der Bewegung stehen und die Einsteinschen Phantasmen unentwegt bekämpften, gebührt der Vortritt. Ehe ich jedoch schließe, noch eine kurze Bemerkung. Ich bin in der

Tagepresse, wie ich schon vorhin erwähnte, von einem hervorragenden deutschen Physiker angegriffen worden. [*Footnote:* Ich habe im Anhang dieses Heftes die Polemik abgedruckt, um sie besser bekannt zu geben.] Mir wurde u. a. entgegengehalten, daß ich annehme, die Ergebnisse mancher Forscher hinsichtlich der Prüfung der Relativitätstheorie könnten durch Voreingenommenheit beeinflußt sein. Dem gegenüber stelle ich fest, daß alle für Einstein sprechenden Gründe in Deutschland besonders aufgebauscht und die gegenteiligen Beweisgründe in angeführter Manier totgeschwiegen wurden. Ferner wird mir meine Behauptung vorgeworfen, Herr Einstein habe eine Formel von Gerber abgeschrieben. Hierzu stelle ich fest, daß das peinlich jahrelange Schweigen von Herrn Einstein über diesen nicht nur von mir, sondern auch von einer ganzen Reihe von Fachgenossen und unvoreingenommenen Beurteilern erhobenen Vorwurf als sehr eigentümlich empfunden wird. Ich stelle fest, daß es doch allgemein üblich ist, sich zu Vorwürfen solcher Art und Schwere selbst und zwar sofort zu äußern.

[*21*]

Abdruck aus: „Tägliche Rundschau", Freitag, 6. August, Abendausgabe.

Einsteins Relativitätstheorie—eine wissenschaftliche Massensuggestion.

Von P a u l   W e y l a n d.

Wir leben in einem Zeitalter des Amerikanismus. Die Geschäftswut Englands ist in Dollarika zur Potenz erhoben, führte dort auf allen Gebieten des wirtschaftlichen und geistigen Lebens zu Rekordleistungen, die rein technischer, zivilisatorischer Art waren, hinter denen kulturelle Bestrebungen zurückstehen mußten. Die Rekordjägerei endigte im Bluff, und wir stehen vor der traurigen Tatsache, daß auch diese Bluffmacherei vor der reinen Wissenschaft nicht Halt machte, so daß die Sache neben der Person verschwand.

Ich erinnere an den bekanntesten Fall dieser Art, an den Entdeckerstreit Cook-Peary, der in der Öffentlichkeit am besten bekannt wurde. In Deutschland erlebte man, nach dem der Amerikanismus hier Eingang fand, gegenüber diesen Reisenbluffs bislang nur Sensatiönchen, die aber so lebhaft von dem Geist Zeugnis ablegten, der gewisse wissenschaftliche Kreise auch unseres Vaterlandes ergriffen hat. Ich erinnere an Friedmanns Tuberkulin, an die Herstellung von Mehl aus Stroh usw., um an diesen Beispielen zu zeigen, daß man es in gewissen Kreisen nicht mehr für nötig hält, die Bestätigung eines Laboratoriumversuches in der Praxis abzuwarten, sondern mit Hilfe einer gefügigen Presse sich mit seiner halbfertigen Sache dem Publikum vorstellt, den werten Namen nebst Photographie in alle Windrichtungen hinausbläst, um einige Zeit später, wenn — wie fast stets — die Hinfälligkeit der Entdeckung durch ernste Forscher beweisen wird, beharrlich zu schweigen. Davon aber erfährt das Publikum natürlich nichts, und die Masse schwört blindlings auf die „großen" Namen.

Mittlerweile hat sich Deutschland — endlich — neben solchen Sensatiönchen auch eine richtige Sensation geleistet. Herr Albertus Magnus ist neu erstanden, guckte in die ernsten Arbeiten stiller Denker wie Riemann, Minkowsky, Lorentz, Mach, Gerber, Palagyi u. a. m., räusperte sich und sprach ein großes Wort gelassen aus. [*Footnote:* Um endlose Wiederholungen zu vermeiden, wird das Relativitätsprinzip beim Leser als bekannt vorausgesetzt.] Die Wissenschaft staunte. Die Öffentlichkeit war starr. Alles [*22*] brach zusammen. Herr Einstein spielte mit der Welt Fangball. Er brauchte nur zu d e n k e n, und flugs relativierte sich alles Geschehen und Werden.

Einsteins Methode war nun so bewußt abstrakt, daß es dem F a c h m a n n ernstliche S c h w i e r i g k e i t e n bereitete, sich hindurchzuarbeiten. Zunächst verquickte er mehrere wissenschaftliche Disziplinen miteinander, ja er errichtete für seine Zwecke ein ganz neues mathematisches Gebäude, so daß der nachprüfende Naturforscher vor lauter Nebensachen zunächst gar nicht an den Kern der Sache heran kam, w e i l d i e s e N e b e n s ä c h l i c h k e i t e n, d i e e r s t g e p r ü f t w e r d e n m u ß t e n, ja den Aufbau seines Theorems bedeuteten. Dieses Drum und Dran ist von Forschern wie P. Lenard, Gehrcke, Kraus u. a. geprüft worden, es stellte sich heraus, d a ß n i c h t e i n m a l d a s S k e l e t t e i n e r k r i t i s c h e n B e t r a c h t u n g s t a n d h i e l t. Was soll da aber erst aus dem Hauptteil werden?

So bemängelt z. B. P. Lenard mit unbedingtem Recht, daß bei Einstein der einfachsten Logik Hohn gesprochen wird. Ich zittiere Lenard wörtlich: [*Footnote:* P. Lenard, Über Relativitätsprinzip, Äther, Gravitation. Verlag S. Hirzel, Leipzig 1920.]

„Man lasse den bekannten Eisenbahn eine deutlich ungleichförmige Bewegung machen. Während hier durch Trägheitswirkung im Zuge alles in Trümmer geht, während draußen alles unbeschädigt bleibt, so wird, meine ich, k e i n g e s u n d e r V e r s t a n d einen anderen Schluß ziehen wollen als den, daß es eben der Zug war, der mit Ruck seine Bewegung geändert hat und nicht die Umgebung. Das verallgemeinerte Relativitätsprinzip verlangt es, seinem einfachen Sinne nach, auch in diesem Falle, zuzugeben, daß es möglicherweise doch die Umgebung sei, welche die Geschwindigkeitsänderung erfahren habe und daß dann das ganze Unglück im Zuge nur Folge dieses Rucks der Außenwelt sei, vermittelt durch eine „Gravitationswirkung'' der Außenwelt auf das Innere des Zuges. Für die naheliegende Frage, warum denn der Kirchturm neben dem Zuge nicht umgefallen sei, wenn er mit der Umgebung den Ruck gemacht habe — warum solche Folgen des Rucks so einseitig nur im Zuge sich zeigen, während dennoch kein einseitiger Schluß auf den Sitz der Bewegungsänderung möglich sein sollte — hat das Prinzip anscheinend keine den einfachen Verstand befriedigende Antwort.''

Hier hat Lenard mit wenigen klar verständlichen, an den Verstand gerichteten Worten den mathematischen Unfug getroffen, der sich aus dem Theorem entwickelte. Was nützt alle hochgelahrte Mathematik, aller verwickelter Formelkram, wenn er — verkehrt aufgebaut wird? Zu obigem Einwand, den Lenard bereits 1918 in dem Jahrbuch für Radioaktivität und Elektronik erhob, hat sich Einstein bis heute nicht geäußert. Mit diesem Einwand oder seiner Widerlegung fällt und steht aber das ganze Prinzip.

Doch sehen wir weiter zu. Einsteins Theorie verlangt, daß infolge der Gravitationswirkung der Sonne ihr Gravitationsfeld passierende Lichtstrahlen [*23*] eine Verzögerung, eine zeitliche Abbremsung erfahren müssen. Die Theorie berechnet eine Verschiebung nach dem roten Teil des Spektrums um 0.01 Angström-Einheiten, d. h. den zehntausendmillionsten Teil eines Millimeters, eine fast unvorstellbare Kleinheit, die aber mit unseren feinen Gitterspektrographen sehr gut zu messen ist. St. Juhn hat („Astrophysik. Journ.'' 46, S. 249, „Nature'' 100, S. 433) an 43 Linien in der Sonnenmitte I 0.00 A.—E., also ein negatives Resultat erzielt, für die Sonnenkorona + 0.0018 A.—E. Ferner hat Schwarzschild (Berl. Ber. 1914 S. 1201) ein ebenfalls negatives Ergebnis festgestellt. Auch andere Forscher von Ruf haben diese Einsteinsche Hauptbedingung nicht bestätigt gefunden. Grebe und Bachem, ausgesprochene „Relativisten'', glauben nun, die gefundenen Werte + 0.0018 für Einstein deuten zu können und ziehen mit einer Kompensationserklärung vom Leder. Einem jungen Forscher, Glaser, ist es aber gelungen, den Nachweis zu führen, daß das Grebe und Bachemsche Ergebnis lediglich auf Beobachtung mit einem fehlerhaften Rowlandschen Gitter zurückzuführen ist. Das Material hierüber wird dem Naturforschertag in Nauheim im September vorgelegt werden. Mit der Verschiebung der Spektrallinien nach Rot ist es also auch nichts. Bleibt somit nur noch die berühmte Ablenkung der Perihelbewegung des Merkur um 41 Sekunden übrig.

Es ist auch hier wieder das Verdienst von Prof. Gehrcke (Berlin), der festgestellt hat, daß Einstein für seine Zwecke eine äußerst schwer zugängliche Arbeit von Gerber benutzte, die bereits vor achtzehn Jahren erschien. Hier gestattete er sich die Abschrift einer Formel, verwendete diese für sich und ließ den wahren Entdecker unerwähnt. Prof. Gehrcke sorgte flugs für zugänglichen Neudruck der seltenen Gerberschen Arbeit, und jedermann kann heute feststellen, wer der Autor dieser Erklärung der Perihel-Abweichung des Merkur ist und ob es nötig ist, dafür ein Relativitätsprinzip zu erfinden.

Unzählige andere Beispiele können noch angeführt werden. Diese wenigen mögen hier genügen. Ein großer Teil deutscher Forscher, der sich zuerst zu Einstein bekannte, sieht den Irrtum ein. Mancher hat schon widerrufen in der richtigen Erkenntnis, daß es ruhmvoller ist, einen Irrtum ehrlich zu bekennen, als in ihm hartnäckig zu verharren. Diese Forscher stellen sich ein ehrenvolles Zeugnis aus, daß sie der Sache, der Wahrheit die Ehre geben und die Person zurückstellen. Noch einige taktische Bemerkungen seien angeführt.

Da, wie gesagt, Einstein eine gewisse Presse, eine gewisse Gemeinde hat, so wird von dieser immer wieder die Oeffentlichkeit im Einsteinschen sinne beeinflußt. So hielt z. B. vor vierzehn Tagen Herr Archenhold im Blüthner-Saal einen Vortrag über dieses Thema. Kundige haben den Kopf geschüttelt, daß Herr Archenhold gar nichts von den Gegengründen erwähnte, sondern sie stillschweigend überging, dagegen die unbedingt strittige Ablenkung des Lichtes um 1.7" im Gravitationsfeld der Sonne postulierte. Herrn Archenhold sei erwidert, daß solche Stellungnahme vor einem Publikum, das in der großen Mehrzahl seine Ausführungen nicht beurteilen [*24*] konnte, entschieden zu verurteilen ist daß Parteinahme wohl politisch gerechtfertigt, wissenschaftlich aber verwerflich ist. Es dürfte Herrn Archenhold als Fachmann und „Sonnenforscher‚‚ wohl nicht unbekannt sein, daß die Sonne eine Atmosphäre besitzt und daß diese für die Ablenkung des Lichtstrahles mit mindestens demselben Recht in Frage kommt wie die sehr hypothetische Wirkung des Gravitationsfeldes, wie das schon Lindemann 1918 festgestellt hat. Daß Einstein den Aether durch ein Dekret abschaffte, ihn aber durch einen anderen Begriff mit gleichen Funktionen wieder einführte, sei hier nur, um mit Einstein selbst zu reden, der „Drolligkeit‚‚ halber erwähnt.

Schließlich sie noch der unzulässigen Art der Propaganda kurz gedacht, die Einstein zum ersten Male in die deutsche Universität einführte. Welcher Mittel sich Einstein zur Verbreitung seiner Ideen bedient, ist an dem Wust von Referaten zu erkennen, von denen die meisten ihn nicht einmal verstehen. Der entzückendste Witz dieser Art ist eine Schrift von Max Hasse, A. Einsteins Relativitätslehre (Magdeburg 1920, Selbstverlag des Verfassers), wo es im Vorwort heißt: „Der Verfasser gesteht freimütig ein, nicht mehr einen Lehrsatz euklidischer Geometrie beweisen zu können — die Zeit hat früher Gelerntes verwischt." Und solch ein Mensch wagt es, über die tollste mathematische Abstraktion, die es je gegeben, zu berichten! Und was sagt Einstein dazu? Es heißt nämlich im Vorwort weiter: „Der Verfasser nahm sich die Freiheit, die Druckbogen Prof. Dr. A. Einstein einzusenden, der ihn mit folgender Antwort erfreute: „Ihre populäre Darstellung scheint mir in der Tat dem Geiste des Nicht-Physikers in glücklicher Weise entgegenzukommen. Ich sende Ihnen die Korrekturbogen mit einigen Randbemerkungen zurück, d a m i t S i e e i n i g e k l e i n e B ö c k e d a r a u s e n t f e r n e n k ö n n e n."

Das ungefähr kennzeichnet Einsteins Methodik. Wenn aber die deutsche Wissenschaft demnächst geschlossen gegen Einstein auftreten wird und mit ihm zu Gericht geht, dann hat er sich diese Wirkung seiner, sagen wir ungewöhnlichen Kampfesweise selbst zuzuschreiben.

[*25*]

Abdruck aus: „Tägliche Rundschau", Mittwoch, 11. August, Abendausgabe.

Zur Erörterung über die Relativitätstheorie.

Entgegnung an Herrn Paul Weyland. Von M. v. L a u e.

In Nr. 171 dieses Blattes ereifert sich Herr Weyland gegen Einsteins allgemeine Relativitätstheorie; gegen die Art ihrer Verbreitung in der größeren Öffentlichkeit sowie gegen ihren Inhalt. Es liegt mir durchaus ferne, alles das decken zu wollen, was kleinere Geister bei der Verbreitung der neuen Lehre durch Ungenauigkeiten, Übertreibungen und Geschmacklosigkeiten gelegentlich gesündigt haben, und die im besonderen herangezogenen Äußerungen von Archenhold und Max Hasse kann ich nicht beurteilen, weil ich sie nicht kenne. Zu einem solchen Angriff auf Einsteins Persönlichkeit, wie ihn Herr Weyland macht, bieten diese Dinge aber doch nicht den mindesten Anlaß.

Welche Einwände richtet aber Weyland gegen den Inhalt? Daß hier reines Denken eine neue Naturauffassung begründet, scheint ihm, wenn ich recht verstehe, gegen die Begründung der Physik in der Erfahrung zu verstoßen. Ist ihm aber nicht bekannt daß Einstein von einer Tatsache ausgeht, die, längst bekannt, noch in den letzten Jahren durch besonders gute Messungen auf das genaueste festgestellt ist? Daß nämlich alle Körper unter der Wirkung der Schwere gleich rasch fallen? Oder fehlt ihm das Verständnis für die Größe einer Leistung, welche uns bei einer so alten Tatsache endlich etwas zu denken lehrt? Bisher galt es doch stets als der größte dem menschlichen Geiste in einer Naturwissenschaft mögliche Triumph, wenn in Umkehrung des gewöhnlichen Ganges die Theorie der Beobachtung erfolgreich voranschritt.

Nun kann man ja freilich noch bestreiten, daß die Folgerungen aus der Theorie, wie die Rotverschiebung der Spektrallinien und die Lichtablenkung an der Sonne durch die Erfahrung endgültig bestätigt sind. Darüber ist in der Tat das letzte Wort nicht gesprochen. Wenn aber Herr Weyland entgegen den sonstigen Gepflogenheiten in wissenschaftlichen Erörterungen andeutet, es könne Voreingenommenheit die Ergebnisse mancher Forscher beeinflußt haben, so möchten wir ihm mitteilen, daß die Engländer, denen wir die Lichtablenkungsmessungen [*26*] verdanken, vorher durchaus nicht Anhänger des Relativitätsgedankens in Einsteinscher Prägung waren. [*Footnote:* Hätte Herr v. Laue die englische Literatur etwas aufmerksamer verfolgt, so hätte er diese Behauptung sicher nicht aufgestellt. Die Tagespresse, wohl meist der Niederschlag der inspirierten öffentlichen Meinung schreibt z. B. darüber: Westminster-Gazette: 14. August 1920: ,,Obwohl die Exped. nach Sobral und Principe in Bezug auf die Bestätigung der Theorie erfolgreich waren, wurde der damals erlangte, etwas dürftige Beweis (*somewhat meagre evidence*) in einem gewissen Grade durch das Versagen des astrographischen Fernrohres in Sobral beeinträchtigt. Aus diesem Grunde sollen eben bei der Sonnenfinsternis am 20. IX. 22 neue Prüfungen vorgenommen werden.''

Hieraus geht z. B. auch hervor, daß die unter atmosphärischen Beeinträchtigungen behinderte Beobachtung auf Principe nicht für einwandsfrei betrachtet wird. Im Übrigen verweise ich auf die schon erwähnte Arbeit von Glaser in Heft 3 dieser Sammlung.]

Unbestreitbar gibt die allgemeine Relativitätstheorie jene minimalen, aber sicher festgestellten Abweichungen der Merkurbahn von der nach der älteren Theorie der Schwere errechneten Form zahlenmäßig richtig wieder. Man mag dies Zusammentreffen als einen Zufall ohne besondere Beweiskraft abtun. Aber man darf Einsteins Ableitung, welche eine entfernte Folgerung einer großen, aus ganz anderen Gesichtspunkten entsprungenen Theorie darstellt, denn doch nicht in einem Atem nennen mit der Arbeit von Gerber, welche nach einer Fülle von Unklarheiten, Mißverständnissen und Ungenauigkeiten die Perihelbewegung aus einem eigens zu diesem Zweck ersonnenen, sonst zu nichts brauchbaren, aus der Geschichte der Wissenschaft nur zu gut verständlichen mathematischen Ansatz errechnet. Hat sich doch auch der Münchener Astronom H. v. Seeliger, ein entschiedener Gegner der Relativitätstheorie, scharf gegen dies Machwerk gewandt. Wie Herr Weyland hier gegen Einstein den Vorwurf erheben konnte, die Gerbersche Formel ,,abgeschrieben'' zu haben, darüber mag er sich einmal selbst Rechenschaft zu geben versuchen.

Etwas näher wollen wir eingehen auf P. Lenards, von Herrn Weyland angeführten Einwand. Einstein hat in der Tat nie auf ihn geantwortet. Man tritt eben einem verdienten Fachgenossen nicht immer entgegen, wenn ihm einmal eine weniger richtige Äußerung entschlüpft; zumal in einem Falle, in welchem der Sachverhalt so leicht zu durchschauen ist, wie hier. Wie steht es denn? Um den Grundgedanken seiner Lehre klarzumachen, knüpft Einstein an das alltägliche Erlebnis einer Eisenbahnfahrt an. Fährt mein Zug auf idealen, stoßfreien Schienen mit unveränderter Geschwindigkeit immer in derselben Richtung a, so sind es zwei physikalisch gleichwertige Annahmen, ob ich mein Abteil als bewegt und die Umgebung als ruhend bezeichne oder umgekehrt verfahre. Das war die Meinung schon seit jeher. Nun aber sagt Einstein, man könne, [*27*] auch wenn der Zug bremst und alle Körper im Abteil das Streben zeigen, sich gegen dessen vordere Wand zu bewegen, die Auffassung in allen ihren physikalischen Folgerungen vertreten, das Abteil bleibe in Ruhe, während die Umgebung, die mir bisher mit konstanter Geschwindigkeit entgegenkam, jetzt in ihrer Bewegung aufgehalten wird. Nur muß dann in dem Bezugsystem, in welchem mein Abteil dauernd ruht, ein Schwerefeld in der Richtung a neu entstanden sein, welches die Umgebung aufhält. Im Innern des ruhenden Abteils bemerke ich das Feld an der erwähnten Bewegungstendenz der Körper. In der Umgebung ruft es außer der gemeinsamen Geschwindigkeitsverminderung aller Gegenstände keine Wirkungen hervor, eben weil a l l e Körper g l e i c h schnell fallen. Geschieht doch auch in einem Aufzug, der sich von der Aufhängung gelöst hat, kein Unheil, s o l a n g e e r f r e i f ä l l t; erst beim Aufschlagen auf den Erdboden wird das anders. Herr Lenard übersieht, daß infolge des gleich raschen Falls aller Körper das neue Schwerefeld im Außenraum keine Lageänderungen der Gegenstände gegeneinander hervorruft, wohl aber im Innenraum die Dinge gegen die ruhenden Wände des Abteils in Bewegung setzt.

Soviel gegen P. Lenard. Herrn Weyland aber möchte ich zum Schluß einen Rat geben, dessen Befolgung in seinem eigensten Interesse liegen dürfte: sollte er sich nämlich noch einmal gegen Einstein wenden, sich über diesen Mann mit etwas mehr Achtung zu äußern. Die Relativitätstheorie mag man für richtig oder falsch halten, es äußert sich auf jeden Fall in ihr eine Genialität, die auf anderen Gebieten der Physik schon zu den schönsten Ergebnissen geführt und ihm verdientermaßen Weltruhm verschafft hat. Die stolze Wissenschaft ist stolz darauf, ihn zu den Ihrigen zählen zu dürfen!

Wir haben Herrn Weyland, wie üblich, von dieser Entgegnung Kenntnis gegeben und erhalten darauf von ihm folgende Zuschrift:

Raummangel verbietet mir, an dieser Stelle eine Erwiderung zu geben, wie sie eine Persönlichkeit wie Herr v. Laue erfordert. Ich werde mich am 24. August im großen Saal der Philharmonie mit Herrn E. Gehrcke zunächst allgemein zur Sache äußern, späterhin im besonderen. Ich bitte Herrn v. Laue, zu diesem Abend anwesend zu sein. Des weiteren werden Herr Kraus (Prag) und Herr Glaser (Berlin) am 2. September im gleichen Saale zum Thema sprechen.

Hier nur soviel: Ich wende mich nicht gegen eine Theorie, sondern gegen mathematische Fiktionen und maßlose Übertreibungen. Daß die Frage der Rotverschiebung für Herrn v. Laue nunmehr ebenfalls keine absolute Tatsache ist, freut mich. Früher, als keine Kritiker, die es kontrollieren konnten, (ich erinnere an Herrn Freundlichs Märzvortrag), da waren, las man's anders. Ferner ist Herr v. Laue anscheinend über den neuesten Stand der englischen und amerikanischen Forschung nicht ganz im Bilde. Anders kann ich seine Bemerkung nicht verstehen. Näheres im Vortrag. Hinsichtlich der Gerberschen [*28*] Formel verweise ich auf die Arbeiten von E. Gehrcke (Verhandlg. d. Deutschen Physikal. Gesellschaft 1918 S. 165, Ann. d. Physik, 4. Folge, Band 51, 1916, S. 119.) Die Sache ist ja für Herrn Einstein sehr peinlich, aber nicht zu ändern. Es wundert mich nur, daß man die ganze Gerbersche Arbeit verdonnert — Schwächen seien zugegeben, aber: wo sind keine? — und g e r a d e d a s E r g e b n i s so s c h ö n f i n d e t, daß man es, sagen wir, verwendet. Hier hilft kein Drehen und Deuteln. Oder soll ich noch deutlicher werden? Ich erinnere an Palagyi, Mach! Weiß Herr v. Laue nicht, wie sich Herr Einstein hinsichtlich der Verwendung, Machscher Gedanken herausgeredet hat?

Zu dem Einwand gegen Herrn L. Lenard äußere ich mich nicht. Dieser hervorragende Heidelberger Gelehrte wird seinerzeit selbst das Wort gegen Einstein ergreifen. [*Footnote:* Herr Lenard teilt mir seine Antwort brieflich mit, die ich hier wiedergeben möchte: „Herrn v. Laues Äußerungen zu meiner Schrift haben mich stark befremdet, insofern sie mir die Sachlage nicht zu treffen scheinen. 1. Trifft es nicht zu, daß Herr Einstein auf meine Einwände nie geantwortet habe. Vielmehr wird seine Antwort in der soeben erschienenen 2. Auflage meiner Schrift „Über Relativitätsprinzip, Äther, Gravitation'' nicht nur genau zitiert, sondern auch besprochen, aber nicht als befriedigend befunden (siehe meine Fußnote auf S. 31) und es wird sogar angegeben, wo Herr Einstein oder einer der Verteidiger der allgemeinen Relativitätstheorie einsetzen müßten, um den Beweis — oder genügenden Hinweis — für die Berechtigung der Verallgemeinerung zu liefern, wobei ich garnicht zweifle, daß es nicht nur mir allein gegenüber lohnend wäre, dies wirklich zu tun, — falls es möglich ist. Es scheint mir hiernach, daß Herr v. Laue die neue Auflage meiner Schrift noch garnicht, die alte aber auch nur unvollkommen kennt, beziehlich überlegt hat. Denn 2. trifft es außerdem auch nicht zu, daß ich das Nichtauftreten von Trägheitswirkungen infolge gleichschnellen Fallens aller Körper bei Wirkung von Gravitation übersehen hätte. Sondern ich finde nur große Schwierigkeiten gegen die Annahme der Einsteinschen Gravitationsfelder und erörtere diese Schwierigkeiten — die sofort auftreten, sobald man einfache Beispielsfälle zu Ende zu überlegen versucht — ausführlich mit dem Resultate, daß eine Einschränkung des verallgemeinerten Relativitätsprinzipes notwendig sei, um es von seinen gegen den Verstand gerichteten Härten zu befreien. — Eine selbst bei Zutreffen der von Herrn Einstein gemachten, experimentell kontrollierbaren Voraussagen irgendwie gesicherte Allgemeingiltigkeit des Relativitätsprinzips kann bisher nicht behauptet werden, womit aber auch jede Betonung einer philosophischen auf die Grundauffassung des Naturgeschehens gerichteten Bedeutung zunächst wegfallen sollte. Gerade weil solche Betonung zu oft zu auffallend vor die Allgemeinheit gebraucht worden ist, schien es und scheint es nun eben nötig, neben den Vorzügen auch die der gegenwärtigen Erfahrung entsprechenden Grenzen des Relativitätsprinzips, oder die Übertreibungen, die man sich mit demselben gestattet hat, hervorzuheben. Wer hierüber im Einzelnen orientiert sein will, wie es meiner Auffassung nach dem wirklichen Stand der Kenntnis entspricht, muß für jetzt auf die erwähnte 2. Auflage meiner Schrift verwiesen werden.] Herr v. Laues Einwand werde ich ihm übermitteln.

[*29*]

Für den mir erteilten Rat danke ich bestens. Ich bin mit anderen Herren so frei, über die Relativitätstheorie meine besondere Meinung zu haben. Die Beweise werden in einer Vortragsreihe, an der erste Physiker und Astronomen teilnehmen, dargelegt werden.

P . W e y l a n d

Tägliche Rundschau Nr. 180.
Zur Erörterung über die Relativitätstheorie.
Entgegnung an Herrn Professor Dr. M. v. Laue.
Von Dr.-Ing. L . C . G l a s e r (Berlin).

In Nummer 175 dieses Blattes sagt M . v . L a u e, daß man E i n s t e i n s Erklärung für die Abweichung der Perihelbewegung der Planetenbahnen, insonderheit des Merkurs, nicht in einem Atem mit der Arbeit von G e r b e r nennen darf, welcher nach seiner Meinung nach einer Fülle von Unklarheiten, Mißverständnissen und Ungenauigkeiten die Perihelbewegung aus einem eigens zu diesem Zweck ersonnenen, sonst zu nichts brauchbaren, aus der Geschichte der Wissenschaft nur zu gut verständlichen, mathematischen Ansatz errechnet. Man ist, wie von P. L e n a r d bereits schon bemerkt ist, mit der Arbeit des verstorbenen Oberlehrers P a u l G e r b e r besonders scharf ins Gericht gegangen. Im Hinblick darauf, daß M. v. Laue sich schützend vor Einstein stellt, ist es Pflicht der Menschlichkeit, das Ergebnis dieser Arbeit des verstorbenen Oberlehrers P a u l G e r b e r gegen die Bezeichnung „M a c h w e r k" in Schutz zu nehmen. Die Ereiferung M. v. L a u e s über die Arbeit von G e r b e r ist unverständlich, zumal diese Arbeit im Auslande auf Grund des Wiederabdruckes in den „Annalen für Physik" von Herrn L. S i l b e r s t e i n, der ja bekanntlich gegen die allgemeine Relativitätstheorie Einsteins eine durchaus ablehnende Stellung einnimmt, gelegentlich einer Arbeit „über die Perihelbewegung des [*30*] Merkurs, abgeleitet nach der klassischen Theorie der Relativität" in den „Monthly Notices" der *Roy. Astr. Soc.* 1917, 503-610, als G e r b e r s F o r m e l aufgeführt und anerkannt wird. Daß nun den Anhängern der Relativitätstheorie das Bestehen der Gerberschen Formel, über deren Ansatz man im einzelnen denken kann, wie man will, recht unbequem ist, ist ja sehr leicht verständlich, zumal die Forderungen und sogenannten Bestätigungen der Einsteinschen Relativitätstheorie im ganzen äußerst beweisbedürftig sind. Da die Arbeit G e r b e r s der Geschichte angehört, das E i n s t e i n s c h e Ergebnis vorwegnimmt, aber gern totgeschwiegen wird, ist es besonders erfreulich, festzustellen, daß diese bereits Aufnahme in der zweiten Auflage des Lehrbuches der Physik von R i e c k e, herausgeben von L e c h e r, gefunden hat.

Tägliche Rundschau Nr. 175, Abendausgabe.
Zur Erörterung über die Relativitätstheorie.
Von M. v. L a u e.

Auf meinem Aufsatz in Nr. 176 dieses Blattes hin haben mich verschiedene Fachgenossen auf Einsteins „Dialog über die Einwände gegen die Relativitätstheorie". [*Footnote:* Diese Arbeit war mir bekannt. Als Einwand habe ich sie nicht gelten lassen. Herr L e n a r d ist lt. seinem Briefe genau derselben Ansicht.] (Naturwissenschaften, **6.** Jahrgang, Seite 6-697, 1918) aufmerksam gemacht, in welchem Einstein selbst zu dem Lenardschen Einwand Stellung nimmt. Was dort steht, deckt sich zwar nicht mit dem, was ich neulich an dieser Stelle — übrigens als die Ansicht sehr vieler — darüber sagte, doch besteht auch kein Widerspruch; ich gebe diesen Hinweis hiermit weiter.

Ein wenig ausführlicher aber möchte ich in Hinblick auf Herrn Glasers Entgegnung in Nr. 178 auf die Gerbersche Erklärung der

Perihelbewegung beim Merkur eingehen. Zwar kann man eine sozusagen philosophische Kritik dieser Arbeit und ihrer Schlußformel nur einem fachmännischen Publikum verständlich machen, so daß ich hier darauf verzichten muß. Aber ich möchte doch einmal fragen, was diese Arbeit denn eigentlich leistet.

Eine Tatsache physikalisch erklären, heißt doch, sie in Beziehung zu anderen physikalischen Tatsachen setzen. Darin bin ich hoffentlich mit den Gegnern der Relativitätstheorie einig. Mit welcher anderen Tatsache setzt nun Gerber die Perihelbewegung in Beziehung? Die Überschrift seiner Veröffentlichung könnte die Antwort nahelegen: M i t d e r (z w a r n i e u n m i t t e l b a r b e o b a c h t e t e n , [*31*] a b e r d o c h s e h r w a h r s c h e i n l i c h e n) A u s b r e i t u n g d e r S c h w e r e m i t e n d l i c h e r , u n d z w a r m i t L i c h t g e s c h w i n d i g k e i t . [*Footnote:* Diese sehr interessante Einschränkung eines der wichtigsten Einstein'schen Postulate werde ich an anderer spezieller Stelle entsprechend würdigen. Daß v . L a u e das Einsteinsche Postulat von der Lichtgeschwindigkeit als äußerste Grenze aller Geschwindigkeiten so einschräkend behandelt, ist aus der Feder diese bedeutendsten Relativisten von außerordentlicher Wichtigkeit.] Aber diese Antwort wäre nicht richtig. Unmittelbar nach dem Wiederabdruck in den Annalen der Physik habe ich an derselben Stelle (Band 53, Seite 214) darauf hingewiesen, daß Gerbers Formeln die Schwere als eine unvermittelte Fernwirkung hinstellen. Einen Widerspruch gegen diesen Nachweis habe ich bisher weder öffentlich noch privatim vernommen. Und welche andere Tatsache ließe sich hier erwähnen? Ich wüßte keine.

Nun lege wir einmal denselben Maßstab an Einsteins Erklärung. Sie bringt die Perihelbewegung in Zusammenhang mit der Äquivalenz der trägen und der schweren Masse, die der Versuch mit einer seltenen Schärfe bewiesen hat; natürlich auch mit der Lichtablenkung und der Verschiebung der Spektrallinien an der Sonne — doch diese Tatsachen sind ja noch bestritten. Sicher aber ist, daß die allgemeine Relativitätstheorie die beschränkte (ich vermeide gern das Fremdwort „spezielle") als fast stets brauchbare Näherung einschließt. Sie setzt damit die Perihelbewegung in Beziehung zu allen den berühmten Versuchen, welche durch Beobachtung auf der Erde deren Bewegung um die Sonne vergeblich nachzuweisen suchten; ferner zu den vielen sicher festgestellten Tatsachen der Elektrodynamik und Optik der bewegten Körper. Weiter: Die beschränkte Relativitätstheorie steht — ich glaube unbestritten — im Einklang zur gesamten mechanischen Erfahrung, einschließlich der verhältnismäßig neuen Beobachtungen über die Dynamik schnell bewegter Elektronen. Kurz: Einsteins Erklärung reiht die Perihelbewegung in den großen Zusammenhang von Tatsachen ein, den wir als das physikalische Weltbild bezeichnen. Der Weg, auf dem das erreicht wird, mag manchem nicht gefallen.

208 Albert Einstein: The Incorrigible Racist

Dafür habe ich durchaus Verständnis. Aber man soll die relativistische Theorie der Perihelbewegung wirklich nicht auf eine Stufe stellen mit der Gerberschen Erklärung, die, abgesehen davon, was sonst über sie zu sagen wäre, überhaupt keine Erklärung ist."

Ernst Gehrcke addressed Albert Einstein to his face in the Berlin Philharmonic on 24 August 1920. Ernst Gehrcke was the second and last speaker at the event. Gehrcke stated, as recorded in a the published transcript of his talk: *Die Relativitätstheorie. Eine Wissenschaftliche Massensuggestion, gemeinverständlich dargestellt*, Volume 1 of the Press of the Arbeitsgemeinschaft deutscher Naturforscher zur Erhaltung reiner Wissenschaft e. V., Köhler, Berlin, (1920); which was reprinted in Gehrcke's booklet *Kritik der Relativitätstheorie*, Hermann Meusser, Berlin, (1924), pp. 54-68:

"Was ist eigentlich die Einsteinsche Relativitätstheorie? Diese Frage wird heute nicht nur in gelehrten Kreisen erörtert, sondern sie beschäftigt sehr viele, denen akademische und gelehrte Dinge sonst fern liegen. Das Thema der Relativitätstheorie, der Streit über ihre Bedeutung und Richtigkeit ist heute bis in die Tagespresse aller möglichen Richtungen gedrungen. Aber um was es sich eigentlich dreht, das dürfte trotz aller Zeitungsartikel und populären Broschüren, die wie Pilze aus der Erde schießen, nur sehr wenigen klar sein. Dem soll im Folgenden abgeholfen werden.

Es wird dabei zu beachten sein, daß die Relativitätstheorie nicht wie ein deus ex machina plötzlich eines Tages da war, sondern dass sie, wie alle geistigen Strömungen, eine längere E n t w i c k l u n g gehabt hat und schrittweise und allmählich gewachsen ist. Daß die Relativitätstheorie eine geistige Strömung darstellt, kann niemand bezweifeln, nur darüber wird man verschiedener Meinung sein können, ob diese Strömung eine gesunde, verheißungsvolle ist, ob sie, kurz gesagt, einen F o r t s c h r i t t darstellt, oder ob das Gegenteil der Fall ist, ob sie ungesund, unfruchtbar und falsch, also kurz gesagt ein Irrlicht der geistigen Entwicklung war. Die Meinungen hierüber sind sehr geteilte. Der Gemeinde der Relativitätsgläubigen steht eine Schar von Zweiflern und Kritikern gegenüber, hüben und drüben haben anerkannte Autoritäten Partei ergriffen, und wie die Dinge liegen, werden nicht allein wissenschaftliche, sondern auch politische und andere Gesichtspunkte in die Debatte hineingetragen. In dieses Chaos der durcheinander wogenden

Behauptungen und Interessen soll hier also hineingeleuchtet werden. Nur unter dem Gesichtspunkt der Entwicklung wird es aber möglich sein, das Durcheinander zu verstehen und sich über das Gewirr der Meinungen ein Urteil zu bilden. Wir fragen im Folgenden n i c h t, was i s t die Relativitätstheorie? sondern: wie hat sie sich entwickelt? und beginnen mit demjenigen Punkte, welcher der Relativitätstheorie den Namen gegeben hat, mit dem

Relativitätsprinzip.

Gemäß dem Obigen werden wir nicht fragen, was ist das Relativitätsprinzip? sondern: wie hat sich das Relativitätsprinzip entwickelt? Erst die Darlegung dieser Entwicklung wird uns zu einem Standpunkt gegenüber dem Relativitätsprinzip führen, der von dem augenblicklichen Tagesurteil frei ist.

Das Relativitätsprinzip ist in der Tat kein erst in unsern Tagen aufgestellter Grundsatz, sondern es hat eine lange Geschichte, die bis in das griechische Altertum und möglicherweise noch weiter zurückreicht. Die voltständige Darstellung seines Werdeganges wäre eine umfangreiche, historisch-kritische Studie, die hier nicht auf kurzem Raum gegeben werden kann und hier auch nicht behandelt zu werden braucht. Es wird genügen, wenn wir deutlich machen, daß das Relativitätsprinzip an sehr einfache, alltägliche Erfahrungen, die schon mancher gemacht hat, anknüpft.

Stellen wir uns etwa vor, daß wir in einem Eisenbahnzuge sitzen, der auf dem Bahnhof hält. Auf der andern Seite des Bahnsteigs soll ebenfalls ein Zug stehen. Wir warten ungeduldig auf Abfahrt, endlich geht es los, der Zug setzt sich in Bewegung, und wir sehen durch das Fenster, wie wir am jenseitigen Zuge uns vorbeibewegen. Aber mit einem Mal entdecken wir, daß wir uns geirrt haben: w i r halten immer noch auf dem Bahnhof, aber der a n d e r e Zug fährt! Dieses unliebsame Erlebnis in seiner Alltäglichkeit und Einfachheit ist geeignet, uns dem Relativitätsprinzip näher zu führen: Wir konnten nicht feststellen, ob w i r fahren oder der a n d e r e Zug, ob w i r in Ruhe blieben oder der andere Zug, das einzige, das wir beobachten konnten, war, daß die beiden Züge r e l a t i v zueinander in Bewegung waren. Man nennt dies die R e l a t i v i t ä t   d e r   B e w e g u n g e n. Alle Bewegung ist r e l a t i v, d. h. bezogen auf irgend etwas, außerhalb des Bewegten Befindliches. Alle Naturkörper in unserer Umgebung, auf der Erde, alle Gestirne am Himmel bewegen sich r e l a t i v zueinander. Man drückt sich auch so aus, daß man sagt, der Bewegungsbegriff sei ein Relationsbegriff, d. h. ein Begriff, der ohne Bezugnahme auf etwas, g e g e n ü b e r w e l c h e m das Bewegte sich bewegt, nicht gedacht werden kann. Aber die Relativität der Bewegungen ist noch nicht das P r i n z i p der Relativität. Hierüber ein anderes, alltägliches Beispiel.

Es soll ein Stück Holz mit einer Säge durchgesägt werden. Das kann auf zweierlei Weisen geschehen: erstens so, daß das Stück Holz f e s t g e h a l t e n wird, z. B. indem man es auf einen Sägebock legt und die Säge hin und her b e w e g t , zweitens so, daß die Säge festgehalten, z. B. zwischen die Knie geklemmt wird, und nun das Stück Holz quer zur Säge hin und her bewegt wird. In beiden Fällen wird das gleiche Ergebnis erzielt: das Holz wird durchgesägt. Ob ich also die Säge bewege und das Holz festhalte, oder umgekehrt die Säge festhalte und das Holz bewege, kommt auf dasselbe hinaus. Die beiden Bewegungsvorgänge: Holz fest, Säge bewegt und: Säge fest, Holz bewegt, sind aber in r e l a t i v e r Hinsicht gleich; es bewegt sich in b e i d e n Fällen das eine i n b e z u g a u f das andere in gleicher Weise. Dieser Spezialfall läßt sich sogleich verallgemeinern, wenn man behauptet, daß bei irgend zwei Bewegungsvorgängen, die r e l a t i v z u e i n a n d e r gleich sind, immer das gleiche Ergebnis herauskommt. Damit wird ein Satz aufgestellt, der durch Beobachtung nahegelegt ist und den man in seiner Allgemeinheit versuchsweise auf a l l e Bewegungsvorgänge in der Natur erstreckt. Die Behauptung, w e n n s i e r i c h t i g i s t , wird damit zu einem allgemeinen Naturprinzip, und man nennt ein solches Naturprinzip das Relativitätsprinzip.

So weit ist die Sache also gar nicht schwierig, und jedermann, der über Beobachtungen an relativ zueinander bewegten Körpern verfügt oder der Holz gesägt hat, kann begreifen, was man unter dem Relativitätsprinzip versteht. Man wird auch begreifen, daß die Gedankengänge, die zum Relativitätsprinzip geführt haben, nicht erst im 20. Jahrhundert von der Menschheit eingeschlagen wurden, sondern erheblich älteren Datums sind. Sonderlich originell ist also das Prinzip n i c h t , das der Relativitätstheorie den Namen gegeben hat. Es taucht nun aber sogleich die Frage auf: ist denn das Prinzip überhaupt richtig?

Diese Frage zu beantworten ist viel verwickelter, als begreiflich zu machen, was man unter dem Relativitätsprinzip versteht. In der sogenannten klassischen Mechanik, die von Galilei und Newton begründet ist, wird das Relativitätsprinzip als in aller Strenge gültig angesehen für gewisse Bewegungen von Naturkörpern, nämlich solche, die derartig verlaufen, daß die relativen Bewegungen g r a d l i n i g sind und mit g l e i c h b l e i b e n d e r   G e s c h w i n d i g k e i t erfolgen, sofern dabei keine andern als rein m e c h a n i s c h e Erscheinungen hervortreten.

Ob das Relativitätsprinzip auch über diesen engen Bereich hinaus   n o c h   i m   R a h m e n   der alten klassischen M e c h a n i k tatsächlich gültig ist, darüber sind sich nicht einmal heute die Gelehrten einig. Namhafte Forscher nehmen an, daß alle Bewegungen in der klassischen Mechanik, in denen die Geschwindigkeiten   n i c h t   gleichbleiben, in denen also sogenannte Beschleunigungen auftreten, das Relativitätsprinzip durchbrechen, andere nehmen an, daß das Relativitätsprinzip auch für u n g l e i c h f ö r m i g e Bewegungsvorgänge gültig bleibt, sofern dabei Drehbewegungen (Rotationen) ausgeschlossen werden. Für Drehbewegungen jedenfalls gilt das Relativitätsprinzip der klassischen Mechanik n i c h t. Wer sich näher für diesen Gegenstand interessiert, mag dies in der Fachliteratur nachlesen. [*Footnote:* Vergl. E. Gehrcke. Verhandlungen der Deutschen Physikalischen Gesellschaft **15** S. 260. 1913.]

Wir werden nun weiter gehen und fragen, ob denn das Relativitätsprinzip auch für solche Naturerscheinungen gilt, welche nicht nur hinsichtlich ihrer Bewegung (z. B. wie zwei relativ zueinander bewegte Eisenbahnzüge) oder mechanisch, wie das Zersägen von Holz, betrachtet werden, sondern ob es auch für elektrische, magnetische, optische und andere Erscheinungen gültig bleibt. Auch hierüber besteht keine Einigkeit unter den Forschern. Besonders trennen sich hier die Parteien nach dem Gesichtspunkt, ob die elektrischen, magnetischen, optischen u. a. Erscheinungen in einem unsichtbaren, untastbaren, unwägbaren, aber doch tatsächlich vorhandenen Medium, genannt Weltäther, vor sich gehen oder nicht. Diejenigen Forscher, welche an den Äther glauben — und zu diesen gehören die bedeutendsten Gelehrten der Vergangenheit und der Gegenwart — müssen das

Relativitätsprinzip, wie es oben für wägbare Naturkörper eingeführt wurde, allgemein ablehnen, auch für völlig gradlinige Bewegungen mit völlig gleichförmiger Geschwindigkeit (sogenannte gleichförmige Translationen). Diejenigen aber, welche nicht an den Äther glauben, haben die Freiheit, die Gültigkeit des Relativitätsprinzips in den verschiedensten Erweiterungen probeweise anzunehmen. Welchen Gültigkeitsbereich nehmen nun die Anhänger der sogenannten Relativitätstheorien für das Relativitätsprinzip an?

Auch diese Frage ist nicht einfach zu beantworten, weil die Meinungen sehr geteilt sind. Der Erfinder der Relativitätstheorie, Einstein, hat hierüber im Laufe der Zeit sehr verschiedene Ansichten gehabt und seinen Standpunkt mehrfach gewechselt. Er hat zunächst behauptet [*Footnote:* A. Einstein, Annalen der Physik **17**, S. 891, 1905. Vgl. ferner die Zusammenstellung von Gehrcke: Die Naturwissenschaften **1**, S. 62, 170, 338, 1913; ebenda 1919, S. 147.], daß das Prinzip auch für optische, elektrische usw. Erscheinungen an wägbaren Körpern g ü l t i g sei wobei stillschweigend vorausgesetzt war, daß die oben von der klassischen Mechanik für m e c h a n i s c h e Erscheinungen zugelassene Bedingung der geradlinigen, gleichbleibenden Geschwindigkeit (gleichförmiger Translation) zutrifft; dann hat er sich zwei Jahre später merkwürdigerweise dahin geäußert, daß das Relativitätsprinzip nur auf beschleunigungs f r e i e (relative) Bewegungen a n g e w a n d t worden sei, und überlegt, ob das Prinzip auch für b e s c h l e u n i g t e Bewegungen gelte. Er kommt zu dem Schluß, daß dies so ist und glaubt, das Prinzip auf den speziellen Fall g l e i c h f ö r m i g e r B e s c h l e u n i g u n g erweitern zu dürfen. Später hat Einstein in einer mehrere Monate nach meinen Einwänden erschienenen Schrift das Relativitätsprinzip wieder b e s c h r ä n k t auf gleichförmige Translationen. Ferner hat Einstein das Relativitätsprinzip ganz allgemein erweitern zu können geglaubt, und es auf s ä m t l i c h e, auch u n gleichförmige Translationen, und sogar auf Rotationen ausdehnen wollen. Er nannte die auf diese Ansicht gegründete Theorie „allgemeine Relativitätstheorie". Schließlich hat Einstein noch einen etwas anderen Standpunkt eingenommen, er hat nämlich das Relativitätsprinzip ersetzt durch ein modifiziertes Prinzip, das sogenannte „Äquivalenzprinzip" [*Footnote:* A. Einstein, Annalen der Physik, Bd. **35**, S. 898,

1911.], und wir stehen vor dem bemerkenswerten Ergebnis, daß dasjenige Prinzip, welches der Relativitätstheorie den Namen gegeben hat, in der neueren Theorie Einsteins einem anderen Prinzip Platz gemacht hat. Einstein hat sich übrigens in der Verteidigung des Relativitätsprinzips nicht glücklich geäußert; dies trifft besonders für seine Polemik mit Lenard [*Footnote:* P. Lenard, Über Relativitätsprinzip, Äther, Gravitation. Verlag von Hirzel, Leipzig 1920. P. Lenard, Über Relativitätsprinzip, Äther, Gravitation. Verlag von Hirzel, Leipzig 1920. Hier findet man viele zugehörige Literaturhinweise.] zu, den er sachlich gar nicht widerlegen kann und an dessen Gegengründen er einfach vorbeiredet.

Es hätten die Schwankungen in der Auffassung Einsteins über eine so grundlegende Frage wie das Relativitätsprinzip eigentlich schon genügen können, um die Fachwelt stutzig zu machen und mit Skepsis gegen die Relativitätstheorie zu erfüllen. Wenn diese Skepsis nicht in dem Maße zutage trat, wie es unter gewöhnlichen Umständen zu erwarten gewesen wäre, so werden hierfür Gründe da sein. Darüber soll später im Zusammenhang mit anderen Dingen einiges gesagt werden. Hier sei noch folgendes zum Relativitätsprinzip bemerkt:

Das Relativitätsprinzip, das in der Relativitätstheorie eine Rolle spielt, betrifft die Relativität von Bewegungs vorgängen. Sachlich gar nichts zu tun hat mit dieser Relativität der Bewegungen alles das, was in der Presse und auch zuweilen in Fachblättern sonst noch mit dem Wort Relativität gemeint wird. Daß „alles relativ'' ist, worunter man sich, je nach dem individuellen Bildungsgrad, das Verschiedenste denken kann, mag auch bei den Anhängern der Relativitätstheorie eine wichtige Rolle, möglicherweise zuweilen nur im Unterbewußtsein, spielen, aber mit der theoretischen Relativitätstheorie als solcher haben derartige Allgemeinheiten sachlich nichts zu schaffen. Als Schlagwort, das auf die Massen wirkt, bei dem jeder glaubt, etwas ihm einigermaßen Bekanntes zu hören und bei dem auch kaum zwei an dasselbe denken, ist aber das „Relative'' zur Einführung und zur Empfehlung der Relativitätstheorie vorzüglich geeignet. Das „Äquivalenzprinzip'' wird niemals so populär werden können wie das „Relativitätsprinzip''. Es liegt eine gewisse Tragik darin, daß die Relativitätstheorie in ihrer allmählichen Entwicklung ihr Hauptschlagwort in den Hintergrund geschoben hat; statt dessen wird, je länger je mehr, der Hauptnachdruck auf ein anderes Gebiet der Relativitätstheorie gelegt: auf die sogenannte

Relativierung von Raum und Zeit.

Die „Relativierung von Raum und Zeit" bildet heute die stolzeste Errungenschaft der Relativitätstheorie, deren Erwähnung die Brust des Relativisten schwellen läßt und durch die die philosophisch-erkenntnistheoretische Umwälzung unserer ganzen Weltauffassung gegeben sein soll. Die Relativierung von Raum und Zeit soll eine geistige Erneuerung und einen Wendepunkt in der menschlichen Denkweise bedeuten, demgegenüber die Taten von Kopernikus, Kepler und Newton verblassen.

Die Relativierung von Raum und Zeit wird in den bekannten Darstellungen der Relativitätstheorie als eine grundgelehrte Sache mathematisch eingekleidet vorgetragen, sodaß vielfach der Nichtmathematiker den Eindruck erhalten hat, er werde nie imstande sein, die Tiefe dieser weltstürzenden Gedanken je zu ermessen und zu begreifen. Und dabei ist kaum ein Gegenstand der ganzen Relativitätstheorie mit so wenig Aufwand an gelehrten Ausdrücken und Formeln klar zu machen, als gerade dieser. Das ist eigentlich von vornherein klar. Denn über Dinge, die so g r u n d l e g e n d sind wie Raum und Zeit, auf denen sich so vieles, Mathematisches und Nichtmathematisches, aufbaut, muß sich der Verstand mit einem Minimum an künstlichem, mathematischen Handwerkszeug klar werden können — wenn er dazu überhaupt imstande ist. Die mathematischen Formeln geben uns ja auch nur Aufschluß darüber, w i e g r o ß im einzelnen die errechneten Effekte sind, sie sagen jedoch nichts aus über den ihnen zugrunde liegenden Standpunkt. Aber die Anhänger der Relativitätstheorie sind anderer Meinung. Ihnen ist der m a t h e m a t i s c h e Aufbau offenbar unlösbar verknüpft mit den a l l g e m e i n e n, erkenntnistheoretischen Grundauffassungen, vor denen sie staunen. An keiner Stelle liegt aber die Wurzel der Relativitätstheorie klarer, als bei der ihr eigentümlichen Auffassung von Raum and Zeit, und an keinem Punkte wird die Lage für die Zukunft der Relativitätstheorie bedenklicher als beim Raum und bei der Zeit.

Einstein hat, wenn auch nicht seine Grundauffassung, so doch seine F o l g e r u n g e n hinsichtlich des raumzeitlichen Geschehens durch allgemein verständliche Bilder zu erläutern gesucht. Hier nur eine Probe.

Einstein erörterte gelegentlich eines Vortrages in Zürich [*Footnote:* A. Einstein, Vierteljahrsschrift der Naturforschenden Gesellschaft Zürich **56**, S. 11 und folgende.] die Vorgänge, die sich nach seiner Theorie in einer hin and her bewegten Uhr angeblich abspielen sollen. Eine solche hin and herbewegte Uhr soll nach Einstein gegenüber einer ruhenden Uhr n a c h gehen. Er äußert sich dann, um recht deutlich and populär zu sein, folgendermaßen: „Wenn wir z. B. einen lebenden Organismus in eine Schachtel hineinbrächten und ihn dieselbe Hin- und Herbewegung ausführen ließen wie vorher die Uhr, so könnte man es erreichen, daß dieser Organismus nach einem beliebig langen Fluge beliebig wenig geändert wieder an seinen ursprünglichen Ort zurückkehrt, während ganz entsprechend beschaffene Organismen, welche an dem ursprünglichen Orte ruhend geblieben sind, bereits längst neuen Generationen Platz gemacht haben. Für den bewegten Organismus war die lange Zeit der Reise nur ein Augenblick, falls die Bewegung annähernd mit Lichtgeschwindigkeit erfolgte! Das ist eine unabweisbare Konsequenz der von uns zugrunde gelegten Prinzipien, die die Erfahrung uns aufdrängt.‘‘

Also kurz gesagt: Die Zeitfolge aller Ereignisse auf einem Naturkörper soll nach Einsteins Theorie abhängig sein vom Bewegungszustand des Körpers, derart, daß die Bewegung des Naturkörpers alle auf ihm sich abspielenden Vorgänge v e r l a n g s a m t : es soll hiernach z. B. ein lebender Organismus durch Schütteln, wegen der dadurch bedingten Verzögerung aller an ihm und in ihm sich abspielenden Prozesse, j u n g e r h a l t e n werden können. Diese Geschichte hat Einstein und ebenso seine Anhänger als „unabweisbare Konsequenz‘‘ der Relativitätstheorie einem staunenden Publikum erzählt! Sie ist von den Relativisten mannigfach variiert and weiter ausgebaut worden: Von zwei Zwillingen wird der eine gleich nach seiner Geburt auf eine lange Reise geschickt, von welcher er als Schuljunge zurückkehrt; er findet dann seinen Bruder als Greis mit weißen Haaren vor! Solche and ähnliche Betrachtungen sind, um es noch einmal hervorzuheben, nicht etwa Märchen oder Witze, sondern „unabweisbare Konsequenzen‘‘ der Relativitätstheorie! Die genannten Konsequenzen muß man mitmachen, wenn man an die Relativitätstheorie glaubt.

Statt auf mathematische Formeln einzugehen, können wir an den genannten Bildern das Wesen der erkenntnistheoretischen Grundlagen der Theorie erfassen. Wir wollen uns fragen: 1. Welche Grundansicht über die Zeit liegt diesen Betrachtungen zugrunde? 2. Was folgt weiter daraus?

Fassen wir jetzt also irgendeine den Folgerungen ins Auge, die den relativistischen Zeitablauf kennzeichnen, z. B. das obige, Einsteinsche Beispiel der gegeneinander bewegten Organismen. Wir wollen tatsächlich annehmen, es wäre experimentell gefunden, daß der b e w e g t e Organismus j ü n g e r geblieben ist als der ruhende; über die Unwahrscheinlichkeit und die technischen Schwierigkeiten einer solchen Feststellung wollen wir uns hinwegsetzen. Dann wäre alles, so sonderlich es wäre, immerhin verständlich, wenn Bewegung als solche die Eigenschaft haben würde, eine Verlangsamung aller auf dem bewegten Körper vor sich gehenden chemischen und physikalischen Prozesse hervorzubringen. Gerade die Bewegung als solche, auch genannt „absolute Bewegung", wird aber von Einstein geleugnet, und er muß daher die gegebene Erklärung für das merkwürdige Jungbleiben des bewegten Organismus von sich weisen. Statt dessen nimmt er eine „Relativierung den Zeit" an; das bedeutet, daß der bewegte Organismus n u r v o m S t a n d p u n k t d e s r u h e n d e n O r g a n i s m u s aus der jüngere ist, daß aber andererseits auch vom Standpunkt des andern Organismus aus der erste Organismus der bewegte und daher der jüngere ist. Nach der Relativitätslehre soll jeder Standpunkt dem andern gleichberechtigt, keiner von dem andern bevorzugt sein. Ein solcher Ausweg führt nun aber zu höchst bedenklichen Folgerungen. Dies ist unschwer einzusehen, wenn wir die beiden Organismen miteinander reden lassen, nachdem die Reise beendet ist und sie beide wieder relativ zueinander ruhen. Der e i n e Organismus wird z. B. behaupten: i c h habe weiße Haare, and Du bist jung geblieben; der a n d e r e Organismus wird ebenfalls behaupten: i c h habe weiße Haare and Du bist jung geblieben, denn i c h bin ja von m e i n e m Standpunkt aus der ruhende, und D u der bewegte! Also die beiden Organismen wenden sich g e g e n s e i t i g für jung und jeder sich selbst für gealtert erklären!

Die beiden kommen also zueinander in Widerspruch. Man könnte auf den Einfall kommen, daß der Widerspruch beseitigt wäre, wenn in der Unterhaltung der eine immer das Gegenteil von dem h ö r e n würde, was der andere s a g t , aber auch das rettet nicht aus der Schwierigkeit. Denn wenn die Reise des bewegten Organismus lange genug gedauert hat, ist der ruhende Organismus tot (vgl. oben Einsteins Worte). Dann ist es aber eine „unabweisbare Konsequenz", wenn der jung gebliebene Organismus zum Toten spricht: N i c h t   D u bist tot, sondern i c h ! Denn vom Standpunkt des jungen Organismus aus war ja e r   s e l b s t   d e r   r u h e n d e , der andere der bewegte [*Footnote:* Der empirische Einwand, daß ein Toter nicht sprechen kann, steht dem Relativisten nicht zu, der selbst als Begründung für seine Behauptungen über Zeit und Raum nichts anderes anzuführen weiß, als daß sich „a priori" nichts gegen sie einwenden ließe.]! Es ist zu bedauern, daß die Relativitätstheoretiker das Einsteinsche Organismenbeispiel nicht gründlich weiter gedacht haben. Vielleicht wären ihnen dann noch einige Zweifel aufgestiegen, ob die Vertauschbarkeit den Standpunkte, die sie hinsichtlich des zeitlichen Geschehens unter der Bezeichnung „Relativierung der Zeit" eingeführt haben, sich durchführen läßt.

Es ist nur eine einzige Möglichkeit ersichtlich, aus den Widersprüchen, zu denen die „Relativierung den Zeit" führt, herauszukommen, wenn man nämlich dazu übergeht, jedem Standpunkt, Organismus, Beobachter, Subjekt oder „Monade" eine e i g e n e   W e l t zuzuordnen, die mit den Welten anderer, bewegter Monaden nichts zu tun hat. Der „Relativierung der Zeit" fügt man so eine „Relativierung des Seins" hinzu, d. h. mit anderen Worten: die E i n d e u t i g k e i t des Naturgeschehens für alle bewegten Monaden wind aufgehoben. Man kann auch so sagen: es wird der Standpunkt eines physikalischen Solipsismus eingenommen. Es weist kein Anzeichen darauf hin, daß die in den erkenntnistheoretischen Fragen sehr unklaren Relativitätstheoretiker einen solchen Ausweg beabsichtigt oder überhaupt nur erwogen haben. Auch Minkowski, der von seiner eigenen „Verwegenheit mathematischer Kultur" spricht, scheint d i e s e Verwegenheit der Relativierung des Seins, zu der er bei konsequentem Festhalten an dem einmal beschrittenen Wege gedrängt wird, nicht im Auge gehabt zu haben. Wie denn überhaupt die Denkrichtung den Relativitätstheoretiker auf den mathematischen Ausbau and die formalistische Struktur der Theorie gerichtet ist, und   n i c h t in die erkenntnistheoretische Vertiefung und Klarstellung.

Immerhin deuten manche Äußerungen Einsteins, gerade in seinen sogenannten „allgemeinverständlichen" Darlegungen, darauf hin, daß ihm die inneren Schwierigkeiten seiner Lehre nicht ganz fremd waren. Wenn er z. B. gelegentlich behauptet hat, daß der Begriff der G l e i c h z e i t i g k e i t zweier Ereignisse keinen Sinn habe, so läßt diese zunächst mystische Ausdrucksweise vermuten, daß Einstein gefühlt hat, etwas Besonderes erfinden zu müssen, um innere Widersprüche zu vermeiden. Bei Klarlegung des erkenntnistheoretischen Standpunkts der Relativitätstheorie als eines Solipsismus erscheint allerdings das Sinnlose der Gleichzeitigkeit als eine zulässige Selbstverständlichkeit. Es ist aber keine Kunst, einen Widerspruch dadurch zu vermeiden, daß man implicite den Grundsatz einführt: es bezieht sich die e i n e Aussage, die einer zweiten Aussage widerspricht, auf eine ganz a n d e r e W e l t als die zweite. Die Sonderbarkeiten der Relativitätstheorie, ihre angebliche Reform der Erkenntnistheorie mündet immer wieder in den oben gekennzeichneten Standpunkt aus, den man p h y s i k a l i s c h e n S o l i p s i s m u s nennen kann. Dieser Standpunkt ist der eines Menschen, welcher in die äußerste Enge getrieben ist, der seine Sache bis aufs letzte verficht, und schließlich, um sich zu retten, die Erklärung abgibt: ich habe nicht, denn Du hast a u c h recht, weil wir beide verschiedenen W e l t e n angehören und deshalb unsere Aussagen gar nicht miteinander vergleichen können! Wenn man den „ Zeitbegriff relativiert", so zerstört man die Idee der einen, a l l g e m e i n e n, o b j e k t i v e n Natur; wenn die eine Monade ihre Eigenzeit, von den Relativisten t genannt, die andere ihre Eigenzeit, t' genannt, hat, so muß auch jede Monade ganz für sich ihre eigene Welt oder Natur haben, und so wenig man den Zeiten t und t' „gleichzeitige" Augenblicke erlaubt, ebensowenig sind auch in den Welten der beiden Monaden ein und dieselben D i n g e vorhanden, höchstens können beide Welten miteinander gewisse Ähnlichkeiten aufweisen. Die Relativitätstheorie führt also nur zu einem alten, abgelebten, skeptischen Standpunkt. Das ist die „neue Revolution des modernen Denkens", die die Relativitätstheorie enzeugt hat!

Wir werden es uns versagen können, nach dem Obigen noch die Relativierung des Raumes in der Relativitätstheorie näher zu erörtern. Wenn Minkowski von sich sagt, er habe Einsteins „Hinwegschreiten über die Zeit" durch ein „Hinwegschreiten über den Raum'' vervollständigt, so hat er damit eine Folgerung gezogen, die ihm nur deshalb bewundernswürdig erschienen ist, weil er selbst sich prinzipiell so unklar war.

Relativitätstheorie und Gravitation. Die erste Relativitätstheorie Einsteins, welche er später „die spezielle'' genannt hat, wurde von ihm ersetzt durch eine zweite „allgemeine'' Relativitätstheorie, die die ursprünglichen Mängel der ersten Theorie nicht haben sollte. Nun ist aber das Verhältnis der beiden Theorien zueinander nur in f o r m a l e r Hinsicht das des Speziellen zum Allgemeinen, während in grundsätzlichen Fragen ein erheblicher, bis zum Widerspruch gesteigerter Unterschied besteht. Die allgemeine Relativitätstheorie ist dadurch gekennzeichnet, daß in ihr die allgemeine Schwere (Gravitation) eine besondere Rolle spielt, ferner ist besonders bezeichnend für sie ein allgemeines Relativitätsprinzip, d. h. die Behauptung den Relativität a l l e r Bewegungen, auch die der Rotationen.

Abgesehen von den mit den „Relativierung von Zeit und Raum'' verbundenen, oben erwähnten Schwierigkeiten sind es auch Bedenken mehr empirischer Natur, die die allgemeine Form der Einsteinschen Relativitätstheorie als undurchführbar erscheinen lassen. Ein Beispiel wird dies deutlich machen können. Angenommen, wir setzen uns auf den in manchen Vergnügungsstätten sehr beliebten Apparat, genannt Drehscheibe, oder wir setzen uns auf eins der altmodischen Karussels, so soll es nach der Relativitätstheorie ebensogut möglich sein zu behaupten, daß das Karussel fährt, als daß das Karussel still steht und die g a n z e A u ß e n w e l t sich um das Karussel dreht. Also der Auffassung des gewöhnlichen Menschen: das Karussel fährt: soll die Behauptung des Relativisten gleichwertig sein: die ganze Welt fährt um das stillstehende Karussel im Kreise herum! Hierbei kommt der Relativist nicht nur nur zu der von seinem eigenen, theoretischen Staudpunkt aus störenden Folgerung, daß er den in großen Abständen vom Karussel stehenden Naturkörpern, wie z. B. allen Fixsternen, ungeheure Geschwindigkeiten beilegen muß, welche die auch der Theorie höchst zulässige Geschwindigkeit, die Lichtgeschwindigkeit, erheblich übersteigen, er muß auch noch besondere, seltsame Naturerscheinungen hinzudichten, um den Ablauf der Erscheinungen, wie er sich abspielt, beschreiben zu können. Er muß nämlich annehmen, daß die bei der Rotation der Welt auftretenden Zentrifugalkräfte durch eine Schwerkraft kompensiert werden, welche proportional dem Abstand von der Drehungsachse des Karussels zunimmt und welche im Raume des Karussels selbst ihr Vorzeichen umkehrt. Für ein solches Schwerkraftfeld ist aber keine Veranlassung erkennbar, abgesehen davon, daß sich auch mathematisch überhaupt keine Massenanordnung ersinnen läßt, die ein Schwerefeld erzeugen können, welches den mathematischen Bedingungen des Problems zu genügen vermöchte. In der Tat ist das Vorgehen des Relativisten, der die ganze Welt in Rotation, um ein Karussel versetzt und der zu diesem Zweck ein physikalisch unmögliches Gravitationsfeld voraussetzt, rein fiktiv, physikalisch unzulässig. Der Standpunkt des Relativisten gleicht dem eines Menschen, welchem ein Geldstück gestohlen worden ist und der behauptet: ich kann entweder annehmen daß der Dieb das Geldstück gestohlen hat, o d e r ich kann annehmen, daß der Dieb d i e g a n z e W e l t gestohlen hat, nur n i c h t das Geldstück. Die zweite „Denkmöglichkeit" scheidet aus Gründen der Erfahrung, „a posteriori", aus, und es ist deshalb n i c h t möglich, hier eine „Relativität" der Standpunkte einzunehmen. Genau so ist es auch mit dem Standpunkt des Relativitätstheoretikers gegenüber der Rotation eines Karussels, er widerspricht aller Erfahrung. Wer sich über diese Seite der Gegnerschaft gegen die Relativitätstheorie näher unterrichten will, dem seien die Schriften von Lenard angelegentlichst empfohlen, besonders die Broschüre: Über Relativitätsprinzip, Äther, Gravitation. Verlag von S. Hirzel, Leipzig 1920, von der ausgehend man auch den Weg zu der übrigen Literatur üben den Gegenstand findet.

Die Grundlage der allgemeinen Relativitätstheorie leidet auch an dem Mangel, keinen i n n e r e Grund für die Annahme eines S c h w e r e feldes für die zur Durchführung der Theorie benötigten Beschleunigungsfelder erkennen zu lassen. Man kann nicht einsehen, warum gerade die G r a v i t a t i o n berufen ist, als Ursache für Beschleunigungen angesehen zu werden, wo doch auch a n d e r e Ursachen für Beschleunigungen denkbar sind, wie Kräfte im Äther, Kapillaritätskräfte usw. Durch die Einführung der Gravitation, also einer empirischen, physikalischen Erscheinung in die Grundgleichungen der Relativitätstheorie, wird jedenfalls der Boden der reinen, mathematischen Konstruktion verlassen und ein physikalisches, empirisches Element hineingezogen. Der Relativist kann sich daher nicht mehr in der Rolle des abstrakten Mathematikers allein verhalten, sondern er muß es sich gefallen lassen, daß der Physiker die Theorie als eine empirisch richtig sein sollende objektiv prüft. Fällt diese Prüfung zu ungunsten des Relativisten aus, so muß dieser seine Theorie aufgeben und kann eventuell eine neue ersinnen. Es geht aber nicht an, daß der Relativist d e s h a l b an seiner Theorie festhält, weil er sie mathematisch schön findet. Abgesehen von allen logischen und erkenntnistheoretischen Erwägungen bleibt die Erfahrung der Hauptprüfstein jeder physikalischen Theorie, und so auch der Relativitätstheorie.

Die experimentelle Prüfung der Theorie.

Wer sich im praktischen Leben oder als Naturforscher betätigt, wird dem theoretischen Unterfangen, e i n e für alle Beobachter gleiche, objektive Natur in ihrer e i n e n Zeit und ihrem e i n e n Raume aufzugeben, wenig Vertrauen entgegenbringen.

Er wird daher auch nicht sonderlich erstaunt sein, wenn sich herausstellt, daß einzelne praktische Folgerungen einer solchen Theorie mit der Erfahrung in Widerspruch geraten. So wenig einerseits die Bestätigung einer F o l g e r u n g die Richtigkeit der T h e o r i e b e w e i s e n würde, — kann man doch häufig von ganz verschiedenen Grundlagen aus zu derselben, sich als richtig erweisenden Folgerung kommen, ohne damit etwas über die Richtigkeit der Grundlagen sagen zu können, — so sicher beweist andererseits eine als falsch sich herausstellende Folgerung, daß auch die Grundlage, aus der sie abgeleitet war, falsch sein muß. Die Relativitätstheorie hat die Prüfung an der Erfahrung schlecht bestanden. Dies soll im Folgenden kurz dargestellt werden.

Zunächst sei bemerkt, daß alle Folgerungen den Relativitätstheorie immer auf so winzige Effekte führen, daß es nicht einfach ist, die experimentelle Prüfung vorzunehmen. Das war bisher in gewissem Sinne ein Glück für die Theorie, die ja dadurch in die Lage versetzt ist, auf die Schwierigkeit des Experiments, die Ungenauigkeit den Beobachtungen hinzuweisen, wenn sich ein vorausgesagter Effekt nicht findet. Es gibt aber heute Beobachtungen, die so genau sind, daß man diesen Schluß nicht mehr ziehen kann.

In ersten Linie ist hier die sogenannte Rotverschiebung der Spektrallinien zu erwähnen. Eine Spektralinie wird durch gewisse Schwingungen in einem Gase erzeugt, das leuchtet. Auch auf unserer Sonne, welche nach den Ergebnissen der Astronomie und Astrophysik ein sehr hoch erhitzter Gasball ist, werden Spektrallinien beobachtet. Nur soll nach der Relativitätstheorie die Zeitdauer irgend eines Vorgangs vom Schwerkraft-(Gravitations-)felde abhängig sein, also sollten auch die Schwingungsvorgänge aller Spektrallinien auf der Sonne vom Gravitationsfeld der Sonne abhängen. Dieses letztere ist aber erheblich stärker als das Gravitationsfeld der Erde, so daß die Spektrallinien eines Gases auf der Sonne gegenüber den Spektrallinien derselben Gasart auf der Erde einen Unterschied zeigen sollten — behauptet die Relativitätstheorie. Für die Größe dieses Unterschiedes und sein Vorzeichen sind Formeln aufgestellt worden. Sie besagen, daß die Spektrallinien der Sonne eine geringe Verschiebung nach der roten Seite des Spektrums erleiden müssen, im Betrage von 0,01 sogenannten Angström-Einheiten. Die Kleinheit dieses Betrages ist für jeden ersichtlich, wenn man ihn in Millimeter ausdrückt: er beträgt ein Milliardstel eines Millimeters. Dieser kleine Effekt, dessen Bestehen die Relativitätstheorie prophezeit hat und fordert, kann aber heutzutage mit den hochentwickelten Meßeinrichtungen gesucht werden und würde den modernen Instrumenten nicht entgehen, wenn er da wäre. Der Effekt ist sorgfältig gesucht worden, hat sich aber n i c h t finden lassen:

Zuerst ist die relativistische Rotverschiebung an Stickstofflinien der Sonne auf dem astrophysikalischen Institut in Potsdam gesucht worden; Schwarzschild [*Footnote:* Sitzungsbericht der Berliner Akademie der Wissenschaft 1914, S. 1201-1213.], der verstorbene Direktor des Instituts, hat das Ergebnis im Jahre 1914 veröffentlicht; er findet k e i n e Rotverschiebung. Dann hat der bekannte amerikanische Astrophysiker St. John nach der Rotverschiebung gesucht und sie ebenfalls nicht gefunden. St. John sagt in seinem Bericht vom Jahre 1917 über das Ergebnis seiner Versuche [*Footnote:* St. John, Carnegie Institution of Washington, Mount Wilson Solar Observatory Communications to the National Academy of Sciences No. 46. Vol. **3**, 450-452, July 1917.]: „Das allgemeine Ergebnis der Untersuchung ist, daß innenhalb der Beobachtungsfehler die Messungen kein Anzeichen eines Effektes von der Größenordnung ergeben, die aus dem Relativitätsprinzip abgeleitet wird." Die Beobachtungsfehler St.

Johns waren nur ein Bruchteil von dem geforderten, nicht vorhandenen Einstein-Effekt. Hale, der bekannte Sonnenforschen und Direktor der Mount-Wilson-Sternwarte, hat sich für die Richtigkeit St. Johns Beobachtungen ausgesprochen [*Footnote:* Z. B. im Annual Report of the Direktor of the Mount Wilson Solar-Observatory, Yearbook, Nr. 16, S. 200, 1917.]. Diese Untersuchungen auf Mount Wilson, mit den besten Instrumenten unter den günstigsten Arbeits- und Beobachtungsbedingungen, wie sie zurzeit kein anderes astrophysikalisches Institut auf der Erde aufweisen kann, hätten den Einstein-Effekt unzweifelhaft feststellen müssen, wenn er existierte. Demgegenüber will es wenig heißen, wenn neuerdings ein Mitarbeiter von Einstein, Herr Freundlich, mit der Behauptung aufgetreten ist, daß die Amerikaner eine Fehlerquelle in ihren Messungen gehabt haben; die Zusammenstellung und kritische Würdigung dieses gesamten Materials wird in einer demnächst von fachmännischer Seite in Aussicht gestellten Druckschrift von. L. C. Glaser gegeben werden, auf die hier verwiesen sei.

Die Rotverschiebung der Spektrallinien auf der Sonne stellt bisher den Haupteffekt der Relativitätstheorie dar, er ist entschieden die wichtigste, weil am genauesten zu prüfende Folgerung, deren Nichtvorhandensein als eine experimentelle Widerlegung der Relativitätstheorie anzusehen ist — wenn es einer solchen überhaupt noch bedurft hätte. Andere Folgerungen der Relativitätstheorie sind für die Theorie weniger charakteristisch, weil sich sofort verschiedene andere Erklärungsmöglichkeiten darbieten. Da ist z. B. die sogenannte Perihelstörung des Planeten Merkur zu nennen. Nach den Beobachtungen der Astronomen dreht sich die Bahnellipse des Merkur um einen sehr kleinen Betrag von 43 Bogensekunden in 100 Jahren. Auch dies ist eine ungeheuer kleine Größe, aber sie ist dank der Feinheit der astronomischen Beobachtungsmethoden feststellbar. Es sind schon seit vielen Jahren Erklärungen für diese Bahnstörung des Merkur gegeben worden, insbesondere muß hier die Formel des Oberlehrers Gerber vom Jahre 1898 genannt werden [*Footnote:* Die schwer zugängliche Veröffentlichung Gerbers ist in den Annalen der Physik Bd. **52**, Seite 415, 1917 im Neuabdruck erschienen.], die dieser aufgestellt hat, als es noch gar keine Relativitätstheorie gab und die völlig mit der aus der Relativitätstheorie von Einstein abgeleiteten Formel übereinstimmt. Hier könnte die Relativitätstheorie nur dann als eine gewisse, und zwar die zuletzt gegebene, Erklärungsmöglichkeit für eine an sich bekannte Sache angesehen werden, wenn sie im übrigen einwandfrei wäre.

Endlich ist noch ein, neuerdings in der Tagespresse mit besonderer Breite behandelter Effekt zu nennen: die Ablenkung der Sternorte in der Nähe der Sonne. Auch hier ist die Sache durchaus nicht so neu, als es auf den ersten Blick den Anschein hat, denn man kennt in der Astronomie schon lange gewisse systematische Abweichungen der Sternorte in Abhängigkeit von der Stellung des Sterns zur Sonne. Diese Erscheinung, die als jährliche Refraktion bezeichnet wird, ist bisher noch nicht erklärt, obschon ein erhebliches Tatsachenmaterial über den Gegenstand vorliegt, das bis in die Mitte des vorigen Jahrhunderts zurückreicht; man kann sich hierüber z. B. aus einer Abhandlung von L. Courvoisier, Beobachtungsergebnisse der Kgl. Sternwarte zu Berlin Nr. 15 vom Jahre 1913 unterrichten. Einstein hat nun ebenfalls eine Abhängigkeit der Sternorte in Abhängigkeit von der Sonne aus seiner Relativitätstheorie gefolgert und es sind Messungen darüber von englischen Expeditionen gelegentlich der Sonnenfinsternis des Jahres 1919 angestellt werden. Die Beurteilung dieser Beobachtungen ist schwierig, da die Originalberichte noch nicht alle gedruckt vorliegen und die Angaben über die in der englischen Akademie in London vorgelegten Mitteilungen der verschiedenen Forscher nicht einheitlich sind. Jedenfalls steht fest, daß die deutsche Fachwelt und Presse bisher in einseitiger, für Einsteins Theorie zu günstiger Weise unterrichtet worden ist. Dies geht z. B. aus Äußerungen des Londoner Astronomen Silberstein hervor, der darauf aufmerksam macht [*Footnote:* Abgedruckt in: Die Naturwissenschaften **8**, 390, 1920.], daß das in der physikalischen Gesellschaft in Berlin erstattete Referat in wesentlichen Punkten Irrtümer enthielt, deren Berichtigung das Ergebnis den Messungen zu Ungunsten von Einsteins Theorie verschiebt. Über den Effekt der Sternorte in der Nähe der Sonne läßt sich also zurzeit nichts Sicheres aussagen. Aber er ist für die Theorie gar nicht so wichtig, da er, selbst wenn die von Einstein angegebene Verschiebung der Sternorte um 1¾ Bogensekunden am Sonnenrande tatsächlich sicher beobachtet wäre, noch eine ganze Reihe anderer Erklärungsversuche, die physikalisch viel verständlicher sind als die Deutung durch die Relativitätstheorie, gegeben werden können. Es ist übrigens hier die Kleinheit des Betrages von nur 1¾ Bogensekunden ein erhebliches Hindernis für das Experiment; um von diesem Betrage eine Vorstellung zu geben, sei erwähnt, daß der kleine Winkel 1¾ Bogensekunden diejenige Größe hat, unter der dem Auge eine Kirsche in 2 Kilometer Entfernung erscheint.

Welches Urteil wird man sich über die Relativitätstheorie zu bilden haben?

Das ist die Frage, die nunmehr zu beantworten ist.

Die Einsteinsche Relativitätstheorie nimmt ihren Ursprung aus einer Theorie des holländischen Physikers Lorentz. Die übereinstimmung mit der Lorentzschen Theorie geht so weit, daß die m a t h e m a t i s c h e Form der Einsteinschen Theorie vom Jahre 1905 wesentlich dieselbe ist, wie die von Lorentz, die Gleichungen dieser Einsteinschen Theorie sind die Gleichungen von Lorentz. Neuartig erschien die D e u t u n g der Theorie, die I n t e r p r e t a t i o n der Grundbegriffe Zeit und Raum. Einstein hat mit dieser Interpretation etwas getan, von dem seine Bewunderer gesagt haben, es stelle alles bisher Dagewesene in den Schatten. Die Interpretation Einsteins war aber gleichfalls weit weniger neu, als es den Anschein hatte. Schon im jahre 1901 hat der ungarische Philosoph Melchior Palágyi in Engelmanns Verlag in Leipzig eine Schrift in deutscher Sprache [*Footnote:* Neue Theorie des Raumes und der Zeit. Von Dr. Melchior Palágyi. Verlag Engelmann, Leipzig 1901.] erscheinen lassen, die wesentliche Gedanken Einsteins und Minkowskis, des begeisterten, mathematischen Anhängers Einsteins, vorwegnahm: so besonders die Idee der „Union zwischen Zeit und Raum‘‘, die Auffassung der „Welt‘‘ in 4 Koordinaten, von denen die eine, die Zeit, mit der imagären Einheit

$$\sqrt{-1}$$

multipliziert auftritt usw. Den Physikern waren diese Vorgänge — zum Teil heute noch—unbekannt, sie nahmen die Relativitätslehre Einsteins teils kopfschüttelnd, teils abwartend auf. Als aber anerkannte Autoritäten sich begeistert für die Relativitätstheorie einsetzten, trat auch im Publikum Begeisterung auf, und nun nahm die Entwicklung ihren unaufhaltsamen Gang. Bei der Verknüpfung mathematischer, physikalischer und philosophischer Gedanken in der Relativitätstheorie war es den Fachleuten in unserer Zeit des hochgesteigerten, wissenschaftlichen Spezialistentums sehr schwer gemacht, zu einem selbständigen Urteil über die Theorie zu gelangen, zumal Einstein sein Werk mit Geschicklichkeit zu verteidigen wußte und den Physikern ihre Bedenken mit mathematischen und philosophischen, den Mathematikern ihre Bedenken mit physikalischen und philosophischen, den Philosophen ihre Bedenken mit mathematischen und physikalischen Gegengründen zerstreute: jeder Fachmann beugte sich vor der Autorität des Kollegen im andern Fach, jeder glaubte das, was er nach andern Fachautoritäten als für bewiesen halten zu sollen vermeinte. **Niemand wollte sich dem Vorwurf aussetzen, er verstände nichts von der Sache!** Und so wurde eine Lage geschaffen, ähnlich der von Andersen geschilderten in seinem Märchen „Des Kaisers neue Kleider": hier sieht ein Kaiser mit seinen Ministern und Untertanen dem Weben eines Gewandes zu, das die Eigenart hat, von denjenigen Menschen n i c h t gesehen zu werden, die dazu nicht klug genug sind, und schließlich stehen a l l e staunend vor den leeren Webstühlen, weil niemand sich getraut zu bekennen, daß er nichts sieht. So hat auch die Relativitätstheorie die Geister gefesselt, sie ist zur Massensuggestion geworden. Aber eine Massensuggestion ist an sich nichts Verwerfliches, die Ausschaltung des klaren Verstandes braucht durchaus kein Beweis dafür zu sein, daß das Streben der Masse ein törichtes ist. Alles hing bei der Relativitätstheorie davon ab, ob sie in ein erkenntnistheoretisch annehmbares Fahrwasser geleitet werden konnte.

Einstein hat die Schwächen seiner Theorie öfters zu verbessern und den Einwänden auszuweichen gesucht, er hat z. B. das Relativitätsprinzip hin und hergeworfen (s. oben S. 57 ff.), er hat schließlich geglaubt, den sicheren Hafen erreicht zu haben und im Jahre 1915 erklärt [*Footnote:* Sitzungsberichte der Berliner Akademie 1915, S. 847.], daß endlich die Relativitätstheorie als logisches Gebäude abgeschlossen sei. Ein Punkt bei all diesen Wandlungen ist noch besonders wichtig, hervorgehoben zu werden: so wenig neuartig die mathematische Form der e r s t e n Relativitätstheorie Einsteins ist, die mit der älteren Lorentzschen Theorie übereinstimmt, so wenig ist auch die im weiteren Verlauf der Entwicklung durch Einstein vollzogene V e r ä n d e r u n g des mathematischen Gewandes der Theorie besonders neuartig gewesen: daß die Relativitätstheorie in die Formeln der nichteuklidischen

Geometrie hineinführt, zeigte zuerst der Mathematiker Varicak; daß die mathematische Komplikation der nichteuklidischen Kontinua von den Mathematikern formal bereits seit langem gelöst war, erkennt sogar Einstein an. Inwieweit Einstein die neueste von Weyl u. a. eingeschlagene, relativitätstheoretische Richtung überhaupt noch mitmacht, ist nicht recht klar. Jedenfalls verbreiten Anhänger von Einstein Nachrichten, die für die Weylschen Arbeiten ungünstig lauten.

Wenn es also feststeht, daß Einstein in seiner Relativitätstheorie keine mathematisch ungewöhnlichen Formen entdeckt hat, wenn die philosophisch-erkenntnistheoretische Grundlage des ganzen Gebäudes unbefriedigend ist, wenn endlich die Experimente der Physiker und Astronomen die Theorie night beweisen können, so wird man fragen, was denn überhaupt noch übrig bleibt, um in der Relativitätstheorie ein Werk zu erblicken, das über die Taten von Kopernikus, Kepler und Newton hinausgeht. Diese Frage werden die heutigen Anhänger und Gegner der Theorie, je nach ihrem persönlichen Gefühl, verschieden beantworten. Eine Antwort, die alle befriedigt, wird sich erst erzielen lassen, wenn die Suggestion der Reklame und der Druckerschwärze, mit welcher die „revolutionäre Relativitätstheorie" arbeitet, von allen als solche erkannt ist. Zu dieser Aufklärung beitragen zu helfen mögen die obigen Zeilen dienen."

Gehrcke effectively accused Einstein of plagiarizing the mathematical formalisms of Lorentz, the space-time concepts of Palágyi,[163] and the non-Euclidean Geometry of Varičak.[164] Albert Einstein's first wife Mileva Marić would have been able to have read *all* of Varičak's works. She also would have been able to have understood all of Smoluchowski's lectures. She could also read English, making her the likely source of many of the works Albert Einstein plagiarized from English-speaking authors.[165] Gehrcke also accused Albert Einstein of masking his plagiarism and the weaknesses of the theory of relativity with irrational Metaphysics. Gehrcke stood up and declared that, "the Emperor has no clothes!"—an admission Einstein had already privately made to Heinrich Zangger on Christmas Eve of 1919.[166] Gehrcke said that people were often afraid to admit that they did not understand the theory of relativity, and were in stupefied awe of that which they did not understand, not in informed appreciation of the theory. Einstein had made the exact same statements in his private correspondence, but shamelessly called Gehrcke anti-Semitic when he reiterated Einstein's own beliefs.

Einstein's only response came days later in a frantic, inappropriately emotional and irrational "hand-waving" *ad hominem* attack against Lenard, Weyland and Gehrcke. Einstein simply appealed to authority—his hangers-on, and those from whom he had plagiarized the theory of relativity. Einstein's response appeared in the *Berliner Tageblatt* on pages 1 and 2 on 27 August 1920.

Nobel Prize laureate Philipp Lenard had had no involvement in the Berlin Philharmonic lectures. Even Einstein's friends condemned Einstein's flippant, inaccurate and racially-charged response. Sommerfeld wrote to Lenard and pleaded with Lenard to forgive Einstein, who had misrepresented Lenard's involvement in the event. Lenard must have been outraged that Sommerfeld should be the one to write to him, not Einstein, and Lenard must have been outraged that Einstein apologized not only through a proxy, but privately.

Nobel Prize laureate Philipp Lenard demanded a personal public apology from Albert Einstein to be attended with as much publicity as Einstein's (and Max von Laue's) cowardly and unscrupulous personal attacks against Lenard. Einstein's apology was not forthcoming.[167] *After* the Bad Nauheim debate, where Lenard destroyed Einstein in a debate, Max Planck and Franz Himstedt stated to the press that Einstein had regretted including Lenard in his personal attack, because Lenard had not granted Weyland leave to place his name on the list of speakers at the Berlin Philharmonic lectures. The *Berliner Tageblatt* morning edition 25 September 1920 ran this story. This was obviously not an adequate apology for Einstein's vicious and deceitful smears.[168]

Einstein could not defend himself or his position other than to change the subject to a personal attack against his opponents. He pouted and whined like a spoiled brat in order to avoid the bulk of accusations made against him and the theory of relativity. Instead of arguing the issues, Einstein wanted to wait for others to speak on his behalf in defense of the theory. He was not competent to defend the theory himself. Einstein, who was himself a racist who believed that anti-Semitism was justified and proper and helpful to Jews, hypocritically tried to change the subject to race in order to attack his opponents as if racists. Albert Einstein wrote in the *Berliner Tageblatt*, Morgen Augabe, 27 August 1920, pp. 1-2:

"Meine Antwort

Ueber die anti-relativitätstheoretische G. m. b. H.

Von
Albert Einstein.

Unter dem anspruchsvollen Namen „Arbeitsgemeinschaft deutscher Naturforscher‟ hat sich eine bunte Gesellschaft zusammengetan, deren vorläufiger Daseinszweck es ist, die Relativitätstheorie und mich als deren Urheber in den Augen der Nichtphysiker herabzusetzen. Neulich haben die Herren Weyland und Gehrke in der Philharmonie einen ersten Vortrag in diesem Sinne gehalten, bei dem ich selber zugegen war. Ich bin mir sehr wohl des Umstandes bewußt, daß die beiden Sprecher einer Antwort aus meiner Feder unwürdig sind; denn ich habe guten Grund zu glauben, daß andere Motive als das Streben nach Wahrheit diesem Unternehmen zugrunde liegen. (Wäre ich Deutschnationaler mit oder ohne Hakenkreuz statt Jude von freiheitlicher, internationaler Gesinnung, so . . .) Ich antworte nur deshalb, weil dies von wohlwollender Seite wiederholt gewünscht worden ist, damit meine Auffassung bekannt werde.

Zuerst bemerke ich, daß es heute meines Wissens kaum einen Forscher gibt, der in der theoretischen Physik etwas Erhebliches geleistet hat und nicht zugäbe, daß die ganze Relativitätstheorie in sich logisch aufgebaut und mit den bisher sicher ermittelten Erfahrungstatsachen im Einklang ist. Die bedeutendsten theoretischen Physiker — ich nenne H. A. Lorentz, M. Planck, Sommerfeld, Laue, Born, Larmor, Eddington, Debye, Langevin, Levi-Civita — stehen auf dem Boden der Theorie und haben meist wertvolle Beiträge zu derselben geleistet. Als ausgesprochenen Gegner der Relativitätstheorie wüßte ich unter den Physikern von internationaler Bedeutung nur Lenard zu nennen. Ich bewundere Lenard als Meister der Experimentalphysik; in der theoretischen Physik aber hat er noch nichts geleistet, und seine Einwände gegen die allgemeine Relativitätstheorie sind von solcher Oberflächlichkeit, daß ich es bis jetzt nicht für nötig erachtet habe, ausführlich auf dieselben zu antworten. Ich gedenke es nachzuholen.

Es wird mir vorgeworfen, daß ich für die Relativitätstheorie eine geschmacklose Reklame betreibe. Ich kann wohl sagen, daß ich zeitlebens ein Freund des wohlerwogenen, nüchternen Wortes und der knappen Darstellung gewesen bin. Vor hochtönenden Phrasen und Worten bekomme ich eine Gänsehaut, mögen sie von sonst etwas oder von Relativitätstheorie handeln. Ich habe mich oft lustig gemacht über Ergüsse, die nun zuguterletzt mir aufs Konto gesetzt werden. Uebrigens lasse ich den Herren von der G. m. b. H. gerne das Vergnügen.

Nun zu den Vorträgen. Herr W e y l a n d, der gar kein Fachmann zu sein scheint (Arzt? Ingenieur? Politiker? Ich konnt's nicht erfahren), hat gar nichts Sachliches vorgebracht. Er erging sich in plumpen Grobheiten und niedrigen Anschuldigungen. Der zweite Redner, Herr Gehrke, hat teils direkte Unrichtigkeiten vorgebracht, teils hat er durch einseitige Auswahl des Materials und Entstellung beim unwissenden Laien einen falschen Eindruck hervorzurufen versucht. Folgende Beispiele mögen das zeigen:

Herr G e h r k e behauptet, daß die Relativitätstheorie zum — Solipsismus führe, eine Behauptung, die jeder Kenner als Witz begrüßen wird. Er stützt sich dabei auf das bekannte Beispiel von den beiden Uhren (oder Zwillingen), deren e i n e in bezug auf das Inertialsystem eine Rundreise durchmacht, die andere nicht. Er behauptet — trotzdem ihm dies von den besten Kennern der Theorie schon oft mündlich und schriftlich widerlegt worden ist —, die Theorie führe in diesem Falle zu dem wirklich unsinnigen Resultat, daß von zwei nebeneinander ruhenden Uhren jede der anderen gegenüber nachgehe. Ich kann dies nur als einen Versuch absichtlicher Irreführung des Laienpublikums auffassen.

Herr Gehrke spielt ferner auf Herrn Lenards Einwände an, die viele auf Beispiele der Mechanik aus dem alltäglichen Leben beziehen. Diese sind schon hinfällig auf Grund meines allgemeinen Beweises, daß die Aussagen der allgemeinen Relativitätstheorie in erster Näherung mit denen der klassischen Mechanik übereinstimmen.

Was Herr Gehrke über die experimentelle Bestätigung der Theorie gesagt hat, ist mir aber der schlagendste Beweis dafür, daß es ihm nicht um die Enthüllung des wahren Sachverhalts zu tun war.

Herr Gehrke will glauben machen, daß die Perihelbewegung des Merkur auch ohne Relativitätstheorie zu erklären sei. Es gibt da zwei Möglichkeiten. Entweder man erfindet besondere interplanetare Massen, die so groß und so verteilt sind, daß sie eine Perihelbewegung von dem wahrgenommenen Betrage ergeben; dies ist natürlich ein höchst unbefriedigender Ausweg gegenüber dem von der Relativitätstheorie gegebenen, welche die Perihelbewegung des Merkur ohne irgendwelche besondere Annahme liefert. Oder aber man beruft sich auf eine Arbeit von Gerber, der die richtige Formel für die Perihelbewegung des Merkur bereits vor mir angegeben hat. Aber die Fachleute sind nicht nur darüber einig, daß Gerbers Ableitung durch und durch unrichtig ist, sondern die Formel ist als Konsequenz der von Gerber an die Spitze gestellten Annahmen überhaupt nicht zu gewinnen. Herrn Gerbers Arbeit ist daher völlig wertlos, ein mißglückter und irreparabler theoretischer Versuch. Ich konstatiere, daß die allgemeine Relativitätstheorie die erste wirkliche Erklärung für die Perihelbewegung des Merkur geliefert hat. Ich habe die Gerbersche Arbeit ursprünglich schon deshalb nicht erwähnt, weil ich sie nicht kannte, als ich meine Arbeit über die Perihelbewegung des Merkur schrieb; ich hätte aber auch keinen Anlaß gehabt, sie zu erwähnen, wenn ich von ihr Kenntnis gehabt hätte. Der diesbezügliche persönliche Angriff, welchen die Herren Gehrke und Lenard auf Grund dieses Umstandes gegen mich gerichtet haben, ist von den wirklichen Fachlauten allgemein als unfair betrachtet worden; ich hielt es bisher für unter meiner Würde, darüber ein Wort zu verlieren.

Herr Gehrke hat die Zuverlässigkeit der meisterhaft durchgeführten englischen Messungen über die Ablenkung der Lichtstrahlen an der Sonne in seinem Vortrage dadurch in einem schiefen Lichte erscheinen lassen, daß er von den d r e i unabhängigen Aufnahmegruppen nur e i n e erwähnte, welche infolge Verzerrung des Heliostatenspiegels fehlerhafte Resultate ergeben mußte. Er hat verschwiegen, daß die englischen Astronomen selbst in ihrem offiziellen Berichte ihre Ergebnisse als eine glänzende Bestätigung der allgemeinen Relativitätstheorie gedeutet haben.

Herr Gehrke hat bezüglich der Frage der Rotverschiebung die Spektrallinien verschwiegen, daß die bisherigen Bestimmungen noch einander widersprechen, und daß eine endgültige Entscheidung dieser Angelegenheit noch aussteht. Er hat nur die Zeugen g e g e n das Bestehen der von der Relativitätstheorie vorhergesagten Linienverschiebung angeführt, hat aber verschwiegen, daß durch die neuesten

Untersuchungen von Grebe und Buchem und von Perot jene früheren Ergebnisse ihre Beweiskraft eingebüßt haben.

Endlich bemerke ich, daß auf meine Anregung hin in Neuheim auf der Naturforscherversammlung eine Diskussion über die Relativitätstheorie veranstaltet wird. Da kann jeder, der sich vor ein wissenschaftliches Forum wagen darf, seine Einwände vorbringen.

Es wird im Auslande, besonders auf meine holländischen und englischen Fachgenossen H. A. Lorentz und Eddington, die sich beide eingehend mit Relativitätstheorie beschäftigt und darüber wiederholt gelesen haben, einen sonderbaren Eindruck machen, wenn sie sehen, daß die Theorie sowie deren Urheber in Deutschland selbst derart verunglimpft wird."

Einstein knew that he had been very publicly exposed as a fraud. He decided to flee Germany. It was obvious to him that all of German science would stand against him for what he had done. Pro-Einstein newspapers came to his rescue and published alarmist nonsense and personal attacks by Einstein's friends. It came as a surprise to Einstein that Laue, Nernst and Rubens would campaign by personal attack in the newspapers to rescue Einstein's reputation.[169]

It was only reluctantly that Einstein then chose to put up any kind of a fight with his undignified rant in the *Berliner Tageblatt*. If his friends had not rescued him, Einstein would have left Germany in total defeat without having spoken a word in his defense. The *Berliner Tageblatt* reported on 27 August 1920, parroting (as opposed to mocking) the nationalistic tone von Laue and Einstein had condemned as "anti-Semitic", and cried out that the sky was falling, and spoke of Einstein as if of a god,

"**Albert Einstein will Berlin verlassen!** Die persönlichen Angriffe, die gegen Dr. Albert Einstein in der an dieser Stelle bereits gekennzeichneten Versammlung der „Arbeitsgemeinschaft deutscher Naturforscher" vorgebracht wurden, haben einen Erfolg gehabt, der für Berlin tief Beschämend ist: Albert Einstein, angewidert von den altdeutschen Anrempelungen und den pseudowissenschaftlichen Methoden seiner Gegner will der Reichshauptstadt den Rücken kehren. So also steht es im Jahre 1920 um die geistige Kultur Berlins! Ein deutscher Gelehrter von Weltruf, den die Holländer als Ehrenprofessor nach Leiden berufen, dem die amerikanische

Columbia-Universität die Große goldene Medaille verleiht, den schwedische und norwegische Gesellschaften zu ihrem Ehrenmitglied ernennen, dessen Werk über die Relativitätstheorie als eines der ersten deutschen Bücher nach dem Kriege in englischer Sprache erscheint: ein solcher Mann wird aus der Stadt, die sich für das Zentrum deutscher Geistesbildung hält, herausgeekelt. Eine Schande!

Wir können es noch nicht glauben, daß in dieser Angelegenheit, die nicht nur für die Welt der Wissenschaft von Bedeutung ist, das letzte Wort gesprochen sein soll. Die Berliner Universität hat die Pflicht, alles zu tun, um diesen hervorragenden Lehrer und Gelehrten sich und Berlin zu erhalten. Und Albert Einstein, der über niedrigen Anwürfen steht, wird hoffentlich nach ruhigerer Ueberlegung seinen Feinden nicht den Gefallen erweisen, vor ihrem sinnlosen Geschrei den Platz zu räumen. Wer die Ehre deutscher Wissenschaft auch in Zukunft hochhalten will, muß jetzt zu diesem Manne stehen."

The report in the *Berliner Tageblatt*, adopting and improving upon Lenard's tactics, sought to make it appear unpatriotic for Germans to enter into a scientific dispute with Einstein—the archangel of Berlin. Einstein had called the *Berliner Tageblatt* a hypocritical newspaper in the context of Socialism.[170] The *Berliner Tageblatt* turned Einstein's cowardly flight from the exposure of his plagiarism, the self-contradictions in relativity theory, and the uncertain evidence used to promote the man and his theory, into the crucifixion of the Messiah by a cabal of ungodly anti-German nationalistic Germans. More effective—more boldly dishonest—propaganda than that used to promote and sell Einstein to the public is hard to find.

Einstein had made his *ad hominem* attacks against the Berlin Philharmonic gathering with the cooperation of some members of the international press not only in an effort to smear his outspoken critics, but also to threaten anyone who dared side with them. The press orchestrated an overwhelming international defamation against Einstein's critics.

Einstein believed the majority of physicists sided with Lenard and Gehrcke and sought to suppress any public sympathy for their position. After the terrible hype of the 1919 eclipse observations, the press used Einstein and Einstein used the press. Einstein wrote to Sommerfeld in this context,

"It is a bad thing that every utterance of mine is made use of by journalists as a matter of business."[171]

Ad hominem attack and smear campaigns were Einstein's and his followers' preferred method of response to challenges to Einstein's priority and to relativity theory, as even Einstein's advocates were forced to concede in 1931,

"Even individual fanatic scientific advocates of the Einsteinian theory seem to have finally abandoned their tactic of cutting off any discussion about it with the threat that every criticism, even the most moderate and scrupulous ones, must be discredited as an obvious effluence of stupidity and malice. But even if these monstrous products of the 'Einstein frenzy' [*Einstein-Taumel*] now belong to history and are thus eliminated from consideration, thoroughly respectable reasons for a certain discomfort with relativity theory still do remain[.]"[172]

This was a response to the charge of such *ad hominem* attacks made in *Hundert Autoren gegen Einstein* (*100 Authors Against Einstein*),

"It is the aim of this publication to confront the terror of the Einsteinians with an overview of the quality and quantity of the opponents and opposing arguments."[173]

Ernst Gehrcke decided to fight propaganda with thoroughly documented fact, but initially came up on the losing side. Einstein's persona, as depicted in the corrupt press, was perhaps too endearing to be successfully countered by the facts. The press also largely made it impossible for Einstein's critics to argue their side to the public. Einstein often opted to hide from criticism, as even his advocates were forced to admit,

"Although Einstein himself, by nature a pure scientist, is uninterested in such academic disputes!"[174]

After decades of misrepresentations which promote Einstein as if he were an angelic figure, it is necessary to show that he was not only capable of plagiarism, but that we know for a fact that he committed far worse moral offenses—Einstein's plagiarism is among the least of his many sins. It is also helpful to know Einstein's habits. Einstein clearly plagiarized the special theory of relativity, as well as many important aspects of the general theory of relativity, from Jules Henri Poincaré and Hendrik Antoon Lorentz. In fact, Einstein evinced a career-long pattern of plagiarism and was often accused of appropriating the work of others. He tried to avoid these accusations and never refuted them.[175] For example, Einstein wrote to Willy Wien in 1916 when Ernst Gehrcke[176] effectively accused Einstein of plagiarizing Paul Gerber's formula for the perihelion motion of Mercury,

"[. . .]I am not going to respond to Gehrcke's tasteless and superficial attacks, because any informed reader can do this himself."[177]

It was clear that Einstein had an ethical obligation to acknowledge Gerber's priority. Einstein's close friends Friedrich Adler and Michele Besso wrote to him and pointed out that Einstein had repeated Gerber's formula.[178] It was terribly unfair, unethical and unprofessional of Einstein to respond to Gehrcke in the manner in which he did. Einstein had an ethical obligation to acknowledge Gerber's priority and explain why he had repeated his formula without an attribution. Einstein instead ridiculed Gerber and Gehrcke and asserted that he had no obligation to cite Gerber's work.

In another instance where Einstein took the coward's way out, a meeting was arranged to discuss Hans Vaihinger's[179] theory of fictions in 1920. Einstein pledged that he would attend this meeting. Knowing that Einstein would be devoured in a debate over his mathematical fictions, which confused induction with deduction, Wertheimer and Ehrenfest helped Einstein to fabricate an excuse to miss the meeting he had agreed to attend. Einstein was proven a liar.[180] He also hid from many other criticisms, and Einstein refused to answer T. J. J. See's many charges of plagiarism,[181] and refused to debate Arvid Reuterdahl or to answer his many charges of plagiarism.[182] When Robert Drill[183] criticized the theory of relativity, Einstein tried to persuade Max Born and Moritz Schlick to not respond to the critique, but if they did so, to hide from his arguments and merely ridicule Drill with insults.[184] Einstein hid from the French Academy of Sciences.[185] Einstein hid from Cardinal O'Connell.[186] Einstein hid from Cartmel.[187] Einstein hid from Dayton C. Miller's falsification of the special theory of relativity.[188] Miller challenged Einstein in the press over the course of many years. *The New York Times Index* lists several articles in which Miller's and William B. Cartmels' falsifications of the special theory of relativity are discussed.[189] Einstein and Lorentz were very worried by Miller's results and could not find fault with them.[190] Einstein told R. S. Shankland not to perform an experiment which might falsify the special theory of relativity,

"[Einstein] again said that more experiments were not necessary, and results such as Synge might find would be 'irrelevant.' [Einstein] told me not to do any experiments of this kind."[191]

Einstein knew he was caught at the Arbeitsgemeinschaft deutscher Naturforscher meeting in the Berlin Philharmonic, and wanted to run away from Germany. Einstein desired to hide from the Bad Nauheim debate, in which he had threatened to devour his opponents,[192] then Einstein—after being talked into appearing and after much hype promoting the event which attracted thousand of visitors—then Einstein, when losing the debate, ran away during the lunch break and again wanted to run away from Germany.[193]

Einstein prospered from hype. Einstein never exhibited his legendary genius in public. Instead, Einstein either appeared like a childish madman in public, or rattled off a script he had been told to recite. The press rescued him again and again, while he and they hid from, and suppressed, legitimate criticism. Einstein was unable to defend "his" theories.

3 EINSTEIN THE RACIST COWARD

Albert Einstein was a genocidal racist Zionist. He was appalled by the fact that most German Jews did not share his racist and segregationist views. Einstein ridiculed Jews who assimilated into German society. Einstein hypocritically and disingenuously dubbed all of his critics "anti-Semites". He was a coward who hid from criticism by smearing his critics. When he was finally forced to debate in Bad Nauheim, he made a fool of himself and ran away in the middle of the argument.

"The General Assembly, [***] Determines that Zionism is a form of racism and racial discrimination."—UNITED NATIONS GENERAL ASSEMBLY RESOLUTION NUMBER 3379[194]

"I get most joy from the emergence of the Jewish state in Palestine. It does seem to me that our kinfolk really are more sympathetic (at least less brutal) than these horrid Europeans. Perhaps things can only improve if only the Chinese are left, who refer to all Europeans with the collective noun 'bandits.'"—ALBERT EINSTEIN [195]

3.1 Introduction

The massive emigration of Eastern European Jews, coupled with the financial might of the Rothschild family and their lesser branches, and with the disproportionate Jewish domination of the press, resulted in tremendous power for the Jewish community, especially in America, England and Germany. Einstein used this organized Jewish power in a cowardly fashion to suppress open debate on the theory of relativity and his career of plagiarism. Einstein, himself a racist, hypocritically and disingenuously accused his critics of racism for saying the same things that Einstein himself had said both publicly and privately. Einstein counted on fellow racist Jews to rush to his defense simply because he was a Jew. His expectations were rewarded.

3.2 The Power of Jewish Tribalism Inhibits the Progress of Science and Deliberately Promotes "Racial" Discord

Just as the "Jewish press" refused to entertain criticism of Judaism in the *Kulturkampf* while they relentlessly ridiculed Catholicism specifically and Christianity generally, they refused to entertain criticism of their Jewish Messiah, Albert Einstein. However, Einstein's Nobel Prize was not awarded for the theory of relativity, because so many were aware of the fact that Albert Einstein had plagiarized the theory. Ernst Gehrcke[196] demonstrated that Paul Gerber had anticipated the general theory of relativity, as had Johann Georg von Soldner, making a Nobel Prize for that theory impossible. It was long known that Einstein had plagiarized the special theory of relativity from Lorentz and Poincaré. Instead of exposing the public to these facts, the Jewish dominated press smeared Einstein's critics, obstructed their access to the public, and shamelessly hyped Albert Einstein and the theory of relativity.

Reassured that corrupt elements in the press would rescue him, Einstein decided to stay in Berlin after the Berlin Philharmonic meeting where he had been publicly humiliated. On 3 September 1920, the *Berliner Tageblatt* proudly reported that Einstein would not run away:

"**Prof. Albert Einstein** wird, wie wir erfahren, einer Berufung ins Ausland nicht Folge leisten, sondern i n B e r l i n b l e i b e n. Dieser erfreuliche Entschluß des Gelehrten ist mit die Folge der zustimmenden Briefe, die infolge der Aktion der sogenannten Gesellschaft der Naturforscher an Einstein gelangt sind. Prof. Einstein wird, ehe er seine Gastvorlesungen an der Universität L e i d e n hält, noch auf der K i e l e r Woche für Kunst und Wissenschaft über die Relativitätstheorie sprechen und auf der Naturforscherversammlung in B a d N a u h e i m seine Theorie zur Diskussion stellen. Ob er im kommenden Wintersemester die angekündigten Vorlesungen an der Berliner Universität halten wird, ist noch nicht sicher."

Einstein recorded his fears and his sudden courage upon learning that he would not have to defend himself, but would instead be defended by sycophants who were more competent than he was, which emboldened him to publish his response in the *Berliner Tageblatt*. Albert Einstein wrote to Arnold Sommerfeld on 6 September 1920:

"Ich hatte in der That jenem Unternehmen gegen mich zu viel Bedeutung zugeschrieben, indem ich glaubte, dass ein grosser Teil unserer Physiker dabei beteiligt sei. So dachte ich wirklich zwei Tage lang an «Fahnenflucht», wie Sie das nennen. Bald aber kam die Besinnung und die Erkenntnis, dass es falsch wäre, den Kreis meiner bewährten Freunde zu verlassen. Den Artikel hätte ich vielleicht nicht schreiben sollen. Aber ich wollte verhindern, dass mein dauerndes Schweigen zu den Einwänden und Beschuldigungen, welche systematisch wiederholt werden, als Zustimmung gedeutet werden. Schlimm ist, dass jede Äusserung von mir von Journalisten geschäftlich verwertet wird. Ich muss mich eben sehr abschliessen."[197]

3.3 A Jew is Not Allowed to Speak Out Against a Jew

Jews have long taught that a good Jew never speaks out against another Jew, and a good Jews does not praise a Gentile unless such praise results in even greater praise for a Jew. We sometimes see Jews deigning to give mild and grudging praise to Hendrik Antoon Lorentz and Jules Henri Poincaré, or to Mileva Marić; but it is almost always so that they can lavish far greater praise on an undeserving Jew, Albert Einstein. The Jewish book of *Leviticus* 19:17-18 states,

"17 Thou shalt not hate thy brother in thine heart: thou shalt in any wise rebuke thy neighbour, and not suffer sin upon him. 18 Thou shalt not avenge, nor bear any grudge against the children of thy people, but thou shalt love thy neighbour as thyself: I *am* the LORD."

In this admonition, "neighbor" refers only to fellow Jews. Jews are also taught to cover up the sins of fellow Jews, lest the tribe suffer as a whole. The Jewish book of *Numbers* 16:22 states,

"And they fell upon their faces, and said, O God, the God of the spirits of all flesh, shall one man sin, and wilt thou be wroth with all the congregation?"

Israel Shahak wrote in his book *Jewish History, Jewish Religion: The Weight of Three Thousand Years*,

"There is also a series of rules forbidding any expression of praise for Gentiles or for their deeds, except where such praise implies an even greater praise of Jews and things Jewish. This rule is still observed by Orthodox Jews. For example, the writer Agnon, when interviewed on the Israeli radio upon his return from Stockholm, where he received the Nobel Prize for literature, praised the Swedish Academy, but hastened to add: 'I am not forgetting that it is forbidden to praise Gentiles, but here there is a special reason for my praise'—that is, that they awarded the prize to a Jew."[198]

Rev. I. B. Pranaitis wrote in his book *The Talmud Unmasked: The Secret Rabbinical Teachings Concerning Christians*, Eugene Nelson Sanctuary, New York, (1939),

"In Abhodah Zarah (20, a, Toseph) it says:

'Do not say anything in praise of them, lest it be said: How good that Goi is!'[Footnote: Maimonides (in Hilkhoth Akum X, 5) adds: 'Moreover, you should seek opportunity to mix with them and find out about their evil doings.']

In this way they explain the words of Deuteronomy (VII, 2) . . . and thou shalt show no mercy unto them [Goim], as cited in the Gemarah. Rabbi S. Iarchi explains this Bible passage as follows:

'Do not pay them any compliments; for it is forbidden to say: how good that Goi is.'

In Iore Dea (151, 14) it says:

'No one is allowed to praise them or to say how good an Akum is. How much less to praise what they do or to recount anything about them which would redound to their glory. If, however, while praising them you intend to give glory to God, namely, because he has created comely creatures, then it is allowed to do so.'"[199]

Jews are taught that non-Jews, the hated Goyim, are "the wicked" and that the names of "the wicked" are to be blotted out of the book of life. There are many Jewish religious writings which call for the name of Amalekites to be forgoten. Jews were simply following their ancient traditions when they promoted Einstein as if he had created the theory of relativity, and when Jews smeared Einstein's predecessors and demanded that their names be forgotten. The Jewish book of *Proverbs* 10:7 states,

"The memory of the just *is* blessed: but the name of the wicked shall rot."

The Jewish book of *Deuteronomy* 7:2 states,

"And when the LORD thy God shall deliver them before thee; thou shalt smite them, *and* utterly destroy them; thou shalt make no covenant with them, nor shew mercy unto them:"

Jews are also taught that a Jew who informs on another Jew must be murdered. Matthew Wagner reported in *The Jerusalem Post* on 18 January 2007,

"A group of rabbis have issued a halachic opinion implying that OC Central Command Maj.-Gen. Yair Naveh deserves to be killed. The rabbis, all connected with a movement to resurrect the Sanhedrin, the ancient Jewish governing body, said in their halachic ruling this week that Naveh was guilty of being a moser, a Hebrew word that can be roughly translated as an informant or traitor."[200]

Israel Shahak and Norton Mezvinsky wrote in their book *Jewish Fundamentalism in Israel,*

"Two additional halachic laws are of special importance both generally and specifically when related to the Rabin assassination. These two laws, employed since talmudic times to kill Jews, were invoked by the assassin, Yigal Amir, as his justification for killing Prime Minister Rabin and are still emphasized by Jews who approved or have barely condemned that assassination. These are the 'law of the pursuer' (din rodef) and the 'law of the informer' (din moser).[Notation: 'Moser,' the Hebrew word for informer, is a terrible insult for Jews, similar to the word 'collaborator' for Palestinians.] The first law commands every Jew to kill or to wound severely any Jew who is perceived as intending to kill another Jew. According to halachic commentaries, it is not necessary to see such a person pursuing a Jewish victim. It is enough if rabbinic authorities, or even competent scholars, announce that the law of the pursuer applies to such a person. The second law commands every Jew to kill or wound severely any Jew who, without a decision of a competent rabbinical authority, has informed non-Jews, especially non-Jewish authorities, about Jewish affairs or who has given them information about Jewish property or who has delivered Jewish persons or property to their rule or authority. Competent religious authorities are empowered to do, and at times have done, those things forbidden to other Jews in the second law. During the long period of incitement preceding the Rabin assassination, many Haredi and messianic writers applied these laws to Rabin and other Israeli leaders. The religious insiders based themselves on later developments in Halacha that came to include other categories of Jews who were defined as 'those to whom the law of the pursuer' applied. Every Jew had a religious duty to kill those Jews who were so included. Historically, Jews in the diaspora followed this law whenever possible, until at least the advent of the modern state. In the Tsarist Empire Jews followed this law until well into the nineteenth century."[201]

The second meeting of the *Arbeitsgemeinschaft deutscher Naturforscher zur Erhaltung reiner Wissenschaft* took place on 2 September 1920. The famous Jewish philosopher Oskar Kraus of Prague was scheduled to deliver a lecture stating his objections to the special theory of relativity. The Czechoslovakian government refused Kraus a visa for "political reasons" thereby preventing his appearance at the meeting and actively obstructing a public expression of anti-relativism by a famous intellectual figure of Jewish descent. Kraus had known Einstein while Einstein lived in Prague. Kraus believed that Einstein was nothing more than an amateurish Metaphysician. Einstein told Leopold Infeld, "I am really more of a philosopher than a physicist."[202] Einstein was a poor philosopher, as well. He argued in redundancies based on unproven assertions.

The pro-Einstein forces—forces so powerful that they were able to deny a man's right to speak and to corrupt the workings of a nation's government—prevented Kraus' speech, which would have been far more interesting and readily understood by a crowd of laymen and news correspondents than was Glaser's technical lecture which replaced it. Kraus' arguments[203] against the metaphysical absurdities in relativity theory make a powerful impression on the lay public—one Einstein's advocates were frantic to prevent. Einstein did not grasp the distinction between Metaphysics and science. He stated in 1930, "Science itself is metaphysics."[204]

This maneuver enabled pro-Einstein newspapers and Max von Laue to:

1. Criticize Weyland for being too popular and allegedly racist. Leopold Infeld stated that Weyland was a, "handsome dark-haired man of about thirty who wore a frockcoat and spoke with enthusiasm about interesting things[. . . .] He said that uproar about the theory of relativity was hostile to the German spirit."[205] Weyland denied that his opposition to Einstein was anti-Semitic.

2. Attack Gehrcke's credibility in handwaving personal attacks which would sound impressive to the lay public. Philipp Frank attacked Gehrcke as, "a competent experimental physicist of Berlin, who criticized the theory from a point of view of a man who, while making no mistakes in his experiments, simply lacks the acute understanding and flight of imagination to pass from individual facts to a synthesis."[206] Frank also stated that Gehrcke was, "a hardworking observer in the laboratory".[207] Shortly before Max von Laue joined the dishonest campaign to smear Gehrcke, Laue wrote to Einstein on 18 October 1919 that Gehrcke was, "a very seasoned optics specialist with a genuine interest in moving bodies."[208] Philipp Lenard, himself a Nobel Prize laureate, nominated Gehrcke for the Nobel Prize. Einstein and his friends tried to destroy Gehrcke's career and censored him on numerous occasions.

3. Attack Lenard as an alleged racist (Arnold Sommerfeld praised Lenard's book in a letter to Einstein,

"In seiner neu aufgelegten Broschüre «Rel[ativität], Äther, Gravit[ation]» hat [Lenard] sich sehr anständig über Sie [Einstein] geäussert."[209]

Lenard, while expressing his patriotism and the dignity and integrity he demanded of German science, did not publicly express racial sentiments until after Einstein had attacked him and smeared his name without grounds around the world.

4. Avoid Glaser's objections as dry and uninteresting pedantic gobbledygook.

5. Prevent Kraus' dramatic public exposition of the fatal flaws in the

theory of relativity, which could not be misconstrued as if "anti-Semitic" even by the shameless pro-Einstein press.

All of this was done to change the subject from Einstein's plagiarism, Einstein's self-promotion and gross exaggeration of the significance of his theories, the relativists' corrupt misrepresentation of the available evidence to the public, and the absurdities of the theory of relativity—all of this was done to change the subject to the irrelevant issue of anti-Semitism. Einstein and his friends were completely unethical. They inhibited the progress of science and took away fundamental human liberties.

Max von Laue reported in the evening edition of *Vossische Zeitung* on 4 September 1920 that the Czechoslovakian government denied Kraus, of Prag, the right to leave the country "for political reasons". Laue, racist Zionist Albert Einstein's "Shabbas Goy", again tried to change the subject to racial issues in a cowardly effort to avoid the relevant facts,

"Der Einstein-Effekt im Spektrum.
Von
Max von Laue.

Professor M a x v o n L a u e, Ordinarius für theoretische Physik an der Berliner Universität, Träger des Nobelpreises für Physik im Jahre 1914, stellt uns folgende Ausführungen zur Verfügung:

Die Arbeitsgemeinschaft deutscher Naturforscher für Rassereinheit der Wissenschaft veranstaltete am 2. 9. ihren zweiten Vortragsabend in der Philharmonie. Zunächst mußte ihr geistiges Haupt, Herr Paul W e y l a n d, das Ausbleiben von Prof. Kraus aus Prag mitteilen, dem die tschecho-slowakische Regierung aus politischen Gründen die Ausreise verweigert hat.

Sodann ergriff Herr Dr.-Ing. G l a s e r das Wort zu dem angekündigten Vortrage, der sich nach ein paar einleitenden Bemerkungen über die Lichtablenkung bei der Sonnenfinsternis 1919 ausführlich mit der Rotverschiebung der Spektrallinien auf der Sonne beschäftigte, deren Dasein die allgemeine Relativitätstheorie notwendig fordern muß. Hier sprach nun ein gescheiter Mann über eine Sache, von der er etwas versteht — ganz im Gegensatz zum ersten Vortragsabend. Schon daraus geht hervor, daß der Physiker viel dabei lernen konnte. Ob auch der Laie? Manchmal schien uns das zweifelhaft.

Der Redner zeigte zunächst in wohlgelungenen-Projektionsbildern die sogenannten Cyanbanden im Sonnenspektrum, an denen die wichtigsten Beobachtungen gemacht sind, und deren Auflösung in einzelne Linien. Er ging dann aus von den Messungen S c h w a r z s c h i l d s , bei denen er selbst mitgearbeitet hat. Deren Ergebnis sprach eher gegen als für den Einsteineffekt. Er führte weiter die langen Messungsreihen vor, die sich in Arbeiten von St. J o h n , E v e r s h e d und R o y d s sowie H a l e befinden. Letztere sind in Deutschland zurzeit schwer zugänglich, und die Mühe, mit der der Vortragende sie sich zu verschaffen gewußt hat, muß sehr anerkannt werden. Mit vollster Bewunderung und einem gewissen Neid muß es erfüllen, wenn man von den großartigen Hilfsmitteln hört, welche die Sternwarte des Mount Wilson für solche Versuche bietet, und dazu die Projektionsbilder sieht. Alle diese Forscher finden V e r s c h i e b u n g e n   d e r S p e k t r a l l i n i e n , doch welchen diese meist in der Größe, manchmal auch in der Richtung vom Einsteineffekt an, auch lassen sich noch manche andere Erklärungen dafür ersinnen, so daß ein einheitliches Bild nicht entsteht.

Sodann ging der Vortragende zu den kurzen Veröffentlichungen zweier Deutscher über. G r e b e und B a c h e m haben nämlich seit 1919 in Bonn mit weit bescheideneren Mitteln dieselben Untersuchungen angestellt. Und sie kommen zu dem Ergebnis, daß man n i c h t w a h l l o s j e d e L i n i e i m S p e k t r u m zur Entscheidung der Frage heranziehen dürfe. Unsymmetrien im Linienbau sowie die unvermeidbaren Unterschiede zwischen Absorptionsspektren, wie wir sie im Sonnenlicht haben, und den irdischen Emissionsspektren, mit denen man sie vergleicht, können nach ihnen das Ergebnis einer genauen Messung vollständig fälschen. Beschränkt man die Untersuchung auf acht Linien, die von solchen Uebelständen frei sind, so findet man aus ihren eigenen Messunggen, s o w i e a u s d e n e n i h r e r V o r g ä n g e r eine Rotverschiebung, welche mit dem von Einstein verlangten Effekt recht gut übereinstimmt.

Hiergegen wandte sich der Redner. Das wesentlichste Instrument der Bonner Untersuchung ist ein Gitter, und die bisherigen Gitter sind nicht hinreichend fehlerfrei, um diese

Untersuchung zu ermöglichen. Er zeigte im Bild vortreffliche photographische Aufnahmen von Gittern und stellte dabei sein eigenes Licht etwas unter den Scheffel, indem er verschwieg, daß solche Aufnahme niemandem vor ihm selbst gesungen sind. Die dabei zutage tretenden Fehler verursachen Schleier um die Spektralanalyse; diese beim Bonner Apparat auftretenden, bei geeigneteren Anordnungen aber fehlenden Schleier sind es nach Glaser, welche Grebe und Bachem zur Ausscheidung der Mehrzahl der bisher untersuchten Linien veranlaßt haben. Glaser hält demgegenüber die älteren Untersuchungen für maßgebend und schloß mit den Worten, er glaube auch die Anhänger der Relativitätstheorie überzeugt zu haben, daß sie von der Rotverschiebung der Spektrallinien nichts mehr zu hoffen hätten.

Darin zeigt sich nun wieder die e i n s e i t i g e P a r t e i n a h m e dieses sonst nicht schlechten Vortrages. Warum verschwieg der Redner, daß, selbst wenn die allgemeine Relativitätstheorie sich an der Erfahrung nicht bestätigen sollte, doch dann immer noch die beschränkte Relativitätstheorie, welche uns Einstein 1905 beschert hat, bestehen bleibt? Warum erwähnte er nicht, daß S c h w a r z s c h i l d , auch nachdem er die theoretische Rotverschiebung nicht hatte finden können, noch kurz vor seinem Tode in zwei höchst wertvollen Untersuchungen an dem mathematischen Ausbau der allgemeinen Relativitätstheorie mitgearbeitet hat? Er muß diese doch wohl noch nicht für ganz erledigt gehalten haben. Ferner haben die Bonner Gelehrten gewiß nicht mit den Mitteln Hales arbeiten können. Aber sie haben dafür einen sehr beachtenswerten Gedanken in die Erörterung geworfen, den ihre englischen und amerikanischen Vorgänger nicht gehabt und deswegen auch nicht mit ihren besseren Mitteln geprüft hatten. Wie denn nun, wenn diese Forscher die Grebe-Bachemsche Prüfung der Spektrallinien auf ihre Braucharbeit wiederholen — was sehr zu wünschen ist — und dabei vielleicht deren Ergebnis bestätigen? Kann man denn diese Möglichkeit von vornherein ausschließen? Der richtige Schluß aus dem vorliegenden Beobachtungsmaterial wäre für einen sehr skeptischen Beurteiler doch wohl der gewesen: Die älteren Untersuchungen sind durch Grebe und Bachem in ihrer Bedeutung zweifelhaft gemacht. Deren eigene Untersuchungen sind bisher von anderer Seite nicht nachgeprüft. Also ist die ganze Frage noch in der Schwebe.

Und noch ein paar allgemeinere Bemerkungen seien hier

gestattet: Hört man die Vorträge der „Arbeitsgemeinschaft", so muß man glauben, mit der Relativitätstheorie wäre der ganze Einstein erledigt. Und dabei ist unter denen, die da gesprochen haben und sprechen wollen, höchstens einer — zur Vorsicht wollen wir sagen, daß wir nicht Herrn W e y l a n d meinen — dessen Leistungen für die Physik sich mit dem messen können, was Einstein a u ß e r d e r R e l a t i v i t ä t s t h e o r i e getan hat. Sein Nachweis der Elektronenbewegung in den Magneten, seine Theorie der Temperaturabhängigkeit der spezifischen Wärme und so manches andere auf dem Gebiete der Quantentheorie sind unvergängliche Ruhmesblätter in der Geschichte der Wissenschaft. Gelänge es der Arbeitsgemeinschaft, was sie — nach der Art ihrer Mittel zu urteilen — anstrebt, nämlich diesen Mann aus Berlin zu vertreiben, so hätte sie damit — ebenfalls unvergängliche Berühmtheit erworben."

Johannes Riem stated that Oskar Kraus had wired him a telegram on 2 September 1920, which informed him that Kraus, "was refused a visa for political reasons."[210] Riem complained that,

"In such a way relativity theory is protected by the immigration service."[211]

The *Berliner Tageblatt* reported in the morning edition of 3 September 1920,

"Im großen Saal der Berliner Philharmonie sollte gestern abend der Vortrag von Professor Dr. K r a u s-Prag, der von der „Arbeitsgemeinschaft deutscher Naturforscher" angekündigt war, stattfinden. Der Beginn des Vortrags war auf ½8 Uhr festgesetzt, um ¼9 Uhr aber erst wurde dem erschienenen Publikum mitgeteilt, daß Professor Dr. Kraus, der über „R e l a t i v i t ä t s t h e o r i e u n d E r k e n n t n i s t h e o r i e" sprechen sollte, n i c h t erscheinen werde."

In the evening edition of 3 September 1920, the *Berliner Tageblatt* wrote,

"*E. V.* **Die Einstein-Kampagne.** Bei den Einstein-Gegnern scheint jetzt doch die Erkenntnis Platz zu greifen, daß die Art, wie die „Arbeitsgemeinschaft deutscher Naturforscher" den Kampf gegen Einstein in dem ersten Vortrag eingeleitet hatte, nicht der richtige ist. Professor Kraus (Prag), der zur Relativitätstheorie vom erkenntnistheoretischen Standpunkt Stellung nehmen wollte, hatte, wie schon im Morgenblatt kurz gemeldet, telegraphisch abgesagt; er verzichtet darauf, sich als Philosoph in den Straßenkampf der allzu persönlich erhitzten Tagesmeinungen zu stellen. Es blieb als Redner des gestrigen Abends in der Philharmonie nur der Physiker Dr. Ing. G l a s e r , ein Gehilfe Schwarzschilds bei dessen früheren experimentellen Studien zur Relativitätstheorie. Und es muß gesagt werden, daß er sich nüchternster Sachlichkeit, man könnte beinahe sagen, Trockenheit, befleißigte. Jedenfalls, wer aus dem Publikum in diesen Vortrag gekommen war, um ein paar billige und tönende Schlagworte für seine Anti- oder Sympathie nach Hause zu tragen, ist Gott sei Dank enttäuscht worden, er saß in einem experimentalphysikalischen Seminar. Glaser begnügte sich damit, die Beobachtungsresultate der aus der Relativitätstheorie gefolgerten und von Einstein errechneten Effekte der L i c h t a b l e n k u n g und der R o t v e r s c h i e b u n g zu untersuchen, um an Hand von Lichtbildern darzutun, das erstens die beobachteten Effekte hinter den errechneten zurückbleiben, und zweitens die beobachteten Phänomen nicht die restlos zwingende Beweiskraft als Relativitätseffekte haben, sondern, zum Beispiel die Differenz in der Verschiebung am Nordrand und am Südrand der Sonne, wie Evershed schon zeigt, sich vorläufig schwer mit dieser Erklärung vereinigen lassen. Glaser untersuchte sehr kritisch die Mittel der Beobachtung und die Möglichkeit, mit den bei den letzten Finsternissen angewandten Apparaten und Methoden ganz einwandfreie Resultate zu erzielen. Wobei zu bedenken ist, daß die Unklarheit der erzielten Bilder doch nicht ohne weiteres zuungunsten der Einsteinschen Effekte ausgelegt werden darf. Es kann auch ein Beobachtungsfehler der unzulänglichen Mittel sein, wenn die beobachteten Effekte hinter den errechneten zurückgeblieben sind.

Es wird uns wohl nichts weiter übrigbleiben, als in Geduld abzuwarten, was am 22. September 1922 die verfinsterte Sonne an den Tag bringen wird, ob die Einsteinsche Sonne aus den kritischen Nebeln, die jetzt mit etwas allzuviel Dunst darum gemacht werden, siegreich hervorgehen wird."

Many years later, Philipp Frank spun things this way and that, and even Max Born felt obliged to state that in the context of the history of the special theory of relativity, Philipp Frank was dishonest and distorted the facts. Frank wrote,

"An invitation had also been extended to a representative of philosophy who was to prove that Einstein's theory was not 'truth,' but only a 'fiction.' He was of Jewish descent and was intended to be the climax of the meeting. Despite his political innocence and urgent telegrams, he declined at the last moment because some friends had explained the purpose of the meeting to him. As a result the first attack took place without the blessing of philosophy."[212]

Max Born said of Frank,

"EINSTEIN's work was the keystone to an arch which LORENTZ, POINCARÉ and others had built and which was to carry the structure erected by MINKOWSKI. I think it wrong to forget these other men, as it can be found in many books. Even PHILIPP FRANK's excellent biography *Einstein, Sein Leben und seine Zeit*, cannot be acquitted of this reproach, e.g., when he says (in Chap. 3, No. 6 of the German edition) that nobody before EINSTEIN had ever considered a new type of mechanical law in which the velocity of light plays a prominent part. Both POINCARÉ and LORENTZ have been aware of this, and the relativistic expression for the mass (which contains c) has rightly been called LORENTZ' formula."[213]

Oskar Kraus was an outspoken critic of the theory of relativity before the Berlin Philharmonic lectures and for many years thereafter. Frank's account does not agree with that of Paul Weyland, Max von Laue and Johannes Riem, who recorded that Kraus wished to attend the meeting, but was refused a visa for political reasons. Einstein's advocates have always relied upon clannish Jewish racism and disproportionate Jewish influence in government, the press and in the universities to prevent a fair and open discussion of the merits of the theory of relativity and of Einstein's career plagiarism. This is but one of many instances of Jewish censorship in the modern world. Jewish organizations have successfully criminalized opinions which deviate from their own. It is today illegal in many countries to offend or obstruct

Jewish racists by revealing their destructive lies and dangerous Messianic aspirations.

3.4 The Bad Nauheim Debate

Nobel Prize winning Physicist Philipp Lenard took great offense at Einstein's defamatory comments. Lenard had said nothing anti-Semitic in public, but instead, in the wake of Germany's defeat in World War I, had simply asserted his national pride and declared that German science stood for high ethical standards and sound scientific practices—as opposed to the wild speculations of the British eclipse observations and the immoderate and self-glorifying advertising of Albert Einstein. Lenard's reaction came at a time when the British and French had openly attempted to destroy German science, with Albert Einstein's help.

In the winter of 1914, Lenard criticized J. J. Thomson and England in a 16 page pamphlet[214] in a nationalistic—not anti-Semitic—tone. Lenard, himself, may have been of Jewish descent and had a classically Jewish appearance.[215] It was common at the time to speak of "German science" and many of Einstein's friends and supporters, many of whom were Jewish, proudly spoke in those exact terms. Lenard supported German efforts in the war, and, like Max Planck, Walter Nernst, Fritz Haber, and many others, signed the pro-German statement of 4 October 1914, as amended, with the signatories broken down by profession, by Goerg Nicolai:

> *"The Manifesto to the Civilized World*
> As representatives of German science and art we protest before the whole civilized world against the calumnies and lies with which our enemies are striving to besmirch Germany's undefiled cause in the severe struggle for existence which has been forced upon her. The course of events has mercilessly disproved the reports of fictitious German defeats. All the more vigorous are the efforts now being made to distort truth and disseminate suspicion. It is against these that we are raising our voices, and those voices shall make the truth known.
> 1.—IT IS NOT TRUE THAT GERMANY WAS GUILTY OF THIS WAR
> Neither the nation nor the Government nor the emperor wanted it. The Germans did everything possible to avert it, documentary evidence of which is before all the world. In the

twenty-six years of his reign William II has frequently shown himself the defender of the world's peace, as has frequently been acknowledged even by our enemies. Indeed, this same emperor, whom they are now presuming to call an Attila, was ridiculed for twenty years and more because of his unswerving devotion to peace. Not until our people was attacked from three sides by superior forces, which had long been lying in wait at the frontier, did it rise as one man.

2.—IT IS NOT TRUE THAT WE CRIMINALLY VIOLATED BELGIAN NEUTRALITY

It can be proved that France and England had resolved to violate it, and it can be proved that Belgium had agreed to this. It would have been suicidal not to have anticipated them.

3.—IT IS NOT TRUE THAT THE LIFE AND PROPERTY OF A SINGLE BELGIAN SUBJECT WERE INTERFERED WITH BY OUR SOLDIERS EXCEPT UNDER THE DIREST NECESSITY

Again and again, despite all warnings, did the population lie in ambush and fire on them, mutilating wounded men, and murdering doctors even while actually engaged in their noble ministrations. There could be no baser misrepresentation than to say nothing about the crime of these assassins and then to call the Germans criminals because of their having administered a just punishment to them.

4.—IT IS NOT TRUE THAT OUR TROOPS BEHAVED BRUTALLY IN REGARD TO LOUVAIN

They were forced to exercise reprisals with a heavy heart on the furious population, which treacherously attacked them in their quarters, by firing upon a portion of the town. The greater portion of Louvain is still standing, and the famous town hall is quite uninjured. It was saved from the flames owing to the self-sacrifice of our soldiers. Every German would regret works of art having been destroyed in this war or their being destroyed in the future. But just as we decline to admit that any one loves art more than we do, even so do we refuse no less decidedly to pay the price of a German defeat for the preservation of a work of art.

5.—IT IS NOT TRUE THAT WE DISREGARD THE PRECEPTS OF INTERNATIONAL LAW IN OUR METHODS OF WARFARE, IN WHICH THERE IS NO UNBRIDLED CRUELTY

But in the East the ground is soaked with the blood of women and children slain by Russian hordes, and in the West the breasts of our soldiers are lacerated with Dumdum bullets. No one has less right to pretend to be defending European civilization than those who are the allies of Russians and Serbians, and are not ashamed to incite Mongolians and negroes to fight against white men.

6.—IT IS NOT TRUE THAT FIGHTING OUR SO-CALLED MILITARISM IS NOT FIGHTING AGAINST OUR CIVILIZATION, AS OUR ENEMIES HYPOCRITICALLY ALLEGE

Without German militarism German civilization would be wiped off the face of the earth. The former arose out of and for the protection of the latter in a country which for centuries had suffered from invasion as no other has done. The German Army and the German people are one, and the consciousness of this makes seventy millions of Germans brothers to-day, without regard to education, rank, or party.

We cannot deprive our enemies of the poisoned weapons of falsehood. All we can do is to cry aloud to the whole world that they are bearing false witness against us. To you who know us, who, together with us, have hitherto been the guardians of man's highest possessions—to you we cry aloud, 'Believe us; believe that to the last we will fight as a civilized nation, to whom the legacy of a Goethe, a Beethoven, and a Kant is no less sacred than hearth and home.'

This we vouchsafe to you on the faith of our name and our honor.

The manifesto was signed by the following seventeen artists actually practising their profession: Peter Behrends, Franz von Defregger, Wilhelm Dörpfeld, Eduard von Gebhardt, Adolf von Hildebrand, Ludwig Hoffmann, Leopold Graf Kalkreuth, Arthur Kampf, Fritz Aug. von Kaulbach, Max Klinger, Max Liebermann, Ludwig Manzel, Bruno Paul, Fritz Schaper, Franz von Stuck, Hans Thoma, Wilh. Trübner.

By these fifteen natural scientists: Adolf von Beyer, Karl Engler, Emil Fischer, Wilhelm Foerster, Fritz Haber, Ernst Haeckel, Gustav Hellmann, Felix Klein, Philipp Lenard, Walter Nernst, Wilhelm Ostwald, Max Planck, Wilhelm Röntgen, Wilhelm Wien, Richard Willstätter.

By these twelve theologians: Adolf Deissmann, Albert Ehrhard, Gerhard Esser, Adolf von Harnack, Wilhelm Herrmann, Alois Knöpfler, Anton Koch, Josef Mausbach,

Sebastian Merkle, Adolf von Schlatter, August Schmidlin, and Reinhold Seeberg.

By these nine poets: Richard Dehmel, Herbert Eulenberg, Ludwig Fulda, Max Halbe, Gerhard and Karl Hauptmann, Hermann Sudermann, Karl Vollmöller, and Richard Voss.

By these seven jurists; Lujo Brentano, Johannes Conrad, Theodor Kipp, Paul Laband, Franz von Liszt, Georg von Mayr, and Gustav von Schmoller.

By these seven medical men: Emil von Behring, Paul Ehrlich, Albert Neisser, Albert Plehn, Max Rubner, Wilhelm Waldeyer, and August von Wassermann.

By these seven historians: Heinrich Finke, J. J. de Groot, Karl Lamprecht, Maximilian Lenz, Eduard Meyer, Karl Robert, and Martin Spahn.

By these five art critics: Wilhelm von Bode, Alois Brandt, Justus Brinkmann, Friedrich von Duhn, and Theodor Wiegand.

By these four philosophers: Rudolf Eucken, Alois Riehl, Wilhelm Windelband, and Wilh. Wundt.

By these four philologists: Andreas Heusler, Heinrich Morf, Karl Vossler, Ulrich von Wilamowitz-Moellendorff.

By these three musicians: Engelbert Humperdinck, Siegfried Wagner, and Felix von Weingartner.

By these two politicians: Friedrich Naumann and Georg Reicke.

By this theatrical manager: Max Reinhardt."[216]

Traitorous Einstein covertly supported the Allies throughout the war. Though he lived in Germany—Einstein was a disloyal agent of Germany's enemies. Einstein became a symbol to many Germans of the Jew who had "stabbed Germany in the back". Many Germans believed that Jewish leaders in the press, the English, and Jewish world finance, had conspired to destroy pan-Germany as it tried to defend Europe from pan-Slavism, and that after the war the Jewish press in Germany sided with the Allies when they sought to punish Germany and break it apart in violation of President Wilson's directives that no nation would lose territory at war's end, which promise had led Germany to surrender in the good faith of that promise.[217] The Allies, and some leading German Jews, betrayed Germany's good faith.

Albert Einstein, together with Wilhelm Förster and Georg Friedrich Nicolai[218] (born Lewinstein)—a crypto-Jew who tried to persuade young Ilse Einstein to accept Albert Einstein's proposal of marriage in 1918, while Albert Einstein was sleeping with her mother, who was Albert Einstein's cousin, Elsa Einstein[219]—drafted their "Call to the Europeans", which anticipated the European Union by calling for peace talks that would destroy the German and Austro-Hungarian Empires and replace them with a yet more universal European block, a Soviet style block that would eliminate personal property and unite the workers in their struggle against the ruling class. This came at a time when Germans were rightly concerned by the attempted takeovers of revolutionary Jewish Communists like Rosa Luxemburg, Karl Liebknecht and Kurt Eisner, which had shaken the German Nation. It was well known that the Bolsheviks under Jewish leadership had mass murdered millions of Christians and had destroyed the Russian Nation. It was also widely known that Jewish financiers had caused the First World War in order to profiteer from it, promote Zionist interests, and to destroy the Europeans' will to fight back against Bolshevism. The Jewish bankers believed that the war would tire the Europeans and leave susceptible to the Jewish propaganda that internationalism and Bolshevism were the solution to war. However, most Europeans realized that these same forces were behind the war and were terrified at the prospect of a Bolshevist Europe.

Raymond Recouly contrasted the French and Russian revolutions, in an article published in 1922, which stated, *inter alia*,

"Since the Bolshevist revolution, the produce of Russia has diminished from 50 to 75 per cent. Famine and the deaths of millions of people have been the consequences of that Russian expropriation.

We have now reached a subject in which a great many people seem to find the chief points of comparison between the two revolutions, namely the question of massacres.

Nothing can excuse a massacre, either in France or in Russia.

The massacres which went on in some of the Paris prisons and certain provincial towns, such as Lyons, Nantes, etc., have branded the French Revolution with bloodstains impossible to wash out.

As to the condemnations pronounced by the revolutionary tribunals during the most active period of the Terror, the very composition of those tribunals, their expeditive and summary manner of delivering the sentence, the wholesale trials and condemnations pronounced by them, were the merest parody of justice.

But between those massacres of the French Revolution and the massacres of the Russian Revolution, there are, however, some capital differences.

First, the number of the victims was in France greatly smaller than it has been in Russia.

About 1,300 people were buried at the cemetery of Picpus in Paris, where the greatest majority of the victims of the guillotine had their sepulchers. Those few thousand victims of the French Revolution seem nearly nothing as compared with the enormous number of people exterminated in Russia.

The Terror in France did not last very long. There came soon a strong reaction and the whole thing was definitely stopped.

Even at the most frightful period of the Terror, the exterior forms of justice were, to a certain extent, observed. If one wished to find extenuating circumstances, they could be found in the violence of the political struggle, especially in the fact of France being invaded, that enemy armies were marching on the capital, that a terrible revolt had broken out in the Vendée province, and insurrections were taking place in the centre and south of France.

In France, the executions were always conducted openly. When Louis XVI and the Queen were beheaded, it was in the middle of the Place de la Concorde in daylight, after they had been publicly judged and condemned.

In the Russian Revolution, on the contrary, no exterior form of justice was even observed. The executions have always taken place secretly. You have only to remember the monstrous manner in which the Czar and all his family were murdered in Ekaterinburg. It was in the middle of the night, in a cellar, by revolver shots, without any judgment whatever.

It has been nearly the same with all the Russian executions.

And what about the Tcheka, that disgusting network of police spies of all kinds, which has something Asiatic, Chinese, in the way of arresting people, of torturing them and putting them to death?

Those Bolshevist massacres have already been going on for several years. There is unfortunately no sign that they are going to decrease.

I have said enough to show you the fundamental differences existing between the two revolutions. The few points of comparison that exist do so only in appearance. They are due to the fact that most of the Russian revolutionaries were wrapped up in the superficialities of the French Revolution.

Their one aim was to imitate, to copy it as much as they could. In spite of that, the two revolutions differ as much as night from day. Nearly all the men at the head of the French Revolution were men of great energy—patriotic, and disinterested; they boldly risked their lives in the struggle; most of them forfeited them.

The French Revolution endowed the country with a far better system of organization, and a far more equitable system of justice than had hitherto existed. It raised the standard of human dignity. The higher material and moral well-being that was its direct creation were immense. The whole of France, and one may truly say a great part of Europe, owes all to those reforms. It abolished all the old privileges, did away with serfdom and feudal rights, founding the liberty and dignity of the human being. It reorganized education, justice, the administering of public affairs, gave a great impulse to the education of the masses, introduced a new system of weights and measures which has been adopted by nearly every country in Europe; it instituted higher education.

That positive, constructive work of the Revolution was, as you can see, immense. When one recalls the conditions under which all those reforms were brought about, when one attempts to conjure up visions of the troubled times rife with political strife, in which the great men of the Revolutionary Assemblies did all that creative work, one cannot help being filled with admiration for their energy and their audacity.

Their virtues far outweighed their old vices.

The Russian Revolution, on the contrary, has produced nothing, it has destroyed everything.

It has not even developed the communist theories. For Lenin, after having wildly proclaimed their inviolability, was forced to abandon them for the greater part.

Bolshevism has for many years laid waste the material, intellectual, and moral forces of Russia.

To draw the conclusion of this article, one could say that while the French Revolution was all the time directed and strongly kept in hand, the Russian Revolution was left without any direction whatever.

Now we must not forget that the leading class in Russia

formed a very small minority, that they were, in some manner, lost in the immensity of that country. The geographical, ethical, historical conditions of Russia were so different from Germany, France, and England that it was very difficult, almost impossible, for the leaders to lead effectively such a big country."[220]

Bolshevik atrocities made the Germans very leery of Jewish Communists—even of Jews in general, especially those calling for the world government foretold in Jewish Messianic prophecies—Jewish Messianic prophecies which called for the overthrow of Kings and Queens, Princes and Princesses; as well as for a world government run by Jews, and the "restoration of the Jews to Palestine"; and for the destruction of Gentile culture, Gentile religions, Gentile nations, and ultimately the extermination of the Gentiles, themselves—all this mass murder justified on the false premise that it was necessary to achieve an era of "peace" and a new world ruled by Jews. The persona of Albert Einstein epitomized these ancient racist and genocidal Jewish objectives and made him a focal point for the legitimate concerns Germans had for their survival, grave concerns that were proven correct by the rise of the Zionist Nazis who destroyed Germany at the behest of Jewish financiers, and the further partition and loss of sovereignty of Germany after the Second World War, when a large section of Germany and Eastern Europe were taken over by the Communists, while Western Zionists who led the Western governments permitted it to happen. Many Germans were disgusted by the Jews who had stabbed Germany in the back in the First World War.

The appeal of Einstein, Förster and Nicolai follows:

"A Manifesto to Europeans
Technical science and intercommunication are clearly tending to force us to recognize the fact that international relations exist, and consequently that a world-embracing civilization exists. Yet never has any previous war caused so complete an interruption of that coöperation which should exist between civilized nations. It may, of course, be that the reason why we are so profoundly impressed by this is only that we were already united by so many ties the severing of which is painful.

That such a state of things should exist must not astonish us. Nevertheless, those who care in the slightest degree for this universal world civilization are under a twofold obligation to strive for the maintenance of these principles. Those who might have been expected to care for such things, in particular men of science and art, have hitherto almost invariably confined their utterances to a hint that the present suspension of direct relations coincided with the cessation of any desire for their continuance.

Such feelings are not to be excused by any national passions. They are unworthy of what every one has hitherto understood by civilization, and it would be a misfortune indeed were they generally to prevail among persons of culture; and not only a misfortune for civilization, but, we are firmly convinced, a misfortune for the very purpose for which, after all, in the last resort all the present hell was let loose—the national existence of the different countries.

Technical achievement has made the world smaller, and to-day the countries of that large peninsula Europe seem brought as near to one another as the cities of each individual small Mediterranean peninsula used to be; and Europe—it might almost be said the world —is already one and indivisible, owing to its multitudinous associations.

Hence it must be the duty of educated and philanthropic Europeans to make, at any rate, an effort lest Europe, owing to her not being sufficiently strongly welded together, should suffer the same tragic fate as ancient Greece. Is Europe gradually to be exhausted by fratricidal war and perish?

The war raging at present will scarcely end in a victory for any one, but probably only in defeat. Consequently, it would seem that educated men in all countries not only should, but absolutely must, exert all their influence to prevent the conditions of peace being the source of future wars, and this no matter what the present uncertain issue of the conflict may be. Above all must they direct their efforts to seeing that advantage is taken of the fact that this war has thrown all European conditions, as it were, into a melting-pot, to mold Europe into one organic whole, for which both technical and intellectual conditions are ripe.

This is not the place to discuss how this new European order is to be brought about. We desire only to assert in principle that we are firmly convinced of the time having come for all Europe to be united together, in order to protect her soil, her inhabitants, and her civilization.

Believing as we do that the desire for such a state of things is latent in many minds, we are anxious that it should everywhere find expression and thus become a force; and with this end in view it seems to us before all else necessary that there should be a union of all in any way attached to European civilization; that is to say, who are what Goethe once almost prophetically called 'good Europeans.' We must never abandon hope that their collective pronouncement may be heard by some one even amidst the clash of arms, most especially if the 'good Europeans' of to-morrow include all those who are esteemed and considered as authorities by their fellow-men.

To begin with, however, it is needful that Europeans should unite, and if, as we hope, there are enough Europeans in Europe,—in other words, enough persons to whom Europe is no mere geographical term, but something which they have profoundly at heart,—then we mean to attempt to found such a union of Europeans. We ourselves wish only to give the first impulse to such a union; wherefore we ask you, should you be in agreement with us, and, like us, bent upon making the determination of Europe as widely known as possible, to send us your signature."[221]

Adolphe Isaac Crémieux, friend to Rothschild and Marx, purportedly stated before the Alliance Israélite Universelle,

"A new Messianic empire, a new Jerusalem, must arise in place of the emperors and popes."[222]

Talmudist Jews, like Karl Marx and the Rothschilds, had always borne a deep-seated hatred of Gentiles. Racist Zionists, like Albert Einstein, also hated Gentiles and wished them dead. Outspoken Zionist Dr. Josef Samuel Bloch was famous for answering August Rohling's criticisms of the Talmud and of anti-Christian rabbinical Talmudic culture.[223] The Talmud and Cabalist literature have been censored to conceal anti-Christian and anti-Gentile passages.[224] Therefore, when discussing Talmudic passages, one must at times make use of very old and difficult to obtain sources and rely upon secondary Christian sources who were highly knowledgeable, such as Martin Luther, Johannes Buxtorf and others.[225] Like Einstein, Bloch later advocated a Continental European union. The Socialist Eduard Bernstein wrote of Bloch,

"With regard to the circle around the *Sozialistische Monatshefte*, one must first speak of the periodical's editor, Dr. Josef Bloch. He is an exceptionally gifted East Prussian of Jewish origin. He is so Prussian-minded that at times he may be mistaken for a German nationalist. Before the war, he favored the defense and colonial policies of the German empire. To him, England was the power which German foreign policy must strive to conquer. During the war he was one of the most enthusiastic defenders of the war credits; today he is the guiding spirit among the socialist proponents of the so-called continental policy, that is, a policy which would tie together Germany, Russia, and France against England and, if necessary, also against the United States. This is not as a result of dislike of the English but because he believes that such a policy is necessary in the interest of Germany's world mission. As a Socialist he is a revisionist and as a Jew he is close to the Zionists."[226]

Though *The Manifesto to the Civilized World* managed to attract 93 signatories, *A Manifesto to Europeans* attracted only one other signatory, Otto Buek. Though Nicolai[227] spoke out against racism and nationalism in the common language of pacifists of the day, Einstein mixed his pacifistic rhetoric with contradictory racist and nationalistic Zionist rhetoric reminiscent of the Talmud. It is odd that Einstein contradicted his Socialistic and Pacifistic leanings with racist Zionist nationalism; and it is unusual that Einstein took such a strong public stance in support of Jews in the East, while most Western Jews—and he was a Western Jew—wanted to assimilate and distance themselves from segregationist Eastern Jews. Einstein was an incestuous sexual deviant like many of the Frankist Jews of the East. Einstein's fame came soon after he became a public spokesman for Eastern Jewish Zionism, which was not a coincidence.

3.4.1 Einstein Desires a "Race" War Which Will Exterminate the European Esau

The proposed union of Europe was perhaps intended by Jews like Nicolai and Einstein to consume itself in a struggle against a united Asia. Einstein often spoke in genocidal and racist terms against Germany, while promoting Jews and England. Einstein had consistently betrayed Germany before, during and after the war. For example, Albert Einstein wrote to Paul Ehrenfest on 22 March 1919,

"[The Allied Powers] whose victory during the war I had felt would be by far the lesser evil are now proving to be *only slightly* the lesser evil. [***] I get most joy from the emergence of the Jewish state in Palestine. It does seem to me that our kinfolk really are more sympathetic (at least less brutal) than these horrid Europeans. Perhaps things can only improve if only the Chinese are left, who refer to all Europeans with the collective noun 'bandits.'"[228]

At the time Einstein made this statement, he likely knew that Bolshevik mass murderers were recruiting large numbers of Chinese.[229] Jews were commonly referred to as Asiatics or Orientals (as opposed to Europeans) at that time, and the context of Einstein's statement was his hope that a Jewish state was about to be formed in Palestine. Einstein differentiates Jews from the Europeans he, like many other Jews, would exterminate.

In an article entitled "The Jews", *The Knickerbocker; or New York Monthly Magazine*, Volume 53, Number 1, (January, 1859), pp. 41-51, at 44-45, wrote,

"Yet the Jews of the Ottoman Empire, notwithstanding their degradation, exhibit a certain intellectual tendency. They live in an ideal world, frivolous and superstitious though it be. The Jew who fills the lowest offices, who deals out *raki* all day long to drunken Greeks, who trades in old nails, and to whose sordid soul the very piastres he bandies have imparted their copper haze, finds his chief delight in mental pursuits. Seated by a taper in his dingy cabin, he spends the long hours of the night in poring over the Zohar, the Chaldaic book of the magic Cabala, or, with enthusiastic delight, plunges into the mystical commentaries on the Talmud, seeking to unravel their quaint traditions and sophistries, and attempting, like the astrologers and alchymists, to divine the secrets and command the powers of Nature. 'The humble dealer, who hawks some article of clothing or some old piece of furniture about the streets; the obsequious mass of animated filth and rags which approaches to obtrude offers of service on the passing traveller, is perhaps deeply versed in Talmudic lore, or aspiring, in nightly vigils, to read into futurity, to command the elements, and acquire invisibility.' Thus wisdom is preferred to wealth, and a Rothschild would reject a family alliance with a Christian prince to form one with the humblest of his tribe who is learned in Hebrew lore.

The Jew of the old world, has his revenge:

'THE pound of flesh which I demand of him
Is dearly bought, is mine, and I will have it.'

Furnishing the hated Gentiles with the means of waging exterminating wars, he beholds, exultingly, in the fields of slaughtered victims a bloody satisfaction of his 'lodged hate' and 'certain loathing,' more gratifying even than the golden Four-per-cents on his Princely loans. Of like significance is the fact that in many parts of the world the despised Jews claim as their own the possessions of the Gentiles, among whom they dwell. Thus the squalid *Yeslir*, living in the Jews' quarter of Balata or Haskeni, and even more despised than the unbelieving dogs of Christians, traffics secretly in the estates, the palaces and the villages of the great Beys and Pachas, who would regard his touch as pollution. What, apparently, can be more absurd? Yet these assumed possessions, far more valuable, in fact, than the best 'estates in Spain,' are bought and sold for money, and inherited from generation to generation."

Einstein's statements attain their full genocidal context in the writings of his friend and political cohort, the crypto-Jew Georg Friedrich Nicolai (Lewinstein), who, together with Einstein called for the "European race" to unite in their *Manifesto to Europeans*—perhaps in Nicolai's mind to fight a preemptive race war of extermination against the "superior race" of Mongols—perhaps in Einstein's mind for the "Mongoloid race" to exterminate the "horrid Europeans"—the "Esau" of Rome.

Nicolai saw Jews as members of the "European race", or he at least pretended to see them as such in his efforts to draw the Europeans into a "race" war with the Asians. Einstein saw Jews as racially distinct from Europeans. Nicolai (Lewinstein) wrote in 1917,

"§ 34.—*What a War of Extermination Means*

Thus to-day the original conception of war is distorted until it has become completely reversed, simply because there is no longer anything natural about war; it is now merely a romantic reminiscence. Now, it might be, and has been said, that the benefits of war come afterward. It might be thought, however, that any one thus contemplating the remote effects of war ought seriously to reflect upon its inevitable results. That is, he ought to think out his ideas to their logical conclusions, which seems easy, but is often very difficult.

The idea of war as a factor likely to favor the selection of the fittest, and thus promote human evolution, is simple enough. War is here looked upon as representing that relentless, or rather that disinterested, justice which allows the fit to survive and destroys the unfit. Those who consider this right should act accordingly, and proceed to draw up rules accordingly. They ought to adopt the usages of war of which we read in ancient history, rules by which old men were killed and also unborn children, but not the seemingly humane (!) rules of modern times—rules which make war a farce in the sense in which a natural scientist uses the word; that is to say, cause it to promote negative selection, and thus convert it into a means of deterioration.

The gulf which apparently separates the selfish human being of to-day from the humane promoter of civilization is merely apparent; and here I would recall what I have already said about struggle between animals and struggle between man and man. Both are justifiable in themselves and both *can* be carried on logically. Difficulties do not arise until we begin to imagine that it is allowable to carry on an animal struggle against human beings and by human methods. This is senseless, and therefore criminal; for war as waged at present can be considered only a justifiable form of struggle for existence if the nations against whom we are waging war are not looked upon as human beings, at any rate not as human beings on a level with ourselves; that is, if it is desired to carry on a war of extermination against barbarians so as to enable true humanity to find room upon and spread over the earth. No European will feel that he is justified in considering another European as a barbarian. The utmost which might be asked is whether we are not entitled to consider ourselves a superior race in comparison with certain undeveloped races, such as the Andamans or Tierra del Fuegans. What will undoubtedly occur is that these people will gradually be exterminated by the white race, though it has long been clear that it would be extremely foolish to make war upon them. They die out of themselves wherever they come in contact with whites, bloodless warfare being always more effectual than bloody.

There is only *one* race for which this question of racial superiority might be profoundly important—the Mongolian. I do not know who are the superior, the Mongolians or we ourselves, but I can quite understand our looking on the Mongolian race as enemies, and that, for instance, Europeans on the highest plane would not easily be induced to have a child by a Mongolian woman, at any rate not to own it. I can therefore also fully understand that we or the Mongolians might say, 'Only one of us two races can rule over the world, and we want that race to be ours.'

In this case the biologically *weaker* race—that is, the one which may rest assured that in ordinary course it would fall a victim to natural selection—might *perhaps* be justified in saying, 'As there is no chance of our getting the upper hand by natural and lawful means, we will try to take by force what nature withholds from us.' This shows very plainly that for the really strong war is superfluous; and as obviously it is generally folly for the weak, it is self-evident that, save in the rarest instances, there can be no possible object whatever in it.

Now, it is possible that one such rare instance may be afforded by the Mongolians, for, unlike all the other colored races, they seem to be in certain respects fitter than Europeans, although it is impossible to know exactly how they will be affected when once they are drawn into the vortex of modern civilization. Meantime, however, the sons of Heaven have the enormous advantage of being able to work equally well under all heavens, whether in the icy wastes of the tundras or under the burning sun of Sumatra. Apparently this is a special Mongolian peculiarity, for even primitive Teutonic peoples simply melted away under the Southern sun to which their impulse led them, and negro races get consumption if transferred to colder climates.

If all this is really the case, then the greater part of the habitable world belongs to the Mongols, and likewise the overlordship thereof; for it seems out of the question, seeing how much going to and fro there already is and how much more there is certain to be in the near future, that two races should live side by side and yet apart. They will mix, and one will prevail over the other.

But perhaps even the most humane of us all would not desire this, and therefore I can imagine our pointing with pardonable pride to our civilization, and saying that we are ready to take up arms in defense of it. You Mongols may be better than we are, we would say, but you are different. We do not want to know anything about your civilization, even supposing it to be superior; we mean to keep our own. From this point of view I can imagine a war, but then it must be really a relentless, merciless war.

There are now in the world five hundred millions of us Europeans or white men originally from Europe, and a thousand millions of various colored races. I believe we have even now the technical means at our disposal for exterminating these thousand millions in the course of the next twenty years. After twenty years, however, we shall no longer be in a position to do this, as soon, that is, as China has armed her whole population, constructs her own dreadnoughts, and manufactures her own cannon and shells, as Japan is already doing.

In the ensuing twenty years, therefore, it is possible that the fate of the world will be decided once and for all, and the responsibility for this decision rests with the five hundred millions of Europeans. The Mongolians need do nothing but wait, for time and space are on their side.

At a time when the fate of so many men is hanging in the balance, Europeans may, perhaps must, be asked whether on careful consideration they mean to declare all colored races barbarians, and then begin a struggle for existence, in other, words a war of extermination, and not a ridiculous war for power, against everything non-European. When once so terrible a conception as that of such a war is grasped, then, if anything save senseless cruelty is to be the result, it also must be thought out to the end, and there would have to be a war *sans trève et sans relâche.*

We must not spare even the child in its mother's womb, and must tolerate no bastards. Such a war would be ghastly, but there would be some object in it. It is useless to talk of the justice of a war, but in a sense this ghastliest of wars is the justest because, at any rate, 'it serves its own particular purpose.'

To me it seems at least conceivable that some such war might succeed, although I certainly do not believe this. History, indeed, proves over and over that the despair of nations fighting for their lives gives rise to strength which enables them to triumph over all technical expedients. Here, again, any attempt to interfere with the justice of history by such brutal methods might only too easily hasten the downfall of Europe. European nations, as I think, would do better to concentrate all their economic, technical, and scientific resources on increasing their internal vital energy, that is, on promoting race hygiene in every respect, and thus endeavor to become the equals and even the superiors of the Mongols.

This opens up vistas of victories not purchased with blood—victories which I am profoundly convinced are within the bounds of possibility. This inextinguishable hope is due to my proud European racial instinct. I will not, and I refuse to, admit that the Mongols have in the long run greater vitality than I. I trust that the majority of Europeans think as I do, and that never shall we show the Asiatics such a sign of weakness as to draw the sword against them. Even if the European nations were faint-hearted, even if they were doubtful of ultimate peaceful victory, and if nothing seemed to stand in the way of their extermination by force, even, then I would shrink from resort to force, and I am convinced that the majority of mankind agree with me.

Every one, however, must compound with his own conscience, and should any one be anxious to proceed to victory by way of force, I will go a step further to please him. I feel that all Europeans belong to the same race, and I am proud of this. But others certainly feel this less keenly than I do, and they let their wholesome race instinct run to waste in all manner of fantastic and useless notions, such as the supposed existence of a Teutonic race.[*Footnote:* Cf. §§ 90-105, about race patriotism.]

But there are those who believe in the Teutons, Germans, or Prussians having a right to predominate. I shall not here discuss the justification for such ideas, but those who would fain lead such small aggregates of human beings to victory must at any rate ask themselves whether they are *able* and, if able, also *willing*, to fight out this fight in the only way in which it can answer its purpose.

As for Teutonism, the question is as follows: take the one hundred million Germans or, properly speaking, the twenty millions more or less pure Teutons living in various parts of Europe, most of whom will have nothing whatever to do with the conception of Teutonism. Do they believe that they *can* with any prospect of success embark upon a struggle against forces from fifteen to a hundred times more numerous, and do they really *mean* to destroy these? If they have made up their minds to this, then let them make the attempt, and they will be fighting for an idea, and for an object which is at least conceivable.

We are therefore faced with the following alternative: we must either resolve to live in peace with the French, Russians, English, and whatever all their names may be, or we must wage a war of extermination upon them, a war whose purpose it is not to leave one of them alive.

Whoever, therefore, decides for war is, at any rate, no fool, and has logic on his side. Nevertheless, I hope and believe that even those who most delight in war will incline toward peace when once they realize what is the inevitable alternative. But this senseless playing at war which is now devastating Europe must be the last of its kind."[230]

The Bolsheviks in Russia had a strong and growing Chinese contingent very early on in the movement. These Chinese Bolsheviks brutally slaughtered Slavic Christians. Jewish leadership had long since scheduled China to become a Communist nation. Zionist Jews sought to establish a "Jewish State" in the far Eastern regions of the Soviet Union, the Jewish Autonomous Oblast in Khabarovsk Krai in the districts of Birobidzhansky, Leninsky, Obluchensky, Oktyabrsky and Smidovichsky.[231] This plan failed, in part, due to the interference of some Zionist Socialists, who insisted that Palestine was the Jews' national home. An even earlier attempt to found a Jewish State in Russia in the districts of Homel, Witebsk and Minsk,[232] also failed, largely due to a lack of Jewish interest. The Zionists insisted that anti-Semitism alone could force the Jews to segregate. When the Zionists put Hitler in power, they had the needed impetus to force Jews to flee Europe and the Zionists attempted to steal Chinese territory for a "Jewish homeland" with the help of the Imperial Japanese under the "Fugu Plan".[233] Zionist Jews sought to establish a "Jewish State" in China, which had been taken over by the Imperial Japanese whom the Jews had been financing since the days when Jacob Schiff loaned them $200,000,000.00 in the Russo-Japanese War. The Zionists used the Imperial Japanese to destroy the Chinese government in preparation for the formation of a Jewish nation in China under the "Fugu Plan" in Manchuria or Shanghai. The Jews even promoted the *Protocols of the Learned Elders of Zion* to the

Japanese as evidence as to how powerful they were. The "Fugu Plan" failed to attract enough Jews, even under Nazi pressure, and die hard Zionists wanted Palestine. The Zionists then arranged for war between the United States and Japan. When America declared war on Japan, Hitler, seemingly inexplicably, declared war on the United States ensuring the ultimate defeat of Germany. Hitler also went to war with the Soviets, which gave him access to large numbers of Jews the Zionists could then segregate and ready for deportation to Palestine.

Albert Einstein's friend Georg Friedrich Nicolai (Lewinstein) stated in 1917,

"Apart from this strange story of Cain, however, murder is forbidden in the Bible, and very sternly forbidden. But—it is only the murder of Jews. As is natural, considering the period from which it dates, the Bible is absolutely national, in character. Only the Jew is really considered as a human being; cattle and strangers might be slain without the slayer himself being slain. In this case there was a ransom. Accordingly, war was of course allowed also, and the Jews were no more illogical than the Moslem who kills the outlander. Of late years the Jews and the Old Testament have often been reproached for their contempt for those who were not Jews; and in practice even Christ acted in precisely the same way."[234]

In a "Letter to the Editor", signed by Isidore Abramowitz, Hannah Arendt, Abraham Brick, Rabbi Jessurun Cardozo, Albert Einstein, Herman Eisen, M. D., Hayim Fineman, M. Gallen, M. D., H. H. Harris, Zelig S. Harris, Sidney Hook, Fred Karush, Bruria Kaufman, Irma L. Lindheim, Nachman Majsel, Seymour Melman, Myer D. Mendelson, M. D., Harry M. Orlinsky, Samuel Pitlick, Fritz Rohrlich, Louis P. Rocker, Ruth Sager, Itzhak Sankowsky, I. J. Schoenberg, Samuel Shuman, M. Znger, Irma Wolpe, Stefan Wolpe; dated "New York. Dec. 2, 1948."; published as: "New Palestine Party; Visit of Menachen Begin and Aims of Political Movement Discussed", *The New York Times*, (4 December 1948), p. 12; it states, *inter alia,*

"Among the most disturbing political phenomena of our time is the emergence in the newly created state of Israel of the 'Freedom Party' (Tnuat Haherut), a political party closely akin in its organization, methods, political philosophy and social appeal to the Nazi and Fascist parties. It was formed out of the membership and following of the former Irgun Zvai Leumi, a terrorist, right-wing, chauvinist organization in Palestine. The current visit of Menachen Begin, leader of this party, to the United States is obviously calculated to give the impression of American support for his party in the coming Israeli elections, and to cement political ties with conservative Zionist elements in the United States. [***] The Deir Yassin incident exemplifies the character and actions of the Freedom Party. Within the Jewish community they have preached an admixture of ultranationalism, religious mysticism, and racial superiority. Like other Fascist parties they have been used to break strikes, and have themselves pressed for the destruction of free trade unions. In their stead they have proposed corporate unions on the Italian Fascist model. [***] This is the unmistakable stamp of a Fascist party for whom terrorism (against Jews, Arabs, and British alike), and misrepresentation are means, and a 'Leader State' is the goal."

Racist Zionist Moses Hess declared that Germans are the genetic enemies of Israel in 1862 (contrast Hess' views with Goldhagen's negative analysis of Germans under Hitler[235] and see Hartmut Stern's response to Goldhagen[236]). Moses Hess' statement must be seen in the context of Jacob and Esau, and Isaac's "blessing" to Esau that Esau should be the servant and the sword of Jacob, of Israel. *Genesis* 25:23 states,

"And the LORD said unto her, Two nations *are* in thy womb, and two manner of people shall be separated from thy bowels; and *the one* people shall be stronger than *the other* people; and the elder shall serve the younger."

Genesis 27:38-41 states,

"38 And Esau said unto his father, Hast thou but one blessing, my father? bless me, *even* me also, O my father. And Esau lifted up his voice, and wept. 39 And Isaac his father answered and said unto him, Behold, thy dwelling shall be the fatness of the earth, and of the dew of heaven from above; 40 And by thy sword shalt thou live, and shalt serve thy brother; and it shall come to pass when thou shalt have the dominion, that thou shalt break his yoke from off thy neck. 41¶ And Esau hated Jacob because of the blessing wherewith his father blessed him: and Esau said in his heart, The days of mourning for my father are at hand; then will I slay my brother Jacob."

Hess may have envisioned the annihilation of the German "race"—referred to by some Jews as the people of the sword. It was clearly better for the Jews to kill off Esau before his descendants "broke his yoke from off his neck" than to let them live and potentially seek revenge on the Jews. Hess' book told his fellow Jews that Germans were the seed of Amalek and must be exterminated. At least as early as the 1860's, Moses Hess argued that the "German race" had a genetically programmed antagonism towards the "Jewish race"—the implication being that one must destroy the other in order to survive. In the Jewish mythology, this confrontation called for the extermination of the Germans. Two World Wars nearly accomplished the destruction of Germany and ended their prominence in world affairs. Two World Wars killed off many of the strongest, smartest and most assertive Germans. Hess wrote in 1862,

"It seems that German education is not compatible with our Jewish national aspirations. Had I not once lived in France, it would never have entered my mind to interest myself with the revival of Jewish nationality. Our views and strivings are determined by the social environment which surrounds us. Every Living, acting people, like every active individual, has its special field. Indeed, every man, every member of the historical nations, is a political, or as we say at present, a social animal; yet within this sphere of the common social world, there are special places reserved by Nature for individuals according to their particular calling. The specialty of the German of the higher class, of course, is his interest in abstract thought; and because he is too much of a universal philosopher, it is difficult for him to be inspired by national tendencies. 'Its whole tendency,' my former publisher, Otto Wigand, once wrote to me, when I showed him an outline of a work on Jewish national aspirations, 'is contrary to my pure human nature.'

The 'pure human nature' of the Germans is, in reality, the character of the pure German race, which rises to the conception of humanity in theory only, but in practice it has not succeeded in overcoming the natural sympathies and antipathies of the race. German antagonism to Jewish national aspiration has a double origin, though the motives are really contrary to each other. The duplicity and contrariety of the human personality, such as we can see in the union of the spiritual and the natural, the theoretical and the practical sides, are in no other nation so sharply marked in their points of opposition as in the German. Jewish national aspirations are antagonistic to the theoretical cosmopolitan tendencies of the German. But in addition to this, the German opposes Jewish national aspirations because of his racial antipathy, from which even the noblest Germans have not as yet emancipated themselves. The publisher, whose 'pure human' conscience revolted against publishing a book advocating the revival of Jewish nationality, published books preaching hatred to Jews and Judaism without the slightest remorse, in spite of the fact that the motive of such works is essentially opposed to the 'pure human conscience.' This contradictory action was due to inborn racial antagonism to the Jews. But the German, it seems, has no clear conception of his racial prejudices; he sees in his egoistic as well as in his spiritual endeavors, not German or Teutonic, but 'humanitarian tendencies'; and he does not know that he follows the latter only in theory, while in practice he clings to his egoistic ideas.

[***]

In 1858, there appeared, at Leipzig, a work written by Otto Wigand under the title *Two discourses concerning the desertion from Judaism*, being an analysis of the views on this question expressed in the recently published correspondence of Dr. Abraham Geiger. The author endeavors to prove that the conclusions of Dr. Geiger are untenable both from a philosophic and from a social standpoint. Here are his social arguments:

'My friend,' says the author, 'there are certain conclusions which you cannot escape. The stamp of slavery, if we may use this expression, which centuries of oppression have deeply impressed upon the Jewish features, might have been obliterated by the blessed hand of regained civil liberty. The gait of the Jews, buoyed up by the happy reminiscences of the victory won in the struggle for the noble possession of liberty, might have been straighter and prouder. The Jewish face may certainly beam with pride, as it views the tremendous progress made by the Jews in a brief time, their mighty flight to the spiritual height upon which they now stand, which is especially notable considering the fact that their poets and writers at whose greatness the nation is astonished, and of whose talents the entire people takes account, have sprung from those who, a generation ago, could hardly converse correctly in the language of the land. Such a state of affairs should undoubtedly call forth admiration in the hearts of the present German generation, and yet, in spite of these achievements, the wall separating Jew and Christian still stands unshattered, for the watchman that guards them is one who will not be caught napping. It is the race difference between the Jewish and Christian populations. If this assertion of mine surprises or astonishes you, I ask you to consider whether it is not almost a rule with the Germans that race differences generate prejudices which cannot be overcome by any manifestation of good-will on the part of the other race. The relations existing between the German and the Slavic populations in Bohemia, in Hungary and Transylvania, between the Germans and the Danes in Schleswig, or between the Irish and the Anglo-Saxon settlers in Ireland, illustrates well the power of race antagonism in the German world. In all these countries the different elements of the population have lived side by side for centuries, sharing equally all political rights, and yet, so strong are the national or racial differences, that a social amalgamation of the various elements of the population is even at the present day quite unthinkable. And what comparison is there between the race differences of a German and Slav, a Celt and Anglo-Saxon, or a German and Dane, and the race antagonism between the children of the Sons of Jacob, who are of Asiatic descent, and the descendants of Teut and Herman, the ancestors of whom have inhabited Europe from time immemorial; between the proud and the tall blond German and the small of figure, black-haired and black-eyed Jew? Races which differ in such a degree oppose each other instinctively and against such opposition reason and good sense are powerless.'

These expressions are certainly frank and sincere in their meaning, though they by no means prove the conclusions to which the author wishes to arrive, namely, the desirability of conversion; for conversion will not turn a Jew into a German. But they at least contain the confession, that an instinctive race antagonism triumphs in Germany above all humanitarian sentiments. The 'pure human nature' resolves itself, according to the Germans, in the nature of pure Germanism. The 'high-born blond race' looks with contempt upon the regeneration of the 'black-haired, quick-moving mannikins,' without regard to whether they are descendants of the Biblical patriarchs, or of the ancient Romans and Gauls.

While other civilized western nations mention the shameful oppression to which the Jews were formerly subjected, only as an act of theirs of which they are ashamed, the German remembers only the 'stamp of slavery' which he impressed upon 'the Jewish physiognomy.'

In a *feuilleton* which appeared recently in the *Bonnerzeitung*, entitled 'Bonn Eighty Years Ago,' the author speaks of the Jews in mocking terms and describes them as people who lived in separate quarters and supported themselves by petty trades. I believe that we should wonder less at the fact that the Jews, who were forbidden to participate in the important branches of industry and commerce, lived on petty trade, than at the fact that they were able to live at all in those centuries of oppression. As a matter of fact, almost every means of existence, including the right of domicile, was denied them. It was only by means of bribes that every Jewish generation could procure anew the 'privilege' not to be driven out of their homes in Bonn, and they felt happy indeed if, in spite of the contract, they were not robbed of their property and exiled, or attacked by a fanatical mob in the bargain. I, also, can tell a story of 'eighty years ago.' A Jew won the high favor of the Kurfuerst of Bonn, that he and his descendants were granted the 'privilege' to settle in Ebendich.

[***]

Gabriel Riesser, the editor of the magazine, *The Jew*, as far as I can recollect, never fell into the error, common to all modern German Jews, that the emancipation of the Jews is irreconcilable with the development of Jewish Nationalism. He demanded emancipation for the Jews on the one condition only, that of their receiving all civil and political rights in return for their assuming all civil and political burdens."[237]

3.4.2 Lenard Sickens of Einstein's Libels

Germany had been very good to the Jews. German Jews were the wealthiest people in the world. In the years following the First World War, the Germans resented the fact that the Jews, Einstein being their chief spokesman, had stabbed the Germans in the back during the war, and then twisted the knife at the peace negotiations in France, where a large contingent of Jews decided Germany's fate, and reneged on Woodrow Wilson's Fourteen Points, one of which assured Germany that it would lose no territory. The Germans had thought that Wilson's pledge would be honored after the Germans had surrendered in good faith. Had not the Germans received this promise of the Fourteen Points, they would not have surrendered and were in a position to continue the war. The promise was broken.

In addition, the Allies insisted that Germany pay draconian war reparations that would forever ruin the nation. Leading Jews in Germany sided with the Allies against their native land. It was obvious that leading Jews were profiteering from the war in every way possible, at the expense of the German nation and its People. Jewish leaders instigated crippling strikes in the arms industry, which left German troops without adequate armaments. Jewish revolutionaries took advantage of Germany's weakened state, which Jews had deliberately caused for the purpose, and created a Soviet Republic in Bavaria and overthrew the monarchy. German-Jewish bankers cut off Germany's access to funds. German-Jewish Zionists moved to London and brought America into the war on the side of the British at the very moment Germany was about to win the war.

Those arms which were produced were often substandard and were peddled by Jews to Jews in the German Government, which also left the German troops without adequate arms, while making Jews immensely wealthy. German-Jewish bankers conspired with German arms manufacturers to produce weapons for both sides. The German-Jewish press, which had initially beat the war drums louder than anyone else, teamed up with leading Jews in the German Government at the end of the war and demanded that Germany submit to the demands of the Allies, give up vast territories and make the reparations payments. The German-Jewish press and Jews in the German Government, many of whom were the same persons who had most boisterously called upon the German People to go to war, insisted that the Germans accept responsibility for causing the war, though they had not caused it. Etc. Etc. Etc.

While millions of Germans were starving to death, many Jews in Germany had never known better times. Whenever anyone revealed the truth of what was happening, the Jewish press immediately smeared them by calling them "anti-Semites". The situation was similar to, though even worse than, the situation in America today.

Many German Jews were very wealthy after the war. They had a great deal of power, and many were very arrogant, especially in their dealings with German Gentiles. A famous German engineer and physicist, who had anticipated many aspects of the theory of relativity, Rudolf Mewes proved that Einstein was a plagiarist. Mewes demonstrated that Albert Einstein had stolen many of his ideas from German scientists.

Albert Einstein made a great show of ridiculing Germans, though he was born in Germany, lived and earned his living in Germany throughout the war, worked for the Prussian Academy of Sciences in Berlin, and published in German journals. Einstein assisted in, and pushed hard for, plans to punish and oppress German scientists after the war—to punish and oppress his German colleagues while he was feted in the British press as the "Swiss Jew". Einstein's ingratitude and treachery were unbearable and he epitomized the Jewish betrayal of Germany in the First World War.

Rudolf Mewes was not afraid to challenge Einstein, or the "Einstein myth" of the "Jewish Newton" which was based on lies, plagiarism, ingratitude, self-glorification and Jewish racism,

> "But then, given the above exposé, one must admit that [Max] Born's contention is correct, that the relativistic ideas were not only first conceived and recorded in the German language, but rather also that they demonstrably derived from pure German scientists, namely Christian Doppler, Wilhelm Weber and Rudolf Mewes, though not from the Semitic Professor and Communist Dr. Albert Einstein. The relationship of Mewes to Einstein can accordingly be briefly characterized by the slogans:
> > 'German versus Jew
> > Increaser of Knowledge versus Fleecer of Knowledge
> > Rightful Ownership versus Plagiarism
> > Monarchist versus Communist'"

> "Dagegen muß man nach den vorstehenden Darlegungen die Behauptung Borns als richtig zugeben, daß die relativistischen Ideen zuerst nicht nur in deutscher Sprache gedacht und aufgezeichnet worden sind, sondern auch von rein deutschen Forschern, nämlich Christian Doppler, Wilhelm Weber und Rudolf Mewes, nachweislich herrühren, aber nicht von dem semitischen Professor und Kommunisten Dr. Albert Einstein. Das Verhältnis von Mewes zu Einstein läßt sich demgemäß kurz

mit den Schlagworten kennzeichnen:
„Deutscher gegen Jude,
Wissensschöpfer gegen Wissensschröpfer,
Eigentum gegen Diebstahl,
Monarchist gegen Kommunist.'""[238]

Germans then knew far more about the genocidal prophecies of Judaism than they do today. They could see them deliberately fulfilled before there eyes. They recognized that Bolshevism and the "Great War", the "War to End All Wars", which prepared the way for the "League of Nations", was largely accomplished under the directorship of Jews and deliberately fulfilled Jewish Messianic prophecy. They knew that leading Jews had lured Germany into the war and then destroyed Germany and profited as much as possible from the destruction.

In addition, an unwise and unproductive rift between British science and German science had existed at least since the time of the Leibnitz-Newton priorities dispute over the invention of calculus, and before that there were strong controversies between the Continent and the Island among Giordano Bruno, Henry More, Isaac Newton, Samuel Clark, René Des Cartes, Christiaan Huyghens, and Gottfried Wilhelm Leibnitz. Einstein sided with the British against the Germans during and after the war, despite the fact he was treated like royalty in Berlin.

Jewish news sources promoted the causes of the Social Democrats, Liberal Democrats, Marxists, Bolsheviks, Anarchists or Chernyshevskiist revolution, and they also promoted Albert Einstein, which inspired suspicion of ethnic bias.[239] The segregationist policies of Albert Einstein, Chaim Weizmann—the political Zionists in general—caused many to suspect that the shameless promotion of Albert Einstein involved a Jewish ethnic bias in favor of Einstein.[240] This unfair and unethical Jewish bias preceded and caused the reactions of Ludwig Glaser, Philipp Lenard, Johannes Stark, Willy Wien, Hugo Dingler, Bruno Thüring, and others who sought to defend themselves, their students and their nation.

Einstein was famously quoted in the forward of the first edition to Lucien Fabre's French book, *Une Nouvelle Figure du Monde: les Théories d'Einstein avec une Préface de M. Einstein*, Payot, Paris, (1921), pp. 15-18; not long after the First World War ended,

"I am a German (Jew) by birth, but I lived in Switzerland from the age of 15 until I was 35, except for brief interruptions. I earned my degree in Zurich; I am a pacifist in favor of an international agreement and have always faithfully conducted myself according to this ideal."

"Je suis Allemand (israélite) de naissance, mais j'ai vécu en Suisse de l'âge de 15 à celui de 35 ans, sauf de courtes interruptions. J'ai conquis mes grades à Zurich; je suis pacifiste, partisan d'une entente internationale et resté toujours fidèle dans ma ligne de conduite à cet idéal."

Einstein's political statements were scripted. He repeated his script and asked others to repeat it. Einstein was quoted in *The Literary Digest* of 16 April 1921, pages 33-34,

"Dr. Einstein asked whether he could not see a copy of my interview with him before it was printed. I told him that I would not write the interview until after my return to America.

'In that event,' he said, 'when you write it, be sure not to omit to state that I am a convinced pacifist, that I believe that the world has had enough of war. Some sort of an international agreement must be reached among nations preventing the recurrence of another war, as another war will ruin our civilization completely. Continental civilization, European civilization, has been badly damaged and set back by this war, but the loss is not irreparable. Another war may prove fatal to Europe.'"

Note that Einstein's scripted statements are classic Jewish propaganda and typify the Jewish method of undermining the sovereignty of the Gentile nations. First, the Zionists caused the war. Then they prolonged it by bringing America into it. Then they threatened the war weary nations with a worse war and offered up what they claimed was the only solution: A world led by Israel with a world government in fulfillment of Judaic Messianic prophecies. The conference Einstein hoped for was a conference where the Zionists could push the Palestine Mandate and demand a nation for the Jews. It was a conference that Einstein knew would be dominated by Jews, who would dictate to the ruined nations their future. Einstein was not concerned for humanity. He was an ardent and thoroughly scripted Jewish Zionist propagandist.

The language used in Einstein's statement in French was somewhat open to interpretation. For example, Stjepan Mohorovičić wrote in 1922,

"Einstein selbst sagt in dem Vorwort des Werkes von L. Fabre (Anmerk. 30) den Franzosen ausdrücklich, daß er nur in Deutschland geboren sei, sonst sei er ein Jude, Pazifist und Mitglied einer internationalen Verbindung.... Es ist nicht schwer zu raten, warum Einstein dies gerade den Franzosen gegenüber gesagt hat (mit eigener Unterschrift), aber lassen wir das, es ist dies nur Geschmacksache...; unsere Arbeit hier ist eine wissenschaftliche. Es ist traurig genug, daß ich gezwungen bin, dies hier zu erwähnen!"[241]

Einstein's use of the word "entente" might also have been interpreted by Germans as a subtle allusion to the Allies. In 1904, England and France entered into an "Entente Cordiale"—an agreement between the two governments; which, while resolving colonial disputes between England and France, created tensions with Germany. In 1906 the "Entente" evolved into a military alliance, which came to include Russia in 1907. This alliance was opposed to the "Triple Alliance" of Germany, Austria-Hungary and Italy. England, France and Russia, who fought against Germany in World War I, were often referred to as the "Entente" and it might have appeared from Einstein's statement that he had always been a devout enemy of Germany and a partisan for the enemies of Germany, though he had lived in Germany throughout the war. We know that this was in fact the case, whether or not it was what Einstein meant to say in his scripted letter to Fabre. It was almost certainly not what Einstein meant to say in that letter.

Einstein used the word "Entente" to describe the Allies in many of his letters and should have been more careful with "his" words. For example, in a letter to Paul Ehrenfest of 6 December 1918,

"Ich werde nächster Tage über die Schweiz nach Paris reisen, um die Entente zu bitten, die hiesige ausgeshungerte Bevölkerung vor dem Hungertod zu retten."[242]

Einstein wrote to Emil Zürcher on 15 April 1919,

"Wenn die Entente gut orientiert[. . . .]"[243]

Einstein wrote to Hedwig Born on 31 August 1919,

"Intervention der Entente in Schlessien"[244]

Einstein wrote to the *Neue Freie Presse* on 6 December 1919,

"[. . .]der Centralmächte und denen der Entente[. . .]"[245]

Einstein wrote to Hedwig and Max Born on 27 January 1920,

"Jedenfalls ist die Wirkekraft ihrer Parole gross, denn die Kriegsgeräte der Entente, welche das deutsche Heer aufgerieben haben, schmelzen in Russland dahin wie der Schnee in der Märzensonne."[246]

Einstein was careless in "his" letter to Fabre, which letter was quoted in Fabre's book.

Einstein did often assert that he was an internationalist and a pacifist, without implying that he had sided with the Allies in the First World War. However, we learn from Einstein's statements to the Frenchman Romain Rolland, as recorded in Rolland's diary after conversations with Einstein in Switzerland on 16 September 1915, that Einstein was indeed loyal to the Entente, not Germany. Rolland wrote,

"What I hear from [Einstein] is not exactly encouraging, for it shows the impossibility of arriving at a lasting peace with Germany without first totally crushing it. Einstein says the situation looks to him far less favorable than a few months back. The victories over Russia have reawakened German arrogance and appetite. The word 'greedy' seems to Einstein best to characterize Germany. [***] Einstein does not expect any renewal of Germany out of itself; it lacks the energy for it, and the boldness for initiative. He hopes for a victory of the Allies, which would smash the power of Prussia and the dynasty. . . . Einstein and Zangger dream of a divided Germany—on the one side Southern Germany and Austria, on the other side Prussia. [***] We speak of the deliberate blindness and the lack of psychology in the Germans."[247]

Einstein often spoke in genocidal and racist terms against Germany and for the Jews and England. He betrayed Germany before, during and after the war. For example, Einstein wrote to Paul Ehrenfest on 22 March 1919,

"[The Allied Powers] whose victory during the war I had felt would be by far the lesser evil are now proving to be *only slightly* the lesser evil. [***] I get most joy from the emergence of the Jewish state in Palestine. It does seem to me that our kinfolk really are more sympathetic (at least less brutal) than these horrid Europeans. Perhaps things can only improve if only the Chinese are left, who refer to all Europeans with the collective noun 'bandits.'"[248]

Einstein almost certainly was not referring to the Allies when referring to an *entente internationale,* but rather to an international agreement. His wording caused further consternation given that there was the soon to appear *Entente Internationale des Partis Radicaux et des Partis Démocratiques similaires,* a group of liberals from many nations who based their movement on the spirit of the *Plan des Libéraux pour recommencer la révolution,* Paris, (1821); probably in the form of the *Carté.* There was also the First International of Marx and Engels, and its offspring: The International Workingmen's Association, the Second International, the Socialist International, the Third International, the Comintern, the Vienna International, the Two-and-a-half International, the Labor and Socialist International, the Fourth International, the Trotsky International, etc. The *Carté* was founded by Communist Henri Barbusse and Einstein's friend and confidant, pacifist Socialist Romain Rolland. In late 1919 and early 1920, Einstein sought to establish a German chapter of the *Clarté* for the purposes of promoting Internationalism.[249] This in itself troubled many Germans, who had come to believe that "Internationalism" was a code word for "Jewish supremacy". Even before the war, the "Proclamation of the Alliance Against the Arrogance of Jewry" of 1912 stated,

"The Reichstag elections of 1912 have taken place under the sign of Jewry—that is, under the sign of open and clandestine republicanism and internationalism. 'National is irrational'. . . was and is the slogan that misled millions of Germans, blinded by the fraudulent Jewish catchwords of international culture and international progress. [***] Jewry is international in the sense of Schopenhauer's phrase: 'The fatherland of the Jews is other Jews.'"[250]

Einstein's declarations of his "tribal"—to use his term—loyalty, his public insults against Germans, and his allegedly privileged Zionist nationalism were viewed as legitimate causes for concern—as was the modern terror of the Internationalism of the Bolsheviks, who had made Bavaria a Soviet Republic for a short span of time.

Many Germans were outraged by Einstein's statement as quoted in Fabre's book,[251] which was an obvious attempt by Einstein to distance himself from Germany (Gentiles) and ingratiate himself to the French, no matter how one translated it—and Einstein and his friends instigated a smear campaign against Fabre in order to deflect attention from Einstein's volatile comments.[252] Einstein's friend Solovine smeared Fabre, claiming that he was an anti-Semite—even though Fabre had written a book which was highly flattering to Einstein.

Einstein charged that Fabre cobbled together the forward from Einstein's statements and published this compilation of quotes without Einstein's approval. Einstein protested that Fabre had no right to designate this compilation as if it were a forward Einstein intended to write for Fabre, because he allegedly had not written it in the form in which it appeared and had not approved its publication as a forward to Fabre's book—though he had made the statements—a fact he appeared to publicly deny. Einstein alleged to Solovine that his words were corrupted in translation though the addition of French *gentillesse* by an acquaintance of his, who Einstein implies wrote the letters.

In the second edition of his book, Fabre stated that he had only given a public expression to Einstein's views to a wanting public, with the best of intentions. Fabre stated that Einstein had repudiated Einstein's own statements. Einstein's friends let Einstein know that Fabre had begun to spread the word after Einstein had attacked Fabre, that Henri Poincaré was the true father of the special theory of relativity. Einstein hid from Fabre's accusation that Einstein had plagiarized Poincaré's theory.[253]

The preface to Fabre's first edition states,

"PRÉFACE

L'ouvrage de M. Fabre est des plus intéressants et fort bien écrit. Ses explications sur l'œuvre de Newton, de Faraday et de Maxwel sont admirablement réussies. L'auteur est un vrai enthousiaste rempli d'un sentiment vibrant pour la beauté scientifique.

L'éloge dont il veut bien honorer mes théories est terriblement exagéré. La théorie de la relativité ne peut ni veut donner aucun système du monde, mais seulement une condition restrictive à laquelle les lois de la nature doivent se soumettre, comme par exemple les deux principaux axiomes de la thermodynamique. Celui-là même qui ne reconnaîtrait pas la théorie de la relativité se voit cependant obligé d'admettre une interprétation physique claire des coordonnées de l'espace et du temps. C'est justement à ce point de vue que pèchent les écrits de certains des savants cités par l'auteur.

L'ouvrage de l'un d'entre eux défend une thèse sans espoir qui, traduite en termes géométriques dirait ceci: «Parmi toutes les directions X possibles dans l'espace, il n'existe qu'une seule direction de coordonnée X absolue» (il s'agit en l'espèce d'un temps absolu devant être préposé aux transformations Lorentz), entreprise sans espoir appuyée sur quelques ambiguïtés involontaires mathématiques.

Un autre de ces savants ne remarque pas — abstraction faite de ce qu'il oublie d'interpréter physiquement l'espace et le temps — que la vitesse de la lumière conformément à l'expérience joue un rôle spécial. Les deux erreurs étroitement liées se cachent sous une enveloppe épaisse de formules mathématiques. Aucun homme raisonnable n'admettra cependant que le son se propage, relativement à l'air en repos, selon les mêmes lois que relativement à l'air en mouvement. L'expérience nous a appris, par contre, que, seule, la vitesse de la lumière est indépendante de l'état de mouvement du système de coordonnées.

On ne peut pas dire non plus que la théorie générale de la relativité ait abandonné, par rapport à la vitesse de la lumière, le principe de la continuité. La vitesse de la lumière, mesurée avec perche et horloge unitaires, dans l'entourage infinitésimal d'un point est toujours, dans la théorie de la relativité aussi, invariablement la même.

Albert EINSTEIN.

Je crois devoir joindre à cette préface quelques extraits d'une lettre de M. Einstein qui me paraissent éclairer la physionomie du savant allemand.

L. F.

Cher Monsieur,   *5-VII-20*

J'ai reçu, par notre ami Oppenheim, au retour d'un long voyage, votre amicale lettre du 19 juin. J'ai étudié votre

intéressant travail et j'y ai pris beaucoup de plaisir (en particulier dans l'exposé du développement historique de la théorie). . . . .
. . . . *Parmi les savants français, Langevin a parfaitement pénétré la théorie de la relativité. C'est un esprit merveilleusement clair et un homme sympathique* . . . .
. . . . *Je joins à ma lettre le* curriculum vitae *que vous souhaitez. — Je suis Allemand (israélite) de naissance, mais j'ai vécu en Suisse de l'âge de 15 à celui de 35 ans, sauf de courtes interruptions. J'ai conquis mes grades à Zurich; je suis pacifiste, partisan d'une entente internationale et resté toujours fidèle dans ma ligne de conduite à cet idéal.*
Agréez, ...
. . . .

A. EINSTEIN.

Voici les renseignements biographiques fournis par M. Einstein:

Albert Einstein est né à Ulm le 14 mars 1879. Il était âgé de six semaines lorsque ses parents émigrèrent vers Munich où il passa son enfance et fréquenta les écoles jusqu'à sa quatorzième année. A quinze aus il se rendit en Suisse, resta un an au collège de Aarau et y obtint son *abiturium*. Il étudia ensuite les mathématiques et la physique à Zurich. En 1902, Einstein fut attaché au bureau des brevets à Berne et prépara simultanément son examen du doctorat auquel il fut admis en 1905. Il fut appelé comme professeur à l'Université de Zurich en 1909, à celle de Prague en 1911 et retourna à Zurich en 1912 comme professeur au Polytechnikum, qu'il quitta en 1914 pour aller occuper un siège à l'académie royale de Prusse à Berlin. Il est également directeur de l'Institut Kaiser-Wilhelm pour la physique."

Einstein wrote in *Die Naturwissenschaften*, Volume 9, Number 13, (1 April 1921), p. 219, giving the false impression that he had not said what he had said,

"Zuschriften an die Herausgeber.
Zur Abwehr.

Herr *Lucien Fabre* hat im Verlage von Payot in Paris ein Buch „Les théories d'Einstein" mit dem Zussatz „Avec une préface de M. Einstein'' herausgegeben. Ich erkläre, daß ich keine Vorrede zu dem Buche geschrieben habe und protestiere gegen diesen Mißbrauch meines Namens. Ich bringe den Protest zu Ihrer Kenntnis in der Hoffnung, daß er aus Ihrer Zeitschrift den Weg in die weitere Öffentlichkeit und im besonderen auch in die Zeitschriften des Auslandes finden wird.

Berlin, 16. März 1921.   *Albert Einstein.*"

According to Ernst Gehrcke, Einstein's statement was indeed reprinted in the popular press. Fabre responded with a statement published in the *Neue Züricher Zeitung* on 9 May 1921, and in many other papers, and Gehrcke quoted the following from it:

"Diese Vorrede besteht aus drei Dokumenten: sie enthält biographische Daten, wissenschaftliche Ansichten und zuletzt ein internationalistisches Glaubensbekenntnis. Ich halte aufs entschiedenste folgende Behauptungen aufrecht: 1. Verfasser dieser Vorrede ist Herr EINSTEIN. 2. Er selbst hat sie mir zugeschickt und zwar in der Form von Briefen und als Antwort auf briefliche Anfragen meinerseits. 3. Sie war ausschließlich dazu bestimmt, meinen Lesern, d. h. dem französischen Publikum, die moralische und wissenschaftliche Persönlichkeit dieses Gelehrten vorzustellen. Ich bin bereit, obige Behauptungen durch unwiderlegliche Schriftstücke zu bezeugen. . ."[254]

Fabre had composed the forward from letters he had received from Einstein, and he still held them as proof that Einstein had made the statements he later disowned.

Fabre wrote in the second edition *Une Nouvelle Figure du Monde: Les Théories d'Einstein. Accrue de notes Liminaires, d'un Exposé des Théories de Weyl, et de Trois Notes de M. M. Guillaume, Brillouin et Sagnac sur Leurs Propres Idées*, Payot, Paris, (1922),

"NOTES LIMINAIRES

La présente édition de cet ouvrage diffère des précédentes.

J'ai procédé à une épuration et à une mise à jour.

*
* *

J'ai d'abord purgé mon livre des déclarations de M. Einstein qui lui servaient de préface. Une partie de la presse et des amis qui me sont chers, avaient critiqué la forme et le fond de ces déclarations. Je ne les avais moi-même insérées que pour permettre au savant israëlite allemand de dire publiquement du haut de cette tribune ce qu'il voulait donner comme vrai sur ses opinions politiques, sa vie, sa nationalité, ses sentiments, en un mot, sa physionomie non scientifique, laquelle, on le sait de reste, est extrêmement discutée.

Bien que j'eusse laissé à M. Einstein la responsabilité de ses déclarations je m'en sentais un peu complice puisque je leur donnais l'hospitalité. Mais je n'en aurais pas purgé ce livre, même si leur teneur m'eût été démontrée mensongère, car elles donnaient sur ce grand savant le témoignage le plus précieux puisqu'il émanait de lui.

L'événement le plus imprévu m'a décidé; M. Einstein a, en effet, renié ses déclarations dans la presse allemand. Je me hâte donc de les retrancher de cet ouvrage qui n'aura à connaître que de la figure purement scientifique du grand théoricien; c'est la seule qu'on puisse considérer avec sérénité et même avec quelque sympathie.

*
* *

Il va sans dire que j'ai également indiqué sur le mode dubitatif, ou même supprimé, les assertions que j'avais, dans le cours de l'ouvrage, avancées sur la foi des paroles d'Einstein, les autographes de celles-ci demeurant entre mes mains pour exercer la sagacité des psychologues futurs.

*
* *

Il m'a semblé indispensable d'ajouter à ce travail un bref exposé des théories de Weyl qui complètent très heureusement celles d'Einstein. Leur audace et leur beauté ne peut guère à l'heure actuelle apparaître qu'aux savants. Il est toutefois dès à présent certain que le disciple égale au moins le maître; et peut-

être le dépasse-t-il.

*

* *

Les nombreuses lettres qui me sont parvenues m'ont aussi convaincu de l'intérêt que présente pour le public la question du temps relatif. J'ai donné avec assez de détails le point de vue einsteinien pour n'y pas revenir. Mais j'ai pensé que le lecteur entendrait avec plaisir sur le même sujet la voix de M. Guillaume dont j'avais brièvement exposé les théories. Le savant bernois a bien voulu écrire, spécialement pour le présent ouvrage, la note qu'on lira en appendice. On trouvera agrément et profit à la méditer.

M. Brillouin a bien voulu également indiquer lui-même son point de vue aux lecteurs du présent ouvrage; on trouvera sa lettre en appendice.

Il faut admirer la sûreté, la clarté de cette belle page bien française. Elle met exactement à sa place scientifique la théorie einsteinienne; elle en dégage la convenance et l'utilité en tant qu'hypothèse; très sobrement, elle met en garde contre les commentaires où se peuvent aventurer ceux qui confondent l'hypothèse et le réel; j'y discerne, sans vouloir engager la pensée de son auteur, une méfiance à l'égard des conceptions philosophiques déduites des travaux einsteiniens.

Il n'est pas possible de ne pas souscrire à un jugement si parfaitement lucide; sa réserve et sa sagesse ne diminuent en rien l'enthousiasme que les théories d'Einstein et celles de Weyl, peuvent, indépendamment de leur adéquation au réel, inspirer à qui y recherche un excitant intellectuel.

*

* *

Enfin M. Sagnac, dont on a pu écrire, en faisant allusion à la phrase qui termine ce livre, qu'il était peut-être le nouveau Poincaré, le seul capable de nous donner une réponse définitive sur la valeur des théories einsteiniennes, a accepté de confier à ce petit ouvrage le sort d'une note originale dont l'extraordinaire importance n'échappera à personne.

Cette note:

—d'une part résume l'effet Sagnac sur la rotation dans

*l'éther (auquel nous avons fait allusion dans notre ouvrage);
—d'autre part institue une théorie générale des champs en
translation par une extension de la pure mécanique des petits
mouvements.*

*Nous sommes extrêmement heureux de pouvoir donner à nos
lecteurs la primeur d'un travail qui nous paraît contenir en
germe les plus belles découvertes. "*

Many interesting and telling facts emerge from the affair—smear tactic and vilification used to rescue Einstein by means of personal attack meant to divert attention from the real issue, and Einstein's dependence upon collaborators to write his statements, as well as Einstein's image. The preface to Fabre's book was only one of many of Einstein's anti-German, pro-Allies, and, elsewhere, Anglophilic, statements made public.[255]

Suspicion also fell upon Einstein because the "war to end all wars", *i. e.* the end of war—pacifism, socialism, revolution and economic hardship—which were great concerns of the Germans in the post-war period—were forecast in Ivan Stanislavovich Bloch's book, *The Future of War in Its Technical, Economic, and Political Relations; Is War Now Impossible?*, Doubleday & McClure Co., New York, (1899). Bolch was a hero and an inspiration to many Jews and to many Socialists. He was part of the culture that inspired H. G. Wells, Russell, Lorentz and Einstein; and Einstein was seen as a believer in, and vocal advocate of, this Blochian philosophy. The concept of the "war to end all wars" is also a prophetic and Apocalyptic one of Jewish world leadership foretold in the period of peace of the book of *Enoch*, with its "elect" and "Elect One" (*see also: Isaiah* 65; 66) and in the final war in the Old Testament in, among other places, *Isaiah 2:1-4*:

"1 The word that Isaiah the son of Amoz saw concerning Judah and Jerusalem. 2 And it shall come to pass in the last days, *that* the mountain of the LORD's house shall be established in the top of the mountains, and shall be exalted above the hills; and all nations shall flow unto it. 3 And many people shall go and say, Come ye, and let us go up to the mountain of the LORD, to the house of the God of Jacob; and he will teach us of his ways, and we will walk in his paths: for out of Zion shall go forth the law, and the word of the LORD from Jerusalem. 4 And he shall judge among the nations, and shall rebuke many people: and they shall beat their swords into plowshares, and their spears into pruninghooks: nation shall not lift up sword against nation, neither shall they learn war any more."

"Pacifists" often promoted the Apocalyptic prophesy of a "war to end all wars", which would establish a "world government" according to prophecy, one run by Jews in Jerusalem. Albert Einstein was one of the many advocates of this plan. "Pacifists" often sought to provoke the most terrible of wars humankind has yet endured on the false premise that it would end war. What these brutal and genocidal wars instead did was weaken the nations making them vulnerable to Jewish revolution, while simultaneously making the Jewish financiers unimaginably wealthy. Thereby, the Jewish financiers could sponsor revolution, dictatorship and genocide, and could buy up the world at reduced rates. The people were intentionally made so weary of war, that they become vulnerable to the sophistical message that the only means to secure peace is to destroy all nations such that there will be no nations left to war with each other. Some Jews press this message in order to bring to fulfillment the Messianic prophecy that the Jews will destroy all nations and religions, and rule the Earth. The false message that the loss of sovereignty leads to peace was a fundamental theme in Communist régimes. The loss of Gentile sovereignty has instead led to the enslavement and extermination of the Gentile peoples, in fulfillment of Judaic Messianic prophecy.

In the era of the German Enlightenment, Moses Mendelssohn asserted that the "Jewish mission" was to convert the world to monotheism and to instill in all peoples the principles of the Jewish moral code, which according to some initially only applied only to Jews, with the ancient Jews viewing Gentiles as subhuman and therefore undeserving of moral treatment. Einstein's friend Georg Friedrich Nicolai (Lewinstein) stated in 1917,

"Apart from this strange story of Cain, however, murder is forbidden in the Bible, and very sternly forbidden. But—it is only the murder of Jews. As is natural, considering the period from which it dates, the Bible is absolutely national, in character. Only the Jew is really considered as a human being; cattle and strangers might be slain without the slayer himself being slain. In this case there was a ransom. Accordingly, war was of course allowed also, and the Jews were no more illogical than the Moslem who kills the outlander. Of late years the Jews and the Old Testament have often been reproached for their contempt for those who were not Jews; and in practice even Christ acted in precisely the same way."[256]

Mendelssohn's message was not very different from that of Jesus Christ, as expressed in the Gospels; or, indeed, that of Islam, "There is no God but God." The political Zionists tended to be secular and racist, and based their beliefs on biological, Darwinistic principles. Albert Einstein saw Judaism as step away from paganistic Polytheism towards utilitarian and scientific morality, with the objectionable premise in the ancient tradition that one is led to morality through fear of the "imaginary" God.[257] However, all of these movements, which meant to lessen the suspicion among Gentiles of Jewish religious aspirations, perpetuated those aspirations which were always more political and racist in nature, than spiritual. Moses of the ten commandments was little different from Moses Mendelssohn.

Einstein followed the line of thought which sponsored European Liberalism, "such as Jacobinism, Fourierism, Owenism, Fabian Socialism, Marxism, and the like",[258] as essentially adopting the moral values of Judaism and replacing the source of these values, "God", with a quasi-Deistic conception of nature. Many critics of the Jews found this irrational, in that the removal of "God" *a priori* removes the fundamental premise of all that can be deduced from this premise, including codes of moral and just conduct, without providing a substitute premise which rationally deduces their conclusions. These critics sought a more synthetic basis for morality than neo-Platonism, and many arrived at pragmatic Darwinism and Metempsychosis, which they argued were logically consistent and empirically justified. In reality, they was less difference between the two points of view than was apparent on the face of the dispute.

Before Bloch were Bertha von Suttner and Alfred Hermann Fried of the *Friedensbewegung* (peace movement) which attracted pacificist physicist and Einstein-supporter Hans Thirring. Suttner published *Die Waffen nieder!*[259] in 1892, which emphasized the harm done to civilians in modern warfare. The American Civil War had demonstrated the destructive force of modern industry applied to warfare. Friedrich Nietzsche, whose work was well known, predicted the massive destruction this would cause in the Twentieth Century.

Unlike Albert Einstein, Philipp Lenard had expressed his loyalty to Germany during and after the First World War. After Einstein smeared him without cause, Nobel Prize laureate Philipp Lenard demanded a very public personal apology from Albert Einstein, which was not forthcoming. Einstein repeatedly made harshly anti-German and warmly Anglophilic statements before and after the Bad Nauheim debate which outraged many Germans.[260] Einstein was member of a commission which intended to investigate and publicize alleged German war atrocities, in 1919, for the purposes of a psychological attack on the German psyche attempting to coerce them into accepting Einstein's view that Germany's defeat was a victory for humanity.[261] Einstein also wanted to increase the hardships on the already starving Germans with foreign boycotts on German products soon after the First World War ended.[262] Many hundreds of thousands, if not millions of Germans had starved to death during a naval blockade in the war. Einstein's, and like minded vindictive spirits', love of punishing Germans made the Germans resentful of the Jews who had stabbed them in the back.

Ethnocentric attacks against German science appeared in America[263] in 1918, and in England[264] in 1919. In addition, English and French scientists, in collusion with traitors like Albert Einstein, took punitive actions against German scientists under the auspices of the International Research Council. Among other punitive sanctions, they excluded German and Austrian nationals from international congresses and banned the Nations of the former Central Powers from membership for a period of ten years. Einstein was marketed to the Allies as a Swiss Jew who had opposed Germany from the beginning of the war and Einstein, the "Swiss Jew", was safe from these vicious attacks on the liberty and dignity of German scientists.

Max Born knew that Hendrik Antoon Lorentz was a friend of the Allies after the First World War and Born disliked him.[265] Einstein, who had lived in Germany throughout the war, in spite of the fact that he hated Germany and wanted to see the nation destroyed, wrote to Lorentz on 1 August 1919,

"Exclusion of German scholars from social international scholarly exchanges for a number of years might perhaps be a lesson in humility for them, which will not do much harm at all—and, it is to be hoped, might even help."[266]

Many German scientists resented Einstein's treachery. Indeed, under pressure from Lenard for his anti-German activities and as a result of the economic conditions in Germany, Einstein published an appeal to ease the punitive measures taken against German science, which he himself had initially sponsored.[267] However, racist Zionist Albert Einstein saw to it that no German scientist would be present at the Solvoy Conference in April of 1921. His friend Hendrik Antoon Lorentz invited only one German scientist to attend the conference, Albert Einstein. Racist Zionist Albert Einstein then refused the invitation with the excuse that he was heading for America to exploit his ill-founded fame to raise money for his fellow racist Zionists. Einstein wrote to Lorentz,

"As this venture lies close to my heart, and as I, as a Jew, feel a duty to contribute, as far as I am able, to its success, I accepted."[268]

Fellow German Jew Fritz Haber was outraged at Albert Einstein's racist treachery and disloyalty. Einstein confirmed that he was disloyal and a racist, and was obligated,

"[. . .] to step in for my persecuted and morally depressed fellow tribesmen, as far as this lies within my power[.]"[269]

In point of fact, Einstein was instead promoting himself and hiding from his critics.

In response to the Berlin Philharmonic lectures, Einstein and his friends arranged for a discussion of the theory of relativity at the Eighty-Sixth Meeting of German Natural Scientists in Bad Nauheim in late September of 1920. These were annual gatherings which had been interrupted by the war. Einstein threatened that Lenard and all critics of the theory of relativity would be humiliated. Einstein was known for his childish and evasive responses to criticism. He was known for hiding from criticism. Einstein responded,

"The best proof that I by no means dodge criticism is that I myself arranged that the theory of relativity be discussed at the meeting of the GDNA in Nauheim."[270]

Einstein stated in his challenge that anyone brave enough should speak in Bad Nauheim.

Einstein, himself, was not brave enough. Contrary to his public bravado, Einstein feared the confrontation he had created and wanted others to speak on his behalf. He knew that he could not defend the theory of relativity and that he had no legitimate defense for his plagiarism. Einstein instead wanted to hide from the criticism directed at him.

Albert Einstein wrote to Arnold Sommerfeld on 6 September 1920 that he wanted to hide from the debate,

"But I do not on any account want to speak myself[.]"[271]

3.4.3 Let the Debate Begin

Einstein, against his better judgement, did speak at Nauheim. The event was highly publicized by Einstein and his supporters and thousands showed up to see the debate. The theory of relativity was hyped beyond all reasonable limits and many were certain that the great hero Einstein would crush his opponents, as advertised. The much anticipated debate between Lenard and Einstein over the general theory of relativity began on Thursday, at 12:45 PM. Einstein's advocates, Max Planck who chaired the session, *et al.*, employed armed police to keep anti-relativists and neutral parties out of the audience and attempted to stack the audience with a pro-Einstein claque. This resulted in a tumultuous protest and unbiased audience members stormed the hall and held their ground.

After long and boring lectures by Einstein and his friends which began at 9:00 AM, the bell sounded at 12:45 PM for the time allotted to Einstein-critics to begin. Einstein and Lenard began to debate.

Though accounts of the meeting are incomplete and vary,[272] Lenard clearly made Einstein look very foolish in a very short time. Einstein was flustered and could not give cogent responses, even though Lenard repeated his questions. In a prearranged maneuver, Max Planck called the session, which had begun at 12:45 PM, to an end at about 1:00 PM, after only a few minutes of debate, so as to let Einstein off the hook and prevent a fuller exposure of Einstein's incompetence. Fifteen minutes before the afternoon session began, Einstein ran away. Gehrcke, who had humiliated Einstein at the Berlin Philharmonic, and whom Einstein had openly challenged to speak at Bad Nauheim, repeatedly demanded time to speak, but Max Planck refused to allow Gehrcke a chance to speak, and delayed Gehrcke until the session was closed. Planck also refused to allow Rudolph, another Einstein critic, time to speak.

Pursuant to Planck's corrupt plan, Einstein's critics were only allotted fifteen minutes to speak, including responses from Einstein and his friends, after hours of pro-Relativity lectures. Planck tried to arrange it so that only pro-Einstein mathematical lectures would occur, which would be entirely uninteresting to the public and to the press.

Max Planck fed Friedrich von Müller, the opening speaker to the Bad Nauheim gathering, a prepared speech Planck and Arnold

Sommerfeld had written lauding Einstein and unfairly degrading his opponents. Planck arranged it so that armed guards would intimidate anti-Einstein participants and prevent them from attending the meeting hall and attempted to stack the audience and the stage with a pro-Einstein claque. Planck not only limited the time of the anti-Relativists at the Thursday meeting to a few minutes, Planck also greatly restricted their time at the Friday meeting to 12 minutes including discussion—a meeting which Einstein and his cronies did not attend. Einstein hid from his opponents and ran away from the debate, even after Max Planck had arranged it so that Einstein would have every conceivable advantage.

Albert Einstein was ashamed of the fact that he had run away. He wrote to Max Born in October of 1920,

"I will live through all that is in store for me like an unconcerned spectator and will not allow myself to get excited again, as in Nauheim. It is quite inconceivable to me how I could have lost my sense of humour to such an extent through being in bad company."[273]

3.4.4 Einstein Disappoints—"Albertus Maximus" is a Laughingstock

Einstein's cowardice and incompetence did not go unnoticed. Johannes Riem ridiculed Albert Einstein,

"Amerika über Einstein
Von
Professor Dr. Johannes Riem.

Es ist kaum anzunehmen, daß Einstein mit reiner Freude an seine amerikanische Rundreise zurückdenken wird. Ein großer Teil der dortigen Physiker und Astronomen stand von vornherein ablehnend da, vor allem der bekannte Michelson, dessen berühmtes Experiment in seiner falschen Deutung mit den Anlaß für die Relativitätstheorie gegeben hat. Vor mir liegen zwei Zeitungsblätter, „The Minneapolis Sunday Tribune", 1921 May 22, und „The St. Pauly Daily News", 1921 May 8. Beide beschäftigen sich mit der Relativitätstheorie und Einsteins Auftreten drüben. Zunächst die Feststellung, daß Einstein gleichzeitig mit der Abordnung der Zionisten drüben ankam, und daß die Presse davon in ausgedehntem Maße Kenntnis nahm. Doch habe man sehr bald dies als bezahlte Mache erkannt, und die ganze Einsteinsche Reise von Beginn an als einen Bluff erfaßt.

Die Amerikaner wären denn doch zu skeptisch gewesen, ihn ohne weitere Beweise für größer als Kopernikus und Newton zu halten, bloß, weil seine Lehre unverständlicher sei. Denn die Wahrheit sei einfach und verständlich. Man habe die Relativitätstheorie deswegen als einen Schwindel zurückgewiesen, und Reuterdahl vom College St. Paul bezeichnet Einstein als den „Barnum der wissenschaftlichen Welt, der die ganze Welt mit seiner mythischen Theorie zum Narren halte". Derselbe Reuterdahl hat Einstein zu einer Erörterung aufgefordert, auch ihm ist es ergangen, wie voriges Jahr den Gegnern Einsteins in Nauheim, denn Einstein zog sich beizeiten zurück, so daß R e u t e r d a h l die ganze Einsteinfahrt für eine von vornherein abgekartete Geschäftsreise erklärt.

Er führt des längeren aus, daß Leute, wie M e w e s , G e h r c k e und andere durchaus recht hätten, wenn sie Einstein des Plagiates beschuldigen. Er hat seine Gedanken zum Teil den Arbeiten Zieglers in Bern entnommen, wo ja Einstein früher wohnte, dessen Gedanken aber von der Wissenschaft unterdrückt seien, ferner von Gerber, dessen Arbeiten auch schwer zugänglich waren. Die Zeitungen sind beide über die Gelehrten bei uns gut unterrichtet, die gegen Einstein arbeiten, L e n a r d , G e h r c k e , F r i c k e .

Der Reklamefeldzug, den die Presse vor einiger Zeit mit und für Einstein machte, wird den Amerikanern als eine Art Film vorgeführt, der aber für die deutsche Wissenschaft, für ihre Ehre und Förderung wenig nützlich gewesen sei. Es sei sehr zu bedauern, daß die Deutsche Wissenschaft durch einen ihrer Vertreter selbst lächerlich gemacht werde. Lodge, Reuterdahl, Heidenreich und andere haben drüben vorher gewarnt, man solle den Einsteinismus nicht so ohne weiteres annehmen. Natürlich zuerst vergeblich, denn dieser neue Ismus rollte wie eine Flutwelle ungehemmt dahin, aber die Ernüchterung kam bald.

Man geht gegen Einstein vor als den Goliat des Skeptizismus. Vorlesungen dagegen werden veranstaltet. In scharfsinniger Weise wird in einem viel gelesenen Buche „Relativität oder innere Abhängigkeit" die Unhaltbarkeit der Relativitätstheorie nachgewiesen. Der Einwand Einsteins, dies sei nur eine besondere Form des Antisemitismus, wird sehr energisch zurückgewiesen, und mit der Anerkennung Spinozols beantwortet.

Man ist sich darüber klar, daß es sich dabei vor allem darum handelt, mit allen Mitteln die Grundlagen der Theorie zu bekämpfen, da diese fehlerhaft, unvollständig und geeignet ist, das Universum in mechanistische Ideen aufzulösen. Es ist eine widerrechtliche Besitzergreifung durch die Mathematik. Der Astronom G l a n v i l l e bezeichnet die Relativitätstheorie als eine neue Droge, die als ein neues Allheilmittel angepriesen wird. Dr. S k i d m o r e hat die Sache richtig erfaßt, wenn er sagt, daß die Relativitätstheorie ausgehe von der Nichteuklidischen, sogenannten Metageometrie, sie bestehe aus rein gedanklichen Konstruktionen, die durchaus subjektiv sind und denen in der Natur nichts entspricht. Sehr hübsch ist folgendes Bild: Man nehme der Relativitätstheorie den mathematischen blauen Dunst, in den sie sich hüllt, dann bleibt nur ein lebloses Skelett und dessen Einsteinscher Schädel grinst andauernd seine Zehen an, die auf der Grundlage Galileis stehen. Man stelle sich das einmal vor!"[274]

On 22 April 1922, the *Luzerner Neueste Nachrichten* ridiculed Einstein's flight from the debate (Einstein would often repeat the cliché that great truths are simple, as if he were the first to make use of it),

"'Americans have too much common sense for that. They know that all the great truths are simple and easily understood, and are, therefore, justly suspicious of the unintelligible theory of relativity of Einstein. More than that they have rejected it as a swindle. Just for example Reuterdahl, dean of engineering of the College of St. Thomas, St. Paul, Minnesota, calls Einstein a 'Barnum of the scientific world who is trying to fool the whole world with a mythical theory.' It is further reported that Reuterdahl has challenged Einstein to a debate, into which he is as likely to enter as in the debate announced last year at the meeting for scientific investigation in Bad Nauheim, where he preferred to withdraw himself quietly before the announced opponents of his theory could say what they had to say. To these opponents was expressed the regret that Mr. Einstein was unable, because of circumstances, to answer them. This, of course, was another prearranged matter of his general trafficking. It is very likely that he is acting in a similar manner towards Reuterdahl. The more so because the latter has accused him of scientific theft, for Reuterdahl maintains that Einstein has taken the fundamentals of his theory from a work which appeared in 1866 under the pseudonym of 'Kinertia.'"[275]

"Dazu haben die Amerikaner noch zu viel gesunden Menschenverstand. Sie sind sich der großen Tatsachen bewußt, daß alle großen Mehrheiten auch einfach und leicht verständlich sind, und bringen daher der unverständlichen Relativitätslehre Einsteins ein durchaus gerechtfertigtes Mißtrauen entgegen. Ja, mehr als das: sie lehnen sie als Schwindel ab. So nennt Reuterdahl, der Dekan des St. Thomas College in Minneapolis, Einstein „einen Barnum in der wissenschaftlichen Welt", der mit seiner mystischen Theorie alle Welt zum Besten halte. Auch soll Reuterdahl Einstein zu einer Disputation aufgefordert haben, zu welcher sich dieser aber wohl ebenso wenig stellen dürfte, wie zu der an der letztjährigen deutschen Naturforscher-Versammlung in Bad Nauheim angekündigten, wo er es vorzog, sich in aller Stille zu drücken, bevor die zum Worte vorgemerkten Gegner seiner Theorie an die Reihe kamen. Man drückte ihnen dann das Bedauern aus, daß ihnen Herr Einstein nicht habe Rede und Antwort stehen können. Das war natürlich eine abgekartete Sache seines Klüngels. Aehnlich dürfte er sich nun auch gegenüber Reuterdahl verhalten, umso mehr, als ihn dieser des wissenschaftlichen Diebstahls bezichtigt. Reuterdahl behauptet nämlich, Einstein habe die Grundlage seiner Theorie einem Werke entlehnt, welches 1866 unter dem Pseudonym „Inertia" erschien."

J. E. G. Hirzel wrote in the *Luzerner Neueste Nachtrichten* of 20 September 1921,

"Albertus Maximus und die Blamage der Schulweisheit.

Warum Maximus? — In Amerika gefeiert und herausgefordert. — Seine Vorläufer als Duellanten: Reuterdahl in Amerika und Dr. J. H. Ziegler in der Schweiz. — Der Reklameturm von Potsdam.

Am 1. April dieses Jahres wurden in Neuyork die letzten Vorbereitungen zum Empfang des größten Genies getroffen, welches die Welt bisher hervorzubringen imstande war. Wenigstens hieß es allgemein, daß alle großen Denker und

Entdecker, denen unsere Wissenschaft und Kultur ihr Dasein verdanken, in Zukunft nur noch als bescheidene Vorläufer oder als Herolde jenes größern Genies gelten könnten, so daß fortan Namen wie die eines Heraklit, Giordano Bruno, Kopernikus, Kepler, Newton und wie sei sonst noch heißen mögen die großen Leuchten des Menschengeschlechts, neben dem seinigen ihren Glanz verlören. Dieses alles überstrahlende Gestirn am Himmel der heutigen Wissenschaft heißt A l b e r t   E i n s t e i n. Ein findiger Berliner Journalist fand jedoch diesen Namen zu bürgerlich und nannte ihn kurz Albertus M a x i m u s. So heißt er jetzt im Hinblick auf jenen berühmten Zeitgenossen des Roger Baco, welcher den Gelehrten seiner Zeit allgemein als doctor mirabilis bekannt war und als der gelehrteste von allen galt, Albertus Magnus: dem großen Lehrer des Kirchenvaters Thomas Aquinas, dem doctor angelicus und eigentlichen Begründer der thomistisch-aristotelischen Philosophie, welche die Wissenschaft das ganze Mittelalter hindurch bis auf die Neuzeit beherrschte. Da diese beiden gewaltigen Männer bekanntlich später von der katholischen Kirche kanonisiert wurden, so erwarteten die Amerikaner den ihnen avisierten ganz Großen mit einer Art heiliger Scheu, auch schon deshalb, weil seine Lehre noch schwerer verständlich sein sollte, als die des heiligen Thomas, welche bereits den gelehrten Theologen schon genug harte Nüsse zu knacken gegeben hatte. Von der Lehre Einsteins hieß es allgemein, sie sei nur für die größten Mathematiker verständlich. Den meisten A m e r i k e r n genügte es darum, den Namen dieser Wunderlehre zu kennen, und man war praktisch genug, sich nicht auch noch um ihren Inhalt zu kümmern. Trotzdem war man allgemein von ihr entzückt, und zwar eben deshalb, weil sie so geheimnisvoll war. Nach ihr sollte es überhaupt nichts Absolutes mehr geben, alles sollte nur noch relativ sein. Aber Einstein sagte nicht, warum. Doch nannte er sie die allgemeine Relativitätstheorie. Sie bedeutet die vollste Freiheit im Denken und Handeln, denn sie befreit alle von jeder absoluten Verpflichtung. Der Glaube an das Absolute ist mit ihr erledigt. Er gehörte zu den Grundirrtümern einer veralteten Weisheit, welche einst durch den Teufel in die Welt gekommen sein mußten. Einstein wollte nun gründlich damit aufräumen. Darum die große Spannung. Man hoffte in ihm den kommenden Erlöser aus der Not des Unverstandes, des Zweifels und Irrtums begrüßen zu dürfen, und den Schlichter jeglichen Streites, den

Friedensfürsten, welcher im Glorienschein schon vollbrachter und noch zu vollbringender Wundertaten der geplagten Menschheit den geistlichen und weltlichen Frieden bringen und das Reich Gottes auf Erden errichten werde. Einstein aber hatte ganz eigene Absichten. Der Verkünder der Relativitätstheorie wußte, daß alles nur relativ sei, also auch seine Messiasmission, und daß es deshalb am klügsten für ihn sei, dies den Amerikanern nicht zu sagen. Er wollte ihnen im Bluff einmal den Meister zeigen.

Am 1. April ließ er sie hangen und bangen, aber am 2. erschien er, vorläufig aber erst im Hafen von Neuyork. Da die Ankunft programmgemäß auf einen Samstag fiel, so halten Einstein und seine Begleiter dadurch Gelegenheit, ihren frommen Landslauten in New-Jerusalem gleich einen Beweis ihrer orthodoxen Frömmigkeit zu geben. Man wartete deshalb mit der Ausschiffung noch bis zum Sabbath-Ende. Dann erst ließ man sich von einem mit der amerikanischen und jüdischen Flagge versehenen, vom Bürgermeister extra zur Verfügung gestellten majors cutter ans Land setzen. Umgeben von einer zionistischen Delegation, unter Führung des Oberzionisten Weizmann und dessen Adjutanten Ussischkin und Mossinsohn betrat der neue Messias den Boden des gelobten Goldlandes Dollarika. Bei der Fahrt durch die Stadt (so berichtet die jüdische Pressezentrale vom 15. April) harrte ihrer eine unabsehbar Menge — ein Bericht spricht sogar von einer Million — von der sie enthusiastisch akklamiert wurde, so daß der E i n z u g   E i n s t e i n s in New-Jerusalem den einfachen von Christus in Alt-Jerusalem vollständig in den Schatten stellte. Offenbar war er viel besser gemanaged. Alles schrie Hosiannah, denn alle Zuschauer waren Juden. Einstein selbst berichtet, er habe in Neuyork zum erstenmal jüdische Volkshaufen gesehen. Aber diese streuten keine Palmblätter, sondern, was den Zionisten viel lieber war, Banknoten und Schecks auf die Bank von England. Denn die jüdische Delegation hatte es nicht auf die Bekehrung der Yankees abgesehen, sondern nur auf die Erleichterung ihrer Börsen. Sie spekulierte nicht auf Seelenfang, sondern auf Gold, und dieses war nach alttestamentlicher Tradition am reichlichsten in Amerika zu finden. Schon Salomo hatte seine Knechte mit denen Hirams nach dem Lande Ophir geschickt, welches nach Mewes mit Peru identisch ist, und sie hatten ihm von dort 450 Zentner Gold zurückgebracht. Jetzt brauchte man es nicht mehr im rohen Zustande. Für die in Jerusalem zu gründende Welt-Universität dienten solide Papiere noch besser, und diese waren in Nordamerika leichter zu beschaffen. Und wirklich brachten die Zionisten hier mit Einstein als „great attraction'' in ebenso viel Monaten, als Salomos Knechte Jahre gebraucht hatten, 23 Millionen Dollars zusammen, womit für derartige Expeditionen ein neuer Weltrekord aufgestellt war. Einstein brauchte dabei nicht einmal zu reden. Erstens geriet so sein Geheimnis weniger in Gefahr und zweitens verstärkte sein Schweigen den Nimbus seiner Theorie. Auch wäre ohnedies niemand genial genug gewesen, ihn zu verstehen. Denjenigen, die ihn durchaus hören wollten, spielte er etwas auf seiner Geige vor. Der Präsident und der Vizepräsident der Union bezeugten ihm für seine Leistungen ihre Anerkennung dadurch, daß sie sich mit ihm zusammen photographieren ließen.

Leider wurde Einstein vor seiner Abreise noch ein schlimmer Streich gespielt, ohne den er seinen lukrativen Aufenthalt wahrscheinlich noch erheblich verlängert hätte. Ich erwähnte bereits, daß seine Mission mehr darin bestand, den Amerikanern einen Propheten zu zeigen, als ihnen seine Theorie auseinanderzusetzen. Reden ist Silber, Schweigen ist Gold. Seine Abneigung gegen das Disputieren hatte Einstein schon an der Naturforscher-Versammlung in Bad Nauheim gezeigt. Ueberhaupt läßt sich kein Prophet, der an sich glaubt, aufs Disputieren ein und einer, der es nicht tut, noch viel weniger. Leider hatte nun aber ein amerikanischer Professor hiefür weder das richtige Verständnis, noch das nötige Zartgefühl. Dieser wollte nicht begreifen, daß eine wertvolle Lehre unverständlich sein müsse, sondern meinte, alle großen Wahrheiten müßten notwendig auch einfach und leicht verständlich sein. Aus diesem Grunde forderte er Herrn Einstein auf, diese Meinungsverschiedenheit mit ihm auf dem Wege einer öffentlichen Disputation auszutragen. Eine derartige Zumutung einem öffentlich beglaubigten Genie gegenüber erscheint etwas brutal und erinnert beinahe an den Boxermatsch Dempsen-Carpentier. Da aber dem Friedensfürsten jede Art von Streit ein Greuel ist, so strafte er die taktlose Herausforderung des Professors Arvid Reuterdahl mit stiller Verachtung. Vielleicht fürchtete er auch, er könnte in der Hitze des Zweikampfes seinem Gegner mit seiner übermenschlich-geistigen Kraft schweren Schaden zufügen. Sei dem, wie ihm wolle, jedenfalls verbot ihm seine Menschenliebe den Zweikampf. Aber die Amerikaner verkannten die hohe Moralität Einsteins und glaubten, er fürchte sich vor Reuterdahl und wäre deshalb vor ihm ausgekniffen. Und so fingen sie an, ihn plötzlich und von allen Seiten so grausam zu verhöhnen und lächerlich zu machen, daß sie dabei sogar den guten Ton verletzten und ihre gute Erziehung vergaßen. Das mußte Einstein noch tiefer schmerzen. Denn jetzt kamen sogar die „guten Eindrücke" in Gefahr, welche er von den Amerikanern empfangen hatte. Um diese zu retten, brach er nun schleunigst seine Tournee ab und schiffte sich so rasch als möglich nach England ein, wo er sich dann von Lord Haldane, einem gefühlvollen Stammesgenossen, über die gehabte Enttäuschung trösten ließ.

So endigte das anfängliche Hosiannah auch bei Einsteins Messiade mit einem Kreuziget ihn! Doch ist es heute nicht mehr Brauch, seine Ueberzeugung durch das Martyrium zu bekräftigen. Darum drückte sich der Prophet, bevor seine Sache eine tragische Wendung nahm. Erst, als er sich in Berlin ganz in Sicherheit wußte, stellte er wieder seinen Mann, machte den Amerikanern eine lange Nase und plimperte mit dem Geld in seiner Tasche. Es klang wie fröhliches Kichern. So endigte sein Triumphzug durch Amerika fast genau so, wie es die „Luzerner Neuesten Nachrichten am 22. April vorausgesagt hatten.

Und R e u t e r d a h l? Nun, Reuterdahl konnte sich darüber trösten, daß ihn Einsteins Flucht um den Triumph gebracht hatte, ihm in öffentlicher Disputation die Richtigkeit seiner famosen Relativitätstheorie zu beweisen und ihm dabei die Denkermaske vom Gesicht zu reißen und dem Publikum nur dasjenige eines schlauen wissenschaftlichen Schiebers zu zeigen. Reuterdahl brauchte diesen Triumph nicht. Als Dekan der Ingenieur- und Architektenabteilung des St. Thomas College in St. Paul (Minnesota) genoß er schon Ansehen genug, auch stand sein Ruf als tiefer Denker und bedeutender Mathematiker längst zu fest, als daß er seiner bedurft hätte. Ernsten Forschern liegt nur die Wahrheit am Herzen und sie verachten die Reklame. Die Flucht Einsteins war das schmachvolle Eingeständnis seiner Niederlage. Nach der hochgeachteten Monatsschrift „The Dearborn Independent" vom 30. Juli sollen bei Einsteins Abfahrt von Neuyork nur noch ein halbes Dutzend Freunde zugegen gewesen sein. Ein stilles Leichenbegängnis! Die Hunderttausende, welche den Ankömmling begrüßt hatten, blieben zu Hause. Viele von ihnen studierten bereits Reuterdahls Werk „Wissenschaftlicher Deismus gegen Materialismus". Die Tendenz dieses Buches ist eine rein absolutistische, radikal antirelativistische, wenn man den Relativismus im Einsteinschen Sinne versteht. Reuterdahl zeigt darin, daß die heutige agnostische Wissenschaft bloß auf vereinbarten Unbestimmtheiten beruht, „scientific unknowns", und daß diesem unsichern Zustande nur durch die sichere Bestimmung der notwendig absolut einfachen Grundlage abgeholfen werden könne. Dieses Absolute nennt er, so wie es die Religion tut, Gott. Aber als Mann der Wissenschaft begnügt er sich nicht mit dem unbestimmten Begriff von Gott. Vielmehr faßt er das Prinzip des allmächtig alles Bewirkenden und Durchwirkenden wieder ähnlich auf, wie es früher die beiden gelehrten Jesuiten Athanasius Kircher und Pater Joseph Boskowich getan hatten. Der letztere starb als Professor der Philosophie, Physik, Astronomie und Mathematik im Jahre 1787 in Mailand. Auch war er Verfasser einer Atomistik. Das ewige Grundprinzip von allen Weltlichen bestand nach ihm aus lauter Kraftzentren. Zu eben diesem Schlusse kam auch Reuterdahl. Er vereinigt aber damit ferner auch die beiden Grundbegriffe von Raum und Zeit. Alle zusammen bilden den absoluten Urgrund, auf dem oder woraus sich dann alles Relativ in verständlicher Weise entwickelt. Damit sichert er diesem von Anfang an ein festes System, während in einer bloßen Relativität ohne Voraussetzung eines bestimmten Absoluten selbstverständlich alles systemlos bleibt, so wie es bei Einstein Lehre der Fall ist. Diese ist darum nicht nur unverständlich, sondern sogar höchst gefährlich. Sie ist absolut ordnungswidrig, nihilistisch und negativ. Beidenkapp nannte sie bolschewistisch. Und sie wirkt deshalb nur zersetzend auf Religion und Wissenschaft ein, anstatt stützend und fördernd. Beiden entzieht sie den festen Boden. Bei Reuterdahl ist das Gegenteil davon der Fall. Darum stimmt er aufs Beste mit den Lehren und Bestrebungen J . H . Z i e g l e r s überein, dessen Werk er in seiner jüngsten Schrift: „Einstein and The New Science" mit unverhehlter Freude rühmt und als grundlegend für die neue und wahre Wissenschaft anerkennt. Zieglers System fußt bekanntlich ebenfalls auf den drei Begriffen von Urkraft, Urraum und Urzeit, deren Einheit nachzuweisen ihm gelungen ist. Einstein spricht dagegen die

Zeit als vierte Dimension des Raumes an! Reuterdahl und Ziegler, der Mathematiker und der Chemiker, ergänzen sich gegenseitig. Einstein dagegen bringt nur mißtönende Anklänge an die Theorie des letztern vor. Immerhin muß man ihm eines lassen. Niemand hat mehr wie er und seine zionistischen und nichtzionistischen Freunde zum Sturze der agnostischen Wissenschaft beigetragen. Denn nichts konnte ihre innere Hohlheit der Menschheit besser zum Bewußtsein bringen, als das marktschreierische Treiben der Einsteinianer. Dieses Treiben lenkte erst die Aufmerksamkeit auf den Schaden und machte sie auf dem ganzen Erdenrund lächerlich und unhaltbar. Das war nun allerdings nicht beabsichtigt, aber es ebnete der neuen, wahren Wissenschaft den Weg. Einstein wurde dadurch nolens volens, zwar nicht zu ihrem Begründer, aber doch wenigstens zu ihrem Herold. Es geht eben oft anders, als man denkt. Das müssen jetzt auch die Koryphäen der alten Wissenschaft erfahren, denn damit, daß sie sich wie ein Mann hinter einen Nachtreter stellen, um mit ihm den ihnen unbequemen H a u p t b e g r ü n d e r der neuen Wissenschaft gemeinsam an die Wand zu drücken, gerieten sie nur noch tiefer in den Sumpf einer bodenlosen Relativität, wobei sie ihre Autorität gänzlich einbüßen. Sie suchen sie jetzt vergeblich zu retten; alle Kniffe werden ihnen nichts mehr helfen. In diesen Tagen tauften sie gelegentlich eines Astronomen-Kongresses in Potsdam ein dort errichtetes Observatorium auf den Namen Einsteins und ließen dieses welterschütternde Ereignis sofort durch den Telegraphen urbi et orbi bekannt machen. Der Einsteinturm paradiert daher schon heute in jeder illustrierten Zeitung als aktuellste Sehenswürdigkeit. Er soll dazu dienen, die öffentliche Aufmerksamkeit von den ruhig und still vor sich gehenden Hauptereignissen abzulenken. Ob er aber den Ruhm des großen Mannes verewigen werde, ist daher noch fraglich. Dieser Reklameturm dürfte meines Erachtens in Zukunft eine weiser gewordene Menschheit an die ungeheure Geistesverwirrung unserer agnostischen Zeit erinnern. Der Einsteinturm wäre demnach nur mehr ein Denkmal für ihre letzte Torheit und größte Blamage.

J. E. G. H i r z e l."

Artur Fürst and Alexander Moszkowski stated in 1916 that Einstein was the Galileo of the Twentieth Century. They suggested that since the designation *Albertus Magnus* was already taken (by Albert Graf von Bollstädt), the title *"Albertus Maximus"*[276] might be reserved for Einstein:

"So ist auch das jenseitige Ufer der neuen Theorie, der Relativität, nur unter Gefahr zu gewinnen. Aber der Wagemutige, der hinüberkommt, sieht sich in einer unermeßlichen neuen Welt, in der auf Schritt und Tritt ungeahnte Wahrheitswunder erblühen. Und mit Bewunderung gedenkt er der Männer, stie ihm diesen Weg wiesen. Zu ihnen gehören die Physiker und Mathematiker L o r e n t z und M i n k o w s k i , vor allen aber der gewaltige Baumeister des neuen Relativitätsgebäudes, der Galilei des zwanzigsten Jahrhunderts: A l b e r t E i n s t e i n.

Vor sieben Jahrhunderten lebte ein Wundermann der Naturlehre, der Graf von Bollstädt, der sich den Namen eines Großen, A l b e r t u s M a g n u s, errang. Die Bezeichnung Albertus Maximus ist noch frei. Es könnte sein, daß dieser Titel für Albert Einstein vorbehalten bleibt und ihm dereinst verliehen wird."[277]

Fürst and Moszkowski were copying Eugen Karl Dühring's pronouncement that Robert Mayer was the "Galileo of the Nineteenth Century" in Dühring's book *Robert Mayer, der Galilei des neunzehnten Jahrhunderts. Eine Einführung in seine Leistungen und Schicksale*, E. Schmeitzner, Chemnitz, (1880).

The feature article Hirzel referred to was published in the *Luzerner Neueste Nachrichten* on 22 April 1921:

"Feuilleton.
Professor Einstein „Triumphzug"
durch Amerika.

In Nr. 164 vom 9. April brachte die „Vosissche Zeitung" folgende überseeische Depesche: „Prof. Albert Einstein und die gleichzeitig mit ihm eingetroffene zionistische Delegation wurden bei ihrer Ankunft in Neuyork sehr warm begrüßt. Die gesamte Neuyorker Presse widmet dem Ereignis als solchem und der Persönlichkeit Einsteins ausführliche Artikel." Man sieht auf den ersten Blich, daß es sich hiebei wieder um eine bestellte Reklame handelt, wie denn überhaupt das ganze Einsteinsche Unternehmen von Anfang an auf den Bluff berechnet war.

Diesmal sollten nun die Amerikaner „dran glauben". Aber die Yankees scheinen weniger naiv zu sein, als die guten Deutschen und Schweizer und sich nicht so leicht zum Glauben an den neuen Propheten kommandieren zu lassen. Sie sind zu skeptisch, um ohne weiteres zu glauben, daß er ein größeres Genie sei, als Kopernikus und Newton, bloß weil er unverständlicher sei als diese. Dazu haben die Amerikaner noch zu viel gesunden Menschenverstand. Sie sind sich der großen Tatsachen bewußt, daß alle großen Mehrheiten auch einfach und leicht verständlich sind, und bringen daher der unverständlichen Relativitätslehre Einsteins ein durchaus gerechtfertigtes Mißtrauen entgegen. Ja, mehr als das: sie lehnen sie als Schwindel ab. So nennt Reuterdahl, der Dekan des St. Thomas College in Minneapolis, Einstein „einen Barnum in der wissenschaftlichen Welt", der mit seiner mystischen Theorie alle Welt zum Besten halte. Auch soll Reuterdahl Einstein zu einer Disputation aufgefordert haben, zu welcher sich dieser aber wohl ebenso wenig stellen dürfte, wie zu der an der letztjährigen deutschen Naturforscher-Versammlung in Bad Nauheim angekündigten, wo er es vorzog, sich in aller Stille zu drücken, bevor die zum Worte vorgemerkten Gegner seiner Theorie an die Reihe kamen. Man drückte ihnen dann das Bedauern aus, daß ihnen Herr Einstein nicht habe Rede und Antwort stehen können. Das war natürlich eine abgekartete Sache seines Klüngels. Aehnlich dürfte er sich nun auch gegenüber Reuterdahl verhalten, umso mehr, als ihn dieser des wissenschaftlichen Diebstahls bezichtigt. Reuterdahl behauptet nämlich, Einstein habe die Grundlage seiner Theorie einem Werke entlehnt, welches 1866 unter dem Pseudonym „Inertia" erschien. Da indessen dieses Werk in Europa kaum bekannt geworden ist, so dürfte Beschuldigung grundlos sein. Aehnliche Beschuldigungen wurden übrigens auch schon von deutschen Gelehrten, wie dem Ingenieur Rudolf Mewes, Prof. E. Gehrke, Paul Weyland u. a. erhoben. Nach ihnen soll sich Einstein aus einer schwer zugänglichen Veröffentlichung vom Jahre 1898 des verstorbenen Oberlehrers Gerber stillschweigend eine Formel angeeignet haben. Wie es sich damit tatsächlich verhält, wird schwer festzustellen sein. Immerhin gibt schon das eigentümliche Gebaren Einsteins und die ungebührliche und auffällige Reklame seines Klüngels genügend Anlaß, seiner Sache nicht ganz zu trauen. Doch scheinen die meisten auf falscher Fährte zu sein, weil sie die Umstände, welche bei der

E n t s t e h u n g d e r E i n s t e i n s c h e n L e h r e herrschten und darauf Einfluß haben konnten, nicht genügend kennen. Und doch können eigentlich nur diese den äußerst verdächtigen Widerspruch erklären, der uns in Einsteins Lehre von Anfang an entgegentritt und darin besteht, daß sie sich einerseits auf eine zwar durchaus richtige, aber von Einstein gar nicht näher begründete, sondern rein hypothetische Annahme abstellt, nämlich auf die Konstanz der Lichtgeschwindigkeit im Vakuum, währenddem anderseits seine weitern Begründungen dermaßen verworren und widerspruchsvoll sind, daß sie einem ganz andern Geiste entslossen zu sein scheinen. Diese sonderbaren Begründungen und die noch sonderbareren daraus gezogenen Schlüsse wurden von vielen Gelehrten, speziell von Prof. Lenard, einem der frühern Nobelpreisträger für Physik, gerügt. Lenard bemerkte ganz richtig, daß sie dem gesunden Menschenverstand direkt ins Gesicht schlügen. Was dagegen die Annahme von der Konstanz der Lichtgeschwindigkeit betrifft, welche Einstein als feststehendes Bezugsobjekt im uferlosen Ozean seiner Relativitätstheorie annimmt, so scheint es damit eine eigene Bewandtnis zu haben. Sie ist schon deshalb verdächtig, weil die Physiker zu jener Zeit die Existenz eines absolut leeren Raumes bestimmt leugneten und als unmöglich hinstellten, sie aber dann mit der Annahme von Einsteins Hypothese ohne weiteres zugaben und ihm diese zudem als eine hervorragende geniale Tat anrechneten. Tatsächlich scheint sie aber eine B e r a u b u n g der nur fünf Jahre f r ü h e r von J. H. Z i e g l e r aufgestellten u n i v e r s e l l e n L i c h t l e h r e zu sein. Das würde den Verzicht Einsteins auf ihre nähere Begründung zur Genüge erklären. Es gibt aber auch noch andere Gründe, welche mit größter Wahrscheinlichkeit darauf hindeuten, daß die Lehre Zieglers der verborgene Quell der Einsteinschen Entdeckung war, u. a. den, daß sie damals besonders in Bern, wo Einstein domiziliert war, stark diskutiert worden war. Zieglers Lehre gründet sich auf den unwiderleglichen Beweis, das die Gundlage der Welt in dem Urgegensatz von der Masse der unbedingt vollen Urlichtatome, dem U r l i c h t, und von der Masse des unbedingt leeren Raumes gebildet ist, deren gegenseitiges aktiv-passives Durchdringungsverhältnis Ziegler als U r z e i t bezeichnet. Ziegler sprach deshalb von einer D r e i e i n i g k e i t v o n K r a f t, R a u m u n d Z e i t, einer Dreieinigkeit, welche dann auch Herr Einstein, allerdings in verschleierter Form, brachte. Da die klare und einfache Lehre Zieglers, wonach alle Wirkungen der e w i g e n W i r k l i c h k e i t, d. h. alle Naturerscheinungen, lediglich Mischformen des strahlenden Urlichts und des bewegten Leeren sind, den Vertretern der offiziellen Physik sehr unbequem war, weil sie so ziemlich das Gegenteil von den lehrte, was diese bis anhin gelehrt hatten, so suchten sie dieselbe von Anfang an zu unterdrücken und totzuschweigen, und schufen so einen Zustand, der einem schlauen und geschickten Plagiator die günstigste Gelegenheit zur Aneignung ihrer Hauptlehren darbieten mußte. Ja, ein solcher konnte dabei sogar des Beifalls und der Unterstützung der Physiker sicher sein, besonders für den Fall, daß er sein Plagiat in einer nur ihrer Zunft verständlichen, dem großen Publikum aber unverständlichen Form vortrug. Dazu eignete sich die Mathematik am besten. Wer in ihrer Sprache schreibt, kann nur vom Mathematiker und Physiker verstanden werden, und diese haben dann volle Freiheit, der Laienwelt davon mitzuteilen, was sie für gut halten. Die gewöhnliche, gebildete Welt ist dann ganz von ihnen abhängig. Der Chemiker und Nichtmathematiker Ziegler aber hatte den „Fehler" gemacht, allgemein verständlich zu schreiben und dadurch auch die heutige Physik öffentlich bloßzustellen. Darum erschien Einstein den Physikern wie ein Deus ex machina. Er wurde zum Retter aus der Not. Kein Wunder, daß man ihn denn auch sofort auf den Schild erhob und ihm vor allem Volke als dem längst ersehnten Messias, d. h. dem wahren Lichtbringer, huldigte. Sein Ruhm wurde durch die Zeitungen in alle Weltteile ausposaunt. Das Volk mußte überall an ihm glauben und glaubte auch schließlich an ihn, weil es seine Lehre ja doch nicht selbst auf ihren Wahrheitsgehalt prüfen konnte. Es sah und hörte nur, wie der große Einstein in der Hierarchie der Physiker mit unglaublicher Schnelligkeit von Stufe zu Stufe stieg. Dies wirkte überzeugend, und die große internationale Presse, welche sich fast ganz in den Händen der Volksgenossen Einsteins befindet, bestärkt es fortwährend in dieser Ueberzeugung. Von dem Schweizer Ziegler hörte dagegen niemand etwas. Und so stände denn alles schön und herrlich für die Einsteinianer, hätte die Sache ihres Helden eben nicht auch ihre Achillesferse. Ziegler hatte seine Lehre nicht immer so ausführlich ausgedrückt, daß sie jeder bei oberflächlicher Kenntnisnahme sofort richtig verstehen könnte.

Dadurch bot sie Anlaß zu allerlei Mißverständnissen. Und so wird es leicht verständlich, woher die vielen Irrtürmer der Relativitätslehre herrühren. Wie sollte sie einheitlich und klar sein können, wenn sie nur einem Mixedpickles aus vielen, mehr oder weniger irrigen Plagiaten gleicht. Daß sie der Zieglerschen Lichtlehre v o n   J a h r   z u   J a h r   ä h n l i c h e r wurde, ist auch kein Gegenbeweis dafür, daß man die letztere nicht als den Urquell für die Einsteinsche Weisheit zu betrachten habe, so wenig als der schon seit zwanzig Jahren andauernde Boykott, in den die Einstein-Presse Ziegler getan hat. Davon wissen nun zwar die Herren Amerikaner nichts. Wenn sie Einstein ablehnen, so dürfte es vielmehr nur aus dem Grunde geschehen, daß sie sich darüber ärgern, für dumm genug gehalten zu werden, um die größten wissenschaftlichen Entdeckungen auch für die unverständlichsten zu halten. Die Amerikaner wissen ganz genau, daß das Gegenteil davon der Fall ist. Und schon darum dürfte sich die Geschäftsreise des falschen Propheten im Lande Dollarika wohl kaum zu einem Triumphzuge gestalten. —G—"

Another newspaper article notable for its mention of the Bad Nauheim debate wrote,

"Wie steht's um Einstein?

Jüdische Propaganda. — Astronomen in Potsdam. — „Silbersteine" des Einsteinturms. — Die Verschobene Rot-Linie. — Konzessionierter Aether. — Kneip-Knippe in Nauheim und Amerika. — Schlichte Presse.

Wie es vom alten Odysseus heißt, daß er der vielgewandte und erfindungsreiche war, der vieler Menschen Länder und Städte gesehen hatte, und dessen Name bis zum Himmel reichte, so haben wir gegenwärtig in E i n s t e i n einen Mann, von dem die ihm nahestehende Presse das gleiche behauptet, — daß er die größten Größen der Wissenschaft, Kopernikus, Kepler Newton bei weitem überträffe, — deren Werke haben bis in die Gegenwart gedauert, das Gedankenwerk Einsteins aber währe in alle Zeiten!

Merkwürdig, daß man das schon voriges Jahr so genau wußte! Jetzt wäre manch' einer froh, es nicht geschrieben zu haben. Vorschußlorbeeren sind immer ein Ding mit zwei verschiedenen Seiten. Denn nachdem die Einsteinpresse das Lob ihres Heros gar zu laut gesungen hatte, so daß die Gegner sich der Sache gründlicher annahmen, da wandte sich das Blatt. Eine lange Reihe von Denkern wurden genannt, bis Descartes zurück, die das, was an der Relativitätstheorie richtig ist, s c h o n l a n g e v o n E i n s t e i n gefunden hatten, daß aber die Theorie in der Form, die ihr Einstein gegeben hat, den allerheftigsten Widerspruch herausfordert.

In Einsteins Gegenwart, und ohne daß dieser oder ein anderer der Seinen etwas dagegen sagen konnte, ist auf der A s t r o n o m e n v e r s a m m l u n g i n P o t s d a m im August dieses Jahres gezeigt worden, daß weder die Beobachtungen der Sterne bei totalen Sonnenfinsternissen, noch die Bewegungen des Planeten Merkur irgendwie eine Beweiskraft für die Relativitätstheorie haben. Die beobachteten Größen finden ihre befriedigende Erklärung auf andere einfache Weise.

Aber hoch ragt jetzt in P o t s d a m d e r E i n s t e i n t u r m, dessen Baugerüst gerade am Tage des Besuches der Astronomenversammlung abgenommen wurde, damit die Fachmänner ihn besuchen konnten. Wie am Vormittag in einem Vortrage gesagt wurde, soll damit eine Messungsreihe gemacht werden, die die Theorie unmittelbar bestätigen würde. Der Turm dient also den Theorien von Einstein, beobachten wird daran F r e u n d l i c h, erbaut hat den Turm der Architekt M e n d e l s o h n, und das Geld soll, wie erzählt wurde, stammen von der Firma S i l b e r s t e i n. So ist es denn auch ein Bauwerk geworden, was den andern einheitlich gestalteten Bauwerken des astrophysikalischen Observatoriums gegenüber sich verhält, wie der Geist Einsteins zum Geiste von Vogel und Lohse, Müller, Kempf und den andern Astronomen, die die Anstalt berühmt gemacht haben. Es sieht aus wie der Vorderteil eines Kriegsschiffes, von der Seite gesehen. Einer nannte es Bismarckturm, da Freundlich gesagt hatte, seine Formgebung entspräche modernen Anschauungen, ein anderer den Tempel Salomonis, denn wir fanden, daß der unterirdische Raum sieben Vorhöfe hatte!

Aber es ist nur gut, daß die Einrichtung vielseitig gebraucht werden kann, denn es ist u n z w e i f e l h a f t n a c h g e w i e s e n, daß der gewünscht Betrag einer V e r s c h i e b u n g d e r S p e k t r a l l i n i e n n a c h R o t n i c h t   v o r h a n d e n. — Sehr peinlich! Denn Einstein sagt, daß mit dieser Verschiebung seine Theorie stehe und falle.

Die ganze Theorie gleicht überhaupt einem Proteus, sie nimmt dauernd neue Formen an: zuerst die spezielle, dann die allgemeine Relativitätstheorie; gegenwärtig hat sie wieder eine neue Gestalt. So ist sie unfaßbar, unverständlich, weil sie nach G e h r c k e unverstehbar ist! E i n e   M a s s e n s u g g e s t i o n!

Bekannt ist die L e u g n u n g   d e s   A e t h e r s. Jetzt hat ihn Einstein unter anderer Form wieder in der Theorie drin. Und L e n a r d   sagt, daß bei einer vernünftigen Aethertheorie überhaupt   gar   k e i n   R a u m   m e h r   f ü r   d i e   R e l a t i v i t ä t s t h e o r i e   i n   d e r   P h y s i k   bleibe; sie habe gewissermaßen von den Lücken in unserer Erkenntnis gelebt. Daher auch das Verhalten Einsteins den Gegnern gegenüber in der Oeffentlichkeit. Man erinnere sich an N a u h e i m   voriges Jahr, wo er versprochen hatte, in öffentlicher Diskussion Rede und Antwort zu stehen. Als es so weit war, erschien er nicht, und die Geschäftsordnung machte die Gegner mundtot. In A m e r i k a   hat er es ebenso gemacht; der als Mathematiker, Physiker und Philosoph bekannte Prof. R e u t e r d a h l   von St. Thomas College hat Einstein bei seiner Amerikafahrt aufgefordert, eine Erörterung öffentlich stattfinden zu lassen. Der Erfolg war der gleiche wie in Nauheim, er paßte nicht in das Reiseprogramm. Dadurch ist die amerikanische Presse sehr ernüchtert worden. Als Einstein drüben ankam, waren gegen 150,000 Menschen am Schiff, darunter zahllose Photographen, b e i   d e r   A b r e i s e   e i n   h a l b e s   D u t z e n d! Es trat eben gar zu kraß hervor, daß die ganze Fahrt eine Verherrlichung das jüdischen Geistes sein sollte. Die Ankunft gleichzeitig mit den Vertretern der Zionisten, der Kreis von jüdischen Lokalkomittees, der den Gefeierten umschloß, die Kritik amerikanischer Zustände durch Einstein nach seiner Rückreise haben bewirkt, daß die dortige Presse mit einer Deutlichkeit sich über den erst Gefeierten ausdrückt, die uns erstaunlich vorkommt. Hält man sich dies vor Augen, dazu die Einblicke in seine Gedankenwelt, wie sie Moszkowski gibt, politisch und wissenschaftlich,   dazu   die   Tatsache,   daß   er   mit   der Sowjetregierung Beziehungen hat und gleichzeitig Mitglied der preußischen Akademie der Wissenschaft ist, so sagt man mit dem echten Berliner: Das ist wirklich allerhand!

R."

Ernst Gehrcke wrote in 1924,

"Auf dem Deutschen Naturforschertag in Nauheim, wo Tausende aus allen Teilen Deutschlands und viele ausländische Besucher zusammenströmten, wurde von den Anhängern der Relativitätstheorie eine ,,Diskussion über die Relativitätstheorie'' in die Wege geleitet. Am 20. September stellte der Vorsitzende der *Gesellschaft Deutscher Naturforscher und Aerzte* in seiner Einführungsrede diese mit neugieriger Spannung erwartete Relativitätsdiskussion in Aussicht, wobei er gleich seine Meinung dahin äußerte, daß die Physik «die größten Veränderungen ihrer wissenschaftlichen Grundlage» erlitten habe, indem «der Begriff des Äthers im Weltall verschwindet und durch die Relativitätstheorie Einsteins die Begriffe von Raum und Zeit wandelbar wurden.» (Bericht der *Frankfurter Zeitung* vom 20. September 1920). Diese Aussprache begann am 23. September. Sie wurde von EINSTEIN eröffnet, der zu drei vorher gehaltenen Vorträgen anderer Redner (WEYL, GREBE, v. LAUE) Stellung nahm: «EINSTEIN lehnte die WEYLsche Theorie» (eine von der Einsteinschen verschiedene, formale Relativitätstheorie) «ab, wogegen dieser von EINSTEIN den Beweis für seine Theorie aus den Naturgesetzen verlangte» (Bericht des *Berliner Lokal-Anzeigers* vom 24. September 1920). Besonderen Eindruck machte der öffentliche Meinungsaustausch zwischen EINSTEIN und dem berühmten Heidelberger Physiker LENARD. «LENARD . . . wandte sich gegen die allgemeine Relativitätstheorie, nach welcher jede Art von Bewegung für uns unerkennbar sein soll, und wir nicht entscheiden können, ob wir uns zum Beispiel in drehender Bewegung befinden oder die gesamte Umwelt sich gegen uns drehe» (aus dem Bericht der *Frankfurter Zeitung* vom 24. September 1920). Eine Einigung zwischen LENARD und EINSTEIN wurde nicht erzielt, und nachdem noch andere Redner für (z. B. Prof. BORN) und wider (Prof. PALAGYI-Budapest) die Relativitätstheorie gesprochen hatten, wurde die weitere Erörterung vertagt, da, wie der Vorsitzende der Sitzung, der berühmte Physiker PLANCK aus Berlin, bemerkte, «die Relativitätstheorie es leider bisher noch nicht fertig gebracht habe, die für die Sitzung verfügbare absolute Zeit von neun bis ein Uhr zu verlängern» *(Kölnische Zeitung* vom 30. September 1920).—Die vertagte Diskussion wurde dann ohne EINSTEIN beendet, der eine Viertelstunde vor

Beginn der Nachmittagssitzung abgereist war. Ein mit großen Erwartungen ins Werk gesetztes Ereignis war vorübergegangen, das Pendel der relativistischen Massenbewegung hatte geschwankt und eine Dämpfung erfahren, ohne aber schon zur Ruhe zu kommen."[278]

Philipp Lenard was surprised by Albert Einstein's poor performance. Lenard was hoping for a stimulating debate that might challenge his beliefs. Einstein was instead evasive and ill-prepared, then ran away. When Einstein hid from Prof. Arvid Reuterdahl's challenge to debate the following year, many likened it to his flight from Bad Nauheim—this after all the hype assuring the public that Einstein would humiliate the opponents of relativity theory. Lenard wrote after the debate,

"Auch sonst war ich schließlich erstaunt, wie wenig Herr E i n s t e i n auf die Beantwortung meiner Fragen vorbereitet zu sein schien — die doch schon zwei Jahre lang mit seiner Kenntnis gedruckt vorgelegen haben, — während von seiner Seite und auch von einem andern Fachmann Zeitungslesern gegenüber ganz ausdrücklich der Anschein der unbedingten Überlegenheit meinen Gedankengängen gegenüber erweckt worden war. Da ich weder Anhänger noch Gegner irgendeines Prinzips bin, sondern nur Naturforscher sein möchte — wie auf S. 12 schon zu erkennen gegeben, — hätte ich den Nachweis, daß und an welcher Stelle meine Überlegungen nicht genügend gründlich waren, als Gewinn entgegennehmen müssen, wenn er geführt worden wäre (vgl. auch Note k, S. 23), zumal in der rein auf die Sache gerichteten Form, in welcher die Nauheimer Aussprache ablief. Die einzige Aufklärung, welche ich von der Diskussion mitgenommen habe, stammt von seiten des Herrn M i e ; sie wird im weiter Folgenden bezeichnet werden."[279]

Einstein lost all credibility at the debate and knew that the scientific community was against him. He undoubtedly wanted only to flee Germany and retreat from the public eye. As happened after Einstein's public humiliation at the Berlin Philharmonic, the Einstein sycophants and the ethnically biased pro-Einstein Jewish press came to his rescue after his public humiliation at Bad Nauheim and carried him through this time of criticism as he traveled the world promoting himself, relativity theory and Zionism, until his second rush of fame, which came with the announcement of the award of his Nobel Prize in late 1922. Many found the award scandalous, given that Einstein was a proven sophist and plagiarist.

Lorentz, Born, von Laue and the others were loyal to Einstein. The acceptance of their fatally flawed theories hinged on the cult of personality which was created for Einstein. If Lorentz exposed Einstein, Lorentz' beliefs and legacy would suffer. The relativists were, and are, so pernicious in their suppression of opposing views, because they were, and are, so insecure and politically motivated. They were, and are, so vicious in their defense of Einstein, because their mythologies are so easily defeated. The theory attacks gullible persons who are willing to accept irrational arguments and who act out of hero worship. Therefore, it is not surprising that these same individuals behave in an unscrupulous and adolescent manner when confronted with the facts.

Knowing they had lost at the debate, Einstein and his friends sought a rapprochement with Lenard which would dull the sting of Einstein's humiliation at Nauheim. Tragically, Lenard and Stark, (Nobel Prize laureates each) who were initially very helpful to Einstein in the early years of the special theory of relativity, after witnessing the corruption in the press and in the German Physical Society, after witnessing the Zionist betrayal of Germany, succumbed to the racial mythologies of the National Socialists and became outspoken advocates of Nazism, and in so doing were yet again the victims of Zionist Jews, though they did not realize it. Einstein's actions played no small rôle in elevating Adolf Hitler to power, in that the Nazis exploited Einstein as an example to stereotype millions of innocent people. The Nazis also exploited Einsteinian racist Zionist mythology to promote their own racial myths, which they imposed on the German People at the behest of Jewish Zionists who wanted assimilating Jews segregated from the allegedly inferior "Goyim".[280]

This was, and is, a common practice among Zionists and anti-Semites. They promote one another's common racism. This compounds the problem by creating an incentive for non-racists to forgive the intolerable behavior of characters like Einstein and to refuse to speak out against it for fear of having that behavior generalized in a sense unfavorable to them. An article in the *Patriot* of 18 July 1929, stated,

"When Ambassador Page was editor of the *Atlantic Monthly* he gave the following advice to a young journalist: *'The most interesting fellow in America is the Jew: but don't write about Jews: without intending it, you may precipitate the calamity America should be most anxious to avoid—I mean Jew-baiting.'*

Incidentally we may mention that an English book which happened to contain that quotation was suppressed, soon after birth, by a very obvious withdrawal of the usual advertising nourishment."[281]

The young journalist was Rollin Lynde Hartt.[282] This censorship further results in a group dynamic whereby one member of the group who speaks out against another is chastised for "betraying" the group which will allegedly be unfairly stereotyped by the exposure of the behavior of an individual like Albert Einstein. *Numbers* 16:22 states,

"And they fell upon their faces, and said, O God, the God of the spirits of all flesh, shall one man sin, and wilt thou be wroth with all the congregation?"

Of course, it is human nature to think in symbols and to generalize, especially when viciously and unfairly attacked and threatened, as were the anti-Relativists Lenard and Stark. Beyond this, Jews have long taught that a good Jew never speaks out against another Jew, and a good Jews does not praise a Gentile. *Leviticus* 19:17-18 states,

"17 Thou shalt not hate thy brother in thine heart: thou shalt in any wise rebuke thy neighbour, and not suffer sin upon him. 18 Thou shalt not avenge, nor bear any grudge against the children of thy people, but thou shalt love thy neighbour as thyself: I *am* the LORD."

3.4.5 Contemporary Accounts of the Bad Nauheim Debate

As many have recognized,[283] Max Born and others gave a very unrealistic portrayal of the events which took place in Germany in the 1920's and 1930's, vilifying Lenard, Gehrcke and Weyland with falsehoods; which accounts, while dramatic and shocking, simply do not agree with the facts. It is probably best to reproduce contemporary accounts from the period in order to obtain a realistic picture of what occurred at Nauheim.

The *Physikalische Zeitschrift*, Volume 21, (1920), pp. 666-668 gave a partial account of the debate between Lenard and Einstein:

"Allgemeine Diskussion über Relativitätstheorie.

L e n a r d : Ich habe mich gefreut, heute in einer Gravitationstheorie vom Äther sprechen gehört zu haben. Ich muß aber sagen, daß, sobald man von der Gravitationstheorie auf andere als massenproportionale Kräfte übergeht, sich der einfache Verstand eines Naturforschers an der Theorie stößt. Ich verweise auf das Beispiel vom gebremsten Eisenbahnzug. Damit das Relativitätsprinzip gilt, werden bei Benutzung nicht massenproportionaler Kräfte die Gravitationsfelder hinzugedacht. Ich möchte sagen, daß man sich im physikalischen Denken zweier Bilder bedienen kann, die ich als Bilder erster und zweiter Art bezeichnet habe. In den Bildern erster Art sprach z. B. Herr W e y l , indem er alle Vorgänge durch Gleichungen ausdrückt. Die Bilder zweiter Art deuten die Gleichungen als Vorgänge im Raume. Ich möchte lieber die Bilder zweiter Art bevorzugen, während Herr E i n s t e i n bei der ersten Art stehen bleibt. Bei den Bildern zweiter Art ist der Äther unentbehrlich. Er war stets eines der wichtigsten Hilfsmittel beim Fortschritt in der Naturforschung, und seine Abschaffung bedeutet das Abschaffen des Denkens aller Naturforscher mittels des Bildes zweiter Art. Ich möchte zuerst die Frage stellen: Wie kommt es, daß es nach der Relativitätstheorie nicht unterscheidbar sein soll, ob im Falle des gebremsten Eisenbahnzuges der Zug gebremst oder die umgebende Welt gebremst wird?

E i n s t e i n : Es ist sicher, daß wir relativ zum Zug Wirkungen beobachten und wenn wir wollen, diese als Trägheitswirkungen deuten können. Die Relativitätstheorie kann sie ebensogut als Wirkungen eines Gravitationsfeldes deuten. Woher kommt nun das Feld? Sie meinen, daß es die Erfindung des Herrn Relativitätstheoretikers ist. Es ist aber keine freie Erfindung, weil es dieselben Differentialgesetze erfüllt wie diejenigen Felder, die wir als Wirkungen von Massen aufzufassen gewohnt sind. Es ist richtig, daß etwas von der Lösung willkürlich bleibt, wenn man einen begrenzten Teil der Welt ins Auge faßt. Das relativ zum gebremsten Zug herrschende Gravitationsfeld entspricht einer Induktionswirkung, die durch die entfernten Massen hervorgerufen wird. Ich möchte also kurz zusammenfassend sagen: Das Feld ist nicht willkürlich erfunden, weil es die allgemeinen Differentialgleichungen erfüllt und weil es zurückgeführt werden kann auf die Wirkung aller fernen

Massen.

L e n a r d : Herrn E i n s t e i n s Ausführungen haben mir nichts Neues gesagt; sie sind auch nicht über die Kluft von den Bildern erster Art zu den anschaulichen Bildern zweiter Art hinweggekommen. Ich meine, die hinzugedachten Gravitationsfelder müssen Vorgängen entsprechen und diese Vorgänge haben sich in der Erfahrung nicht gemeldet.

E i n s t e i n : Ich möchte sagen, daß das, was der Mensch als anschaulich ansieht, und was nicht, gewechselt hat. Die Ansicht über Anschaulichkeit ist gewissermaßen eine Funktion der Zeit. Ich meine, die Physik ist begrifflich und nicht anschaulich. Als Beispiel über die wechselnde Ansicht über Anschaulichkeit erinnere ich Sie an die Auffassung über die Anschaulichkeit der galileischen Mechanik zu den verschiedenen Zeiten.

L e n a r d : Ich habe meine Meinung in der Druckschrift „Über Relativitätsprinzip, Äther, Gravitation" zum Ausdruck gebracht, daß der Äther in gewissen Beziehungen versagt hat, weil man ihn noch nicht in der rechten Weise behandelt hat. Das Relativitätsprinzip arbeitet mit einem nichteuklidischen Raum, der von Stelle zu Stelle und zeitlich nacheinander verschiedene Eigenschaften annimmt; dann kann nun eben in dem Raum ein Etwas sein, dessen Zustände diese verschiedenen Eigenschaften bedingen, und dieses Etwas ist eben der Äther. Ich sehe die Nützlichkeit des Relativitätsprinzips ein, solange es nur auf G r a v i t a t i o n s k r ä f t e   a n g e w a n d t   w i r d .   F ü r   n i c h t massenproportionale Kräfte halte ich es für ungültig.

E i n s t e i n : Es liegt in der Natur der Sache, daß von einer Gültigkeit des Relativitätsprinzips nur dann gesprochen werden kann, wenn es bezüglich a l l e r Naturgesetze gilt.

L e n a r d : Nur wenn man geeignete Felder hinzudichtet. Ich meine, das Relativitätsprinzip kann auch nur über Gravitation neue Aussagen machen, weil die im Falle der nichtmassenproportionalen Kräfte hinzugenommenen Gravitationsfelder gar keinen neuen Gesichtspunkt hinzufügen, als nur eben den, das Prinzip gültig erscheinen zu lassen. Auch macht die Gleichwertigkeit aller Bezugssysteme dem Prinzip Schwierigkeiten.

E i n s t e i n : Es gibt kein durch seine Einfachheit prinzipiell bevorzugtes Koordinatensystem; deshalb gibt es auch keine Methode, um zwischen „wirklichen" und „nichtwirklichen" Gravitationsfeldern zu unterscheiden. Meine zweite Frage lautet:

Was sagt das Relativitätsprinzip zu dem unerlaubten Gedankenexperiment, welches darin besteht, daß man z. B. die Erde ruhen und die übrige Welt um die Erdachse sich drehen läßt, wobei Überlichtgeschwindigkeiten aufheben?

Der erste Satz ist keine Behauptung, sondern eine neuartige Definition für den Begriff „Äther".

Ein Gedankenexperiment ist ein prinzipiell, wenn auch nicht faktisch ausführbares Experiment. Es dient dazu, wirkliche Erfahrungen übersichtlich zusammenzufassen, um aus ihnen theoretische Folgerungen zu ziehen. Unerlaubt ist ein Gedankenexperiment nur dann, wenn eine Realisierung p r i n z i p i e l l unmöglich ist.

L e n a r d : Ich glaube zusammenzufassen zu können: 1. Daß man doch besser unterläßt, die „Abschaffung des Äthers" zu verkünden. 2. Daß ich die Einschränkung des Relativitätsprinzips zu einem Gravitationsprinzip immer noch für angezeigt halte, und 3., daß die Überlichtgeschwindigkeiten dem Relativitätsprinzip doch eine Schwierigkeit zu bereiten scheinen; denn sie heben bei der Relation jedes beliebigen Körpers auf, sobald man dieselbe nicht diesem, sondern der Gesamtwelt zuschreiben will, was aber das Relativitätsprinzip in seiner einfachsten und bisherigen Form als gleichwertig zuläßt.

R u d o l p h : Daß sich die allgemeine Relativitätstheorie glänzend bewährt hat, ist kein Beweis gegen den Äther. Die E i n s t e i n sche Theorie ist richtig, nur ihre Ansicht über den Äther ist nicht richtig. Auch wird sie erst annehmbar mit der W e y l schen Ergänzung, geht dann aber sogar aus der Ätherhypothese h e r v o r , wenn zwischen den beim Fließen verschobenen Ätherwänden L ü c k e n bleiben, die durch Schleuderkraft infolge Richtungsänderung der Sternfäden l e e r gehalten werden.

P a l a g y i : Die Diskussion zwischen E i n s t e i n und L e n a r d hat auf mich einen tiefen Eindruck gemacht. Man begegnet hier wieder den alten historischen Gegensätzen zwischen experimentaler und mathematischer Physik, wie sie schon z. B. zwischen F a r a d a y und M a x w e l l bestanden. Herr E i n s t e i n sagt, daß es kein ausgezeichnetes Koordinatensystem gibt. Es gibt eins. Lassen Sie mich biologisch denken. Dann trägt jeder Mensch sein Koordinatensystem in sich. In der Verfolgung dieses Gedankens ist eine Widerlegung der Relativitätstheorie enthalten.

E i n s t e i n weist darauf hin, daß kein Gegensatz zwischen Theorie und Experiment besteht.

B o r n : Die Relativitätstheorie bevorzugt sogar die Bilder zweiter Art. Ich betrachte als Beispiel die Erde und die Sonne. Wäre die Anziehung nicht, liefe die Erde geradlinig davon usw.

M i e : Daß die Ansicht, der Äther sei der greifbaren Materie wesensgleich, erst durch die Relativitätstheorie als unmöglich erkannt sein solle, habe ich nie verstehen können. Das war doch schon lange vorher durch L o r e n t z in seinem Buch „Elektrische und optische Erscheinungen in bewegten Körpern" geschehen. Auch A b r a h a m hat in seinem Lehrbuch schon damals, als er der Relativitätstheorie noch ablehnend gegenüberstand, gesagt: „Der Äther ist der leere Raum."

Ich bin der Ansicht, daß man auch bei Annahme der E i n s t e i n schen Gravitationstheorie doch ganz scharf unterscheiden muß zwischen den bloß fingierten Gravitationsfeldern, die man nur durch die Wahl des Koordinatensystems in das Weltbild hineinbringt, und den wirklichen Gravitationsfeldern, die durch den objektiven Tatbestand gegeben sind. Ich habe kürzlich einen Weg gezeigt, wie man zu einem „bevorzugten" Koordinatensystem kommen kann, in welchem von vornherein alle bloß fingierten Felder ausgeschlossen sind.

E i n s t e i n : Ich kann nicht einsehen, wieso es ein bevorzugtes Koordinatensystem geben soll. Höchstens könnte man daran denken, solche Koordinatensysteme zu bevorzugen, in bezug auf welche der M i n k o w s k i sche Ausdruck für ds^2 a n n ä h e r n d gilt. Aber abgesehen davon, daß es für große Räume solche Systeme gar nicht geben dürfte, sind diese Koordinatensysteme sicherlich nicht exakt, sondern nur approximater definierbar.

K r a u s weist auf eine erkenntnistheoretische Differenz zwischen den Bildern erster und zweiter Art hin, indem er die Bilder erster Art für höherwertig als die Bilder zweiter Art hält.

L e n a r d : Es ist soeben das Schwerpunktsprinzip hineingebracht worden; ich glaube jedoch, daß das auf prinzipielle Fragen keinen Einfluß haben kann."

The *Berliner Tageblatt* published a report on 24 September 1920, which fills in some of the gaps in the incomplete account presented in the *Physikalische Zeitschrift,*

"Die Einstein-Debatte auf dem Naturforschertag.

Vier physikalisch-mathematische Vorträge. — Ein Rededuell Einstein-Lenard.

(Telegramm unseres Sonderkorrespondenten.)

G. G. Bad Nauheim, 23. September.

Vorläufiger Bericht. Heute vormittag fand vor dichtgefülltem Saale unter dem Vorsitze des Geheimrats Planck und in Gegenwart sämtlicher großen Physiker und auch der Berliner Einstein-Gegner die E i n s t e i n - S i t z u n g   d e r   m a t h e m a t i s c h e n   u n d   p h y s i k a l i s c h e n   A b t e i l u n g des Naturforschertages statt. Die Vorträge behandelten zumeist den Gegenstand in streng mathematischer Weise. Es sprachen hintereinander: **Weyl** (Zürich), **Mie** (Halle), **Laue** (Berlin), **Grebe** (Bonn). Dieser berichtete über V e r g l e i c h s m e s s u n g e n   d e r   S o n n e n s p e k t r e n   u n d   i r d i s c h e r   S p e k t r e , die sich auf die d r i t t e   e x p e r i m e n t e l l e   B e s t ä t i g u n g der Relativitätstheorie beziehen. Bei der Diskussion, in welcher u. a. L a u e und M i e eingriffen, entspann sich **ein lebhaftes Rededuell zwischen Einstein und Lenard.** Dieser warf ein, daß die Einsteinsche Theorie der Anschaulichkeit für den gesundes Menschenverstand entbehre. Seine E i n z e l a r g u m e n t e, die Einstein die willkürliche Annahme irrealer Gravitationsfeldes vorwarfen und Widerspruch der Theorie in sich über die Lichtgeschwindigkeit behaupteten, w i d e r l e g t e   E i n s t e i n . Die spannende Diskussion zog sich durch mehrere Stunden hin. (Siehe auch Seite 4.)

[***]

Ein neuer Beweis für die Einstein-Theorie.

Das Rededuell Einstein-Lenard.

Die Rotverschiebung im Sonnenspektrum.

(Telegramm unseres Sonderberichterstatters.)

G. S. Bad Nauheim, 23. September.

Wie wir schon gemeldet haben, spielte sich heute unter

ungeheuerem Interesse die mit Spannung erwartete große E i n s t e i n - D e b a t t e des Naturforscherkongresses ab. Der Saal des Badehauses war bis auf die letzte Ecke gefüllt.

Alle unsere großen Physiker, auch die Physikochemiker und eine Menge Interessierter aus anderen Wissensgebieten hatten sich eingefunden. Der scharfe Mathematikerkopf P l a n c k s blickt vom Vorstandstich her. Ihm gegenüber sitzt in der vordersten Reihe der, um dessen Werk es geht, E i n s t e i n. Was die Physiker in Erwartung und zur abwehr des kolossalen Ansturms angekündigt hatten, bewahrheitete sich: „Die Sitzung wird die Theorie in rein wissenschaftlicher, s t r e n g m a t h e m a t i s c h e r F o r m behandeln." Die Einzelheiten der Darlegungen und der vorgebrachten Beweisführung entziehen sich denn auch der summarischen Wiedergabe in eiliger Berichterstattung. Als erster spricht **Weyl** (Zürich) über seine Theorie von „Elektrizität und Gravitation", dann Professor **Mie** (Halle) über „das elektrische Feld eines um ein Gravitationszentrum rotierenden geladenen Partikelchens", endlich **v. Laue** (Berlin) über „neue Versuche zur Optik bewegter Körper". Es hagelt jetzt Differentiale, Koordinateninvarianz, elementare Wirkungsquanten, Transformationen, Vectorialsysteme usw. Gespannt lauschen die Fachleute, E i n s t e i n seelenruhig, R u b e n s mit seinem bezeichnenden Kopfnicken, N e r n s t erhobenen Hauptes, F r a n k interessiert lächelnd, H a b e r in bequemer Stellung die Decke betrachtend. Dem Laien aber graut es. Einzelne verlassen den Saal, die meisten aber harren in der Schwüle tapfer der Dinge, die da kommen sollen. Und sie werden nicht betrogen.

Professor **Grebe** aus Bonn ergreift jetzt das Wort. Und was er berichtet, ist des Aufhorchens wert: „Einsteins Theorie hat ihre vorläufige B e s t ä t i g u n g erfahren durch die gelungene Berechnung der Merkurbahn und der Lichtablenkung im Gravitationsfeld der Sonne. Es fehlte noch **der Nachweis der von Einstein geforderten Rotverschiebung der Spektrallinien der Sonne.** Dazu muß das Absorptionsspektrum der Sonne mit einem irdischen Emissionsspektrum verglichen werden. Mannigfache Einflüsse machen die Messungen schwierig. Wir fanden aber schließlich im B a n d e n s p e k t r u m d e s S t i c k s t o f f e s, dem früher so genannten Cyanspektrum, ein gut verwertbares Spektrum. Unser V e r g l e i c h s s p e k t r u m wurde im Kohlenlichtbogen erzeugt. An jeder einzelnen Linie wurden zwanzig bis vierundzwanzig Messungen gemacht." Es folgt ein P r o j e k t i o n s b i l d , das in mehreren Linienpaaren die Abweichungen zwischen Sonnen- und irdischen Spektrallinien, zugleich aber auch die Schwierigkeiten der Beobachtung und die vielfachen gegenseitigen Störungen der Linien zeigt. Redner fährt fort: „Der von uns gefundene Unterschied in der Lage der Linien stimmt gut überein mit dem anderer, amerikanischer Beobachtungen. Jedoch war die Verschiebung bei den einzelnen Linien verschieden. Berücksichtigt man aber die gegenseitigen Beeinflussungen, so kommt man zu einem Wert von etwa 0,66, der mit dem Einsteinschen Wert für die Verschiebung von 0,62 bis 0,68 übereinstimmt. Zweifellos müssen auch noch weitere Experimente gemacht werden. Aber wir haben jetzt schon guten Grund zu der Annahme, daß die von der Einsteinschen Theorie verlangte Rotverschiebung wirklich vorhanden ist."

Nun eröffnet Planck die D i s k u s s i o n . Einstein ist der erste Redner. Unwillkürlich tritt feierliche stille ein. Einstein bespricht die Weylsche Theorie. Weyl, Mie, Laue sprechen weiterhin. Es handelt sich zuerst um die vorhin gehaltenen Vorträge. Dann kommt die Generaldiskussion über die Relativitätstheorie überhaupt. Sie ist ein Zwiegespräch zwischen Geheimrat **Lenard** (Heidelberg) und Einstein, der sein eigener Anwalt ist. Jetzt kann auch der nicht auf den Höhen der Wissenschaft Thronende wieder leidlich folgen. Es kommt Leben in die Menge. Die zerstreuten Blicke konzentrieren sich jetzt auf die beiden Gegner. Es ist wie ein Turnier. Lenard läßt nicht locker, aber Einstein pariert vorzüglich. Hinter mir steht W e y l a n d , der Berliner Einstein-Töter. Auf dem Boden dieser w i s s e n s c h a f t l i c h e n Versammlung hält er sich im Hintergrunde der Ereignisse und gibt sein Interesse nur durch nervöses Schütteln der Mähne und leise Beifallsrufe bei **Lenards** worten zu erkennen. Dieser sagt: „Ich bewege mich nicht in Formeln, sondern in den tatsächlichen Vorgängen im Raume. Daß ist die Kluft zwischen Einstein und mir. Gegen seine s p e z i e l l e Relativitätstheorie habe ich gar nicht. Aber seine Gravitationslehre? Wenn ein fahrender Zug brennt, so tritt doch die Wirkung tatsächlich nur im Zuge auf, nicht draußen, wo alle Kirchtürme stehen bleiben!"

Einstein: „Die Erscheinungen im Zuge sind die Wirkungen eines G r a v i t a t i o n s f e l d e s , das induziert ist durch die

Gesamtheit der näheren und ferneren Massen.

Lenard: „Ein solches Gravitationsfeld müßte doch auch anderweitig noch Vorgänge hervorrufen, wenn ich mir sein Vorhandensein a n s c h a u l i c h machen will!"

Einstein: „Was der Mensch als a n s c h a u l i c h betrachtet, ist großen Aenderungen unterworfen, ist e i n e F u n k t i o n d e r Z e i t. Ein Zeitgenosse Galileis hätte dessen Mechanik auch für sehr unanschaulich erklärt. Diese „anschaulichen" Vorstellungen haben ihre Lücken, genau wie der viel zitierte „gesunde Menschenverstand". (Heiterkeit.)

Lenard: „Diese Diskussion wird unfruchtbar. Eine andere Frage: Wenn die Erde rotiert, so sagt Einstein, man könne genau so gut sagen, die Erde ruhe, und alle Materie rotiere um sie. Dann kommt man aber für die fernsten Gestirne zu G e s c h w i n d i g k e i t e n, d i e w e i t ü b e r L i c h t g e s c h w i n d i g k e i t liegen. Diese soll nach der Theorie aber eine Grenzgeschwindigkeit sein. Das ist ein W i d e r s p r u c h i n s i c h."

Einstein: Nein, die Lichtgeschwindigkeit ist Grenzgeschwindigkeit nur für die geradlinig gleichförmigen Bewegungen der speziellen Relativität; bei beliebig bewegten Systemen können beliebige Geschwindigkeiten des Lichts auftreten."

Es griffen dann noch verschiedene Herren in die Debatte ein, der Wert und Sinn von Gedankenexperimenten, die „Kluft" zwischen mathematischen und praktischen Physikern, philosophische und erkenntnistheoretische Fragen werden gestreift. Da aber, wie Professor Planck humorvoll bemerkt, die Versammlung nicht beschließen kann, daß die absolute Zeit von 9-1 länger als vier Stunden dauert, so muß man sich schließlich trennen."

Vossische Zeitung reported on 24 September 1920,

"Der Kampf um Einstein.
Die Auseinandersetzung

auf dem Naturforschertag.

Dr. B. Bad Nauheim, 23. September.

Die Einzelheiten der Relativitätstheorie führen in schwierige Gebiete, die nur mit der Kenntnis der höheren Mathematik zu bewältigen sind. Man sollte daher glauben, einer Diskussion über ihre Grundlagen würden andere, als Fachphysiker und Mathematiker, kein besonderes Interesse entgegenbringen. Aber durch die bekannten Vorgänge in Berlin, wo man die Leistungen Einsteins in öffentlichen Versammlungen angreift und sich auch zu persönlichen Beschimpfungen des Gelehrten versteigt, ist die allgemeine Aufmerksamkeit noch mehr, als durch die Erfolge der Theorie bei der jüngsten Sonnenfinsternis, auf sie gelenkt worden.

Kein Wunder, daß auch auf der Naturforscherversammlung die Sitzung der Physikalischen und Mathematischen Abteilung, in der über Dinge, die mit der Relativitätstheorie zusammenhängen, gesprochen werden sollte, das größte Interesse erregte. Um zu verhindern, daß die Physiker und Mathematiker selbst von einem Publikum verdrängt würden, dessen Sensationsluft bei dieser wissenschaftlichen Behandlung sicher nicht befriedigt werden konnte, wurden zunächst nur Mitglieder der Physikalischen und Mathematischen Gesellschaft als Hörer zugelassen und dann erst der Eingang für weitere Besucher geöffnet. Schnell war der große Raum völlig gefüllt, der zusammen mit der Galerie wohl 500 bis 600 Personen faßte.

In nüchtern fachlicher Weise, seine Ausführungen reichlich mit mathematischen Formeln erläuternd, trug nun W e y l-Zürich seine Erweiterung der allgemeinen Relativitätstheorie vor, durch die er neben der Gravitation auch die elektrischen Erscheinungen umfassen will. Es folgte M i e-Greifswald, der das allgemeine Relativitätsprinzip lieber durch ein Prinzip der Relativität der Gravitation ersetzen will. Dann leitet L a u e-Berlin rechnerisch aus den Grundlagen der Theorie die bekannte Folgerung ab, daß ein Lichtstrahl in einem Gravitationsfeld sich krümmen müsse, also z. B. beim Vorbeipassieren an der Sonne, und daß die Spektrallinien in einem solchen Gravitationsfeld sich nach dem roten Ende des Spektrums verschieben müßten. Schließlich berichtete G r e b e-Bonn über seine gemeinsam mit Herrn Bachem angestellten Versuche, diese Rotverschiebung der Spektrallinien als wirklich zu erweisen.

Nachdem einige Einzelheiten dieser Vorträge noch

besprochen waren, wurde die a l l g e m e i n e E r ö r t e r u n g
ü b e r d i e R e l a t i v i t ä t s t h e o r i e eröffnet. In ihrer Art
erinnerte sie an die Wettkämpfe mittelalterlicher Gelehrter, denn
in ihrem Hauptteil gestaltete sie sich zu einer Zwiesprache
zwischen dem bedeutenden Experimentalphysiker L e n a r d-
Heidelberg und E i n s t e i n. Sie konnte, wie vorauszusehen war,
zu keinem Ergebnis führen. Lenard stellte zum Schluß fest, daß
weder er überzeugt sei, noch wohl auch seinen Gegner überzeugt
habe. Es handle sich um den Gegensatz zwischen
experimentellen und mathematischen Physikern, der nicht zu
überbrücken sei, wenn der mathematische Physiker nicht von
den Bildern erster Art, nach Lenards Ausdruck, in denen er zu
denken gewohnt sei, zu den Bildern zweiter Art übergehe, den
anschaulichen Bildern, in denen der Experimentalphysiker
denke.

Von anderen Rednern wurde das Vorhandensein eines
solchen Gegensatzes lebhaft bestritten; der mathematische
Physiker fasse vielmehr die Erscheinungen, die der
Experimentalphysiker erforsche, unter einheitlichen
Gesichtspunkten zusammen. M i e hob lebhaft hervor, daß
Einstein keineswegs nur als Mathematiker zu betrachten sei,
sondern durchaus als Physiker, der seine bedeutende
mathematische Geschicklichkeit mit großem physikalischen
Blick verbinde.

E i n s t e i n selbst bemerkte, die Meinung, was anschaulich
oder was nicht anschaulich sei, habe sich im Wechsel der Zeit
sehr beträchtlich gewandelt, sie sei im wahrsten Sinne selbst eine
Funktion der Zeit. Die Physik sei eben ihrem Wesen nach
b e g r e i f l i c h und nicht anschaulich. Den Zeitgenossen
Galileis war dessen Mechanik gewiß recht wenig anschaulich,
heute aber, und zwar schon lange vor Begründung der
Relativitätstheorie betrachtet man die elektrischen Felder als die
elementarsten Gebilde, mit denen man arbeitet. Es gibt sogar
Elektriker, die sich mechanische Vorgänge erst mit Hilfe der
elektrischen Felder anschaulich machen können. L e n a r d führte
das Beispiel des plötzlich gebremsten Eisenbahnzuges an, in
dem der darin Sitzende eine gewaltige Erschütterung erleide; es
würde jedem gesunden Menschenverstand widersprechen, wenn
man annehmen wollte, nicht der Mensch sei in Bewegung
gewesen, sondern die gesamte Umwelt.

E i n s t e i n warnte vor dem Operieren mit dem „gesunden

Menschenverstand", der sehr leicht in die Irre gehe; es komme darauf an, ein für die Rechnung bequemes Koordinatensystem zu wählen, an sich gäbe es in der Welt kein bevorzugtes Koordinatensystem. Das erwiderte er auch auf den Vorhalt, daß bei der Annahme, die Erde ruhe und um sie bewege sich die gesamte Umwelt, man für gar nicht so weit entfernte Massen zu Ueberlichtgeschwindigkeiten kommen müsse. Einstein scheut sich nicht vor diesen Geschwindigkeiten, die keineswegs dem allgemeinen Relativitätsprinzip widersprächen, er sieht in ihnen keinen Grund, ein Koordinatensystem zu verwerfen, wenn nur sonst bei seiner Wahl die Rechnung einfach werde.

In diesem Punkte trat M i e den Einwänden Lenards bei; auch er will die fingierten Gravitationsfelder fortlassen. Sie haben, meint er, keinen Erkenntniswert; ihm kämen diese Dinge als „zu feinspintisiert" vor, er wolle demgegenüber doch lieber an dem gesunden Menschenverstand festhalten. Er glaube auch, daß es tatsächlich ein bevorzugtes Koordinatensystem gäbe. Aber auf die Frage Einsteins, wodurch denn eine solche Bevorzugung eines Koordinatensystmes verständlich gemacht werden sollte, mußte er die Antwort schuldig bleiben.

Am deutlichsten wird für den Leser der Gegensatz der Anschauungen vielleicht, wenn man sich erinnert, daß Lenard immer und immer wieder betont, an dem „A e t h e r" müsse f e s t g e h a l t e n werden, der Aether könne gar nicht abgeschafft werden, der „Aether" sei keine H y p o t h e s e, sondern W i r k l i c h k e i t, denn wenn es keinen „Aether" gäbe, könne man ja die Welt nicht mechanisch begreifen, dann könne man nicht alle physikalischen Erscheinungen auf Bewegungsvorgänge zurückführen. Demgegenüber muß doch betont werden, daß fast alle modernen Physiker die Forderung von der mechanischen Begreifbarkeit der Natur längst aufgegeben haben — es sei nur an den glänzenden Vortrag Plancks auf der Königsberger Naturforscherversammlung vor 10 Jahren erinnert. Es ist eben eine unbegründete Forderung, daß die Natur mechanisch begreifbar sein s o l l. Der Physiker hat an die Natur keine F o r d e r u n g e n, sondern nur F r a g e n zu stellen und zu sehen, was die Natur auf diese Fragen antwortet. In Verkennung dieses Verhältnisses hat man lange Jahre von der Natur ihre mechanische Begreifbarkeit gefordert. Die Natur ist aber nicht so liebenswürdig gewesen, diese Forderung zu erfüllen.

Im Verfolg der Erörterungen hob M i e mit Nachdruck hervor, daß die Abschaffung des Aethers ja gar nichts mit der Relativitätstheorie zu tun habe, er sei vielmehr schon in den 80er Jahren des vorigen Jahrhunderts durch die grundlegenden Arbeiten von Lorenth beseitigt worden.

Professor B o r n-Göttingen meinte, daß gerade die Relativitätstheorie das Bedürfnis nach Anschaulichkeit befriedige. Nach der Newtonschen Auffassung werde die Erde bei den Lauf um die Sonne von der Anziehung der Sonne und der Trägheit in ihrer Bahn gehalten, denke man sich die Sonne weg, so müßte die Erde in grader Linie weitergehen. Warum aber denn in g r a d e r Linie und w o h i n, müss man doch fragen. Hier sage nun die Einsteinsche Theorie, selbst wenn die Sonne weggedacht wird, so bleibt in der Umwelt noch eine große Massenverteilung übrig, und diese wirkt auf der Erde, so daß die Erde in eine gradlinige Bahn gezwungen wird. Im Grunde gebe die Newtonschen Anschauung dem leeren Raum bestimmte Eigenschaften, während die Einsteinsche Theorie nur Wechselwirkungen kennt. Daß die Einsteinsche Theorie darüber hinaus noch zu den Beziehungen der Anziehung zwischen Sonne und Erde komme, und sie erklären könne, obwohl sie gar nicht ihren Voraussetzungen stecke, sei eine glänzende Leistung.

So weit das Wesentliche der Erörterungen.

Ein dem Berichterstatter nahestehendes Lehrbuch aus dem Jahre 1892 beginnt mit den Worten „Die Physik hat die Aufgabe, die Erscheinungen der Natur als Bewegungsvorgänge zu beschreiben". Auf Grund der seitherigen Erfahrungen über Elektrizität hat der Verfasser diese Auffassung preisgegeben. Aus dem Festhalten an ihr kann man die Gegnerschaft gegen Einsteins Theorie verstehen. Aus ihrer Preisgabe leiten sich die Denkrichtungen Einsteins und seiner Anhänger ab.

*

Einsteins Ernennung zum Leydener Professor. Aus dem H a a g meldet „Holl. Nieuwsbüro'': Die Regierung genehmigte die Ernennung von Professor Dr. Einstein zum „außerordentlichen Professor'' der Naturwissenschaften an der Universität in L e y d e n. (Die Meldung ist in der vorliegenden Form geeignet, Anlaß zu Mißverständnissen zu geben. Prof. Einstein hat sich, wie bereits vor längerer Zeit berichtet, auf Ersuchen der Leydener Universität bereit erklärt, dort in jedem Jahre während einiger Frühjahrswochen Vorlesungen über

Relativitätstheorie und andere Kapitel der theoretischen Physik zu halten. Wohl um diese Verpflichtung äußerlich zu kennzeichnen, hat man die Form der Ernennung zum Honorarprofessor gewählt; von einer dauernden Uebersiedelung des berühmten Gelehrten an die holländische Hochschule kann kein Rede sein. D. Red.)"

The *Frankfurter Zeitung* reported,

"86. Versammlung deutscher Naturforscher und Aerzte.

Bad Nauheim, 24. September.

Die E i n s t e i n s c h e   R e l a t i v i t ä t s t h e o r i e wurde gestern vor dem zuständigen Forum, in den vereinigten mathematischen und physikalischen Abteilungen der deutschen Naturforscher- und Aerzteversammlung behandelt. Da es bekannt war, daß Professor E i n s t e i n selbst das Wort zu den Referaten den Professoren Dr. W e y l-Zürich, L a u e-Berlin, M i e-Halle und G r e b e-Bonn über seine Theorie in der Aussprache nehmen werde, hatte sich eine zahlreiche Zuhörerschaft eingefunden. Der geräumige Saal des Badehauses 8 und die Galerie waren gedrängt voll. Ganz auf dem Standpunkt Einsteins stand das Referat von Mie und auch Grebe-Bonn vertrat die Ansicht, daß sich für die von ihm angestellten Spezialstudien über die Cyanbande des Sonnenspektrums die Eisnteinsche Theorie mit den von ihm gefundenen Werten decken. Professor Weyl-Zürich und Lau-Berlin stimmten zwar nicht vollständig mit Einstein überein, lehnten ihn aber keineswegs prinzipiell ab. Das tat nur Professor L e n a r d-Heidelberg. Einstein selbst ging auf jeden erhobenen Einwand der Reihe nach ein und tat das in vornehmer, bescheidener, ja fast schüchterner und gerade dadurch überlegener Weise. Zum Schluß trat noch der erst jüngst von Frankfurt nach Göttingen berufene Physiker Professor Dr. B o r n in entschiedener Weise für Einstein ein, der auf alle Fälle die große Mehrheit der Versammlung auf seiner Seite hatte. Wir geben aus der Aussprache Folgendes wieder:

W e y l-Zürich sprach über eine von ihm vorgenommene Erweiterung der allgemeinen Relativitätstheorie, die auch die elektrischen Erscheinungen mitumfassen und aus allgemeinen

Grundlagen erklären will. Dann trug M i e die Durchrechnung eines Spezialproblems vor, demzufolge er lieber von der Relativität der Gravitation als von der allgemeinen Relativität sprechen will. Hierauf leitete L a u e-Berlin die Ablenkung eines Lichtstrahls durch ein Gravitationsfeld und die Rot-Verschiebung der Spektrallinien in einem solchen aus der Theorie her, und schließlich berichtete G r e b e-Bonn über seine gemeinsam mit B a c h e m ausgeführten Messungen, die diese von der Theorie geforderte Rot-Verschiebung der Spektrallinien auf der Sonne wirklich zeigen. Die sich anschließende Diskussion mußte streng auf diese Vorträge selbst beschränkt bleiben. Erst nach ihrer Erledigung wurde in eine allgemeine Diskussion über die Relativitätstheorie eingetreten. Sie gestaltete sich sehr lebendig, in der Hauptsache zu einer Diskussion zwischen Einstein und Professor Lenard. Lenard bekannte sich zu einem Anhänger der speziellen Relativitätstheorie, nach welcher eine vollkommen gleichförmige Translationsbewegung durchaus unerkennbar sein muß, dagegen wandte er sich gegen die allgemeine Relativitätstheorie, nach welcher jede Art von Bewegung für uns unerkennbar sein soll und wir nicht entscheiden können, ob wir uns zum Beispiel in drehender Bewegung befinden oder die gesamte Umwelt sich gegen uns drehe, oder ob wir, wenn wir in einem plötzlich gebremsten Eisenbahnzug eine schwere Erschütterung erleiden, diese erleiden zufolge einer Veränderung der Bewegung des Eisenbahnzuges oder nicht vielmehr durch die entsprechend entgegengesetzte Bewegung der Erde. Das letztere widerspricht nach seiner Meinung jedem gesunden Menschenverstand, den der Physiker gerade so gut braucht und anwenden muß wie jeder andere. Auch die Abschaffung des Aethers durch die Relativitätstheorie lehnt Lenard ab, er hält seine Existenz vielmehr für durchaus erwiesen, weil wir ohne ihn die physikalischen Erscheinungen nicht restlos als mechanische Bewegungsvorgänge erklären können — eine Forderung, die notwendig sei, um die Erscheinungen anschaulich begreifen zu können. In Bezug auf diese letzte Bemerkung erwiderte Einstein, was der Mensch als anschaulich oder nicht anschaulich betrachtet, das hat im Laufe der Zeit beträchtlich gewechselt, die Physik ist eben ihrem Wesen nach begrifflich und nicht anschaulich. Den Zeitgenossen Galileis war dessen Mechanik gewiß recht unanschaulich, heute aber, und zwar schon lange vor der Relativitätstheorie betrachtet man die elektrischen Felder als die elementarsten Gebilde, mit denen man arbeitet; dem Elektriker ist das elektrische Feld das anschaulichste, was nicht überholen werden kann, und es gibt Elektriker, die sich mechanische Vorgänge erst mit Hilfe der elektrischen Felder anschaulich machen können. Was den gebremsten Eisenbahnzug betrifft, so handelt es sich eben um die Wechselwirkung zwischen diesem und allen übrigen in der Welt vorhandenen Massen, wobei es ganz gleichgültig ist, welche von beiden gegen die andere bewegt wird. Mit dem gesunden Menschenverstand zu operieren, sei sehr gefährlich. Für die mathematische Behandlung gibt es eben kein an sich bevorzugtes Koordinatensystem und man wird daher jedesmal das für die Durchführung der Rechnung bequemste wählen. Das gleiche gilt von den Rotationsbewegungen. Wenn man bei der Annahme, die Umwelt bewege sich rotierend, und die Erde stehe still, zu Ueberlicht-Geschwindigkeiten komme, so sei das auch kein Widerspruch gegen die allgemeine Relativitätstheorie, die garnicht wie die spezielle eine konstante Lichtgeschwindigkeit fordere. In Bezug auf die Abschaffung des Aethers betonte Professor Mie, daß sie nichts mit der Relativitätstheorie zu tun habe. Schon in den 80er Jahren ist der Aether durch die grundlegenden Arbeiten von L o r e n t z abgeschafft worden. Im übrigen bekannte sich Mie zwar als begeisterten Anhänger der Relativitätstheorie, trat aber in einem Punkte Herrn Lenard bei, nämlich, daß er glaube es gäbe wirklich ein bevorzugtes Koordinatensystem und man könne fingierte Gravitationsfelder fortlassen. Es scheine ihm nicht als ob ihre Einführung erkenntnistheoretischen Wert habe, es komme ihm vor, als ob man da zu sein spintisiere demgegenüber lobt er sich doch immer unseren gesunden Menschenverstand. Inwiefern es aber ein bevorzugtes Koordinatensystem in der Welt geben soll, konnte er Herrn Einstein nicht sagen. Lenard meinte, die Diskussion habe zu einer Einigung der abweichenden Anschauungen und zu einer gegenseitigen Ueberzeugung ihrer Vertreter nicht führen können, weil der Gegensatz der experimentellen und mathematischen Physiker hier zum Ausdruck komme, eine Meinung, der von anderer Seite lebhaft widersprochen wurde, denn der mathematische Physiker stehe nicht im Gegensatz zum Experimentalphysiker, sondern stelle die von diesem erforschten Erscheinungen unter einheitlichen

Gesichtspunkten dar."

The *Frankfurter Zeitung*, on 21 September 1921, and the *Berliner Tageblatt*, Evening Edition, 20 September 1920, had reported on the Eighty-Sixth Meeting of German Natural Scientists. In the opening address to the meeting of natural scientists, Friedrich von Müller performed a staged and scripted homage to Einstein, and slandered anyone and everyone who disagreed with Einstein. Max Planck and Arnold Sommerfeld provided Müller with the speech. Planck and Sommerfeld also made certain that their personal attacks against Einstein's critics would be accompanied by scripted applause from Einstein's friends.[284] The *Frankfurter Zeitung* stated on 21 September 1920, first morning edition:

"Versammlung deutscher Naturforscher und Aerzte.
(Privattelegramm der „Frankfurter Zeitung".)

L—z Bad Nauheim, 20. Septbr.
Mit einem phantastischen Schmuck bunter Herbstfarben hat sich das mit Naturreizen so überaus reich versehene Bad Nauheim bekleidet, um die Teilnehmer der 86. Versammlung Deutscher Naturforscher und Aerzte zu begrüßen. Der große Saal des Konzerthauses und seine Galerien sind dicht besetzt mit Männern und Frauen, als bald nach 9 Uhr der Geschäftsführer der 86. Versammlung, Prof. Dr. G r ö d e l (Bad Nauheim) die Erschienenen begrüßt. Dabei gedenkt er nicht nur der Auslandsdeutschen, sondern auch der wenigen Ausländer, die zur Versammlung gekommen sind, und betont, daß die Wissenschaft bei uns keine nationalen Grenzen kenne. Zugleich weist er auf den Unterschied dieser Versammlung gegenüber den früheren hin, der in der veränderten allgemeinen Lage begründet ist. Diese Tagung soll eine Tagung des E r n s t e s sein. — Als zweiter Redner begrüßte der Präsident des hessischen Bildungsamtes Dr. S t r e c k e r die Versammlung. Er bezeichnet die Versammlung als ein Symbol des Aufbaus. Insbesondere sei eine der wichtigsten Aufgaben der deutschen Aerzteschaft, den physischen Wiederaufbau der Bevölkerung zu leiten und zu ermöglichen. Dem Naturforscher und Wissenschaftler im allgemeineren Sinne liegt der geistige Wiederaufbau ob. Die

Bedeutung der Natur als Lehrerin bei unserm Nachwuchs zur Geltung zu bringen, sei seine wichtigste Aufgabe. Aus den allgemeinen Betrachtungen heraus fällt das Wort, daß wir nicht nur die Kräfte der Natur beherrschen lernen müssen, sondern auch die im Menschen lebenden Naturkräfte. — Hatte diese politische Anspielung schon den Beifall der Versammlung hervorgerufen, so nimmt die Teilnahme der Zuhörer außerordentlich zu, als nach einigen kurzen Begrüßungsworten des Ministerialrats B a l s e n als Vertreter des hessischen Finanzministeriums, des Hausherrn der Versammlung als Besitzerin des staatlichen Bades Nauheim, und des Bürgermeisters der Stadt Nauheim Dr. K a i s e r der Rektor der hessischen Landesuniversität Gießen im Namen der vier benachbarten Hochschulen Marburg, Gießen, Frankfurt und Darmstadt das Wort ergreift. Er nennt als führenden Namen der Hochschulen auf dem Gebiete der Naturwissenschaften Ehrlich für Frankfurt, Behring für Marburg, Liebig für Gießen und Merck für Darmstadt und löst den ersten Beifall aus, als er wünscht, daß nun auch ein leider scheinbar abhanden gekommenes Gefühl sich wieder einstellen möge, d a s G e f ü h l d e s S t o l z e s, e i n D e u t s c h e r z u s e i n. Deutsche Forschung und Wissenschaft kann uns nicht genommen werden; sie müssen zwar darben, aber können nicht untergehen. Helmholtz, Virchow und Haber kann man nicht wegleugnen und annektieren.

Der Vorsitzende der Gesellschaft Deutscher Naturforscher und Aerzte, Prof. Dr. Friedrich v. M ü l l e r (München), der nunmehr die eigentlichen Arbeiten der Versammlung einleitet, gedenkt zunächst der zahlreichen Toten, die die Gesellschaft, besonders der Vorstand, in den sechs Fahren, in denen die Versammlungen unterbrochen waren, zu beklagen hat. Er bezeichnet dann den Beschluß, schon in diesem Jahre eine Naturforscherversammlung abzuhalten, als eine mutige Tat, deren Ausführung besonders durch Ernährungs- und Unterkunftsschwierigkeiten in Gefahr geriet. Deshalb mußte Hannover als Versammlungsort aufgegeben werden, und dem hessischen Staat wie der Stadt Nauheim sei besonderer Dank dafür abgestattet, daß sie die Abhaltung der Versammlung durch ihr außerordentliches Entgegenkommen ermöglicht haben. Der Redner streift dann die Aufgaben der Versammlung und deren besondere Bedeutung in den heutigen Tagen. Die

S e u c h e n b e k ä m p f u n g ist während des Krieges dank unserer medizinischen Wissenschaft und den Männern des Kriegssanitätsdienstes in großem Maße möglich gewesen, so daß wir vor schweren Seuchen bewahrt geblieben sind. Aber drei furchtbare Seuchen gilt es zu bekämpfen: Grippe, Schlafkrankheit und Syphilis. Diesen Krankheiten werden die Arbeiten der Versammlung besonderes Augenmerk widmen. Unter den Naturwissenschaften haben Chemie und Physik in dieser Zeit die größten Veränderungen ihrer wissenschaftlichen Grundlage erlitten: die Chemie dadurch, daß der Grundsatz der Unteilbarkeit der Atome zu Fall gekommen ist, die Physik dadurch, daß der Begriff des Aethers im Weltall verschwindet und durch die Relativitätstheorie E i n s t e i n s die Begriffe von Raum und Zeit wandelbar wurden. Damit ist dem Redner Gelegenheit gegeben, in ausdrucksvollen Worten g e g e n d i e B e r l i n e r V o r g ä n g e z u p r o t e s t i e r e n. Die außerordentlichen geistigen Taten eines Einstein gehören nicht vor das Forum einer mit Schlagworten und aus politischen Motiven arbeitenden öffentlichen Versammlung, sondern eines Berufskreises von Gelehrten. — Diese offene und deutliche Ehrung Einsteins erweckt lauten Beifall. Müller kommt dann auf die weiteren großen Probleme, deren Behandlung der Versammlung obliegt, zu sprechen: Stickstoff und Eiweiß und die Fragen des Unterrichts. Er betont den Wert der humanistischen Bildung und warnt vor einer Geichmachung des geistigen Besitzes in Anlehnung an die Bestrebungen zur Ausgleichung materiellen Besitzes. Die Beziehungen zum Ausland bezeichnet der Redner als noch gering. Die Zeit für internationale Kongresse ist noch nicht für uns gekommen. Diese sind auch nicht so nötig wie die fremde Literatur. Die Zeitschriften- und Büchernot ist eine große Gefahr für die Wissenschaft. Die Aufrichtung einer absperrenden Mauer gegen unsere geistigen Erzeugnisse erscheint dem Redner weniger gefährlich. Sie spreche eher für eine eistige Armut dessen, der sie aufrichtet. Denn geistig positive Völker vertragen keinen Abschluß, sie brauchen die andern Völker für die Publikation ihrer geistigen Tätigkeit. Von den allgemeinen Betrachtungen gleitet der Redner dann aber ab, als er auf die frühere Gewohnheit, des Landesherrn bei solchen Anlässen zu gedenken, hinweist. Diese Gewohnheit habe nun in Fortfall kommen müssen. Aber er halte es für seine Pflicht, der deutschen Fürsten als Förderer der Wissenschaften zu gedenken. Setzt bei diesen Worten schon ein starker Beifall ein, so steigert er sich noch, als der Redner sagt, die Monarchie pflege, die Republik schütze die Wissenschaft, die Revolution zerstöre. Er erinnert dabei an die Hinrichtung L a v o i s i e r s während der französischen Revolution und die sie begleitenden Worte des Richters: *nous n'avons plus besoin de savants.* Aber er hofft, ebenso wie im Frankreich der Revolution ein gewaltiger geistiger Aufschwung folgte, daß auch wir neben dem materiellen einen geistigen Aufschwung erreichen. — Der langdauernde Beifall der Versammlung sprach dafür, daß der Redner mit seiner kleinen Abschweifung auf politisches Gebiet doch sehr den Zuhörern aus dem Herzen gesprochen hat, und das mag bei einer Versammlung von wissenschaftlich gebildeten Zuhörern doch von Bedeutung sein.

Im Anschluß an diese einführenden Worte sprachen Dr. B o s c h, der Direktor der Badischen Anilin- und Sodafabriken, Prof. E h r e n b e r g (Göttingen) und Geheimrat R u b n e r (Berlin) zu dem Thema des Stickstoffes, worüber weiterer Bericht folgt."

Paul Weyland redressed the dishonest press reports disseminated by Einstein's friends in a statement Weyland published in "Die Naturforschertagung in Nauheim. Erdrosselung der Einsteingegner!", *Deutsche Zeitung,* Number 449, (26 September 1920), Morgen-Ausgabe, 1. Beiblatt, p. 1;[285] reprinted as "Die Naturforschertagung in Nauheim", *Politisch-Anthropologische Monatsschrift für praktische Politik, für politische Bildung und Erziehung auf biologischer Grundlage,* Volume 19, (1920), pp. 365-370:

"Die Naturforschertagung in Nauheim.

W e y l a n d.

Begünstigt von blendend schönem Wetter, gefördert durch den Opfersinn von Bevölkerung und Badeverwaltung, tagte in dieser Woche in dem unvergleichlich schönen Bad Nauheim die 86. Versammlung Deutscher Naturforscher und Ärzte. Seit der 85., die in Wien stattfand, wo im Jahre 1913 der greise Kaiser Franz Joseph es sich nicht nehmen ließ, den wissenschaftlichen Gästen seine Hofburg zur Verfügung zu stellen, liegt der

Weltkrieg, der hemmend in die Wissenschaft eingriff und nur die Gebiete der Kriegs-Chirurgie und Kriegsmedizin befruchtend beeinflußte. Lediglich die Physik hatte neben der Medizin eine Frage von weitgehender wissenschaftlicher Bedeutung zu erörtern, und dieses war die Relativitäts-Theorie, die seit 1911 und 1915 von Einstein eingeführt wurde. So ist es denn kein Wunder, daß sich mangels jeder anderen wissenschaftlichen Ausbeute dieser fünf Jahre das Hauptinteresse auf die Donnerstag- und Freitags-Sitzung konzentrierte, in welcher Einstein seiner wachsenden Opposition Rede und Antwort zu stehen hatte.

Um es gleich vorweg zu nehmen: er hat nicht sehr glänzend abgeschnitten, wenngleich die unter Einsteinschem Einfluß stehenden Presse-Referate der Deutschen physikalischen Gesellschaft völlig entstellte Berichte in die Welt jagten, die natürlich ein einseitiges Bild der Situation geben. Wir wollen versuchen, so kurz wie möglich die wichtigsten Vorträge herauszugreifen und müssen dabei leider bemerken, daß tatsächlich in diesen fünf Jahren außer der mathematischen Abstraktion der Relativitätstheorie nichts Neues hervorgebracht wurde, es sei denn, daß man als Fortschritt feststellt, daß die physikalische Forschung im Sinne ihrer jetzigen geistigen Leitung völlig zum Sklaven mathematischer Abstraktionen herabgesunken ist und jedes vernunftgemäße Forschen ausschaltet. Einstein hat denn auch eine Art Glaubensbekenntnis abgelegt, indem er die denkwürdigen Worte aussprach: „Gesunden Menschenverstand in die Physik einzuführen, ist gefährlich.'' Der einzige positive Gewinn dieser Naturforschertagung ist denn auch der, daß die Scheidung der Geister sich vollzogen hat und unter der Leitung L e n a r d s die Vergewaltigung der Physik durch mathematische Dogmen abgelehnt wird, während auf der anderen Seite die Einsteinophilen auf ihrem Standpunkt beharren und hurtig den Parnaß ihres Formelkrames zu erklimmen versuchen . . . bis sie von ihren „eisigen Höhen'' einmal jäh herabfallen werden.

Schon in der Eröffnungssitzung wies Herr v o n M ü l l e r darauf hin, das diese Versammlung im Zeichen der Relativitätstheorie steht, indem er in einem ihm von dem Einsteinleuten unterschobenen Konzept bemerkte, daß von Einstein eine der größten Geistestaten geschehen ist: er hat ja den Äther abgeschafft. Im übrigen wies Herr von Müller in seiner glänzenden Rede auf die Errungenschaften der Kriegsmedizin und Chirurgie hin, gedachte der Toten der deutschen Naturforscher und leitete in taktvoll feinen Worten die Versammlung ein. Als Vertreter der Regierung Hessens sprach der ehemalige Patriot und jetzige Linksmann Professor S t r e c k e r einige Begrüßungsworte, indem er um sich einige Phrasen verbreitete, daß die Naturforscher der Wahrheit dienen sollen und nun auch dafür zu sorgen hätten, daß die Wahrheit auch in uns Deutschen selbst einzudringen hat, daß nicht wieder durch deutsches Verschulden ein solcher Krieg entsteht. Diese versuchte Politisierung wurde merkwürdigerweise schweigend hingenommen und von einem Teil der Versammlung beklatscht. Als aber der Rektor der Gießener Universität K a l b f l e i s c h sich in einer kernigen deutschen Rede an das Auditorium wandte und den famosen Vorredner glatt abfallen ließ, brauste ein nicht endenwollender Beifall durch das Haus. Ein erhebendes Bekenntnis zum Deutschtum lag in dieser Akklamation, und als ferner Herr von Müller in einem weiteren Referat mit Wehmut feststellte, daß man zum ersten Male, so lange die deutschen Naturforscher tagen, nicht mehr des Kaisers gedenken darf und es der Versammlung anheimstellte, in Dankbarkeit der deutschen Fürsten zu gedenken, unter deren Fürsorge die deutsche Wissenschaft blühte und gedieh, zog es wie schmerzlich durch die so zahlreich erschienenen aufrechten deutschen Männer, und mancher gedachte der schönen Zeiten, wo deutsche Wissenschaft an der Spitze aller Wissenschaft stand und die deutschen Institutsleiter nicht von Herrn Haenisch mit Androhung von Disziplinarstrafen belästigt wurden, wenn sie nicht mit ihrem Friedensetat auskamen. Wohl selten hat der Theatersaal einen derartigen Sturm des Beifalls erlebt, wie er durch die Worte von Müllers, der deutschen Fürsten zu gedenken, ausgelöst wurde.

Die allgemeinen Vorträge behandelten die Atom- und Molekulartheorie, welche hauptsächlich von D e b y e , F r a n k und K o s s e l referiert wurden. Das Ernährungsproblem wurde von B o s c h , E h r e n b e r g , v o n G r u b e und P a u l behandelt.

Neue fundamentale Tatsachen wurden in diesen Vorträgen nicht verkündet. Lediglich des jungen D e b y e s blendender Vortragskunst gelang es, auch den Wissenden zu fesseln und sein Sammelreferat über Atomstruktur als Plus zu verbuchen. Er gipfelte *summa summarum* in der Andeutung, daß sich die Welt wahrscheinlich aus Vielheiten des Wasserstoffatoms zusammensetzt, wie dies die letzten Rutherfordschen Untersuchungen gezeigt haben, so daß also mit Wahrscheinlichkeit anzunehmen ist, daß die mehr als hundertjährige Proutsche Hypothese wieder zu Ehren gelangt und wahrscheinlich auch Goethes Standpunkt in der Farbenlehre von seinem oppositionellen Standpunkt gegen Newton wieder zur Anerkennung gelangt. Die Vorträge von F r a n k und K o s s e l bewegten sich in ähnlichem Rahmen und bestätigten auf anderem Wege die Ausführungen Debyes. In der Medizin war es besonders S u d h o f f, dessen greiser Charakterkopf überall in der Versammlung auffiel, der durch eine mit seltener Liebe und Sorgfalt zusammengebrachte Vesal-Ausstellung zu Ehren des 400 jährigen Geburtstages des Begründers der deutschen Anatomie fesselte. L e h m a n n erfreute sein dankbares Auditorium mit kinematographischen Aufnahmen über die neuesten Ergebnisse in der Forschung der flüssigen Kristalle, und R i n n e löste Beifallsstürme seiner Zuhörerschaft aus, die er in seiner liebenswürdigen humoristischen Art mit blendendem Material an sein Thema über Kristallgitter fesselte.

Sehr zu erwähnen ist ferner der von außerordentlicher Fachkenntnis getragene Vortrag von S t e u e r über die Geologie der Nauheimer Quellen.

Es waren dies ungefähr die Höhepunkte der allgemeinen Vorträge, wenn man von den naturwissenschaftlichen Filmen absehen will, welche die „Ufa" durch A d a m vortragen ließ, auf die wir vom pädagogischen Standpunkt aus noch einmal zurückkommen werden. Mittwoch nachmittag begannen die Spezialsitzungen der einzelnen Fakultäten, welche der Öffentlichkeit nichts Bemerkenswertes boten und über die zu referieren zu weit führen würde. Es sei nur bemerkt, daß allein die Physiker z. B. 56 solcher Vorträge zu erledigen hatten, die jedoch samt und sonders nicht über den Rahmen üblicher Laboratoriumstätigkeit hinausgingen und auch ohne Naturforschertag in Zeitschriften ihre Erledigung hätten finden können. So nahte der Donnerstag nachmittag mit seiner Hauptsitzung heran, wo sich zahlreiche Opponenten gegen Einstein gemeldet hatten. Diese Sitzung ist nun wohl eine von den denkwürdigsten, die in der Geschichte der deutschen Naturforschung stattgefunden hat. Obwohl es jedem

Tagesteilnehmer freistand, mit seinem Ausweis jeden Vortrag zu besuchen, hatte der Vorstand der Deutschen physikalischen Gesellschaft die Stirn, an der Eingangstür eine scharfe Siebung vorzunehmen, um nur diejenigen hineinzulassen, welche ihm genehm waren. Es erhob sich ein gewaltiger Tumult, das empörte Auditorium schob die wissenschaftliche Polizei beiseite, stürmte den Saal und behauptete sich. Auf diesem Wege gelangten auch andere als Einstein-Freunde hinein. Und nun geschah das Unglaubliche. Statt daß es zu einer wissenschaftlichen Auseinandersetzung kam, wurde von der Vorstandsleitung unter dem Vorsitz von M a x P l a n c k dafür gesorgt, daß die Opposition einfach mundtot gemacht wurde. In stundenlangen Reden verbreiteten sich W e y l , M i e , v o n L a u e und G r e b e über das Relativitätsprinzip, während den gegnerischen Rednern einschließlich Diskussion 15 Minuten zugebilligt wurden. Um 1 Uhr sollte die Sitzung beendet sein, um $^3/_4$ 1 Uhr war man noch mit der Diskussion der Einstein-Vorträge beschäftigt, und der Apparat der Erdrosselung klappte so vorzüglich, daß tatsächlich die Diskussion ausschließlich von Einstein-Leuten geführt wurde, hauptsächlich von Einstein selbst. G e h r c k e-Berlin, der sich mehrfach energisch zum Wort meldete, wurde bis zuletzt gelassen, um ihm dann mitzuteilen, daß die Diskussion geschlossen sei. R u d o l p h-Koblenz versuchte, wenigstens im Wege einer Geschäftsordnungsbemerkung zu Worte zu kommen: ihm wurde von Planck bedeutet, daß er nicht das Wort habe. L e n a r d-Heidelberg wurde schon nach drei Sätzen von Planck in die Parade gefahren, so daß Lenard auf das Wort verzichtete. P a l a g y i-Ofenpest, von dem hauptsächlich neben Mach Einstein seine Weisheit bezog, wurde $^1/_2$ Minute Redezeit bewilligt (in Worten eine halbe Minute), die dann auf 3 Minuten ausgedehnt wurde (!!!) und ähnlich Anmutigkeiten mehr. Der ehrwürdigen und geachteten Persönlichkeit Lenards, über den sich selbst ein Planck nicht hinwegzusetzen vermochte, gelang es schließlich, sich mit aller Energie Gehör zu verschaffen und Einstein zur Rede zu stellen. Er führte kurz aus, daß es nach seiner Auffassung wohl zwei Möglichkeiten physikalischer Forschung gäbe, nämlich die logisch verständliche und die mathematisch abstrakte. Er richtete an Einstein die klar präzisierte Frage und die dringende Bitte, ihm vernünftig zu erklären, wie es denn komme, daß beim plötzlichen Anrücken des berühmten Eisenbahnzuges nicht der Kirchturm des benachbarten Dorfes umfalle, sondern der Mann im Zuge, welche Voraussetzungen durch die Einsteinsche Theorie gegeben seien. Einstein drückte sich in seinen bekannten gewundenen Erklärungen und billigen Witzeleien um die Beantwortung der Frage herum, was Lenard zu weiterer zweimaliger Anfrage an Einstein veranlaßte, ihm Rede und Antwort zu stehen. Als es ihm nicht gelang, von Einstein eine sachliche Antwort zu erlangen, verzichtete Lenard auf das Wort mit der Feststellung, daß es ihm nicht gelungen sei, eine Übereinstimmung zwischen Einstein und ihm in dem Sinne zu erzielen, daß Einstein eine an ihn klar gerichtete Frage ebenso klar beantworten konnte. M i e trat Lenard zur Seite und erklärte, daß die vernünftige Anschauungsweise nicht ausgeschaltet werden dürfe. Hierauf gefiel sich Einstein in der denkwürdigen Bemerkung, daß es gefährlich sei, mit dem menschlichen Verstand zu operieren, womit er vor aller Welt kundgab, daß er mit der Vernunft nichts mehr zu tun hat. Die im vorhergehenden mitgeteilten Tatsachen finden sich nun nicht in dem offiziellen Pressebericht der Naturforschertagung, der selbstverständlich von den Einsteinleuten herausgegeben wurde. Es verdient hiermit festgenagelt zu werden, in welcher geradezu korrupten Art und Weise die Berichterstattung dieser Leute vonstatten geht und die freie wissenschaftliche Meinung systematisch geknebelt wird. Daß ein Max Planck sich zu derartigen Machenschaften hergab, ist bedauerlich, aber wohl dadurch verständlich, daß er sich, wie die anderen Spitzen der deutschen physikalischen Gesellschaft, mit Einstein wissenschaftlich und noch anders zu eng liiert hat, um anders handeln zu können.

Die zu Wort gemeldeten Gegner Einsteins wurden auf den Freitag versetzt, wo ihnen 12 Minuten Redezeit einschließlich Diskussion bewilligt wurde. Selbstverständlich war es am Freitag nachmittag nicht möglich, fünf Vorträge in einer Stunde à 12 Minuten wissenschaftlich zu erledigen, sie gaben nur Bruchstücke oder wurden schon in der Einleitung vom Vorsitzenden abgesetzt. Wir werden die Berichte jedoch nach dem Manuskript an dieser Stelle später behandeln.

Zu bemerken ist ferner, daß weder Einstein noch seine Freunde diesen Vorträgen beiwohnten.

Zusammenfassend kann man sagen, daß die Art und Weise

der freien Forschung, wie sie von der Deutschen physikalischen Gesellschaft verstanden wird, ein in der Geschichte der deutschen Wissenschaft beispielloser Skandal ist und daß es wohl die höchste Zeit wird, daß in dieses Rattennest wissenschaftlicher Korruption einmal frische Luft kommt. Wenn man bedenkt, daß Einstein sogar Weyl ablehnt, weil dessen Mathematik wieder zur einfachen euklidischen Geometrie hinüberführt, so versteht man wohl, daß es sich nicht darum handelt, in der Deutschen physikalischen Gesellschaft der Wissenschaft noch zu dienen, sondern daß es nur gilt, ihrem Papste Einstein die Tiara zu erhalten. Mit einem Gefühl tiefster Beschämung mußte man diese Versammlung verlassen, und auf der Kurpromenade und allen Gängen, wo das Thema besprochen wurde, gab es nur ein Wort der Entrüstung über das unerhörte Gebaren des Vorstandes, besonders seines Vorsitzenden Max Planck. Forscher von Ruf versichern mir, in dieser Gesellschaft kein Wort mehr zu sprechen.

Im übrigen verlief die Tagung in vollster Harmonie, kleine technische Mängel, die ja schließlich überall vorkommen, waren vorhanden. Die Ausstellung war glänzend beschickt, besonders von den optischen Firmen. Hier ragten insbesondere die Stände von Goerz, Leitz und Winkel hervor. Besonders Leitz fesselte durch ein neues dermatologisches Mikroskop, welches durch einfaches Aufsetzen auf den menschlichen Organismus, z. B. durch einfaches Auftragen einer Immersionsflüssigkeit das Leben des Gewebes erkennen ließ und die Blutkörperchen in Vene und Arterie deutlich machte. Höchst beachtenswert war ferner der neue Helldunkelfeldkondensator, welcher der biologisch-bakteriologischen Forschung neue Wege zu weisen berufen ist."

Franz Kleinschrod, who had a theory and an agenda of his own to promote, wrote,

"Die Einsteinsche Relativitätslehre ist bereits zur *cause celèbre* der Wissenschaft geworden. Noch vor wenigen Monaten nur der nächsten Umgebung bekannt, ist heute der Name Einstein im Munde, man darf sagen, wohl der gesamten Wissenschaft. Es dürfte wohl wenig wissenschaftliche Persönlichkeit geben, die in so kurzer Zeit den höchsten Gipfel wissenschaftlicher Popularität ersteigen. Man kann es verstehen, wenn man die Behauptungen und die schrankenlose Begeisterung seiner Anhänger liest: „Damit ist aber die alte Newtonsche Mechanik durch das Relativitätsprinzip über den Haufen geworfen. Das RP greift somit in alle durch Alter geheiligten Denkgewohnheiten ein, es zerstört alle Begriffe, mit denen wir aufgewachsen sind, und es verlangt von uns außerdem eine Fähigkeit zur Abstraktion, gegen die selbst die Anforderungen der vierdimensionalen Mathematik ein Kinderspiel sind. Aber als Gegengabe beschert uns das RP eine Fülle neuer Einsichten; es beschert uns Tag, wo vordem Dämmerung oder Nacht war. K u r z , e s   i s t   e i n e   g e i s t i g e B e f r e i u n g ,   w i e   d i e   T a t   d e s   K o p e r n i k u s .“ (Das Einsteinsche Relativitätsprinzip. A. Pflüger. 2. Aufl. 1920. Cohen-Bonn.) Im ähnlichen Tone ergehen sich alle Anhänger.—

Aber bald erhob sich auch dagegen, wie vorauszusehen war, die Kritik und setzte mächtig ein. Mit großer Spannung erwartete man auf der Naturforscherversammlung in Nauheim die Aussprache der Gegner mit Einstein. Sie verlief, wie auch hier vorauszusehen war, resultatlos. Es stand wohl der größere Teil der Gelehrten auf Seite von Einstein, aber Einstein konnte seine Gegner, besonders seinen Hauptgegner, Lenard (Heidelberg), nicht widerlegen, — aber die Gegner konnten auch Einstein nicht widerlegen. So blieb der Streit unentschieden und wird es auch bleiben, denn beide Parteien schossen mit ihren Angriffen immer dicht an dem Ziel vorbei. Keiner traf den andern richtig. [***] „Ja, selbst die Begriffe von Raum und Zeit, die wir seit Jahrtausenden als feststehend anzusehen gewohnt sind, sind w a n d e l b a r geworden durch die Relativitätstheorie.“ Mit diesen Worten eröffnete Friedr. von Müller die 86. Naturforscherversammlung deutscher Naturforscher und Aerzte zu Nauheim 1920."[286]

Philipp Lenard commented on the Bad Nauheim debate in the third edition of his booklet *Über Relativitätsprinzip, Äther, Gravitation*, S. Hirzel, Leipzig, (1921), pp. 36-44:

"Zusatz,
betreffend die Nauheimer Diskussion über das Relativitätsprinzip.

W ährend der Vorbereitung der vorliegenden Neuauflage hat am 23. Sept. d. J. die Diskussion über das Relativitätsprinzip bei der Nauheimer Naturforscherversammlung stattgefunden. Es hat dabei Herr E i n s t e i n auf die in dieser Schrift hervorgehobenen Schwierigkeiten einzugehen und die dabei sich ergebenden Fragen zu beantworten versucht, nachdem die Herren W e y l und M i e in ihren Vorträgen über Elektrizität und Gravitation besondere Anregungen gegeben hatten.

Der Eindruck, welchen die Aussprache hinterließ, an welcher außer den genannten Herren auch andere Vertreter der Mathematik und der Physik sich beteiligten, ging nach meinem Urteil im allgemeinen dahin, daß in der Tat an den in dieser Schrift gekennzeichneten Stellen Schwierigkeiten und Fragen vorliegen, deren Erledigung nicht ohne weiteres in befriedigender Weise gelingt und deren Hervorhebung also wohl berechtigt war. Es darf wohl scheinen, daß das Weitereingehen auf dieselben bei Überwindung der vorhandenen Hindernisse eine Weiterführung der Theorie mit Beseitigung ihrer gegenwärtigen Härten ergeben sollte, wie denn auch besonders die von Herrn M i e gelieferten Beiträge nach einer Weiterführung strebten, und zwar nicht ohne teilweises Abgehen von Herrn E i n s t e i n s ursprünglichem Wege [*Footnote:* Vgl. in verwandtem Sinne auch E. W i e c h e r t, Astron. Nachr. Bd. 211, Nr. 5054, S. 275, 1920, woselbst auch auf eine bevorstehende weitergehende Veröffentlichung desselben Verfassers über Gravitation in den Annalen der Physik hingewiesen wird. (Erschienen während der Drucklegung des Vorliegenden in Bd. 63, S. 301.)]. Die Hindernisse gegen volles Eingehen auf die von mir hervorgehobenen Schwierigkeiten und Fragen liegen, wie auch bei der Diskussion wieder erkennbar wurde, in der Kluft, welche für gewöhnlich zwischen den Benutzern der beiden auf Seite 25 des Vorliegenden erläuterten Bilderarten besteht.

[*Page 25:* Daß Andere den Äther in ihrem Gesamtbilde und auch bei ihrer Arbeit entbehren können, beweist nichts gegen den Äther, sondern ist vollkommen selbstverständlich, wenn man die Z w e i f a c h h e i t d e r B i l d e r bedenkt, die der Menschengeist von der (unbelebten) Natur bisher sich zu machen verstand. Es sei gestattet, diese Zweifachheit hier mit schon einmal gebrauchten Worten zu erläutern [*Footnote:* „Über Äther und Materie", Heidelberg (C. Winter) 1911, S. 5.]: „Nun sind aber diese Bilder des Naturforschers doch von zweierlei Art. Quantitativ sind sie immer; sie können aber — und das ist die erste Art — sich sogar ganz darin erschöpfen, quantitative Beziehungen zwischen beobachtbaren Größen zu sein. In diesem Falle sind sie vollkommen darstellbar in Gestalt mathematischer Formeln, meist Differentialgleichungen. Dies ist der Weg, den K i r c h o f f und H e l m h o l t z bevorzugt haben, von K i r c h o f f die mathematische Beschreibung der Natur genannt. Die denknotwendigen Folgen der Bilder, in deren Entwicklung die Benutzung und zugleich die Prüfung der Bilder besteht, sind dann die mathematischen Folgen jener Gleichungen, und auch weiter nichts. Man kann aber weitergehen — und dies ergibt die z w e i t e A r t der Bilder —, indem man sich von einer Überzeugung leiten läßt, ohne welche die Naturforschung sicherlich nie Erfolg gehabt hätte. Von der Überzeugung nämlich, daß alle Vorgänge in der Natur — in der unbelebten Natur wenigstens — bloße Bewegungsvorgänge sind, d. i. nur in Ortsveränderungen ein für allemal gegebenen Stoffes bestehen. Dann würde es sich in jedem Falle um Mechanismen handeln, und die Gleichungen, welche wir uns als Bilder erster Art gemacht haben, müssen Gleichungen der Mechanik sein, sie müssen ganz bestimmten Mechanismen entsprechen, und dann können wir auch geradezu diese Mechanismen als die Bilder betrachten, die wir uns von den Naturvorgängen gemacht haben. Wir haben dann mechanische Modelle, dynamische Modelle der Dinge als Bilder derselben in unserem Geiste. Die mechanischen Modelle und die Gleichungen, also die beiden Bildarten, sind, wenn die beide richtige Bilder sind, einander in den Resultaten, welche sie ergeben, vollkommen gleichwertig" [*Footnote:* Man sieht aus dieser Erörterung, daß ich die Bilder zweiter Art als höherstehend betrachte, gegenüber denen erster Art, da sie, wenn vollendet, eine Weiterentwicklung der letzteren sind, obgleich sie in den Anfängen auch umgekehrt oft einleitend diesen letzteren vorausgehen. Allerdings kommt es aus diesem in der Entwickelung liegenden Grunde stellenweise vor, daß bereits gute Bilder erster Art vorhanden sind, wo die Herstellung vollendeter Bilder zweiter Art noch nicht gelungen ist, und dies verleiht den Bildern erster Art an solchen Stellen Überlegenheit.]]

Die Benutzer der Bilder erster Art, zu welchen besonders auch Herr E i n s t e i n zählt, scheinen zumeist nicht geneigt, sich nach dem Standpunkt der Bilder zweiter Art zu begeben, um die Schwierigkeiten und Fragen, die von dort aus am deutlichsten zu erkennen sind, überhaupt genügend ins Auge zu fassen. Unzweifelhaft ist es aber, daß eine Theorie, mag sie auf Bilder erster oder zweiter Art gegründet sein, erst dann als einwandfrei gelten kann, wenn sie von beiden Standpunkten aus standhält; denn beide Standpunkte haben sich im Fortschreiten der Naturforschung als voll berechtigt gezeigt, und alle bisherigen gut bewährten Theorien sind von beiden Standpunkten aus widerspruchsfrei erschienen. Wer freilich die „Abschaffung des Äthers" verkündet

[*Footnote:* Die „Abschaffung des Äthers" wurde in Nauheim in großer Eröffnungssitzung wieder als Resultat verkündet (zur früheren Verkündung in Salzburg, von Herrn E i n s t e i n selbst, siehe das Zitat in Note 17, S. 27). {*Footnote 17, Pages 27-28:* Als das Überspringen eines Abgrundes konnte wohl seinerzeit die Entdeckung der L i c h t q u a n t e n erscheinen: Auf der einen Seite waren die Wellen des Lichtes, auf der anderen die neuartigen Lichtquanten, und die Kluft zwischen ihnen wurde leer gelassen, was allerdings dem kühnen Springer selber niemand verdenken wird. Weitergehend war aber, nach der negativen Seite hin, der an diese Entdeckung geknüpfte Ausspruch (Naturforscherversammlung zu Salzburg am 21. September 1909, Verh. d. D. Phys. Ges. S. 482, Physik. Zeitschr. Bd. 10, S. 817, 1909): „Heute aber müssen wir wohl die Ätherhypothese als einen überwundenen Standpunkt ansehen", was zu einer nachträglichen Überbrückung der Kluft, die doch im Interesse der Wissenschaften zu wünschen war, nicht eben ermunterte. Ich habe dennoch eine solche Überbrückung versucht und bin dabei zu dem Resultat gelangt, daß die Lichtquanten dasselbe seien, was man als kohärente Lichtwellenzüge schon lange vorher ins Auge gefaßt hatte, allerdings mit dem wesentlichen neuen Zusatze der Konzentrierung der Energie auf einen Strahl von bestimmter Richtung, welches letztere ich durch die auch sonst naheliegende Annahme nur e i n e s elektrischen Kraftlinienringes (gedacht als diskreter Ätherwirbelring) in jeder durch die Schwingung e i n e s e i n z e l n e n E l e k t r o n s emittierten Lichtwelle erklärte (S. „Über Äther und Materie'', Heidelberg 1911, S. 19 u. f. und die Untersuchung über Phosphoreszenz, Heidelb. Akad. 1913 A 19, S. 34 Fußnote 61. Als kohärente Wellenzüge hat, wie ich nachträglich finde, auch bereits H. A. L o r e n t z die Lichtquanten erklärt; Physikal. Zeitschr. Bd. 11, S. 353, 1910). Man sieht aus solcher Erklärungsmöglichkeit, was für das Gesamtbild des Naturforschers doch nicht unwichtig ist, daß die Lichtquanten nichts Umstürzendes für die Theorie des Lichtes sind, namentlich auch, daß sie für oder gegen die „Ätherhypothese'' überhaupt gar nichts aussagen, sondern daß sie in der Hauptsache eine besondere, bis dahin unbekannt gewesene Eigenschaft der lichtemittierenden Atome betreffen, nämlich die, auf kohärente Wellenzüge von bestimmtem mit der Schwingungsdauer zusammenhängenden Energieinhalt eingerichtet zu sein.

Die Vorstellung, daß das Lichtquant ein kohärenter Wellenzug sei, dessen Länge demnach in jedem Falle durch optische Interferenzversuche feststellbar wäre, hat durch neuartige Versuche von Herrn W. W i e n (Annalen d. Phys., Bd. 60, S. 597, 1919) eine augenfällige Bestätigung erfahren, indem die Zeitdauer der Emission des Lichtquants gemessen wurde. Sehr bemerkenswert ist dabei die hier als unmittelbares Beobachtungsergebnis auftretende Erkenntnis, daß die Energie des Lichtquants ungleichmäßig über die Länge des Wellenzugs verteilt ist, indem ein allmähliches Abklingen des emittierenden Atoms stattfindet (nach einer Exponentialfunktion, wie beim akustischen Wellenzuge einer angeschlagenen Glocke), so daß eine bestimmte Länge des Wellenzuges nur dann sich ergibt, wenn man festsetzt, in welchem Stadium des Abklingens man das Ende als erreicht ansehen will. Setzt man beispielswelse das Ende bei 1/7 (genauer $1/e^2$) der Anfangsintensität fest, so ergibt sich nach Herrn W. W i e n s Messungen die Länge des Lichtquants zu rund 10 m, und zwar gilt diese Länge — was an sich wieder sehr bemerkenswert ist — nach den bisherigen Messungen für Lichtquanten aller Wellenlängen, trotz des verschiedenen Energieinhalts der Lichtquanten verschiedener Wellenlänge. Es käme das darauf hinaus (wenn man bei diesen neuartigen Versuchen schon jetzt verallgemeinern darf), daß die Energie jeder einzelnen Welle irgendeines Lichtquants bei gleichem Abstande vom Anfange des Wellenzuges die gleiche ist. Der verschiedene Energieinhalt verschieden weit vom

Anfange abstehender Wellen bestünde dabei in unserer Vorstellung in verschieden großer senkrecht zum Strahl gemessener Breite des elektrischen Kraftlinienringes dieser Wellen.} Man hat nicht dazu gelacht. Ich weiß nicht, ob es anders gewesen wäre, wenn die Abschaffung der Luft verkündet worden wäre.]

und vertritt, der will die Bilder zweiter Art hinwegleugnen (vgl. S. 27); er kann dann allerdings nicht in der Lage sein, auf deren Standpunkt sich zu begeben, und von ihm ist dann die Lösung der Schwierigkeiten und der damit verbundene Fortschritt auch nicht zu erwarten. Es wäre unnütz, hierauf weiter eingehen zu wollen, und es war dankenswert, daß die Aussprache an diesem Punkte in Nauheim von selber abbrach;

[*Footnote:* Die Frage des vierdimensionalen Raumzeitbegriffes war in der Diskussion von vornherein außer Spiel geblieben. Es wäre in Gegenwart so vieler Mathematiker (die oft dem mathematischen Hilfsmittel ebensoviel Bedeutung beilegen, als dem physikalischen Sinn) nicht förderlich gewesen, den mir als Naturforscher (der aber nicht nur die materielle Welt sehen will) allein annehmbar erscheinenden diesbezüglichen Standpunkt (vgl. S. 7 u. Anm. 7, S. 14) zu betonen, da es als Geschmackssache betrachtet werden kann, wieviel Denkfreiheit man zugunsten der „Relativierung der Zeit" opfern will.]

man findet sich hier von der zu Bescheidenheit mahnenden Erkenntnis der ganz außerordentlichen Ansprüche, welche an dieser Stelle der Entwicklung an den Geistesumfang des Naturforschers gestellt werden. Große mathematische Begabung, welche die Bilder erster Art mit Leichtigkeit meistert, scheint nicht oft in demselben Kopfe mit der Leichtigkeit der inneren dynamischen, physikalischen Anschauung verbunden zu sein, welche mehr Vorliebe für die Bilder zweiter Art verleiht, — und umgekehrt [*Footnote:* Man kann hieraus wohl auch ermessen, wie wenig Zweck es hat, wenn volkstümliche Schriften oder Vortragende von einseitigem Standpunkt aus das Relativitätsprinzip vor die Öffentlichkeit bringen, wobei auch der Verdacht kaum abzuweisen ist, daß die Einseitigkeit um des größeren Aufsehens willen, das sie hervorbringt, geliebt wird. Es ist das eine bedauerliche Erscheinung; aber sie besteht, und es wäre ein ungesundes Zeichen, und als solches sicherlich noch viel bedauerlicher, wenn darauf nicht Gegenwirkung einträte. Die „Relativisten" müßten aber eine von ihnen selbst hervorgerufene Gegenwirkung jederzeit ruhig hinzunehmen wissen.].

Im Einzelnen ergab die Aussprache etwa das Folgende:

Es wurden zwei Fragen gesondert diskutiert, deren Zusammenhang aber doch so wesentlich sich zeigte, daß wir sie hier der Kürze halber teilweise zusammenfassen können, nämlich 1. die Frage (vgl. S. 15, 16): Wie ist es im Beispiel des gebremsten Eisenbahnzuges, wo die Folgen der ungleichförmigen Bewegung nur innerhalb des Zuges sich zeigen, möglich, den Sitz der ungleichförmigen Bewegung trotz dieser Einseitigkeit der Erscheinung für unauffindbar erklären zu wollen, wie es die allgemeine Relativitätstheorie tut? Und 2. die Frage des unerlaubten Gedankenexperiments (vgl. Note 10, S. 16, 17): Bedeutet nicht das Auftreten von Überlichtgeschwindigkeiten im Falle einer Drehung der Gesamtwelt, z. B. um die Erde, die von der allgemeinen Relativitätstheorie als eine mit der Drehung irgendeines Körpers, z. B. der Erde, bei ruhender Gesamtwelt gleichwertige Annahme angesehen wird, einen inneren Widerspruch, da doch Überlichtgeschwindigkeiten nach eben derselben Theorie ausgeschlossen seien?

Es wurde von Herr E i n s t e i n s Seite selbstverständlich Gewicht auf die Gravitationsfelder gelegt, welche in seiner Theorie jeden Fall ungleichförmiger Bewegung begleiten müssen; aber es blieb doch dabei, daß diese Felder zunächst nur zu dem Zwecke hinzugenommen seien, um das Relativitätsprinzip allgemeingültig erscheinen zu lassen und auf alle Fälle anwenden zu können, woraus aber noch nicht hervorgeht, daß diese Felder weitere Beziehungen zur Wirklichkeit haben, die die Notwendigkeit ihrer Einführung den sie begleitenden Härten gegenüber erweisen (vgl. S. 22). Dabei sollte nicht bezweifelt sein, daß jedes Auftreten einer ungleichförmigen Bewegung mit gewissen Zuständen des Äthers (des „Raumes" liebt die Relativitätstheorie zu sagen, vgl. S. 28) in ihrer Umgebung verbunden sei; aber so lange die E i n s t e i n schen Gravitationsfelder mit ihrem Zubehör den gesunden Verstand nicht befriedigen, wird man zweifeln dürfen, ob sie diese Zustände des Äthers ganz allgemein richtig abbilden. Vergeblich mahnt hierbei Herr E i n s t e i n zu Mißtrauen gegenüber dem gesunden Verstand: Eine Theorie, die nicht in der Lage ist, auf so einfache Fragen, wie die obigen beiden es sind, eine entsprechende einfache, den gewöhnlichen Verstand befriedigende Antwort zu geben, ist nicht einwandfrei. Sie kann Erfolge haben und man kann solche bewundern, sie kann verbesserungsfähig, ja vielleicht schon in Verbesserung begriffen sein, aber sie darf nicht mit den üblichen weit gesteigerten Ansprüchen auftreten, welche wir in der vorliegenden Schrift getadelt haben, und sie darf das am allerwenigsten vor der Allgemeinheit tun, die als nicht sachkundig leicht beliebig irre zu führen ist. Es ist besser, der Allgemeinheit neben den Resultaten auch die Zweifel vorzuführen, um ihr den Ernst der Forschung zu zeigen, — oder aber gar nichts.

Auf die zweite Frage ist übrigens überhaupt keine entscheidende Antwort erfolgt [*Footnote:* Auch sonst war ich schließlich erstaunt, wie wenig Herr E i n s t e i n auf die Beantwortung meiner Fragen vorbereitet zu sein schien — die doch schon zwei Jahre lang mit seiner Kenntnis gedruckt vorgelegen haben, — während von seiner Seite und auch von einem andern Fachmann Zeitungslesern gegenüber ganz ausdrücklich der Anschein der unbedingten Überlegenheit meinen Gedankengängen gegenüber erweckt worden war. Da ich weder Anhänger noch Gegner irgendeines Prinzips bin, sondern nur Naturforscher sein möchte — wie auf S. 12 schon zu erkennen gegeben, — hätte ich den Nachweis, daß und an welcher Stelle meine Überlegungen nicht genügend gründlich waren, als Gewinn entgegennehmen müssen, wenn er geführt worden wäre (vgl. auch Note k, S. 23), zumal in der rein auf die Sache gerichteten Form, in welcher die Nauheimer Aussprache ablief. Die einzige Aufklärung, welche ich von der Diskussion mitgenommen habe, stammt von seiten des Herrn M i e ; sie wird im weiter Folgenden bezeichnet werden.], und man darf daher wohl sagen, daß die Überlichtgeschwindigkeiten des unerlaubten Gedankenexperiments der allgemeinen Relativitätstheorie in der Tat eine Schwierigkeit bereiten [*Footnote:* Man muß immer bedenken, daß jeder beliebige rotierende Körper auf Erden, mag er auch nur eine Umdrehung in 3000 Jahren ausführen, Überlichtgeschwindigkeit schon der Orionsterne, vielhundertfache Lichtgeschwindigkeit der vielhundertfach ferneren Nebelsysteme ergibt, sobald man die Rotation nicht a b s o l u t dem Körper, sondern also der Umwelt zuschreiben will.]. Dies bedeutet aber nicht weniger, als daß diese Theorie in sich selbst — ganz abgesehen von ihrer Übereinstimmung oder Nichtübereinstimmungen mit der Wirklichkeit, — d. i. logisch nicht in Ordnung ist. Der innere Widerspruch, welchen sie enthält, fällt weg, wenn man nach Herrn M i e s Vorschlag gewisse, von ihm ,,vernunftgemäß" genannte Koordinatensysteme für bevorzugt erklärt [*Footnote:* Vgl. G . M i e , Physikal. Zeitschr. 18, S. 551, 574, 596, 1917 und Annalen d. Physik 62, S. 46, 1920.] und die anderen möglichen Koordinatensysteme ausschließt [*Footnote:* Ganz im Sinne der auf S. 15 des Vorliegenden Gesagten; vgl. besonders auch die Note 8a.] Gleichzeitig wäre damit auch die erste Frage erledigt; man braucht nur ein mit dem Eisenbahnzug verbundenes Koordinatensystem als ruhend gedachtes Bezugssystem auszuschließen und dafür das mit dem Erdboden verbundene Koordinatensystem als vernunftgemäß in Benutzung zu nehmen, um der Schwierigkeit der Frage enthoben zu sein. Aber dieser Ausweg bedeutet nicht eine Rettung, sondern eine Vernichtung des Relativitätsprinzips in seiner allgemeinsten, von Herrn E i n s t e i n aufgestellten, einem einfachen und zugleich allumfassenden Naturgesetz entsprechenden und daher das besondere philosophische Interesse in Anspruch nehmenden Form. Denn das Prinzip sagt in dieser Form aus, daß der Ablauf allen Naturgeschehens — die Formulierung der allgemeinen Naturgesetze — unabhängig ist von der Wahl des Bezugssystems [*Footnote:* Dies ist auch wirklich nach dem Ursprung des Prinzips sein einfacher Sinn, wenn überhaupt einer vorhanden ist. Es nützte in philosophischer Beziehung nichts, kompliziertere, verklausulierte Fassungen einzuführen; sind solche notwendig, so hat damit das Prinzip nicht zwar seinen möglichen Wert als Hilfmittel der Naturforschung, aber doch seine Ansprüche auf Wichtigkeit für das allgemeine Denken, für die Naturauffassung im Ganzen verloren.], wodurch es in allen Fällen unmöglich würde, durch irgendwelche Naturbeobachtungen absolut über Vorhandensein von Ruhe oder Bewegung zu entscheiden. Es müßten dann alle Bezugsysteme durchaus gleichwertig sein für die Schlüsse die sie ergeben (weshalb auch Herr E i n s t e i n die verschiedenen Koordinatensysteme, auch die, welche zu den offensichtlichsten

Schwierigkeiten oder zu inneren Widersprüchen führen, immer wieder als prinzipiell gleichwertig hinstellen will), [*Footnote:* Nur praktische, nicht prinzipielle Gründe sollten nach Herrn E i n s t e i n s Äußerung von der Wahl gewisser Koordinatensysteme abhalten. Hierin liegt aber, wenn man sich vergegenwärtigt, daß gewisse, durch das Prinzip selbst gar nicht gekennzeichnete Koordinatensysteme in die Irre führen, eben der (wenn auch versteckte) Hinweis auf die Nichtigkeit der höchsten theoretischen Ansprüche des Prinzips; ganz unbeschadet natürlich seines etwaigen heuristischen und auch entwicklungsfördernden Wertes.] was aber nicht der Fall ist, wie die Beispielsfälle unserer beiden Fragen und in strengerer Form Herrn M i e s Untersuchungen zeigen.

Man kann dann also — wie die Sache bis heute steht — das allgemeine Relativitätsprinzip nicht als Naturgesetz in strengem Sinne hinnehmen, und zwar, wie aus den Untersuchungen von Herrn M i e hervorzugehen scheint — und was hier als über den Inhalt der vorstehenden Teile dieser Schrift hinausgehend besonders hervorzuheben ist, — selbst dann nicht, wenn man seine behauptete Allgemeingültigkeit einschränken will auf massenproportionale Kräfte (Gravitationsprinzip, vgl. S. 18);

[*Footnote:* Das allgemeine Relativitätsprinzip ohne Einschränkung scheitert, wenn wirklich ernst genommen, an b e i d e n oben ausgesprochenen Fragen. Das Gravitationsprinzip (die von mir vorgeschlagene Einschränkung des allgemeinen Relativitätsprinzips) ist dagegen allerdings fern von jeder Schwierigkeit der e r s t e n Frage gegenüber (da es sich auf deren Fall gar nicht bezieht), zeigt aber doch der zweiten Frage gegenüber den inneren Widerspruch, der, wie es nun scheint, jeder Anwendung des Relativitätsprinzips auf ungleichförmige Bewegungen gefährlich werden muß, wenn nicht geeignete Kunstgriffe dagegen schützen. Man könnte danach sagen, daß das Gravitationsprinzip zwar in höherem Grade einwandfrei erscheint als das allgemeine Relativitätsprinzip, daß es aber doch ebenfalls nicht völlig und ohne weiteres einwandfrei ist. Immerhin erscheint der Unterschied in den Mängeln der beiden Prinzipien groß genug, um die in der vorliegenden Schrift geschehene Einführung und Hervorhebung des Gravitationsprinzips zu rechtfertigen.]

sondern man kann es — will man Irreführung vermeiden — nur als ein heuristisches Prinzip hinstellen (vgl. Note 11, S. 17), dessen Anwendung von der Hinzunahme nicht in dem Prinzip liegender Festsetzungen oder von besonderem Geschick oder Glück in Nebenannahmen begleitet sein muß, um das Ausmünden in falsche Resultate zu vermeiden, als ein Prinzip also, das unter Umständen richtige, wertvolle, ganz neue Zusammenhänge beobachtbarer Dinge liefern kann, wobei aber doch der wirkliche Beweis für die Richtigkeit der so vorausgesagten Zusammenhänge nur in noch hinzuzunehmender Erfahrung zu suchen wäre, mit der sie besonders verglichen werden müssen, nicht in mathematisch noch so einwandfreier Ableitung aus dem Prinzip.

[*Footnote:* Man bemerkt hier einen Unterschied gegenüber den sonstigen physikalischen Prinzipien, beispielweise dem Energieprinzip. Die aus solchen Prinzipien bei richtiger Beachtung der zugehörigen Begriffe mathematisch fehlerlos gezogenen Schlüsse darf man ohne weiteres für ebenso zutreffend halten wie die Gesamtheit der Erfahrungen, welche dem Prinzip zugrunde liegen und an welchen es bereits bewährt ist. Der Unterschied mag an der Neuheit des Relativitätsprinzips liegen (vgl. S. 14), die noch nicht genügend Klarheit hat aufkommen lassen über Gültigkeitsbereich oder über Zusatzbedingungen, welche bei der Anwendung einzuhalten und also als wesentlich zum Prinzip gehörig zu betrachten sind. Jedenfalls scheint mir bei dieser Sachlage im Falle der Perihelverschiebung des Merkur doch immer noch G e r b e r s „Ableitung" des richtigen quantitativen Zusammenhanges (sei sie auch nur Scheinableitung gewesen) mit Berücksichtigung der Frühzeitigkeit nennenswert zu bleiben gegenüber der nach dem Gesagten doch auch nur scheinbar aus strenger Anwendung eines Prinzips allein hervorgegangenen Ableitung E i n s t e i n s (vgl. S. 10-12 u. 30). Ganz abgesehen ist dabei inbezug auf G e r b e r davon, daß es mir durchaus unzulässig erscheint, einem längst Verstorbenen, der einen für richtig gehaltenen Zusammenhang (nämlich die Endgleichung für die Perihelverschiebung), also etwas Nützliches gebracht hat (mit dem Ungeschick der Hinzufügung eines anfechtbaren Beweises, aber auch ohne jedes Streben damit hervorzutreten), Pfuscherei oder dergleichen vorzuwerfen, wie es geschehen ist. Ich glaube, daß man den Pythagoräischen Lehrsatz, wenn ihn Pythagoras bloß veröffentlich und nicht bewiesen hätte, doch heute noch nach ihm benennen würde — damaliges genügend schnelles Bekanntwerden des Satzes angenommen, — da er richtig und wertvoll ist.]

Ein möglicherweise praktisch wertvolles Prinzip ist das Relativitätsprinzip also, aber keines, auf das eine neue Weltanschauung sich gründen ließe, oder das berufen sein könnte, bewährte anders geartete Wege der Naturforschung nun auf einmal als abgetan erscheinen zu lassen, wenn es auch selber einen neuen, augenblicklich vielbeschrittenen Weg eröffnet hat.

[*Footnote:* Man kann dann auch wohl sagen, daß es sich beim verallgemeinerten Relativitätsprinzip um ein durch Mathematik in quantitative Bahnen gedämmtes System des Erratens von Naturvorgängen handelt. Solches Erraten unter Aufwand eines ziemlich ausgedehnten mathematischen Apparats spielt auch sonst in der gegenwärtigen Physik eine früher nicht in gleichem Maße dagewesene Rolle, z. B. bei den quantentheoretischen Betrachtungen, und das Verfahren hat sich als sehr förderlich erwiesen, insofern die Kontrolle durch die Beobachtung nicht fehlte. Aber es wäre doch falsch, wenn man — wie einige Mathematiker es tun — nun eine Verwandlung der Physik in einen Nebenzweig der Mathematik als Endziel der Entwicklung vor sich sehen wollte. Die Natur, deren Erforschung Aufgabe der Physik ist, wird mit ihren Wundern, die jederzeit auch tiefsinnigste Forscher überrascht haben, noch nicht so bald zu Ende sein. — Offenbar ist es auch nur Geschmackssache, ob man lieber mit oder ohne mathematische Ableitung sich auf neue, der erfahrungsmäßigen Prüfung wert erscheinende Thesen bringen läßt, wenn die Ableitung nicht exakten Anschluß der Thesen an Erfahrungsresultate und an Annahmen von einfacher physikalischer Bedeutung liefert.]

Der mögliche praktische Wert des Prinzips kann umso höher bemessen werden, als es vielleicht richtige Zusammenhänge hat angeben helfen, die auf die Gravitation sich beziehen, auf eine Kraft, der man seit N e w t o n und C a v e n d i s h, also über 100 Jahre lang nicht mehr weiter systematisch hat beikommen können [*Footnote:* Wozu, wenn solche Leistungen in Frage stehen, noch — genau besehen — übertriebene Ansprüche stellen?] Es liegen in dieser Beziehung bekanntlich drei Resultate vor: Die (schon von G e r b e r angegebene) Perihelverschiebungsgleichung, die Lichtstrahlenkrümmung und die Rotverschiebung der Spektrallinien bei Gravitationszentren, und es handelt sich um deren Prüfung an der Erfahrung, die auch über den mehr oder weniger großen Wert der Theorie entscheiden muß.

Der gegenwärtige Stand dieser Prüfung ist für die beiden erstgenannten Zusammenhänge, Perihelverschiebung und Lichtstrahlenkrümmung, im Vorliegenden bereits besprochen worden (S. 19, 20), und es kann hier der Lage der Sache nach auch nicht so schnell neue Erfahrung hinzukommen. Die Frage des drittgenannten Zusammenhangs, der Rotverschiebung (vgl. Note 6, S. 19), ist dagegen augenblicklich mehr in Fluß. Es scheint dabei fast, als ob die mit besten Mitteln und von bewährtesten Seiten bisher ausgeführten Beobachtungen zu negativem Resultat sich vereinigten. [*Footnote:* Siehe die reichhaltige Zusammenstellung der in Betracht kommenden Veröffentlichungen in der auf S. 36 zitierten, soeben in den Annalen der Physik erschienenen Arbeit von E . W i e c h e r t.] Jedenfalls erschien es bei der hierauf bezüglichen Diskussion in Nauheim nicht günstig für einwandfreien Überblick, daß nur die Bonner Beobachter (mit positivem Resultat) zu Wort kommen konnten, deren Hilfsmittel, so weit bekannt, weniger vollkommen waren als die der amerikanischen Beobachter, deren Resultat ebenso wie das kürzlich noch hinzugekommene von J u l i u s in Utrecht [*Footnote:* W . H . J u l i u s u. P . H . v a n C i t t e r t, Kon. Akad. van Wetenschappen te Amsterdam, 29. Mai 1920.] aber negativ war. [*Footnote:* Die in bezug auf die Bonner Beobachtungen noch vorhandenen Zweifel erinnern mich an zwei Fälle, die zeigen, daß im Bonner Physikalischen Institut bei spektralanalystischen Beobachtungen nicht gerade traditionelles Glück vorhanden ist. Man vergleiche die gänzlich unrichtigen Angaben über die räumliche Verteilung der spektralen Lichtemission in den Alkalibogenflammen, die noch heute in nicht genügend kritisch bearbeiteten Werken eine irreführende Rolle spielen (s. dazu Heidelb. Akad. 1914 A 17, Fußnote 94, S. 48, auch S t a r k s Jahrb. 13, S. 234, 1916) und ebenso die Beobachtungen über spektrale Erregungsverteilungen von Phosphoreszenzbanden, die ebenfalls mit der Annahme in die Irre gingen, bereits vorhandene Beobachtungen an Feinheit übertroffen zu haben (siehe dazu Heidelb. Akad. 1913 A 19, Fußnote 1, S. 3.]

Man kann daher bei der Rotverschiebung gegenwärtig noch von keiner experimentellen Bestätigung reden. Die beiden anderen Zusammenhänge sind zwar bestätigt, jedoch — wie auf S. 19, 20 erläutert — so, daß es noch fraglich blieb, ob diese Bestätigung überhaupt auf das Gravitationsprinzip sich beziehen läßt. Weiteres muß erst die Zukunft zeigen. Man wird dann sehen können, wie weit das Gravitationsprinzip — neben dem schon durch einfachste alltäglich Erfahrung widerlegten allgemeinen Relativitätsprinzip — wenigstens heuristischen Wert bewährt."

Hermann Weyl defended Einstein, though Einstein did not agree with Weyl's work.[287] Weyl repeatedly demonstrated dishonesty and his unscientific, unfair and adolescent pro-Einstein bias. In addition to being unfair to Gehrcke, Weyl intentionally underrated David Hilbert's priority for the generally covariant field equations of gravitation of the general theory of relativity. Though Weyl acknowledged Hilbert's work, he failed to emphasize Hilbert's priority as the first to deduce the generally covariant field equations of gravitation of the general theory of relativity. Weyl committed this vile act over Hilbert's objections, in Weyl's book *Space-Time-Matter*.[288]

Weyl published an article in *Die Umschau*, Volume 24, Number 42, (23 October 1920) pp. 609-610, which was not accessible to your author up to time of this publication. Other references to contemporary accounts which do not appear herein include: "Einladung zur 86. Vers. Dt. Naturforscher.", *Die Naturwissenschaften*, Volume 37, IV; and *Deutsche Allgemeine Zeitung*, 25 September 1920) Morning edition, p. 2.

Ernst Gehrcke redressed Hermann Weyl's (and Kleinschrod's) statement regarding the Bad Nauheim debate,

"Der in der Umschau vom 23. Oktober 1920, Seite 610, erstattete Bericht von WEYL über die Relativitätssitzung in Nauheim bedarf in mehrfacher Hinsicht der Ergänzung.

Ein nicht ganz unwichtiger Punkt, der auf der Nauheimer Tagung mit bemerkenswerter Deutlichkeit hervortrat, ist dem Berichte von Herrn WEYL nachzutragen: EINSTEIN hat nämlich unzweideutig und klar in der Diskussion seine

M i ß b i l l i g u n g der WEYLschen Theorie zum Ausdruck gebracht und die Erklärung abgegeben, daß eine aus rein mathematischen Forderungen der Symmetrie aufgebaute Theorie, wie die von WEYL, a b z u l e h n e n sei. Wenn Herr WEYL es unternimmt, seine Gedanken der Öffentlichkeit näher zu führen, so sollte er einen so interessanten Punkt wie den der Stellungnahme EINSTEINs zur WEYLschen Theorie nicht unerwähnt lassen, damit in der Öffentlichkeit von vornherein keine irrige Meinung darüber entstehen kann, wie der Urheber der Relativitätstheorie zur species Relativismus von WEYL steht.

Herr WEYL glaubt in seinem Bericht konstatieren zu dürfen, daß LENARD den Sinn der Relativitätstheorie nicht erfaßt habe. Dies ist nur eine Zurückgabe der von LENARD auf der Nauheimer Tagung gemachten Feststellung, daß die Relativisten k e i n V e r s t ä n d n i s f ü r d i e E r f o r d e r n i s s e d e r Wirklichkeitsforschung in der Physik gezeigt hätten, und daß sie keinen Versuch machen, die „Kluft" zu überbrücken. WEYL sollte bedenken, daß auch wenn jemand als Mathematiker virtuose Geschicklichkeit in der Handhabung mathematischer Symbole besitzt, er doch für a n d e r e Abstraktionen als Größenbeziehungen der Mathematik einen Mangel an Verständnis bezeigen kann, von dem universeller begabte Naturen frei sind. An Hand der WEYLschen Schriften würde sich leicht eine Liste von erkenntnistheorestischen Schnitzern und begrifflichen Wirrnissen anlegen lassen; es sei in diesem Zusammenhang übrigens auch auf die kürzlich erschienene Schrift von RIPKE-KÜHN: KANT contra EINSTEIN, Verlag von KEYSER-Erfurt, verwiesen.

Der von Herrn WEYL in seinem Bericht näher ausgeführte Punkt in der Diskussion zwischen EINSTEIN und LENARD hinsichtlich dessen Beispiel des gebremsten Eisenbahnzuges läßt den wesentlichen, von LENARD näher erläuterten Einwand vermissen, daß zur Erzeugung eines Gravitationsfeldes doch nach unseren heutigen physikalischen Kenntnissen M a s s e n da sein sollten, die das Gravitationsfeld hervorbringen. Im Falle des Eisenbahnunglücks, wo nach Angabe des Relativisten n i c h t der Zug, sondern die g a n z e U m g e b u n g gebremst worden sein soll, ist keine Massenanordnung und nichts ersichtlich, was das zur Bremsung der Umgebung erforderliche Gravitationsfeld erzeugt haben könnte. Der Relativist wurde denn auch in

N a u h e i m veranlaßt, ausdrücklich Gravitationsfelder ohne erzeugende, gravitierende Massen anzunehmen, wobei er allerdings u. a. offen ließ, woher die Energie dieser Gravitationsfelder genommen wird. Von all dem berichtet uns Herr WEYL nichts.

Endlich hat die Diskussion in Nauheim die Erklärung EINSTEINs gezeitigt, daß nach der allgemeinen Relativitätstheorie der Körper j e d e b e l i e b i g e Geschwindigkeit, größer als die Lichtgeschwindigkeit, besitzen dürfen. Auch diese in ihren Folgerungen hier nicht weiter zu behandelnde Angelegenheit erwähnt Herr WEYL nicht. „Ergebnislos" war die Debatte in Nauheim also keineswegs."[289]

Weyl answered *Die Umschau* a.k.a.*Die Umschau; Wochenschrift über die Fortschritte in Wissenschaft und Technik*; a. k. a. *Umschau in Wissenschaft und Technik*, Volume 25, (1921), p. 123.

Ernst Gehrcke wrote,

"Ich möchte hier zum Ausdruck bringen, daß EINSTEIN auf der Nauheimer Naturforscherversammlung die Möglichkeit der Überlichtgeschwindigkeiten vom Standpunkt seines allgemeinen Relativitätsprinzips zugestanden hat. Wenn Herr WEYL dies leugnen zu können glaubt, so ist nur ein neuer Widerspruch zwischen ihm und EINSTEIN — wenigstens zur Zeit der Nauheimer Tagung — festzustellen. Die Erklärung EINSTEINs über die Überlichtgeschwindigkeiten, so unbefriedigend sie sein mag, ist tatsächlich abgegeben worden, und Herr WEYL hätte besser getan, das Beweismaterial zu prüfen, als einen Irrtum LENARDS anzunehmen."[290]

Hermann Weyl wrote in 1921:

"Die Relativitätstheorie auf der Naturforscherversammlung in Bad Nauheim.

Von H. WEYL in Zürich.

Auf Veranlassung der Deutschen Mathematikervereinigung war auf der letztjährigen Naturforscherversammlung in Bad Nauheim die Relativitätstheorie in einer kombinierten Sitzung der mathematischen und physikalischen Sektion zum

Mittelpunkt einer Reihe von Vorträgen und einer allgemeinen Diskussion gemacht worden; darüber sei hier — nach reichlich langer Zeit, die aber vielleicht der Klärung und ruhigen Beurteilung der Sachlage zugute kommt — Bericht erstattet.

Den ersten Teil der Sitzung bildeten vier Vorträge aus dem Gebiete der Relativitätstheorie: 1. H. W e y l , Elektrizität und Gravitation; 2. G. M i e , Das elektrische Feld eines um ein Gravitationszentrum rotierenden geladenen Partikelchens; 3. M. v. L a u e , Theoretisches über neuere optische Beobachtungen zur Relativitätstheorie; 4. L. G r e b e , Über die Gravitationsverschiebung der Fraunhoferschen Linien. Den vier Vorträgen folgte die auf ihren Inhalt sich beziehende „Spezial"-Diskussion. Der letzte und dramatischste Teil, die allgemeine Diskussion über die Relativitätstheorie, gestaltete sich im wesentlichen zu einem Zweikampf zwischen E i n s t e i n und L e n a r d. Mit großem Geschick, Strenge und Unparteilichkeit waltete P l a n c k seines Amtes als Vorsitzender; ihm war es nicht zum wenigsten zu danken, daß dieses „Nauheimer Relativitätsgesprach", in welchem entgegengesetzte erkenntnistheoretische Grundauffassungen der Wissenschaft aufeinanderstießen, einen würdigen Verlauf nahm.

Auf den Inhalt der Vorträge werde hier nur insoweit eingegangen, als er mit den prinzipiellen Fragen der Relativitätstheorie in Zusammenhang steht. Nach der speziellen Relativitätstheorie beruht der *Dopplereffekt* auf den folgenden beiden Tatsachen: 1. Die Frequenzen der von zwei Atomen der gleichen Konstitution, etwa zwei Wasserstoffatomen, ausgesendeten Spektrallinien sind einander gleich, wenn jede von ihnen gemessen wird in der dem Atom eigentümlichen *Eigenzeit*. 2. Die Frequenz einer Lichtwelle ist im ganzen Raum überall die gleiche, wenn sie gemessen wird in der „kosmischen" Zeit t, die zusammen mit den drei Raumkoordinaten ein System linearer Koordinaten für die ganze Welt bildet. Wie übertragen sich diese beiden T a t s a c h e n in die allgemeine Relativitätstheorie? Hier wird die Eigenzeit nach E i n s t e i n definiert durch die „metrische Fundamentalform"

$$ds^2 = \sum g_{ik}\, dx_i\, dx_k,$$

eine quadratische Differentialform der vier willkürlichen Weltkoordinaten x_i vom Trägheitsindex 3; und das Analogon zu 1. lautet: für zwei Atome gleicher Konstitution hat das Integral $\int ds$, erstreckt über eine volle Periode, den gleichen Wert. Fragt man indes danach — um der Sache etwas mehr auf den Grund zu gehen —, wodurch das ds^2 physikalisch bestimmt ist, wodurch insbesondere der Vergleich der Maßeinheiten des ds an verschiedenen Weltstellen ermöglicht wird, so antwortet E i n s t e i n , daß dazu die Atomuhren das Mittel bilden (auch starre Maßstäbe oder, physikalisch etwas strenger gesprochen, die Gitterabstände in einem Kristall können zum gleichen Zwecke dienen): kommt die Atomuhr im Laufe ihrer Geschichte vom Weltpunkt O nach dem Weltpunkt O' und legt sie beim Passieren von O während einer Periode die unendlichkleine Weltstrecke s, beim Passieren von O' während einer Periode die unendlichkleine Weltstrecke s' zurück, so hat *definitionsgemäß* s' die gleiche Länge ds wie s. 1. ist danach keine erklärungsbedürftige Tatsache, sondern ds ist physikalisch so definiert, daß 1. zutrifft. Dennoch schließt die Möglichkeit dieser Festsetzung über den Transport der Maßeinheit eine physikalische Grundtatsache ein, nämlich die folgende: Haben zwei Atomuhren, die sich an derselben Weltstelle O befinden, dort die gleiche Frequenz und treffen sie, nachdem sie verschiedene Wege in der Welt durchlaufen haben, in einem anderen Weltpunkt O' wieder zusammen, so haben sie auch dort gleiche Frequenz. Meine Theorie von Elektrizität und Gravitation, auf einer Weltgeometrie beruhend, in welcher die Übertragung einer Strecke durch kongruente Verpflanzung längs eines Weges vom Wege abhängig ist, war von den Physikern meist dahin mißverstanden worden, als wolle ich an dieser Tatsache rütteln. Der Hauptzweck meines Vortrages in Nauheim war, dem entgegenzutreten. Ich akzeptiere jene Grundtatsache so gut wie E i n s t e i n ; wir weichen voneinander ab in ihrer theoretischen Deutung. Nach E i n s t e i n ist die metrische Struktur des Äthers von der Art, wie sie R i e m a n n annimmt, die Streckenübertragung vom Wege unabhängig. Die Frequenzen der Atomuhren folgen dieser kongruenten Verpflanzung; die Erhaltung der Frequenz beruht also auf einer von Augenblick zu Augenblick infinitesimal wirksamen *Beharrungstendenz*. Im Gegensatz dazu scheint mir die einzig mögliche physikalische Deutung jener Grundtatsache die zu sein, daß sich die Frequenz durch *Einstellung* auf eine gewisse Feldgröße (von der Dimension einer Länge) bestimmen muß: zufolge ihrer *Konstitution* hat die Atomuhr an einer beliebigen Feldstelle eine Periode, die im Verhältnis zu jener Feldgröße einen bestimmten numerischen Gleichgewichtswert besitzt. [*Footnote:* In einer jüngst erschienenen Note (Berliner Sitzungsberichte 1921, S. 261). akzeptiert E i n s t e i n, wenn ich ihn recht verstehe, diesen Standpunkt, nicht aber meine weltgeometrische Deutung der Elektrizität.] In der Tat ergeben die Naturgesetze, daß sich die materiellen Körper so verhalten, und zwar ist die Feldgröße, auf welche sich die Längen einstellen, der aus der skalaren Krümmung des Feldes zu berechnende Krümmungsradius. Die aus dem Verhalten der materiellen Körper in der geläufigen Weise abgelesene Maßgeometrie ist also mit der metrischen Struktur des Äthers nicht identisch, sondern geht aus ihr hervor, indem die kongruente Verpflanzung ersetzt wird durch die Einstellung auf den Krümmungsradius. In der anschließenden Diskussion wurde der beiderseitige Standpunkt klar und knapp zum Ausdruck gebracht, ohne daß einer den andern zu bekehren oder zu widerlegen suchte. [*Footnote:* Eine ausführliche Darstellung meiner Auffassung wurde von mir gerade jetzt veröffentlicht in zwei Arbeiten in den Ann. d. Physik **65** und der Physik. Zeitschrift **22** unter den Titeln: „Feld und Materie", „Über die physikalischen Grundlagen der erweiterten Relativitätstheorie".]

Ich komme zu der oben erwähnten Tatsache 2. und ihrer Übertragung in die allgemeine Relativitätstheorie. Davon handelte der Lauesche Vortrag. Ein *statisches* Gravitationsfeld ist dadurch gekennzeichnet: man kann die vier Weltkoordinaten

$$x_0 = t, \; x_1 \, x_2 \, x_3$$

(statische Koordinaten) so wählen, daß sich Zeit (t) und Raum ($x_1 \, x_2 \, x_3$) vollständig trennen und die Beschaffenheit des Feldes zeitlich konstant ist; d. h. es wird

$$ds^2 = f^2 dt^2 - d\sigma^2,$$

wo f, die Lichtgeschwindigkeit, und $d\sigma^2$, die metrische Fundamentalform des Raumes, nur von dem Raumkoordinaten $x_1 \, x_2 \, x_3$ abhängen; $d\sigma^2$ ist positiv-definit. In einem solchen statischen Gravitationsfeld haben die Maxwellschen Gleichungen (komplexe) Lösungen von folgender Art: das elektromagnetische Feld ist gleich einem zeitlich konstanten Felde multipliziert mit dem von der Zeit abhängigen rein periodischen Term e^{ivt}; v ist die konstante Frequenz. Sind derartige „einfache Schwingungen", wie wir es annehmen wollen, für den tatsächlichen Vorgang der Lichtausbreitung maßgebend, so heißt das: 2. In einem statischen Gravitationsfeld ist die Frequenz der von einem ruhenden Körper ausgesendeten Lichtwelle überall im Raum die gleiche, gemessen in der kosmischen Zeit t, der Zeitkoordinate im System der vier statischen Koordinaten. Aus den beiden Tatsachen 1. und 2. ergibt sich mit Notwendigkeit die von E i n s t e i n behauptete *Rotverschiebung der Spektrallinien* in der Nähe großer Massen, die ja nach dem Äquivalenzprinzip mit dem Dopplerschen Prinzip auf engste zusammenhängt; denn im statischen Gravitationsfeld hat f in der Nähe großer Massen einen kleineren Wert als fern von ihnen. — Außerdem leitete L a u e in seinem Vortrag nach dem Muster des von D e b y e für die klassische Elektrodynamik vorgeschlagenen Verfahrens aus den Maxwellschen Gleichungen als erste Näherung für hohe Frequenzen das Grundgesetz der geometrischen Optik her, daß ein Lichtsignal eine geodätische Nullinie beschreibt. Man macht den Ansatz, daß alle Feldkomponenten multiplikativ den Term e^{ivE} enthalten mit einem sehr großen konstanten v, und erhält dann für die „Eikonalfunktion" E die partielle Differentialgleichung

$$\sum_{ik} g^{ik} \frac{\partial E}{\partial x_i} \frac{\partial E}{\partial x_k} = 0,$$

deren Charakteristiken die geodätischen Nullinien sind.

An das eben aufgestellte Prinzip 2. sei es gestattet, hier eine kritische Bemerkung anzuknüpfen. Das Prinzip ist eindeutig, wenn durch die Forderung der statischen Koordinaten die Zeit t bis auf eine lineare Transformation in sich, die drei Raumkoordinaten $x_1 x_2 x_3$ bis auf eine willkürliche Transformation untereinander festgelegt sind. Im allgemeinen ist das der Fall, aber nicht immer. Die gravitationslose Welt der speziellen Relativitätstheorie:

$$ds^2 = dt^2 - \left(dx_1^2 + dx_2^2 + dx_3^2\right)$$

ist ein Beispiel dafür. Doch wird hier unter den linearen Koordinatensystemen eine bestimmte kosmische Zeit t dadurch ausgezeichnet, daß man fordert, der licht-aussendende Körper solle ruhen; und so gestatten in diesem Falle unsere beiden Forderungen 1. und 2. die Lichtwellen zu vergleichen, die von zwei relativ zueinander bewegten Körpern ausgehen (Dopplersches Prinzip). Ein anderes wichtiges Beispiel ist die leere Welt, wie sie sich ergibt, wenn man in den Gravitationsgleichungen das Einsteinsche kosmologische Glied mitberücksichtigt. Nach d e S i t t e r [*Footnote:* On Einsteins theory of gravitation and its astronomical consequences III, Monthly Notices of the R. Astron. Society, Nov. 1917.] ist diese leere Welt ein „Kegelschnitt"

$$\Omega(x) = a^2$$

in einem 5-dimensionalen Euklidischen Raum mit dem Linienelement

$$ds^2 = -\Omega(dx);$$

$$\Omega(x) = x_1^2 + x_2^2 + x_3^2 + x_4^2 - x_5^2.$$

Durch die Substitution

(*) $$x_4 = z \cdot Cos\, \frac{t}{a}, \quad x_5 = z \cdot Sin\, \frac{t}{a}$$

kommt man hier auf statische Koordinaten

$$t,\, x_1\, x_2\, x_3;$$

es wird nämlich

$$-ds^2 = \left(dx_1^2 + dx_2^2 + dx_3^2 + dz^2\right) - \frac{z^2}{a^2}\, dt^2$$

mit $$z^2 = a^2 - r^2, \quad r^2 = x_1^2 + x_2^2 + x_3^2.$$

$$f^2 = 1 - \left(\frac{r}{a}\right)^2$$

nimmt vom Werte 1 im Nullpunkt bis zum Werte 0 auf dem Äquator ab. Ist diese statische Zeit für die Ausbreitung des Lichtes maßgebend, so würden also die Spektrallinien von Sternen um so stärker nach dem Rot verschoben sein, je weiter sie vom Nullpunkt entfernt liegen. D e S i t t e r hat die Möglichkeit erwogen, auf diese Weise die tatsächlich vorhandene systematische starke Rotverschiebung in den Spektren der Spiralnebel kosmologisch zu deuten. Nun ist aber t offenbar keineswegs die einzige „statische Zeit"; zu dem Spiralnebel als Nullpunkt wird ebenso eine solche Zeit gehören wie zu der bisher als Nullpunkt angenommenen Sonne. In der Tat kann man ja vor Ausführung der Substitution (*) die Koordinaten $x_1 .. x_5$ einer willkürlichen linearen Transformation unterwerfen, welche $\Omega(x)$ invariant läßt; dann bekommt man ein ganz anderes t. Welches soll nun nach dem Prinzip 2. maßgebend sein für die Ausbreitung des Lichtes? Die durch (*) eingeführten statischen Koordinaten stellen nicht den ganzen de Sitterschen Kegelschnitt, sondern nur den Keil

$$x_4^2 - x_5^2 > 0$$

reell dar. Ist die wirkliche Welt der ganze de Sittersche Kegelschnitt, so ist also das Prinzip 2. völlig unberechtigt. Wenn aber die Welt nur aus einem derartigen Keil besteht, wie E i n s t e i n es annimmt, ist natürlich dasjenige, bis auf eine lineare Transformation eindeutig bestimmte t zu nehmen, welches diesem Keil entspricht. Steht das im Einklang mit der Wirklichkeit, so ist also auf die Ausbreitung einer Lichtwelle vom Moment ihrer Entstehung an der Zusammenschluß der Welt im Ganzen von Einfluß, während man doch erwarten sollte, daß die Lichtwelle darauf erst reagieren kann, wenn sie den ganzen Weltraum durchlaufen hat. Mit der in den retardierten Potentialen zum Ausdruck kommenden alten Hertzschen Vorstellung von der Entstehung einer Lichtwelle ist das gewiß unverträglich. So bedarf das Prinzip 2., der Mechanismus der Übertragung der Frequenz in einer Lichtwelle, noch sehr der physikalischen Aufklärung.

Inwieweit die nach E i n s t e i n zu erwartende *Rotverschiebung* der Fraunhoferschen Linien im Sonnenspektrum gegenüber den von irdischen Lichtquellen stammenden Linien durch die *Experimente* bestätigt wird, darüber berichtete G r e b e. Die Messungen sind angestellt worden von S c h w a r z s c h i l d, dann von E v e r s h e d und R o y d s, später von S t . J o h n, schließlich von B a c h e m und G r e b e. Namentlich die mit den schärfsten Hilfsmitteln ausgeführten Beobachtungen von S t . J o h n sprachen *gegen* das Vorhandensein des Einsteineffektes. Alle Beobachter stellen aber übereinstimmend fest, daß verschiedene Linien verschiedene Verschiebungen aufweisen. G r e b e und

B a c h e m machten nun darauf aufmerksam, daß für die Erklärung dieser Unregelmäßigkeiten vor allem der Umstand in Betracht fällt, daß unmittelbar benachbarte Linien sich gegenseitig in der Lage ihrer Intensitätsmaxima stören. Sie sonderten deshalb auf Grund mikrophotometrischer Aufnahmen aus den von ihnen gemessenen 36 Linien der sogenannten Cyanbande 11 aus, die sie als störungsfrei glaubten in Anspruch nehmen zu dürfen; diese zeigen nun im Mittel eine Rotverschiebung, welche dem Einsteineffekt ungefähr entspricht. Ebenso ergab sich als Mittel der Verschiebungen von 100 *aufeinanderfolgenden* Cyanbandenlinien *ohne jede Auswahl* — wo man erwarten darf, daß die gegenseitigen Störungen sich ausgleichen — nahezu derselbe Wert. Wenn man diese Untersuchungen auch noch kaum als eine definitive experimentelle Bestätigung des Einsteineffektes ansprechen darf, so verstärken sie doch die Wahrscheinlichkeit seines wirklichen Vorhandenseins erheblich. In der seit der Nauheimer Tagung verflossenen Zeit hat sich die Situation in dieser Hinsicht durch neue Beobachtungen noch weiter verbessert.

Um Sinn und Tragweite des Einsteinschen *Äquivalenzprinzips* durch ein vollständig zu übersehendes, nicht triviales Beispiel zu illustrieren, berechnete M i e nach diesem Prinzip das elektrische Feld eines geladenen Teilchens, das um ein elektrisch neutrales Gravitationszentrum unter dem Einfluß der Gravitation eine Kreisbahn beschreibt. Die statischen Koordinaten, in welchen das kugelsymmetrische Gravitationsfeld die von S c h w a r z s c h i l d angegebene Form besitzt, bezeichnet M i e als das vernünftige Koordinatensystem. In einem gewissen „künstlichen" Koordinatensystem, in welchem sowohl das Teilchen ruht wie auch das Gravitationsfeld stationär ist, haben die Maxwellschen Gleichungen eine von der Zeit unabhängige Lösung, welche in der unmittelbaren Nähe des Teilchens mit der elektrostatischen Lösung identisch ist. Transformiert man sie auf das vernünftige Koordinatensystem, so erhält man diejenige Lösung des Problems, welche nach dem Äquivalenzprinzip dem elektrostatischen Feld eines ruhenden Teilchens gleichwertig ist. Das Feld ist in unendlichgroßer Entfernung nicht von solcher Art, daß eine Ausstrahlung von Energie stattfindet, sondern man erhält es dort, wenn einem nach den Liénard-Wiechertschen Formeln berechneten ausstrahlenden Feld ein einstrahlendes von gleicher Stärke superponiert wird.

Zweifellos ist das eine mit den uns bekannten Feldgesetzen verträgliche Lösung; dennoch ist es sicher, daß das wirkliche Verhalten eines elektrisch geladenen Körpers, der um ein Gravitationszentrum rotiert, nicht ihr entspricht, sondern eine elektromagnetische Welle ausstrahlt und dadurch selber in seiner Bewegung modifiziert wird. Die *tatsächlichen* Vorgänge bei Ruhe und Rotation sind also *nicht* einander äquivalent. M i e äußert sich darüber so: Man denke sich ein Einsteinsches Kupee, welches auf einer Kreisbahn um das Gravitationszentrum herumfährt; die Beobachter stellen an einem mitgeführten elektrischen Teilchen Beobachtungen an. Bestehen die Wandungen des Kupees aus Metall, so daß das von dem Teilchen erregte elektrische Feld dort endigt, so gilt das Äquivalenzprinzip; bestehen die Wandungen jedoch aus isolierendem Material, so können die Beobachter im Kupee ihre Bewegung feststellen; die Feldlinien des Teilchens sind sozusagen Fühler, die sie aus dem Kupee heraus ins Unendliche strecken. Damit kann man sich sehr wohl auch vom Einsteinschen Standpunkt aus einverstanden erklären. Solange man mit einem unendlichen Raum operiert, hat man immer den unendlich fernen Saum dieses Raumes zu berücksichtigen, über den gewissermaßen ein das Feld bestimmendes Agens ebenso herüberwirkt wie über die inneren Feldsäume, welche den verschiedenen Materieteilchen entsprechen. Mathematisch äußert sich das darin, daß nur solche Koordinaten zulässig sind, für welche im Unendlichen das ds^2 die Gestalt der speziellen Relativitätstheorie hat. In Einsteins geschlossenem Raum aber fällt der unendlich ferne Saum weg, an seine Stelle treten die weit entfernten Massen.

Der Durchrechnung dieses speziellen Problems schickte M i e einige grundsätzliche Bemerkungen voraus, welche zeigen, daß er in einigen Punkten einen andern Standpunkt einnimmt als Einstein. Insbesondere glaubt er an ein ausgezeichnetes „vernunftgemäßes" Koordinatensystem. Nun ist ja zuzugeben, daß sich in speziellen Problemen oft aus der Beschaffenheit des metrischen Feldes heraus ein besonders einfaches und zweckmäßiges Koordinatensystem definieren läßt. So kann man im Schwarzschildschen Fall des statischen kugelsymmetrischen Gravitationsfeldes die Raumkoordinaten x_1 x_2 x_3 derart wählen, daß, wenn man mit ihrer Hilfe den wirklichen Raum auf einen Cartesischen abbildet, das lineare Vergrößerungsverhältnis für

Linienelemente, welche senkrecht zu den Radien im Bildraum stehen, = 1 wird (für radiale Linienelemente wird es dann, wie aus den Gravitationsgleichungen hervorgeht,

$$= 1/f, \text{ und } f^2 \text{ ist } = 1 - \frac{2\alpha}{r} ; \alpha$$

eine Konstante, r die im Bildraum gemessene Entfernung von Zentrum). Aber gerade in diesem Fall kann man über die radiale Maßskala z. B. doch auch so verfügen, daß die Abbildung auf den Cartesischen Bildraum konform ist (dann wird das Vergrößerungsverhältnis für alle Linienelemente

$$= \left(1 + \frac{\alpha}{r} \right)^2, \text{ und } f \text{ ist } = \frac{r - \alpha/2}{r + \alpha/2} \right).$$

Hier ist gar nicht abzusehen, warum man das eine dieser beiden Koordinatensysteme als „vernunftgemäßer" ansprechen soll denn das andere. Die Frage nach der Existenz eines vernunftgemäßen Koordinatensystems hängt aufs engste mit der andern zusammen, inwiefern es berechtigt ist, zu behaupten: die wahre Geometrie des Raumes sei die *euklidische;* daß materielle Maßstäbe nicht die Relationen erfüllen, welche diese Geometrie für den idealen starren Körper angibt, liege daran, daß die materiellen Körper durch das Gravitationsfeld in bestimmter Weise deformiert werden. Dieser Standpunkt, den z. B. D i n g l e r und H a m e l vertreten [*Footnote:* D i n g l e r : Der starre Körper, Physik. Zeitschr. 1920 S. 487; H a m e l : Sitzungsber. d. Berl. Mathem. Gesellschaft 1921. S. 65.], ist zunächst natürlich gegenüber der Gravitation physikalisch ebenso berechtigt wie gegenüber der Temperatur (E i n s t e i n selbst zieht diese Parallele in seiner populären Schrift über die Relativitätstheorie): kein Mensch behauptet, daß auf einer ungleichförmig erwärmten Platte eine nichteuklidische Geometrie gilt, sondern daß die zur Ausmessung verwendeten Maßstäbe durch die verschiedenen Temperaturen verschiedene Ausdehnungen erfahren. Aber in diesem Fall existiert eine absolut ausgezeichnete Reduktion, die Reduktion auf „gleiche Temperatur", durch welche das Verhalten der Maßstäbe mit der euklidischen Geometrie in Einklang gebracht wird. Im Fall der Gravitation existiert zwar auch eine „Reduktion auf Euklid" (das ist sogar selbstverständlich), aber unter den unendlich vielen möglichen derartigen Korrekturvorschriften, deren jede zu andern Resultaten führt, ist keine physikalisch so ausgezeichnet, daß sie sich zwingend als die „einzig richtige" aufdrängt. Darum ist es hier wertlos, den an den materiellen Körpern abgelesenen Maßzahlen durch Korrektur eine euklidische Geometrie zu supponieren. Vielleicht hat der Philosoph immer noch Recht mit seiner Ansicht, daß man ohne einen idealen euklidischen Anschauungsraum nicht auskomme; ihm entspräche in der mathematischen Darstellung die Notwendigkeit, ein Koordinatensystem zu verwenden. Aber seine Beziehung auf das Ordnungsschema der physikalischen Ereignisse ist wie die Wahl des Koordinatensystems in hohem Maße willkürlich. Die universelle Konstruktion, welche M i e selber für· das vernunftgemäße Koordinatensystem andeutet (mit Hilfe einer Einbettung des vierdimensionalen wirklichen Raumes in einen zehndimensionalen euklidischen) ist vieldeutig und ohne inneres Vorzugsrecht. Es ist gar nicht einzusehen, welche Erleichterung dadurch für die Beschreibung der physikalischen Vorgänge geschaffen werden soll; sie läßt sich ja immer mittels invarianter Begriffe vollziehen. — Noch in einem andern Punkte weicht M i e von E i n s t e i n ab; er meint, man dürfe nicht von allgemeiner Relativität, sondern nur von einer Relativität der Gravitationswirkungen sprechen, da man nach der Einsteinschen Theorie das Verhalten eines beschleunigt bewegten materiellen Systems aus dem des ruhenden nur dann berechnen kann, wenn die wirkende Kraft die eines Gravitationsfeldes ist. Mir scheint, das ist kein Einwand gegen die Allgemeinheit des Relativitätsprinzips, sondern eine Bemerkung über seine Tragweite: nur für die im „Führungsfeld" neben der Trägheit mitenthaltenen Kräfte (Zentrifugalkraft, Gravitation), die man an ihrer Massenproportionalität erkennt, ist dieses Prinzip ausreichend, ihre Wirkungsweise a p r i o r i aus dem Galileischen Trägheitsprinzip abzuleiten.

Die beiden zuletzt erörterten Punkte kamen auch in der *allgemeinen Diskussion,* die vor allem von L e n a r d benutzt wurde, zwischen L e n a r d und E i n s t e i n zur Sprache. Es sei um der Übersichtlichkeit willen gestattet, aus diesem Wechselgespräch zunächst noch zwei weitere Streitfragen herauszuschälen, die neben der am Schluß zu besprechenden Hauptdifferenz nur von nebensächlicher Bedeutung sind. Das ist erstens die *Existenz des Äthers.* L e n a r d meint, E i n s t e i n habe, bei Aufstellung der speziellen Relativitätstheorie, allzu voreilig die Abschaffung des Äthers verkündet. In der Tat kann er ja darauf hinweisen, daß E i n s t e i n heute wieder in der allgemeinen Relativitätstheorie von einem Äther spricht. [*Footnote:* Siehe namentlich die Leidener Antrittsvorlesung E i n s t e i n s über Äther und Relativitätstheorie, Springer 1920.] Man darf sich doch aber durch das gleichlautende Wort nicht über die Verschiedenheit der Sache täuschen lassen! Der alte Äther der Lichttheorie war ein *substantielles* Medium, ein dreidimensionales Kontinuum, von welchem sich jede Stelle *P* in jedem Augenblick *t* in einem bestimmten Raumpunkt *p* (oder an einer bestimmten Weltstelle) befindet; die Wiedererkennbarkeit derselben Ätherstelle zu verschiedenen Zeiten ist dabei das Wesentliche. Durch diesen Äther löst sich die vierdimensionale Welt auf in ein dreifach unendliches Kontinuum von eindimensionalen Weltlinien; infolgedessen gestattet er, *Ruhe* und *Bewegung* absolut voneinander zu unterscheiden. *In diesem Sinne,* etwas anderes hat E i n s t e i n nicht behauptet, ist der Äther durch die spezielle Relativitätstheorie abgeschafft; er wurde ersetzt durch die affingeometrische Struktur der Welt, welche nicht den Unterschied zwischen Ruhe und Bewegung festlegt, sondern die *gleichförmige Translation* von allen andern Bewegungen absondert. Der substantielle Äther war von seinen Erfindern als etwas Reales, den ponderablen Körpern Vergleichbares gedacht. In der Lorentzschen Elektrodynamik hatte er sich in eine rein geometrische, d. h. ein für allemal feste, von der Materie nicht beeinflußte Struktur verwandelt. In E i n s t e i n s spezieller Relativitätstheorie trat an ihre Stelle eine andere, die affingeometrische Struktur. In der allgemeinen Relativitätstheorie endlich verwandelte sich die letztere, als „affiner Zusammenhang" oder „Führungsfeld", wieder zurück in ein mit der Materie in Wirkungszusammenhang stehendes Zustandsfeld von physikalischer Realität. Und darum hielt es E i n s t e i n für angezeigt, das alte Wort Äther für den vollständig gewandelten Begriff wieder einzuführen; ob das zweckmäßig war oder nicht, ist weniger eine physikalische als eine philologische Frage.

Zweitens: die *Überlichtgeschwindigkeit.* L e n a r d meint, die allgemeine Relativitätstheorie führe die Überlichtgeschwindigkeit wieder ein, da sie als Bezugssystem z. B. die rotierende Erde zuläßt; in hinreichend großen Entfernungen treten dabei Überlichtgeschwindigkeit auf. Dies ist ein offenbares Mißverständnis. Sind $x_1 x_2 x_3$ die in bezug auf die rotierende Erde gemessenen Raumkoordinaten, x_0 die zugehörige „Zeit" (auf ihre präzise Definition kommt es jetzt nicht an), so werden die Koordinatenlinien x_0, auf denen bei konstanten $x_1x_2x_3$ nur x_0 variiert, nicht alle zeitartige Richtung haben, d. h. es wird in diesen Koordinaten nicht überall $g_{00} > 0$ sein. Nun behauptet E i n s t e i n allerdings, daß auch solche Koordinatensysteme zulässig sind; auch in solchen Koordinatensystemen gelten seine allgemein invarianten Gravitationsgesetze. Dagegen hält er durchaus daran fest, daß die *Weltlinie eines materiellen Köpers* stets zeitartige Richtung besitzt, daß an einem materiellen Körper (und als „Signalgeschwindigkeit") keine Überlichtgeschwindigkeit auftreten kann. Ein Koordinatensystem von der oben angegebenen Art läßt sich infolgedessen nicht in seiner ganzen Ausdehnung durch einen „Bezugsmollusken" wiedergeben, d. h. man kann sich kein materielles Medium denken, dessen einzelne Elemente die Koordinatenlinien x_0 jenes Koordinatensystems als Weltlinien beschreiben.—

Aber es wird Zeit, daß ich auf den entscheidenden Gegensatz zwischen L e n a r d und E i n s t e i n zu sprechen komme. L e n a r d behauptet, daß die Einsteinsche Theorie mit *fingierten Gravitationsfeldern* operiere, zu denen sich keine erzeugende Materie nachweisen ließe und welche nur dem Relativitätsprinzip zuliebe eingeführt würden. Das anschauliche Lenardsche Beispiel des durch einen entgegenfahrenden Zug plötzlich gebremsten Eisenbahnzuges diene auch hier als Unterlage der Diskussion. Warum, fragt L e n a r d , geht der Zug in Trümmer und nicht der Kirchtum neben dem Zug, da doch nach E i n s t e i n ebensogut von ihm wie von dem Eisenbahnzug gesagt werden kann, daß er gebremst werde? Hierauf scheint mir die Antwort leicht. In der Einsteinschen Theorie gibt es so gut wie nach alter Auffassung das *Führungsfeld,* dem ein Körper nach dem Galileischen Prinzip folgt, solange auf ihn keine Kräfte wirken. Die Katastrophe ereignet sich am Zuge und nicht am Kirchturm, weil der erstere durch die Molekularkräfte des entgegenfahrenden Zuges aus der Bahn des Führungsfeldes herausgeworfen wird, der Kirchturm hingegen nicht. Diese Antwort ist auch vollkommen im Einklang mit dem „gesunden Menschenverstand", der von Herzen damit einverstanden ist, die sich den Kräften entgegenstemmende Beharrungstendenz des Führungsfeldes mit E i n s t e i n als eine physikalische Realität anzusehen. Die Frage ist jetzt aber weiter die: ist dieses Führungsfeld eine Einheit oder lassen sich in ihr zwei Bestandteile, die „Trägheit" und die „Gravitation", grundsätzlich voneinander trennen, derart daß die erste von selber ein für allemal vorhanden ist als affinlineare Struktur der vierdimensionalen Welt und nur die zweite durch die Materie erzeugt wird? Hier, für die Gleichberechtigung aller Bewegungszustände, ist die Sachlage eine ganz analoge wie für die Gleichberechtigung aller Richtungen im Raum. Nach D e m o k r i t gibt es an sich ein absolutes Oben-Unten; die wirkliche Fallrichtung eines Körpers setzt sich zusammen aus dieser absoluten Richtung und einer aus physikalischen Ursachen entspringenden Abweichung davon. D e m o k r i t könnte etwa gegen N e w t o n, der die Fallrichtung als Einheit ansieht, genau so argumentieren wie L e n a r d gegen E i n s t e i n : Macht man eine andere als jene wahre Richtung zur Normalrichtung, so muß man außer ihr und der wirklichen Abweichung drittens noch eine überall gleiche und nicht in der Materie verankerte fingierte Abweichung einführen; und das nur, um dem Prinzip von der Gleichberechtigung aller Richtungen im Raume zu genügen. Sobald man die absolute Richtung Oben-Unten zugibt, kann man scheiden zwischen wirklicher und fingierter Abweichung; sobald man ein ausgezeichnetes, „vernunftgemäßes" Koordinatensystem annimmt, muß man (mit M i e und L e n a r d) scheiden zwischen wirklichen und fingierten Gravitationsfeldern. Auf dem Relativitätsstandpunkt hingegen wird eine solche Scheidung unmöglich. Wenn wir aber mit N e w t o n gegen D e m o k r i t die Unzerlegbarkeit der wirklichen Fallrichtung in ein absolutes Oben-Unten und eine Abweichung davon behaupten, so müssen wir auch nicht nur für die *Abweichung,* sondern für die *Fallrichtung als Ganzes eine physikalische Ursache* angeben; genau so hat E i n s t e i n die Verpflichtung, zu zeigen, *wie und nach welchem Gesetz das Führungsfeld als Ganzes durch die Materie erzeugt wird.* Das verlangt L e n a r d mit vollem Recht von ihm, und das ist der tiefste und eigentlich entscheidende Punkt seiner Einwände. Es muß unverhohlen zugegeben werden, daß hier für die Relativitätstheorie bei ihrer jetzigen Formulierung noch ernstliche Schwierigkeiten vorliegen. E i n s t e i n weist zur Beantwortung auf seine *Kosmologie* der räumlich geschlossenen Welt hin; er erwidert L e n a r d : Das Feld ist nicht willkürlich erfunden, weil es die allgemeinen Differentialgleichungen erfüllt und weil es zurückgeführt werden kann auf die Wirkung aller fernen Massen. Solange man überhaupt an dem Gegensatz von Materie und Feld festhält (und nur dann ist ja die Forderung, daß die Materie das Feld erzeuge, sinnvoll und berechtigt), bedeutet die Einsteinsche Kosmologie dies, daß neben den inneren Säumen des Feldes, über welche die einzelnen Materieteilchen feldbestimmend herüberwirken, nicht noch ein weiterer unendlichferner Saum als ein das Feld im Unendlichen bestimmendes Agens hinzukommt; an seine Stelle ist die Gesamtheit der fernen Massen getreten. Das Mitdrehen der Ebene des Foucaultschen Pendels mit dem Fixsternhimmel macht das ganz sinnfällig. Behoben ist damit die Schwierigkeit aber noch nicht. Erstens ist zu sagen, daß von E i n s t e i n nur die Gesetze angegeben werden, welche den inneren differentiellen Zusammenhang des Feldes binden, aber noch keine klare Formulierung der Gesetze vorliegt, nach welchen die Materie das Feld determiniert (das liegt übrigens beim elektromagnetischen Feld nicht wesentlich anders). Zweitens aber und vor allem ist es sogar ganz ausgeschlossen, daß die Materie das Feld eindeutig bestimmen kann, wenn man als Charakteristika der Materie, wie kaum anders möglich, *Masse, Ladung* und *Bewegungszustand* ansieht. Man kann nämlich in der Welt ein solches Koordinatensystem einführen, daß für die dadurch bewirkte Abbildung der Welt auf einen vierdimensionalen Cartesischen Bildraum nicht nur der Weltkanal *eines* Teilchens, sondern *aller* Teilchen simultan vorgegebene Gestalt annimmt, z. B. alle diese Kanäle vertikale Geraden werden. Im Vergleich zu M a c h , dessen Bezugskörper stets ein starrer Körper ist, hat sich bei E i n s t e i n das Koordinatensystem so „erweicht", daß es sich simultan den Bewegungen aller Teilchen anschmiegen kann, daß man alle Teilchen zugleich auf Ruhe transformieren kann; es hat also hier nicht einmal einen Sinn mehr, vom *relativen* Bewegungszustand verschiedener Körper gegeneinander zu sprechen. Diese Schwierigkeit hat neuerdings R e i c h e n b ä c h e r deutlicher hervorgehoben. [*Footnote:* Schwere und Trägheit, Physik. Zeitschr. **22** (1921), S. 234-243.] Das Prinzip, daß die Materie das Feld erzeuge, wird sich danach nur aufrechterhalten lassen, wenn der Begriff der Bewegung ein dynamisches Moment mit in sich aufnimmt; nicht um den Gegensatz *absolut* oder *relativ*, sondern *kinematisch* oder *dynamisch* dreht es sich bei der Analyse des Bewegungsbegriffs. —

In einer zweiten Sitzung am andern Tage demonstrierte F . P . L i e s e g a n g (Düsseldorf) einige treffliche Schaubilder zur Darstellung der Zeitraumverhältnisse in der speziellen Relativitätstheorie, und es verlas H. D i n g l e r (München), wie es schien nur zu formalem Protest gegen die Relativitätstheorie, ohne sich um das Publikum zu kümmern, seine kritischen Bemerkungen zu den Grundlagen der Theorie; es ist sonderbar, daß sich bei D i n g l e r mit seinem an P o i n c a r é orientierten konventionalistischen Standpunkt die dogmatische Halsstarrigkeit des geborenen Apriorikers verbindet. Daß der Tragödie am Schluß das Satyrspiel nicht fehle, entwickelte H r . R u d o l p h eine phantastische Äthertheorie mit „Lücken" zwischen fließenden Ätherwänden, Sternfäden usw., mit Hilfe deren er aus Nichts die Sonnenmasse auf eine beliebige Anzahl von Dezimalen genau bestimmte . . .

Ich habe hier in freier Weise die Fragen kennzeichnen wollen, die in der Nauheimer Diskussion zur Sprache kamen, nicht aber einen objektiven Bericht über den Verlauf der Sitzung erstatten wollen; für eine gekürzte, aber sinngetreue Wiedergabe der Vorträge und der Diskussion sei der Leser auf das Dezemberheft 1920 der Physikalischen Zeitschrift verwiesen.

(Eingegangen am 29. 8. 21.)"[291]

Bruno Thüring wrote,

"Im selben Jahre 1920 fand in Bad Nauheim auf der dortigen Naturforschertagung die berühmt gewordene Diskussion zwischen Philipp Lenard und Albert Einstein statt. In dieser Diskussion, welche in echt jüdischer Weise zu einer Sensation aufgebauscht wurde, verglich Einstein sein Werk mit demjenigen Galileis und tat, als sich Lenard auf den gesunden Menschverstand berief, die Äußerung, daß es gefährlich sei, den gesunden Menschenverstand in der Physik zur Anwendung zu bringen. Diese seltsame Argumentation ist dann auch in die populärwissenschaftliche Literatur eingegangen.

Im übrigen kam es bei dieser Tagung auch zu tumultuarischen Szenen. Der Vorsitzende Max Planck sah es als seine Hauptaufgabe an, die Einsteinpartei gegen ihre wissenschaftlichen Gegner möglichst gleich durch organisatorische Maßnahmen zu schützen. Er ließ, wie aus Presseveröffentlichungen hervorgeht, an der Eingangstüre eine Siebung vornehmen, um ihm nicht genehme Personen fernzuhalten. Darauf erhob sich zwar ein großer Tumult, und das empörte Auditorium stürmte den Saal. Planck erreichte seinen Zweck schließlich dadurch, daß er die Relativisten in stundenlangen Vorträgen sich verbreiten ließ, während den antirelativistischen Rednern einschließlich Diskussion insgesamt nur 15 Minuten zugebilligt werden sollten. Unter den Rednern dieser Tagung befand sich auch der im Kampf gegen Einstein an vorderster Stelle stehende Hugo Dingler.

Freilich erlag die Opposition gegen den relativistischen Wissenschaftsbetrieb in der Folgezeit der Übermacht der jüdischen Pressepropaganda und der staatlichen Schutzmaßnahmen. Bald wurde Einsteins Lehre als eine „Selbstverständlichkeit" bezeichnet, und die maßgebenden Männer der internationalen Gelehrtenrepublik hielten nach Möglichkeit jeden von einem Lehrstuhl fern, der sich gegen das relativistische Dogma — sei es auch in der wissenschaftlich-sachlichsten Weise — ausgesprochen hatte. So wurden diese Dogmatismen an die junge Physikergeneration so gut wie widerspruchslos weitergegeben."[292]

3.5 Einstein the Genocidal Racist

Albert Einstein was himself a racist; and, therefore, a hypocrite when criticizing the racism of others. John Stachel wrote,

"While he lived in Germany, however, Einstein seems to have accepted the then-prevalent racist mode of thought, often invoking such concepts as 'race' and 'instinct,' and the idea that the Jews form a race."[293]

On 8 July 1901, Einstein wrote to Winteler,

"There is no exaggeration in what you said about the German professors. I have got to know another sad specimen of this kind — one of the foremost physicists of Germany."[294]

Einstein wrote to Besso sometime after 1 January 1914,

"A free, unprejudiced look is not at all characteristic of the (adult) Germans (blinders!)."[295]

After the war Einstein and some of his friends alluded to much earlier conversations with Einstein, where he had correctly predicted the eventual outcome of the war. In his diaries, Romain Rolland recorded his conversations with Einstein in Switzerland at their meeting of 16 September 1915,

"What I hear from [Einstein] is not exactly encouraging, for it shows the impossibility of arriving at a lasting peace with Germany without first totally crushing it. Einstein says the situation looks to him far less favorable than a few months back. The victories over Russia have reawakened German arrogance and appetite. The word 'greedy' seems to Einstein best to characterize Germany. [***] Einstein does not expect any renewal of Germany out of itself; it lacks the energy for it, and the boldness for initiative. He hopes for a victory of the Allies, which would smash the power of Prussia and the dynasty. . . . Einstein and Zangger dream of a divided Germany—on the one side Southern Germany and Austria, on the other side Prussia. [***] We speak of the deliberate blindness and the lack of psychology in the Germans."[296]

Jews often sought to Balkanize nations so as to weaken the power of any faction within a nation and to created perpetual agitation between the nations which could be exploited for profit and other Jewish gains. For example, the Rothschilds created the American Civil War and profited from the debts it generated. They hoped to divide America into two nations and to pit these against one another. They were successful. Jews had long been pitting North German Protestants against South German and Austrian Catholics. Jews were the motive force behind the *Kulturkampf*. After creating these divides and promoting perpetual agitations amongst neighbors, Jewry could then fund one side against the other to destroy it whenever Jewry decided to wreck a given nation.

Einstein's dreams during the First World War remind one of the "Carthaginian Peace" of the Henry Morgenthau, Jr. plan for the destruction of Germany following the Second World War. Morgenthau worked with Lord Cherwell (Frederick Alexander Lindemann), Churchill's friend and advisor, who planned to bomb German civilian populations into submission. Lindemann studied under Einstein's friend,

372   Albert Einstein: The Incorrigible Racist

Walther Nernst, who worked with Fritz Haber, a Jewish developer of poisonous gas. James Bacque argues that the Allies, under the direction of General Eisenhower, starved hundreds of thousands, if not millions of German prisoners of war to death. Dwight David Eisenhower was called "the terrible Swedish-Jew" in his yearbook for West Point, *The 1915 Howitzer*, West Point, New York, (1915), p. 80. He was also called "Ike", as in. . . Eisenhower? The Soviets also abused and murdered countless German POW's after the Second World War.[297]

Einstein often spoke in genocidal and racist terms against Germany, and for the Jews and England, and he betrayed Germany before, during and after the war. Einstein wrote to Paul Ehrenfest on 22 March 1919,

"[The Allied Powers] whose victory during the war I had felt would be by far the lesser evil are now proving to be *only slightly* the lesser evil. [***] I get most joy from the emergence of the Jewish state in Palestine. It does seem to me that our kinfolk really are more sympathetic (at least less brutal) than these horrid Europeans. Perhaps things can only improve if only the Chinese are left, who refer to all Europeans with the collective noun 'bandits.'"[298]

While responsible people were trying to preserve some sanity in the turbulent period following World War I, Zionists like Albert Einstein sought to validate and encourage the racism of anti-Semites. The Dreyfus Affair taught them that anti-Semitism had a powerful effect to unite Jews around the world. The Zionists were afraid that the "Jewish race" was disappearing through assimilation. They wanted to use anti-Semitism to force the segregation of Jews from Gentiles and to unite Jews, and thereby preserve the "Jewish race". They hoped that if they put a Hitler-type into power—as Zionists had done in the past, they could use him to herd up the Jews and force the Jews into Palestine against their will. This would also help the Zionists to inspire distrust and contempt for Gentile government, while giving the Zionists the moral high-ground in international affairs, despite the fact that the Zionists were secretly behind the atrocities. In 1896, Theodor Herzl wrote his book *The Jewish State*,

"Great exertions will not be necessary to spur on the movement. Anti-Semites provide the requisite impetus. They need only do what they did before, and then they will create a love of emigration where it did not previously exist, and strengthen it where it existed before. [***] I imagine that Governments will, either voluntarily or under pressure from the Anti-Semites, pay certain attention to this scheme; and they may perhaps actually receive it here and there with a sympathy which they will also show to the Society of Jews."[299]

Albert Einstein wrote to Max Born on 9 November 1919. Einstein encouraged anti-Semitism and advocated segregation (one must wonder what rôle Albert's increasing racism played in his divorce from Mileva Marić—a Gentile Serb),

"Antisemitism must be seen as a real thing, based on true hereditary qualities, even if for us Jews it is often unpleasant. I could well imagine that I myself would choose a Jew as my companion, given the choice. On the other hand I would consider it reasonable for the Jews themselves to collect the money to support Jewish research workers outside the universities and to provide them with teaching opportunities."[300]

In 1933, the Zionists publicly declared their allegiance to the Nazis. They wrote in the *Jüdische Rundshau* on 13 June 1933,

"Zionism recognizes the existence of the Jewish question and wants to solve it in a generous and constructive manner. For this purpose, it wants to enlist the aid of all peoples; those who are friendly to the Jews as well as those who are hostile to them, since according to its conception, this is not a question of sentimentality, but one dealing with a real problem in whose solution all peoples are interested."[301]

On 21 June 1933, the Zionists issued a declaration of their position with respect to the Nazi régime, in which they expressed a belief in the legitimacy of the Nazis' racist belief system and condemned anti-Fascist forces.[302]

Michele Besso wrote that it might have been Albert Einstein's racism and bigotry which caused him to separate from his first wife Mileva Marić in 1914. Besso wrote to Einstein on 17 January 1928,

"[. . .]perhaps it is due in part to me, with my defense of Judaism and the Jewish family, that your family life took the turn that it did, and that I had to bring Mileva from Berlin to Zurich[.]"[303]

The hypocrisy of racist Zionists often manifested itself. As another example, consider the fact that racist Zionist Moses Hess was married to a Christian Gentile prostitute named Sybille Pritsch.

Einstein may have been affected by his mother's early racist opposition to his relationship with Marić. Another factor in the Einsteins' divorce was, of course, Albert's incestuous relationship with his cousin Else Einstein, and his desire to bed her daughters, as well as Albert's general promiscuity—some believe he was a whore monger. Albert Einstein opposed his sister Maja's marriage to the Gentile Paul Winteler on racist grounds and thought they should divorce. Albert Einstein wrote to Michele Besso on 12 December 1919 and stated that, "No mixed marriages are any good (Anna says: oh!)"[304] Besso, himself, was married to a Gentile, Anna Besso-Winteler. Denis Brian wrote,

"When asked what he thought of Jews marrying non-Jews, which, of course, had been the case with him and Mileva, [Albert Einstein] replied with a laugh, 'It's dangerous, but then all marriages are dangerous.'"[305]

On 3 April 1920, Einstein wrote, criticizing assimilationist Jews,

"And this is precisely what he does *not* want to reveal in his confession. He talks about religious faith instead of tribal affiliation, of 'Mosaic' instead of 'Jewish' because the latter term, which is much more familiar to him, would emphasize affiliation to his tribe."[306]

After declaring that Jewish children segregate due to natural forces and that they are "different from other children",[307] not due to religion or tradition, but due to genetic features and "heritage", Einstein continued his 3 April 1920 statement,

"With adults it is quite similar as with children. Due to race and temperament as well as traditions (which are only to a small extent of religious origin) they form a community more or less separate from non-Jews. [***] It is this basic community of race and tradition that I have in mind when I speak of 'Jewish nationality.' In my opinion, aversion to Jews is simply based upon the fact that Jews and non-Jews are different. [***] Where feelings are sufficiently vivid there is no shortage of reasons; and the feeling of aversion toward people of a foreign race with whom one has, more or less, to share daily life will emerge by necessity."[308]

Einstein made similar comments in a document dated sometime "after 3 April 1920". Einstein was in agreement with Philipp Lenard that a "Jewish heritage" (read for "heritage", "racial instinct") could be seen in intellectual works published by Jews. Einstein stated,

"The psychological root of anti-Semitism lies in the fact that the Jews are a group of people unto themselves. Their Jewishness is visible in their physical appearance, and one notices their Jewish heritage in their intellectual works, and one can sense that there are among them deep connections in their disposition and numerous possibilities of communicating that are based on the same way of thinking and of feeling. The Jewish child is already aware of these differences as soon as it starts school. Jewish children feel the resentment that grows out of an instinctive suspicion of their strangeness that naturally is often met with a closing of the ranks. [***] [Jews] are the target of instinctive resentment because they are of a different tribe than the majority of the population."[309]

Albert Einstein often referred to Jews as "tribesmen" and Jewry as the "tribe". Fellow German Jew Fritz Haber was outraged at Albert Einstein's racist treachery and disloyalty. Einstein confirmed that he was disloyal and a racist, and was obligated,

"[. . .] to step in for my persecuted and morally depressed fellow tribesmen, as far as this lies within my power[.]"[310]

Einstein bore no such loyalty to Germans, who had feed him and made him famous. In fact, Einstein wanted to exterminate the Germans.

In a draft letter of 3 April 1920, Einstein wrote that children are conscious of "racial characteristics" and that this alleged "racial" gulf between children results in conflicts, which instill a sense of foreignness in the persecuted child. Einstein wrote,

"Unter den Kindern war besonders in der Volksschule der Antisemitismus lebendig. Er gründete ich auf die den Kindern merkwürdig bewussten Rassenmerkmale und auf Eindrücke im Religionsunterricht. Thätliche Angriffe und Beschimpfungen auf dem Schulwege waren häufig, aber meist nicht gar zu bösartig. Sie genügten immerhin, um ein lebhaftes Gefühl des Fremdseins schon im Kinde zu befestigen."[311]

Einstein's racism was perhaps a defense mechanism to depersonalize the attacks he faced as a child and to counter the hurt with a sense of communal love and communal hatred, which was sponsored by his racist mother. Like Adolf Stoecker before him,[312] Albert Einstein advocated the segregation of Jewish students. Peter A. Bucky quoted Albert Einstein,

"I think that Jewish students should have their own student societies. [***] One way that it won't be solved is for Jewish people to take on Christian fashions and manners. [***] In this way, it is entirely possible to be a civilized person, a good citizen, and at the same time be a faithful Jew who loves his race and honors his fathers."[313]

Einstein stated,

"We must be conscious of our alien race and draw the logical conclusions from it. [***] We must have our own students' societies and adopt an attitude of courteous but consistent reserve to the Gentiles. [***] It is possible to be [***] a faithful Jew who loves his race and honours his fathers."[314]

On 5 April 1920, Einstein repeated what he had heard from his political Zionist friends who believed that anti-Semitism was necessary to the preservation of the "Jewish race",

"Anti-Semitism will be a psychological phenomenon as long as Jews come in contact with non-Jews—what harm can there be in that? Perhaps it is due to anti-Semitism that we survive as a race: at least that is what I believe."[315]

and,

"I am neither a German citizen, nor is there in me anything that can be described as 'Jewish faith.' But I am happy to belong to the Jewish people, even though I don't regard them as the Chosen People. Why don't we just let the Goy keep his anti-

Semitism, while we preserve our love for the likes of us?"[316]

This letter was published in the *Israelitisches Wochenblatt für die Schweiz*, on 24 September 1920, on page 10. It became famous and was widely discussed in newspapers and was used as a political issue. Einstein's racism had already become a weapon for Jewish critics to wield against German Jews who were loyal to the Fatherland. Einstein ridiculed the *Central-Verein deutscher Staatsbürger jüdischen Glaubens*, an organization that combated anti-Semitism and vigorously defended and celebrated Jews, because Einstein sought to promote anti-Semitism and because Einstein believed that being "Jewish" was a racial, not a religious, state. Einstein knew quite well that the letter had been published. The *C. V.* contacted him about it and published a statement regarding it in their periodical *Im deutschen Reich* in March of 1921,

"So wurde auch in einzelnen Versammlungen der b e k a n n t e B r i e f des Naturforschers P r o f e s s o r E i n s t e i n, den dieser an den Central-Verein gerichtet hat, und in welchem er die Bestrebungen des Central-Vereins ablehnt, weil sie zu national-deutsch und zu wenig jüdisch orientiert seien, zum Gegenstand der Erörterungen gemacht. Dieser Brief hat in der öffentlichen Erörterung der jüdischen und judengegnerischen Presse in den letzten Monaten und auch bei den Wahlen eine gewisse Rolle gespielt und Anlaß zu den verschiedenartigsten Betrachtungen je nach der Parteistellung der Versammlungsredner und der verschiedenen Zeitungen gegeben. So hat sich z. B. die jüdisch-nationale „Wiener Morgenzeitung" veranlaßt gesehen, den Central-Verein in wenig vornehmer Weise anzugreifen und ihn wegen seines nationaldeutschen Standpunktes zu verdächtigen. Diese Angriffe würden durch die Auffassung von Professor Einstein nicht gedeckt worden sein, wenn die „Wiener Morgenzeitung" gewußt hätte, daß Professor Einstein ohne nähere Kenntnis der Bestrebungen und der Arbeit des Central-Vereins seinen Brief geschrieben und keineswegs an eine Veröffentlichung, die nur durch eine Indiskretion erfolgt ist, gedacht hat. Erst n a c h der Veröffentlichung hat er von der Art und Weise der Tätigkeit des Central-Vereins Kenntnis erhalten und hat, w i e m i t g u t e m G r u n d v e r s i c h e r t w e r d e n k a n n, i n f o l g e d i e s e r K e n n t n i s e i n e w e s e n t l i c h a n d e r e A u f f a s s u n g v o m W e r t e d e r

Arbeit unseres Central-Vereins gewonnen. Auch dieser Vorfall sollte Anlaß geben, Urteile in der Oeffentlichkeit erst dann zu fällen, wenn die Sachlage einigermaßen geklärt ist."[317]

On 24 May 1931, the *Sunday Express* of London published an interview it claimed it had had with Einstein while he was visiting Oxford. The interview contained inflammatory statements similar to those published in the *Israelitisches Wochenblatt für die Schweiz* on 24 September 1920. These statements were repeated in several German language newspapers across Europe together with scathing editorial indictments of Einstein. Einstein claimed that no interview had taken place and the quotations were taken from a letter he had written eleven years prior. Einstein stated in a letter to Michael Traub of 22 August 1931 that this letter had never been published,[318] though it had been published and Einstein knew quite well that it had been published.

Einstein accused the *Central-Verein deutscher Staatsbürger jüdischen Glaubens e. V.* of instigating the "forgery". The C.V. denied that it was behind the publication in the *Sunday Express* and invited Einstein to respond in their official organ the *Central-Verein Zeitung.* Einstein took the opportunity and stated, "Es wurden mir schon wiederholt Auszüge aus einem Artikel der „S u n d a y   E x p r e ß" zugesandt, aus denen ich ersehe, daß es sich **um eine glatte Fälschung** handelt. Ich habe in O x f o r d überhaupt kein einziges Zeitungsinterview gegeben. Der Inhalt ist eine böswillige Entstellung eines vor elf Jahren geschriebenen, nicht für die Oeffentlichkeit bestimmten Briefes."[319] He affirmed in 1931 that he had made the statements in 1920 and did not repudiate them.

In 1932, Einstein stated, referring to the "deplorably high development of nationalism everywhere"—his own rabid Zionism apparently excepted,

"The introduction of compulsory service is therefore, to my mind, the prime cause of the moral collapse of the white race, which seriously threatens not merely the survival of our civilization but our very existence. This curse, along with great social blessings, started with the French Revolution, and before long dragged all the other nations in its train."[320]

Einstein had a reputation as a rabid anti-assimilationist—here again Einstein merely parroted the racist anti-assmilationism of his Zionist predecessors, like Solomon Schechter who dreaded assimilation more than pogroms—and Zionists encouraged pogroms in order to discourage assimilation.

Zionists were by no means alone in the anti-assimilationist panic that struck the western world at the end of the Nineteenth Century. In 1906, Chaim Weizmann had persuaded Arthur James Balfour to become a racist Zionist.[321] In 1908, Balfour published a racist and nationalistic lecture on the subject of race degeneration and stagnation called *Decadence*.[322] In America, Theodore Roosevelt had an enduring interest in racial questions and feared "racial suicide" and the decline of a race like the decline of an organism in old age.[323] On 5 March 1908, Roosevelt wrote to Balfour, later signatory of the Balfour Declaration,

"Most emphatically there is such a thing as 'decadence' of a nation, a race, a type; and it is no less true that we cannot give any adequate explanation of the phenomenon. Of course there are many partial explanations, and in some cases, as with the decay of the Mongol or Turkish monarchies, the sum of these partial explanations may represent the whole. But there are other cases, notably, of course, that of Rome in the ancient world, and, as I believe, that of Spain in the modern world, on a much smaller scale, where the sum of all the explanations is that they do not wholly explain. Something seems to have gone out of the people or peoples affected, and what it is no one can say."[324]

The London Times wrote on 12 February 1919 on page 9, confirming that Balfour's Declaration was based on precisely the same racist myths of "Blut und Boden" the Nazis would later assert to justify the racism of Nazi Germany,

"MR. BALFOUR ON ZIONISM.
THE CASE FOR A NATIONAL HOME.

Mr. Balfour, in whose hands has been placed the interests of Palestinian Jewry at the Peace Conference, has written a preface to the History of Zionism, shortly to be published from the pen of M. Sokolow, one of the four leaders of the Zionist Executive Committee.

Mr. Balfour says that convinced by conversations with Dr. Weizmann in January, 1906, that if a home was to be found for the Jewish people, homeless now for nearly 1900 years, it was vain to seek it anywhere but in Palestine. Answering the question why local sentiment is to be more considered in the case of the Jew than (say) in that of the Christian or the Buddhist, Mr. Balfour says:—'The answer is, that the cases are not parallel. The position of the Jews is unique. For them race, religion, and country are interrelated, as they are interrelated in the case of no other race, no other religion, and no other country on earth. By a strange and most unhappy fate it is this people of all others which, retaining to the full its racial self-consciousness, has been severed from its home, has wandered into all lands and has nowhere been able to create for itself an organized social commonwealth. Only Zionism—so at least Zionists believe—can provide some mitigation of this great tragedy.

'Doubtless there are difficulties, doubtless there are objections—great difficulties, very real objections. . . . Yet no one can reasonably doubt that if, as I believe, Zionism can be developed into a working scheme, the benefit it would bring to the Jewish people, especially perhaps to that section of it which most deserves our pity, would be great and lasting.'

The criticism that the Jews use their gifts to exploit for personal ends a civilization which they have not created, in communities they do little to maintain, Mr. Balfour declares to be false. He admits, however, that in large parts of Europe their loyalty to the State in which they dwell is (to put it mildly) feeble compared with their loyalty to their religion and their race. How, indeed, could it be otherwise? he asks. 'In none of the regions of which I speak have they been given the advantages of equal citizenship; in some they have been given no right of citizenship at all.'

'It seems evident that Zionism will mitigate the lot and elevate the status of no negligible fraction of the Jewish race. Those who go to Palestine will not be like those who now migrate to London or New York. . . . They will go in order to join a civil community which completely harmonizes with their historical and religious sentiments; a community bound to the land it inhabits by something deeper even than custom; a community whose members will suffer from no divided loyalty nor any temptation to hate the laws under which they are forced to live. To them the material gain should be great; but surely the spiritual gain will be greater still.'

Mr. Balfour goes on to consider the position of those, though Jews by descent, and often by religion, who desire wholly to identify themselves with the life of the country wherein they have made their home, many of them distinguished in art, medicine, politics, and law. 'Many of this class,' he says, 'look with a certain measure of suspicion and even dislike upon the Zionist movement. They fear that it will adversely affect their position in the country of their adoption. The great majority of them have no desire to settle in Palestine. Even supposing a Zionist community were established, they would not join it. . . .

'I cannot share these fears. I do not deny that, in some countries where legal equality is firmly established, Jews may still be regarded with a certain measure of prejudice. But this prejudice, where it exists, is not due to Zionism, nor will Zionism embitter it. The tendency should surely be the other way. Everything which assimilates the national and international status of the Jews to that of other races ought to mitigate what remains of ancient antipathies; and evidently this assimilation would be promoted by giving them that which all other nations possess—a local habitation and a national home."

Others repeated Theodor Herzl's theme, that Jews could not assimilate, because the presence of Jews in a host nation ultimately led to anti-Semitism due to Jewish parasitism—according to Herzl. Hilaire Belloc was a strong advocate of the view that Jews should not integrate. Belloc published a book on the subject entitled *The Jews* in 1922, and expressed similar convictions in *G. K.'s Weekly* in the 1930's. Belloc wrote biographies of men who had fallen under the influence of Zionists, like Oliver Cromwell and Napoleon. Belloc, however, was strongly opposed to Nazism. Douglas Reed took a similar Zionist stance on the alleged unassimilability of Jews in the late 1930's,[325] though he later opposed Zionism.

Racist Zionist Solomon Schecter stated, in harmony with numerous political Zionists, though in opposition to the vast majority of Jews,

"It is this kind of assimilation [the death of a "race" through integration], with the terrible consequences indicated, that I dread most; even more than pogroms."[326]

On 15 March 1921, Kurt Blumenfeld wrote to Chaim Weizmann,

"Einstein [***] is interested in our cause most strongly because of his revulsion from assimilatory Jewry."[327]

Einstein stated in 1921,

"To deny the Jew's nationality in the Diaspora is, indeed, deplorable. If one adopts the point of view of confining Jewish ethnical nationalism to Palestine, then one, to all intents and purposes, denies the existence of a Jewish people. In that case one should have the courage to carry through, in the quickest and most complete manner, entire assimilation. We live in a time of intense and perhaps exaggerated nationalism. But my Zionism does not exclude in me cosmopolitan views. I believe in the actuality of Jewish nationality, and I believe that every Jew has duties towards his coreligionists. [***] [T]he principal point is that Zionism must tend to strengthen the dignity and self-respect of the Jews in the Diaspora. I have always been annoyed by the undignified assimilationist cravings and strivings which I have observed in so many of my friends."[328]

In 1921, Einstein declared, referring to Eastern European Jews,

"These men and women retain a healthy national feeling; it has not yet been destroyed by the process of atomisation and dispersion."[329]

Einstein wrote in the *Jüdische Rundschau*, on 21 June 1921, on pages 351-352,

"This phenomenon [*i. e.* Anti-Semitism] in Germany is due to several causes. Partly it originates in the fact that the Jews there exercise an influence over the intellectual life of the German people altogether out of proportion to their number. While, in my opinion, the economic position of the German Jews is very much overrated, the influence of Jews on the Press, in literature, and in science in Germany is very marked, as must be apparent to even the most superficial observer. This accounts for the fact that there are many anti-Semites there who are not really anti-Semitic in the sense of being Jew-haters, and who are honest in their arguments. They regard Jews as of a nationality different from the German, and therefore are alarmed at the increasing

Jewish influence on their national entity. [***] But in Germany the judgement of my theory depended on the party politics of the Press[.][330]

Einstein also stated,

"The way I see it, the fact of the Jews' racial peculiarity will necessarily influence their social relations with non-Jews. The conclusions which—in my opinion—the Jews should draw is to become more aware of their peculiarity in their social way of life and to recognize their own cultural contributions. First of all, they would have to show a certain noble reservedness and not be so eager to mix socially—of which others want little or nothing. On the other hand, anti-Semitism in Germany also has consequences that, from a Jewish point of view, should be welcomed. I believe German Jewry owes its continued existence to anti-Semitism."[331]

Nazi Zionist Joseph Goebbels, sounding very much like political Zionist Albert Einstein, was quoted in *The New York Times*, on 29 September 1933, on page 10,

"It must be remembered the Jews of Germany were exercising at that time a decisive influence on the whole intellectual life; that they were absolute and unlimited masters of the press, literature, the theatre and the motion pictures, and in large cities such as Berlin, 75 percent of the members of the medical and legal professions were Jews; that they made public opinion, exercised a decisive influence on the Stock Exchange and were the rulers of Parliament and its parties."

On 1 July 1921, Einstein was quoted in the *Jüdische Rundshau* on page 371,

"Let us take brief look at the *development of German Jews* over the last hundred years. With few exceptions, one hundred years ago our forefathers still lived in the Ghetto. They were poor and separated from the Gentiles by a wall of religious tradition, secular lifestyles and statutory confinement and were confined in their spiritual development to their own literature, only relatively weakly influenced by the forceful progress which intellectual life in Europe had undergone in the Renaissance. However, these little noticed, modestly living people had one thing over us: *Every one of them belonged with all his heart to a community*, into which he was incorporated, in which he felt a worthwhile member, in which nothing was asked of him which conflicted with his normal processes of thought. Our forefathers of that era were pretty pathetic both bodily and spiritually, but—in social relations—in an enviable state of mental equilibrium. Then came emancipation. It offered undreamt of opportunities for advancement. The isolated individual quickly found their way into the upper financial and social circles of society. They eagerly absorbed the great achievements of art and science which the Occidentals[332] had created. They contributed to the development with passionate affection, and themselves made contributions of lasting value. They thereby took on the lifestyle of the Gentile world, turning away from their religious and social traditions in growing masses—took on Gentile customs, manners and mentality. It appeared as if they were being completely dissolved into the numerically superior, politically and culturally better organized host peoples, such that no trace of them would be left after a few generations. The complete eradication of the Jewish nationality in Middle and Western Europe appeared to be inevitable. However, it didn't turn out that way. It appears that racially distinct nations have instincts which work against interbreeding. The adaptation of the Jews to the European peoples among whom they have lived in language, customs and indeed even partially in religious practices *was unable to eliminate all feelings of foreigness* which exist between Jews and their European host peoples. In short, this spontaneous feeling of foreignness is ultimately due to a loss of energy.[333] For this reason, *not even well-meant arguments can eradicate it*. Nationalities do not want to be mixed together, rather they want to go their own separate ways. A state of peace can only be achieved by mutual tolerance and respect."

Einstein stated that Jews should not participate in the German Government,

"I regretted the fact that [Rathenau] became a Minister. In view of the attitude which large numbers of the educated classes in Germany assume towards the Jews, I have always thought that their natural conduct in public should be one of proud reserve."[334]

Einstein merely parroted the Zionist Party line. Werner E. Mosse wrote,

"While the leaders of the CV saw it as their special duty to represent the interests of the German Jews in the active political struggle, Zionism stood for. . . systematic Jewish non-participation in German public life. It rejected as a matter of principle any participation in the struggle led by the CV."[335]

In 1925, Einstein wrote in the official Zionist organ *Jüdische Rundschau*,

"By study of their past, by a better understanding of the spirit [Geist] that accords with their race, they must learn to know anew the mission that they are capable of fulfilling. [***] What one must be thankful to Zionism for is the fact that it is the only movement that has given many Jews a justified pride, that it has once again given a despairing race the necessary faith, if I may so express myself, given new flesh to an exhausted people."[336]

On 12 October 1929, Albert Einstein wrote to the *Manchester Guardian*,

"In the re-establishment of the Jewish nation in the ancient home of the race, where Jewish spiritual values could again be developed in a Jewish atmosphere, the most enlightened representatives of Jewish individuality see the essential preliminary to the regeneration of the race and the setting free of its spiritual creativeness."[337]

Einstein's public racism eventually waned, but he continued to publicly express his segregationist philosophy in the same terms as anti-Semites, as well as his belief that Jews "thrived on" and owed their "continued existence" to anti-Semitism. Einstein stated in December of 1930 to an American audience,

"There is something indefinable which holds the Jews together. Race does not make much for solidarity. Here in America you have many races, and yet you have the solidarity. Race is not the cause of the Jews' solidarity, nor is their religion. It is something else—which is indefinable."[338]

Einstein's confusing public statement perhaps resulted from his desire to promote multi-culturalism in America, which had the benefit of freeing up Jewish immigration to the United States.[339] Einstein was also likely parroting, or trying to parrot, a fellow anti-assimilationist political Zionist whose pamphlet was well known in America, Solomon Schechter and his *Zionism: A Statement*, Federation of American Zionists, New York, (1906), in which Schechter states, among other things, "Zionism is an ideal, and as such is indefinable."[340]
Einstein stated in 1938,

"JUST WHAT IS A JEW?

The formation of groups has an invigorating effect in all spheres of human striving, perhaps mostly due to the struggle between the convictions and aims represented by the different groups. The Jews, too, form such a group with a definite character of its own, and anti-Semitism is nothing but the antagonistic attitude produced in the non-Jews by the Jewish group. This is a normal social reaction. But for the political abuse resulting from it, it might never have been designated by a special name.

What are the characteristics of the Jewish group? What, in the first place, is a Jew? There are no quick answers to this question. The most obvious answer would be the following: A Jew is a person professing the Jewish faith. The superficial character of this answer is easily recognized by means of a simple parallel. Let us ask the question: What is a snail? An answer similar in kind to the one given above might be: A snail is an animal inhabiting a snail shell. This answer is not altogether incorrect; nor, to be sure, is it exhaustive; for the snail shell happens to be but one of the material products of the snail. Similarly, the Jewish faith is but one of the characteristic products of the Jewish community. It is, furthermore, known that a snail can shed its shell without thereby ceasing to be a snail. The Jew who abandons his faith (in the formal sense of the word) is in a similar position. He remains a Jew.

[***]

WHERE OPPRESSION IS A STIMULUS

[***]
Perhaps even more than on its own tradition, the Jewish group has thrived on oppression and on the antagonism it has forever met in the world. Here undoubtedly lies one of the main reasons for its continued existence through so many thousands of years."[341]

Albert Einstein was parroting racist political Zionist leader Theodor Herzl, who wrote in his book *The Jewish State,*

"Oppression and persecution cannot exterminate us. No nation on earth has survived such struggles and sufferings as we have gone through. Jew-baiting has merely stripped off our weaklings; the strong among us were invariably true to their race when persecution broke out against them. This attitude was most clearly apparent in the period immediately following the emancipation of the Jews. Later on, those who rose to a higher degree of intelligence and to a better worldly position lost their communal feeling to a very great extent. Wherever our political well-being has lasted for any length of time, we have assimilated with our surroundings. I think this is not discreditable. Hence, the statesman who would wish to see a Jewish strain in his nation would have to provide for the duration of our political well-being; and even Bismarck could not do that. [***] The Governments of all countries scourged by Anti-Semitism will serve their own interests in assisting us to obtain the sovereignty we want. [***] Great exertions will not be necessary to spur on the movement. Anti-Semites provide the requisite impetus. They need only do what they did before, and then they will create a love of emigration where it did not previously exist, and strengthen it where it existed before. [***] I imagine that Governments will, either voluntarily or under pressure from the Anti-Semites, pay certain attention to this scheme; and they may perhaps actually receive it here and there with a sympathy which they will also show to the Society of Jews."[342]

In 1938, Einstein stated in his essay "Our Debt to Zionism",

"Rarely since the conquest of Jerusalem by Titus has the Jewish community experienced a period of greater oppression than prevails at the present time. [***] Yet we shall survive this period too, no matter how much sorrow, no matter how heavy a loss in life it may bring. A community like ours, which is a community purely by reason of tradition, can only be strengthened by pressure from without."[343]

Einstein avowed *circa* 3 April 1920, that,

"If what anti-Semites claim were true, then indeed there would be nothing weaker, more wretched, and unfit for life, than the German people".[344]

Einstein often avowed that the anti-Semites' beliefs were true, and, hence, Einstein wished the Germans dead. When discussing the meaning of life, Einstein spoke to Peter A. Bucky about persons and creatures who "[do] not deserve to be in our world" and are "hardly fit for life."[345] Einstein's language is quite similar to the language of Hitler's "T4" "*Euthanasia-Programme*".

After siding with Germany's enemies in the First World War—while living in Germany, and after intentionally provoking Germans into increased anti-Semitism, which he thought was good for Jews, and after defaming German Nobel Prize laureates in the international press to the point where they felt obliged to join Hitler's cause, which cause eventually resulted in the genocide of Europe's Jews; Einstein sponsored the production of genocidal weapons to mass murder Germans, whom he had hated all of his life, in the famous letter to President Roosevelt that Einstein signed urging Roosevelt to begin the development of atomic bombs—before the mass murder of Jews had begun.[346]

Einstein callously asserted that the use of atomic bombs on civilian populations was "morally justified". I quote Einstein without delving into the question of who first bombed civilian centers,

"It should not be forgotten that the atomic bomb was made in this country as a preventive measure; it was to head off its use by the Germans, if they discovered it. The bombing of civilian centers was initiated by the Germans and adopted by the Japanese. To it the Allies responded in kind—as it turned out, with greater effectiveness—and they were morally justified in doing so."[347]

Einstein advocated genocidal collective punishment,

"The Germans as an entire people are responsible for these mass murders and must be punished as a people if there is justice in the world and if the consciousness of collective responsibility in the nations is not to perish from the earth entirely."[348]

and,

"It is possible either to destroy the German people or keep them suppressed; it is not possible to educate them to think and act along democratic lines in the foreseeable future."[349]

Albrecht Fölsing has assembled a compilation of post-WW II quotations from Einstein, which evince Einstein's lifelong habit of stereotyping people based on their ethnicity. Einstein expressed his hatred in the horrific post-Holocaust context—a temptation Max Born had resisted,

"With the Germans having murdered my Jewish brethren in Europe, I do not wish to have anything more to do with Germans, not even with a relatively harmless Academy. [***] The crimes of the Germans are really the most hideous that the history of the so-called civilized nations has to show. [***] [It was] evident that a proud Jew no longer wishes to be connected with any kind of German official event or institution. [***] After the mass murder committed by the Germans against my Jewish brethren I do not wish any publications of mine to appear in Germany."[350]

Einstein wrote to Born on 15 September 1950 that his views towards Germans predated the Nazi period,

"I have not changed my attitude to the Germans, which, by the way, dates not just from the Nazi period. All human beings are more or less the same from birth. The Germans, however, have a far more dangerous tradition than any of the other so-called civilized nations. The present behavior of these other nations towards the Germans merely proves to me how little human beings learn even from their most painful experiences."[351]

and on learning that Born would return to Germany, Einstein wrote on 12 October 1953,

"If anyone can be held responsible for the fact that you are migrating back to the land of the mass-murderers of our kinsmen, it is certainly your adopted fatherland — universally notorious for its parsimony."[352]

3.6 Racist Jewish Hypocrisy, Intimidation and Censorship

Sigmund Freud used prominent Gentiles, or "Goyim" as Freud called them, to promote his theories of psychology. He did this to give himself and the theories he plagiarized from Plato and others credibility in the broader "Gentile world". Though Freud thought that Gentiles were inferior to Jews, Freud was after fame.

Freud was another feted Jewish racist, who believed that the Jews were a superior race. Kevin MacDonald wrote in his book *The Culture of Critique*,

"Freud's powerful racial sense of ingroup-outgroup barriers between Jews and gentiles may also be seen in the personal dynamics of the psychoanalytic movement. We have seen that Jews were numerically dominant within psychoanalysis, especially in the early stages when all the members were Jews. 'The fact that these were Jews was certainly not accidental. I also think that in a profound though unacknowledged sense Freud wanted it that way' (Yerushalmi 1991, 41). As in other forms of Judaism, there was a sense of being an ingroup within a specifically Jewish milieu. 'Whatever the reasons—historical, sociological—group bonds did provide a warm shelter from the outside world. In social relations with other Jews, informality and familiarity formed a kind of inner security, a 'we-feeling,' illustrated even by the selection of jokes and stories recounted within the group' (Grollman 1965, 41). Also adding to the Jewish milieu of the movement was the fact that Freud was idolized by Jews generally. Freud himself noted in his letters that 'from all sides and places, the Jews have enthusiastically seized me for themselves.' 'He was embarrassed by the way they treated him as if he were 'a God-fearing Chief Rabbi,' or 'a national hero,'' and by the way they viewed his work as 'genuinely Jewish' (in Klein 1981, 85; see also Gay 1988, 599).
As in the case of several Jewish movements and political activities reviewed in Chapters 2 and 3 (see also *SAID*, Ch. 6), Freud took great pains to ensure that a gentile, Jung, would be

the head of his psychoanalytic movement—a move that infuriated his Jewish colleagues in Vienna, but one that was clearly intended to deemphasize the very large overrepresentation of Jews in the movement during this period. To persuade his Jewish colleagues of the need for Jung to head the society, he argued, 'Most of you are Jews, and therefore you are incompetent to win friends for the new teaching. Jews must be content with the modest role of preparing the ground. It is absolutely essential that I should form ties in the world of science' (in Gay 1988, 218). As Yerushalmi (1991, 41) notes, 'To put it very crudely, Freud needed a goy, and not just any goy but one of genuine intellectual stature and influence.' Later, when the movement was reconstituted after World War I, another gentile, the sycophantic and submissive Ernest Jones, became president of the International Psychoanalytic Association."[353]

The aggressive rôle that the "Shabbas Goy" Max von Laue played in personally attacking Einstein's critics was a part of this pattern.[354] He put a Gentile face on the assault against the rights of Einstein's critics to hold their own opinions and express them in public. Laue championed a smear campaign against Einstein's critics in the full knowledge that Einstein had plagiarized the works of Poincaré and Lorentz, and in full knowledge of the fact that the experimental evidence which had allegedly confirmed the general theory of relativity, did not confirm it, but rather disproved it.

Laue must have known that Einstein was an outspoken Jewish racist, but instead of condemning Einstein for his racism, Laue let himself be used to miscast the scientific and ethical critique of Einstein as if it were an expression of anti-Jewish racism. Einstein played a central rôle in corrupting the universities, the journals and the popular press of his day with Jewish racists and sycophantic Gentiles, who would promote him and the theories he appropriated from others.

Freud did not invent the field of psychology. He was a career plagiarist and he largely deprived the field of its synthetic scientific basis, which appeared in the earlier work of Spencer and James. Freud converted psychology into an introspective metaphysical analysis of his own mental maladies. Freud abused the pseudoscientific doctrines he plagiarized, and the fame he had achieved through the Jewish community, to make political attacks against persons whom he hated, and against Rome—against the Catholic Church. Largely under the directorship of Jews, the field of psychology degenerated into a sadistic house of tortures and mutilation. It was exploited as a means to suppress dissent, especially in Marxist countries, and particularly in the hands of Jews. Psychology, under Freud, also become a means to enrich psychiatrists by providing sick persons with someone with whom they could talk, and giving them the false hope that this panacea of talk would cure them of their physical ailments.

Max Born intimated in his 16 July 1955 lecture in Bern (as had Moszkowski and Freundlich) that the hype promoting Einstein in 1919 was intended, in part, as a *rapprochement* between Great Britain and Germany after the war. Eddington wrote to Einstein on 1 December 1919,

> "It is the best possible thing that could have happened for scientific relations between England and Germany. I do not anticipate rapid progress towards official reunion, but there is a big advance towards a more reasonable frame of mind among scientific men, and that is even more important than the renewal of formal associations. [***] [T]hings have turned out very fortunately in giving this object-lesson of the solidarity of German and British science even in time of war."[355]

Others wrote of their excitement that the eclipse sensation would promote better international relations.[356]

This indicates that the eclipse "observations" signified a political maneuver, not a legitimate experiment. At the time much was made of the fact that Einstein's book had been translated into English and was the first book to be translated from German to English after the war.[357] Einstein's correspondence regarding this translation and his article for the *The London Times* also reveal some of the political motives of *rapprochement* behind the Einstein hype of 1919, and beyond.[358]

In 1955, Born stated that the eclipse expeditions of 1919 created an undescribable stir around the world,

> "EINSTEIN became at once the most famous and popular figure, the man who had broken through the wall of hatred and united the scientists to a common effort, the man who had replaced ISAAC NEWTON's system of the world by another and better one. But at the same time an opposition, which had already been apparent while I was in Berlin, grew under the leadership of PHILIPP LENARD and JOHANNES STARK. It was springing from

the most absurd mixture of scientific conservatism and prejudice with racial and political emotions, due to EINSTEIN's Jewish descent and pacifistic, antimilitaristic convictions."[359]

Born also stated,

"[. . .]EINSTEIN's theory was new and revolutionary, an effort was needed to assimilate it. Not everybody was able or willing to do so. Thus the period after EINSTEIN's discovery was full of controversy, sometime of bitter strife."[360]

Nobel Prize laureates Philipp Lenard (1905 Nobel Prize for Physics) and Johannes Stark (1919 Nobel Prize for Physics) had initially sponsored Einstein and his work, and it was only after Einstein played the race card—publicly and internationally smearing Philipp Lenard without cause, that race became an issue in the debate over relativity theory—mostly for Einstein, Max von Laue and Max Born, who had a financial interest in the Einstein myth, and for the press people who smeared Einstein's opponents. They desperately wanted to change the subject from the legitimate claims of Einstein's plagiarism, legitimate arguments against the irrationality of the theory of relativity and the shameless hype and misrepresentation of experimental evidence by Einstein and his friends, to name-calling and racial strife provoked by them.

Lenard and Stark initially opposed Einstein on purely scientific and ethical grounds related to Einstein's sophistry, self-promotion and plagiarism. They later embraced Nazism and its racial mythologies.

Einstein eventually succeeded in bringing racial politics into the debate, though it was initially a larger issue for him than for his opponents. Einstein most often outright refused to discuss his plagiarism or purely scientific, non-political critiques of the theory of relativity; but he did not hesitate to name-call and smear his critics. He could not win in a dispute over the scientific and historical facts, so he provoked a race war over relativity theory in order to avoid legitimate criticism. It was a war everyone would ultimately lose.

Einstein's complaints were hypocritical. He   himself sought ethnically segregated educational institutions and an ethnically segregated society and often stated that anti-Semitism was both correct and good for Jews. Einstein had bad experiences early in his youth[361] and always bore a stereotypical prejudice against Gentile Germans, which is consistent with the racism inherent in genocidal Judaism.

Max Born, himself, "played the race card" and misrepresented events at the Bad Nauheim debate. Born stated,

"[Philipp Lenard] directed sharp, nasty attacks against Einstein, with a blatantly anti-Semitic tendency. Einstein became agitated and answered him sharply, and I believe I remember that I supported him."[362]

Born took pride in his biased and unfair efforts to quash any opposition to Einstein's mythologies. Born stated,

"There appeared attacks against EINSTEIN by well-known scientists and philosophers in the *Frankfurter Zeitung* which aroused my pugnacity. I answered in a rather sharp article."[363]

Born's contradictory claim that Einstein had concurrently united and divided scientists indicates Born's blindness to his own hypocrisy and the magnitude of the zealotry he felt for his political cause, which he believed would make him rich. While Born and his ilk boasted of their opposition to anti-Semitism, they themselves were elements in the atmosphere which created Hitler's tragic ascent to power, and for them to pretend to victory among that horror, greatly dishonors the innocent lives lost in the Holocaust. Political Zionists, Einstein among them—Born not, saw anti-Semitism as a good thing and promoted segregation and racial tension. Some even delighted in the fact that forced segregation would bring more Jews into the political Zionist camp.

Albert Einstein was one of the world's leading political Zionists. Political Zionism was a new form of racism that emerged at the end of the Nineteenth Century. It held that Jews were a pure race that could not coexist with non-Jews. Einstein had many powerful friends in the Zionist and Socialist press. Einstein's friends and supporters, in what political Zionist founder Theodor Herzl called the "Jewish papers",[364] libeled those who opposed Einstein or the theory of relativity and deflected attention from Einstein's plagiarism by misrepresenting any criticism of Einstein as if it were anti-Semitism, *per se*.[365]

There was also an anti-Einstein press and an unbiased press which documented Einstein's plagiarism and his scientific and philosophical defeats. Like radicals in general, radical Socialists, Zionists and Communists had well-deserved reputations as defamers, which manifested itself in their vitriolic attacks on Jewish leaders who refused to fund their schemes; or, in the case of Zionism, opposed their racist agenda. Einstein stated, "But in Germany the judgement of my theory depended on the party politics of the Press[.]"[366] German newspapers had well-deserved reputations as being organs for the many political parties which were active in Germany in the Teens of the Twentieth Century. They brought politics into science in a way not previously known.

Einstein took advantage of the political climate after World War I to change the subject from the accusations of plagiarism against him, which were easily proven, to racial politics, which were explosive at the time. It is tragic that the search for the truth in Physics, and in Ethics related to priorities, became a political issue centered on "the Jewish question", but Einstein succeeded in making it one.

Political Zionists, Einstein and his friends among them, have earned a reputation throughout their history for preventing free and open public dialog about important issues they would rather not see discussed. They have often had open access to the press to publish their smears and the means to largely prevent those who have been wronged from responding. They accomplish these feats by: spuriously presuming to speak for all persons of Jewish descent, organized intimidation, boycott, smear tactic, intensive letter writing campaigns which give an inflated appearance that their views are widely held, threats and acts of violence, etc.

Even the disciples of Christ are said to have feared Jewish tribalism and Jewish religious intolerance, for example *John* 7:1 tells that,

"After these *things* Jesus walked in Galilee: for he would not walk in Jewry, because the Jews sought to kill him."

John 7:13 states:

"Howbeit no *man* spake openly of him for fear of the Jews."

John 19:38 states:

"And after this Joseph of Arimathaea, being a disciple of Jesus, but secretly for fear of the Jews, besought Pilate that he might take away the body of Jesus: and Pilate gave *him* leave. He came therefore, and took the body of Jesus."

John 20:19 states:

"Then the same day at evening, being the first *day* of the week, when the doors were shut where the disciples were assembled for fear of the Jews, came Jesus and stood in the midst, and saith unto them, Peace *be* unto you."

In 1914, Edward Alsworth Ross, a Professor of Sociology at the University of Wisconsin, wrote in his book, *The Old World in the New: The Significance of Past and Present Immigration to the American People*, The Century Co., New York, (1914), pages 143 and 165,

"IN his defense of Flaccus [*Pro Flaccus*, Chapter 28], a Roman governor who had 'squeezed' his Jewish subjects, Cicero lowers his voice when he comes to speak of the Jews, for, as he explains to the judges, there are persons who might excite against him this numerous, clannish and powerful element. With much greater reason might an American lower his voice to-day in discussing two million Hebrew immigrants united by a strong race consciousness and already ably represented at every level of wealth, power, and influence in the United States. [***] This cruel prejudice—for all lump condemnations are cruel—is no importation, no hang-over from the past. It appears to spring out of contemporary experience and is invading circle after circle of broad-minded. People who give their lives to befriending immigrants shake their heads over the Galician Hebrews. It is astonishing how much of the sympathy that twenty years ago went out to the fugitives from Russian massacres has turned sour. Through fear of retaliation little criticism gets into print; in the open the Philo-semites have it all their way. The situation is: Honey above, gall beneath. If the Czar, by keeping up the pressure which has already rid him of two million undesired subjects, should succeed in driving the bulk of his six million Jews to the United States, we shall see the rise of the Jewish question here, perhaps riots and anti-Jewish legislation. No doubt thirty or forty thousand Hebrews from eastern Europe might be absorbed by this country each year without any marked growth of race prejudice; but when they come in two or three or even four times as fast, the lump outgrows the leaven, and there will be trouble."

Cicero's *Pro Flaccus*, Chapter 28, states,

"XXVIII. The next thing is that charge about the Jewish gold. And this, forsooth, is the reason why this cause is pleaded near the steps of Aurelius. It is on account of this charge, O Lælius, that this place and that mob has been selected by you. You know how numerous that crowd is, how great is its unanimity, and of what weight it is in the popular assemblies. I will speak in a low voice, just so as to let the judges hear me. For men are not wanting who would be glad to excite that people against me and against every eminent man; and I will not assist them and enable them to do so more easily. As gold, under pretence of being given to the Jews, was accustomed every year to be exported out of Italy and all the provinces to Jerusalem, Flaccus issued an edict establishing a law that it should not be lawful for gold to be exported out of Asia. And who is there, O judges, who cannot honestly praise this measure? The senate had often decided, and when I was consul it came to a most solemn resolution that gold ought not to be exported. But to resist this barbarous superstition were an act of dignity, to despise the multitude of Jews, which at times was most unruly in the assemblies in defence of the interests of the republic, was an act of the greatest wisdom. 'But Cnæus Pompeius, after he had taken Jerusalem, though he was a conqueror, touched nothing which was in that temple.' In the first place, he acted wisely, as he did in many other instances, in leaving no room for his detractors to say anything against him, in a city so prone to suspicion and to evil speaking. For I do not suppose that the religion of the Jews, our enemies, was any obstacle to that most illustrious general, but that he was hindered by his own modesty. Where then is the guilt? Since you nowhere impute any theft to us, since you approve of the edict, and confess that it was passed in due form, and do not deny that the gold was openly sought for and produced, the facts of the case themselves show that the business was executed by the instrumentality of men of the highest character. There was a hundredweight of gold, more or less, openly seized at Apamea, and weighed out in the forum at the feet of the prætor, by Sextus Cæsius, a Roman knight, a most excellent and upright man; twenty pounds weight or a little more were seized at Laodicea, by Lucius Peducæus, who is here in court, one of our judges; some was seized also at Adramyttium, by Cnæus Domitius, the lieutenant, and a small quantity at Pergamus. The amount of the gold is known; the gold is in the treasury; no theft is imputed to him; but it is attempted to render him unpopular. The speaker turns away from the judges, and addresses himself to the surrounding multitude. Each city, O Lælius, has its own peculiar religion; we have ours. While Jerusalem was flourishing, and while the Jews were in a peaceful state, still the religious ceremonies and observances of that people were very much at variance with the splendour of this empire, and the dignity of our name, and the institutions of our ancestors. And they are the more odious to us now, because that nation has shown by arms what were its feelings towards our supremacy. How dear it was to the immortal gods is proved by its having been defeated, by its revenues having been farmed out to our contractors, by its being reduced to a state of subjection."[367]

United States Army Captain Montgomery Schuyler reported on 1 March 1919,

"It is probably unwise to say this loudly in the United States but the Bolshevik movement is and has been since its beginning guided and controlled by Russian Jews of the greasiest type[. . .]"[368]

Senator Ernest F. Hollings argued before the United States that his position was being mischaracterized, when he put America's interests ahead of the Neo-Conservatives' plan for providing Israel with hegemony in the Mid-East and was called "anti-Semitic". Senator Hollings' comments appear in the *Congressional Record* (Proceedings and Debates of the 108th Congress, Second Session), Volume 150, Number 72, (20 May 2004), pages S5921-S5925; which includes Senator Hollings' article, "Bush's Failed Mideast Policy is Creating More Terrorism", *Charleston Post and Courier*, 6 May 2004, which article has appeared in several websites. The *Congressional Record* is also available online. At pages S5921-S5925, Senator Hollings states, *inter alia*,

"Mr. HOLLINGS. Mr. President, I thank my distinguished colleagues. I have, this afternoon, the opportunity to respond to being charged as anti-Semitic when I proclaimed the policy of President Bush in the Mideast as not for Iraq or really for democracy in the sense that he is worried about Saddam and democracy. If he were worried about democracy in the Mideast, as we wanted to spread it as a policy, we would have invaded Lebanon, which is half a democracy and has terrorism and terrorists who have been problems to the interests of Israel and the United States. [***] I want to read an article that appeared in the Post and Courier in Charleston on May 6; thereafter, I think in the State newspaper in Columbia a couple days later; and in the Greenville News—all three major newspapers in South Carolina. You will find that there is no anti-Semitic reference whatsoever in it. [***] But in any event, the better way to do it is go right in and establish our predominance in Iraq and then, as they say, and I have different articles here I could refer to, next is Iran and then Syria. And it is the domino theory, and they genuinely believe it. I differ. I think, frankly, we have caused more terrorism than we have gotten rid of. That is my Israel policy. You can't have an Israel policy other than what AIPAC [American Israel Public Affairs Committee] gives you around here. I have followed them mostly in the main, but I have also resisted signing certain letters from time to time, to give the poor President a chance. I can tell you no President takes office— I don't care whether it is a Republican or a Democrat—that all of a sudden AIPAC will tell him exactly what the policy is, and Senators and members of Congress ought to sign letters. I read those carefully and I have joined in most of them. On some I have held back. I have my own idea and my own policy. I have stated it categorically. [***] Again, let me read: Bush thought tax cuts would hold his crowd together and that spreading democracy in the Mideast to secure Israel would take the Jewish vote from the Democrats. Is there anything wrong with referring to the Jewish vote? Good gosh, every 1 of us of the 100, with pollsters and all, refer to the Jewish vote. That is not anti-Semitic. It is appreciating them. We campaigned for it. I just read about President Bush's appearance before the AIPAC. He confirmed his support of the Jewish vote, referring to adopting Ariel Sharon's policy, and the dickens with the 1967 borders, the heck with negotiating the return of refugees, the heck with the settlements he had objected to originally. They had those borders, Resolution No. 242—no, no, President Bush said: I am going along with Sharon, and he was going to get that and he got the wonderful reception he got with the Jewish vote. There is nothing like politicizing or a conspiracy, as my friend from Virginia, Senator ALLEN, says—that it is an anti-Semitic, political, conspiracy statement. That is not a conspiracy. That is the policy. I didn't like to keep it a secret, maybe; but I can tell you now, I will challenge any 1 of the other 99 Senators to tell us why we are in Iraq, other than what this policy is here. It is an adopted policy, a domino theory of The Project For The New American Century. Everybody knows it because we want to secure our friend, Israel. If we can get in there and take it in 7 days, as Paul Wolfowitz says, then we would get rid of Saddam, and when we got rid of Saddam, now all they can do is fall back and say: Aren't you getting rid of Saddam? Let me get to that point. What happens is, they say he is a monster. We continued to give him aid after he gassed his own people and everything else of that kind. George Herbert Walker Bush said in his book All The Best in 1999, never commit American GIs into an unwinnable urban guerrilla war and lose the support of the Arab world, lose their friendship and support. That is a general rephrasing of it. The point is, my authority is the President's daddy. I want everybody to know that. I don't apologize for this column. I want them to apologize to me for talking about anti-Semitism. They are not getting by with it. I will come down here every day—I have nothing else to do—and we will talk about it and find out what the policy is. [***] We are losing the terrorism war because we thought we could do it militarily under the domino policy of President Bush, going into Iraq. That is my point. That is not anti-Semite or whatever they say in here about people's faith and ethnicity. I never referred to any faith. I should have added those other names from the Project For The New American Century, but I picked out the names I had quotes for. And for space, I left other things out. Mr. President, on May 12 of this year, I had printed in the RECORD the article in its entirety. I diverted from the reading of the article several times, so for the sake of accuracy I wanted the whole article printed. This particular op-ed piece appeared in the Post and Courier. Never would they have thought, having read it, if it was anti-Semitic, that they would have ever put it in there. Nor would the Knight Ridder newspapers in Columbia, SC. Nor would the Metro Media newspapers in Greenville, SC. But the Anti-Defamation League picked it up and now they have given it to my good friend, Senator ALLEN of Virginia. I have his particular admonition how I am anti-Semitic and I cannot let that stay there. [***] Come on. So we have to go out and not speak sense with respect to policy, and when you want to talk about policy, they say it is anti-Semitic. Well, come on the floor, let's debate it. Because my friend from Virginia admonishes me. Referring to me he says, 'I suggest he should learn from history before making accusations.' I didn't make any accusations. I stated facts. That is their policy. That is not my policy."

Former Illinois Congressman Paul Findley experienced first hand the ability and willingness of Zionists in more recent times to defame those who call for open public debate on issues the Zionists would rather suppress, or would have told from their heavily biased perspective and from their perspective only. Findley has written several books exposing the Zionists' ability to unfairly smear him and others, and to force silence through intimidation on any who would otherwise side with Findley in his efforts to involve the American people in an honest and open dialog about the rights of Palestinians.[369] Just as the Zionists have often sought to suppress public discussion of the Palestinians' rights and an honest discussion of what is in America's best interests, as opposed to the Zionists' perceived self-interests, political Zionists—and indeed like minded Marxist-leaning Socialists—have often obstructed public debate about Einstein's plagiarism from the moment Einstein became their most famous and important spokesman.

Congressman Paul Findley stated, among his many revealing remarks about Zionist influence,

"Journalist Harold R. Piety observes that 'the ugly cry of anti-Semitism is the bludgeon used by the Zionists to bully non-Jews into accepting the Zionist view of world events, or to keep silent.' In late 1978 Piety, withholding his identity in order not to irritate his employer, wrote an article on 'Zionism and the American Press' for *Middle East International* in which he decried 'the inaccuracies, distortions and— perhaps worst—inexcusable omission of significant news and background material by the American media in its treatment of the Arab-Israeli conflict.'

Piety traces the deficiency of U.S. media in reporting on the Middle East to largely successful efforts by the pro-Israel lobby to 'overwhelm the American media with a highly professional public relations campaign, to intimidate the media through various means and, finally, to impose censorship when the media are compliant and craven.' He lists threats to editors and advertising departments, orchestrated boycotts, slanders, campaigns of character assassination, and personal vendettas among the weapons employed against balanced journalism."[370]

Former Mossad agent Victor Ostrovsky wrote in his book *The Other Side of Deception: A Rogue Agent Exposes the Mossad's Secret Agenda* (note that a "Sayanim" is a disloyal and deceitful Jew, who is prepared to betray his or her neighbors at any time in order to advance a perceived Israeli interest),

"The American Jewish community was divided into a three-stage action team. First were the individual *sayanim* (if the situation had been reversed and the United States had convinced Americans working in Israel to work secretly on behalf of the United States, they would be treated as spies by the Israeli government). Then there was the large pro-Israeli lobby. It would mobilize the Jewish community in a forceful effort in whatever direction the Mossad pointed them. And last was B'nai Brith. Members of that organization could be relied on to make friends among non-Jews and tarnish as anti-Semitic whomever they couldn't sway to the Israeli cause. With that sort of one-two-three tactic, there was no way we could strike out."[371]

Prof. Norman G. Finkelstein writes in his book, *Beyond Chutzpah: On the Misuse of Anti-Semitism and the Abuse of History*, University of California Press, Berkeley, (2005), pp. 21-22, 32, and 66,

"**THE LATEST PRODUCTION** of Israel's apologists is the 'new anti-Semitism.' [***] The main purpose behind these periodic, meticulously orchestrated media extravaganzas is not to fight anti-Semitism but rather to exploit the historical suffering of Jews in order to immunize Israel against criticism. [***] Finally, whereas in the original *New Anti-Semitism* marginal left-wing organizations like the Communist Party and the Socialist Workers Party were cast as the heart of the anti-Semitic darkness, in the current revival Israel's apologists, having lurched to the right end of the political spectrum, cast mainstream organizations like Amnesty International and Human Rights Watch in this role. [***] **WHAT'S CURRENTLY CALLED** the new anti-Semitism actually incorporates three main components: (1) exaggeration and fabrication, (2) mislabeling legitimate criticism of Israeli policy, and (3) the unjustified yet predictable spillover from criticism of Israel to Jews generally. **EXAGGERATION AND FABRICATION** The evidence of a new anti-Semitism comes mostly from organizations directly or indirectly linked to Israel or having a material stake in inflating the findings of anti-Semitism."[372]

In 2006, Professors John J. Mearsheimer and Stephen M. Walt wrote in their paper, "The Israel Lobby and U. S. Foreign Policy",

"No discussion of how the Lobby operates would be complete without examining one of its most powerful weapons: the charge of anti-Semitism. Anyone who criticizes Israeli actions or says that pro-Israel groups have significant influence over U. S. Middle East policy—an influence that AIPAC celebrates—stands a good chance of getting labeled an anti-Semite. In fact, anyone who says that there is an Israel Lobby runs the risk of being charged with anti-Semitism, even though the Israeli media themselves refer to America's 'Jewish Lobby.' In effect, the Lobby boasts of its power and then attacks anyone who calls attention to it. This tactic is very effective, because anti-Semitism is loathsome and no responsible person wants to be accused of it."[373]

Jimmy Carter, Thirty-Ninth President of the United States of America, wrote in his book *Palestine: Peace not Apartheid*, Simon & Schuster, New York, (2006), page 209,

"Two other interrelated factors have contributed to the perpetuation of violence and regional upheaval: the condoning of illegal Israeli actions from a submissive White House and U.S. Congress during recent years, and the deference with which other international leaders permit this unofficial U.S. policy in the Middle East to prevail. There are constant and vehement political and media debates in Israel concerning its policies in the West Bank, but because of powerful political, economic, and religious forces in the United States, Israeli government decisions are rarely questioned or condemned, voices from Jerusalem dominate in our media, and most American citizens are unaware of circumstances in the occupied territories. At the same time, political leaders and news media in Europe are highly critical of Israeli policies, affecting public attitudes. Americans were surprised and angered by an opinion poll, published by the *International Herald Tribune* in October 2003, of 7,500 citizens in fifteen European nations, indicating that Israel was considered to be the top threat to world peace, ahead of North Korea, Iran, or Afghanistan."

Jimmy Carter also stated,

"You and I both know the powerful influence of AIPAC, which is not designed to promote peace. I'm not criticizing them, they have a perfect right to lobby, but their purpose in life is to protect and defend the policies of the Israeli government and to make sure those policies are approved in the United States and in our Congress—and they're very effective at it. I have known a large number of Jewish organizations in this country [that] have expressed their approval for the book and are trying to promote peace. But their voices are divided and they're relatively reluctant to speak out publicly. And any member of Congress who's looking to be re-elected couldn't possibly say that they would take a balanced position between Israel and the Palestinians, or that they would insist on Israel withdrawing to international borders, or that they would dedicate themselves to protect human rights of Palestinians—it's very likely that they would not be re-elected."[374]

In an interview with George Stephanopoulos on ABC television, in February of 2007, President Carter stated,

"It's almost politically suicidal in the United States for a member of the Congress who wants to seek reelection to take any stand that might be interpreted as anti-policy of the conservative Israeli government, which is equated, as I've seen it myself, as anti-Semitism."[375]

There is nothing new about fabricated accusations of anti-Semitism. The Judeans who fabricated the Old Testament fabricated a history of Egyptian tyranny which never occurred, and which fictions recklessly defamed the Egyptians as anti-Semites. Esau was defamed as an hereditary anti-Semite for daring to be angry at Jacob for stealing the Covenant from him.[376] Jewish historians defamed Caligula for not tolerating Judean intolerance (etc. etc. etc.).

Douglas Reed, who was a British journalist, but was forced out of the profession, because he reported on Zionist brutality, wrote in December of 1950,

"More important still, during all that period and to the present time, it was not possible freely to report or discuss a third vital matter: Zionist Nationalism. In this case the freedom of the press has become a fallacy during the past two decades. Newspaper-writers have become less and less free to express any criticism, or report any fact unfavourable to this new ambition of the Twentieth Century. When I eventually went to America I found that this ban, for such it is in practice, prevailed even more rigidly there than in my own country.

Today an awakening is supposed to have occurred in the matter of Communism. During the most fateful and decisive years of the Second War, when the things were being done which obviously set the stage for a third one, it was in fact almost impossible for any independent writer to publish any reasonable criticism, supported by no matter what evidence, about Soviet Communism and its intentions. Now, when the damage is done, Communism is much attacked, but even so the mass of Communist writers who were planted in the American and British press during those years has by no means been displaced; and the attentive newspaper-reader in either country may see for himself how the most specious Communist sophistries are daily injected into the editorial arguments and the news-columns of newspapers professing the most respectable principles.

In the matter of Zionist Nationalism, which I hold to be allied in its roots to Soviet Communism, the ban is much more severe. In my own adult lifetime as a journalist, now covering thirty years, I have seen this secret ban grow from nothing into something approaching a law of lèse majesté at some absolute court of the dark past. In daily usage, no American or British newspaper, apparently, now dares to print a line of news or comment unfavourable to the Zionist ambition; and under this thrall matters are reported favourably or non-committally, if they are reported at all, which if they occurred elsewhere would be denounced with the most piteous cries of outraged morality. The inference to me is plain: the Zionist Nationalists are powerful enough to govern governments in the great countries of the remaining West!

I believe Zionist Nationalism to be a political movement organized in all countries, which aims to bring all Jews under its thrall just as Communism enslaved the Russians and National Socialism the Germans. I hold it to be as dangerous as both of those, and when I recall the results that came of the subtle suppression of information in the cases of Stalinism and Hitlerism, I judge that the consequences of this even more rigorous suppression will not be less grave.

I think it a cardinal error to identify 'Jews' with Zionist Nationalism, 'Russians' with Communism, or 'Germans' with National Socialism. I saw the enslavement of Germans and Russians and know different. I believe that the astonishingly powerful attempt to prevent any discussion of Zionist Nationalism by dismissing it as the expression of an aversion to Jews, as Jews, is merely meant to stop any public discussion of its objects, which seem to me to be as dangerous to Jew as to Gentile. Of the three groups which have appeared, like stormy petrels, to presage the tempests of our century, the Zionist Nationalists appear to me the most powerful. National Socialism, I think, was but a stooge or stalking horse for the pursuit of Communist aims. Communism is genuinely tigerish, and was strong enough to infest governments everywhere and distort the policies which were pursued behind the screen of military operations; but, if forced into a corner by the rising unease of their peoples, Western politicians are prepared in the last resort to turn against it.

But Zionist Nationalism! . . . That is a different matter. Today American Presidents and British Prime Ministers, and all their colleagues, watch it as anxiously as Muslim priests watch for the crescent moon on the eve of Ramadan, and bow to it as the faithful prostrating themselves in the mosque at Mecca. The thing was but a word unknown to the masses forty years ago; today Western politicians hardly dare take the seals of office without first, or immediately afterwards, making public obeisance towards this strange new ambition."[377]

Gore Vidal wrote,

"Currently, there is little open debate in the United States on any of these matters. The Soviet Union must be permanently demonized in order to keep the money flowing to the Pentagon for 'defense,' while Arabs are characterized as subhuman terrorists. Israel may not be criticized at all. (Ironically, the press in Israel is far more open and self-critical than ours.) We do have one token Palestinian who is allowed an occasional word in the press, Professor Edward Said, who wrote (*Guardian*, December 21,1986): since the '1982 Israeli invasion of Lebanon . . . it was felt by the Zionist lobby that the spectacle of ruthless Israeli power on the TV screen would have to be effaced from memory, by the strategy of incriminating the media as anti-Semitic for showing these scenes at all.' A wide range of Americans were then exuberantly defamed, including myself."[378]

Robert I. Friedman wrote in 1987,

"Indeed, Americans have very little idea about how severely troubled Israel is, or how critical many Israelis are of their own government's policies, such as arming the contras, Khomeini's Iran, and South Africa. And some prominent U.S. editors and publishers who have dropped all pretense of objectivity to become public-relations advisors for the Israeli government hope to keep it that way. [***] And many others who have tried to defy this orthodoxy have come under unrelenting attack from the Israel lobby—a coalition of editors and publishers, pro-Israel PACs, and wealthy businessmen—which tries to silence dissidents with accusations of anti-Israel bias or anti-Semitism. [***] Yet these tactics of intimidation in the service of Israel may backfire. 'It is precisely the fact that it is the job of the national press to be fair and objective that gets these superoverheated Jews foaming,' said the *Washington Post's* Stephen Rosenfeld. 'They want 100 percent. They don't want fairness: they want unfairness on their side, and when they don't get it they accuse the press of being unfair. Most journalists get so much uninformed, unfair whining from the organized Jews that Jewish organizations—and ultimately Israel—may lose their credibility.'"[379]

Arvid Reuterdahl wrote to William L. Fisher on 17 October 1931,

"My dear Mr. Fisher,

Dr. Erich Ruckhaber recently sent you a letter of Aug. 29, 1931, addressed here to me for consideration.

Having lived through the Einstein Battle, I am well aware of all the difficulties which opposition to Einsteinism meets with everywhere, and not the least in the United States. I have had articles refused by Scientific Societies of which I am a member, because they clearly exposed the Einsteinian Sham.

It would be a great stroke for truth if we could find the means of getting '100 Autoren Gegen Einstein' published in the English. I managed to get a reference in a St. Paul Paper, and another indirect reference in the Kansas City Star, on the occasion of a visit to Kansas City. I enclose a copy of the latter. Through friends, elsewhere, I tried to get newspaper notices, but without success.

The forces behind Einstein have excellent control over the press and scientific journals. They control our mathematical and scientific departments (indirectly) in our universities and colleges—a most deplorable condition. I know, by actual experience, whereof I speak.

I fear that no American publishing house will lend its name to '100 Autoren', because of possible boycott and persecution (financial). Hence the publication involves raising the required funds independently and creating a marketing organization. Where the funds can be raised, at the present time of depression, is a stupendous problem. I too know Dr. Dayton C. Miller through correspondence—a splendid gentleman and true scientist. I have had correspondence with Dr. Charles Lane Poor and he knows of my efforts against Einsteinism. But,—are they in a position to back such a venture? My prolonged illness has incapacitated me financially.

I have seen references to the stand taken by Dr. L. J. Moore of Cincinnati, and he is sound on the Einstein fiasco. There are others. There are other U[niversity] scientists—a few besides these three—who are aware of the Einsteinian nonsense, but many are afraid of losing scientific caste, and perhaps their positions.

Since you are personally acquainted with Dr. Dayton C. Miller, it may be possible for you to approach him on the subject in order to learn his reaction. From his answer, conclusions may be drawn which will be of solid and practical value.

If you will kindly take this step, then we can confer again by correspondence. You may, of course, mention my name to Dr. Miller, stating my position in reference to the urgent need of an English translation of '100 Autoren --'.

If a fearless champion can be found who has the financial resources, then '100 Autoren --' can be gotten to the intelligent public and the days of Einsteinism in the U. S. will soon be numbered—such is the power of '100 Autoren' as I appraise it.

Of course, I am ready to serve in such way as Dean in order to bring this most desirable purpose to a realization.

With best wishes, I remain,
Most cordially yours,"[380]

Stjepan Mohorovičić wrote,

"Eine vorzügliche und sehr scharfsinnige Kritik veröffentlichte G. v. GLEICH 1930, wo er alle seine diesbezüglichen Arbeiten gesammelt und geordnet hatte, obwohl das 'Relativitätssyndikat' mit allen Mitteln trachtete, das Erscheinen dieses Werkes zu verhindern. Nun es war sehr schwer die Kritik gänzlich zu unterdrücken, da man in der Wahl der Mittel nicht kleinlich war. Alle, für die Relativitätstheorie ungünstigen Arbeiten wurden einfach kurzerhand als unrichtig, fehlerhaft oder falsch bezeichnet oder als u n w i c h t i g (heutzutage ein sehr beliebtes Wort!) oder wenigstens als u n i n t e r e s s a n t verschwiegen. Von den Philosophen erhielten nur die Applaudierenden das Wort, den kritisch Gesinnten warf man ihre mathematischen Unkenntnisse vor; wer sich darüber unterrichten will, sollte die offenen Briefe des bekannten Philosophen O. KRAUS nachlesen,

[*Endnote*: Vgl. Lit. [*O s k a r   K r a u s : Offene Briefe an Albert Einstein u. Max v. Laue über die gedanklichen Grundlagen der speziellen und allgemeinen Relativitätstheorie. Wien u. Leipzig 1925.*] S. 78 u. ff., dann S. 96 u. ff. So sagte beispielsweise O. KRAUS wörtlich S. 94-95: 'Herr EINSTEIN selbst ist philosophisch Laie. . . Mit der Zuwendung zu Reichenbachs radikalem Konventionalismus hat er, scheint es, nun den Standpunkt erreicht, der seiner Theorie kongenial ist. . . D e r   K o n v e n t i o n a l i s m u s   f ä l s c h t   d e n   W a h r h e i t s b e g r i f f   p r a g m a t i s t i s c h .   D i e s e m

Niveau entspricht die Relativitätstheorie vom philosophischen Standpunkt aus.' (O. KRAUS war Professor an der deutschen Universität in Prag zu gleicher Zeit wie auch A. EINSTEIN).]

und doch haben die Philosophen die Grundlage der Rechnung, nicht aber die Rechnung selbst untersucht. Aber die Relativisten haben übersehen, daß die modernen Relativitätstheorien, ähnlich wie die moderne Musik, voll von Dissonanzen sind, (eine solche Musik entzückt den heutigen Snob außerordentlich und er kann nicht begreifen, daß es gebildete Leute gibt, welche die moderne Musik nicht ausstehen können, aber dafür muß man das Ohr und die richtige musikalische Erziehung haben!). O. KRAUS hat besonders den Umstand hervorgehoben (1. c. S. 96.), 'daß jeder Quark, der für die Theorie zu sein scheint, von den Relativisten mit freundlicher Gebärde begrüßt wird. . . wahrend eine ernste Kritik mißhandelt wird'.

[*Endnote:* Ein erschreckendes Beispiel ist z. B. der beschleunigte Tod des verdienstvollen 80-jährigen Physikers. C. ISENKRAHE, (vgl. 317 [*O s k a r   K r a u s   :   Offene Briefe an Albert Einstein u. Max v. Laue über die gedanklichen Grundlagen der speziellen und allgemeinen Relativitätstheorie. Wien u. Leipzig 1925.*] S. 96-97); dann wie M. ABRAHAM behandelt wurde; oder, wenn man einen Physiker als den Gegner der modernen Relativitätstheorien bezeichnet, so sind dann alle seine wissenschaftlichen Verdienste umsonst u n d   e i n   j e d e r   S t ü m p e r   b i l d e t   s i c h   e i n ,   e r   h a b e   d a s   R e c h t   i h n   z u   v e r l e u m d e n.— Ein anderes Beispiel ist der weltbekannte und große deutsche Philosoph HUGO DINGLER; in [*H a n s   W a g n e r   :   Hugo Dinglers Beitrag zur Thematik der Letztbegründung. Kantstud. 47, 148-167, 1955-56. Sonderdruck, Köln 1956.*] S. 1. lesen wir folgendes über den von ibm geführten Kampf für die strenge Wissenschaft: '. . .ein Kampf, der unter schweren äußeren Bedingungen hatte geführt werden müssen — erst unter dem Vorwurf des Antisemitismus, seit er der Einsteinschen Relativitätstheorie entgegengetreten war, nach 1933 unter dem Vorwurf der Semitophilie, welcher ihn alsbald auch seinen Darmstädter Lehrstuhl kostete, 1945 unter dem Vorwurf einer Verbundenheit mit dem Ungeist des Hitlerreichs, der ihn abermals von der Lehrtätigkeit verwies und über ihn die aktuelle Gefahr eines buchstäblichen Hungertodes heraufführte, schließlich nach seiner Rehabilitierung unter der Last eines schweren Augenleidens.' usw. usw. Der Verfasser könnte noch vieles aus eigener Erfahrung beifügen, aber man wird das alles nach seinem Tode erfahren... (vgl. Anm. 90 [Dies alles sage ich aus eigener Erfahrung. Was ich z. B. persönlich in dieser Beziehung erlebt und zu ertragen habe, wird man erst nach meinem Tode erfahren. Dies wird eine wahre Anklage gegen die relativistischen unerhörten Kampfmethoden sein, welche nur mit der mittelalterlichen Inquisition verglichen werden können.])). Siehe auch [*Wilhelm Krampf : Die Philosophie Hugo Dinglers. München 1955.*] u. [A. FRITSCH, G. BARTH, S. MOHOROVIČIĆ: Hugo Dingler Gedenkbuch zum 75. Geburtstag. Wissen im Werden 2, H. 4, 169-183, 1958 (und als selbständige Broschüre München 1959).].

Dies wirkte aber verhängnisvoll und diese modernen Theorien wurden größtenteils ein Tätigkeitsfeld p o u r   c e u x   q u i   s a v e n t   v i v r e . . . oder wie ein lachender Philosoph sagte:

[*Endnote:* ∗ * ∗ Demokritos oder hinterlassene Papiere eines lachenden Philosophen. 4. Aufl. Bd. VII., Stuttgart 1853., S. 322.—Wir müßten ebenfalls mit JULIAN APOSTATA eine Rede gegen die ungebildeten... halten.—Siehe auch [*C l y d e R . M i l l e r : Kunstgriffe der Propaganda (Das Institut für Propaganda-Analyse d. Columbia University). Neue Auslese 3, 93-97; 1948 (übersetzt aus d. Jb. 'New Directions', New York).—Hier lesen wir folgendes (S. 96): 'Mit falschen Karten spielen ist ein Kunstgriff, bei dem der Propagandist alle Künste der Täuschung und des Truges anwendet, um unsere Unterstützung für sich selbst, seine G r u p p e ,   N a t i o n ,   R a s s e ,   P o l i t i k ,   M e t h o d e n und Ideale zu gewinnen. Er entstellt bewusst die Wahrheit. Er übertreibt oder 'untertreibt', um sich um Diskussionen zu drücken und den Tatsachen aus dem Weg zu gehen. Er 'vernebelt' eine peinlich Angelegenheit, indem er mit grossem Trara eine neue Streitfrage aufs Tapet bringt. E r   l i e f e r t   H a l b w a h r h e i t e n   u n t e r   d e r   M a s k e   d e r   W a h r h e i t   (v o n   u n s   u n t e r s t r i c h e n). Durch den Kunstgriff der 'falschen Karten' wird ein mittelmässiger Kandidat als ein Genie hingestellt; . . . Zu dieser Art von Falschspielerei gehören Täuschung, Heuchelei und*

Unverschämtheit'.]

'. . . an Höfen ist Höflichkeit der Verstand und die Münze. .
. .' „381

3.7 Einstein's Trip to America

Einstein was discredited in Germany in late 1920. In early 1921, Einstein desperately needed a boost and a break. Zionist Kurt Blumenfeld arranged for Einstein to take a trip to America in order to spread propaganda for political Zionism and to raise money for the cause, on the deceitful premise that the money would go to fund an university in Jerusalem, the "Jewish university"[382] or "Hebrew University". Einstein was deceived. The real goal of the Zionists who took advantage of him was to exploit Einstein's fame for profit.

Elements of the American press again promoted Einstein as the greatest genius of all time. For Jewish racists, this provided helpful racist propaganda claiming that all important contributions to the world of thought were made by Jews. The racist political Zionist United States Supreme Court Justice Louis Dembitz Brandeis wrote in a letter dated 1 March 1921,

"You have doubtless heard that the Great Einstein is coming to America soon with Dr. Weizmann, our Zionist Chief. Palestine may need something more now than a new conception of the Universe or of several additional dimensions; but it is well to remind the Gentile world, when the wave of anti-Semitism is rising, that in the world of thought the conspicuous contributions are being made by Jews."[383]

Viktor G. Ehrenberg, Hedwig Born's father, wrote to Einstein on 23 November 1919,

"So it uplifts the heart and strengthens one's faith in the future of mankind when one sees the researchers of all nations prostrating themselves before a man of Jewish blood, who thinks and writes in the German language, in full recognition of his greatness."[384]

Paul Ehrenfest wrote to Einstein that he had heard that the Zionists were using Einstein to promote the myth that he was a "Jewish Newton" and a Zionist. Ehrenfest was tortured by the fact that his character would not allow him to participate in the dishonest promotion of Einstein to the public. He believed it would ultimately be destructive to Jews. Ehrenfest committed suicide in 1933.

In 1905 and 1906, Paul Ehrenfest considered Lorentz' 1904 paper[385] on special relativity and Poincaré's 1905 Rendiconti paper[386] on space-time to be the most significant work (both historically and scientifically) on the subject of the principle of relativity. Ehrenfest and his wife Tatiana attended David Hilbert's 1905 Göttingen seminars on electron theory, which described Lorentz' and Poincaré's work on special relativity. They knew that Einstein did not create the theory of relativity. Paul Ehrenfest wrote to Albert Einstein on 9 December 1919,

"I hear, for ex., that your accomplishments are being used to make propaganda, with the 'Jewish Newton, who is simultaneously an ardent Zionist' (I personally haven't *read* this yet, but only *heard* it mentioned). [***] But I cannot go along with the propagandistic fuss with its *inevitable* untruths, precisely *because* Judaism is at stake and *because* I feel myself so thoroughly a Jew."[387]

Immediately upon his arrival at America's shores, Einstein mischaracterized any and all opposition to him and the theory of relativity as if it were anti-Semitism, *per se*.[388] After Einstein returned to Europe and after these Zionists bilked many generous Americans in the name of ethnic pride and duty, the promised funding of the university did not materialize. The nationalists allegedly could not agree on the final form this ethnically segregated school should take.[389] We learn from American Zionist Louis Dembitz Brandeis' letters that the University was nothing but a "side show",

"The University, important & dear to us, is merely a side show. It can wait. Nothing must be done in relation to it which would embarrass or confuse the main issue. It should be taken up—if and only if it would be helpful in furthering our fight on the main issue."[390]

And where did the money go, which good-hearted Americans had donated for a university? Again, Brandeis' letters provide us with some likely answers,

"In telling [Einstein] of the misappropriation of which we learned in London, I mentioned the diversion also of a University Fund & our apprehension as to further diversion."[391]

The editors of Brandeis' letters wrote,

"It was L[ouis] D[embitz] B[randeis]'s belief that the funds earmarked for the Hebrew University had been used for various projects in the Haifa area, and he wanted deHaas to provide whatever information they had on the matter to Einstein."[392]

Zionist racists set the tone for the racist "Aryan Physics" movement that would soon follow the political Zionists' smear campaigns against Germans, which followed centuries of active discrimination against Jews which was only then beginning to lessen, and so the cycle of hatred continued. These political Zionists had little respect for the truth or for the innocents they bilked. Einstein's "secretary" on the trip, Salomon Ginzberg, later wrote,

"It was also hoped that the University, being a non-political institution of great spiritual appeal, would find supporters among the wealthier non-Zionist Jews who might not contribute to Zionist funds proper."[393]

Salomon Ginzberg, a. k. a. Simon Ginsberg, was the son of the famous Zionist Ha'am. Ginzberg apparently thought that Einstein was a somewhat ridiculous person. Ginzberg mocked Einstein's "speech"—a Goebbels-like plea for ethnic unity behind a lone *Führer*.[394] Einstein declared to the Zionists of America,

"You have one leader — Weizmann. Follow him and no other!"[395]

Jewish lore had long inspired a desire among Jews for a charismatic leader, be it another Moses, or the Messiah King. In the 1600 and 1700's many would-be messiahs appeared and some, like Shabbatai Zevi and Jacob Frank, attracted large followings numbering in the millions. Graetz famously called for a charismatic leader to the lead the Jews in the modern world. On the Zionists' quest to find a "great man" to be their "dictator" and on the naturalness of dictatorships to Zionists, *see:* N. Goldman, "Zionismus und nationale Bewegung", *Der Jude*, Volume

5, Number 4, (1920-1921), pp. 237-242, at 240-242; which was part of a series including: "Zionismus und nationale Bewegung", *Der Jude*, Volume 5, Number 1, (1920-1921), pp. 45-47; and "Zionismus und nationale Bewegung", *Der Jude*, Volume 5, Number 7, (1920-1921), pp. 423-425.

When Albert Einstein traveled to America in April of 1921 to promote his Zionist agenda he had received a triumphant welcome, but soon met with great and growing opposition. Einstein was lampooned and humiliated in certain segments of the international press. Einstein left America in defeat. He expressed his bitterness towards America in an interview for the *Nieuwe Rotterdamsche Courant*. Einstein stated, as reported in *The New York Times* on 8 July 1921 on page 9,

"BERLIN, July 7.—Dr. Albert Einstein, the famous scientist, made an amazing discovery relative to America on his trip which he recently explained to a sympathetic-looking Hollander as follows:

'The excessive enthusiasm for me in America appears to be typically American. And if I grasp it correctly the reason is that the people in America are so colossally bored, very much more than is the case with us. After all, there is so little for them there!' he exclaimed.

Dr. Einstein said this with vibrant sympathy. He continued:

'New York, Boston, Chicago and other cities have their theatres and concerts, but for the rest? There are cities with 1,000,000 inhabitants, despite which what poverty, intellectual poverty! The people are, therefore, glad when something is given them with which they can play and over which they can enthuse. And that they do, then, with monstrous intensity.

'Above all things are the women who, as a literal fact, dominate the entire life in America. The men take an interest in absolutely nothing at all. They work and work, the like of which I have never seen anywhere yet. For the rest they are the toy dogs of the women, who spend the money in a most unmeasurable, illimitable way and wrap themselves in a fog of extravagance. They do everything which is the vogue and now quite by chance they have thrown themselves on the Einstein fashion.

'You ask whether it makes a ludicrous impression on me to observe the excitement of the crowd for my teaching and my theory, of which it, after all, understands nothing? I find it funny and at the same time interesting to observe this game.

'I believe quite positively that it is the mysteriousness of what they cannot conceive which places them under a magic spell. One tells them of something big which will influence all future life, of a theory which only a small group, highly learned, can comprehend. Big names are mentioned of men who have made discoveries, of which the crowd grasps nothing. But it impresses them, takes on color and the magic power of mystery, and thus one becomes enthusiastic and excited.

'My impressions of scientific life in America? Well, I met with great interest several extraordinarily meritorious professors, like Professor Milliken [sic]. I unfortunately missed Professor Michelson in Chicago, but to compare the general scientific life in America with Europe is nonsense.'"[396]

This is but a part of a longer polemic interview, in which Einstein also smeared all Germans as corrupt. Einstein repeated some of what Gehrcke had said, though Einstein had called Gehrcke "anti-Semitic" for saying the same thing. The full interview of 29 June 1921 is reproduced in Dutch and English, together with an interpretation initially published in German in the *Berliner Tageblatt* on 7 July 1921, in *The Collected Papers of Albert Einstein*, Volume 7, Appendix D, (2002), pp. 620-627.

Einstein's comments met with much criticism and a damage control apparatus quickly began to repair the harm he had done to his reputation, by denying that he had said what he had said.[397] Some Americans stepped forward to say, "I told you so!" *The Minneapolis Evening Tribune* wrote on 8 July 1921,

"Einstein Has No Valid Cause to Congratulate Self, Reuterdahl Says

In Calling Americans 'Lot of Bored Low Brows,' He Forgets the Ungullible.

Makes No Mention of Terrific Lampooning He Received at Hands of His Critics.

Professor Albert Einstein's lofty conception of the American people as a lot of bored lowbrows who couldn't find intellectual amusement elsewhere and so turned to his theory of relativity without understanding it, drew a sharp rejoinder today from Prof. Arvid Reuterdahl, dean of the department of engineering and architecture at St. Thomas college. The remarks by the scientist whose recent visit to the United States attracted nation-wide attention, were cabled last night from Berlin.

'Doctor Einstein has omitted all reference to the terrific lampooning to which he was subjected by the Eastern newspapers during the last week of his sojourn with us,' Professor Reuterdahl remarked. 'He has no valid reason to congratulate himself while smiling at the unsophistication and gullibility of the American people.

Einstein Appeared Amused.

'The radio dispatch from Berlin, which appeared in The Minneapolis Morning Tribune today, conveys the impression that Doctor Einstein was greatly amused by his recent reception in the United States,' he continued. 'He attributes the exaggerated enthusiasm shown him to the fact that our people are bored. In that connection he points out that we have theaters to alleviate the weariness of our dull existence but he intimates that we, nevertheless, welcome new thrills. His remarks indicate that he believes that he furnished us with a new 'thrill,' which accounts for the alleged enthusiasm.

'Professor Einstein found this attitude very comical and consequently confirmative of his pre-established conviction that Americans are lacking in intelligence. However, Doctor Einstein did not hesitate to come to our shores in order to lend zest to the financial campaign of the Zionists, who do not underestimate the advertising value of an international celebrity. This remark is not intended to be derogatory to the Zionist movement, which, undoubtedly is a worthy cause. Nevertheless, we cannot avoid feeling like a man who, having been outwitted in a trade, must remain impassive while the victor laughs at him.

Entire Tale Untold.

'Dr. Einstein, however, has not told the entire tale. He has adroitly omitted all reference to the terrific lampooning to which he was subjected by the eastern newspapers during the last week of his sojourn with us. Never before has a man been subjected to such colossal ridicule. He was even likened to the notorious Dr. Cook and Friedmann.

'Mr. Nelson Robbins, in the Baltimore Evening Sun, April 29, 1921, says: 'But the proletariat having forgotten Friedmann and his unexplainable discoveries, it hasn't forgotten a host of men like him. Remembering them, the proletariat will be ding-busted if it will swear allegiance to any idea that it cannot understand and which is labeled unexplainable by the 'mentally equipped,' who tap the individual inquirer on the head and, with kindly smile, tell him to run along and not bother his little brain about things he cannot understand.'

'Dr. Einstein, therefore, has no valid reason to congratulate himself enthusiastically while smiling outwardly at the unsophistication and gullibility of the American people.'"

Einstein's feigned amusement is belied by his bitterness at being mocked in America. Contrast Einstein's later remarks, after he had left America, with an interview he gave to *The New York Times* while in America, which was published in *The New York Times Book Review and Magazine* on 1 May 1921 on page 50. In this interview Einstein appears as an especially odd and childlike man, who had wondered from his script. On 15 March 1921, Zionist Kurt Blumenfeld had warned Zionist Chaim Weizmann that it would be unwise to let Einstein make speeches during his trip to America, "Einstein is a poor speaker and often says things out of naiveté that are unwelcome to us[.]"[398] The "secretary" who broke into the conversation during the interview was the son of Zionist Ha'am, Salomon Ginzberg. Many of Einstein's comments are reminiscent of the spirit of Zionist Israel Zangwill's play *The Melting-Pot: Drama in Four Acts*, Macmillan, New York, (1909); and Einstein may have been encouraged to promote the melting-pot idea in order to promote the immigration of Eastern European Jews to America. Einstein's interview:

"Einstein on Irrelevancies
By DON ARNALD

How comfortable you make everything in the hotel! Every door, every window, is perfect; nothing is out of order. It is all so well planned and well organized. I never saw such rooms; such care for details; such hotel lobbies, with so many to serve you. Everything—everything is systematized, down to the bathrooms. You people in America are very practical. I like the way you light up the windows with the signs. I like the cheerful way you arrange the electricity up and down the streets.'

So spoke Professor Albert Einstein, apostle of relativity, in the course of a talk about his experiences in New York.

'What was it that impressed you most when you arrived?' the interviewer asked.

'Ah! I see so many nationalities living together so well. America is a country of many different peoples at peace with one another. Then, too, I like the restaurants with the 'color' of the nations in the air. Each has its own atmosphere. It is like a zoological garden of nationalities, when you go from one to the other.

'Are you a bit disappointed not to find some beer in our dining rooms?'

'I cannot say alcohol is as bad as people think it is,' replied the professor. 'It may not be so good for men to spend all their wages on drinking. But it is more an economic question than a question of health. Some workmen must have liquor, it seems. We must not take everything away. Prohibition shows the strength of your democratic Government against private interests. In a corrupt State this could not be done.'

'Do you consider it against personal liberty to take liquor away?'

'How could that be in America? You have a republic. You have no dictator who makes slaves of people. Nothing is done by a democratic Government could be done against freedom. I think you will find it best for the economic welfare of the people in the end.'

'How about tobacco?' was the next question. 'Some people want to take that away, too.'

Dr. Einstein drew back in surprise. 'Oh, my, no! I never heard of it. So some one is starting this? Who is doing this?'

'Some temperance organization here in the United States.'

The professor said: 'If I do not wish to smoke, I say it is

excellent to take my tobacco away. But I do wish to smoke, so I say I do not like you to do that.'

'But they say it is not healthful.'

'If you take our tobacco and everything else away, what have you left?' cried Professor Einstein. 'It may be healthful to take away tobacco, but it is mighty lonesome.' He thought a moment. 'But this is economic, too,' he said at last. 'The men spend too much money on cigars, and their wives kick; therefore, they take it way. They say it costs too much money to smoke. I do not know! I have never heard of such a thing as taking away a man's smoking! I'll stick to my pipe. I do not care who will not smoke. I will! If you take everything away, life is not worth while!'

'And the blue laws—how about them?'

'Blue laws? Blue laws? I never heard of those blue laws in my life. What are you saying?' The professor fairly blazed with consternation.

'They want to pass laws to close up all places of amusement on Sunday,' the interviewer explained. 'All theatres, music shows, baseball and other places will be shut down, including everything for relaxation, even amusement parks and the movies.'

'For Heaven's sake. More laws? I never heard of such a thing. Here's what I say: Men must have rest, yes? But what is the right rest? You cannot make a law to tell people how to do it. See—some people have rest when they lie down and go to sleep. Others have rest when they are wide awake and are stimulated. They must work or write or go to amusements to find rest. If you pass one law to show all people how to rest, that means you make everybody alike. But everybody is not alike. No, I do not care for these blue laws. They will do no good for the country or the people.

'Many workmen want to go to movies on Sunday because they have no time during the week days, so they find rest there,' he continued. 'And that is very good.'

'What do you think of our movies and the theatres?'

'I've been so busy that I haven't had much time, but I have never in my life seen such theatres—everything for your taste, all sorts of plays, comedy, tragedy, romance, pageants. And the movies? I am enthusiastic about them—I mean for the presentation of living moving things. They will develop more and more. In general, the pictures shown now are not so artistic, but they will get better, very much better, all the time. The art is not high enough now, but soon you will have science through this art, as well as you are now having art through this science. I see how the movies will be used in the future for science in bacteriology and technology. Perhaps not so soon for astronomy, because the motions of the heavenly bodies are too quick for measurement. But the movies must only be fitted well, and they can be used most adequately for instruction in all science! I think, all in all, the movies are only in their infancy. They are very beautiful, but they will get better, until the best plays can be shown. You deserve much credit for doing such fine pictures. I compliment you, and I hope for more artistic plays right along.'

At this point his wife, a charming little gray-haired lady, slipped into the room and sat by her husband's side.

'Maybe I can help you,' she said kindly. 'I speak English, and I can interpret for him.' The interview up to that point had been in German.

'Perhaps you can tell me something about the professor's life,' I asked. Dr. Einstein laughed heartily.

'He does not want my life,' said he. 'That is of no use to him. Why should he care for that. He is asking what I think of New York. I tell him glorious! I tell him I see here the greatest city in the world, like Paris, like London, only better! I tell him here all people of all nationalities are melted together—and are happy. I tell him the stranger comes here and is full of joy because he goes to his people at once and feels at home.'

'But your book on relativity translated into English, maybe he wants that,' queried Mrs. Einstein.

'No, why that?' said the professor. 'He doesn't come here for relativity. He comes here to see me. I want to say something to the people, how I like the restaurants and the theatres and the movies and the hotels, and how I do not like the blue laws—and if they take away my tobacco—I do not know what I'll do, but I'll take America anyway, no matter what they do.'

At this the secretary arrived. He wanted to add a word on the professor's mission in America. He said:

'I suppose you know Professor Einstein is here to help the University of Palestine. Its foundation stone was laid by Dr. Weizmann in 1918, and since then the university site has been expanded. There is also a library with more than 3,000 volumes and rapidly growing. Plans have been worked out both for the complete university of the future and for a comparatively modest beginning. The time has now come for us to make a foundation fund, part of which will go to the university. American people play a great part in world politics, showing that their aspirations are noble, and we have come from sick and suffering Europe with feelings of hope, convinced that our spiritual aims will command the full sympathy of the American Nation.'

Dr. Einstein broke in: 'We will receive their enthusiastic approval, we are sure, but the people know all this. This gentleman asks me other things, and I tell him what I think of New York.'

He slapped me on the back and added: 'You greet for me all the good people of America and you say, 'I feel at home here among people, many different people from all the nations in the world.'''

3.7.1 Einstein Hides from Reuterdahl's Challenge to Debate

Though Einstein had hoped to run away from his critics, he had an international reputation as a coward, a plagiarist and a scientific fraud. Things were not as easy for Einstein in America as he had hoped they would be. On 10 April 1921, *The Minneapolis Sunday Tribune* reported Prof. Arvid Reuterdahl's charges against Einstein,

"Einstein Branded Barnum of Science, Minnesota Man Calls Relativity 'Bunk'

St. Thomas Dean of Engineering Challenges German to Debate.

Teuton's Pet 'Cult' Born 13 Years Before Him, Says Professor.

Reuterdahl Cites Passages in 1914 Treatise to Back Assertions.

Branding Prof. Albert Einstein as a sophist, a dealer in 'might-have-beens' and the Barnum of the scientific world, Prof. Arvid Reuterdahl, dean of the Engineering school of St. Thomas

College, St. Paul, yesterday challenged the German savant to a written debate on his theory of relativity.

Professor Reuterdahl, who has been exploring the worlds conquered by Einstein since 1902, declared that he was willing to meet the much-heralded mathematician at any time in a written debate, and that he was prepared to prove that Einstein's theory is largely 'bunk.' Professor Reuterdahl used the scientific word for it, but that is what he meant.

'Work Antedated by Another.'

Coupled with his challenge to a debate, Professor Reuterdahl declared Einstein was not only deceiving scientists with a mythical theory, but that he was either a plagiarist, or his work has been antedated by another without his knowledge.

'Einstein is at liberty to accept either horn of the dilemma,' he said.

That the Einstein theory of relativity in its gravitational aspects was advanced in 1866, 13 years before Einstein was born, by a scientist known under the pen name of 'Kinertia' is the contention of Professor Reuterdahl, in a statement in which he gives the life history of both men, and gives references and dates to prove his charge. While not accepting the theory, he gives 'Kinertia' credit for its origin.

American Scientists 'Jolted.'

Professor Reuterdahl, however, gives credit to Einstein for one thing, which, he says, more than justifies his claim to prominence. The German savant, he says, has broken down the barriers of set ideas in science, and made it possible for a hearing for new ideas.

'The American scientists,' said Professor Reuterdahl, 'are the most clannish and orthdox in the world. In the Old World the scientific journals publish articles advancing new theories. Here they will not consider anything except that which is based on their own knowledge and belief. If Einstein has done anything, he has jolted American scientists into accepting something new.' Professor Reuterdahl paid tribute to Einstein's genius as a mathematician, declaring him to be one of the greatest in the world.

Magazine Articles Cited.

Professor Reuterdahl refers to 11 articles which appeared in Harper's Weekly in 1914 giving 'Kinertia' credit for originating the so-called Einstein theory of gravitation.

'If it is true that 'Kinertia' actually considered the Einsteinian problem in these essays,' he says, 'then the question of priority is inevitably raised and the unparalleled originality claimed for Einstein's work becomes a debatable matter.'

Einstein's investigation of his theory is traced by articles which appeared in German publications.

'The year 1905 is considered, by most authorities on Einstein's work,' he says, 'as the birth year of the theory of relativity.

Theory Announced in 1915.

'Careful search, however, has revealed a paper on this subject which was published in Berlin during the year 1904 in the journal 'Sitzungsberichte.' That portion of Einstein's theory which deals with the phenomenon of gravitation is a later development. Einstein first gave his attention to the problem of gravitation in 1911, when he developed the principle of equivalence of gravitational and accelerative fields.

'Other phases of this subject were dealt with in papers which appeared in the years 1912 and 1913. A further elaboration, the joint work of Einstein and Marcel Grossman, appeared in 1914. The theory in its final and complete form was announced in the year 1915.

Historical Summary.

'A brief historical summary of the work of 'Kinertia' is now in order. Lord Kelvin first aroused 'Kinertia's' interest in the problem of gravitation. That was in the year 1866, when 'Kinertia' was a student under Lord Kelvin. 'Kinertia' even then did not agree with the Newtonian theory of force as presented by Lord Kelvin. Incidentally, we desire to call the reader's attention to the fact that Albert Einstein was born in 1879 in Ulm, Germany, 13 years later.

'During the period from 1877 to 1881, 'Kinertia' became convinced that acceleration was the basic cause of what we generally speak of as 'weight.'

'Kinertia' Ridiculed in U. S.

'The reader undoubtedly is aware of the fact that acceleration plays the fundamental role in Einstein's theory of gravitation. 'Kinertia' corresponded with Kelvin, Tait and Niven of Cambridge with the hope that he would be able to interest these men in his startling theory. This attempt met with little or no sympathy.

'His attempts, dating from the year 1899, to persuade our stubborn American scientists that the Newtonian theory of gravitation must be revised met with nothing but ridicule and indifference. To Harper's Weekly and its managing editor, Mr H. D. Wheeler, belongs the credit of having published 'Kinertia's' series of articles entitled 'Do Bodies Fall?' The first article appeared in the issue of August 29, 1914, Vol. 59.

Similarity of Views Pointed Out.

The final article is dated November 7, 1914. From the preceding it is evident that 'Kinertia' derived his norm of gravitation before Einstein was born.

Professor Reuterdahl quotes from the writing of Einstein and 'Kinertia' to prove the similarity of their views, and says:

'It is noteworthy that the only real difference between these two citations is that Einstein derives his conclusions from a hypothetical case, whereas 'Kinertia' draws his conclusions from an actual experiment upon himself.'

Further quotations are from Prof. A. S. Eddington's 'Space Time Gravitation,' published by the Cambridge University Press in 1920; from an article by Prof. Edwin B. Wilson of the Massachusetts Institute of Technology, and from 'Kinertia's' articles.

Striking Similarity.

These quotations, he says. 'show the striking similarity existing between Einstein and 'Kinertia' when they consider the relation between acceleration and gravitation, a similarity which extends not only to intent but affects even the very words.'

The following quotation from Einstein's 'Relatively' illustrates that scientist's theory as to the relation between acceleration and gravitation, according to Professor Reuterdahl:

'We imagine a large portion of empty space, so far removed from stars and other appreciable masses that we have before us aproximately the conditions required by the fundamental law of Galilei.

Hypothetical Example.

As reference body let us imagine a spacious chest resembling a room with an observer inside who is equipped with apparatus. Gravitation naturally does not exist for this observer. He must fasten himself with strings to the floor, otherwise the slightest impact against the floor will cause him to rise slowly toward the ceiling of the room.

'To the middle of the lid of the chest is fixed externally a hook with rope attached, and now a 'being' (what kind of a 'being' is immaterial to us) begins pulling at this with a constant force. The chest, together with the observer, then begins to move upwards with a uniformly accelerated motion. In course of time their velocity will reach unheard of values, provided that we are viewing all this from another reference body which is not being pulled with a rope.

Viewpoint of Man in Chest.

'But how does the man in the chest regard the process? The acceleration of the chest will be transmitted to him by the reaction of the floor of the chest. He must therefore take up this pressure by means of his legs if he does not wish to be laid out full length on the floor. He is then standing in the chest in exactly the same way as anyone stands in a room of a house on our earth. If he releases a body which he previously had in his hand, the acceleration of the chest will no longer be transmitted to this body, and for this reason the body will approach the floor of the chest with an accelerated motion.

The observer will further convince himself that the acceleration of the body towards the floor of the chest is always of the same magnitude, whatever kind of body he may happen to use for the experiment.'

'Kinertia' Quoted.

'Kinertia's' theory of the relation between acceleration and gravitation is set forth in the following quotation from 'Do Bodies Fall?' and is used by Professor Reuterdahl in building up his argument:

'I set to work to find out by experiment whether bodies actually did fall with the acceleration which the force of attraction was said to produce. Years before that, when in England, where some of our coal mines had vertical shafts about 1,500 feet deep, I had studied the cause of weight by having the hoisting engine drop me down with the full acceleration for about 500 feet. Then, by retardation during the lowest 500 feet, I could experience increase of weight all over me so marked that my legs could hardly support me.

Weight Not a Force.

'That taught me that acceleration was the proximate cause of weight, but at the time of these experiments I still thought the acceleration of the falling cage was really caused by the earth's attraction.

'Weight is not a kinetic force because it cannot produce acceleration. If a body were accelerated in proportion to its weight, then weight would be a force.'

'Laying aside the right of Einstein to claim originality for his theory,' said Professor Reuterdahl yesterday, 'he is a sophist, and the world will know him as such in due time. He is dealing with mythical beings. They are 'might-have-beens.'

'His fourth dimension is a composite of time and space. That cannot be, because time and space never can be one. Space may be referred to as the distance between two points, A and B. We may travel from A and B, and return to find the same permanent objects in their places. We may require a certain amount of time to make the journey, but when we turn back that time is gone.

'I demand that Einstein show me his proof. I believe in dealing in the physical things of this world. In other words, I am from Missouri. I shall be glad to meet Professor Einstein at any time or place and debate this subject. But I shall demand an actual demonstration of his theory, not a journey into the realm of the mythical. That demonstration he can never give.'"

The story of Reuterdahl's challenge to Einstein was covered by newspapers around the world. *The New York Times* reported on 10 April 1921,

"CHALLENGES PROF. EINSTEIN

St. Paul Professor Asserts Relativity Theory Was Advanced in 1866.

Special to The New York Times.

MINNEAPOLIS, April 9.—Professor Arvid Deuterdahl, Dean of the College of Engineering of St. Thomas College, St. Paul, yesterday challenged Prof. Albert Einstein to a written debate on his theory of relativity.

That the Einstein theory was advanced in 1866, thirteen years before he was born, by a scientist known under the pen name of 'Kinertia,' is the contention of Professor Reuterdahl, in a statement in which he gives the life history of both men, and gives references and dates to support his contention.

Professor Reuterdahl, however, says the fact that Professor Einstein has broken down the barriers of set ideas in science and made it possible for a hearing for new ideas more than justifies his claim to prominence.

'The American scientists,' said Professor Reuterdahl, 'are the most clannish, I should say the most pig-headed, in the world. In the Old World the scientific journals publish articles advancing new theories. Here they will not accept anything that is not based on their own knowledge and belief. If Einstein has done anything he has jolted American scientists into accepting something new.'

Professor Reuterdahl refers to eleven articles which appeared in Harper's Weekly in 1914, in giving 'Kinertia' credit for originating the Einstein theory.

'Kinertia,' Professor Reuterdahl says, is the nom de plume of a professor believed to be living in California now."

The Chicago Tribune (European Edition, Paris) reported on 11 April 1921,

"AMERICAN CALLS EINSTEIN 'BARNUM'

(Special Cable to **The Tribune.**)
MINNEAPOLIS, April 10.—Professor Arvid Reuterdahl, dean of the college of engineers at St. Thomas college, has styled Dr. Einstein, discoverer of the theory of relativity, 'the Barnum of the scientific world' and challenges him to a written debate on his theory.

Dr. Reuterdahl asserted that Einstein is not only 'fooling scientists with his mystical theory' but is a plagiarist. He declares the 'Einstein theory' was advanced in 1866 by a scientist under the pen name of 'Inertia.'"

On 11 April 1921, The Sun of New York reported,

"Challenges Einstein, Calls Him Plagiarist

MINNEAPOLIS, April 11. — Not only has Einstein's theory of relativity been challenged but the scientist himself has been charged with being a plagiarist and the 'Barnum of Science' by Prof. Arvid Reuterdahl, dean of the Engineering School of St. Thomas's College, St. Paul. He has issued a challenge to the German scientist to meet him in a written debate.

The gravitational aspects of the Einstein theory were presented in 1866 in *Harper's Weekly* by a writer who called himself 'Kinertia,' Prof. Reuterdahl asserts. But the professor does give Prof. Einstein credit for blazing a new trail in thought for American scientists whom Dr. Reuterdahl declares to be more orthodox than European scientists."

On 11 April 1921, the *New York American* wrote,

"EINSTEIN CHARGED WITH PLAGIARISM

St. Paul Educator Says Theory of Relativity Was Advanced in Harper's Weekly in 1866.

Special Dispatch to the New York American.

MINNEAPOLIS, April 10.—That the Albert Einstein theory of relativity in its gravitational aspects was advanced in 1866, thirteen years before Einstein was born, by a scientist known under pen name of 'Kinertia' was the assertion made to-day by Professor Arvid Reuterdahl, dean of the engineering school of St. Thomas College in St. Paul. He challenged the German savant to defend his theories in a written debate.

Professor Reuterdahl declared Einstein was not only deceiving scientists with a mythical theory, but that he was either a plagiarist or his work had been antedated by another without his knowledge.

He then cited 'Kinertia,' whose theory was expounded in eleven articles running in Harper's Weekly in 1914, according to Professor Reuterdahl. These give 'Kinertia' credit for the so-called Einstein theory of gravitation, which is a later development of the theory of relativity.

The theory of relativity itself, says Einstein's challenger, was made public exactly one year before authorities on Einstein's work credit him with having made the discovery. In 1904, says Professor Reuterdahl, there was a paper on this subject, published in Berlin in the Journal Sitzungsberichte."

On 12 April 1921, the *New York American* reported,

"EINSTEIN REFUSES TO DEBATE THEORY

Dean Reuterdahl's Challenge to Discuss Relativity Declined as Detraction from Mission.

Dr. Albert Einstein was interviewed yesterday in his headquarters at the Hotel Commodore regarding the attack on his theory of relativity made by Dean Arvid Renterdahl, of St. Thomas College, St. Paul, Minn.

Dr. Einstein smilingly listened to newspaper accounts of the Reuterdahl attack. Through his secretary he said:

'I came here with one object—the promotion of the establishment of the Hebrew University in Jerusalem. I will not be led into a discussion of my theory with persons who may not understand. There may be some personal intent in the remarks of this gentleman, whom I have not the honor of knowing.

'The great purpose of my mission to this country must not be overshadowed by my theory. I will be here a short time, and all of that time must be devoted to the great Palestine reconstruction project.

'I have consented to deliver a few lectures, but beyond that I do not wish to encroach upon my limited time. It must be seen plainly that I cannot enter into newspaper discussions with persons who doubt or misunderstand my theories or question my integrity.

'I have not had the opportunity to look into this challenge to debate issued by Dean Reuterdahl. Being without knowledge of the person called 'Kinertia' who is said to have written on the subject, I am not prepared to express any opinion.

It was further said for Dr. Einstein that he had no desire to popularize his theory of relativity; that he had writ- [*Unfortunately your author's photocopy of this article lacks the remainder.*]"

Segments of the press came to Einstein's defense. The *World* of New York wrote on 12 April 1921, quoting Einstein,

"EINSTEIN AMUSED BY A NEW ATTACK

'Being Called P. T. Barnum of
Scientific World Only What
I Get at Home.'

DECLINES REUTERDAHL'S CHALLENGE TO A DEBATE.

He, Prof. Weizmann and Others
to Be Guests at Jewish
Mass Meeting To-Night.

Prof. Albert Einstein was not greatly disturbed yesterday when he learned that Prof. Arvid Reuterdahl, dean of the engineering school of St. Thomas College, St. Paul, Minn., had called him the 'P. T. Barnum of the scientific world.' In fact, Prof. Einstein was amused.

'It reminds me of home,' he said, 'In Germany I am quite accustomed to being called names by persons who disagree with me.'

Prof. Einstein said he had never heard of Prof. Reuterdahl and that he was not in the least interested in the latter's challenge to a written debate on the subject of relativity. He intimated that he might read an article written by Prof. Reuterdahl if he happened to come across it, but as for entering a controversy, he couldn't waste the time.

The professor's mail is flooded with letters from persons who have pet theories which they wish to put before him, or who wish to argue on the subject of relativity. Several letters have been received from 'Messiahs' with plans for leading the Jews back to Palestine.

Prof. Chaim Weizmann, President of the World Zionist Organization, Prof. Einstein, M. M. Ussishkin, Chairman of the Zionist Commission to Palestine, Dr. Ben Zion Mosesohn, Principal of the Hebrew High School in Jaffe, and Dr. Schmaya Levine, member of the International Zionist Committee, will be the principal guests at an all-Jewish mass meeting to-night in the 69th Regiment Armory, 25th Street and Lexington Avenue. This reception is in charge of a committee of 100, representing more than 1,800 local Jewish organizations of every variety and type.

Senator Calder and Dr. Butler, President of Columbia University, will be the principal speakers. In addition there will be addresses by prominent Jewish leaders representing the various elements in Jewry. Morris Rothenberg will welcome the guests in behalf of the American Jewish Congress.

Tickets are free and the seats will be reserved for ticket holders until 8 P. M., and after that all the seats will be thrown open to the public. Reservations have been made for a large delegation of Jewish wounded veterans of the World War. They will be brought from the nearby hospitals under an escort of Jewish legionnaires who fought in Palestine under Gen. Allenby."

3.7.2 Cowardly Einstein Caught in a Lie

Einstein hypocritically called his critics name-callers, when in fact Einstein had been recklessly defaming his critics for years, and had encouraged others to not respond to criticism of relativity theory other than by way of personal attack. The newspaper tried to deflect attention away from Einstein's evasiveness, but their story also unwittingly revealed that Albert Einstein was dishonest. E. Lee Heidenreich wrote in the *Minneapolis Morning Tribune*, on 16 May 1921,

"Calls Einstein's Statements Irreconcilable.

To the Editor of The Tribune:
The scientific world has lately been much entertained and somewhat mystified by the increasing doubts, which have gradually crept into the press, regarding both the authenticity and the reliability of Professor Einsteins much-vaunted theory of relativity.

Professor Arvid Reuterdahl of St. Thomas college has challenged Professor Einstein to a written debate on the latter's theory, but has so far only been met with more or less evasive statements by Professor Einstein, some of which appear to the writer simply irreconcilable.

Thus, the New York World of April 12, 1921, says: 'Professor Einstein said he never heard of Professor Reuterdahl, and that he was not in the least interested in the latter's challenge to a written debate on the subject of relativity. He intimated that he might read an article written by Professor Reuterdahl, if he happened to come across it, but as for entering a controversy, he could not waste his time.'

The writer spent four months in Norway in 1920, and took occasion to give to 'Aftenposten' in Christiania a brief synopsis of Professor Reuterdahl's theory of interdependence, containing also considerable adverse criticism of both the authenticity and reliability of Professor Einstein's theory of relativity. The latter at that time was in Christiania, where he gave a lecture on his relativity.

'Aftenposten,' Christiania, of June 18, 1920, says: 'But what does Professor Einstein say to this? It would be interesting to know whether he is acquainted with the product of Professor Reuterdahl's pen. 'No,' answers Professor Einstein at our question, 'I do not know the name of Professor Reuterdahl and have never heard mentioned that he is said to have worked on the theory of relativity. I have often corresponded with Professor Mittag-Leffler, but he never mentioned any such work'.'

And later, in the same interview, Professor Einstein continues: 'Ein rechter mensch (a man of justice) would not have made the public announcement which Professor Reuterdahl has made through the American press.'

During the 'frequent correspondence' between Professor Mittag-Leffler and Professor Einstein, the original manuscript by Professor Reuterdahl of his space-time potential remained in the hands of Professor Mittag-Leffler for about four years, sometime between 1914 and 1918, and we have to take Professor Einstein's word for it that no discussion of the space-time potential took place during this 'frequent correspondence'—it would not have mattered much—except for the peculiar fact that Professor Einstein so carefully disclaims any notice of Reuterdahl's existence.

In spite of this, on the 12th day of April, 1921, Professor Einstein, in an interview, stated that 'he had never heard of Professor Reuterdahl.'

One might ask why the professor is afraid of admitting that he has heard of Reuterdahl? Does a ghost of a MS held by Mittag-Leffler lurk around somewhere? Have we here a sword of Damocles?

Professor Einstein denies that he has heard of Reuterdahl on April 12, 1921, in New York World, whereas he did hear of him and discussed his statements in Christiana to Aftenposten June 18, 1920, nearly a year earlier!

Either his memory has slipped away into the four dimensional space-time continuum, or for some reason he misrepresents facts.

As one of the remaining champions of materialistic and atheistic science, why does not the professor bravely come forth to defend the moss-grown theories against the onslaught of Scientific theism, and valiantly charge into the shrinking form of his adversary, right in the arena of the public eye? Does it behoove a world acclaimed scientist, a giant of mathematics, to say: 'My arguments you will not understand, I cast not my pearls before swine.'

It reminds one of the old fairy tale by H. C. Anderson, 'The Emperor's New Clothes,' which were so intricately and fearfully spun that they could not be seen by persons who were not wise, or who could not properly serve his majesty—and thus the visibility of the emperor's new clothes became a criterion of intellect of his subjects—only to have the bubble pricked by an unsophisticated street gamin, who cried out in astonishment: 'But the emperor is stark naked!'—tableau!

If someone has said that only seven, or was it twelve, men in the whole world would understand Einstein's theory of relativity, he should add 'as Einstein dresses it'—for relativity with common sense and logic instead of a lot of sophistic embellishments is not such a formidable study.

The writer was amazed at the spectacular ascendancy of Professor Einstein in the public view and the acquiescent attitude of a seemingly bewildered lot of scientific institutions—an attitude almost similar to the impulsive reception of Dr. Cook of North Pole fame.

When the reaction comes, when Professor Einstein has left the United States, covered with decorations, the professor probably will realize that it were better had he met the questions squarely in the spirit in which they were made, because they now will stand as though cut in granite: Relativity or Interdependence? And must sooner or later be met without beating the devil around a bush with evasive and irreconcilable statements.—E. Lee Heidenreich, Kansas City, Mo."

As Heidenreich had affirmed, the *Aftenposten* of Oslo, Norway wrote on 18 June 1920,

"Diskussionen om relativitetstheorien.

En amerikansk professor, som gjør krav paa at være theoriens skaber.

En udtalelse af professor Einstein.

Vi har liggende foran os et eksemplar af den amerikanske avis »St. Paul Sunday Pioneer Press«, som udkommer i St. Paul, Minnesota. Numeret er dateret 1ste februar 1920 og indeholder bl. a. en længere artikel om relativitetstheorien. Bladet giver en fremstilling af det arbeide, som den amerikanske professor Arvid R e u t e r d a h l har nedlagt til udforskning af den saa meget omtalte relativitetstheori. Det dreier sig om en meget mystisk affære, idet det heder, at professor Reuterdahl saa tidlig som i 1902 har skapt theorien, men paa en lidt usandsynlig maade er hans manuskript kommet paa afveie. Hvordan? Jo, historien lyder som følgende i »St. Pauls Pioneer«:

Professor Einstein offentliggjorde sin teori i »Annalen der Physik« for 1905. Reuterdahl foredrog sin theori den 5te april 1902 i »The American Elektrochemical society« ved dets aabningstnøde i Philadelphia. Udviklingen af theorien beskjæftigede ham helt til 1914, da han var færdig med udarbeidelsen. Hans theori vakte straks stor interesse og i februar

1915 gav han forelæsninger over sin theori ved Kansas State Agricultural College og senere ved Kansas universitet.

Den 19de februar 1915 blev professor Reuterdahls manuskript sendt til Norge, hvor det var meningen, at redaktør O p p e d a l skulde offentliggøre det i »Verdens Gang«. Redaktør Oppedal refererede professor Reuterdahls arbeide til professor S t ø r m e r; men presserende arbeide hindrede en undersøgelse og overveielse. Det blev saa refereret for professor M i t t a g - L e f f l e r i Stockholm. Her mister man ethvert spor af manuskriptet.

Albert Einstein er nu medlem af en tysk videnskabelig kommission. Hans sidste arbeide hader »Time, Space and Gravitation«. Reuterdahls manuskript bærer titelen »Space, Time Potential, a new concept of Gravitation and Electricity«. Postprotokoller viser, at manuskriptet var et sted i Europa i hænde hos en tysk professor i begyndelsen af 1915.

Professor Reuterdahl har nu under udarbeidelse en ny bog om sin theori og denne bog vil blive hans livsverk.

Saavidt vor amerikanske kilde. Alle de forsøg vi har sat igang for at finde sporet efter det forsvundne manuskript er mislykket og nogen berettiget mening om den mystiske affæres vitterlighed skal vi ikke driste os til at have.

Men hvad siger professor Einstein til dette. Det vilde have sin interesse at vide, om han kjender professor Reuterdahls arbeider. »Nei«, svarer professor Einstein paa vor forespørgsel. »Jeg kjender ikke professor Reuterdahls navn og har aldrig hørt tale om, at han skal have arbeidet paa relativitetstheorien. Jeg har ofte korresponderet med professor Mittag-Leffler, men han omtalte aldrig noget saadant arbeide. Jeg vil ikke bestemt paastaa umuligheden i det, som nævnes i den amerikanske avis, men jeg finder det hele lidet sandsynlig. Hvis professor Reuterdahl virkelig har opdaget relativitetstheorien, vilde vi med stor sandsynlighed have faaet underretning om det. Jeg kjender størstedelen af den literatur om dette emne, men noget arbeide af Reuterdahl har jeg ikke truffet paa. Dette er jo ikke bevis«, slutter professor Einstein, og tilføier: »Ein rechter Mensch vilde ikke have gjort den reklame, som professor Reuterdahl har gjort gjennem den amerikanske avis«.

Det var Einsteins svar, som ikke stiller professor Reuterdahls paastand i noget godt lys. Et moment, som taler for den samme antagelse, ligger deri, at hvis professor Reuterdahl havde ret, vilde et universitet som University of Columbia have tildet ham sin store guldmedalje. Som vi tidligere har meddelt, har Columbiauniversitetet tildelt professor Einstein denne medalje."

3.7.3 Reuterdahl Pursues Einstein, Who Continues to Run

Heidenreich was right, Einstein's refusal to respond to charges that he was a plagiarist haunted Einstein around the world and throughout his lifetime. The *Minneapolis Evening Tribune* wrote on 15 April 1921,

"Einstein, Jolted Out of Silence, Defends Theory

Challenged by St. Thomas Mentor,
Scientist Goes Deeper Into
Relativity Explanation.

Mathematician Ignores Charge
That He Is Not Originator of
Deductions Reached.

Professor Albert Einstein has been jolted out of a silence he has maintained since his arrival in America by the challenge of Professor Arvid Reuterdahl of St. Thomas college, according to dispatches today from New York.
Plagiarism Charge Ignored.
The charge that the famous mathematician is a plagiarist or at least not the originator of the theory which upset the scientific world is ignored, on the ground that it is not important. Professor Reuterdahl, however, has succeeded in bringing out a specific statement as to a test of the Einstein theory of relativity, and today the St. Thomas professor declared he was ready to meet the assertions concerning that test, and would make a statement later.

Einstein's Test Stated.

Professor Einstein's test, upon which he declares he is willing to rest his whole theory, was stated as follows:

'You know the solar spectrum. Everybody has seen it in the rainbow. You have also seen it when the sunlight passes through a triangular glass prism and falls upon a screen.

'Any light-giving body produces a spectrum, but the spectra from a different bodies are not alike. The spectrum from sodium for instance, shows only two yellow lines. The hydrogen spectrum shows only four colors.

Band With Seven Colors.

'The solar spectrum is a colored band, showing seven primary and secondary colors, ranging from red at one side to violet at the other.

'My theory demands that the spectrum of solar light, as compared with similar spectra from all other bodies, must be different in this respect.

'The lines of the solar spectrum must be found displaced—that is out of line—in the direction of red. If my theory of relativity is true, then this must be true. Why? Because of the nearness of the original solar light to the great mass which is the sun. If my theory is true, that mass must affect the spectral lines as I have said.'"

The *Minneapolis Morning Tribune* reported on 16 April 1921,

"Relativity Hit Counter Blow By Reuterdahl

Twin City Man Says Einstein Cult Has Not Attained Dignity of Theory.

Conceding that Prof. Albert Einstein, famous mathematician, whose theory of relativity startled the scientific world, has been supported by the results of one experiment, but contending that his theory still is a mere hypothesis without a foundation in fact, Prof. Arvid Reuterdahl of St. Thomas college yesterday renewed his attack upon the theory.

Replying to Professor Reuterdahl's challenge, Professor Einstein gave out a statement in New York, the first since his arrival in America, in which he declared that he was willing to rest his whole theory upon one experiment.

'Admission Proves Contention.'

In turn, Professor Reuterdahl declared that the mathematicians' admission that the theory had not been proved substantiated his contention that relativity had not been established and never would be.

One effect of the challenge by Professor Reuterdahl was that the man whom he had called the Barnum of the scientific world was jolted out of a profound silence. To the charge of plagiarism Professor Einstein gave no heed, but he did rush to the defense of his pet theory.

Einstein's Test Stated.

Professor Einstein's test, upon which he declares he is willing to rest his whole theory, was stated as follows:

'You know the solar spectrum. Everybody has seen it when the sunlight passes through a triangular glass prism and falls upon a screen.

'Any light-giving body produces a spectrum, but the spectra from different bodies are not alike. The spectrum from sodium, for instance, shows only two yellow lines. The hydrogen spectrum shows only four colors.

Band With Seven Colors.

'The solar spectrum is a colored band, showing seven primary and secondary colors, ranging from red at one side to violet at the other.

'My theory demands that the spectrum of solar light, as compared with similar spectra from all other bodies, must be different in this respect.

'The lines of the solar spectrum must be found displaced—that is out of line—in the direction of red. If my theory of relativity is true, then this must be true. Why? Because of the nearness of the original solar light to the great mass which is the sun. If my theory is true, that mass must affect the spectral lines as I have said.'

Professor Reuterdahl's answer to this statement follows:

'Professor Einstein refuses to enter into a written debate with me concerning the correctness of the basic tenets of the theory of relativity for the reason that he is willing to risk the validity of the entire theory on the result of an experiment. The theory of relativity assumes the displacement of the solar spectral lines toward the red will take place when the original solar light is near to a great mass like the sun. Professor Einstein admits that if this displacement does not take place then the general theory of relativity must be abandoned as untenable.

'Upon the results of this experiment Dr. Einstein rests the validity of his entire theory. Many experiments intended to discover this displacement have already been made. Had these experiments been successful Professor Einstein would not have made the statement which has this very day been transmitted to me by The Minneapolis Tribune.

'Professor Einstein's admission of the absence of this verification transforms the entire situation and leaves the theory as an hypothesis yet to be verified.

'Furthermore, Professor Einstein has admitted that it is extremely difficult to observe the deflection, even if it does exist, because of the fact that the predicted displacement is extremely small.

'Moreover, Professor Einstein has conceded the further fact that it is very difficult to make any calculations whatsoever, because of the indefiniteness of the involved facts.

'Now Professor Einstein himself admits that he rests the validity of his entire intellectual structure upon the future results of this extremely delicate experiment involving conditions difficult of realization.

'Professor Einstein, in his reply to my challenge, makes no mention of the significance of the observations made by the English solar expedition and the observed motion of the planet Mercury.

'Apparently he magnanimously waives the right to contend that the result of his predictions and calculations concerning the bending of light rays and the perihelion-perturbation of Mercury has bearing upon the validity of his theory.

'I gladly grant the importance and bearing of these

mathematical deductions of Professor Einstein. The granting of these contentions, however, in no way modifies my conviction that the theory of relativity is grounded upon fallacious assumptions, and therefore cannot survive. The history of science shows that one mathematic-physical theory after another has been abandoned because of inadequacy, unnecessary complexities, and untenability in the light of wider knowledge.

'It is true, of course, that this is the price which must be paid for intellectual advancement.

'Nevertheless it is also true that an hypothesis based upon fallacious assumptions contains the leaven of its own ultimate dissolution, despite the fact that some of the results of its applications to physical phenomena may be approximately correct.

'This I am prepared to prove is the status of Professor Einstein's theory of relativity. I am, indeed, surprised that Professor Einstein, while claiming that he had written his book from scientific motives and not for the sake of notoriety, lightly brushes to one side a challenge to a debate upon the validity of his theory. In no better way can the cause of science be served.

'A theory which so completely upsets all common-sense deductions concerning realities cannot hope forever to go unchallenged. Certainly it is not in keeping with the scientific motives of which Professor Einstein claims to be so ardent an exponent, continuously to reiterate the platitude that those who do not accept his theory are incapable of comprehending its alleged profundities.

'I desire to disabuse Professor Einstein of the correctness of the inference that any ulterior personal motive caused me to issue my challenge to him. The matter of nationality of an earnest investigator or any other ulterior motive never has had and never will have any bearing upon my attitude toward the significance and value of his work.'"

The Kansas City Post reported on 17 April 1921,

"DUBS EINSTEIN 'BARNUM OF SCIENCE' AND 'KIDDER'

German Savant Challenges
Theorist to Written Debate on Relativity.

Charges Feted Jew With
Having Plagiarized Material From the Past.

A 'Barnum of science.'

Thus is Prof. Albert Einstein, German scientist, who at present is making a triumphal visit to the United States, branded by a former Kansas City public school professor, Dr. Arvid Reuterdahl, dean of the engineering school of St. Thomas colege, St. Paul.

While New York hands the celebrated discoverer of the theory of relativity the key to the city, and while savants, scholars, bankers, butchers, hang on his non-understandable words, Dr. Reuterdahl steps out and boldly calls him names.

A 'sophist,' a dealer in 'might have beens,' says Dr. Reuterdahl of Einstein.

The former Kansas City teacher then challenges the widely heralded mathematician to a written debate.

Dr. Reuterdahl, speaking of course in scientific language, has said in effect that he is prepared to prove the Einstein theory largely 'bunk,' and a borrowing from older scientists. It is easy enough, he insinuates, to set forth a theory of any kind, so long as you make it sufficiently abstruse not to be understood.

Long before Einstein announced his visit to America, Dr. Reuterdahl and he had become involved in an international dispute over his theory. The controversy has attracted wide attention in the old world from Norway to Italy.

Dr. Reuterdahl, who was an instructor at the Polytechnic institute here, left Kansas City in 1915. In the fall of the same year he gave lectures at the Kansas State Agricultural college at Manhattan and at Kansas university on 'Space-Time-Potential,' in which he set forth some of the same views enunciated by Einstein, crediting them to scientists who lived before Einstein was born.

At that time Dr. E. Lee Heidenreich of the Heidenreich Engineering company of Kansas City, a friend of Dr. Reuterdahl, wrote the Carnegie institute of Dr. Reuterdahl's lectures, saying: 'It takes a scientific giant to gainsay a Newton and such a giant we have with us today.'

Coupled with his challenge to a debate, Dr. Reuterdahl now asserts that Einstein is deceiving scientists with a mythical theory and that he is a plagiarist, his works being antedated by another.

Dr. Reuterdahl points out that the Einstein theory of relativity in its gravitational aspects was advanced in 1866 by a scientist who wrote under the pen name of 'Kinertia.' The latter, when a student under Lord Kelvin, is said to have questioned the Newton theory of force.

Dr. Reuterdahl gives Einstein credit for breaking down the barriers of set ideas in science and making it possible for hearing new ideas.

'The American scientists,' says Dr. Reuterdahl, 'are the most clannish and orthodox in the world. They will not consider anything but what is based on their own knowledge and belief.'

Dr. Reuterdahl, while giving Einstein credit for being one of the greatest mathematicians in the world, 'calls' him on many parts of his theory.

'I demand that Einstein show me his proof,' says the American professor. 'I believe in dealing in the physical things in the world. In other words, I am from Missouri. I shall be glad to meet Professor Einstein at any time or place and debate this subject. But I shall demand an actual demonstration of his theory, not a journey into the realm of the mythical. That demonstration he can never give.'"

Ernst Gehrcke noted in his book *Die Massensuggestion der Relativitätstheorie: Kulturhistorisch-psychologische Dokumente*, Hermann Meusser, Berlin, (1924), pp. 29-30; that the *Neue Preußische (Kreuz-) Zeitung* wrote on 11 April 1921, together with many other papers,

"E I N S T E I N a l s P l a g i a t o r h e r a u s g e f o r d e r t. Aus Paris, 11. April, wird gedrahtet: Aus Minneapolis erfährt die „Chicago Tribune" Prof. ARVID REUTERDAUL, der

Präsident der Ingenieure der St. Thomas-Universität, erklärt über die Theorie des Professor EINSTEIN, daß dieser der „BARNUM" der Wissenschaft für die Welt sei. Professor REUTERDAUL fordert EINSTEIN zu einer schriftlichen Debatte über die Relativitätstheorie heraus. REUTERDAUL nennt EINSTEIN nicht nur einen verrückten Wissenschaftler mit mystischer Theorie, sondern auch einen Plagiator und behauptete, daß die EINSTEINsche Theorie bereits 1866 von einem Gelehrten unter dem Namen „INERTIA" entdeckt worden sei."

Gehrcke further notes that the *Vorwärts* wrote on 18 April 1921,

"Ein amerikanischer Professor hat die Theorie des Prof. EINSTEIN für eitel Humbug erklärt und ihn als einen Mann hingestellt, der einfach die wissenschaftliche Welt an der Nase herumführe. EINSTEIN ist der Schöpfer von etwas Neuem, nicht Dagewesenem, der Menge vor der Hand Unbegreiflichem, und daß alle neuen und großen Entdeckungen ihre Gegner haben und in der Geschichte stets hatten, scheint beinahe eine Notwendigkeit zu sein."

According to Gehrcke, the *Dresdner Anzeiger* reported on 18 April 1921,

"Professor EINSTEIN äußerte mit Bezug auf das Urteil des amerikanischen Prof. REUTERDAHL vom Thomas-College über seine Relativitätstheorie, sie sei die Leistung eines „Barnum der Wissenschaft", daß solche Angriffe ihn sehr an seine deutsche Heimat gemahnten . . . Prof. EINSTEIN lehnte es formell ab, mit Professor REUTERDAHL sich in eine wissenschaftliche Aussprache einzulassen."

Die Hamburger Woche wrote on 9 June 1921,

"Jenseits des großen Teiches hat A l b e r t   E i n s t e i n , der mit seiner Relativitätstheorie raschen Weltruhm gewann, große Ehrungen erfahren. Beim Besuch der Princeton-Universität wurde er in Anwesenheit vieler Gelehrter anderer amerikanischer Hochschulen zum Ehrendoktor ernannt. Von einer anderen amerikanischen Hochschulseite dagegen ist

Einstein ein neuer scharfer Gegner erstanden. Professor A r v i d R e u t e r d a h l , der Präsident der Ingenieure der St. Thomas-Universität, erklärte über die Theorie des Professors Einstien, daß dieser der „Barnum der Wissenschaft'' für die Welt sei. Professor Reuterdahl fordert Einstein zu einer schriftlichen Debatte über die Relativitätstheorie heraus. Reuterdahl nennt Einstein nicht nur einen „verrückten Wissenschaftler mit hysterischer Theorie'', sondern auch einen P l a g i a t o r und behauptet, daß die Einsteinsche Theorie bereits 1866 von einem Gelehrten unter dem Namen „I n e r t i a'' entdeckt worden sei.

Man darf gespannt sein, welches objektive Endergebnis sich aus den Kämpfen für und wider Einstein die Wissenschaft schließlich herausdestillieren wird! . . ."

3.7.4 Einstein All Hype

On 27 April 1921, Gertrude Besse King wrote about the publicity campaign for Einstein in *The Freeman* of New York,

"ALADDIN EINSTEIN. THE popular interest in America in Professor Einstein's theories has astonished the professor. The public who does not know whether the theory of relativity has accounted for the alteration of mercury or of Mercury, waylays his steps, and delights, with the exception of a mere alderman or two, to do him honour. Gifted newspaper-reporters herald him as the originator of the theory of relativity, which, by the way he is not, and question him as to the ultimate nature of space, though only a mathematical physicist who is also a philosopher could understand the professor's answers.

This general interest in an extremely difficult science is not quite what it seems. Probably Professor Einstein does not realize how sensationally and cunningly he has been advertised. From the point of view of awakening popular curiosity, his press-notices could hardly have been improved. The newspapers first announced his discovery as revolutionizing science. This sounds well, but its meaning, after all, is rather vague. Then they printed a series of entertaining oddities, supposedly deducible from his hypothesis, although most of them could have been equally well deduced from the conclusions of Lorentz or Poincaré: for example, moving objects are shortened in the direction of their motion. This is a gay novelty until one learns the proportion of the reduction, which is calculated to divest the statement of interest to any but scientists. Further, our newspapers told us that if we were to travel from the earth with the speed of light, and could see the clock we left behind, it would always remain at the same moment, permanently pausing, unable to reach the next tick. But we should be unable to travel at the rate of light for a number of reasons, the most interesting and perhaps the most decisive being that such a speed would cause our mass to be infinite! Finally, our informants assert that no point in space, no moment of time can serve as a permanent base for measurement; we can measure only the relations of space, the relations of time, never absolute space or time; and even to measure space-relations, we have to take into account time! What a fascinating dervish-dance of what we used to regard as immutable fixities! Is it possible that these delicious contradictions are serious and accredited doctrines among those who know? Yet so they appear, for though Professor Einstein is always careful in stating that his hypothesis enjoys as yet only a tentative security, his methods are vouched for by the experts, his procedure is according to Hoyle, and the crowd is at liberty to gorge its appetite for marvels untroubled by the ogres of scientific orthodoxy.

Aside from the fact that Professor Einstein comes as a distinguished and somewhat mysterious foreigner to partake of our insatiable hospitality, his popular welcome is to be accounted for by the spell of wizardry that the press has cast upon his interpretations. For it is the necromancy of these strange theories, not their science, that catches the gaping crowd. Reporters are often good, practical psychologists. Instinctively they have divined the public eagerness for miracles, without grasping the factors that feed this taste. They know that most of us are essentially children still clamouring for fairy tales. Man is congenitally restless with the prison-house of this too, too solid world. He is always looking for short-cuts to power. Since he can not find them to his mental satisfaction as once he could through the miracles and divine dispensations of the Church, or through the magic and occultism that were his legitimate resources in the Middle Ages, he now turns to the wonders of science and philosophy. Here, even in theories that he does not understand, he can find release for his cramped position, here he can taste the intoxicating freedom of a boundless universe, and renew his sense of personal potency. [. . .]"[399]

Thomas Jefferson Jackson See wrote in *The San Francisco Journal* on 27 May 1923,

"If anyone should ask how Einstein managed to get such vast publicity in the matter of relativity, we may observe that he has the habit of a promoter. Mark Twain humorously wrote to the president of the St. Louis exposition in 1904, that he 'would like to attend the exposition and exhibit himself.' So also does Einstein contrive constantly to be seen among men in conspicuous places. When he came to America, with the Zionist committee, some two years ago, he had to go to the White House at Washington and talk relativity to President Harding. The President, with becoming modesty, said he could not understand the subject.

Things in Europe afterwards became uncomfortable for Einstein, and he sought refuge in an Oriental trip. When in Tokyo he called upon the emperor of Japan, and it was advertised over the world that he was without a dress suit. This report is spectacular and like that of a skillful advertiser.

His return trip is duly chronicled by the press. Thus he finally arrives in Egypt, and on reaching Spain addresses the Academy of Science, at a session held in the presence of the king of Spain. If this is not the trumpeting of an organized press agency, what is it?

Einstein is not liked in Germany. A year or so ago, the students at the University of Berlin hooted him down. It was reported that he was in fear of assassination—but it probably was only a ruse to gain public sympathy."[400]

The Minneapolis Sunday Tribune published a letter from Arvid Reuterdahl on 22 May 1921, which, while not the best work on the subject, is notable for its ridicule of Einstein for running away from the Bad Nauheim debate, as well as Einstein's refusal to debate Reuterdahl. It quotes a Swiss newspaper's statement that Einstein's flight from the Nauheim debate, "was another prearranged matter of his general trafficking." The alleged corruption is proven by Philipp Frank, who described Max Planck's biased control over the debate and his abuse of his power to censor speakers, intimidate the would-be audience and anti-Einstein speakers with armed guards, and restrict the topics of discussion in a way that would favor Einstein and prevent Einstein's having to face criticisms of the Metaphysics in the theory of relativity.[401] Frank wrote,

"[Max Planck] arranged it so that the greatest part of the available time was filled with papers that were purely mathematical and technical. Not much time remained for Lenard's attack and the debate that would ensue. The entire arrangement was made to prevent any dramatic effects. [***] The armed policemen who had watched the building were withdrawn."[402]

The theory of relativity is largely a metaphysical theory, not a scientific theory. In order to oppose the Metaphysics of relativity theory one must, of course, discuss Metaphysics. Proponents of relativity theory often refuse to discuss Metaphysics claiming that Metaphysics has nothing to do with science, and they thereby insulate their theory from criticism. Einstein did not grasp the distinction between Metaphysics and science. He stated in 1930, "Science itself is metaphysics."[403]

Hugo Dingler, a critic of relativity theory, confirmed that severe time restrictions were placed on the opponents of relativity theory at the Bad Nauheim debate. Others complained that Einstein's followers had stacked the audience with a pro-Einstein claque and tried to prevent the admission of neutral "unauthorized" persons into the forum.[404] Philipp Frank admitted that the corruption backfired—every fairminded person smelled a rat, and knew that Einstein and the relativists were avoiding the facts and dodging the issues. Just when Nobel Prize winner Philipp Lenard, Einstein's primary opponent, had cornered Einstein at the debate, Einstein ran away. Max Planck stopped the discussion for a break, and Einstein never returned. It is difficult to believe that this was not a prearranged maneuver to save face for Einstein.

Reuterdahl's article published in *The Minneapolis Sunday Tribune* on 22 May 1921,:

"Science's 'Baby Guy' Was Simple Child Till Einstein Adopted It

Clothed in a Garbled Dress of Mathematical Theories,

the Youngster, 'Relativity,' Joined Ranks of Unintelligible Genii—Swiss Paper Backs Reuterdal.

By Arvid Reuterdahl.

Dean Department of Engineering and Architecture
the College of St. Thomas.

In a signed statement published in The Minneapolis Morning Tribune, issue of May 16, Dr. E. Lee Heidenreich, the eminent engineer, mathematician, and philosopher of Kansas City, Mo., points out that Dr. Einstein does not hesitate to make irreconcilable statements in order to avoid facing issues squarely. I now have in my possession a copy of the 'Aftenposten' article which was cited by Dr. Heidenreich in his communication to The Tribune. I also have a copy of the New York World interview with Dr. Einstein. The date of the 'Aftenposten" article is June 18, 1920, and the New York World interview is dated April 12, 1921.

There is only one verdict possible when a comparison is made of these two conflicting statements of Professor Einstein, either his statements are relativistic conveniences or his memory has been weakened by relativistic sophistries. Dr. Einstein, it seems, is permitted to say anything he pleases without being held accountable.

Access to Ziegler's Work.

From abroad I have received copies of publications which convey the idea, in no uncertain terms, that while Dr. Einstein was in Switzerland he had access to the work of Dr. J. H. Ziegler and that he used the results of this able investigator's work without giving him any credit whatsoever.

I have now in my possession evidence furnished by 'Kinertia,' which shows conclusively that in the year 1903, copies of certain contributions of 'Kinertia' were in the hands of the imperial Prussian academy of science in Berlin. Did Dr. Einstein avail himself of those easily accessible records? Moreover in September, 1904, a well-known American journal published a statement setting forth 'Kinertia's' theory of gravitation.

Swiss Paper on Einstein.

The following quotations from the well known Swiss paper, 'the Lucerne Daily News,' of April 22, 1921, should have been interesting reading to Dr. Einstein under the heading, 'Professor

Einstein's Triumphal March Through America,' a translation of the article reads:

'Professor Albert Einstein and the Zionist delegation which arrived simultaneously with him, was accorded a very warm welcome on its arrival in New York. The entire New York press devoted a good deal of space to this happening, as well as to the personality of Einstein. One can clearly see that there is again question here of the previously ordered advertising, just as the whole Einstein undertaking has been from its very beginning a bluff. This time the Americans were supposed to believe, but the good Yankee seemed to be less naive than the good Germans and Swiss, and were not so easily forced into a belief in the new prophet. They are too skeptical to believe without a further proof that he is a greater genius than Copernicus and Newton, simply because he is more unintelligible.

Too Much Common Sense.

'Americans have too much common sense for that. They know that all the great truths are simple and easily understood, and are, therefore, justly suspicious of the unintelligible theory of relativity of Einstein. More than that they have rejected it as a swindle. Just for example Reuterdahl, dean of engineering of the College of St. Thomas, St. Paul, Minnesota, calls Einstein a 'Barnum of the scientific world who is trying to fool the whole world with a mythical theory.' It is further reported that Reuterdahl has challenged Einstein to a debate, into which he is as likely to enter as in the debate announced last year at the meeting for scientific investigation in Bad Nauheim, where he preferred to withdraw himself quietly before the announced opponents of his theory could say what they had to say. To these opponents was expressed the regret that Mr. Einstein was unable, because of circumstances, to answer them. This, of course, was another prearranged matter of his general trafficking. It is very likely that he is acting in a similar manner towards Reuterdahl. The more so because the latter has accused him of scientific theft, for Reuterdahl maintains that Einstein has taken the fundamentals of his theory from a work which appeared in 1866 under the pseudonym of 'Kinertia.'

Work Little Known In Europe.

'As this work is scarcely known in Europe, the accusation may possibly be groundless. Similar accusations have been made by German scientists, such as the Engineer Rudolph Mewes,

Professors E. Gehrke and Paul Weyland, etc. According to them, Emstein is supposed to have secretly taken a formula from a publication of the deceased Professor Gerber which appeared in 1898, and was very inaccessible, and to have made it his own. The facts in the matter are, of course, difficult to prove, nevertheless, the peculiar conduct of Einstein and his sensational advertising campaign lead one to believe that his whole business is very suspicious. However, most of these opponents seem to be upon a wrong scent, because they do not understand the circumstances which existed at the time of the origination of the Einsteinian teaching, and do not sufficiently understand the influences that may have been at work in regard to his theory. He seems to have started with the correct notion of the constancy of the velocity of light, and of vacuum; which potion, however, he did not test out further, but simply accepted hypothetically; whereas, the other teachings of his theory are so tangled and contradictory that they seem to have come from an entirely different source.

Deductions Criticized.

'These other peculiar assumed proofs, and the still more peculiar deductions made from them have been criticized by many scientists, notably by Professor Lenard, a former Nobel Prize winner in physics. Lenard calls attention to the fact that these suppositions and deductions are contradictory to common sense. Einstein's acceptance of constancy of the velocity of light, which he makes the one stable concept in the shoreless ocean of his theory of relativity, seems to be a special case. It is already suspicious, because the physicists at that time denied the existence of absolute empty space, and regarded such a thing as impossible, but then conceded it without more adieu when they accepted Einstein's hypotheses, and in addition regarded him as having performed a very acceptable thing. As a matter of fact Einstein's theory of velocity of light seems to be a direct theft of the universal theory of light given out by J. H. Ziegler five years previous. There are reasons that seem to point with great probability to the fact that the teaching of Ziegler was the hidden spring of Einstein's discovery.

The Unmoved Emptiness.

'Just to mention one of them, the findings of Ziegler were very much discussed in Berne, which was at the time Einstein's domicile. Ziegler speaks of the trinity of energy, space and time, a trinity which Mr. Einstein then brought forth in a modified form. The clear and simple teaching of Ziegler, according to which all natural phenomena are mixed forms of radiating source light (urilcht), and unmoved (unergized) emptiness, were very inconvenient to the exponents of accepted physics, and so they tried from the beginning to suppress it. Thus they created an opportunity for a clever and foxy plagiarist to possess himself of these principle teachings. He would get all the greater hearing and support from those physicists if he would proffer his plagiarism in a manner intelligible to them, but unintelligible to the general public. Mathematics served as an excellent medium. The chemist (not the mathematician) Ziegler, had made the mistake of writing intelligibly and of revealing the mistakes in modern physics, thus Einstein appeared to these physicists as a Deus ex Machina, he was a friend in need. It is no wonder that he was hailed as long-expected Messiah of the world of physics, the true bringer of light.

Ziegler's Name Forgotten.

'Ziegler's name was forgotten in the great propaganda which the papers carried on for Einstein. Ziegler has not always propounded his teachings so clearly that superficial study would lead to a great understanding of it. Thus, there was occasion of all sorts of misconception. Hence the many mistakes of the theory of relativity. How could this theory of relativity be unified and clear when it was only a mixed pickle affair of erroneous plagiarisms. The fact that Einstein's theory approached the Ziegler light theory more and more every year does not disprove that the Ziegler theory is a source of Einsteinian wisdom, even though the Einsteinian press has carefully boycotted Ziegler for 20 years. The Americans, of course, know nothing of this. It they reject Einstein, it is rather because they are angry to be considered so stupid as to regard the greatest scientific discovery as the most unintelligible. The Americans know well enough that the opposite is the case, and for this reason the business trip of the false prophet in the United States will scarcely constitute a triumphal march.

From German Journal.

The following excerpts from the Scientific journal 'Weltwissen,' May, 1921, published in Munich, Germany, is significant:

'From numerous sources we have previously received

various printed articles and manuscripts directed against Einstein, among others, one from the 'Regierungsrat,' Dr. H. Fricke, 'The Error In Einstein's Theory of Relativity' and from the Engineer A. Patschke, 'The Overthrow of the Einsteinian Theory of Relativity.' The tremendous advertising campaign, which Einstein has for some time conducted throughout the world has been carried on to such an extent as to throw a sort of protective film over his work. Such procedure does not redound to the honor and furtherance of science, in special letters, at the beginning of the year 1920, we called the attention of the University of Berlin and of the minister of education to this horn-tooting for Einstein. It is a very deplorable fact that German science should be laid open to ridicule by one of Germany's own scientists.'

This statement emanated from Dr. Johannes Zacharias of the editorial department of the journal 'Weltwissen.'"[405]

3.8 Assassination Plots

Though Theodor Wolff, editor of the *Berliner Tageblatt*, had stated that there was no anti-Semitic movement in the German government in 1915, Wolff spread the rumor in 1922 (which was denied by the German police) that assassins were out to murder him and Albert Einstein. Wolff's pronouncement followed on the heels of the assassination of Walter Rathenau. Rathenau was a German Jew who found a way around the Treaty of Versailles (which he had supported—profiteering off of the reparations payments made by Germany) by restoring Germany's military in Russia with the Rapallo Treaty. It was alleged that he and his friends could financially profit from this venture and that they sought to sponsor Bolshevism. Bolshevism itself stole the wealth of Russia and channeled it other hands. Rathenau was preparing the way for the Second World War.

Wolff's baseless claims of assassination plots may have been a pretext for Einstein's withdrawal from the meetings of the League of Nations, where he would have had to have met with his critic Henri Bergson, and been publicly challenged to debate his positions. Instead of running this risk, Einstein ran around the world promoting himself and advertising the theory of relativity—and Zionism, at a critical point in the history of the Zionist Movement. In this same period, Wickham Steed prevented Lord Northcliffe, principal owner of *The London Times* and outspoken critic of Zionism, from voicing his objections to the

League of Nations Mandate for Palestine of 24 July 1922 (reproduced in the endnote[406]). Perhaps the Zionists sought sympathy for their cause by spreading rumors that Einstein was in danger from those who had murdered Rathenau. They failed to explain how exposing himself in public and traveling abroad safeguarded Einstein.

Einstein's Internationalism and his anti-Germanism did indeed cause some Germans to wish him dead; and a year earlier, in 1921, Rudolph Leibus put a bounty on Einstein's head and Leibus was prosecuted for it. *The New York Times* carried the story reported by the *Chicago Tribune*,

"Urged Murder of Einstein,
Pays $16 Fine in Berlin Court

Copyright, 1921, by The Chicago Tribune Co.

BERLIN, April 7.—Charged with attempting to incite the murder of Professor Albert Einstein, who is now in America on a lecture tour, Rudolph Leibus, an anti-Semitic leader, was assessed a fine of $16 by a Berlin Judge.

Leibus recently offered a reward for the murder of Einstein, Professor Foerster and Maximilian Harden, saying that it was a patriotic duty to shoot these leaders of pacifist sentiment."

Jewish anti-Zionist Walter Rathenau was assassinated on 24 June 1922. Both nationalist Germans and political Zionists hated Rathenau. The political Zionists resented Rathenau for being an advocate for, and prime example of, the possibility of assimilation; and for being a vocal anti-Zionist who believed that assimilation was the best means to end anti-Semitism. Rathenau published an article in Maximilian Harden's newspaper *Die Zukunft* in 1897, in which Rathenau called on Jews to assimilate by adopting the Teutonic values of honesty, manhood and integrity, because they were allegedly not an integral part of German society, but were instead an "alien organism in its body."[407] He famously wrote, *inter alia*,

"What a peculiar sight! Amidst German life, a segregated and heterogeneous tribal race, glitteringly and gaudily garnished, with a hot-blooded and restless temperament. An Asiatic horde on the soil of Brandenburg."

"Seltsame Vision! Inmitten deutschen Lebens ein abgesondert fremdartiger Menschenstamm, glänzend und auffällig staffiert, von heißblütig beweglichem Gebaren. Auf märkischem Sand eine asiatische Horde."[408]

Rathenau also famously stated that there was a committee of 300 persons, known to each other, who effectively ruled the world. Some believed that Rathenau was one of them, and that they were the "Elders of Zion". Rathenau was considered one of the many leading Jews who stabbed Germany in the back in the First World War.

The Zionists had stated that it was *impossible* for Jews to assimilate in a Gentile nation and Rathenau's murder bolstered their contention and lent sympathy to their cause. German nationalists believed that Rathenau, who had numerous connections to big business and was the son of the founder of AEG and became its chairman in 1915, had profiteered from the war in his role as Director of Economic Mobilization in control of military spending in the German War Ministry, and had bought inferior goods from Jewish merchants at inflated prices, then at war's end sold off Germany's machinery of war to his Jewish friends. They quoted statements by Rathenau, in which Rathenau declared that he wanted Germany to lose the war. German nationalists resisted Rathenau, who became Minister of Reconstruction in 1921 and Foreign Minister in 1922, because he had sponsored the punitive Versailles Treaty and had demanded that Germany pay the oppressive reparations it imposed. Furthermore, they thought that the Rapallo Treaty was but another opportunity for Jews to profit from war and that it aided the Bolshevists.

Anti-Communist *Freikorps* soldier Ernst von Salomon, who served a five year prison sentence for conspiring to assassinate Rathenau, may have believed that Rathenau was one of the alleged Elders of Zion, who wanted to bring Bolshevism to Germany. Rathenau brought about the Rapallo Treaty with the Bolsheviks, and Rathenau had alleged that 300 men controlled the economic destiny of Europe, which 300 some German nationalists assumed were the alleged Elders of Zion. The murder of Rathenau on 24 June 1922, no matter who had committed it and irregardless of the reasons behind it, served as a convenient propaganda tool for the Zionists' promotion of the adoption of the League of Nations Mandate for Palestine on 24 July 1922.

Racist-segregationist and genocidal-Zionist Albert Einstein stated,

"I regretted the fact that [Rathenau] became a Minister. In view of the attitude which large numbers of the educated classes in Germany assume towards the Jews, I have always thought that their natural conduct in public should be one of proud reserve."[409]

Chaim Weizmann wrote,

"[Rathenau's] attitude was, of course, all too typical of that of many assimilated German Jews; they seemed to have no idea that they were sitting on a volcano; they believed quite sincerely that such difficulties as admittedly existed for German Jews were purely temporary and transitory phenomena, primarily due to the influx of East European Jews, who did not fit into the framework of German life, and thus offered targets for anti-Semitic attacks."[410]

The *Berliner Tageblatt*, Morgen-Ausgabe, reported on 5 August 1922,

"Einsteins Absage an den Naturforschertag.
Auf der Liste der Mörderorganisation.
(T e l e g r a m m   u n s e r e s   K o r r e s p o n d e n t e n.)

Leipzig, 4. August.
Die „Leipziger Neuesten Nachrichten" bringen in ihrer Sonnabendnummer vom 5. August folgende Aufsehen erregende Meldung aus Naturforscherkreisen: Professor A l b e r t E i n s t e i n hatte zugesagt, auf der H u n d e r t j a h r f e i e r d e r G e s e l l s c h a f t d e u t s c h e r N a t u r f o r s c h e r u n d A e r z t e in Leipzig einen Vortrag über die Relativitätstheorie zu halten. Kurz nach der E r m o r d u n g R a t h e n a u s teilte aber Einstein dem Vorsitzenden der Gesellschaft, Geheimrat P l a n c k, mit, daß er seine Beteiligung an der Hundertjahrfeier a b s a g e n müsse, weil er für mehrere Monate ins A u s l a n d gehe. Diesen plötzlichen Entschluß faßte Einstein, als er erfuhr, daß auch s e i n N a m e a u f d e r L i s t e d e r O p f e r stehe, die von der M ö r d e r o r g a n i s a t i o n beseitigt werden sollten, der schon Rathenau zum Opfe gefallen ist. Der Entschluß Einsteins, unter diesen Umständen auf längere Zeit ins Ausland zu gehen, war vollkommen zu begreifen. Inzwischen hat sich durch das tatkräftige Eingreifen der Regierung die Lage im Reich erfreulicherweise bedeutend gebessert. Die Mörderorganisation ist aufgedeckt. Alle Schuldigen und

Verdächtigen sind in Gewahrsam gebracht worden, so daß nun hoffentlich dem schädlichen Treiben dieser Kreise ein für allemal ein Ende bereitet worden ist. Der Vorsitzende der Gesellschaft deutscher Naturforscher und Aerzte hat nun den Versuch unternommen, Einstein zur Rückkehr nach Deutschland und zur Teilnahme an der Leipziger Hundertjahrfeier zu bewegen, und er bedauert sehr, daß es seinen Bemühungen bisher noch nicht gelungen ist, E i n s t e i n z u r R ü c k k e h r z u b e w e g e n. Es scheint, daß ein den Gelehrten umgebender engerer Kreis von Freunden und Bewunderern besorgter ist als Einstein selbst. Denn von dieser Seite wird alles getan, die Rückkehr des Gelehrten nach Deutschland zu verhindern oder doch h i n a u s z u s c h i e b e n. Hoffentlich aber lassen sich noch diese Schwierigkeiten rechtzeitig überwinden, damit Einstein seinen Vortrag über die R e l a t i v i t ä t s t h e o r i e in Leipzig doch noch persönlich halten kann.

*

Wie wir erfahren, trifft es zu, daß Professor Einstein an der Leipziger Hundertjahrfeier der Gesellschaft deutscher Naturforscher und Aerzte nicht teilnehmen wird. Gewiß ist es ein tief bedauerlicher Vorgang, daß einer der ersten Gelehrten unserer Zeit an einer Veranstaltung von dem Range der Leipziger Tagung deshalb nicht teilnehmen kann, weil er befürchten muß, in Deutschland, seiner Heimat, statt der Ehrungen, die ihm in der ganzen Welt entgegengebracht worden sind, d e r K u g e l e i n e s M e u c h e l m ö r d e r s ausgesetzt zu sein. Die Meldung, die das Leipziger Blatt aus Naturforscherkreisen veröffentlicht, ist gewiß sehr gut gemeint. Wir vermögen auch nicht zu beurteilen, in welchem Grade das Leben und die Sicherheit des großen Gelehrten gefährdet sind. Aber wenn sich auch durch das tatkräftige Eingreifen der Regierung die Lage gebessert hat, so ist doch die Behauptung, daß a l l e Schuldigen und Verdächtigen in Gewahrsam gebracht seien, etwas kühn und schwerlich zu verantworten. Der Mordbube, der den Anschlag auf Maximilian Harden ausgeführt hat, ist beispielsweise noch nicht gefaßt und Erzbergers Mörder leben in Freiheit und in Saus und Braus. Es ist auch sehr begreiflich, daß die Freunde des Gelehrten in höherem Maße besorgt sind, als er selbst, und es ist sehr bedauerlich, das R a t h e n a u trotz vielfacher Warnung so wenig besorgt gewesen ist. Vielleicht dient dieser Vorgang, dessen t i e f b e s c h ä m e n d e r   C h a r a k t e r niemandem entgehen kann, endlich dazu, der moralischen Verwilderung, die aus den genügend gekennzeichneten Gründen in weiten Kreisen des Rechtsradikalismus eingerissen ist, durch die entschiedene Abwehr der anständigen Elemente aus allen Lagern im Interesse des deutschen Namens und der deutschen Ehre Einhalt zu tun."

The *Rheinisch-Westfalische Zeitung* (Essen a. Ruhr) reported on 5 August 1922 that the whole affair was contrived as a means to advertize Einstein, whose stardom was fading,

"Die flüchtige Relativität

Eine Teilnahme E i n s t e i n s am deutschen Naturforscherkongreß in Leipzig ist, wie das B. T. meldet, nicht zu erwarten. Einstein sollte dort einen Vortrag über seine Relativitätstheorie halten. Nach dem Morde Rathenaus ist er aber ins Ausland gereist, da er, wie er erklärte, auf der schwarzen Liste stände.

*

Die Propagierung der Einsteinschen allgemeinen Relativitätstheorie hat zwar einen für das deutsche Kulturleben gemeingefährlichen Charakter, doch hat Einsteins Person damit nichts zu tun. Seine Flucht und die erdachte schwarze Liste sind eins der vielen jetzt auftauchenden republikanischen Propagandamittel, die man sachlich nicht ernst zu nehmen hat. Einsteins Person ist viel zu unwichtig, als daß jemand um ihretwillen sein Leben aufs Spiel setzen wollte. Daß die von ihm in Szene gesetzte Flucht als Reklame auszulegen ist, die seinen schon merklich verblaßten Stern in neuem Glanze erstrahlen lassen soll, dürfte wohl des Pudels Kern in dieser Affäre bedeuten."

Thomas Jefferson Jackson See wrote in *The San Francisco Journal* on 27 May 1923,

"If anyone should ask how Einstein managed to get such vast publicity in the matter of relativity, we may observe that he has the habit of a promoter. Mark Twain humorously wrote to the president of the St. Louis exposition in 1904, that he 'would like to attend the exposition and exhibit himself.' So also does Einstein contrive constantly to be seen among men in conspicuous places. When he came to America, with the Zionist committee, some two years ago, he had to go to the White House at Washington and talk relativity to President Harding. The President, with becoming modesty, said he could not understand the subject.

Things in Europe afterwards became uncomfortable for Einstein, and he sought refuge in an Oriental trip. When in Tokyo he called upon the emperor of Japan, and it was advertised over the world that he was without a dress suit. This report is spectacular and like that of a skillful advertiser.

His return trip is duly chronicled by the press. Thus he finally arrives in Egypt, and on reaching Spain addresses the Academy of Science, at a session held in the presence of the king of Spain. If this is not the trumpeting of an organized press agency, what is it?

Einstein is not liked in Germany. A year or so ago, the students at the University of Berlin hooted him down. It was reported that he was in fear of assassination—but it probably was only a ruse to gain public sympathy."[411]

The Associated Press spread Theodor Wolff's rumors of assassination plots. *The New York Times* wrote on 6 August 1922 in Section 2, on page 1,

"Einstein Has Fled Temporarily From Germany
Because of Threats That He Will Be Killed

LEIPSIC, Aug. 5 (Associated Press).—Professor Albert Einstein, originator of the theory of relativity, has fled from Germany temporarily because he was threatened with assassination by the group that caused the murder of Dr. Walter Rathenau, German Foreign Minister, according to a letter from Professor Einstein canceling an engagement to address a meeting here.

Efforts to induce the noted scientist to return, in view of the Government's success in coping with the situation, are said to have so far proved unavailing.

Receipt of the letter was announced by the President of the

German Physicists' Association, before which Dr. Einstein was to discuss his relativity theory at the organization's 100th anniversary meeting. It was received soon after Dr. Rathenau's assassination, and stated that Dr. Einstein had learned that he also was listed to be killed and had, therefore, decided to go abroad.

It appears that Dr. Einstein's friends and admirers had been more concerned in keeping the scientist safe in this manner than was he himself, and were doing their utmost to prevent, or at least postpone, his return. Dr. Einstein is not accompanying the expedition to Christmas Island, contrary to previously announced plans.

Considerable comment was caused in Geneva early last week by the absence of Dr. Einstein from the meeting of the members of the Intellectual Committee of the League of Nations to begin the work of organization. He had been designated to represent Germany, but did not appear. It was said he was unable to leave his work at the University of Berlin.

Dispatches from Germany soon after the Rathenau murder quoted police authorities there as accusing the notorious 'Consul' organization of having marked twelve leading politicians, editors and financiers of Jewish extraction for assassination, including Dr, Rathenau, Theodor Wolff, editor of the Berliner Tageblatt, and Max Warburg, the Hamburg banker."

The New York Times wrote on 8 August 1922 on page 7,

"URGE EINSTEIN TO HIDE.

Friends Fear Because He Is on Anti-Semite Blacklist.

BERLIN, Aug. 7 (Jewish Telegraph Agency).—Friends of Professor Albert Einstein insist upon his remaining abroad, where he is understood to be hiding from the 'Deutsche Nationale' plotters, by whom he has been blacklisted, together with a number of other leading German Jews.

The fear of Professor Einstein's friends is justified, in the opinion of the Berliner Tageblatt, whose editor, Theodor Wolff, is included in the monarchists' blacklist.

'Professor Einstein's continued concealment is advisable,' the Tageblatt says, 'because the assailants of Maximilian Harden and Mathias Erzberger have not been apprehended. Professor

Einstein's enforced absence is a blot on the German name and honor.'"

The New York Times published a statement on 9 August 1922 on page 10, that perpetuated the myth that anyone who disagreed with Einstein did so out of envy and resultant malice,

"His Offense Can Be Imagined.
It takes not a little thought to arrive at even a suspicion why anybody wants to assassinate Dr. EINSTEIN. Whoever has seen his picture knows how unlikely he is to excite angry passions in any minds. He is gentleness personified, and it is incredible that he ever gave anybody any of the ordinary forms of offense.
   But wait! Not long ago he announced, or at least allowed somebody else, without denial, to announce, that there were not more than twelve people in the world who could understand his new theory of relativity. That, come to think of it, did waken something of animosity in every mind whose possessor lacked the self-confidence to number himself among the so exceptional dozen. Humiliation is an unpleasing sensation, and few if any turn more readily to dislike of him who causes it, and hatred is not far away.
   This may not be the basis of the rumored plot against Dr. EINSTEIN, but it is a working hypothesis that will stand until facts are brought forward to prove it untenable."

The German police refuted Wolff's alarmist claims. The *Casseler Allgemeine Zeitung* reported on 12 August 1922, that the alleged "blacklist" did not exist and that the pro-Einstein press was corrupt:

"E i n e   n i c h t   v o r h a n d e n e   M o r d l i s t e. Nach der Ermordung RATHENAUs lief die Meldung durch die Presse, es sei eine Liste der Mörderorginsation aufgefunden worden, auf der . . . . . die Namen . . . . . Prof. EINSTEINs u. a. verzeichnet gewesen sein sollen. Jetzt endlich wird von der zuständigen Berliner Stelle versichert, daß die polizeilichen Erhebungen . . . . . eine derartige Liste   n i c h t   ans Licht gefördert haben. Daß die amtlichen Stellen der Veröffentlichung dieser Gerüchte in der gesamten Presse nicht sofort ein Dementi entgegengesetzt haben, kann selbst in der politischen Verwirrung jener Tage keine zureichende Erklärung finden."[412]

There were many more reasons why some suspected that Einstein's flight from the League of Nations, and the Hundertjahrfeier der Gesellschaft Deutscher Naturforscher und Aerzte in Leipzig, on the pretext of unsubstantiated murder plots against him, was a contrived affair to create a false panic over anti-Semitism and to promote sympathy for Einstein, the theory of relativity and Zionism in anticipation of a grand world tour. German science had turned against Einstein. Philipp Lenard and others promised to again embarrass Einstein at the Leipzig meeting as they had done in Bad Nauheim. The racist coward Albert Einstein wanted to hide from them, as Ernst Gehrcke recorded in his book *Die Massensuggestion der Relativitätstheorie: Kulturhistorisch-psychologische Dokumente*, Hermann Meusser, Berlin, (1924), pp. 62-64. Though Einstein was scheduled to deliver a lecture at the centenary of the Association of German Scientists and Physicians in Leipzig, which was overseen by the corrupt sycophant Max Planck, Einstein again took the coward's way out. Max Planck and Max von Laue again rescued Albert Einstein from certain embarrassment. Laue, who was far more competent, though no less childish, than Einstein, delivered a lecture on the theory of relativity, while Einstein again hid from his critics.

Several top Physicists, Mathematicians and Philosophers joined Nobel Prize laureate Philipp Lenard in protesting Max Planck's attempt to deceive the German Public into believing that the scientific community had accepted the theory of relativity as if it were the climax of modern science. These scholars joined together to protect the lay public from the self-aggrandizement and lies of Max Planck and Albert Einstein. Their published protest revealed that the majority of Physicists, Mathematicians and Philosophers considered the theory of relativity to be an unproven hypothesis and a fundamentally flawed, irrational and untenable fiction,

"Die Leitung der „Gesellschaft Deutscher Naturforscher und Ärzte" hat es für richtig gehalten, unter den wissenschaftlichen Darbietungen der Leipziger Jahrhundertfeier Vorträge über R e l a t i v i t ä t s t h e o r i e auf die Tagesordnung einer großen, allgemeinen Sitzung aufzunehmen. Es muß und soll dadurch wohl der Eindruck erweckt werden, als stelle die Relativitätstheorie einen Höhepunkt der modernen wissenschaftlichen Forschung dar.

Hiergegen legen die unterzeichneten Physiker, Mathematiker und Philosophen e n t s c h i e d e n e   V e r w a h r u n g   e i n . Sie beklagen aufs tiefste die Irreführung der öffentlichen Meinung, welcher die Relativitätstheorie als Lösung des Welträtsels angepriesen wird, und welche man über die Tatsache im Unklaren hält, daß viele und auch sehr angesehene Gelehrte der drei genannten Forschungsgebiete die Relativitätstheorie nicht nur als eine unbewiesene Hypothese ansehen, sondern sie sogar als eine im Grunde verfehlte und logisch unhaltbare Fiktion ablehnen. Die Unterzeichneten betrachten es als unvereinbar mit dem Ernst und der Würde deutscher Wissenschaft, wenn eine im höchsten Maße anfechtbare Theorie voreilig und marktschreierisch in die Laienwelt getragen wird, und wenn die Gesellschaft Deutscher Naturforscher und Ärzte benutzt wird, um solche Bestrebungen unterstützen."

After his crushing defeat at Bad Nauheim and humiliation at the Berlin Philharmonic, Einstein elected to run away and hide from Lenard and Gehrcke at the Hundertjahrfeier der Gesellschaft Deutscher Naturforscher und Aerzte in Leipzig.

The First World War had emancipated all the Jews of the world. Kerensky and the the Bolsheviks had completely liberated the Jews of Russia. Political Zionism was dying a political death. Would not a world tour expose Einstein to greater danger, not less? Einstein had written to the Generalsekretär des Volkerbundes in Genf in July that he was planning to visit Japan.

The Zionist movement was fractionalizing.[413] Even Louis Brandeis was coming to realize that the Jews did not want to emigrate to the Palestinian desert in large enough numbers to form a majority population and American Zionists were softening. Weizmann and Einstein had a tense relationship. Zionism needed a common enemy, real or manufactured, to hold it together. *The New York Times* reported on 20 July 1922 on page 19,

"JERUSALEM, June 22 (Correspondence of the Associated Press).—The inhabitants of Palestine, both Moslem and Christian, are immeasurably pleased that the British House of Lords yesterday passed the Islington motion disapproving the Balfour declaration of 1917. The native press is jubilant; pan-Arab demonstrations are being held and the local cable office is swamped with congratulatory messages from Arabs to the House of Lords.

The Balfour declaration pledged the erection of a Jewish homeland in Palestine. The resolution passed yesterday by a vote of 60 to 29 set forth that 'the mandate for Palestine in its present form is unacceptable to this House, because it directly violates the pledges made by his Majesty's Government to the people of Palestine in the declaration of October, 1915, and again in the declaration of November, 1918 (pledges given to the Arabs), and is as at present framed opposed to the sentiments and wishes of the great majority of the people of Palestine. That, therefore, its acceptance by the Council of the League of Nations should be postponed until such modifications have therein been effected as will comply with pledges given by his Majesty's Government.'

The Arabs regard this incident as a great victory. 'It is the bounden duty,' says an Arab call to a demonstration of celebration, 'of all of us to set forth our gratitude to the House of Lords for having proved to the world that God and justice still live in Great Britain.'

Miraat el Shark, a Jerusalem newspaper, says: 'We will win our fight for freedom; we have God and right on our side.' Beit el Makdes, another local paper, says: 'Our victory in the House of Lords is the beginning of the end of political Zionism.'

The Zionists are correspondingly disappointed at the news. They have not failed to cable strong protests to London. The Chairman of the Zionist organization here said to the Associated Press:

'All our hopes have been shattered on the rocks of political expediency. If the House of Commons follows the lead of the House of Lords, then Jews of the world will have been dealt a more staggering blow than that administered by the Emperor Hadrian 1,800 years ago, when his persecutions brought about the last dispersion of the Jewish race.'"

The New York Times reported on 26 August 1922, on page 4,

"ARABS COMING HERE TO OPPOSE ZIONISM
Declaring Against Palestine Mandate, They Seek American and British Support.

CAIRO, Egypt, Aug. 25.—Following the news last night that the Mesopotamian Ministry had resigned because it was unable to agree with the British regarding the Anglo-Irak treaty comes the news today that the situation in the Irak is restive, due to the efforts of extremists to stir anti-British feeling, while excitement is spreading. The Arab delegation meeting in Congress at Nablus reports that hopes for the success of their Palestine cause against the Jews depend largely on sympathetic action from America and England. Feeling in these two countries is to be aroused for protests against Zionism in Palestine, which will be sent from different Moslem countries if the Arab propagandists succeed in inducing the Moslems to produce protests.

America may be interested to learn that the Nablus Congress has decided to send an Arab mission to the United States to collect subscriptions for the Arab organization to enable it to continue the campaign against a Jewish national home in Palestine on the present conditions.

A message from Mecca, which is confirmed by Pilgrims recently at Mecca, says Moslems from all Arab countries met there recently and agreed to organize a movement throughout the Moslem Arab world for the elimination of all foreign political and commercial influence from Moslem Arab countries in the Mid-East. Details of the preliminary organization are to be submitted to the Congress which reassembles at Mecca on the occasion of next year's pilgrimage. The native press of Egypt does not favor the Mecca Congress policy on the ground that an exclusively Ismalic policy nowadays is doomed to react on Islam and to the advantage of Islam's opponents.

JERUSALEM, Aug. 25 (Jewish Telegraphic Agency).—The Arab Congress, meeting at Nablus, 33 miles north of here, has adopted a resolution, rejecting the League of Nations mandate plan for Palestine, refusing Palestinian nationality and declining participation in the elections to the Legislature Council.

The congress instructed the political committee to prepare a national covenant and send missions to all Arab settlements in order to create a union of eastern nations. It was also decided to establish propaganda headquarters in London.

The congress was attended by over 100 delegates from all parts of the country. The deliberations ran quietly, undisturbed by demonstrations. Most of the speakers in a determined tone advised the policy of non-co-operation with the British

Administration in Palestine.
ZIONISTS URGE UNION.
Karlsbad Congress Seeks to Reconcile
Two American Factions.
KARLSBAD, Aug. 25 (Jewish Telegraph Agency)—Many more delegates to the World Zionist Congress are arriving, the total number now reaching over 150, besides many visitors from Europe and America. Dr. Chaim Weizmann, President of the World Zionist Organization, was to preside at the formal opening today, which follows the meetings of executive committees.

A determined effort is being made to effect a reconciliation between the two Zionist factions in the United States. The delegates chiefly interested in this movement are from Germany, France, Holland and Belgium. It is fostered by the strong sentiment for peace existing among the delegates.

Nahum Sokolow, Chairman of the World Zionist Executive Committee, is said to be advocating an immediate settlement of the differences between the two American groups in order to unite all the Zionist forces in the task of upbuilding Palestine."

It is clear that the Zionists needed a common enemy to unite them, and the alleged murder threats against Einstein, real, contrived or imagined, played a rôle in the promotion of that goal. The Zionists then worked to create economic conditions which would make Germany ripe for a Zionist dictator named Adolf Hitler. The history of the political Zionists' involvement in German wartime politics is discussed in Isaiah Friedman's *Germany, Turkey, and Zionism, 1897-1918*, Clarendon Press, Oxford, (1977).

3.9 Wolff Crying, Dirty Tricks, Censorship, Smear Campaigns and Anonymous Threats in the Name of Einstein

The promoters of Einstein and the theory of relativity have employed many of the same tactics and strategies common to such corrupt Jewish political movements as Zionism and Bolshevism. Charles Lane Poor worked hard to expose Einstein as a fraud.[414] Poor complained of terrible censorship of his efforts to expose Einstein and the experiments taken as evidence in support of the theory of relativity. This was and is a common complaint among those who raise concerns about the shameless promotion of the plagiarist Albert Einstein, and who question the metaphysical fallacies and internal contradictions of the theory of relativity.

In 1930, C. L. Poor wrote,

"Thus the claim of Einstein to have found a new law of gravitation and the many assertions that the theory of relativity has worked in accounting for the motions of Mercury and has been conclusively proved by the eclipse observations and by the displacement of spectral lines are all merely unproved, and, so far, really unsupported illusions. Einstein and his followers have been dwelling in the 'pleasing land of drowsyshed—'; in the land 'Of dreams that wave before the half shut eye.'"[415]

Though the theory of relativity was hyped in the 1920's as a well-proven and perfectly exact, perfectly logical theory, such claims were just that, just hype. There were few people who were competent to try to defend the theory, and the nonexistence of empirical justification for its fantastical claims led to a great insecurity in the academic community—some members of which had stretched out their necks when the press promoted Einstein as the new and improved "Jewish Newton"—and which was worried that the public might discover that Einstein was a fraud and his theories had no rational justification.

Those brave enough to speak out against the degeneration of science into bizarre mysticism, and the demise of professional integrity in science, faced intimidation, censorship, and the classic pernicious political tactics of crowd manipulation by Einstein's supporters. Einstein and his followers were not above employing dirty tricks to suppress opposition and the public disclosure of the truth.

Hubert Goenner tells the story of how Oskar Kraus was scheduled to deliver a speech in Berlin against the theory of relativity on 2 September 1920. Kraus was not able to give his speech, because he was not allowed to go to Germany. Johannes Riem stated that Kraus had wired him a telegram on 2 September 1920, which informed him that Kraus, "was refused a visa for political reasons."[416] Riem complained that,

"In such a way relativity theory is protected by the immigration service."[417]

Goenner notes that Ernst Gehrcke believed that he was censored at Einstein's request[418] from publishing Einstein's verbal assertion that accelerations are absolute in the theory of relativity. Gehrcke, who was a well published and well respected physicist, attempted to draw attention to Einstein's beliefs in the journal *Die Naturwissenschaften*, a Julius Springer publication edited by Einstein's friend and supporter Arnold Berliner,[419] which was quick to provide Einstein with an outlet to attack Lucien Fabre,[420] and which published *ad hominem* attacks against anti-relativists in the form of polemic book "reviews" written by Einstein's friends of anti-relativistic literature.[421] Einstein once commented that Springer had "powerful advertising resources",[422] and indeed the publishing house was large, influential and long-lived. Einstein was very well connected and most of his friends looked to him for letters of recommendation and for his intervention to obtain them positions, grants and increased salaries.[423]

Arvid Reuterdahl wrote of the political atmosphere surrounding the corrupt promotion of Einstein,

"The Academy of Nations—Its Aims and Hopes
World-Wide Organization of Learned Men Will Study
Scientific Questions for the Benefit of All Mankind
By ARVID REUTERDAHL
Dean, Department of Engineering and Architecture, the College of St. Thomas. St. Paul, Minn.

W E ARE emerging from a period of material and intellectual chaos. Nations have clashed in war. The intellectual world is still in conflict on the fields of knowledge. Never before has the demarcation between intellectual camps been so clearly defined. The meteoric rise of Einstein marks the beginning of this division in the modern kingdom of intellect. The history of civilization shows us that there is nothing exceptional in this condition of things. There were distinct schools of philosophy in ancient India and Greece. The Middle Ages tell the same story of intellectual diversity. In more recent times we find the schools of Descartes, Spinoza, Locke, Berkeley, Hume, Kant, Hegel, Schopenhauer, Comte, Mill, Spencer, Darwin, Lotze, Nietzsche, Bergson and Haeckel.

Now the intellectual world is divided broadly into the Relativistic and Anti-Relativistic schools. Einstein has served as a chemical reagent which has precipitated relativity from the present content of knowledge as a mass insoluble to the average man. Never before has the attention of the entire world been drawn to an intellectual system in so short a time. What are the reasons for this unprecedented occurrence? Does the theory of Einstein contain elements of unique value to the human race? These and many other questions come to us as we ponder over the almost miraculous and sudden advent of Einsteinism. No one will dispute the truth of the statement that, as far as the general public is concerned, the theory of Einstein has little or no value. The intricacies of its mathematics and the subtleties of its sophistries are beyond the average man.

How Einsteinism Was 'Put Over'

WE DO not deny that certain features of Einstein's theory cannot fail to fascinate the general public. The world's greatest masters of the art of appeal have, with infallible accuracy, provided sufficient potions from the 'world-of-make-believe' to excite the imagination and interest of even the most prosaic and matter-of-fact individual. Effective advertising when coupled with equally potent measures of suppression of all that might be inimical to the propaganda, together constitute a moving force capable of converting the world in a very brief time. By these doubtful means Einsteinism has conquered the world.

Were the Theory of Relativity sound, upright men must, nevertheless, protest against such questionable means of forcing its acceptance. Hidden forces, inimical to the frank and open discussion of alleged merits of this theory, have been at work in every civilized land.

I am in possession of letters from eminent European scientists describing the deplorable methods employed to hinder and, if possible, completely prevent an unbiased and free discussion of the problem of relativity. In addition to this evidence my own experience is proof conclusive that the known evil effects are not due to accidental causes, but arise from a well defined and strongly organized plan.

Scientific journals and societies in the United States have been loath to accept articles which even mildly criticized Einstein's theories. The advertisement of a book which contains a criticism of relativity, written by a well-known opponent of Einstein, was refused by a journal known for its vigorous publicity campaign in favor of Einsteinism. Two leading

American journals, whose main alleged purpose is the unbiased presentation of both sides of every question, have until recently refrained from publishing any statements inimical and detrimental to the theory of relativity. The change of attitude is undoubtedly due to the potent fact that despite the attempted suppression of free discussion, the entire world is now fearlessly and openly challenging the foundations of Einsteinism. A reaction against relativity, of unprecedented proportions and intensity, has set in and Einstein now finds himself on the defensive.

Discrimination Against Scientists

THE writer's article entitled 'Kinertia Versus Enstein' was rejected by a well-known eastern journal. The editor of this journal, after admitting that I had presented a strong case against Einstein, one that would cause something of a sensation, confided that after many misgivings, he, nevertheless, felt that he must return my article.

To draw certain inevitable inferences concerning the real reason for the rejection of the article was undoubtedly justifiable. It was then that THE DEARBORN INDEPENDENT accepted the article for publication.

Many of our scientific societies have discriminated against comparatively unknown scientists. Their papers have been returned without even a hasty perusal, because the writers were not members of the inner controlling circle. This criticism is, moreover, true also in the case of many scientific journals. In certain instances material has been appropriated from the articles before being returned. No credit has, in these cases, been given to the original contributors. The sacred unwritten law that credit should always be freely given to a contributor for even the smallest addition made to our quota of knowledge has been entirely ignored in many cases. The writer does not desire to convey the impression that these corrupt practices are universal; on the contrary, the splendid standards of purity and integrity of some scientific societies and journals constitute ideals which all should emulate.

There is, at the present time, a distressful lack of co-operation between learned societies. This unsound condition inevitably retards intellectual progress. International intellectual co-operation is, as yet, entirely unknown. Many years are required to transmit, through the laborious machinery of scientific approval, results and discoveries made in one country to another isolated from the former by language and geographical location. No common clearing house exists in which the appraisal and valuation of theories may be expeditiously effected. Organized attempts at unification, co-ordination and standardization of systems of knowledge to expedite educational progress are entirely lacking. The general public must oftentimes wait many years before receiving even a small measure of benefit from valuable discoveries because of the absence of organized means of systematic dissemination of accurate knowledge in a simple and easily understood form.

Many of these unfortunate conditions and deficiencies have been emphasized by the arrival of the theory of relativity. The rapid advent of Einsteinism, however, has taught us the lesson that a theory can be speedily 'promoted' by systematic publicity, fortified by a campaign of suppression of honest criticism. There is a twofold aspect to the lesson taught:

First, a benevolent aspect, consisting in the exemplified truth that knowledge can be rapidly disseminated by systematic co-operation.

Second, a malevolent aspect, involving the imposition of unproved hypotheses on the public by coercive means.

The intellectual world should benefit by both aspects of the lesson taught by the rise of relativity. The intellectual world must organize, sanely and safely, for co-operative derivation and dissemination of knowledge by dignified, simple, and accurate means. The world of intellect must protect itself from the evil effects of coercive effort in the 'promotion' of hypotheses.

The crucial question which now faces us may be briefly stated as follows: Can the errors and deficiencies of the *modus operandi* of the intellectual world, forcibly brought to our attention by the advent of Einsteinism, be eliminated and overcome? Have we the remedy at hand which will make impossible the recurrence of these unfortunate and lamentable conditions?

Would Keep World Informed

THE writer herewith presents for the serious consideration of the thinking world a brief outline of the purposes, scope and organization of The Academy of Nations, with the firm conviction that this instrument, when wielded co-operatively by the intellectual world, will transform the existing intellectual chaos into a cosmos of knowledge, advance the general status of education, protect the public against fallacious theories, disseminate knowledge of value to mankind, and enrich the world by the development of the common good.

Before a synopsis of this significant and important movement is presented, it is eminently fitting that a short statement be made concerning its origin.

Dr. Robert T. Browne, one of America's greatest thinkers, and author of the most profound work ever written on the hyperspace movement (The Mystery of Space) in a letter, May 9, 1921, to the writer, indicated that a renaissance in the field of education was not only necessary but inevitable at the present time. This conviction of Dr. Browne's was particularly gratifying to the writer because he had held the same view since that memorable day in 1919, when it became known here that Einstein's theory *seemed* to be confirmed by the results of the observations of the English Solar Expedition.

After some correspondence I submitted a plan for an international organization which met with the unqualified approval of Dr. Browne. At the request of the writer Dr. Browne proceeded to amplify the original outline of the plan with the result that an epoch-making document has been produced. The following excerpts from the original document will convey a brief idea of the causes, purposes and scope of the plan:

'The intellectual world is passing through a period of reconstruction. The entire body of knowledge is being reconstituted. New and radical developments are becoming manifest in science, philosophy, religion, and art; and these are approaching a synthesis hitherto undreamed of, being brought to this consummation by the advent of a movement of far-reaching significance and importance.

'A powerful creative spirit is at work in the world energizing and illumining the minds of men everywhere. The energies of humankind are seeking new and advanced avenues of expression, demanding freedom, certainty, security and the opportunity for the peaceful pursuit of the highest good.

'In the mind of man a new consciousness is broadening; the

foundations of a new race of superior men are being laid; the seeds of a higher and better civilization which may bless the nations of the earth are beginning to germinate. The development and fruition of these mighty factors in the advancement of mankind demand the earnest intellectual co-operation of strong men throughout the world to give direction and tendance to the new impulses, which as yet are without adequate determination and means of expression.

'This new order in the world should not and must not be allowed to lose its regenerating power on account of the lack of intelligent co-operation and conscious direction and guidance. The stream of potent human energies must be harnessed and its power utilized for the enrichment of the common good.'

To meet 'the urgency of the call for the accomplishment of these high purposes' an international organization known as *The Academy of Nations* has been formed.

The principal purposes of this organization are:

1. Unification of national effort in the world of knowledge.

2. Discovery, investigation and dissemination of truth.

3. Classification, standardization. and evaluation of the data of science, philosophy, religion and art.

4. Dialectic treatment of data with the view of arriving at synthetic judgment thereon.

5. Publication of findings under the impress of The Academy of Nations.

6. Announcement at prescribed intervals of the status of knowledge in the four major branches, viz: science, philosophy, religion, art.

Note—This to be equivalent to the charting of the bounds of material knowledge.

7. Recognition and encouragement of individual effort amid contributions to the body of knowledge.

Will Seek Co-operation

UNDER the plan each national unit will publish a journal at suitable intervals. The most important of these contributions will appear in the journal of the academy, which will be published in the languages of all the nations represented. The Year Book of the Academy of Nations will contain announcement of the advance of knowledge (the knowledge status) for the current year of publication. It will be compiled by an international board composed of members elected by the nation units.

The results of this organized work will be made available to the general public, in simple form, through the medium of the public press and by other suitable means.

The Academy of Nations will function in the unification and co-ordination of systems of knowledge, thus procuring the development of synthesized body of knowledge as against the highly specialized conditions now existing. The methods, aims and programs of education will be standardized. Another important function of the academy will be the promotion of the co-operative commonwealth of man in which the wealth-producing energies, the civilizing energies and the energies inherent in the social heritage of humanity shall be co-ordinated and made to yield the maximum value for the welfare of all mankind. Moreover, the academy will promote the use of scientific knowledge as a guiding principle in every department of human endeavor and it will encourage and develop the application of the principles of scientific human engineering to the problems of humanity and to the shaping of its destiny. There will be instituted a world tribunal for the adjudication of controversies in matters connected with theories, philosophical systems, hypotheses, and so on. The academy will be a powerful instrumentality for effecting international solidarity and for the promotion of good will and accord among the nations of the world. It will function also as a supreme centralized authority for the conferring of honors, merits, prizes, degrees, and so on, for distinguished services and for contributions to the body of knowledge. Heretofore, there has been no world society or authority which could bestow academic honors or recognitions on individuals. Affiliations with governments and other national agencies will be established to advance the cause of knowledge and the execution of its programs.

Organization Meeting Is Held

THE above consists in the main of direct quotations, suitably rearranged, from the original classic document.

In this great academy intellectual freedom will be reborn.

There will be no arbitrary exclusion of hypotheses, theories, views and beliefs. The academy will ever function as an open and free forum for the discussion of all the great problems of humanity.

One of the first duties to be assigned to the academy will be the adjudication and appraisal of the precise value and merit of the Theory of Relativity definitely to fix its 'knowledge status.'

The organization meeting of the College of Fellows of the Academy of Nations was held December 28 and 30, 1921, in Brooklyn. National institutes of the Academy of Nations are now being formed in Sweden, Germany. Switzerland, Czecho-Slovakia and Spain. Steps are being taken for the organization of institutes in Norway, Denmark, England, Holland, France and Italy. Within the ensuing year national institutes will be organized in every civilized country of the world.

The field of the academy embraces every general and special class of knowledge and its interests will, therefore, be universal."[424]

In the spring of 1922, Edouard Guillaume gave Einstein fair warning that he would debate him in Paris. Guillaume and others had published their findings that the special theory of relativity derives from a particular light sphere in a preferred frame of reference, and that in translational frames of reference this sphere becomes an ellipsoid.[425] Jánossy and others have since published works which also favor Lorentz' physical interpretation of light speed anisotropy in "moving" frames of reference, without relying solely upon the paradox of the twins.[426]

The Chicago Tribune reported on 31 March 1922,

"EINSTEIN FACES
IN PARIS GRAVE
BLOW AT THEORY

[Chicago Tribune Foreign News Service.]

BERNE, March 30.—Edmond Guillaume says he has discovered a fundamental error in the Einstein theory and is en route to Paris to attend the savant's lecture and to challenge the relativity discoverer.

M. Guillaume hopes for a public debate in which he can use

his ellipsoid to demonstrate Prof. Einstein's error.

Former Premier Painleve, a celebrated mathematician, has reached the same conclusions as M. Guillaume, but through a different process. M. Guillaume is a cousin of Charles Albert Guillaume, a recent Nobel Prize winner."

The Minneapolis Journal wrote on 9 April 1922,

"DR. GUILLAUME'S PROOFS OF EINSTEIN THEORY'S FALLACY REVEALED TO THE JOURNAL

Professor Reuterdahl of St. Thomas Makes Public Correspondence With Swiss Savant Disclosing Latter's Weapons of Attack on Relativity

BARES FACTS FOR WHICH SCIENTIFIC WORLD NOW EAGERLY WAITS AT PARIS

Simple Experience of Every Day Railroad Operation Relied On to Show That Man Who Upset Accepted Laws of Nature Is All Wrong

With the scientific world awaiting Dr. Edmund Guillaume's appearance in Paris to challenge and attempt to destroy the very foundation of the Einstein theory of relativity, Professor Arvid Reuterdahl, dean of the department of engineering and architecture at the College of St. Thomas, Midway, last night revealed to The Journal the purported proof of the fallacy of 'Einsteinism' which Dr. Guillaume will use in his Paris attack.

Professor Reuterdahl all along has contended the Einstein theory was all wrong and is now preparing a book, 'Fallacies of Einstein.' When Einstein was in America Reuterdahl challenged him to a debate without avail. He has been in correspondence with Dr. Guillaume and has received from the noted Swiss scientist a special contribution for his book containing the very matter which Guillaume will use in his forthcoming Paris attack on relativity. Until Professor Reuterdahl disclosed Dr.

Guillaume's proofs to The Journal last night, the St. Thomas dean was the only man in the United States who possessed the explanation that is expected by its advocate to knock the whole Einstein theory of relativity into a cocked hat when Professor Einstein is confronted with it at his forthcoming lecture in Paris.

According to a special cable dispatch published in The Journal March 31, Dr. Guillaume claims that the matter now in possession of Professor Reuterdahl and revealed to the public today, discloses a fundamental error in the Einstein theory. The cable dispatch stated that Dr. Guillaume hoped for a public debate with Einstein in which he would have a chance to hurl his proofs at the author of the relativity theory.

'The final death blow to Einsteinism is about to be delivered by the eminent Swiss physicist and mathematician. Dr. Edouard Guillaume when the scientists convene at Paris,' said Professor Reuterdahl last night. 'Dr. Guillaume in two letters written to me and dated July 25 and Aug. 13, 1921, pointed out a fundamental error in the mathematical speculations of Einstein which explodes the entire theory proving that relativity is the greatest scientific fiasco of all times. Dr. Guillaume shows that Einstein, in his first article entitled, 'Zur Elektrodynamik bewegter Koeper,' which appeared in 1905 in Annalen der Physik, volume 17, commits 'the greatest scientific blunder of modern times.'

Swiss Savant's Proofs Revealed

'Einsteinism stands or falls upon the socalled postulate of the absolute velocity of light. Dr. Guillaume in a brilliant analysis, shows that this very postulate is destroyed by a fatal error in Einstein's mathematics.'

The following is a translation of Professor Guillaume's final summary communicated to Professor Reuterdahl:

'Einstein considers a luminous signal produced, for instance, on a track by means of an electric pocket lamp. A brief signal gives rise to a wave which moves through space and in all directions with a velocity of 300,000 kilometers per second. This wave forms at each moment a spherical surface, the ray of which increases with this velocity and the center of which is motionless. Let us inquire now how the wave appears to an observer carried along with the train. Let us apply the transformation of Lorentz. What is found? Einstein maintains that the wave appears also as a sphere with its center motionless as regards the train, and whose ray grows likewise with the velocity of 300,000 kilometers a second.

Simple Test Cited

"Die betrachtete Welle,' says Einstein in conclusion, 'ist auch in bewegten System (Wagon) betrachtel eine Kugelwelle von der Ausbreitungsgeschwindigkeit 300,000 km-sec.' But if we look more closely we detect an error in the famous physicist's calculation: the wave seen from the train is not a sphere, but rather an ellipsoid, and the famous principle of the absolute constancy of light vanishes! At the same time collapse all the paradoxes, and at last we are clear of this inextricable web and beyond the reach of the entangling challenges that Einstein has hurled at our good sense, free from what Americans have so well termed 'Einsteinism.''

'Einstein has been challenged to meet Dr. Guillaume at Paris,' said Professor Reuterdahl last night. 'The evidence presented by Dr. Guillaume is so conclusive that Einstein will hasten the death of the already dying theory of relativity by accepting the challenge. If Einstein uses the same caution that he exhibited when challenged by me he will again carefully avoid the issue by veiling himself in sphynx like silence.'"

On 22 April 1922, Edouard Guillaume complained to Arvid Reuterdahl, in a letter which was reproduced in *The Minneapolis Journal*, which newspaper wrote on 14 May 1922,

"Guillaume, Barred in Move To Debate Einstein, Calls Meeting Political Reunion

Savant, in letter to Professor Reuterdahl of St. Thomas, Says Ideals of Science Were Treated With Ignominy in Paris

Failing in an attempt to force a public debate which they hoped would disclose fundamental errors in the Einstein theory of relativity, scientists in the antirelativity group will continue their fight on 'Einsteinism,' Professor Arvid Reuterdahl of St. Thomas college said last night.

Dean of the department of engineering and architecture at St. Thomas, a prominent figure in the scientific world because of his research work, Professor Reuterdahl has collaborated with Dr. Edouard Guillaume, Swiss savant, in disputing the theory which has brought fame to Einstein.

When Einstein visited the United States Professor Reuterdahl challenged him to an open debate.

Guillaume Meets Einstein

In Paris recently Dr. Guillaume faced Dr. Einstein on a platform, before French scientists convened at the College of France. His appearance had been awaited eagerly by scientists throughout the world.

'In a letter which I just have received,' Professor Reuterdahl said, 'Dr. Guillaume gives a vivid picture of the scene which ever will remain a blot on the fair escutcheon of science.

Dr. Guillaume had lectured only a few minutes when he was silenced peremptorily in order to give way to the illustrious man of the hour, Einstein, who dismissed the entire matter with the gesture of a conqueror.'

Floor Given to Einstein

'I had hoped to be permitted quietly to present the results of my researches,' reads the letter from Dr. Guillaume to Professor Reuterdahl. Unfortunately, I had barely lectured for five minutes when I was interrupted in order to give the floor to Einstein, who was forced to acknowledge the fact that an ellipsoid results from his own mathematics.

(Einstein's theory is that a wave surface of light, traveling outward from any luminous body, such as an electric light, is a spherical surface. Dr. Guillaume and Professor Reuterdahl contend that this surface is ellipsoidal under certain conditions.)

'Einstein dismissed the matter,' the letter continues, 'by saying that he was not interested. At this statement of Einstein's the large audience present applauded vociferously. I then saw that it was absolutely impossible to carry on a scientific discussion under these conditions.

'That, my dear Professor Reuterdahl, is the ignominious treatment which the high ideals of science receive at the present time.

Called Political Reunions

'Scientific congresses of this kind are nothing more than political reunions. It is urgent that all honest men unite to fight against these deplorable methods, which can only lead to the death of science. You may say definitely in America that all discussion was prevented and made impossible by the fanatic attitude of the relativists.'

When Professor Reuterdahl revealed April 9, through The Journal, the points to be used by Dr. Guillaume in his Paris debate, he predicted that that attempt to force Einstein into an honest discussion of his own theory would prove a total failure.

Professor Reuterdahl now is preparing a book, 'Fallacies of Einstein,' to which Dr. Guillaume has made a contribution. Dr. Guillaume issued a public statement March 31, which was cabled to The Journal, in which he said a fundamental error had been found in the Einstein theory."

Guillaume's letter, which was also reproduced in *The New York Times*, Arvid Reuterdahl, "The Origin of Einsteinism", (12 August 1923), Section 7, p. 8:

"I had hoped to be permitted quietly to present the results of my researches. Unfortunately, I had barely lectured for five minutes when I was interrupted in order to give the floor to Einstein, who was forced to acknowledge that an ellipsoid results from his own mathematics. Einstein dismissed the matter by saying that he was not interested. At this statement of Einstein's the large audience present applauded vociferously. I then saw that it was absolutely impossible to carry on a scientific discussion under these conditions. That, my dear Professor Reuterdahl, is the ignominious treatment which the high ideals of science receive at the present time. Scientific congresses of this kind are nothing more than political reunions. It is urgent that all honest men unite to fight against these deplorable methods, which can only lead to the death of science. You may say definitely in America that all discussion was prevented and made impossible by the fanatic attitude of the relativists."[427]

William Cardinal O'Connell, who had written a letter condemning anti-Semitism and who had signed John Spargo's protest against anti-Semitism,[428] accused Einstein and his clique of promoting atheism in a lecture the Cardinal had given. Cardinal O'Connell was quoted in the 12 April 1929 issue of the *Boston Evening American*,

"That there is in certain quarters such a heated defense of an unprovable, certainly unproved hypothesis, only again makes it doubly clear that what I said to the students was true—the claque is applauding noisily so as to drown honest criticism. But that has been from all accounts the Einstein method of answer to all who disagree with him."

Other such staged interruptions as happened to Guillaume took place in defense of the indefensible, in defense of Einstein and his metaphysical nonsense. For example, when Arvid Reuterdahl spoke at the University of Wisconsin, Madison, in March of 1926 about the Einstein swindle, the faculty there allegedly disrupted his lecture.[429] The University's newspaper, *The Daily Cardinal*, reported,

"Not even a tithe of courtesy is being shown Prof. Reuterdahl [***] At the lecture Wednesday night instructors of the mathematics department interfered with the lecturer so that he was unable to finish his talk. [***] **Staff Tries To Stop Talk** [***] members of the instructional staff of the mathematical department tinkered with the water pressure apparatus which operates the projection screen [***] and made it impossible for the lecturer to continue [***] the members of the department also blinked the lights in the auditorium while the speaker was lecturing, putting the auditorium in darkness temporarily. This is said to have occurred three times."[430]

Johannes Stark alleged that Ernst Gehrcke was denied a full professorship in Germany, because he had argued against the theory of relativity,

"G e h r c k e ist der Kampf gegen die Relativitätstheorie übel bekommen; trotz seiner zahlreichen hervorragenden experimentellen Arbeiten wird er von Fakultäten nicht für ein physikalisches Ordinat vorgeschlagen."[431]

In 1882, Franz Mehring quoted a Jewish author who criticized Jews for, among other things, "the malicious gloating when veritable conspiracies deprived of their livelihoods people who were suspected of anti-Jewish feelings[.]"[432] Einstein and his friends sought to stigmatize *any* criticism of him or of the theory of relativity as if it were "anti-Semitism" *per se*.[433] They thereby threatened anyone who dared speak out with career infringement or the absolute inability to find work. Whether or not significant numbers of people interfered with the careers of persons suspected of anti-Jewish feelings for merely questioning Einstein or discussing the facts, the impression that they would existed and had a chilling effect on Einstein's opposition in the debate over the merits of relativity theory and Einstein's obvious plagiarism. This has been very detrimental to the progress of Physics.

Hugo Dingler's alloted time to speak against the theory of relativity at the Bad Nauheim meeting was severely restricted. Ernst Mach wrote of his admiration for Dingler,

> "I myself—seventy-four years old, and struck down by a grave malady—shall not cause any more revolutions. But I hope for important progress from a young mathematician, Dr. Hugo Dingler, who, judging from his publications, has proved that he has attained to a free and unprejudiced survey of *both* sides of science."[434]

Gehrcke's accusations that Einstein was a plagiarist were fully justified by the facts, and Dingler correctly pointed out several fatal flaws in the metaphysical formulation of the theory of relativity.[435]

Hubert Goenner wrote,

> "[Gehrcke] blame[d] Einstein's reply of 27 August [1920] for arousing political and racial instincts and deflecting public attention from the facts of relativity theory."

Paul Weyland made the same charge, that Einstein's defense of his theory and his claims of originality were so weak that he was forced to run away from Germany, and to change the subject to fabricated accusations of anti-Semitism. Arvid Reuterdahl made a similar claim when the *Scientific American* raised the issue of anti-Semitism in the context of Reuterdahl's questioning of Einstein's priority, while being forced to concede that Reuterdahl was factually correct in his arguments.[436] Reuterdahl responded, stating on 18 June 1921, *inter alia*:

> "IN AN article published in this journal, April 30, 1921, Professor Arvid Reuterdahl presented definite evidence proving the similarity between the work of the unknown scientist 'Kinertia' and the much-advertised Einsteinian Theory of Relativity. The similarity is so pronounced that any fair-minded person at once must wonder if the alleged contributions of Dr. Einstein rest upon borrowed foundations. It is a fact that 'Kinertia's' work antedates that of Einstein. It is difficult to prove a direct charge of plagiarism. This is

particularly true whenever the person involved is surrounded by a veritable host of protectors who refuse to permit an honest investigation.

Professor Reuterdahl's reply to his critics follows in part:

In the case of 'Kinertia' Versus Einstein the present writer did not state that Einstein is a plagiarist. To make such a bald statement one must have indisputable proofs. I did state and again repeat the statement: 'If Einstein was aware of 'Kinertia's' discovery then the appellation 'plagiarist,' bestowed upon him by his German professional colleagues, is eminently fitting. If, on the contrary, Einstein was unaware of this work, then he is, nevertheless, antedated by the work of 'Kinertia'. Einstein is at liberty to choose either horn of the dilemma.'

Referring to an editorial criticism in the *Scientific American* of May 14, Professor Reuterdahl continues: 'The *Scientific American* is particularly disturbed by my article entitled ''Kinertia' Versus Einstein.' On the cover of this issue the following question appeared in bold type 'Is Einstein a Plagiarist?' In reference to this question the *Scientific American* states: 'It will be at once understood that according to Professor Reuterdahl he is.' What I actually stated in my article has been again recorded above in order to refresh the memory of the editorial writer. After this perversion of truth a subtle atmosphere is created in order to link, by contrastive suggestion, both the present writer and THE DEARBORN INDEPENDENT with the ambitions of the former Kaiser of Germany. A diversion is thereby adroitly produced which removes the reader's attention from the actual question in hand, that is, ''Kinertia' Versus Einstein,' to an entirely different issue. Moreover, another irrelevant issue is deftly imposed, that is, anti-Semitism.

The present writer emphatically denies and resents both insinuations created in this questionable manner. I am a loyal citizen of the United States. I was born in Sweden. I came to the United States when I was six and a half years of age. Furthermore, the allegation, also by innuendo, that my attack upon the theories of Einstein are due to anti-Semitic feeling, I brand as a gross misrepresentation.

The *Scientific American* editorial then becomes a plea for Professor Einstein's mathematical product. There seems to be urgent need to show that although Einstein has benefitted by 'ideas which have had a rather nebulous existence before him' nevertheless in the hands of this master craftsman they have been mathematically welded into a 'crowning achievement' which 'has never been approached or approximated in any way.'

Suppose, for the sake of argument, that we grant that this concession in no way affects the real issue which we may state in the form of a question: Has Einstein given proper credit to the creators of the 'nebulous ideas' which he used in constructing this supreme masterpiece of the human intellect? We are not aware that he has ever referred to their humble contributions to his stupendous structure. It seems that he has ruthlessly discarded the scaffolding which he used in building his edifice without paying for its use. Do we find the name of Dr. J. H. Ziegler mentioned in any of his writings? Is there any reference to the contributions of 'Kinertia'? Has he ever answered the charges made by Engineer Rudolph Mewes, Professors E. Gehrke and Paul Weyland that he appropriated a formula which appeared in a work published by the late Professor Gerber in the year, 1898? If perchance Professor Einstein should plead ignorance of these contributions at the time when he developed his mathematical analysis, then we demand that he publicly admit their previous existence and definite worth. It remains to be seen if Dr. Einstein will even condescend to comply with this eminently just demand. We trust that we may be permitted to state that what we have granted in the above, for the sake of argument, we do not admit as an actual fact. The writer is prepared to show that Einsteinism is a pernicious fallacy."[437]

Below is the article in *Scientific American*, which Reuterdahl rejoined. The author of the *Scientific American* article dubbed the practice of standing up for ethical practices and giving due credit to those who deserve it, "picking the bones". The author sought to characterize anyone who would assert their priority for ideas Einstein repeated without an attribution, as if a "vulture". Whereas Reuterdahl focused on the facts, the author of the *Scientific American* article launched a hand-waving personal attack against Reuterdahl, *conceding that he was factually correct*, and mischaracterized the general theory of relativity as an exposition on the mechanism and cause of gravitation, which it is not. The author asserted that, "Nobody would claim that Einstein's entire structure is novel[. . . .]" However, that is exactly what Einstein did do by publishing papers completely devoid of references to the work of his predecessors. Daniel Kennefick wrote in his article,

"Einstein Versus the *Physical Review*", *Physics Today*, (September, 2005), pp. 43-48, at 46:

"Although it now bears Einstein and Rosen's names, the solution for cylindrical gravitational waves had been previously published by the Austrian physicist Guido Beck in 1925. But Beck's paper was completely unknown to relativists with the single exception of his student Peter Havas, who entered the field in the late 1950's. In a 1926 paper by the English mathematicians O. R. Baldwin and George B. Jeffery, and in the referee's report on Einstein's paper, there was discussion of the fact that singularities in the metric coefficients are unavoidable when describing plane waves with infinite wavefronts. But although such a wave shows some distortion, in the words of the referee, 'the field itself is flat' at infinity.[9]

Clearly, the referee's familiarity with the literature exceeded Einstein's, but then Einstein was notoriously lax in that regard. The published Einstein-Rosen paper contains no direct reference to any other paper whatsoever and only two other authors are even mentioned by name. In response to Infeld's suggestion that he search the literature for previous work, Einstein laughed and said, 'Oh yes. Do it by all means. Already I have sinned too often in this respect.'[5,438]

The *Scientific American* of 14 May 1921 stated:

"The Anti-Einstein Campaign

THE intellectual world moves slowly in the matter of extending recognition to those who have consecrated their lives to the cause of reason. Mendel had been dead many years before the remarkable nature of his work was recognized. When we contrast Mendel's case with that of Einstein we are forced to admit that the German physicist's sensational rise is the most extraordinary in the history of science. Barnum, king of advertisers, could not have staged a more effective or expeditious advertising campaign."

With so much of Professor Reuterdahl's article in the *Dearborn Independent* we suppose anyone will agree. But this article is given its real place by the scare-head of the cover, which asks, in ¾-inch letters, "IS EINSTEIN A PLAGIARIST?"

It will be at once understood that according to Professor Reuterdahl he is. We expect this sort of thing from the anti-Semites of Germany, and from those of the former Kaiser's loyal supporters who resent Dr. Einstein's refusal to have anything to do with the celebrated Manifesto of the 93 Immortals. But from a reputable American source—even one celebrated for its anti-Semitism—we should look for something a little different.

It is not easy for a layman to form a just estimate of Einstein's work. And whatever temptation to error is presented to him will be in the direction of underestimation. The phrase "relativity of motion" is not new. The Greeks had it, Newton had it, every popular explanation of Einstein starts by reminding us that this is something we have always known but chosen to ignore. It is easy to overlook that Einstein has taken this familiar notion, applied it with a rigor and a consistency and a generality which it has never before enjoyed, given it a significance and got results out of it which it had never before been dreamed lay in it.

Again with the problem of gravitation. We all know that Newton solved this problem empirically only. We all know that he said nothing about the causes or the mechanism of gravitation—for the excellent reason that he could learn nothing of these. We all know that since his time thousands of scientists have searched for the cause and the mechanism. We do not all know what is equally true, that many of these searchers have been led to propose slight modifications in Newton's mathematical law—modifications which were in agreement with this or that observed fact.

All this makes it very easy to accuse Einstein of plagiarism. Not alone is everyone acquainted with classical relativity apt to judge the contents by the label on the container and assume that Einstein's relativity is the same old stuff, but the claim may with some show of plausibility be made that any investigator of gravitation has anticipated Einstein. This claim gains color in the far-from-rare case that its beneficiary can be shown to have attained results which are included in Einstein's, or to have supplied Einstein with some of his material. Nobody would claim that Einstein's entire structure is novel—the sum total of human knowledge is today too large to make it possible for a contribution like his to be made out of whole cloth.

Everyone who possesses enough mathematics to follow

Einstein knows that he has made a very material original contribution—that he has formulated mathematically and as a concrete whole ideas which have had a rather nebulous existence before him, cementing the structure with ideas to which he has himself given birth. His crowning achievement is the precise mathematical formulation; this has never been approached or approximated in any way.

We can paraphrase Professor Reuterdahl with some profit. Never in the history of science has anyone ever made an epoch-marking advance, but what the vultures have flocked about his trail, demanding credit for what he has done and claiming ownership of the work which he has put out. But never before has it been the case that the really big men of science have accepted an advance so promptly and so whole-heartedly, and left this business of picking the bones to the small fry whose names will be forgotten fifty years from now."

In 1846, an author in the *Scientific American* had demonstrated an interest in Zionist affairs,

"THE ISRAELITES IN GERMANY are in great commotion. At Berlin and Frankfort two-thirds of them have separated from the synagogues, to form new societies, and it is thought that their example will be generally followed. The new school are supported by the government; they celebrate the Sabbath of the Christians, and worship with chaunts, the music of the organ, and sermons. Sir Moses Montefiore, backed by the Rothschilds, is about establishing a Jewish colony in Palestine, and has obtained an ukase from the Emperor Nicholas, authorising the emigration thither of ten thousand Russian Jews."[439]

The maltreatment of anyone who disagreed with Einstein, pointed out his plagiarism or questioned the theory of relativity, reminds one of the fanatical and truly vicious abuse political Zionists inflicted upon anyone who dared disagree with them. Albert T. Clay documented the methods of the political Zionists in Palestine in 1921, in an article, "Political Zionism", *The Atlantic Monthly*, Volume 127, Number 2, (February, 1921), pp. 268-279, at 276-277,

"The old resident Jews of Palestine certainly have other than religious grounds for their indifference toward the efforts of the

Political Zionists. Last winter the Council of Jerusalem Jews appointed a commission of representative men holding leading positions, to visit parents who were sending their children to proscribed schools, in order to secure their withdrawal. Among these schools, which included those conducted by the convents and churches, some of which have existed in Jerusalem for a long time, are the British High School for Girls, the English College for Boys, and the Jewish School for Girls. In the latter, conducted by Miss Landau, an educated English Jewess, all the teachers are Jewish; most of the teaching is in the English language. This school, which is financed by enlightened Jews of England, was denounced more severely than the others, because, not being in sympathy with the programme of the Political Zionists, Miss Landau refused to teach the Zionist curriculum. She was even informed that her school would be closed.

In a series of articles that appeared in *Doar Hayom*, the Hebrew daily paper, last December, it was stated that the parents who refused to comply with the requests of the Commission [of the Council of Jerusalem Jews] were to be boycotted, cast out from all intercourse with Jews, denied share in Zionist funds, and deprived of all custom for their shops and hotels. 'Anyone who refused, let him know that it is forbidden for him to be called by the name of Jew; and there is to be for him no portion or inheritance with his brethren.' They were given notice that they would 'be fought by all lawful means.' Their names were to be put 'upon a monument of shame, as a reproach forever, and their deeds writte unto the last generation.' 'If they are supported, their support will cease; if they are merchants, the finger of scorn will be pointed at them; if they are rabbis, they will be moved far from their office; they shall be put under the ban and persecuted, and all the people of the world shall know that there is no mercy in justice.'

A month later the results of this 'warfare' were reviewed. We were informed that some Jews had been influenced, 'but others—and the greater number, and those of the Orthodox,—those who fear God—having read the letters [signed by the head of its delegates and the Zionist Commission] became angry at the 'audacity' of the Council of Jerusalem Jews 'which mix themselves up in private affairs,' have torn the letter up, and that finished it.'

Then followed a long diatribe against these parents, boys,

and girls, in which it was demanded that the blacklist of traitors to the people be sent to 'those who perform circumcision, who control the cemeteries and hospitals'; that an order go forth so that 'doctors will not visit their sick, that assistance when in need, if they are on the list of the American Relief Fund, will not be given to them.' 'Men will cry to them, 'Out of the way, unclean, unclean.' . . . They are in no sense Israelites.'

It is to be regretted that only these few paraphrases and quotations from the series of articles published can be presented here.

The work of the Councils Committee met with not a little success; pupils left schools, and teachers gave up their positions. Two instructors in the English College, whose fathers were rabbis, and a third, whose brother was a teacher in a Zionist school, resigned. Another refused to do so, and declared himself ready, in the interests of the Orthodox Jews, who were suffering under this tyranny, which they deplored, to give the fullest testimony to the authorities concerning this persecution. The administration, under Governor Bols, finally intervened, and at least no further public efforts to carry out their programme were made.

If, in this early stage of the development of Political Zionism, even the Palestinian Religious Jews already find themselves under such a tyranny, what will happen if these men are allowed to have full control of the government? And what kind of treatment can the Christian and th Moslem expect in their efforts to educate their children, if the Political Zionists are allowed to develop their Jewish state to such a point that they can dispense with their mandatory and tell the British to clear out? When such things happen under British administration, what will take place if the Jewish State is ever realized, and such men are in full control?"

Prof. Arvid Reuterdahl was quoted in *The St. Paul Daily News* on 8 May 1921,

"Einstein's Theory of Relativity Upset by St. Paul Scientist Whose New Book Charges Gross Errors

World Has Gone Mad About Mythical Unrealities, Declares Prof. Arvid Reuterdahl, Dean of Engineering and Architecture at St. Thomas College—Offers to Debate Question.

Editor's Note.—The visit to the United States of Prof. Einstein has brought on a countrywide discussion of his theory of relativity. Not many persons know anything about relativity, but nevertheless, they are talking about it and Einstein. In St. Paul there is a man, Prof. Arvid Reuterdahl, dean, department of engineering and architecture, St. Thomas college, who disputes the Einstein theory. He is writing a book now called 'The Fallacies of Einstein.' Prof. Reuterdahl is a distinguished scientist, both in America and abroad. He is the author of various scientific works and a frequent contributor to magazines. At the request of The Daily News he has written the following article dealing with the Einstein theory of relativity.

* * *

BY ARVID REUTERDAHL,
Dean, Department of Engineering and Architecture,

The College of St. Thomas.

AT THE present time we often hear this question asked:
'What is the theory of relativity?'
Whenever the question is asked Einstein's name is invariably mentioned.
To be exact this question should take the following form:
'What Is Einsteinism?'
A complete answer would require a book of many pages.
However, we may answer the latter question briefly as follows:
Einsteinism is a mind-product produced by combining a few consistent concepts with numerous mythical unrealities into a mental world system with the hope it will correspond with the real physical universe.

'SWEPT ENTIRE COUNTRY.'
We may say Einsteinism in the United States began with the

publication of a dispatch cabled from Berlin Dec. 2, 1919, to the New York Times.

Like an enormous tidal wave Einsteinism then swept from the Atlantic to the Pacific coast.

Mr. Average Man soon began talking about the theory of relativity. Humorous publications gave versions of Einsteinism which for accuracy in presentation oftentimes surpassed the mathematical outbursts of over-enthusiastic savants.

Nowhere could one hear a dissenting voice.

EXPOSED LAST YEAR.

The first brief exposition of the fallacies of Einstein, published in the United States, appeared in my work, 'Scientific Theism Versus Materialism: the Space-Time Potential.' This book was published in the fall of 1920 by the Devin-Adair Co., New York. Sir Oliver Lodge a few months previously, however, had issued a warning against the too ready acceptance of Einsteinism.

His warning went unheeded and the great wave of Einsteinism rolled on unchecked. I found myself almost alone in the fight against the greatest and most pernicious scientific fallacy of modern times.

However, I was not entirely alone at this time in my battle against the great sophist of all times.

AIDED BY HEIDENREICH.

In fact, since the year 1914 my dear friend, Dr. E. Lee Heidenreich, the eminent engineer, mathematician and philosopher, had espoused my cause. With the clear vision of a seer, Dr. Heidenreich realized that the old science must give way before a broader cosmic theory based upon sound philosophic principles grounded in fact.

He courageously and fearlessly championed the cause of my Space-Time Potential. He was instrumental in arranging lectures for me at the Kansas state agricultural college and the University of Kansas.

The commendatory letters concerning these lectures which I received from Dr. A. A. Potter, then dean of the agricultural college, and Dr. H. E. Rice, Kansas state university, have been a source of great encouragement to me during my long and arduous fight for the recognition of a broader and more universally consistent view of the physical universe.

Dr. Heidenreich, being a descendant of the Vikings, gloried

in the single combat.

Persistently and fearlessly he has championed my cause both in the United States and in Norway.

When Einsteinism overran the world Dr. Heidenreich refused to accept its fallacious tenets and gave vigorous battle to this new intellectual Frankenstein.

In the early part of the year 1921 an able and fearless writer championed my cause in an article entitled 'Relativity or Interdependence.' This article has since been referred to, time and again, as a classic.

Its author, Rev. Prof. John T. Blankart, in no uncertain terms and with keen acumen points out the inherent inconsistencies in Einsteinism. He brings his masterly article to a close with the following statement:

'Einstein has stated, 'If any deduction from it (the theory of relativity) should prove untenable it must be given up. A modification of it seems impossible without destruction of the whole.'

MORE AID NECESSARY.

'If this article has indicated to the reader that by that statement Einstein has perhaps signed the death warrant of his theory of relativity, the writer shall feel that part of his purpose has been accomplished.'

This exceptionally meritorious contribution exercised a beneficent influence in limited circles. However, one could hardly expect that a lone volume and a single article, without proper publicity, could stem the onrush of the Einsteinistic heresy.

Now, however, the tide is turning. After I issued my challenge to Einstein to a written debate on the theory of relativity I have received letters from prominent scientists and thinkers who assure me they will do their utmost to help vanish this Goliah of skepticism. Prof. Einstein has insinuated that my attack on his theory of relativity is merely a form of anti-Semitic propaganda.

This insinuation is absolutely without foundation in fact.

REVERES BARUCH SPINOZA.

If the originator of the theory of relativity had been born in Sweden, my native land, I would have denounced the tenets of his theory with no less vigor. The fact that Dr. Einstein is of Jewish extraction is not the reason for my attack on his theory.

I desire that this be distinctly understood now and for all future time.

My challenge to Prof. Einstein is based upon purely intellectual grounds. I contend his theory is a monstrous and dangerous fallacy which leads to absolute skepticism. I have profound reverence for Baruch Spinoza, the great philosopher. Spinoza was a Jew.

Certain erroneous inferences and unjust insinuations have been made concerning the appearance of my article entitled 'Kinertia Versus Einstein' in the Dearborn Independent.

Before I submitted this article to the Dearborn Independent I sent it to a well-known eastern journal.

MANUSCRIPT RETURNED.

The editor of this journal finally returned my manuscript with a most courteously worded letter in which he expressed his regret that he could not risk its publication, despite the fact he felt confident I had made out a particularly strong case against Einstein. In fact, he went so far as to state my article would create a sensation if published. Evidently it would have been unwise for this eastern journal to publish my article. The path of truth is beset with many thorns.

It grieves me to be forced into the admission that our scientific journals, while professing to be the free and untramelled vehicles of truth for its own sake, generally manage by means of plausible excuses to permanently prevent the publication of contributions which do not conform with the intellectual welfare of the clique in control.

The journals which are free from this destructive influence are generally too timid to assert their own independence.

FREEDOM IN DAILY PRESS.

This latter class is composed of journals which depend upon the European scientists to put the stamp of approval or disapproval upon that which is new or disturbing. It would seem there is much more genuine freedom in the daily press.

The spirit of revolt against this czar of science is growing.

Many independent thinkers have joined the anti-Einsteinism ranks. I believe Einstein himself is now beginning to see the handwriting on the wall.

One may be permitted, not without considerable show of justice, to infer his persistent refusal to enter into any controversial discussion is an indication he tacitly admits the relativity bubble is practically ready to collapse.

The following quotation from a letter which I have recently received from Dr. Robert T. Browne, author of the truly great work, 'The Mystery of Space,' is indeed noteworthy:

'The gods of science have placed their imprimatur upon the theory of relativity and consequently it will be exceedingly difficult to break through the iron ring.

BROWNE PLEDGES AID.

'Primarily, however, I should think with you, as with me, the consideration of greatest importance is not so much with the incidentals of this movement itself. The theory of relativity is but a phase of that deeper and broader movement of mechanistic conceptualism against which you have argued so incontrovertibly in 'Scientific Theism.' The task, then, is not so much to combat the theory, as I see it, as it is to strike with might and main at the vitals, the fundamental premises of that erroneous, fragmentary and biased view which seeks to interpret the universe in terms of mechanistic concepts.'

Dr. Browne concludes his letter to me with the following assurance:

'Please be assured that should the opportunity come my way I shall be allied with you in the fight against this mathematical usurpation.'

COMPARED TO DRUG.

Dr. W. E. Glanville, the eminent astronomer of Baltimore, who is a member of British, French and American astronomical societies, states:

'The Einstein theory is like a newly discovered drug which is brought forth and acclaimed as a universal scientific panacea.'

Dr. Sydney T. Skidmore of Philadelphia writes:

'It (Einsteinism) is shapen from non-Euclidean, otherwise called meta-geometry, and this consists entirely of mental constructions that are purely subjective and correspond to nothing in nature.'

'Kinertia' states: 'Science wants more than agnosticism; it wants to know the absolute truth before accepting any such theory; even if D'Alembert's ghost is dressed in Hamiltonian functions.'

QUOTES SWISS BOOK.

I have just received a complimentary copy of an exceptionally meritorious work written by Dr. Edouard

Guillaume of the University of Lausanne, Switzerland. The title of this work is 'La Theorie de la Relativite, Et Sa Signification.' I quote the following from this work: 'We have gradually come to substitute for Descarte's rigid system of relation, systems of unheard of subtleness, to which Einstein has given the picturesque name of 'mollusk systems.' Our mathematical constructions become, as it were, devilfish which strive, while adapting themselves to fasten upon subtle natural manifestations.'

Note the keen rapier thrusts against Einsteinism by this famous scientific 'maitre d'armes.'

WORK NEARS COMPLETION.

Dr. Guillaume has not been hoodwinked by the delicate sophism of Einstein.

My work entitled 'The Fallacies of Einstein' is now nearing completion.

In this work I have stripped Einsteinism of its mathematical adornment.

Without this mathematical camouflage Einsteinism is scarcely more than a mere devitalized skeleton whose Einsteinian skull is forever grinning at its Galileian toes."

While it is true that THE DEARBORN INDEPENDENT published broad criticisms of Jews, Reuterdahl's article was not in any way anti-Semitic and an allegation of ethnic bias is not a racist attack, but is rather a defense against racism. Reuterdahl first sought to publish his article elsewhere and it was refused without stated grounds. Reuterdahl asserted that the circulation of Henry Ford's paper was about 750,000 readers, which offered Reuterdahl the opportunity he had been denied elsewhere to bring his message to a wide audience. Jewish racists ought not to be allowed to censor out all open debate on issues they want suppressed and Reuterdahl had a right and an obligation to express his views wherever he could.

Frederick Drew Bond raised the issue of Reuterdahl's publication of articles in THE DEARBORN INDEPENDENT in a polemic against Reuterdahl in *The New York Times* in 1923.[440] Bond's second and then current wife was first cousin of the racist Zionist blackmailer United States Supreme Court Justice Louis D. Brandeis, who was an ardent and politically influential Zionist with close connections to President Wilson and Chaim Weizmann, and who attained his seat in the Supreme Court by blackmailing President Woodrow Wilson. Bond, perhaps speaking from a guilty conscience, denied that his connection to Brandeis had anything to do with his attack on Reuterdahl, in private correspondence with Reuterdahl.[441] However, it was Bond who raised the issue of his connection to Brandeis, which was not known to Reuterdahl, and Bond's denial was made as an unsolicited confession. Brandeis had expressed an interest in promoting Einstein. The racist Zionist blackmailer United States Supreme Court Justice Louis Dembitz Brandeis wrote in a letter dated 1 March 1921,

"You have doubtless heard that the Great Einstein is coming to America soon with Dr. Weizmann, our Zionist Chief. Palestine may need something more now than a new conception of the Universe or of several additional dimensions; but it is well to remind the Gentile world, when the wave of anti-Semitism is rising, that in the world of thought the conspicuous contributions are being made by Jews."[442]

The series of letters exchanged in *The New York Times* began with a letter from Dr. Harris A. Houghton, M. D., of No. 97/100 Riverside Drive, New York City, dated 13 April 1923; which accused Einstein of publishing a "Newtonian Duplication".[443] Houghton was involved with U. S. Army Intelligence and had called the attention of the U. S. Government to the *Protocols of the Learned Elders of Zion* in 1918, informing President Wilson and his cabinet of an alleged plot by Zionists to overthrow the governments of the world and to destroy Christianity.[444] Brandeis, who controlled Wilson, assured the U. S. Government that the document was a forgery.[445] Houghton published the "Beckwith" English translation of the *Protocols* in 1920.[446] Dr. Houghton also wrote to John Spargo, about Louis Marshall's letter to Max Senior of 26 September 1918, in an effort to convince Spargo that Marshall feared Zionists and believed Zionism was a part of a larger Jewish plot—which accusations Marshall denied.[447] Boris Brasol[448] may have been the one who brought the *Protocols* to U. S. Army Intelligence and convinced them of their authenticity, *viz.* Dr. Harris Houghton and Natalie De Bogory.[449] Houghton wrote to Arvid Reuterdahl on 15 July 1923.[450]

Racist Zionist United States Supreme Court Justice Louis Dembitz Brandeis was a Frankist Jew. Frankist Jews were committed to the destruction of Gentile society. They deliberately wormed their way into positions of power in order to subvert Gentile religions and governments and bring them into war and ruin. Brandeis brought America into the

First World War in a *quid pro quo* deal with the British in exchange for the Zionist Balfour Declaration by blackmailing Woodrow Wilson with love letters Wilson had written to Mrs. Peck. Brandeis and his leading Jewish friends instituted Rothschild's banking system in America, which led to the Great Depression. Brandeis was known as the most deceitful lawyer in America. His appointment to the United States Supreme Court was the most scandalous event in the Court's history. Like all Frankist Jews, Brandeis returned Gentile generosity with treachery. Arthur Hertzberg discussed Brandeis' Frankist roots,

"On the surface Brandeis was a strange kind of leader for the Zionists. Born in Louisville, Kentucky, in 1856 to recent immigrants from Bohemia, who were not much involved in Jewish life, Brandeis had a brilliant career at Harvard Law School, and by the late 1880s had become a successful Boston lawyer. True, many of his initial clients were 'German Jews' to whose social set he inevitably belonged, but he was even more peripheral to the Jewish community than the most assimilated among them. There was some memory in his family of its origins in Prague in a circle that still harbored loyalty to the memory of Jacob Frank, the false messiah who had appeared in Poland in the latter half of the eighteenth century. Brandeis's mother was very opposed to Jewish particularism. In his earliest Boston years, he was to be found, at least once, on the list of contributors to the First Unitarian Church. On the other hand, he had been deeply influenced in his earliest years by an uncle, Louis Dembitz (whose family name he adopted as his own middle name), a learned, Orthodox Jew."[451]

Here is Reuterdahl's 30 April 1921 article, to which an author responded in the *Scientific American* with an obnoxious *ad hominem* attack,

"'Kinertia' Versus Einstein
By ARVID REUTERDAHL
Dean, Department of Engineering and Architecture.
The College of St. Thomas, St. Paul. Minnesota
Citations That Raise Delicate Question
on Age of Theory of Relativity

THE intellectual world generally moves slowly in the matter of extending recognition to those who have consecrated their lives to the cause of reason. Mendel had been dead many years before the remarkable nature of his work was recognized. When we contrast Mendel's case with that of Einstein we are forced to admit that the German physicist's sensational rise is the most extraordinary in the history of science. Barnum, the king of advertisers, could not have staged a more effective and expeditious advertising campaign. Within the brief period of a few months, Einstein's name became known in every civilized country in the world. The Theory of Relativity afforded cartoonists material for humorous sketches, and the doctor and his doctrine became subjects for mirth and merriment.

After the first volcanic outburst of scientific approval and humorous recognition, rumblings of discontent were heard from Einstein's native land. A group of German scientists, in no uncertain terms, expressed their doubts concerning the precise value and originality of Einstein's theory. There were even those who boldly charged the author with deliberate plagiarism. In England Sir Oliver Lodge and a few other able men cautioned the world against a too hasty acceptance of the new doctrine of relativity. In the United States, however, Einstein's theory met with immediate and complete success. Even at the present time we rarely hear a dissenting voice. This is particularly strange for the reason that in the year 1914 a well-known American journal published a series of articles by an unknown investigator who discussed the very same problem which brought fame to Einstein. We refer to the eleven articles written by the unknown 'Kinertia,' which appeared in *Harper's Weekly* under the caption 'Do Bodies Fall?' If it is true that 'Kinertia' actually considered the Einsteinian problem in these essays, then the question of priority is inevitably raised and the unparalleled originality claimed for Einstein's work becomes a debatable matter. Indeed, the presentation of the very facts which raise these questions is the main purpose of this article. Since the matter of priority is involved, the introduction in this article of a brief chronological survey of the work of both Einstein and 'Kinertia' is of the utmost importance.

The most significant contributions of Albert Einstein have been published in *Annalen Der Physik*. His papers deal with the

Special Theory of Relativity, Theory of the Brownian Movements, Inertia of Energy, the Quantum Law of the Emission and Absorption of Light, Theory of the Specific Heat of Solid Bodies, and the General Theory of Relativity. The year 1905 is considered, by most authorities on Einstein's work, as the birth-year of the Theory of Relativity. Careful search, however, has revealed a paper on this subject which was published in Berlin during the year 1904 in the journal *Sitsungsberichte*. That portion of Einstein's theory which deals with the phenomenon of gravitation is a later development. Einstein first gave his attention to the problem of gravitation in 1911, when he developed the Principle of Equivalence of gravitational and accelerative fields. Other phases of this subject were dealt with in papers which appeared in the years 1912 and 1913. A further elaboration, the joint work of Einstein and Marcel Grossman, appeared in 1914. The theory in its final and complete form was announced in the year 1915.

'Kinertia's' contribution deals principally with the problem of gravitation. The question of priority of 'Kinertia' over Einstein consequently involves the phenomenon of gravitation in particular. It must be admitted, however, that 'Kinertia' has also considered Einstein's earlier problem which involved the significance of motion in reference to an observer. Einstein distinguishes this earlier problem from his theory of gravitation by the separate designation, 'Special Theory of Relativity.' A brief historical summary of the work of 'Kinertia' is now in order.

Lord Kelvin first aroused 'Kinertia's' interest in the problem of gravitation. That was in the year 1866 when 'Kinertia' was a student under Lord Kelvin. 'Kinertia' even then did not agree with the Newtonian theory of force as presented by Lord Kelvin. Incidentally, we desire to call the reader's attention to the fact that Albert Einstein was born in 1879 in Ulm, Germany, thirteen years later. It is a curious coincidence that both 'Kinertia' and Einstein were engineers. During the period of time from 1877 to 1881, 'Kinertia' became convinced that *acceleration* was the basic cause of what we generally speak of as 'weight.' The reader is undoubtedly aware of the fact that *acceleration* plays the fundamental role in Einstein's theory of gravitation. 'Kinertia' corresponded with Kelvin, Tait, and Niven, of Cambridge, with the hope that he would be able to interest these men in his startling theory. This attempt met with little or no sympathy. Some years later, through an accident, 'Kinertia' was unfortunately deprived of his hearing. This misfortune forced him to abandon his engineering profession for a rancher's life in the state of California. This new occupation gave 'Kinertia' the requisite leisure to complete his investigations which resulted in confirming his supposition that *acceleration* was the great norm of the phenomenon of gravitation. His attempts, dating from the year 1899, to persuade our stubborn American scientists that the Newtonian theory of gravitation must be revised met with nothing but ridicule or indifference. To *Harper's Weekly* and its managing editor (1914), Mr. H. D. Wheeler, belongs the credit of having published 'Kinertia's' series of articles entitled, 'Do Bodies Fall?' The first article appeared in the issue of August 29, 1914, Vol. 59. The final article is dated November 7, 1914. From the preceding it is evident that 'Kinertia' derived his norm of gravitation before Einstein was born. The question of priority is therefore definitely and irrefutably established in favor of 'Kinertia' in the case of the General Theory of Relativity considered as a discussion of the problem of gravitation and acceleration.

We turn our attention now to the content of these two gravitational theories. We propose, by means of direct quotations from the works of these two men, to set forth their remarkable similarity. In the case of Einstein we shall quote from his recent book, 'Relativity' (Henry Holt and Company, 1920), and in 'Kinertia's' case our quotations will be from the *Harper's Weekly* articles.

The following comparative quotations show the striking similarity existing between Einstein and 'Kinertia' when they consider the relation between acceleration and gravitation, a similarity which extends not only to intent but affects even the very words.

Einstein.

'We imagine a large portion of empty space, so far removed from stars and other appreciable masses that we have before us approximately the conditions required by the fundamental law of Galilei.—As reference-body let us imagine a spacious chest resembling a room with an observer inside who is equipped with apparatus. Gravitation naturally does not exist for this observer.

He must fasten himself with strings to the floor, otherwise the slightest impact against the floor will cause him to rise slowly toward the ceiling of the room.

'To the middle of the lid of the chest is fixed externally a hook with rope attached, and now a 'being' (what kind of a being is immaterial to us) begins pulling at this with a constant force. The chest together with the observer then begin to move 'upwards' with a uniformly accelerated motion. In course of time their velocity will reach unheard of values—provided that we are viewing all this from another reference-body which is not being pulled with a rope.

'But how does the man in the chest regard the process? The acceleration of the chest will be transmitted to him by the reaction of the floor of the chest. He must therefore take up this pressure by means of his legs if he does not wish to be laid out full length on the floor. He is then standing in the chest in exactly the same way as anyone stands in a room of a house on our earth. If he release a body which he previously had in his hand, the acceleration of the chest will no longer be transmitted to this body, and for this reason the body will approach the floor of the chest with an accelerated motion. The observer will further convince himself *that the acceleration of the body toward the floor of the chest is always of the same magnitude, whatever kind of body he may happen to use for the experiment.'*— (*'Relativity,'* pages 78 and 79.)

'Kinertia.'

'I set to work to find out by experiment whether bodies actually did fall with the acceleration which the force of attraction was said to produce. Years before that, when in England, where some of our coal mines had vertical shafts about 1,500 feet deep, I had studied the cause of weight by having the hoisting engine drop me down with the full acceleration for about 500 feet. Then, by retardation during the lowest 500 feet, I could experience increase of weight all over me so marked that my legs could hardly support me. That taught me that acceleration was the proximate cause of weight, but at the time of these experiments I still thought the acceleration of the falling cage was really caused by the earth's attraction.' —('Do Bodies Fall?' *Harper's Weekly,* August 29, 1914, page 210). 'Weight is not a kinetic force because it cannot produce acceleration. *If a body were accelerated in proportion to its weight, then weight would be a force.'*—('Do Bodies Fall ?' Harper's Weekly, October 17, 1914, page 383).

It is noteworthy that the only real difference between these two citations is that Einstein derives his conclusions from an hypothetical case, whereas 'Kinertia' draws his conclusions from an actual experiment upon himself.

The interpreters of Einstein furnish us with further corroborative material which we submit as additional evidence in the case of 'Kinertia' versus Einstein. Professor A. S. Eddington's interpretation of Einstein's theory is authoritative. The following quotations are from his work, 'Space, Time and Gravitation' (Cambridge University Press, 1920). These quotations from Eddington's work also consider the equivalence of acceleration and gravitation.

Eddington.

'The nature of gravitation has seemed very mysterious, yet it is a remarkable fact that in a limited region it is possible to create an artificial field of force which imitates a natural gravitational field so exactly that, so far as experiments have yet gone, no one can tell the difference. Those who seek for an explanation of gravitation naturally aim to find a model which will reproduce its effects; *but no one before Einstein seems to have thought of finding the clue in these artificial fields, familiar as they are.*

'When a lift starts to move upward the occupants feel a characteristic sensation, which is actually identical with a sensation of increased weight.—In fact, the upward acceleration of the lift is in its mechanical effects exactly similar to an additional gravitational field superimposed on that normally present.'—('Space, Time and Gravitation,' page 64.)

On the eminent authority of Eddington we may therefore state with absolute certainty that Einstein found his clue to the nature of gravitation in the *artificial field* created by acceleration. Eddington's statement, however, that Einstein was the first scientist to think of this *clue* is evidently erroneous in view of the preceding quotations from the work of 'Kinertia.'

The remarkable similarity in thought of the following

quotations pertaining to the relative effects produced by accelerated and uniform motion, is of high evidential interest.

Eddington.
'The observer in the accelerated lift travels upward in a straight line, say 1 foot in the first second, 4 feet in two seconds, 9 feet in three seconds, and so on. If we plot these points as x and t on a diagram we obtain a curved track. Presently the speed of the lift becomes uniform and the track in the diagram becomes straight. So long as the track is curved (accelerated motion) a field of force is perceived; it disappears when the track becomes straight (uniform motion) .'— ('Space, Time and Gravitation,' page 66.)

'Kinertia.'
'The proof that matter can exist without weight depends on the first law of motion; because if a mass moves uniformly in a straight line in space, it cannot have weight. If weight is caused by the mutual attraction of matter, then a mass subject to attraction must move in a curve. If weight is caused by acceleration then it cannot follow Newton's law and move with uniform velocity in a straight line.'—('Do Bodies Fall ?' *Harper's Weekly*, October 10, 1914, page 350.)

The conclusions of Einstein and 'Kinertia' concerning the very existence of the force of gravitational attraction are identical in content. This is apparent from the following citations from an article by Professor Edwin B. Wilson, (Massachusetts Institute of Technology) and 'Kinertia's' basic articles.

Wilson.
'But just suppose that somebody tells us that the force of gravity is physically non-existing quite as much as the centrifugal or Coriolis force, and that the reason we think that gravity is real is essentially the same that leads the untutored mind to believe there is a physical force acting to move objects to one side when a train goes around a curve—namely, an unhappily ignorant view of Nature. This is what Einstein asserts.' —('Space, Time and Gravitation,' the *Scientific Monthly*, March, 1920, page 226.)

'Kinertia.'

'But now, since it can be proved that there is no such force in the universe as attraction and that the supposed fall of bodies toward the earth *by that force* is only an illusion of the senses, there will be new ground upon which theologians can meet the Laplace attractionists, and Haeckel and his materialists.'—('Do Bodies Fall?' *Harper's Weekly*, September 19, 1914, page 285.)

The preceding citations are sufficient to establish conclusively the fact that, in underlying essence, 'Kinertia's' theory of gravitation is identical with Einstein's. Both men find the crux of the problem in acceleration, and the development of both theories is based upon the very same experiment.

It will be particularly interesting to compare the conclusions of the two men concerning the nature of the path of the earth's motion in space.

Eddington.

'Consider, for example, two events in space-time, namely, the position of the earth at the present moment, and its position a hundred years ago. Call these events P^2 and P^1. In the interim the earth (being undisturbed by impacts) has moved so as to take the longest possible track from P^1 to P^2—or, if we prefer, so as to take the longest possible proper-time over the journey. In the weird geometry of the part of space-time through which it passes (a geometry which is no doubt associated in some way with our perception of the existence of a massive body, the sun) this longest track is a *spiral*—a circle in space drawn out into a spiral by continuous displacement in time. Any other course would have had a shorter interval-length.'—('Space, Time and Gravitation,' page 72.)

Wilson.

'Draw from the sun perpendicular to the plane of the earth's orbit a line which shall represent the time-axis and disregard the third spatial dimension. Now for each kilometer that the earth moves around in its orbit, it must be considered to move in time by 10,000 kilometers. The path of the earth in space and time on this diagram is therefore a *helix* with an extremely steep pitch winding once a year about the cylinder standing in the earth's orbit but advancing ten thousand billion kilometers while 'circulating' one billion kilometers.'— ('Space, Time and Gravitation.' The *Scientific Monthly*, March, 1920, page 227.)

'Kinertia.'
'The possible motion of the sun in space, as adrift with the planets, was anticipated by Newton; but the laws of motion prevented him from reaching the true *corkscrew* path of the planets in space as they revolve round the sun.'—('Do Bodies Fall?' *Harper's Weekly*, September 19, 1914, page 285.)

In this connection we submit as corroborative evidence of the highest import, the illustration of this *corkscrew* path of the earth and moon which was used to elucidate 'Kinertia's' article in *Harper's Weekly*, September 19, 1914, page 285.
This illustration, taken in conjunction with 'Kinertia's' statement, quoted above, proves conclusively that the unknown 'Kinertia' derived the same type of path for the earth's motion in space that Einstein claims as his original contribution.
We introduce the following final quotation in order definitely to fix the date of 'Kinertia's' contribution:

'Kinertia.'
'This statement is concerning a discovery in natural science and the ordinary phenomena of daily life, which I discovered about fifteen years ago while engaged in carrying on some experiments to verify what I had previously suspected to be the true physical cause of *Elasticity, Gravity, Weight and Energy.'*—('Do Bodies Fall?' *Harper's Weekly*, August 29, 1914, page 210.)

Since this article bears the date 1914, it is clear that the year 1899, fifteen years earlier, is the date which can safely be regarded as the birth-year of 'Kinertia's' theory of gravitation. We have seen that Einstein's first work on gravitation was done in the year 1911; consequently 'Kinertia' antedates Einstein by twelve years.
We rest the case of 'Kinertia' Versus Einstein on the evidence submitted in this article. If Einstein was aware of 'Kinertia's' discovery then the appellation 'plagiarist,' bestowed upon him by his German professional colleagues, is eminently fitting. If, on the contrary, Einstein was unaware of this work,

then he is, nevertheless, antedated by the work of 'Kinertia.' Einstein is at liberty to choose either horn of the dilemma."[452]

On 12 February 1920, Einstein gave a speech at the University of Berlin. He allowed non-students to attend, in direct violation of the University's rules. A similar situation had occurred a year earlier at the University of Zürich, where persons not entitled to attend Einstein's lectures did attend, and those who had purchased tickets, but whose seats were taken by those without tickets, requested a refund.[453] During his lecture in Berlin, Einstein called the student council the "dregs of humanity". Einstein was met again and again with applause and left to general applause.[454] The only disturbance of any kind was the reaction of the crowd of Eastern European Jews when Einstein spoke of cancelling future lectures should non-students not be permitted to attend, and returning their fees. Eastern European Jews created a series of disturbances,[455] because they wanted to attended the lectures, which the rules would not allow them to attend. Eastern European Jews were noted for producing Zionists, prostitutes, Frankist revolutionaries and for their pronounced tribalism[456]—their appearance and actions identified them, as the *Deutsche Zeitung* noted,

"[The audience had] a predominantly Asiatic imprint. One saw distinguished matrons, young ladies of questionable quality, schoolboys with the sacred colors of Zion on the blazonry of the Jewish wandering club[.]"[457]

According to Einstein, and the newspaper *Berliner Tageblatt* (14 February 1920), and a petition signed by almost 300 students, nothing anti-Semitic was said or done at the meeting.[458] A young Jewish student, Hans Toby Cohn, wrote to Einstein to apologize for his and his fellow Jews actions, because they were too young to decipher yet whether to be,

"a Communist or a Monarchist, whether an atheist or a nationalistic Jew."[459]

The uproar did not involve any anti-Semitic statements, but according to Cohn did include such statements as, "'Socialist' and 'money refund' or 'Are we still students?!'"[460] which were made by young Jews. Despite these facts, numerous sources have misrepresented the events which took place and misrepresented the disorderly outbursts of Eastern European Jews, as if anti-Semitic attacks by German Gentiles. As with the Berlin Philharmonic affair, it was Einstein and his friends who made an issue of anti-Semitism, where it was not a legitimate issue. It was yet another example of their Jewish racism and Jewish tribalism. Recall that Einstein called the Student Council, the "refuse of humankind".[461]

The newspaper *Vorwärts* published an article on 13 February 1920 and wrote of alleged "excesses of an anti-Semitic student mob" "Exzessen eines antisemitischen Studentenpöbels".[462] The newspaper *8-Uhr Abentblatt* wrote on 13 February 1920,

"Tumultszenen bei einer Einstein-Vorlesung.
Professor Einstein verzichtet auf weitere Vorlesungen an der Universität. — Rückzahlung der Kollegien an die Studenten.

Bei der gestrigen Vorlesung des Universitätsprofessors Einstein über seine Relativitätstheorie and der Berliner Universität kam es zu unliebsamen Szenen, die eine Unterbrechung der Vorlesung bewirkten und Professor Einstein zwangen, die Studenten aufzufordern, sich die eingezahlten *Kollegiengelder zurückzahlen* zu lassen. Nach einer uns übermittelten Darstellung dieses Zwischenfalles wollte der Studentenausschuß es nicht zulassen, daß die Vorlesungen des Professors *Einstein* außer den imatrikulierten [*sic*] Studenten auch von *Richtstudenten* besucht werden. Als nun Professor Einstein die gestrige Vorlesung dazu benutzte, um an die Studentenschtft [*sic*] die Bitte zu richten, ihren Standpunkt zu verlassen, wurde dieses Ersuchen mit einem Tumult beantwortet, bei dem auch *Aeußerungen antisemitischen Charakters* fielen. Professor Einstein sah sich infolge dieses unqualifizierbaren Verhaltens der Studentenschaft gezwungen, die Vorlesung abzubrechen und an seine studentische Zuhörerschaft die Aufforderung zu richten, sich die *Kollegiengelder zrückzahlen* [*sic*] zu lassen.

Eine Erklärung Professor Einsteins.

Auf unsere Anfrage teilte uns Herr Professor Einstein über den gestrigen Vorfall folgendes mit:
„Meine populär gehaltenen Vorträge über die Relativitätstheorie besuchten nicht nur Studenten, sondern auch

viele andere Leute, die dazu eigentlich nicht berechtigt sind. Der Studentenausschuß erklärte deshalb, dies nicht länger zulassen zu wollen. Ich machte darauf aufmerksam, daß der große Saal für alle Platz habe, die zuhören wollen und daß es dadurch zu keinen Unzulänglichkeiten kommen müsse. Der Studentenausschuß hat sich damit jedoch nicht zufrieden gegeben, sondern sich in dieser Frage an den *Rektor* gewandt. Der Rektor schrieb mir einen *Brief*, in dem er darauf hinwies, daß nach der bestehenden Vorschrift jene Leute nicht die Berechtigung haben, den Saal zu betreten. Dies ist *formellrichtig*. Ich habe mich jedoch auf den Standpunkt gestellt, daß es mir widerstrebe, ohne inneren Grund es Leuten unmöglich zu machen, weiter zu hören, und ich habe deswegen gestern, statt zu lesen, eine Besprechung mit meiner Zuhörerschaft veranstaltet, die jedoch zu einem bestimmten Ergebnis nicht führte. Ich habe mich daher veranlaßt gesehen, auf meine weiteren Vorlesungen zu verzichten und der Studentenschaft erklärt, sie könne ihre eingezahlten Kollegiengelder sich zurückzahlen lassen. Ich habe aber nicht die Absicht, meine Vorlesungen überhaupt zu unterlassen, ich werde sie vielmehr in anderer Form wieder aufnehmen. In welchem Saal ist aber noch unbestimmt. Sollte es noch einmal zu solchen Szenen wie gestern kommen, dann höre ich überhaupt auf. Von einem *Skandal*, der sich gestern abgespielt haben soll, kann nicht die Rede sein, immerhin bewiesen manche Aeußerungen, die fielen, eine gewisse animose Gesinnung mir gegenüber. *Antisemitische Äußerungen* als solche fielen nicht, doch konnte ihr *Unterton* so gedeutet werden."

Eduard Meyer, Rector of the University of Berlin, was astonished by these reports of anti-Semitism, which he knew were utterly false. On 13 February 1920, Meyer wrote to the Ministry of Culture, stating, *inter alia*,

"Vorausschicken muß ich, daß ich zu meinem größten Erstaunen durch Herrn Seeberg erfuhr, daß behauptet wird, dabei habe der Antisemitismus eine Rolle gespielt und sei von Judentum u. ä. dei Rede gewesen. Demgegenüber muß ich erklären, daß das völlig unbegründet ist und ich gar nicht begreife, wie solche Behauptungen haben entstehen können. Das Gespräch, das ich gestern mit Herrn Kollegen Einstein über die Sache hatte, ist in der friedlichsten Weise ganz glatt verlaufen, und ebenso erklärt mir der offizielle Vertreter des studentischen Ausschusses, den ich darum befragt habe, daß in den Diskussionen in der gestrigen Vorlesung, an denen er selbst Anteil genommen hat, mit keinem Wort von Antisemitismus, Judentum usw. die Rede gewesen ist."[463]

In 1962, Peter Michelmore conveyed an even more alarming, though also purely fictional, account of the events at the University of Berlin, than had the Jewish newspapers,

"A group of black-shirted students broke up one of Einstein's lectures at the University of Berlin. A blond youth screamed above the din, 'I'm going to cut the throat of that dirty Jew.'"[464]

This alarmist script, this Jewish canard, appeared many times and was attributed to many different events. Ernst Gehrcke recorded that the newspaper *Freiheit* changed its story repeatedly after the events at the Berlin Philharmonic of 24 August 1920:

"[. . .]So sprach die *Freiheit*, das Parteiorgan EINSTEINS, am 26. August noch von «wissenschaftlichen Einwänden», am 27. August von der «auf ihre Urheber zurückfallenden, schimpflichen Art, in der der Kampf gegen Professor EINSTEIN und seine Relativitätstheorie geführt wird», am 31. August setzte sich das Blatt über gesellschaftliche und parlamentarische Formen der Berichterstattung hinweg, indem es «einen studentischen Rowdy» sagen läßt, er wolle dem «Saujud EINSTEIN an die Gurgel», und am 4. September: «Die ernsthafte exakte Wissenschaft ist also ein Geschäft, das mit Schiebergewinnen abschließt»."

Die Umschau, Volume 24, (1920), page 554, alleged that someone said,

"man sollte diesem Juden an die Gurgel fahren."[465]

Vossische Zeitung reported on 29 August 1920, Morning Edition, Supplement 4, front page, that someone loudly stated,

"Diesem Saujuden müßte man eigentlich an die Gurgel springen."[466]

Yet another account, again by interested pro-Einstein parties, in 1927, places the alleged incident at an unnamed "public meeting in the spring of 1919."[467]

Johannes Riem, who was not bashful, wrote on 1 July 1921, in reference to Reuterdahl,

> "Man geht gegen Einstein vor als den Goliat des Skeptizismus. Vorlesungen dagegen werden veranstaltet. In scharfsinniger Weise wird in einem viel gelesenen Buche „Relativität oder innere Abhängigkeit" die Unhaltbarkeit der Relativitätstheorie nachgewiesen. Der Einwand Einsteins, dies sei nur eine besondere Form des Antisemitismus, wird sehr energisch zurückgewiesen, und mit der Anerkennung Spinozols beantwortet."[468]

Physicist Stjepan Mohorovičić declared that he was intimidated out of opposing Einstein's myths and plagiarism, through fear of being labeled an anti-Semite and by anonymous threats. Johannes Jürgenson writes,

> "Ein weiterer Punkt war, daß es Einstein, der selbst Jude war, geschickt verstand, seinen Gegnern Antisemitismus zu unterstellen:
> 'Die erste Opposition der wissenschaftlichen Welt gegen die neuen Relativitätstheorien hat man einfach gebrochen, indem man sie als eine Folge des Antisemitismus dem breiten Publikum vorgestellt hat' sagte Mohorovicic 1962. Auch er hatte in jener Zeit in Zagreb seine Kritik zurückgestellt, um nicht als Antisemit zu gelten."[469]

Mohorovičić wrote in 1962 in the second volume of *Kritik der Relativitätstheorie*,

> "The initial opposition in the scientific world against the new theory of relativity was easily crushed by convincing the general public that it was a product of anti-Semitism, although no one could reliably make such an accusation against M. ABRAHAM, O. KRAUS, O. D. CHWOLSON, etc.! But it disgusts me to speak further of such things; those wanting to learn more about it can glean the facts from many sources, for example [269-270] through [316-317] and others."

"Die erste Opposition in der wissenschaftlichen Welt gegen die neuen Relativitätstheorien hat man einfach gebrochen, indem man sie als eine Folge des Antisemitismus dem breiten Publikum vorgestellt hat, obwohl man dies sicher nicht einem M. ABRAHAM, O. KRAUS, O. D. CHWOLSON, etc. vorwerfen konnte! (usw.). Aber es ekelt mir, über solche Verhältnisse weiter zu sprechen; wer sich darüber unterrichten will, müßte vieles nachlese, wie z. B. [269-270] bis [316-317] und manches andere."[470]

Mohorovičić also stated that the "Relativity Syndicate" vehemently obstructed the publication of works which criticized the theory of relativity (your author has personally witnessed such corrupt practices):

"Eine vorzügliche und sehr scharfsinnige Kritik veröffentlichte G. v. GLEICH 1930, wo er alle seine diesbezüglichen Arbeiten gesammelt und geordnet hatte, obwohl das 'Relativitätssyndikat' mit allen Mitteln trachtete, das Erscheinen dieses Werkes zu verhindern. Nun es war sehr schwer die Kritik gänzlich zu unterdrücken, da man in der Wahl der Mittel nicht kleinlich war. Alle, für die Relativitätstheorie ungünstigen Arbeiten wurden einfach kurzerhand als unrichtig, fehlerhaft oder falsch bezeichnet oder als unwichtig (heutzutage ein sehr beliebtes Wort!) oder wenigstens als uninteressant verschwiegen. Von den Philosophen erhielten nur die Applaudierenden das Wort, den kritisch Gesinnten warf man ihre mathematischen Unkenntnisse vor; wer sich darüber unterrichten will, sollte die offenen Briefe des bekannten Philosophen O. KRAUS nachlesen [108]), und doch haben die Philosophen die Grundlage der Rechnung, nicht aber die Rechnung selbst untersucht. Aber die Relativisten haben übersehen, daß die modernen Relativitätstheorien, ähnlich wie die moderne Musik, voll von Dissonanzen sind, (eine solche Musik entzückt den heutigen Snob außerordentlich und er kann nicht begreifen, daß es gebildete Leute gibt, welche die moderne Musik nicht ausstehen können, aber dafür muß man das Ohr und die richtige musikalische Erziehung haben!). O. KRAUS hat besonders den Umstand hervorgehoben (l. c. S. 96.), 'daß jeder Quark, der für die Theorie zu sein scheint, von den Relativisten mit freundlicher Gebärde begrußt wird... während eine ernste Kritik mißhandelt wird' [109]). Dies wirkte aber verhängnisvoll und diese modernen Theorien wurden größtenteils ein Tätigkeitsfeld pour ceux qui savent vivre... oder wie ein lachender Philosoph sagte [110]: '...an Höfen ist Höflichkeit der Verstand und die Münze...'."[471]

Mohorovičić stated in 1922 that he had received anonymous threats for opposing relativity theory,

"Viele wurden von der Behauptung geblendet, daß diese Theorie sich mit der Erfahrung in Übereinstimmung befinde (vgl. II, 4), was von den Anhängern der Einsteinschen Theorie sehr geschickt zu Propagandazwecken ausgenutzt wurde. Das letzte (nämlich diese gewissenlose Reklame) ist gerade auch die dunkelste Seite des erwähnten Kampfes, welcher nie in einer so scharfen Form ausgebrochen wäre, wenn nicht diese unglückliche und unerhörte Propaganda gewesen wäre, welche in der Geschichte fast aller Wissenschaften beispiellos ist [*Footnote deleted*]. Alles dies wird noch durch die Tatsache verschärft, daß Einstein und die Mehrzahl seiner ersten Anhänger Juden sind — (ich hätte keinen Grund, die Rasse Einsteins zu erwähnen, wenn nicht Einstein *selbst* so häufig betont hätte, daß er ein Jude sei) [*Footnote:* Einstein selbst sagt in dem Vorwort des Werkes von L. Fabre (Anmerk. 30) den Franzosen ausdrücklich, daß er nur in Deutschland geboren sei, sonst sei er ein Jude, Pazifist und Mitglied einer internationalen Verbindung.... Es ist nicht schwer zu raten, warum Einstein dies gerade den Franzosen gegenüber gesagt hat (mit eigener Unterschrift), aber lassen wir das, es ist dies nur Geschmacksache...; unsere Arbeit hier ist eine wissenschaftliche. Es ist traurig genug, daß ich gezwungen bin, dies hier zu erwähnen!] —, und da die letzteren fast die ganze Weltpresse in den Händen haben, so bereiteten sie für Einstein eine kolossale Reklame und haben fast jede Arbeit, welche gegen diese Theorie gerichtet wurde, zu unterdrücken gesucht. Zu diesem religiös-sozialen Moment kommt noch ein politisches Moment hinzu, worüber ich hier nicht zu reden wünsche. *Ich bin nur überzeugt, daß wir, die wir uns ziemlich welt von diesem Kampfe befinden, viel ruhiger und objektiver über diese neue Richtung urteilen können, und daß wir nicht sofort blind und kritiklos jede neue Richtung, welche zu uns aus dem Ausland gelangt, anzunehmen brauchen.* [*Footnote:* Leider sind diese »Methoden« des Streits auch zu uns gekommen. Mitglieder einer philosophischen Fakultät, die in ihrem fanatischem Abscheu gegen jede sachliche, kritische Stellungnahme zur Relativitätstheorie offenbar ganz vergessen hatten, daß die Wissenschaft eine *über* den Parteien stehende Sache ist, haben sich nicht gescheut, persönliche Gehässigkeit gegen mich als Kritiker der Relativitätstheorie an den Tag zu legen, wie ich mehrfach erfahren mußte. Einige Herren Relativisten haben mir *anonyme Drohbriefe* zugestellt und sich anderer, sonst in wissenschaftlichen Kreisen sehr ungewöhnlicher Mittel bedient. Es ist die höchste Zeit, mit solchen Methoden endlich aufzuhören!]"[472]

Einstein, too, was attacked by lunatics—who made death threats and plots against him, but these were political attacks which were not directly related to the theory of relativity. In the spring of 1921, Rudolph Leibus offered a reward to anyone who murdered Einstein, Harden or Foerster. Theodor Wolff, editor of the *Berliner Tageblatt*, spread the false rumor that Einstein and he were targets of assassins after the murder of Walter Rathenau in 1922. This may have been a pretext to give Einstein an excuse to back away from his commitment with the League of Nations and the police denied Wolff's charges. *The New York Times* reported on the front page on 19 February 1923 that Prof. Herzen of Lausanne University told a meeting of the Brussels Engineering Association in a discussion on the theory of relativity that Einstein was on a death list. *The New York Times* reported on 1 February 1925 on page 13 that Marie Evgenievna Dickson was arrested after she showed up at the Einstein's home and frightened Mrs. Einstein. Dickson had been expelled from France for planning to murder the Soviet Ambassador Leonid Krassin. Years later, after the World Committee for Help for Victims of German Fascism, for which Einstein was a figurehead, published *The Brown Book of the Hitler Terror*,[473] the rumor spread that the Nazis had put a bounty on Einstein's head.[474]

Ad hominem attack and smear campaigns were Einstein's preferred method of response to challenges to Einstein's priority and challenges to relativity theory, as even Einstein's advocates were forced to concede in 1931. Von Brunn, a defender of Einstein, wrote,

"Even individual fanatic scientific advocates of the Einsteinian theory seem to have finally abandoned their tactic of cutting off any discussion about it with the threat that every criticism, even the most moderate and scrupulous ones, must be discredited as an obvious effluence of stupidity and malice. But even if these monstrous products of the 'Einstein frenzy' [*Einstein-Taumel*] now belong to history and are thus eliminated from consideration, thoroughly respectable reasons for a certain discomfort with relativity theory still do remain[.]"[475]

This was published in a pro-Einstein "review" of *Hundert Autoren gegen Einstein*, which anti-Einstein book stated,

"It is the aim of this publication to confront the terror of the Einsteinians with an overview of the quality and quantity of the opponents [of the theory of relativity] and opposing arguments."[476]

Sadly, the *ad hominem* attacks against anyone who criticized Einstein or relativity theory were not relegated to history, despite Brunn's claims; and, ironically, one need only read his "review" of *Hundert Autoren gegen Einstein* to see that the so-called "review" was itself an *ad hominem* attack against the authors. *One Hundred Authors Against Einstein* was a response to personal attacks from Einstein and his followers, and largely contained philosophical objections to relativity theory, some better than others.

Charles Lane Poor complained of severe censorship.

Einstein liked to smear his critics. Henri Bergson published a book, which was, according to Abraham Pais, not included in his collected works, and which was a negative critique of relativity theory titled *Duration and Simultaneity*. Pais wrote,

"In his presentation speech on December 10, 1922, Arrhenius said, 'Most discussion [of Einstein's oeuvre] centers on his theory of relativity. This pertains to epistemology and has therefore been the subject of lively debate in philosophical circles. It will be no secret that the famous philosopher Bergson in Paris has challenged this theory, while other philosophers have acclaimed it wholeheartedly'.

Bergson's collected works appeared in 1970 [B3]. The editors did not include his book *Durée et Simultanéité: A Propos de la Théorie d'Einstein*. Einstein came to know, like, and respect Bergson. Of Bergson's philosophy he used to say, 'Gott verzeih ihm,' God forgive him."[477]

In the 1965 English translation of Bergson's book, *Duration and Simultaneity*, physicist Herbert Dingle wrote an introductory piece detailing the suppression of criticisms of relativity theory. Dingle warned of the dangers of the anti-rational state of awareness induced by Logical Positivism in its pseudo-relativistic adherents, with its celebration of the denial of physical reality, its solipsism, hypocrisy, numerology, and semantics; with the positivists' acceptance of metaphysical fallacy as if fact.

Dingle asked us all to consider the fact that we place our lives in the hands of a class of scientists who see as their goal the denial of the physical world, as for them it is an illusion supplanted by numbers, and who corruptly pursue the unchecked promotion of their myths. Herbert Dingle, whose words were often suppressed, stated, *inter alia*,

"The facts must be faced. To a degree never previously attained, the material future of the world is in the hands of a small body of men, on whose not merely superficially apparent but absolute, intuitive (in Bergson's sense of the word) integrity the fate of all depends, and that quality is lacking. Where there was once intellectual honesty they have now merely the idea that they possess it, the most insidious and the most dangerous of all usurpers; the substitution is shown by the fruits, which are displayed in unmistakable clarity in the facts described here. After years of effort I am forced to conclude that attempts with the scientific world to awaken it from its dogmatic slumber are in vain. I can only hope that some reader of these pages, whose sense of reality exceeds that of the mathematicians and physicists and who can command sufficient influence, might be able from the outside to enforce attention to the danger before it is too late."[478]

Under the headline "When a scientist challenges dogma, he's the one who gets mauled", Scott LaFee wrote in the *The San Diego Union-Tribune* of 2 November 1994,

"But unfortunate things can still happen when a novel contention challenges the perceived or popular 'truth.' Instead of receiving an honest but critical evaluation, the new idea can be ridiculed or, worse, ignored, its creator punished professionally and personally.

'I wouldn't do it again,' says Wallace Kantor, a retired local physicist who questioned Einstein's Special Theory of Relativity in several scientific papers and a book. 'Reaction to my work ranged from intense rage to contemptuous pity. It was career-damaging. It wasn't worth it.'"

3.9 Zionists Declare that Anti-Semitism is the Salvation of the "Jewish Race"

Albert Einstein's anti-German rhetoric in the post-war period especially irked many Germans, because they knew that Zionist traitors like Einstein had betrayed Germany to England and Russia in exchange for a deal with the British to take Palestine from Turkey and make it available to the Jews for a homeland. This stab in the back came after Germany had done so much for Jews and it betrayed the generally very positive relationship between Jews and Germany. Albert Einstein stated in 1938,

> "When the Germans had lost the World War hatched by their ruling class, immediate attempts were made to blame the Jews, first for instigating the war and then for losing it. In the course of time, success attended these efforts. The hatred engendered against the Jews not only protected the privileged classes, but enabled a small, unscrupulous, and insolent group to place the German people in a state of complete bondage."[479]

Albert Einstein told Peter A. Bucky,

> "For instance, after the First World War, many Germans accused the Jews first of starting the war and then of losing it. This is nothing new, of course. Throughout history, Jews have been accused of all sorts of treachery, such as poisoning water wells or murdering children as religious sacrifices. Much of this can be attributed to jealousy, because, despite the fact that Jewish people have always been thinly populated in various countries, they have always had a disproportionate number of outstanding public figures."[480]

Einstein's opinion that many Germans blamed Jews for the First World War, and for Germany's defeat in that war, is correct. Hitler wrote in his unpublished sequel to *Mein Kampf,*

"The war against Germany was fought by an overpowering world coalition in which only a part of the states could have a direct interest in Germany's destruction. In not a few countries the shift to war was brought by influences which in no way sprang from the real domestic interests of these nations or even which could also be to their benefit. A monstrous war propaganda began to befog public opinion of these peoples and to stir it into enthusiasm for a war which for these very peoples in part could not bring any gain at all and indeed sometimes ran downright counter to their real interests.

International world Jewry was the power which instigated this enormous war propaganda. For as senseless as the participation in the war by many of these nations may have been, seen from the viewpoint of their own interests, it was just as meaningful and logically correct seen from the viewpoint of the interests of world Jewry."[481]

4 ZIONISM IS RACISM

Jews have always been tribalistic and racist. Ancient Jews dubbed themselves the "chosen people" of a racist and genocidal God, and in so doing justified their racism and bloodlust with religion. Institutionalizing their racism as a religion guaranteed them that their progeny would remain forever segregated from the outside world of sub-human "cattle". The racism must have come before the religious mythology, because Jewish religious mythology is based upon supremacist racism.

"The General Assembly [***] Determines that Zionism is a form of racism and racial discrimination."—UNITED NATIONS GENERAL ASSEMBLY RESOLUTION NUMBER 3379[482]

"For thou *art* an holy people unto the LORD thy God: the LORD thy God hath chosen thee to be a special people unto himself, above all people that *are* upon the face of the earth."—*DEUTERONOMY* 7:6

4.1 Introduction

Deuteronomy, Chapter 7, states,

"When the LORD thy God shall bring thee into the land whither thou goest to possess it, and hath cast out many nations before thee, the Hittites, and the Girgashites, and the Amorites, and the Canaanites, and the Perizzites, and the Hivites, and the Jebusites, seven nations greater and mightier than thou; 2 And when the LORD thy God shall deliver them before thee; thou shalt smite them, *and* utterly destroy them; thou shalt make no covenant with them, nor show mercy unto them: 3 Neither shalt thou make marriages with them; thy daughter thou shalt not give unto his son, nor his daughter shalt thou take unto thy son. 4 For they will turn away thy son from following me, that they may serve other gods: so will the anger of the LORD be kindled against you, and destroy thee suddenly. 5 But thus shall ye deal with them; ye shall destroy their altars, and break down their images, and cut down their groves, and burn their graven images with fire. **6 For**

thou *art* an holy people unto the LORD thy God: the LORD thy God hath chosen thee to be a special people unto himself, above all people that *are* upon the face of the earth. 7 The LORD did not set his love upon you, nor choose you, because ye were more in number than any people; for ye *were* the fewest of all people: 8 But because the LORD loved you, and because he would keep the oath which he had sworn unto your fathers, hath the LORD brought you out with a mighty hand, and redeemed you out of the house of bondmen, from the hand of Pharaoh king of Egypt. 9 Know therefore that the LORD thy God, he *is* God, the faithful God, which keepeth covenant and mercy with them that love him and keep his commandments to a thousand generations; 10 And repayeth them that hate him to their face, to destroy them: he will not be slack to him that hateth him, he will repay him to his face. 11 Thou shalt therefore keep the commandments, and the statutes, and the judgments, which I command thee *this* day, to do them. 12 Wherefore it shall come to pass, if ye hearken to these judgments, and keep, and do them, that the LORD thy God shall keep unto thee the covenant and the mercy which he sware unto thy fathers: 13 And he will love thee, and bless thee, and multiply thee: he will also bless the fruit of thy womb, and the fruit of thy land, thy corn, and thy wine, and thine oil, the increase of thy kine, and the flocks of thy sheep, in the land which he sware unto thy fathers to give thee. 14 Thou shalt be blessed above all people: there shall not be male or female barren among you, or among your cattle. 15 And the LORD will take away from thee all sickness, and will put none of the evil diseases of Egypt, which thou knowest, upon thee; but will lay them upon all *them* that hate thee. 16 And thou shalt consume all the people which the LORD thy God shall deliver thee; thine eye shall have no pity upon them: neither shalt thou serve their gods; for that *will be* a snare unto thee. 17 If thou shalt say in thine heart, These nations *are* more than I; how can I dispossess them? 18 Thou shalt not be afraid of them: *but* shalt well remember what the LORD thy God did unto Pharaoh, and unto all Egypt; 19 The great temptations which thine eyes saw, and the signs, and the wonders, and the mighty hand, and the stretched out arm, where*by* the LORD thy God brought thee out: so shall the LORD thy God do unto all the people of whom thou *art* afraid. 20 Moreover the LORD thy God will send the hornet among them, until they that are left, and hide themselves from thee, be destroyed. 21 Thou shalt not be affrighted at them: for the LORD thy God *is* among you, a mighty God and terrible. 22 And the LORD thy God will put out those nations before thee by little and little: thou mayest not consume them at once, lest the beasts of the field increase upon thee. 23 But the LORD thy God shall deliver them unto thee, and shall destroy them *with* a mighty destruction, until they be destroyed. 24 And he shall deliver their kings into thine hand, and thou shalt destroy their name from under heaven: there shall no man *be able to* stand before thee, until thou have destroyed them. 25 The graven images of their gods shall ye burn with fire: thou shalt not desire the silver or gold *that is* on them, nor take *it* unto thee, lest thou be snared therin: for it *is* an abomination to the LORD thy God. 26 Neither shalt thou bring an abomination into thine house, lest thou be a cursed thing like it: *but* thou shalt utterly detest it, and thou shalt utterly abhor it; for it *is* a cursed thing."

Rabbi Dr. J. Loeph wrote in an article entitled, "Jüdischer Volksbegriff", in the *Central-Verein Zeitung*, Volume 1, Number 2, (11 May 1922), p. 29,

"Jüdischer Volksbegriff.

Von Rabbiner Dr. J. L o e p h.

Der Begriff des „Jüdischen Volkes" leidet in seiner Bedeutung unter derselben Unklarheit, die in der Regel mit dem Begriffe „Volk" überhaupt verbunden ist. Man muß hier scharf zwischen sprachlicher Herleitung und dem herausgebildeten, mit Synonymen arbeitenden Sprachgebrauch unterscheiden, obwohl nicht zu leugnen ist, daß häufig im sprachlichen Ursprung schon der scheinbar weit davon entfernte Sinn des späteren Sprachgebrauchs verdeckt enthalten ist.

Beim Herausschälen der ursprünglichen Bedeutung von „Jüdischem Volk" tut man am besten, auf die hebräischen Bezeichnungen für „Volk" zurückzugehen. Es scheiden zunächst aus als Sammelbegriffe engerer Art *Mischpacha*=Familie, *Beth-aboth*=Sippe, *Schebet*=Stamm. Für „Volk" hat die hebräische Sprache zwei Bezeichnungen, die häufig als Synonyma miteinander abwechseln, im Grunde aber ganz verschieden in ihrer Herleitung und rechten Anwendung sind: *Goj* und *Am*. G o j hängt mit der Wurzel *Gew*=Rücken,

Rückgrat, aram. *Gew.*=das Innerste zusammen. Wies dieses ein von Natur fest zusammenhängendes homogenes Ganzes ist (Skelett), als wenig veränderlicher Halt für das angeschlossene, ständig Veränderliche, so stellt das Wort *Goj* zweifellos in seiner ursprünglichen Bedeutung den Begriff des von einem Ahnherrn ausgehenden, in fortlaufender Geschlechtsfolge sich ausbreitenden und abzweigenden Stammes dar, der zum Volke sich weitet. Das Kennzeichnende ist die A b s t a m m u n g oder gemeinsamer ererbter Landbesitz, letzteres besonders in der Mehrzahl. Die Zusammengehörigkeit ist eine natürliche und braucht nicht bewußt zu sein. Es ist das griechische *Ethnos*—Volksstamm, Menschenklasse, wie die Septuaginta *Goj* stets übersetzt.

A m hängt grammatisch mit *Im*—„mit" zusammen und bedeutet einen bewußten, auf K u l t u r und S c h i c k s a l s g e m e i n s c h a f t beruhenden Zusammenschluß stammlich oft ganz verschiedener Individuen und Körperschaften. Die Septuaginta übersetzt es regelmäßig mit *laos*—Volkshaufe, Masse, Menge von zusammengekommenen Menschen. Daher nennt Gott Israel selten *Goj*, wenn er nämlich den seinem Dienste geweihten Stamm (*Kadosch*) meint oder ihn als solchen mit anderen Völkerschaften vergleicht, meistens aber *Am*, wenn er sein persönliches Verhältnis zu der freiwillig ihm sich anschließenden, seinem Schutze anvertrauten, seiner Liebe oder Strafe im Schicksal zugewiesenen Gemeinschaft hervorheben will. Die jüdische Religions- und Schicksalsgemeinschaft „Israel" wird nie als *Goj*, sondern stets als *Am* bezeichnet, weshalb auch Gott sein Volk niemals *Goji* (die einzige widersprechende Stelle im Zephanja, II, 9 ist ohne Bedeutung, da es hier ganz deutlich nicht auf die Bedeutung, sondern lediglich auf die Herstellung des Parallelismus ankommt), sondern stets *Ammi*, „mein Volk", nennt, weil die Zugehörigkeit zu Gott weniger auf der Abstammung von Abraham beruht—wenn diese auch nicht ganz außer acht gelassen ist—, als auf dem Wandel in Gottes Wegen, der durch den Gehorsam gegen seine besonderen, dem Volke Israel gegebenen Gebote zum Ausdruck kommt.

Im gegenwärtigen Sprachgebrauch verstehen die verschiedenen jüdischen Richtungen unter „Jüdischem Volk" je nach ihrer Stellungnahme zum Rasse-, Glaubens- und jüdisch-politischen Standpunkt verschiedenes. Man muß also immer wissen, wer der Sprecher ist, um zu wissen, was mit „Jüdischem Volk" gemeint ist."

4.2 Political Zionism is a Form of Racism

Political Zionism has often been condemned as a form of racism by Jew and Gentile alike. The United Nations General Assembly passed a resolution number 3379 condemning Zionism as racism on 10 November 1975:

"3379 (XXX). Elimination of all forms of racial discrimination

The General Assembly,

Recalling its resolution 1904 (XVIII) of 20 November 1963, proclaiming the United Nations Declaration on the Elimination of All Forms of Racial Discrimination, and in particular its affirmation that 'any doctrine of racial differentiation or superiority is scientifically false, morally condemnable, socially unjust and dangerous' and its expression of alarm at 'the manifestations of racial discrimination still in evidence in some areas in the world, some of which are imposed by certain Governments by means of legislative, administrative or other measures',

Recalling also that, in its resolution 3151 G (XXVIII) of 14 December 1973, the General Assembly condemned, *inter alia*, the unholy alliance between South African racism and zionism,

Taking note of the Declaration of Mexico on the Equality of Women and Their Contribution to Development and Peace, 1975,[4] proclaimed by the World Conference of the International Women's Year, held at Mexico City from 19 June to 2 July 1975, which promulgated the principle that 'international co-operation and peace require the achievement of national liberation and independence, the elimination of colonialism and neo-colonialism, foreign occupation, zionism, *apartheid* and racial discrimination in all its forms, as well as the recognition of the dignity of peoples and their right to self-determination',

Taking note also of resolution 77 (XII) adopted by the Assembly of Heads of State and Government of the Organization of African Unity at its twelfth ordinary session,[5] held in Kampala from 28 July to 1 August 1975, which considered 'that the racist régime in occupied Palestine and racist régimes in Zimbabwe and South Africa have a common imperialist origin, forming a whole and having the same racist structure and being organically linked in their policy aimed at repression of the dignity and integrity of the human being',

Taking note also of the Political Declaration and Strategy to Strengthen International Peace and Security and to Intensify Solidarity and Mutual Assistance among Non-Aligned Countries,[6] adopted at the Conference of Ministers for Foreign Affairs of Non-Aligned Countries held at Lima from 25 to 30 August 1975, which most severely condemned zionism as a threat to world peace and security and called upon all countries to oppose this racist and imperialist ideology,

Determines that Zionism is a form of racism and racial discrimination.

2400th plenary meeting

10 November 1975"[483]

This resolution was revoked in 1991, when the Zionist influence increased in the United Nations, in part due to the fall of the Soviet Union.

When confronted with the facts some racist Zionists and some of their advocates, including Einstein and many of Einstein's advocates, too often resort to smear tactics in lieu of reasoned arguments. The *Executive Council of the International Organization for the Elimination of All Forms of Racial Discrimination* stated,

"On 10 November 1975 the General Assembly of the United Nations adopted resolution 3379 (XXX) determining 'that Zionism is a form of racism and racial discrimination.' The response of Zionists and their supporters to this resolution was, not to attempt to demonstrate that the finding was in error, but to mount a campaign designed to discredit the UN and to impugn the motives of the 72 member states voting in support of it."[484]

Dr. Fayez A. Sayegh stated,

"[. . .]I am not chagrined by verbal abuse—by the insolent railing, the name-calling, to which the Delegation of the United States has resorted, both inside and outside the United Nations, ever since 3 October. 'Perverse,' 'obscene,' 'indecent,' 'lies'—these words have graced and punctuated the statements of the representatives of the United States. I am not chagrined and I am not disconcerted. Long, long ago, in my first elementary course in philosophy, I was told by my professors: Only he who has no argument resorts to name-calling.[47] Name-calling is no substitute for rational discourse; name-calling is an admission of intellectual bankruptcy."[485]

The Zionists later used Einstein, then a celebrity, as an attraction to lure in crowds, and with them, cash, just as Herzl had planned. In return, Einstein, Herzl's proposed prize horse, was able to bask in the limelight he so loved. Einstein, as a political personality, was especially vulnerable to Herzl's racist belief system. Einstein generally hated Gentile Germans and was an impressionable and simplistic absolutist, who sought his opinions in the writings of others, and who formed generalized, stereotypical opinions expressed in absolutes. Einstein spoke of the "common destiny" of Jews in all of the countries of the world, of "our race", of Jews "sticking together", of ties of "blood", of the "Gentile world", of the "whole Jewish people", of the "salvation for the race", etc.[486] While asserting his Zionist racism, Einstein would sometimes soften his statements, and mask his Jewish racism and supremacism, by asserting that he would prefer a world in which all human beings were brothers in the spirit of internationalism, but such a world did not exist because of anti-Semitism and he had to face facts and so practiced racism in order to protect himself from racism. Some anti-Semites had already justified segregation in the same terms as Einstein. Some anti-Semites claimed that they would prefer a Utopian world with universal brotherhood in the true Christian spirit, but that Zionist racism made such a world impossible and they just had to face facts and protect themselves from Jewish racists.[487]

Weizmann, Blumenfeld and Ginsberg ordered Einstein around, and he dutifully followed them until tensions and divisions arose among the Zionists. It is a myth that all Zionists were Communists or, alternatively, that all were right-wing extremists, though many did tend towards extremes as was natural for a fledgling movement caught in the tumult of turbulent times. There was a great deal of infighting among the political Zionists. The most common theme among Zionists was racism. Ber Borochov, a Marxist Zionist, cited Marx and Engel's materialistic racism in an effort to justify Zionism.[488] Racist Zionist Moses Hess, who was condemned to death in the German Revolution of 1848 and who had worked with Marx and Engels, opposed the dogmatic approach of communistic materialistic determinism, and preferred nationalistic Socialism—like the Nazis later would.

The Zionists were able to corrupt the press and to promote anti-Semitism, so that the anti-Semites would force European governments to force the Jews to leave Europe and assist in the expulsion of Jews to Palestine. Herzl, even before the Russian revolution, but after the French Revolution and the revolutions of 1848, played on the fear European governments had of the Jewish mission to rule the world by deposing monarchies through revolution, and in so doing the political Zionists reinforced anti-Semitism. Herzl unwisely believed that he could threaten the governments of the world,

"The governments will give us their friendly assistance because we relieve them of the danger of a revolution which would start with the Jews—and stop who knows where!"[489]

Herzl wrote in his book *The Jewish State*,

"When we sink, we become a revolutionary proletariat, the subordinate officers of the revolutionary party; when we rise, there rises also our terrible power of the purse. [***] Again, people will say that I am furnishing the Anti-Semites with weapons. Why so? Because I admit the truth? Because I do not maintain that there are none but excellent men amongst us? Again, people will say that I am showing our enemies the way to injure us. This I absolutely dispute. My proposal could only be carried out with the free consent of a majority of Jews. Individuals or even powerful bodies of Jews might be attacked, but Governments will take no action against the collective nation. The equal rights of Jews before the law cannot be withdrawn where they have once been conceded; for the first attempt at withdrawal would immediately drive all Jews rich and poor alike, into the ranks of the revolutionary party. The first official violation of Jewish liberties invariably brings about economic crisis. Therefore no weapons can be effectually used against us, because these cut the hands that wield them."[490]

However, it is clear from Herzl's book *The Jewish State* of 1896, that Herzl knew that the Jews of various nations were loyal to their homelands and would never leave Europe and America in large enough numbers of their own volition. Herzl took it upon himself, as self-appointed pseudo-Messiah, to generate political conditions whereby the Jews would have no choice but to leave. This political Zionist policy of provoking anti-Semitism fit in well with Einstein's desire to avoid criticism by dangerously stigmatizing scientific disagreement as if anti-Semitism, *per se*.[491] In this way Einstein accomplished two ends with one tactic. He generated and increased anti-Semitic sentiments in academia and he publicly smeared anyone who disagreed with him or threatened to expose him.

4.3 Albert Einstein Becomes a Cheerleader for Racist Zionism

Albert Einstein actively campaigned for Herzl's racism and traveled to America in April of 1921 in order to promote it. Einstein brought a "secretary", Salomon Ginzberg, the son of the famous Zionist leader Ha-Am. Ginzberg apparently had little respect for Einstein. He ridiculed Einstein for one of Einstein's "speeches"—a pre-Goebbels-like plea for ethnic unity behind a lone *Führer*,[492]

> "You have one leader — Weizmann. Follow him and no other!"[493]

Ginzberg and Einstein's second wife failed to persuade Albert to return to his rehearsed lines, when Einstein was interviewed by *The New York Times Book Review* quoted herein. Note that Einstein's "secretary" repeated lines from Einstein's Zionist arrival speech—much to Einstein's annoyance. This speech was covered in *The New York Times* in a story which began on the front page and spilled over onto page 13, on 3 April 1921, reprinted herein. The interview in the *New York Times Book Review* was arranged for Einstein to promote his book, and to raise money for Zionists, not for Einstein to babble and boast.

But why, in contrast to his pro-American attitude in that interview, was Einstein so bitter after he had left America? The Zionists quibbled among themselves in America and the trip turned out to be a disappointment for them. The American Zionists wanted to proceed slowly and to maintain the bonds Jews had to the many nations of the world. Few wanted to venture from their comfortable mansions in America to tame the deserts of Palestine. European Zionists were more militant and isolationist, and resented the fact that masses of Jews could not be persuaded to voluntarily emigrate to Palestine.

4.3.1 While Zionists and Sycophants Hailed Einstein, Most Scientists Rejected Him and "His" Theories

In addition to Zionist strife and infighting, which caused Einstein problems during his trip to America, Einstein's scientific work was not so well-received, nor so perfect, as his present day advocates would have us believe. As a result, Albert Einstein had quite a rough time in America, where he was again and again challenged for his plagiarism and for his irrationality.[494] The same was true in Germany. The same was true in England. Louis Essen wrote,

"But there have always been its critics: Rutherford treated it as a joke: Soddy called it a swindle: Bertrand Russell suggested that it was all contained in the Lorentz transformation equations and many scientists commented on its contradictions. These adverse opinions, together with the fact that the small effects predicted by the theory were becoming of significance to the definition of the unit of atomic time, prompted me to study Einstein's paper. I found that it was written in imprecise language, that one assumption was in two contradictory forms and that it contained two serious errors."[495]

John T. Blankart stated in 1921,

"The 'Kinertia' articles offer food for thought when considered in connection with the colossal claims made by Einstein's supporters concerning his almost super-human originality. In fact, one begins to doubt the justice of these claims and to wonder if the charges made by a fast growing group of German scientists who, like E. Gehrcke, P. Lenard, and Paul Weyland, hold that Einstein is both a plagiarist and a sophist, are not, after all, true. We have done little justice in the above to the rare dialectic skill with which Dr. Einstein has applied his intellectual anæsthesia to the minds of his readers. All intellectual obstructions have been removed, and the reader is prepared to venture forth boldly into the mysterious realm of 'curved' space *whose geometrical properties depend upon the matter present.* This most curious inference of Einstein is the master stroke in his skillful massing of inconsistent sophistries."[496]

Einstein once asked,

"Do I have something of a charlatan or a hypnotist about me that draws people like a circus clown?"[497]

Paul Weyland[498] and Ernst Gehrcke[499] proved that Einstein's rise to fame was a "mass suggestion" fed by the insecurities of some of the authorities, and by the press, who would frequently misrepresent the facts, and misrepresented the views of many leading authorities, who were in reality mostly opposed to relativity theory. Weyland pointed out that Einstein obviously could not defend himself or "his" theories, because Einstein relied upon the *ad hominem* attack of calling his opponents "anti-Semites", instead of refuting their arguments in a rational manner.

Ernst Gehrcke and Stjepan Mohorovičić pointed out that Einstein rose to prominence, not because "his" theories were sound, but rather because his hangers-on, his connections in the press, and his racist smears intimidated the scientific community and deliberately inhibited the debate, with their frenzied personal attacks and their proven threats of violence, smears and career infringement against any who would question Einstein. Bruno Thüring, in 1941, stated that the acceptance of the theory of relativity resulted from a "mass psychosis" brought about by Jewish led propaganda, intimidation and the career infringement of anyone who opposed the dogmatism of Einstein.[500] Ernst Mach considered Einstein a charlatan, and Mach, too, categorized the theory of relativity as a "mass suggestion"—even before the terrible hype of the 1919 eclipse observations.

We know Mach's opinion from a letter which Čeněk Dvořák wrote to Mach on 19 August 1915,

"The best contemporary physicists would agree with you about the exaggerated speculation, mass suggestion, and modish tendencies in modern physics."[501]

Arvid Reuterdahl was quoted in the *Minneapolis Sunday Tribune* on 20 November 1921, after Einstein's humiliating departure from America,

"Einstein Foes
Prove Theory
False Claim

530   Albert Einstein: The Incorrigible Racist

Twin Cities Mathematical Association Hears Talk on Relativity.
Former Exponents Are Now Sorry, Says St. Thomas Engineering Dean.

Einstein's theory of relativity, which created a stir in the scientific world when first promulgated, is rapidly being rejected by the leading scholars of Europe and America. Prof. Arvid Reuterdahl told members of the Twin Cities Mathematical association last night at the Minnesota Union, University of Minnesota.

Professor Reuterdahl, who has been a vigorous opponent of Einsteinism since its inception, is dean of the department of engineering and architecture at St. Thomas college.

'Seething in Revolt.'

'It is literally true that Europe is seething in revolt against the yoke of Einsteinism,' Professor Reuterdahl declared. 'The eminent thinkers of Europe emphatically object to the steam roller methods used by the Einsteinian propagandists.

'The affair of Einstein was overdone and as a result the entire world is united, not only against a palpable fallacy, but also against the questionable methods by which this fallacy was flaunted before an unsuspecting public as a super-truth.'

A score of eminent scientists of both Europe and America were named by Professor Reuterdahl as actively opposed to the Einstein theory.

'Even in England where Einsteinism has been firmly entrenched since the findings of the English polar expedition were made known, the rebellion is gaining strength,' he said. 'In the front rank of the English expedition we find Prof. W. D. Ross of Oxford, and the celebrated mathematicians Gaynor and Whitehead.'

Professor Reuterdahl asserted that the leading astronomers of the United States are now either directly denying the truth of Einstein's theory or openly doubting the correctness of its contentions.

Majority Opposed.

'It is no longer an intellectual misdemeanor to doubt the validity of his speculations,' he said, "Undoubtedly the great majority of American scientists are today solidly opposed to the theories of Einstein. Many of those scientists who succumbed to the mass psychology of his trumpet blasts now sincerely wish that they had remained discreetly neutral.

Doctor T. J. J. See, professor of mathematics, United States navy, and director of the Mare island observatory, California, was said by Professor Reuterdahl to be one of the leading opponents of the theory in America.

'It is truly a sad ending to a perfect Einsteinian day,' he said, 'A camouflaged formula successfully used to gather renown is finally shown by an American scientist to be contrary to that great law which serves as the basic foundation of the entire structure of science.'"

The *Minneapolis Evening Tribune* of 5 May 1921 wrote,

"Scientists Rally to Support Reuterdahl in Fight on Einstein

Mysterious 'Kinertia' Attacks Theory and Thanks Minnesota Man.

'Fantastic Jazz of Mathematical Symbols,' Says Dr. S. P. Skidmore.

American scientists are rallying to the support of Professor Arvid Reuterdahl of St. Thomas college in his fight against Doctor Albert Einstein, including the mysterious 'Kinertia,' to whom Professor Reuterdahl gives credit for originating the theory of relativity.

Professor Reuterdahl has received a statement signed by 'Kinertia,' through an intermediary in New York, in which the scientist again attacks Einsteinism and thanks the St. Thomas dean for his efforts to prove the theory false.

All Write to Reuterdahl.

Doctor Sydney P. Skidmore of Philadelphia, Dr. W. E. Glanville, noted astronomer of Baltimore, and Dr. Robert P. Browne, author of 'Mystery of Space,' are others who have communicated with Professor Reuterdahl.

Doctor Skidmore says:

'Einsteinism is a fantastic jazz of mathematical symbols, devoid of quanta, in a dance hall floored by a parquetry of ifs, supposings and assumptions, and has no application to anything in the realm of objective truth.'

Doctor Glanville likens the Einstein theory to a newly discovered drug which is brought forth and acclaimed as a universal scientific panacea. He also compares Einsteinism to a great deflated scientific bubble. Doctor Brown assures Professor Reuterdahl that he will be allied in the fight 'against the mathematical usurpations of Einstein and relativity.'

Doubts Efficiency of Test.

'In the critical portion of the article just sent me by 'Kinertia' he points out some of the outstanding errors in Einstein's theory,' said Reuterdahl today. 'He expresses serious doubt that the solar spectrum test proposed by Einstein to prove his theory will be confirmative in its result. 'Kinertia' states:

''In dynamics, acceleration and weight are not forces or physical causes. This is the dangerous ground Einstein assumes in his apparent anxiety to relegate forces to the waste basket because they disappear in the parallelogram law; he proposes to substitute uniform antecedents in place of natural causation.'

''Kinertia,' moreover, demands that Einstein be consistent in his application of the motion of acceleration. In order to be consistent, 'Kinertia' holds, Einstein must develop a law which provides that bodies at the earth's surface be pushed from its center with the same acceleration with which falling bodies are apparently drawn toward it.

What Differentials Show.

''Kinertia' further states:

'Einstein's differentials only show that either case would suffice if the acceleration was the same.'

He concludes his article with this pertinent statement:

'Science wants more than agnosticism; it wants to know the absolute truth, before accepting any such theory; even if d'Alembert's static ghost is dressed in Hamiltonian functions.'''

Hubert Goenner contended that,

"Also, a majority of theoretical physicists in Germany moved away from a theory with little potential for experiments and testable consequences."[502]

This view is supported by the record, for example the *St. Paul Dispatch* wrote on 3 April 1921, that Einstein had run away from Germany to America to hide from his critics,

"EINSTEIN ON RUN, SAYS LETTER TO REUTERDAHL
Albert Einstein, denounced by the opponents of his alleged 'discoveries,' is on the run, according to a letter received from Dr. Hermann Fricke, physicist and astronomer of Berlin, dated August 19, by Prof. Arvid Reuterdahl, dean of the department of engineering and architecture at St. Thomas college, and author of 'Einstein and the New Science,' an attack on the Einstein theory, recently published.
Einstein's popularity has waned, the Berlin scientist writes, and he says also that a large edition of Prof. Reuterdahl's book is to be published in the German capital.
Dr. J. G. A. Goedhart, astronomer at Amsterdam, writes that Einstein has left Germany and has taken a professorship at the university in Leiden Holland. Circulation of Prof. Reuterdahl's book in Holland, and also in Sweden, is to he undertaken by foreign scientists opposed to the Einstein theory."

Nobel Prize laureate Johannes Stark wrote in 1922,

"V o r w o r t
Die deutsche Physik macht gegenwärtig eine Krisis durch. Es kämpfen in ihr zwei Richtungen miteinander. E i n s t e i n s und durch den Dogmatismus der Quantentheorie hat eine theoretische Richtung einen beherrschenden Einfluß gewonnen, welcher die physikalische Wissenschaft grundsätzlich zu schädigen begonnen hat, indem sie deren Quellen mehr in der gedanklichen Konstruktion als in der Erfahrung sucht und diese zur Dienerin der Formel machen will. Ihr gegenüber findet sich die experimentelle Richtung in der Verteidigungsstellung; sie sieht die Quelle der Physik in der Beobachtung und Messung und in der Theorie ein heuristisches und systematisches Hilfsmittel für die Gewinnung und Darstellung der physikalischen Erkenntnis. Es kann kein Zweifel darüber bestehen, welche Richtung schließlich die Oberhand gewinnen

wird. Die vorliegende Schrift hat die Aufgabe, durch die rückhaltlose Kritik von experimenteller Seite her die Entwicklung der gegenwärtigen Krisis in der deutschen Physik zu beschleunigen.

[***]

Die vorstehenden Ausführungen über das Verhältnis der physikalischen Theorie zur Erfahrung enthalten nichts Neues und in späterer Zeit mag einem Leser ihre Wiederholung als überflüssig erscheinen. In der gegenwärtigen Zeit ist es aber gegenüber dem anspruchsvollen Auftreten moderner Theorien notwendig, an sie zu erinnern. Für die Überschätzung der Theorie und die Unterschätzung der Beobachtung ist ein Ausspruch E i n s t e i n s, des Schöpfers der allgemeinen Relativitätstheorie, kennzeichnend. Anfangs dieses Jahres hielt Herr E i n s t e i n in Berlin vor einem auserwählten Kreis von Wissenschaftern, Wirtschaftern und Politikern einen Vortrag über die neuere Entwicklung der physikalischen Forschung. Gegen den Schluß desselben äußerte er sich zusammenfassend über die Quantentheorie des Atoms folgendermaßen: man dürfe erwarten, daß die Theorie bald imstande sein werde, die Eigenschaften der chemischen Atome und ihre Reaktionen vorauszuberechnen, so daß sich die mühevollen zeitraubenden experimentellen Arbeiten der Chemiker erübrigen würden. Als ich diese lobpreisende Überschätzung der Theorie mitanhörte, mußte ich aus Höflichkeit gegen den Gastgeber an mich halten, um nicht in Lachen auszubrechen. Aber danach war ich über die Leichtfertigkeit empört, mit welcher Herr E i n s t e i n, der von dem breiten Publikum herausgestellt wird, eine Auffassung verbreitet, welche auf die Dauer großen Schaden stiften muß. Herr E i n s t e i n sollte sich einmal eingehender mit der Erfahrung der anorganischen und organischen Chemie befassen, dann würde ihm klar werden, wie ungeheuer übertrieben seine theoretischen Erwartungen im Gebiete der Chemie sind und wie wenig gerade diese Wissenschaft die immer erneute Erfahrung entbehren kann. Es würde auch lehrreich für ihn sein, zu sehen, wie erstaunlich weit sich diese Wissenschaft fast allein auf Grund der Erfahrung ohne die mathematische Hilfe der Theorie entwickelt hat.

II. Die Stellung der allgemeinen Relativitätstheorie

Einsteins in der Physik
und die Propaganda für sie.

Wenn die Bedeutung einer Theorie proportional der Zahl der Abhandlungen, Bücher und Vorträge über sie wäre, so müßte die allgemeine Relativitätstheorie E i n s t e i n s als die weitaus bedeutendste Theorie aller Zeiten gewertet werden. Denn über keine Theorie in der Physik ist bisher von berufener und unberufener Seite soviel geschrieben und geredet worden wie über sie; es ist für sie seit Jahren in aller Welt sowohl in wissenschaftlichen Zeitschriften wie in Flugschriften und in der Tagepresse eine Propaganda getrieben worden, wie sie bisher unbekannt in der physikalischen Wissenschaft war. Diese Propaganda und der Einfluß des E i n s t e i n schen Kreises ist in erster Linie für das Überwuchern der Theorie in der gegenwärtigen Physik, für die Unterschätzung der experimentellen Forschung und für die Vernachlässigung der angewandten Physik in Unterricht und Forschung verantwortlich zu machen. Mit Recht haben bereits L e n a r d [*Footnote:* P. L e n a r d, Über Relativitätstheorie, Äther, Gravitation, S. Hirzel, Leipzig 1921.] und G e h r c k e Einspruch gegen die Fiktionen der E i n s t e i n schen Relativitätstheorie erhoben und auch W. Wien [*Footnote:* W. W i e n, Die Relativitätstheorie, Joh. Ambr. Barth, Leipzig 1921.] hat zu physikalischer Besinnung in dem Für und Wider um sie gemahnt. Aber L e n a r d s und G e h r c k e s Kritik wurde von der Seite E i n s t e i n s als persönliche Beleidigung aufgefaßt und in unsachlicher Weise beantwortet. Und trotzdem die Auseinandersetzungen über die E i n s t e i n s c h e Theorie auf der N a u h e i m e r Naturforscherversammlung in persönlicher Hinsicht höchst unerquicklich und in sachlicher Hinsicht unfruchtbar waren, und obwohl seitdem kein unbestrittener Fortschritt in der experimentellen Prüfung der Theorie erfolgt ist, soll auf der diesjährigen Naturforscherversammlung in Leipzig die E i n s t e i n sche Theorie wieder einem Kreise vorgeführt werden, der nur zu einem kleinen Teile aus Physikern besteht.

Bei dieser Lage der Dinge ist eine kritische Auseinandersetzung mit der allgemeinen Relativitätstheorie hinsichtlich ihrer physikalischen Bedeutung und der Propaganda für sie dringend geboten.

Von einer physikalischen Theorie ist zu verlangen, daß sie an ihre Spitze eine grundlegende Aussage über eine Beziehung zwischen physikalischen Großen stellt. So liegt der mechanischen Wärmetheorie der Gedanke von der wechselseitigen Umwandelbarkeit von Wärme und Arbeit zugrunde, der M a x w e l l schen Theorie der Gedanke der raumzeitlichen Verknüpfung von elektrischer und magnetischer Feldstärke. Welche grundlegende Aussage über eine zahlreiche Erscheinungen umfassende Beziehung zwischen physikalischen Größen stellt nun E i n s t e i n an die Spitze seiner allgemeinen Relativitätstheorie? Er selbst versteht unter „allgemeinem Relativitätsprinzip" die Behauptung: „Alle Bezugskörper K, K' usw. sind für die Naturbeschreibung (Formulierung der allgemeinen Naturgesetze) gleichwertig, welches auch deren Bewegungszustand sein mag." An einer anderen Stelle derselben Schrift bezeichnet E i n s t e i n als exakte Formulierung seines allgemeinen Relativitätsprinzips folgende Aussage: „Alle Gaussschen Koordinatensysteme sind für die Formulierung der allgemeinen Naturgesetze prinzipiell gleichwertig."

Wie selbst der Nichtphysiker erkennt, macht das so formulierte allgemeine Relativitätsprinzip keine Aussage über eine Beziehung zwischen physikalischen Größen, sondern über die formal-mathematische Darstellung von physikalischen Gesetzen. Entsprechend seinem formal-mathematischen Grundgedanken ist es darum überhaupt nicht unter die physikalischen Theorien in dem oben umschriebenen Sinne zu rechnen, sondern gehört in das Grenzgebiet zwischen Physik, Mathematik und Erkenntnistheorie. In dem formal-mathematischen Grundgedanken der allgemeinen Relativitätstheorie ist es denn auch gelegen, daß Nichtphysiker, vor allem Erkenntnistheoretiker und Mathematiker, sie mit Eifer aufgegriffen und in zahlreichen Abhandlungen und dicken Schriften auf ihre Weise ausgearbeitet haben. Wenn ich dieser Art Relativitätsliteratur, welche vorzügliche philosophische oder mathematische Leistungen darstellen mögen, jeglichen Wert für die physikalische Wissenschaft abspreche, so werde ich zwar von den Einsteinianern als armseliger Banause abgetan werden, dies kann mich aber nicht hindern, meinerseits als Physiker mein Urteil über die physikalische Bedeutung des allgemeinen Relativitätsprinzips zu bekennen und sogar folgende Blasphemie auszusprechen: Wäre E i n s t e i n mit seiner Theorie doch von Anfang unter die Mathematiker und Philosophen gegangen! Die deutsche Physik wäre dann vielleicht von dem lähmenden Gift des Gedankens verschont geblieben, man könne aus geistreichen Fiktionen („Gedankenexperimenten") mit Hilfe mathematischer Operationen physikalische Erkenntnisse oder, wie es in der Regel heißt, das „Weltbild" gewinnen.

Der Vorwurf der physikalischen Inhaltslosigkeit trifft die allgemeine Relativitätstheorie Einsteins ins Herz und diejenigen ihrer Verteidiger, welchen mein Urteil nicht von vornherein gleichgültig ist, werden sich beeilen mir entgegenzuhalten, daß die Relativitätstheorie doch zu bestimmten Folgerungen von sachlich-physikalischem Inhalt gelange, so zu einer Aussage über den Einfluß des Gravitationsfeldes auf die Lichtpflanzung und auf die optischen Eigenfrequenz chemischer Atome. Ist bis jetzt der Ausgangspunkt der Relativitätstheorie vom physikalischen Standpunkt aus beurteilt worden, so kommen wir mit der Antwort auf den vorstehenden Einwand zur physikalischen Beurteilung der methodischen Seite der Theorie. Ich gebe vorweg zu, daß die allgemeine Relativitätstheorie zu sachlich-physikalischen Folgerungen gelangt. Indes haben diese ihre Wurzel nicht allein in ihrem formal-mathematischen Grundgedanken, sondern auch in den sachlich-physikalischen Zutaten bei seiner mathematischen Verarbeitung, so vor allem in der Verknüpfung des Gravitationsfeldes mit der beschleunigten Bewegung und in der Verwertung der Tatsache von Proportionalität der schweren und der trägen Masse.

Die Art der Verarbeitung des Grundgedankens der Relativitätstheorie entsprecht ebensowenig den an eine physikalische Theorie zu stellenden Forderungen wie ihr Grundgedanke selbst. Wie oben dargelegt wurde, ist eine physikalische Theorie in erster Linie für den experimentellen Physiker bestimmt; sie soll da, wo sie nicht seine Messungen zusammenfassend beschreibt, sondern Vorhersagen macht, auch für denjenigen Experimentalphysiker verständlich sein, welcher nicht die Kenntnisse des Fachmathematikers besitzt. Wie steht es in dieser Hinsicht mit E i n s t e i n s allgemeiner Relativitätstheorie? Zwar E i n s t e i n glaubte seine Theorie selbst dem Nichtphysiker verständlich machen zu können; seiner „gemeinverständlicher" Schrift [*Footnote:* A. E i n s t e i n, Über die spezielle und die allgemeine Relativitätstheorie, 51.-55. Tausend. F. Vieweg & Sohn, Braunschweig.] über sie, die in mehr als 50,000 Stück verbreitet ist, schickt er nämlich folgende

Sätze voraus: „Das vorliegende Büchlein soll solchen eine möglichst exakte Einsicht in die Relativitätstheorie vermitteln, die sich vom allgemein wissenschaftlichen, philosophischen Standpunkt für die Theorie interessieren, ohne den mathematischen Apparat der theoretischen Physik zu beherrschen. Die Lektüre setzt etwa Maturitätsbildung und — trotz der Kürze des Büchleins — ziemlich viel Geduld und Willenskraft beim Leser voraus."

E i n s t e i n war also der Meinung, daß für das Verständnis seiner Relativitätstheorie die Kenntnis der höheren Mathematik nicht nötig sei. In Wirklichkeit ist wohl noch keine Theorie in der physikalischen Literatur mitgeteilt worden, welche so schwer verständlich gewesen wäre wie die E i n s t e i n sche Relativitätstheorie. Hierfür zeugt schon die Tatsache, daß man es für nötig hielt, sie durch zahlreiche Bücher selbst dem physikalischen und mathematischen Fachmann verständlich zu machen. Und auf der Seite ihrer Verteidiger hat man sich heute gegenüber der Kritik von Experimentalphysikern hinter die bequeme Ausrede zurückgezogen, sie besäßen nicht die höhere mathematische Bildung, welche zum Verständnis der allgemeinen Relativitätstheorie notwendig sei. Diejenigen Physiker, welche an ihr Kritik üben, verfügen nach ihnen nicht über dies nötige mathematische Begabung, um sie zu verstehen; sie werden gegenüber den Relativitätstheoretikern in eine tiefere Klasse verwiesen. Diese Behandlung ist selbst einem Physiker von den experimentellen Leistungen und mathematischen Kenntnissen L e n a r d s von Seite E i n s t e i n s und seiner Anhänger widerfahren. Indes sprechen diese Theoretiker, welche so überlegen nicht bloß die höhere, sondern die höchste mathematische Bildung für das Verständnis der allgemeinen Relativitätstheorie fordern, dieser selbst das Urteil. Sie vergessen in Selbsteingenommenheit, daß die Theorie in der Physik nicht Selbstzweck, nicht allein für den Theoretiker und den Mathematiker da ist, sondern daß sie eine Hilfe für den Experimentalphysiker sein, seine Arbeit anregen oder formal abschließen soll. Für eine Theorie, welche dieser Forderung nicht genügt, sollte in physikalischen Zeitschriften kein Platz sein.

Die Übertreibung ins Abstrakte und Formale, die Beschränkung auf das intellektuelle Spiel mit den mathematischen Definitionen und Formeln kommt in der

E i n s t e i n schen Relativitätstheorie vor allem in der absichtlichen Ignorierung des Äthers zum Ausdruck. Gewiß kann man physikalische Beziehungen zwischen materiellen Körpern in mathematischen Formeln unter Absehen vom Äther zwischen ihnen darstellen. Wird aber damit der Begriff des Äthers überflüssig, wird damit die Tatsache der Existenz des Äthers aus der Welt geschafft? In einer der Ansprachen auf der Nauheimer Naturforscherversammlung wurde es von einem Nichtphysiker als eine naturwissenschaftliche Großtat E i n s t e i n s gefeiert, daß er den Äther abgeschafft habe. Soll man lachen über diese Wertschätzung einer vermeintlichen Großleistung E i n s t e i n s, oder soll man empört sein über die von seinen Fiktionen angerichtete Verwüstung. Nein, die gefeierte Abschaffung des Äthers durch E i n s t e i n ist nicht eine Großtat, sondern der Versuch zu einem verheerenden Rückschritt in der physikalischen Wissenschaft. Die Einführung des Äthersbegriffes in die Optik und in die Elektrodynamik, das anschauliche Denken mit ihm hat sich in der Physik als außerordentlich fruchtbar erwiesen; der Äther ist durch die physikalische Forschung eines Jahrhunderts aus einer Hypothese zu einer Tatsache geworden. Eine Physik ohne den Äther ist keine Physik. E i n s t e i n ist wohl selbst ob seiner Großtat der Abschaffung des Äthers bange geworden; denn in neuerer Zeit scheint er in einem Vortrag den Äther wieder einführen zu wollen, freilich ist es nicht der alte abgeschaffte Äther, sondern eine Art E i n s t e i n scher Relativitätsäther.

Man mag nun zugeben, daß die allgemeine Relativitätstheorie weder in ihrem Grundgedanken noch in ihrer Entwicklung den Anforderungen genügt, welche von physikalischer Seite an eine physikalische Theorie zu stellen sind. Es könnte aber doch sein, daß ihr das große Verdienst zuzusprechen wäre, die Entdeckung neuer Erscheinungen veranlaßt zu haben und daß ihre Folgerungen experimentell bestätigt worden sind. Es ist darum zu prüfen, ob dies für die allgemeine Relativitätstheorie zutrifft. Drei Erscheinungen sind es, welche in dieser Hinsicht in Betracht kommen.

Da ist zunächst die Anomalie in der Perihelbewegung des Merkurs; sie war bereits vor Aufstellung der Relativitätstheorie aus der astronomischen Beobachtung bekannt. Ihr Betrag schien früher genau mit der Rechnung nach der Relativitätstheorie übereinzustimmen; dies ist indes nach einer kürzlich erschienenen Nachprüfung durch G r o ß m a n n zum mindesten fraglich geworden. Aber selbst wenn die Übereinstimmung vorhanden wäre, könnte durch sie die Richtigkeit der Relativitätstheorie noch nicht als erwiesen gelten. Denn es gibt noch eine andere Möglichkeit (Annahme interplanetarer Massen) zur Deutung jener Anomalie.

Denn soll die Relativitätstheorie durch den Nachweis der Ablenkung des Fixsternlichtes beim Vorbeigang an der Sonne bestätigt worden sein. Es muß zugestanden werden, daß der Gedanke eines Einflusses des Gravitationsfeldes auf die Lichtbewegung ursprünglich und wertvoll ist. Es erfordert allerdings die geschichtliche Gerechtigkeit, die Priorität dieses Gedankens S o l d n e r zuzuerkennen, der ihn bereits vor hundert Jahren, wenn auch auf Grund einer anderen Annahme über das Wesen des Lichtes zur Grundlage einer theoretischen Abhandlung in den Annalen der Physik und Chemie gemacht hat. Wie steht es aber mit der experimentellen Bestätigung dieser zweiten Folgerung der Relativitätstheorie? Bisher liegen nur Beobachtungen bei einer einzigen Sonnenfinsternis vor. Wer die für derartige Messungen notwendige Meßtechnik zu beurteilen und den Wert von Meßdaten, welche nahe der Grenze der Meßgenauigkeit liegen, abzuwägen versteht, der wird erklären, daß durch jene Beobachtungen lediglich wahrscheinlich gemacht ist, daß Lichtstrahlen, wenn sie nahe bei der Sonne verlaufen, aus ihrer anfänglichen Richtung etwas abgelenkt werden. Von einer quantitativen Bestätigung der allgemeinen Relativitätstheorie durch jene Beobachtungen kann jedoch nicht die Rede sein. Die Ablenkung von Lichtstrahlen in der Nähe der Sonne kann einen anderen Grund haben, als in der Relativitätstheorie angenommen wird.

Die dritte Folgerung der Relativitätstheorie behauptet, daß durch die Wirkung eines Gravitationsfeldes, z. B. durch dasjenige an der Sonne, die optischen Eigenfrequenzen der chemischen Atome etwas verkleinert, also die ihnen entsprechenden Spektrallinien etwas nach Rot verschoben werden. Die bis jetzt in dieser Hinsicht vorliegenden Messungen widersprechen sich in ihrem Ergebnis hinsichtlich der Relativitätstheorie. Amerikanische und deutsche Beobachter, welche mit einer guten Technik arbeiteten, erklären, daß eine Rotverschiebung von Sonnenlinien in dem von der Theorie geforderten Betrag nicht vorhanden ist. Wieder andere deutsche

Beobachter und ein französischer behaupten, sie hätten die von
E i n s t e i n gefolgerte Rotverschiebung der Sonnenlinien
gefunden. Es steht also Behauptung wider Behauptung und es
kann nur durch neue, mit besonderer Umsicht durchgeführte
Messungen die Entscheidung gebracht werden. Diese neuen
Messungen sollten ohne jegliche Voreingenommenheit für und
wider die Theorie unternommen werden. Bei dem Lesen des
Berichtes über sie sollte man nicht den Eindruck haben, daß sie
in der Absicht durchgeführt und zurechtgemacht wurden, um die
Theorie zu bestätigen. Und der spektralanalytische Fachmann
wird mit Zurückhaltung und theoretischer Skepsis an die
Deutung einer geringen Verschiebung von Linien im
Sonnenspektrum gegenüber ihrer Lage im Spektrum irdischer
Lichtquellen herangehen. Weiß er doch, daß es eine Reihe von
Wirkungen gibt, welche geringe Verschiebungen von
Spektrallinien hervorbringen, und da uns die Bedingungen an der
Oberfläche der Sonne nicht genügend bekannt sind, so wird er
an die Beweisführung zugunsten einer besonderen Wirkung hohe
Anforderungen stellen.

In keinem der drei Fälle, welche in der Regel als Beweise für
die Richtigkeit der allgemeinen Relativitätstheorie angeführt
werden, liegen also die Verhältnisse so, daß ein vorsichtiger
Physiker anerkennen könnte, daß die Richtigkeit der
E i n s t e i n schen Relativitätstheorie erwiesen sei; er kann
höchstens zugeben, daß es nicht ausgeschlossen ist, daß weitere
verfeinerte Messungen eine Übereinstimmung zwischen den
Folgerungen der Theorie und den Beobachtungen ergeben. Und
es kann der Relativitätstheorie darum noch nicht das Verdienst
zugesprochen werden, neue Entdeckungen veranlaßt zu haben.

Bedenkt man, daß die „Bestätigung" der E i n s t e i n schen
Theorie noch aussteht, nimmt man dazu, daß ihr Grundgedanke
formal-mathematisch ist und das Verständnis ihrer Entwicklung
hohe mathematische Kenntnisse erfordert, so versteht man nicht,
wie mit einer solchen Theorie eine so unerhörte Propaganda
getrieben werden konnte, wie es bisher mit keiner anderen
Theorie der Fall gewesen ist. Weit über den Kreis der wenigen
physikalischen und mathematischen Fachleute hinaus, welche sie
zu beurteilen vermögen, wurde sie dem urteilslosen Publikum in
angeblich gemeinverständlichen Schriften, in der Tagespresse,
in öffentlichen Vorträgen und im Salon als höchste und tiefste
naturwissenschaftliche Weisheit angepriesen. Und zuletzt

scheute man nicht einmal vor dem Unfug zurück, Illustrationen zur Relativitätstheorie im Film dem Kinopublikum vorführen zu lassen. Diese Propaganda fand in der Zeit der politischen und sozialen Revolution einen fruchtbaren Boden, redete sie doch von dem Umsturz unserer bisherigen Anschauungen von Raum und Zeit und von einer die Welt umspannenden Theorie. Sie lag auch insofern dem Geiste der letzten Jahre, als ihre jüngsten Jünger mit großen Worten ihre Weisheit vortragen konnten, ohne auf die Wirklichkeit Rücksicht nehmen zu brauchen.

E i n s t e i n ist der Vorwurf nicht zu ersparen, daß er sich dem Hinauszerren seiner Theorie auf den Jahrmarkt nicht entgegengesetzt hat, die Propaganda seiner Freunde und Anhänger gewähren ließ, ja Schriften von Dilettanten zum Ruhme seiner Theorie ermunterte. Er mag es entrüstet zurückweisen, mit seinen Vortragsreisen ins Ausland selbst Propaganda für seine Theorie getrieben zu haben. Gut. Aber hinsichtlich seiner Auslandsreisen halte ich es für notwendig, daß ihm bei dieser Gelegenheit folgender Hinweis gegeben wird.

In einem Artikel im Berliner Tageblatt hat sich Einstein zu internationaler Gesinnung bekannt. Gleichwohl ist es nicht zu verstehen, daß er ohne Rücksicht auf die furchtbare Bedrückung des deutschen Volkes durch die Franzosen einer französischen Einladung zu einem Vortrag in Paris in diesem Frühjahre Folge geleistet, ja im Anschluß daran sogar darauf gehalten hat, auf einer Automobilfahrt sich die „verwüsteten" Gegenden (les régions dévastées) zeigen zu lassen. E i n s t e i n lebt doch in Deutschland, und ist Mitglied amtlicher deutscher Ausschüsse, vor allem Direktor eines Kaiser-Wilhelm-Instituts; da hätte er mit Rücksicht darauf soviel Takt haben müssen, die Reise nach Paris zu einer Zeit zu unterlassen, wo der französische Druck besonders stark war. Und wenn er dies nicht von selbst einsah, so hätten es ihm seine Freunde, die ihm sonst so rasch beispringen, bedeuten sollen. Daß über die Franzosenreise E i n s t e i n s große deutsche Tageszeitungen telegraphisch berichteten, daß sie nicht von selbst daran Kritik übten, ja nicht einmal einen Einspruch dagegen aus physikalischen Kreisen aufnahmen, ist ein trauriges Zeichen von dem deutschen Verfall.

Doch zurück zur Propaganda für die Relativitätstheorie! Während sie sich selbst keine Schranken setzte, nahmen E i n s t e i n und seine Anhänger sogar eine Kritik aus Fachkreisen sehr übel auf. So warf er L e n a r d, einem unserer tiefsten und gewissenhaftesten Denker, im Berliner Tageblatt (27. Aug. 1920) Oberflächlichkeit vor und G e h r c k e s [*Footnote:* G e h r c k e ist der Kampf gegen die Relativitätstheorie übel bekommen; trotz seiner zahlreichen hervorragenden experimentellen Arbeiten wird er von Fakultäten nicht für ein physikalisches Ordinat vorgeschlagen.] Kritik unterstellte er unsachliche Motive.

Auch der Fernerstehende erkennt beim Lesen der vorstehenden Ausführungen, daß durch die allgemeine Relativitätstheorie ein Zwiespalt zwischen den Physikern aufgerissen worden ist. Experimentell gerichtete Physiker lehnen sich gegen den nach ihrer Meinung unphysikalischen Geist der Relativitätstheorie und gegen die maßlose Propaganda für sie auf; deren Anhänger werfen ihnen dafür Beschränktheit, Mangel an mathematischer Bildung oder gar unsachliche Motive vor. Ferner fühlt selbst der Fernerstehende, daß die experimentelle Begründung einer so umstrittenen Theorie noch nicht gesichert sein kann und daß es unangebracht ist, eine Theorie, über welche selbst die physikalischen und mathematischen Fachleute noch im Streit liegen, vor den weiten Kreis der Laien bis herab zum Kinopublikum zu bringen.

Bei dieser Lage der Dinge muß es auf physikalischer Seite als ein bedauerlicher Mißgriff bezeichnet werden, daß für die Hundertjahr-Feier der Gesellschaft deutscher Naturforscher und Ärzte in diesem Jahre in Leipzig als Thema für die erste allgemeine Sitzung die Relativitätstheorie in Aussicht genommen wurde. Daß dies nach den Auseinandersetzungen in Nauheim geschehen konnte, ist, wie ich bereits bemerkte, ein Zeichen für das Überwuchern der Theorie. Man lasse uns Physiker endlich eine Zeitlang in Ruhe mit der bis zum Überdruß abgehandelten E i n s t e i n schen Relativitätstheorie! Man warte endlich einige Jahre mit der Propaganda für sie, bis ihre Folgerung durch zuverlässige Beobachtungen geprüft sind!"[503]

The New York Times stated in 1923,

"It was reported in January from Berlin that fifty German physicists, mathematicians and philosophers were 'seriously grieved' to see public opinion misled by the suggestion that the Theory of Relativity is the solution of the problems of the universe, and by the concealment of the fact that many savants, 'including the most distinguished,' do not accept this theory as a proved hypothesis, but look upon it as fiction."[504]

This was quoted in a press release Thomas Jefferson Jackson See issued to the *Associated Press* on 18 April 1923. It appears to paraphrase a flier distributed at the meeting of the *Gesellschaft Deutscher Naturforscher und Ärtze* in Leipzig in 1922.[505] T. J. J. See concluded his press release with the rhetorical question,

"Under the circumstances is it any wonder that some of us who owe a duty of Truth to the Public, should be obliged to vigorously contest the unauthorized and indefensible conclusion that the observed refraction of starlight near the Sun is a confirmation of the discredited Doctrine of Relativity?"

See later published similar statements in *The San Francisco Journal* on 20 May 1923 in an article entitled, "Einstein a Second Dr. Cook?"

Ones sees that it wasn't just the Germans who were disgusted with Einstein, his theories, his self-promotion and his plagiarism. As Einstein himself professed, it was only in America that his theories were generally accepted and where he was loved, a fact he found comical. Einstein made a scathing, ethnocentric, misogynist and hateful denouncement of America and American scientists.[506] However, in America, See, Reuterdahl and Poor wrote several articles exposing Einstein as a fraud. Each complained of censorship of their efforts to expose Einstein.

French savants had little love for Einstein. *The New York Times* reported on 4 April 1922 on page 21:

"*Einstein Breaks Engagement In Paris, Fearing Hostility*
PARIS, April 3.—Professor Albert Einstein of the University of Berlin, who recently delivered his first lecture here under the auspices of the College of France and had a notable reception, canceled an engagement to attend the session of the Academy of Sciences today in order to avoid a hostile manifestation.

Some of the members of the academy had decided as a protest against his presence to rise and leave the hall as soon as he entered."

The New York Times reported on 5 April 1922 on page 21:

"PLEDGED TO SNUB EINSTEIN.
30 French Scientists Would Have Left if He Had Attended Meeting.

PARIS, April 4.—The failure of Professor Albert Einstein to pay his formal visit to the French Academy of Sciences yesterday was due to the fact that he had received a friendly warning that the occasion would be made embarrassing by a certain element of that distinguished body. This statement is in L'Oeuvre. Scoring French scientists for their unbelievable narrowness, L'Oeuvre declares that thirty members had pledged themselves, if Professor Einstein made his appearance, to leave the hall in a body."

The New York Times reported on 16 November 1922 on the front page that the Russians had condemned Einstein's theory:

"Einstein Theory 'Bourgeois' And Dangerous, Say Russians

PARIS, Nov. 15.—A message from Moscow to the Echo de Paris says that Professor Albert Einstein has been solemnly excommunicated by the Russian Communists.

At a special council meeting held in order to examine the question the Russian Communist Party condemned the Einstein theory as being 'reactionary of nature, furnishing support for counter-revolutionary ideas'; also as being 'the product of the bourgeois class in decomposition.'

Professor Timirazeff presented a long report to the council in which he discussed whether Einstein's theories could be reconciled with the theory of materialism. He decided that they could not, and because, in his opinion, they led to 'pure idealism,' the council pronounced condemnation."

Irving Levy published the following comment in *The New York Times*, on 2 March 1936, page 16,

"The relativity theory advanced by Professor Einstein is held in such uncomprehending awe by the vast majority of people that it is not generally known there exists a far from unanimous acceptance of it in the scientific world."

So we see that, contrary to the popular history told today, Einstein was internationally known as a sophist and a plagiarist when he came to

America in 1921. Einstein tried to head off any criticism he might face in America by stigmatizing any criticism of him, or of the theory of relativity as if "anti-Semitism" *per se* before he even stepped off the boat onto America's shores.[507] He was a coward who hid behind the power of Jewish tribalism.

4.3.2 Hypocritical and Cowardly Einstein Plays the "Race Card" and Cripples Scientific Progress

Like his cowardly Zionist comrades, hypocritical Einstein "played the race card." In an effort to change the subject from his plagiarism and fallacious theories, which subject was beginning to destroy his fame, Einstein smeared anyone and everyone who would dare question him or the theory of relativity as if an anti-Semite *per se* in *The New York Times* on 3 April 1921 on pages 1 and 13, and bear in mind that *The New York Times*, itself, reported that relativity theory was "much-debated",

"PROF. EINSTEIN HERE, EXPLAINS RELATIVITY

'Poet in Science' Says It Is a
Theory of Space and Time,
But It Baffles Reporters.

SEEKS AID FOR PALESTINE

Thousands Wait Four Hours to
Welcome Theorist and His
Party to America.

A man in a faded gray raincoat and a flopping black felt hat that nearly concealed the gray hair that straggled over his ears stood on the boat deck of the steamship Rotterdam yesterday, timidly facing a battery of cameramen. In one hand he clutched a shiny briar pipe and with the other clung to a precious violin.

He looked like an artist—a musician. He was.

But underneath his shaggy locks was a scientific mind whose deductions have staggered the ablest intellects of Europe. One of his traveling companions described him as an 'intuitive physicist' whose speculative imagination is so vast that it senses great natural laws long before the reasoning faculty grasps and defines them.

The man was Dr. Albert Einstein, propounder of the much-debated theory of relativity that has given the world a new conception of space, and time and the size of the universe.

Dr. Einstein comes to this country as one of a group of prominent Jews who are advocating the Zionist movement and hope to get financial aid and encouragement for the rebuilding of Palestine and the founding of a Jewish university. He is of medium height, with strongly built shoulders, but an air of fragility and self-effacement. Under a high, broad forehead are large and luminous eyes, almost childlike in their simplicity and unworldliness.

Thousands Welcome Him.

With him as fellow-travelers were Professor Chaim Weizmann, President of the Zionist World Organization, discoverer of trinitrotoluol, and head of the British Admiralty laboratories during the war; Michael Ussichkin, a member of the Zionist delegation to the Paris Peace Conference and now Resident Chairman of the Zionist Commission in Palestine, and Dr. Benzion Mossinson, President of the Hebrew Teachers Organization in Palestine.

The party was welcomed at the Battery by thousands of fellow-Jews who had waited there for hours.

The crowds were packed deeply along the Battery wall, waving Jewish flags of white with two blue bars, wearing buttons with Zionist inscriptions, and cheering themselves hoarse as the police boat John F. Hylan drew near. Dozens of automobiles were parked near the landing, and when the welcoming committee and the visitors had entered them they started uptown to the Hotel Commodore, preceded by a police escort. They turned into Second Avenue, where the sidewalks were lined nearly all the way uptown with thousands who waved hands and handkerchiefs and shouted welcome to the visitors.

Professor Einstein was reluctant to talk about relativity, but when he did speak he said most of the opposition to his theories was the result of strong anti-Semitic feeling. He was amused at attempts by reporters to get some idea of his theory by questioning him, and he did his best to make his answers as simple as possible. He spoke through an interpreter.

A Theory of Space and Time.

The interview took place in the Captain's cabin, where Professor Einstein was almost surrounded by seekers after knowledge. He was asked to define his theory.

'It is a theory of space and time, so far as physics are concerned,' he said.

'How long did it take you to conceive your theory?" he was asked.

'I have not finished yet,' he said with a laugh. 'But I have worked on it for about sixteen years. The theory consists of two grades or steps. On one I have been working for about six years and on the other about eight or nine years.

'I first became interested in it through the question of the distribution and expansion of light in space; that is, for the first grade or step. The fact that an iron ball and a wooden ball fall to the ground at the same speed was perhaps the reason which prompted me to take the second step.'

He was asked about those who oppose his theory, and said:

'No man of culture or knowledge has any animosity toward my theories. Even the physicists opposed to the theory are animated by political motives.'

When asked what he meant, he said he referred to anti-Semitic feeling. He would not elaborate on this subject, but said the attacks in Berlin were entirely anti-Semitic.

Dr. Einstein said the theory was a step in the further development of the Newtonian theory. He hoped to lecture at Princeton on relativity before he left the country, he said, as he felt grateful to the Faculty of Princeton, which was the first college to become interested in his work.

Poses for Moving Picture Men.

As the questioners gave up their attempts to seek further elucidation of the Einstein principles, the professor laughed and said:

'Well, I hope I have passed my examination.'

Professor Einstein's interview came soon after he had escaped the moving picture men. As they ground away at their machines, ordering him about, he seemed at first bewildered, then amused. He posed with other members of his party and with Mrs. Einstein for nearly half an hour, and then almost ran away, shaking his head in exasperation and refusing to do any more.

'Like a prima donna,' he exclaimed.

'He does not like to be, what you call it, a showcase,' said Mrs. Einstein. 'He does not like society, for he feels that he is on exhibition. He would rather work and play his violin and walk in the woods.'

'Do you understand his theory?' Mrs. Einstein was asked.

'Oh, no,' she said, laughing, 'although he has explained it to me so many times. I understand it in a general way, but in its details it is too much for a woman to grasp. But it is not necessary for my happiness.'

Dr. Einstein was an inspirational worker, she said. When he was engaged on some problem, 'there was no day and no night,' but in his periods of relaxation he went for weeks without doing anything in particular but dream and play on his violin. Whenever he became weary in the midst of his work he went to the piano or picked up his violin and rested his mind with music.

'He improvises,' she explained. 'He is really an excellent musician.'

Mozart and Brahms His Favorites.

On the ship, when a concert was held Dr. Einstein played selections from Mozart, of whose work he is particularly fond, on the violin. Brahms is another of his favorites.

'I never met Professor Einstein before this voyage,' said Professor Weizmann, who is a great admirer of his fellow-scientist. 'He has a singularly sweet and lovable nature, and is exceedingly simple in his habits of life. I have talked with him many times about his work, and he is glad to speak of it when he can find some one who is interested and at least partly capable of understanding it. I do not entirely, for when I get beyond the atom I am lost.

'When he was called 'a poet in science' the definition was a good one. He seems more an intuitive physicist, however. He is not an experimental physicist, and although he is able to detect fallacies in the conceptions of physical science, he must turn his general outlines of theory over to some one else to work out. That would be readily understandable to a man of science. He first became interested in mathematics when he was 14 years old, and his work is his life. He spends most of his time reading and thinking when he is not playing his violin.'

Professor Weizmann also is accompanied by his wife. He and the other Zionist visitors, during their visit of several weeks, will endeavor to interest American Jews in the Zionist movement and obtain money and moral support for both the national Zionist idea and for the university.

Dr. Weizmann Explains Mission.

'It is a great satisfaction to me as President of the Zionist Organization to find myself for the first time in the Union States,' said Dr. Weizmann. 'The cause of the Jewish national home in Palestine has from the first appealed to the generous instincts of the American people and owes much to the sympathetic support it has consistently received from leaders of public opinion in the United States.

'Our primary object is to confer with the American Zionists who have, under the distinguished leadership of Justice Brandeis, Judge Mack and other representative American Jews, rendered invaluable services to the Zionist movement during the past few critical years. In the task of reconstruction in Palestine, for which the time has now arrived, it is confidently expected that the American Zionists will play an equally conspicuous and honorable part. In this connection we hope to enlist the active interest of American Jews in the Keren Hayesod, or Foundation Fund, the central fund for the building up of the Jewish National Home, to which Jews throughout the world are being called upon to contribute to the utmost limit of their resources.

'Professor Einstein has done us the honor of accompanying us to America in the interest of the Hebrew University of Jerusalem. Zionists have long cherished the hope of creating in Jerusalem a centre of learning in which the Hebrew genius shall find full self-expression and which shall play its part as interpreter between the Eastern and Western worlds. Professor Einstein attaches the utmost importance to the early inauguration of the Jerusalem university and is prepared when the time arrives personally to associated himself within its activities—a course in which there is reason to hope he will be followed by other Jewish scholars and scientists of world-wide reputation.'

Einstein to Work for University.

Professor Einstein will devote most of his time while here to advocating support of the university by American Jews.

'The establishment of such a university has been for a long

time one of the most cherished plans of the Zionist organization,' he said. 'But for the outbreak of the war it would have materialized in 1914, when a site was actually purchased on the Mount of Olives. In 1918 the foundation stone was laid by Dr. Weizmann. Since then the university site has been extended and a building purchased in which it will be possible for a beginning to be made. There is also a library of 30,000 volumes which is rapidly growing.

'Plans have been worked out both for the complete university of the future and for a comparatively modest beginning. The time has now come to insure the immediate realization of the latter. Such is the importance attached by the Zionist Organization to the spiritual values in the Zionist national home that even at this moment, when the organization is faced with tremendous tasks of immigration and colonization, and is concentrating all efforts upon the Palestine Foundation Fund, an exception is made in favor of the university to which a special branch of the fund is devoted.

'I know of no public event which has given me such delight as the proposal to establish a Hebrew university in Jerusalem. The traditional respect for knowledge which Jews have maintained intact through many centuries of severe hardship made it particularly painful for us to see so many talented sons of the Jewish people cut off from higher education and study, and knocking vainly at the doors of universities of Eastern and Central Europe.

Home For Spiritual Life.

'Others who have gained access to the regions of free research only did so by undergoing a painful, even dishonoring, process of assimilation which crippled and robbed them again and again of their cultural leaders. The time has now come when our spiritual life will find a home of its own. Distinguished Jewish scholars in all branches of learning are waiting to go to Jerusalem, where they will lay the foundation of a flourishing spiritual life and will promote the intellectual and economic development of Palestine.

'Notwithstanding the crude political realism of our times and the materialistic atmosphere in which it has enveloped us, there are visible none the less glimmerings of a nobler conception of human aspirations, such as were expressed in the part played by the American people in world politics. And so we come from sick and suffering Europe with feelings of hope, being convinced that our spiritual aims will command the full sympathy of the American nation and will receive enthusiastic approval and powerful support from our Jewish brethren in the United States.'

The Zionists were met down the bay by a delegation from the Mayor's committee of welcome, Captain Abraham Tulin, who served as American liason officer with General Mangin's army in the war; Dr. Schmarya Levin, who was member of the first Russian Duma and of the Cadet Party in Russia, and Magistrate Bernard Rosenblatt. They were delayed by the quarantine examination and were not able to board the Rotterdam until nearly 1 o'clock. On the way up the bay they had lunch with Professor Einstein, Professor Weizmann and others in the party, and remained with them on the ship until sundown. As it was the Sabbath their religion prevented them from leaving until that time.

Crowd Waits Four Hours at Pier.

At the pier were several hundred welcomers, although the ship was more than four hours late in reaching her pier. They gave the Zionists a rousing welcome before they went aboard the police boat John F. Hylan, which landed them at the Battery. The boat flew the Jewish flag in honor of the party. On board were L. Lipsky, Secretary of the Zionist Organization of America; L. Robison of the National Executive Committee; B. G. Richards, Secretary of the American Jewish Congress; M. Rothenberg, Chairman of the American Jewish Congress; J. Fishman, managing editor of The Jewish Morning Journal; W. Edlin, editor of The Day; Rabbi M. Berlin; David Pinski, editor of Die Zeit; John F. Sinnott, Secretary to Mayor Hylan; Henry H. Klein, Commissioner of Accounts; Judge Gustave Hartman, the Rev. H. Masliansky, Judge Jacob S. Strahl and many others.

An official meeting of welcome will be held at the City Hall on Tuesday at which Mayor Hylan, Frank L. Polk, George W. Wickersham, Magistrate Rosenblatt, Professor Einstein and Professor Weizmann will speak.

Among those on the Committee of Welcome are Nathan Straus, Arthur Brisbane, Chancellor E. E. Brown, Judge Benjamin Cardoza, Abram I. Elkus, James A. Foley, F. H. LaGuardia, Justice Samuel Greenbaum, William D. Guthrie, Mrs. William R. Hearst, Adolph Lewisohn, Alfred E. Smith, Leon Kaimaky, Judge Otto A. Rosalsky, Benjamin Schlessinger,

Oscar S. Straus, Senator Nathan Straus Jr., Marcus Loew, Dr. Bernard Flexner, Colonel Robert Grier Monroe, Herman Bernstein, Samuel Koenig and George Gordon Battle.

A meeting also will be held at the Metropolitan Opera House on April 10. Professor Einstein will not touch on relativity at these meetings, but it is expected that before he leaves the city he will speak before some scientific gathering, at which he will discuss his discovery."

Einstein prevented an uninhibited debate over the merits of the theory of relativity. His shrill cries of "anti-Semitism" had a chilling effect, which froze Twentieth Century Physics in a mythology of metaphysical "Space-Time" and physical gravitation via mathematical abstraction and imaginary dimensions.

The Chicago Tribune reported on 3 April 1921 on page 5 (and note that Einstein was careful to not offend the lovers of Newton as was done in 1919),

"EINSTEIN IN N. Y.; EVEN WIFE CAN'T GRASP THEORIES

Hopes to Lecture at Princeton, He Says.

New York, April 2.—[Special]—A man in a faded gray raincoat, topped off by a flopping black felt hat, which nearly concealed straggling gray hair that fell over his ears, stood on the boat deck of the steamship Rotterdam today, timidly facing a battery of camera men. In one hand he clutched a shiny briar pipe and the other clung to a violin.

Dr. Albert Einstein, discoverer of the famous theory of relativity, which has given the world a new conception of space and time, looks like a musician, and he is.

Dr. Einstein comes to this country as one of a group of prominent Jews, advocating the Zionist movement. They hope to get financial aid and encouragement for the rebuilding of Palestine and the founding of a Jewish university.

Amused by Questions.

The scientist was reluctant to talk about relativity. He was greatly amused at the attempts of reporters to search out by their questions some idea of what his theory is, and did his best to make his answers as simple as possible. He does not speak English and answered through an interpreter.

'It is a theory of space and time, so far as physics are concerned,' he said.

'How long did it take you to conceive your theory?' he was asked.

'I have not finished yet,' he said with a laugh. 'But I have worked on it for about sixteen years. The theory consists of two grades or steps. On one I have been working for about six years and on the other about eight or nine years.'

Iron and Wooden Balls.

'I first became interested in it through the question of the distribution and expansion of light in space. That is, for the first grade or step. The fact that an iron ball and a wooden ball fall to the ground at the same speed was perhaps the reason which prompted me to take the second step.'

He was asked about those who opposed his theory, and said:

'No man of culture or knowledge has any animosity toward my theories. Even the physicists opposed to the theory are animated by political motives.'

Asked what he meant, he said he referred to anti-semitic feeling. He would not elaborate on this subject, but said that the attacks in Berlin were entirely anti-semitic.

Develops Newton's Theory.

Dr. Einstein said that the theory is a step in the further development of the Newtonian theory. He hopes to lecture at Princeton on relativity before he leaves the country, as he feels grateful to the faculty of Princeton, which was the first college to become interested in his work.

'Do you understand his theory,' Mrs. Einstein was asked.

'O, no,' she said, 'although he has explained it to me so many times. I understand it in a general way, but it is too subtle for a woman to grasp. Still it is not necessary for my happiness.'"

Einstein called anti-Semitic, among other things, the thesis of Gehrcke and Weyland that: Einstein's promotion mirrored Hans Christian Andersen's fairy tale *The Emperor's New Clothes*; that, the overblown public reaction to the theory of relativity was a "mass suggestion" and a "mass psychosis"; and Gehrcke and Weyland's criticism that theory of relativity had not been proven correct and was instead contradicted by St. John's experiments; and Gehrcke and Weyland's accusation that Einstein's theory, while promoted as a radically new development, was not a new idea, but was derived from Lorentz and others. Einstein, himself, had complained to Heinrich Zangger on 24 December 1919,

> "[T]his business reminds one of the tale of 'The Emperor's New Clothes,' but it is harmless tomfoolery."[508]

Einstein endorsed and plagiarized Gehrcke and Weyland's other views, which he had called anti-Semitic in 1920, on 3 April 1921, and would again plagiarize Gehrcke and Weyland's ideas when Einstein returned to Europe and was again interviewed by the press. *The Chicago Tribune* reported on 4 April 1921 on page 6,

"EINSTEIN, TOO, IS PUZZLED; IT'S AT PUBLIC INTEREST

Can't See Why Theories Are Widely Discussed.

New York, April 3.—[Special]—Prof. Albert Einstein, the German scientist, who is visiting this country, today discussed his famous 'relativity' theory with reporters.

Before going into details with the reporters, Prof. Einstein exploded the accepted story that he had said only twelve men in the world were capable of understanding it. He thinks most scientists understand his theories and added that his students in Berlin understand them perfectly.

No theory can be susceptible of absolute proof, he added, and mentioned that an American scientist, St. John, is now conducting experiments which seem to give results at variance with the Einstein theory.

'The two theories, that of St. John and my own, have not yet been brought into harmony,' Prof. Einstein said. 'The subject dealt with is that of the wave lengths in the spectrum. It is impossible at the present stage of the experiments to say what the result will be.'

Calls for Psychologist.

Prof. Einstein was rather puzzled to account for the public interest in his conception of time and space, and said the public attitude seemed to call for a psychologist who could determine why persons who are not generally interested in scientific work should be interested in him.

'It seems psycho-pathological,' he said, with a laugh.

When it was suggested that perhaps people were interested because he seemed to give a new conception of the universe, which, next to the idea of God, has been the subject of the most fascinating speculations of the mind, he agreed that such might be the case.

'The theory has a certain bearing in a philosophical sense on the conception of the universe,' he said, 'but not from the scientific point of view. Its great value lies in the logical simplicity with which it explains apparently conflicting facts in the operation of natural law. It provides a more simple method. Hitherto science has been burdened by many general assumptions of a complicated nature.'

Not a Radical Departure.

Two of the great facts explained by the theory are the relativity of motion and the equivalence of mass of inertia and mass of weight, said Prof. Einstein.

'There has been a false opinion widely spread among the general public,' he said, 'that the theory of relativity is to be taken as differing radically from the previous developments in physics from the time of Galileo and Newton—that it is violently opposed to their deductions. The contrary is true. Without the discoveries of every one of the great men of physics, those who laid down preceding laws, relativity would have been impossible to conceive and there would have been no basis for it. Psychologically, it is impossible to come to such a theory at once without the work which must be done before. The four men who laid the foundations of physics on which I have been able to construct my theory are Galileo, Newton, Maxwell, and Lorenz.'

Man in Street Needn't Worry.

Whatever the value of relativity, it will not necessarily change the conceptions of the man in the street, said Prof. Einstein.

'The practical man does not need to worry about it,' he said.

'From the philosophical aspect, however, it has importance, as it alters the conceptions of time and space which are necessary to philosophical speculations and conceptions. Up to this time the conceptions of time and space have been such that if everything in the universe were taken away, if there was nothing left, there would still be left to man time and space. But under this theory even time and space would cease to exist, because they are unalterably bound up with the conceptions of matter.'

The reporters did not argue the point."

The New York Times responded to Einstein's "PSYCHOPATHIC RELATIVITY" on 5 April 1921 on page 18, and quoted Einstein on 8 July 1921 on page 9,

"'You ask whether it makes a ludicrous impression on me to observe the excitement of the crowd for my teaching and my theory, of which it, after all, understands nothing? I find it funny and at the same time interesting to observe this game.

'I believe quite positively that it is the mysteriousness of what they cannot conceive which places them under a magic spell. One tells them of something big which will influence all future life, of a theory which only a small group, highly learned, can comprehend. Big names are mentioned of men who have made discoveries, of which the crowd grasps nothing. But it impresses them, takes on color and the magic power of mystery, and thus one becomes enthusiastic and excited."

Einstein wrote to Max Born on 15 September 1950, in the context of politics,

"And the idiotic public can be talked into anything."[509]

Among those who actively opposed relativity theory, as it was expressed by Einstein—who, according to Einstein's assertions, must have been uncultured, ignorant anti-Semites—we find Hendrik Antoon Lorentz, Max Abraham, Alfred North Whitehead, Ernst Mach, Albert Abraham Michelson, Friedrich Adler, Henri Bergson, Oskar Kraus, Melchior Palágyi, [etc. etc. etc.]. Clearly, Einstein lied about a very serious matter, and, what is worse, Einstein was himself a racist instigator and a political agitator; and, therefore, a hypocrite and a deliberate inciter of "racial" discord.

4.3.3 What is Good for the Goose is not Good for the Goyim

The political Zionists emphasized their mistaken belief that Jews are a distinct race incapable of assimilation, and that Jews constitute a foreign nation within Germany. Einstein's anti-assimilationist rhetoric would later find its match in Philipp Lenard's segregationist belief in "Aryan Physics". Nobel Prize laureate Philipp Lenard was reacting to the Jews' bigoted assertions of their distinct racial characteristics and the Zionists' open declarations of their disloyalty to Germany.[510] Many Jews viewed Physics in expressly racist terms long before Lenard joined their ranks.[511]

Following the racial mythologies of Gobinaeu and Renan, Philipp Lenard joined the Jewish movement to segregate science and wrote of "Aryan Physics". Like many Jews before him, Lenard artificially distinguished between "German Physics" and "Jewish Physics" in 1936. Johannes Stark and Wilhelm Müller adopted this nomenclature in 1941 at the behest of the Zionist Nazis.[512]

Racist Jews provided the segregationist dogma. For example, there was the segregated "Jüdisch-Russisch Wissenschaftliches Verein" (Russian-Jewish Scientific Society) which participated in the foundation of the modern Zionist movement with its leaders Shmarya Levin, Leo Motzkin, Nachman Syrkin, Victor Jacobson, Arthur Hantke, Heinrich Löwe, Zelig Soskin, Willi Bambus, and many others.[513] In the late 1800's men like Theodor Mommsen and Anatole Leroy-Beaulieu were criticizing segregated Jewish associations, which they rejected as bigoted and segregated institutions.[514]

Just as some Christians felt uncomfortable around Eastern Jews, some Eastern Jews felt uncomfortable around Christians and found them dirty and disgusting. These Jews refused to eat at the same table with Christians, who did not oblige their Kosher laws.

In the early 1800's there was an influential movement to promote "Jewish science". At the time, some Jews were forced to feign Christian conversion if they wished to become university professors. In 1822, Gans, Zunz and Moser created the *Verein für Kultur und Wissenschaft der Juden,* a segregated Jewish institution which offered Jews an alternative to an insincere and degrading baptism. They published a journal on "Jewish science", the *Zeitschrift für die Wissenschaft des Judenthums* published from 1822-1823.[515] There was also the *Jeschurun. Zeitschrift für die Wissenschaft des Judenthums* published from 1856-1870 by Joseph Kobak in German and Hebrew; and the *Monatsschrift für Geschichte und Wissenschaft des Judenthums* published from 1851-

1939 by Rudolf Kuntze of the *Gesellschaft zur Förderung der Wissenschaft des Judentums*, Dresden.

Albert Einstein traveled to America in order to raise money[516] for an ethnically segregated "Jewish university"[517] or "Hebrew University" in Jerusalem. Many Zionists asserted that Jews had to be segregated in order to manifest their superior Jewish racial characteristics, which had lain dormant in the Diaspora. In accord with Jewish Messianic prophecy, they asserted that the Jewish race would again shine and lead the world of thought if only they could be "restored" to Palestine and segregated and at long last be permitted to be "Jews" and be relieved of the burden of being pseudo-Gentiles. Even after the Holocaust, Einstein was still calling for the segregation of Jewish students from Gentile students, which he argued was the only solution to the problem of anti-Semitism. Peter A. Bucky quoted Albert Einstein,

"I think that Jewish students should have their own student societies. [***] One way that it won't be solved is for Jewish people to take on Christian fashions and manners. [***] In this way, it is entirely possible to be a civilized person, a good citizen, and at the same time be a faithful Jew who loves his race and honors his fathers."[518]

Shortly after World War One, Zionist Shmuel Hugo Bergmann wrote to Einstein,

"[. . .]whether you, Professor, whom the world rightly calls the greatest Jewish scientist, but above all whom we love and value also as a person—whether you would be willing to participate in this conference and help us with its preparation. I do not need to say how happy the Jewish people would be if *you* could be appointed to its university, but that is a question for the future."[519]

Albert Einstein stated,

"Antisemitism must be seen as a real thing, based on true hereditary qualities, even if for us Jews it is often unpleasant. I could well imagine that I myself would choose a Jew as my companion, given the choice. On the other hand I would consider it reasonable for the Jews themselves to collect the money to support Jewish research workers outside the universities and to provide them with teaching opportunities."[520]

and,

> "The psychological root of anti-Semitism lies in the fact that the
> Jews are a group of people unto themselves. Their Jewishness is
> visible in their physical appearance, and one notices their Jewish
> heritage in their intellectual works, and one can sense that there
> are among them deep connections in their disposition and
> numerous possibilities of communicating that are based on the
> same way of thinking and of feeling. The Jewish child is already
> aware of these differences as soon as it starts school. Jewish
> children feel the resentment that grows out of an instinctive
> suspicion of their strangeness that naturally is often met with a
> closing of the ranks. [***] [Jews] are the target of instinctive
> resentment because they are of a different tribe than the majority
> of the population."[521]

Maja Winteler-Einstein wrote in her biography of her brother Albert
Einstein,

> "His later advocacy of Zionism and his activities on its behalf
> came from this impulse: less in accordance with and on the basis
> of Jewish teachings than from an inner sense of obligation
> toward those of his race for whom an independent working place
> for scholarly activity in the sciences should be created, where
> they would not be discriminated against as Jews."[522]

Albert Einstein wrote to Paul Ehrenfest on 8 November 1919,

> "This university will contribute toward making less Jewish
> talent, particularly in Poland and Russia, have to go wretchedly
> to waste."[523]

4.3.4 It is Alright for Jews to Claim that "Einstein's Theories" are "Jewish", but Goyim Dare Not Say It

Immediately after Einstein's humiliating retreat from America and at a
critical moment in the Zionist movement, *The London Times* wrote on
14 June 1921 on page 8, referring to the occasion of Einstein's lecture
at King's College:

"LORD HALDANE, who presided, said they were there to give a British welcome to a man of genius. (Cheers.) The highest knowledge was a possession of which the world at large was proud, and genius knew no frontier. That morning he had been touched to observe that his distinguished guest had left his house to gaze on the tomb of Newton in Westminster Abbey. What Newton was to the 18th century Einstein was to the 20th century. In the lecture they were about to hear they would find a new point in the theory of relativity which had never been so definitely stated. Einstein had given a new conception of the universe, a conception, he thought, more revolutionary than that of Galileo, Copernicus, or Newton. He had taught them to think of the universe of externality as relative in its reality to knowledge. Reality was relative, not merely our knowledge of it. He had given a view which brought us back to the deeper meaning of knowledge itself.

The new doctrine, added Lord Haldane, had come from a man distinguished by his desire, if possible, to efface himself and yet impelled by the unmistakable power of genius which would allow the individual of whom it had taken possession to rest for one moment. Professor Einstein had two great qualities for his task. He had a command of the tremendous instrument of mathematics as complete, at least, as that of any man alive. He had something more, a creative imagination akin to that of the poet. He fashioned creations apparently out of nothing in the way that genius alone could do. He was, too, a musician who played with a feeling and insight not always found in even the very best professionals. He was a master of the violin as well as of mathematics. The 20th century had produced one of the greatest thinkers that the last 500 years had seen and they were proud to be there to welcome him. (Cheers.)"

Einstein, himself, admitted that he was no mathematician. He was an absolutist and his ideas were not original and others expressed these ideas far more cogently than he was ever able to express them.

Even before Wagner, long before Wagner, Jews suffered under false accusations that they were incapable of creative thought. Josephus wrote in his ancient polemic in defense of the Jews, *Against Apion*,

"Hence hath arisen that accusation which some make against us, that we have not produced men that have been the inventors of new operations, or of new ways of speaking; for others think it a fine thing to persevere in nothing that has been delivered down from their forefathers, and these testify it to be an instance of the sharpest wisdom when these men venture to transgress those traditions; whereas we, on the contrary, suppose it to be our only wisdom and virtue to admit no actions nor supposals that are contrary to our original laws; which procedure of ours is a just and sure sign that our law is admirably constituted; for such laws as are not thus well made are convicted upon trial to want amendment."[524]

Jews did suffer from the rigid dogmatism of Judaism, which inhibited their progress in the ancient world and during the Enlightenment (see, for example, *Babylonian Talmud*, Tractate Menahoth, folio 99*b*, which discourages the study of "Greek science"). The uncreative indoctrination of Jewish scholars in the beliefs of the Talmud and in the learning of the Hebrew language also tended to destroy their ability to think independently and creatively.

Adolf Hitler attacked Jews as if uncreative and parasitic in many of his speeches. Following Rathenau's murder in 1922, Hitler spent a month in jail. When he was released, he stated,

"That is the lurking danger, and the Jew can meet it in one way only—by destroying the hostile national intelligentsia. That is the inevitable ultimate goal of the Jew in his revolution. And this aim he must pursue; he knows well enough his economics brings no blessing: his is no master-people: he is an exploiter: the Jews are a people of robbers. He has never founded any civilization, though he has destroyed civilizations by the hundred. He possesses nothing of his own creation to which he can point. Everything that he has is stolen. Foreign peoples, foreign workmen build him his temples, it is foreigners who create and work for him: it is foreigners who shed their blood for him. He knows no 'people's army': he has only hired mercenaries who are ready to go to death on his behalf. He has no art of his own: bit by bit he has stolen it all from the other peoples or has watched them at work and then made his copy. He does not even know how merely to preserve the precious things which others have created: as he turns the treasures over in his hand they are transformed into dirt and dung. He knows that he cannot maintain any State for long. [***] All that the Jew cannot do.

And because he cannot do it, therefore all his revolutions must be 'international'. They must spread as a pestilence spreads. He can build no State and say 'See here! Here stands the State, a model for all. Now copy us!' He must take care that the plague does not die, that it is not limited to one place, or else in a short time this plague-hearth would burn itself out. So he is forced to bring every mortal thing to an international expansion. For how long? Until the whole world sinks in ruins and brings him down with it in the midst of the ruins."[525]

At the Nuremberg *Parteitag* in 1937, Hitler stated,

"The people which has thus through Jewish agitators been driven into madness, reinforced by non-social elements liberated from the prisons, now destroys its own national intelligentsia on the scaffold and the Jew without scruple and without conscience is supreme. The Jew is himself completely uncreative: he may in many countries hold 90 per cent. of the positions in the intellectual world, but he never discovered, formed, or conceived the elements of knowledge, culture, or art, and the same is true in trade. Therefore of necessity, if he wishes to hold power for any length of time in a country, he must proceed to a bloody annihilation of the former intellectual upper class; otherwise he would soon be conquered once more by this superior intelligence."[526]

The Jewish Bolsheviks made it a priority to mass murder the intellectual elite of the Gentiles in the nations they conquered, while elevating educated and intelligent Jews into positions of power and comparative wealth. Hitler, as a good Bolshevist, did much to destroy the intellectual class of Germany, and to ruin its educational institutions.

The charge that Jews are incapable of producing great minds in the arts and science has resulted in an unnecessary insecurity among Jews. This may be why some have a pro-Einstein ethnic bias and so violently oppose the exposure of the truth which results in the loss of one of "their" supposed greats. This is not only a mistake on their part, it is unnecessary, as there have been many great minds of Jewish descent in history, and even were there not, the insecurity which results in zealous hero worship is artificial and destructive and ultimately results in arrogance and cultural stagnation, as was recognized even before the time of Josephus.

Albert Einstein realized that the cult of personality surrounding him was destructive to science and to progress. He was very much aware of the fact that people believed in what he said out of blind faith—not because it was true or because it was logical, but merely because the miraculous "Einstein" had said it and the press had applauded it. It worried him that people had surrendered their individuality, their ability to make their own judgements, to his authority; but he worried privately and enjoyed the limelight.[527]

The shameless hype of Einstein as if equal to, or greater than, Copernicus, Galileo, Kepler, Huyghens and Newton,[528] was begun by Alexander Moszkowski, who was familiar with Eugen Karl Dühring's work, and favored by Einstein,[529] who was also familiar with Dühring's work. Dühring's book *Robert Mayer, der Galilei des neunzehnten Jahrhunderts. Eine Einführung in seine Leistungen und Schicksale*, E. Schmeitzner, Chemnitz, (1880); provided Moszkowski with the inspiration to call Einstein the Galileo of the Twentieth Century. Moszkowski's shameless hype was likely a direct response to Dühring's accusation of 1881,

"If one surveys the history of the Jewish tribe as a whole, one finds immediately how it has not managed a fibre of real science in its national existence. [***] Where, however, is — to recall only the development of science since Copernicus, Kepler, Galilei, Huyghens, etc. — the Jew, to whom, in these significant centuries too, even a single natural scientific discovery is due?"[530]

Houston Stewart Chamberlain later repeated the insult. Ironically, Jewish litterateurs countered the charge that Jews were uncreative, by plagiarizing their critics.

Paul Ehrenfest, who opposed the dishonest promotion of Einstein as the "Jewish Newton", wrote to him on 9 December 1919,

"I hear, for ex., that your accomplishments are being used to make propaganda, with the 'Jewish Newton, who is simultaneously an ardent Zionist' (I personally haven't *read* this yet, but only *heard* it mentioned). [***] But I cannot go along with the propagandistic fuss with its *inevitable* untruths, precisely *because* Judaism is at stake and *because* I feel myself so thoroughly a Jew."[531]

Communist Zionist Nachman Syrkin thought that Jews had an innate "national character". He wrote in 1898,

"The peculiar literature, thought, and sentiment of the Jewish masses, which stamp them unmistakably with a well-defined national character, are clearly reflected in Jewish socialism."[532]

The pro-Jewish promoter A. A. Roback wrote in his book *Jewish Influence in Modern Thought*, that racial characteristics happily gave Jews the edge in creating the theory of relativity; which, according to Roback, was a Jewish creation, one might even say, according to Roback, a racially predetermined Jewish physics resulting from uniquely Jewish biological forces. Roback even thought it a shame that Lorentz was not Jewish, made much of the fact that most everyone considered Lorentz to be Jewish, stated that Lorentz looked Jewish, and then demeaned Lorentz' contribution to the theory. Roback wrote in 1929,

"It is common knowledge that the man whose name is most intimately associated with the theory of relativity is a Jew of unmistakable Semitic origin and avowedly nationalistic tendencies. Albert Einstein has already taken his place with Galileo, Kepler, Copernicus and Newton in the forefront of scientific achievement. But it is not generally known that the doctrine of relativity has been reared, so to speak, on a Jewish foundation. [***] If Michelson, Minkowski, Levi-Civita, and other Jews all had a hand with Einstein in the establishment of the great principle, only as a result of chance or coincidence, then the line between a coincidence and a miracle almost vanishes. In self-defense for broaching this delicate subject, I may call attention to the fact that the issue between the House of Israel and the principle of relativity has already been picturesquely and good-humoredly brought up by a non-Jew. [***] It is my belief that a theory, principle or even law, *must be in us before we can discover it in nature.* [***] In the development of the relativity theory, it is perhaps significant that the Jewish stamp is found at almost every turn. Were Einstein, alone of all Jewry, responsible for the vast physical transformation, the connection between relativity and the Jews could be regarded as wholly fortuitous, but where the names of Michelson, Levi-Civita, Minkowski, Born, and Silberstein are all associated, in a more or less intimate way, with Einstein's achievement, one begins to feel that the 'Elders of Zion' have unwittingly conspired to explain the world's most baffling phenomena, and apparently have met with success."[533]

Roback and Lenard were kindred spirits. Some have asserted that Lenard was a crypto-Jew.[534]

Roback was inspired by L. Roth, who also went too far in 1927 in his essay *Jewish Thought in the Modern World*,

"In the same way, what is perhaps the most remarkable of modern intellectual movements, the development in mathematical physics, is largely the result of the labours of the Jews Michelson, Minkowski, Einstein, and Weyl, while its philosophical interpretation (as a part of a vast body of other fruitful work in the general history and evaluation of the sciences) is being furthered by the insight of Cassirer, Brunschvicg, and Meyerson. Yet truth is its own witness and its own judge, and it is absurd to discuss it in terms of its discoverers. Like many other pioneers these men are of Israel, but their work is for the whole world."[535]

These statements were made at a time when Jews were characterized by anti-Semitic Jewish Zionists as "parasites" feeding off of the nations. Many Jews began to doubt their ability to live independently of a "host".[536] One can certainly understand the need to correct that injustice and self-doubt, but it would more than have sufficed to have simply told the truth without distorting and exaggerating the facts in a way that did gross injustice not only to history and to the public which was lied to, but also to the many philosophers, mathematicians and scientists whose legacies were stolen and whose good reputations were destroyed for the sake of promoting mediocre Jewish minds.

Racist Jews tried to justify themselves by claiming that if race is the standard, then the Jews are a superior race. For example, Ignatz Zollschan stated at least as early as 1914, referring to his book, *Das Rassenproblem unter besonderer Berücksichtigung der theoretischen Grundlagen der jüdischen Rassenfrage*, W. Braumüller, Wien, (1910),

"JEWISH QUESTIONS
I.
The Cultural Value of the Jewish Race
The cultural value of the Jewish race has long been

established by students of history and philosophy. A race whose genius has created all prevailing religions among all civilized nations, a race whose spiritual heroes have given to the world the principles of freedom and justice, a race whose sons have for thousands of years made vast contributions to the advance of civilization—such a race unquestionably represents a useful member in the family of nations. And yet a minute, scientific investigation of this problem, from the point of view of anthropology and biology, is urgently needed.

For, at the present time, some writers are busily engaged in disseminating the view that the Jews are no race at all; that modern Jews are not descendants of the ancient Hebrews, and are accordingly no Jews, but merely adherents of the Mosaic creed. Should this opinion prove to be correct, we would naturally have no right to appeal to the achievements of the Jewish intellect in ancient times. If this view is right, then all the facts enumerated above must be eliminated, when we consider the cultural value of the Jewish race. This opinion, however, can easily be refuted by anthropological arguments. But far more serious and more dangerous are the theories of a different kind, which pretend to be the result of strictly scientific research.

These theories do not deny that the Jews of to-day are the descendants of the Jews of ancient times, but assert that both modern and ancient Jews represent an inferior racial element, and that they are injurious to the State and Society in whose midst they dwell. The anti-Semitic theories, of which H. Stewart Chamberlain is now the foremost exponent, are as follows:

The Jewish race has developed its characteristics on lines diametrically opposed to those of the rest of mankind. The inoculation of the characteristics of the Jewish race in other nations would be a great menace to the latter. Above all, however, the Jews deserve to be contemned and despised for their spiritual inferiority. The Semites have never created anything great and comprehensive. They never founded a great organized State. Loyalty, respect for the great, and nobility of character in general, are entirely unknown among the Jews. In all these thousands of years they have not rendered any exceptionally great service in the domain of philosophy, science and art. There are a number of talented Jews, but they have no surpassing genius. The Semitic race, accordingly, is far below the Aryan race. Even the religious genius, which has been, ascribed to the Jews, does not exist, according to Chamberlain. It is just the Jews, he maintains, who are the least gifted in matters of religion. Even the Negro is above them in this respect.

Now anyone familiar with modern tendencies and with the latest literature, will recognize the reality of these disgraceful attacks, and will understand that should such theories be allowed to remain unanswered, they would become a great political danger. It is very desirable, therefore, that we should employ the same weapons as our opponents: that is to say, the weapons of anthropology, sociology and natural science, to investigate the social value of the Jews.

It is unfortunately impossible, you realize, to solve this problem in a single lecture. In the short time allotted to me, I can only give a rough outline of a sketch, to show the manner in which our opponents argue in order to attain such results, and to point out the method we are to choose in our refutation.

It has hitherto been the commonly accepted theory, that in remote antiquity all the nations, from the East Indians to the Britons, from the Greeks to the Norwegians, formed one common race—the Aryan. The great historians of human culture, and especially Renan, propounded the theory, that all great things that were achieved by German industry, British energy, Roman power, Greek art and Indian philosophy, were due to this common Aryan spirit. With these they compared the cultural achievements of the Semites, and arrived at the conclusion that the Semites have indeed achieved much in the field of religion, but have been surpassed by far by the Aryans, in all other domains. To this Aryan theory, which was important enough in itself, there has, in the course of the last decade, been added another one, which is of infinitely greater significance. What is the purport of this new theory, and what relation does it bear to our subject?

The well-known migration of natives, which entirely devastated the south of Europe at the end of classical antiquity was, according to this theory, not an isolated event, but the last link of a chain of such migrations from the Germanic North. These migrations were the consequence of the overcrowded population of these countries, the soil of which became diminished on account of the encroachment of the sea and through glaciation. The severity of the glacial period made the struggle for existence very strenuous, and only the fittest survived. This struggle made it necessary to exert all bodily and mental power. And thus arose in these cold regions a blond, well-built nation, endowed to the highest degree with vitality and mental activity.

When the population became overcrowded, part of this race crossed the Alps, and inhabited in prehistoric times all countries in Southern Europe, the northern coast of Africa, and the western and southern parts of Asia. Some of these stocks even came to China and Japan, and even further. We indeed find to-day in all these countries, men of high stature, blue eyes, blond hair, and long heads. These men are considered the descendants of those men of the prehistoric migrations.

Many problems now appear to be solved. In the first place, we understand why the Aryan speech is so widely spread. For these wanderers brought their language along with them. Hence all the languages, of all the kindred nations from India to the Atlantic Ocean, are related. But this is not the only problem that is solved. It was discovered that the blood-relationship reaches much further. A reason was finally found for the phenomenon that there are so many blond and dolichocephalic, that is, longheaded people, in the South. The explanation was simple. Anthropologically, they belonged to the nations that hailed from the North. This newly won experience is even applied to the Jews. For instance, Esau was red; King David was blond; Jesus, too, as it is sometimes claimed, was blond—hence those men, as well as modern blond Jews, were not pure Semites, but descendants of the Amorites; that is to say, of a race that hailed from the North and which, according to Chamberlain, had a great share in the composition of the Jewish race.

It is claimed, that scientific inquiry has succeeded in demonstrating that great achievements, which history ascribes to the Jews, are due to these non-Jewish elements. Furthermore, that scientific inquiry appears to establish the fact that many of these great achievements were not at all produced by the Jews, but were borrowed by them from the neighboring nations. Thus the most important elements of Jewish culture are supposed to be derived from Babylon and Egypt; and the bulwarks of their religion are supposed to be borrowed from the Sumero-Accadians. But, according to Chamberlain and the politico-anthropological school, these Sumero-Accadians were dolichocephalic—longheaded—and hence of Aryan; of Northern origin.

All these Aryan Germanic natives, according to this theory, had in common, certain characteristics of soul and mind, as well as of creative genius. And in consequence of those creative characteristics, all the enumerated nations had already, in remotest antiquity, attained their high classical culture. To-day, however, all these Oriental countries are almost entirely excluded from cultural creations. The historian of human culture has often occupied himself with this question. But the solution of this problem is only apparently difficult. For in our own times also, only the Germanic nations are politically, economically, spiritually and artistically, the standard-bearers of idealism and progress. These anthropologists find that all the great and important achievements have proceeded from men of Germanic extraction. An explanation was thus found for nearly all striking phenomena.

For through these migrations in remote antiquity, not only Germanic blood, but also Germanic power and energy, and Germanic intellectual productivity were imported to the South. Along with their blood and language these Northern hordes, also brought, according to this theory, to the South, their high and gigantic cultural ability; while the primitive inhabitants of the latter countries had lived in an intellectual lethargy. Thanks to these invasions, all the oriental nations of antiquity were enabled to attain the loftiest summit of civilization. But as the northern blood of that uncultured primitive population was slowly and gradually waning, these primitive nations fell back to their present-day inactivity and sluggishness. Their cultural value was reduced, in proportion to the dilution of the quality of their blood. The decline of Greece and Rome is thus easily explained by the anthropologists, through the waning of the fair-complexioned race elements. For the cultural value of a nation stands in direct relations to its racial value. And this racial value depends on the quantity of northern blood which still flows in its veins. Hence the racial value of the Jews is very insignificant, according to the teaching of Gobineau, the politico-anthropological school and Chamberlain.

According to Chamberlain, the Jews are, apart from this, a bastard nation, which arose through the mingling of racially different nations: Semitic Arabs, Aryan Amorites and Syrian Hittites. It is this bastard character which is responsible for the unusual inferiority of the Jewish race.

I am extremely sorry that I am not in a position to discuss here in detail the anthropology of the Semites. For, although theories explained here appear far-fetched at first sight, they are, nevertheless, important. It would by far lack due emphasis, were I merely to explain to you that these theories are incorrect. It is necessary to enter deeply into this question, in order to see how furidamentally wrong these theories are, and that in many cases just the opposite is true. But one must enter into linguistic and pre-historical, as well as into sociological and anthropological investigation, and into a study of the laws of heredity, if one wishes even to begin to criticize this system. By investigating the history of human cultute we find, to take only a single example, that no Aryans ever existed at all, and that identity of language does not permit us to draw any conclusions about identity of race. For, according to this language theory, all negroes in South America would be pure Spaniards and all negroes of North America would be pure Anglo-Saxons! Languages are altered and transformed through political and social influences, so that two neighboring and kindred nations may by chance speak different languages. Thus the Jews of to-day collectively speak all the languages of the world except their own. And thus, also, the Persian or the Armenian, who is supposedly Aryan, is, according to all anthropological characteristics without any doubt, more akin to the Semitic Syrian than to the Iberian or Norwegian. For this reason alone, it is impossible to speak of the contrast between the Semites and the Aryans.

But more significant than these linguistic considerations are the anthropological investigations themselves, of too technical a nature to be discussed here in detail, concerning which I must refer you to my book on this subject. The researches about this matter force upon us the conclusion that the Germanic race theory is from beginning to end untenable and without foundation.

All this is, however, only a part of that which an impartial investigation into the material reveals, but even this is sufficient to prove the whole proud edifice of these theorists to be only a house of cards, which can offer no resistance to a keen critic. But anthropological inquiry yields still more important results. For the division of the races of man, according to their historical development—and this is the only division possible to-day—arrives at conclusions diametrically opposed to those maintained by these theorists.

When we enter into the study of anthropology, we find an entirely different grouping of nations. On account of the glaciation of the Alps, the entire white Caucasian race was, for many thousand years after the glacial period, divided into two unequal groups of nations differing, therefore, from each other, in their development and physiognomy; the land in the cold regions north of the Alps was inhabited by the fair-complexioned group —the Xanthochroic or light-haired—and the land south of the Alps was populated by a darker-haired group—the Melanochroic. To the Xanthochroic belong the Slavonic-Keltic-Germanic nations; while to the Melanochroic, south of the Alps, belong the nations of Southern Europe, North Africa, and the white nations of Asia. To the southern group belong, accordingly, the Jews and other Semites, as well as the East Indians, Persians, Sumero-Accadians, Egyptians, Greeks, Romans, etc.

According to the dogma of the race theorists, innate ability is determined by birth, and nations of the same race must necessarily be equally gifted. The Jews, according to this division, are of the same race as the nations enumerated above, and hence their innate ability must in no respect differ from that of the Indians, Sumero-Accadians and Greeks. The racial value of the Jews must, therefore, be the same as that of those nations of which the race theory treated; namely, of all Aryan nations except those of the Germanic group. For just as the Germanic nations distinguished themselves among the Xanthochroic group, so did the Jews excel among the Melanochroic types. That group to which the Germans belong, entered the stage of civilization only as late as the 13th century, and it is only in the very late periods that it assumed a leading role in the advance of European culture. The nations of the other group had a high state of civilization in remotest ages, and some of them, for instance, the Egyptians and Babylonians, stood thousands of years ago, at the highest stage of classical development. As Greeks and Romans they created the classical culture, and as Moors, Byzantines and Italians, they were the authors of post-classical civilization.

Is it, however, at all true, that innate ability depends upon race, and that every race has its specific racial peculiarities which invariably adhere to it forever, under all conditions and circumstances? Is there an innate racial soul which never changes? Are the psychical bases of various races really fundamentally different? It is true that there are different racial characteristics and abilities. But do these fundamental racial peculiarities remain the same throughout all ages or are they subject to the laws of change?

This is a problem with which Science has interested itself for more than a century. Formerly it was merely a subject for philosophic speculation, but it has now entered into the field of experimental investigation. In the field of heredity two views are now current, that of Lamarck, who insists upon the adaptability and changeability of characteristics in the entire organic world, and that of Weissmann, who maintains that the specific character always remains the same. However interesting it may be to pursue this theme in detail, I must confine myself to a brief resume of the results obtained from a historico-philosophical analysis and further study of the laws of heredity. The theory that acquired characteristics are not transmissible and that the specific character is absolutely constant, can now be regarded as exploded. As it is impossible to give details on this point in a single lecture, I must again refer you to my book for a fuller discussion. What applies to the entire organic world applies with greater force to man. It is therefore not true that we are justified in assuming specific racial psychical powers for each race. It is indeed true that the Greeks distinguished themselves by their artistic sense and the Romans by their energy, and that the peculiarities of the Italians differed from those of the Scandinavians. But the reason for these differences are to be found in their historical and social environment. The inductive method of historical investigation shows that the internal character of these nations changed, when the external conditions altered fundamentally. Thus the so-called innate family virtues of the Jews may be lost, when they come in disturbing environments. It is equally untrue that the essential psychical differences of the various races can be demonstrated by natural science, in the sense that all pre-eminent Frenchmen must distinguish themselves by their *esprit*, and Germans can only excel as poets and thinkers, and that the specific ability of the ancient Greeks lay only in art, that of the ancient Indians only in philosophy, that of the Romans only in conquest and control, and that of the Jews only in Commerce.

The psychology of a people changes at the various stages of culture through which it passes. Most people pass through the same stages of 'Volkspsychologie,' at one stage or another of their existence, and this 'Volkspsychologie' is the product of the particular stage. There is a peculiar psychology of hunters and husbandmen, of scholars and merchants; a distinct psychology of the inhabitants of the country and of the inhabitants of the city. This is the same among all races. There would accordingly be more justification to speak of a psychology of stages than of a psychology of races. The quality of the capability of a nation does not depend upon its race, but upon environment, the stage of development through which it at the moment happens to be passing, and upon the influences of tradition.

And yet when we consider the capacity and psychical intellectual ability of a nation, we cannot say that it is immaterial from which race it descended. The descendants of one race may indeed be more gifted than those of another. The explanation is to be found in the past experience of that stock. In the entire organic world, we find that every being developed and perfected those organs which were mostly employed. The limb which is most exercised, grows best. When it was necessary, therefore, for a certain species to develop its brain to the highest perfection—when a certain race, by its own free-will or by force of circumstances, devoted itself to work which required it to perfect the brain, it necessarily follows that the descendants of such a race have the advantage over the descendants of another race. The quality of their ability, as was remarked above, depends upon environment, the stage of development and the influences of tradition; but the quantity of their capacity, the magnitude and intensity of their ability does not depend upon environment, but upon race, or rather upon the cultural activity of their ancestors. This is, therefore, a factor of heredity.

Now with what people and with what race was the cultural activity of their ancestors greater than with the Jews? For with the Jews study was a religious duty, and those among them who did not possess a high degree of intellectual activity were not fit for the struggle for existence. In consequence of the intensive cultural activity of their ancestors, the Jews must possess the maximum sum of innate ability.

This result is obtained from the theory of heredity.

Anthropology, as we have shown, points to the contrast between the Xanthochroic and Melanochroic. But this contrast also led us to a conclusion different from that taught in the schools. All those nations which achieved the great things, and created the intellectual monuments, belong to the same groups of races to which the Jews belong. This would be the inference from the mode of distributing the intellectual ability, if we are to maintain with the race theorists, that nations derived from the same race are equally gifted. I merely wish to hint at this conclusion.

But the racial pride of the Semites does not require them to employ any speculative demonstration and logical deductions, which may perhaps be considered as sophistry. The simple, but forceful historical facts in themselves render all other demonstrations unnecessary. The principal reproach cast upon the Jews by their foes, that the Semitic race lacks creative genius, stands self-condemned in the light of the result of modern research, which considers Mesopotamia, the cradle of all the Semites, as the place where civilization originated. And furthermore, no period of history is more neglected by these theorists than the golden age of Semitic culture in Spain. They pass over in silence the influence that that period had on the development of modern Europe. There is an unbroken chain of evidence to prove that the origin of Humanism and of the Renaissance of which Europe is so proud, can be traced to the Semites, Jews and Arabs, in Spain The Jew indeed among the nations, who draw upon his resources and in whose midst he lives, is only one of the heirs of his own past achievements.

There is, however, another important question which waits an answer. We have seen that the Jews and the other Semitic nations were the torch-bearers of civilization. In ancient times the Babylonians, Phoenicians, and Carthaginians took an active part in advancing human culture, while in mediaeval times the Arabs achieved wonders, and were the leading and creative genius of all that is great. How is it that now, as it seems, the Jews are merely receptive and reproductive, but do not produce anything really new? An explanation of this phenomenon is to be found in the social structure of presentday Jewry.

In Mesopotamia, Palestine, and finally in Spain, these nations lived in accordance with their own culture. They did not confine themselves to one branch of industry, but, like all other nations of the earth, cultivated all sorts of trades. But the unnatural historical development of the Jews, and the quite unnatural distribution of professions of to-day must inevitably produce unnatural results. The social structure of present-day Jewry is unsound. The keen struggle for existence stifles much that is really great and profound, so that for the most part only those that are commercially fit are able to rise. In consequence of the present-day development, which is contrary to the law of natural selection, Judaism of to-day cannot fully bring out its dormant powers, and its cultural energies cannot be brought into complete action.

The development of great talents finds a favorable field among such nations, ashaving grown to fruition with their soil—owing to their calm and stable pursuits, have the necessary leisure to think and contemplate for its own sake. But in a commercial community where the struggle for existence is still more intensified by political and economic conditions, such talents are crippled or lie fallow and rusty. It is due to this influence, which is contrary to the law of natural selection, that the Jews are extremely ambitious. Prof. Werner Sombart erroneously takes this as the principal characteristic of the Jewish race. In addition to those disadvantages, we must take account of the destruction of the old religious and Ghetto environment, in which the people were at least complete after their fashion. Ours is a period of hollow and empty transition. The inner distraction and disruption of our people in this transition, have caused this characteristic to be considered as the principal feature of the Jewish race. It is very unfortunate that, owing to exceedingly superficial reasoning, the noble personalities are left out of account. The mediocre and obtrusive Jews are in evidence, and they form the criterion for the entire Jewry. The gross, misleading picture which arose through the social structure of Jewry in the diaspora depicted the Jew as the type opposed to all that is lofty in humanity.

The peculiar environment brought it about, that the actual conditions could not have been different from what they are to-day. Under the conditions existing at present, the Jews cannot attain that richly productive activity which in remote antiquity their ancestors developed in Mesopotamia, and later on in the Pyrhenean peninsula. And yet even to-day, under the most discouraging circumstances, the Jews have created not only the modern system of capital, or not only a large number of prominent workers in purely intellectual domains, but they are also the creators of the new currently dominant tendencies of knowledge. One at once thinks—to mention only a few—of Hertz and Ehrlich, of Marx and Stahl, of Spinoza and Bergson, and of Georg Kantor in mathematics. One sees that your profound thinkers have very often created also in heterogeneous cultures, a transvaluation of all intellectual, ethical and religious values, a radical change and renewal of the whole spiritual life. One wonders what their cultural value would be under healthy and normal circumstances. We fear to draw any definite conclusion on this point, lest it should sound exaggerated and speculative, to say the least.

Through the conscious efforts of numerous generations of thinkers and statesmen and through the influence of religion, a nation of pure blood, not tainted by diseases of excess or immorality, of a highly developed sense of family purity, and of deeply rooted, virtuous habits, would develop an exceptional intellectual activity. Furthermore, the prohibition against mixed marriage provided that these highest ethnical treasures should not be lost, through the admixture of less carefully bred races. This prohibition brought it about that heredity, which is the first factor in the formation of a race, should exercise its power in a most beneficial way, and thus the racial qualities are not only transmitted from generation to generation, but are gradually heightened.

Thus from the striving after eternal existence (which was likewise a commandment of the Deity), there resulted that natural selection which has no parallel in the history of the human race. In the struggle for existence imposed upon this nation, which was shaken by fire and sword, by the hardest economic and moral oppression, and by constant enticements to fall away, only those individuals who were morally and physically strong could survive and propagate.

Thus the Jews form an ancient, chaste race of a maximum cultural value. If a race that is so highly gifted were to have the opportunity of again developing its original power, nothing could equal it as far as cultural value is concerned.

We thus admit that, despite the extraordinary share that the modern Jews contribute to the advance of civilization, their achievements are only an insignificant part of that which they could have produced under normal conditions. The philosopher

Eduard von Hartmann, who can by no means be regarded as a friend of the Jews, has admirably expressed himself on this point when he says:

The conflicting position of Judaism makes it impossible for the Jews to produce anything new in the field of a Jewish national culture, which does not exist, or in the field of the national culture of other nations. But the versatility of Judaism and the originality of its comprehension are sufficiently large to enable it to adapt itself to alien national cultures of various kinds, and by good fortune sometimes to reach as far as that borderline, which divides talent from genius.' This proves, at least, there is nothing against the assumption, that should a Jewish national culture exist, the old productivity of Judaism would manifest itself once more.

I have made no reference in this lecture to the enormous influence of the religions to which Judaism gave birth. There is hardly any parallel for such activity in the cultural world. Nor have I spoken of the Jewish spirit, that is to say, Judaism in a broader sense, that lies hidden in these religions and in the most important intellectual movements of modern times, as, for instance, in Philosophy and Socialism. I have purposely confined myself to the services rendered by the Sernites in other domains, to the material culture, and to the investigation of our problem from the point of view of pure Natural Science.

I am satisfied if I have been able to show you, that even if the Jewish people should prove itself unequal to the task of carrying out its wonderful mission, namely, to realize its dormant potentialities, no stigma of belonging to an inferior race can be attached to it in the name of Science."[537]

In agreement with Philipp Lenard's later view that "Jewishness" could be seen in intellectual works published by Jews, Einstein stated sometime "after 3 April 1920",

"The psychological root of anti-Semitism lies in the fact that the Jews are a group of people unto themselves. Their Jewishness is visible in their physical appearance, and one notices their Jewish heritage in their intellectual works, and one can sense that there are among them deep connections in their disposition and numerous possibilities of communicating that are based on the same way of thinking and of feeling. The Jewish child is already aware of these differences as soon as it starts school. Jewish children feel the resentment that grows out of an instinctive suspicion of their strangeness that naturally is often met with a closing of the ranks. [***] [Jews] are the target of instinctive resentment because they are of a different tribe than the majority of the population."[538]

Viktor G. Ehrenberg, Hedwig Born's father, wrote to Einstein on 23 November 1919,

"So it uplifts the heart and strengthens one's faith in the future of mankind when one sees the researchers of all nations prostrating themselves before a man of Jewish blood, who thinks and writes in the German language, in full recognition of his greatness."[539]

The Zionist United States Supreme Court Justice Louis Dembitz Brandeis wrote in a letter dated 1 March 1921,

"You have doubtless heard that the Great Einstein is coming to America soon with Dr. Weizmann, our Zionist Chief. Palestine may need something more now than a new conception of the Universe or of several additional dimensions; but it is well to remind the Gentile world, when the wave of anti-Semitism is rising, that in the world of thought the conspicuous contributions are being made by Jews."[540]

Brandeis' racist views were, in part, a reaction to the views of the ancients who asserted that the Judeans produced nothing new, and men like Bauer, Marx, Wagner, Dühring and Houston Stewart Chamberlain, who asserted that Jews, with their dogmatic and obedient monotheism, detested anything new and repressed science and art. Ada Sterling wrote in *The Jew and Civilization* published in 1924,

" NOTWITHSTANDING the honor which the world of scientists yields to their Jewish confrères, the Messrs. Michaelson, Bergson, Einstein, and a host of lesser men, who, nevertheless, have made and are making continually, great discoveries toward improving conditions of life for humanity, there have been published, and recently, a vast amount of deliberate mispraisement of the Jew in science as in other departments of life, and ingenious arguments, the purpose of which is to minimize his present-day worth, and to deny his race a position among the pioneers in the field of physics. It is not surprising if the uninformed, overwhelmed by the dogmatic positiveness of such a rabid foe to the Jews as Mr. Chamberlain—who angrily deplores that 'Walhalla and Olympus became depopulated because the Jewish priests wished it so'—should take on similar prejudice and beliefs; or that they should accept his violent assertions when he declares that it was the Jews' scorn of science which long retarded the spread of knowledge along scientific lines. Nor is it to be wondered at if the uneducated, seeing in a news-sheet a belittling allusion to the uselessness of star-measuring should find themselves repeating such idle estimates of the scientific seekers, especially in connection with the measuring of Betelgueuse.

Mr. Chamberlain's statement is an interesting admission in more ways than one. It ascribes to a people strictly 'inferior', and he so names them over and over again, powers which only a distinctly superior people could possess. This contradiction is a common characteristic, as has been pointed out in another connection, of the resolute anti-Semite; but few so often display it as does the writer just referred to. He pronounces the Jews 'mentally sterile', and presently shows them to be the most mentally active people in the world, dangerously creative in fact; he undertakes to prove them the most money-worshipping race in the world—by means of a characteristic with which he invests the matriarch Rebekah—and denies them wit enough to invent numerals.

To prove their stupidity he says that in sharp business transactions 'one Armenian is a match for three Jews.' He resorts, as well, to quoting Apion's time-worn accusation—ascribing it to Wellhausen—that 'the Jews never invented anything,' and he attaches a deal of indexed learning to prove that the race has never even been near to 'grasping the eel of science'; to prove, as well, that all the Jewish people knew—they with a known history of three thousand years, and a traditional one of many thousands more—they borrowed, he says, from their young neighbors, the Greeks, who came into existence 800 B. C."[541]

The dangers of a racist Jewish reaction to any criticism of Jews are many, and the racism of Brandeis and his ilk only serve to inhibit the progress of science and the uninhibited criticism of scientific theories. Brandeis and Sterling are wrong to make a "racial" defense and to assume that all criticisms are completely false, merely because they are false in their "racial" aspects. Ironically, Brandeis and Sterling reinforce the racism they ought to have attempted to discredit. Sterling continued, arrogantly parroting the lies many racist Jews told to promote Einstein,

"As each new ascent in knowledge is made possible by the plane attained by our predecessors, so it has been said that the Morley-Michelson experiments are the starting-point whence arises the Einstein theories on Equivalents and Relativity, which latest discovery of the Jewish mind, though yet to be proven, have been greeted by the scientists of the age as 'probably the most profound and far- reaching application of mathematics to the phenomena of the material universe that the world has ever known'; one which 'takes us behind our present ideas about space, time and matter to the primitive reality out of which we have built up those ideas'. Professor Thomson says Mr. Wells had a pretty clear idea of it all before Einstein's theory appeared; but, he adds, Einstein takes us a big step farther. He asked a question which nobody had asked before him: 'Is the space and time interval which separates two events the same for everybody'?

[***]

The Einstein Theory, while still, in part, under experiment, nevertheless has already solved problems that had worried great mathematicians for generations. To test it, England sent out an important expedition, for the purpose of photographing the stars whose light passed near the sun, when it was in eclipse. The 'Theories' stood the test; more, strikingly verified them. 'Einstein's Theory', say the editors of 'The Outline of Science', shows, further, 'that there is something in the nature of an ultimate entity in the universe' though even yet we know nothing intelligible about it; but, these authorities believe it will presently be made clear through the Einstein discoveries that the whole universe has been . . . . created by the mind itself.

To what insignificant proportions do fanatical critics shrink before the blaze of scientific accomplishment which haloes the modern Jew, and this, not alone because of his exploration of the spaces of the sky, not alone for setting back of the horizon to take in undreamed of worlds, but because, too, great men of the race, regardless alike of fame, and of profit, work on in the secret quiet of 'Science's holy cell', seeking tirelessly and often finding panaceas for the relief of humanity's ills!

But, great as are the findings of the race in the broader fields of physics, to the individual they are of less instant value than are the mysteries of life which chemists, physicians and other scientists of the race may be credited with. At these, too, we will now glance."[542]

4.4 All the Best Zionists are Anti-Semites

The worst enemy of the common Jew has always been the Zionist.

In 1932, Einstein stated, referring to the "deplorably high development of nationalism everywhere"—his own rabid Zionism excepted,

> "The introduction of compulsory service is therefore, to my mind, the prime cause of the moral collapse of the white race, which seriously threatens not merely the survival of our civilization but our very existence. This curse, along with great social blessings, started with the French Revolution, and before long dragged all the other nations in its train."[543]

Einstein complained to Lorentz on 12 January 1920 that even well-educated persons fell victim to "the illiberal nationalistic standpoint."[544] Einstein called "Nationalism" an "ugly name".[545] Einstein's Zionist hypocrisy did not go unnoticed. He was asked why he stood firmly against Gentile nationalism, while making Zionist nationalism his primary purpose in life. According to Thüring, the *Jüdische Presse* reported on 29 May 1929,

> "Man fragte [Einstein], warum er als Verfechter aller internationalen Interessen, als Gegner aller nationalistischen Bestrebungen die jüdische nationale Sache zu seiner eigenen mache. Er erklärte seinen Standpunkt durch ein Gleichnis: Wer einen rechten Arm hat und davon spricht und immer davon spricht, ist ein Narr. Wem aber rechte Arm fehlt, der darf alles tun, um sich das fehlende Glied zu ersetzen. Daher sei er in einer Welt, in der jedes Volk die Bedingungen des nationalen Lebens hat, ein Feind des Nationalismus, als Jude aber ein Anhänger der

jüdisch-nationalen Idee, weil den Juden die notwendige und natürliche Voraussetzung ihres nationalen Lebens fehlt."

This clearly elucidates Einstein's nationalistic perspective, which mirrored the Nazis' nationalistic perspective. The Nazis simply pursued the same false reasoning as Einstein and asserted that their right arm was infected with Einstein's self-described foreign and disloyal nationalists. Einstein agreed with the Nazis and saw them as the salvation of the Jews.

Therein lies the potential danger of Einstein's segregationism. Segregationist nationalism is bound to lead to genocidal nationalism. Einstein's tacit premise that citizenry and nationhood be based on ancient territory, ethnicity, race and religion—on *Blut und Boden*, instead of the sovereignty of a group of living persons in a territory, whether homogenous or heterogeneous in its ethnicities and religions, was racist bigotry—commonly held bigotry, but bigotry nonetheless. Einstein's Zionist nationalism, which was no different from Nazi nationalism, would disconnect Jews around the world from the nations in which they were citizens. His racist nationalism definitely did not conform with his internationalist views, which were premised upon a community of nations, which implies a human family. In addition, Einstein voluntarily amputated his right arm, though he pretended that his self-inflicted wound was a congenital defect. Einstein was born a German, not a Palestinian. But Einstein's hypocrisy, his system of double standards, his desire that the Gentiles be consumed in wars and that the Jews reestablish a State and rule the world, were nothing new. They were Judaism.

Einstein was an advocate of world government and a segregated "Jewish State". While this seemed a contradiction to many, including many Jews, especially many secular Jews, Einstein was merely expressing his loyalty to Jewish Messianic myth. Given Einstein's racist Zionism, it is clear that Einstein wished for a day when Jews would rule a world devoid of Gentile government and that they would be segregated from, and reign over, the "Goyim", to use Einstein's term. "Internationalism" was a code word for a world devoid of Gentile government—a Jewish Messianic prophecy. "Zionism" was a code word for Jewish supremacy reigning over the world from Jerusalem in the Jewish Nation. Einstein's "Internationalism" and Einstein's "Zionism" need no reconciliation, they are one in the same objective—Judaism. Rather those who are confused by Einstein's apparent contradictions need only read the Hebrew Bible, where the Jewish prophets tell the

Jews to reconstruct the Jewish State and at the same time destroy all the Gentile governments of the world.

After World War II had ended, Einstein's friend Peter A. Bucky also questioned the apparent contradiction in Einstein's political philosophy. Bucky asked Einstein how he reconciled his Zionism with his anti-Nationalism. As a good racist Zionist Jew was wont to do, Einstein exploited modern anti-Semitism to legitimize racist Jewish Nationalism which is at least 2,500 years old,

"I think that [nationalism] is justified in this special case because the world has forced the Jews to entrench themselves with the continued existence of anti-Semitism."[546]

Einstein felt that Jews owed anti-Semites a great debt of appreciation for forcing Jews to "entrench themselves". He must also have known that the Zionists created the Nazis to force reluctant assimilating Jews to Palestine. Einstein dreaded a world without anti-Semitism, without segregation and without segregated racist Jews like himself. The incentive for Jews to create anti-Semitism is clear. There is abundant evidence that leading Jews have again and again down through history created and sponsored anti-Semitism. In the racist Zionist's view, racist segregationist Judaism and the Jewish tribe cannot continue to exist without manufacturing anti-Semitism to keep them alive.

Given that the vast majority of German Jews during Einstein's lifetime vehemently opposed his bigotry, it is especially odd that Einstein was so unenlightened and so racist. His own children were assimilated Jews, and he hated them for it.[547] Whereas most German Jews considered the racism of Zionist Eastern Jews primitive and uncivilized, Einstein considered assimilation uncivilized and inhuman, because Einstein believed that European Gentiles were sub-human and incapable of civilization. His Zionist sponsors created wars for, among other things, the purpose of discrediting Gentile government. Einstein owed his fame to Zionists, who used him to publicize their cause. Einstein was more loyal to the Zionists' racism, than he was to his own children. Racism buttered Einstein's bread, his children wanted eat it, though he wouldn't let them—they were sub-human. Fellow Jewish racists kept Einstein in the spotlight and shielded him from criticism.

Einstein, himself, echoed and endorsed the views of the anti-Semites in an interview in which he again revealed himself to be a racist and a segregationist. Zionists intentionally provoked and sought to inspire anti-Semitism, and anti-Semites welcomed the openly racist positions of the Zionists.[548] Einstein went along with the crowd of prominent political Zionists who openly stated that anti-Semitism is welcomed, encouraged and useful to the Zionists. They based their myth on Spinoza's declaration that emancipation leads to assimilation and that the Jews only exist in modern times because glorious anti-Semitism kept them segregated.[549]

Prominent Zionist and author of the *Encyclopaedia Judaica; das Judentum in Geschichte und Gegenwart*, Jakob Klatzkin stated in 1925,

> "The national viewpoint taught us to understand the true nature of antisemitism, and this understanding widens the horizons of our national outlook. [***] In the age of enlightenment antisemitism was included among the phenomena that are likely to disappear along with other forms of prejudice and iniquity. The antisemites, so the rule stated, were the laggard elements in the march of progress. Hence, our fate is dependent on the advance of human culture, and its victory is our victory. [***] In the period of Zionism, we learned that antisemitism was a psychic-social phenomenon that derives from our existence as a nation within a nation. Hence, it cannot change, until we attain our national end. But if Zionism had fully understood its own implications, it would have arrived, not merely as a psycho-sociological explanation of this phenomenon, but also as a justification of it. It is right to protest against its crude expressions, but we are unjust to it and distort its nature so long as we do not recognize that essentially it is a defense of the integrity of a nation, in whose throat we are stuck, neither to be swallowed nor to be expelled. [***] And when we are unjust to this phenomenon, we are unfair to our own people. If we do not admit the rightfulness of antisemitism, we deny the rightfulness of our own nationalism. If our people is deserving and willing to live its own national life, then it is an alien body thrust into the nations among whom it lives, an alien body that insists on its own distinctive identity, reducing the domain of their life. It is right, therefore, that they should fight against us for their national integrity. [***] Know this, that it is a good sign for us that the nations of the world combat us. It is proof that our national image is not yet utterly blurred, our alienism is still felt. If the war against us should cease or be weakened, it would indicate that our image has become indistinct and our alienism softened. We shall not obtain equality of rights anywhere save

at the price of an explicit or implied declaration that we are no longer a national body, but part of the body of the host-nation; or that we are willing to assimilate and become part of it. [***] Instead of establishing societies for defense against the antisemites, who want to reduce our rights, we should establish societies for defense against our friends who desire to defend our rights. [***] When Moses came to redeem the children of Israel, their leaders said to him, 'You have made our odor evil in the eyes of Pharaoh and in the eyes of his servants, giving them a sword with which to kill us.' Nevertheless, Moses persisted in worsening the situation of the people, and he saved them."[550]

Klaus J. Herrmann has collected a great deal of evidence related to Zionist racism in his presentation, "Historical Perspectives on Political Zionism and Antisemitism", *Zionism & Racism: Proceedings of an International Symposium*, International Organization for the Elimination of All Forms of Racial Discrimination, Tripoli, (1977), pp. 197-210. At page 197, Herrmann states, [quoting   Constantin Brunner, *Der Judenhass und die Juden*, Berlin, (1918), p. 112; and Ernst Ludwig Pinner, "Meine Abkehr vom Zionismus", *Los vom Zionismus*, J. Kauffmann, Frankfurt, (1928), pp. 32-33; and referencing Houston Stewart Chamberlain, *Die Grundlagen des neunzehnten Jahrhunderts*, F. A. Bruckmann, München, (1899), English translation by John Lees, *Foundations of the Nineteenth Century*, John Lane, New York, (1910)—*see:* F. Kahn, "H. St. Chamberlain (Eine Charakteristik)", *Jüdische Rundschau*, Volume 25, Nummer 63/64, (10 September 1920), pp. 499-500, for a contemporary view of the impact on Jews of Chamberlain's much-read book. His book was popular among Zionists and the English translation of it received a long and favorable review in the *Times Literary Supplement* of 15 December 1910, pp. 500-501.]:

"Jews,' wrote Brunner, 'have been taken in by the racial theories of the Jew-haters;' and he accused the Zionists of having taken as their teacher the notorious racist and forger of scholarly documentation Houston Stewart Chamberlain, whose 'confused nonsense revelations' had been 'restammered' in a Zionist book on the subject of race. 'How could Germans of Jewish background begin to talk of a Jewish nation, and to fashion of the worst calumny the dream of their greatest nonsense!'[1]
One of Brunner's disciples, Ernst Ludwig Pinner, who had been a Zionist earlier, bitterly accused the Zionists of having

taken up Europe's newest nonsense, namely racial theory as the justification of national emotion. Racial arrogance and racial hate poison national emotion, as did previously religious arrogance and religious hatred. Today it is race which is exalted as the banner in whose name everything is justified.

Pinner also designated the Zionists as 'Jews infected by the sickness of racial insanity . . . because, similar to the Jew-haters, they drew political consequences out of race-consciousness.'[2] Pinner did absolve Zionists of 'preaching arrogance and hatred;'[3] whether or not he would have done so in later years remains open to conjecture."

At pages 204-205, Klaus J. Herrmann quotes the Zionist ideologist Jakob Klatzkin who stated, among other things, in his book of 1921 *Krisis und Entscheidung im Judentum; der Probleme des modernen Judentums*, Second Enlarged Edition, Jüdischer Verlag, Berlin, pages 61-63, and 118:

"[I applaud] the contribution of our enemies in the continuance of Jewry in eastern Europe. [***] We ought to be thankful to our oppressors that they closed the gates of assimilation to us and took care that our people were concentrated and not dispersed, segregatedly united and not diffusedly mixed [***] One ought to investigate in the West and note the great share which antisemitism had in the continuance of Jewry and in all the emotions and movements of our national rebirth . [***] Truly our enemies have done much for the strengthening of Judaism in the diaspora . [***] Experience teaches that the liberals have understood better than the antisemites how to destroy us as a nation. [***] We are, in a word, naturally foreigners; we are an alien nation in your midst and we want to remain one."[551]

"Man vergegenwärtige sich, wie groß der Anteil unserer Feinde am Fortbestand des Judentums im Osten ist. [. . .] Wir müßten beinahe unseren Bedrängern dankbar sein, wenn sie die Tore der Assimilation vor uns schlossen und dafür Sorge trugen, daß unsere Volksmassen konzentriert und nicht zerstreut, abgesondert geeint und nicht zerklüftet vermischt werden[. . . .] Man untersuche es im Westen, welchen hohen Anteil der Antisemitismus am Fortbestand des Judentums und an all den Regungen und Bewegungen unserer nationalen Wiedergeburt hat. [. . .] Wahrlich, unsere Feinde haben viel zur Stärkung des Judentums in der Diaspora beigetragen. [. . .] Und die Erfahrung lehrt, daß die Liberalen es besser als die Antisemiten verstanden haben, uns als Volk zu vernichten. [. . .] Wir sind schlechthin Wesensfremde, sind — wir müssen es immer wiederholen — ein Fremdvolk in eurer Mitte und wollen es auch bleiben."

Some Jews, and some critics of the Jews, have for thousands of years asserted that Jews always form a separate state within the nations they inhabit. This they attribute to the Jewish religion, with its one God to rule over all—Jews being the chosen people who will one day receive the Messiah who will assist them in ruling the world after all other nations are destroyed, which fatalistic belief system inspires the nationalism many Jews have expressed in the Diaspora.

When Zionists like Herzl, Klatzkin and Rabbi Meir Bar-Ilan, who stated in 1922,

"We have no 'church' that is not also concerned with matters of state, just as we have no state which is not also concerned with 'church' matters—in Jewish life these are not two separate spheres."[552]

confirmed that these ancient religious, nationalistic and political aspirations were current in modern Europe, where Jews had been emancipated, it caused many to view Jews not only with suspicion, but with contempt, most especially so because radical revolutionary organizations were often led by, and populated with, Jews in disproportionate numbers to Gentiles. Many leading figures warned the public that the Bolshevik Jews were seeking world domination. They wanted to end the immigration of Eastern European Jews to Germany, and to expel Eastern European Jews from Germany. The Bolshevik Jews had already conducted successful, though short-lived, revolutions in German territory. Many of the Jews emigrating to Germany from the East were the descendants of the Frankists, who had pledged themselves to destroy the Gentile nations by means of deception and revolution. Frankist Jews were often crypto-Jews who hid their Jewish ethnicity in order to deceive Christians who might not otherwise trust them, to place the blame for their actions on other peoples so as to cause an unjust hatred towards those innocent peoples, and to prevent a backlash against Jews for the vile actions Jews were taking against other peoples. The Talmud teaches the Jews that they can sin against others with immunity if they hide the fact that they are Jewish such that Jews will not be attacked in retaliation. *Moed Katan* 17*a* states,

"R' IL'AI SAYS: [***] IF A PERSON SEES THAT HIS evil INCLINATION IS OVERWHELMING HIM, [***] HE SHOULD GO TO A PLACE WHERE THEY DO NOT RECOGNIZE HIM [***] AND CLOTHE HIMSELF IN BLACK AND WRAP HIMSELF IN BLACK, [***] AND HE SHOULD DO WHAT HIS HEART DESIRES, [***] AND HE SHOULD NOT DESECRATE THE NAME OF HEAVEN OPENLY."[553]

An alternative translation:

"For R. Il'ai says, If one sees that his [evil] *yezer*[5] is gaining sway over him, let him go away where he is not known; let him put on sordid[6] clothes, don a sordid wrap and do the sordid deed that his heart desires rather than profane the name of Heaven openly.[7]"[554]

Albert Einstein stated in the *Berliner Tageblatt* on 30 December 1919,

"It is quite likely that there are Bolshevist agents in Germany, but they undoubtedly hold foreign passports, have at their disposal ample funds and cannot be seized by any administrative measures. The big profiteers among the Eastern European Jews have certainly, long ago, taken precautions to elude arrest by officials. The only [Jews] affected would be *those poor and unfortunate ones*, who in recent months made their way to Germany under inhumane privations, in order to look for work here."[555]

Albert Einstein was himself a racist; and, therefore, a hypocrite when criticizing the racism of others. John Stachel wrote,

"While he lived in Germany, however, Einstein seems to have accepted the then-prevalent racist mode of thought, often invoking such concepts as 'race' and 'instinct,' and the idea that the Jews form a race."[556]

On 8 July 1901, Einstein wrote to Winteler,

"There is no exaggeration in what you said about the German professors. I have got to know another sad specimen of this kind — one of the foremost physicists of Germany."[557]

Einstein wrote to Besso sometime after 1 January 1914,

"A free, unprejudiced look is not at all characteristic of the (adult) Germans (blinders!)."[558]

After the war Einstein and some of his friends alluded to much earlier conversations with Einstein where he had correctly predicted the eventual outcome of the war. In his diaries, Romain Rolland recorded his conversations with Einstein in Switzerland at their meeting of 16 September 1915,

"What I hear from [Einstein] is not exactly encouraging, for it shows the impossibility of arriving at a lasting peace with Germany without first totally crushing it. Einstein says the situation looks to him far less favorable than a few months back. The victories over Russia have reawakened German arrogance and appetite. The word 'greedy' seems to Einstein best to characterize Germany. [***] Einstein does not expect any renewal of Germany out of itself; it lacks the energy for it, and the boldness for initiative. He hopes for a victory of the Allies, which would smash the power of Prussia and the dynasty. . . . Einstein and Zangger dream of a divided Germany—on the one side Southern Germany and Austria, on the other side Prussia. [***] We speak of the deliberate blindness and the lack of psychology in the Germans."[559]

Jews often sought to Balkanize nations so as to weaken the power of any faction within a nation and to created perpetual agitation between the nations which could be exploited for profit and other Jewish gains. For example, the Rothschilds created the American Civil War and profited from the debts it generated. They hoped to divide America into two nations and to pit these against one another. They were successful. Jews had long been pitting North German Protestants against South German and Austrian Catholics. Jews were the motive force behind the *Kulturkampf.* After creating these divides and promoting perpetual agitations amongst neighbors, Jewry could then fund one side against the other to destroy it whenever Jewry decided to wreck a given nation.

Einstein's dreams during the First World War remind one of the "Carthaginian Peace" of the Henry Morgenthau, Jr. plan for the destruction of Germany following the Second World War. Morgenthau worked with Lord Cherwell (Frederick Alexander Lindemann), Churchill's friend and advisor, who planned to bomb German civilian populations into submission. Lindemann studied under Einstein's friend, Walther Nernst, who worked with Fritz Haber, a Jewish developer of poisonous gas. James Bacque argues that the Allies, under the direction of General Eisenhower, starved hundreds of thousands, if not millions of German prisoners of war to death. Dwight David Eisenhower was called "the terrible Swedish-Jew" in his yearbook for West Point, *The 1915 Howitzer*, West Point, New York, (1915), p. 80. He was also called "Ike", as in. . . Eisenhower? The Soviets also abused countless German POW's after the Second World War.[560]

Einstein often spoke in genocidal and racist terms against Germany, and for the Jews and England, and he betrayed Germany before, during and after the war. Einstein wrote to Paul Ehrenfest on 22 March 1919,

> "[The Allied Powers] whose victory during the war I had felt would be by far the lesser evil are now proving to be *only slightly* the lesser evil. [***] I get most joy from the emergence of the Jewish state in Palestine. It does seem to me that our kinfolk really are more sympathetic (at least less brutal) than these horrid Europeans. Perhaps things can only improve if only the Chinese are left, who refer to all Europeans with the collective noun 'bandits.'"[561]

While responsible people were trying to preserve some sanity in the turbulent period following World War I, Zionists like Albert Einstein sought to validate and encourage the racism of anti-Semites. The Dreyfus Affair taught them that anti-Semitism had a powerful effect to unite Jews around the world. The Zionists were afraid that the "Jewish race" was disappearing through assimilation. They wanted to use anti-Semitism to force the segregation of Jews from Gentiles and to unite Jews, and thereby preserve the "Jewish race". They hoped that if they put a Hitler into power—as Zionists had done in the past, they could use him to herd up the Jews and force the Jews into Palestine against their will. This would also help the Zionists to inspire distrust and contempt for Gentile government, while giving the Zionists the moral high-ground in international affairs, despite the fact that the Zionists were secretly behind the atrocities. Theodor Herzl wrote in his book *The Jewish State*,

> "Oppression and persecution cannot exterminate us. No nation on earth has survived such struggles and sufferings as we have gone through. Jew-baiting has merely stripped off our weaklings; the strong among us were invariably true to their race when persecution broke out against them. This attitude was most clearly apparent in the period immediately following the emancipation of the Jews. Later on, those who rose to a higher degree of intelligence and to a better worldly position lost their communal feeling to a very great extent. Wherever our political well-being has lasted for any length of time, we have assimilated with our surroundings. I think this is not discreditable. Hence, the statesman who would wish to see a Jewish strain in his nation would have to provide for the duration of our political well-being; and even Bismarck could not do that. [***] The Governments of all countries scourged by Anti-Semitism will serve their own interests in assisting us to obtain the sovereignty we want. [***] Great exertions will not be necessary to spur on the movement. Anti-Semites provide the requisite impetus. They need only do what they did before, and then they will create a love of emigration where it did not previously exist, and strengthen it where it existed before. [***] I imagine that Governments will, either voluntarily or under pressure from the Anti-Semites, pay certain attention to this scheme; and they may perhaps actually receive it here and there with a sympathy which they will also show to the Society of Jews."[562]

Albert Einstein wrote to Max Born on 9 November 1919, and encouraged anti-Semitism and advocated segregationism (one must wonder what rôle Albert's increasing racism played in his divorce from Mileva Marić—a Gentile Serb),

> "Antisemitism must be seen as a real thing, based on true hereditary qualities, even if for us Jews it is often unpleasant. I could well imagine that I myself would choose a Jew as my companion, given the choice. On the other hand I would consider it reasonable for the Jews themselves to collect the money to support Jewish research workers outside the universities and to provide them with teaching opportunities."[563]

In 1933, the Zionists publicly declared their allegiance to the Nazis. They wrote in the *Jüdische Rundshau* on 13 June 1933,

"Zionism recognizes the existence of the Jewish question and wants to solve it in a generous and constructive manner. For this purpose, it wants to enlist the aid of all peoples; those who are friendly to the Jews as well as those who are hostile to them, since according to its conception, this is not a question of sentimentality, but one dealing with a real problem in whose solution all peoples are interested."[564]

On 21 June 1933, the Zionists issued a declaration of their position with respect to the Nazi régime, in which they expressed a belief in the legitimacy of the Nazis' racist belief system and condemned the anti-Fascist forces.[565]

Michele Besso wrote that it might have been Albert Einstein's racism and bigotry which caused him to separate from his first wife Mileva Marić in 1914. Besso wrote to Einstein on 17 January 1928,

"[. . .]perhaps it is due in part to me, with my defense of Judaism and the Jewish family, that your family life took the turn that it did, and that I had to bring Mileva from Berlin to Zurich[.]"[566]

The hypocrisy of racist Zionists often manifested itself in this way. Many had "intermarried". Racist Zionist Moses Hess was married to a Christian Gentile prostitute named Sybille Pritsch.

Einstein may have been affected by his mother's early racist opposition to his relationship with Marić. Another factor in the Einsteins' divorce was, of course, Albert's incestuous relationship with his cousin Else Einstein, and his desire to bed her daughters, as well as his general promiscuity. Albert Einstein opposed his sister Maja's marriage to Gentile Paul Winteler on racist grounds, and Albert thought they should divorce. Albert Einstein wrote to Michele Besso on 12 December 1919, "No mixed marriages are any good (Anna says: oh!)"[567] Besso, himself, was married to a Gentile, Anna Besso-Winteler. Denis Brian wrote,

"When asked what he thought of Jews marrying non-Jews, which, of course, had been the case with him and Mileva, [Albert Einstein] replied with a laugh, 'It's dangerous, but then all marriages are dangerous.'"[568]

On 3 April 1920, Einstein wrote, criticizing assimilationist Jews,

"And this is precisely what he does *not* want to reveal in his confession. He talks about religious faith instead of tribal affiliation, of 'Mosaic' instead of 'Jewish' because the latter term, which is much more familiar to him, would emphasize affiliation to his tribe."[569]

Albert Einstein often referred to Jews as "tribesmen" and Jewry as the "tribe". Fellow German Jew Fritz Haber was outraged at Albert Einstein's racist treachery and disloyalty. Einstein confirmed that he was disloyal and a racist, and was obligated,

"[. . .] to step in for my persecuted and morally depressed fellow tribesmen, as far as this lies within my power[.]"[570]

Einstein bore no such loyalty to Germans, who had feed him and made him famous. In fact, Einstein wanted to exterminate the Germans.

After declaring that Jewish children segregate due to natural forces and that they are "different from other children",[571] not due to religion or tradition, but due to genetic features and "heritage", Einstein continued his 3 April 1920 statement,

"With adults it is quite similar as with children. Due to race and temperament as well as traditions (which are only to a small extent of religious origin) they form a community more or less separate from non-Jews. [***] It is this basic community of race and tradition that I have in mind when I speak of 'Jewish nationality.' In my opinion, aversion to Jews is simply based upon the fact that Jews and non-Jews are different. [***] Where feelings are sufficiently vivid there is no shortage of reasons; and the feeling of aversion toward people of a foreign race with whom one has, more or less, to share daily life will emerge by necessity."[572]

Einstein made similar comments in a document dated sometime "after 3 April 1920". Einstein was in agreement with Philipp Lenard that a "Jewish heritage" could be seen in intellectual works published by Jews. Einstein stated,

"The psychological root of anti-Semitism lies in the fact that the

Jews are a group of people unto themselves. Their Jewishness is visible in their physical appearance, and one notices their Jewish heritage in their intellectual works, and one can sense that there are among them deep connections in their disposition and numerous possibilities of communicating that are based on the same way of thinking and of feeling. The Jewish child is already aware of these differences as soon as it starts school. Jewish children feel the resentment that grows out of an instinctive suspicion of their strangeness that naturally is often met with a closing of the ranks. [***] [Jews] are the target of instinctive resentment because they are of a different tribe than the majority of the population."[573]

In a draft letter of 3 April 1920, Einstein wrote that children are conscious of "racial characteristics" and that this alleged "racial" gulf between children results in conflicts, which instill a sense of foreignness in the persecuted child. Einstein wrote,

"Unter den Kindern war besonders in der Volksschule der Antisemitismus lebendig. Er gründete [s]ich auf die den Kindern merkwürdig bewussten Rassenmerkmale und auf Eindrücke im Religionsunterricht. Thätliche Angriffe und Beschimpfungen auf dem Schulwege waren häufig, aber meist nicht gar zu bösartig. Sie genügten immerhin, um ein lebhaftes Gefühl des Fremdseins schon im Kinde zu befestigen."[574]

Einstein's racism was perhaps a defense mechanism to depersonalize the attacks he faced as a child and to counter the hurt with a sense of communal love, and communal hatred. Like Adolf Stoecker before him,[575] Albert Einstein advocated the segregation of Jewish students. Peter A. Bucky quoted Albert Einstein,

"I think that Jewish students should have their own student societies. [***] One way that it won't be solved is for Jewish people to take on Christian fashions and manners. [***] In this way, it is entirely possible to be a civilized person, a good citizen, and at the same time be a faithful Jew who loves his race and honors his fathers."[576]

Einstein stated,

"We must be conscious of our alien race and draw the logical conclusions from it. [***] We must have our own students' societies and adopt an attitude of courteous but consistent reserve to the Gentiles. [***] It is possible to be [***] a faithful Jew who loves his race and honours his fathers."[577]

On 5 April 1920, Einstein repeated what he had heard from his political Zionist friends, who believed that anti-Semitism was necessary to the preservation of the "Jewish race",

"Anti-Semitism will be a psychological phenomenon as long as Jews come in contact with non-Jews—what harm can there be in that? Perhaps it is due to anti-Semitism that we survive as a race: at least that is what I believe."[578]

and,

"I am neither a German citizen, nor is there in me anything that can be described as 'Jewish faith.' But I am happy to belong to the Jewish people, even though I don't regard them as the Chosen People. Why don't we just let the Goy keep his anti-Semitism, while we preserve our love for the likes of us?"[579]

This letter was published in the *Israelitisches Wochenblatt für die Schweiz*, on 24 September 1920, on page 10. It became famous and was widely discussed in newspapers and was used as a political issue. Einstein's racism had already become a weapon for critics of the Jews to wield against German Jews loyal to the Fatherland. Einstein ridiculed the *Central-Verein deutscher Staatsbürger jüdischen Glaubens*, an organization that combated anti-Semitism and vigorously defended and celebrated Jews, because Einstein sought to promote anti-Semitism and because Einstein believed that being "Jewish" was a racial, not a religious, condition. Einstein knew quite well that the letter had been published. The *C. V.* contacted him about it and published a statement regarding it in their periodical *Im deutschen Reich* in March of 1921,

"So wurde auch in einzelnen Versammlungen der b e k a n n t e B r i e f des Naturforschers P r o f e s s o r E i n s t e i n, den dieser an den Central-Verein gerichtet hat, und in welchem er die Bestrebungen des Central-Vereins ablehnt, weil sie zu national-deutsch und zu wenig jüdisch orientiert seien, zum Gegenstand der Erörterungen gemacht. Dieser Brief hat in der öffentlichen Erörterung der jüdischen und judengegnerischen Presse in den letzten Monaten und auch bei den Wahlen eine gewisse Rolle gespielt und Anlaß zu den verschiedenartigsten Betrachtungen je nach der Parteistellung der Versammlungsredner und der verschiedenen Zeitungen gegeben. So hat sich z. B. die jüdisch-nationale „Wiener Morgenzeitung" veranlaßt gesehen, den Central-Verein in wenig vornehmer Weise anzugreifen und ihn wegen seines nationaldeutschen Standpunktes zu verdächtigen. Diese Angriffe würden durch die Auffassung von Professor Einstein nicht gedeckt worden sein, wenn die „Wiener Morgenzeitung" gewußt hätte, daß Professor Einstein ohne nähere Kenntnis der Bestrebungen und der Arbeit des Central-Vereins seinen Brief geschrieben und keineswegs an eine Veröffentlichung, die nur durch eine Indiskretion erfolgt ist, gedacht hat. Erst n a c h der Veröffentlichung hat er von der Art und Weise der Tätigkeit des Central-Vereins Kenntnis erhalten und hat, w i e m i t g u t e m G r u n d v e r s i c h e r t w e r d e n k a n n , i n f o l g e d i e s e r K e n n t n i s e i n e w e s e n t l i c h a n d e r e A u f f a s s u n g v o m W e r t e d e r A r b e i t u n s e r e s C e n t r a l - V e r e i n s g e w o n n e n. Auch dieser Vorfall sollte Anlaß geben, Urteile in der Oeffentlichkeit erst dann zu fällen, wenn die Sachlage einigermaßen geklärt ist."[580]

On 24 May 1931, the *Sunday Express* of London published an interview it claimed it had had with Einstein while he was visiting Oxford. The interview contained inflammatory statements similar to those published in the *Israelitisches Wochenblatt für die Schweiz* on 24 September 1920. These statements were repeated in several German language newspapers across Europe together with scathing editorial indictments of Einstein. Einstein claimed that no interview had taken place and the quotations were taken from a letter he had written eleven years prior. Einstein stated in a letter to Michael Traub of 22 August 1931 that this letter had never been published,[581] though it had been published and Einstein knew quite well that it had been published. Einstein accused the *Central-Verein deutscher Staatsbürger jüdischen Glaubens e. V.* of instigating the "forgery". The *C.V.* denied that it was behind the publication in the *Sunday Express* and invited Einstein to respond in their official organ the *Central-Verein Zeitung*. Einstein took the opportunity and stated, "Es wurden mir schon wiederholt Auszüge aus einem Artikel der „S u n d a y   E x p r e ß" zugesandt, aus denen ich ersehe, daß es sich **um eine glatte Fälschung** handelt. Ich habe in O x f o r d überhaupt kein einziges Zeitungsinterview gegeben. Der Inhalt ist eine böswillige Entstellung eines vor elf Jahren geschriebenen, nicht für die Oeffentlichkeit bestimmten Briefes."[582] He affirmed in 1931 that he had made the statements and did not repudiate them.

In 1932, Einstein stated, referring to the "deplorably high development of nationalism everywhere"—his own rabid Zionism excepted,

"The introduction of compulsory service is therefore, to my mind, the prime cause of the moral collapse of the white race, which seriously threatens not merely the survival of our civilization but our very existence. This curse, along with great social blessings, started with the French Revolution, and before long dragged all the other nations in its train."[583]

Einstein had a reputation as a rabid anti-assimilationist, which is to say that Einstein was a rabid racist segregationist. On 15 March 1921, Kurt Blumenfeld wrote to Chaim Weizmann,

"Einstein [***] is interested in our cause most strongly because of his revulsion from assimilatory Jewry."[584]

Einstein stated in 1921,

"To deny the Jew's nationality in the Diaspora is, indeed, deplorable. If one adopts the point of view of confining Jewish ethnical nationalism to Palestine, then one, to all intents and purposes, denies the existence of a Jewish people. In that case one should have the courage to carry through, in the quickest and most complete manner, entire assimilation. We live in a time of intense and perhaps exaggerated nationalism. But my Zionism does not exclude in me cosmopolitan views. I believe in the actuality of Jewish nationality, and I believe that every Jew has duties towards his coreligionists. [***] [T]he principal point is that Zionism must tend to strengthen the dignity and self-respect of the Jews in the Diaspora. I have always been annoyed by the undignified assimilationist cravings and strivings which I have observed in so many of my friends."[585]

In 1921, Einstein declared, referring to Eastern European Jews,

"These men and women retain a healthy national feeling; it has not yet been destroyed by the process of atomisation and dispersion."[586]

Einstein wrote in the *Jüdische Rundschau*, on 21 June 1921, on pages 351-352,

"This phenomenon [*i. e.* Anti-Semitism] in Germany is due to several causes. Partly it originates in the fact that the Jews there exercise an influence over the intellectual life of the German people altogether out of proportion to their number. While, in my opinion, the economic position of the German Jews is very much overrated, the influence of Jews on the Press, in literature, and in science in Germany is very marked, as must be apparent to even the most superficial observer. This accounts for the fact that there are many anti-Semites there who are not really anti-Semitic in the sense of being Jew-haters, and who are honest in their arguments. They regard Jews as of a nationality different from the German, and therefore are alarmed at the increasing Jewish influence on their national entity. [***] But in Germany the judgement of my theory depended on the party politics of the Press[.]"[587]

Einstein also stated,

"The way I see it, the fact of the Jews' racial peculiarity will necessarily influence their social relations with non-Jews. The conclusions which—in my opinion—the Jews should draw is to become more aware of their peculiarity in their social way of life and to recognize their own cultural contributions. First of all, they would have to show a certain noble reservedness and not be so eager to mix socially—of which others want little or nothing. On the other hand, anti-Semitism in Germany also has consequences that, from a Jewish point of view, should be welcomed. I believe German Jewry owes its continued existence to anti-Semitism."[588]

Nazi Zionist Joseph Goebbels, sounding very much like political Zionist Albert Einstein, was quoted in *The New York Times*, on 29

September 1933, on page 10,

> "It must be remembered the Jews of Germany were exercising at that time a decisive influence on the whole intellectual life; that they were absolute and unlimited masters of the press, literature, the theatre and the motion pictures, and in large cities such as Berlin, 75 percent of the members of the medical and legal professions were Jews; that they made public opinion, exercised a decisive influence on the Stock Exchange and were the rulers of Parliament and its parties."

On 1 July 1921, Einstein was quoted in the *Jüdische Rundshau* on page 371,

> "Let us take brief look at the *development of German Jews* over the last hundred years. With few exceptions, one hundred years ago our forefathers still lived in the Ghetto. They were poor and separated from the Gentiles by a wall of religious tradition, secular lifestyles and statutory confinement and were confined in their spiritual development to their own literature, only relatively weakly influenced by the forceful progress which intellectual life in Europe had undergone in the Renaissance. However, these little noticed, modestly living people had one thing over us: *Every one of them belonged with all his heart to a community*, into which he was incorporated, in which he felt a worthwhile member, in which nothing was asked of him which conflicted with his normal processes of thought. Our forefathers of that era were pretty pathetic both bodily and spiritually, but—in social relations—in an enviable state of mental equilibrium. Then came emancipation. It offered undreamt of opportunities for advancement. The isolated individual quickly found their way into the upper financial and social circles of society. They eagerly absorbed the great achievements of art and science which the Occidentals[589] had created. They contributed to the development with passionate affection, and themselves made contributions of lasting value. They thereby took on the lifestyle of the Gentile world, turning away from their religious and social traditions in growing masses—took on Gentile customs, manners and mentality. It appeared as if they were being completely dissolved into the numerically superior, politically and culturally better organized host peoples, such that

no trace of them would be left after a few generations. The complete eradication of the Jewish nationality in Middle and Western Europe appeared to be inevitable. However, it didn't turn out that way. It appears that racially distinct nations have instincts which work against interbreeding. The adaptation of the Jews to the European peoples among whom they have lived in language, customs and indeed even partially in religious practices *was unable to eliminate all feelings of foreignness* which exist between Jews and their European host peoples. In short, this spontaneous feeling of foreignness is ultimately due to a loss of energy.[590] For this reason, *not even well-meant arguments can eradicate it*. Nationalities do not want to be mixed together, rather they want to go their own separate ways. A state of peace can only be achieved by mutual tolerance and respect."

Einstein stated that Jews should not participate in the German Government,

"I regretted the fact that [Rathenau] became a Minister. In view of the attitude which large numbers of the educated classes in Germany assume towards the Jews, I have always thought that their natural conduct in public should be one of proud reserve."[591]

Einstein merely parroted the Zionist Party line. Werner E. Mosse wrote,

"While the leaders of the CV saw it as their special duty to represent the interests of the German Jews in the active political struggle, Zionism stood for. . . systematic Jewish non-participation in German public life. It rejected as a matter of principle any participation in the struggle led by the CV."[592]

In 1925, Einstein wrote in the official Zionist organ *Jüdische Rundschau,*

"By study of their past, by a better understanding of the spirit [Geist] that accords with their race, they must learn to know anew the mission that they are capable of fulfilling. [***] What one must be thankful to Zionism for is the fact that it is the only movement that has given many Jews a justified pride, that it has once again given a despairing race the necessary faith, if I may so express myself, given new flesh to an exhausted people."[593]

On 12 October 1929, Albert Einstein wrote to the *Manchester Guardian*,

"In the re-establishment of the Jewish nation in the ancient home of the race, where Jewish spiritual values could again be developed in a Jewish atmosphere, the most enlightened representatives of Jewish individuality see the essential preliminary to the regeneration of the race and the setting free of its spiritual creativeness."[594]

Einstein's public racism eventually waned, but he continued to publicly express his segregationist philosophy in the same terms as anti-Semites, as well as his belief that Jews "thrived on" and owed their "continued existence" to anti-Semitism.

Einstein stated in December of 1930 to an American audience,

"There is something indefinable which holds the Jews together. Race does not make much for solidarity. Here in America you have many races, and yet you have the solidarity. Race is not the cause of the Jews' solidarity, nor is their religion. It is something else—which is indefinable."[595]

Einstein's confusing public statement perhaps resulted from his desire to promote multi-culturalism in America, which had the benefit of freeing up Jewish immigration to the United States.[596] Einstein was also likely parroting, or trying to parrot, a fellow anti-assimilationist political Zionist whose pamphlet was well known in America, Solomon Schechter and his *Zionism: A Statement*, Federation of American Zionists, New York, (1906), in which Schechter states, among other things, "Zionism is an ideal, and as such is indefinable."

Einstein stated in 1938,

"JUST WHAT IS A JEW?

The formation of groups has an invigorating effect in all spheres of human striving, perhaps mostly due to the struggle between the convictions and aims represented by the different groups. The Jews, too, form such a group with a definite character of its own, and anti-Semitism is nothing but the antagonistic attitude produced in the non-Jews by the Jewish group. This is a normal social reaction. But for the political abuse resulting from it, it might never have been designated by a special name.

What are the characteristics of the Jewish group? What, in the first place, is a Jew? There are no quick answers to this question. The most obvious answer would be the following: A Jew is a person professing the Jewish faith. The superficial character of this answer is easily recognized by means of a simple parallel. Let us ask the question: What is a snail? An answer similar in kind to the one given above might be: A snail is an animal inhabiting a snail shell. This answer is not altogether incorrect; nor, to be sure, is it exhaustive; for the snail shell happens to be but one of the material products of the snail. Similarly, the Jewish faith is but one of the characteristic products of the Jewish community. It is, furthermore, known that a snail can shed its shell without thereby ceasing to be a snail. The Jew who abandons his faith (in the formal sense of the word) is in a similar position. He remains a Jew.

[***]

WHERE OPPRESSION IS A STIMULUS

[***]

Perhaps even more than on its own tradition, the Jewish group has thrived on oppression and on the antagonism it has forever met in the world. Here undoubtedly lies one of the main reasons for its continued existence through so many thousands of years."[597]

Albert Einstein was parroting racist political Zionist leader Theodor Herzl, who wrote in his book *The Jewish State*,

"Oppression and persecution cannot exterminate us. No nation on earth has survived such struggles and sufferings as we have gone through. Jew-baiting has merely stripped off our weaklings; the strong among us were invariably true to their race when persecution broke out against them. This attitude was most clearly apparent in the period immediately following the emancipation of the Jews. Later on, those who rose to a higher degree of intelligence and to a better worldly position lost their communal feeling to a very great extent. Wherever our political well-being has lasted for any length of time, we have assimilated

604 Albert Einstein: The Incorrigible Racist

with our surroundings. I think this is not discreditable. Hence, the statesman who would wish to see a Jewish strain in his nation would have to provide for the duration of our political well-being; and even Bismarck could not do that. [***] The Governments of all countries scourged by Anti-Semitism will serve their own interests in assisting us to obtain the sovereignty we want. [***] Great exertions will not be necessary to spur on the movement. Anti-Semites provide the requisite impetus. They need only do what they did before, and then they will create a love of emigration where it did not previously exist, and strengthen it where it existed before. [***] I imagine that Governments will, either voluntarily or under pressure from the Anti-Semites, pay certain attention to this scheme; and they may perhaps actually receive it here and there with a sympathy which they will also show to the Society of Jews."[598]

Einstein's statements and those of other like-minded racist Zionists threw fuel on the fire and were reflective of the spirit and tone enunciated in *Protocols of the Learned Elders of Zion*, Number 9, which states (no matter who wrote it),

"Nowadays, if any States raise a protest against us, it is only *pro forma* at our discretion, and by our direction, for their anti-Semitism is indispensable to us, for the management of our lesser brethren."[599]

Many Zionist leaders espoused racist nationalism, which made them the darlings of the Nazis, the Nazis they had put into power. Joachim Prinz wrote, among other things, a racist polemic against assimilation in his book published in Germany in the Hitler-era, *Wir Juden* of 1934,

"Die Theorie der Assimilation ist zusammengebrochen. Kein Schlupfwinkel birgt uns mehr. Wir wünschen an die Stelle der Assimilation das Neue gesetzt: *das Bekenntnis zur jüdischen Nation und zur jüdischen Rasse.* Ein Staat, der aufgebaut ist auf dem Prinzip der Reinheit von Nation und Rasse, kann nur vor dem Juden Achtung und Respekt haben, der sich zur eigenen Art bekennt. Nirgendwo kann er in diesem Bekenntnis mangelnde Loyalität dem Staate gegenüber erblicken. Er kann keine anderen Juden wollen, als die Juden des klaren Bekenntnisses zum eigenen Volk. Er kann keine liebedienerischen, kriecherischen

Juden wollen. Er muß von uns das Bekenntnis zur eigenen Art fordern. Denn nur jemand, der *eigene* Art und *eigenes* Blut achtet, wird den Respekt vor dem *nationalen Wollen anderer Nationen* haben können.

In dem Bekenntnis des Juden zu seiner eigenen Nation, in seiner Gewißheit, in sich sein eigenes Blut zu tragen, seine eigene Vergangenheit und seine eigene Art — wird er erst beginnen, die Distanz vor den Erlebnissen der anderen Nationen zu wahren, die notwendig ist, um ein ehrliches Miteinander und eine anständige Nachbarschaft zu halten. In dem Augenblick, in dem dieses Bekenntnis zur jüdischen Nationalität die Mehrheit der Judenheit ergreift, beginnt *die erste ehrliche Aussprache zwischen Juden und Nichtjuden.*"[600]

Prinz wrote of the supposed suicide of the emancipated Jews through assimilation in *liberal* states, and he despised liberalism. His goal was to preserve the alleged purity of the Jewish race in a Jewish nation, *i. e.* the expulsion of the Jews to a new territory which allowed the Zionists to enforce racial segregation. Prinz wrote,

"The brochure of the baptized Jew Karl *Marx* on the Jewish question is an anti-Jewish pamphlet and an autobiographical entry in the chapter of Jewish self-hatred."

"Die Broschüre des getauften Juden Karl *Marx* über die Judenfrage ist ein antijüdisches Pamphlet und ein autobiographischer Beitrag zum Kapitel des jüdischen Selbsthasses."[601]

Prinz was not alone in his condemnation of Karl Marx's anti-Semitism.[602] Hitler and Prinz had much in common. Lenni Brenner documents Prinz' and the Zionists' *kinship* with the Nazis' nationalistic and racial views in his book *Zionism in the Age of the Dictators.*[603]

Dietrich Bronder and Hennecke Kardel[604] state that the top leadership of the Nazi Party and the orchestrators of the "final solution" were of Jewish descent, including Adolf Hitler,[605] Adolf Eichmann, Reinhard Heydrich, Rudolf Hess (member of the *Thule-Gesellschaft*, an organization Zionists created to promote anti-Semitism in order to force Jews to accept Zionism), Dietrich Eckart (member of the *Thule-Gesellschaft*), Alfred Rosenberg (member of the *Thule-Gesellschaft*), Julius Streicher (member of the *Thule-Gesellschaft*), Joseph Goebbels, and Hans Frank (member of the *Thule-Gesellschaft*). Dietrich Bronder wrote in 1964,

"Aus den eigenen Untersuchungen des Verfassers über die führenden Nationalsozialisten sei hier nur mitgeteilt, daß sich unter 4000 Männern der Reichsführung 120 Ausländer von Geburt befanden, viele mit einem oder zwei Elternteilen ausländischer Herkunft und ein Prozent sogar jüdischer Abkunft — also im Sinne der NS-Rassengesetze „untragbar".

a) So rechnen zu den Auslandsgeborenen:
   Reichsminister und Führerstellvertreter Rudolf Heß (Ägypten); Reichsminister Darré (Argentinien); Gauleiter und Staatssekretär E. W. Bohle und der Reichskommissar Herzog von Sachsen-Coburg (England); Generaloberst Löhr (Jugoslawien); General der Waffen-SS Phleps (Rumänien); Reichsärzteführer und Staatssekretär Dr. Conti und der Berliner Oberbürgermeister Lippert (Schweiz); NSKK-Obergruppenführer G. Wagner (Frankreich); sowie aus Rußland: Reichsminister und Reichsleiter Alfred Rosenberg und die NS-Reichshauptamtsleiter Brockhausen, Dr. von Renteln und Schickedanz, Reichsminister Backe, Präsident Dr. Neubert, Staatsrat Dr. Freiherr von Freytag-Loringhoven und Bischof J. Beermann.

b) Darüber hinaus stammten von einem oder beiden ausländischen Elternteilen (u. v. a.):
   Der Reichsjugendführer Baldur von Schirach, Generaloberst Rendulic sowie der Generaldirektor Gustav Krupp von Bohlen-Halbach.

c) Selbst jüdischer Abkunft bzw. mit jüdischen Familien verwandt waren:
   der Führer und Reichskanzler Adolf Hitler; seine Stellvertreter, die Reichsminister Rudolf Heß und Reichsmarschall Hermann Göring; die Reichsleiter der NSDAP Gregor Strasser, Dr. Josef Goebbels, Alfred Rosenberg, Hans Frank und Heinrich Himmler; die Reichsminister von Ribbentrop (der mit dem berühmten Zionisten Chaim Weizmann, dem 1952 verstorbenen ersten Staatsoberhaupt von Israel, einst Brüderschaft getrunken hatte) und von Keudell; die Gauleiter Globocznik (der Judenvernichter), Jordan und Wilhelm Kube; die hohen SS-Führer und z. T. in der Judenvernichtung tätigen Reinhard

Heydrich, Erich von dem Bach-Zelewski und von Keudell II; die Bankiers und alten Förderer Hitlers vor 1933 Ritter von Stauß (Vizepräsident des NS-Reichstages) und von Stein; der Generalfeldmarschall und Staatssekretär Milch, der Unterstaatssekretär Gauß; die Physiker und Alt-Pg.'s Philipp von Lenard und Abraham Esau; die Uralt-Pg.'s Hanffstaengel (NS-Auslandspressechef) und Prof. Haushofer (s. S. 190)."[606]

Inferences can be drawn that these crypto-Jewish Nazi leaders were either motivated by self-hatred, or they were front men under the control of Herzlian political Zionists. Both may have been true of the genocidal Nazi Party leaders. Bryan Mark Rigg estimates the total number of Jewish soldiers and sailors in the Nazi military perhaps ranged upwards to 150,000.[607]

Many Zionists hated themselves and Jews in general and defamed Jews in their literature, especially the relatively impoverished and uneducated Jews of the East, whom the Zionists tried to bribe into migrating to Palestine, though they only largely succeeded in capturing ne'er-do-wells. Herzl considered himself to be a sleazy ultra-Jew in the most pejorative sense of which he could conceive to use the term "Jew". Herzl justified himself by generalizing his character flaws as if they were a racial "Jewish" trait. He hated the masses of poor Jews from the East and the rich Jews of the West, who wanted to assimilate.

In 1845, *The North American Review* wrote of the snobbish class hatred common among Jews, the inter-Jewish racism which has long plagued Jews, and the various dogmatic Jewish sects hatefully at odds with one another (note the misogyny and dogmatic indoctrination of Jews, which continues to this day,[608] and which manifests itself in, among other things, virulent Jewish censorship of others),

"As the Jews were anciently divided into several religious sects,—the Pharisees, the Sadducees, the Essenes,—so we find them distinguished at the present day. Their chief modern denominations, some of which represent the more ancient, are the Caraites, the Zabathaites, the Chasidim, the Rabbinists, or Talmudists, and the Reformed Jews. The Samaritans

[*Footnote:* Mixed descendants of a remnant of the ten tribes left in their own land, and of the Assyrians colonized among them. 2 Kings, xvii. 24, &c. In Christ's time they had a temple on

Mount Gerizim, which they held more sacred than Mount Zion and its temple. They receive only the Pentateuch, and perhaps the Books of Joshua and Judges, which are found among them; but confidently wait for the Messiah, and observe the Mosaic laws more strictly than even the Jews. Wolff found fifty families of them at the foot of Gerizim, and they have also been met with in other parts of Palestine and in Egypt.]

are not to be classed among them, though akin to them in many respects. The main point of difference between most of these sects, though not the only one, respects the Talmud. The *Talmud*—a word that means *doctrine*—is a voluminous work of two parts,—the *Mishna*, that is the *second law*, and the *Gemara*, or *completion*. The former, consisting of a divine interpretation of the written law, say the Talmudists, was given to Moses at the same time with that delivered on Mount Sinai, together with rules for its exegesis, all to be orally handed down; and by him it was made known to the whole people, and specially committed to his successors. These traditions were collected in the Mishna, a work ascribed to Judah Hannasi,—the Holy, as he is usually called,—about the middle of the second century. Many glosses upon this text soon accumulated, which the Rabbi Jochanan, about the year 230, threw together in the form of a perpetual commentary upon it, entitled the Gemara; and this, with the Mishna, is called the Jerusalem Talmud; though sometimes the Mishna, and sometimes the Gemara alone, is, by synecdoche, called the Talmud. About a century later, Ashi and Abhina, distinguished Babylonian rabbins, compiled a much larger collection of opinions, which, with the Mishna, is styled the Babylonian Talmud, a work held in much higher esteem than the other, and generally understood when the Talmud, without further specification, is mentioned. It has commonly been published in twelve large folios. The other is comprised in a single folio. The Talmud has been justly described as 'containing things frivolous and superstitious, impieties and blasphemies, absurdities and fables.' As an example of all these in one,—God is represented as having contracted impurity by the burial of Moses, and as washing in fire to cleanse himself. These traditions, many of them the same by which, in Christ's time, the Jews 'made the commandment of God of none effect,' since then, in accumulated instances, have been used to destroy the force of the Old Testament Scriptures; which, indeed, Rabbinists consider of very little importance.

[***]

Rabbinism is the Catholic faith, from which all these sects are, in modern phrase, dissenters. It is the lineal descendant of Pharisaism, and distinguished by its blind adherence to the Talmud. The estimation in which strict Rabbinists hold this book is unbounded. 'He that has learned the Scripture, and not the Mishna,' says the Gemara, 'is a blockhead.' Isaac, a distinguished rabbi, says, 'Do not imagine that the written law is the foundation of our religion, which is really founded on the oral law.' The Rabbinical doctrine is, ' The Bible is like water, the Mishna like wine, and the Gemara like spiced wine.' [*Soferim* 13*b*] Some even say, that 'to study the Bible is but a waste of time.' [*Baba Mezia* 33*a*] For strict Rabbinism, a melancholy compound of superstition and fanaticism, we must look to Poland, Russia, Hungary, and Palestine, of which we speak, in describing the system. In those countries, the Rabbinists, or Talmudists, discountenance as profane all other study than that of the Bible and Talmud, but are very careful to educate their sons in their religious lore. The Talmud forbids teaching females more than their appropriate domestic arts. 'Whoever instructs his daughter in the Bible is as if he instructed her in abominations.' But it is a disgrace, if boys are not taught to read the Hebrew Bible. The rich provide teachers for their own children, and either permit the poorer to share this provision, or aid them in obtaining masters. So honorable is the office of teacher made, that a bare support is enough generally to secure a competent one. The ordinary method of instruction is very simple. The child, when four years old, is taught the Hebrew letters, and then to pronounce words, the meaning of which he afterwards learns from his tutor; and thus proceeds, without grammar or dictionary, until he can translate the Pentateuch with tolerable ease. Then he begins at Genesis to study exegetically, surrendering his mind, however, entirely to the guidance of some Jewish commentator; and, from first to last, never forming an independent judgment, but implicitly following tradition, and of course never detecting its gross perversions of the Bible. Some stop short of this commentary, with which others conclude their education; while others still, whose parents can afford it, especially if they display quickness in study and fondness for it, pass on to the Talmud,—first the Mishna, then the Gemara, each with its rabbinical commentaries. As an evidence of the ardor sometimes manifested in these studies, and of complete devotion to them, we are told, that a traveller, some years ago, met three young educated rabbins, who 'were born and lived to manhood in the middle of Poland, and yet knew not one word of its language.' A Jewish youth, distinguished for proficiency in Talmudical learning, is anxiously sought in marriage for the daughters of wealthy parents; who look not only at the certain honor of such an alliance, but also at the chance, thus increased, of the Messiah's coming in their line. On the other hand, the Talmud designates by the name of 'people of the land,' equivalent to *peasantry*, those educated in the Bible alone, or not at all; and represents them as an inferior class, fit only for servile labor, with whom others may not intermarry; applying Deut. xxvii. 21,—'Cursed be he that lieth with any manner of beast.' Indeed, the Talmud authorizes every species of oppression towards such, giving them the hope of heaven only if they submit. The Jewish 'peasant' is a servant of servants, ground down by those who have learned, by being oppressed, the art of oppression. In Russia and Poland, where the Jews collect the government taxes among themselves, the rabbins make the peasantry pay nearly the whole. This class, too, where the Jews regulate the conscription, must furnish all the soldiers required.

Some other characteristics of the strict Rabbinists may be briefly noticed. They are the lowest of the Jews in point of morals, and this is sufficiently accounted for by the gross immorality of many Talmudical precepts. On the great yearly *Day of Atonement*, complete absolution from all past sins is pronounced, and from all religious vows, bonds, and oaths taken since the last preceding, and until the next, atonement. This latter absolution, contained in a prayer denominated *col nidre*, being supposed by Christians to extend to all oaths and obligations, civil as well as religious, which the Jews deny, has caused them much trouble in some parts of Europe. The Talmud teaches, moreover, that no respect is due to a Gentile's, or an unlearned Jew's, rights of property; and it accumulates other abominable doctrines, too numerous, and some of them too vile, to mention. Indeed, the modern Rabbinical Jews are generally, in practice, superior to the precepts of the Talmud. They believe in a purgatory, and pray for the souls of the dead; they hold that all Hebrews will rise in the Holy Land, those dying elsewhere rolling painfully under ground until they reach that soil; and that 'all Israel hath part in eternal life.' The dead buried in the Holy Land are expected to be the first to rise in the Messiah's day; [*Kethuboth* 111a-b. *Yerushalmi Kilayim* 9, 3. *Ezekiel* 37. *Genesis* 50:25] and so strong has been the desire of burial there, that in the seventeenth century large quantities of Jewish bones were yearly sent thither to be interred. Ship-loads of this melancholy freight might often be seen at Joppa. They believe that a council properly constituted is infallible, and practically, by their implicit confidence in the Talmud, they make the ancient rabbins their 'fathers.' They place a high estimate on the merits of good works, especially those of a ceremonial kind. Thus, though the reading of the Bible is considered hardly a good act, and even as a positive waste of time, the act of taking out the Pentateuch from its depository in the synagogue, and the duty of standing on the left side of the reader, and of closing and removing the roll after service, are considered highly meritorious, and the privilege of performing them is often sold to the highest bidder. A pilgrimage to the Holy Land, much more to pass one's life there, is a superlative merit. They place great confidence in the supererogatory merits of their ancient saints, especially of Abraham, Isaac, and Jacob, for the males, and of Sarah, Rebekah, and Leah, for females. They have daily morning and evening prayer in the synagogue; and all the prayers for public and private devotion are prescribed, and in Hebrew; for the Talmud affirms, that the angels who receive them understand no other language. Women, servants, and children under twelve years of age, are not required to observe the hours of prayer. The Jews of the Holy Land are, perhaps, singular in praying to saints, and honoring and even worshipping relics. They never approach the supposed stones of the temple, some of which are much worn by kissing, without removing their shoes. Every spot where a saint is supposed to be buried is a place of prayer and pilgrimage. The Talmudists do not allow women to attend the synagogue, until they are married; and then, in Poland, Russia, and the East, they occupy a separate apartment.

Public worship among the Talmudical Jews is, for the most part, where the civil power has not interfered, very irreverent and disorderly. A missionary at Beyroot saw comfits thrown among the people in the synagogue, when particular portions of the service were read, *to show the sweetness of the law!* and the audience—some of the adults, and all the boys—tumbling over one another in the scramble for them on the floor. The Talmud declares, that, in observing the feast of Purim, 'Every man must get so drunk, that he cannot distinguish between the phrases, *Blessed be Mordecai*, and *Cursed be Haman.*' While the Talmud imposes many burdensome ceremonies in addition to the Mosaic institutions, it also furnishes multiplied expedients for lightening the latter; and a fertile ingenuity, newly exercised for each emergency, or perpetuated in legendary rules, has extended the dispensation to every desirable point. Stephens, in his travels in the Holy Land, lodged with a Jew, who would not suffer a lamp, lighted the day before, to be extinguished on the Sabbath; but 'described an admirable contrivance he had invented for reconciling appetite with duty;—an oven, heated the night before to such a degree, that the process of cooking was continued during the night, and the dishes were ready when wanted on the Sabbath.' Yet even the Talmudical Jews are generally superior in morals to their Christian neighbours, especially in the point of female purity. No wonder they hate the New Testament, reading it only through the profligate and intolerant conduct of their persecutors.

Hospitality and alms-giving to their brethren are sacred duties among all the Jews. A large majority of those in Palestine are paupers, and, for their support, contributions, averaging fourteen thousand dollars a year, are made in different parts of Europe, deposited at Amsterdam, and thence transmitted to Beyroot. Jerusalem, Hebron, Tiberias, and Saphet are holy cities in Jewish esteem, and in all the Italian synagogues money-boxes are kept, marked, 'For Jerusalem,' 'For Saphet,' &c. The largest collections are in Amsterdam. Leghorn sends about four thousand dollars. But the poor unlearned Jews of Palestine are greatly oppressed by the rabbins, and generally defrauded, wholly or in part, of their share in these charities. When the Hebrew quarter at Smyrna was destroyed by fire, in 1841, Mr. Rothschild, of Vienna, gave 20,000 francs for the sufferers. He and his brothers have lately offered 100,000 francs for founding a Jewish hospital at Jerusalem. Sir Moses Montefiori, during his late visit to Palestine, contributed munificently to the wants of his poor brethren there."[609]

Lenni Brenner cites numerous examples of defamations against Jews by the Jewish Zionists Maurice Samuel, Ben Frommer, Micah Yosef Berdichevsky, Yosef Chaim Brenner[610] and Aaron David Gordon.[611] One could add Theodor Herzl's, Berl Katzenelson's[612] and Vladimir Jabotinsky's[613] names to the list. Mussolini called Jabotinsky a "Jewish Fascist" and David Ben-Gurion found Adolf Hitler's writings reminiscent of Jabotinsky's.[614] Lenni Brenner wrote, quoting Chaim Greenberg,

"In March 1942 Chaim Greenberg, then the editor of New York's Labour Zionist organ, *Jewish Frontier*, painfully admitted that, indeed, there had been:

a time when it used to be fashionable for Zionist speakers (including the writer) to declare from the platform that 'To be a good Zionist one must be somewhat of an anti-Semite'. . . To this day Labor Zionist circles are under the influence of the idea that the Return to Zion involved a process of purification from our economic uncleanliness. Whosoever doesn't engage in so-called 'productive' manual labor is believed to be a sinner against Israel and against mankind."[615]

The essentially meaningless term "anti-Semitism", a term for anti-Jewish which is employed as a weapon by hypocritical racist Jews with which to smear and threaten, was coined by an "anti-Semitic" crypto-Jew named Wilhelm Marr after Jewish corruption imploded the stock markets of Europe. In its article entitled "ANTI-SEMITISM", *The Universal Jewish Encyclopedia*, Volume 1, The Universal Jewish Encyclopedia, Inc., New York, (1939), pp. 341-409, at 341; states:

"The word was probably first used by Wilhelm Marr, said to have been a converted Jew, in Der Sieg des Judentums ueber das Germanentum, a pamphlet which he published in 1879, the same year in which he founded the Anti-Semitic League; two years later he began publication of Zwanglose antisemitische Hefte."

In 1945, Einstein wrote, among other things,

"[The Jews'] status as a uniform political group is proved to be a fact by the behavior of their enemies. Hence in striving toward a stabilization of the international situation they should be considered as though they were a nation in the customary sense of the word. [***] In parts of Europe Jewish life will probably be impossible for years to come. In decades of hard work and voluntary financial aid the Jews have restored the soil of Palestine to fertility. All these sacrifices were made because of trust in the officially sanctioned promise given by the governments in question after the last war, namely that the Jewish people were to be given a secure home in their ancient Palestinian country. To put it mildly, the fulfillment of this promise has been but hesitant and partial. Now that the Jews—especially the Jews in Palestine—have in this war too rendered a valuable contribution, the promise must be forcibly called to mind. The demand must be put forward that Palestine, within the limits of its economic capacity, be thrown open to Jewish immigration. If supranational institutions are to win that confidence that must form the most important buttress for their endurance, then it must be shown above all that those who, trusting to these institutions, have made the heaviest sacrifices are not defrauded."[616]

Einstein's statements prove that the human sacrifice of Jewish lives in the Zionist Holocaust had not changed the nationalistic racism of the political Zionists at all, but rather had strengthened their hand—in fulfillment of the Zionists' expressed plans. The racist Zionists had no regrets over their mass murder of Jews and they rejoiced at their slaughter of Gentiles. In the 1890's, Bernard Lazare iterated the Zionist mantra:

"It is because the Jews are a nation that anti-Semitism exists. [***] If the cause of anti-Semitism is the existence of the Jews as a nationality, its effect is to make this nationality more tangible for the Jews, to make them more aware of the fact that they are a people."[617]

Albert Einstein told Peter A. Bucky that the Holocaust had the benefit of uniting "all the Jews in the world":

"But the suffering had not been in vain, in Einstein's view. He felt that the Jews who died in Hitler's pogroms had strengthened the bond uniting all of the Jews in the world."[618]

Einstein was simply repeating the Zionist party line, as expressed by Rabbi Abba Hillel Silver in 1943,

> "Should not, I ask you fellow Jews, ought not, the incalculable and unspeakable suffering of our people and the oceans of blood which we have shed in this war and in all the wars of the centuries; should not the myriad martyrs of our people, as well as the magnificent heroism and the vast sacrifices of our brave soldier sons who are today fighting on all the battle fronts of the world—should not all this be compensated for finally and at long last with the re-establishment of a free Jewish Commonwealth?"[619]

Did it occur to no one that the world, including the Jews, would be far better off if racist Zionism and Jewish tribalism were eradicated, rather than further justified, as a result of yet another massive Jewish tragedy? What, other than Jewish racism, prevented a massive drive for assimilation world-wide after the Holocaust?

4.5 Einstein Lulls Jews into Complacency—The Zionist Trap

After the Second World War and the Holocaust were over, few Jews wanted to emigrate to Palestine, despite the racist Zionists' best efforts to destroy their lives and make it impossible for them to live anywhere else. They had had enough of racist segregation. The Zionists then again employed corruption and the manipulation of public opinion to coerce Jews into moving to Palestine against their will and better natures.[620]

Einstein had long known that the Zionists would put a Hitler into power to attack European Jewry. Paul Ehrenfest made an interesting comment in an 8 February 1920 letter to Albert Einstein—a racist political Zionist who believed that anti-Semitism was the salvation of the Jews. Ehrenfest stated that the Zionists had commissioned a Hitler, a Haman, to save them from assimilation,

> "Something quite discontinuous is about to happen in Europe now, isn't that true?—And on this occasion a devil will surely come, on special commission to grab all Jews in Europe *uniformly* and *synchronously* by the scruff of the neck and give them a tremendous shake. Will the great miracle then happen that our prophets foresee, which will awaken and unite us all, orthodox and atheists alike, to a new living faith?—Maybe you

have already seen something of it, even just a hint? I can't see it anywhere yet."[621]

The Babylonian Talmud states in *Sanhedrin* folio 97*b*,

"R. Joshua said to him, if they do not repent, will they not be redeemed! But the Holy One, blessed be He, will set up a king over them, whose decrees shall be as cruel as Haman's, whereby Israel shall engage in repentance, and he will thus bring them back to the right path."[622]

The Jews put Hitler into power to fulfill this Talmudic commandment, to punish the Jews and thereby win them atonement and the return to Palestine.

Ehrenfest had earlier written to Einstein that an old and very influential Zionist Prof. Oppenheim had warned him that Zionists ought not to mix with secular Jews, who were not, in his view, Jews at all.[623] A sorry fate awaited secular Jews at the hands of the anti-Semites the Zionists had commissioned on special order. After stating that it was not in his nature to lie to the public with the dishonest Zionist propaganda claiming that Einstein was a "Jewish Newton", Ehrenfest expressed doubts about acting immorally and wrote to Einstein on 9 December 1919,

"But God only knows, this old man may be right: maybe salvation of the masses can only be bought by the *hardest* sacrifice—sacrificing the last remnants of 'purity.' [Please don't read this as elegant empty words!]—Well, maybe that's how it is—but then my powers do not suffice."[624]

Disturbed that Jews were perpetually defining themselves by a persecution myth—this many years, decades, centuries, before the appearance of the Holocaust the Zionists themselves created—a myth which made their lives easier in that it gave them unfair advantages in society and unburdened them from an existential quest for *Self;* Ralph Philip Boas identified many of the circumstances in America in 1921, which led to the Holocaust in Europe, including Jewish racism, the Jewish love of manufactured martyrdom, the lack of a genuine *raison d'être* for Judaism in the Twentieth Century, and the need of a common enemy to prevent the Jews from extinction through assimilation—the glorification of the myth that Gentile kindness is the worst enemy of the

Jews and that anti-Semitism is the Jews' salvation from integration:

"DESPITE the fact that we are ceasing to persecute people who disagree with us in religion or politics, we only dimly realize that one of the greatest evils of persecution is the fact that it saves its victims the trouble of justifying themselves. Persecution begets martyrdom, a glory as lacking in reason as its progenitor. Whether Sir Roger Casement was right or not is now only an academic question; his execution, by enshrining him forever in the Pantheon of Irish martyrs, makes the heart rather than the mind his judge. So it is with the Jews. Jews have not troubled themselves to justify, on any rational ground, the tenacious fight of their race against the storms of nineteen centuries of persecution. The fight has been its own justification. Obviously, a race that has endured what theirs has withstood must have some glorious mission to perform; to define that mission would be an element of positive weakness, since their enemies would then have a chance to meet them on the ground of reason, where their peculiar virtues, tenacity, single-mindedness, and pliant heroism, would avail them nothing.

It is, therefore, a happy chance for the American Jew that his age-long persecution has either ended or has degenerated into petty social discrimination. For he must now realize that the day has gone when he could justify himself by recalling his heroic miseries. In other days and other countries he faced only the problems of existence. New ideas and opportunities could not pass the walls of the ghetto; custom made adherence to old ceremonies and beliefs not only easy but imperative. The Sabbath was the one day on which the Jew could be a man instead of a thing; the recurrent holidays gave him his one outlet for the emotions rigidly suppressed in daily life; the study and analysis of the Law and the Talmud furnished the intellectual exercise that his eager mind was denied in the schools and the learned circles of the country which tolerated him. The very fact that he was confined within a pale, therefore, made it easy for him to keep his race a distinct entity.

But now, if he is unable to find a rational ground for his religious and racial unity, he will meet a foe more insidious than persecution—the gradual disintegration of race and religious consciousness within the faith. Ironically enough, what pales, pogroms, and ghettos could not accomplish, freedom promises to bring to pass. So the time has come when the Jew in America must decide what he is going to do with and for himself; his enemies can no longer save him the effort of decision.

[***]

What is true of Europe is true also of the United States: the Jew occupies a position the importance of which is out of all proportion to his numbers. Hence the problem of Judaism is of real interest in America, because the influence which the Jew can have upon social life and the current political and financial situation depends almost entirely upon his mode of life and manner of thought. [***] What the Jew is going to do with this self-consciousness may, to Christians, seem of little moment. It is not of that loyal kind which moves men to blow up munition factories, or to plant bombs in steamships. For others, doubtless, its implications are not of great importance. For himself, however, they are everything. His self-consciousness colors his whole point of view. It is not a simple thing. It is compounded of many factors. It is both racial and religious; it makes him both hopeful and despondent; it gives cause both for pride and for a feeling of inferiority; it makes him clannish, and it makes him long for a wider field of acquaintance. [***] Judaism is clannish. Jews undoubtedly hang together. The combination of persecution with its inevitable concomitant, self-justification, acts as a centripetal force in driving Jews upon themselves. Just as Jews have the almost grotesque notion that a man will make his philosophic and religious convictions 'jibe' with his birth, so they have the wholly grotesque notion that a man should choose his friends and his wife from the small group among whom he happens to be born, though later education and environment may move him a thousand miles away. The results of this clannishness are paradoxical. For instance, the average Jew is sure that the chief reason why Anti-Semitism is everywhere ready to show its ugly head, is jealousy of the splendid history and the extraordinary business ability of the race. At the same time he subconsciously assumes the inferiority which has long been attributed to him, covering his feelings, however, by uncalled-for justification and bitter opposition to all criticism. It is torture to him, for example, that *The Merchant of Venice* should be read in the public schools. Who can blame him? For Shylock, although undoubtedly an exaggerated character, nevertheless makes concrete those qualities the portrayal of which hurts because it bears the sting of truth.

The development of committees 'On Purity of the Press' in Jewish societies, and the extraordinary wire-pulling over the Russian treaty and the Immigration bill, show to what lengths this consciousness can go. It is impossible for the Jew to be entirely at ease in the world. He is introspective and suspicious, often unhappy, always sure that, for good or ill, he is a marked man among men.

There are three attitudes which Jews in this country take toward their problem—a few as a result of having thought it through, the majority as a result of the forces of inertia, environment, or chance, forces of which they themselves are perhaps not aware. Some Jews attempt to get rid of their self-consciousness by separating from the group. They deliberately set out to convince themselves that there is no difference between them and other men, and that they can act and live in all respects like other American citizens. A second group find their fellow Jews entirely satisfactory. They are conscious of a difference between themselves and others, but, living as they do in large cities where the Jewish community numbers hundreds of thousands, they feel no need of association with non-Jews other than that which they get in business. They are rich, or at least well-to-do; they have all the comforts that money can buy; they occupy fine streets and build expensive synagogues. They are willing, not only to accept their group-consciousness, but to develop it to the fullest extent by means of societies and fraternal orders. In the third place, there is a small group of Jews keenly conscious of their race, who would like to make Judaism vital as a great religion and a great tradition. They differ from the second group in that they not only accept their individuality but try to justify it. It is not sufficient for them that there should be enough Jewish organizations and undertakings to make a respectable year-book: they are interested in showing why such organizations should exist They not only *are* Jews, but they *want to be* Jews; they want to feel that Judaism really has a mission to fulfill and a message to carry to the questioning world.

The Jew who attempts to solve his problem by separating from his community must leave the great centres of Jewish life and go to some small town where he may make a fresh start. There he will find himself in an anomalous position. He will have neither the support that comes from rubbing elbows with one's own kind, nor the mental and moral stiffening that comes from active opposition. He will be simply an odd fish, and as such will be subject, not to antagonism, but to curiosity. What cordiality he meets with is the cordiality of curiosity. He is a strange creature, similar—on a far lower scale of interest—to a Chinese traveler or a Hindu student. He is engaged in conversation on the 'Jewish problem,' or Jewish customs and history, until he sickens with trading on the race-consciousness that he is striving to forget. With cruel kindliness his friends impress upon him that his Judaism 'makes no difference,' with the result that he finds himself anticipating every imminent friendship by a clear statement of his race, lest the friendship be built upon the sands of prejudice. His social relations must be above reproach. A hasty word, an ill-considered action, in other men to be put down to idiosyncracy, in him is attributed to his birth. Even when there exists the frankest and most open friendship, he is continually seeing difficulties. The fathers have eaten a sour grape and the children's teeth are set on edge. The self-consciousness that he learned in youth reappears in maturity. Whether he will or no, a Jew he remains.

If he finds his situation intolerable he may, of course, utterly and completely deny his Jewish affiliation. He may consort with Christians, join a Christian church, marry a Christian wife, and tread under foot the old associations that will occasionally cast a disagreeable shadow across his life Unfortunately for such a solution, a cloud still hangs about the idea of apostasy. Such a refuge seems to a man of honor despicable. It is a cowardly procedure, surely, to deny one's birth and sail under false colors, the more so since, though it does no harm to others, it gains advantage for one's self. Why ii should it be treason for a Jew to abandon his religion and forget his birth any more than for a Frenchman or a Swede to do so? Probably for the reason that no one cares whether a man was born in France or not, whereas in certain circles it makes a great deal of difference if a man was born in Jewry. Furthermore, Christians feel strongly that the Jew who forsakes the religion into which he was born, does so, not because his eyes have been opened upon the truth, but because he sees in apostasy definite material advantages. The Jew who would take this means of obtaining peace, therefore, would find himself cursed by an irrational idealism which can disturb while it cannot fortify and achieve.

If, however, he returns to some great centre of Jewish life and attempts to affiliate with his own people, he is in a perilous position. He is more than likely to meet with distrust where he seeks sympathy. Jews are so extremely sensitive to criticism and so keenly conscious of the social discrimination which they encounter from Christians, that they can hardly believe that a man who seems to have lived for several years on an equal footing with Christians has not either denied his birth, in which case he has been a traitor, or has not certain qualities of mind which, since they have been palatable to Christians, must be severely critical of Jews.

And, indeed, they have, perhaps, a measure of justice in their position. It is impossible for a Jew to live apart from his race for several years without looking upon his people with a new light. For one thing, distance has enabled him to focus. He has learned to sympathize more than a little with those hotel-keepers whose ban upon Jews is a terrible thorn in the flesh of the man whose money ought to take him anywhere. He has come to see that the clannishness of Jews serves only to intensify what social discrimination may exist, and to make present in the imagination much that does not. He has realized that persecution is not necessarily justification, and that because a Jew was blackballed at a fashionable club does not prove that he was a man of first-rate calibre. And finally, he has perceived that there is an arrogance of endurance as well as an arrogance of persecution, and that for a man to be continually assuming that people are taking the trouble to despise him for his birth, is to postulate an importance that does not exist.

On the other hand, he has, because of his distance, idealized Judaism. In his retirement he studied the history of his people; he thrilled with their martyrdom; he marveled at their tenacity and their fortitude. He built up for himself on the cobweb foundation of boyhood memories, visions of the simple nobility of Jewish ritual and ceremonies, and vague ideals of an inspiring religious faith. He may, perhaps, have met, far more frequently than ill-will, a sentimental and unbalanced adulation of Jews. The cult of the new is with us, and the history, the folk-lore, the literature, and the customs of Judaism have, for many people who pride themselves on their social liberality, the fascination of novelty. It is the easiest thing in the world for a Jew to yield to this sentimental tolerance, and to view his people in a rosy light.

It is, therefore, something of a shock to him when he reënters a great Jewish community, for he finds that the great mass of American Jews have sunk into a comfortable materialism. What persecution could not accomplish, success in business has brought to pass. The innate qualities of the Jew could not save him from the fate of the Christian who has become rich in a hurry—grossness and self-conceit. That Jeshurun waxed fat and kicked is as true now as it ever was, and there is little reason to expect that the race which was hopelessly cankered by national prosperity in the days of Solomon can escape a similar fate in the twentieth century. [***] The sad result is that in prosperity the Jewish self-consciousness ceases to be religious and becomes merely racial.

[***]

The number of immigrants, or children of immigrants, from countries where for centuries they have been trained in an atmosphere of slavish cunning and worship of money, who become rich, is almost incredible. In Russia, Galicia, or Roumania, they cultivated a self-respect by rigid adherence to dignified and beautiful customs; in America the florid exuberance of newly acquired wealth cannot be dignified. Clannishness, exclusion from circles of good taste and good breeding, the infiltration of the parvenu East-European Jews, and imitation of the most obvious aspects of Americanism—its flamboyant and tasteless materialism—all combine to make the thoughtful Jew sadly question what hope lies in the bulk of the Jews who live in the great American cities.

[***]

[Zionism] is actuated by a spirit of helpfulness and by an ideal of racial unity. [***] Aided by persecution and poverty, [American Judaism] furnished admirable discipline to a race naturally stubborn and tenacious. Persecution, poverty, and discipline gone, what is left?—an indistinct monotheism joined to an ethical tradition never formulated into a system, and only vaguely defined. None of the great Jewish philosophers ever succeeded in establishing a Jewish creed; indeed, there was no need of one when common suffering wrought so effectual a bond. [***] At all events it must be remembered that, since the problem of Judaism comes from intense self-consciousness, persecution and sentimental tolerance are both bad for the Jew. The one saves him the trouble of seeking out his reason for existence; the other flatters him into a belief that there is no necessity for the search. If men will treat Jews like other people, instead of nourishing their age-long notions of peculiarity, they will make it easier for time to settle the Jewish problem as it settles all others."[625]

Kurt G. W. Ludecke wrote in 1937 of Moses Pinkeles, a. k. a. Trebitsch Lincoln, a. k. a. Arthur Trebitsch, a Jew who marched with anti-Semites in the streets of Berlin, scripted their statements, and who funded Adolf Hitler and paid in part for his purchase of the newspaper *Münchener Beobachter* from the Thule Society, which became the Nazi Party's official organ the *Völkischer Beobachter*,

> "Another encounter in Vienna lives in my memory as something even more extraordinary. Some one introduced me to Arthur Trebitsch, and I spent a whole evening with him. His name was somewhat known through his books, *Geist und Judentum* and *Deutscher Geist oder Judentum?*, but I for my part had never heard of him; so I found myself quite unprepared for the strange discussion which ensued.
>
> Arthur Trebitsch was a peculiar and pathetic personality, a full-blooded Jew who was an apostate from his people and his religion; who uncompromisingly attacked the Jew and the Jewish spirit in his speeches and writings, yet could not enter into the Gentile world with which he strove to ally himself. Whether the attitude which turned his life into a tragedy sprang from his mind or his emotions, I cannot say. This was the first time I had talked at length with an intellectual and erudite Jew about the German-Jewish problem, and though even among Gentiles I was now discovering a widespread doubt of the Nazi program, I was amazed to find that Trebitsch still passionately endorsed it.
>
> Trebitsch did not consider himself a Jew, either spiritually or physically, in spite of his two Jewish parents. Convinced that he was the result of a phenomenon which biologists call "mutation,' he presented himself as a Gentile. Seriously believing that he looked very much like Houston Stewart Chamberlain, the declared scientific enemy of the Jewish people, he produced as proof one of his pamphlets which showed their pictures facing each other. Looking at his eyes and fair hair, I had to agree that the photographs bore a striking resemblance.

Never before had I considered the Jewish problem from the standpoint of the individual Jew who finds much to condemn in his own people and dares to say so. Trebitsch was an extreme case; yet some of his findings were sound. Discovering that his people were resentful of criticism, he had turned his coat—without finding it any warmer. My mind reverted at once to the two famous apostates, Spinoza and Uriel de Acosta, who were excommunicated from the synagogues, and I reflected that there is no more sorrowful destiny than that which overtakes those who alienate their own people without making friends elsewhere.

Trebitsch sought to convince me that he could be a valuable ally in the Nazi struggle. Intuition and reason told me to remain reserved. But it was distressing to witness the despair of this exhausted and high-strung man, who beyond question was sincere. Ostracized on one side and rejected on the other, he was indeed an outcast. The tragic overtones of our interview made a deep impression on me, and at the earliest moment I spoke about him at length with Rosenberg. Needless to say, there was no place for him in the Party."[626]

Douglas Reed wrote in 1938 of Moses Pinkeles, a. k. a. Ignatz (Ignatius) Trebitsch-Lincoln, a Jew who financed Hitler, and of Zionists who sponsored Hitler,

"Oblivion for a few years, and then came the Kapp Putsch in Germany, the first of the Nationalist conspiracies to overthrow the democratic liberal regime that was so kind to the Jews, and reinstate the big business men, big landlords, monarchists, militarists, in the seats of the mighty in Germany. Who was a leading figure in this short-lived seizure of power? Trebitsch Lincoln, now a German die-hard. Among the other sympathizers was a relatively unknown man, one Adolf Hitler. Trebitsch Lincoln on the side of the anti-Semites? Of course, he was a Christian. [***] If you doubt me, think of Trebitsch Lincoln leading the anti-Semites down the Wilhelmstrasse to the seat of power. But I can show you the modern counterpart of Trebitsch Lincoln, and I don't mean those pro-Hitler Jews who were said by rumour to have marched round Berlin in the early Nazi days carrying a banner with the legend 'Hinaus mit uns!'—'Chuck us out!'"[627]

Eustace Mullins, Ezra Pound's authorized biographer, stated on Daryl Bradford Smith's radio program *The French Connection*, that the German-Jewish bankers Warburg and Oppenheimer marched with the Nazis carrying signs that read "throw us out".

Prominent Zionist and author of the *Encyclopaedia Judaica; das Judentum in Geschichte und Gegenwart*, Jakob Klatzkin stated in 1925,

> "The national viewpoint taught us to understand the true nature of antisemitism, and this understanding widens the horizons of our national outlook. [***] In the age of enlightenment antisemitism was included among the phenomena that are likely to disappear along with other forms of prejudice and iniquity. The antisemites, so the rule stated, were the laggard elements in the march of progress. Hence, our fate is dependent on the advance of human culture, and its victory is our victory. [***] In the period of Zionism, we learned that antisemitism was a psychic-social phenomenon that derives from our existence as a nation within a nation. Hence, it cannot change, until we attain our national end. But if Zionism had fully understood its own implications, it would have arrived, not merely as a psycho-sociological explanation of this phenomenon, but also as a justification of it. It is right to protest against its crude expressions, but we are unjust to it and distort its nature so long as we do not recognize that essentially it is a defense of the integrity of a nation, in whose throat we are stuck, neither to be swallowed nor to be expelled. [***] And when we are unjust to this phenomenon, we are unfair to our own people. If we do not admit the rightfulness of antisemitism, we deny the rightfulness of our own nationalism. If our people is deserving and willing to live its own national life, then it is an alien body thrust into the nations among whom it lives, an alien body that insists on its own distinctive identity, reducing the domain of their life. It is right, therefore, that they should fight against us for their national integrity. [***] Know this, that it is a good sign for us that the nations of the world combat us. It is proof that our national image is not yet utterly blurred, our alienism is still felt. If the war against us should cease or be weakened, it would indicate that our image has become indistinct and our alienism softened. We shall not obtain equality of rights anywhere save at the price of an explicit or implied declaration that we are no longer a national body, but part of the body of the host-nation;

or that we are willing to assimilate and become part of it. [***] Instead of establishing societies for defense against the antisemites, who want to reduce our rights, we should establish societies for defense against our friends who desire to defend our rights. [***] When Moses came to redeem the children of Israel, their leaders said to him, 'You have made our odor evil in the eyes of Pharaoh and in the eyes of his servants, giving them a sword with which to kill us.' Nevertheless, Moses persisted in worsening the situation of the people, and he saved them."[628]

Who was the "devil" the political Zionists commissioned to shake up the Jews of Europe? When Hitler came to power, some Zionists asked all Jews to let him do as he wished. Some Zionists even hailed him as their savior.

Leon Simon wrote in the introduction to a collection of Einstein's Zionist works, that emancipation posed a greater threat to the Jewish "race" than the problems of the unemancipated. Hitler soon thereafter unemancipated the Jews. Simon wrote in 1930, *inter alia*,

> "THERE are two main ways of approach to Zionism. One starts from those Jews who are made to suffer for being Jews, the other from the smaller number who are not. In the one case Zionism means the transfer of masses of Jews from countries in which they are obviously not wanted to a country which they might call their own; in the other case it means the re-creation in Palestine of a Hebraic type of life, which will be regarded by all Jews as the embodiment of their own distinctive outlook and ideals, and will thus help to counteract the inevitable tendency of the Jews, when they are not driven back on themselves by external restrictions, to lose their sense of being a separate people.
>
> Of these two conceptions of Zionism, the former has the more direct and obvious appeal. The fact that masses of Jews are made to suffer for the crime of being Jews and wishing to remain Jews is too patent to call for demonstration; and, while it is true that in some countries Jewish disabilities have been removed so far as that can be done by statute, bitter experience engenders a sceptical attitude towards the idea that universal emancipation will provide a panacea for the Jew's troubles. In the first place, the countries with the largest numbers of Jews are not all eager to admit them to full equality; and in the second place, even

where equality has been accorded, dislike of the Jew often makes itself felt too strongly for his liking or comfort. Hence, from the point of view of a Jew who wishes to see his people better off in the world than it is to-day, or has been these many centuries, there is much to commend a scheme which sets out to cut at the root of the trouble by removing all the victims of anti-Semitism to a land of their own. By contrast with this perfectly simple and intelligible idea, the other conception of Zionism appears abstruse, almost other-worldly. The problem to which it offers a solution is one of which the existence, let alone the urgency, is not, readily realised by ordinary men and women. It requires no great exercise of thought or imagination to appreciate the unenviable position of the Jewish masses, or the desirability of transporting them to a safe home of refuge. It is less easy to recognise that the emancipated Jew presents, from the point of view of Jewish survival, at least as difficult a problem as the unemancipated; that the very removal of restrictions on the political and economic freedom of the Jews in this or that country creates conditions which are more inimical than persecution to the maintenance of whatever is worthily distinctive of the Jew as such; that the consequent disintegration of an ancient people, involving the disappearance of one of the world's great cultures, is even more tragic than the material ills of the Jewish masses; and that the paramount need of the hour is a safe home of refuge for the Jewish spirit."[629]

4.6 Einstein a Subtle Hitler Apologist

When the "Hitlerites" showed their strength in the elections, political might paid for by Jewish financiers, Einstein and some other Zionist leaders told Jews not worry but to close ranks and unite. Of course, should Hitler lead the country into war, it would benefit bankers, investors, and factory owners. Hitler's anti-Semitism benefitted the political Zionists. An article entitled "Fascists Walk Out of Berlin Council", *The New York Times* on 19 September 1930 on page 9 quoted the *Jewish Telegraphic Agency*, which quoted Albert Einstein,

"There is no reason for despair,' declared Professor Einstein, 'for the Hitler vote is only a symptom, not necessarily of anti-Jewish hatred but of momentary resentment caused by economic misery and unemployment within the ranks of misguided

628 Albert Einstein: The Incorrigible Racist

German youth. I hope that the momentary fever and wave will rapidly fall.

'During the more dangerous Dreyfus period almost the entire French nation was to be found in the anti-Semitic camp. I hope that as soon as the situation improves the German people will also find their road to clarity."

Einstein acted as a Nazi apologist and tried to subvert any organized Jewish reaction to Hitler—he effectively promoted Hitler at a critical time in history. Many Jews in Germany failed to respond to Hitler's victory with an organized reaction, in part because treacherous Jews like Albert Einstein led them to believe that Hitler would soon be unseated and that Nazism was an ephemeral malady they need not bother too much about.

At a time when anti-Zionist Jews were desperately trying to organize all Jews to fight against the Fascists, while many Zionists were encouraging the Fascists,[630] Einstein wanted to remove Jews from Germany and was confused by his own racist hypocrisy. Following Hitler's election victory in 1933, Albert Einstein commented, merely parroting the Zionist Party line,[631]

"For the time being, I see the National Socialist movement as merely a product of the current economic crisis and the teething pains of the Republic. The solidarity of the Jews is for me an eternal commandment, but I feel a specific reaction to the election results would be entirely inappropriate."

"Ich sehe in der nationalsozialistischen Bewegung einstweilen nur eine Folgeerscheinung der momentanen wirtschaftlichen Notlage und eine Kinder-Krankheit der Republik. Solidarität der Juden halte ich immer für geboten, aber eine besondere Reaktion auf das Wahlergebnis für ganz unzweckmässig."[632]

At the time Einstein made this cavalier statement, he knew that the Nazis were going to annihilate the Jews of Europe—as did Zionist Nazi apologist Ludwig Lewisohn, the dear friend, and the lover, of the famous Hitler-promoter George Sylvester Viereck.[633] Albert Einstein wrote to Gustav Bucky on 15 July 1933,

"I really do believe that any action aimed at keeping Jews in Germany would have the effect of speeding up their annihilation."[634]

In 1933, Einstein told British Prime Minister (1923-1929, 1935-1937) Stanley Baldwin of Hitler's plan for world conquest and that Hitler would perhaps cause a new world war. Baldwin, who was later criticized for not preparing England to face Germany, told Einstein that Great Britain had her allies.[635] Einstein did take a firmer stand against the Nazis and against the Prussian Academy of Sciences in 1933 than many Zionists, and was accused of public anti-Germanism by that Academy. In this exchange, Einstein fought for the rights of Jews to human dignity and the right to equality under the law. What Einstein meant by "annihilation" in 1933 is not necessarily clear. He may have meant the rooting out of Jews from Germany by cutting off their means of earning a living and forcing them to Palestine—as the Nazis and Zionists had planned,[636] or he may have meant mass murder.

4.7 Einstein's Seething Racist Hatred and Rabid Nationalism

The smear tactics of Zionists are well known. Einstein's smear tactics gained him and his defenders an international reputation as agitators and reckless defamers. A "Biographical Sketch" issued to U. S. Army Intelligence sometime in 1940 stated,

> "The origin of the case is that in Berlin, even in the political free and easy period of 1923 to 1929, the Einstein home was known as a Communist center and clearing house. Mrs. and Miss Einstein were always prominent at all extreme radical meetings and demonstrations. When the German police tried to bridge some of the extreme Communist activities, the Einstein villa at Wannsee was found to be the hiding place of Moscow envoys, etc. The Berlin conservative press at the time featured this, but the authorities were hesitant to take any action, as the more radical press immediately accused these reporters as being Anti-Semites."[637]

The historic record bears out the accusation that Einstein and his sponsors had the means and the will to smear innocents in their efforts to redirect public attention away from their own vile actions. It had become a habit for them, and they took every opportunity, no matter how unjustified, to raise the issue of race, paint themselves as victims of racist oppression, and often went so far as to accuse innocent persons of racism. The ridiculous extremes of this political maneuvering were manifest long before the Holocaust, and reached across the English Channel.

In 1919, hypocritical, racist, ethnocentric and insulting Einstein smeared all Germans, all English, and the reporter who had helped to promote him,

> "A final comment. The description of me and my circumstances in *The Times* shows an amusing feat of imagination on the part of the writer. By an application of the theory of relativity to the taste of readers, today in Germany I am called a German man of science, and in England I am represented as a Swiss Jew. If I come to regarded as a *bête noire*, the descriptions will be reversed, and I shall become a Swiss Jew for the Germans and a German man of science for the English!"[638]

Einstein, either directly, or through someone else, took his line from Bernard Lazare's *L'Antisémitisme: Son Histoire et Ses Causes* of 1894,

> "In general the Jews, even the revolutionaries, have kept the Jewish spirit, and if they have given up religion and faith, they have nevertheless been formed, thanks to their ancestry and their education, by the influence of Jewish nationalism. This is true in a very special fashion of the Jewish revolutionaries who lived in the first half of this century. Heinrich Heine and Karl Marx are two typical examples. Heine is held to be German in France. In Germany he is accused of being French. He was above all a Jew."[639]

A couple of years after Einstein made his comment, in June of 1921, *The Jewish Chronicle* reported,

> "The *Times* of Monday last, by the by, published an interview with Einstein. The interviewer gave minute personal descriptions of the remarkable scientist, and yet did not venture to suggest that he was a Jew. If (the *Jewish World* comments) he had been a Bolshevik or a reprehensible character of any kind, we doubt not the fact would have dawned upon the *Times* correspondent that he was a Jew, and would have found place in what he had to say. Strange how circumstances alter one's point of view!"[640]

Strange, indeed, that no matter what a *Times* correspondent said about Einstein; either Einstein, or some extremist among his supporters, would viciously smear that correspondent as a bigot, without any grounds whatsoever. And for what purpose? This appears to have been a habit for them, a pernicious habit and a divisive habit meant to perpetuate, intensify and generate hatred, fear and conflict—for political Zionist purposes.

Einstein's ardent nationalism became so extreme, that it played into the hands of his political foes, and became an example for their generalizations. Max Nordau described the pernicious habits of racists, with no small measure of hypocrisy, in his address to the First Zionist Congress in 1897,

"No one has ever tried to justify these terrible accusations by facts. At most, now and then, an individual Jew, the scum of his race and of mankind, is triumphantly cited as an example, and contrary to all laws of logic, the example is made general. This tendency is psychologically correct. It is the practice of human intellect to invent for the prejudices, which sentiment has called forth, a cause seemingly reasonable. Probably wisdom has long been acquainted with this psychological law, and puts it in fairly expressive words: 'If you have to drown a dog,' says the proverb, 'you must first declare him to be mad.' All kinds of vices are falsely attributed to the Jews, because one wishes to convince himself that he has a right to detest them. But the pre-existing sentiment is the detestation of the Jews."[641]

Einstein detested Germans throughout his life. He hated Germans long before the Nazi Party was formed. Einstein's racist nationalism rivaled and perhaps even surpassed Physics in Einstein's self-image, making him the ideological twin of the Nazis—one who wanted to exterminate the Germans—one who wanted to exterminate all Gentile Europeans. He was described in the *Daily Graphic* as,

"A man of the most simple tastes, he lives in a lofty flat in Berlin. He is an indifferent linguist, and will lecture in German, but he has a passion for music, and beyond this his scientific pursuits and his work for Zionism comprise his sole interests."[642]

While hiding from Arvid Reuterdahl's challenge to a public debate,[643] Einstein announced through his secretary Salomon Ginzberg during his famous stay in America,

> "I came here with one object—the promotion of the establishment of the Hebrew University in Jerusalem. [***] The great purpose of my mission to this country must not be overshadowed by my theory. I will be here a short time, and all of that time must be devoted to the great Palestine reconstruction project."[644]

Einstein stated in an interview following his visit to America,

> "I really went on behalf of the Jewish cause. Yes, I have placed my name and indeed my self in the service of the Zionist movement to make propaganda for Palestine, and the true purpose of the America trip was to collect money for a fund to establish a university in Jerusalem."[645]

Nationalism became so consuming a personal passion for Einstein, that he took advantage of his fraudulently-based fame to promote the political cause. R. S. Shankland stated,

> "About publicity Einstein told me that he had been *given* a publicity value which he did not *earn*. Since he had it he would use it if it would do good; otherwise not. [*Emphasis found in the original*]"[646]

His famous trip to America was not made to promote or celebrate the theory of relativity, but to promote his personal vision of nationalism and to raise money for this cause. Though this was absolutely his right, many found Einstein's exploitation of his scientific fame for political purposes distasteful—to the point of being disgraceful.

As early as February of 1914, loyal German Jews publicly protested against anti-German Zionism. Albert Einstein was a virulently racist oddity among German Jews. German Jews knew quite well that the Zionists were planning to deliberately place all Jews in harm's way and ruin Germany. *The New York Times* wrote on 8 February 1914, Section 3, page 3,

"PROTEST AGAINST ZIONISTS.

German-Jewish Organizations Say They Harm Jews and Fatherland.

Special Cable to THE NEW YORK TIMES.

BERLIN, Feb. 7.—Several Jewish organizations of Germany have joined in a protest against what they call the 'insidious German national Chauvinism,' which is being carried on in the name of German Jews by German Zionists.

It is alleged that the Zionists are resorting to methods that must bring the whole Jewish cause into disrepute at home and abroad and sow seeds of discord between Christians and Jews in Germany itself.

The protest, which has taken the form of a strong public statement, addressed to the press of the country, urges that the mere matter of faith which separates German Jews from their fellow-citizens must not be exploited by overzealous co-religionists to the disadvantage of both Jews and the Fatherland."

In 1930, some German Jews demanded that Albert Einstein stop using his scientific fame to promote racism, disloyalty and "interracial" strife. *The New York Times* reported on 7 December 1930 on page 11,

"The National German-Jewish Union, a small group of extreme nationalist and anti-Zionist Jews, protested against Professor Einstein using his world-fame as a scientist for 'propagating Zionism.'"

After the Second World War, Jews again criticized Einstein for his nationalistic Zionism. Einstein responded,

"In my opinion condemning the Zionist movement as 'nationalistic' is unjustified. [***] Thus already our precarious situation forces us to stand together irrespective of our citizenship."[647]

Einstein parroted the Zionist dogma that ethnic, racial and religious unity among peoples of Jewish descent around the world constituted a sovereignty without physical borders, which should be organized around a community in Palestine, but which sovereign status should be intrinsic to anyone of Jewish descent anywhere in the world—since a Jewish dispersion had allegedly taken place two thousand years ago. Theodor

Herzl stated that anti-Semitism was justified and that the only means to end it was segregation. Chaim Weizmann made it very clear that Zionism is not a form of self-defense against prejudice, but is instead an indefensible product of Jewish bigotry. Weizmann proclaimed,

> "The sufferings of Russian Jewry never were the cause of Zionism. The fundamental cause of Zionism was, and is, the ineradicable national striving of Jewry to have a home of its own—a national center, a national home with a national Jewish life."[648]

German Jews around the world had largely assimilated into various nations and cultures and were often quite successful. They were leading and highly productive members of their societies. Eastern European Jews were often living in intolerable conditions and sought to emigrate to the West. They looked to their religious brethren in the West for help, but were often resented and rejected, because they clung to their ancient Jewish racism, and their desire to flee their neighbors and their call to other Jews in other countries was itself a manifestation of their racist tribalism.

Many German Jews feared that these clannish Easterners would inspire anti-Semitism and resented their presence.[649] Weizmann feared that the Russian Revolution would put an end to Zionism, because it achieved the freedom of Russian Jews,

> "At that time the whole world—and the Jews more than anyone else—had been thrilled by the overthrow of the czarist regime in Russia, and the establishment of the liberal Kerensky regime."[650]

Weizmann was a rabid anti-assimilationist.[651] He wasn't simply after social justice for Jews. Weizmann was after self-imposed segregation of the Jews.

The Zionists are the product of an ancient racist and genocidal religious mythology. This religious mythology is largely political and racist, and it affects even secular Jews, some of whom view it as the product of Jewish genes, and therefore of intrinsic value in defining Jews and their actions. The prophets need not have been inspired by God, for they were inspired by a yet more divine source, Jewish blood. The creation myth was turned on its head such that some secular Jews stated that the Jews created a fellow Jew, "God", to express the urges of their "Jewish blood"—their "Jewish soul". Those many secular Jews who rejected this racist viewpoint, also could not have helped but have been somewhat affected by the legacy of centuries of Jewish culture which had evolved in the continuing presence of religious Jewish racism.

The Hebrew Bible contains numerous stories of the segregation, punishment and genocide of assimilationist Jews by anti-assimilationist Jews. For example, *Numbers*, Chapter 25, states:

"And Israel abode in Shittim, and the people began to commit whoredom with the daughters of Moab. 2 And they called the people unto the sacrifices of their gods: and the people did eat, and bowed down to their gods. 3 And Israel joined himself unto Baal-peor: and the anger of the LORD was kindled against Israel. 4 And the LORD said unto Moses, Take all the heads of the people, and hang them up before the LORD against the sun, that the fierce anger of the LORD may be turned away from Israel. 5 And Moses said unto the judges of Israel, Slay ye every one his men that were joined unto Baal-peor. 6 ¶ And, behold, one of the children of Israel came and brought unto his brethren a Midianitish woman in the sight of Moses, and in the sight of all the congregation of the children of Israel, who *were* weeping *before* the door of the tabernacle of the congregation. 7 And when Phinehas, the son of Eleazar, the son of Aaron the priest, saw *it*, he rose up from among the congregation, and took a javelin in his hand; 8 and he went after the man of Israel into the tent, and thrust both of them through, the man of Israel, and the woman through her belly. So the plague was stayed from the children of Israel. 9 And those that died in the plague were twenty and four thousand. 10 ¶ And the LORD spake unto Moses, saying, 11 Phinehas, the son of Eleazar, the son of Aaron the priest, hath turned my wrath away from the children of Israel, while he was zealous for my sake among them, that I consumed not the children of Israel in my jealousy. 12 Wherefore say, Behold, I give unto him my covenant of peace: 13 and he shall have it, and his seed after him, even the covenant of an everlasting priesthood; because he was zealous for his God, and made an atonement for the children of Israel. 14 Now the name of the Israelite that was slain, *even* that was slain with the Mid'i-anitish woman, *was* Zimri, the son of Salu, a prince of a chief house among the Simeonites. 15 And the name of the Midianitish woman that was slain *was* Cozbi, the daughter of

Zur; he *was* head over a people, *and* of a chief house in Midian. 16 And the LORD spake unto Moses, saying, 17 Vex the Midianites, and smite them: 18 for they vex you with their wiles, wherewith they have beguiled you in the matter of Peor, and in the matter of Cozbi, the daughter of a prince of Midian, their sister, which was slain in the day of the plague for Peor's sake."

Since many Zionists were atheists, or pretended to be atheists to assuage Christian and Moslem concerns, as well as secular and religious Jewish fears, and since Herzl and others had made Zionism a political question rather than a religious question, Zionism became strictly a matter of racist segregation.

There was a definite rift between Eastern European Jews and German Jews, who feared that the presence of these Easterners, especially when led by rabidly racist Zionists, would inspire and intensify anti-Semitism. Einstein and Weizmann wanted to force Western European Jews into sponsoring the emigration of Eastern European Jews—who appeared in Western Europe like peoples from another time—and who would make a suitable slave labor force for the Zionists.[652] In turn, these highly racist Eastern European Jews resented the assimilationist Western Jews. Many of the Jews of Palestine also resented the Eastern European Jews for creating conflicts in Palestine, where Jews, Moslems and Christians had been living together in peace.

A racist unity among Jews had long been a goal of the political Zionists despite the resistence they encountered from Jews around the world. Max Nordau wrote, soon after the First Zionist Congress in Basel in August of 1897:

"Die Voraussetzung des politischen Zionismus ist, dass es ein jüdisches Volk gibt. Das gerade leugnen die Assimilationsjuden und die von ihnen besoldeten geistlosen, salbungsvoll schwatzenden Rabbiner."

and,

"{*Margin Note:* Die Assimilanten} Viele Juden, namentlich des Westens, haben innerlich vollkommen mit dem Judenthum gebrochen und sie werden es wahrscheinlich bald auch äusserlich thun, und wenn nicht sie, dann ihre Kinder oder Enkel. Diese wünschen ganz unter ihren christlichen Landsleuten aufzugehen. Sie empfinden es als schwere Störung, dass andere Juden neben ihnen ihr besonderes Volksthum laut verkünden und reinlich Scheidung zwischen sich und den anderen Völkern fordern. Ihre grosse Angst ist, in ihrem Geburtslande, dessen freie Bürger sie sind, als Fremde bezeichnet zu werden. Sie fürchten, dass man dies mehr als je vorher thun wird, wenn ein grosser Theil des jüdischen Volkes offen die Rechte eines selbständigen Volkes für sich fordert, und nun gar, wenn erst irgendwo in der Welt wirklich ein politisches und culturelles Centrum des Judenthums entsteht, um das sich Millionen national geeinigter Juden gruppieren.

{*Margin Note:* Zwei Millionen gegen zehn} Alle diese Gefühle der Assimilationsjuden sind verständlich. Sie sind auch von ihrem Standpunkt aus berechtigt. Aber sie haben keinen Anspruch darauf, dass der Zionismus ihnen zu Liebe Selbstmord begehe. Die Juden, die in ihrem Geburtslande zufrieden und glücklich sind und die Zumuthung, es aufzugeben, empört zurückweisen, sind etwa ein Sechstel des jüdischen Volkes, sagen wir 2 Millionen von zwölf. Die übrigen fünf Sechstel, zehn Millionen, fühlen sich in ihrem Aufenthaltsorte sehr unglücklich und sie haben auch allen Grund dazu. Diesen zehn Millionen ist nicht zuzumuthen, dass sie sich für immer widerstandlos in ihre Knechtschaft fügen, dass sie jedes Streben nach Erlösung aus ihrer Noth aufgeben, bloss damit das Behagen der zwei Millionen glücklicher und zufriedener Juden nicht gestört werde."[653]

Theodor Herzl wrote of the utility of using Eastern European Jewish peasants as a slave labor force in his book *The Jewish State* and in his diaries. The Zionist Nazis helped the political Zionists to train this slave labor force and to condition them to accept their fate. After the Holocaust, Chaim Weizmann tried to blame assimilatory Jews for the tragic events the Zionists deliberately caused,

"[Rathenau's] attitude was, of course, all too typical of that of many assimilated German Jews; they seemed to have no idea that they were sitting on a volcano; they believed quite sincerely that such difficulties as admittedly existed for German Jews were purely temporary and transitory phenomena, primarily due to the influx of East European Jews, who did not fit into the framework of German life, and thus offered targets for anti-Semitic attacks."[654]

Joachim Prinz explored the issue in his book *Wir Juden,* Erich Reiss, Berlin, (1934), pp. 50-55. Albert Einstein wrote to Max Born on 22 March 1934 that the same impediments Western European Jews had placed against the immigration of Eastern European Jews during their migration to the West were now being instituted against German Jews by the Jews of America, France and England,

> "It is particularly unfortunate that the satiated Jews of the countries which have hitherto been spared cling to the foolish hope that they can safeguard themselves by keeping quiet and making patriotic gestures, just as the German Jews used to do. For the same reason they sabotaged the granting of asylum to German Jews, just as the latter did to Jews from the East. This applies just as much in America as in France and England."[655]

Einstein's personality interfered with his attempts to open up immigration for Eastern European Jews and his bigoted hatred worked against his cause. In the long run, Einstein's racism and provocative statements proved horrifically counter-productive and deliberately aided anti-Semitic racists in their ascent to power in Europe, which might have been his goal all along. Einstein later avowed that the plan for the inhuman carnage of which many Europeans and European governments eventually proved capable under Zionist leadership, appeared in Hitler's *Mein Kampf,* which was written in the 1920's.[656] He knew well what to expect.

Hitler's mentor, Dietrich Eckart, who was a member the Zionists' anti-Semitic propaganda school the *Thule-Gesellschaft,* exploited Jewish racism and anti-Germanism for propaganda purposes. Dietrich Eckart wrote, quoting Hitler, in Eckart's *Der Bolschewismus von Moses bis Lenin: Zwiegespräch zwischen Adolf Hitler und mir,*

> "'Send me a box full of German soil, so that I can at least symbolically defile the accursed country,' wrote the German Jew, Börne; [*Notation:* Ludwig Börne (alias Löb Baruch), *Briefe aus Paris* (Hamburg, 1832), I.] and Heinrich Heine sniffed out Germany's future from a toilet bowl. [*Notation:* Heinrich (alias Chaim) Heine, *Deutschland, ein Wintermärchen* (1844).] The physicist, Einstein, whom the Jewish publicity agents celebrate as a second Kepler, explained he would have nothing to do with German nationalism. He considered 'deceitful' the custom of the Central Association of German Citizens of Jewish Faith

[*Notation: Zentralverein deutscher Staatsbürger jüdischen Glaubens.* {Translator}] of concerning themselves only with the religious interests of the Jews and not with their racial community also. A rare bird? No, only one who believed his people already safely in control, and thus considered it no longer necessary to keep up pretenses. In the Central Association itself, the mask has already fallen. A Dr. Brünn frankly admitted there that the Jews could have no German national spirit. [*Notation:* Artur Brünn, *Im Deutschen Reich* (the periodical of the *Zentralverein*) 1913, No. 8.] We always mistake their unprincipled exertions to accommodate themselves to all and everyone for impulses of the heart. Whenever they see an advantage to be gained by adopting a certain pose, they never hesitate, and certainly wouldn't let ethical considerations stand in their way. How many Galician Jews have first become Germans, then Englishmen, and finally Americans! And every time in the twinkling of an eye. With startling rapidity they change their nationality back and forth, and wherever their feet touch, there resounds either the 'Watch on the Rhine,' or the 'Marsellaise,' or 'Yankee Doodle.' Dr. Heim does not once question the fact that our Warburgs, our Bleichroders, or our Mendelssohns are able to transfer their patriotism as well as their residence of today to London or to New York on the morrow. 'On the sands of Brandenburg an Asiatic horde!' Walther Rathenau once blurted out about the Berlin Jews. [*Notation:* Walther Rathenau, *Berliner Kulturzentren*, 1913. Rathenau was a Jewish war profiteer in World War I and later a minister in the Weimar government. He was executed by German patriots in 1922. {Translator}] He forgot to add that the same horde is on the Isar, the Elbe, the Main, the Thames, the Seine, the Hudson, the Neva, and the Volga. And all of them with the same deceit toward their neighbors."[657]

Should Albert Einstein be forgiven as an ethnocentric and racist victim of his time and political affiliations, who defended "his people" from what appeared to him to be a threat to their very existence—the dangers of assimilation and philo-Semitism? Early on, Jews with far more sense than Einstein organized to defend themselves from the fanatical and racist Zionists, knowing that the political games of the racists on both sides of the "Jewish question" would result in tragedy and trauma for the world's Jews. Klaus J. Herrmann wrote,

"To counter the coalition of antisemites and Zionists, in 1912, within the Association for Liberal Judaism, a number of distinguished leaders of Germany's Jewish communities decided to form an *Anti-Zionist Committee*. This Committee [***] took on the task of 'enlightening the German Jews on and combating Zionism.'"[658]

Paul Ehrenfest saw the harm racist and segregationist Zionist Jews were doing to his fellow Jews.[659] Since all reasonable Jews knew the destruction that would inevitably follow from Einstein's ideology, Einstein should have known it, and indeed he did know it. One outgrowth of these anti-Zionist organizations, which formed to protect themselves, is Neturei Karta. Rabbi Moshe Shonfeld documented the collaboration of the Zionists with the Nazis and the deliberate human sacrifice of innocent Jews in order to establish the "Jewish State".[660] Numerous other Jewish authors have chastised Zionist Jews for their behavior towards other Jews during the Holocaust.[661] Rabbi E. Schwartz published a statement on behalf of the American Neturei Karta in *The New York Times* on 18 May 1993,

"To achieve the goal of statehood the Zionists have always deliberately provoked anti-Semitism. [***] Their interest was not to save Jews, on the contrary, more spilling of Jewish blood would strengthen their demand of the nations for the creation of their state."[662]

Albert Einstein, the "Person of the Century" who sought to promote and foment anti-Semitism wherever he went, stated in 1921,

"On the other hand, anti-Semitism in Germany also has consequences that, from a Jewish point of view, should be welcomed. I believe German Jewry owes its continued existence to anti-Semitism."[663]

Contrast this with Nobel Peace Prize laureate Elie Wiesel's statement in 1968,

"Every Jew, somewhere in his being, should set apart a zone of hate—healthy, virile hate—for what the German personifies and for what persists in the German. To do otherwise would be a betrayal of the dead."[664]

Lieutenant General Rafael Eytan, outgoing Chief of Staff of the Israeli Army, stated on 12 April 1983,

> "When we have settled the land, all the Arabs will be able to do about it will be to scurry around like drugged roaches in a bottle."[665]

In an article entitled, "An Israeli Mayor Is Under Scrutiny", *The New York Times* reported on 6 June 1989, on page 5,

> "Rabbi Yitzhak Ginsburg had offered biblical justification for the view that the spilling of non-Jewish blood was a lesser offense than the spilling of Jewish blood. 'Any trial based on the assumption that Jews and goyim are equal is a total travesty of justice,' he said."

Rabbi Yaacov Perrin was quoted by Clyde Haberman, in an article entitled, "Arafat Dismisses Rabin's Moves as 'Hollow'", *The New York Times*, (28 February 1994), p. 1. Rabbi Perrin stated,

> "One million Arabs are not worth a Jewish fingernail[.]"

Wiesel has stressed his view that the Holocaust should be seen as a uniquely tragic event in History. However, this exclusivist view of Jewish History predates the Holocaust by at least a century, for example in a statement from 1845,

> "The sufferings of the Jews—whether the 'wringing out of the dregs of a cup of trembling' from Jehovah, or not—have far exceeded all other experience, and the common measure of human endurance."[666]

After the First World War Einstein and some of his friends alluded to much earlier conversations with Einstein where he had correctly predicted the eventual outcome of the war. In his diaries, Romain Rolland recorded his conversations with Einstein in Switzerland at their meeting of 16 September 1915,

> "What I hear from [Einstein] is not exactly encouraging, for it shows the impossibility of arriving at a lasting peace with Germany without first totally crushing it. Einstein says the

642   Albert Einstein: The Incorrigible Racist

situation looks to him far less favorable than a few months back. The victories over Russia have reawakened German arrogance and appetite. The word 'greedy' seems to Einstein best to characterize Germany. [***] Einstein does not expect any renewal of Germany out of itself; it lacks the energy for it, and the boldness for initiative. He hopes for a victory of the Allies, which would smash the power of Prussia and the dynasty. . . . Einstein and Zangger dream of a divided Germany—on the one side Southern Germany and Austria, on the other side Prussia. [***] We speak of the deliberate blindness and the lack of psychology in the Germans."[667]

Jews often sought to Balkanize nations so as to weaken the power of any faction within a nation and to created perpetual agitation between the nations which could be exploited for profit and other Jewish gains. For example, the Rothschilds created the American Civil War and profited from the debts it generated. They hoped to divide America into two nations and to pit these against one another. They were successful. Jews had long been pitting North German Protestants against South German and Austrian Catholics. Jews were the motive force behind the *Kulturkampf*. After creating these divides and promoting perpetual agitations amongst neighbors, Jewry could then fund one side against the other to destroy it whenever Jewry decided to wreck a given nation.

Einstein's dreams during the First World War remind one of the "Carthaginian Peace" of the Henry Morgenthau, Jr. plan for the destruction of Germany following the Second World War. Morgenthau worked with Lord Cherwell (Frederick Alexander Lindemann), Churchill's friend and advisor, who planned to bomb German civilian populations into submission. Lindemann studied under Einstein's friend, Walther Nernst, who worked with Fritz Haber, a Jewish developer of poisonous gas. James Bacque argues that the Allies, under the direction of General Eisenhower, starved hundreds of thousands, if not millions of German prisoners of war to death. Dwight David Eisenhower was called "the terrible Swedish-Jew" in his yearbook for West Point, *The 1915 Howitzer*, West Point, New York, (1915), p. 80. He was also called "Ike", as in. . . Eisenhower? The Soviets also abused countless German POW's after the Second World War.[668]

Einstein often spoke in genocidal and racist terms against Germany, and for the Jews and England, and he betrayed Germany before, during and after the First World War. Einstein wrote to Paul Ehrenfest on 22 March 1919,

"[The Allied Powers] whose victory during the war I had felt would be by far the lesser evil are now proving to be *only slightly* the lesser evil. [***] I get most joy from the emergence of the Jewish state in Palestine. It does seem to me that our kinfolk really are more sympathetic (at least less brutal) than these horrid Europeans. Perhaps things can only improve if only the Chinese are left, who refer to all Europeans with the collective noun 'bandits.'"[669]

Einstein avowed *circa* 3 April 1920, that,

"If what anti-Semites claim were true, then indeed there would be nothing weaker, more wretched, and unfit for life, than the German people".[670]

Einstein avowed that the anti-Semites' beliefs were true. Therefore, Einstein must have believed at least as early as 1920 that the Germans ought to be exterminated. When discussing the meaning of life, Einstein spoke to Peter A. Bucky about persons and creatures who "[do] not deserve to be in our world" and are "hardly fit for life."[671] Einstein's language is quite similar to the language of Hitler's "T4" *"Euthanasia-Programme"*.

After siding with Germany's enemies in the First World War—while living in Germany, and after intentionally provoking Germans into increased anti-Semitism, which he thought was good for Jews, and after defaming German Nobel Prize laureates in the international press to the point where they felt obliged to join Hitler's cause, which cause eventually resulted in the genocide of Europe's Jews; Einstein sponsored the production of genocidal weapons to mass murder Germans, whom he had hated all of his life, in the famous letter to President Roosevelt that Einstein signed urging Roosevelt to begin the development of atomic bombs. Einstein signed this letter before the alleged mass murder of Jews had begun.[672]

Genocidal Einstein callously asserted that the use of atomic bombs on civilian populations was "morally justified". I quote Einstein without delving into the question of who first bombed civilian centers,

"It should not be forgotten that the atomic bomb was made in this country as a preventive measure; it was to head off its use by the Germans, if they discovered it. The bombing of civilian centers was initiated by the Germans and adopted by the

Japanese. To it the Allies responded in kind—as it turned out, with greater effectiveness—and they were morally justified in doing so."[673]

Einstein advocated genocidal collective punishment,

"The Germans as an entire people are responsible for these mass murders and must be punished as a people if there is justice in the world and if the consciousness of collective responsibility in the nations is not to perish from the earth entirely."[674]

and,

"It is possible either to destroy the German people or keep them suppressed; it is not possible to educate them to think and act along democratic lines in the foreseeable future."[675]

Albrecht Fölsing has assembled a compilation of post-WW II quotations by Albert Einstein, which evince Einstein's lifelong habit of stereotyping people based on their ethnicity. Einstein again expressed his hatred after the war—a temptation Max Born had resisted,

"With the Germans having murdered my Jewish brethren in Europe, I do not wish to have anything more to do with Germans, not even with a relatively harmless Academy. [***] The crimes of the Germans are really the most hideous that the history of the so-called civilized nations has to show. [***] [It was] evident that a proud Jew no longer wishes to be connected with any kind of German official event or institution. [***] After the mass murder committed by the Germans against my Jewish brethren I do not wish any publications of mine to appear in Germany."[676]

Einstein wrote to Born on 15 September 1950 that his pathological hatred towards Germans predated the Nazi period,

"I have not changed my attitude to the Germans, which, by the way, dates not just from the Nazi period. All human beings are more or less the same from birth. The Germans, however, have a far more dangerous tradition than any of the other so-called civilized nations. The present behavior of these other nations towards the Germans merely proves to me how little human beings learn even from their most painful experiences."[677]

and on learning that Born would return to Germany, Einstein wrote on 12 October 1953,

"If anyone can be held responsible for the fact that you are migrating back to the land of the mass-murderers of our kinsmen, it is certainly your adopted fatherland — universally notorious for its parsimony."[678]

Einstein wanted to carry out the extermination of the Germans he had been planning for many decades before the Holocaust. Einstein could not forgive the fact that other nations forgave the Germans and did not take the opportunity the Zionists had created for the complete extermination of the German People, the extermination of Amalek.

4.8 The Final Solution of the Jewish Question is Zionism, but the Final Solution of the German Question is Extermination

The generally accepted history of the Wannsee-Konferenz of 20 January 1942 holds that the Nazis first proposed the party policy of the genocidal extermination of Jews on this date. Lesser known today is the fact that a Jewish American named Theodor Newman Kaufman advocated the genocidal sterilization of all Germans as a "final solution" in 1941 in his book *Germany Must Perish!*, Argyle Press, Newark, New Jersey, (1941), for which an ad was posted in *The New York Times* on 1 March 1941 on page 13. Kaufman had called for the sterilization of all Americans in 1939.

Kaufman promoted his book by sending out small black cardboard coffins with a note inside which read, "Read GERMANY MUST PERISH! Tomorrow you will receive your copy," to leading figures and persons in the media. This was followed by a copy of the book the next day. This book was briefly noted in "Latest Books Received", *The New York Times*, (16 March 1941), Book Reviews Section, pp. 28-30, at 29; which simply states, "A plan for permanent peace among civilized nations." *Time Magazine*, under the heading "A Modest Proposal", described the odd book, the strange method by which Kaufman had promoted it, and the peculiar history of Theodor Newman Kaufman, who claimed to have known members of Winston Churchill's family.[679] In an interesting aside, Albert Einstein's personal physician, Professor

Janos Plesch, became Winston Churchill's personal physician.[680]

Kaufman's book advocating the genocide of Germans was known to most Germans. *Germany Must Perish!* was condemned in German publications, which alleged that President Roosevelt had sponsored it and had even written passages in it. The book, which proposed the genocide of the Germans, provoked attacks on Jews in Germany.[681] To the Germans, *Germany Must Perish!* represented the climax of the generalized vilification of all Germans propagandized by enemies of Germany in the First World War, like Émile Durkheim.[682] At least as early as the 1860's, recalling the myth of Esau and Amalek, Zionist racist and National Socialist Moses Hess[683] argued that the "German race" had a genetically programmed antagonism towards the "Jewish race"—the implication being that one must destroy the other in order to survive. Hess cushions his blows by mentioning enlightened Germans who have supposedly overcome their alleged genetic compulsions to destroy Jews, but his genocidal hatred of Germans is clear.

Hess was an interesting figure. He married a Christian prostitute. He wrote together with Marx, then criticized him. Hess created many of the elements of National Socialism that would eventually become the National Socialist German Worker's Party, or "Nazi" Party.

With Kaufman's *Germany Must Perish!* as evidence, the Nazis told the German public that the Americans, under the direction of Jews, planned to exterminate the "German race" if the Allies won the war. This life and death struggle between the "German race" and the "Jewish race" was foretold in Hess' book of 1862, *Rom und Jerusalem: die letzte Nationalitätsfrage*, Eduard Wengler, Leipzig, (1862); English: *Rome and Jerusalem: A Study in Jewish Nationalism*, Bloch, New York, (1918).

Goebbels proclaimed that the inhumane crimes Germans had committed against Jews compelled Germany to fight to the very end, thereby maximizing German and Allied and European casualties and the destruction of Europe. At the end of the war, Hitler called for Germans to kill themselves, because they had proven themselves unworthy to live in the fight for survival. Some have alleged that Hitler was sent to destroy Germans, who many Jews had alleged were genetic or cultural enemies of Jews predisposed to destroy them. Hitler destroyed Europe with perpetual war and he destroyed "Red Assimilationist" Jews in order to punish them and to shock American Jews into embracing Zionism.

Einstein's genocidal statements hint at the proposed measures advocated in Kaufman's book of 1941. Among other things, Kaufman wrote,

"A final solution: Let Germany be policed forever by an international armed force? *Even if such a huge undertaking were feasible life itself would not have it so. As war begets war, suppression begets rebellion. Undreamed horrors would unfold.* Thus we find that there is no middle course; no act of mediation, no compromise to be compounded, no political or economic sharing to be considered. There is, in fine, no other solution except one: That Germany must perish forever from this earth! [***] There remains then but one mode of ridding the world forever of Germanism — and that is to stem the source from which issue those war-lusted souls, by preventing the people of Germany from ever again reproducing their kind. This modern method, known to science as Eugenic Sterilization, is at once practical, humane and thorough. Sterilization has become a byword of science as the best means of ridding the human race of its misfits: the degenerate, the insane, the hereditary criminal. [***] The population of Germany, excluding conquered and annexed territories, is about 70,000,000, almost equally divided between male and female. To achieve the purpose of German extinction it would be necessary to only sterilize some 48,000,000—a figure which excludes, because of their limited power to procreate, males over 60 years of age, and females over 45. [***] Reviewing the foregoing case of sterilization we find that several factors resulting from it firmly establish its advocacy. Firstly, no physical pain will be imposed upon the inhabitants of Germany through its application, a decidedly more humane treatment than they will have deserved. As a matter of fact it is not inconceivable that after Germany's defeat, the long-suffering peoples of Europe may demand a far less humane revenge than that of mere sterilization. Secondly, execution of the plan would in no way disorganize the present population nor would it cause any sudden mass upheavals and dislocations The consequent gradual disappearance of the Germans from Europe will leave no more negative effect upon that continent than did the gradual disappearance of Indians upon this."[684]

Perhaps inspired by the accusations against Jews of poising the wells in the 1300's, some Jews unsuccessfully attempted revenge against the Germans for the Holocaust after the Second World War by poisoning the water supply of Germany. Tom Segev wrote in his book *The Seventh Million: The Israelis and the Holocaust*,

"Kovner therefore set six million German citizens as his goal. He thought in apocalyptic terms: revenge was a holy obligation that would redeem and purify the Jewish people. The group divided into cells, each with a commander. Their primary goal, Plan A, was 'to poison as many Germans as possible.' Plan B was to poison several thousand former SS men in the American army's POW camps. Reichman succeeded in infiltrating some members of the group into the Hamburg and Nuremberg water companies. Kovner went to Palestine to bring the poison—and, he hoped, to receive the blessing of the Haganah."[685]

It is often alleged that a group of high ranking Nazi officials met at a conference in Wannsee and settled on a plan to exterminate the Jews of Europe in concentration camps. There is a purported transcript of this meeting. Some have disputed the authenticity of the minutes of the Wannsee-Konferenz. At any rate, the minutes of the Wannsee Conference do not contain any statements plotting the deliberate murder of the Jews or the extermination of all Jews. The "final solution of the Jewish question" proposed in the purported minutes of the Wannsee Conference was not murder or complete extermination; but was instead the deportation of Jews to the East in conformity with the wishes of the Zionist Jews.[686]

Zionist Nazi propagandist Julius Streicher affirmed at the Nuremberg Trials that the Nuremberg Laws of 1935 were patterned after Jewish Law,

"Yes, I believe I had a part in it insofar as for years I have written that any further mixture of German blood with Jewish blood must be avoided. I have written such articles again and again; and in my articles I have repeatedly emphasized the fact that the Jews should serve as an example to every race, for they created a racial law for themselves—the law of Moses, which says, 'If you come into a foreign land you shall not take unto yourself foreign women.' And that, Gentlemen, is of tremendous importance in judging the Nuremberg Laws. These laws of the Jews were taken as a model for these laws. When, after centuries, the Jewish lawgiver Ezra discovered that notwithstanding many Jews had married non-Jewish women, these marriages were dissolved. That was the beginning of Jewry which, because it introduced these racial laws, has survived throughout the centuries, while all other races and civilizations have perished."[687]

Dr. Marx asked Julius Streicher,

"Were you of the opinion that the 1935 legislation represented the final solution of the Jewish question by the State?"[688]

Streicher responded that Zionism was the final solution of the Jewish question,

"With reservations, yes. I was convinced that if the Party program was carried out, the Jewish question would be solved. The Jews became German citizens in 1848. Their rights as citizens were taken from them by these laws. Sexual intercourse was prohibited. For me, this represented the solution of the Jewish problem in Germany. But I believed that another international solution would still be found, and that some day discussions would take place between the various states with regard to the demands made by Zionism. These demands aimed at a Jewish state."[689]

Nazi Secretary of State in the Interior Ministry Wilhelm Stuckart, who attended the Wannsee-Konferenz, was questioned by Robert M. W. Kempner at his Nuremberg trial and denied that the extermination of the Jews was discussed,

"No, I don't believe that I am wrong in saying that there was no discussion of the final solution of the Jewish question, in the sense in which it is now understood.

KEMPNER: Heydrich related clearly, in your presence, what it was about?

STUCKART: That is absolutely out of the question—otherwise I would have known what it meant."[690]

Refer to the Nuremberg trial transcripts of 22 November 1945, where Stuckart was quoted as referring to the "final solution" in the late 1930's, as a political solution, some years before the Wannsee-Konferenz occurred, meaning the formation of a "Jewish State". This quotation was cited prior to the first appearance of the purported "Protocols of the

Wannsee Conference". Again, some have called into questions the authenticity of these "Protocols".

Though Eichmann stated that the "final solution" had always meant a Zionistic political solution to him, Eichmann alleged many years after the war that he had heard from third party sources that Hitler changed course in the middle of the war and planned to exterminate the Jews.[691] David Irving has argued that Hitler never had any such plan.

Accusations that Hitler was out to exterminate the Jews predated the Holocaust by many years, and served the interests of the Zionists, just as the Holocaust served and serves the interests of the Zionists. *The New York Times* reported on 8 February 1923, on page 3, in an article entitled,"SAYS FORD AIDS ROYALISTS. Auer Charges Financial Help to Bavarian Anti-Semites.":

> "Henry Ford was accused of financing a Bavarian monarchist revolution by Herr Auer, Vice President of the Bavarian Diet, who came to Berlin today to report to President Ebert on the situation. Herr Auer informed The Tribune that Henry Ford's financial as well as moral backing had been given to Bavarian revolution-makers during the past year because a part of the program of Herr Hitler, leader of the Monarchists, is the extermination of the Jews in Germany."

It would be interesting to determine the exact German word used, which had been translated as "exterminate". Was it *Ausrottung*, or perhaps *Vernichtung*? There has been a dispute over the meaning of Hitler's many statements against the Jews in the original German, which hinges on whether or not he meant to simply rid Germany of Jews by deporting them, or whether he was out to exterminate all Jews. At the time, Hitler was calling for the expulsion of Jews from Bavaria and from all German lands. The money scandal drew attention in the newspapers in Germany, but most attention was paid to the French connection. Hitler's agent Kurt G. W. Ludecke failed in his attempts to solicit monies for the Nazis from Henry Ford.[692]

The "Hamburg Resolutions of the German Social Reform Party" proclaimed in 1899,

> "The strivings of Zionism are a fruit of the antisemitic movement. [***] Unfortunately [any hope that all Jews will emigrate to Palestine] appears to be infeasible. [***] As such, [the Jewish question] should be solved in common with other

nations and result finally in full separation, and—if self-defense demands—in final annihilation [*Vernichtung*] of the Jewish race."[693]

Adolf Hitler wrote in an article entitled "Staatsmänner oder Nationalverbrecher" in the *Völkischer Beobachter*, Volume 35, Number 22, (15 March 1921), p. 1-2, that the fight against Bolshevism in Russia entailed the rooting out (*Ausrottung*) of the Jews. On 30 January 1939 Hitler famously threatened before the Reichstag that if Jewish finance again led the world into war, it would not mean a victory for "world Jewry", but "the annihilation [*Vernichtung*] of the Jewish race in Europe",

"[I want to be a prophet again today:] If international finance Jewry in and outside Europe succeeds in plunging the peoples into another world war, then the end result will not be the Bolshevization of the earth and the consequent victory of Jewry but the annihilation of the Jewish race in Europe."[694]

"Ich will heute wieder ein Prophet sein: Wenn es dem internationalen Finanzjudentum in und außerhalb Europas gelingen sollte, die Völker noch einmal in einen Weltkrieg zu stürzen, dann wird das Ergebnis nicht die Bolschewisierung der Erde und damit der Sieg des Judentums sein, sondern die Vernichtung der jüdischen Rasse in Europa!"[695]

The Jewish Zionist Nazi tyrant of Poland, Dr. Hans Frank, stated at a Cabinet Session on 16 December 1941,

"As far as the Jews are concerned, I want to tell you quite frankly, that they must be done away with in one way or another. The Fuehrer said once: should united Jewry again succeed in provoking a world war, the blood of not only the nations which have been forced into the war by them, will be shed, but the Jew will have found his end in Europe"[696]

Did Zionists Adolf Hitler and Hans Frank mean that they would exterminate the Jews of Europe in death camps, or did they mean that they would deport the Jews of Europe to Palestine as a final solution to the Jewish question? Frank was a long-term Zionist who wanted to segregate the Jews in Polish concentration camps and then ship them to

Palestine—not to say that he did not intend to kill off a large percentage of his brethren in the process. In the fall of 1933 in Nuremberg on *Reichsparteitag*, Frank stated that his goal was to secure a "Jewish State",

> "Unbeschadet unseres Willens, uns mit den Juden auseinanderzusetzen, ist die Sicherheit und das Leben der Juden in Deutschland staatlich, reichsamtlich und juristisch nicht gefährdet. Die Judenfrage ist rechtlich nur dadurch zu lösen, dass man an die Frage eines jüdischen Staates herangeht."[697]

The expression "final solution of the Jewish question (*or:* "problem")" was a commonplace in the parlance of the Zionists long before the Wannsee Konferenz.[698] Jewish Zionist Nahum Sokolow wrote in the introduction of his *History of Zionism* of 1919,

> "The progress of modern civilization has come to be regarded as a sort of 'Messiah' for the final solution of the Jewish problem."[699]

Sokolow spoke in reference to the "Jewish mission" of reformed Jews under the influence of Moses Mendelssohn. The Zionists believed this "final solution of the Jewish problem" resulted in fatal assimilation, whereas the Zionists were pitching Palestine as the "final solution of the Jewish problem". Many others believed that assimilation was the only viable "final solution to the Jewish question".[700]

Boris Brasol wrote in 1921,

> "When the Zionist claim was first established, and Theodore Hertzl, in 1897, came out with his specific program of a Jewish State, the world at large gave a sigh of relief as it was trusted that henceforth the Jews would have a country of their own where they would be able to develop freely and unhampered their racial peculiarities, their cultural traditions and their religious thought. Christian countries have been so accustomed to innumerable complaints made by the Jews of their oppression, of anti-Semitism breeding throughout the world, of pogroms ravaging the Jewish masses, that there was every reason to hope that the Jews would dash to Palestine, leaving those cruel Christians to their own destinies. What better scheme for a fair solution of the Jewish problem could be hoped for by both

Gentiles and Jews?"[701]

The Zionists wrote in the official organ of the German Zionist Organization, *Jüdische Rundshau*, on 13 June 1933, shortly after Hitler assumed power,

"Zionism recognizes the existence of the Jewish question and wants to solve it in a generous and constructive manner. For this purpose, it wants to enlist the aid of all peoples; those who are friendly to the Jews as well as those who are hostile to them, since according to its conception, this is not a question of sentimentality, but one dealing with a real problem in whose solution all peoples are interested."[702]

Jewish Zionist Joachim Prinz stated in 1937,

"Everyone in Germany knew that only the Zionists could responsibly represent the Jews in dealings with the Nazi government. We all felt sure that one day the government would arrange a round table conference with the Jews, at which—after the riots and atrocities of the revolution had passed—the new status of German Jewry could be considered. The government announced very solemnly that there was no country in the world which tried to solve the Jewish problem as seriously as did Germany. Solution of the Jewish question? It was our Zionist dream! We never denied the existence of the Jewish question! Dissimilation? It was our own appeal! . . . In a statement notable for its pride and dignity, we called for a conference."[703]

In 1917, Jewish Zionist Elisha M. Friedman made several references to the "solution of the Jewish question",

"Recent events have served to accentuate Zionism as an attempt at the solution of the Jewish question. [***] And only yesterday, as it were, Adolph Lewinsohn, whose activities transcend creed, has likewise joined those that see in Zionism a solution to the Jewish question. [***] Insofar as it affords no relief to the assimilationist and intensifies the loyalty of the great mass of a dispersed people, the policy of partial assimilation defeats its own ends. It is purposeless. It has been tested out, as a solution of the Jewish question, and has proven an eloquent failure."[704]

In 1911, Jewish Zionist Israel Zangwill made reference to the "solution of the Jewish Question",

> "But if the prospect of a territorial solution of the Jewish Question, whether in Palestine or in the New World appears remote, it must be admitted that the Jewish race, in abandoning before the legions of Rome the struggle for independent political existence, in favor of spiritual isolation and economic symbiosis, discovered the secret of immortality, if also of perpetual motion."[705]

In 1898, an American Jewish Zionist, Richard Gottheil, proposed a Zionist "final solution of the Jewish question". Gottheil feared the "extermination" of the Jewish race, not through violent genocide, but by "a final solution of the Jewish question" of "assimilation". Gottheil proposed that Jews form a nation in Palestine in order to maintain the Jewish race. Note that Gottheil mentions "those Jews who are forced to go" to Palestine. Gottheil's speech appeared in *The World's Best Orations*, Volume 6, F. P. Kaiser, St. Louis, (1899), pp. 2294-2298:

"THE JEWS AS A RACE AND AS A NATION

(Peroration of the Address, ‹The Aims of Zionism,› Delivered in New York City, November 1st, 1898)

I KNOW that there are a great many of our people who look for a final solution of the Jewish question in what they call «assimilation.» The more the Jews assimilate themselves to their surroundings, they think, the more completely will the causes for anti-Jewish feeling cease to exist. But have you ever for a moment stopped to consider what assimilation means? It has very pertinently been pointed out that the use of the word is borrowed from the dictionary of physiology. But in physiology it is not the food which assimilates itself into the body. It is the body which assimilates the food. The Jew may wish to be assimilated; he may do all he will towards this end. But if the great mass in which he lives does not wish to assimilate him — what then? If demands are made upon the Jew which practically mean extermination, which practically mean his total effacement from among the nations of the globe and from among the religious forces of the world, — what answer will you give? And the demands made are practically of that nature.

I can imagine it possible for a people who are possessed of an active and aggressive charity which it expresses, not only in words, but also in deeds, to contain and live at peace with men of the most varied habits. But, unfortunately, such people do not exist; nations are swayed by feelings which are dictated solely by their own self-interests; and the Zionists in meeting this state of things, are the most practical as well as the most ideal of the Jews.

It is quite useless to tell the English workingman that his Jewish fellow-laborer from Russia has actually increased the riches of the United Kingdom; that he has created quite a new industry, — that of making ladies' cloaks, for which formerly England sent £2,000,000 to the continent every year. He sees in him some one who is different to himself, and unfortunately successful, though different. And until that difference entirely ceases, whether of habit, of way, or of religious observance, he will look upon him and treat him as an enemy.

For the Jew has this especial disadvantage. There is no place where that which is distinctively Jewish in his manner or in his way of life is *à la mode.* We may well laugh at the Irishman's brogue; but in Ireland, he knows, his brogue is at home. We may poke fun at the Frenchman as he shrugs his shoulders and speaks with every member of his body. The Frenchman feels that in France it is the proper thing so to do. Even the Turk will wear his fez, and feel little the worse for the occasional jibes with which the street boy may greet it. But this consciousness, this ennobling consciousness, is all denied to the Jew. What he does is nowhere *à la mode;* no, not even his features; and if he can disguise these by parting his hair in the middle or cutting his beard to a point, he feels he is on the road towards assimilation. He is even ready to use the term «Jewish» for what he considers uncouth and low.

For such as these amongst us, Zionism also has its message. It wishes to give back to the Jew that nobleness of spirit, that confidence in himself, that belief in his own powers which only perfect freedom can give. With a home of his own, he will no longer feel himself a pariah among the nations, he will nowhere hide his own peculiarities, — peculiarities to which he has a right as much as any one, — but will see that those peculiarities carry with them a message which will force for them the admiration of the world. He will feel that he belongs somewhere and not everywhere. He will try to be something and not everything. The great word which Zionism preaches is conciliation of conflicting aims, of conflicting lines of action; conciliation of Jew to Jew. It means conciliation of the non-Jewish world to the Jew as well. It wishes to heal old wounds; and by frankly confessing differences which do exist, however much we try to explain them away, to work out its own salvation upon its own ground, and from these to send forth its spiritual message to a conciliated world.

But, you will ask, if Zionism is able to find a permanent home in Palestine for those Jews who are forced to go there as well as those who wish to go, what is to become of us who have entered, to such a degree, into the life around us, and who feel able to continue as we have begun? What is to be our relation to the new Jewish polity? I can only answer: Exactly the same as is the relation of people of other nationalities all the world over to their parent home. What becomes of the Englishman in every corner of the globe? What becomes of the German? Does the fact that the great mass of their people live in their own land prevent them from doing their whole duty towards the land in which they happen to live? Is the German-American considered less of an American because he cultivates the German language and is interested in the fate of his fellow-Germans at home? Is the Irish-American less of an American because he gathers money to help his struggling brethren in the Green Isle? Or are the Scandinavian-Americans less worthy of the title Americans, because they consider precious the bonds which bind them to the land of their birth, as well as those which bind them to the land of their adoption?

Nay! it would seem to me that just those who are so afraid that our action will be misinterpreted should be among the greatest helpers in the Zionist cause. For those who feel no racial and national communion with the life from which they have sprung should greet with joy the turning of Jewish immigration to some place other than the land in which they dwell. They must feel, for example, that a continual influx of Jews who are not Americans is a continual menace to the more or less complete absorption for which they are striving.

But I must not detain you much longer. Will you permit me to sum up for you the position which we Zionists take in the following statements: —

We believe that the Jews are something more than a purely religious body; that they are not only a race, but also a nation; though a nation without as yet two important requisites — a common home and a common language.

We believe that if an end is to be made to Jewish misery and to the exceptional position which the Jews occupy, — which is the primary cause of Jewish misery, — the Jewish nation must be placed once again in a home of its own.

We believe that such a national regeneration is the fulfillment of the hope which has been present to the Jew throughout his long and painful history.

We believe that only by means of such a national regeneration can the religious regeneration of the Jews take place, and they be put in a position to do that work in the religious world which Providence has appointed for them.

We believe that such a home can only naturally, and without violence to their whole past, be found in the land of their fathers — in Palestine.

We believe that such a return must have the guarantee of the great powers of the world in order to secure for the Jews a stable future.

And we hold that this does not mean that all Jews must return to Palestine.

This, ladies and gentlemen, is the Zionist program. Shall we be able to carry it through? I cannot believe that the Jewish people have been preserved throughout these centuries either for eternal misery or for total absorption at this stage of the world's history. I cannot think that our people have so far misunderstood their own purpose in life, as now to give the lie to their own past and to every hope which has animated their suffering body.

Bear with me but a few moments longer while I read the words which a Christian writer puts into the mouth of a Jew. «The effect of our separateness will not be completed and have its highest transformation, unless our race takes on again the character of a nationality. That is the fulfillment of the religious trust that molded them into a people, whose life has made half the inspiration of the world. . . . Revive the organic centre; let the unity of Israel which has made the growth and form of its religion be an outward reality. Looking toward a land and a polity, our dispersed people in all the ends of the earth may share the dignity of a national life which has a voice among the peoples of the East and the West — which will plant the wisdom and skill of our race so that it may be, as of old, a medium of transmission and understanding. Let that come to pass, and the living warmth will spread to the weak extremities of Israel. Let the central fire be kindled again, and the light will reach afar. The degraded and scorned of the race will learn to think of their sacred land, not as a place for saintly beggary to await death in loathsome idleness, but as a republic, where the Jewish spirit manifests itself in a new order founded on the old, purified, enriched by the experiences which our greatest sons have gathered from the life of the ages. A new Judea, poised between East and West — a covenant of reconciliation. The sons of Judah have to choose, that God may again choose them. The Messianic time is the time when Israel shall will the planting of the national ensign. The divine principle of our race is action, choice, resolved memory. Let us help to will our own better future of the world — not renounce our higher gift and say: ‹Let us be as if we were not among the populations,› but choose our full heritage, claim the brotherhood of our nation, and carry into it a new brotherhood with the nations of the Gentiles. The vision is there; it will be fulfilled.»

These are the words of the non-Jewish Zionist, George Eliot. We take hope, for has not that Jewish Zionist said: «We belong to a race that can do everything but fail.»"

On 22 August 1897, on page 12, in an article entitled, "Jews Against Zionism", *The New York Times* wrote,

"Many of them thought that a purely philanthropic movement would always be but a palliative, and would never lead to a solution of the Jewish question."

Like countless other Jewish Zionists, Theodor Herzl spoke of Zionism as the "solution of the Jewish question". In fact the very title of Herzl's seminal book makes the reference, *Der Judenstaat; Versuch einer modernen Lösung der Judenfrage*, M. Breitenstein, Leipzig, Wien, (1896). English translation: *A Jewish State: An Attempt at a Modern Solution of the Jewish Question*, The Maccabæan Publishing Co., New York, (1904). Herzl stated in this book,

"This guard of honour would be the great symbol of the solution of the Jewish Question after eighteen centuries of Jewish suffering."[706]

In an article entitled "Zionist Congress in Basel", *The New York Times* quoted Theodor Herzl, on 31 August 1897, on page 7,

"I think we shall find Palestine at our disposal sooner than we expected. Last year I went to Constantinople and had two long conferences with the Grand Vizier, to whom I pointed out that the key to the preservation of Turkey lay in the solution of the Jewish question."

In his opening address to the First Zionist Congress, Herzl stated,

"Wir Zionisten wünschen zur Lösung der Judenfrage nicht etwa einen internationalen Verein, sondern die internationale Diskussion."[707]

Herzl's statements were recorded in, "The Zionist Congress: Full Report of the Proceedings", *The Jewish Chronicle*, (3 September 1897), pp. 10-15, at 11, 12 and 15,

"We Zionists desire for the solution of the Jewish Question. [***] But it is not the solution of the Jewish Question, and cannot be so in its present form. [***] The financial help which the Jews are able to offer to Turkey is not small, and would serve to put an end to many an evil from which the country is suffering. If a part of the Oriental question can be solved, together with the Jewish question, this surely is in the interest of all nations. [***] In this way we understand, we expect the solution of the Jewish Question. [***] On the day when the Jews again held the plough in Palestine, on that day would the Jewish Question be solved."

In examining the history of expressed threats of genocide, it should be mentioned that long before Kaufman's genocidal book *Germany Must Perish!* advocated the extermination of Gentile Germans, anti-Semite Eugen Karl Dühring implicitly advocated the genocide of Jews in the 1901 edition of his *Die Judenfrage*, Chapter 5, Sections 4-9, which concludes with the statement:

"Precisely this situation must however urge the determined component of better humanity only so much more to act in order to create communities and communal life whose principles extend over the earth and thereby also, obviously, do not leave any room for Hebrew life."[708]

Jörg Lanz-Liebenfels advocated the deportation and sterilization of "inferior races" in his book *Theozoologie, oder Die Kunde von den Sodomsäfflingen und dem Götter-Elektron eine Einführung in die älteste und neueste Weltanschauung und eine Rechtfertigung des Fürstentums und des Adels. . .*, Moderner Verlag, Wien, (1905).[709] Hitler's racial views came in part from Lanz-Liebenfels, who promoted the procreation of blond-haired people and the sterilization of the "ape-men" of the "inferior races"—he was also a Zionist who encouraged the formation of a Jewish State, and his mythologies may have been derived from the Jewish myth that angels bred with humans to produce a unique race. One example of the political Zionists' equivalent of Liebenfels prescriptions for the ideal "Aryan", was Elias Auerbach's article "Rassenkunde" in Zionist Martin Buber's journal *Der Jude*, Volume 5, Number 1, (1920-1921), pp. 49-57, which discusses eye and hair color, skeletal proportions, etc. of the average Jew. In 1909, Buber himself romanticized that a Jew awakening to his heritage undergoes many stages of racial self-awareness,

"He perceives then what commingling of individuals, what confluence of blood, has produced him, what round of begettings and births has called him forth. He senses in this immortality of the generations a community of blood, which he feels to be the antecedents of his I, its perseverance in the infinite past. To that is added the discovery, promoted by this awareness, that blood is a deep rooted nurturing force within individual man; that the deepest layers of our being are determined by blood ; that our innermost thinking and our will are colored by it. Now he finds that the world around him is the world of imprints and influences, whereas blood is the realm of a substance capable of being imprinted and influenced, a substance absorbing and assimilating all into its own form. And he therefore senses that he belongs no longer to the community of those whose constant elements of experience he shares, but to the deeper-reaching community of those whose substance he shares. [***] Whoever, faced with the choice between environment and substance, decides for substance will henceforth have to be a Jew truly from within, to live as a Jew with all the contradiction, all the tragedy, and all the future promise of his blood."[710]

Josef Ludwig Reimer published *Ein pangermanisches Deutschland. Versuch über die Konsequenzen der gegenwärtigen wissenschaftlichen Rassenbetrachtung für unsere politischen und religiösen Probleme*, F. Luckhardt, Berlin, Leipzig, (1905); which advocated dividing human beings into three categories with the rulers being blond-haired, blue-eyed supermen, who ruled the "mixed-race" and middle class, and the lowest grouping, the non-Germanics.[711] The non-Germanics would be sterilized or prevented by law from bearing children. Extremist and violent Social Darwinism appeared in Germany in the Nineteenth Century in the writings of Friedrich von Hellwald, and Ernst Haeckel advocated Eugenics.[712]

The "Eugenics" of Sir Fancis Galton[713] has a long and complex history dating back to the Greeks and includes such famous persons as Charles Darwin and Alexander Graham Bell. Prior to the Nazi regime, Eugenics was most enthusiastically promoted in the United States, where there was active governmental interest in the field, and where Eugenics influenced legislation. It was also welcomed in England. The colonial powers sought scientific justification for their un-Christian treatment of their fellow human beings, as if inferior. America sought to limit the immigration and political power of the so-called "inferior races". The Nazis instituted their "T4" *"Euthanasie-Programme"* in 1939.

Under the sponsorship of the Jewish bankers, Richard Koudenhove-Kalergi called for the extermination of Europeans through miscegenation with Africans and Asians in his book of 1925, *Praktischer Idealismus*. He advocated making the Jews a master race to rule over Europe and all of humanity in conformity with Jewish messianic prophecy.

Richard Couvenhove-Kalergi was the father of the genocidal EU. Kalergi admitted in his autobiography that he was funded by jewish bankers Rothschild, Warburg and Baruch. In a NSDAP publication, Dieter Schwarz exposed Jewish Freemasonry in 1938 and revealed that Kalergi's plot to genocide Europeans and destroy the races and make jews the rulers over all the World was openly endorsed by Kalergi's fellow masons.[714]

German Jews had endured increasingly hostile agitations since the end of the First World War, and the Hitler regime enacted discriminatory laws against the Jews long before Kaufman's book found its way into print, which segregationist laws had an ancient history in Europe and were endorsed by Heinrich Class under the *nom de plume* Daniel Frymann, *Wenn ich der Kaiser wär': politische Wahrheiten und Notwendigkeiten*, Dieterich, Leipzig, (1912); even before the First World War.

In naming the important historical incidents of genocidal propaganda and acts, it must also be mentioned that Biblical passages in the Old Testament and the New, as well as Talmudic and Cabalistic writings, prophesied the genocide and enslavement of Gentiles and the ascent of a master race of Jews. Writing on Thomas Jefferson's religious views, William D. Gould wrote,

> "Jefferson praised the philosophers of antiquity for their insistence on the necessity of governing the passions, but found that they did not deal adequately with social duties. They taught well the obligation of being just in dealing with one's neighbor or countryman, but felt under no constraint to cultivate a love for all mankind. Even the Jews in Jesus' day, he believed, entertained many erroneous ideas concerning religion and morality. In addition to the fact that he felt that a number of their conceptions of God were incorrect, their ethics, in respect to other nations, were, he thought, decidedly antisocial."[715]

Jefferson criticized ancient philosophers and the ancient Jews in his *Syllabus*. He wrote, *inter alia*, in a letter to Dr. Benjamin Rush of 21 April 1803 responding to rumors that he was not a Christian,

> "*Syllabus of an Estimate of the Merit of the Doctrines of Jesus, Compared with Those of Others.*
> In a comparative view of the Ethics of the enlightened nations of antiquity, of the Jews and of Jesus, no notice should be taken of the corruptions of reason among the ancients, to wit, the idolatry and superstition of the vulgar, nor of the corruptions of Christianity by the learned among its professors.
> Let a just view be taken of the moral principles inculcated by the most esteemed of the sects of ancient philosophy, or of their individuals; particularly Pythagoras, Socrates, Epicurus, Cicero, Epictetus, Seneca, Antoninus.
> I. Philosophers. I. Their precepts related chiefly to ourselves, and the government of those passions which, unrestrained,

would disturb our tranquillity of mind.[*Footnote:* To explain, I will exhibit the heads of Seneca's and Cicero's philosophical works, the most extensive of any we have received from the ancients. Of ten heads in Seneca, seven relate to ourselves, viz. *de ira, consolatio, de tranquilitate, de constantia sapientis, de otio sapientis, de vita beata, de brevitate vitae*; two relate to others, *de clementia, de beneficiis*; and one relates to the government of the world, *de providentia*. Of eleven tracts of Cicero, five respect ourselves, viz. *de finibus, Tusculana, academica, paradoxa, de Senectute*; one, *de officiis*, relates partly to ourselves, partly to others; one, *de amicitia*, relates to others; and four are on different subjects, to wit, *de natura deorum, de divinatione, de fato*, and *sommium Scipionis*.] In this branch of philosophy they were really great.

> 2. In developing our duties to others, they were short and defective. They embraced, indeed, the circles of kindred and friends, and inculcated patriotism, or the love of our country in the aggregate, as a primary obligation: towards our neighbors and countrymen they taught justice, but scarcely viewed them as within the circle of benevolence. Still less have they inculcated peace, charity and love to our fellow men, or embraced with benevolence the whole family of mankind.
>
> II. Jews. ı. Their system was Deism; that is, the belief in one only God. But their ideas of him and of his attributes were degrading and injurious.
>
> 2. Their Ethics were not only imperfect, but often irreconcilable with the sound dictates of reason and morality, as they respect intercourse with those around us; and repulsive and anti-social, as respecting other nations. They needed reformation, therefore, in an eminent degree."[716]

Ancient Jewish myths enunciate a nationalistic and destructive racism by a master nation of Israel on a holy mission to mercilessly subjugate the other nations of the world, supposedly pursuant to God's will. For example, *Deuteronomy*, Chapter 7, states,

> "When the LORD thy God shall bring thee into the land whither thou goest to possess it, and hath cast out many nations before thee, the Hittites, and the Girgashites, and the Amorites, and the

Canaanites, and the Perizzites, and the Hivites, and the Jebusites, seven nations greater and mightier than thou; 2 And when the LORD thy God shall deliver them before thee; thou shalt smite them, *and* utterly destroy them; thou shalt make no covenant with them, nor show mercy unto them: 3 Neither shalt thou make marriages with them; thy daughter thou shalt not give unto his son, nor his daughter shalt thou take unto thy son. 4 For they will turn away thy son from following me, that they may serve other gods: so will the anger of the LORD be kindled against you, and destroy thee suddenly. 5 But thus shall ye deal with them; ye shall destroy their altars, and break down their images, and cut down their groves, and burn their graven images with fire. 6 For thou *art* an holy people unto the LORD thy God: the LORD thy God hath chosen thee to be a special people unto himself, above all people that *are* upon the face of the earth. 7 The LORD did not set his love upon you, nor choose you, because ye were more in number than any people; for ye *were* the fewest of all people: 8 But because the LORD loved you, and because he would keep the oath which he had sworn unto your fathers, hath the LORD brought you out with a mighty hand, and redeemed you out of the house of bondmen, from the hand of Pharaoh king of Egypt. 9 Know therefore that the LORD thy God, he *is* God, the faithful God, which keepeth covenant and mercy with them that love him and keep his commandments to a thousand generations; 10 And repayeth them that hate him to their face, to destroy them: he will not be slack to him that hateth him, he will repay him to his face. 11 Thou shalt therefore keep the commandments, and the statutes, and the judgments, which I command thee this day, to do them. 12 Wherefore it shall come to pass, if ye hearken to these judgments, and keep, and do them, that the LORD thy God shall keep unto thee the covenant and the mercy which he sware unto thy fathers: 13 And he will love thee, and bless thee, and multiply thee: he will also bless the fruit of thy womb, and the fruit of thy land, thy corn, and thy wine, and thine oil, the increase of thy kine, and the flocks of thy sheep, in the land which he sware unto thy fathers to give thee. 14 Thou shalt be blessed above all people: there shall not be male or female barren among you, or among your cattle. 15 And the LORD will take away from thee all sickness, and will put none of the evil diseases of Egypt, which thou knowest, upon thee; but will lay them upon all *them* that hate thee. 16 And thou shalt consume all the people which the LORD thy God shall deliver thee; thine eye shall have no pity upon them: neither shalt thou serve their gods; for that *will be* a snare unto thee. 17 If thou shalt say in thine heart, These nations *are* more than I; how can I dispossess them? 18 Thou shalt not be afraid of them: *but* shalt well remember what the LORD thy God did unto Pharaoh, and unto all Egypt; 19 The great temptations which thine eyes saw, and the signs, and the wonders, and the mighty hand, and the stretched out arm, whereby the LORD thy God brought thee out: so shall the LORD thy God do unto all the people of whom thou art afraid. 20 Moreover the LORD thy God will send the hornet among them, until they that are left, and hide themselves from thee, be destroyed. 21 Thou shalt not be affrighted at them: for the LORD thy God *is* among you, a mighty God and terrible. 22 And the LORD thy God will put out those nations before thee by little and little: thou mayest not consume them at once, lest the beasts of the field increase upon thee. 23 But the LORD thy God shall deliver them unto thee, and shall destroy them with a mighty destruction, until they be destroyed. 24 And he shall deliver their kings into thine hand, and thou shalt destroy their name from under heaven: there shall no man be able to stand before thee, until thou have destroyed them. 25 The graven images of their gods shall ye burn with fire: thou shalt not desire the silver or gold *that is* on them, nor take *it* unto thee, lest thou be snared therein: for it *is* an abomination to the LORD thy God. 26 Neither shalt thou bring an abomination into thine house, lest thou be a cursed thing like it: *but* thou shalt utterly detest it, and thou shalt utterly abhor it; for it *is* a cursed thing."

Deuteronomy, Chapter 28, proclaims the punishment to befall the assimilate Jewsd,

"And it shall come to pass, if thou shalt hearken diligently unto the voice of the LORD thy God, to observe *and* to do all his commandments which I command thee this day, that the LORD thy God will set thee on high above all nations of the earth: 2 And all these blessings shall come on thee, and overtake thee, if thou shalt hearken unto the voice of the LORD thy God. 3 Blessed *shalt* thou *be* in the city, and blessed *shalt* thou *be* in the field. 4 Blessed *shall be* the fruit of thy body, and the fruit of thy ground, and the fruit of thy cattle, the increase of thy kine, and the flocks of thy sheep. 5 Blessed *shall be* thy basket and thy store. 6 Blessed *shalt* thou *be* when thou comest in, and blessed *shalt* thou *be* when thou goest out. 7 The LORD shall cause thine enemies that rise up against thee to be smitten before thy face: they shall come out against thee one way, and flee before thee seven ways. 8 The LORD shall command the blessing upon thee in thy storehouses, and in all that thou settest thine hand unto; and he shall bless thee in the land which the LORD thy God giveth thee. 9 The LORD shall establish thee an holy people unto himself, as he hath sworn unto thee, if thou shalt keep the commandments of the LORD thy God, and walk in his ways. 10 And all people of the earth shall see that thou art called by the name of the LORD; and they shall be afraid of thee. 11 And the LORD shall make thee plenteous in goods, in the fruit of thy body, and in the fruit of thy cattle, and in the fruit of thy ground, in the land which the LORD sware unto thy fathers to give thee. 12 The LORD shall open unto thee his good treasure, the heaven to give the rain unto thy land in his season, and to bless all the work of thine hand: and thou shalt lend unto many nations, and thou shalt not borrow. 13 And the LORD shall make thee the head, and not the tail; and thou shalt be above only, and thou shalt not be beneath; if that thou hearken unto the commandments of the LORD thy God, which I command thee this day, to observe and to do *them*: 14 And thou shalt not go aside from any of the words which I command thee this day, *to* the right hand, or *to* the left, to go after other gods to serve them. 15 But it shall come to pass, if thou wilt not hearken unto the voice of the LORD thy God, to observe to do all his commandments and his statutes which I command thee this day; that all these curses shall come upon thee, and overtake thee:16 Cursed *shalt* thou *be* in the city, and cursed *shalt* thou *be* in the field. 17 Cursed *shall be* thy basket and thy store. 18 Cursed *shall be* the fruit of thy body, and the fruit of thy land, the increase of thy kine, and the flocks of thy sheep. 19 Cursed *shalt* thou *be* when thou comest in, and cursed *shalt* thou *be* when thou goest out. 20 The LORD shall send upon thee cursing, vexation, and rebuke, in all that thou settest thine hand unto for to do, until thou be destroyed, and until thou perish quickly; because of the wickedness of thy doings, whereby thou hast forsaken me. 21 The LORD shall make the pestilence cleave unto thee, until he have consumed thee from off the land, whither thou goest to possess it. 22 The LORD shall smite thee with a consumption, and with a fever, and with an inflammation, and with an extreme burning, and with the sword, and with blasting, and with mildew; and they shall pursue thee until thou perish. 23 And thy heaven that *is* over thy head shall be brass, and the earth that is under thee *shall be* iron. 24 The LORD shall make the rain of thy land powder and dust: from heaven shall it come down upon thee, until thou be destroyed. 25 The LORD shall cause thee to be smitten before thine enemies: thou shalt go out one way against them, and flee seven ways before them: and shalt be removed into all the kingdoms of the earth. 26 And thy carcase shall be meat unto all fowls of the air, and unto the beasts of the earth, and no man shall fray *them* away. 27 The LORD will smite thee with the botch of Egypt, and with the emerods, and with the scab, and with the itch, whereof thou canst not be healed. 28 The LORD shall smite thee with madness, and blindness, and astonishment of heart: 29 And thou shalt grope at noonday, as the blind gropeth in darkness, and thou shalt not prosper in thy ways: and thou shalt be only oppressed and spoiled evermore, and no man shall save *thee*. 30 Thou shalt betroth a wife, and another man shall lie with her: thou shalt build an house, and thou shalt not dwell therein: thou shalt plant a vineyard, and shalt not gather the grapes thereof. 31 Thine ox *shall be* slain before thine eyes, and thou shalt not eat thereof: thine ass *shall be* violently taken away from before thy face, and shall not be restored to thee: thy sheep *shall be* given unto thine enemies, and thou shalt have none to rescue *them*. 32 Thy sons and thy daughters *shall be* given unto another people, and thine eyes shall look, and fail *with longing* for them all the day long: and *there shall be* no might in thine hand. 33 The fruit of thy land, and all thy labours, shall a nation which thou knowest not eat up; and thou shalt be only oppressed and crushed alway: 34 So that thou shalt be mad for the sight of thine eyes which thou shalt see. 35 The LORD shall smite thee in the knees, and in the legs, with a sore botch that cannot be healed, from the sole of thy foot unto the top of thy head. 36 The LORD shall bring thee, and thy king which thou shalt set over thee, unto a nation which neither thou nor thy fathers have known; and there shalt thou serve other gods, wood and stone. 37 And thou shalt become an astonishment, a proverb, and a byword, among all nations whither the LORD shall lead thee. 38 Thou shalt carry much seed out into the field, and shalt gather *but* little in; for the locust shall consume it. 39 Thou shalt plant vineyards, and dress *them*, but shalt neither drink *of* the wine, nor gather *the grapes*; for the worms shall eat them. 40 Thou shalt have olive trees throughout all thy coasts, but thou shalt not anoint *thyself* with the oil; for thine olive shall cast *his fruit*. 41 Thou shalt beget sons and daughters, but thou shalt not enjoy them; for they shall go into captivity. 42 All thy trees and fruit of thy land shall the locust consume. 43 The stranger that *is* within thee shall get up above thee very high; and thou shalt come down very low. 44 He shall lend to thee, and thou shalt not lend to him: he shall be the head, and thou shalt be the tail. 45 Moreover all these curses shall come upon thee, and shall pursue thee, and overtake thee, till thou be destroyed; because thou hearkenedst not unto the voice of the LORD thy God, to keep his commandments and his statutes which he commanded thee: 46 And they shall be upon thee for a sign and for a wonder, and upon thy seed for ever. 47 Because thou servedst not the LORD thy God with joyfulness, and with gladness of heart, for the abundance of all *things*; 48 Therefore shalt thou serve thine enemies which the LORD shall send against thee, in hunger, and in thirst, and in nakedness, and in want of all *things*: and he shall put a yoke of iron upon thy neck, until he have destroyed thee. 49 The LORD shall bring a nation against thee from far, from the end of the earth, *as swift* as the eagle flieth; a nation whose tongue thou shalt not understand; 50 A nation of fierce countenance, which shall not regard the person of the old, nor show favour to the young: 51 And he shall eat the fruit of thy cattle, and the fruit of thy land, until thou be destroyed: which *also* shall not leave thee *either* corn, wine, or oil, *or* the increase of thy kine, or flocks of thy sheep, until he have destroyed thee. 52 And he shall besiege thee in all thy gates, until thy high and fenced walls come down, wherein thou trustedst, throughout all thy land: and he shall besiege thee in all thy gates throughout all thy land, which the LORD thy God hath given thee. 53 And thou shalt eat the fruit of thine own body, the flesh of thy sons and of thy daughters, which the LORD thy God hath given thee, in the siege, and in the straitness, wherewith thine enemies shall distress thee: 54 *So that* the man *that is* tender among you, and very delicate, his eye shall be evil toward his brother, and toward the wife of his bosom, and toward the remnant of his children which he shall leave: 55 So that he will not give to any of them of the flesh of his children whom he shall eat: because he hath nothing left him in the siege, and in the straitness, wherewith thine enemies shall distress thee in all thy gates. 56 The tender and delicate woman among you, which would not adventure to set the sole of her foot upon the ground for delicateness and tenderness, her eye shall be evil toward the husband of her bosom, and toward her son, and toward her daughter, 57 And toward her young one that cometh out from between her feet, and toward her children which she shall bear: for she shall eat them for want of all *things* secretly in the siege and straitness, wherewith thine enemy shall distress thee in thy gates. 58 If thou wilt not observe to do all the words of this law that are written in this book, that thou mayest fear this glorious and fearful name, THE LORD THY GOD; 59 Then the LORD will make thy plagues wonderful, and the plagues of thy seed, *even* great plagues, and of long continuance, and sore sicknesses, and of long continuance. 60 Moreover he will bring upon thee all the diseases of Egypt, which thou wast afraid of; and they shall cleave unto thee. 61 Also every sickness, and every plague, which *is* not written in the book of this law, them will the LORD bring upon thee, until thou be destroyed. 62 And ye shall be left few in number, whereas ye were as the stars of heaven for multitude; because thou wouldest not obey the voice of the LORD thy God. 63 And it shall come to pass, *that* as the LORD rejoiced over you to do you good, and to multiply you; so the LORD will rejoice over you to destroy you, and to bring you to nought; and ye shall be plucked from off the land whither thou goest to possess it. 64 And the LORD shall scatter thee among all people, from the one end of the earth even unto the other; and there thou shalt serve other gods, which neither thou nor thy fathers have known, *even* wood and stone. 65 And among these nations shalt thou find no ease, neither shall the sole of thy foot have rest: but the LORD shall give thee there a trembling heart, and failing of eyes, and sorrow of mind: 66 And thy life shall hang in doubt before thee; and thou shalt fear day and night, and shalt have none assurance of thy life: 67 In the morning thou shalt say, Would God it were even! and at even thou shalt say, Would God it were morning! for the fear of thine heart wherewith thou shalt fear, and for the sight of thine eyes which thou shalt see. 68 And the LORD shall bring thee into Egypt again with ships, by the way whereof I spake unto thee, Thou shalt see it no more again: and there ye shall be sold unto your enemies for bondmen and bondwomen, and no man shall buy *you*."

Isaiah, Chapter 34,

"Come near, ye nations, to hear; and hearken, ye people: let the earth hear, and all that is therein; the world, and all things that come forth of it. 2 For the indignation of the LORD *is* upon all nations, and *his* fury upon all their armies: he hath utterly destroyed them, he hath delivered them to the slaughter. 3 Their slain also shall be cast out, and their stink shall come up out of their carcases, and the mountains shall be melted with their blood. 4 And all the host of heaven shall be dissolved, and the heavens shall be rolled together as a scroll: and all their host shall fall down, as the leaf falleth off from the vine, and as a falling *fig* from the fig tree. 5 For my sword shall be bathed in heaven: behold, it shall come down upon Idumea, and upon the people of my curse, to judgment. 6 The sword of the LORD is filled with blood, it is made fat with fatness, *and* with the blood of lambs and goats, with the fat of the kidneys of rams: for the LORD hath a sacrifice in Bozrah, and a great slaughter in the land of Idumea. 7 And the unicorns shall come down with them, and the bullocks with the bulls; and their land shall be soaked with blood, and their dust made fat with fatness. 8 For *it is* the day of the LORD's vengeance, *and* the year of recompenses for the controversy of Zion. 9 And the streams thereof shall be turned into pitch, and the dust thereof into brimstone, and the land thereof shall become burning pitch. 10 It shall not be quenched night nor day; the smoke thereof shall go up for ever: from generation to generation it shall lie waste; none shall pass through it for ever and ever. 11 But the cormorant and the bittern shall possess it; the owl also and the raven shall dwell in it: and he shall stretch out upon it the line of confusion, and the stones of emptiness. 12 They shall call the nobles thereof to the kingdom, but none *shall be* there, and all her princes shall be nothing. 13 And thorns shall come up in her palaces, nettles and brambles in the fortresses thereof: and it shall be an habitation of dragons, *and* a court for owls. 14 The wild beasts of the desert shall also meet with the wild beasts of the island, and the satyr shall cry to his fellow; the screech owl also shall rest there, and find for herself a place of rest. 15 There shall the great owl make her nest, and lay, and hatch, and gather under her shadow: there shall the vultures also be gathered, every one with her mate. 16 Seek ye out of the book of the LORD, and read: no one of these shall fail, none shall want her mate: for my mouth it hath commanded, and his spirit it hath gathered them. 17 And he hath cast the lot for them, and his hand hath divided it unto them by line: they shall possess it for ever, from generation to generation shall they dwell therein."

Isaiah, Chapter 60:12, 16,

"For the nation and kingdom that will not serve thee shall perish; yea, *those* nations shall be utterly wasted. [***] Thou shalt also suck the milk of the Gentiles, and shalt suck the breast of kings: and thou shalt know that I the LORD *am* thy Saviour and thy Redeemer, the mighty One of Jacob."

Isaiah, Chapter 61,

"The spirit of the Lord GOD *is* upon me; because the LORD hath anointed me to preach good tidings unto the meek; he hath sent me to bind up the brokenhearted, to proclaim liberty to the captives, and the opening of the prison to *them that are* bound; 2 To proclaim the acceptable year of the LORD, and the day of vengeance of our God; to comfort all that mourn; 3 To appoint unto them that mourn in Zion, to give unto them beauty for ashes, the oil of joy for mourning, the garment of praise for the spirit of heaviness; that they might be called trees of righteousness, the planting of the LORD, that he might be glorified. 4 And they shall build the old wastes, they shall raise up the former desolations, and they shall repair the waste cities, the desolations of many generations. 5 And strangers shall stand and feed your flocks, and the sons of the alien *shall be* your plowmen and your vinedressers. 6 But ye shall be named the Priests of the LORD: *men* shall call you the Ministers of our God: ye shall eat the riches of the Gentiles, and in their glory shall ye boast yourselves. 7 For your shame *ye shall have* double; and *for* confusion they shall rejoice in their portion: therefore in their land they shall possess the double: everlasting joy shall be unto them. 8 For I the LORD love judgment, I hate robbery for burnt offering; and I will direct their work in truth, and I will make an everlasting covenant with them. 9 And their seed shall be known among the Gentiles, and their offspring among the people: all that see them shall acknowledge them, that they *are* the seed *which* the LORD hath blessed. 10 I will greatly rejoice in the LORD, my soul shall be joyful in my God; for he hath clothed me with the garments of salvation, he hath covered me with the robe of righteousness, as a bridegroom decketh *himself* with ornaments, and as a bride adorneth *herself* with her jewels. 11 For as the earth bringeth forth her bud, and as the garden causeth the things that are sown in it to spring forth; so the Lord GOD will cause righteousness and praise to spring forth before all the nations."

The Nazis' infamous *Lebensborn* program, the program to breed "Aryan" children for the Reich, was perhaps instead a means for racist Jews to interject Jewish blood into the German "race" so as to dilute the blood of Esau. This is pure speculation, but it is based upon the fact that the Jews viewed Germans as Esau, wanted to destroy or weaken Esau, had control over the Third Reich, and had numerous Jewish members in the *SS* who could have fathered these children.

After the war, many people began to notice that a large number of children in Israel were tall, blond and blue eyed. They could have passed for Swedes. The entire Holocaust may well have been a eugenics program for racist Jews to clean up their blood, which they believed had been damaged by the Ghetto system of Europe. Jewish prophecy and lore teaches that in the Messianic Era Jews will be tall, fair-skinned (radiant: *Isaiah* 60:5) and handsome.

The especially interesting thing about these tall, blond, blue-eyed children in Israel, is that many were allegedly orphans—orphans who believed that they were Gentiles and who were shocked when told that their parents had been Jewish. This has led some to conclude that Jews kidnaped Gentile children and brought them to Israel.[717] This leads to speculation that after anointing their Messiah, racist Jews will use Gentile slaves to breed them children, so that they can populate the world with the children of breeding slaves and completely kill off Gentiles born and raised by Gentiles. They may plan to steal the children fathered and mothered by Gentiles, and they may plan to use Gentile woman as surrogate mothers to bear children of Jewish parents on a massive scale. This speculation is based on many Jewish writings, including, but not limited to, *Isaiah*, Chapter 49,

"Listen, O isles, unto me; and hearken, ye people, from far; The LORD hath called me from the womb; from the bowels of my mother hath he made mention of my name. 2 And he hath made my mouth like a sharp sword; in the shadow of his hand hath he hid me, and made me a polished shaft; in his quiver hath he hid me; 3 And said unto me, Thou *art* my servant, O Israel, in whom I will be glorified. 4 Then I said, I have laboured in vain, I have spent my strength for nought, and in vain: *yet* surely my judgment *is* with the LORD, and my work with my God. 5 And now, saith the LORD that formed me from the womb *to be* his servant, to bring Jacob again to him, Though Israel be not gathered, yet shall I be glorious in the eyes of the LORD, and my God shall be my strength. 6 And he said, It is a light thing that thou shouldest be my servant to raise up the tribes of Jacob, and to restore the preserved of Israel: I will also give thee for a light to the Gentiles, that *thou* mayest be my salvation unto the end of the earth. 7 Thus saith the LORD, the Redeemer of Israel, *and* his Holy One, to him whom man despiseth, to him whom the nation abhorreth, to a servant of rulers, Kings shall see and arise, princes also shall worship, because of the LORD that *is* faithful, *and* the Holy One of Israel, and he shall choose thee. 8 Thus saith the LORD, In an acceptable time have I heard thee, and in a day of salvation have I helped thee: and I will preserve thee, and give thee for a covenant of the people, to establish the earth, to cause to inherit the desolate heritages; 9 That *thou* mayest say to the prisoners, Go forth; to *them* that *are* in darkness, Shew yourselves. They shall feed in the ways, and their pastures *shall be* in all high places. 10 They shall not hunger nor thirst; neither shall the heat nor sun smite them: for he that hath mercy on them shall lead them, even by the springs of water shall he guide them. 11 And I will make all my mountains a way, and my highways shall be exalted. 12 Behold, these shall come from far: and, lo, these from the north and from the west; and these from the land of Sinim. 13 Sing, O heavens; and be joyful, O earth; and break forth *into* singing, O mountains: for the LORD hath comforted his people, and will have mercy upon his afflicted. 14 But Zion said, The LORD hath forsaken me, and my Lord hath forgotten me. 15 Can a woman forget her sucking child, that *she* should not have compassion on the son of her womb? yea, they may forget, yet will I not forget thee. 16 Behold, I have graven thee upon the palms of *my* hands; thy walls *are* continually before me. 17 Thy children shall make haste; thy destroyers and they that made thee waste shall go forth of thee. 18 Lift up thine eyes round about, and behold: all these gather themselves together, *and* come to thee. *As* I live, saith the LORD, thou shalt surely clothe thee with them all, as with an ornament, and bind them *on thee*, as a bride *doth*. 19 For thy waste and thy desolate places, and the land of thy destruction, shall even now be too narrow by reason of the inhabitants, and they that swallowed thee up shall be far away. 20 The children which thou shalt have, after thou hast lost the other, shall say again in thine ears, The place *is* too strait for me: give place to me that I may dwell. 21 Then shalt thou say in thine heart, Who hath begotten me these, seeing I have lost my children, and *am* desolate, a captive, and removing to and fro? and who hath brought up these? Behold, I was left alone; these, where *had* they *been?* 22 Thus saith the Lord GOD, Behold, I will lift up mine hand to the Gentiles, and set up my standard to the people: and they shall bring thy sons in *their* arms, and thy daughters shall be carried upon *their* shoulders. 23 And kings shall be thy nursing fathers, and their queens thy nursing mothers: they shall bow down to thee *with their* face *toward* the earth, and lick up the dust of thy feet; and thou shalt know that I *am* the LORD: for they shall not be ashamed that wait for me. 24 Shall the prey be taken from the mighty, or the lawful captive delivered? 25 But thus saith the LORD, Even the captives of the mighty shall be taken away, and the prey of the terrible shall be delivered: for I will contend with him that contendeth with thee, and I will save thy children. 26 And I will feed them that oppress thee with their own flesh; and they shall be drunken with their own blood, as with sweet wine: and all flesh shall know that I the LORD *am* thy Saviour and thy Redeemer, the mighty One of Jacob."

Isaiah, Chapter 60:12, 16,

"For the nation and kingdom that will not serve thee shall perish; yea, *those* nations shall be utterly wasted. [***] Thou shalt also suck the milk of the Gentiles, and shalt suck the breast of kings: and thou shalt know that I the LORD *am* thy Saviour and thy Redeemer, the mighty One of Jacob."

There are many instances in the Old Testament of the use of slaves taken from other nations to bear the ancestors of the Jews young, for example Abraham and Hagar. *Isaiah* 66 states, note that the "Lord" who is speaking is the voice of genocidal Jewish racism and absolute Jewish religious intolerance,

> "1 Thus saith the LORD, The heaven *is* my throne, and the earth *is* my footstool: where *is* the house that ye build unto me? and where *is* the place of my rest? 2 For all those *things* hath mine hand made, and all those *things* have been, saith the LORD: but to this *man* will I look, *even* to *him that is* poor and of a contrite spirit, and trembleth at my word. 3 He that killeth an ox *is as if* he slew a man; he that sacrificeth a lamb, *as if* he cut off a dog's neck; he that offereth an oblation, *as if he offered* swine's blood; he that burneth incense, *as if* he blessed an idol. Yea, they have chosen their own ways, and their soul delighteth in their abominations. 4 I also will choose their delusions, and will bring their fears upon them; because when I called, none did answer; when I spake, they did not hear: but they did evil before mine eyes, and chose *that* in which I delighted not. 5¶ Hear the word of the LORD, ye that tremble at his word; Your brethren that hated you, that cast you out for my name's sake, said, Let the LORD be glorified: but he *shall* appear to your joy, and they shall be ashamed. 6 A voice of noise from the city, a voice from the temple, a voice of the LORD that rendereth recompence to his enemies. 7 Before she travailed, she brought forth; before her pain came, she was delivered of a man child. 8 Who hath heard such *a thing?* who hath seen such *things?* Shall the earth be made to bring forth in one day? *or* shall a nation be born at once? for as soon as Zion travailed, she brought forth her children. 9 Shall I bring to the birth, and not cause to bring forth? saith the LORD: shall I cause to bring forth, and shut *the womb?* saith thy God. 10 Rejoice ye with Jerusalem, and be glad with her, all ye that love her: rejoice for joy with her, all ye that mourn for her: 11 That ye may suck, and be satisfied with the breasts of her consolations; that ye may milk out, and be delighted with the abundance of her glory. 12 For thus saith the LORD, Behold, I will extend peace to her like a river, and the glory of the Gentiles like a flowing stream: then shall ye suck, ye shall be borne upon *her* sides, and be dandled upon *her* knees. 13 As one whom his mother comforteth, so will I comfort you; and ye shall be comforted in Jerusalem. 14 And when ye see *this,*

your heart shall rejoice, and your bones shall flourish like an herb: and the hand of the LORD shall be known toward his servants, and *his* indignation toward his enemies. 15 For, behold, the LORD will come with fire, and with his chariots like a whirlwind, to render his anger with fury, and his rebuke with flames of fire. 16 For by fire and by his sword will the LORD plead with all flesh: and the slain of the LORD shall be many. 17 They that sanctify themselves, and purify themselves in the gardens behind one *tree* in the midst, eating swine's flesh, and the abomination, and the mouse, shall be consumed together, saith the LORD. 18 For I *know* their works and their thoughts: it shall come, that I will gather all nations and tongues; and they shall come, and see my glory. 19 And I will set a sign among them, and I will send those that escape of them unto the nations, *to* Tarshish, Pul, and Lud, that draw the bow, *to* Tubal, and Javan, *to* the isles afar off, that have not heard my fame, neither have seen my glory; and they shall declare my glory among the Gentiles. 20 And they shall bring all your brethren *for* an offering unto the LORD out of all nations upon horses, and in chariots, and in litters, and upon mules, and upon swift beasts, to my holy mountain Jerusalem, saith the LORD, as the children of Israel bring an offering in a clean vessel *into* the house of the LORD. 21 And I will also take of them for priests *and* for Levites, saith the LORD. 22 For as the new heavens and the new earth, which I *will* make, *shall* remain before me, saith the LORD, so shall your seed and your name remain. 23 And it shall come to pass, *that* from one new moon to another, and from one sabbath to another, shall all flesh come to worship before me, saith the LORD. 24 And they shall go forth, and look upon the carcases of the men that have transgressed against me: for their worm shall not die, neither shall their fire be quenched; and they shall be an abhorring unto all flesh."

NOTES:

1. A. Einstein, A. Engel translator, "How I became a Zionist", *The Collected Papers of Albert Einstein*, Volume 7, Document 57, Princeton University Press, (2002), pp. 234-235, at 235.

2. A. Einstein, "Jewish Nationalism and Anti-Semitism", *The Jewish Chronicle*, (17 June 1921), p. 16.

3. J. Stachel, "Einstein's Jewish Identity", *Einstein from 'B' to 'Z'*, Birkhäuser, Boston, Basel, Berlin, (2002), pp. 57-83, at 68.

4. A. Moszkowski to A. Einstein, translated by A. M. Hentschel, *The Collected Papers of Albert Einstein*, Volume 8, Document 292, Princeton University Press, (1998), p. 281.

5. Letter from A. Einstein to H. Zangger of 15 or 22 December 1919, English translation by A. Hentschel, *The Collected Papers of Albert Einstein*, Volume 9, Document 217, Princeton University Press, (2004), pp. 185-186, at 186.

6. Letter from A. Einstein to H. Zangger of 24 December 1919, English translation by A. Hentschel, *The Collected Papers of Albert Einstein*, Volume 9, Document 233, Princeton University Press, (2004), pp. 197-198.

7. Letter from A. Einstein to H. Zangger of 3 January 1920, English translation by A. Hentschel, *The Collected Papers of ALbert Einstein*, Volume 9, Document 242, Princeton University Press, (2004), pp. 204-205, at 204.

8. Letter from A. Einstein to H. A. Lorentz of 19 January 1920, English translation by A. Hentschel, *The Collected Papers of Albert Einstein*, Volume 9, Document 265, Princeton University Press, (2004), p. 220.

9. Adelbert von Chamisso:

Die Sonne bringt es an den Tag

Gemächlich in der Werkstatt saß
Zum Frühtrunk Meister Nikolas,
Die junge Hausfrau schenkt' ihm ein,
Es war im heitern Sonnenschein. —
Die Sonne bringt es an den Tag.

Die Sonne blinkt von der Schale Rand,
Malt zitternde Kringeln an die Wand,
Und wie den Schein er ins Auge faßt,
So spricht er für sich, indem er erblaßt :
"Du bringst es doch nicht an den Tag" —

"Wer nicht? was nicht?'. die Frau fragt gleich,
"Was stierst du so an? was wirst du so bleich?"
Und er darauf: "Sei still, nur still !
Ich's doch nicht sagen kann noch will.
Die Sonne bringt's nicht an den Tag."

Die Frau nur dringender forscht und fragt,
Mit Schmeicheln ihn und Hadern plagt,
Mit süßem und mit bitterm Wort;
Sie fragt und plagt ihn Ort und Ort :
"Was bringt die Sonne nicht an den Tag?"

"Nein nimmermehr!" — "Du sagst es mir noch."
"Ich sag es nicht." — "Du sagst es mir doch."
Da ward zuletzt er müd und schwach
Und gab der Ungestümen nach. —
Die Sonne bringt es an den Tag.

"Auf der Wanderschaft, 's sind zwanzig Jahr,
Da traf es mich einst gar sonderbar.
Ich hatt nicht Geld, nicht Ranzen, noch Schuh,
War hungrig und durstig und zornig dazu. —
Die Sonne bringt's nicht an den Tag.

Da kam mir just ein Jud in die Quer,
Ringsher war's still und menschenleer,
'Du hilfst mir, Hund, aus meiner Not!
Den Beutel her, sonst schlag ich dich tot!'
Die Sonne bringt's nicht an den Tag.

Und er: 'Vergieße nicht mein Blut,
Acht Pfennige sind mein ganzes Gut!'
Ich glaubt ihm nicht und fiel ihn an ;
Er war ein alter, schwacher Mann —
Die Sonne bringt's nicht an den Tag.

So rücklings lag er blutend da;
Sein brechendes Aug in die Sonne sah;
Noch hob er zuckend die Hand empor,
Noch schrie er röchelnd mir ins Ohr.
'Die Sonne bringt es an den Tag!'

Ich macht ihn schnell noch vollends stumm
Und kehrt ihm die Taschen um und um:
Acht Pfenn'ge, das war das ganze Geld.
Ich scharrt ihn ein auf selbigem Feld —
Die Sonne bringt's nicht an den Tag.

Dann zog ich weit und weiter hinaus,
Kam hier ins Land, bin jetzt zu Haus. —
Du weißt nun meine Heimlichkeit,

So halte den Mund und sei gescheit!
Die Sonne bringt's nicht an den Tag.

Wann aber sie so flimmernd scheint,
Ich merk es wohl, was sie da meint,
Wie sie sich müht und sich erbost, —
Du, schau nicht hin und sei getrost :
Sie bringt es doch nicht an den Tag."

So hatte die Sonn eine Zunge nun,
Der Frauen Zungen ja nimmer ruhn. —
"Gevatterin, um Jesus Christ!
Laßt Euch nicht merken, was Ihr nun wißt!" —
Nun bringt's die Sonne an den Tag.

Die Raben ziehen krächzend zumal
Nach dem Hochgericht, zu halten ihr Mahl.
Wen flechten sie aufs Rad zur Stund?
Was hat er getan? wie ward es kund?
Die Sonne bracht es an den Tag.

10. E. Halley, in Newton's *Principia* in the translation by A. Motte, revised and annotated by F. Cajori, "Ode to Newton", *Principia*, Volume 1, University of California Press, Berkeley, Los Angeles, London, (1962), pp. XIII-XV.
11. Racist political Zionist Theodor Herzl wrote on 12 June 1895,

"Jewish papers! I will induce the publishers of the biggest Jewish papers (*Neue Freie Presse, Berliner Tageblatt, Frankfurter Zeitung,* etc.) to publish editions over there, as the *New York Herald* does in Paris."—T. Herzl, English translation by H. Zohn, R. Patai, Editor, *The Complete Diaries of Theodor Herzl*, Volume 1, Herzl Press, New York, (1960), p. 84.

THE DEARBORN INDEPENDENT, praised the *New York Herald*. "When Editors Were Independent of the Jews", THE DEARBORN INDEPENDENT, (5 February 1921). *See also:* T. Herzl, English translation by H. Zohn, R. Patai, Editor, *The Complete Diaries of Theodor Herzl*, Volumes 1 and 2, Herzl Press, New York, (1960), pp. 37, 97, 170, 455, 457, 480. *See also:* A. Elon, *Herzl*, Holt, Rinehart and Winston, New York, (1975), pp. 167-168. *See also: The Collected Papers of Albert Einstein*, Volume 7, Document 35, Princeton University Press, (2002), pp. 296-297, note 8.
12. Letter from H. Zangger to A. Einstein of 22 October 1919, English translation by A. Hentschel, *The Collected Papers of Albert Einstein*, Volume 9, Document 148, Princeton University Press, (2004), pp. 126-128, at 127.

13. F. K. Wiebe, *Deutschland und die Judenfrage*, M. Müller & Sohn, Hrsg. im Auftrage des Instituts zum Studium der Judenfrage, Berlin, (1939); **English** translation, *Germany and the Jewish Problem*, Published on behalf of the Institute for the Study of the Jewish Problem, Berlin, (1939); **French** translation, *L'Allemagne et la Question Juive*, Berlin, Edité sous les auspices de l'Institut pour l'étude de la question juive, (1939); **Spanish** translation, *Alemania y la Cuestión Judía*, Publicado por encargo del Instituto para el Estudio de la Cuestión Judía, Berlín, (1939).

14. Racist political Zionist Theodor Herzl wrote on 12 June 1895,

> "Jewish papers! I will induce the publishers of the biggest Jewish papers (*Neue Freie Presse, Berliner Tageblatt, Frankfurter Zeitung,* etc.) to publish editions over there, as the *New York Herald* does in Paris."—T. Herzl, English translation by H. Zohn, R. Patai, Editor, *The Complete Diaries of Theodor Herzl,* Volume 1, Herzl Press, New York, (1960), p. 84.

THE *DEARBORN INDEPENDENT*, praised the *New York Herald.* "When Editors Were Independent of the Jews", THE *DEARBORN INDEPENDENT*, (5 February 1921). *See also:* T. Herzl, English translation by H. Zohn, R. Patai, Editor, *The Complete Diaries of Theodor Herzl,* Volumes 1 and 2, Herzl Press, New York, (1960), pp. 37, 97, 170, 455, 457, 480. *See also:* A. Elon, *Herzl*, Holt, Rinehart and Winston, New York, (1975), pp. 167-168. *See also: The Collected Papers of Albert Einstein,* Volume 7, Document 35, Princeton University Press, (2002), pp. 296-297, note 8.

15. S. E. Weltmann, "Germany, Turkey, and the Zionist Movement, 1914-1918", *The Review of Politics,* Volume 23, Number 2, (April, 1961), pp. 246-269, at 266.

16. A. Myerson and I. Goldberg, *The German Jew: His Share in Modern Culture,* A. A. Knopf, New York, (1933), pp. 140-142.

17. Letter from H. K. Onnes to A. Einstein of 8 February 1920, A. Hentschel, translator, *The Collected Papers of Albert Einstein,* Volume 9, Document 304, Princeton University Press, (2004), pp. 254-255, at 255.

18. E. Gehrcke, *Die Massensuggestion der Relativitätstheorie: Kuturhistorisch-psychologische Dokumente,* Berlin, Hermann Meusser, (1924), pp. 19-22, 25, 56.

19. English translation by I. Born, *The Born-Einstein Letters,* Walker and Company, New York, (1971), pp. 34-52.

20. M. Born, *Die Relativitätstheorie Einsteins und ihre physikalischen Grundlagen: gemeinverständlich dargestellt,* J. Springer, Berlin, (1920).

21. P. Rogers, "Another *Annus Mirabilis?*", *Physics World,* (August, 2004); posted on *Physics Web,* <http://physicsweb.org/articles/world/17/8/1>

22. P. Rogers, "History Revisited", *Physics World,* (September, 2003); posted on *Physics Web,* <http://physicsweb.org/articles/world/16/9/1>

23. P. Rogers, "Do's and don'ts [*sic*] for authors", *Physics World*, (November, 2003); posted on *Physics Web*, <http://physicsweb.org/articles/world/16/11/1>

24. Letter from A. Eliasberg to A. Einstein of 27 January 1920, A. Hentschel, translator, *The Collected Papers of Albert Einstein*, Volume 9, Document 286, Princeton University Press, (2004), pp. 238-239, at 239.

25. Letter from P. Epstein to A. Einstein of 31 January 1920, A. Hentschel, translator, *The Collected Papers of Albert Einstein*, Volume 9, Document 290, Princeton University Press, (2004), pp. 240-241.

26. Letter from A. Einstein to H. and M. Born of 27 January 1920, A. Hentschel, translator, *The Collected Papers of Albert Einstein*, Volume 9, Document 284, Princeton University Press, (2004), pp. 235-238, at 236.

27. Letter from V. G. Ehrenberg to A. Einstein of 23 November 1919, English translation by A. Hentschel, *The Collected Papers of Albert Einstein*, Volume 9, Document 173, Princeton University Press, (2004), p. 145.

28. Letter from P. Oppenheim to A. Einstein of 27 November 1919, English translation by A. Hentschel, *The Collected Papers of Albert Einstein*, Volume 9, Document 179, Princeton University Press, (2004), pp. 153-154, at 153. *See also:* Editor's note 3 in the German ed.

29. P. L. Rose, *Revolutionary Antisemitism in Germany from Kant to Wagner*, Princeton University Press, (1990).

30. E. K. Dühring, *Die Judenfrage als Racen-, Sitten- und Culturfrage: mit einer weltgeschichtlichen Antwort*, H. Reuther, Karlsruhe, (1881); English translation by A. Jacob, *Eugen Dühring on the Jews*, Nineteen Eighty Four Press, Brighton, England, (1997), pp. 133-134, 138-139, 178-179.

31. B. Disraeli, *Coningsby; or, The New Generation*, H. Colburn, London, (1844), here quoted from The Century Co. edition of 1904, New York, pp. 231-232.

32. M. Born, *The Born-Einstein Letters*, Walker and Company, New York, (1971), p. 16. A. Einstein, *The World As I See It*, Citadel Press, New York, (1993), p. 89.

33. S. G. Bloom, *Postville: A Clash of Cultures in Heartland America*, Harcourt, Inc., New York, (2000), pp. 63-64.

34. H. Dukas and B. Hoffmann, *Albert Einstein: The Human Side*, Princeton University Press, (1979), p. 55.

35. M. Janssen, *et al.*, Editors, *The Collected Papers of Albert Einstein*, Volume 7, Note 7, Princeton University Press, (2002), pp. 124-125.

36. M. Born, *My Life: Recollections of a Nobel Laureate*, Charles Scribner's Sons, New York, (1975), p. 185.

37. *See, for example: The Collected Papers of Albert Einstein*, Volume 9, Documents 44 and 64, Princeton University Press, (2004).

38. D. Fahey, *The Mystical Body of Christ in the Modern World*, Browne and Nolan Limited, London, (1935), pp. 273-275, *see also:* 275-280, *especially* points 2 and 16, at pp. 277-279.

39. "Consul Investigated Charge", *The New York Times*, (6 December 1933), p. 6.

40. J. Stachel, *Einstein from 'B' to 'Z'*, Birkhäuser, Boston, (2002), p. 71.

41. A. Einstein, "Why Socialism?", *Monthly Review*, (May, 1949); reprinted in *Ideas and Opinions*, Crown, New York, (1954), pp. 151-158.

42. M. Janssen, *et al.*, Editors, *The Collected Papers of Albert Einstein*, Volume 7, Princeton University Press, Volume 7, Note 7 (2002), pp. 124-145.

43. Letter from A. Einstein to the Borns of 27 January 1920, *The Collected Papers of Albert Einstein*, Volume 9, Document 284, Princeton University Press, (2004).

44. A. Ha-Am, "The Law of the Heart", in A. Hertzberg, *The Zionist Idea*, Harper Torchbooks, New York, (1959), pp. 251-255.

45. H. N. Bialik, "Bialik on the Hebrew University", in A. Hertzberg, *The Zionist Idea*, Harper Torchbooks, New York, (1959), pp. 281-288, at 282-283.

46. D. Ben-Gurion, *Ba-Maarachah*, Volume 3, Tel-Aviv, (1948), pp. 200-211, English translation in A. Hertzberg, *The Zionist Idea*, Harper Torchbooks, New York, (1959), pp. 606-619, at 618.

47. A. Einstein, *Ideas and Opinions*, Crown, New York, (1954), p. 181.

48. "Prof. Einstein Here, Explains Relativity", *The New York Times*, (3 April 1921), pp. 1, 13, at 1.

49. A. Leroy-Beaulieu, *Israel chez les nations: Les Juifs et l'antisémitisme*, C. Lévy, Paris, (1893); English translation by F. Hellman, *Israel among the Nations: A Study of the Jews and Antisemitism*, G. P. Putnam's Sons, New York, W. Heinemann, London, (1895), pp. 60-61.

50. P. Findley, *They Dare to Speak Out: People and Institutions Confront Israel's Lobby*, Lawrence Hill, Westport, Connecticut, (1985); **and** *Deliberate Deceptions: Facing the Facts about the U.S.-Israeli Relationship*, Lawrence Hill Books, Chicago, (1993); **and** *Silent No More: Confronting America's False Images of Islam*, D : Amana Publications, Beltsville, Maryland, (2001). *See also:* R. I. Friedman, "Selling Israel in America: The Hasbara Project Targets the U.S. Media", *Mother Jones*, (February/March, 1987), pp. 1-9; reprinted "Selling Israel to America", *Journal of Palestine Studies*, Volume 16, Number 4, (Summer, 1987) , pp. 169-179.

51. P. Michelmore, *Einstein: Profile of the Man*, Dodd, Mead, New York, (1962), p. 3.

52. Letter from A. Einstein to E. Zürcher of 15 April 1919, English translation by A. Hentschel, *The Collected Papers of Albert Einstein*, Volume 9, Document 23, Princeton University Press, (2004), p. 19.

53. P. Frank, *Einstein: His Life and Times*, Alfred A. Knopf, New York, (1967), p. 145.

54. A. Leroy-Beaulieu, *Israel chez les nations: Les Juifs et l'antisémitisme*, C. Lévy, Paris, (1893); English translation by F. Hellman, *Israel among the Nations: A Study of the Jews and Antisemitism*, G. P. Putnam's Sons, New York, W. Heinemann, London, (1895), pp. 246-247.

55. On the myth among Einstein supporters, *see:* D. E. Rowe, "'Jewish Mathematics' at Göttingen in the Era of Felix Klein", *Isis*, Volume 77, Number 3, (September, 1986), pp. 422-449; **and** "Science in Germany: The Intersection of Institutional and Intellectual Issues", *Osiris*, Series 2, Volume 5, (1989), pp. 186-213. *See also:* A. Fölsing, *Albert Einstein: A Biography*, Viking, New York, (1997), p. 203. On the myth among Einstein's adversaries, *see:* K. Hentschel, *Physics and National Socialism: An Anthology of Primary Sources*, Basel, Boston, Birkhäuser, (1996). On Einstein's anti-intuition / anti-induction stance, *see:* A. Moszkowski, *Einstein: The Searcher*, E. P. Dutton, New York, (1921), pp. 179-182. *See also:* A. Einstein, "Antrittsreden des Hrn. Einstein", *Sitzungsberichte der Königlich Preussischen Akademie der Wissenschaften zu Berlin*, (1914), pp. 739-742; English translation by A. Engel, "Inaugural Lecture of Mr. Einstein", *The Collected Papers of Albert Einstein*, Volume 6, Document 3, Princeton University Press, (1997), pp. 16-18; **and** "Motive des Forschers", *Zu Max Plancks sechzigstem Geburtstag. Ansprachen, gehalten am 26. April 1918 in der Deutschen Physikalischen Gesellschaft von E. Warburg, M. v. Laue, A. Sommerfeld und A. Einstein*, C. F. Müllersche Hofbuchhandlung, (1918), pp. 29-32; English translation by A. Engel, "Motives for Research", *The Collected Papers of Albert Einstein*, Volume 7, Document 7, Princeton University Press, (2002), pp. 41-45; **and** "Time, Space, and Gravitation / Theories of Principle", *London Times*, (28 November 1919), p. 13-14, English translation corrected: "Einstein on His Theory", *London Times*, (2 December 1919), p. 17; **and** "Induktion und Deduktion in der Physik", *Berliner Tageblatt*, Morning Edition, 4. Beiblatt, (25 December 1919), p. 1; English translation by A. Engel, "Induction and Deduction", *The Collected Papers of Albert Einstein*, Volume 7, Document 28, (2002), pp. 108-109; "Physics and Reality", *The Journal of the Franklin Institute*, Volume 221, Number 3, (March, 1936), reprinted: A. Einstein, *Ideas and Opinions*, Crown Publishers, Inc., New York, (1954), pp. 290-323, *see especially:* Section 4, "The Theory of Relativity", p. 307. Maurice Solovine quotes Einstein as supporting intuition, "Physics,' he said, 'is essentially an intuitive and concrete science. Mathematics is only a means for expressing the laws that govern phenomena.'" Quoted in, *Einstein: A Centenary Volume*, International Commission on Physics Education, U. S. A., (1979), p. 9. *The New York Times* reported on 3 April 1921 on the front page, "One of his traveling companions described him as an 'intuitive physicist' whose speculative imagination is so vast that it senses great natural laws long before the reasoning faculty grasps and defines them."

56. *La Vieille* (Paris), Number 272, (20 April 1922), p. 15.

57. "Prof. Einstein Here, Explains Relativity", *The New York Times*, (3 April 1921), pp. 1, 13, at 1.

58. "Prof. Einstein Here, Explains Relativity", *The New York Times*, (3 April 1921), pp. 1, 13, at 1.

59. "Prof. Einstein Here, Explains Relativity", *The New York Times*, (3 April 1921), pp. 1, 13.

60. Letter from A. Einstein to P. Nathan of 3 April 1920, *The Collected Papers of Albert Einstein*, Volume 9, Document 366, Princeton University Press, (2004), p. 492. Also: *The Collected Papers of Albert Einstein*, Volume 1,

Princeton University Press, (1987), p. *lx*, note 44. J. Stachel, "Einstein's Jewish Identity", *Einstein from 'B' to 'Z'*, Birkhäuser, Boston, Basel, Berlin, (2002), pp. 57-83, at 69. *See also:* P. A. Bucky, Einstein, and A. G. Weakland, *The Private Albert Einstein*, Andrews and McMeel, Kansas City, (1992), pp. 83, 86.

61. H. Goenner, "The Reaction to Relativity Theory. I: The Anti-Einstein Campaign in Germany in 1920", *Science in Context*, Volume 6, Number 1, (1993), pp. 107-133, at 112. "Kleinert (1979, 501-6) and Elton (1986, 95)" refers to: A. Kleinert, in H. Nelkowski, et. al. Editors, *Einstein Symposium Berlin 1979*, pp. 501-506; **and** L. Elton, "Einstein, General Relativity and the German Press", *Isis*, Volume 79, (1986), p. 95.

62. P. Michelmore, *Einstein: Profile of the Man*, Dodd, Mead, (1962), p. 87.

63. H. Dukas and B. Hoffmann, *Albert Einstein: The Human Side*, Princeton University Press, (1979), pp. 55-56.

64. A. Einstein quoted in A. Fölsing, English translation by E. Osers, *Albert Einstein, a Biography*, Viking, New York, (1997), p. 494; which cites speech to the *Central-Verein Deutscher Staatsbürger Jüdischen Glaubens*, in Berlin on 5 April 1920, in D. Reichenstein, *Albert Einstein. Sein Lebensbild und seine Weltanschauung*, Berlin, (1932). This letter from Einstein to the Central Association of German Citizens of the Jewish Faith of 5 April 1920 is reproduced in *The Collected Papers of Albert Einstein*, Volume 9, Document 368, Princeton University Press, (2004).

65. T. Herzl, English translation by H. Zohn, R. Patai, Editor, *The Complete Diaries of Theodor Herzl*, Volume 1, Herzl Press, New York, (1960), p. 196.

66. A. Einstein, "Our Debt to Zionism", *Out of My Later Years*, Carol Publishing Group, New York, (1995), pp. 262-264, at 262.

67. R. P. Boas, "The Problem of American Judaism", *The Atlantic Monthly*, Volume 119, Number 2, (February, 1917), pp. 145-152.

68. "The Modern Jews", *The North American Review*, Volume 60, Number 127, (April, 1845), pp. 329-368, at 348.

69. "LURIA, ISAAC BEN SOLOMON, *Encyclopaedia Judaica*, Volume 11 LEK-MIL, Macmillan, Jerusalem, (1971), cols. 572-578, at 576. J. A. Eisenmenger, *The Traditions of the Jews, Contained in the Talmud and other Mystical Writings*, Volume 1, J. Robinson, London, (1748), pp. 277-338.

70. B. J. Hendrick, "The Jews in America: II Do the Jews Dominate American Finance?", *The World's Work*, Volume 44, Number 3, (January, 1923), pp. 266-286, at 282.

71. R. I. Friedman, *The False Prophet: Rabbi Meir Kahane: from FBI Informant to Knesset Member*, Lawrence Hill Books, Brooklyn, New York, (1990), p. 38.

72. *Cf.* "Gentile", *The Jewish Encyclopedia*, Funk and Wagnalls Company, New York, (1903), pp. 615-626, at 618.

73. H. Dukas and B. Hoffmann, *Albert Einstein: The Human Side*, Princeton University Press, (1979), p. 55.

74. Letter from A. Einstein to "Berlin-Schöneberg Office of Taxation" of 10 February 1920, *The Collected Papers of Albert Einstein*, Volume 9, Document

306, Princeton University Press, (2004), pp. 256-257, at 257.

75. D. Overbye, *Einstein in Love: A Scientific Romance*, Viking, New York, (2000), pp. 343, 404, note 22. *See:* A. Einstein to Ilse Einstein, *The Collected Papers of Albert Einstein*, Volume 8, Document 536, Princeton University Press, (1998); **and** Ilse Einstein to Georg Nikolai, *The Collected Papers of Albert Einstein*, Volume 8, Document 545, Princeton University Press, (1998).

76. B. Thüring, "Albert Einsteins Umsturzversuch der Physik und seine inneren Möglichkeiten und Ursachen", *Forschungen zur Judenfrage*, Volume 4, (1940), pp. 134-162, at 142. Republished as: *Albert Einsteins Umsturzversuch der Physik und seine inneren Möglichkeiten und Ursachen*, Dr. Georg Lüttke Verlag, Berlin, (1941).

77. H. Dukas and B. Hoffmann, *Albert Einstein: The Human Side*, Princeton University Press, (1979), p. 55.

78. Quoted in B. Thüring, "Albert Einsteins Umsturzversuch der Physik und seine inneren Möglichkeiten und Ursachen", *Forschungen zur Judenfrage*, Volume 4, (1940), pp. 134-162, at 156-157. Republished as: *Albert Einsteins Umsturzversuch der Physik und seine inneren Möglichkeiten und Ursachen*, Dr. Georg Lüttke Verlag, Berlin, (1941).

79. P. Frank, *Einstein, His Life and Times*, Alfred A. Knopf, New York, (1947), pp. 182-183.

80. C. Weizmann, *Trial and Error: The Autobiography of Chaim Weizmann*, Harper & Brothers, New York, (1949), p. 266.

81. *Compare, for example:* Letter from A. Einstein to the League of German Scholars and Artists of 13 January 1920, *The Collected Papers of Albert Einstein*, Volume 9, Document 258, Princeton University Press, (2004); *to:* A. Einstein, *The World As I See It*, Citadel Press, New York, (1993), p. 89. *See also:* G. J. Whitrow, Editor, *Einstein: The Man and his Achievement*, Dover, New York, (1967), pp. 17-18. H. Dukas and B. Hoffmann, *Albert Einstein: The Human Side*, Princeton University Press, (1979), pp. 6-11. A. Fölsing, *Albert Einstein: A Biography*, Viking, New York, (1997), pp. 30, 39-41, 52, 58, 80-82, 83, 273, 327, 334-335, 346, 394, 426, 502, 515, 539-541, 643, 661, 667, 687, 714. A. Pais, *Subtle is the Lord*, Oxford University Press, (1982), p.504. R. Schulmann, *et al.*, Editors, *The Collected Papers of Albert Einstein*, Volume 8, Part A, Note 3, Princeton University Press, (1998), pp. 166-167. Letter from A. Einstein to A. S. Eddington of 2 February 1920, *The Collected Papers of Albert Einstein*, Volume 9, Document 293, Princeton University Press, (2004), p. 245. Letter from A. Einstein to "Berlin-Schöneberg Office of Taxation" of 10 February 1920, *The Collected Papers of Albert Einstein*, Volume 9, Document 306, Princeton University Press, (2004), pp. 256-257, at 256.

82. J. Stachel, *Einstein from 'B' to 'Z'*, Birkhäuser, Boston, (2002), pp. 60-61.

83. "Text of Untermyer's Address", *The New York Times*, (7 August 1933), p. 4. *See also:* "Untermyer Back, Greeted in Harbor", *The New York Times*, (7 August 1933), p. 4.

84. A. Einstein, "Jewish Nationalism and Anti-Semitism", *The Jewish Chronicle*, (17 June 1921), p. 16.

85. A. Einstein, A. Engel translator, "How I became a Zionist", *The Collected Papers of Albert Einstein*, Volume 7, Document 57, Princeton University Press, (2002), pp. 234-235, at 235.

86. M. Samuel, "Diaries of Theodor Herzl", in: M. W. Weisgal, *Theodor Herzl: A Memorial*, The New Palestine, New York, (1929), pp. 125-180, at 129. T. Herzl, English translation by H. Zohn, R. Patai, Editor, *The Complete Diaries of Theodor Herzl*, Volume 1, Herzl Press, New York, (1960), pp. 4, 111.

87. P. W. Massing, *Rehearsal for Destruction: A Study of Political Anti-Semitism in Imperial Germany*, Howard Fertig, New York, (1967), pp. 311-312.

88. R. H. Fife, Jr., *The German Empire Between Two Wars: A Study of the Political and Social Development of the Nation Between 1871 and 1914*, Macmillan, New York, (1916), pp. 177-199 and 359-388:

"CHAPTER IX

THE PROLETARIAN IN POLITICS

IF we were obliged to cover with one word the development of Germany in the four decades between the two great wars, that word would certainly be "socialism." It is not merely that in philosophy, literature and art the welfare of the masses is the leading motif running through the eighties and nineties until it became lost after 1900 in the swelling music of national ambition. In the field of political economy also socialistic ideas marked the age. They began by conquering the professorial chairs in the universities in the seventies, where such "socialists of the chair" as Adolf Wagner of the university of Berlin set their stamp on the generation of political economists which followed the war with France, and they found expression in the compulsory insurance measures and similar legislation of the following decade. Such ideas were indeed nothing new in Germany since the sixteenth century, when cities such as Augsburg and Strasburg were models of a hard and fast organization, in which capital played a small part and the workers formed the commonwealth on the principle of a closed shop, where communal undertakings largely supplanted private enterprise and every detail of life, including the details of food and dress, was fixed by law. The paternalism of the petty despotisms which preceded German unity had disciplined the Germans to live under efficient supervision, and the ideals of the Manchester school of British economists did not take lasting hold on German economic life.

Socialism then grew in Germany on well-prepared soil. State ownership of railroad and telegraph had come naturally soon after the coming of these utilities, and municipal control of many forms of enterprise descended as a tradition from the later middle ages. That the individual should look to the government to provide for his welfare and that state and communal funds should supplant private capital in many undertakings had long been the case when Bismarck undertook his compulsory insurance policy in the eighties. This program was, as we have seen, an effort to strike the ground from beneath the Social Democrats by removing some of the causes of proletarian dissatisfaction. Here and there Bismarck's successors went further on the road, with such measures as the purchase of the *Hercynia* potash mine (cf. page 166). That they did not go still further in this and other fields of state socialism was due in large measure to the existence of the Social Democratic party. This Ishmael in Germany's political life by its very advocacy of measures made them impossible for the government.

What is it that has made the Socialist unfitted to be an ally and unwelcome as a coworker with nearly all other parties? What is there in the advocacy by the Social Democrats of any reform that has caused not only the East Elbian *Junker* and the Westphalian manufacturer, but even the National Liberal physician and shopkeeper to look askance at it? The answer is to be found both in the doctrinaire character of the party and in the violence of Socialist editors and orators. Karl Lamprecht has shown that all German political parties are antiquated in that all cling to formulas and doctrines that have outlived their applicability to present-day affairs. In this sense the Social Democratic party is the most antiquated and the least opportunist. In this has lain its strength as a class party and its weakness in electoral and parliamentary strategy. Beginning with the removal of the coercive laws in 1890, it cast at all national elections the largest vote of any party, and after 1903 held under its discipline nearly one-third of all the electors to the national parliament, more than all the other Liberal fractions combined. Nevertheless it exercised less influence on legislation than any other of the major groups in the empire. To understand the reason for this one must glance at the development of socialism as a political force.

When in 1867 Friedrich Liebknecht and August Bebel were elected to the first *Reichstag* of the new-born North German Confederation, they found ready at hand both the gospel of socialism in the works of Karl Marx and the needed fighting force in the German Workingmen's Party (*Allgemeiner Deutscher Arbeiter-Verein*), which had been founded four years earlier by Ferdinand Lassalle. Two years later at the famous Eisenach Convention Liebknecht and Bebel called the Social Democratic Workingmen's Party into existence, on a platform built of Marx' theory of the destructive rule of capital and his call to the workingmen of all lands to unite, and finally in 1875 the followers of Lassalle forsook their nationalistic ideals and were won over to the internationalism of the Marxists. Immediately the triumphal march of the Social Democrats began, a march which has continued with few halts since. Aided by the hardships brought on by the financial crises of the seventies, the Marxian theories of the misery caused by the capitalistic state and the exploitation of the working class through the capitalistic organization of society found eager acceptance in all quarters of industrial Germany. Already in 1876 there were twenty-four papers and journals published in the interest of the party with nearly one hundred thousand subscribers: by the next year the number of party periodicals had increased to forty-one, and that year the party cast nearly half a million votes and elected twelve members to the national legislature. From that time the Social Democracy kept pace closely with the forward movement of industrial Germany. Wherever factories sprang up and workmen came to live together, the theories of Marx took root. The workingmen were organized into Socialist unions, which became at once fighting units in the industries and the elections; with the capacity for organization so characteristic of an industrial age and of German society in particular, the Social Democracy was solidified by the establishment of central bureaus under the control of secretaries. These latter quickly developed into a class of experienced leaders, at once clever agitators in the industries and skillful strategists in political campaigns.

Bismarck watched the rise of the party and its often unscrupulous means of agitation with growing distrust. He put no confidence in the alleged peaceful program of socialism: for him the party bore nothing but red revolution on its banners. In 1878 two attempts were made on the life of Emperor William which were unjustly ascribed to the effect of socialist agitation; and the Chancellor took advantage of the popular outcry to dissolve the Liberal *Reichstag* and appeal to the electors on an anti-socialist program. The result was the enactment of rigid laws forbidding Socialist propaganda. The following ten years, 1880 to 1890, were for the party a period of almost subterranean existence. Clubs were suppressed, newspapers and journals confiscated, many of the leaders, Liebknecht and Bebel among them, went to prison. In spite of prosecution and imprisonment, however, the propaganda went straight ahead. Political clubs were reorganized as singing societies and bowling clubs and the party organization was perpetuated by these and by the trade unions, which continued to spread like a vast network throughout industrial Germany. During the ten years of the anti-socialist laws the total vote of the party increased, a larger number of deputies was chosen to the *Reichstag*, and more important still, the inner organization and solidity of the party gained tremendously under persecution. This was shown immediately on the expiration of the anti-socialist laws in 1890. In that year the party cast nearly one and one-half million votes in the national elections, and became thereby the strongest party in the empire. In 1898 the Social Democratic vote had risen to two millions, in 1907 to three and one quarter millions, in 1912 to more than four and one-quarter millions, more than one-third of all votes cast in the imperial elections of that year.

The great Chancellor was, however, too far-seeing a statesman to think that the mere forbidding of socialist propaganda would stop the growth of socialism, which to his mind was only revolution in disguise. He set out, as we have seen, to cut the ground from beneath the feet of the proletarian agitators by a system of legislation which should ban from the empire the direst poverty by insuring to the working class compensation in case of injury and care in sickness and old age. These needs, which were outlined in an imperial message of 1881, formed the basis of debate and experiment through the following eight years and were finally met in the various compulsory insurance measures which, so to speak, set their stamp upon Germany's internal politics in the eighties. In the Workingmen's Compensation or Accident Insurance Act of

1884, the burden of insurance was laid entirely upon the employer; the cost of the Sick Insurance Act of 1883 fell upon both employer and employee; for carrying out the provisions of the Old Age Pension Act of 1889, the empire joined with both capital and labor in providing for the veterans of labor. By this legislation, which though several times amended in minor parts, has remained essentially the same, Germany took a long step in the direction of state socialism and assumed the first place among nations in the protection of its army of labor. Both Radical and Socialist have found much to criticise in the laws, and the amendments which reformers suggested should long ago have received attention at the hands of the government; nevertheless, with all of their imperfections, the compulsory insurance acts have been a guiding star for the social legislation of other lands and one of the brightest decorations on the bosom of modern Germania. They are no less a superb monument to the liberal view and modern spirit of Bismarck in social legislation.

But they did not win over the Socialists. The representatives of the fourth estate accepted the socialistic laws of the eighties not as a gift from the hands of benevolent capital, but as a right conceded through the fear of the rising strength of the proletariat. There is evidence that the old Chancellor had wearied of the struggle to win the working classes to a national and patriotic spirit and that at the expiration of the anti-socialist laws in 1890 he was preparing a stroke against the constitution, which by the abolition of manhood suffrage should undo the work of 1866 and exclude the non-propertied classes from a share in government (cf. page 127). However, young Emperor William thought otherwise, and with the fall of Bismarck, legislation against the Social Democracy was dropped and the Emperor sought to accomplish by conciliation what suppressive laws had failed to do. He summoned an international congress in Berlin to consider measures for the further welfare of the working classes, and outlined for adoption various propositions, such as a complete Sunday holiday, which had been advocated in the Socialist platform. But the effort to win the workingmen to fealty to monarch and Fatherland by kindness broke against the hard class consciousness of the fourth estate. No royal enticements could prevail against the teachings of Marx, ably and speciously interpreted by Socialist speakers, no words of the sovereign could make progress against the class feeling which had been bred in the industrial proletariat for two decades in trade union, tavern debating club and Socialist journal. From that day on the crown and indeed all of the upper classes and a large part of the middle classes in Germany parted company with the proletariat. Henceforth every representative of the existing organization of society from the sovereign to the Rhenish crockery dealer denounced the Social Democrats as enemies of the Fatherland. But whether ridiculed as a "transitory phase" or threatened with a holy war of extermination by "all lovers of God and Fatherland," the Socialist forces marched on in ever increasing numbers, a solid phalanx of industrial workers, soaked with the doctrines of Marx and Engel and ably led by labor secretary and editor.

In his opposition to the monarchy and the entire capitalistic state, the

Social Democrat included of course the army, under feudal and capitalistic leadership. Nowhere, however, has the German military spirit found better expression than in the organization and discipline of the Social Democratic party. Who could watch the orderly, shoulder to shoulder march of tens of thousands of workingmen through the streets of Berlin on the occasion of the burial of a leader or on the anniversary of the "victims of March," the revolutionists who fell in the street fighting of March 1848, without seeing in imagination these same men clad in the blue and red or khaki of active soldiers? And who could see the eyes-to-the-front, fingers-on-the-trouser-seam carriage with which the individual workman follows his leader in strike or electoral campaign without recalling the Prussian military discipline? In August 1911 at Treptow, a suburb of Berlin, a mighty Socialist demonstration was made against the threatened war with France and England over the Morocco affair. A vast crowd of men and women, estimated at eighty thousand, gathered on a Sunday afternoon about a tribune to hear their leaders denounce war as a diabolical game at which the capitalist must win and the proletarian lose. Only a few of the mighty audience could hear a word of the orators, but all stood at respectful attention in the intense heat until the speeches were over and then at a given signal waved their arms in a mighty storm wave, voting affirmatively on a resolution which protested in the name of labor against the threatened war. And throughout the day not one case of disorder, scarcely even a chance hard word at an over-officious policeman, among the tens of thousands of workingmen and working women who spent the hot Sunday journeying back and forth from their homes in almost all parts of Greater Berlin!

The same iron discipline that has taught moulder and stoker and street paver that he owes it to his class to suppress even a natural outburst of resentment, because it may give the representatives of feudalism and capitalism an advantage, holds sway over leader and editor. The annual party convention, the *Parteitag*, is the court of last resort, before which even those highest in the councils of the party must appear and justify their actions. Prominent Socialists, including some of the leading parliamentarians of the party and the editors of such journals as *Vorwärts* and the *Sozialistische Monatshefte*, have been called upon to defend the orthodoxy of their faith, and prominent leaders have been unceremoniously thrust out of the party. It became an accepted canon that when a man found that his position, reached after scientific inquiry, was no longer that of the party, and when he could not persuade the party to accept his position, he was by that very fact no longer a Social Democrat. This tyranny of the majority was due not merely to a democratic intolerance of strong individualities, it proceeded also from the extreme doctrinarianism of the party.

This doctrinarianism is the very bone of the Social Democracy. No orthodox theologian of years agone ever clung to the verbal inspiration of Holy Writ with greater zeal than Socialist orator and editor and private soldier have held to every jot and tittle of the Erfurt Platform. This declaration of faith was adopted in 1891, soon after the expiration of the anti-socialist laws, and has had no official revision since. It could not be expected, however, that the Marxian theories, as enunciated in that instrument, would stand unimpaired by the experience of the passing years, and even the most devout Socialist must acknowledge that some planks in the Erfurt Platform have been shown to be fallacies by the industrial history of the past few decades in Germany. Of none is this more strikingly true than of the so-called "iron law of wages," according to which the condition of the workingman under the capitalistic system must constantly grow worse. This dogma has been absolutely contradicted by the facts. The general condition of industrial labor in Germany has constantly grown better, and as the years have passed not a few of the proletariat have become themselves members of the capitalistic class.

These conditions were recognized quite early by Social Democrats of more liberal training. The first bold reformer to attempt to bring socialism down from the domain of dreams to economic reality was Edward Bernstein in a memorable brochure published in 1899 (*Die Voraussetzungen des Sozialismus und die Aufgaben der Sozialdemokratie*).[*Footnote: The Basis of Socialism and the Task of the Social Democracy.*] The author, who had suffered in his own person for his adherence to the Marxian faith in the days of the anti-Socialist laws, proposed a revision of the old Marxian theories in the light of present day economic and social life, "the development of the theory and practice of the Social Democracy in an evolutionistic sense." The first point of his attack was the time-honored premise of the "iron law of wages." The condition of the working classes, he contended, is not growing worse but better. Furthermore, not all means of production are to be socialized, as is demanded in the Erfurt Platform, but only land and the larger means of production, and as a very important reservation, one must avoid anything which would injure the nation in its competition for trade with foreign countries. This attack on the major premise of the Erfurt Platform and this modification of its first article instantly called into the ring a host of defenders of socialistic orthodoxy. August Bebel, the parliamentary generalissimo, Karl Kautsky, the learned dogmatist, and others rushed to arms in defense of the Marxian theories and the battle was on between "Radicals" and "Revisionists," the former ably led by Kautsky in the *Neue Zeit*, the latter by Bernstein in the *Sozialistische Monatshefte*. The struggle reached its culmination in the Dresden convention of 1903, a convention which will long be remembered in German political annals as the highwater mark of violence and "rough-house" tactics. The result was a defeat for the "Revisionists," less on scientific than on tactical grounds, the "Radicals" claiming that any concession to the "middle-class parties," whether in theory or practice, would result in weakening the feeling of class consciousness upon which the Social Democracy is built.

In the meantime, however, practice ran away with theory. The exigencies of electoral and parliamentary struggles drew the party more and more into coöperation with the Liberal Left, and tended more and more to transform the revolutionary Socialists, despite themselves, into political democrats. Liebknecht, the founder, with truly doctrinaire consistency, had held that the party existed as a protest against the capitalistic organization of society and should therefore take no part in parliamentary affairs, except in protest. In the days of the anti-socialist laws, the Social Democratic members of the *Reichstag* refused to accept membership on committees. The first break in this policy of simple negation came from South Germany, where as a result of more democratic constitutions, the working classes had been accustomed to a share in governmental responsibilities. A Bavarian deputy, Vollmar, as early as 1891, came out strongly against the attitude of sulking, and demanded that the party, deferring its ultimate aim, the socialization of industry, should coöperate with the middle-class parties in winning immediate advantages for the working class. In spite of the bitter opposition of the Prussian irreconcilables, a revision of the party's program in this respect actually took place. With the growth of Socialist representation in the *Reichstag*, their work on the committees became more and more important, and at the beginning of the session of 1912 a Socialist presided for a time over the national parliament. While the fraction continued to vote steadily against all military and naval supplies and against the prosecution of colonial development, signs multiplied that the opposition to these national undertakings had lost its ferocity, and Socialist votes in committee repeatedly brought about modifications in military and naval bills.

When finally under the shadow of a great national danger in May 1913 the Social Democrats accepted the national Defense Bill, which in its system of direct property taxation coincided with their theories, it was plain that a considerable breach had at last been made in the doctrinarian internationalism of the party and that it had at last begun to catch the national spirit. That this was true found complete confirmation at the outbreak of the war, when disappointment came to those who had counted upon socialism as a weakness in Germany's hour of trial. The Social Democratic workman threw down his tools and rushed to obey the order of mobilization with the same patriotic enthusiasm as inspired shopkeeper and reserve officer. The party leaders, speaking through their papers, reaffirmed the faith of the Socialists in the ideals of peace and international brotherhood among workers, but put the defense of German culture from Russian barbarism as a first life-consideration; and the Socialist members of the *Reichstag* followed the direction of the party councils in voting with practical unanimity for the government war measures. The same hail which had resounded so often with attacks on the spirit of militarism, and Prussian militarism in particular, now heard from the Social Democratic leaders words of patriotic devotion scarcely less ardent than those which came from Conservative and Liberal benches. That there were still elements of dissent and that the hatred of feudalism and capitalism still burned brightly could not be doubted, but for the present these were lost to view in the national enthusiasm which made many Socialist leaders answer the first call for volunteers.

In South Germany, indeed, even before the "revision" crusade the Socialists had become to all intents and purposes a national party. In Würtemberg, Baden and Bavaria they repeatedly voted for the budget, including the supplies for the royal family, a proceeding which stirred the radical Socialists to the bitterest attacks. In Baden in 1906 the leader of the party in the Chamber paid a visit of respect to the Grand Duke on the birth of a prince; in the Grand Duchy of Hesse in 1907 the fraction voted an address to the sovereign. In the diminutive principality of Schwarzburg-Rudolstadt the Socialists had in 1912 a majority of the Chamber and elected one of their number president. In the same year in nineteen states of the empire one hundred and eighty-eight Socialist deputies sat in the legislative chambers. The increasing participation in government which such a large number of representatives must bring with it on more than one occasion excited the Prussian radicals to the boiling point and more than one national party convention resounded with wild scenes of disorder over the struggle as to how far a Social Democrat might participate in government. Under the sting of the radical lash the South German delegates revolted at the Nuremberg Convention of 1908 and announced their intention of proceeding independently of the party in state affairs, submitting themselves to the national convention only in matters of national issue.

That the process of *Mauserung* of the Social Democrats, that is, a gradual conversion to the practical coworking with other liberal groups, did not go further and faster was chiefly due to conditions in Prussia. It is not an accident that most of the radicals among the Social Democratic leaders have been Prussians and that the worship of an idea among the serried thousands of followers has gone further and the collisions between the proletarian and propertied classes have been more numerous in Prussia than elsewhere in the empire. It is true that the Prussian, whether capitalist or proletarian, has a real gift for discipline, whether it be the discipline of the drill sergeant, of the manufacturers' association, or the Social Democratic party leader. But the existence of a sharp and obdurate class feeling in Prussia is to be explained most of all by the constitution of the kingdom. Under the provisions of this constitution, as we have seen, a property qualification for the vote exists, and the working classes are almost entirely excluded from participation in government, whether it be the government of parish, province or kingdom. Of the three classes (cf. page 143) which by indirect means choose the representatives in local and municipal council, in provincial assembly and national *Landtag*, the first class has included in the elections since 1903 from three to five per cent of the total vote, the second class from ten to fourteen per cent, the third class from eightyone to eighty-seven per cent. Since the Socialists from the nature of things fall almost entirely in the third class, it will be seen what a small chance they have of securing adequate representation in any elective body. The industrial workers are placed at a further disadvantage in elections to the *Landtag* by a system of electoral districts which has remained, with minor alterations, that of sixty years ago. Thus while in the agrarian districts of East Prussia in 1908, 63,000 persons elected a deputy, in Berlin the average was one deputy to 170,000. It is not surprising that the Conservative agrarians, who are most bitterly opposed to the interests of the industrial workers, have a far greater number of seats than their vote entitles them to. In 1903 the Conservatives, polling 19.4 per cent of the vote, elected 33 per cent of the deputies in the *Landtag*.

It is not to be wondered at that when in 1908 for the first time Social Democrats, seven in number, found their way into the lower house of the Prussian parliament, they were received with scant courtesy. The Conservative *Kreuzzeitung* protested against their being assigned to any committees, and in fact something very like a boycott was exercised against them. The election of 1913 brought only a slight increase in numbers; but the Socialist deputies made up in noise what they lacked in voting strength, and in spite of the iron rod of Conservative presiding officers, they made themselves as obnoxious as ever did the Irish Nationalists at Westminster in the palmy days of Parnell and Healy. Thus in the spring of 1912 a scandalous scene was precipitated on the floor of the *Landtag*, during which the presiding officer was obliged to send for the police. The minions of the law forcibly removed a refractory Herr Borchardt and played hide-and-seek a while with him in the corridors, a comical scene which found its epilogue in the law courts, where the liberties of the house were finally vindicated by Herr Borchardt paying a small fine. During the same session a Socialist was called to order for saying that "war is a mockery against God" on the ground that this was "an insult to the memory of Emperor William the Great, who waged three wars, and to the chivalrous and patriotic spirit of the German people." The Socialist members are obliged to hear from the ministerial benches that the government regards all Socialists as enemies of God and Fatherland, and that any official, civil or military, breaks his oath to the sovereign when he affiliates himself in any way with the anti-monarchical party.

It was the same bitter impatience against the Prussian constitution that accounted for many of the violent outbreaks of representatives of the fourth estate in the *Reichstag*. Here, backed by crowded benches of applauding colleagues, the fiery champions of the proletariat have reaped a harvest of calls to order in every session for their attacks on the sovereign, the ministry, the army, the Prussian constitution and the entire Prussian system. Some of the party manifestations have been even less excusable, and their childishness can only be explained by political immaturity or demagogery run mad, as the habit which the Socialist members have had of leaving the hall of parliament when the obligato *Hoch!* is given in honor of the Kaiser at the close of the session. When with the Liberal-Radical-Socialist victory of 1912 the Clerical party was obliged to resign to Radical hands the presidency of the *Reichstag*, attacks on the Emperor himself became less restrained than ever. Each public speech of the monarch found its echo in some choice epigram from the Socialist benches. Thus in the debate on the Kaiser's threat against the constitution of Alsace-Lorraine the printer Scheidemann, erstwhile president of the assembly, aroused an uproar by characterizing the Emperor as a "crowned dilettante," and the intellectual free lance Ledebour earned a call to order by declaring that if the king of England had spoken as Kaiser Wilhelm did, he would be straightway shut up in Balmoral, like the crazy king of Bavaria or Abdul Hamid of Turkey. It was not merely by their attacks on the monarch and by their unceasing diatribes against army and bureaucracy that Social Democratic editors and orators won applause in tavern and workshop or wherever their eager constituents gathered to read the party press. Were a stupid recruit in Jüterbog or Gumbinnen overdrilled by a zealous sergeant until he fell from exhaustion, then one might be certain that the case would be illuminated down to its furthest cranny in the next issue of *Vorwärts* or by a vitriol-tongued Liebknecht or Ledebour in the *Reichstag*. Did a Conservative government official in some remote Silesian district snort at Social Democratic voters at a bye-election, the party press and the *Reichstag* hall would ring with denunciation. Every case of judicial error had a merciless searchlight turned upon it, every instance of official discrimination against those suspected of being Socialists became the theme for attacks in which coarseness and brutality of language often crossed the limits prescribed by the German libel law. Whatever political errors may be charged to the Socialists, the weakness of turning the other cheek to the smiter is something of which the party's representatives cannot be accused. While one must credit Social Democratic representatives in press and parliament with sincerity of motive in the defense of the politically and socially weak and defenseless, it cannot be overlooked that it is mainly due to them that a spirit of undisciplined coarseness and vituperation has found its way into German public life.

There is no denying that they have bad provocation enough. The government from the sovereign down has always made no secret of its determination to fight the Socialists as a foreign enemy in the Fatherland. As believers in "internationalism" and enemies of the existing state, they have been as a matter of course ineligible to any office in the government, whether in the army, navy or in the civil service, although they represent more than one-third of the voting strength of the nation. At the elections all government officials have been expected to exert every legitimate influence against the Social Democratic candidate. Recruits who attended Socialist gatherings or frequented taverns known to be Socialist rendezvous were liable to severe punishment. Especially in Prussia, although the basic ideas of socialism had for years been freely taught in the universities, any teacher in an elementary school who was suspected of Socialist sympathies exposed himself to loss of promotion or might even be removed from the service. The same fate awaited any postal or customs employee who identified himself in any way with the Socialist cause; and it has often been charged by the Socialists and never disproved that the workmen on public works have been practically forced to enroll their children in clubs where a sort of "hurra-patriotism" was taught and where the youngsters were trained to regard the Social Democrats as the most dangerous enemies of God and native land. Naturally a state of affairs like this leads to deceit, to cringing, tale-bearing and denunciation. Unfortunately also, while the German courts are usually models of fairness and inaccessible to political, social or financial influences, the Social Democrat has not always had an impartial hearing. The Jena students demonstrated against the Socialist convention held in that little Athens on the Saale in 1911, and the Weimar *Volkszeitung* was fined for calling one of the student leaders a *Mistfink*, a somewhat intensified equivalent of "mucker." A laborer in the Kiel district in 1912 gave his daughter the euphonious name of Lassalline. When the registrar refused to record a name so full of danger to the Fatherland, the magistrate's court finally ordered him to do so, but attached to this confirmation of the parent's right to denominate his offspring a long oration against socialism.

The Socialist workman replied to this boycott by exercising in his way a terrorism which the government, aided by all the conservative forces in the state, has striven in vain to suppress. He has vented on the non-socialist worker his dissatisfaction with the government, and, as might be expected, often with brutality and violence. That during a political strike, such as the coal strike in the Ruhr district in 1912 (cf. page 167), the Catholic labor unions should suffer bloody attacks from the striking miners is not surprising: even the non-political Hirsch-Duncker unionists have more than one tale to tell of similar mistreatment during labor troubles. But it is not merely the strike breakers in strike times who have suffered. Every non-Socialist brick mason or carpenter must look for a continuous hazing. If he were so unfortunate as to be obliged to work with a Socialist unionist, he might consider himself lucky if he got off with the occasional loss of tools or dinner bucket or an accidental fall into a horse-pond and did not have his hand permanently maimed by the slip of a chisel or his head cracked by the premature topple of a hod of bricks. Against such petty cases of tyranny of course both government and employer have been helpless. In past years the government has eagerly sought from the *Reichstag* sharper weapons for the suppression of strike violence and the protection of strike breakers; but in spite of the personal influence of the Emperor in their favor, no one of these special measures for the protection of the workers has been able to find a majority in parliament. The fear that they might be used as a weapon for further strengthening the great industrialists has always frightened off enough Clericals to cause their defeat.

It must not be supposed that the feeling against the Socialists has been confined to feudal squires and factory owners. It pervades the entire middle class in Germany, for except the extreme Radicals, all Germans, whether they thrive by land, trade or manufacture, have been taught to regard the Social Democrat as an enemy of the Fatherland. The Rhenish shopkeeper, the Black Forest clockmaker, the Pomeranian peasant farmer, — all have shuddered alike at the growing power and influence of the Social Democracy and regarded almost any means as holy that would tend to defeat its ultimate success. It was only when the excessive demands of agrarian and clerical interests aroused the alarm of those who live by commerce and industry that these classes considered the possibility of a league, and the coworking of Radicals and Social Democrats at the polls in 1912 broke ground in that direction. The Socialist leaders, however, have been well aware that any modification of their extreme radical attitude toward the middle classes would not only endanger their hold on the working class, with its sharp class feeling, but that a large number of the discontented from all classes would fall away from them. For the growth of socialism's vote in Germany has been due by no means merely to the rising demands of the industrial workers. It has been distinctly the party of discontent and protest. Every discontented and disappointed man is liable at any time to express his dissatisfaction with society in general by voting the Social Democratic ticket. Has the young medical student failed of an appointment, has the citizen soldier been given a verbal castigation by the officer during his drill with the reserve, has a postal clerk been docked in his pay, has the grocer's wife had a snub from the factory owner's, — each sufferer can give vent to his private grievance against society by voting for the Social Democrat and thus making trouble for the powers that be. None of these persons has the slightest sympathy with the ultimate socialist program, and none of them would think of overthrowing the present state of society, except in a moment of ill humor. This habit of "voting to the Left" has attacked large classes of democratically inclined persons of the lower middle class following such a period of reaction as that which ended with the election of the *Reichstag* of 1912.

It is indeed unfortunate that this is so, and the lovers of Germany have often asked themselves what the end would be, if so strangely constituted a party continued to grow in voting strength. Largely through its own choice the Social Democracy, although representing one-third of the voters in the empire, has been deprived of any considerable share in government and remained in an attitude of sullen hostility to the state. So well have the class organizers of past decades done their work that they have developed among the industrial workers who make up the Social Democratic party a class feeling that is nothing more nor less than an independent class culture. It is not merely a political gulf which the Socialist leaders have fixed between the workman and every other class in Germany. Through constant teaching in young men's clubs, trade unions and political societies the industrial worker has become to a certain extent a different creature from his middle class neighbor, a member of a nation within the German nation. A striking characteristic of the German the world over is the love of Fatherland. The Socialist workman has claimed to be an international and to feel as one, and in program at least he has professed to be more strongly drawn to his fellow proletarian in France and England than to the shopkeepers and peasant proprietors of his native district. The North German is by tradition strongly monarchical; the Socialist frankly detests monarchy and monarch. While the German, north and south, may not approve of all the methods of the Evangelical and Roman Catholic churches, he is held by mighty roots to a deep religiosity; the Socialist claims to regard religion as a private matter, nevertheless he cannot forget that the church has been the handmaid of reaction and oppression, and the attitude of intellectual leader and proletarian follower is frankly and openly and-religious. Many of the most brilliant Social Democratic leaders with tongue and pen are Jews, it need hardly be said, unorthodox Jews, who have cut loose entirely from the religion of Moses and the prophets. Anyone who is at all familiar with the anti-Semitic feeling among the upper and middle classes in Germany can understand how much the prejudice against the Socialists is deepened by this Jewish alliance. Furthermore, in spite of the casehardening of the modern struggle for existence, the average German has remained a romanticist, full of hero-worship and with a deep enthusiasm for the poetry of the nation's past; the Social Democrat has been taught to view the past under the hard light of Marx' theory as a battle-ground of economic forces, where without mercy the strong has preyed upon the weak.

When the war came the attitude of the Social Democracy toward it showed at once that much of the so-called "internationalism" of the German industrial worker is purely academic. All the doctrinarianism of the tavern benches and the nobler enthusiasm of such demonstrations as that of Treptow could not affect the age-old roots which bind him to the Fatherland. It is improbable that the Socialists, were they to command a majority in Germany's parliament and so succeed in changing Germany's constitution as to have a free hand in legislation, would do anything to weaken the nation's defenses, either by a change in the military system or a destruction of protective duties. It seemed, indeed, as if even old-line leaders, like the late August Bebel, had caught something of the enthusiasm for Germany's world-empire. After the so-called "Hottentot election" of 1907, when Socialists and Clericals alike suffered severely at the hands of the voters for their opposition to colonial expansion, there began to show itself in the Social Democratic press a tendency toward increasing patriotic expression with regard to the national honor and defenses. Here again South Germany led the way, for here the "revisionists" were stronger. Among the first prominent men to fall in the invasion of France in August 1914 was Dr. Frank of Mannheim, a widely known Social Democratic leader; and indeed the blood of Socialist patriots has reddened every battlefield where German armies have fought. Under these the attitude of the party towards the nation's inner life cannot fail to undergo a change. In later years indeed the Social Democrats had already accomplished much that was positive. By their constant and searching criticisms they held a searchlight constantly fixed on the weak spots and the sore spots in the courts and the army. In the field of social legislation, such as the extension of compulsory insurance, the fixing of a shorter working day, and the protection of women and children in the industries, they kept high ideals before the country. In their work for universal peace, in their opposition to immoderate military expenditures and to duels and other manifestations of the feudal spirit in the army, they offered a valuable counterbalance to the militarism-run-mad spirit. In their pleas for a judiciary free from influence of every kind, schools free from religious bigotry, for a system of taxation which should fall directly upon the propertied classes, for a strong central control of great industries and for woman's suffrage, they accomplished much toward the inner upbuilding of the state. These affirmative policies have been pushed by a class of leaders who are very different from those who led the serried thousands of the fourth estate in the nineties or even at the beginning of the present century. The really advanced men in the Social Democratic party are no longer the narrow Marxian enthusiasts or class fanatics who grew up under the anti-socialist laws or when the party was still in the fledgling period of political strategy. They are often men of the highest university training, occasionally with inherited wealth and culture, who know the history of the party and are filled with the optimism of success. They have shown an increasing power to lead the party farther away from a sterile doctrinarianism toward a really practical democracy.

[***]

CHAPTER XVII
THE PRESS AND PUBLIC OPINION

SINCE the day when the bankrupt Mayence genius invented movable types, Germany has with few interruptions held the first place among printing and publishing nations. Her annual output in books surpasses the combined production of France, England and the United States; and even if we subtract pamphlets, which in German statistics are rated as books, and which bring into the world many things that appear in other countries in magazines, the Fatherland exceeds in its contribution to this "paper age" any two other nations. The explanation is to be found not merely in the high culture of the nation, but also in the methodical spirit, which drives the German to analyze, correlate and formulate, seeking not merely apostles for his patiently won ideas but often clearness for the writer through the very formulation of his ideas. In no land is access to the press so cheap and easy, in no land are the rewards for the author proportionately so large. Unfortunately also in no land are there so many worthless books brought into the world, from the machine-made doctor dissertation with its pathetic testimony to years of youthful vigor wasted in counting the hairs in Homer's beard down to the penny manuals on "How to learn French in Three Weeks." The Germans pay the penalty of a nation which produces each year a mass of creative scholarly research with the by-products of boneless pedantry and speculative dilettanteism.

Besides the book press, the periodical press rolls up each month and each day its vast flood. Every science, art and industry, every branch of commerce, every political fraction has its press; every handicraft, yes, almost every forceful personality in the country has its periodical exponent. The press directory of 1913 mentions 11 periodicals devoted to the continuation school system alone. The *Schornsteinfeger*, published monthly in Berlin, ministers to the literary needs of chimney sweeps; the *Allgemeine deutsche Käseblatt* to those of the cheese workers: a specialization in the printed representatives of Germany's multifarious industries confronts us as hairsplit and bewildering as in the industrial branches themselves. Only indeed in a land where the division of industry and the organization of commerce are carried as far as in Germany could this vast array of trade periodicals live and flourish.

On the other hand the number of popular periodicals dealing with history, political science and geography is small: the *Deutsche Rundschau*, founded by the late Julius Rodenberg, the *Süddeutsche Monatshefte* and the

Deutsche Revue are the only ones which deserve to be put beside half a dozen or more great British reviews. In the field of artistic and literary criticism there is none which in the variety and brilliance of its contents appeals to so large a public as the *Revue des deux Mondes*. Nor do the more popular *Westermanns* or *Velhagen und Klasings Monatshefte, Nord und Süd* or the time-honored *Gartenlaube* attain to the vivid contemporary interest of a few of the best American illustrated magazines. The out-of-door element, so attractive a part of British and American magazines, has only recently made its appearance in German periodicals and is to be found mainly in publications devoted to Alpine, automobile and aviation clubs or other special sports. If, however, the German press has something less to offer to the leisure hours of the man of general culture than that of the western nations, to the specialist and scholar, whether he be a specialist in Sanscrit, stamp collecting or soap boiling, it brings each year a wealth of material which serves later on as a reservoir for the writers of other nations.

The spirit of the German press is then that of German scholarship. It shows the same enthusiasm for truth, the same conscientiousness in the search for it and the same honesty in proclaiming it as have set their stamp on German scholarship everywhere. The reverse of this in pedantry of manner and boring tediousness of portrayal is not lacking. The daily press, to which this chapter is chiefly devoted, shows these characteristics in an even greater degree. The most popular child of the printing press, the newspaper, had also its birth in Germany, and so far as numbers are concerned, Germany is still above all its home. Exact statistics are lacking, but in 1908 the number of daily papers was estimated by competent authorities at four thousand, of which Dr. Robert Brunhuber,[*Footnote: Das deutsche Zeitungswesen.*] an expert in this field, counts about four hundred organs of considerable importance. Of these perhaps 35 are papers of great influence of which over one-half appear in Berlin and less than half a dozen outside of Prussia. In the aggregate the German daily press rises then to tremendous figures. The post-office department acts as the agent of the press, receiving subscriptions at all offices and distributing the papers, and reckoning by post-office statistics, German observers set the distribution of papers in the year 1906 at between twelve and twenty million copies per day. This mighty flood, which pours itself daily over all parts of Germany, rippling to the most distant dune villages of the Baltic coast and the eeriest nests of the Bavarian highlands, flows most densely in the Rhine valley. Here the Cologne, Düsseldorf and Dortmund papers find their way into every hamlet and in the industrial centres into every house. In the Rhine Palatinate the average is one daily newspaper to every fifteen thousand inhabitants in the entire district.

Through this great flood, from the Berlin and Frankfort journals down to the provincial *"General Anzeiger"* ("Official Gazette") is a long journey past all sorts of newspaper undertakings. Most of the larger papers maintain correspondence bureaus in the greater German cities, and the largest also in foreign capitals, but as in the case of other lands, by far the greater part of the news comes to them through press associations. The great German press association is Wolff's Telegraphic Bureau, which differs from international bureaus like Reuter's and the Agence Havas in that it is mainly national in its scope, and differs from the American press agencies in being directly under government control. Wolff's Bureau counts among its subscribers practically all the important papers in Germany, its despatches are forwarded over the imperial telegraph system toll free and have a certain precedence over private messages, and it is used, as we shall see, to disseminate governmentally edited news. Besides Wolff's, there are in Berlin and other larger capitals other news agencies which send out information, — telegraphed, printed, mimeographed, — flooding the newspaper world with official, semi-official, political or colorless news items, which play a great part in the make-up of the provincial press. The pirating of news from the larger journals is carried on by the provincial papers in Germany in a way that is absolutely conscienceless, possibly because, as will be shown below, the reading public seems less eager for news than for editorial comments thereon.

This borrowing of news items is not, however, confined to the provincial press. As we have seen, the larger papers maintain correspondents in foreign capitals; but only in a few cases is this correspondence forwarded by telegraph, since the papers, apparently following the desires of the reading public, prefer to spend their money on literary essays and scientific treatises rather than on telegraph and cable tolls. For their daily news from abroad they depend on Wolff's Bureau, which has a limited staff abroad, but derives most of its information through the great international agencies like Reuter's. The cheapest and readiest source of information is the French and British dailies, whose news columns even the largest Berlin papers do not hesitate to use, reproducing with a generous hand news items from the *Times*, the *Daily Chronicle* and the *Standard* forty-eight hours after publication in London.

The effect on Germany's relations with the outside world of this dependence on British-influenced news agencies has already been noted (cf. page 73 ff.). Even more important for the development of public sentiment at home is the lack of an adequate, independent system of telegraphic correspondence from foreign countries. The greater metropolitan papers which do maintain foreign correspondents have not succeeded in placing in the foreign capitals men who are able to give a true picture of foreign feeling or through personal influence and adroitness to fill the semi-diplomatic mission of their office, with the result that the readers of even such high-class journals as the *Kölnische* or *Frankfurter Zeitung* or the *Berliner Tageblatt* are often uninformed as to the real condition of public affairs and public feeling in France, England and America. The result has been that each succeeding international crisis has found the German reading public living in a fool's paradise of misinformation with regard to the mighty forces of public sentiment which sway cabinet decisions in London, Paris, Washington and to some extent Rome. Some of the greater German dailies, like the *Kölnische*, have spent vast sums in sending experts to spy out the highlands of Thibet or the savage stretches of the upper Congo and spread before their readers a wealth of information regarding the economic possibilities of southern Brazil or the valleys of Mesopotamia or the fauna and flora of the strangest islands of the southern seas. Of everything that has a scientific interest they render account with characteristic German enthusiasm for truth: in political matters their information is usually neither complete nor accurate and their correspondence from neighboring French and Italian cities or even from Alsace or the Prussian East is often but valorous vaporing of the tap-room sort.

The weakness of the German papers as international newsgatherers is partly to be explained through the personnel of the German newspaper office. This seldom has at its command men of the standing of those who represent the great London papers in foreign capitals, a lack that is directly traceable to the inferior standing of the journalist in Germany as compared with Western lands. In the Fatherland, as elsewhere, the newspaper man does not as a rule freely elect the profession which he practises, but gravitates into it as a result of circumstances. Here, however, the result is worse than elsewhere, not only for the training of the journalist, but for the social status of the profession. In this land of specialization every aspirant for a professional career selects or is supposed to select, or have his parents select for him, his life career before he goes to the university, and he is expected to follow it up with all his force and enthusiasm from that time forth forevermore. Few, very few, select journalism, for while the financial rewards of the successful journalist are not inconsiderable, the social prestige belonging to the profession is still almost as lacking and the professional pride among journalists as undeveloped as half a century ago, when Gustav Freytag wrote his charming comedy *Die Journalisten* to prove that German editors could be men of honor.

The editorial chairs of Germany contain some brilliant men, who, feeling an inner call to journalism, have deserted the teacher's chair or even the lawyer's desk or surgeon's case. Besides these and others, whose lives have been given to a special training for the periodical press, there are a very great number who have found their way into the newspaper office simply because they have failed as lawyers or as teachers or in some other calling where success means *official* position. Hard-and-fast conditions of society in Germany admit a fall in the social scale, but seldom a rise. There is no such thing as working for a while in a minor or menial position and then entering one of the learned professions: the educational system forbids it. The dark side of German efficiency is that those who have through temperament or other causes made a failure in the profession for which they have prepared, have thereafter small chance of success in any calling of equal social rank or even in the close in-fighting of business competition. To a good many such journalism offers the only field where they can still hope for a remunerative activity without entire loss of social position.

In addition to the lack of preparation for their profession under which so many German newspaper men suffer, they are not permitted, as in France, to sign their articles. Not a few leading articles and summaries are signed by the chief editor; but as a rule the German newspaper man is hidden behind the same impenetrable veil of anonymity that shrouds his colleagues in England and America. His work, be it ever so faithfully done, brings him no personal advertisement. On the other hand, the lack of liberal institutions condemns the editor to something like political impotence; and except among the Social Democrats, where newspaper editors are frequently elected to legislative office, he rarely gets anything in the way of political reward. The positions in the consular and even the diplomatic service that now and then recompense the American editor for faithful service to the party cause and the titles and distinctions which successful British journalists receive have no counterpart in Germany. With the exception of the two groups with the best developed political sense, the Conservatives and the Social Democrats, the journalist plays but a small part in the active life of the party and is practically never rewarded by the gift of political office. The effect of this upon the ambition of newspaper men can well be imagined. Thus cut off from adequate preparation, shut in behind a paralyzing anonymity, ineligible for political rewards, the German journalist cannot, save in the case of a few great papers, lay claim to an enviable social or political position. As a rule he does his duty faithfully within the limits allowed him by the laws and by the business considerations of his office.

These considerations play a no more important part in Germany than in more democratic lands, where the cashier's office is too often permitted to dominate the editorial rooms. Absolute independence of the advertising columns and similar considerations is an ideal rather than a fact in every part of the newspaper world, though here the German publisher may be said to be less exposed to temptation because of the rigid laws which govern business competition and because by education the German is opposed to unfair play in business life. The treatment of the editor as a hireling who must echo the policy of the publisher and guard the latter's political and financial interests is a sacrifice which the editorial profession makes everywhere to the capitalistic organization of society, and it is no more common in Germany than abroad, although it must be said that anything that in any way diminishes the importance and standing of the press as a tribune of the people must increase the temptation of publisher and editor to sell their influence to the highest bidder.

The dignity of the press is then directly dependent upon the liberty allowed it, and this liberty in turn upon the habit of free institutions. It follows that those statesmen who have shown themselves most hostile to these institutions have in the history of present-day Germany done the most to prostitute the press. Bismarck, according to his press secretary, Moritz Busch, frequently expressed himself with cynical contempt on the subject of the honesty of the German press and its value as a representative of the people. "German papers," he declared in 1876, "are bound to be amusing reading, for they are meant to be glanced over while drinking a mug of beer and to furnish topics of lively conversation, usually about something which has taken place a long way off in foreign parts." The Iron Chancellor, however, himself made constant use of the newspapers to influence public opinion both at home and abroad, maintaining at the foreign office, in addition to the official literary bureau, a private bureau under the adroit management first of Busch and later of Professor Aegidi. Through these men he played upon public opinion by means of articles inspired by himself and often prepared under his dictation, which were published not only in the semi-official *Norddeutsche Zeitung*, the *Kölnische Zeitung* or the *Kreuzzeitung*, but in papers issued in remote cities of the provinces, whose connection with the government would not be guessed. Sometimes under the direction of their wily chief his lieutenants would put the Chancellor's ideas in the form of a letter from a German long resident in Paris or a Prussian close to Vatican circles in Rome, playing upon the various keys and stops of prejudice and sentiment as the national or international situation demanded. By his Press Ordinances of 1863 Bismarck had shown himself quite willing to throttle a free press, later on he assured himself of adequate newspaper support by means of a cleverness and an insincerity a little more than diplomatic. That these means were at times highly immoral, no one who reads Busch's biography of the Chancellor can deny. From the income of the sequestrated property of the King of Hanover and the Landgrave of Hesse, who had been deposed on the annexation of these countries by Prussia in 1866, the Chancellor drew the so-called "reptile funds," by which the imperial government maintained an influence over the press which extended into the remotest corners of Germany and made itself felt in London, Paris and Rome.

All of this was justified by Bismarck and his apologists as a measure of war. It is certain that the Iron Chancellor had to face all of his life the bitterest opposition on the part of a few independent newspapers, the most relentless from the *Kreuzzeitung*, which under its brilliant editor Hammerstein forced the fighting in the most violent manner whenever Bismarck showed the slightest inclination toward liberal ideas. Confronted by bitter enemies not only in the Liberal and Clerical ranks but among his own class, the conservative aristocracy, as well, Bismarck did not hesitate to assure himself of press support by means which were sometimes, as has been pointed out, of doubtful morality. He believed that his enemies were poisoning the wells of public opinion; he himself disdained no weapons of deceit and bribery in his newspaper campaigns, furnishing false information to draw the fire of his opponents, or introducing misleading articles into the trusted organs of the opposition. The success of this policy for the Chancellor's aims cannot be denied; its final result was to weaken for decades the political influence of the German press at home and abroad.

Bismarck's successors in the home and foreign offices inherited something of his cynical contempt for the press without the great Chancellor's skill in using it for his purposes. Indeed the attitude of the government officials in Germany toward the representatives of the fourth estate has been one of arrogance, not unmixed with fear. Often the feeling seems to be that the press represents an improper curiosity on the part of the masses about government doings, a curiosity which must be checked if possible, and if that is not possible, satisfied with such meagre news as the government may find fit for popular consumption. The result is, that the same feeling is cultivated in the German newspapers that one finds often among German citizens toward public affairs: they have been told so often that the governing classes can manage things without their help that they have grown to believe it, and the press thus frequently accepts without hesitation government leadership and voluntarily resigns its rights as a tribune of the people. Two instances will illustrate this, both taken from the exciting days at the end of July, 1914, just before Germany declared war against Russia. On July 30 the air was full of rumors and the Berlin *Lokalanzeiger* published an extra announcing that war had been declared against Russia. This was followed immediately by a governmental denial and a disavowal and the withdrawal of its issue by the offending paper. The premature news reached Munich, where it was published in various extra issues and caused the greatest excitement. At the height of this the newspapers, which were unable to communicate with Berlin on account of the overloading of the wires, applied to the Bavarian government to know the truth of the situation. For hours they were kept waiting, and finally with the greatest reluctance the Bavarian officials gave the information that they had not been advised of a declaration of war, which as a matter of fact did not take place till two days later. As showing how dependence on the government has become a matter of habit in crises, on the same day on which the press representatives were treated so superciliously by the Bavarian government when making inquiries regarding a matter of the highest public concern, the Munich *Zeitung*, a Radical paper, called urgently upon the imperial officials, in view of the disturbed state of the public mind, to "take charge of public opinion!"

As a rule the papers have no right to find fault with the government for not attempting to mould public opinion. Since Bismarck's day, however, with the growth of healthfulness in German political life, ministerial efforts to control the public view have become less insidious, although they are not yet always sincere and devoid of trickery. At the present time governmental influence finds its way to the public mind through papers which are directly "official" and papers whose utterances are known as "semi-official" and also by means of articles in journals where government influences are least suspected. The directly and openly "official" papers, such as the *Reichsanzeiger* and the organs of the army and navy and the various *Anzeiger* to be found in the Prussian provincial capitals and the capitals of the other German states, are merely organs of governmental announcement, and have no more influence on public opinion than departmental announcements in Washington. Aside from these organs of the imperial and state governments, the various departments of the federal government contain officials whose duty it is to furnish information to the press, the most important bureau of that kind being found in the Foreign Office. The organization of these bureaus is as efficient as the German bureaucracy always is, and their work includes not only the furnishing of information to the press, but the preparation of editorial leaders and all sorts of articles intended to work upon public sentiment, which find publication in some of the "semi-official" papers.

As has been noted, the most important agency for disseminating news throughout Germany is Wolff's Telegraphic Bureau, an institution which may be called a governmentally owned press association. It antedates the foundation of the new German empire, having been organized in 1865 as a joint stock company, with the Prussian government in control of a majority of the stock. Like Reuter's Bureau, the Agence Havas and other national news agencies, the Wolff Bureau claims an international character. It maintains correspondents in foreign capitals and has in peace times affiliations with other great news agencies. It practically controls the news field in Germany, although its known governmental character causes German readers to discount its despatches to some extent, less because there is any possibility of Wolff's Bureau falsifying the actual facts furnished from the world outside of Germany than from the feeling that other facts may be suppressed. To the American in Germany the tone of the Wolff messages, when they concern royalty, smacks not a little of unctuous servility. Good or bad, it forms the first means by which the German reader learns his foreign news: that it has not developed further in past years as a real newsgatherer is due less to governmental control than to the traditional lack of interest among Germans in international affairs.

Next to Wolff's Bureau come the information bureaus of the government offices, referred to above, and that brings up the question of "semi-official" papers. Just which papers deserve this title is hard to say, the German press itself being often in the dark as to how far government influence extends over certain papers. Universally recognized as the government mouthpiece is the *Norddeutsche Allgemeine Zeitung* of Berlin, which has been in the service of the Prussian and the imperial government since the sixties. Bismarck used it from the early days of his chancellorship, and since that time it has published the government's views, particularly on foreign affairs, prepared in the government offices and under the direction of the imperial chancellor and occasionally of the emperor himself. The statements of the rather old-fashioned *Norddeutsche* are recognized as having the highest authority. At the other end of the scale stands the rural daily which champions the government program and especially at election time rages against the Social Democrats with eager zeal in return for the local government advertising given by the all-powerful local administrator, the *Landrat*. Between the two there extends a whole line of papers, whose articles are regularly or occasionally inspired by the federal or state officials. Certain journals, like the *Kölnische Zeitung*, the *Tägliche Rundschau* of Berlin and the *Hannoverische Courier*, have been regularly used to express government opinion on domestic or foreign affairs, the actual subject-matter or the general ideas being furnished from the Home or Foreign Office. Frequently the reading public is hard put to it to know whether articles in these papers represent the ideas of the government or not, for even the staid *Norddeutsche* occasionally kicks over the traces and treats the topics of the day in a manner which is quite opposed to all theories of feudal-conservative administration. In proportion, however, as the news matter concerns the person or entourage of the Emperor or one of the rulers of the major states or a foreign crisis the articles in the papers in question are apt to reflect the feeling in government circles, for the value of the proper public treatment of such subjects is well understood by the governing class. The public and semi-public utterances of the Emperor are regularly reported by an official stenographer and carefully edited by the Foreign Office before publication.

"One cannot carry on international politics without a press." This statement of the late Marschall von Bieberstein, formerly German foreign minister, is undoubtedly confirmed by the practice of every civilized land. But there is considerable difference between the information furnished the national press in London, Paris and Washington and the press articles which find their way into the German "semi-official" papers, a difference peculiar to the German government. In the more democratic countries the press is taken sufficiently into the government's confidence as to facts to enable it to fulfil its mission as the mouthpiece of the nation. In Germany the imperial and Prussian government by the use of its system of anonymous inspiration has been accustomed to play upon the various organs in which the government's views are wont to appear so as to control public opinion, fanning or restraining the fires of national enthusiasm as the foreign situation demands. This was illustrated in the careful management of the press in the Morocco crisis of 1911, when the anti-French and anti-British feeling was alternately stimulated and checked; incontestibly also in the days preceding the outbreak of war in 1914, when a series of "hands off!" articles following Austria's ultimatum to Serbia was well adapted to steel and inspire the national spirit for the approaching crisis.

Occasionally, however, public opinion in Germany gets very much out of hand. This was the case during the Boer War, when the waves of enthusiasm for the South African republics rolled high in spite of all efforts of the governmentally inspired press to pour oil upon them, and in 1906 when through the Kaiser's interview with the *Daily Telegraph* correspondent the last phases of the pro-British attitude of the imperial government at the time of the struggle with the Boers were laid bare. On such occasions as this, when German ideals are strongly touched, the press arrays itself with force and remarkable unanimity on the popular side and leads an outbreak of Teutonic fury that echoes in every home and hall of the Fatherland. Such unanimity is, however, rare. Some of the strongest papers are handicapped in their influence on public opinion by the suspicion of government inspiration. All tend to suffer, so far as they are not the mouthpieces of the Foreign Office, from a lack of a feeling of responsibility, passing in their leading articles from an unmotivated exultation over Germany's present and future situation to an equally unfounded despair.

Much more than in foreign matters has the system of governmental influence been harmful to the German press in matters of domestic policy. While the ministry no longer poisons the wells of public opinion as in

Bismarck's day, it does greatly impair the influence of a great section of the press. During crises like that before the *Reichstag* election of 1907 or the discussions preceding the passage of the Defense Bill in 1913, the imperial ministry constantly played upon the keys and stops of the press. Here, however, there has grown up in the great National Liberal and Radical papers, not to speak of the vast network of Socialist organs, led by the Berlin *Vorwärts*, an array of popular tribunes, who guard jealously the interests of the economic groups which they represent and are themselves free from all suspicion of unfair government influence.

Almost all of the great papers of Germany are in fact strict party organs, only a few like the *Lokalanzeiger* of Berlin professing to be impartial in matters political. Political interests have, as we have seen, combined with economic interests in Germany, so that journals represent not merely a party, but an economic group as well. Thus the *Kreuzzeitung*, the old organ of the Conservative party, is likewise the most influential representative of agrarian interests, while Radical organs like the *Frankfurter Zeitung* have their constituency among the financial and commercial classes of the cities and the great National Liberal papers, like the *Kölnische Zeitung*, the *Tägliche Rundschau* of Berlin and the *Hamburger Nachrichten*, represent the industrial interests and those of the upper middle class. It is but natural that those political parties which are most closely identified with economic groups should be represented by the most aggressive press. Thus the two groups which occupy opposite ends of the political scale, the Conservatives and the Socialists, whose organizations rest on a strong community of economic interest, have an aggressive and well-disciplined press; and as a result it is chiefly among the Conservative and Socialist editors that one finds men of strong personal influence on the counsels of the party. Next to them comes the press of the Centre party, led by the powerful *Germania* in Berlin, a journal which was founded in 1870 with the first leap into power of the ultramontane party and which has valiantly led the firing line in defense of Roman Catholic interests ever since. Between these extremes stands a long line of papers with liberal and radical leanings. It is remarkable indeed that by far the greater number of journals of national and international standing in Germany are National Liberal in faith or tendency, just as this party, with all of its trimming and irresolution in program, contains a vastly greater proportion of the brains of the empire than its electoral figures would lead one to suppose. Papers like the *Kölnische Zeitung*, the *Münchner Neueste Nachrichten*, the *Schwäbische Merkur* of Stuttgart, the *Hannoverische Courier* or the *Tägliche Rundschau* of Berlin, with their Radical contemporaries, the *Berliner Tageblatt*, the *Vossische Zeitung* of Berlin and the *Frankfurter Zeitung*, represent the very best that German journalism has to offer, both as newsgatherers and in the national-patriotic tone of their policies. In Germany as elsewhere the more narrow the political attitude of a paper, the less its importance as a gatherer of news.

Every political, social and economic direction then has its own press, which watches jealously over the interests of its group and presents them with more or less passion and narrowness. From the wild chauvinism of the Berlin *Deutsche Tageszeitung* or *Post* to the bitter class appeals of the Socialistic *Vorwärts*, each strikes its own peculiar note and plays the pipe for its party's dancing. It seldom happens indeed that a newspaper ties itself completely to the fortunes of a political leader, as in France, nevertheless the party press reflects in striking fashion the individualism and separatism of German politics as well as the pettiness and narrowness which is a part of factional strife. The fulminations of the agrarian aristocrat against the inheritance tax, those of the manufacturer against the income tax or the radical against the tariff on food-stuffs and the appeals of the Social Democrat to class feeling echo and reecho harshly and shrilly according as the acoustic space furnished by the individual sheet is large or small.

The German, whether country squire, townsman or peasant-farmer, demands that the paper which he reads beside the family lamp or the restaurant table shall support first of all Germany's claims abroad and secondly, the program of his particular party, with loyalty, which is the trait which he most reveres. In no country is a newspaper more clearly tagged with its party name, and in no country does the reader insist more strongly that it shall remain true to its colors. Through thick and thin, right or wrong, in disaster or success, the paper must be the defender, apologist and conserver of the party's traditions. Every act of the party's leaders must be championed, every move of the party's opponents must be attacked or given an unflattering interpretation. Characteristic of this is the attitude of the papers in reporting political debates. "I always took care that the Whig dogs should not get the best of it," said Dr. Johnson in speaking of his parliamentary reporting, and something like this has become the motto of the German press. Even journals of the highest standing almost always have their party's representative emerge from a political discussion covered with honor "for his clear and practical demonstration of the facts," while his opponent invariably "seeks to confuse the matter and takes refuge in excuses and hedging."

The result of this attitude on public opinion is still further to narrow and to embitter political life. The unfortunate side of this life, already pointed out, is that it splits the nation into factions and creates among these factions the feeling that the government is a hostile force with which in various crises the best terms possible are to be made. The result is that the German citizen gets very little help from the press in laying aside the swaddling clothes of political separatism. He swears by his *Frankfurter* or *Magdeburger* or *Kölnische* and avoids other papers like the pest. This attitude toward the newspapers is characteristic of the narrow partisan in every country. An especially unfortunate result in Germany, however, is the weakening of liberalism through the dissipation of its energies in factional controversies. Radical and National Liberal papers have found it as impossible to make common cause against feudal pressure and agrarian demands in the press as in parliament, and the Social Democratic papers attack the middle-class Berlin *Tageblatt* as fiercely as they do the feudal *Kreuzzeitung*.

Unfortunately then political factionalism and blind subserviency to the party program harm the independence of the press and damage its influence as an organizer of public opinion. On the other hand it seems that the sources of public opinion are kept purer from strictly financial and business contamination in Germany than elsewhere. Such bribery as there is, is usually backed in some way by government influence, which dominates many a petty provincial or rural sheet. In the various "districts" and "circles" into which Prussia is divided some one of the local newspapers enjoys the official advertising and is regarded as the governmental mouthpiece. This provincial sheet, which assumes the proud title of "Official Gazette" (*Amtsund Kreisblatt*), is a private undertaking, of course, but is strongly under the influence of the local crown official, the *Landrat*, who has the privilege of withdrawing at any time the official titles and official advertising. Naturally the paper is expected to support the government, and particularly the policies of the Conservative party, with all vigor, and the *Landrat* sees to it that it goes for the Social Democrats without gloves and he permits nothing to pass uncensured that might be construed as a reflection on the ruler or the monarchy. During electoral campaigns the editor of such a paper must do his utmost to prevent any increase in the Radical or the Socialist vote in his district, if he would avoid a vigorous bullying from the all-powerful *Landrat*, who is nearly always a member of the feudal class.

Aside from such instances of official terrorism, it is not usual to find German journals listening to financial seduction. Certain papers, it is true, represent particular business interests, as the *Rheinwestfälische Zeitung* of Düsseldorf those of the Westphalian mine operators and iron and steel manufacturers. The big business interests, indeed, have their own press, which is in great measure independent of party, although supporting of course Conservative or National Liberal policies. Thus the Krupps and iron and steel interests are said to own the Berlin *Neueste Nachrichten*, which represents most adequately those industries and the financiers behind them, while individuals identified with the Agrarian League own the Berlin *Tageszeitung*. It is, however, extremely rare when a newspaper modifies its understood political policy as a result of financial considerations. Especially in the case of the Social Democratic press is the influence of the advertising columns on the papers' policy negligible.

Of all the influences then which work upon the press, the government through its various open and subterranean agencies is far and away the strongest. Even in peace times the Berlin ministry may hold a heavy hand on public information through its control of the only great news agency, Wolff's Bureau, to which every German paper is in a sense tributary, from the metropolitan journal with its four editions daily to the "patent outside" of the East Prussian or Bavarian village. The result is a marked lack of enterprise in seeking news on the part of the individual journals, greatly in contrast with the papers of western Europe and America. To begin with, in the very arrangement of the greater number of German papers the news plays a much less important part than the editorial and essay, for the telegraphic news is usually relegated to the inside pages, the first page being given over to discursive articles, which in the greater journals may concern the most recent news, but in the smaller papers usually limp twenty-f our hours behind it. More often the first columns in the morning or evening editions are devoted to an essay on some political or sociological subject or to a résumé, such as would be found in the Sunday issue of an American paper. Even some of the best German newspapers put the latest news in the last columns of the inside of the last page, the place which seems to foreign readers the least conspicuous in the whole paper. News is indeed furnished with startling frequency by the greater German papers, such journals as the *Kölnische Zeitung* putting out four editions daily, with a specialization that is characteristic of other sides of German industry, one edition containing general news, another especially market reports, etc. The wealth of material which such a daily offers, including social and political philosophy, fiction, poetry, travel, biography and literary criticism, much of it of considerable scientific and literary value, is confusing to the American, who seeks first of all the news in his daily paper.

There are other confusing sides in the German attitude towards the day's news when approached with British or American prejudices. One of the most striking is the habit of even the best papers of interlarding news despatches with editorial comment. Provincial sheet and metropolitan daily alike are apt to introduce telegraphic news which is favorable to the cause which they represent with salvos of editorial applause, while unfavorable items are emasculated by constant interlinear comments signed "D.R." (*Der Redakteur*, the editor), such as, "We doubt that!" "Well, we shall wait and see!" or even "This is an open falsehood!" or "Such a campaign of lies!" and similar remarks. Or passages of crucial importance in the text may be interrupted by a bracketed row of question marks or points of exclamation. This confusing mixture of editorial opinion with the day's news is not countenanced by some prominent publishers, like Louis Ullstein, the owner of the Berlin *Morgenpost* and other publications, who have tried to make head against it. Like most newspaper sins, this is also to be laid at the door of the reader, for it must be said that the German reader likes to have his news served up in a way which shall spice the attractiveness of welcome announcements and soften the bitterness of unwelcome things. The German, it must never be forgotten, embraces a cause with his whole soul, whether it be the cause of the whole Fatherland, or that of his economic class or political party, or even his side in the teapot tempest of local politics. He is a devoted champion and good fighter, but also a hard loser, and his tendency to romanticism often permits him to revel in a paradise of dreams even when the enemy is at the gate. This characteristic of the great body of Germans is not of course a weakness of the politically trained classes nor of those aggressive men who guided Germany's industry to the front. But it must not be forgotten that the great majority of German citizens are just emerging from a state of political immaturity. They devote themselves with patient conscientiousness and enthusiasm to the daily duties of home and family, handiwork or profession, and leave political leadership to those who make a profession of ruling, quite willing to accept their orders so long as their patriotism seems trustworthy.

If the liking for news flavored with the sauce of editorial comment indicates a weakness in German public opinion, the distaste for a directly sensational treatment of news is a strength. Germany has, to be sure, its political press of a sensational sort. The wild chauvinism of some of the Berlin and provincial journals is not to be outdone in Paris or Petrograd; but in all that does not concern politics, the most sensational of German journals is as mild when compared with certain French or American dailies as the poems of Felicia Hemans with the early effusions of Swinburne. In the whole field of personalities and in the matter of crime especially, the German papers show a decency and reserve all the more refreshing in view of the flood of impure books which has risen to such a height in Germany. There are, to be sure, yellow journals in Berlin and Munich, and especially certain comic weeklies, the clever *Simplicissimiss* at their head, show a coarseness of tone which has on more than one occasion shut them out from the mails in those countries where puritanism is still a strong tradition; but the German demands that the news columns of his daily paper shall be clean, and the law backs him up in it. For here as elsewhere in German life, the correction of abuses is not left simply to the force of public opinion. Court proceedings must be reported in such a way that they cannot possibly educate to crime; certain classes of cases are entirely shut out of the papers, and it may be said in general that the atmosphere of the German court room does not lend itself to yellow journalism. Offenders against the press laws are invariably punished, often with a severity which seems really out of proportion to the offense.

Especially does the German journalist have to walk carefully to avoid conflict with the rigid libel laws. Even the most innocent remark about the behavior of some public servant or a news item which permits of a construction placing some private individual in an unflattering light may call forth a demand for a public retraction or provoke an expensive libel suit. The German law, indeed, goes very far in protecting the individual in all the rights of personality, especially in the right of avoiding publicity. The retractions published from time to time in German papers are one of the most enlightening chapters in a study of the German press, illustrating as they do how fully the rights of the individual are guarded. The feeling seems to prevail that the doings of no person or group of persons shall be dragged before the public without the consent of those concerned. It goes without saying that the interviewer plays no considerable rôle in the German newspaper world, and that the position of the reporter is much less important than in those countries where an unrestricted license of the press prevails. Indeed the German law goes so far that in many ways the importance of the press as a sanitary agent is taken away. A newspaper is sometimes forced by threats or legal sentence to retract a statement when the retraction is practically a falsehood, for the mere fact that a news item is true does not by any means serve as a defense against a libel suit, if the item may be construed as a reflection on the behavior of any person or group of persons. Thus a case is recorded where an editor was convicted for publishing a statement reflecting on a hospital, although it was shown in the court proceedings that the statement had been made in a public medical gathering. In this case the law guaranteed to the physician the right of criticism, but denied to the editor the right of publicity.

The libel laws are the constant burden of editorial complaint in Germany. Especially the Social Democratic press has had to suffer under their administration at the hands of their political opponents. The German bench is far above any suspicion of bias except that which comes with the belief held in official circles that the Socialists are public enemies, combined with a reverence for those in authority which degenerates at times into servility. This, the Socialist press has contended, was hardly the right source from which it might expect a square deal. In the nineties and the earliest years of the present century heavy sentences, often from three to five years in prison, were pronounced against Social Democratic editors for *lèse majesté*. The modification of the law in 1908 (cf. page 108) did much to soften the tone of the Socialist and Radical press towards royalty in Prussia; but prosecutions for libel still occur when the press of these parties breaks the bounds prescribed by conservative feeling in its criticism of some municipal official or even of a minister of state. Such cases are usually fought bitterly up through the various courts and usually result in a conviction. With the increase of the number and influence of the Socialist press — the party had by 1910 established daily newspapers in more than 68 cities — the watchfulness of prosecuting officers under the inspiration of the higher provincial officials is kept constantly alert. All of this has not tended to soften the tone of the Socialist editor, who never turns the other cheek to the smiter. This unfortunate state of affairs has done much to lower the tone of political discussion in Germany to a bitterness and brutality, which, especially in electoral campaigns, swells into a crescendo of billingsgate and presents a most unattractive side of the German press. No stronger evidence could be presented that the cure for the shrill outbreaks of political immaturity is to be found in liberty and not in constant paternal correction.

In spite of these false notes, the lack of sensationalism in the treatment of news is one of the most refreshing characteristics of the German press. The fact that in Prussia and in some other German states every issue must show the names of the persons responsible for the news and editorial portions and for the advertising columns is a guarantee; and the innate German love of truth and hatred of sham hangs heavy on the success of those metropolitan sheets which show a dangerous tendency to rival the yellow papers of France and America. That these tendencies are manifest in some of the Berlin papers is not to be denied, and it is to be expected that they will continue to grow in proportion as the Americanization of the imperial capital emancipates the individual spirit from the traditions of the past. But the whole spirit of German public opinion is opposed to this hectic demoralization of the press. A few years ago, when an enterprising Berlin firm established an illustrated weekly on the model of those British and American papers which have a maximum of the personal in pictures and articles and a minimum of news and literature, the undertaking was received with a shaking of heads everywhere. "This personal advertisement is against the genius of our people," remarked a prominent Leipsic business man concerning it. "It is an importation from America and is fostering a spirit which Germany has never known." It must be said in defense of America, however, that the German press admits without hesitation advertisements and a sort of humor which in America would be impossible in any paper using the mails.

The reformation of the libel laws cannot long be delayed in Germany, and the result will almost certainly be an improvement in the tone of political and public discussion. It is, however, very improbable that the tone of the German daily papers will be much brightened thereby. The staring headlines which form such a feature of the foreign press the German newspaper reader knows only in a mild form: he demands that he be given that which is true or at least that which is in accord with his ideas of the truth, and wants no trifling with his news in order to make it sensational. The interesting "write-up" of the American or English reporter cannot therefore find a place in a paper which takes itself and its functions so seriously. The editor may himself destroy the effect of the news by critical interpolations, but these spring in most cases from soul convictions which are those of the reader himself. The latter disdains any attempt to make either news or editorial matter interesting, and this paired with the German lack of feeling for literary form makes the German press dull reading for those who seek in it anything like the sparkle and crisply classical presentation of the Paris journals. The dull and formal narration of the news, fortified usually by editorial comment, political résumés, rhodomontades of doubtful inspiration, accurate but colorless police and market reports, with here and there an outburst of Teutonic rage against foreign competitors or political opponents, — these make up the current parts of the newspapers, and certainly do not appeal to those who read the journals for the froth of life or expect from them models of literary excellence.

Since Schopenhauer's day, indeed, "newspaper German" has been a term of contempt. "Pig German, — I beg pardon, — newspaper German!" exclaimed the celebrated pessimist more than half a century ago in a memorable essay on "The Butchery of the German Language." "The linguistic debauch," he exclaimed in his customary gentle style, "to which no other nation can show a parallel, seems to proceed in the main from the political newspapers, the lowest form of literature, and go from them into the literary journals and finally into books." It is certain that newspaper German has done nothing to remove this reproach since Schopenhauer's day; indeed, the style of German prose, which seems to grow more cumbersome and unwieldy every year, can charge much of its degeneracy to the daily and weekly press. An illustrated journal of the highest standing introduces to its readers a series of pictures "from the by-the-Russians-temporarily-occupied-and-by-the German-army-under-the brilliant leadership-of-General-von-Hindenburg-gloriously-reconquered province of East Prussia," and similar sins against all of the muses may be found in the best journals. Of recent years a reaction has been observable, led by papers like the *Vossische Zeitung* of Berlin, "Auntie Voss," as it is humorously called by its contemporaries, which looks back on a century and three-quarters of literary history since no less a stylist than young Gotthold Ephraim Lessing contributed to its early numbers, or the *Frankfurter Zeitung*, which commands some very able pens.

Such criticisms of the German newspaper as literature, however, apply only to its news and editorial columns. Besides these transient expressions of the popular spirit which are written day by day and exist only for a day, the German journals, provincial and metropolitan alike, offer each day a mass of material, which is not merely literature in the strict sense of the word, but which for richness and variety of literary and scientific material has no equal anywhere in the world's press. It is the custom for most papers to maintain a *feuilleton*, separated from news and editorial matter by a type-bar, which reserves the lower half of the page for matters of more lasting content, non-contemporaneous or quasi-contemporaneous in their interest. This essay was a French invention developed in Germany early in the nineteenth century by the Jewish prose virtuoso Heinrich Heine, and it has cultivated a lightness and gracefulness of style which is strikingly in contrast to the soggy editorial or news paragraph. In light essays on science, literature or art, the whole field of modern culture is laid under tribute with a style which recalls the conversational tone of the drawing room or club. The *feuilleton* writers of Germany lack the grace which marks the best salon literateurs of the French press; but they count among them some of the most brilliant stylists of the nation and maintain a high standard in the wealth and variety of their scientific material.

To these articles of critical and conversational tone are to be added literary works, such as novels by the best authors of Germany, published serially in the daily papers. Gerhart Hauptmann's *Atlantis* first appeared in the daily edition of the Berlin *Tageblatt*, and other names scarcely less well known on the German Parnassus are to be found in the daily press of the larger cities. Articles of more solid import appear in special supplements, forming a weekly or semi-weekly part of the larger papers. Some of these command the ablest pens in Germany in the field of literature, art and science, and become an indispensable reference material for investigators and critics. Indeed, the literary criticism of such papers as the Berlin *Tag* and the *Vossische Zeitung* or the Cologne *Volkszeitung* is among the best that appears anywhere in Germany. The well-nigh inexhaustible wealth of material offered in this way may be shown by a résumé of the various supplements issued within one week to accompany the morning and afternoon news and editorial matter and market reports of a large Berlin newspaper: a technical supplement of eight pages; a supplement containing essays on legal subjects, four pages; a literary review, two pages; an illustrated supplement, six pages; a comical supplement, six pages; a household supplement, six pages; and a page each for women's affairs, for art and drama criticism and for tourists. In addition the regular issues contained a letter from China on politico-economic subjects, a sketch of the Hungarian drama, and essays on the teaching of pedagogics in the universities and on the sleeping sickness in the African colonies, and one page daily devoted to a review of sports, mostly horse racing and aeronautics.

It is evident that while the German newspaper does not as a newsgatherer satisfy western demands, it brings to its readers each day a wealth of material which in other lands would find its way into the "heavier" magazines or into scientific periodicals. It is evident also that while the German who reads his chosen newspaper may be insufficiently informed or biassed regarding that which is called in press parlance "live news," he is schooled in scientific methods of observation and inquiry and in accuracy of reporting regarding those things which can be divorced from the ephemeral passions of the day. He finds in his daily or weekly journal not so much a raconteur of the day's doings as a pedagogue and staid mentor, who delights to lead him into the devious paths of science or the romantic world of ideas and ideals. The pedagogical instinct and the enthusiasm for knowledge for its own sake, the love of truth and the careful accuracy in method, narrowness of political view and passionate insistence on the personal standpoint: these ingredients of German character are nowhere more clearly exemplified than in the nation's press."

89. F. S. Meyer, *The Moulding of Communists: The Training of the Communist Cadre*, Harcourt, Brace and Co., New York, (1961). *See also:* W. Chambers, *Witness*, Random House, New York, (1952). *See also:* D. A. Hyde, *Dedication and Leadership Techniques*, Mission Secretariat, Washington, (1963); **and** *Dedication and Leadership: Learning from the Communists*, University of Notre Dame Press, (1966).

90. E. Bernstein, "Jews and German Social Democracy", *Die Tukunft* (New York), Volume 26, (March, 1921), pp. 145ff.; English translation in: P. W. Massing, *Rehearsal for Destruction: A Study of Political Anti-Semitism in Imperial Germany*, Howard Fertig, New York, (1967), pp. 322-330. *See also:* H. Hirsch, "The Ugly Marx: Analysis of an 'Outspoken Anti-Semite'", *Philosophical Forum*, Volume 8, (1978), pp.150-162. *See also:* P. L. Rose, *Revolutionary Antisemitism in Germany from Kant to Wagner*, Princeton University Press, (1990), pp. 296-305. *See also:* R. Grooms, "The Racism of Marx and Engels", *The Barnes Review*, Volume 2, Number 10, (October, 1996), pp. 3-8.

91. Quoted in V. I. Lenin, "What is to be Done?", *V. I. Lenin: Collected Works*, Volume 5, Foreign Languages Publishing House, Moscow, (1961), pp. 347-530, at 347; **and** *What is to be Done? Burning Questions of Our Movement*, International Publishers, New York, (1969), p. 5. Note that the title of Lenin's work, "What is to be Done?", was a repetition of revolutionary Nikolai Gavrilovich Chernyshevsky's work of 1873, *What is to be Done?*

92. H. E. Barnes, *The Genesis of the World War: An Introduction to the Problem of War Guilt*, A.A. Knopf, New York, London, (1927), pp. 590-653;

and *In Quest of Truth and Justice: De-bunking the War Guilt Myth*, National Historical Society, Chicago, (1928), pp. 30-34, 98-105. *See also:* A. Ponsonby, *Falsehood in War-Time, Containing an Assortment of Lies Circulated Throughout the Nations During the Great War*, G. Allen & Unwin, ltd. London, E. P. Dutton, New York, (1928). A. J. Dawe, Letter to the Editor, "The Crime Of Louvain. Vivid Account By An Eye-Witness. *See also:* A Ruthless Holocaust. The Real Horrors Of War", *The London Times*, (3 September 1914), p. 4. *See aslo:* J. Bryce, *Report of the Committee on alleged German outrages appointed by His Britannic Majesty's Government and presided over by the Right Hon. Viscount Bryce. Evidence and Documents laid before the Committee on alleged German outrages: (appendix to the Report).*, Printed Under the Authority of His Majesty's Stationery Office, London, (1915); **French** *Rapport de la Commission d'Enquête sur les Atrocités Allemandes*, Darling & Son, London, (1915); **Italian** *Relazione della Commissione d'Inchiesta sulle Atrocità Tedesche*, Vincenzo Bartelli, Perugia, (1915), **Portugese** *Relatorio da Commissão sobre as Barbaridades Attribuidas aos Allemães, nomeada pelo Governo de Sua Magestade Britannica presidida pelo Visconde Bryce*, Thomas Nelson & Sons, Paris, Edimburgo, (1915); **Spanish** *Informe Acerca de los Atentados Atribuidos á los Alemanes, Emitido por la Comisión Nombrada por el Gobierno de su Majéstad Británica y Presidida por el muy Honorable Vizconde Bryce*, Thomas Nelson & Sons, Paris, Edimburgo, (1915).

93. G. Parker, "The United States and the War", *Harper's Magazine*, Volume 136, Number 814, (March, 1918), pp. 521-531, at 521-522.

94. Letter from M. Planck to A. Einstein of 4 October 1919, *The Collected Papers of Albert Einstein*, Volume 9, Document 121, Princeton University Press, (2004). Letter from H. Zangger to A. Einstein of 22 October 1919, *The Collected Papers of Albert Einstein*, Volume 9, Document 148, Princeton University Press, (2004).

95. A. Moszkowski, *Einstein: The Searcher*, E. P. Dutton, New York, (1921), pp. 12-15.

96. A. Moszkowski, *Einstein: The Searcher*, E. P. Dutton, New York, (1921), p. 19.

97. *The Collected Papers of Albert Einstein*, Volume 9, Documents 110, 112, 113, 117, 121,124, 127, 149, 151, 164, 165, etc., Princeton University Press, (2004). R. W. Clark, *Einstein: The Life and Times*, World Publishing, New York, (1971), pp. 230-231.

98. A. Einstein, "Vom Relativitäts-Prinzip", *Vossische Zeitung*, Morning Edition, (26 April 1914), pp. 1-2; reproduced in *The Collected Papers of Albert Einstein*, Volume 6, Document 1, Princeton University Press, (1996), pp. 3-5.

99. The published lecture was: A. Einstein, "Motive des Forschens", *Zu Max Plancks sechzigstem Geburtstag. Ansprachen, gehalten am 26. April 1918 in der Deutschen Physikalischen Gesellschaft von E. Warburg, M. v. Laue, A. Sommerfeld und A. Einstein*, C. F. Hofbuchhandlung, Karlsruhe, (1918), pp. 29-32; reprinted in *The Collected Papers of Albert Einstein*, Volume 7,

Document 7, Princeton University Press, (2002), pp. 54-59.

100. *See:* Letter from A. Einstein to A. Sommerfeld of 2 February 1916, *The Collected Papers of Albert Einstein*, Volume 8, Document 186, Princeton University Press, (1998).

101. E. Freundlich, *Die Grundlagen der Einsteinschen Gravitationstheorie*, J. Springer, Berlin, (1916); English translation: *The Foundations of Einstein's Theory of Gravitation*, Cambridge University Press, (1920). *See also:* M. Schlick, *Raum und Zeit in der gegenwärtigen Physik. Zur Einführung in das Verstandnis der allgemeinen Relativitätstheorie*, Springer, Berlin, (1917); English translation: *Space and Time in Contemporary Physics: An Introduction to the Theory of Relativity and Gravitation*, Oxford University Press, New York, (1920). *See also:* The Collected Papers of Albert Einstein, Volume 9, Documents 105, 119, 222, 228, 234, 240, 249, 275, 285, 392, 393, Princeton University Press, (2004).

102. Letter from E. Freundlich to A. Einstein of 15 September 1919, *The Collected Papers of Albert Einstein*, Volume 9, Document 105, Princeton University Press, (2004).

103. Letter from A. Einstein to E. Freundlich of 19 September 1919, English translation by A. Hentschel, *The Collected Papers of Albert Einstein*, Volume 9, Document 106, Princeton University Press, (2004), pp. 89-90, at 89. Freundlich's fortunes changed after Einstein began to spread word of Lorentz's news that the English confirmed that a deflection of light at the limb of the sun had been measured. *See: The Collected Papers of Albert Einstein*, Volume 9, Documents 119, 168 and 194, Princeton University Press, (2004).

104. A. Einstein quoted in "Einstein, Too, Is Puzzled; It's at Public Interest", *The Chicago Tribune*, (4 April 1921), p. 6.

105. R. S. Shankland, "Conversations with Albert Einstein", *American Journal of Physics*, Volume 31, Number 1, (January, 1963), pp. 47-57, at 56. Also see Einstein's letters to Zangger of late December, 1919, and of January, 1920, in which he discusses the cult surrounding him.

106. A. Einstein, "On Receiving the One World Award", *Out of My Later Years*, Philosophical Library, New York, (1950); here quoted from: *Ideas and Opinions*, Crown, New York, (1954), pp. 146-147.

107. P. A. Bucky, Einstein, and A. G. Weakland, *The Private Albert Einstein*, Andrews and McMeel, Kansas City, (1992), p. 32, *see also:* pp. 110, 116-117.

108. Letter from A. Einstein to M. Besso of 12 December 1919, English translation by A. Hentschel, *The Collected Papers of Albert Einstein*, Volume 9, Document 207, Princeton University Press, (2004), pp. 178-179, at 178.

109. "The Zionist Congress: Full Report of the Proceedings", *The Jewish Chronicle*, (3 September 1897), pp. 10-15, at 11.

110. Letter from P. Ehrenfest to A. Einstein of 9 December 1919, English translation by A. Hentschel, *The Collected Papers of Albert Einstein*, Volume 9, Document 203, Princeton University Press, (2004), pp. 173-175, at 174.

111. *The Collected Papers of Albert Einstein*, Volume 9, Documents 227, 238, and 283, Princeton University Press, (2004).

112. *The Collected Papers of Albert Einstein*, Volume 9, Documents 186, 187 and 216, Princeton University Press, (2004). *See also: The Collected Papers of Albert Einstein*, Volume 5, Documents 492 and 506, Princeton University Press, (1993). *See also:* Letter from A. Einstein to P. Ehrenfest of 19 August 1914, *The Collected Papers of Albert Einstein*, Volume 8, Part A, Document 34, Princeton University Press, (1998), pp. 56-57, *especially* p. 57, note 4. *See also:* E. Freundlich, "Über einen Versuch, die von A. Einstein vermutete Ablenkung des Lichtes in Gravitationsfeldern zu prüfen", *Astronomische Nachrichten*, Volume 193, (1913), cols. 369-372; **and** "Zur Frage der konstanz der Lichtgeschwindigkeit", *Physikalische Zeitschrift*, Volume 14, (1913), pp. 835-838; **and** "Über die Verschiebung der Sonnenlinien nach dem roten Ende auf Grund der Hypothesen von Einstein und Nordström", *Physikalische Zeitschrift*, Volume 15, (1914), pp. 369-371; **and** "Über die Verschiebung der Sonnenlinien nach dem roten Ende des Spektrums auf Grund der Äquivalenzhypothese von Einstein", *Astronomische Nachrichten*, Volume 198, (1914), cols. 265-270; **and** *Astronomische Nachrichten*, Volume 199, (1915), cols. 363-365; **and** "Über die Gravitationsverschiebung der Spektrallinien bei Fixsternen", *Physikalische Zeitschrift*, Volume 16, (1915), pp. 115-117; **and** *Beobachtungs-Ergebnisse der Königlichen Sternwarte zu Berlin*, Number 15, (1915), p. 77; **and** "Über die Erklärung der Anomalien im Planeten-System durch die Gravitationswirkung interplanetarer Massen", *Astronomische Nachrichten*, Volume 201, (1915), cols. 49-56; **and** "Über die Gravitationsverschiebung der Spektrallinien bei Fixsternen", *Astronomische Nachrichten*, Volume 202, (1915), cols. 17-24; **and** "Über die Gravitationsverschiebung der Spektrallinien bei Fixsternen", *Astronomische Nachrichten*, Volume 202, (1916), cols. 17-24; **and** *Astronomische Nachrichten*, Volume 202, (1916), col. 147; **and** "Die Grundlagen der Einsteinschen Gravitationstheorie", *Die Naturwissenschaften*, Volume 4, (1916), pp. 363-372, 386-392; **and** *Die Grundlagen der Einsteinschen Gravitationstheorie*, Multiple Revised and Enlarged Editions; **and** "Über die singulären Stellen der Lösungen des n-Körper-Problems", *Sitzungsberichte der Königlich Preussischen Akademie der Wissenschaften zu Berlin*, (1918), pp. 168-188; **and** "Zur Prüfung der allgemeine Relativitätstheorie", *Die Naturwissenschaften*, Volume 7, (1919), pp. 629-636, 696; **and** "Über die Gravitationsverschiebung der Spektrallienien bei Fixsternen. II. Mitteilung", *Physikalische Zeitschrift*, Volume 20, (1919), pp. 561-570.

113. Letter from M. Born to D. Hilbert of 23 November 1915, Niedersächische Staats- und Universitätsbibliothek Göttingen, Cod. Ms. D. Hilbert 40 A: Nr. 11; the relevant part of which is reproduced in D. Wuensch, *„zwei wirkliche Kerle": Neues zur Entdeckung der Gravitationsgleichungen der Allgemeinen Relativitätstheorie durch Albert Einstein und David Hilbert*, Termessos, Göttingen, (2005), pp. 73-74.

114. A. Einstein, "Die Feldgleichungen der Gravitation", *Sitzungsberichte der Königlich Preussischen Akademie der Wissenschaften zu Berlin der physikalisch-mathematischen Classe*, (1915), pp. 844-847.

115. H. A. Lorentz, "Electromagnetische Verschijnselen in een Stelsel dat Zich met Willekeurige Snelheid, Kleiner dan die van Het Licht, Beweegt", *Koninklijke Akademie van Wetenschappen te Amsterdam, Wis- en Natuurkundige Afdeeling, Verslagen van de Gewone Vergaderingen*, Volume 12, (23 April 1904), pp. 986-1009; translated into English, "Electromagnetic Phenomena in a System Moving with any Velocity Smaller than that of Light", *Proceedings of the Royal Academy of Sciences at Amsterdam (Noninklijke Nederlandse Akademie van Wetenschappen te Amsterdam)*, 6, (May 27, 1904), pp. 809-831; reprinted *Collected Papers*, Volume 5, pp. 172-197; a redacted and shortened version appears in *The Principle of Relativity*, Dover, New York, (1952), pp. 11-34; a German translation from the English, "Elektromagnetische Erscheinung in einem System, das sich mit beliebiger, die des Lichtes nicht erreichender Geschwindigkeit bewegt," appears in *Das Relativitätsprinzip: eine Sammlung von Abhandlungen*, B. G. Teubner, Leipzig, (1913), pp. 6-26.

116. H. Poincaré, "Sur la Dynamique de l'Électron", *Rendiconti del Circolo matimatico di Palermo*, Volume 21, (1906, submitted July 23rd, 1905), pp. 129-176; reprinted in H. Poincaré, *La Mécanique Nouvelle: Conférence, Mémoire et Note sur la Théorie de la Relativité / Introduction de Édouard Guillaume*, Gauthier-Villars, Paris, (1924), pp. 18-76; reprinted *Œuvres*, Volume IX, pp. 494-550; redacted English translation by H. M. Schwartz with modern notation, "Poincaré's Rendiconti Paper on Relativity", *American Journal of Physics*, Volume 39, (November, 1971), pp. 1287-1294; Volume 40, (June, 1972), pp. 862-872; Volume 40, (September, 1972), pp. 1282-1287; English translation by G. Pontecorvo with extensive commentary by A. A. Logunov with modern notation, *On the Articles by Henri Poincaré ON THE DYNAMICS OF THE ELECTRON*, Publishing Department of the Joint Institute for Nuclear Research, Dubna, (1995), pp. 15-78.

117. W. de Sitter, "On the Bearing of the Principle of Relativity on Gravitational Astronomy", *Monthly Notices of the Royal Astronomical Society*, Volume 71, (March, 1911), pp. 388-415.

118. Letter from A. Einstein to H. and M. Born of 27 January 1920, *The Collected Papers of Albert Einstein*, Volume 9, Document 284, Princeton University Press, (2004).

119. L. Pyenson, *The Young Einstein: The Advent of Relativity*, Adam Hilger, Boston, (1985), p. 82.

120. Racist political Zionist Theodor Herzl wrote on 12 June 1895,

"Jewish papers! I will induce the publishers of the biggest Jewish papers (*Neue Freie Presse, Berliner Tageblatt, Frankfurter Zeitung,* etc.) to publish editions over there, as the *New York Herald* does in Paris."—T. Herzl, English translation by H. Zohn, R. Patai, Editor, *The Complete Diaries of Theodor Herzl*, Volume 1, Herzl Press, New York, (1960), p. 84.

THE DEARBORN INDEPENDENT, praised the New York Herald. "When Editors Were Independent of the Jews", THE DEARBORN INDEPENDENT, (5 February 1921). *See also:* T. Herzl, English translation by H. Zohn, R. Patai, Editor, *The Complete Diaries of Theodor Herzl*, Volumes 1 and 2, Herzl Press, New York, (1960), pp. 37, 97, 170, 455, 457, 480. *See also:* A. Elon, *Herzl*, Holt, Rinehart and Winston, New York, (1975), pp. 167-168. *See also: The Collected Papers of Albert Einstein*, Volume 7, Document 35, Princeton University Press, (2002), pp. 296-297, note 8.

121. R. D. Carmichael, *The Theory of Relativity*, Mathematical Monographs No. 12, John Wiley & Sons, Inc., New York, Chapman & Hall, Limited, London, (1920).

122. M. Schlick, *Space and Time in Contemporary Physics*, Oxford University Press, New York, (1920).

123. R. Drill, "Die Kultur der Haeckel-Zeit", *Frankfurter Zeitung*, (18 August 1919); **and** "Nachwort", *Frankfurter Zeitung*, (2 September 1919); **and** "Ordnung und Chaos. Ein Beitrag zum Gesetz von der Erhaltung der Kraft. I-II", *Frankfurter Zeitung*, (30 November 1919 / 2 December 1919).

124. F. Kleinschrod, "Das Lebensproblem und das Positivitätsprinzip in Zeit und Raum und das Einsteinsche Relativitätsprinzip in Raum und Zeit", *Frankfurter Zeitgemäße Broschuren*, Volume 40, Number 1-3, Breer & Thiemann, Hamm, Westphalen, (October-December, 1920), pp. 17, 47.

125. H. Dingler, *Die Grundlagen der Physik; synthetische Prinzipien der mathematischen Naturphilosophie*, Second Edition, Walter de Gruyter & Co., Berlin, (1923); **and** *Physik und Hypothese Versuch einer induktiven Wissenschaftslehre nebst einer kritischen Analyse der Fundamente der Relativitätstheorie*, Walter de Gruyter & Co., Berlin, Leipzig, (1921); **and** "Kritische Bemerkungen zu den Grundlagen der Relativitätstheorie", *Physikalische Zeitschrift*, Volume 21, (1920), pp. 668-669.

126. F. A. Hayek, edited by S. Kresge and L. Wenar, *Hayek on Hayek: An Autobiographical Dialogue*, University of Chicago Press, (1994), pp. 48-49, 50-51.

127. J. Leveugle, *La Relativité, Poincaré et Einstein, Planck, Hilbert: Histoire véridique de la Théorie de la Relativité*, L'Harmattan, Paris, (2004).

128. M. Born, *My Life: Recollections of a Nobel Laureate*, Charles Scribner's Sons, New York, (1975), pp. 98, 130; **and** *The Born-Einstein Letters*, Walker and Company, New York, (1971), p. 1; **and** "Physics and Relativity", *Physics in my Generation*, second revised edition, Springer, New York, (1969), p. 101. *See also:* J. Leveugle, "Hilbert et Poincaré", *Poincaré et la Relativité : Question sur la Science*, Chapter 10, (2002), ISBN: 2-9518876-1-2, pp.147-230; **and** *La Relativité, Poincaré et Einstein, Planck, Hilbert: Histoire véridique de la Théorie de la Relativité*, L'Harmattan, Paris, (2004). *See also:* L. Pyenson, *The Young Einstein and the Advent of Relativity*, Bristol, Adam Hilger, (1985), pp. 103-104. *See also:* C. Reid, *Hilbert*, Springer Verlag, Berlin, Heidelberg, New York, (1970), pp. 100, 105.

129. *See, for example:* M. Born, "Zur Kinematik des starren Körpers im System des Relativitätsprinzips", *Nachrichten von der Königlichen Gesellschaft der Wissenschaften und der Georg-Augusts-Universität zu Göttingen*, (1910), pp. 161-179, at 161.

130. *See, for example:* M. Born, "Eine Ableitung der Grundgleichungen für die elektromagnetischen Vorgänge in bewegten Körpern vom Standpunkte der Elektronentheorie. Aus dem Nachlaß von Hermann Minkowski", *Mathematische Annalen*, Volume 68, (1910), pp. 526-551; **and** "Zur Kinematik des starren Körpers im System des Relativitätsprinzips", *Nachrichten von der Königlichen Gesellschaft der Wissenschaften und der Georg-Augusts-Universität zu Göttingen*, (1910), pp. 161-179.

131. Letter from M. Born to D. Hilbert of 23 November 1915, Niedersächische Staats- und Universitätsbibliothek Göttingen, Cod. Ms. D. Hilbert 40 A: Nr. 11; the relevant part of which is reproduced in D. Wuensch, *„zwei wirkliche Kerle": Neues zur Entdeckung der Gravitationsgleichungen der Allgemeinen Relativitätstheorie durch Albert Einstein und David Hilbert*, Termessos, Göttingen, (2005), pp. 73-74.

132. M. Born, *The Born-Einstein Letters*, Walker and Company, New York, (1971), p. 5.

133. *See:* Letter from P. Lenard to J. Stark 8 September 1920 in A. Kleinert and C. Schönbeck, "Lenard und Einstein. Ihr Briefwechsel und ihr Verhältnis vor der Nauheimer Diskussion von 1920", *Gesnerus*, Volume 35, Number 3/4, (1978), pp. 318-333, at 328-329.

134. D. Bronder, *Bevor Hitler kam: Eine historische Studie*, Hans Pfeiffer Verlag, Hannover, (1964), p. 204 (p. 211 in the 1974 edition). H. Kardel, *Adolf Hitler, Begründer Israels*, Verlag Marva, Genf, (1974); English translation *Adolf Hitler: Founder of Israel*, Modjeskis' Society Dedicated to Preservation of Cultures, San Diego, (1997), pp. 4, 73.

135. "Personal-Glimpses: Einstein Finds the World Narrow", The Literary Digest, (16 April 1921), pp. 33-34.

136. M. Born, *The Born-Einstein Letters*, Walker and Company, New York, (1971), p. 41.

137. Letter from A. Einstein to Cambridge University Press of 27 January 1920, *The Collected Papers of Albert Einstein*, Volume 9, Document 285, Princeton University Press, (2004).

138. M. Born, *Die Relativitätstheorie Einsteins und ihre physikalischen Grundlagen: gemeinverständlich dargestellt*, J. Springer, Berlin, (1920).

139. M. Born, *The Born-Einstein Letters*, Walker and Company, New York, (1971), pp. 39-40.

140. M. Born, "Preface", *Einstein's Theory of Relativity*, Revised and Enlarged Edition, Dover, New York, (1962/1965).

141. "Die Einsteinsche Relativitätstheorie" *Frankfurter Zeitung*, Number 46, (18 January 1920), p. 2; Number 61, (23 January 1920), p. 2; Number 82, (31 January 1920), p. 2.

142. M. Born, *Einstein's Theory of Relativity*, Revised and Enlarged Edition, Dover, New York, (1962/1965), p. 246.

143. M. Born, *My Life: Recollections of a Nobel Laureate*, Charles Scribner's Sons, New York, (1975), pp. 195-196.

144. Letter from F. Ehrenhaft to A. Einstein of 6 December 1919, English translation by A. Hentschel, *The Collected Papers of Albert Einstein*, Volume 9, Document 196, Princeton University Press, (2004), pp. 166-167, at 166. Einstein rejected the offer *ibid.* Document 211; and expressed reservations about Ehrenhaft's personality, *ibid.* Documents 269 and 270.

145. I. Shahak, Jewish History, Jewish Religion: The Weight of Three Thousand Years, Pluto Press, London, (1997/2002), p. 93.

146. English translation of I. B. *Pranaitis, Christianus in Talmude Iudaeorum sive, Rabbinicae doctrinae de Christianis secreta: quae patere fecit, Officina Typographica Academiae Caesarae Scientiarum*, Petropoli, (1892).

147. "Gentile", *The Jewish Encyclopedia*, Funk and Wagnalls Company, New York, (1903), pp. 615-626, at 619-620.

148. M. Higger, *The Jewish Utopia*, Lord Baltimore Press, Baltimore, (1932), pp. 12-13, 57.

149. J. Crelinsten, "Einstein, Relativity, and the Press", *The Physics Teacher*, (February, 1980), pp. 115-122; **and** "Physicists Receive Relativity: Revolution and Reaction", *The Physics Teacher*, (March, 1980), pp. 187-193. On the reaction of the British to the idea that Newton had been defeated, see A. F. Lindemann's letter to A. Einstein of 23 November 1919, *The Collected Papers of Albert Einstein*, Volume 9, Document 174, Princeton University Press, (2004).

150. "Introduction to the Abridged Edition", in A. Einstein, *The World As I See It*, translated by A. Harris, Citadel, New York, (1993), p. vii.

151. O. Lodge, "The New Theory of Gravity", *Nineteenth Century*, (December, 1919); and "The Ether Versus Relativity", *Fortnightly Review*, (January, 1920). *Cf.* "A New Physics Based on Einstein", *The New York Times*, (25 November 1919), p. 17. *The London Times*, (8 November 1919), p. 12, col. *d*; (25 November 1919), p.16, col. *d*; (29 November 1919), p. 9, col. *d*; (13 December 1919), p. 13, col. *a*. Lodge also published an article in *Nature*, Volume 106, (17 February 1921). *Confer:* J. Crelinsten, "Physicists Receive Relativity: Revolution and Reaction", *The Physics Teacher*, (March, 1980), pp. 187-193.

152. Letter from A. Einstein to H. A. Lorentz of 21 September 1919, English translation by A. Hentschel, *The Collected Papers of Albert Einstein*, Volume 9, Document 108, Princeton University Press, (2004), pp. 92-93, at 93.

153. Letter from A. Einstein to H. A. Lorentz of 21 September 1919, English translation by A. Hentschel, *The Collected Papers of Albert Einstein*, Volume 9, Document 108, Princeton University Press, (2004), pp. 92-93, at 93.

154. D. K. Buchwald, *et al.*, Editors, *The Collected Papers of Albert Einstein*, Volume 7, Princeton University Press, (2002), p. 106.

155. A. Einstein quoted in M. Born, *The Born-Einstein Letters*, Walker and Company, New York, (1971), p. 8.

156. Ilse Einstein to Georg Nikolai, English translation by A. M. Hentschel, *The Collected Papers of Albert Einstein*, Volume 8, Document 545, Princeton University Press, (1998), p. 565. *See also:* D. Overbye, *Einstein in Love: A Scientific Romance*, Viking, New York, (2000), pp. 343, 404, note 22. *See also:* A. Einstein to Ilse Einstein, *The Collected Papers of Albert Einstein*, Volume 8, Document 536, Princeton University Press, (1998).

157. Letter from P. Ehrenfest to A. Einstein of 2 September 1919, English translation by A. Hentschel, *The Collected Papers of Albert Einstein*, Volume 9, Document 98, Princeton University Press, (2004), pp. 81-82, at 82.

158. Letter from A. Einstein to H. A. Lorentz of 19 January 1920, English translation by A. Hentschel, *The Collected Papers of Albert Einstein*, Volume 9, Document 265, Princeton University Press, (2004), p. 220.

159. Letter from A. S. Eddington to A. Einstein, *The Collected Papers of Albert Einstein*, Volume 9, Document 271, Princeton University Press, (2004), pp. 224-225, at 224.

160. *The Collected Papers of Albert Einstein*, Volume 9, Documents 146 and 177, Princeton University Press, (2004).

161. B. Russell, *The A B C of Relativity*, Harper & Brothers, New York, London, (1925).

162. Letter from A. Einstein to H. Delbrück of 26 January 1920, *The Collected Papers of Albert Einstein*, Princeton University Press, (2004), p. 235.

163. Menyhért (Melchior) Palágyi, *Neue Theorie des Raumes und der Zeit*, Engelmanns, Leipzig, (1901); reprinted in *Zur Weltmechanik, Beiträge zur Metaphysik der Physik von Melchior Palágyi, mit einem Geleitwort von Ernst Gehrcke*, J. A. Barth, Leipzig, (1925).

164. V. Varičak, "Primjedbe o jednoj interpretaciji geometrije Lobačevskoga", *Rad Jugoslavenska Akademija Znanosti i Umjetnosti*, Volume 154, (1903), pp. 81-131; **and** "O transformacijama u ravnini Lobačevskoga" *Rad Jugoslavenska Akademija Znanosti i Umjetnosti*, Volume 165, (1906), pp. 50-80; **and** "Opcéna jednadzba pravca u hiperbolnoj ravnini", *Rad Jugoslavenska Akademija Znanosti i Umjetnosti*, Volume 167, (1906), pp. 167-188; **and** "Bemerkung zu einem Punkte in der Festrede L. Schlesingers über Johann Bolyai", *Jahresbericht der Deutschen Mathematiker-Vereinigung*, Volume 16, (1907), pp. 320-321; **and** "Prvi osnivači neeuklidske geometrije", *Rad Jugoslavenska Akademija Znanosti i Umjetnosti*, Volume 169, (1908), pp. 110-194; **and** "Beiträge zur nichteuklidischen Geometrie", *Jahresbericht der Deutschen Mathematiker-Vereinigung*", Volume 17, (1908), pp. 70-83; **and** "Anwendung der Lobatschefskijschen Geometrie in der Relativitätstheorie", *Physikalische Zeitschrift*, Volume 11, (1910), pp. 93-96; **and** "Die Relativtheorie und die Lobatschefskijsche Geometrie", *Physikalische Zeitschrift*, Volume 11, (1910), pp. 287-294; **and** "Die Relexion des Lichtes an bewegten Spiegeln", *Physikalische Zeitschrift*, Volume 11, (1910), pp. 586-587; **and** "Zum Ehrenfestschen Paradoxon", *Physikalische Zeitschrift*, Volume 12, (1911), pp. 169-170; **and** "Интерпретација теорије релативности у геометрији Лобачевскова", *Glas, Srpska Kraljevska Akademija*, Volume 83,

(1911), pp. 211-255; **and** *Glas, Srpska Kraljevska Akademija*, Volume 88, (1911); **and** "Über die nichteuklidische Interpretation der Relativitätstheorie", *Jahresbericht der Deutschen Mathematiker-Vereinigung*, Volume 21, (1912), pp. 103-127; **and** *Rad Jugoslavenska Akademija Znanosti i Umjetnosti*, (1914), p. 46; (1915), pp. 86, 101; (1916), p. 79; (1918), p. 1; (1919), p. 100.

165. *Cf.* J. Stachel, Ed., *The Collected Papers of Albert Einstein*, Volume 2, Princeton University Press, (1989), p. 110.

166. Letter from A. Einstein to H. Zangger of 24 December 1919, English translation by A. Hentschel, *The Collected Papers of Albert Einstein*, Volume 9, Document 233, Princeton University Press, (2004), pp. 197-198.

167. A. Kleinert and C. Schönbeck, "Lenard und Einstein. Ihr Briefwechsel und ihr Verhältnis vor der Nauheimer Diskussion von 1920", *Gesnerus*, Volume 35, Number 3/4, (1978), pp. 318-333.

168. D. K. Buchwald, *et al.* Editors, *The Collected Papers of Albert Einstein*, Volume 7, Princeton University Press, (2002), p. 110.

169. A. Hermann, *Briefwechsel. Sechzig Briefe aus dem goldenen Zeitalter der modernen Physik*, Schwabe & Co., Basel, Stuttgart, (1968), p. 65.

170. Letter from A. Einstein to A. Stodola of 31 March 1919, *The Collected Papers of Albert Einstein*, Volume 9, Document 16, Princeton University Press, (2004).

171. A. Einstein quoted in R. W. Clark, *Einstein: The Life and Times*, The World Publishing Company, (1971), p. 261; referencing A. Einstein to A. Sommerfeld, in A. Hermann. *Briefwechsel. 60 Briefe aus dem goldenen Zeitalter der modernen Physik*, Schwabe & Co., Basel, Stuttgart, (1968), p. 69.

172. A. v. Brunn, quoted in: K. Hentschel, Ed., A. Hentschel, Ed. Ass. and Trans., *Physics and National Socialism: An Anthology of Primary Sources*, Birkhäuser, Basel, Boston, Berlin, (1996), p. 11.

173. From the preface of *Hundert Autoren gegen Einstein* translated by: H. Goenner, "The Reaction to Relativity Theory in Germany, III: 'A Hundred Authors against Einstein'", J. Earman, M. Janssen, J. D. Norton, Eds., *The Attraction of Gravitation: New Studies in the History of General Relativity*, Birkhäuser, Boston, Basel, Berlin, (1993), p. 251.

174. A. v. Brunn, quoted in: K. Hentschel, Ed., A. Hentschel, Ed. Ass. and Trans., *Physics and National Socialism: An Anthology of Primary Sources*, Birkhäuser, Basel, Boston, Berlin, (1996), p. 14.

175. C. J. Bjerknes, *Albert Einstein: The Incorrigible Plagiarist*, XTX Inc., Downer Grove, Illinois, (2002). *See also:* P. Langevin, "Le Physicien", *Revue de Métaphysique et de Morale*, Volume 20, Number 5, (September, 1913), pp. 675-718. *See also:* H. A. Lorentz, "Deux mémoires de Henri Poincaré sur la physique mathématique", *Acta Mathematica*, Volume 38, (1921), pp. 293-308; reprinted in *Œuvres de Henri Poincaré*, Volume 9, Gautier-Villars, Paris, (1954), pp. 683-695; and Volume 11, (1956), pp. 247-261. *See also:* W. Pauli, "Relativitätstheorie", *Encyklopädie der mathematischen Wissenschaften mit Einschluss ihrer Anwendungen*, Volume 5, Part 2, Chapter 19, B. G. Teubner, Leipzig, (1921), pp. 539-775; English translation by G. Field, *Theory of*

Relativity, Pergamon Press, London, Edinburgh, New York, Toronto, Sydney, Paris, Braunschweig, (1958). *See also:* H. Thirring, "Elektrodynamik bewegter Körper und spezielle Relativitätstheorie", *Handbuch der Physik*, Volume 12 ("Theorien der Elektrizität Elektrostatik"), Springer, Berlin, (1927), pp. 245-348, *especially* 264, 270, 275, 283. *See also:* S. Guggenheimer, *The Einstein Theory Explained and Analyzed*, Macmillan, New York, (1929). *See also:* J. Mackaye, *The Dynamic Universe*, Charles Scribner's Sons, New York, (1931). *See also:* J. Le Roux, "Le Problème de la Relativité d'Après les Idées de Poincaré", *Bulletin de la Société Scientifique de Bretagne*, Volume 14, (1937), pp. 3-10. *See also:* Sir Edmund Whittaker, *A History of the Theories of Aether and Electricity*, Volume II, Philosophical Library Inc., New York, (1954), *especially* pp. 27-77; and "Albert Einstein", *Biographical Memoirs of Fellows of the Royal Society*, Volume 1, (1955), pp. 37-67. *See also:* G. H. Keswani, "Origin and Concept of Relativity, Parts I, II & III", *The British Journal for the Philosophy of Science*, Volume 15, Number 60, (February, 1965), pp. 286-306; Volume 16, Number 61, (May, 1965), pp.19-32; Volume 16, Number 64, (February, 1966), pp. 273-294; and Volume 17, Number 2, (August, 1966), pp. 149- 152; Volume 17, Number 3, (November, 1966), pp. 234-236. *See also:* G. H. Keswani and C. W. Kilmister, "Intimations of Relativity before Einstein", *The British Journal for the Philosophy of Science*, Volume 34, Number 4, (December, 1983), pp. 343-354. *See also:* G. B. Brown, "What is Wrong with Relativity?", *Bulletin of the Institute of Physics and the Physical Society*, Volume 18, Number 3, (March, 1967), pp. 71-77. *See also:* C. Cuvaj, "Henri Poincaré's Mathematical Contributions to Relativity and the Poincaré Stresses", *American Journal of Physics*, Volume 36, (1968), pp. 1109-1111. *See also:* C. Giannoni, "Einstein and the Lorentz-Poincaré Theory of Relativity", *PSA: Proceedings of the Biennial Meeting of the Philosophy of Science Association*, Volume 1970, (1970), pp. 575-589. JSTOR link:

<http://links.jstor.org/sici?sici=0270-8647%281970%291970%3C575%3AE ATLTO%3E2.0.CO%3B2-Z>

See also: J. Mehra, *Einstein, Hilbert, and the Theory of Gravitation*, Reidel, Dordrecht, Netherlands, (1974). *See also:* W. Kantor, *Relativistic Propagation of Light,* Coronado Press, Lawrence, Kansas, (1976). *See also:* R. McCormmach, "Editor's Forward", *Historical Studies in the Physical Sciences*, Volume 7, (1976), pp. xi-xxxv. *See also:* H. Ives, D. Turner, J. J. Callahan, R. Hazelett, *The Einstein Myth and the Ives Papers*, Devin-Adair Co., Old Greenwich, Connecticut, (1979). *See also:* J. Leveugle, "Henri Poincaré et la Relativité", *La Jaune et la Rouge*, Volume 494, (April, 1994), pp. 29-51; **and** *La Relativité, Poincaré et Einstein, Planck, Hilbert: Histoire véridique de la Théorie de la Relativité*, L'Harmattan, Paris, (2004). *See also:* A. A. Logunov, *On the Articles by Henri Poincaré ON THE DYNAMICS OF THE ELECTRON*, Publishing Department of the Joint Institute for Nuclear Research, Dubna, (1995); and *The Theory of Gravity*, Nauka, Moscow, (2001); **and** Анри

Пуанкаре и ТЕОРИЯ ОТНОСИТЕЛЬНОСТИ, Наука, Москва, (2004). An English translation of this book will soon appear as: *Henri Poincaré and the Theory of Relativity*. *See also:* E. Gianetto, "The Rise of Special Relativity: Henri Poincaré's Works before Einstein", *ATTI DEL XVIII CONGRESSO DI STORIA DELLA FISICA E DELL'ASTRONOMICA*, pp. 172-207; URL:

<http://www.brera.unimi.it/Atti-Como-98/Giannetto.pdf>

See also: S. G. Bernatosian, *Vorovstvo i obman v nauke*, Erudit, St. Petersburg, (1998), ISBN: 5749800059. *See also:* U. Bartocci, *Albert Einstein e Olinto De Pretto: La vera storia della formula piu famosa del mondo*, Societa Editrice Andromeda, Bologna, (1999). *See also:* Jean-Paul Auffray, *Einstein et Poincaré: sur les Traces de la Relativité*, Le Pommier, Paris, (1999). Y. Brovko, "Einshteinianstvo—agenturnaya set mirovovo kapitala", Molodaia Gvardiia, Number 8, (1995), pp. 66-74, at 70. Юрий Бровко, "Эйнштейнианство — агентурная сеть Мирового капитала", Молодая гвардия, № 8, (1995), cc. 66-74; **and** Y. Brovko, "Razgrom einshteinianstvo", Priroda i Chelovek. Svet, Number 7, (2002), pp. 8-10. Юрий Бровко, "Разгром эйнштейнианства", Природа и Человек. Свет, № 7, (2002), cc. 8-10. URL:

<http://medograd.narod.ru/einstein.html>

176. E. Gehrcke, "Zur Kritik und Geschichte der neueren Gravitationstheorien", *Annalen der Physik*, Volume 51, (1916), pp. 119-124; reprinted *Kritik der Relativitätstheorie*, Hermann Meusser, Berlin, (1924), pp.40-44.

177. Letter from A. Einstein to W. Wien of 17 October 1916, translated by A. M. Hentschel, *The Collected Papers of Albert Einstein*, Volume 8, Document 267, Princeton University Press, (1998), p. 255.

178. M. Besso letter to Einstein of 5 December 1916, translated by A. M. Hentschel, *The Collected Papers of Albert Einstein*, Volume 8, Document 283, Princeton University Press, (1998), p. 271. F. Adler letter to Einstein of 23 March 1917, translated by A. M. Hentschel, *The Collected Papers of Albert Einstein*, Volume 8, Document 316, Princeton University Press, (1998), p. 308.

179. H. Vaihinger, *Die Philosophie des Als Ob, System der theoretischen, praktischen und religiosen Fiktionen der Menschheit auf Grund eines idealistichen Positivismus. Mit einem Anhang über Kant und Nietzsche*, Reuther & Reichard, Berlin, (1911); English translation by C. K. Ogden, *The Philosophy of 'As If'*, Harcourt, Brace & Company, Inc., New York, (1925); reprinted Routledge & K. Paul, London, (1965). *See also:* C. K. Ogden, *Bentham's Theory of Fictions*, K. Paul, Trench, Trubner & Co. Ltd., (1932).

180. H. Goenner, "The Reaction to Relativity Theory. I: The Anti-Einstein Campaign in Germany in 1920", *Science in Context*, Volume 6, Number 1, (1993), pp. 107-133, at 111.

181. "Einstein Ignores Capt. See", *The New York Times*, (18 October 1924), p. 17.

182. "Challenges Prof. Einstein: St. Paul Professor Asserts Relativity Theory Was Advanced in 1866", *The New York Times*, (10 April 1921), p. 21. *See also:* "Einstein Charged with Plagiarism", *New York American*, (11 April 1921). *See also:* "Einstein Refuses to Debate Theory", *New York American*, (12 April 1921).

183. R. Drill, "Die Kultur der Haeckel-Zeit", *Frankfurter Zeitung*, (18 August 1919); **and** "Nachwort", *Frankfurter Zeitung*, (2 September 1919); **and** "Ordnung und Chaos. Ein Beitrag zum Gesetz von der Erhaltung der Kraft. I-II", *Frankfurter Zeitung*, (30 November 1919 / 2 December 1919).

184. *The Collected Papers of Albert Einstein*, Volume 9, Documents 198, 199 and 222, Princeton University Press, (2004).

185. *The New York Times*, (4 April 1922), p. 21.

186. "Cardinal Doubts Einstein", *The New York Times*, (8 April 1929), p. 4. *See also:* "Einstein Ignores Cardinal", *The New York Times*, (9 April 1929), p. 10. *See also:* "Cardinal Opposes Einstein", *The Chicago Daily Tribune*, (8 April 1929), p. 33. *See also:* "Cardinal Hits at Einstein Theory", *The Minneapolis Journal*, (8 April 1929). *See also:* "Cardinal Gives Further Views on Einstein", *Boston Evening American*, (12 April 1929). *See also:* "Cardinal Warns Against Destructive Theories", *The Pilot* [Roman Catholic Newspaper, Boston], (13 April 1929), pp. 1-2. *See also:* "Vatican Paper Praises Critic of Dr. Einstein", *The Minneapolis Morning Journal*, (24 May 1929).

187. *The New York Times*, (24 February 1936), p. 7. *See also:* "Calls Ether Reality; Differs with Einstein; Proof is Submitted", *The Chicago Tribune*, (23 February 1936).

188. M. Polanyi, *Personal Knowledge*, University of Chicago Press, (1958), p. 13. *See also:* A. Pais, *Subtle is the Lord*, Oxford University Press, (1982), pp. 113-114. *See also:* W. Broad and N. Wade, *Betrayers of the Truth: Fraud and Deceit in the Halls of Science*, Simon & Schuster, New York, (1982), p. 139.

189. *See also:* "Einstein Theory will be Refuted by an American", *The Chicago Tribune*, (24 October 1929), p. 18. *See also:* "Calls Ether Reality; Differs with Einstein; Proof is Submitted", *The Chicago Tribune*, (23 February 1936).

190. R. S. Shankland, "Conversations with Albert Einstein", *American Journal of Physics*, Volume 31, Number 1, (January, 1963), pp. 47-57; **and** "Conversations with Albert Einstein. II", *American Journal of Physics*, Volume 41, Number 7, (July, 1973), pp. 895-901.

191. R. S. Shankland, "Conversations with Albert Einstein", *American Journal of Physics*, Volume 31, Number 1, (January, 1963), pp. 47-57, at 54.

192. A. Einstein quoted in R. W. Clark, *Einstein: The Life and Times*, The World Publishing Company, (1971), p. 261; referencing A. Einstein to A. Sommerfeld, in A. Hermann. *Briefwechsel. 60 Briefe aus dem goldenen Zeitalter der modernen Physik*, Schwabe & Co., Basel, Stuttgart, (1968), p. 69.

193. A. Einstein, *Neues Wiener Journal*, (29 September 1920). C. Kirsten and H. J. Treder, *Albert Einstein in Berlin 1913-1933*, Akademie Verlag, Berlin,

Volume 2, (1979), pp. 139, 205.

194. "3379 (XXX). Elimination of All Forms of Racial Discrimination", General Assembly—Thirtieth Session, Resolutions adopted on the reports of the Third Committee, 2400th Plenary Meeting, (10 November 1975), pp. 83-84. URL:

http://www.un.org/documents/ga/res/30/ares30.htm

Confer: Zionism & Racism: Proceedings of an International Symposium, International Organization for the Elimination of All Forms of Racial Discrimination, Tripoli, (1977), pp. 249-250. *Cf.* F. A. Sayegh, *Zionism: A Form of Racism And Racial Discrimination" Four Statements Made at the U.N. General Assembly*, Office of the Permanent Observer of the Palestine Liberation Organization to the United Nations, (1976), pp. 40-41. URL:

http://www.ameu.org/uploads/sayegh_march1_03.pdf

After the fall of the Soviet Union, which had long sponsored racial integration (*see:* "Circus" a motion picture released in 1936 directed by Grigori Alexandrov starring Lyubov Orlova), the U. N. withdrew this resolution under great pressure from Zionists.

195. Letter from A. Einstein to P. Ehrenfest of 22 March 1919, English translation by A. Hentschel, *The Collected Papers of Albert Einstein*, Volume 9, Document 10, Princeton Univsersity Press, (2004), pp. 9-10, at 10.

196. E. Gehrcke, *Annalen der Physik*, Volume 51, (1916), pp. 119-124; **and** "Über den Äther", *Verhandlungen der Deutschen Physikalischen Gesellschaft*, Volume 20, (1918), pp. 165-169; **and** "Zur Diskussion über den Äther", *Verhandlungen der Deutschen Physikalischen Gesellschaft*, Volume 21, (1919), pp. 67-68; **and** "Was beweisen die Beobachtungen über die Richtigkeit der Relativitätstheorie?", *Zeitschrift für technische Physik*, Volume 1, (1920), p. 123; **and** "Die Relativitätstheorie, eine wissenschaftliche Massensuggestion", Lecture Delivered in the Berlin Philharmonic on August 24th, 1920, published in *Kritik der Relativitätstheorie*, Hermann Meusser, Berlin, (1924), pp. 54-68; **and** "Zur Frage der Relativitätstheorie", *Kosmos*, Special Edition on the Theory of Relativity, (1921), pp. 296-298.

197. A. Einstein to A. Sommerfeld, in A. Hermann, Ed., *Albert Einstein / Arnold Sommerfeld: Briefwechsel: Sechzig Briefe aus dem goldenen Zeitalter der modernen Physik*, Schwabe & Co., Basel, Stuttgart, (1968), p. 69.

198. I. Shahak, *Jewish History, Jewish Religion: The Weight of Three Thousand Years*, Pluto Press, London, (1997/2002), p. 93.

199. English translation of I. B. Pranaitis, *Christianus in Talmude Iudaeorum sive, Rabbinicae doctrinae de Christianis secreta: quae patere fecit*, Officina Typographica Academiae Caesarae Scientiarum, Petropoli, (1892).

200. M. Wagner, "Rabbis: Naveh Deserves to be Killed", *The Jerusalem Post*, http://www.jpost.com/servlet/Satellite?c=JPArticle&cid=1167467765105&p

agename=JPost%2FJPArticle%2FShowFull, (18 January 2007).
201. I. Shahak and N. Mezvinsky, *Jewish Fundamentalism in Israel*, Pluto Press, London, (1999), pp. 137-138.
202. L. Infeld, *Quest—An Autobiography*, Chelsea, New York, (1980), p. 258.
203. O. Kraus, "Zum Kampf gegen Einstein und die Relativitätstheorie", *Bohemia*, Prag, (2 September 1920); **and** "Zur Lehre vom Raum und Zeit" Nachlaß Brentano, *Kantstudien*, Volume 25, (1920); **and** "Fiktion und Hypothese in der Relativitätstheorie", Schmidt's *Annalen der Philosophie*, Volume 2, Number 3, (1921), pp. 335-396; **and** "Die Verwechslungen von 'Beschreibungsmittel' und 'Beschreibungsobjekt' in der Einsteinschen speziellen und allgemeinen Relativitätstheorie", *Kantstudien, Philosophische Zeitschrift der Kant-Gesellschaft, Berlin*, Volume 26, (1921), pp. 454-486; **and** "Einwendungen gegen Einstein: Philosophische Betrachtungen gegen die Relativitätstheorie", *Neue Freie Presse*, Wien, (11 September (192?), Number 20130, pp. 2ff.; **and** "Die Unmöglichkeit der Einsteinschen Bewegungslehre", *Die Umschau*, Volume 25, (12 November 1921), pp. 681-684; **and** *Zur Relativitäts Theorie*, Meiner, Leipzig, (1921); **and** *Lotos*, Volume 70, (1922), pp. 333ff.; **and** *Offene Briefe an Albert Einstein und Max von Laue über die gedanklichen Grundlagen der allgemeinen Relativitätstheorie*, Braumüller, Wien, (1925); **and** "Zur Relativitätstheorie", *Frankfurter Zeitung*, Number 163, 3, Volume 3, reprinted in *Hundert Autoren gegen Einstein*, R. Voigtländers Verlag, Leipzig, (1931), pp. 17-19.
204. A. Einstein quoted in "Einstein on Arrival Braves Limelight for Only 15 Minutes", *The New York Times*, (12 December 1930), pp. 1, 16, at 16.
205. L. Infeld, quoted in R. W. Clark, *Einstein: The Life and Times*, World Publishing, New York, (1971), pp. 256-257; Clark cites: L. Infeld, *Die Wahrheit*, (March 15-16, 1969).
206. P. Frank, *Einstein: His Life and Times*, Alfred A. Knopf, New York, (1947), p. 161.
207. P. Frank, *Einstein: His Life and Times*, Alfred A. Knopf, New York, (1947), p. 167.
208. Letter from M. v. Laue to A. Einstein of 18 October 1919, English translation by A. Hentschel, *The Collected Papers of Albert Einstein*, Volume 9, Document 145, Princeton University Press, (2004), pp. 122-124, at 123.
209. A. Sommerfeld to A. Einstein, in A. Hermann, *Briefwechsel. 60 Briefe aus dem goldenen Zeitalter der modernen Physik*, Schwabe & Co., Basel, Stuttgart, (1968), p. 71. Prof. Lewis Elton stresses this point.
210. H. Goenner, "The Reaction to Relativity Theory. I: The Anti-Einstein Campaign in Germany in 1920", *Science in Context*, Volume 6, Number 1, (1993), pp. 107-133, at 118.
211. H. Goenner, "The Reaction to Relativity Theory. I: The Anti-Einstein Campaign in Germany in 1920", *Science in Context*, Volume 6, Number 1, (1993), pp. 107-133, at 118-119.
212. P. Frank, *Einstein: His Life and Times*, Alfred A. Knopf, New York, (1967), p. 161.

213. M. Born, "Physics and Relativity", *Physics in my Generation*, second revised edition, Springer, New York, (1969), p. 106.

214. P. Lenard, *England und Deutschland zur Zeit des grossen Krieges*, Heidelberg, (1914).

215. D. Bronder, *Bevor Hitler kam: Eine historische Studie*, Hans Pfeiffer Verlag, Hannover, (1964), p. 204 (p. 211 in the 1974 edition). H. Kardel, *Adolf Hitler, Begründer Israels*, Verlag Marva, Genf, (1974); English translation *Adolf Hitler: Founder of Israel*, Modjeskis' Society Dedicated to Preservation of Cultures, San Diego, (1997), pp. 4, 73.

216. G. Nicolai, *Die Biologie des Krieges, Betrachtungen eines deutschen Naturforschers*, O. Füssli, Zürich, (1917); English translation: *The Biology of War*, Century Co., New York, (1918), pp. xi-xiv.

217. F. K. Wiebe, *Deutschland und die Judenfrage*, M. Müller & Sohn, Hrsg. im Auftrage des Instituts zum Studium der Judenfrage, Berlin, (1939); **English** translation, *Germany and the Jewish Problem*, Published on behalf of the Institute for the Study of the Jewish Problem, Berlin, (1939); **French** translation, *L'Allemagne et la Question Juive*, Berlin, Edité sous les auspices de l'Institut pour l'étude de la question juive, (1939); **Spanish** translation, *Alemania y la Cuestión Judía*, Publicado por encargo del Instituto para el Estudio de la Cuestión Judía, Berlín, (1939).

218. W. W. Zuelzer, *The Nicolai Case: A Biography*, Wayne State University Press, Detroit, (1982). Christoph Friedrich Nicolai was a friend of Gotthold Ephraim Lessing and Moses Mendelssohn; and a critic of Kant, Fichte, Goethe and Schiller. I do know if Georg Friedrich Nicolai was a namesake.

219. Letter from Ilse Einstein to Georg Nikolai of 22 May 1918, *The Collected Papers of Albert Einstein*, Volume 8, Document 545, Princeton University Press, (1998). *See also:* D. Overbye, *Einstein in Love: A Scientific Romance*, Viking, New York, (2000), pp. 343, 404, note 22. *See also:* A. Einstein to Ilse Einstein, *The Collected Papers of Albert Einstein*, Volume 8, Document 536, Princeton University Press, (1998).

220. R. Recouly, "Contrasts Between the French and Russian Revolutions", *The World's Work*, Volume 44, Number 1, (November, 1922), pp. 67-80, at 78-80.

221. G. Nicolai, *Die Biologie des Krieges, Betrachtungen eines deutschen Naturforschers*, O. Füssli, Zürich, (1917); English translation: *The Biology of War*, Century Co., New York, (1918), pp. xvii-xix.

222. P. W. Massing, *Rehearsal for Destruction: A Study of Political Anti-Semitism in Imperial Germany*, Howard Fertig, New York, (1967), p. 284. *See also:* L. Fry, *Waters Flowing Eastward: The War Against the Kingship of Christ*, TBR Books, Washington, D. C., (2000), pp. 30, 98, 101-105.

223. A. Rohling, *Der Talmudjude: zur beherzigung für Juden und Christen aller Stände*, Adolph Russel, Münster, (1871); English translation: *The Jew According to the Talmud*, Sons of Liberty, Metairie, Louisiana, (1978); **and** *Der Antichrist und das Ende der Welt: Zur Erwägung für alle Christen*, B. Herder, St. Louis, (1875); **and** *Der Katechismus des neunzehnten*

Jahrhunderts, für Juden und Protestanten, den auch Katholiken lesen dürfen,
F. Kirchheim, Mainz, (1877); **and** *Franz Delitzsch und die Judenfrage, Antwortlich beleuchtet. . . ,* J.B. Reinitz, Prag, (1881); **and** *Fünf Briefe über den Talmudismus und das Blutritual der Juden,* Prag, (1881); **and** *Die Polemik das Menschenopfer des Rabbinismus; eine wissenschaftliche Antwort ohne Polemik für die Rabbiner und ihre Genossen,* Bonifacius-Druckerei, Paderborn, (1883); **and** *Meine Antworten an die Rabbiner, oder Fünf Briefe über den Talmundismus und das Blut-Ritual der Juden,* Cyrillo-Method'sche Buchdruckerei, Prag, (1883); **and** *Die Ehre Israels: Neue Briefe an die Juden,* Prag, (1889); **and** *Erklärung der Apokalypse des h. Johannes des grossen Propheten von Patmos,* Verlag der Liebfraumen-Druckerei (Dr. W. Wingerth), München, (1895); **and** *Auf nach Zion!: oder die grosse Hoffnung Israels und aller Menschen,* Jos. Kosel'schen Buchhandlung, Kempten, (1901); **and** *Das Judentum nach neurabbinischer Darstellung der Hochfinanz Israels,* G. Schuh, München, (1903). *See also:* A. Rohling and M. de Lamarque, *Le juiftalmudiste,* A. Vromant, Paris, Bruxelles, (1888). *See also:* A. Rohling and E. A. Drumont, *Le juif selon le Talmud,* Albert Savine, Paris, (1889); German translation: *Prof. Dr. Aug. Rohling's Talmud-Jude,* T. Fritsch, Leipzig, (1891). *See also:* J. A. Eisenmenger, A. Rohling and J. Ecker, *Die Sittenlehre des Juden. Auszug aus dem Talmud (Schulchan-Aruch),* Deutschen Schutz- und Trutz-bund, Landesverein Bayern, Nürnberg, (1920).

Rohling's work is derivative of J. A. Eisenmenger, *Des bey 40. Jahr von der Judenschafft mit Arrest bestrickt gewesene, nunmehro aber durch Autorität eines hohen Reichsvicariats relaxirte Johann Andreä Eisemengers. . . Endecktes Judenthum, oder: Gründlicher und warhaffter Bericht: welchergestalt die verstockte Juden die hochheilige Dreyeinigkeit, Gott Vater, Sohn und Heiligen Geist, erschrecklicher Weise lästern und verunehren, die heil. Mutter Christi verschmähen, das Neue Testament, die Evangelisten und Aposteln, die christliche Religion spöttlich durchziehen, und die gantze Christenheit auf das äusserste verachten und verfluchen; dabey noch viele andere, bishero unter den Christen entweder gar nicht, oder nur zum Theil bekant-gewesene Dinge und grosse Irrthüme der jüdischen Religion und Theologie, wie auch viel lächerliche und kurtzweilige Fabeln und andere ungereimte Sachen an den Tag kommen,* Frankfurt, (1700); **and** *Entdecktes Judenthum oder, Gründlicher und warhaffter Bericht, welchergestalt die verstockte Juden die hochheilige Drey-einigkeit. . . verunehren, die heil. Mutter Christi verschmähen. . . die christliche Religion spöttisch durchziehen, und die gantze Christenheit. . . verachten und verfluchen; dabey noch viel andere. . . nur zum Theil bekant gewesene Dinge und grosse Irrthüme der jüdischen Religion und Theologie, wie auch viel lächerliche und kurtzweilige Fabeln. . . . an den Tag kommen. Alles aus ihren eigenen. . . Büchern. . . kräfftiglich erwiesen, und in zweyen Theilen verfasset. . . Allen Christen zur treuhertzigen Nachricht verfertiget, und mit volkommenen Registern versehen,* Königsberg in Preussen, (1711); English translation by J. P. Stehelin, *The Traditions of the Jews: With the Expositions and Doctrines of the Rabbins Contain'd in the*

Talmud and Other Rabbinical Writings, Volume 1, Printed for G. Smith, London, (1732); **and** *The Traditions of the Jews: Or the Doctrines and Expositions Contain'd in the Talmud and other Rabbinical Writings*, Printed for G. Smith, London, (1742-1743). *See also:* E. L. Roblik J. A. Eisenmenger, *Jüdische Augen-Gläser, das ist: Ein. . . denen Juden zur Erkanntnuss des wahren Glaubens vorgesteltes Buch. Allwo in dem ersten Theil (wider die jüdische irrende Lehr) durch die heil. Schrifft des Alten und Neuen Testaments, gantz klar bewiesen wird, dass Jesus Christus seye ein wahrer Sohn des lebendigen Gottes. . . In dem anderten Theil aber, wird aus dem jüdischen Buch (Talmud genannt) bewiesen, dass der jetzige jüdische Glauben, ein falscher und gottslästerlicher Glauben seye. . .* , Gedruckt bey M.B. Swobodin, Brünn, (1741-1743). *See also:* C. Anton and J. A. Eisenmenger, *Einleitung in die rabbinischen Rechte, dabey insonderheit von einem Judeneide, wie solchen eine christliche Obrigkeit am verbindlichsten abnehmen kann umständlich ist gehandelt worden*, F.W. Meyer, Braunschweig, (1756).

Bloch accused Rohling of forging sources, and Rohling sued Bloch for libel, though the suit was dropped: A. Rohling and J. S. Bloch, *Acten und Gutachten in dem Prozesse Rohling contra Bloch*, Volume 1, M. Breitenstein, Wien, (1890); **and** *Anhang zum ersten Bande der Acten und Gutachten in dem Prosezze Rohling contra Bloch*, W. Breitenstein's Verlagsbuchhandlung, Wien, (1890).

Rohling had numerous critics: J. S. Bloch, *Gegen die Anti-semiten. Eine Streitschrift*, D. Löwy, Wien, (1882); and *Prof. Rohling und das Wiener Rabbinat: oder, "Die arge Schelmerei"*, Im Selbstverlage des Verfassers, Wien, (1882); and *Des k.k. prof. Rohling neueste Fälschungen*, Wiener Allgemeine Zeitung, Wien (1883); and *Einblicke in die Geschichte der Entstehung der talmudischn Literatur*, D. Löwy, Wien, (1884); and *Einblicke in die Geschichte der Entstehung der talmudischen Literatur*, D. Löwy, Wien, (1884); and *Talmud und Judenthum in der Oesterr. Volksvertretung*, Oesterreichische Wochenschrift, Wien, (1900); and *Talmud und Judenthum in der Oesterr Volksvertretung*, Oesterreichische Wochenschrift, Wien, (1900); and *"Kol Nidre" und seine Entstehungsgeschichte*, Löwit, Wien, (1918); and *Erinnerungen aus meinem Leben*, R. Löwit, Wien, Leipzig, (1922); English translation: *My Reminiscences*, Arno Press, New York, (1973). See also: M. L. Rodkinson and J. S. Bloch, *Wahrheit gegen Lüge*, Wien, (1886). *See also:* Rabbiner Dr. Kroner, *Entstelltes Unwahres und Erfundenes in dem „Talmudjuden" Professor Dr. August Rohling's*, E. Obertüschen, Münster, (1871); which is described in: "Litarischer Wochenbericht", *Allgemeine Zeitung des Judenthums*, Volume 35, Number 34, (22 August 1871), pp. 673-674, at 674. *See also:* J. E. Fraenkel, P. Mansch, Philipp and A. Rohling, *Erwiederung auf die vom Professor Dr. Aug. Rohling Verfasste Schrift der Talmudjude*, Kugel, Lemberg, (1874). *See also:* P. Bloch, *Prof. Rohling's Falschmünzerei auf talmudischem Gebiet*, L. Merzbach, Posen, (1876). *See also:* F. Delitzsch, *Rohlings Talmudjude beleuchtet*, Dörffling & Franke, Leipzig, (1881); **and** *Schachmatt den Blutlügnern Rohling & Justus*, A.

Deichert, Erlangen, (1883); **and** *Was d. Aug. Rohling beschworen hat und beschwören will*, Dörffling & Franke, Leipzig, (1883). *See also:* J. Kopp, *Zur Judenfrage nach den Akten des Prozesses Rohling-Bloch*, Leipsic, (1886). *See also:* C. A. Victor, *Prof. Dr. Rohling, die Judenfrage und die öffentliche Meinung*, T. Fritsch, Leipzig, (1887). *See also: Acten und Gutachten in dem Prozesse Rohling contra Bloch*, M. Breitenstein, Wien, (1890). *See also: Jüdische Presse*, Number 46, (1902).

224. *See:* D. Kimhi, *Hesronot ha-Shas: ve-hu sefer kevutsat ha-hashmatot: kolel kol ha-devarim ha-haserim be-Talmud Bavli ve-Rashi ve-Tosafot ve Rosh veha-G. a. u-fe. ha-mishnayot leha-Rambam; mini az nidpesu ʿal yede ʿEmanuʾel Bambashti be-ʾAmsterdam shenat 410 ve-khen hashlamat ha-hisaron hidushe halakhot. . .* , Jos. Schlesinger, Budapest, (1865). *See also:* G. Dalman, *Jesus Christ in the Talmud, Midrash, Zohar, and the Liturgy of the Synagogue*, Deighton Bell, Cambridge, (1893). *See also:* W. Popper, *The Censorship of Hebrew Books: Submitted in Partial Fulfilment of the Requirements for the Degree of Doctor of Philosophy, Columbia University*, Knickerbocker Press, New York, (1899). *See also:* M. A. Hoffman II, *Judaism's Strange Gods*, Independent History and Research, Coeur d'Alene, Idaho, (2000), pp. 70-72.

225. M. Luther, *Von den Juden und ihren Lügen*, Hans Lufft, Wittenberg, (1543); Reprinted, Ludendorffs, München, (1932); English translation by Martin H. Bertram, "On the Jews and Their Lies", *Luther's Works*, Volume 47, Fortress Press, Philadelphia, (1971), pp. 123-306. *See also:* J. Buxtorf, *Synagoga Judaica: Das ist Jüden Schul ; Darinnen der gantz Jüdische Glaub und Glaubensubung. . . grundlich erkläret*, Basel, (1603); English edition, *The Jewish Synagogue: Or An Historical Narration of the State of the Jewes, At this Day Dispersed over the Face of the Whole Earth*, Printed by T. Roycroft for H. R. and Thomas Young at the Three Pidgeons in Pauls Church-Yard, London, (1657). *See also:* J. A. Eisenmenger, *Des bey 40. Jahr von der Judenschafft mit Arrest bestrickt gewesene, nunmehro aber durch Autorität eines hohen Reichsvicariats relaxirte Johann Andreä Eisemengers. . . Endecktes Judenthum, oder: Gründlicher und wahrhaffter Bericht: welchergestalt die verstockte Juden die hochheilige Dreyeinigkeit, Gott Vater, Sohn und Heiligen Geist, erschrecklicher Weise lästern und verunehren, die heil. Mutter Christi verschmähen, das Neue Testament, die Evangelisten und Aposteln, die christliche Religion spöttlich durchziehen, und die gantze Christenheit auf das äusserste verachten und verfluchen; dabey noch viele andere, bishero unter den Christen entweder gar nicht, oder nur zum Theil bekant-gewesene Dinge und grosse Irrthüme der jüdischen Religion und Theologie, wie auch viel lächerliche und kurtzweilige Fabeln und andere ungereimte Sachen an den Tag kommen*, Frankfurt, (1700); **and** *Entdecktes Judenthum oder, Gründlicher und wahrhaffter Bericht, welchergestalt die verstockte Juden die hochheilige Drey-einigkeit. . . verunehren, die heil. Mutter Christi verschmähen. . . die christliche Religion spöttisch durchziehen, und die gantze Christenheit. . . verachten und verfluchen; dabey noch viel andere. . .*

nur zum Theil bekant gewesene Dinge und grosse Irrthüme der jüdischen Religion und Theologie, wie auch viel lächerliche und kurtzweilige Fabeln. . . an den Tag kommen. Alles aus ihren eigenen. . . Büchern. . . kräfftiglich erwiesen, und in zweyen Theilen verfasset. . . Allen Christen zur treuhertzigen Nachricht verfertiget, und mit volkommenen Registern versehen, Königsberg in Preussen, (1711); English translation by J. P. Stehelin, *The Traditions of the Jews: With the Expositions and Doctrines of the Rabbins Contain'd in the Talmud and Other Rabbinical Writings,* Volume 1, Printed for G. Smith, London, (1732); **and** *The Traditions of the Jews: Or the Doctrines and Expositions Contain'd in the Talmud and other Rabbinical Writings,* Printed for G. Smith, London, (1742-1743). *See also:* E. L. Roblik J. A. Eisenmenger, *Jüdische Augen-Gläser, das ist: Ein. . . denen Juden zur Erkanntnuss des wahren Glaubens vorgesteltes Buch. Allwo in dem ersten Theil (wider die jüdische irrende Lehr) durch die heil. Schrifft des Alten und Neuen Testaments, gantz klar bewiesen wird, dass Jesus Christus seye ein wahrer Sohn des lebendigen Gottes. . . In dem anderten Theil aber, wird aus dem jüdischen Buch (Talmud genannt) bewiesen, dass der jetzige jüdische Glauben, ein falscher und gottslästerlicher Glauben seye. . . ,* Gedruckt bey M.B. Swobodin, Brünn, (1741-1743). *See also:* C. Anton and J. A. Eisenmenger, *Einleitung in die rabbinischen Rechte, dabey insonderheit von einem Judeneide, wie solchen eine christliche Obrigkeit am verbindlichsten abnehmen kann umständlich ist gehandelt worden,* F.W. Meyer, Braunschweig, (1756). *See also:* A. Rohling, *Der Talmudjude: zur beherzigung für Juden und Christen aller Stände,* Adolph Russel, Münster, (1871); English translation: *The Jew According to the Talmud,* Sons of Liberty, Metairie, Louisiana, (1978); **and** *Der Antichrist und das Ende der Welt: Zur Erwägung für alle Christen,* B. Herder, St. Louis, (1875); **and** *Der Katechismus des neunzehnten Jahrhunderts, für Juden und Protestanten, den auch Katholiken lesen dürfen,* F. Kirchheim, Mainz, (1877); **and** *Franz Delitzsch und die Judenfrage, Antwortlich beleuchtet. . . ,* J.B. Reinitz, Prag, (1881); **and** *Fünf Briefe über den Talmudismus und das Blutritual der Juden,* Prag, (1881); **and** *Die Polemik das Menschenopfer des Rabbinismus; eine wissenschaftliche Antwort ohne Polemik für die Rabbiner und ihre Genossen,* Bonifacius-Druckerei, Paderborn, (1883); **and** *Meine Antworten an die Rabbiner, oder Fünf Briefe über den Talmundismus und das Blut-Ritual der Juden,* Cyrillo-Method'sche Buchdruckerei, Prag, (1883); **and** *Die Ehre Israels: Neue Briefe an die Juden,* Prag, (1889); **and** *Erklärung der Apokalypse des h. Johannes des grossen Propheten von Patmos,* Verlag der Liebfraumen-Druckerei (Dr. W. Wingerth), München, (1895); **and** *Auf nach Zion!: oder die grosse Hoffnung Israels und aller Menschen,* Jos. Kosel'schen Buchhandlung, Kempten, (1901); **and** *Das Judentum nach neurabbinischer Darstellung der Hochfinanz Israels,* G. Schuh, München, (1903). *See also:* A. Rohling and M. de Lamarque, *Le juif-talmudiste,* A. Vromant, Paris, Bruxelles, (1888). *See also:* A. Rohling and E. A. Drumont, *Le juif selon le Talmud,* Albert Savine, Paris, (1889); German translation: *Prof. Dr. Aug. Rohling's Talmud-Jude,* T. Fritsch, Leipzig, (1891). *See also:* J. A. Eisenmenger, A.

Rohling and J. Ecker, *Die Sittenlehre des Juden. Auszug aus dem Talmud (Schulchan-Aruch)*, Deutschen Schutz- und Trutz-bund, Landesverein Bayern, Nürnberg, (1920). *See also:* I. B. Pranaitis (also: J. B. Pranaitis), *Christianus in Talmude Judaeorum sive rabbinicae doctrinae de christianis secreta*, Academia caesarea scientiarum, Petropoli, (1892); **English:** *The Talmud Unmasked: The Secret Rabbinical Teachings Concerning Christians*, Eugene Nelson Sanctuary, New York, (1939); **German:** *Das Christenthum im Talmud der Juden oder die Geheimnisse der rabbinischen Lehre über die Christen, enthüllt*, Verlag des "Sendboten des hl. Joseph", Wien, (1894); **Russian:** *Khristianin v Talmudie Evreiskom ili tainy ravvinskago ucheniia o khristianakh*, Tip. M.A. Aleksandrova, St. Petersburg, (1911); **Polish:** *Chrzescijanin w Talmudzie zydowskim = Christianus in Talmude Iudaeorum*, Instytut Wydawniczy "Pro Fide", Warszawa, (1937); **Spanish:** *El Talmud desenmascarado!: las enseñanzas rabinicas secretas sobre los cristianos*, La Verdad, Buenos Aires, (1981). *See also:* G. Dalman, *Jesus Christ in the Talmud, Midrash, Zohar, and the Liturgy of the Synagogue*, Deighton Bell, Cambridge, (1893). *See also:* E. K. Dilling, *The Plot Against Christianity*, Elizabeth Dilling Foundation, Lincoln, Nebraska, (1964); *the Jewish Religion: Its Influence Today: Formerly Titled the Plot Against Christianity*, Noontide Press, Torrance, California, (1983). *See also:* M. A. Hoffman II, *Judaism's Strange Gods*, Independent History and Research, Coeur d'Alene, Idaho, (2000).

226. P. W. Massing, *Rehearsal for Destruction: A Study of Political Anti-Semitism in Imperial Germany*, Howard Fertig, New York, (1967), p. 326.

227. G. Nicolai, *Die Biologie des Krieges, Betrachtungen eines deutschen Naturforschers*, O. Füssli, Zürich, (1917); English translation: *The Biology of War*, Century Co., New York, (1918).

228. Letter from A. Einstein to P. Ehrenfest of 22 March 1919, English translation by A. Hentschel, *The Collected Papers of Albert Einstein*, Volume 9, Document 10, Princeton Univsersity Press, (2004), pp. 9-10, at 10.

229. Letter from A. Einstein to E. Zürcher of 15 April 1919, *The Collected Papers of Albert Einstein*, Volume 9, Document 23, Princeton Univsersity Press, (2004).

230. G. Nicolai, *Die Biologie des Krieges, Betrachtungen eines deutschen Naturforschers*, O. Füssli, Zürich, (1917); English translation: *The Biology of War*, Century Co., New York, (1918), pp. 84-89.

231. "Jews", *Great Soviet Encyclopedia: A Translation of the Third Edition*, Volume 2, Macmillan, New York, (1973), pp. 292-293, at 293.

232. I. Zangwill, "Is Political Zionism Dead? Yes", *The Nation*, Volume 118, Number 3062, (12 March 1924), pp. 276-278, at 276.

233. M. Tokayer and M. Swartz, *The Fugu Plan: The Untold Story of the Japanese and the Jews During World War II*, Paddington Press, New York, (1979). D. Goodman and M. Miyazawa, *Jews in the Japanese Mind: The History and Uses of a Cultural Stereotype*, Free Press, New York, (1995).

234. G. Nicolai, *Die Biologie des Krieges, Betrachtungen eines deutschen Naturforschers*, O. Füssli, Zürich, (1917); English translation: *The Biology of War*, Century Co., New York, (1918), p. 531.

235. D. J. Goldhagen, *Hitler's Willing Executioners: Ordinary Germans and the Holocaust*, Knopf, New York, (1996). *See also:* É. Durkheim, *"Germany above All" The German Mental Attitude and the War*, Librairie Armand Colin, Paris, (1915). *See also:* "By a German", *I Accuse! (J'Accuse!)*, Grosset & Dunlap, New York, (1915). *See also:* W. F. Barry, *The World's Debate: An Historical Defence of the Allies*, George H. Doran, New York, (1917). *See also:* W. T. Hornaday, *A Searchlight on Germany: Germany's Blunders, Crimes and Punishment*, American Defense Society, New York, (1917). *See also:* D. W. Johnson, *Plain Words from America: A Letter to a German Professor*, London, New York, Toronto, Hodder & Stoughton, (1917).

236. H. Stern, *KZ-Lügen: Antwort auf Goldhagen*, FZ-Verlag, München, Second Edition, (1998), ISBN: 3924309361; **and** *Jüdische Kriegserklärungen an Deutschland: Wortlaut, Vorgeschichte, Folgen*, FZ-Verlag, München, Second Edition, (2000), ISBN: 3924309507.

237. M. Hess, *Rom und Jerusalem: die letzte Nationalitätsfrage*, Eduard Wengler, Leipzig, (1862); English: "Fourth Letter", "Note III" and "Note IV", *Rome and Jerusalem: A Study in Jewish Nationalism*, Bloch, New York, (1918), pp. 56-57, 240-244.

238. R. Mewes, "Geschichtliche Entwicklung der Relativitäts- oder Raumzeitlehre", Chapter 4, "Wissenschaftliche Begründung der Raumzeitlehre oder Relativitätstheorie (1884-1894) mit einem geschichtlichen Anhang", *Gesammelte Arbeiten von Rudolf Mewes*, Volume 1, Rudolf Mewes, Berlin, (1920), pp. 48-78, at 78.

239. *See, for example*, On the occasion of Einstein's 50th birthday, "Die Relativitätstheorie und der dialektische Materialismus", *Arbeiterstimme*, (1929), which is quoted by B. Thüring, "Albert Einsteins Umsturzversuch der Physik und seine inneren Möglichkeiten und Ursachen", *Forschungen zur Judenfrage*, Volume 4, (1940), pp. 134-162, at 144-145. Republished as: *Albert Einsteins Umsturzversuch der Physik und seine inneren Möglichkeiten und Ursachen*, Dr. Georg Lüttke Verlag, Berlin, (1941).

240. *Cf.* C. Weizmann, *Trial and Error: The Autobiography of Chaim Weizmann*, Harper & Brothers, New York, (1949).

241. S. Mohorovičić, *Die Einsteinsche Relativitätstheorie und ihr mathematischer, physikalischer und philosophischer Charakter*, Walter de Gruyter & Co., Berlin, Leipzig, (1923), pp. 52-53.

242. A. Einstein to P. Ehrenfest, (6 December 1918), *The Collected Papers of Albert Einstein*, Volume 8, Part B, Document 664, Princeton University Press, (1998), pp. 960-961.

243. A. Einstein to E. Zürcher, (15 April 1919), *The Collected Papers of Albert Einstein*, Volume 9, Document 23, Princeton University Press, (2004), pp. 35-36, at 36.

244. A. Einstein to H. Born, (31 August 1919), *The Collected Papers of Albert Einstein*, Volume 9, Document 97, Princeton University Press, (2004), pp. 142-144, at 143.

245. A. Einstein to the *Neue Freie Presse*, *The Collected Papers of Albert Einstein*, Volume 9, Document 193, Princeton University Press, (2004), p. 273.

246. Letter from A. Einstein to the Borns of 27 January 1920, *The Collected Papers of Albert Einstein*, Volume 9, Document 284, Princeton University Press, (2004), pp. 386-390, at 387.

247. R. Romain, *La Conscience de l'Europe*, Volume 1, pp. 696ff. English translation from A. Fölsing, *Albert Einstein: A Biography*, Viking, New York, (1997), pp. 365-367. *See also:* Letter from A. Einstein to R. Romain of 15 September 1915, *The Collected Papers of Albert Einstein*, Volume 8, Document 118, Princeton University Press, (1998); **and** Letter from A. Einstein to R. Romain of 22 August 1917, *The Collected Papers of Albert Einstein*, Volume 8, Document 374, Princeton University Press, (1998).

248. Letter from A. Einstein to Paul Ehrenfest of 22 March 1919, English translation by A. Hentschel, *The Collected Papers of Albert Einstein*, Volume 9, Document 10, Princeton University Press, (2004), pp. 9-10, at 10.

249. Letter from A. Einstein to R. W. Lawson of 26 December 1919, *The Collected Papers of Albert Einstein*, Volume 9, Document 234, Princeton University Press, (2004). *See also:* A. Einstein, "Welcoming Address to Paul Colin", *The Collected Papers of Albert Einstein*, Volume 7, Document 27, Princeton University Press, (2002). *See also: The Collected Papers of Albert Einstein*, Volume 9, Documents 222, 230, 237, 249, 275, 297 and 331, Princeton University Press, (2004).

250. R. S. Levy, *Antisemitism in the Modern World: An Anthology of Texts*, D. C. Heath and Company, Toronto, (1991), pp. 129-130, at 129.

251. *Cf.* S. Mohorovičić, *Die Einsteinsche Relativitätstheorie und ihr mathematischer, physikalischer und philosophischer Charakter*, Walter de Gruyter & Co., Berlin, Leipzig, (1923), p. 53. Einstein stated in the *Jüdische Pressezentral*, Number 111, (21 September 1920), that it irked him to read that he was a German citizen of Jewish faith. He stated that he was not a German citizen, but was a Jew. *Cf.* B. Thüring, *Albert Einsteins Umsturzversuch der Physik und seine inneren Möglichkeiten und Ursachen*, Dr. Georg Lüttke Verlag, Berlin, (1941), pp. 24-25.

252. D. K. Buchwald, et al., Editors, *The Collected Papers of Albert Einstein*, Volume 7, Princeton University Press, (2002), pp. 417-419. A. Einstein, "Zuschriften an die Herausgeber: Zur Abwehr", *Die Naturwissenschaften*, Volume 9, (1921), p. 219. *See also:* L. Fabre's response to A. Einstein's objections: L. Fabre, *Une Nouvelle Figure du Monde: Les Théories d'Einstein*, Payot, Paris, (1922), pp. 15-16.

253. D. K. Buchwald, et al., Editors, *The Collected Papers of Albert Einstein*, Volume 7, Princeton University Press, (2002), pp. 417-419.

254. E. Gehrcke, *Die Massensuggestion der Relativitätstheorie: Kulturhistorisch-psychologische Dokumente*, Hermann Meusser, Berlin,

(1924), p. 67.

255. "Time, Space, and Gravitation", *The London Times*, (28 November 1919), pp. 13-14. *See also:* "Meine Antwort", *Berliner Tageblatt*, Morgen Ausgabe, (27 August 1920), pp. 1-2. *See also:* "Einstein and Newton", *The London Times*, (14 June 1921), p. 8. *See also:* "Wie ich Zionist wurde", *Jüdische Rundschau*, (21 June 1921), pp. 351-352; English translation by A. Engel, "How I became a Zionist", *The Collected Papers of Albert Einstein*, Volume 7, Document 57, Princeton University Press, (2002), pp. 234-237. Einstein stated in the *Jüdische Pressezentral*, Number 111, (21 September 1920), that it irked him to read that he was a German citizen of Jewish faith. He stated that he was not a German citizen, but was a Jew. *Confer:* B. Thüring, *Albert Einsteins Umsturzversuch der Physik und seine inneren Möglichkeiten und Ursachen*, Dr. Georg Lüttke Verlag, Berlin, (1941), pp. 24-25.

256. G. Nicolai, *Die Biologie des Krieges, Betrachtungen eines deutschen Naturforschers*, O. Füssli, Zürich, (1917); English translation: *The Biology of War*, Century Co., New York, (1918), p. 531.

257. A. Einstein, *The World As I See It*, Citadel, New York, (1993), p. 91.

258. R. P. Oliver, "Liberalism", *America's Decline: The Education of a Conservative*, Londinium Press, London, (1981).

259. English translation, B. v. Suttner, *Ground Arms!" = "Die Waffen nieder!" A Romance of European War*, A.C. McClurg & Co., Chicago, (1906). *See also:* B. v. Suttner, *Martha's Kinder: eine Fortsetzung zu "Die Waffen nieder!"*, E. Pierson, Dresden, (1903).

260. "Time, Space, and Gravitation", *The London Times*, (28 November 1919), pp. 13-14. *See also:* "Meine Antwort", *Berliner Tageblatt*, Morgen Ausgabe, (27 August 1920), pp. 1-2. *See also:* L. Fabre, *Une Nouvelle Figure du Monde: Les Théories d'Einstein*, Payot & Cie, Paris, (1921), pp. 15-18. *See also:* "Einstein and Newton", *The London Times*, (14 June 1921), p. 8. *See also:* "Wie ich Zionist wurde", *Jüdische Rundschau*, (21 June 1921), pp. 351-352; English translation by A. Engel, "How I became a Zionist", *The Collected Papers of Albert Einstein*, Volume 7, Document 57, Princeton University Press, (2002), pp. 234-237. Einstein stated in the *Jüdische Pressezentral*, Number 111, (21 September 1920), that it irked him to read that he was a German citizen of Jewish faith. He stated that he was not a German citizen, but was a Jew. *Confer:* B. Thüring, *Albert Einsteins Umsturzversuch der Physik und seine inneren Möglichkeiten und Ursachen*, Dr. Georg Lüttke Verlag, Berlin, (1941), pp. 24-25. *See also Einstein's private correspondence, for example:* The Collected Papers of Albert Einstein, Volume 9, Documents 10, 28, 36, 78, 79, 80, 92, 94, 96 and 108, Princeton University Press, (2004).

261. Letter from A. Einstein to H. A. Lorentz of 26 April 1919, *The Collected Papers of Albert Einstein*, Volume 9, Document 28, Princeton University Press, (2004). Letter from A. Einstein to W. de Haas of 9 May 1919, *The Collected Papers of Albert Einstein*, Volume 9, Document 36, Princeton University Press, (2004).

262. Letter from A. Einstein to H. A. Lorentz of 21 September 1919, *The Collected Papers of Albert Einstein*, Volume 9, Document 108, Princeton University Press, (2004).

263. P. G. Nutting, "National Prestige in Scientific Achievement", *Science*, Volume 48, (1918), pp. 605-608.

264. "America and German Science", *Nature*, Volume 102, (1919), pp. 446-447.

265. Letter from M. Born to A. Einstein of 28 October 1920, M. Born, *The Born-Einstein Letters*, Walker and Company, New York, (1971), pp. 43-45.

266. Letter from A. Einstein to H. A. Lorentz of 1 August 1919, English translation by A. Hentschel, *The Collected Papers of Albert Einstein*, Volume 9, Document 80, Princeton University Press, (2004), pp. 67-68, at 68. See also Document 108, the letter from Einstein to Lorentz of 21 September 1919, at pages 92–93.

267. A. Einstein, *Thoughts on Reconciliation*, Deutscher Gesellig-Wissenschaftlicher Verein von New York, New York, (1920), pp. 10-11; facsimile republished in *The Collected Papers of Albert Einstein*, Volume 7, Document 47, Princeton University Press, (2002), pp. 360-364.

268. A. Einstein quoted in: H. Gutfreund, "Albert Einstein and the Hebrew University", J. Renn, Editor, *Albert Einstein Chief Engineer of the Universe: One Hundred Authors for Einstein*, Wiley-VCH, Berlin, (2005), pp. 314-318, at 315.

269. A. Einstein quoted in: H. Gutfreund, "Albert Einstein and the Hebrew University", J. Renn, Editor, *Albert Einstein Chief Engineer of the Universe: One Hundred Authors for Einstein*, Wiley-VCH, Berlin, (2005), pp. 314-318, at 316.

270. A. Einstein quoted in *Vossische Zeitung*, Morning Edition, Supplement 4, (29 August 1920), p. 1. English translation from, D. K. Buchwald, et. al. Editors, *The Collected Papers of Albert Einstein*, Volume 7, Princeton University Press, (2002), Note 1, p. 357.

271. A. Einstein quoted in R. W. Clark, *Einstein: The Life and Times*, The World Publishing Company, (1971), p. 261; referencing A. Einstein to A. Sommerfeld, in A. Hermann, *Briefwechsel. 60 Briefe aus dem goldenen Zeitalter der modernen Physik*, Schwabe & Co., Basel, Stuttgart, (1968), p. 69.

272. A biased and heavily redacted version of the discussion appeared in: *Physikalische Zeitschrift*, Volume 21, (1920), pp. 666-668. That this version is incomplete and biased is proven in: P. Lenard, *Über Relativitätsprinzip, Äther, Gravitation*, Third Edition, S. Hirzel, Leipzig, (1921); **and** "Zur zweiten Auflage. Ein Mahnwort an deutsche Naturforscher.", *Über Äther und Uräther*, Second Edition, S. Hirzel, Leipzig, (1922), pp. 5-10. E. Gehrcke, "Die Relativitätstheorie auf dem Naturforschertage in Nauheim", *Umschau, Wochenschrift über die Fortschritte in Wissenschaften und Technik*, Volume 25, (1921), p. 99; **and** "Zur Relativitätsfrage", *Die Umschau*, Volume 25, (1921), p. 227. *Berliner Tageblatt*, Evening Edition, (24 September 1920), p. 3. *Vossische Zeitung*, Evening Edition, (24 September 1920), p. 1-2.

273. M. Born, *The Born-Einstein Letters*, Walker and Company, New York, (1971), p. 41.

274. J. Riem, "Amerika über Einstein", *Deutsche Zeitung*, Abend Ausgabe, (1 July 1921).

275. From A. Reuterdahl, *The Minneapolis Sunday Tribune*, (22 May 1921). Reuterdahl translates parts of "Professor Einsteins „Triumphzug" durch Amerika", *Luzerner Neueste Nachrichten*, (22 April 1921).

276. Rudolf Peters picked up on the ridiculous title "Albertus Maximus". *See: The Collected papers of Albert Einstein*, Volume 9, Document 388, Princeton University Press, (2004), p. 523, note 2.

277. A. Fürst and A. Moszkowski, *Das Buch der 1000 Wunder*, A. Langen, München, (1916), pp. 263-264.

278. E. Gehrcke, *Die Massensuggestion der Relativitätstheorie*, Hermann Meusser, Berlin, (1924), pp. 16-17.

279. P. Lenard, *Über Relativitätsprinzip, Äther, Gravitation*, Third Edition, S. Hirzel, Leipzig, (1921), Note 1, p. 39.

280. D. Eckart and A. Hitler, *Der Bolschewismus von Moses bis Lenin: Zwiegespräch zwischen Adolf Hitler und mir*, Hoheneichen-Verlag, München, (1924); English translation by W. L. Pierce, "Bolshevism from Moses to Lenin", *National Socialist World*, (1966). URL: <http://www.jrbooksonline.com/DOCs/Eckart.doc> p. 7. J. Klatzkin, *Krisis und Entscheidung im Judentum; der Probleme des modernen Judentums*, Jüdischer Verlag, Berlin, (1921). Heinrich Class under the pseudonym Daniel Frymann, *Wenn ich der Kaiser wär': politische Wahrheiten und Notwendigkeiten*, Dieterich, Leipzig, (1912); English translation, R. S. Levy, "If I were the Kaiser / Daniel Freymann", *Antisemitism in the Modern World: An Anthology of Texts*, Chapter 14, D.C. Heath, Toronto, (1991).

281. D. Fahey, *The Mystical Body of Christ in the Modern World*, Browne and Nolan Limited, London, (1935), p. 254.

282. R. L. Hartt, "New York and the Real Jew", *Independent* (New York), (25 June 1921). *Cf.* "Jews Are Silent, the National Voice Is Heard", *THE DEARBORN INDEPENDENT*, (30 July 1921).

283. *Confer:* A. Unsöld, "Albert Einstein — Ein Jahr danach", *Physikalische Blätter*, Volume 36, (1980), pp. 337-339; **and** Volume 37, Number 7, (1981), p. 229. L. R. B. Elton, "Einstein, General Relativity, and the German Press, 1919-1920", *Isis*, Volume 77, Number 1, (March, 1986), pp. 95-103; **and** "Letters: Einstein and Germany", *Physics Today*, Volume 40, Number 7, (July, 1987), pp. 15, 106. W. Krause, "Letters: Einstein and Germany", *Physics Today*, Volume 40, Number 7, (July, 1987), pp. 106, 108. H. Goenner, "The Reaction to Relativity Theory I: The Anti-Einstein Campaign in Germany in 1920", *Science in Context*, Volume 6, (1993), pp. 107-133. M. Janssen *et al*, Editors, "Einstein's Encounters with German Anti-Relativists", *The Collected Papers of Albert Einstein*, Volume 7 (Hardbound), Princeton University Press, (2002), pp. 101-113.

284. *Cf.* D. K. Buchwald, et al. Editors, *The Collected Papers of Albert Einstein*, Volume 7, Princeton University Press, (2002), p.108.

285. S. Grundmann, "Das moralische Antlitz der Anti-Einstein-Liga", Wissenschaftliche Zeitschrift der Technischen Universität Dresden, Volume 16, pp. 1623-1626.

286. F. Kleinschrod, "Das Lebensproblem und das Positivitätsprinzip in Zeit und Raum und das Einsteinsche Relativitätsprinzip in Raum und Zeit", *Frankfurter Zeitgemäße Broschuren*, Volume 40, Number 1-3, Breer & Thiemann, Hamm, Westphalen, (October-December, 1920), pp. 1-2, 63-64.

287. *See, for example: The Collected Papers of Albert Einstein*, Volume 9, Documents 26, 52, 59, 189, 207, 216, Princeton University Press, (2004).

288. T. Sauer, "The Relativity of Discovery: Hilbert's First Note on the Foundations of Physics", *Archive for History of Exact Sciences*, Volume 53, Number 6, (1999), pp. 529-575, at 568, note 156.

289. E. Gehrcke, "Die Relativitätstheorie auf dem Naturforschertage in Nauheim", *Die Umschau*, Volume 25, (1921), p. 99.

290. E. Gehrcke, "Zur Relativitätsfrage", *Die Umschau*, Volume 25, (1921), p. 227.

291. H. Weyl, "Die Relativitätstheorie auf der Naturforscherversammlung in Bad Nauheim", *Jahresbericht der Deutschen Mathematiker-Vereinigung*, Volume 31, (1922), pp. 51-63.

292. B. Thüring, "Albert Einsteins Umsturzversuch der Physik und seine inneren Möglichkeiten und Ursachen", *Forschungen zur Judenfrage*, Volume 4, (1940), pp. 134-162, at 159. Republished as: *Albert Einsteins Umsturzversuch der Physik und seine inneren Möglichkeiten und Ursachen*, Dr. Georg Lüttke Verlag, Berlin, (1941), pp. 59-60.

293. J. Stachel, "Einstein's Jewish Identity", *Einstein from 'B' to 'Z'*, Birkhäuser, Boston, Basel, Berlin, (2002), pp. 57-83, at 68.

294. A. Einstein to J. Winteler, English translation by A. Beck, *The Collected Papers of Albert Einstein*, Volume 1, Document 115, Princeton University Press, (1987), pp. 176-177, at 177.

295. A. Einstein, English translation by A. Beck, *The Collected Papers of Albert Einstein*, Volume 5, Document 499, Princeton University Press, (1995), pp. 373-374, at 374.

296. R. Romain, *La Conscience de l'Europe*, Volume 1, pp. 696ff. English translation from A. Fölsing, *Albert Einstein: A Biography*, Viking, New York, (1997), pp. 365-367. *See also:* Letter from A. Einstein to R. Romain of 15 September 1915, *The Collected Papers of Albert Einstein*, Volume 8, Document 118, Princeton University Press, (1998); **and** Letter from A. Einstein to R. Romain of 22 August 1917, *The Collected Papers of Albert Einstein*, Volume 8, Document 374, Princeton University Press, (1998).

297. J. Bacque, *Other Losses: An Investigation into the Mass Deaths of German Prisoners at the Hands of the French and Americans after World War II*, Stoddart,Toronto, (1989).

298. Letter from A. Einstein to Paul Ehrenfest of 22 March 1919, English translation by A. Hentschel, *The Collected Papers of Albert Einstein*, Volume 9, Document 10, Princeton Univsersity Press, (2004), pp. 9-10, at 10.

299. T. Herzl, *A Jewish State: An Attempt at a Modern Solution of the Jewish Question*, The Maccabæan Publishing Co., New York, (1904), pp. 68, 93.

300. M. Born, *The Born-Einstein Letters*, Walker and Company, New York, (1971), p. 16.

301. English translation in: K. Polkehn, "The Secret Contacts: Zionism and Nazi Germany, 1933-1941", *Journal of Palestine Studies*, Volume 5, Number 3/4, (Spring-Summer, 1976), pp. 54-82, at 59.

302. L. S. Dawidowicz, "The Zionist Federation of Germany Addresses the New German State", *A Holocaust Reader*, Behrman House, Inc., West Orange, New Jersey, (1976), pp. 150-155. *See also:* H. Tramer, Editor, S. Moses, *In zwei Welten: Siegfried Moses zum fünfundsiebzigsten Geburtstag*, Verlag Bitaon, Tel-Aviv, (1962), pp. 118.ff; cited in K. Polkehn, "The Secret Contacts: Zionism and Nazi Germany, 1933-1941", *Journal of Palestine Studies*, Volume 5, Number 3/4, (Spring-Summer, 1976), pp. 54-82, at 59.

303. English translation quoted from J. Stachel, "Einstein's Jewish Identity", *Einstein from 'B' to 'Z'*, Birkhäuser, Boston, Basel, Berlin, (2002), pp. 57-83, at 78. Stachel cites M. Besso, A. Einstein, *Correspondance, 1903-1955*, Hermann, Paris, (1972), p. 238.

304. Letter from A. Einstein to M. Besso of 12 December 1919, English translation by A. Hentschel, *The Collected Papers of Albert Einstein*, Volume 9, Document 207, Princeton University Press, (2004), pp. 178-179, at 179.

305. D. Brian, *The Unexpected Einstein: The Real Man Behind the Icon*, Wiley, Hoboken, New Jersey, (2005), p. 42.

306. A. Einstein, English translation by A. Engel, *The Collected Papers of Albert Einstein*, Volume 7, Document 34, Princeton University Press, (2002), pp. 153-155, at 153.

307. A. Einstein, English translation by A. Engel, *The Collected Papers of Albert Einstein*, Volume 7, Document 34, Princeton University Press, (2002), pp. 153-155, at 153.

308. A. Einstein, English translation by A. Engel, *The Collected Papers of Albert Einstein*, Volume 7, Document 34, Princeton University Press, (2002), pp. 153-155, at 153-154.

309. A. Einstein, English translation by A. Engel, *The Collected Papers of Albert Einstein*, Volume 7, Document 35, Princeton University Press, (2002), pp. 156-157.

310. A. Einstein quoted in: H. Gutfreund, "Albert Einstein and the Hebrew University", J. Renn, Editor, *Albert Einstein Chief Engineer of the Universe: One Hundred Authors for Einstein*, Wiley-VCH, Berlin, (2005), pp. 314-318, at 316.

311. Letter from A. Einstein to P. Nathan of 3 April 1920, *The Collected Papers of Albert Einstein*, Volume 9, Document 366, Princeton University Press, (2004), p. 492. Also: *The Collected Papers of Albert Einstein*, Volume

1, Princeton University Press, (1987), p. *lx*, note 44.

312. P. W. Massing, *Rehearsal for Destruction: A Study of Political Anti-Semitism in Imperial Germany*, Howard Fertig, New York, (1967), pp. 278-294.

313. P. A. Bucky, Einstein, and A. G. Weakland, *The Private Albert Einstein*, Andrews and McMeel, Kansas City, (1992), p. 88.

314. A. Einstein, *The World As I See It*, Citadel, New York, (1993), pp. 107-108.

315. A. Einstein, English translation by A. Engel, *The Collected Papers of Albert Einstein*, Volume 7, Document 37, Princeton University Press, (2002), p. 159.

316. A. Einstein quoted in A. Fölsing, English translation by E. Osers, *Albert Einstein, a Biography*, Viking, New York, (1997), p. 494; which cites speech to the *Central-Verein Deutscher Staatsbürger Jüdischen Glaubens*, in Berlin on 5 April 1920, in D. Reichenstein, *Albert Einstein. Sein Lebensbild und seine Weltanschauung*, Berlin, (1932). This letter from Einstein to the Central Association of German Citizens of the Jewish Faith of 5 April 1920 is reproduced in *The Collected Papers of Albert Einstein*, Volume 9, Document 368, Princeton University Press, (2004).

317. "Zeitschau", *Im deutschen Reich*, Volume 27, Number 3, (March, 1921), pp. 90-97, at 92.

318. D. K. Buchwald, *et al.*, Editors, *The Collected Papers of Albert Einstein*, Volume 7, Document 37, Princeton University Press, (2002), p. 304, note 8.

319. "Professor Einstein erklärt das ,,Sunday Expreß''-Interview für gefälscht", *Central-Verein Zeitung*, Volume 10, Number 37, (11 September 1931), p. 443.

320. A. Einstein, translated by A. Harris, "The Disarmament Conference of 1932. I." *The World As I See It*, Citadel, New York, (1993), pp. 59-60.

321. "Mr. Balfour on Zionism", *The London Times*, (12 February 1919), p. 9.

322. Arthur James Balfour, Earl of Balfour, *Decadence: Henry Sidgwick Memorial Lecture*, Cambridge, University Press, (1908).

323. T. G. Dyer, *Theodore Roosevelt and the Idea of Race*, Louisiana State University Press, Baton Rouge, (1992).

324. *The Works of Theodore Roosevelt*, Volume 24, Memorial Edition, C. Scribner's Sons, New York, (1923-1926), p. 122. J. B. Bishop, *Theodore Roosevelt and His Time Shown in His Own Letters*, Volume 2, Charles Scribner's Sons, New York, (1920), pp. 104-110, at 105.

325. D. Reed, *Disgrace Abounding*, Jonathan Cape, London, (1939).

326. S. Schechter, *Zionism: A Statement*, Federation of American Zionists, New York, (1906); reprinted in the relevant part in A. Hertzberg, *The Zionist Idea*, Harper Torchbooks, New York, (1959), p. 507.

327. J. Stachel, *Einstein from 'B' to 'Z'*, Birkhäuser, Boston, (2002), p. 79, note 41.

328. A. Einstein, "Jewish Nationalism and Anti-Semitism", *The Jewish Chronicle*, (17 June 1921), p. 16.

329. J. Stachel, "Einstein's Jewish Identity", *Einstein from 'B' to 'Z'*, Birkhäuser, Boston, (2002), p. 65. Stachel cites, *About Zionism: Speeches and Letters*, Macmillan, New York, (1931), pp. 48-49. For Zionist Ha-Am's use of the image of atomisation and dispersion, *see:* A. Hertzberg, *The Zionist Idea*, Harper Torchbooks, New York, (1959), p. 276.

330. A. Einstein, "Jewish Nationalism and Anti-Semitism", *The Jewish Chronicle*, (17 June 1921), p. 16.

331. A. Einstein, A. Engel translator, "How I became a Zionist", *The Collected Papers of Albert Einstein*, Volume 7, Document 57, Princeton University Press, (2002), pp. 234-235, at 235.

332. At the time Einstein made his statement, Jews and Gentiles often referred to Jews as "Orientals".

333. Einstein repeatedly spoke of the Germans as "greedy" to acquire territory and of the "loss of energy" when different "races" attempted to live together. He have been speaking literally. Georg Friedrich Nicolai wrote of the struggle of life to aquire the energy of the sun and he applied this struggle to humanity. G. Nicolai, *Die Biologie des Krieges, Betrachtungen eines deutschen Naturforschers*, O. Füssli, Zürich, (1917); English translation: *The Biology of War*, Century Co., New York, (1918), pp. 36-39, 44-53.

334. R. W. Clarck, *Einstein, the Life and Times*, World Publishing Company, USA, (1971), p. 292. Clarck refers to: *Neue Rundschau*, Volume 33, Part 2, pp. 815-816.

335. W. E. Mosse, "Die Niedergang der deutschen Republik und die Juden", *The Crucial Year 1932*, p. 38; English translation in: K. Polkehn, "The Secret Contacts: Zionism and Nazi Germany, 1933-1941", *Journal of Palestine Studies*, Volume 5, Number 3/4, (Spring-Summer, 1976), pp. 54-82, at 56-57.

336. English translation by John Stachel in J. Stachel, "Einstein's Jewish Identity", *Einstein from 'B' to 'Z'*, Birkhäuser, Boston, (2002), p. 67. Stachel cites, "Botschaft", *Jüdische Rundschau*, Volume 30, (1925), p. 129; French translation, *La Revue Juive*, Volume 1, (1925), pp. 14-16.

337. J. Stachel, "Einstein's Jewish Identity", *Einstein from 'B' to 'Z'*, Birkhäuser, Boston, (2002), p. 65. Stachel cites, *About Zionism: Speeches and Letters*, Macmillan, New York, (1931), pp. 78-79.

338. A. Einstein quoted in "Einstein on Arrival Braves Limelight for Only 15 Minutes", *The New York Times*, (12 December 1930), pp. 1, 16, at 16.

339. E. A. Ross, *The Old World in the New: The Significance of past and Present Immigration to the American People*, Century Company, New York, (1914), p. 144.

340. Reprinted in the relevant part in A. Hertzberg, *The Zionist Idea*, Harper Torchbooks, New York, (1959), p. 505.

341. A. Einstein, "Why do They Hate the Jews?", *Collier's*, Volume 102, (26 November 1938); reprinted in *Ideas and Opinions*, Crown, New York, (1954), pp. 191-198, at 194, 196. Einstein expressed himself in a similar way to Peter A. Bucky, P. A. Bucky, Einstein, and A. G. Weakland, *The Private Albert Einstein*, Andrews and McMeel, Kansas City, (1992), p. 87.

342. T. Herzl, *A Jewish State: An Attempt at a Modern Solution of the Jewish Question*, The Maccabæan Publishing Co., New York, (1904), pp. 5-6, 25, 68, 93.

343. A. Einstein, "Our Debt to Zionism", *Out of My Later Years*, Carol Publishing Group, New York, (1995), pp. 262-264, at 262.

344. A. Einstein, English translation by A. Engel, *The Collected Papers of Albert Einstein*, Volume 7, Document 35, Princeton University Press, (2002), pp. 156-157.

345. P. A. Bucky, Einstein, and A. G. Weakland, *The Private Albert Einstein*, Andrews and McMeel, Kansas City, (1992), p. 111.

346. A. Unsöld, "Albert Einstein — Ein Jahr danach", *Physikalische Blätter*, Volume 36, (1980), pp.337-339; **and** Volume 37, Number 7, (1981), p. 229.

347. A. Einstein, "Atomic War or Peace", *Atlantic Monthly*, (November, 1945, and November 1947); *as reprinted in:* A. Einstein, *Ideas and Opinions*, Crown, New York, (1954), p. 125.

348. A. Einstein, "To the Heroes of the Battle of the Warsaw Ghetto", *Bulletin of the Society of Polish Jews*, New York, (1944), reprinted in *Ideas and Opinions*, Crown, New York, (1954), pp. 212-213.

349. A. Einstein, quoted in O. Nathan and H. Norton, *Einstein on Peace*, Avenel Books, New York, (1981), p. 331.

350. A. Einstein quoted in A. Fölsing, *Albert Einstein: A Biography*, Viking, New York, (1997), pp. 727-728.

351. M. Born, *The Born-Einstein Letters*, Walker and Company, New York, (1971), p. 189.

352. M. Born, *The Born-Einstein Letters*, Walker and Company, New York, (1971), p. 199.

353. K. MacDonald, *The Culture of Critique*, Praeger, Westport, Connecticut, London, (1998), pp. 113-114; *citing:* E. A. Grollman, *Judaism in Sigmund Freud's World*, Bloch, New York, (1965); **and** D. B. Klein, *Jewish Origins of the Psychoanalytic Movement*, Praeger, New York, (1981); **and** P. Gay, *Freud: A Life for Our Time*, W. W. Norton, New York, (1988); **and** Y. H. Yerushalmi, *Freud's Moses: Judaism Terminable and Interminable*, Yale University Press, (1991); **and** K. MacDonald, *Separation and Its Discontents: Toward an Evolutionary Theory of Anti-Semitism*, Praeger, Westport, Connecticut, (1998).

354. See: Letter from M. Planck to W. Wien of 9 July 1922 in J. L. Heilbron, *Max Planck: Ein Leben für die Wissenschaft 1858-1947. Mit einer Auswahl der allgemeinverstänlichen Schriften von Max Planck*, S. Hirzel, Stuttgart, (1988), p. 127.

355. Letter from A. S. Eddington to A. Einstein of 1 December 1919, *The Collected Papers of Albert Einstein*, Volume 9, Document 186, Princeton University Press, (2004), pp. 262-263, at 263.

356. *The Collected Papers of Albert Einstein*, Volume 9, Documents 203, 220, 227, 238, 249, 253, Princeton University Press, (2004).

357. *See, for example:* "Literarische Mitteilungen", *Jüdische Rundschau*, Volume 25, Number 33, (21 May 1920), p. 254.

358. *The Collected Papers of Albert Einstein*, Volume 9, Documents 177, 180, 182, 185, 186 and 194, Princeton University Press, (2004).

359. M. Born, "Physics and Relativity", *Physics in my Generation*, second revised edition, Springer, New York, (1969), p. 110-111.

360. M. Born, "Physics and Relativity", *Physics in my Generation*, second revised edition, Springer, New York, (1969), p. 100.

361. J. Stachel, "Einstein's Jewish Identity", *Einstein from 'B' to 'Z'*, Birkhäuser, Boston, Basel, Berlin, (2002), pp. 57-83, at 59.

362. M. Born quoted and translated in: D. A. Buchwald, *et al.* Editors, "Einstein's Encounters with German Anti-Relativists", *The Collected Papers of Albert Einstein*, Volume 7, Princeton University Press, (2002), p. 109, footnote 52.

363. M. Born, "Physics and Relativity", *Physics in my Generation*, second revised edition, Springer, New York, (1969), p. 112.

364. Racist political Zionist Theodor Herzl wrote on 12 June 1895,

"Jewish papers! I will induce the publishers of the biggest Jewish papers (*Neue Freie Presse, Berliner Tageblatt, Frankfurter Zeitung*, etc.) to publish editions over there, as the *New York Herald* does in Paris."—T. Herzl, English translation by H. Zohn, R. Patai, Editor, *The Complete Diaries of Theodor Herzl*, Volume 1, Herzl Press, New York, (1960), p. 84.

THE DEARBORN INDEPENDENT, praised the *New York Herald*. "When Editors Were Independent of the Jews", THE DEARBORN INDEPENDENT, (5 February 1921). *See also:* T. Herzl, English translation by H. Zohn, R. Patai, Editor, *The Complete Diaries of Theodor Herzl*, Volumes 1 and 2, Herzl Press, New York, (1960), pp. 37, 97, 170, 455, 457, 480. *See also:* A. Elon, *Herzl*, Holt, Rinehart and Winston, New York, (1975), pp. 167-168. *See also: The Collected Papers of Albert Einstein*, Volume 7, Document 35, Princeton University Press, (2002), pp. 296-297, note 8.

365. "Prof. Einstein Here, Explains Relativity", *The New York Times*, (3 April 1921), pp. 1, 13, at 1.

366. A. Einstein, "Jewish Nationalism and Anti-Semitism", *The Jewish Chronicle*, (17 June 1921), p. 16.

367. M. T. Cicero, *Pro Flaccus*, Chapter 28; translated by C. D. Yonge, *The Orations of Marcus Tullius Cicero*, Volume 2, George Bell & Sons, London, (1880), pp. 454-455.

368. K. A. Strom, Editor, *The Best of Attack! and National Vanguard Tabloid*, National Alliance, Arlington, Virginia, (1984), p. 66.

369. P. Findley, *They Dare to Speak Out: People and Institutions Confront Israel's Lobby*, Lawrence Hill, Westport, Connecticut, (1985); **and** *Deliberate Deceptions: Facing the Facts about the U.S.-Israeli Relationship*, Lawrence Hill Books, Chicago, (1993); **and** *Silent No More: Confronting America's*

False Images of Islam, D : Amana Publications, Beltsville, Maryland, (2001).

370. P. Findley, *They Dare to Speak Out: People and Institutions Confront Israel's Lobby*, Lawrence Hill & Company, Westport, Connecticut, (1985), p. 296.

371. V. Ostrovsky, *The Other Side of Deception: A Rogue Agent Exposes the Mossad's Secret Agenda*, Harper Collins, New York, (1994), p. 32.

372. *See also:* N. G. Finkelstein, *The Holocaust Industry: Reflections on the Exploitation of Jewish Suffering*, Second Edition, Verso, London, New York, (2003).

373. J. J. Mearsheimer and S. M. Walt, *The Israel Lobby and U. S. Foreign Policy*, Faculty Research Working Papers Series, Harvard University, John F. Kennedy School of Government, (March, 2006), p. 23.

374. J. Carter, as quoted by E. Clift, "Last Word: Jimmy Carter Revisiting 'Apartheid'", *Newsweek International*, (25 December 2006—1 January 2007). <http://www.msnbc.msn.com/id/16240761/site/newsweek/>

375. Jimmy Carter, Thirty-Ninth President of the United States of America, in an interview on, "This week with George Stephanopoulos," ABC, as quoted by Yitzhak Benhorin, "Balanced stand on ME is political suicide, says Carter", www.ynetnews.com, http://www.ynetnews.com/articles/0,7340,L-3369679,00.html, (26 February 2007).

376. D. Duke, *Jewish Supremacism: My Awakening on the Jewish Question*, Free Speech Press, Covington, Louisiana, (2002), pp. 200-205.

377. D. Reed, *Somewhere South of Suez*, Devin-Adir, U. S. A., (1951), pp. 8-10.

378. G. Vidal, *Imperial America*, Nation Books, New York, (2004), pp. 76-77; originally, *The Observer*, London, (15 November 1987), "But written as of March 1987 In *The Nation*."

379. R. I. Friedman, "Selling Israel in America: The Hasbara Project Targets the U.S. Media", *Mother Jones*, (February/March, 1987), pp. 1-9; reprinted "Selling Israel to America", *Journal of Palestine Studies*, Volume 16, Number 4, (Summer, 1987), pp. 169-179, at 170, 178.

380. Courtesy of the Department of Special Collections, University of St. Thomas, St. Paul, MN.

381. S. Mohorovičić, "Raum, Zeit und Welt", in two parts in K. Sapper, Editor, *Kritik und Fortbildung der Relativitätstheorie*, Akademische Druck- u. Verlagsanstalt, Graz, (1958/1962), Part 1 in Volume 1, (1958), pp. 168-281, at 277, 279, notes 317, 352, 364, 365; Part 2 in Volume 2, (1962), pp. 219-352, at 273, 317, 319, 329, notes 90, 108, 109, 110, 637.

382. Letter from A. Einstein to H. Bergman of 5 November 1919, English translation by A. Hentschel, *The Collected Papers of Albert Einstein*, Volume 9, Document 155, Princeton University Press, (2004), pp. 132-133, at 132. *See also:* H. N. Bialik, "Bialik on the Hebrew University", in A. Hertzberg, *The Zionist Idea*, Harper Torchbooks, New York, (1959), pp. 281-288, at 284-285.

383. L. D. Brandeis, M. I. Urofsky and D. W. Levy, Editors, *Letters of Louis D. Brandeis* Volume 4, State University of New York Press, Albany, New York, (1975), pp. 536-537.

384. Letter from V. G. Ehrenberg to A. Einstein of 23 November 1919, English translation by A. Hentschel, *The Collected Papers of Albert Einstein*, Volume 9, Document 173, Princeton University Press, (2004), p. 145.

385. H. A. Lorentz, "Electromagnetische Verschijnselen in een Stelsel dat Zich met Willekeurige Snelheid, Kleiner dan die van Het Licht, Beweegt", *Koninklijke Akademie van Wetenschappen te Amsterdam, Wis- en Natuurkundige Afdeeling, Verslagen van de Gewone Vergaderingen*, Volume 12, (23 April 1904), pp. 986-1009; translated into English, "Electromagnetic Phenomena in a System Moving with any Velocity Smaller than that of Light", *Proceedings of the Royal Academy of Sciences at Amsterdam (Noninklijke Nederlandse Akademie van Wetenschappen te Amsterdam)*, 6, (May 27, 1904), pp. 809-831; reprinted *Collected Papers*, Volume 5, pp. 172-197; a redacted and shortened version appears in *The Principle of Relativity*, Dover, New York, (1952), pp. 11-34; a German translation from the English, "Elektromagnetische Erscheinung in einem System, das sich mit beliebiger, die des Lichtes nicht erreichender Geschwindigkeit bewegt," appears in *Das Relativitätsprinzip: eine Sammlung von Abhandlungen*, B. G. Teubner, Leipzig, (1913), pp. 6-26.

386. H. Poincaré, "Sur la Dynamique de l'Électron", *Rendiconti del Circolo matimatico di Palermo*, Volume 21, (1906, submitted July 23rd, 1905), pp. 129-176; reprinted in H. Poincaré, *La Mécanique Nouvelle: Conférence, Mémoire et Note sur la Théorie de la Relativité / Introduction de Édouard Guillaume*, Gauthier-Villars, Paris, (1924), pp. 18-76; reprinted *Œuvres*, Volume IX, pp. 494-550; redacted English translation by H. M. Schwartz with modern notation, "Poincaré's Rendiconti Paper on Relativity", *American Journal of Physics*, Volume 39, (November, 1971), pp. 1287-1294; Volume 40, (June, 1972), pp. 862-872; Volume 40, (September, 1972), pp. 1282-1287; English translation by G. Pontecorvo with extensive commentary by A. A. Logunov with modern notation, *On the Articles by Henri Poincaré ON THE DYNAMICS OF THE ELECTRON*, Publishing Department of the Joint Institute for Nuclear Research, Dubna, (1995), pp. 15-78.

387. Letter from P. Ehrenfest to A. Einstein of 9 December 1919, English translation by A. Hentschel, *The Collected Papers of Albert Einstein*, Volume 9, Document 203, Princeton University Press, (2004), pp. 173-175, at 174.

388. "Prof. Einstein Here, Explains Relativity", *The New York Times*, (3 April 1921), pp. 1, 13, at 1.

389. *Cf.* Schlomo Ginossar, a. k. a. Simon Ginsburg, a. k. a. Salomon Ginzberg, "Early Days", *The Hebrew University of Jerusalem, 1925-1950*, Universitah ha-'uvrit bi-Yerushalayim, Jerusalem, (1950), pp. 71-74.

390. L. D. Brandeis, M. I. Urofsky and D. W. Levy, Editors, *Letters of Louis D. Brandeis* Volume 4, State University of New York Press, Albany, New York, (1975), p. 555.

391. L. D. Brandeis, M. I. Urofsky and D. W. Levy, Editors, *Letters of Louis D. Brandeis* Volume 4, State University of New York Press, Albany, New York, (1975), p. 556.

392. L. D. Brandeis, M. I. Urofsky and D. W. Levy, Editors, *Letters of Louis D. Brandeis* Volume 4, State University of New York Press, Albany, New York, (1975), p. 556.

393. *Cf.* Schlomo Ginossar, a. k. a. Simon Ginsburg, a. k. a. Salomon Ginzberg, "Early Days", *The Hebrew University of Jerusalem, 1925-1950*, Universitah ha-'uvrit bi-Yerushalayim, Jerusalem, (1950), pp. 71-74, at 72.

394. *See, for example,* J. Goebbels, "Der Führer", *Aufsätze aus der Kampfzeit*, Zentralverlag der NSDAP, Munich, (1935), pp. 214-216; **and** "Goldene Worte für einen Diktator und für solche, die es werden wollen", *Der Angriff*, (1 September 1932); reprinted in: *Wetterleuchten: Aufsätze aus der Kampfzeit*, Zentralverlag der NSDAP., Franz Eher Nachf., München, (1939), pp. 325-327. On the Zionists' quest to find a "great man" to be their "dictator", *see:* N. Goldman, "Zionismus und nationale Bewegung", *Der Jude*, Volume 5, Number 4, (1920-1921), pp. 237-242, at 240-242; which was part of a series including: "Zionismus und nationale Bewegung", *Der Jude*, Volume 5, Number 1, (1920-1921), pp. 45-47; and "Zionismus und nationale Bewegung", *Der Jude*, Volume 5, Number 7, (1920-1921), pp. 423-425.

395. *Cf.* Schlomo Ginossar, a. k. a. Simon Ginsburg, a. k. a. Salomon Ginzberg, "Early Days", *The Hebrew University of Jerusalem, 1925-1950*, Universitah ha-'uvrit bi-Yerushalayim, Jerusalem, (1950), pp. 71-74, at 73. *See also:* J. Stachel, *Einstein from 'B' to 'Z'*, Birkhäuser, Boston, (2002), p. 79, note 41.

396. *The New York Times*, (8 July 1921), p. 9.

397. N. Robbins, *Baltimore Evening Sun*, (29 April 1921). "Americans Tremendously Bored, Einstein Says, Explaining 'Exaggerated Welcome'", *Minneapolis Morning Tribune*, (8 July 1921). "Einstein Has No Valid Cause to Congratulate Self, Reuterdahl Says", *Minneapolis Evening Tribune*, (8 July 1921), p. 10. "The Amused Mr. Einstein", *Minneapolis Morning Tribune*, (9 July 1921). "Reuterdahl Sees No Cause for Einstein's Slurs on Americans", *The Minneapolis Morning Tribune*, (9July 1921). "Chicago Women Resent Einstein's Opinions", *The New York Times*, (9 July 1921), p. 7. "Probably He Did Say It All", *The New York Times*, (9 July 1921), p. 8. K. W. Payne, "Einstein on Americans, wherein the Eminent Scientist Failed to Understand Us", *The New York Times*, Section 2, (10 July 1921), p. 2. Response, "Einsteins amerikanische Eindrücke. Was er wirklich sah", *Vossische Zeitung*, Morning Edition, Supplement 1, (10 July 1921), Front Page. A transcription is found in *The Collected Papers of Albert Einstein*, Volume 7, Appendix E, Princeton University Press, (2002), pp. 628-630. "A Product of His Education", *The New York Times*, (11 July 1921), p. 10. "Explanation Rather than Denial", *The New York Times*, (12 July 1921), p. 12. "Prohibition Stays, Says Dr. Einstein", *The New York Times*, Section 2, (31 July 1921), p. 4. An anti-Semitic article appeared in *The Dearborn Independent*, "Relatively Unimportant, Extremely Typical", (30 July 1921), p. 14. Einstein had declared America "violently" "anti-German", which statement also brought criticism. *See:* "Dr. Einstein Found America Anti-German. Violently So, He Says, Though He Noted That a Reaction Was Setting In", *The New York Times*, (2 July 1921), p. 3. "A Genius Makes a Mistake", *The New York Times*, (4 July 1921), p. 8. *New York Herald Magazine*, (26 June 1921). J. Riem, "Amerika über Einstein", *Deutsche Zeitung*, (Berlin), (1 July 1921); and "Zu Einsteins Amerikafahrt", *Deutsche Zeitung*, (Berlin), (13 September 1921).

398. J. Stachel, *Einstein from 'B' to 'Z'*, Birkhäuser, Boston, (2002), p. 79, note 41.

399. "Aladdin Einstein", *The Freeman* (New York), Volume 3, Number 59, (27 April 1921), pp. 153-154.

400. T. J. J. See, "EINSTEIN A TRICKSTER?", *The San Francisco Journal*, (27 May 1923). Peter A. Bucky recalls that others intimated that Einstein's disheveled appearance was meant to attract publicity. Bucky discounted the notion, as did Einstein. P. A. Bucky, Einstein, and A. G. Weakland, *The Private Albert Einstein*, Andrews and McMeel, Kansas City, (1992), p. 4, 111.

401. P. Frank, *Einstein: His Life and Times*, Alfred A. Knopf, New York, (1947), pp. 163-166.

402. P. Frank, *Einstein: His Life and Times*, Alfred A. Knopf, New York, (1947), p. 163.

403. A. Einstein quoted in "Einstein on Arrival Braves Limelight for Only 15 Minutes", *The New York Times*, (12 December 1930), pp. 1, 16, at 16

404. *Cf.* H. Goenner, "The Reaction to Relativity Theory. I: The Anti-Einstein Campaign in Germany in 1920", *Science in Context*, Volume 6, Number 1, (1993), pp. 107-133, at 125.

405. A. Reuterdahl, *The Minneapolis Sunday Tribune*, (22 May 1921). Reuterdahl translates parts of "Professor Einsteins „Triumphzug" durch Amerika", *Luzerner Neueste Nachrichten*, (22 April 1921).

406.

The Palestine Mandate
The Council of the League of Nations:
July 24, 1922
Whereas the Principal Allied Powers have agreed, for the purpose of giving effect to the provisions of Article 22 of the Covenant of the League of Nations, to entrust to a Mandatory selected by the said Powers the administration of the territory of Palestine, which formerly belonged to the Turkish Empire, within such boundaries as may be fixed by them; and

Whereas the Principal Allied Powers have also agreed that the Mandatory should be responsible for putting into effect the declaration originally made on November 2nd, 1917, by the Government of His Britannic Majesty, and adopted by the said Powers, in favor of the establishment in Palestine of a national home for the Jewish people, it being clearly understood that nothing should be done which might prejudice the civil and religious rights of existing non-Jewish communities in Palestine, or the rights and political status enjoyed by Jews in any other country; and

Whereas recognition has thereby been given to the historical connection of the Jewish people with Palestine and to the grounds for reconstituting their national home in that country; and

Whereas the Principal Allied Powers have selected His Britannic Majesty as the Mandatory for Palestine; and

Whereas the mandate in respect of Palestine has been formulated in the following terms and submitted to the Council of the League for approval; and

Whereas His Britannic Majesty has accepted the mandate in respect of Palestine and undertaken to exercise it on behalf of the League of Nations in conformity with the following provisions; and

Whereas by the afore-mentioned Article 22 (paragraph 8), it is provided that the degree of authority, control or administration to be exercised by the Mandatory, not having been previously agreed upon by the Members of the League, shall be explicitly defined by the Council of the League Of Nations; confirming the said Mandate, defines its terms as follows:

ARTICLE 1. The Mandatory shall have full powers of legislation and of administration, save as they may be limited by the terms of this mandate.

ART. 2. The Mandatory shall be responsible for placing the country under such political, administrative and economic conditions as will secure the establishment of the Jewish national home, as laid down in the preamble, and the development of self-governing institutions, and also for safeguarding the civil and religious rights of all the inhabitants of Palestine, irrespective of race and religion.

ART. 3. The Mandatory shall, so far as circumstances permit, encourage local autonomy.

ART. 4. An appropriate Jewish agency shall be recognised as a public body for the purpose of advising and co-operating with the Administration of Palestine in such economic, social and other matters as may affect the establishment of the Jewish national home and the interests of the Jewish population in Palestine, and, subject always to the control of the Administration to assist and take part in the development of the country. The Zionist organization, so long as its organization and constitution are in the opinion of the Mandatory appropriate, shall be recognised as such agency. It shall take steps in consultation with His Britannic Majesty's Government to secure the co-operation of all Jews who are willing to assist in the establishment of the Jewish national home.

ART. 5. The Mandatory shall be responsible for seeing that no Palestine territory shall be ceded or leased to, or in any way placed under the control of the Government of any foreign Power.

ART. 6. The Administration of Palestine, while ensuring that the rights and position of other sections of the population are not prejudiced, shall facilitate Jewish immigration under suitable conditions and shall encourage, in co-operation with the Jewish agency referred to in Article 4, close settlement by Jews on the land, including State lands and waste lands not required for public purposes.

ART. 7. The Administration of Palestine shall be responsible for enacting a nationality law. There shall be included in this law provisions framed so as to facilitate the acquisition of Palestinian citizenship by Jews who take up their permanent residence in Palestine.

ART. 8. The privileges and immunities of foreigners, including the benefits of consular jurisdiction and protection as formerly enjoyed by Capitulation or usage in the Ottoman Empire, shall not be applicable in Palestine. Unless the Powers whose nationals enjoyed the afore-mentioned privileges and immunities on August 1st, 1914, shall have previously renounced the right to their re-establishment, or shall have agreed to their non-application for a specified period, these privileges and immunities shall, at the expiration of the mandate, be immediately reestablished in their entirety or with such modifications as may have been agreed upon between the Powers concerned.

ART. 9. The Mandatory shall be responsible for seeing that the judicial system established in Palestine shall assure to foreigners, as well as to natives, a complete guarantee of their rights. Respect for the personal status of the various peoples and communities and for their religious interests shall be fully guaranteed. In particular, the control and administration of Wakfs shall be exercised in accordance with religious law and the dispositions of the founders.

ART. 10. Pending the making of special extradition agreements relating to Palestine, the extradition treaties in force between the Mandatory and other foreign Powers shall apply to Palestine.

ART. 11. The Administration of Palestine shall take all necessary measures to safeguard the interests of the community in connection with the development of the country, and, subject to any international obligations accepted by the Mandatory, shall have full power to provide for public ownership or control of any of the natural resources of the country or of the public works, services and utilities established or to be established therein. It shall introduce a land system appropriate to the needs of the country, having regard, among other things, to the desirability of promoting the close settlement and intensive cultivation of the land. The Administration may arrange with the Jewish agency mentioned in Article 4 to construct or operate, upon fair and equitable terms, any public works, services and utilities, and to develop any of the natural resources of the country, in so far as these matters are not directly undertaken by the Administration. Any such arrangements shall provide that no profits distributed by such agency, directly or indirectly, shall exceed a reasonable rate of interest on the capital, and any further profits shall be utilised by it for the benefit of the country in a manner approved by the Administration.

ART. 12. The Mandatory shall be entrusted with the control of the foreign relations of Palestine and the right to issue exequaturs to consuls appointed by foreign Powers. He shall also be entitled to afford diplomatic and consular protection to citizens of Palestine when outside its territorial limits.

ART. 13. All responsibility in connection with the Holy Places and religious buildings or sites in Palestine, including that of preserving existing rights and of securing free access to the Holy Places, religious buildings and sites and the free exercise of worship, while ensuring the requirements of public order and decorum, is assumed by the Mandatory, who shall be responsible solely to the League of Nations in all matters connected herewith, provided that nothing in this article shall prevent the Mandatory from entering into such arrangements as he may deem reasonable with the Administration for the purpose of carrying the provisions of this article into effect; and provided also that nothing in this mandate shall be construed as conferring upon the Mandatory authority to interfere with the fabric or the management of purely Moslem sacred shrines, the immunities of which are guaranteed.

ART. 14. A special commission shall be appointed by the Mandatory to study, define and determine the rights and claims in connection with the Holy Places and the rights and claims relating to the different religious communities in Palestine. The method of nomination, the composition and the functions of this Commission shall be submitted to the Council of the League for its approval, and the Commission shall not be appointed or enter upon its functions without the approval of the Council.

ART. 15. The Mandatory shall see that complete freedom of conscience and the free exercise of all forms of worship, subject only to the maintenance of public order and morals, are ensured to all. No discrimination of any kind shall be made between the inhabitants of Palestine on the ground of race, religion or language. No person shall be excluded from Palestine on the sole ground of his religious belief. The right of each community to maintain its own schools for the education of its own members in its own language, while conforming to such educational requirements of a general nature as the Administration may impose, shall not be denied or impaired.

ART. 16. The Mandatory shall be responsible for exercising such supervision over religious or eleemosynary bodies of all faiths in Palestine as may be required for the maintenance of public order and good government. Subject to such supervision, no measures shall be taken in Palestine to obstruct or interfere with the enterprise of such bodies or to discriminate against any representative or member of them on the ground of his religion or nationality.

ART. 17. The Administration of Palestine may organise on a voluntary basis the forces necessary for the preservation of peace and order, and also for the defence of the country, subject, however, to the supervision of the Mandatory, but shall not use them for purposes other than those above specified save with the consent of the Mandatory. Except for such purposes, no military, naval or air forces shall be raised or maintained by the Administration of Palestine. Nothing in this article shall preclude the Administration of Palestine from contributing to the cost of the maintenance of the forces of the Mandatory in Palestine. The Mandatory shall be entitled at all times to use the roads, railways and ports of Palestine for the movement of armed forces and the carriage of fuel and supplies.

ART. 18. The Mandatory shall see that there is no discrimination in Palestine against the nationals of any State Member of the League of Nations (including companies incorporated under its laws) as compared with those of the Mandatory or of any foreign State in matters concerning taxation, commerce or navigation, the exercise of industries or professions, or in the treatment of merchant vessels or civil aircraft. Similarly, there shall be no discrimination in Palestine against goods originating in or destined for any of the said States, and there shall be freedom of transit under equitable conditions across the mandated area. Subject as aforesaid and to the other provisions of this mandate, the Administration of Palestine may, on the advice of the Mandatory, impose such taxes and customs duties as it may consider necessary, and take such steps as it may think best to promote the development of the natural resources of the country and to safeguard the interests of the population. It may also, on the advice of the Mandatory, conclude a special customs agreement with any State the territory of which in 1914 was wholly included in Asiatic Turkey or Arabia.

ART. 19. The Mandatory shall adhere on behalf of the Administration of Palestine to any general international conventions already existing, or which may be concluded hereafter with the approval of the League of Nations, respecting the slave traffic, the traffic in arms and ammunition, or the traffic in drugs, or relating to commercial equality, freedom of transit and navigation, aerial navigation and postal, telegraphic and wireless communication or literary, artistic or industrial property.

ART. 20. The Mandatory shall co-operate on behalf of the Administration of Palestine, so far as religious, social and other conditions may permit, in the execution of any common policy adopted by the League of Nations for preventing and combating disease, including diseases of plants and animals.

ART. 21. The Mandatory shall secure the enactment within twelve months from this date, and shall ensure the execution of a Law of Antiquities based on the following rules. This law shall ensure equality of treatment in the matter of excavations and archaeological research to the nationals of all States Members of the League of Nations.

(1) "Antiquity" means any construction or any product of human activity earlier than the year 1700 A. D.

(2) The law for the protection of antiquities shall proceed by encouragement rather than by threat. Any person who, having discovered an antiquity without being furnished with the authorization referred to in paragraph 5, reports the same to an official of the competent Department, shall be rewarded according to the value of the discovery.

(3) No antiquity may be disposed of except to the competent Department, unless this Department renounces the acquisition of any such antiquity. No antiquity may leave the country without an export licence from the said Department.

(4) Any person who maliciously or negligently destroys or damages an antiquity shall be liable to a penalty to be fixed.

(5) No clearing of ground or digging with the object of finding

antiquities shall be permitted, under penalty of fine, except to persons authorised by the competent Department.

(6) Equitable terms shall be fixed for expropriation, temporary or permanent, of lands which might be of historical or archaeological interest.

(7) Authorization to excavate shall only be granted to persons who show sufficient guarantees of archaeological experience. The Administration of Palestine shall not, in granting these authorizations, act in such a way as to exclude scholars of any nation without good grounds.

(8) The proceeds of excavations may be divided between the excavator and the competent Department in a proportion fixed by that Department. If division seems impossible for scientific reasons, the excavator shall receive a fair indemnity in lieu of a part of the find.

ART. 22. English, Arabic and Hebrew shall be the official languages of Palestine. Any statement or inscription in Arabic on stamps or money in Palestine shall be repeated in Hebrew and any statement or inscription in Hebrew shall be repeated in Arabic.

ART. 23. The Administration of Palestine shall recognise the holy days of the respective communities in Palestine as legal days of rest for the members of such communities.

ART. 24. The Mandatory shall make to the Council of the League of Nations an annual report to the satisfaction of the Council as to the measures taken during the year to carry out the provisions of the mandate. Copies of all laws and regulations promulgated or issued during the year shall be communicated with the report.

ART. 25. In the territories lying between the Jordan and the eastern boundary of Palestine as ultimately determined, the Mandatory shall be entitled, with the consent of the Council of the League of Nations, to postpone or withhold application of such provisions of this mandate as he may consider inapplicable to the existing local conditions, and to make such provision for the administration of the territories as he may consider suitable to those conditions, provided that no action shall be taken which is inconsistent with the provisions of Articles 15, 16 and 18.

ART. 26. The Mandatory agrees that, if any dispute whatever should arise between the Mandatory and another member of the League of Nations relating to the interpretation or the application of the provisions of the mandate, such dispute, if it cannot be settled by negotiation, shall be submitted to the Permanent Court of International Justice provided for by Article 14 of the Covenant of the League of Nations.

ART. 27. The consent of the Council of the League of Nations is required for any modification of the terms of this mandate.

ART. 28. In the event of the termination of the mandate hereby conferred upon the Mandatory, the Council of the League of Nations shall make such arrangements as may be deemed necessary for safeguarding in perpetuity, under guarantee of the League, the rights secured by Articles 13 and 14, and shall use its influence for securing, under the guarantee of the League, that the Government of Palestine will fully honour the financial obligations legitimately incurred by the Administration of Palestine during the period of the mandate, including the rights of public servants to pensions or gratuities. The present instrument shall be deposited in original in the archives of the League of Nations and certified copies shall be forwarded by the Secretary-General of the League of Nations to all members of the League.

Done at London the twenty-fourth day of July, one thousand nine hundred and twenty-two.

407. H. Kessler, *Walter Rathenau: His Life and Work*, Harcourt, Brace, New York, (1930).

408. W. Hartenau (W. Rathenau), "Höre, Israel!", *Die Zukunft*, Volume 18, (6 March 1897), pp. 454-462.

409. R. W. Clarck, *Einstein, the Life and Times*, World Publishing Company, USA, (1971), p. 292. Clarck refers to: *Neue Rundschau*, Volume 33, Part 2, pp. 815-816.

410. C. Weizmann, *Trial and Error: The Autobiography of Chaim Weizmann*, Harper & Brothers, New York, (1949), p. 289.

411. T. J. J. See, "EINSTEIN A TRICKSTER?", *The San Francisco Journal*, (27 May 1923).

412. *Casseler Allgemeine Zeitung*, (12 August 1922), as recorded by Ernst Gehrcke in his book: *Die Massensuggestion der Relativitätstheorie: Kulturhistorisch-psychologische Dokumente*, Hermann Meusser, Berlin, (1924), p. 63.

413. H. Morgenthau, "Zionism a Surrender, Not a Solution", *The World's Work*, Volume 42, Number 3, (July, 1921), pp. i-viii. "Mr. Zangwill on Zionism", *The London Times*, (16 October 1923), p. 11. I. Zangwill, "Is Political Zionism Dead? Yes", *The Nation*, Volume 118, Number 3062, (12 March 1924), pp. 276-278.

414. C. L. Poor, "Planetary Motions and the Einstein Theories", *Scientific American Monthly*, Volume 3, (June, 1921), pp. 484-486; **and** "Alternative to Einstein: How Dr. Poor Would Save Newton's Law and the Classical Time and Space Concept", *Scientific American*, Volume 124, (11 June 1921), p. 468; **and** "Motions of the Planets and the Relativity Theory", *Science*, New Series, Volume 54, (8 July 1921), pp. 30-34; **and** "Test for Eclipse Plates", *Science*, New Series, Volume 57, (25 May 1923), pp. 613-614; **and** C. L. Poor and A. Henderson, "Is Einstein Wrong? A Debate", *Forum*, Volumes 71 & 72, (June/July, 1924), pp. 705-715, 13-21; replies *Forum*, Volume 72, (August 1924), pp. 277-281; **and** C. L. Poor, "Relativity and the Motion of Mercury", *Annals of the New York Academy of Sciences*, Volume 29, (15 July 1925), pp. 285-319; **and** "The Deflection of Light as Observed at Total Solar Eclipses", *Journal of the Optical Society of America*, Volume 20, (1930), pp. 173-211; **and** "What Einstein Really Did", *Scribner's Magazine*, Volume 88, (July-December, 1930), pp. 527-538; discussion follows in *Commonweal*, Volume 13, (24 December 1930, 7 January 1931, 11 February 1931), pp. 203-204, 271-272, 412-413. *See also:* "Alternative to Einstein; How Dr. Poor would Save

Newton's Law and the Classical Time and Space Concept", *Scientific American*, Volume 124, (11 June 1921), p. 468.

415. C. L. Poor, "What Einstein Really Did", *Scribner's Magazine*, Volume 88, (July-December 1930), pp. 527-538, at 538.

416. H. Goenner, "The Reaction to Relativity Theory. I: The Anti-Einstein Campaign in Germany in 1920", *Science in Context*, Volume 6, Number 1, (1993), pp. 107-133, at 118.

417. H. Goenner, "The Reaction to Relativity Theory. I: The Anti-Einstein Campaign in Germany in 1920", *Science in Context*, Volume 6, Number 1, (1993), pp. 107-133, at 118-119.

418. E. Gehrcke, *Kritik der Relativitätstheorie*, Hermann Meusser, Berlin, (1924), pp. 34-35. *Cf.* H. Goenner, "The Reaction to Relativity Theory. I: The Anti-Einstein Campaign in Germany in 1920", *Science in Context*, Volume 6, Number 1, (1993), pp. 107-133, at 112.

419. A. Einstein, "In Honour of Arnold Berliner's Seventieth Birthday", *The World As I See It*, Citadel, New York, (1993), p. 14.

420. A. Einstein, "Zuschriften an die Herausgeber. Zur Abwehr", *Die Naturwissenschaften*, Volume 9, Number 13, (1 April 1921), p. 219.

421. *Die Naturwissenschaften* exhibited a long history of personal attack by "book review". *See, for example: Die Naturwissenschaften*, Volume 11, Number 2, (12 January 1923), pp. 252-256; **and** *Die Naturwissenschaften*, Volume 19, Number 11, (13 March 1931), pp. 252-256.

422. Letter from A. Einstein to W. Dällenbach of 27 September 1919, English translation by A. Hentschel, *The Collected Papers of Albert Einstein*, Volume 9, Document 112, Princeton University Press, (2004), pp. 97-98, at 97.

423. See, as but one of countless examples, the letter from W. Dällenbach to A. Einstein of 19 September 1919, *The Collected Papers of Albert Einstein*, Volume 9, Document 107, Princeton University Press, (2004).

424. A. Reuterdahl, "The Academy of Nations—Its Aims and Hopes", *The Dearborn Independent*, (7 January 1922), p. 14.

425. E. Guillaume's letter, translated by A. Reuterdahl, "Guillaume, Barred in Move To Debate Einstein, Calls Meeting Political Reunion", *Minneapolis Journal*, (14 May 1922), p. 14; reprinted with slight modifications, "The Origin of Einsteinism", *The New York Times*, (12 August 1923), Section 7, p. 8. *See also:* "Einstein Faces in Paris Grave Blow at Theory", *The Chicago Tribune*, (31 March 1922). *See also:* "Dr. Guillaume's Proofs of Einstein Theory's Fallacy Revealed to the Journal", *Minneapolis Journal*, (9 April 1922). *See also:* E. Guillaume, "Un Résultat des Discussions de la Théorie d'Einstein au Collège de France", *Revue Générale des Sciences Pures et Appliquées*, Volume 33, Number 11, (15 June 1922), pp. 322-324. *See also:* "Les Bases de la Physique moderne", *Archives des Sciences Physiques et Naturelles*, Series 4, Volume 43, (1917), pp. 5-21, 89-112, 185-198; **and** "Sur le Possibilité d'Exprimer la Théorie de la Relativité en Fonction du Temps Universel", *Archives des Sciences Physiques et Naturelles*, Series 4, Volume 44, (1917), pp. 48-52; **and** "La Théorie de la Relativité en Fonction du Temps Universel",

Archives des Sciences Physiques et Naturelles, Series 4, Volume 46, (1918), pp. 281-325; **and** "Sur la Théorie de la Relativité", *Archives des Sciences Physiques et Naturelles*, Series 5, Volume 1, (1919), pp. 246-251; **and** "Représentation et Mesure du Temps", *Archives des Sciences Physiques et Naturelles*, Series 5, Volume 2, (1920), pp. 125-146; **and** "La Théorie de la Relativité et sa Signification", *Revue de Métaphysique et de Morale*, Volume 27, (1920), pp. 423-469; **and** "Relativité et Gravitation", *Bulletin de la Société Vaudoise des Sciences Naturelles*, Volume 53, (1920), pp. 311-340; **and** "Les Bases de la Théorie de la Relativité", *Revue Générale des Sciences Pures et Appliquées*, (15 April 1920) pp. 200-210; **and** C. Willigens, "Représentation Géométrique du Temps Universel dans la Théorie de la Relativité Restreinte", *Archives des Sciences Physiques et Naturelles*, Series 5, Volume 2, (1920), p. 289; **and** E. Guillaume, *La Théorie de la Relativité. Résumé des Conférences Faites à l'Université de Lausanne au Semestre d'été 1920*, Rouge & Co., Lausanne, (1921); **and** E. Guillaume and C. Willigens, "Über die Grundlagen der Relativitätstheorie", *Physikalische Zeitschrift*, Volume 22, (1921), pp. 109-114; **and** E. Guillaume, "Graphische Darstellung der Optik bewegter Körper", *Physikalische Zeitschrift*, Volume 22, (1921), pp. 386-388; **and** Guillaume's Appendix II, "Temps Relatif et Temps Universel", in L. Fabre, *Une Nouvelle Figure du Monde: les Théories d'Einstein*, Second Edition, Payot, Paris, (1922); **and** E. Guillaume, "Y a-t-il une Erreur dans le PremierMémoire d'Einstein?", *Revue Générale des Sciences Pures et Appliquées*, Volume 33, (1922), pp. 5-10; **and** "La Question du Temps d'après M. Bergson, à Propos de la Théorie d'Einstein", *Revue Générale des Sciences Pures et Appliquées*, Volume 33, (1922), pp. 573-582; **and** Guillaume's introduction in H. Poincaré, *La Mécanique Nouvelle: Conférence, Mémoire et Note sur la Théorie de la Relativité / Introduction de Édouard Guillaume*, Gauthier-Villars, Paris, (1924), pp. V-XVI; **and** H. Bergson, *Durée et Simultanéité, à Propos de la Théorie d'Einstein*, English translation by L. Jacobson, *Duration and simultaneity, with Reference to Einstein's Theory*, The Library of Liberal Arts, Bobbs-Merrill, Indianapolis, (1965); which contains a bibliography at pages xliii-xlv. *See also:* P. Painlevé, "La Mécanique Classique et la Théorie de la Relativité", *Comptes rendus hebdomadaires des séances de L'Académie des sciences*, Volume 173, (1921), pp. 677-680. *See also:* S. Mohorovičić, "Raum, Zeit und Welt. II Teil", in K. Sapper, Editor, *Kritik und Fortbildung der Relativitätstheorie*, Akademische Druck- u. Verlagsanstalt, Graz, Volume 2, (1962), pp. 219-352, at 273-275. *See also:* K. Hentschel, *Interpretationen und Fehlinterpretationen der speziellen und der allgemeinen Relativitätstheorie durch Zeitgenossen Albert Einsteins*, Birkhäuser, Basel, Boston, Berlin, (1990). *See also:* A. Genovesi, *Il Carteggio tra Albert Einstein ed Edouard Guillaume. "Tempo Universale" e Teoria della Relativtà Ristretta nella Filosofia Francese Contemporanea*, Franco Angeli, Milano, (2000). *See also:* Letter from A. Einstein to E. Guillaume of 24 September 1917, *The Collected Papers of Albert Einstein*, Volume 8, Part A, Document 383, Princeton University Press, (1998). *See also:* Letter from E. Guillaume to A. Einstein of 3 October

1917, *The Collected Papers of Albert Einstein*, Volume 8, Part A, Document 385, Princeton University Press, (1998). *See also:* Letter from A. Einstein to E. Guillaume of 9 October 1917, *The Collected Papers of Albert Einstein*, Volume 8, Part A, Document 387, Princetone University Press, (1998). *See also:* Letter from E. Guillaume to A. Einstein of 17 October 1917, *The Collected Papers of Albert Einstein*, Volume 8, Part A, Document 392, Princeton University Press, (1998). *See also:* Letter from A. Einstein to E. Guillaume of 24 October 1917, *The Collected Papers of Albert Einstein*, Volume 8, Part A, Document 394, Princeton University Press, (1998). *See also:* Letter from E. Guillaume to A. Einstein of 25 January 1920, *The Collected Papers of Albert Einstein*, Volume 9, Document 280, Princeton University Press, (2004). *See also:* Letter from M. Grossmann to A. Einstein of 5 February 1920, *The Collected Papers of Albert Einstein*, Volume 9, Document 300, Princeton University Press, (2004). *See also:* Letter from A. Einstein to E. Guillaume of 9 February 1920, *The Collected Papers of Albert Einstein*, Volume 9, Document 305, Princeton University Press, (2004). *See also:* Letter from E. Guillaume to A. Einstein of 15 February 1920, *The Collected Papers of Albert Einstein*, Volume 9, Document 316, Princeton University Press, (2004). *See also:* Letter from A. Einstein to M. Grossmann of 27 February 1920, *The Collected Papers of Albert Einstein*, Volume 9, Document 330, Princeton University Press, (2004). *See also:* Letter from A. Einstein to P. Oppenheim of 29 April 1920, *The Collected Papers of Albert Einstein*, Volume 9, Document 399, Princeton University Press, (2004).

426. L. Jánossy, "Über die physikalische Interpretation der Lorentz-Transformation", *Annalen der Physik*, Series 6, Volume 11, (1953), pp. 293-322; **and** *Theory of Relativity Based on Physical Reality*, Akademiai Kiadó, Budapest, (1971). *See also:* S. J. Prokhovnic, *The Logic of Special Relativity*, Cambridge University Press, (1967). *See also:* K. Sapper, Editor, *Kritik und Fortbildung der Relativitätstheorie*, In Two Volumes, Akademische Druck- u. Verlagsanstalt, Graz, Austria, (1958/1962).

427. E. Guillaume's letter, translated by A. Reuterdahl, "Guillaume, Barred in Move To Debate Einstein, Calls Meeting Political Reunion", *Minneapolis Journal*, (14 May 1922), p. 14; reprinted with slight modifications, "The Origin of Einsteinism", *The New York Times*, (12 August 1923), Section 7, p. 8. *See also:* "Einstein Faces in Paris Grave Blow at Theory", *The Chicago Tribune*, (31 March 1922). *See also:* "Dr. Guillaume's Proofs of Einstein Theory's Fallacy Revealed to the Journal", *Minneapolis Journal*, (9 April 1922). *See also:* E. Guillaume, "Un Résultat des Discussions de la Théorie d'Einstein au Collège de France", *Revue Générale des Sciences Pures et Appliquées*, Volume 33, Number 11, (15 June 1922), pp. 322-324. *See also:* "Les Bases de la Physique moderne", *Archives des Sciences Physiques et Naturelles*, Series 4, Volume 43, (1917), pp. 5-21, 89-112, 185-198; **and** "Sur le Possibilité d'Exprimer la Théorie de la Relativité en Fonction du Temps Universel", *Archives des Sciences Physiques et Naturelles*, Series 4, Volume 44, (1917), pp. 48-52; **and** "La Théorie de la Relativité en Fonction du Temps Universel",

Archives des Sciences Physiques et Naturelles, Series 4, Volume 46, (1918), pp. 281-325; **and** "Sur la Théorie de la Relativité", *Archives des Sciences Physiques et Naturelles*, Series 5, Volume 1, (1919), pp. 246-251; **and** "Représentation et Mesure du Temps", *Archives des Sciences Physiques et Naturelles*, Series 5, Volume 2, (1920), pp. 125-146; **and** "La Théorie de la Relativité et sa Signification", *Revue de Métaphysique et de Morale*, Volume 27, (1920), pp. 423-469; **and** "Relativité et Gravitation", *Bulletin de la Société Vaudoise des Sciences Naturelles*, Volume 53, (1920), pp. 311-340; **and** "Les Bases de la Théorie de la Relativité", *Revue Générale des Sciences Pures et Appliquées*, (15 April 1920) pp. 200-210; **and** C. Willigens, "Représentation Géométrique du Temps Universel dans la Théorie de la Relativité Restreinte", *Archives des Sciences Physiques et Naturelles*, Series 5, Volume 2, (1920), p. 289; **and** E. Guillaume, *La Théorie de la Relativité. Résumé des Conférences Faites à l'Université de Lausanne au Semestre d'été 1920*, Rouge & Co., Lausanne, (1921); **and** E. Guillaume and C. Willigens, "Über die Grundlagen der Relativitätstheorie", *Physikalische Zeitschrift*, Volume 22, (1921), pp. 109-114; **and** E. Guillaume, "Graphische Darstellung der Optik bewegter Körper", *Physikalische Zeitschrift*, Volume 22, (1921), pp. 386-388; **and** Guillaume's Appendix II, "Temps Relatif et Temps Universel", in L. Fabre, *Une Nouvelle Figure du Monde: les Théories d'Einstein*, Second Edition, Payot, Paris, (1922); **and** E. Guillaume, "Y a-t-il une Erreur dans le PremierMémoire d'Einstein?", *Revue Générale des Sciences Pures et Appliquées*, Volume 33, (1922), pp. 5-10; **and** "La Question du Temps d'après M. Bergson, à Propos de la Théorie d'Einstein", *Revue Générale des Sciences Pures et Appliquées*, Volume 33, (1922), pp. 573-582; **and** Guillaume's introduction in H. Poincaré, *La Mécanique Nouvelle: Conférence, Mémoire et Note sur la Théorie de la Relativité / Introduction de Édouard Guillaume*, Gauthier-Villars, Paris, (1924), pp. V-XVI; **and** H. Bergson, *Durée et Simultanéité, à Propos de la Théorie d'Einstein*, English translation by L. Jacobson, *Duration and simultaneity, with Reference to Einstein's Theory*, The Library of Liberal Arts, Bobbs-Merrill, Indianapolis, (1965); which contains a bibliography at pages xliii-xlv. *See also:* P. Painlevé, "La Mécanique Classique et la Théorie de la Relativité", *Comptes rendus hebdomadaires des séances de L'Académie des sciences*, Volume 173, (1921), pp. 677-680. *See also:* S. Mohorovičić, "Raum, Zeit und Welt. II Teil", in K. Sapper, Editor, *Kritik und Fortbildung der Relativitätstheorie*, Akademische Druck- u. Verlagsanstalt, Graz, Volume 2, (1962), pp. 219-352, at 273-275. *See also:* K. Hentschel, *Interpretationen und Fehlinterpretationen der speziellen und der allgemeinen Relativitätstheorie durch Zeitgenossen Albert Einsteins*, Birkhäuser, Basel, Boston, Berlin, (1990). *See also:* A. Genovesi, *Il Carteggio tra Albert Einstein ed Edouard Guillaume. "Tempo Universale" e Teoria della Relativtà Ristretta nella Filosofia Francese Contemporanea*, Franco Angeli, Milano, (2000). *See also:* Letter from A. Einstein to E. Guillaume of 24 September 1917, *The Collected Papers of Albert Einstein*, Volume 8, Part A, Document 383, Princeton University Press, (1998). *See also:* Letter from E. Guillaume to A. Einstein of 3 October

1917, *The Collected Papers of Albert Einstein*, Volume 8, Part A, Document 385, Princeton University Press, (1998). *See also:* Letter from A. Einstein to E. Guillaume of 9 October 1917, *The Collected Papers of Albert Einstein*, Volume 8, Part A, Document 387, Princetone University Press, (1998). *See also:* Letter from E. Guillaume to A. Einstein of 17 October 1917, *The Collected Papers of Albert Einstein*, Volume 8, Part A, Document 392, Princeton University Press, (1998). *See also:* Letter from A. Einstein to E. Guillaume of 24 October 1917, *The Collected Papers of Albert Einstein*, Volume 8, Part A, Document 394, Princeton University Press, (1998). *See also:* Letter from E. Guillaume to A. Einstein of 25 January 1920, *The Collected Papers of Albert Einstein*, Volume 9, Document 280, Princeton University Press, (2004). *See also:* Letter from M. Grossmann to A. Einstein of 5 February 1920, *The Collected Papers of Albert Einstein*, Volume 9, Document 300, Princeton University Press, (2004). *See also:* Letter from A. Einstein to E. Guillaume of 9 February 1920, *The Collected Papers of Albert Einstein*, Volume 9, Document 305, Princeton University Press, (2004). *See also:* Letter from E. Guillaume to A. Einstein of 15 February 1920, *The Collected Papers of Albert Einstein*, Volume 9, Document 316, Princeton University Press, (2004). *See also:* Letter from A. Einstein to M. Grossmann of 27 February 1920, *The Collected Papers of Albert Einstein*, Volume 9, Document 330, Princeton University Press, (2004). *See also:* Letter from A. Einstein to P. Oppenheim of 29 April 1920, *The Collected Papers of Albert Einstein*, Volume 9, Document 399, Princeton University Press, (2004).

428. "Issue a Protest on Anti-Semitism", *The New York Times*, (17 January 1921), p. 10.

429. "Reuterdahl Gives Mathematic Lectures", *The Daily Cardinal* (University of Wisconsin, Madison), (11 March 1926). "Prof. Reuterdahl Talks Despite All Faculty Efforts", *The Daily Cardinal* (University of Wisconsin, Madison), (12 March 1926), Front Page. "St. Paulite Piqued by Badger Faculty", *The St. Paul Daily News*, Final Pink, (12 March 1926), Front Page. "Intolerance", *The St. Paul Daily News*, (13 March 1926), Front Page or page 2???. "Everything Fine, Reuterdahl Says of Badger Antics", *St. Paul Dispatch*, (13 March 1926), Front Page. "Reuterdahl Says He Had a 'Bully' Time in Madison", *The Minneapolis Sunday Tribune*, (14 March 1926). "Wisconsin U Mathematics Professors 'Act Like Children' Says Reuterdahl; Had a Fine Time", *The St. Paul Daily News*, (14 March 1926), Front Page. "Reuterdahl Takes Fling at Madison", *St. Paul Dispatch*, (19 March 1926), p. 17. "Intellectual Despotism Is Menace to Honest Research in Science, Dr. Reuterdahl Declares", *St. Paul Daily News*, (19 March 1926), p. 2.

430. "PROF. REUTERDAHL TALKS DESPITE ALL FACULTY EFFORTS: Instructors Place Auditorium in Darkness in Attempt to Stop Lecture", *The Daily Cardinal* (University of Wisconsin, Madison), (12 March 1926).

431. *Cf.* H. Goenner, "The Reaction to Relativity Theory in Germany, III: 'A Hundred Authors against Einstein", *The Attraction of Gravitation: New Studies in the History of General Relativity*, Birkhäuser, Boston, Basel, Berlin, (1993),

p. 250. J. Stark, *Die gegenwärtige Krisis in der Deutschen Physik*, Johann Ambrosius Barth, Leipzig, (1922), p. 16.

432. English translation from: P. W. Massing, *Rehearsal for Destruction: A Study of Political Anti-Semitism in Imperial Germany*, Howard Fertig, New York, (1967). p. 315.

433. "Prof. Einstein Here, Explains Relativity", *The New York Times*, (3 April 1921), pp. 1, 13, at 1.

434. E. Mach, *The Science of Mechanics*, Open Court, La Salle, Illinois, (1960), p. xxviii.

435. H. Dingler, *Die Grundlagen der Physik; synthetische Prinzipien der mathematischen Naturphilosophie*, Second Edition, Walter de Gruyter & Co., Berlin, (1923); **and** *Physik und Hypothese Versuch einer induktiven Wissenschaftslehre nebst einer kritischen Analyse der Fundamente der Relativitätstheorie*, Walter de Gruyter & Co., Berlin, Leipzig, (1921); **and** "Kritische Bemerkungen zu den Grundlagen der Relativitätstheorie", *Physikalische Zeitschrift*, Volume 21, (1920), pp. 668-669.

436. "The Anti-Einstein Campaign", *Scientific American*, (14 May 1921). *See also:* "Getting Back at Einstein", *The Literary Digest*, (4 June 1921).

437. A. Reuterdahl, quoted in "The Pro-Truth Campaign", *The Dearborn Independent*, (18 June 1921).

438. Kennefick cites: Note 9, "G. Beck, *Z. Phys.* **33**, 713 (1925); O. R. Baldwin, G. B. Jeffery, *Proc. Phys. Soc. London, Sect. A.* **111**, 95 (1926)"; **and** Note 5, "L. Infeld, *Quest: An Autobiography*, Chelsea, New York, (1980)", p. 277.

439. *Scientific American*, Volume 1, Number 42, (9 July 1846), p. 3.

440. A. Reuterdahl, "The Origin of Einsteinism", *The New York Times*, Section 7, (12 August 1923), p. 8. Reply to F. D. Bond's response, "Reuterdahl and the Einstein Theory", *The New York Times*, Section 7, (15 July 1923), p. 8. Response to A. Reuterdahl, "Einstein's Predecessors", *The New York Times*, Section 8, (3 June 1923), p. 8. Which was a reply to F. D. Bond, "Relating to Relativity", *The New York Times*, Section 9, (13 May 1923), p. 8. Which was a response to H. A. Houghton, "A Newtonian Duplication?", *The New York Times*, Section 1, Part 1, (21 April 1923), p. 10.

441. F. D. Bond, 24 Manhattan Avenue, New York City, letter to A. Reuterdahl dated 10 July 1923, Department of Special Collections, O'Shaughnessy-Frey Library, University of St. Thomas, Minnesota.

442. L. D. Brandeis, M. I. Urofsky and D. W. Levy, Editors, *Letters of Louis D. Brandeis* Volume 4, State University of New York Press, Albany, New York, (1975), pp. 536-537.

443. H. A. Houghton, "A Newtonian Duplication?", *The New York Times*, Section 1, Part 1, (21 April 1923), p. 10.

444. H. Bernstein, *The Truth about 'The Protocols of Zion'*, Ktav Publishing House, New York, (1971), pp. 43-44.

445. Letters from L. Brandeis to J. W. Mack, *et al.* of 26 November 1918, 22 March 1920, 17 November 1920 and 18 November 1920, L. D. Brandeis, M.

I. Urofsky and D. W. Levy, Editors, *Letters of Louis D. Brandeis* Volume 4, State University of New York Press, Albany, New York, (1975), pp. 365, 452-453, 506-508.

446. *The Protocols of the Wise Men of Zion*, Beckwith, New York, (1920). H. Bernstein, *The Truth about 'The Protocols of Zion'*, Ktav Publishing House, New York, (1971), p. 55.

447. L. Marshall to J. Spargo, *Louis Marshall: Champion of Liberty; Selected Papers and Addresses*, Volume 1, The Jewish Publication Society of America, Philadelphia, (1957), pp. 351-353.

448. B. Brasol, *The Protocols and World Revolution, Including a Translation and Analysis of the "Protocols of the Meetings of the Zionist Men of Wisdom"*, Small, Maynard & Company, Boston, (1920); **and** *Socialism Vs. Civilization*, C. Scribner's Sons, New York, (1920); **and** *The World at the Cross Roads*, Small, Mayhard & Co., Boston, (1921); **and** *The Balance Sheet of Sovietism*, Duffield, New York, (1922).

449. S. G. Marks, "Destroying the Agents of Modernity: Russian Antisemitism", *How Russia Shaped the Modern World*, Chapter 5, Princeton University Press, (2003), pp. 140-175; notes 354-358.

450. Houghton's letter is found in the Department of Special Collections, University of St. Thomas, St. Paul, Minnesota.

451. A. Hertzberg, *The Jews in America: Four Centuries of an Uneasy Encounter: A History*, Simon and Schuster, New York, (1989), p. 218.

452. A. Reuterdahl, "'Kinertia' Versus Einstein", *The Dearborn Independent*, 30 April 1921, pp. 2 and 14.

453. Letter from T. Vetter to A. Einstein of 28 January 1919, *The Collected Papers of Albert Einstein*, Volume 9, Document 4, Princeton University Press, (2004).

454. D. K. Buchwald, *et al.*, Editors, *The Collected Papers of Albert Einstein*, Volume 9, Document 312, Princeton University Press, (2004), pp. 426-427, at 427, note 3.

455. *Deutsche Zeitung*, (17 February 1920), p. 5. *Deutsche Zeitung*, (19 February 1920).

456. E. A. Ross, "The East European Hebrews", *The Old World in the New: The Significance of Past and Present Immigration to the American People*, Chapter 7, The Century Co., New York, (1914), pp. 143-167. *See also:* B. J. Hendrick, "The Jews in America: I How They Came to This Country", *The World's Work*, Volume 44, Number 2, (December, 1922), pp. 144-161; **and** "The Jews in America: II Do the Jews Dominate American Finance?", *The World's Work*, Volume 44, Number 3, (January, 1923), pp. 266-286; **and** "The Jews in America: III The Menace of the Polish Jew", *The World's Work*, Volume 44, Number 4, (February, 1923), pp. 366-377; **and** "Radicalism among the Polish Jews", *The World's Work*, Volume 44, Number 6, (April, 1923), pp. 591-601.

457. D. K. Buchwald, *et al.*, Editors, *The Collected Papers of Albert Einstein*, Volume 9, Document 311, Princeton University Press, (2004), pp. 425-426, at

426, note 2.

458. *Cf.* M. Janssen, *et al*, Editors, *The Collected Papers of Albert Einstein*, Volume 7, Princeton University Press, (2002), pp. 284-288.
459. Letter from H. T. Cohn to A. Einstein of 12 February 1920, English translation by A. Hentschel, *The Collected Papers of Albert Einstein*, Volume 9, Document 309, Princeton University Press, (2004), pp. 258-259, at 258.
460. Letter from H. T. Cohn to A. Einstein of 12 February 1920, English translation by A. Hentschel, *The Collected Papers of Albert Einstein*, Volume 9, Document 309, Princeton University Press, (2004), pp. 258-259, at 258.
461. Letter from Eduard Meyer to A. Einstein of 13 February 1920, A. Hentschel, translator, *The Collected Papers of Albert Einstein*, Volume 9, Document 312, Princeton University Press, (2004), p. 260.
462. C. Kirsten and Hans-Jürgen Treder, Editors, *Albert Einstein in Berlin, 1913-1933 : Teil I, Darstellung und Dokumente*, Akademie-Verlag, Berlin, (1979), p. 202.
463. C. Kirsten and Hans-Jürgen Treder, Editors, *Albert Einstein in Berlin, 1913-1933 : Teil I, Darstellung und Dokumente*, Akademie-Verlag, Berlin, (1979), p. 201.
464. P. Michelmore, *Einstein: Profile of the Man*, Dodd, Mead, New York, (1962), p. 88.
465. M. Janssen, *et al.*, Editors, *The Collected Papers of Albert Einstein*, Volume 7, Princeton University Press, (2002), p. 348, note 3.
466. M. Janssen, *et al.*, Editors, *The Collected Papers of Albert Einstein*, Volume 7, Princeton University Press, (2002), p. 348, note 3.
467. H. Goenner, "The Reaction to Relativity Theory. I: The Anti-Einstein Campaign in Germany in 1920", *Science in Context*, Volume 6, Number 1, (1993), pp. 107-133, at 112.
468. J. Riem, "Amerika über Einstein", *Deutsche Zeitung*, (1 July 1921).
469. J. Jürgenson, "Es lebe die Theorie - oder das Recht auf freie Phantasie", *Die lukrativen Lügen der Wissenschaft*, Ewert, (1998), ISBN: 389478699X.

URL:<http://www.unglaublichkeiten.info/unglaublichkeiten/htmlphp/erfind ungeneslebedietheorie.html>

This is likely a reference to: S. Mohorovičić, "Raum, Zeit und Welt. II Teil", in K. Sapper, Editor, *Kritik und Fortbildung der Relativitätstheorie*, Akademische Druck- u. Verlagsanstalt, Graz, Volume 2, (1962), pp. 219-352.
470. S. Mohorovičić, "Raum, Zeit und Welt", in two parts in K. Sapper, Editor, *Kritik und Fortbildung der Relativitätstheorie*, Akademische Druck- u. Verlagsanstalt, Graz, (1958/1962), Part 1 in Volume 1, (1958), pp. 168-281; Part 2 in Volume 2, (1962), pp. 219-352, at 317, note 89.
471. S. Mohorovičić, "Raum, Zeit und Welt", in two parts in K. Sapper, Editor, *Kritik und Fortbildung der Relativitätstheorie*, Akademische Druck- u. Verlagsanstalt, Graz, (1958/1962), Part 1 in Volume 1, (1958), pp. 168-281; Part 2 in Volume 2, (1962), pp. 219-352, at 273.

766 Albert Einstein: The Incorrigible Racist

472. S. Mohorovičić, *Die Einsteinsche Relativitätstheorie und ihr mathematischer, physikalischer und philosophischer Charakter*, Walter de Gruyter & Co., Berlin, Leipzig, (1923), pp. 52-53.

473. "Einstein Denies Part in Book on Hitlerism", *The New York Times*, (4 September 1933), p. 2.

474. "Price Declared Put on Einstein's Head", *The New York Times*, (7 September 1933), p. 8. "Wants Only Peace", *The New York Times*, (11 September 1933), p. 9.

475. A. v. Brunn, quoted in: K. Hentschel, Ed., A. Hentschel, Ed. Ass. and Trans., *Physics and National Socialism: An Anthology of Primary Sources*, Birkhäuser, Basel, Boston, Berlin, (1996), p. 11.

476. From the preface of *Hundert Autoren gegen Einstein* translated by: H. Goenner, "The Reaction to Relativity Theory in Germany, III: 'A Hundred Authors against Einstein'", J. Earman, M. Janssen, J. D. Norton, Eds., *The Attraction of Gravitation: New Studies in the History of General Relativity*, Birkhäuser, Boston, Basel, Berlin, (1993), p. 251.

477. A. Pais, *Subtle is the Lord*, Oxford University Press, New York, (1982), p. 510.

478. H. Dingle, in his introduction to H. Bergson's, *Duration and Simultaneity*, Bobbs-Merrill Company, Inc., Indianapolis, New York, Kansas City, (1965), p. xlii. *See also*: H. Dingle, *Science at the Crossroads*, Martin, Brian and O'Keefe Ltd., London, (1972).

479. A. Einstein, "Why do They Hate the Jews?", *Collier's*, Volume 102, (26 November 1938); reprinted in *Ideas and Opinions*, Crown, New York, (1954), p. 192.

480. P. A. Bucky, Einstein, and A. G. Weakland, *The Private Albert Einstein*, Andrews and McMeel, Kansas City, (1992), p. 87.

481. A. Hitler, translated by S. Attanasio, *Hitler's Secret Book*, Bramhall House, New York, (1962), p. 211.

482. "3379 (XXX). Elimination of All Forms of Racial Discrimination", General Assembly—Thirtieth Session, Resolutions adopted on the reports of the Third Committee, 2400th Plenary Meeting, (10 November 1975), pp. 83-84. URL:

http://www.un.org/documents/ga/res/30/ares30.htm

Confer: Zionism & Racism: Proceedings of an International Symposium, International Organization for the Elimination of All Forms of Racial Discrimination, Tripoli, (1977), pp. 249-250. *Cf.* F. A. Sayegh, *Zionism: A Form of Racism And Racial Discrimination" Four Statements Made at the U.N. General Assembly*, Office of the Permanent Observer of the Palestine Liberation Organization to the United Nations, (1976), pp. 40-41. URL:

http://www.ameu.org/uploads/sayegh_march1_03.pdf

After the fall of the Soviet Union, which had long sponsored racial integration (*see:* "Circus" a motion picture released in 1936 directed by Grigori Alexandrov starring Lyubov Orlova), the U. N. withdrew this resolution under great pressure from Zionists.

483. "3379 (XXX). Elimination of All Forms of Racial Discrimination", General Assembly—Thirtieth Session, Resolutions adopted on the reports of the Third Committee, 2400th Plenary Meeting, (10 November 1975), pp. 83-84. URL:

http://www.un.org/documents/ga/res/30/ares30.htm

Confer: Zionism & Racism: Proceedings of an International Symposium, International Organization for the Elimination of All Forms of Racial Discrimination, Tripoli, (1977), pp. 249-250. *Cf.* F. A. Sayegh, *Zionism: A Form of Racism And Racial Discrimination" Four Statements Made at the U.N. General Assembly*, Office of the Permanent Observer of the Palestine Liberation Organization to the United Nations, (1976), pp. 40-41. URL:

http://www.ameu.org/uploads/sayegh_march1_03.pdf

After the fall of the Soviet Union, which had long sponsored racial integration (*see:* "Circus" a motion picture released in 1936 directed by Grigori Alexandrov starring Lyubov Orlova), the U. N. withdrew this resolution under great pressure from Zionists.

484. F. A. Sayegh, *Zionism: A Form of Racism And Racial Discrimination" Four Statements Made at the U.N. General Assembly*, Office of the Permanent Observer of the Palestine Liberation Organization to the United Nations, (1976), pp. 51-52.

<http://www.ameu.org/uploads/sayegh_march1_03.pdf>

485. Preface, *Zionism & Racism: Proceedings of an International Symposium*, International Organization for the Elimination of All Forms of Racial Discrimination, Tripoli, (1977), p. vii.

486. A. Einstein, *The World As I See It*, Citadel, New York, (1993), pp. 92-97, 103, 106, 108.

487. P. W. Massing, *Rehearsal for Destruction: A Study of Political Anti-Semitism in Imperial Germany*, Howard Fertig, New York, (1967), pp. 303-305.

488. B. Borochov, *Nationalism and Class Struggle*, New York, (1935), pp. 135-136, 183-205; quoted in A. Hertzberg, *The Zionist Idea*, Harper Torchbooks, New York, (1959), pp. 355-360, at 356.

489. T. Herzl, English translation by H. Zohn, R. Patai, Editor, *The Complete Diaries of Theodor Herzl*, Volume 1, Herzl Press, New York, (1960), p. 183.

490. T. Herzl, *A Jewish State: An Attempt at a Modern Solution of the Jewish Question*, The Maccabæan Publishing Co., New York, (1904), pp. 23, 99.

491. "Prof. Einstein Here, Explains Relativity", *The New York Times*, (3 April 1921), pp. 1, 13, at 1.

492. *See, for example*, J. Goebbels, "Der Führer", *Aufsätze auf der Kampfzeit*, Zentralverlag der NSDAP, Munich, (1935), pp. 214-216; **and** "Goldene Worte für einen Diktator und für solche, die es werden wollen", *Der Angriff*, (1 September 1932); reprinted in: *Wetterleuchten: Aufsätze aus der Kampfzeit*, Zentralverlag der NSDAP., Franz Eher Nachf., München, (1939), pp. 325-327. On the Zionists' quest to find a "great man" to be their "dictator", *see:* N. Goldman, "Zionismus und nationale Bewegung", *Der Jude*, Volume 5, Number 4, (1920-1921), pp. 237-242, at 240-242; which was part of a series including: "Zionismus und nationale Bewegung", *Der Jude*, Volume 5, Number 1, (1920-1921), pp. 45-47; and "Zionismus und nationale Bewegung", *Der Jude*, Volume 5, Number 7, (1920-1921), pp. 423-425.

493. *Cf.* Schlomo Ginossar, a. k. a. Simon Ginsburg, a. k. a. Salomon Ginzberg, "Early Days", *The Hebrew University of Jerusalem, 1925-1950*, Universitah ha-'uvrit bi-Yerushalayim, Jerusalem, (1950), pp. 71-74, at 73. *See also:* J. Stachel, *Einstein from 'B' to 'Z'*, Birkhäuser, Boston, (2002), p. 79, note 41.

494. *See, for example:* A. Lynch, *The Case Against Einstein*, P. Allan, London, (1932). H. Dingler, *Die Grundlagen der Physik; synthetische Prinzipien der mathematischen Naturphilosophie*, Second Edition, Walter de Gruyter & Co., Berlin, (1923); **and** *Physik und Hypothese Versuch einer induktiven Wissenschaftslehre nebst einer kritischen Analyse der Fundamente der Relativitätstheorie*, Walter de Gruyter & Co., Berlin, Leipzig, (1921); **and** "Kritische Bemerkungen zu den Grundlagen der Relativitätstheorie", *Physikalische Zeitschrift*, Volume 21, (1920), pp. 668-669. H. Nordenson, *Relativity, Time and Reality: A Critical Investigation of the Einstein Theory of Relativity from a Logical Point of View*, Allen and Unwin, London, (1969).

495. L. Essen, "Relativity — Joke or Swindle?", *Electronics and Wireless World*, (February, 1988), pp. 126-127. URL: <http://www.cfpf.org.uk/articles/scientists/essen.html>

496. J. T. Blankart, "Relativity or Interdependence", *Catholic World*, Volume 112, (February, 1921), pp. 588- 610, at 606.

497. K. Sugimoto, translated by B. Harshav, *Albert Einstein, A Photographic Biography*, Schocken Books, New York, (1989), p. 74.

498. P. Weyland, "Einsteins Relativitätstheorie—eine wissenschaftliche Massensuggestion", *Tägliche Rundschau*, (August 6, 1920).

499. E. Gehrcke, "Die gegen die Relativitätstheorie erhobenen Einwände", *Die Naturwissenschaften*, Volume 1, Number 3, (1 January 1913), pp. 62-66; republished *Kritik der Relativitätstheorie*, Hermann Meusser, Berlin, (1924), pp. 20-28, "Massensuggestion" appears at page 28; Gerhcke also delivered a lecture, which Einstein attended, on 24 August 1920 in the Berlin Philharmonic, *Die Relativitätstheorie eine wissenschaftliche Massensuggestion*, Arbeitsgemeinschaft Deutscher Naturforscher zur Erhaltung reiner

Wissenschaft, Berlin, (1920); republished in *Kritik der Relativitätstheorie*, pp. 54-68. *See also: Die Massensuggestion der Relativitätstheorie*, Hermann Meusser, Berlin, (1924). The editors of *The Collected Papers of Albert Einstein*, Volume 7, Princeton University Press, (2002), p. 102; cite the earliest appearance by Gehrcke of this charge as: E. Gehrcke, Ed., P. Drude, *Lehrbuch der Optik*, Third Edition, S. Hirzel, Leipzig, (1912), p. 470. Reference is also had to this fact in H. Goenner, "The Reaction to Relativity Theory. I: The Anti-Einstein Campaign in Germany in 1920", *Science in Context*, Volume 6, Number 1, (1993), pp. 107-133.

500. B. Thüring, "Albert Einsteins Umsturzversuch der Physik und seine inneren Möglichkeiten und Ursachen", *Forschungen zur Judenfrage*, Volume 4, (1940), pp. 134-162. Republished as: *Albert Einsteins Umsturzversuch der Physik und seine inneren Möglichkeiten und Ursachen*, Dr. Georg Lüttke Verlag, Berlin, (1941).

501. Č. Dvořák quoted in J. T. Blackmore, *Ernst Mach: His Work, Life, and Influence*, University of California Press, Berkeley, Los Angeles, London, (1972), p. 279.

502. H. Goenner, "The Reaction to Relativity Theory in Germany, III: 'A Hundred Authors against Einstein'", J. Earman, M. Janssen, J. D. Norton, Editors, *The Attraction of Gravitation: New Studies in the History of General Relativity*, Birkhäuser, Boston, Basel, Berlin, (1993), p. 249.

503. J. Stark, *Die gegenwärtige Krisis in der Deutschen Physik*, Johann Ambrosius Barth, Leipzig, (1922), Forward and pp. 6-16.

504. "Einstein's Triumph", *The New York Times*, (13 April 1923), p. 16.

505. *See:* C. Schönbeck, "Albert Einstein und Philipp Lenard", *Schriften der mathematisch-naturwissenschaftliche Klasse der Heidelberger Akademie der Wissenschaften*, Volume 8, (2000), pp. 1-42, at 37.

506.C. Brown, *The New York Times*, (8 July 1921), p. 9.

507. "Prof. Einstein Here, Explains Relativity", *The New York Times*, (3 April 1921), pp. 1, 13, at 1.

508. A. Einstein to H. Zangger of 24 December 1919, English translation by A. Hentschel, *The Collected Papers of Albert Einstein*, Volume 9, Document 233, Princeton University Press, (2004), pp. 197-198, at 197.

509. A. Einstein, *The Born-Einstein Letters*, Walker and Company, New York, (1971), p. 188.

510. J. Klatzkin, *Krisis und Entscheidung im Judentum; der Probleme des modernen Judentums*, Jüdischer Verlag, Berlin, (1921). Heinrich Class under the pseudonym Daniel Frymann, *Wenn ich der Kaiser wär': politische Wahrheiten und Notwendigkeiten*, Dieterich, Leipzig, (1912); English translation, R. S. Levy, "If I were the Kaiser / Daniel Freymann", *Antisemitism in the Modern World: An Anthology of Texts*, Chapter 14, D.C. Heath, Toronto, (1991).

511. T. Lessing, *Der jüdische Selbsthaß*, Zionistischer Bücherbund, Berlin, (1930).

512. P. Lenard, *Deutsche Physik in vier Bänden*, J. F. Lehmann, München, (1936-1937); **and** *Philipp Lenard, der deutsche Naturforscher: sein Kampf um nordische Forschung: Reichssiegerarbeit*, J. F. Lehmanns Verlag, München, (1937). J. Stark and W. Müller, *Jüdische und deutsche Physik, Vorträge zur Eröffnung des Kolloquiums für theoretische Physik an der Universität München*, Helingsche Verlagsanstalt, (1941). *See also:* P. Lenard and J. Stark, "Hitlergeist und Wissenschaft", *Großdeutsche Zeitung. Tageszeitung für nationale und soziale Politik und Wirtschaft*, Volume 1, Number 81, (8 May 1924), pp. 1-2; reprinted *Nationalsozialistische Monatshefte*, Volume 7, Number 71, (February, 1936), pp. 110-111; annotated English translation, K. Hentschel, "Philipp Lenard & Johannes Stark: The Hitler Spirit and Science [May 8, 1924]" *Physics and National Socialism: An Anthology of Primary Sources*, Basel, Boston, Birkhäuser, (1996), pp. 7-10; which book also contains numerous other Nazi-era texts in English translation.

513. *Cf.* C. Weizmann, *Trial and Error: The Autobiography of Chaim Weizmann*, Harper & Brothers, New York, (1949), p. 35.

514. J. B. Agus, *The Meaning of Jewish History*, Volume 2, Abelard-Schuman, New York, (1963), pp. 407-408. Agus cites: A. Leroy-Beaulieu, *Israel among the Nations: A Study of the Jews and Antisemitism*, G.P. Putnam's sons, New York, W. Heinemann, London, (1895), pp. 45, 131, 134; and T. Mommsen, *Auch ein Wort über unser Judenthum*, Weidmannsche Buchhandlung, Berlin, (1880), pp. 5, 7, 15-16.

515. M. Hess, English translation by M. Waxman, *Rome and Jerusalem: A Study in Jewish Nationalism*, Bloch, New York, (1918/1943), pp. 17-18, 24.

516. A. Einstein, *The World As I See It*, Citadel, New York, (1993), p. 98.

517. Letter from A. Einstein to H. Bergman of 5 November 1919, English translation by A. Hentschel, *The Collected Papers of Albert Einstein*, Volume 9, Document 155, Princeton University Press, (2004), pp. 132-133, at 132. *See also:* H. N. Bialik, "Bialik on the Hebrew University", in A. Hertzberg, *The Zionist Idea*, Harper Torchbooks, New York, (1959), pp. 281-288, at 284-285.

518. P. A. Bucky, Einstein, and A. G. Weakland, *The Private Albert Einstein*, Andrews and McMeel, Kansas City, (1992), p. 88.

519. Letter from A. Einstein to H. Bergman of 5 November 1919, English translation by A. Hentschel, *The Collected Papers of Albert Einstein*, Volume 9, Document 155, Princeton University Press, (2004), pp. 132-133, at 132.

520. M. Born, *The Born-Einstein Letters*, Walker and Company, New York, (1971), p. 16.

521. A. Einstein, English translation by A. Engel, *The Collected Papers of Albert Einstein*, Volume 7, Document 35, Princeton University Press, (2002), pp. 156-157.

522. M. Winteler-Einstein, English translation by A. Beck, "Albert Einstein—A Biographical Sketch", *The Collected Papers of Albert Einstein*, Volume 1, Princeton University Press, (1987), pp. xv-xxii, at xx.

523. Letter from A. Einstein to P. Ehrenfest of 8 November 1919, English translation by A. Hentschel, *The Collected Papers of Albert Einstein*, Volume

9, Document 160, Princeton University Press, (2004), pp. 135-136, at 136.

524. Josephus, "Flavius Josephus Against Apion", *The Works of Flavius Josephus: Comprising the Antiquities of the Jews; a History of the Jewish Wars; and Life of Flavius Josephus, Written by Himself*, Book 2, S. S. Scranton Co., Hartford, Connecticutt, (1916), pp. 917-918.

525. A. Hitler, *The Speeches of Adolf Hitler April 1922-August 1939*, Volume 1, Howard Fertig, New York, (1969), pp. 30-31.

526. A. Hitler, *The Speeches of Adolf Hitler April 1922-August 1939*, Volume 1, Howard Fertig, New York, (1969), p. 699.

527. P. A. Bucky, Einstein, and A. G. Weakland, *The Private Albert Einstein*, Andrews and McMeel, Kansas City, (1992), pp. 32, 110, 116-117.

528. It should be noted that Arnold Sommerfeld stated at the end of 1915, that Einstein was the greatest spirit since Gauss and Newton. *See:* Letter from A. Sommerfeld to K. Schwarzschild of 28 December 1915, Niedersächische Staats- und Universitätsbibliothek Göttingen, Cod. Ms. K. Schwarzschild 743. Sommerfeld was one of the first to profit by promoting Einstein while demeaning the deceased Poincaré in Sommerfeld's annotations for *Das Relativitätsprinzip*, B. G. Teubner, Berlin, Leipzig, (1913)—a book published shortly after Poincaré died, which failed to include any of Poincaré's works, but obviously helped to promote Sommerfeld.

529. P. A. Bucky, Einstein, and A. G. Weakland, *The Private Albert Einstein*, Andrews and McMeel, Kansas City, (1992), p. 31.

530. E. K. Dühring, *Die Judenfrage als Racen-, Sitten- und Culturfrage: mit einer weltgeschichtlichen Antwort*, H. Reuther, Karlsruhe, (1881); English translation by A. Jacob, *Eugen Dühring on the Jews*, Nineteen Eighty Four Press, Brighton, England, (1997), pp. 96-97.

531. Letter from P. Ehrenfest to A. Einstein of 9 December 1919, English translation by A. Hentschel, *The Collected Papers of Albert Einstein*, Volume 9, Document 203, Princeton University Press, (2004), pp. 173-175, at 174.

532. N. Syrkin, under the nom de plume "Ben Elieser", *Die Judenfrage und der socialistische Judenstaat*, Steiger, Bern, (1898); English translation in A. Hertzberg, *The Zionist Idea*, Harper Torchbooks, New York, (1959), pp. 333-350, at 344.

533. A. A. Roback, *Jewish Influence in Modern Thought*, Sci-Art Publishers, Harvard Square, Cambridge, Massachusetts, (1929), pp. 237-238, 245-246, 250-251.

534. D. Bronder, *Bevor Hitler kam: Eine historische Studie*, Hans Pfeiffer Verlag, Hannover, (1964), p. 204 (p. 211 in the 1974 edition). H. Kardel, *Adolf Hitler, Begründer Israels*, Verlag Marva, Genf, (1974); English translation *Adolf Hitler: Founder of Israel*, Modjeskis' Society Dedicated to Preservation of Cultures, San Diego, (1997), pp. 4, 73.

535. L. Roth, "Jewish Thought in the Modern World", *The Legacy of Israel*, Clarendon Press, Oxford, (1927), pp. 433-463 at 463.

536. L. Pinsker, "Auto-Emancipation", in A. Hertzberg, *The Zionist Idea*, Harper Torchbooks, New York, (1959), pp. 181-198, at 193. H. N. Bialik,

"Bialik on the Hebrew University", in A. Hertzberg, *The Zionist Idea*, Harper Torchbooks, New York, (1959), pp. 281-288, at 284. A. D. Gordon, *Kitve A. D. Gordon*, In Five Volumes, Tel-Aviv, ha-Va'ad ha-merkazi shel mifleget ha-Po'el ha-tsa'ir, (1927-1930), parts translated to English in A. Hertzberg, *The Zionist Idea*, Harper Torchbooks, New York, (1959), pp. 371-386, at 376. S. H. Landau, *Kithe*, Warsaw, (1935), pp. 36-43; translated to English in A. Hertzberg, *The Zionist Idea*, Harper Torchbooks, New York, (1959), pp. 434-439, at 437-438.

537. I. Zollschan, "The Cultural Value of the Jewish Race", *Jewish Questions: Three Lectures*, New York, Bloch Pub. Co., (1914), pp. 3-19.

538. A. Einstein, English translation by A. Engel, *The Collected Papers of Albert Einstein*, Volume 7, Document 35, Princeton University Press, (2002), pp. 156-157.

539. Letter from V. G. Ehrenberg to A. Einstein of 23 November 1919, English translation by A. Hentschel, *The Collected Papers of Albert Einstein*, Volume 9, Document 173, Princeton University Press, (2004), p. 145.

540. L. D. Brandeis, M. I. Urofsky and D. W. Levy, Editors, *Letters of Louis D. Brandeis* Volume 4, State University of New York Press, Albany, New York, (1975), pp. 536-537.

541. A. Sterling, *The Jew and Civilization*, Aetco, New York, (1924), pp. 202-203.

542. A. Sterling, *The Jew and Civilization*, Aetco, New York, (1924), pp. 221-222.

543. A. Einstein, translated by A. Harris, "The Disarmament Conference of 1932. I." *The World As I See It*, Citadel, New York, (1993), pp. 59-60.

544. Letter from A. Einstein to H. A. Lorentz of 12 January 1920, English translation by A. Hentschel, *The Collected Papers of Albert Einstein*, Volume 9, Document 256, Princeton University Press, (2004), pp. 214-215, at 214.

545. A. Einstein, *The World As I See It*, Citadel, New York, (1993), p. 109.

546. P. A. Bucky, Einstein, and A. G. Weakland, *The Private Albert Einstein*, Andrews and McMeel, Kansas City, (1992), pp. 88-89.

547. P. A. Bucky, Einstein, and A. G. Weakland, *The Private Albert Einstein*, Andrews and McMeel, Kansas City, (1992), pp. 107-108.

548. *Cf.* K. J. Herrmann, "Historical Perspectives on Political Zionism and Antisemitism", *Zionism & Racism: Proceedings of an International Symposium*, International Organization for the Elimination of All Forms of Racial Discrimination, Tripoli, (1977), pp. 197-208.

549. J. Wellhausen, *Sketch of the History of Israel and Judah*, Third Edition, Adam and Charles Black, London, (1891), pp. 201-203.

550. J. Klatzkin, *Tehumim: Ma'amarim*, Devir, Berlin, (1925). English translation in J. B. Agus, *The Meaning of Jewish History*, Volume 2, Abelard-Schuman, New York, (1963), pp. 425-426.

551. K. J. Herrmann, "Historical Perspectives on Political Zionism and Antisemitism", *Zionism & Racism: Proceedings of an International Symposium*, International Organization for the Elimination of All Forms of

Racial Discrimination, Tripoli, (1977), pp. 197-210, at 204-205. A lengthy quotation from Klatzkin, in English translation, appears in: M. Menuhin, *The Decadence of Judaism in Our Time*, Exposition Press, New York, (1965), pp. 482-483.

552. M. Bar-Ilan, *Kitve Rabi Me'ir Bar-Ilan*, Volume 1, Mosad ha-Rav Kuk, Jerusalem, (1950), pp. 5-16; English translation in A. Hertzberg, *The Zionist Idea*, Harper Torchbooks, New York, (1959), pp. 548-555, at 548.

553. *Moed Katan 17a*, Rabbi Y. S. Schorr, *et al.*, Editors, "Tractate Moed Katan", *Talmud Bavli: the Schottenstein edition: the Gemara: the classic Vilna edition, with an annotated, interpretive elucidation, as an aid to Talmud study / elucidated by a team of Torah scholars under the general editorship of Hersh Goldwurm and Nosson Scherman.*, Volume 21, Mesorah Publications, Ltd., Brooklyn, New York, (1999), p. 17a[2].

554. Mo'ed Katan, Rabbi I. Epstein, Editor, "Seder Mo'ed", *The Babylonian Talmud*, Volume 14, The Soncino Press, (1938), p. 107.

555. A. Einstein, translated by A. Engel, *The Collected Papers of Albert Einstein*, Volume 7, Document 29, Princeton University Press, (2002), pp. 110-111.

556. J. Stachel, "Einstein's Jewish Identity", *Einstein from 'B' to 'Z'*, Birkhäuser, Boston, Basel, Berlin, (2002), pp. 57-83, at 68.

557. A. Einstein to J. Winteler, English translation by A. Beck, *The Collected Papers of Albert Einstein*, Volume 1, Document 115, Princeton University Press, (1987), pp. 176-177, at 177.

558. A. Einstein, English translation by A. Beck, *The Collected Papers of Albert Einstein*, Volume 5, Document 499, Princeton University Press, (1995), pp. 373-374, at 374.

559. R. Romain, *La Conscience de l'Europe*, Volume 1, pp. 696ff. English translation from A. Fölsing, *Albert Einstein: A Biography*, Viking, New York, (1997), pp. 365-367. *See also:* Letter from A. Einstein to R. Romain of 15 September 1915, *The Collected Papers of Albert Einstein*, Volume 8, Document 118, Princeton University Press, (1998); **and** Letter from A. Einstein to R. Romain of 22 August 1917, *The Collected Papers of Albert Einstein*, Volume 8, Document 374, Princeton University Press, (1998).

560. J. Bacque, *Other Losses: An Investigation into the Mass Deaths of German Prisoners at the Hands of the French and Americans after World War II*, Stoddart,Toronto, (1989).

561. Letter from A. Einstein to Paul Ehrenfest of 22 March 1919, English translation by A. Hentschel, *The Collected Papers of Albert Einstein*, Volume 9, Document 10, Princeton Univsersity Press, (2004), pp. 9-10, at 10.

562. T. Herzl, *A Jewish State: An Attempt at a Modern Solution of the Jewish Question*, The Maccabæan Publishing Co., New York, (1904), pp. 5-6, 25, 68, 93.

563. M. Born, *The Born-Einstein Letters*, Walker and Company, New York, (1971), p. 16.

564. English translation in: K. Polkehn, "The Secret Contacts: Zionism and Nazi Germany, 1933-1941", *Journal of Palestine Studies*, Volume 5, Number 3/4, (Spring-Summer, 1976), pp. 54-82, at 59.

565. L. S. Dawidowicz, "The Zionist Federation of Germany Addresses the New German State", *A Holocaust Reader*, Behrman House, Inc., West Orange, New Jersey, (1976), pp. 150-155. *See also:* H. Tramer, Editor, S. Moses, *In zwei Welten: Siegfried Moses zum fünfundsiebzigsten Geburtstag*, Verlag Bitaon, Tel-Aviv, (1962), pp. 118.ff; cited in K. Polkehn, "The Secret Contacts: Zionism and Nazi Germany, 1933-1941", *Journal of Palestine Studies*, Volume 5, Number 3/4, (Spring-Summer, 1976), pp. 54-82, at 59.

566. English translation quoted from J. Stachel, "Einstein's Jewish Identity", *Einstein from 'B' to 'Z'*, Birkhäuser, Boston, Basel, Berlin, (2002), pp. 57-83, at 78. Stachel cites M. Besso, A. Einstein, *Correspondance, 1903-1955*, Hermann, Paris, (1972), p. 238.

567. Letter from A. Einstein to M. Besso of 12 December 1919, English translation by A. Hentschel, *The Collected Papers of Albert Einstein*, Volume 9, Document 207, Princeton University Press, (2004), pp. 178-179, at 179.

568. D. Brian, *The Unexpected Einstein: The Real Man Behind the Icon*, Wiley, Hoboken, New Jersey, (2005), p. 42.

569. A. Einstein, English translation by A. Engel, *The Collected Papers of Albert Einstein*, Volume 7, Document 34, Princeton University Press, (2002), pp. 153-155, at 153.

570. A. Einstein quoted in: H. Gutfreund, "Albert Einstein and the Hebrew University", J. Renn, Editor, *Albert Einstein Chief Engineer of the Universe: One Hundred Authors for Einstein*, Wiley-VCH, Berlin, (2005), pp. 314-318, at 316.

571. A. Einstein, English translation by A. Engel, *The Collected Papers of Albert Einstein*, Volume 7, Document 34, Princeton University Press, (2002), pp. 153-155, at 153.

572. A. Einstein, English translation by A. Engel, *The Collected Papers of Albert Einstein*, Volume 7, Document 34, Princeton University Press, (2002), pp. 153-155, at 153-154.

573. A. Einstein, English translation by A. Engel, *The Collected Papers of Albert Einstein*, Volume 7, Document 35, Princeton University Press, (2002), pp. 156-157.

574. Letter from A. Einstein to P. Nathan of 3 April 1920, *The Collected Papers of Albert Einstein*, Volume 9, Document 366, Princeton University Press, (2004), p. 492. Also: *The Collected Papers of Albert Einstein*, Volume 1, Princeton University Press, (1987), p. *lx*, note 44.

575. P. W. Massing, *Rehearsal for Destruction: A Study of Political Anti-Semitism in Imperial Germany*, Howard Fertig, New York, (1967), pp. 278-294.

576. P. A. Bucky, Einstein, and A. G. Weakland, *The Private Albert Einstein*, Andrews and McMeel, Kansas City, (1992), p. 88.

577. A. Einstein, *The World As I See It*, Citadel, New York, (1993), pp. 107-108.

578. A. Einstein, English translation by A. Engel, *The Collected Papers of Albert Einstein*, Volume 7, Document 37, Princeton University Press, (2002), p. 159.

579. A. Einstein quoted in A. Fölsing, English translation by E. Osers, *Albert Einstein, a Biography*, Viking, New York, (1997), p. 494; which cites speech to the *Central-Verein Deutscher Staatsbürger Jüdischen Glaubens*, in Berlin on 5 April 1920, in D. Reichenstein, *Albert Einstein. Sein Lebensbild und seine Weltanschauung*, Berlin, (1932). This letter from Einstein to the Central Association of German Citizens of the Jewish Faith of 5 April 1920 is reproduced in *The Collected Papers of Albert Einstein*, Volume 9, Document 368, Princeton University Press, (2004).

580. "Zeitschau", *Im deutschen Reich*, Volume 27, Number 3, (March, 1921), pp. 90-97, at 92.

581. D. K. Buchwald, *et al.*, Editors, *The Collected Papers of Albert Einstein*, Volume 7, Document 37, Princeton University Press, (2002), p. 304, note 8.

582. "Professor Einstein erklärt das „Sunday Expreß‘‘-Interview für gefälscht", *Central-Verein Zeitung*, Volume 10, Number 37, (11 September 1931), p. 443.

583. A. Einstein, translated by A. Harris, "The Disarmament Conference of 1932. I." *The World As I See It*, Citadel, New York, (1993), pp. 59-60.

584. J. Stachel, *Einstein from 'B' to 'Z'*, Birkhäuser, Boston, (2002), p. 79, note 41.

585. A. Einstein, "Jewish Nationalism and Anti-Semitism", *The Jewish Chronicle*, (17 June 1921), p. 16.

586. J. Stachel, "Einstein's Jewish Identity", *Einstein from 'B' to 'Z'*, Birkhäuser, Boston, (2002), p. 65. Stachel cites, *About Zionism: Speeches and Letters*, Macmillan, New York, (1931), pp. 48-49. For Zionist Ha-Am's use of the image of atomisation and dispersion, *see:* A. Hertzberg, *The Zionist Idea*, Harper Torchbooks, New York, (1959), p. 276.

587. A. Einstein, "Jewish Nationalism and Anti-Semitism", *The Jewish Chronicle*, (17 June 1921), p. 16.

588. A. Einstein, A. Engel translator, "How I became a Zionist", *The Collected Papers of Albert Einstein*, Volume 7, Document 57, Princeton University Press, (2002), pp. 234-235, at 235.

589. At the time Einstein made his statement, Jews and Gentiles often referred to Jews as "Orientals".

590. Einstein repeatedly spoke of the Germans as "greedy" to acquire territory and of the "loss of energy" when different "races" attempted to live together. He have been speaking literally. Georg Friedrich Nicolai wrote of the struggle of life to aquire the energy of the sun and he applied this struggle to humanity. G. Nicolai, *Die Biologie des Krieges, Betrachtungen eines deutschen Naturforschers*, O. Füssli, Zürich, (1917); English translation: *The Biology of War*, Century Co., New York, (1918), pp. 36-39, 44-53.

591. R. W. Clarck, *Einstein, the Life and Times*, World Publishing Company, USA, (1971), p. 292. Clarck refers to: *Neue Rundschau*, Volume 33, Part 2, pp. 815-816.

592. W. E. Mosse, "Die Niedergang der deutschen Republik und die Juden", *The Crucial Year 1932*, p. 38; English translation in: K. Polkehn, "The Secret Contacts: Zionism and Nazi Germany, 1933-1941", *Journal of Palestine Studies*, Volume 5, Number 3/4, (Spring-Summer, 1976), pp. 54-82, at 56-57.

593. English translation by John Stachel in J. Stachel, "Einstein's Jewish Identity", *Einstein from 'B' to 'Z'*, Birkhäuser, Boston, (2002), p. 67. Stachel cites, "Botschaft", *Jüdische Rundschau*, Volume 30, (1925), p. 129; French translation, *La Revue Juive*, Volume 1, (1925), pp. 14-16.

594. J. Stachel, "Einstein's Jewish Identity", *Einstein from 'B' to 'Z'*, Birkhäuser, Boston, (2002), p. 65. Stachel cites, *About Zionism: Speeches and Letters*, Macmillan, New York, (1931), pp. 78-79.

595. A. Einstein quoted in "Einstein on Arrival Braves Limelight for Only 15 Minutes", *The New York Times*, (12 December 1930), pp. 1, 16, at 16.

596. E. A. Ross, *The Old World in the New: The Significance of past and Present Immigration to the American People*, Century Company, New York, (1914), p. 144.

597. A. Einstein, "Why do They Hate the Jews?", *Collier's*, Volume 102, (26 November 1938); reprinted in *Ideas and Opinions*, Crown, New York, (1954), pp. 191-198, at 194, 196. Einstein expressed himself in a similar way to Peter A. Bucky, P. A. Bucky, Einstein, and A. G. Weakland, *The Private Albert Einstein*, Andrews and McMeel, Kansas City, (1992), p. 87.

598. T. Herzl, *A Jewish State: An Attempt at a Modern Solution of the Jewish Question*, The Maccabæan Publishing Co., New York, (1904), pp. 5-6, 25, 68, 93.

599. L. Fry, *Waters Flowing Eastward: The War Against the Kingship of Christ*, TBR Books, Washington, D. C., (2000), p. 137.

600. J. Prinz, *Wir Juden*, Erich Reiss, Berlin, (1934), pp. 154-155.

601. J. Prinz, *Wir Juden*, Erich Reiss, Berlin, (1934), p. 44.

602. E. Bernstein, "Jews and German Social Democracy", *Die Tukunft* (New York), Volume 26, (March, 1921), pp. 145ff.; English translation in: P. W. Massing, *Rehearsal for Destruction: A Study of Political Anti-Semitism in Imperial Germany*, Howard Fertig, New York, (1967), pp. 322-330. On Marx's alleged "self-hatred", *see:* H. Hirsch, "The Ugly Marx: Analysis of an 'Outspoken Anti-Semite'", *Philosophical Forum*, Volume 8, (1978), pp.150-162. *See also:* P. L. Rose, *Revolutionary Antisemitism in Germany from Kant to Wagner*, Princeton University Press, (1990), pp. 296-305. *See also:* R. Grooms, "The Racism of Marx and Engels", *The Barnes Review*, Volume 2, Number 10, (October, 1996), pp. 3-8. Communists have always been opportunistic Jew baiters.

603. *See especially* Chapter 5: L. Brenner, *Zionism in the Age of the Dictators*, Croom Helm, London, L. Hill, Westport, Connecticut, (1983).

<http://www.aaargh-international.org/engl/zad/zad.html>

604. D. Bronder, *Bevor Hitler kam: Eine historische Studie*, Hans Pfeiffer Verlag, Hannover, (1964), p. 204 (p. 211 in the 1974 edition). H. Kardel, *Adolf Hitler, Begründer Israels*, Verlag Marva, Genf, (1974); English translation *Adolf Hitler: Founder of Israel*, Modjeskis' Society Dedicated to Preservation of Cultures, San Diego, (1997).

605. H. Koehler, *Inside the Gestapo: Hitler's Shadow Over the World*, Pallas Pub. Co. Ltd., London, (1940). *See aslo:* H. Frank, *Im Angesicht des Galgens; Deutung Hitlers und seiner Zeit auf Grund eigener Erlebnisse und Erkenntnisse. Geschrieben im Nürnberger Justizgefängnis*, F. A. Beck, München-Gräfelfing, (1953), pp. 330-331. *See aslo:* D. Bronder, *Bevor Hitler kam: Eine historische Studie*, Hans Pfeiffer Verlag, Hannover, (1964), p. 204 (p. 211 in the 1974 edition). *See aslo:* H. Kardel, *Adolf Hitler, Begründer Israels*, Verlag Marva, Genf, (1974); English translation *Adolf Hitler: Founder of Israel*, Modjeskis' Society Dedicated to Preservation of Cultures, San Diego, (1997).

606. D. Bronder, *Bevor Hitler kam: Eine historische Studie*, Hans Pfeiffer Verlag, Hannover, (1964), pp. 203-204 (pp. 210-211 in the 1974 edition).

607. "Who Were Hitler's Jewish Soldiers", *The Jewish Chronicle*, (6 December 1996), p. 1. *See also:* W. Hoge, "Rare Look Uncovers Wartime Anguish of Many Part-Jewish Germans", *The New York Times*, (6 April 1997), p. 16. *See also:* B. M. Rigg, *Hitler's Jewish Soldiers: The Untold Story of Nazi Racial Laws and Men of Jewish Descent in the German Military*, University Press of Kansas, Lawrence, Kansas, (2002); **and** *Rescued from the Reich: How One of Hitler's Soldiers Saved the Lubavitcher Rebbe*, Yale University Press, New Haven, (2004).

608. E. Kaye, *The Hole in the Sheet: A Modern Woman Looks at Orthodox and Hasidic Judaism*, L. Stuart Inc., Secaucus, New Jersey, (1987).

609. "The Modern Jews", *The North American Review*, Volume 60, Number 127, (April, 1845), pp. 329-368, at 353-354, 357-361.

610. J. H. Brenner, "Self-Criticism", in A. Hertzberg, *The Zionist Idea*, Harper Torchbooks, New York, (1959), pp. 307-312. Brenner cites Mendele Moher Sefarim's works (Mendele's real name was Shalom Jacob Abramowitz).

611. A. D. Gordon, *Kitve A. D. Gordon*, In Five Volumes, Tel-Aviv, ha-Va'ad ha-merkazi shel mifleget ha-Po'el ha-tsa'ir, (1927-1930), parts translated to English in A. Hertzberg, *The Zionist Idea*, Harper Torchbooks, New York, (1959), pp. 371-386, *see especially* pp. 372, 376, 377, 379.

612. B. Katzenelson, *Ba-Mivhan*, Tel-Aviv, (1935); parts translated to English in A. Hertzberg, *The Zionist Idea*, Harper Torchbooks, New York, (1959), pp. 390-395, *see especially* pp. 390-391.

613. V. Jabotinsky, *Evidence Submitted to the Palestine Royal Commission*, London, (1937), pp. 10-29; in A. Hertzberg, *The Zionist Idea*, Harper Torchbooks, New York, (1959), pp. 559-570, 1t 560-561.

614. M. Bar-Zohar, *Ben-Gurion: A Biography*, Delacorte Press, New York, (1978), p. 67.

615. L. Brenner, *Zionism in the Age of the Dictators*, Chapter 2, Croom Helm, London, L. Hill, Westport, Connecticut, (1983), p. 24. *Brenner cites:* C. Greenberg, "The Myth of Jewish Parasitism", *Jewish Frontiers*, (March, 1942), p. 20. Brenner also refers to Yehezkel Kaufman, "Hurban Hanefesh: A Discussion of Zionism and Anti-Semitism", *Issues*, (Winter, 1967), p.106.

616. A. Einstein, "Unpublished Preface to a Blackbook", *Out of My Later Years*, Philosophical Library, New York, (1950), pp. 258-259, at 259.

617. B. Lazare, "Jewish Nationalism and Emancipation (1897-1899)", in A. Hertzberg, *The Zionist Idea: A Historical Analysis and Reader*, Garden City, N.Y. Doubleday, (1959), pp. 471-476, at 471.

618. P. A. Bucky, Einstein, and A. G. Weakland, *The Private Albert Einstein*, Andrews and McMeel, Kansas City, (1992), p. 84.

619. A. H. Silver, *Vision and Victory*, Zionist Organization of America, New York, (1949); in A. Hertzberg, *The Zionist Idea*, Harper Torchbooks, New York, (1959), pp. 592-600, at 597.

620. A. M. Lilienthal, *What Price Israel*, Henry Regnery Company, Chicago, (1953), pp. *vi-viii*, 239. *See also:* "Israel's Flag Is Not Mine", *Reader's Digest*, (September, 1949), pp. 49-53. "The State of Israel and the State of the Jew", *Vital Speeches of the Day*, Volume 16, Number 13, (15 April 1950). *See also:* R. Garaudy, *Les Mythes Fondateurs de la Politique Israélienne*, Samiszdat, Paris, (1996); English translations: *The Founding Myths of Israeli Politics*, and *The Mythical Foundations of Israeli Policy*, Studies Forum International, London, (1997) and *The Founding Myths of Modern Israel*, Institute for Historical Review, Newport Beach, California, (2000). *See also:* B. Kimmerling, "Israel's Culture of Martyrdom", *The Nation*, (10-17 January 2005), pp. 29-30, 33-34, 36, 38, 40; which is a review of I. Zertal, *Israel's Holocaust and the Politics of Nationhood*, Cambridge University Press, (2005); and Y. Grodzinsky, *In the Shadow of the Holocaust: The Struggle Between Jews and Zionists in the Aftermath of World War II*, Common Courage Press, Monroe, Maine, (2004).

621. Letter from P. Ehrenfest to A. Einstein of 8 February 1920, English translation by A. Hentschel, *The Collected Papers of Albert Einstein*, Volume 9, Document 303, Princeton University Press, (2004), pp. 251-254, at 254.

622. I. Epstein, Editor, "Sanhedrin 20*b*", *The Babylonian Talmud*, Volume 27, The Soncino Press, London, (1935).

623. Letter from P. Ehrenfest to A. Einstein of 9 December 1919, English translation by A. Hentschel, *The Collected Papers of Albert Einstein*, Volume 9, Document 203, Princeton University Press, (2004), pp. 173-175, at 174.

624. Letter from P. Ehrenfest to A. Einstein of 9 December 1919, English translation by A. Hentschel, *The Collected Papers of Albert Einstein*, Volume 9, Document 203, Princeton University Press, (2004), pp. 173-175, at 175.

625. R. P. Boas, "The Problem of American Judaism", *The Atlantic Monthly*, Volume 119, Number 2, (February, 1917), pp. 145-152.

626. K. G. W. Ludecke, *I Knew Hitler: The Story of a Nazi A Who Escaped the Blood Purge*, Charles Scribner's Sons, New York, (1937), pp. 191-218.

627. D. Reed, *Disgrace Abounding*, Jonathan Cape, London, (1939), pp. 249, 251.

628. J. Klatzkin, *Tehumim: Ma'amarim*, Devir, Berlin, (1925). English translation in J. B. Agus, *The Meaning of Jewish History*, Volume 2, Abelard-Schuman, New York, (1963), p. 425-426.

629. L. Simon, Introduction to A. Einstein, Edited by L. Simon, *About Zionism: Speeches and Letters by Professor Albert Einstein*, Macmillan, New York, (1931), pp. 9-12.

630. *Central-Verein Zeitung*, Volume, 9, Number 28, (11 July 1930); and Volume 9, Number 37, (12 September 1930); and Volume 9, Number 38, (19 September 1930). K. Polkehn, "The Secret Contacts: Zionism and Nazi Germany, 1933-1941", *Journal of Palestine Studies*, Volume 5, Number 3/4, (Spring-Summer, 1976), pp. 54-82.

631. K. Polkehn, "The Secret Contacts: Zionism and Nazi Germany, 1933-1941", *Journal of Palestine Studies*, Volume 5, Number 3/4, (Spring-Summer, 1976), pp. 54-82, at 56-57.

632. P. W. Fabry, *Mutmassungen über Hitler: Urteile von Zeitgenossen*, Droste, Düsseldorf, (1969), p. 130. Fabry cites: *Israelischen Familienblatt*.

633. L. Lewisohn, "A Year of Crisis", in A. Hertzberg, *The Zionist Idea*, Harper Torchbooks, New York, (1959), pp. 488-492, at 489. Hertzberg cites: L. Lewisohn, *Rebirth* (editor), New York, (1935), pp. 290-296.

634. P. A. Bucky, Einstein, and A. G. Weakland, *The Private Albert Einstein*, Andrews and McMeel, Kansas City, (1992), p. 61.

635. P. A. Bucky, Einstein, and A. G. Weakland, *The Private Albert Einstein*, Andrews and McMeel, Kansas City, (1992), p. 62.

636. Letter from A. Einstein to the Prussian Academy of Sciences of 5 April 1933, *The World As I See It*, Citadel, New York, (1993), pp. 82-84, at 83.

637. *Reproduced in:* F. Jerome, *The Einstein File*, St. Martin's Press, New York, (2002), second plate following page 170.

638. A. Einstein, "Time, Space and Gravitation", *The Times* (London), (28 November 1919), pp. 13-14; reprinted in *Science* and in E. E. Slossen, *Easy Lessons in Einstein*, Harcourt Brace and Howe, New York, (1920), pp. 109-114. Einstein was perhaps inspired to make this remark by a letter from A. F. Lindemann of 23 November 1919, *The Collected Papers of Albert Einstein*, Volume 9, Document 174, Princeton University Press, (2004). Einstein told Ehrenfest of his joke in a letter of 4 December 1919, *The Collected Papers of Albert Einstein*, Volume 9, Document 189, Princeton University Press, (2004).

639. D. Fahey, *The Mystical Body of Christ in the Modern World*, Browne and Nolan Limited, London, (1935), p. 77.

640. *The Jewish Chronicle*, (17 June 1921), p. 26.

641. M. Nordau, "Max Nordau on the General Situation of the Jews", *The Jewish Chronicle*, (3 September 1897), pp. 7-9, at 8.

642. *Daily Graphic* as quoted in *The Jewish Chronicle*, (17 June 1921), p. 26.

643. *See:* "Challenges Prof. Einstein: St. Paul Professor Asserts Relativity Theory Was Advanced in 1866", *The New York Times*, (10 April 1921), p. 21.

644. "Einstein Refuses to Debate Theory: Dean Reuterdahl's Challenge to Discuss Relativity Declined as Detraction from Mission", *New York American*, (12 April 1921).

645. A. Einstein, "Een interview met Prof. Einstein", *Nieuwe Rotterdamsche Courant*, (4 July 1921). English translation found in, M. Janssen, *et al* Editors, *The Collected Papers of Albert Einstein*, Volume 7, Appendix D, Princeton University Press, (2002), pp. 623.

646. R. S. Shankland, "Conversations with Albert Einstein", *American Journal of Physics*, Volume 31, Number 1, (January, 1963), pp. 47-57, at 56.

647. H. Dukas and B. Hoffmann, *Albert Einstein: The Human Side*, Princeton University Press, (1979), p. 55.

648. C. Weizmann, *Trial and Error: The Autobiography of Chaim Weizmann*, Harper & Brothers, New York, (1949), p. 201.

649. J. Prinz, *Wir Juden*, Erich Reiss, Berlin, (1934), pp. 50-55. Letter from A. Einstein to M. Born of 22 March 1934, in M. Born, *The Born-Einstein Letters*, Walker and Company, New York, (1971), pp. 121-122.

650. C. Weizmann, *Trial and Error: The Autobiography of Chaim Weizmann*, Harper & Brothers, New York, (1949), p. 201. We must be careful not to confuse Kerensky and his "liberalism" with Lenin, Chernyshevsky and "Bolshevism".

651. C. Weizmann, *Trial and Error: The Autobiography of Chaim Weizmann*, Harper & Brothers, New York, (1949), pp. 31-35, 42, 47, 50-53, 65, 82, 156-163, 200-207, 288-289.

652. C. Weizmann, *Trial and Error: The Autobiography of Chaim Weizmann*, Harper, New York, (1949), p. 289.

653. M. Nordau, *Der Zionismus*, Jüdischen Volksstimme, Brünn, (ca. 1898), pp. 8, 14. *See also:* M. Nordau, *Die Tragödie der Assimilation*, Berlin, Wien, R. Löwit, (1920).

654. C. Weizmann, *Trial and Error: The Autobiography of Chaim Weizmann*, Harper & Brothers, New York, (1949), p. 289.

655. Letter from A. Einstein to M. Born of 22 March 1934, in M. Born, *The Born-Einstein Letters*, Walker and Company, New York, (1971), pp. 121-122.

656. A. Einstein, *Ideas and Opinions*, Crown, New York, (1954), p. 213. *See also:* P. A. Bucky, Einstein, and A. G. Weakland, *The Private Albert Einstein*, Andrews and McMeel, Kansas City, (1992), p. 63.

657. D. Eckart and A. Hitler, *Der Bolschewismus von Moses bis Lenin: Zwiegespräch zwischen Adolf Hitler und mir*, Hoheneichen-Verlag, München, (1924); English translation by W. L. Pierce, "Bolshevism from Moses to Lenin", *National Socialist World*, (1966). URL: <http://www.jrbooksonline.com/DOCs/Eckart.doc> p. 7.

658. K. J. Herrmann, "Historical Perspectives on Political Zionism and Antisemitism", *Zionism & Racism: Proceedings of an International Symposium*, International Organization for the Elimination of All Forms of

Racial Discrimination, Tripoli, (1977), pp. 197-210, at page 208.
659. Letter from P. Ehrenfest to A. Einstein of 9 December 1919, *The Collected Papers of Albert Einstein*, Volume 9, Document 203, Princeton University Press, (2004).
660. M. Shonfeld, *The Holocaust Victims Accuse: Documents and Testimony on Jewish War Criminals*, Neturei Karta of U.S.A., Brooklyn, (1977).
661. Rabbi M. D. Weissmandel, *Min ha-metsar: zikhronot mi-shenot 702-705*, Hotsa'at Emunah, New York, (1960); **and** *Ten Questions to the Zionists*, (1974). *See also:* L. Brenner, *Zionism in the Age of the Dictators*, Croom Helm, London, L. Hill, Westport, Connecticut, (1983); **and** *51 Documents: Zionist Collaboration with the Nazis*, Barricade Books Inc., Fort Lee, New Jersey, (2002). *See also:* M. J. Nurenberger, *The Scared and the Doomed: The Jewish Establishment Vs. The Six Million*, Mosaic Press, Oakville, New York, (1985). *See also:* W. R. Perl, *The Holocaust Conspiracy: An International Policy of Genocide*, Shapolsky Publishers, New York, (1989). *See also:* T. Segev, *The Seventh Million: The Israelis and the Holocaust*, Hill and Wang, New York, (1993).
662. Rabbi E. Schwartz, "WHY DO YOU VIOLATE G'D'S ORDER? IT WILL NOT SUCCEED", *The New York Times*, (18 May 1993), p. A16.
663. A. Einstein, A. Engel translator, "How I became a Zionist", *The Collected Papers of Albert Einstein*, Volume 7, Document 57, Princeton University Press, (2002), pp. 234-235, at 235.
664. E. Wiesel, *Legends of Our Time*, Schocken Books, New York, (1982), p. 142.
665. D. K. Shipler, "Most West Bank Arabs Blaming U. S. for Impasse", *The New York Times*, (14 April 1983), p. A3; **and** "Israel's Military Chief Retires and Is Replaced by His Deputy", *The New York Times*, (20 April 1983), p. A8; **and** "The Israeli Army Signs a Political Truce", *The New York Times*, Section 4, (15 May 1983), p. 3. *See also:* A. Lewis, "Hope Against Hope", *The New York Times*, Section 4, (17 April 1983), p. 19; and "The New Israel; Away from the Early Zionist Dream", *The New York Times*, (30 July 1984), p. A21. *See also:* J. Kuttab, "West Bank Arabs Foresee Expulsion", *The New York Times*, (1 August 1983), p. A15. *See also:* A. Cowell, "Israel Frees More Prisoners, But Arabs Are Not Mollified", *The New York Times*, (4 March 1994), p. A10. *See also:* Y. M. Ibrahim, "Palestinians See a People's Hatred in a Killer's Deed", *The New York Times*, (6 March 1994), p. E16.
666. "The Modern Jews", *The North American Review*, Volume 60, Number 127, (April, 1845), pp. 329-368, at 330.
667. R. Romain, *La Conscience de l'Europe*, Volume 1, pp. 696ff. English translation from A. Fölsing, *Albert Einstein: A Biography*, Viking, New York, (1997), pp. 365-367. *See also:* Letter from A. Einstein to R. Romain of 15 September 1915, *The Collected Papers of Albert Einstein*, Volume 8, Document 118, Princeton University Press, (1998); **and** Letter from A. Einstein to R. Romain of 22 August 1917, *The Collected Papers of Albert Einstein*, Volume 8, Document 374, Princeton University Press, (1998).

668. J. Bacque, *Other Losses: An Investigation into the Mass Deaths of German Prisoners at the Hands of the French and Americans after World War II*, Stoddart,Toronto, (1989).

669. Letter from A. Einstein to Paul Ehrenfest of 22 March 1919, English translation by A. Hentschel, *The Collected Papers of Albert Einstein*, Volume 9, Document 10, Princeton Univsersity Press, (2004), pp. 9-10, at 10.

670. A. Einstein, English translation by A. Engel, *The Collected Papers of Albert Einstein*, Volume 7, Document 35, Princeton University Press, (2002), pp. 156-157.

671. P. A. Bucky, Einstein, and A. G. Weakland, *The Private Albert Einstein*, Andrews and McMeel, Kansas City, (1992), p. 111.

672. A. Unsöld, "Albert Einstein — Ein Jahr danach", *Physikalische Blätter*, Volume 36, (1980), pp.337-339; **and** Volume 37, Number 7, (1981), p. 229.

673. A. Einstein, "Atomic War or Peace", *Atlantic Monthly*, (November, 1945, and November 1947); *as reprinted in:* A. Einstein, *Ideas and Opinions*, Crown, New York, (1954), p. 125.

674. A. Einstein, "To the Heroes of the Battle of the Warsaw Ghetto", *Bulletin of the Society of Polish Jews*, New York, (1944), reprinted in *Ideas and Opinions*, Crown, New York, (1954), pp. 212-213.

675. A. Einstein, quoted in O. Nathan and H. Norton, *Einstein on Peace*, Avenel Books, New York, (1981), p. 331.

676. A. Einstein quoted in A. Fölsing, *Albert Einstein: A Biography*, Viking, New York, (1997), pp. 727-728.

677. M. Born, *The Born-Einstein Letters*, Walker and Company, New York, (1971), p. 189.

678. M. Born, *The Born-Einstein Letters*, Walker and Company, New York, (1971), p. 199.

679. "A Modest Proposal", *Time Magazine*, Volume 37, Number 12, (24 March 1941), pp. 95-96.

680. P. A. Bucky, Einstein, and A. G. Weakland, *The Private Albert Einstein*, Andrews and McMeel, Kansas City, (1992), p. 56.

681. W. Diewerge, *Das Kreigsziel der Weltplutokratie: dokumentarische Veröffentlichung zu dem Buch des Präsidenten der amerikanischen Friedensgesellschaft Theodore Nathan Kaufman "Deutschland muss sterben"* ("Germany must perish"), Zentral Verlag der NSDAP, F. Eher Nachf., Berlin, (1941). *See also: Wenn Du dieses Zeichen siehst. . .*, NSDAP Propaganda Brochure, (November, 1941). *See also:* H. Goitsch, *Niemals!*, Zentral Verlag der NSDAP, F. Eher Nachf., Berlin, (1944). *See also: Der Angriff*, (23 July 1941). *See also: Das Reich*, (3 August 1941). *See also:* "Nazis Attack Roosevelt", *The New York Times*, (24 July 1941), p. 8. *See also:* "Jews of Hanover Forced from Homes", *The New York Times*, (9 September 1941), p. 4; and Kaufman's response, p. 4.

682. É. Durkheim, *"Germany above All" The German Mental Attitude and the War*, Librairie Armand Colin, Paris, (1915). *See also:* "By a German", *I Accuse! (J'Accuse!)*, Grosset & Dunlap, New York, (1915). *See also:* W. F.

Barry, *The World's Debate: An Historical Defence of the Allies*, George H. Doran, New York, (1917). *See also:* W. T. Hornaday, *A Searchlight on Germany: Germany's Blunders, Crimes and Punishment*, American Defense Society, New York, (1917). *See also:* D. W. Johnson, *Plain Words from America: A Letter to a German Professor*, London, New York, Toronto, Hodder & Stoughton, (1917).

683. M. Hess, *Rom und Jerusalem: die letzte Nationalitätsfrage*, Eduard Wengler, Leipzig, (1862); English: *Rome and Jerusalem: A Study in Jewish Nationalism*, Bloch, New York, (1918).

684. T. N. Kaufman, *Germany Must Perish!*, Argyle Press, Newark, New Jersey, (1941), pp. 88-89, 93, 94, 96.

685. T. Segev, *The Seventh Million: The Israelis and the Holocaust*, Hill and Wang, New York, (1993), p. 142.

686. An English translation of the minutes appears in: R. S. Levy, "Wannsee Conference on the Final Solution of the Jewish Question", *Antisemitism in the Modern World: An Anthology of Texts*, D.C. Heath, Toronto, (1991), pp. 252-258; *see also:* pp. 250-252.

687. *Trial of the Major War Criminals Before the International Military Tribunal, Nuremberg, 14 November 1945 — 1 October 1946*, Volume 12, Secretariat of the Tribunal, Nuremberg, Germany, p. 315.

688. *Trial of the Major War Criminals Before the International Military Tribunal, Nuremberg, 14 November 1945 — 1 October 1946*, Volume 12, Secretariat of the Tribunal, Nuremberg, Germany, p. 316.

689. *Trial of the Major War Criminals Before the International Military Tribunal, Nuremberg, 14 November 1945 — 1 October 1946*, Volume 12, Secretariat of the Tribunal, Nuremberg, Germany, p. 316.

690. M. Roseman, *The Wannsee Conference and the Final Solution: A Reconsideration*, Henry Holt, New York, (2002), p. 105. Roseman cites: R. M. W. Kempner, *Eichmann und Komplizen*, Europa Verlag, Zürich, (1961), pp. 152-153.

691. Refer to Eichmann's testimony at trial, and: A. Eichmann, "Eichmann Tells His Own Damning Story", *Life Magazine*, Volume 49, Number 22, (28 November 1960), pp. 19-25, 101-112; and "Eichmann's Own Story: Part II", *Life Magazine*, (5 December 1960), pp. 146-161.

692. K. G. W. Ludecke, *I Knew Hitler: The Story of a Nazi A Who Escaped the Blood Purge*, Charles Scribner's Sons, New York, (1937), pp. 191-218.

693. English translation in: R. S. Levy, *Antisemitism in the Modern World: An Anthology of Texts*, D. C. Heath and Company, Toronto, (1991), pp. 127-128, at 128.

694. English translation in: R. S. Levy, *Antisemitism in the Modern World: An Anthology of Texts*, D. C. Heath and Company, Toronto, (1991), pp. 222-223, at 223. An alternative translation appears in: "Holocaust", *Encyclopaedia Judaica*, Volume 8, Macmillan, Jerusalem, (1971), col. 852.

695. A. Hitler in M. Domarus, Editor, *Hitler: Reden und Proklamationen, 1932-1945: Kommentiert von einem deutschen Zeitgenossen*, Süddeutscher

Verlag, München, (1965), pp. 1057-1058.

696. H. Frank, (16 December 1941), quoted in: *Nazi Conspiracy and Aggression*, Volume 2, United States, Office of Chief of Counsel for the Prosecution of Axis Criminality, Washington, D. C., United States Government Printing Office, (1946), p. 634. *See also:* Y. Arad, Yitzhak, I. Gutman, A. Margaliot, Abraham,Editors, *Documents on the Holocaust: Selected Sources on the Destruction of the Jews of Germany and Austria, Poland, and the Soviet Union*, Yad Vashem in cooperation with the Anti-Defamation League and Ktav Pub. House, Jerusalem, (1981).

697. H. Frank quoted in H. Kardel, *Adolf Hitler, Begründer Israels*, Verlag Marva, Genf, (1974).

698. The exact phrasing depends upon translation, but one finds such phrases in: A. Ha-Am, "The Negation of the Diaspora", in A. Hertzberg, *The Zionist Idea*, Harper Torchbooks, New York, (1959), pp. 270-277, at 272-273, 277.

699. N. Sokolow, *History of Zionism 1600-1918*, Volume 1, Longmans, Green and Co., New York, (1919), p. xvii.

700. P. S. Mowrer, "The Assimilation of Israel", *The Atlantic Monthly*, Volume 128, Number 1, (July, 1921), pp. 101-110.

701. B. L. Brasol, *The World at the Cross Roads*, Small, Mayhard & Co., Boston, (1921), pp. 371-379.

702. English translation in: K. Polkehn, "The Secret Contacts: Zionism and Nazi Germany, 1933-1941", *Journal of Palestine Studies*, Volume 5, Number 3/4, (Spring-Summer, 1976), pp. 54-82, at 59.

703. J. Prinz, "Zionism under the Nazi Government", *Young Zionist* (London), (November, 1937), p. 18; *as quoted in:* L. Brenner, *Zionism in the Age of the Dictators*, Chapter 5, Croom Helm, London, L. Hill, Westport, Connecticut, (1983), p. 47.

704. E. M. Friedman, "Zionism and the American Spirit", *Forum*, Volume 58, (July, 1917), pp. 67-80; *reprinted as: Zionism and the American Spirit: A New Perspective*, University Zionist Society, New York, (1917).

705. I. Zangwill, *The Problem of the Jewish Race*, Judaen Publishing Company, New York, (1914), p. 18; which was first published as an article, "The Jewish Race", *The Independent*, Volume 71, Number 3271, (10 August 1911), pp. 288-295, at 294.

706. T. Herzl, *A Jewish State: An Attempt at a Modern Solution of the Jewish Question*, The Maccabæan Publishing Co., New York, (1904), p. 29.

707. L. Kellner, "Eröffnungsrede zum ersten Kongress", *Theodor Herzls Zionistische Schriften*, Jüdischer Verlag, Berlin, (1920), p. 139-144, at 140.

708. E. K. Dühring, *Die Judenfrage als Racen-, Sitten- und Culturfrage: mit einer weltgeschichtlichen Antwort*, H. Reuther, Karlsruhe, (1881); English translation by A. Jacob, *Eugen Dühring on the Jews*, Nineteen Eighty Four Press, Brighton, England, (1997), pp. 211-212. *See also:* E. K. Dühring, *Der Werth des Lebens: Eine Denkerbetrachtung im Sinne heroischer Lebensauffassung*, Fifth Edition, Reisland, Leipzig, (1894), p. 9.

709. *Confer:* W. Daim, *Der Mann, der Hitler die Ideen gab: Jörg Lanz von Liebenfels*, Third Improved Edition, Ueberreuter, Wien, (1994).

710. M. Buber, "Das Judentum und die Juden", *Drei Reden über das Judentum*, Rütten & Loening, Frankfurt a. M., (1911); English translation:"Judaism and the Jews", *On Judaism*, Schocken Books, New York, (1967), pp. 11-21, at 15, 19.

711. J. R. Marcus, *The Rise and Destiny of the German Jew*, The Union of American Hebrew Congregations, Cincinnati, (1934), pp. 61-62.

712. F. v. Hellwald, *Culturgeschichte in ihrer natürlichen Entwicklung bis zur Gegenwart*, Lampart & Comp., Augsburg, (1875); **and** "Der Kampf ums Dasein im Menschen- und Völkerleben", *Das Ausland*, Volume 45, (1872), pp. 105ff., *see also: Das Ausland*, (1872), 901ff., 957ff. *See also:* R. Weikart, *The Human Life Review*, Volume 30, Number 2, (Spring 2004), pp. 29-37; **and** *From Darwin to Hitler: Evolutionary Ethics, Eugenics, and Racism in Germany*, Palgrave Macmillan, New York, (2004).

713. F. Galton, *Hereditary Genius: An Inquiry into its Laws and Consequences*, Macmillan, London, (1869); **and** *Inquiries into Human Faculty and its Development*, Macmillan and Co., London, (1883); **and** *The Possible Improvement of the Human Breed under the Existing Conditions of Law and Sentiment*, Washington, D. C., (1902). *See also:* The journal *Biometrika*.

714. D. Schwartz, *Die Freimaurerei. Weltanschauung, Organisation und Politik*, Zentral Verlag der NSDAP, Berlin, (1938), pp. 38-40.

715. W. D. Gould, "The Religious Opinions of Thomas Jefferson", *The Mississippi Valley Historical Review*, Volume 20, Number 2, (September, 1933), pp. 191-208, at 202.

716. Letter from T. Jefferson to B. Rush of 21 April 1803, *The Writings of Thomas Jefferson*, Volume 10, Issued Under the Auspices of the Thomas Jefferson Memorial Association of the United States, Washington, D.C., (1905), pp. 379-385, at 381-382.

717. R. H. Williams, *The Ultimate World Order—As Pictured in "The Jewish Utopia"*, CPA Book Publisher, Boring, Oregon, (1957?), pp. 43-47.

CPSIA information can be obtained
at www.ICGtesting.com
Printed in the USA
BVHW041056120619
550833BV00014B/265/P

9 781523 458875